Sloyan

WORD FREQUENCY DICTIONARY

Louis J. Hampton
17. VII. 67

AN ENGLISH-FRENCH-GERMAN-SPANISH WORD FREQUENCY DICTIONARY

(formerly titled: *Semantic Frequency List for English, French, German, and Spanish*)

A CORRELATION OF THE FIRST SIX THOUSAND WORDS IN FOUR SINGLE-LANGUAGE FREQUENCY LISTS

COMPILED BY

HELEN S. EATON

Sometime Research Assistant, Division of Psychology,
Institute of Educational Research, Teachers College, Columbia University,
Visiting Instructor in Spanish and Comparative Philology, the University of New Mexico

DOVER PUBLICATIONS, INC.
NEW YORK

Published in Canada by General Publishing Company, Ltd., 30 Lesmill Road, Don Mills, Toronto, Ontario.
Published in the United Kingdom by Constable and Company, Ltd., 10 Orange Street, London, W.C. 2.

This new Dover edition, first published in 1961, is an unabridged and unaltered republication of the work first published by The University of Chicago Press in 1940 under the former title: *Semantic Frequency List for English, French, German, and Spanish.*

The original edition was issued by the Committee on Modern Languages of the American Council on Education.

Library of Congress Catalog Card Number: 61-4487

Manufactured in the United States of America

Dover Publications, Inc.
180 Varick Street
New York, N. Y. 10014

PREFACE

Miss Eaton has done a notable service by preparing this semantic frequency list. The frequency lists hitherto published will be more useful as a result of her careful and scholarly compendium of parts of them. Teachers of the languages represented will find her list of prime importance in deciding how to treat the words in texts which their pupils are reading, and in their own choice of words in speaking. Teachers of other European languages (for example, Italian and Russian) may well consult the list until it is extended by adequate counts for the languages concerned. If used reasonably, the list can do nothing but good to teaching, testing, and textbook making.

I commend it also to the attention of psychologists, anthropologists, and students of what has been called the psycho-biology of language. The vocabulary, active and passive, of any group is as truly an index of its nature and culture as are its tools, monuments, customs, and myths. This list gives a useful base-line for comparisons of many sorts.

E. L. THORNDIKE

TEACHERS COLLEGE
COLUMBIA UNIVERSITY

FOREWORD

The present work is an effort in a field of inquiry that has engaged the attention of students of language through many generations. Only those who have examined the history of linguistic theory can appreciate the full significance of an experiment which employs a technique recently developed to establish in relative frequency of use the common conceptions of mankind as they find expression in four languages of the present day. In a former, metaphysical age, when men believed in the existence of innate ideas, philosophers like Leibnitz thought that it would be possible to assemble the basic concepts of the human mind and put them into mathematical formulas. Such an effort to bind mentality in a logical strait jacket was discarded long ago, for the operations of the mind are too complex to be brought into categories in this way. The empirical method seeks to approach the problem of inner experience from the opposite end—through language itself. Here is the activity that gives the key to man's inner reflection of the world of phenomena.

In recent years American investigators have discovered a new method of approach to the problem, that of frequency of use. This is based on the assumption that the words and locutions which appear most often are those which are most necessary for the concerns of life, and efforts have been made to establish a scale of frequency. These resulted in the English Word List by Thorndike and the word and idiom counts in the foreign languages compiled for the American and Canadian committees on modern languages after 1925, as well as the syntax count in Spanish by Hayward Keniston, published in 1937, and similar investigations of syntax usage in French and German which are now in progress. Obviously, the basis of these undertakings must be limited to a sampling of the written languages; but the validity of the selection of sources for the studies mentioned has been widely accepted, and the results are being used for the teaching of English and foreign languages to a degree that no one could have antici pated a decade ago.

A word has two factors of equal importance: form and meaning. These are inseparable in the mind of the user; but while the word-form is a relatively stable phenomonon in the written languages of civilized peoples, word-meaning includes a number of possibilities, varying with the individual word. Some words, like "sun," have one universally understood meaning, which can be extended only in metaphorical usage; others stand at the opposite end of the scale, such as the common verbs "get" and "make," each of which includes a great bundle of possibilities. On the other hand, even words with a wide range of semantic values, often determinable only by the context in which they are used, have a certain semantic focus about which the meanings cluster. Evidence of such a basic idea appears plainly when we find words of complex meaning with a similar semantic focus in several languages. The correlation of the word frequencies in a group of languages may then show an interlingual relationship among the concepts measurable by a scale of frequency of use.

This is precisely what the compiler of the present work, Miss Eaton, has done for English, French, German, and Spanish. The result is an arrangement which shows the relative importance of approximately six thousand basic concepts as they appear in the four languages. The work of investigation and alignment has gone on, with interruptions, during a decade. Five years ago a preliminary list, based on the first thousand words in each of the source lists, was published by the Committee on Modern Languages in the volume *Experiments and Studies in Modern Language Teaching* (Chicago: University of Chicago Press, 1934), pages 244–79, and aroused considerable interest. The same Committee now undertakes the publication of the completed study. It is convinced that it offers herewith an important contribution of material for research and teaching, as well as for application to the practical use of language.

The Semantic Frequency List opens, indeed, a wide field of possibilities. To the psychologist and the student of civilization it furnishes material for a comparison of the basic ideologies of the peoples of four linguistic areas, as reflected in vocabulary, and thus brings light to a problem that has had little investigation. The linguist will find in it a basis for examining the most urgent linguistic needs of the several peoples in order to express their culture. The educationist and the teacher of English and the modern foreign languages has in this comparative semantic list a guide for selecting vocabularies graded to meet the various age levels and intelligence levels. This is of particular importance for those working with pupils in two languages, where it often happens that a concept which is quite usual in one of them may find expression in the other only by means of a word of lower frequency and therefore less likely to be familiar to the learner. For practical purposes the List gives important hints for vocabulary usage in its relation to ease of general understanding, as measured by the coincidence of concepts among peoples employing four languages. Like the frequency lists for word, idiom, and syntax that have appeared, the material contained in the Semantic Frequency List is, of course, raw material, to be adapted for research, pedagogical, and other uses in accordance with the needs of investigators, textbook makers, examiners, or those seeking objective criteria for a style that is to be widely understood. All those who use the work—whether students, teachers, or writers—have in it a reliable measure of simplicity and intelligibility and a means of avoiding expressions which have shown themselves to be of limited range.

Thanks are due the International Auxiliary Language Association for financial support given to the research and to the publication of this List.

ROBERT HERNDON FIFE, *Chairman*
Committee on Modern Languages of the American Council on Education

515 WEST ONE HUNDRED AND SIXTEENTH STREET
NEW YORK CITY

TABLE OF CONTENTS

INDEXES

APPENDIXES

APPENDIX I

APPENDIX II

"Experience and study confirm the observation that no word of one language (not considering terms which stand for purely physical objects) coincides in meaning fully with a word of another language. . . . . Each language expresses the concept somewhat differently, adding this or that connotation. . . . . A synonymy of the major languages has never been attempted, although pertinent fragments are to be found in many authors. However, an imaginative treatment of it would surely lead to a most appealing work."—Translation from WILHELM VON HUMBOLDT, *Gesammelte Schriften* (Berlin, 1909), VII, 129.

INTRODUCTION

The Semantic Frequency List presented herewith attempts to correlate the first six thousand entries in English, French, German, and Spanish frequency lists. The List will serve as a practical tool in ascertaining a basic vocabulary for any language—at least any European language—for, if users of four different languages concur in the need of a means of expressing these concepts most frequently, it is justifiable to suppose that people using still other languages would also feel the same need. The List should be of especial value to textbook makers, vocabulary-test makers, and compilers of small bilingual dictionaries by guiding them in their selection of the meanings of words on a basis of actual frequency. It should be of assistance in determining, especially for the user of a single-language frequency list, the most frequent meaning or meanings of a given word-form. It should be helpful as a basis for objective measurement tests, as well as for regular examinations in language, and as a guide to the selection of practice material in language classes, in order to insure that this material does not contain words used in rare meanings.[1]

Source lists.—The source lists in the four languages used are: for English, the Thorndike *Teacher's Word Book of 20,000 Words,* which contains 20,000 words taken from a count of 9,565,000 in 279 sources and categories of sources (not given separately); for French, the *French Word Book,* compiled by Vander Beke, which contains 6,067 words taken from a count of over 1,000,000 in 88 sources divided into 9 categories; for German, the *Häufigkeitswörterbuch der deutschen Sprache,* compiled by Kaeding, which contains 79,716 words taken from a count of 10,910,777 in 299 sources divided into 11 categories; for Spanish, the *Graded Spanish Word Book,* compiled by Buchanan, which contains 6,702 words taken from a count of 1,200,000 in 40 sources divided into 7 categories.[2]

Semantics.—The source lists were compiled before the present-day emphasis on semantics in linguistic science became so prominent. With a few exceptions, in the French list, they do not, therefore, give definitions or translations of any words. For this reason one cannot be sure as to which meanings of a word-form are included in the aggregate sum which provides the basis for allocating the word-form in a frequency list. It seems reasonable to suppose that, in most cases, correlating the words in the four languages serves as a reliable criterion for determining the prevalent meaning (semantic value) of any given word-form. At first glance the objection may be made that a false position is accorded to a word by giving to each individual meaning listed

[1] In this Introduction, *word-form* is used to mean simply a combination of letters written together. *Semantic value* refers to one of the specific meanings contained in a word-form of a given language.

[2] For more detailed information regarding sources see: *Teacher's Word Book of 20,000 Words,* by Edward L. Thorndike (New York City: Bureau of Publications, Teachers College, Columbia University, 1932); *French Word Book,* by George E. Vander Beke (New York City: Macmillan Co., 1929); *Häufigkeitswörterbuch der deutschen Sprache,* by F. W. Kaeding (Berlin: handled by E. S. Mittler & Sohn, 1898); *Graded Spanish Word Book,* by Milton A. Buchanan (Toronto: University of Toronto Press, 1927). Permission was kindly given by the publishers to use these lists in the present study.

the position which the word-form has attained in the source list through the adding together of the various meanings. For example, *present* in English has to be considered as meaning "gift" and also as indicating "time"; as meaning "give" and also "introduce"; as an equivalent of "here" in "(be) here"; and signifying "current" in, e.g., "the present trend." All these meanings are used to correlate it with the various word-forms in the other language lists which convey these meanings. It is, of course, the aggregate of these meanings that allocates the word-form *present* to its position among the first five hundred in the English frequency list, and naturally, one has no right to presume that any one of these meanings would be of sufficiently frequent occurrence to give it such a high rank. It is to be noted, however, that (*a*) the other language lists, using, for the most part, different word-forms for these different meanings, have these six semantic values listed separately, each in its proper thousand; and (*b*) that the position of a word in the present List is determined by all four of the thousand-numbers of the word with the same semantic value in the separate source lists. It would therefore seem that these factors are a sufficient check to determine the proper *relative* position in the List of a word-form used in more than one of its meanings.

Indexes.—The indexes in all four languages permit the List to be used conveniently by any person having a knowledge of any one of the four. Since English is the key language used, the other language indexes give the English word with which a foreign-language word is correlated and the number(s) of the section(s) where the word will be found.

METHODOLOGY

Frequency.—The superior figure "1" after a word indicates that it occurs among the first thousand words in the source list; "2," among the second thousand; etc. The letters "a" and "b" after the figures indicate, respectively, the first and the second five hundred of that thousand.

Weighting of the source lists.—As the number of words counted, as well as the range of material, for the English and the German lists is much greater than for the other two source lists, the English and the German words used in this study have been given more weight than the other two, in the proportion of four to one. For example: a word that occurs among the first thousand in all four languages is allocated as follows: English is reckoned 4, plus French 1, plus German 4, plus Spanish 1; this equals 10, which, divided by 10, places the word in Section 1. Similarly, a word that occurs among the first thousand in English, French, and Spanish, and among the second thousand in German, is allocated as follows: English 4, plus French 1, plus German 8, plus Spanish 1, equals 14; divided by 10, this sum places the word in Section 1.4.

Omission of complete phrases in each language.—In order to save space, a complete phrase in each language has not been set down, but only the key word which would be used in the sense indicated in the English; anyone using the List will be able to supply the whole phrase in any of the other languages with which he is familiar. It happens sometimes that the parts of speech are not the same in all four languages; for example: *hungry* and *faim*, etc., are considered as equivalents.

Proper nouns omitted.—As proper names of peoples, countries, etc., are not included in the French and Spanish lists, they have been omitted entirely; and the blanks thus created in the English and German lists have been filled from the next-following thousand words.[3] This accounts for the fact that some words numbered "2a" in the Thorndike list are numbered "1b" in the present study, etc. Adjectives derived from names of countries and used as the designation of the language or of an inhabitant of the country, and a few other words that are capitalized in English, have been included, since they are in all four source lists and are not considered proper adjectives or proper nouns in French and in Spanish. In the English list, 4 words have been moved up from the second thousand into the first; 23 (19+4) from the third to the second; 59 (36+23) from the fourth to the third; 93 (34+59) from the fifth to the fourth; 157 (64+93) from the sixth to the fifth; and 233 (76+157) from the seventh to the sixth. This process of moving words from one thousand to the next above would naturally entail shifting into the "a" (first 500) group of each thousand words from the "b" (second 500) group a number corresponding to that deleted from "a." But, as the choice of such words would, of necessity, be arbitrary, and as it would have no effect on the position of the word in the present work (which does not arrange the words in groups of five hundred), this has not been done. As the frequencies of individual English words are not given in the source list, the selection of the words in English to be moved up has been made in the following manner: the entries in each section of the present List are arranged in alphabetical order according to the key word, which is an English word; the requisite number of words to be moved have been taken in this order. In the German list no words have been moved up from the second thousand into the first; 5 have been moved from the third into the second; 10 (5+5) from the fourth to the third; 22 (12+10) from the fifth to the fourth; 33 (11+22) from the sixth to the fifth; 51 (18+33) from the seventh to the sixth. The frequency of the individual German words is given in the source list; so, in making these necessary transfers of German words, they were taken in order.[4]

Division of the List.—The Frequency List is divided into seven parts, each containing approximately 1,000 words (except the seventh, with about 500) and into 115 sections, running from 1. to 13. As the combination of thousands did not produce any of the following figures: 10.7, 11.1, 11.6, 11.8, 11.9, 12.3, these sections are omitted. A word not present in any of the three foreign-language lists (French, German, Spanish) is counted as belonging to the eighth thousand. As the English list goes up to 20,000, the actual position of a word can almost always be ascertained in English. If it is not among the 20,000, it is reckoned as in the twenty-first thousand. These words, not given in the several language lists, are not followed by a number. In the headings of each section where the various combinations of thousands in the four languages are given, the 8 and the 21 are marked by an asterisk to show that they are estimated figures. It is obvious that any word with a blank number space necessarily affects

[3] The proper names omitted from the English and German lists, as well as the words that have been transferred, are given in Appendix I.

[4] In the case of names of the languages and the people of a nation, the following method has been used: corresponding to the English entry *English* are given *français, deutsch, español,* in the other three languages, respectively. *English* is considered the native language and the name of the person using it; the native language of a speaker of French is, of course, *français;* etc. The same method has been used for units of money: *pound, dollar, franc, Mark,* and *peseta,* being used as corresponding; and *penny, cent, centime, Pfennig,* and *centavo.*

the whole entry of that concept and renders it conjectural as far as its proper position in the study is concerned; but here, too, the relative position in the List is probably fairly accurate.

Locutions.—Some locutions (composed of more than one word) are given in the source lists. These are entered in our List with the thousand-number of the source list after the last word. On some other occasions it was necessary to use a familiar locution in one or more of the languages in order to indicate a definite meaning for a word-form. In such cases the proper position-number is put after each word of the locution. The expressions in parentheses accompanying English words simply provide an explanation of the senses in which those words are used. It is, of course, impossible to go into the use of prepositions in their various meanings. They are therefore listed singly only under the general meaning. The frequency number has been omitted after prepositions and after some other words used in locutions, when they have already been listed separately and obviously belong to the first thousand. In such cases these words do not appear in the indexes.[5]

Latin and Anglo-Saxon words in English.—In English the Latin-derived words, which are cognates of the French and Spanish words exclusively used in those languages to express a certain concept, are often not in as frequent use for these concepts as are equivalents of Anglo-Saxon origin. These latter are sometimes made up of more than one word. But it has seemed more in keeping with the aim of the present work to use the Anglo-Saxon equivalent, such as "make use of" for "utilize," or as "catch sight of" for "perceive." It is possible, however, to simplify so many words of this type that the question arose as to where to draw the line. As a *modus operandi*, if such a Latin derivative occurs among the same thousand in English as the corresponding word in French and Spanish, that derivative has been used to express the concept.

Treatment of synonyms.—In cases where synonyms or quasi-synonyms for a listed word are found in different thousands in one language, they are listed together, each with its thousand-number, the most frequent being taken as the guide for allocating the word in our study; but where such quasi-synonyms have their equivalents in all four or in three of the languages, each is listed separately in its proper place. Synonyms listed together which are in a different thousand in the source list from the key word in the entry are put in parentheses.

Separable prefixes in German.—It is impossible from the Kaeding list to tell the actual frequency of verbs with separable prefixes, as the prefixes are given separately with no indication of what they belong to. In a few cases, such as *anfangen*, where the compound forms are so numerous as to place these verbs in the first five hundred of the second thousand, it has seemed justifiable to estimate that these verbs in their total count would be among the first thousand words. Hence, they have been so considered; and such entries are noted by an asterisk. As it is impossible in the Kaeding list to distinguish between such compounds as *úbersetzen* and *übersétzen*, the other languages have had to serve as a check.

[5] A few interjections occur in the French and the Spanish lists. The equivalents of these in English and in German are often common words whose use as interjections is not separately computed. It seems obvious that the credit given them by our system of weighting is too high, but there was no other method of evaluating them for position.

Compounds in German.—A great many of the compound words in the German source list would be translated into the other languages by a simple word plus a qualifying word or by a locution. The simple word which forms the nuclear element of the compounds is generally also present in the German list. It seemed wisest to list such compounds along with the simple word in the same entry. As each compound has its thousand-number following it, one can easily reckon, according to the explanation already given of the system of allocation used, where each would fall in the present List. This will probably be of use only to persons wanting to draw from this study a graded vocabulary in German. The same procedure noted here as applying to compounds in German was used also in the case of some French words with the prefix *re-*.

Spelling.—The spelling in the Kaeding list has been changed to conform to modern usage.

Treatment of divergencies in the source lists.—The German list enters separately each form of every verb, noun, and adjective. The English list gives separately the various forms of the verb "to be" and some different forms of certain other verbs and nouns. The French and the Spanish lists, with one or two exceptions, give only one form of each part of speech. Therefore, all the forms of the verb have been entered in the present List under the infinitive—in English, listed separately with their thousand-number; in German, all added together. In the few exceptional cases in the French and the Spanish lists, just mentioned, the equivalent forms in German have been computed separately, and a distinct entry has been made, with the English form, if separately given, as it appears in the source list.

In the case of adverbs, (*a*) none are given in Spanish, but presumably they are included in the adjective; (*b*) in German the adverb and the adjective are generally the same word; (*c*) in English a few adverbs are listed separately, although by no means all; (*d*) in French the adverbs seem to be listed separately. Consequently, such adverbs as are given in a source list are entered uniformly under the adjective. There are a few exceptions to this rule in cases where the adverb has taken on a special meaning.

In German, when a certain form is common to two words, such as the common forms of *brauchen* and *gebrauchen*, the method of treatment has been to add together all the frequencies of all the forms that could belong to only one of these words, and to allot proportionately the frequencies of the common form or forms. In the case of one or two words, such as *ihr*, "her," and *ihr*, "their," identical in all forms, the total frequencies have been arbitrarily divided evenly.

In French, in certain cases, such as *son*, "bran," where it seems obvious that the word with this semantic value would not come within the first six thousand, it has been reckoned as not coming within the ascertainable limits of the List, although *son* in its other meanings naturally appears in the List.

In Spanish, as the source list includes all numerals in an "etc." after "one," the Spanish word designating a numeral has been given a frequency corresponding to the average of the equivalent words in the other three languages. The same applies to personal and to possessive pronouns.

There are certain apparent inconsistencies in the arrangement of the items in some entries. This is due to the fact that each item is copied exactly from the source lists, which use different methods of entering the material.

Selection of words of the same frequency in French and in Spanish.—The French list contains 6,067 words, the last 146 entries having the same frequency and range. As 79 of these are enough to make up the total of 6,000, it has seemed justifiable to take any 79 of this lot that best fit in with the other languages. The Spanish list gives 6,702 words. A number of these—133—that have the same range and frequency cluster about the 6,000 point. So here also, of these 133, the most suitable 110 have been taken to fill up the 6,000.

ASSISTANCE

Checking by native experts.—The compiler has made every effort to be as objective as possible in this investigation. An element of subjectivity is necessarily involved in assigning some word-forms to given concepts. As an added precaution, therefore, each language column has been checked by a native expert linguist who, besides his own language, knows well two of the other languages included in the work. These experts for French, German, and Spanish are, respectively, Messrs. Pierre Gault (New York City), Alexander Gode-von Aesch (University of Chicago), Eugene Delgado-Arias (Townsend Harris High School, New York City).

Checking with the English semantic count.—The List has in part been checked with a semantic list in English in process of being compiled at the Institute of Educational Research. Owing to the unfinished state of the latter and to other factors, an accurate comparison of all entries in the present List was not possible. However, among the 416 comparable entries, taken from the second five hundred of the first thousand entries of the present List, about an 85 per cent accord was found in the relative frequency rating. It is gratifying to discover from this result that the aim of the Semantic Frequency List seems to have been realized in so far as is possible at the present stage of activities on this line in the science of semantics.

Mechanics of the study.—In working out the mechanics of index-making, etc., the part-time services of Dr. Irving Lorge, of the Institute of Educational Research, were provided by Teachers College, Columbia University.

Financial support of the work.— The International Auxiliary Language Association, later disbanded, supplied the funds for the entire undertaking as a part of its linguistic research program. A grant from the Association to Teachers College, Columbia University, made possible the completion of the List in the Division of Psychology, Institute of Educational Research; and another grant provided funds for publication.

ACKNOWLEDGMENTS

Sincere gratitude is here expressed to Dr. Robert Herndon Fife, chairman of the Committee on Modern Languages of the American Council on Education, who gave many hours to going over the manuscript of the List and made many helpful suggestions for clarification of the arrangement. The late Dr. Algernon Coleman, of the same Committee, also made several suggestions for the wording of the Introduction—suggestions which were received with deep appreciation. Sincere thanks go also to Dr. Edward L. Thorndike, of Teachers College, Columbia University, who gave much helpful advice on the original setting-up of the project, which, without his encouraging words, would probably never have got under way. Thanks are also tendered to Mrs. Mary C. Bray, executive secretary of the International Auxiliary Language Association, for her help in reading proof. The compiler is especially happy to have the opportunity of expressing the deepest gratitude to Dr. Gode-von Aesch for his painstaking and untiring labor in reading proof for the entire book; and also for the continued support of the project by the International Auxiliary Language Association.

Helen S. Eaton

NOTE FOR THE USER

Organization of the List.—The 6,474 concepts contained in the following pages are arranged on a scale of descending frequency, as determined by their frequency position in the four individual languages examined: English, French, German, and Spanish. As one language had to be selected for the "key words" or "finding words" for the concepts, English was chosen; and the other languages follow in the order given above. This does not mean, however, that the List was made entirely from the English approach. The English source list was examined first, and equivalents for the English words in the other three language lists were sought. A relatively large number fell naturally and easily into place. Then the French source list was used as the language of approach for the words not already allotted. After that the German and the Spanish source lists were taken in turn in the same manner.

The correlated concepts are divided into seven units or groups of diminishing frequency—the first six units containing approximately 1,000 entries each and the seventh group approximately 500. Thus, Part I includes the first thousand, Part II, the second thousand, and so on to Part VII, which embraces only the first half of the seventh thousand. The parts are further subdivided into groups of diminishing frequency within each thousand. These sections vary in number in accordance with the formula, set forth in the Introduction, for determining the frequency series. Thus, in Part I, Sections 1., 1.1, 1.2, 1.3, and 1.4 contain 1,018 concepts appearing in the first thousand in two or more of the four languages, and in the first to the fifth thousand in the others. These subdivisions are numbered decimally. For example: Part I, Section 1.3, concepts 785–806, includes those words which occur in the first thousand in English and in German; in the first thousand either in French or in Spanish, and in the fourth thousand in the fourth language; *or* in the second thousand in French or in Spanish, and in the third thousand in the fourth language.

The Semantic List is therefore finally arranged in 115 subdivisions, called "sections," each of which consists of an alphabetical list of English key words followed by the words which represent a similar thought-content in the other three languages.

How to use the List.—For relative frequency of concepts, the arrangement by thousands in the seven parts, with their subdivisions in sections, shows the diminishing relationship in 115 stages as it appears in the alphabetical groups found in the sections. For locating a given concept in its serial position, reference should be made to the indexes. Here the word will be found in separate English, French, German, and Spanish groups, provided it occurs among the 6,474 items listed, and its position will be given in the section where it occurs. This will also disclose its frequency relationship to words having a similar semantic character in the other three languages. Thus, for any word coming into the semantic frequency range of the List, it is possible to determine its conceptual analogues in the other languages, and the frequency relation of these to each other and to the entire List.

EXPLANATION OF THE CODE AT THE BEGINNING OF EACH SECTION

At the beginning of each section there is a block of letters with numbers underneath. These letters stand for the four languages with which this book is concerned: *E* for English, *F* for French, *G* for German, and *S* for Spanish. In order to allocate the concepts expressed by the words in the book according to their frequency of use, as explained in the second paragraph of the section "Methodology" of the Introduction, the thousand position of the words (as determined by the thousand position of each word in the appropriate single-language frequency list) is indicated by numbers directly beneath the italic letters. For example, in Section 1.1:

E - *F* - *G* - *S*

1 - 1 - 1 - 2

1 - 2 - 1 - 1

shows that some of the words in the section occur among the first thousand in English, French, and German, but among the second thousand in Spanish, and that the other words in the section occur among the first thousand in English, German, and Spanish, but among the second thousand in French.

PART I

THE FIRST THOUSAND CONCEPTS

SECTION 1. CONCEPTS 1 THROUGH 662

E F G S

1-1-1-1

Read: English, first thousand; French, first thousand;
German, first thousand; Spanish, first thousand

English	French	German	Spanish
a[1a], an[1a]	un[1a]	ein[1a]	un, uno[1a]
(be) able[1b], can[1a], could[1a], cannot[1b], (can't[2b]), (couldst[3a]), (canst[3a]), (couldn't[3b])	pouvoir[1a]	können[1a], vermögen[1a]	poder[1a]
about[1a], (concerning[4a])	de[1a], (touchant[4a])	von[1a], über[1a], betreffend[1b], ([in] Betreff[4a]), (betreffs[5a]), (was[1a] . . . . anbetrifft[5a])	de[1a]
about[1a] (approximately)	environ[1b], (à peu près[5b])	etwa[1a], (ungefähr[2a]), (zirka[4a])	como[1a], cerca[1a]
(be) about[1a] (to), (just going to)	(être sur le) point (*n.*)[1a] de	(im) Begriff[1b] sein, (bevorstehen[6b])	estar[1a] a[1a] punto[1a] de[1a], estar[1a] para[1a]
above[1a] (*prep.*), over[1a], (o'er[3a])	au-dessus de[1b], supérieur[1b] à[1a], (par-dessus[3b])	über[1a], darüber[1a], (hierüber[3b]), (hinüber[4a]), (worüber[4b])	arriba[1a] de[1a], sobre[1a], encima[1b]
above[1a] (*adv.*), (overhead[4b]), (aloft[6])	supérieur[1b], (dessus[2b]), (par-dessus[3b]), (là-haut[3b]), (au-dessus[5a])	oben[1a], (oberhalb[5a])	arriba[1a]
above[1a] all[1a], especially (especial[2a]), (chiefly[6*]), (specially[6])	surtout[1a], avant[1a] tout[1a], (notamment[3a]), (spécialement[4a]), (principalement[4b])	besonders[1a], hauptsächlich[1b], insbesondere[1b], namentlich[1a], (ausdrücklich[2a]), (speziell[2b]), (zumal[2b]), (vorzugsweise[3b]), (vornehmlich[4b])	sobre[1a] todo[1a], especialmente (especial[1b]), (ante[5a] todo[1a])
accept[1b]	accepter[1a], (agréer[5b])	annehmen[1a], (akzeptieren[4b])	aceptar[1b]
account[1b] (*n.*), bill[1b]	compte[1a], (note[2b]), (facture[7a])	Rechnung[1b], (Konto[4b]), (Nota[4b]), (Rechenschaft[5a]), (Zeche[5b])	cuenta[1a], (factura[6b])
account[1b] for[1a], (explain[2a])	expliquer[1a]	erklären[1a], (deuten[3a]), (begreiflich[4a] machen[1a]), (erläutern[5b]), (auslegen[6a])	explicar[1b]
(be) across[1a], over[1a] there[1a]	en[1a] face[1a], de[1a] l'[1a]autre[1a] côté[1a], (vis à vis[3b])	gegenüber[1a], (hinüber[4a]), (herüber[5a]), (drüben[5a])	al[1a] otro[1a] lado[1a], frente[1a] a[1a]
act[1b] (take action)	agir[1b]	handeln[1a], wirken[1a]	proceder[1b], (obrar[2b]), (actuar[4b])
act[1b], (behave[4a])	se[1a] conduire[1a], (se[1a] comporter[3a])	handeln[1a], sich[1a] tragen[1a], sich[1a] führen[1a], (sich[1a] betragen[2a]), (sich[1a] anstellen[2b]), (sich[1a] aufführen[2b]), (sich[1a] benehmen[5a])	conducir[1b] se[1a], (portar[4a] se[1a])

English	French	German	Spanish
act[1b] (*n.*), (action[2b]), (deed[2a]), (doings[3b])	acte[1b], action[1b]	Handlung[1b], Tat[1a], (Akt[3b]), (Tun[5a])	acto[1a], hecho[1b], acción[1a]
(be) afraid[1b], fear[1a], (dread[2b]), ([be] fearful[3a]), ([be] affright[ed][5a])	craindre[1a], avoir[1a] peur[1b], (redouter[2a])	fürchten[1b], (Angst[2b] haben[1a]), (Furcht[2a] haben[1a]), (befürchten[3b])	temer[1a], tener[1a] miedo[1b]
after[1a], (hereafter[4b])	après[1a], (après que[5a])	nach[1a], nachdem[1a], (danach[2b]), (wonach[3b])	después[1a], tras[1b], ([en] pos[4b])
again[1a]	encore[1a] (une fois), de[1a] nouveau[1a]	wieder[1a], (wiederum[2a]), (nochmal[s][2b]), (abermals[3a])	de[1a] nuevo[1a], otra (otro[1a]) vez[1a], volver[1a] a[1a] . . . .
against[1a]	contre[1a]	gegen[1a], dagegen[1a], entgegen[1b], (wider[2a]), (wogegen[5b])	contra[1a]
age[1b] (years old)	âge[1b]	Alter[1b]	edad[1a]
ago[1b]	il[1a] y[1a] a (avoir[1a])	vor[1a]	ha, hace (hacer[1a])
air[1a] (to breathe)	air[1a]	Luft[1a], (Äther[6a])	aire[1a], (aura[5a])
all[1a] (*adv.*), quite[1b], (fully[3a]), (altogether[3b]), (wholly[4b]), (completely[6]*)	tout (*adv.*)[1a], tout à fait[1b], (complètement[2a]), (entièrement[2b]), (totalement[5b]), (pleinement[5b])	all[1a], ganz[1a], durchaus[1a], gar[1a], (vollends[4a])	todo[1a], completamente (completo[1a]), enteramente (entero[1a]), (totalmente [total[2a]]), (plenamente [pleno[2b]])
(not[1a] at[1a]) all[1a], in[1a] no[1a] way[1a]	(pas[1a] du[1a]) tout[1a], (nullement[2b]), (aucunement[5a])	überhaupt[1a] nicht[1a], (keineswegs[2a]), (garnicht[3b])	nada[1a] de[1a] eso[1a], de[1a] ningún[1a] modo[1a], (de ninguna) manera[1a], (de ninguna) forma[1a]
all[1a] right[1a]	bien[1a]	gut[1a], schön[1a]	bien[1a], bueno[1a]
allow[1b], let[1a], (permit[2a]), (let's[6]), (vouchsafe[6])	permettre[1a], laisser[1a]	erlauben[1b], gestatten[1b], lassen[1a], (zulassen[2b]), (anheim[4b] stellen), (belassen[5b])	permitir[1a], dejar[1a]
almost[1a], (nearly[3b]*)	presque[1a], (quasi[4b])	fast[1a], (ungefähr[2a]), (beinah[e][2b]), (nahezu[4b])	casi[1a]
alone[1a]	seul[1a]	allein[1a]	solo[1a]
already[1b]	déjà[1a]	schon[1a], bereits[1a]	ya[1a]
also[1a], too[1a]	aussi[1a], également[1b]	auch[1a], ebenfalls[1b], (gleichfalls[2b])	también[1a], igualmente (igual[1a]), además[1a]
although[1b], though[1a], (tho'[5a])	bien que[1b], (quoique[2b])	obgleich[1b], wenn[1a] auch[1a], (obwohl[2a]), (obschon[4b]), (wenngleich[5a]), (wiewohl[5a])	aunque[1a], aun[1a] cuando[1a]
always[1a], ever[1a], (forever[3b]), (e'er[4a]), (ay[5a]), (evermore[5b])	toujours[1a]	immer[1a], stets[1a], (jederzeit[4a]), (allemal[4b]), (von[1a] jeher[4b]), (allezeit[5b])	siempre[1a]
among[1a], (midst[3a]), (mid[4a]), (amid[5a]), (amongst[6])	parmi[1a], entre[1a]	unter[1a], zwischen[1a], (mitten[2a]), (dazwischen[4a]), (inmitten[5a])	entre[1a]
amount[1b], (quantity[2a]), (sum[2a])	somme[1b], (quantité[2b]), (montant [*n.*][6a])	Anzahl[1b], Menge[1b], Summe[1b], Betrag[1b], (Quantität[4a]), (Summa[6b]), (Quantum[6a])	cantidad[1b], (suma[2a]), (importe[5a]), (magnitud[6b])
and[1a]	et[1a]	und[1a]	e[1a], y[1a]
another[1a]	un[1a] autre[1a]	andere[1a]	otro[1a]
another's (another[1a])	(d')un[1a] autre[1a], ([d']autrui[6a])	eines (ein[1a]) anderen (andere[1a])	ajeno[1b]
answer[1a] (*vb.*), reply[1b], (respond[5a])	répondre[1a], (repartir[2b]), (répliquer[3a]), (riposter[6b])	antworten[1b], erwidern[1b], (beantworten[3a]), (entgegnen[4b])	responder[1a], contestar[1a], (replicar[2a])

English	French	German	Spanish
any[1a], some[1a]	quelque[1a], en[1a]	einige[1a], welche[1a], etwas[1a]	alguno[1a]
any[1a] (whatever)	n'[1a] importe (importer[1b])	irgend[1a], (beliebig[3b]), (jeglich[4b]), (jedweder[6b])	cualquier(-a)[1a]
anything[1b], something[1a], (aught[6])	quelque[1a] chose[1a]	etwas[1a]	algo[1a], alguna (alguno[1a]) cosa[1a]
appear[1b] (come into view), (loom[5a])	paraître[1a], apparaître[1a], (reparaître[3b]), (comparaître[7a])	erscheinen[1a], vorkommen[1b], (auftreten[2b]), ([zum] Vorschein[6a] [kommen]), (sich[1a] einfinden[6b])	aparecer[1a], asomar[1b], (comparecer[5b]), (despuntar[5b])
appear[1b], look[1a], seem[1a]	sembler[1a], paraître[1a]	scheinen[1a], (aussehen[3a])	parecer[1a]
arm[1a] (part of body)	bras[1a]	Arm[1a]	brazo[1a]
arm[1a], (weapon[3a])	arme[1b]	Waffe[1b], (Gewehr[2b])	arma[1b]
art[1b]	art[1b]	Kunst[1a]	arte[1a]
as[1a], since[1a]	puisque[1a], (d'autant que[5a])	da[1a], denn[1a]	pues[1a], puesto (poner[1a]) que[1]
as[1a], like[1a] *(prep.)*	comme[1a]	wie[1a], gleich[1a], (gleichwie[6b])	como[1a]
as[1a] (e.g., I was walking)	comme[1a]	als[1a], indem[1a]	al[1a], (a) medida[1b] (a)
as[1a] for[1a], as[1a] to[1a], ([with] regard[2a] [to]), (concerning[4a])	quant à[1b], ([à l']égard[2a] [de]), (à propos de[3a])	(in) Bezug[1b] (auf), (mit) Rücksicht[1b] (auf), (in) Beziehung[1b] (auf), (bezüglich[2a]), (anlangend [anlangen[2b]]), (hinsichtlich[3a]), ([in] Hinblick[5a] [auf]), ([was . . . .] anbelangt[6a])	en[1a] cuanto[1a] a[1a], (en) atención[1b] (a), respecto (respe[c]to[1a]), (acerca[2a])
as[1a] soon[1a] as[1a]	dès que[1b], (aussitôt que[5a])	sobald[1b]	tan[1a] pronto[1a] como[1a]
ask[1a] (a question), (inquire[3a]), (enquire[5b])	demander[1a]	fragen[1a], (sich[1a] erkundigen[4b])	preguntar[1a], (averiguar[2b]), (inquirir[4b])
ask[1a] (a favor), (beg[2a]), (bid[2a]), (pray[2a]), (request[2b]), (bade[3a]), (solicit[5a])	prier[1b], (solliciter[4a]), (requérir[5a]), (interpeller[6a])	bitten[1a], (ersuchen[3a]), (erbitten[3b])	pedir[1a], rogar[1a], (solicitar[2a])
at[1a]	à[1a]	an[1a], zu[1a], daran[1a], (woran[4a]), (hieran[6b])	a[1a], en[1a]
away[1a], off[1a]	loin[1a], (parti [partir[1a]])	fort[1a], ab[1a], (weg[2a]), (hinweg[3a])	lejos[1a], fuera[1a]
(in) back[1a] (of), behind[1a]	derrière[1a]	hinter[1a], (dahinter[6a])	tras[1b], detrás[1b]
back[1a] (be back)	de[1a] retour[1b]	zurück[1a]	de[1a] vuelta[1b], (de[1a] regreso[3b])
bad[1a]	mauvais[1a], mal[1a], (fichu [*adj.*][6b])	schlecht[1b], (schlimm[2a]), (arg[4a])	mal(o)[1a], (vicioso[5b])
be[1a], am[1a], are[1a], been[1a], being[1a], is[1a], was[1a], were[1a], (I'm[2b]), ('tis[3a]), ('twas[3b]), (it's[4b]), (you're[4b]), ('twere[4b]), (wast[4b]), (wert[4b]), (wasn't[5a]), (isn't[6]), (he's[6])	être[1a], se[1a] trouver[1a], (figurer[6b])	sein[1a]	estar[1a], ser[1a]
bear[1a], stand[1a], (borne[3b]), (endure[3a]), (undergo[5b])	souffrir[1a], supporter[1a], subir[1b], (tolérer[4b])	leiden[1b], (dulden[3b]), (vertragen[4b]), (aushalten[4a]), (durchmachen[6a]), (leidlich[6a])	sufrir[1a], sostener[1b], (aguantar[3b]), (soportar[3a]), (tolerar[4a]), (resistir[2a])
beat[1b] (in a game), win[1b]	battre[1a], gagner[1a]	schlagen[1a], gewinnen[1a]	ganar[1a]

English	French	German	Spanish
beautiful[1a], (handsome[2b]), (beauteous[6])	beau[1a]	schön[1a]	bello[1a], hermoso[1a], (guapo[2b]), (vistoso[4b])
because[1a], for[1a] (*conj.*)	parce que[1a], car[1a], (aussi bien[6a])	weil[1a], denn[1a], da[1a]	porque[1a], pues[1a]
because[1a] of [1a], on[1a] account[1b] of	à[1a] cause[1a] de[1a]	wegen[1a], (infolge[2a])	a[1a] causa[1a] de[1a]
become[1a], get[1a], got[1a], grow[1a], grew[1b], (became[2a])	devenir[1a], (redevenir[2b])	werden[1a], (geraten[2a])	hacer[1a] se, llegar[1a] (a ser)
before[1a] (time) (*prep.* and *adv.*), (ere[2a]), (heretofore[6])	avant[1a], avant de[1b], (auparavant[2b])	vor[1a], ehe[1a], vorher[1b], (bevor[2b]), (vorhin[3b])	antes[1a], anteriormente (anterior[1b])
before[1a], (in) front[1a] (of)	devant[1a]	vor[1a], (voraus[2a])	delante[1a] (de), frente[1a] (a), (ante[5a])
begin[1a], start[1a], began[1b], (begun[2b]), (commence[3b]), (launch[5a]), (beginning[5b]*)	commencer[1a], se mettre à[1b], (débuter[4b])	beginnen[1a], in[1a] Angriff[1b] nehmen[1a], anfangen[1a]*, (eingreifen[3a]), (einsetzen[3b]), (ansetzen[5a])	empezar[1a], comenzar[1a], (estrenar[3b]), (principiar[3b]), (iniciar[3b]), (entablar[4a])
begin[1a] again[1a], (resume[4a])	recommencer[1b]		
being[1a] (*n.*)	être[1b]	Wesen[1a]	ser[1b]
believe[1a]	croire[1a]	glauben[1a]	creer[1a]
belong[1b], (pertain[6])	appartenir[1b]	gehören[1b], (angehören[2b]), (zustehen[3b])	pertenecer[1b]
beside[1b]	auprès de[1b], à[1a] côté[1a] de[1a]	neben[1a], bei[1a], nächst (nah[1a])	al[1a] lado[1a] de[1a], junto[1a] (a)
best[1a]	(le) meilleur[1a], (le) mieux[1a]	beste[1a], (Beste[2b]) (bestens[6a])	(el) mejor[1a]
better[1a]	meilleur[1a], mieux[1a]	besser[1a]	mejor[1a]
between[1a]	entre[1a]	zwischen[1a], unter[1a]	entre[1a]
big[1a], large[1a], (massy[6])	grand[1a], gros[1a]	groß[1a]	gran(de)[1a], (corpulento[6b] [person])
black[1a], (sable[6])	noir[1a]	schwarz[1b]	negro[1a]
blood[1b], (gore[5b])	sang[1b]	Blut[1b]	sangre[1a]
body[1a]	corps[1a]	Körper[1b], (Leib[2a])	cuerpo[1a]
book[1a]	livre[1b]	Buch[1a]	libro[1a]
(be) born[1b]	naître[1a], (renaître[4a]), (né [*adj.*][6b])	geboren (gebären[1b]) (werden)	nacer[1a], (renacer[4a])
both[1a]	l'[1a]un[1a] et[1a] l'[1a]autre[1a], (tous[5b] [les] deux[1a])	beide (B)[1a]	ambos[1a], (entrambos[3b])
bottom[1b]	fond[1a], bas[1b]	Boden[1a], Grund[1a]	fondo[1a]
(be) brave[1b], (gallant[4a]), (valiant[4b]), (heroic[4b]), (fearless[5b]), (courageous[6]), (stout[3a] hearted[6])	avoir[1a] du[1a] courage[1b], (être) brave[1b], (vaillant[4a]), (courageux[4a]), (intrépide[6b]) (bravement[5a]), (courageusement[5b]), (hardiment[6a])	Mut[1b] haben[1a], (brav[2b] sein), (kühn[2b]), (tapfer[3a]), (wacker[4a]), (mutig[4b])	(ser) valiente[1b], (bravo[2b]), (guapo[2b]), (valeroso[4a]), (intrépido[5a]), (animoso[6a])
bring[1a], brought[1a]	apporter[1a], amener[1b], (emmener[2b])	bringen[1a], (einbringen[3b]), (mitbringen[4a]), (hineinbringen[6b])	traer[1a]
brother[1a], (brethren[4a])	frère[1b]	Bruder[1a], (Geschwister[5a])	hermano[1a]
business[1b]	affaire[1a]	Geschäft[1a], Handel[1b], (Terminhandel[3a]), (Handelsgeschäft[4b]), (Termingeschäft[5a]), (Handelssache[6b])	asunto[1b], negocio[1b]

English	French	German	Spanish
busy[1b]	occupé (occuper[1a]), (s'occuper[2a]), (affairé[4b])	beschäftigt (beschäftigen[1b]), schaffen[1a], wirken[1a], (obliegen[4b])	ocupado (ocupar[1a])
(busily[6])			
but[1a]	mais[1a]	aber[1a], sondern[1a]	mas[1a], pero[1a], sino[1a]
by[1a] (agent-instrument), (whereby[4b])	de[1a], par[1a]	von[1a], durch[1a], (per[2b])	por[1a]
by[1a], (according[2a] [to]), ([as] per[2b]), ([in] accordance[6] [with])	selon[1b], suivant[1b], (d'après[2a])	nach[1a], (gemäß[2b]), (demgemäß[3b]), (hiernach[3b]), (zufolge[4a])	según[1a], (conforme[2a]), ([de] acuerdo[2a]), ([con] arreglo[3a])
call[1a] (*vb.*)	appeler[1a]	rufen[1a]	llamar[1a]
care[1a], (solicitude[10])	soin[1b], (sollicitude[6a])	Sorge[1b], (Pflege[3b]), (Besorgnis[3b]), (Sorgfalt[3b]), (Fürsorge[4b]), (Aufsicht[5a]), (Schonung[5b])	cuidado[1a], (solicitud[3a]), (esmero[4a]), (cautela[6a]), (recato[6a]), (miramiento[6b])
(take[1a]) care[1a] (of[1a]), care[1a] for[1a], mind[1a], attend[1b], (nurse[2a])	prendre[1a], avoir[1a] soin[1b] de[1a], (soigner[2a])	pflegen[1b], (sorgen[2a]), (achten[2a]), (besorgen[2a]), (schonen[3b]), (vorsehen[3b]), (nachsehen[4b])	atender[1b], cuidar[1b]
carry[1a], (convey[4b])	porter[1a]	tragen[1a], bringen[1a]	cargar[1a], llevar[1a]
carry[1a] out[1a], carry[1a] through[1a], (accomplish[2b]), (perform[2b]), (execute[4a]), (fulfil[l][4a]), (achieve[4b])	remplir[1a], (accomplir[2a]), (exécuter[2a]), (accompli[3b])	erfüllen[1b], ausführen[1b], (zur) Ausführung[1b] (bringen), (erzielen[2a]), (durchführen[2b]), (vollziehen[2b]), ([in] Erfüllung[2b] [bringen]), (vollbringen[4b]), (verrichten[5a]), (ausrichten[5b])	cumplir[1a], (ejecutar[2a]), (desempeñar[2b])
case[1a]	cas[1a]	Fall[1a]	caso[1a]
(in any) case[1a], (anyway[4b]), (anyhow[6])	(en tout) cas[1a]	jedenfalls[1b], (immerhin[2b]), (ohnehin[4a])	(de todos) modos (modo[1a]), (en todo) caso[1a], (en cualquier) caso[1a]
cause[1a] (*n.*)	cause[1a]	Grund[1a], Ursache[1b], (Anlaß[2b]), (Veranlassung[2b]), (Motiv[2b])	causa[1a], motivo[1b]
cause[1a], make[1a], (render[2b])	causer[1b], faire[1a]	lassen[1a], machen[1a], (bewirken[2a]), (veranlassen[2a]), (herbeiführen[6a]), (verursachen[3a]), (zufügen[3b]), (gereichen[5a])	hacer[1a], causar[1b], (ocasionar[2b]), (motivar[5a])
center[1b], middle[1b] (place)	milieu[1a], (centre[2a])	Mitte[1b], Mittelpunkt[1b], (Zentrum[3a])	medio[1a], centro[1b]
chance[1b], (occasion[2a]), (opportunity[2b])	occasion[1a], chances (chance[1b])	Gelegenheit[1a]	ocasión[1a], (oportunidad[3b])
character[1b]	caractère[1a]	Charakter[1b]	carácter[1b]
chief[1a] (*adj.*), head[1a], (main[2a]), (principal[2b]), (major[4a]), (prime[4a]), (foremost[4b])	chef[1b], principal[1b], (capital [*adj.*][4a]), (majeur[4a]), (prime[5a])	hauptsächlich[1b], (Haupt-[2a]), (Hauptsache[2a]), (Hauptgrund[4b]), (Hauptaufgabe[5b])	mayor[1a], principal[1a], (máximo[5a])
child[1a], children[1a], (infant[3b]), (offspring[5b])	enfant[1a]	Kind[1a], Kleine[1a]	niño[1a], (párvulo[6a])

English	French	German	Spanish
choose[1b], pick[1b] (out[1a]), (chose[2a]), (select[2b])	choisir[1b]	wählen[1b], (erwählen[4b]), (aussuchen[5b]), (auswählen[6a])	escoger[1b]
church[1a]	église[1b]	Kirche[1b]	iglesia[1b]
city[1a], town[1a]	ville[1a], (cité[2a])	Stadt[1a], (Städtchen[5a])	ciudad[1a], (villa[2b])
class[1b] (*n.*)	classe[1b]	Klasse[1b]	clase[1b]
clean[1b] (*adj.*)	net[1b], (propre[2b])	rein[1a], (sauber[4b])	limpio[1b]
clear[1a], plain[1a], (distinct[3a]), (vivid[5b])	clair[1a], net[1b], (distinct[3a])	klar[1a], deutlich[1b], (erkennbar[5a]), (anschaulich[6a])	claro[1a], (cristalino[4a]), (límpido[6b])
	(nettement[2b]), (clairement[4b])	([mit] Entschiedenheit[6a])	
close[1a], shut[1b]	fermer[1a], (clos[3a]), (refermer[3a])	schließen[1a], (zufallen[5a])	cerrar[1a], (cerrado[5b])
cold[1a] (*adj.*)	froid[1b] (froidement[3b])	kalt[1b]	frío[1a], (yerto[6b])
color[1a] (*n.*)	couleur[1b]	Farbe[1b]	color[1a], (colorido[6a])
come[1a], came[1a], coming[1b]	venir[1a]	kommen[1a]	venir[1a]
come[1a] from[1a], (proceed[2a]), (arise[3a]), (arose[3a]), (derive[4a])	venir[1a] de[1a], ([avoir son] origine[2a] [dans]), (provenir[4a]), (émaner[5a])	entstehen[1a], kommen[1a], (entspringen[3a]), (stammen[3a]), (ableiten[5a]), (herrühren[5a]), (erstehen[6b])	venir[1a] de[1a], nacer[1a], proceder[1b], (originar[3a]), (derivado+derivar[4b]), (provenir[4b]), (emanar[5a]), (procedente[6b])
company[1a] (business), firm[1b], (society[2b]), (association[4b])	société[1b], (compagnie[2a]), (association[3a])	Gesellschaft[1a], (Firma[2a]), (Kompagnie[2a]), (Handelsgesellschaft[4a]), (Korporation[6b])	compañía[1b], sociedad[1b], (firma[2b]), (asociación[5a])
company[1a] (social), (society[2b]), (association[4b])	monde[1a], société[1b]	Gesellschaft[1a], Verein[1b], (Genossenschaft[2b]), (Berufsgenossenschaft[6b])	compañía[1b], sociedad[1b], (asociación[5a])
complete[1b], entire[1b], whole[1a]	tout[1a], complet[1b], entier[1b], (intact[4a])	ganz[1a], gesamt[1b], sämtlich[1b], völlig[1b], vollkommen[1b], vollständig[1b], (gänzlich[2a])	completo[1a], entero[1a], (harto[2a]), (íntegro[4b])
complete[1b],(conclude[3a])	achever[1b], (conclure[2a]), (consommer[3a]), (compléter[3a]), (accompli[3b])	vollenden[1b], (ergänzen[4a]), (ausarbeiten[5a])	concluir[1b], (completar[3b]), (consumar[4a]), (rematar[4a])
condition[1b]	condition[1b]	Zustand[1a], Umstand[1a], Bedingung[1b]	condición[1a]
contain[1b]	contenir[1b]	enthalten[1a]	contener[1b], encerrar[1b]
continue[1b]	continuer[1a]	dauern[1b], (fortsetzen[2a]), (fortfahren[4a]), (fortdauern[4b]), (fortführen[5b])	continuar[1b], (proseguir[2a])
count[1b] (*vb.*)	compter[1a]	rechnen[1b], (zählen[2a])	contar[1a]
count[1b] on[1a], (depend[2b] on), (rely[6] on)	compter[1a] sur[1a], (avoir) confiance[1b] (en), (s'attendre[4b]), (se fier[6b] à)	rechnen[1b] auf[1a], (sich) verlassen[1a] auf, (vertrauen[2b] auf)	contar[1a] con[1a], (depender[2b] de), (confiar[2a])
country[1a] (geographical)	pays[1a]	Land[1a]	país[1a], tierra[1a]
country[1a] (not town)	campagne[1a]	Land[1a]	campo[1a], (campaña[2a]), (campiña[4a])
(of) course[1a]	bien[1a] sûr[1a], (bien[1a] entendu[2a]), naturellement[1b]	natürlich[1a], nämlich[1a], gewiß[1a], (selbstverständlich[2b]), (bekanntlich[2b])	por[1a] supuesto (+suponer)[1a], naturalmente (natural[1a]), claro[1a], seguro[1a]

English	French	German	Spanish
court[1b] (royal)	cour[1a]	Hof[1b]	corte[1b]
court[1b], (woo[4a])	faire[1a] la[1a] cour[1a], (courtiser[6b])	Hof[1b] machen[1a], (werben[5a])	hacer[1a] la[1a] corte[1b], enamorar[1b], (cortejar[7a])
cover[1a] (*vb.*)	couvrir[1b], (recouvrir[2a]), (draper[6b])	decken[1b], (bedecken[2a]), (belegen[3b]), (überziehen[4a])	cubrir[1a], (tapar[2b])
cross[1a], go[1a] across[1a], (traverse[5b])	traverser[1a], (franchir[2a])	über[1a] . . . . gehen[1a], (übergehen[2a]), (hinüber[4a] gehen[1a]), (kreuzen[5b])	cruzar[1b], atravesar[1b], (traspasar[3a])
crowd[1b], (throng[3b]), (multitude[3b])	foule[1b], (multitude[4a])	Menge[1b], Masse[1b]	gente[1a], (multitud[2b]), (muchedumbre[2b]), (tropel[4b])
cry[1b], cried[1b], shout[1b], (scream[3a]), (shriek[3b]), (cries[4a]), (yell[4a]), (hoot[6])	crier[1b]	rufen[1a], (schreien[2b]), (zurufen[5b])	gritar[1b], (clamar[3a]), (chillar[5b])
dare[1b], (daring[6])	oser[1a]	wagen[1b]	atreverse[1a], (osar[2b])
dark[1a] (*adj.*)	sombre[1b], (obscur[2a])	dunkel[1b], (finster[3a]), (düster[4a])	obscuro[1a], (tenebroso[3b])
daughter[1b]	fille[1a]	Tochter[1a]	hija (hijo[1a])
day[1a], (daytime[5b])	jour[1a], journée[1b]	Tag[1a]	día[1a]
(the) day[1a] (after), (morrow[4b])	lendemain[1b]	(der nächste) Tag[1a]	el[1a] día[1a] siguiente[1a]
dear[1a] (in affection)	cher[1a]	lieb[1a], teuer[1b]	querido[1b], (caro[3b])
death[1a]	mort[1a], (décès[5b])	Tod[1a]	muerte[1a]
decide[1b], (doom[3b]), (resolve[3a])	décider[1b], (se décider[4a]), (s'aviser de[5a])	entscheiden[1a], beschließen[1b], bestimmen[1b], (entschließen[2a])	decidir[1b], decidir (se)
deep[1a], (profound[5a])	profond[1a] (profondément[2b])	tief[1a]	profundo[1a], (hondo[2a])
delight[1b], joy[1b], (gladness[6])	joie[1b], (allégresse[6a])	Freude[1a], (Entzücken[4b]), (Jubel[5b])	alegría[1b], (delicia[3a]), (gozo[3a]), (deleite[3b]), (regocijo[3b])
demand[1b], (exact[2a])	réclamer[1b], (exiger[7a]), (requérir[5a])	fordern[1b], verlangen[1b], (in) Anspruch[1b] (nehmen)	exigir[1b], (requerir[2b]), (demandar[3b])
desire[1b] (*n.*), wish[1a]	désir[1b], envie[1b], (souhait[6a])	Wunsch[1a], (Begierde[5a])	deseo[1a]
desire[1b] (*vb.*), want[1a], wish[1a]	désirer[1b], vouloir[1a], (souhaiter[2a])	wünschen[1a], (begehren[3b]), (erwünschen[3b])	desear[1a], querer[1a], ([tener] gana[2a]), (antojarse[3b]), (apetecer[4a])
die[1a], (expire[4b]), (decease[5b])	mourir[1a], (décéder[5a])	sterben[1a]	morir[1a], (fallecer[3b]), (fenecer[6a])
different[1b], (various[2a]), (unlike[4b])	autre[1a], différent[1b], divers[1b]	anders[1a], verschieden[1a], (mancherlei[3a]), (verschiedenartig[4b]), (zweierlei[6b])	vario[1a], diferente[1b], distinto[1b], diverso[1b]
direct[1b], (boss[6])	diriger[1a]	richten[1a], weisen[1b], (lenken[3a])	dirigir[1a]
direct[1b], straight[1b]	droit (*adj.*)[1a], (direct[3a])	gerade[1a], direkt[1b], unmittelbar[1b]	derecho[1a], (directo[2a]), (recto[2b])
direction[1b] (toward)	sens[1a], (direction[2a])	Richtung[1a]	dirección[1b], (rumbo[2b])
do[1a], did[1a], does[1a], done[1a], don't[1b], (didn't[3a]), (doth[3a]), (doesn't[3b]), (dost[4a])	faire[1a]	machen[1a], tun[1a], leisten[1b]	hacer[1a], cumplir[1a]
do[1a] (auxiliary)	(within the verb)	(within the verb)	(within the verb)

English	French	German	Spanish
doctor[1b], (physician[3a]), (Dr.[5b])	médecin[1b], (docteur[2b]), (chirurgien[6a])	Doktor[1a], (Arzt[2a])	doctor[1b], (médico[2a])
door[1a]	porte[1a]	Tür[1b], (Haustür[3b])	puerta[1a]
doubt[1b] (*n.*)	doute[1a]	Zweifel[1b], (Bedenken[2a]), (Unsicherheit[5b]), (Ungewißheit[6b])	duda[1a]
(without[1a]) doubt[1b], (doubtless[4a])	sans[1a] (aucun) doute[1a]	ohne[1a] Zweifel[1b], (zweifellos[3b]), (unzweifelhaft[3b])	sin[1a] duda[1a], (indudable[3a])
down[1a] (*adv.*)	en[1a] bas[1a]	nieder[1b], unten[1b], (herab[2b]), (hinab[3a]), (herunter[4a]), (hinunter[4b])	abajo[1b]
drive[1a] (*intr. vb.*), (drove[2b]), ride[1a] (Amer.), (rode[2b])	aller[1a] en[1a] voiture[1b], se[1a] promener[1b] en voiture	fahren[1a], (auffahren[6b])	ir[1a]
drive[1a] (car, etc.), (drove[2b])	conduire[1a]	fahren[1a] (mit)	conducir[1b], (manejar[3b])
drive[1a] (horse), (drove[2b])	conduire[1a]	treiben[1b]	conducir[1b]
drive[1a] (*tr. vb.*) (force)	pousser[1a]	treiben[1b]	echar[1a]
drop[1a] (*tr. vb.*)	laisser[1a] tomber[1a]	fallen[1a] lassen[1a]	dejar[1a] caer[1a]
during[1a]	pendant[1a], (durant[2a])	während[1a]	durante[1a]
duty[1b] (obligation)	devoir[1b]	Pflicht[1b], (Verpflichtung[2a]), (Schuldigkeit[6a])	deber[1b]
each[1a] (*adj.*)	chaque[1a]	jeder[1a]	cada[1a]
each[1a] (*pron.*), (apiece[5a])	chacun[1a]	jeder[1a]	cada[1a] uno[1a]
each[1a] other[1a], one[1a] another[1a]	se[1a], l'[1a]un[1a] l'[1a]autre[1a]	sich[1a], einander[1a]	se[1a], el[1a] uno[1a] al[1a] otro[1a]
earth[1a], soil[1b]	terre[1a], sol[1b]	Erde[1a], Boden[1a]	tierra[1a], suelo[1a]
easy[1b], (easier[4b])	facile[1b], (aisé[3b]) (aisément[4a])	leicht[1a]	fácil[1a]
either[1b] (*conj.*)	ou[1a]	entweder[1b]	o[1a], u[1a]
either[1b] (one)	l'[1a]un[1a] ou[1a] l'[1a]autre[1a]	der[1a] eine[1a] oder[1a] der[1a] andere[1a]	el[1a] uno[1a] o[1a] el[1a] otro[1a]
end[1a] (*tr. vb.*), finish[1b], (ending[4b])	finir[1a], terminer[1b], (fini [*adj.*][3b])	fertig[1b] machen[1a], schließen[1a], (enden[3a]), (fertigen[4a]), (endigen[5a])	acabar[1a], terminar[1a]
end[1a], (ending[4b]), (conclusion[4b])	fin (*n.*)[1a], bout[1a], terme[1b], (conclusion[3b]), (consommation[4b])	Ende[1a], Schluß[1b]	fin[1a], término[1a], cabo[1b], (conclusión[3a]), (remate[5b]), (terminación[5b])
enemy[1b], (foe[2b])	ennemi[1a]	Feind[1a]	enemigo[1a]
English[1b] (native language and person), American[1b], (British[2b]), (Englishman[4a]), (Englander[4a]), (Briton[6])	français[1a], (Français [*n.*][5a])	deutsch[1a], Deutsche[1b]	español[1a]
(subdivisions) Indian[1b], (Irish[4b]), (Scotch[4b]), (Scot[5a])	(basque[5b]), (gaulois[5b]), (breton[6a])	(sächsisch[3b]), (westfälisch[5a]), (böhmisch[5b]), (hessisch[6a]), (württembergisch[6a]), (schlesisch[6b])	castellano[1b], (andaluz[3a]), (gallego[3a]), (madrileño[4a]), (vizcaino[4a]), (catalán[4b]), (chileno[5a]), (aragonés[5b]), (asturiano[6b]), (manchego[6b]), (navarro[6b]), (valenciano[6b])
enough[1a]	assez[1a]	genug[1a], ([zur] Genüge[5a]), (genugsam[6b])	bastante[1a]

English	French	German	Spanish
(be) enough[1a], (suffice[3b])	suffire[1a]	genügen[1b], langen[1b], (ausreichen[2b]), (hinreichen[3a])	bastar (+basta)[1a]
enter[1b]	entrer[1a], rentrer[1a], pénétrer[1b]	eintreten[1a], eingehen[1b], (einkommen[2a]), (betreten[3a]), (herein[3a] kommen[1a]), (einziehen[3b]), (einlaufen[6a])	entrar[1a], penetrar[1b], (internar[5b] se)
equal[1b] (*adj.*)	égal[1b]	gleich[1a], ebenso[1a], (gleichmäßig[2b])	igual[1a]
(equally)	également[1b]	ebenfalls[1b]	por[1a] igual
even[1a] (*adv.*)	même[1a], (voire[4b])	selbst[1a], sogar[1a], (mal[2b])	aun, aún[1a]
evening[1b]	soir[1a], (soirée[2a])	Abend[1a]	tarde[1a], (velada[5b])
ever[1a], (e'er[4a]) (e.g., have you – seen . . . .)	jamais[1a]	je[1a], (jemals[3a])	jamás[1a], nunca[1a]
every[1a]	chaque[1a], tout[1a]	all[1a], jeder[1a]	cada[1a]
expect[1b]	attendre[1a], (s'attendre[3a] à)	erwarten[1a], (harren[4a]), (entgegensehen[5b])	aguardar[1b], esperar[1a]
express[1b] (*vb.*)	exprimer[1b]	darstellen[1b], äußern[1b], (ausdrücken[2b])	expresar[1b], (denotar[6b])
extend[1b], (stretch[2a]), (rack[3a]), (span[5a]), (expand[6])	étendre[1b], tendre (*vb.*)[1a]	reichen[1b], langen[1b], (ausdehnen[2a]), (erstrecken[3a]), (erweitern[6a]), (spannen[3b]), (strecken[3b]), (dehnen[5b]), (ausstrecken[6a])	extender[1b], (ensanchar[3b]), (estirar[3b])
eye[1a] (*n.*)	œil (yeux)[1a]	Auge[1a]	ojo[1a]
face[1a] (part of head)	figure[1a], visage[1a], face[1a]	Gesicht[1b], (Angesicht[3b])	cara[1a], rostro[1b], (semblante[2b]), (faz[3a])
fact[1b]	fait[1a]	Tatsache[1b]	hecho[1b], realidad[1b]
(in) fact[1b]	(en) effet[1a], (de) fait[1a], (en) fait[1a]	(in der) Tat[1a]	(en) efecto[1a]
fall[1a], fell[1b], (tumble[3a]), (fallen[3b])	tomber[1a], (dégringoler[6a])	fallen[1a], (sinken[2a]), (stürzen[2b])	caer[1a], (desplomar[4b])
family[1a]	famille[1a]	Familie[1b]	familia[1a]
far[1a], (distant[2a]), (farther[2a]), (remote[4b]), (farthest[5a]), (afar[5b]), (far-off[6])	loin[1a], (lointain[2a]), (éloigné[4a]), (distant[5a])	weit[1a], fern[1a], (weiterhin[6a]), (weithin[6b])	lejos[1a], (a[1a] legua[2a]), (lejano[2a]), (remoto[2a]), (distante[2b]), (en[1a] lontananza[5b]), (distar[6b] [to be –])
fast[1a], quick[1a], rapid[1b], (swift[2a]), (fleet[2b]), (hasty[4b]), (speedy[4b]), (brisk[5a]), (hastily[5a])	vite[1a], vif[1b], rapide[1b], (rapidement[2a]), (vivement[2b]), (précipitamment[5b])	schnell[1a], rasch[1b], (eilig[3b]), (geschwind[6b]), (schleunig[4b])	pronto[1a], vivo[1a], rápido[1b], (apresurado [apresurar[2b]]), (presto[2b]), (precipitado[3a]), (veloz[3a]), (vertiginoso[6a])
father[1a], (sire[3b])	père[1a]	Vater[1a]	padre[1a]
feel[1a], felt[1b], feeling[1b]	sentir[1a], éprouver[1b]	fühlen[1a], empfinden[1b], (spüren[5b])	sentir[1a]
feeling[1b], (sentiment[5b]), (emotion[5b])	sentiment[1b], émotion[1b], (attendrissement[5a])	Gefühl[1a], Gemüt[1b], (Gesinnung[2a]), (Rührung[5b])	sentimiento[1a], sentir[1a], (emoción[2a])
(a) few[1a]	peu[1a], plusieurs[1a], quelques (quelque[1a])	wenige (wenig[1a]), einige[1a], (ein[1a] paar[2a]), (etliche[4a])	pocos (poco[1a])
field[1a]	champ[1b]	Feld[1b], (Acker[5a])	campo[1a]
figure[1b] (*n.*), form[1a], shape[1b]	forme[1a], taille[1b]	Figur[1b], Form[1a], Gestalt[1b]	figura[1a], forma[1a], (talle[3a]) (of person)

English	French	German	Spanish
find^{1a}, found^{1a}	trouver^{1a}, retrouver^{1a}	finden^{1a}, (auffinden^{4b}), (vorfinden^{5a}), (ausmitteln^{6b})	hallar^{1a}, encontrar^{1a}
fine^{1a} (*adj.*) (not coarse)	fin (*adj.*)^{1b}	fein^{1b}	fino^{1b}
fire^{1a} (*n.*)	feu^{1a}, (incendie^{4b})	Feuer^{1b}, (Brand^{3b})	fuego^{1a}, (lumbre^{2b}), (incendio^{3a}), (hoguera^{4a})
first^{1a}, (foremost^{4b}), (primary^{5b})	premier^{1a}	erste (E)^{1a}	primero^{1a}, (delantero^{4a}), (primario^{6b})
(at) first^{1a}	d'abord^{1a}, (en) premier^{1a} lieu^{1a}	zuerst^{1a}, (am) Anfang^{1b}, (anfangs^{2b}), (anfänglich^{4b}), (erstens^{5a}), (zuvörderst^{5b}), (vorerst^{6b})	primero^{1a}, (al) principio^{1a}, (en primer) lugar^{1a}
fit^{1b} (*vb.*), suit^{1b}, (be) fit (for), (suitable^{4b})	convenir^{1a}	sich^{1a} eignen^{1b}, (passen^{2a}), (sich^{1a} anpassen^{5a}), (taugen^{6a})	convenir^{1b}, caber^{1b}, (conformar^{4a}), (cuadrar^{4b}), (encajar^{6b})
five^{1a}	cinq^{1a}	fünf^{1b}	cinco^{1*}
fix^{1b} (make fast)	fixer^{1b}, (fixe [*adj.*]^{3a})	fest^{1a} machen^{1a}, (befestigen^{2a}), (fixieren^{6a})	asegurar^{1b}, fijar^{1b}, afirmar^{1b}, (afianzar^{6b})
follow^{1a}, following^{1b}, (ensue^{5a})	suivre^{1a}, (s'ensuivre^{7a})	folgen^{1a}, (nachgehen^{6a})	seguir^{1a}
foot^{1a}, feet^{1a}	pied^{1a}	Fuß^{1a}	pie^{1a}
for^{1a} (*prep.*), ([in] behalf^{4b}), (therefor^{6})	pour^{1a}	für^{1a}, dafür^{1a}, (hierfür^{4a}), (wofür^{4b})	para^{1a}, por^{1a}, ([en] pro^{6a})
for^{1a}, (in) favor^{1b} (of)	pour^{1a}, (en) faveur^{1b} (de)	für^{1a}, dafür^{1a}	por^{1a}, (a) favor^{1a} (de)
force^{1b}, (oblige^{2b}), (compel^{3a}), (enforce^{5b}), (constrain^{6})	obliger^{1a}, forcer^{1b}, (contraindre^{3b})	zwingen^{1b}, (nötigen^{2a}), (erzwingen^{5b})	obligar^{1a}, (forzar^{3b})
force^{1b}, strength^{1b}, (vigor^{3b})	force^{1a}, (vigueur^{5a}), (solidité^{6a})	Macht^{1a}, Kraft^{1a}, Gewalt^{1b}, (Stärke^{2b})	fuerza^{1a}, (vigor^{3a}), (fortaleza^{3b}), (entereza^{5b})
forest^{1b}, wood^{1a}, (grove^{2b}), (woodland^{4b}),	bois^{1a}, (forêt^{2a})	Wald^{1b}, (Waldung^{6a}), (Gehölz^{6b})	monte^{1b}, (bosque^{2a}), (selva^{3b}), (floresta^{4b})
forget^{1b}, (forgot^{2b}), (forgotten^{2b})	oublier^{1a}	vergessen^{1b}	olvidar^{1a}, (dar^{1a} al^{1a} olvido^{2b})
form^{1a} (*vb.*)	former^{1a}	bilden^{1a}, (gestalten^{2a}), (ausbilden^{3a}), (formen^{5a}), (formieren^{6a})	formar^{1a}
former^{1b}	celui(-ci, -là)^{1a}, ceux(-ci, -là)^{1a}, celle(-ci, -là)^{1a}, celles(-ci, -là)^{1b}	jener^{1a}	aquél^{1a}
forth^{1b}	en^{1a} avant^{1a}	hervor^{1b}	adelante^{1b}
four^{1a}	quatre^{1a}	vier^{1b}	cuatro^{1*}
free^{1a} (*adj.*), (freeman^{5b}), (exempt^{6}), (unbound^{6})	libre^{1a} (librement^{3b})	frei (F)^{1a}, (ohne^{1a} Zwang^{3b})	libre^{1a}, (exento^{4b}), (sin^{1a} reserva^{5a})
(foreign person and language of List) French^{1b}, (German^{2a}), (Spanish^{2a}), (Spaniard^{4b}), (Frenchman^{6})	anglais^{1b}, (allemand^{2a}), (américain^{2b}) (espagnol^{3a})	französisch^{1a}, englisch^{1b}, (Franzose^{2a}), (spanisch^{3a}), (amerikanisch^{3b}), (Engländer^{4b})	francés^{1a}, inglés^{1b}, (americano^{2a}), (alemán^{2b}), (hispanoamericano^{5a}), (yanqui^{5a}), (gabacho^{5b})
friend^{1a}	ami^{1a}	Freund^{1a}, (Freundin^{2a}), (Hausfreund^{5b})	amigo^{1a}
from^{1a}, (fro^{4b})	de^{1a}	aus^{1a}, von^{1a}, (woraus^{4b})	de^{1a}
full^{1a}	plein^{1a}	voll^{1a}	lleno^{1a}, (pleno^{2b})
gain^{1b}, win^{1b}, (won^{2a}), (earn^{2a})	gagner^{1a}	gewinnen^{1a}, erwerben^{1b}, verdienen^{1b}, (erringen^{3a}), (abgewinnen^{6b})	ganar^{1a}

English	French	German	Spanish
general[1a] (*adj.*)	général[1b]	allgemein[1a], (abstrakt[6a])	general[1a]
(in) general[1a], usually (usual[1b]), (generally[6*])	(en) général[1b], (d')habitude[1b], (d')ordinaire[1b], (généralement[4a]), (ordinairement[4b]), (habituellement[5a])	(im) allgemeinen (allgemein[1a]) gewöhnlich[1a]	(en, por lo) general[1a]
gentleman[1b]	monsieur[1a]	Herr[1a]	caballero[1a]
get[1a], got[1a], receive[1a]	recevoir[1a], (accueillir[2a])	annehmen[1a], erhalten[1a], bekommen[1b], empfangen[1b]	recibir[1a], admitir[1b], cobrar[1b], (acoger[2b])
get[1a], got[1a], (obtain[2a]), (acquire[3b]), (procure[4a])	obtenir[1b], (acquérir[2a]), (procurer[3a]), (accaparer[6a])	erhalten[1a], bekommen[1b], empfangen[1b], (erlangen[2a]), (beschaffen[3b]), (kriegen[5b])	adquirir[1b], conseguir[1b], lograr[1b], (obtener[2a])
girl[1a], (maid[2a]), (maiden[2b]), (damsel[5a]), (lass[5b])	jeune[1a] fille[1a], (vierge[3a]), (fillette[5b])	junges (jung[1a]) Mädchen[1b], (Jungfrau[3b]), (Jungfer[5b])	muchacha (muchacho[1a]), chica (chico[1b]), (virgen[2a]), (doncella[2b])
give[1a], gave[1a], given[1a]	donner[1a]	geben[1a], (schenken[2a]), (hingeben[3a])	dar[1a]
glad[1a], happy[1a], (content[2a])	heureux[1a], content[1b]	glücklich[1a], gern[1a], sich[1a] freuen[1b], (froh[2a]), (zufrieden[2a]), (beglücken[5a])	feliz[1a], alegre[1b], contento[1b], (dichoso[2a])
glass[1b] (drinking)	verre[1b]	Glas[1b]	vaso[1b]
go[1a], went[1a], going[1b], gone[1b], (goes[2b])	aller[1a]	fahren[1a], gehen[1a], (schreiten[2a]), (hingehen[5a])	ir[1a]
go[1a] away[1a], leave[1a], (depart[2a])	partir[1a], (s'en aller[2a]), (s'absenter[6b])	sich[1a] entfernen[1b], (fortfahren[4a]), (aufbrechen[5b]), (fortgehen[5b])	ir[1a]se, partir[1a], marchar[1b] (se), (ausentarse[5a])
go[1a] up[1a], mount[1b], (ascend[3a]), (upward[s][3a])	monter[1a], remonter[1a]	steigen[1b], (hinauf[2b]), (empor[3a]), (aufwärts[4b])	subir[1a], (ascender[3b])
go[1a] with[1a], (accompany[2b])	accompagner[1a]	mit[1a] . . . . gehen[1a], begleiten[1b]	acompañar[1a]
God (g)[1a]	dieu[1a]	Gott[1a]	dios[1a]
God[1a] grant[1a] . . . . (may[1a] . . . .!)	plaise (plaire[1a]) (à Dieu)	Gott[1a] gebe (geben[1a])	Dios[1a] quiera (querer[1a]) Dios[1a] permita (permitir[1a]), (ojalá[4a])
gold[1a]	or[1b]	Gold[1b]	oro[1a]
good[1a] (*adj.*)	bon[1a], brave[1b], (sage[2a])	gut[1a], (artig[5a])	buen(o)[1a]
grant[1b], (afford[3b]), (bestow[3b]), (accord[4a]), (confer[4a]), (endue[6])	accorder[1b], (conférer[5b]), (concéder[6a]), (départir[6a]), (adjuger[6b]), (allouer[6b]), (octroyer[6b])	gestatten[1b], gewähren[1b], (bewilligen[2b]), (verleihen[2b]), (belassen[5b]), (vergönnen[5b])	conceder[1b], (dispensar[3a]), (otorgar[3b]), (conferir[6a]), (deparar[6a])
great[1a] (physical), (huge[2a]), (enormous[3a]), (immense[3b]), (tremendous[5a])	grand[1a], énorme[1b], immense[1b], (gigantesque[4a]), (colossal[5b])	groß[1a], (ungeheuer[2a]), (enorm[3a]), (kolossal[5a]), (riesig[5b])	enorme[1b], inmenso[1b], (colosal[3b]), (gigantesco[3b]), (descomunal[6a])
great[1a] (a – man)	grand[1a]	groß[1a]	gran(de)[1a]
ground[1a] (*n.*)	terre[1a], sol[1b]	Erde[1a], Grund[1a], Boden[1a]	suelo[1a], (terreno[2a])
guard[1b] (*vb.*)	garder[1a]	schützen[1b], (hüten[3b]), (bewachen[5b])	guardar[1a]
hair[1a]	cheveu[1b], (chevelure[4a]), (poil[4b])	Haar[1b]	pelo[1b], (cabello[2a]), (cabellera[4a]), (cana[4a]) (white)
half[1a] (*adj.*)	demi[1a]	halb[1b]	medio[1a]
half[1a] (*n.*)	moitié[1b]	Hälfte[1b]	mitad[1b]

English	French	German	Spanish
hand[1a] (*n.*)	main[1a]	Hand[1a]	mano[1a]
happen[1b], (occur[2b]), (befall[4a])	arriver[1a], se[1a] passer[1a], (survenir[4a]), (échoir[6b])	geschehen[1a], (eintreffen[2a]), (sich[1a] begeben[2a]), (passieren[3a]), (zugehen[3b]), (widerfahren[4b]), (sich[1a] ereignen[5a]), (verlaufen[5a])	suceder[1a], ocurrir[1b], (acontecer[3a]), (acaecer[5a]), (sobrevenir[5a])
hard[1a] (not soft)	dur[1b]	hart[1b]	duro[1a]
hard[1a], (difficult[2a])	difficile[1b] (difficilement[5a])	schwer[1a], (schwierig[2a])	difícil[1b], (arduo[5a])
have[1a], had[1a], has[1a], (hast[3b]), (I've[3b]), (hadst[4a]), (hath[4a]), (hasn't[6])	avoir[1a]	haben[1a]	haber[1a], tener[1a]
have[1a] (to do with), (concern[2b])	regarder[1a], (concerner[2b])	betreffen[1b], (angehen[3b])	importar[1a], (interesar[2a])
he[1a], him[1a]	il[1a], le[1a], lui[1a]	er[1a], etc.	él[1a], etc.
head[1a] (part of body)	tête[1a]	Kopf[1a], (Haupt[2a])	cabeza[1a]
hear[1a], heard[1b]	entendre[1a]	hören[1a]	oír[1a]
heart[1a]	cœur[1a]	Herz[1a]	corazón[1a], (entraña[2b])
heaven[1b], sky[1b], (firmament[5b])	ciel[1a]	Himmel[1a]	cielo[1a], (firmamento[4b])
Heavens! (heaven[1b]), ([the] devil[2b]!)	mon[1a] Dieu[1a]!, (le[1a] diable[2a]!), (bah![3b])	ach[1b] Gott[1a]!, (der[1a] Teufel[2a]!)	¡dios[1a]!, (caramba[5a]), (diantre[5b])
heavy[1a] (heavily[4b])	lourd[1b], (pesant [*adj.*][4a]) (lourdement[5b])	schwer[1a]	pesado (pesar[1a])
help[1a], (aid[2a]), (assist[2b]), (accommodate[5b])	aider[1b], (assister[4b]), (secourir[5b])	helfen[1b], (nützen[3a]), (mitwirken[4b]), (beistehen[5b])	ayudar[1b], (auxiliar[3a]), (socorrer[3a])
her[1a] (*adj.*)	son[1a]	ihr[1a]	su[1]*
here[1a], (hither[3a])	ici[1a], voici[1a], (çà[3a])	hier[1a], her[1a], (hierher[2b]), (hieher[6b])	acá[1a], aquí[1a]
hide[1b] (*tr. vb.*), (hid[2b]), (hidden[4b]), (conceal[3b])	cacher[1b], (voiler[5a])	verbergen[1b], (bergen[4a]), (verstecken[5a]), (verschweigen[5a]), (verhehlen[5b]), (verdecken[6a])	esconder[1b], (ocultar[2a]), (oculto[2a]), (encubrir[3b]), (recatar[4b]), (embozado[5b] [*adj.*])
hide[1b] (*intr. vb.*), (lurk[4a])			
high[1a], (lofty[3b])	haut[1a]	hoch[1a], (allerhöchst[6b])	alto[1a]
higher (high[1a])	supérieur[1b]	höher (hoch[1a])	superior[1b]
his[1a] (*adj.*)	son[1a]	sein[1a]	su[1]*
hold[1a], held[1b]	tenir[1a], (se tenir[6a])	halten[1a], fassen[1a], (festhalten[2a])	tener[1a], (sujetar[2b])
(at) home[1a], (at the) home (of), (homeward[5a])	chez[1a], à[1a] la[1a] maison[1a]	bei[1a], zu[1a] Hause (Haus[1a]), (daheim[5a]), (heim[5a]), nach[1a] Hause	en[1a] casa[1a]
honor[1b] (*n.*)	honneur[1a]	Ehre[1b]	honor[1a], (honra[2a]), (decoro[3a])
hope[1a] (*vb.*)	espérer[1a]	hoffen[1a], (hoffentlich[3a])	esperar[1a]
hope[1a] (*n.*)	espoir[1b], (espérance[2a])	Hoffnung[1b]	esperanza[1a]
horse[1a], (pony[3a]), (mare[4b]), (steed[4b])	cheval[1b], (jument[5a])	Pferd[1b], (Roß[4a])	caballo[1a]
hour[1a]	heure[1a]	Stunde[1a]	hora[1a]

English	French	German	Spanish
house[1a]	maison[1a], hôtel[1b]	Haus[1a]	casa[1a], (hotel[3b])
how[1a]	comment[1a]	wie[1a]	como[1a], cómo[1a]
however[1b], still[1a], yet[1a], (nevertheless[4a]), (notwithstanding[5b]), (howe'er[6])	cependant[1a], pourtant[1a], (toutefois[2a]), (néanmoins[2b]), (tout de même[4b])	doch[1a], jedoch[1a], dennoch[1b], jedenfalls[1b], (indes[2a]), (trotzdem[2b]), (gleichwohl[3b]), (ungeachtet[4b])	sin embargo[1a], (no[1a] obstante[2b]), (empero[5b])
husband[1b], (mate[2b]), (spouse[5a]), (consort[6])	mari[1b], (époux[4a])	Mann[1a], (Gatte[3a]), (Gemahl[4a]), (Ehegatte[6b]), (Ehemann[6b])	esposo[1a], marido[1a]
I[1a], me[1a]	je[1a], moi[1a], me[1a]	ich[1a]	yo[1a]
if[1a]	si[1a]	wenn[1a], (falls[2a])	si[1a]
important[1b]	important[1b]	wichtig[1a], erheblich[1b], (ansehnlich[4b]), (gewichtig[6a]), (einflußreich[6b])	importante[1b]
in[1a], (wherein[4a]), (herein[6]), (therein[6])	dans[1a], en[1a]	in[1a], darin[1a], (hierbei[2a]), (worin[2a]), (hierin[3b])	en[1a]
indeed[1b]	en[1a] effet[1a], (certes[2a]), (tiens![3a]), (parbleu[3b]), (va![5b]), (allez![5a])	ja[1a], zwar[1a], wirklich[1a], allerdings[1a], (mal[2b]), (wahrlich[3a]), (fürwahr[6b])	verdaderamente (verdadero[1a]), en[1a] efecto[1a]
instead[1b] (of)	au[1a] lieu[1a] (de)	statt[1a], (anstatt[3a])	(en) lugar[1a] (de)
interest[1b] (*n.*), (concern[2b])	intérêt[1a]	Interesse[1a], (Anklang[6b])	interés[1b]
interest[1b], (percent[illegible])	intérêt[1a], pour[1a] cent[1a], (usure[5b])	Interessen (Interesse[1a]), Prozent[1b], (Zins[2b]), (Dividende[4b])	intereses (interés[1b])
into[1a]	dans[1a]	in[1a], hinein[1b], (herein[3a]), (darein[6b])	en[1a], dentro[1a]
it[1a]	il[1a]	es[1a]	lo[1a], etc.
its[1a]	son[1a]	sein[1a]	su[1]*
join[1b], (connect[2a]), (fasten[2b]), (attach[3b])	attacher[1b], (joindre[2a]), (accrocher[2b]), (rattacher[4b])	verbinden[1a], (fügen[2a]), (anschließen[2b]), (zusammenhängen[6b] [be joined]), (gesellen[5b])	añadir[1a], juntar[1b], (incorporar[3a]), (enlazar[4a])
journey[1b], trip[1b], (voyage[3a])	voyage[1b]	Reise[1b], (Fahrt[3a])	viaje[1a], (jornada[2b]), (pasaje[3a]), (navegación[5a]), (travesía[5b])
judge[1b] (*vb.*)	juger[1b]	richten[1a], befinden[1a], (beurteilen[2b]), (urteilen[4a])	juzgar[1b]
just[1a] (past time)	venir[1a] de[1a], (à l')instant[1a], (justement[2a])	eben[1a], gerade[1a], (soeben[3b])	acabar[1a] de[1a], (hace) poco[1a]
keep[1a], save[1a], kept[1b]	garder[1a], retenir[1a], conserver[1b]	erhalten[1a], behalten[1b]	guardar[1a], conservar[1a]
kind[1a], sort[1b]	sorte[1a], espèce[1b], genre[1b]	Art[1a], (allerlei[3a]), (derart[3b]), (Gattung[3b]), (Sorte[3b]), (allerhand[6a])	clase[1b], especie[1b], género[1b], (tenor[6a])
kind[1a], (thoughtful[4b])	(avoir) bon[1a] cœur[1a], bon[1a], (bienfaisant[4b]), (complaisant[6b])	freundlich[1b], (gnädig[2a]), (gütig[2b]), (liebenswürdig[2b]), (wohlwollend[3b]), (gutmütig[6a])	bueno[1a], (bondadoso[3b]), (benéfico[4a]), (benévolo[4b])
king[1a]	roi[1b]	König[1a]	rey[1a]
know[1a], known[1a], knew[1b], ([be] acquainted [acquaint[3b]] [with])	connaître[1a]	kennen[1a]	conocer[1a]

English	French	German	Spanish
know[1a], etc. (have knowledge of), ([be] conscious[4b] [of]), ([be] aware[5b] [of])	savoir[1a]	wissen[1a], (bewußt[2b]), (gewahr[5b])	saber[1a]
(let) know[1a], (inform[2b]), (acquaint[3b]), (impart[4b]), (notify[5b])	faire[1a] part[1a], prévenir[1b], (aviser[2a]), (avertir[2a]), (informer[2b]), (renseigner[3a]), (mander[5a])	wissen[1a] lassen[1a], mitteilen[1b], (verkünden[4a]), (verkündigen[4b]), (benachrichtigen[5b]), (Einblick[5b] verschaffen[2a])	advertir[1a], (avisar[2a]), (enterar[2a]), (informar[2b]), (prevenir[2b]), (notificar[6a])
(not) know[1a], ([be] ignorant[3b] [of])	ignorer[1b]	(nicht) wissen[1a]	desconocer[1b], ignorar[1b]
lady[1b], (ladies[2b]), (dame[3b])	dame[1a], (châtelain[-e][4b])	Dame[1b]	señora (señor[1a]), dama[1b]
land[1a] (*n.*) (not sea)	terre[1a]	Land[1a]	tierra[1a]
(on) land[1a], (ashore[4a])			
last[1a] (*adj.*)	dernier[1a]	letzte[1a]	último[1a], (postrero[3a])
(at) last[1a], (finally[2a])	enfin[1a], (finalement[4b])	endlich[1a], (zum) Beschluß[1b], schließlich[1b], zuletzt[1b]	al[1a] fin[1a], por[1a] fin[1a], por[1a] último[1a], al[1a] cabo[1b], (a[1a] la[1a] postre[3b]), (por[1a] remate[5b])
late[1a], (tardy[4b])	tard[1a], (tardif[4a])	spät[1a], (spätestens[6a])	tarde[1a], (tardo[5b])
laugh[1a] (*vb.*), (chuckle[6])	rire[1a]	lachen[1b]	reír[1b]
law[1a], (statute[5b])	loi[1b], (code[3b])	Gesetz[1a], (Einkommensteuergesetz[4b]), (Landrecht[5a]), (Reichsgesetz[5a]), (Naturgesetz[6a])	ley[1a], (código[5b]), (estatuto[6b])
lay[1a], laid[1b]	coucher[1b]	legen[1a], (lagern[3b])	echar[1a], poner[1a]
lead[1a], led[1b], (conduct[2b])	conduire[1a], mener[1a], amener[1b]	führen[1a], leiten[1b], (anführen[2a]), (dirigieren[6a]), (herleiten[6b])	llevar[1a], conducir[1b]
learn[1a]	apprendre[1a]	lernen[1a], erfahren[1a]	aprender[1b]
least[1b]	(le) moins[1a], moindre[1b]	geringste (gering[1a]), wenigste (wenig[1a]), mindeste (minder[1b])	(lo) menos[1a]
(at) least[1b]	(au) moins[1a]	wenigstens[1a], (mindestens[2a])	a[1a] lo[1a] menos[1a], al[1a] menos[1a], siquiera[1b]
leave[1a], left[1a], (quit[2b])	laisser[1a], quitter[1a]	lassen[1a], überlassen[1b]	dejar[1a]
leave[1a], left[1a], (desert[2a]), (forsake[3b]), (abandon[4a])	abandonner[1b], (délaisser[4a]), (déserter[4b])	verlassen[1a], (aufgeben[2b]), (preisgeben[5b])	abandonar[1b], (desamparar[4b])
left[1a] (*adj.* and *adv.*)	gauche[1b], (à gauche[2b])	linke[1b], links[1b], (Linke[4a])	izquierdo[1b], (siniestro[3b])
less[1a], (lesser[6])	moins[1a]	weniger (wenig[1a]), minder[1b]	menos[1a], (menor[6a])
letter[1a] (epistle)	lettre[1b]	Brief[1a], (Zuschrift[6a])	carta[1a], (epístola[6b])
lie[1b] (*vb.*), lay[1a], (lying[2a]), (lain[6])	être[1a] couché (coucher[1b])	liegen[1a]	echar[1a] se[1a]
life[1a]	vie[1a]	Leben[1a], (Dasein[2a]), (Menschenleben[3a])	vida[1a], ser[1b]
(full of) life[1a], (lively[3a])	vif[1b], (vivant [*adj.*][2a]), (animé [animer[2b]])	lebhaft[1b], (lebendig[2a]), (rege[3b])	vivo[1a], (brioso[6a] [horse])
lift[1b], raise[1a], (rear[2b]), (heave[3b]), (elevate[4b]), (uplift[6])	élever[1a], lever[1a], relever[1a], dresser[1b], soulever[1b], (hausser[2b]), (hisser[5a])	erheben[1a], heben[1b], (erhöhen[2a]), (steigern[2a]), (aufziehen[6b])	levantar[1a], alzar[1b], elevar[1b], (erigir[3a]), (empinar[6b])
light[1a] (*n.*)	lumière[1b]	Licht[1b], (Licht[2b] [luminary])	luz[1a], (resplandor[3a])

English	French	German	Spanish
light[1a] (*adj.*) (weight)	léger[1b] (légèrement[2b])	leicht[1a]	ligero[1b], (leve[2a]), (liviano[5a])
like[1a], care[1a] for[1a], ([be] fond[2b] [of])	aimer[1a], ([avoir de la] sympathie[2b] [pour])	gern[1a] haben[1a], mögen[1a], (sympathisch[5b])	gustar[1a], querer[1a], (tener [simpatía[2b]] por)
like[1a] (*adj.*), (alike[2b])	pareil[1a], semblable[1b]	gleich[1a], ähnlich[1a], (überein[4b])	semejante[1a]
(look[1a]) like[1a], (resemble[4a])	ressembler[1b]	ähnlich[1a] sein[1a], (gleichen[3b])	parecer[1a] se[1a], (semejar[3b])
line[1a]	ligne[1b]	Linie[1b], (Zeile[2b])	línea[1b], (renglón[5b]) (written)
little[1a], small[1a], (slight[2a]), (tiny[2b]), (wee[3a])	petit[1a], (mignon[4a]), (menu[6a]), (minuscule[6a])	gering[1a], klein[1a]	pequeño[1a], chico[1b], (menudo[2a]), (diminuto[6b])
little[1a] (*n.*), bit[1b]	peu[1a]	wenig[1a], (ein[1a] bißchen[5a])	poco[1a], poquito[1a]
little[1a] (*adv.*), (somewhat[2b])	un[1a] peu[1a], quelque[1a] peu[1a]	etwas[1a]	algo[1a]
little[1a] by[1a] little, (by[1a] degrees [degree[2a]]), (gradual[3a])	peu[1a] à[1a] peu, (successivement[3b])	allmählich[1b]	poco[1a] a[1a] poco, (gradual[6b])
live[1a], (be[1a] alive[2a])	vivre[1a]	leben[1a]	vivir[1a]
long[1a] (*adj.*)	long[1a]	lang[1a]	largo[1a], (luengo[5a])
long[1a] (*adv.*) (time)	longtemps[1a]	lang[1a], längst (lang[1a]), (langjährig[6b])	mucho[1a] tiempo[1a]
look[1a] (*n.*), (peep[2b]), (glance[2b]), (glimpse[5a])	regard[1a], coup[1a] d'[1a]œil[1a]	Blick[1a]	mirada[1b], (mirar[5b]), (ojeada[6b]), (vislumbre[6b])
look[1a] at[1a], (scan[6])	regarder[1a]	ansehen[1b], (blicken[2a]), (schauen[2a]), (umsehen[6a])	mirar[1a]
look[1a] for[1a], hunt[1b] for[1a], seek[1b], (search[2a]), (sought[2b])	chercher[1a], (rechercher[2b])	suchen[1a], (aufsuchen[3a]), (nachsehen[4b])	buscar[1a], (registrar[3b])
looks (*n.*) (look[1a]), (appearance[2b]), (aspect[5b])	air[1a], (apparence[2a]), (aspect[2a]), (mine[2b])	Erscheinung[1b], (Schein[2b]), (Anschein[5a]), (Aussehen[5b])	aire[1a], (apariencia[2b]), (parecer[3a]), (viso[6a])
lose[1b], lost[1a]	perdre[1a]	verlieren[1a], (einbüßen[5b]), (zusetzen[6a])	perder[1a]
(out) loud[1b], (aloud[3a])	à[1a] haute (haut [*adj.*][1a]) voix[1a], (haut [*adv.*][2a])	laut[1b]	alto[1a]
love[1a] (*vb.*)	aimer[1a]	lieben[1a], lieb[1a] haben[1a]	amar[1a], querer[1a]
love[1a] (*n.*)	amour[1a]	Liebe[1a], (Lieben[5a])	amor[1a], cariño[1b]
make[1a], made[1a]	faire[1a]	machen[1a], tun[1a]	hacer[1a], (confeccionar[5b])
man[1a], men[1a]	homme[1a]	Mann[1a], Mensch[1a]	hombre[1a]
many[1a]	beaucoup[1a]	manch[1a], viele (viel[1a])	muchos (mucho[1a])
mark[1a] (*vb.*)	marquer[1b]	bezeichnen[1a], zeichnen[1b], (kennzeichnen[5b])	señalar[1b], (marcar[2a])
master[1b] (*n.*)	maître[1a]	Meister[1b]	amo[1a], dueño[1a]
matter[1a], thing[1a], question[1b], (affair[2b]), (concern[2b])	affaire[1a], chose[1a], question[1a]	Sache[1a], Angelegenheit[1b]	cosa[1a], asunto[1b], cuestión[1b], (achaque[5a])
matter[1a] (what's the matter), (ail[6])	avoir[1a] (qu'est-ce qu'il y a)	vorliegen[1b], (los[2a] sein[1a])	qué[1a] pasa (pasar[1a])
matter (negative)	(ne rien) faire[1a], importer[1b]	gleich[1a] sein[1a], (ausmachen[3b])	importar[1a]
may[1a], might[1a], (mayst[6])	pouvoir[1a]	dürfen[1a], mögen[1a]	poder[1a]
mean[1a] (*vb.*), (meant[2b]), (signify[5b])	vouloir[1a] dire[1a], (signifier[2a])	bedeuten[1a], heißen[1a], meinen[1a], (besagen[5a])	querer[1a] decir[1a], (significar[2a])

English	French	German	Spanish
means (mean[1a]) (*n.*), (medium[4b])	moyen[1a]	Mittel[1b]	medio[1a]
measure[1a], (measurement[5b])	mesure[1a]	Maß[1b], (Maßnahme[5a])	medida[1a], (compás[3a]), (tasa[6a])
meet[1a], met[1b]	rencontrer[1a]	treffen[1a], begegnen[1b], (antreffen[4b]), (zusammentreffen[5a])	encontrar[1a]
miss[1a] (*vb.*)	manquer[1b], (rater[5a]), (manqué[5b])	fehlen[1b], (verfehlen[4a]), (vermissen[4b])	echar[1a] (de) menos[1a], faltar[1a]
moment[1b]	moment[1a]	Augenblick[1a], (Moment[2a])	momento[1a]
money[1a]	argent[1a]	Geld[1a]	dinero[1a], plata[1b]
month[1a]	mois[1a]	Monat[1b]	mes[1a]
more[1a]	plus[1a], davantage[1a]	mehr[1a]	más[1a]
morning[1a], (forenoon[4a]), (morn[4a])	matin[1a], (matinée[3b])	Morgen[1a], (Vormittag[5a])	mañana[1a]
most[1a]	(le) plus[1a], plupart[1b]	meist[1a], (Meiste[6a])	lo[1a] más[1a]
mother[1a], (ma[6])	mère[1b]	Mutter[1a]	madre[1a]
mouth[1b]	bouche[1b], (gueule[6a])	Mund[1a], (Maul[5b])	boca[1a]
Mr.[1b], sir (S)[1b], (mister (M)[6])	monsieur[1a]	Herr[1a], (monsieur[4b]), (Mister[6b])	don, D.[1a], señor[1a], señorito[1a]
Mrs.[1b], (madam[3b])	madame[1b]	Frau[1a], (Madame[4a])	doña, Da.[1a], señora (señor[1a])
much[1a], a[1a] lot[1b], a[1a] great[1a] deal[1b]	beaucoup[1a], (grand'chose[6a])	viel[1a]	mucho[1a]
must[1a], have[1a] (to)	devoir[1a], falloir[1a]	müssen[1a], sollen[1a]	deber[1a]
my[1a]	mon[1a]	mein[1a]	mi[1a]
name[1a] (*n.*)	nom[1a]	Name[1a], (Bezeichnung[2b]), (Benennung[6b])	nombre[1a], (apellido[3a])
name[1a] (give – to), (entitle[4a])	nommer[1b], (intituler[4b])	nennen[1a]	nombrar[1b], (titular[2b]), (denominar[4a])
name[1a], (appoint[2a])	nommer[1b], (désigner[2a]), (définir[3b]), (nommé [*adj.*][5a])	bestimmen[1b], (ernennen[2b]), (benennen[5a])	nombrar[1b], (designar[2b])
(what is your) name[1a]	s'[1a]appeler[1a]	heißen[1a]	llamar[1a]
narrow[1b]	étroit[1b] (étroitement[4b])	eng[1b], (schmal[3a])	estrecho[1b], (angosto[4a])
natural[1b]	naturel[1a] naturellement[1b]	natürlich[1a], (naturgemäß[2b])	natural[1a]
nature[1b]	nature[1a]	Natur[1a]	naturaleza[1a]
nature[1b], character[1b], soul[1b]	caractère[1a], nature[1a], âme[1a], (qualité[2a])	Wesen[1a], (Beschaffenheit[3a])	carácter[1b], (genio[2a]), (índole[3a]), (temperamento[4a])
near[1a] (*adj.* and *adv.*), close[1a], (nigh[4a]), (adjacent[6])	voisin(-e)[1a], près[1b], (auprès[2b]), (proche[3a])	dabei[1a], nah[1a], neben[1a], (in der) Nähe[1b], (herbei[3b]), (nebenbei[3b]), (baldig[4b]), (bevorstehend[5a])	cerca[1a], junto[1a], vecino[1b], (cercano[2a]), (próximo[2a]), (contiguo[6a])
near[1a] (*prep.*), (nigh[4a])	près de[1a], auprès de[1b]	neben[1a], bei[1a], (wobei[2a])	cerca[1a] de[1a]
necessary[1b], (needful[5b])	nécessaire[1a]	notwendig[1a], nötig[1a], erforderlich[1b]	necesario[1a], preciso[1a]
need[1a] (*n.*), want[1a]	besoin[1a]	Mangel[1b], Not[1b], (Bedarf[3a])	necesidad[1a], (menester[2a])
need[1a] (*vb.*), require[1b]	avoir[1a] besoin[1a] de[1a]	brauchen[1a], (bedürfen[2a]), (erfordern[2b])	hacer[1a] falta[1a], necesitar[1a], (haber[1a] menester[2a])
neither[1b] . . . . nor[1b]	ni[1a] . . . . ni[1a]	weder[1b] . . . . noch[1a]	ni[1a] . . . . ni[1a]
neither[1b] (*adv.*), nor[1b]	non[1a] plus[1a]	auch[1a] nicht[1a]	tampoco[1b]

English	French	German	Spanish
neither[1b] (one)	ni[1a] l'[1a] un[1a] ni[1a] l'[1a] autre[1a]	weder[1b] der[1a] eine[1a] noch[1a] der[1a] andere[1a]	ni[1a] el[1a] uno[1a] ni[1a] el[1a] otro[1a]
never[1a], (ne'er[5b])	jamais[1a]	nie[1a], niemals[1b], (nimmermehr[4b])	jamás[1a], nunca[1a]
new[1a]	nouveau[1a], (neuf[2a])	neu[1a]	nuevo[1a]
next[1a], following[1b], (subsequent[5b])	prochain[1b], suivant[1b]	folgend[1a], nächst (nah[1a]), zunächst[1a]	siguiente[1a], inmediato[1b], (próximo[2a]), (sucesivo[2b]), (venidero[4b])
night[1a]	nuit[1a]	Nacht[1a]	noche[1a]
no[1a], (nay[4a])	non[1a]	nein[1a]	no[1a]
no[1a] (*adj.*)	aucun[1a], nul[1b]	kein[1a]	ninguno[1a]
no[1a] longer (long[1a]), no[1a] more[1a]	(ne) . . . . plus[1a]	nicht[1a] mehr[1a], (nimmer[3b])	ya[1a] no[1a]
no[1a] one[1a], (nobody[2b])	personne[1a]	niemand[1a]	nadie[1a]
none[1b]	(ne) . . . . point[1a], (ne) . . . . aucun[1a], nul[1b]	kein[1a]	ningún[1a], nada[1a] (de)
not[1a]	ne . . . . pas[1a], pas[1a]	nicht[1a]	no[1a]
nothing[1a], (nought[5a]), (naught[6])	rien[1a], (néant[5a])	nichts[1a]	nada[1a]
now[1a], at[1a] present[1a]	maintenant[1a], (à présent[2b]), (actuellement[2b])	jetzt[1a], nun[1a], nunmehr[1b], (diesmal[2b]), (vorläufig[2b]), (heutzutage[4b]), (jetzo[6a])	ahora[1a], (en[1a] la[1a] actualidad[5b])
now[1a] (*conj.*)	or[1b]	nun[1a]	ahora[1a] bien[1a]
number[1a] (*n.*) (quantity)	nombre[1a]	Zahl[1a]	número[1a]
of[1a], (thereof[3b]), (whereof[6])	de[1a], en (*pron.*)[1a]	von[1a], davon[1a], (wovon[3a]), (hiervon[4a])	de[1a], del[1a]
offer[1b] (*vb.*)	offrir[1a]	bieten[1a], (darbieten[3a]), (anbieten[3b]), (darbringen[6b])	ofrecer[1a], (brindar[3a])
often[1a], (frequently [frequent[2a]]), (oft[3b])	souvent[1a], (fréquemment[5a])	oft + öfter(s)[1a], häufig[1b]	muchas (mucho[1a]) veces (vez[1a]), (a[1a] menudo[2a]), (frecuentemente [frequente[2a]]), (con[1a] frecuencia[2b])
old[1a], (elder[4b]), (eldest[4a]), (aged[6]), (senior[6])	vieux (*adj.* and *n.*)[1a], ancien[1a], vieille (*adj.* and *n.*)[1b], (vieil[2a]), (âgé[3a]), (aîné[3a])	alt[1a], (uralt[5a])	antiguo[1a], viejo[1a]
on[1a], upon[1a], (thereon[4b]), (whereon[6])	sur[1a]	auf[1a], darauf[1a], (worauf[2a]), (hinauf[2b]), (herauf[5a])	sobre[1a], al[1a]
once[1a] (one time + once upon a time)	une[1a] fois[1a], jadis[1b]	einmal[1a], einst[1b]	una[1a] vez[1a]
(at) once[1a], right[1a] off[1a] (Amer.), (immediately [immediate[2a]]), (instantly [instant[2b]]), (forthwith[5b]), (straightway[5b])	à[1a] l'[1a]instant[1b], aussitôt[1b], tout de suite[1b], (immédiatement[2a])	sogleich[1b], (augenblicklich[2b]), (als[o]bald[3a]), (unverzüglich[6b])	ahora[1a] mismo[1a], al[1a] instante[1a], luego[1a], ya[1a] mismo[1a], en[1a] seguida[1b], inmediato[1b]
one[1a] (*indef. pron.*), they[1a], you[1a]	on[1a]	man[1a]	se[1a], uno[1a]
one[1a] (numeral)	un[1a]	ein[1a]	uno[1a]
only[1a] (*adv.*)	seulement[1a], (uniquement[3b]), (ne . . . . que[5b])	bloß[1a], erst[1a], nur[1a], lediglich[1b], (lauter[3a])	sólo[1a]
only[1a] (*adj.*), single [1b], (mere[2a]), (sole[2b]), (lone[3a])	seul[1a], simple[1a], unique[1b]	einzeln[1a], einzig[1a], (einmalig[6a])	solo[1a], único[1a], (mero[5a])

English	French	German	Spanish
open[1a], (uncover[5a]), (unlock[6])	ouvrir[1a], ouvert[1b], (entr'ouvrir[3a]), (rouvrir[5a])	offen[1b], öffnen[1b], (zugänglich[4a]), (aufschlagen[5b]), (auftun[5b]), (erschließen[5b])	abrir[1a], (entreabrir[4b])
or[1a]	ou[1a]	oder[1a], (beziehungsweise[2b])	u[1a], o[1a]
(in) order[1a] (to), so[1a] as[1a], so[1a] that[1a], that[1a]	pour[1a], pour que[1b], (afin de[2a]), (afin que[3a])	damit[1a], sowie[1a], um[1a] . . . . zu[1a], (sodaß[4a])	para[1a]
order[1a], command[1b], (commandment[6])	ordre[1a], (commandement[4a]), (commande[4b])	Befehl[1b], (Auftrag[2a]), (Gebot[2b]), (Erlaß[3a]), (Anweisung[4a]), (Ordre[4b]), (Bestellung[5a]), (Weisung[5a])	orden[1a], (encargo[2b]), (mandato[4a]), (mandamiento[6b])
other[1a]	autre[1a], (autrui[6a])	andere[1a], (sonstig[2a]), (anderweitig[5a])	demás[1a], otro[1a]
ought[1b]	devoir[1a]	sollen[1a]	deber[1a]
our[1a]	notre, nos[1a]	unser[1a]	nuestro[1*]
out[1a], outside[1b]	dehors[1a]	aus[1a], außer[1a], daraus[1b], heraus[1b], hinaus[1b], (hieraus[4a])	fuera[1a], (afuera[4a])
own[1a] (*adj.*)	propre[1a]	eigen[1a]	propio[1a]
own[1a] (*vb.*), (possess[2a])	posséder[1b]	besitzen[1b]	poseer[1a]
pain[1b] (*n.*), (ache[3b]), (pang[4a])	peine[1a], douleur[1b], (souffrance[2b])	Schmerz[1b]	dolor[1a], (dolencia[5b])
paper[1a]	papier[1b]	Papier[1b]	papel[1a]
paper[1a], (newspaper[2b])	journal[1b]	Zeitung[1b], (Wochenblatt[6b])	diario[1a], (periódico[2a]), (gaceta[6b])
part[1a] (*n.*)	part[1a], partie[1a], parti[1b]	Teil[1a]	parte[1a]
(in) part[1a], (partly[2b]), (partial[5b])	en[1a] partie[1a]	teils[1b], (teilweise[2b])	en[1a] parte[1a], (parcialmente [parcial[5b]])
part[1a] (of country), (region[2a]), (area[3a])	environs (environ[1b]), (ronde[2b]), (alentours [les][5a])	Gegend[1b]	región[1b], (comarca[3a]), (contorno[3a])
party[1b], (festival[4b]), (celebration[5b]), (jubilee[6])	fête[1b]	Gesellschaft[1a], Fest[1b]	fiesta[1b]
pay[1a], (paid[2a])	payer[1a]	bezahlen[1a], zahlen[1b], (entrichten[4a])	pagar[1a], (abonar[3a])
peace[1b]	paix[1b]	Friede[1b]	paz[1a]
people[1a] (race)	peuple[1b]	Volk[1a]	pueblo[1a]
people[1a] (persons), (folk[2a])	gens[1a], monde[1a]	Leute[1a]	gente[1a]
people[1a] (common[1b])	peuple[1b]	Volk[1a]	pueblo[1a], (vulgo[3a]), (plebe[6a]), (proletario[6b]) (one of –)
perfect[1b] (*adj.*)	parfait[1b], (accompli[3b]) parfaitement[1b]	vollkommen[1b]	perfecto[1b], (cabal[3b])
perhaps[1b], (maybe[4a]), (perchance[5b]), (haply[6]), (possibly[6*])	peut-être[1a]	vielleicht[1a], (eventuell[2b]), (allenfalls[5a]), (womöglich[5b]), (tunlichst[6a])	quizá(s)[1a], tal vez[1a]
person[1a], self[1b]	personne[1a], (individu[2a])	Mensch[1a], Person[1a]	persona[1a]
piece[1a], (chip[4b]), (fragment[5b])	morceau[1b], pièce[1a], (bribe[6b])	Stück[1a]	pedazo[1b], (pieza[2a]), (trozo[2b]), (fragmento[4a]), (mendrugo[6b])

English	French	German	Spanish
place[1a], (position[2b]), (location[4b]), (site[4b]), (stead[5a])	lieu[1a], endroit[1b], place[1a], (position[2a]), (site[4b]), (localité[5b])	Ort[1a], Platz[1a], Raum[1b], Stand[1a], Stelle[1a], Stellung[1a], (Ortschaft[4a]), (Stätte[4a]), (Statt[6b])	lugar[1a], puesto[1a], sitio[1a], (posición[2a]), (paraje[3a]), (colocación[3b]), (local[3b]), (recinto[5b]), (localidad[6a])
place[1a], put[1a], set[1a]	mettre[1a], poser[1a], déposer[1b], placer[1b], (fourrer[4b])	legen[1a], setzen[1a], stellen[1a], herstellen[1b], (stecken[2a]), (hinstellen[4a]), (unterstellen[5a]), (niedersetzen[6a])	colocar[1a], meter[1a], poner[1a], (situar[2a]), (depositar[3b]), (anteponer[5b]), (posar[6a])
(take) place[1a]	(avoir) lieu[1a]	stattfinden[1b]	suceder[1a], ocurrir[1b]
play[1a] (*vb.*)	jouer[1a]	spielen[1b]	tocar[1a], jugar[1b], (tañer[6a])
please[1a]	plaire[1a], faire[1a] plaisir[1a] à[1a], (complaire[6b])	bitte (bitten[1a]), (gefallen[2a]), (belieben[3a]), (ergötzen[6a])	placer[1a], (agradar[2a]), (complacer[2a])
point[1a], (dot[2b])	point[1a]	Punkt[1a]	punto[1a]
point[1a] of[1a] view[1b]	point[1a] de[1a] vue[1a]	Gesichtspunkt[1b], (Standpunkt[2a])	punto[1a] de[1a] vista[1a]
poor[1a] (not rich)	pauvre[1a]	arm[1a]	pobre[1a]
possible[1b]	possible[1a]	möglich[1a], (etwaig[3b]), (denkbar[4a]), (ausführbar[6a])	posible[1a], (dable[6b])
pound[1b] (money), (dollar[2a]), (guinea[6])	franc (*n.*)[1b], (sterling[6b])	Mark[1a], (Taler[2b]), (Gulden[3b]), (Franken[4b]), (Rubel[4b]), (Dollar[6b]), (Sterling[6b])	peso[1a], peseta[1b], (franco[2a]), (ducado[4b]), (doblón[6b]), (maravedí[6b])
power[1a], might[1a]	puissance[1b], (pouvoir [*n.*][2a])	Kraft[1a], Macht[1a], Gewalt[1b]	fuerza[1a], poder[1b], (potencia[2b]), (dominio[3a]), (poderío[5a])
pretty[1a], (goodly[3b]), (comely[6])	joli[1a]	schön[1a], (hübsch[2a])	bonito[1a], (lindo[2a])
	(joliment[4b])		
pretty[1a], quite[1a], rather[1b] (moderately)	assez[1a]	ganz[1a], ziemlich[1b]	bastante[1a], (asaz[4b])
price[1b], cost[1b], (fee[4a])	prix[1a], (frais [*n.*][2a])	Kosten[1b], Preis[1b], (Unkosten[6a])	precio[1b]
promise[1b] (*vb.*)	promettre[1b]	versprechen[1b], (zusagen[4b])	prometer[1b]
prove[1b]	prouver[1b]	beweisen[1b], erweisen[1b], (bewähren[2b]), (dartun[4b]), (bekunden[5a])	probar[1b]
public[1b] (*adj.*)	public[1b]	öffentlich[1a]	público[1a]
pull[1b], draw[1a], (drag[2b]), (drew[2b]), (drawn[4b]), (tug[4b]), (haul[5a]), (tow[6])	tirer[1a], attirer[1b]	ziehen[1a], (zuziehen[5b]), (hineinziehen[6b])	sacar[1a], arrastrar[1b], tirar[1b]
pure[1b]	pur[1b]	bloß[1a], rein[1a]	puro[1a]
purpose[1a], (aim[2b]), (goal[4b])	but[1b], (objectif[4b])	Ziel[1a], Zweck[1a], (Vorsatz[4a])	fin[1a], propósito[1a], (designio[4b]), (objetivo[4b])
(to be a) question[1b] (of), (have to) do[1a] (with)	s'agir de[1b]	sich[1a] handeln[1a] um[1a], betreffen[1b]	tratar[1a] se
quiet[1b], still[1a], (calm[2b]), (serene[5a]), (tranquil[6]), (undisturbed[6])	calme[1a], tranquille[1b], (serein [*adj.*][6a])	ruhig[1b], still[1b]	tranquilo[1b], (sereno[2a]), (quieto[4a]), (plácido[4b]), (quedo[5a])
	(tranquillement[3b])		
quiet[1b], (calm[2b]), (hush[3a]), (stillness[5a]), (tranquillity[6])	calme[1a],(tranquillité[4a]), (sérénité[6a])	Ruhe[1b], (Stille[2b])	calma[1b], silencio[1b], (quietud[3a]), (serenidad[3a]), (tranquilidad[3a]), (sosiego[5a])
rather[1b]	plutôt[1b]	ehe[1a], vielmehr[1b]	antes[1a]

English	French	German	Spanish
reach[1a], (attain[3b])	arriver à[1a], atteindre[1b], parvenir[1b]	erreichen[1a], gelangen[1a], (ankommen[2a])	alcanzar[1a]
read[1a]	lire[1a], (relire[5a])	lesen[1a], (vorlesen[5a])	leer[1a]
real[1b] (veritable)	vrai[1a], véritable[1b], (réel[2a]) (véritablement[5b])	eigentlich[1a], wirklich[1a], (echt[2a]), (tatsächlich[2a])	real[1a], verdadero[1a]
reason[1a] (*n.*) (for something)	raison[1a]	Grund[1a], Ursache[1b]	razón[1a]
red[1a], (scarlet[3b]), (crimson[4b]), (ruby[5b]), (ruddy[6])	rouge[1a], (roux[4a]), (rougeâtre[6a])	rot[1b]	rojo[1b], (colorado[3b]), (encarnado[4a]), (grana[5a])
remain[1a], stay[1a], (abide[4a])	rester[1a]	bleiben[1a], (zurückbleiben[3a])	quedar[1a], permanecer[1b]
remain[1a] (be left over) (mathematical)	rester[1a]	bleiben[1a]	quedar[1a], (restar[5a])
remember[1a], (recollect[6])	se rappeler[1b], se souvenir[1b]	erinnern[1b], (gedenken[2b]), (besinnen[3b])	recordar[1a]
report[1b] (*n.*)	rapport[1b]	Bericht[1b]	relación[1a], (informe[2b])
rest[1a] (*vb.*), (repose[3b])	reposer[1b]	ruhen[1b]	descansar[1b], (reposar[2a]), (holgar[4b])
rich[1a], (wealthy[3b])	riche[1a]	reich[1a], (wohlhabend[5a])	rico[1a], (opulento[3b])
right[1a], (correct[2a])	droit (*adj.*)[1a], juste[1a], (correct[5a]) (correctement[6a])	recht[1a], richtig[1a], (korrekt[6a])	justo[1b], (correcto[3b])
right[1a] (hand)	droit (*adj.*)[1a]	recht[1a]	derecha (-o + -a[1a]), (diestra[3a])
(be) right[1a]	(avoir) raison[1a]	Recht[1a] (haben)	(tener) razón[1a]
road[1a], way[1a], (route[3a]), (highway[4a])	chemin[1a], route[1a], voie[1b], (chaussée[5b])	Weg[1a], Bahn[1b], (Chaußee[4b])	camino[1a], (vía[2b]), (carretera[3b]), (ruta[5a])
room[1a], (chamber[2a])	chambre[1a], (pièce[2a])	Zimmer[1b], (Kammer[2b]), (Stube[3b]), (Gemach[4b]), (Nebenzimmer[6b])	cuarto[1a], (sala[2a]), (cámara[2b])
room[1a], space[1b]	place[1a], (espace[2a])	Platz[1a], Raum[1b]	espacio[1a], lugar[1a]
rule[1b], (govern[3a])	dominer[1b], (gouverner[4b]), (régir[6a])	herrschen[1b], (beherrschen[2b]), (walten[3b])	dominar[1b], (gobernar[2a]), (regir[3a]), (imperar[4b])
run[1a], ran[1b]	courir[1a], (accourir[2a])	laufen[1b], (rennen[5a])	correr[1a]
safe[1b], (secure[2a])	sûr[1b], (sauf [*adj.*][3b])	sicher[1a]	seguro[1a], ([en] salvo[2b])
same[1a], very[1a], (selfsame[5a])	même (*adj.*)[1a]	derselbe[1a], etc., (nämliche[3b]), (derselbige[4a]), (selbige[6a])	mismo[1a], propio[1a]
(all the) same[1a], (not) care[1a], (indifferent[6])	égal[1b], (indifférent[2b])	gleich[1a], (gleichgültig[2b]), (einerlei[5a]), (gleichviel[5b])	igual[1a], (indiferente[2a])
save[1a], (rescue[3b])	sauver[1b]	retten[1b]	salvar[1b]
say[1a], said[1a], (quoth[5b])	dire[1a], (dit [*adj.*][6a])	sagen[1a], (angeblich[3b] . . . . sein[1a] [said to be . . . .])	decir[1a]
say[1a] again[1a], (repeat[2a])	répéter[1a], (redire[3b])	wiederholen[1b]	repetir[1b], (reiterar[6b])
school[1a], (schoolhouse[3b])	école[1b], (secondaire[5a]), (lycée[5a])	Schule[1b], (Gymnasium[4a]), (Volksschule[4a]), (Lehranstalt[6a])	escuela[1b], ([escuela] secundaria [secundario[5b]])
sea[1a]	mer[1b]	Meer[1b], (See [*f.*][3a])	mar[1a]
seat[1b] (*vb.*)	(faire) asseoir[1b]	setzen[1a]	sentar[1a]
seat[1b] (*n.*)	place[1a], siège[1b]	Platz[1a], (Sitz[2b])	plaza[1a], (asiento[2a])
second[1a] (*adj.*)	second[1a], (deuxième[2b])	zweite[1a]	segundo[1a]
see[1a], saw[1a], seen[1a], (lo[4b])	voir[1a], revoir[1b]	sehen[1a], (wiedersehen[4b])	ver[1a]

English	French	German	Spanish
self[1b] (*refl.*), himself[1a], herself[1b], myself[1b], themselves[1b], (itself[2a]), (yourself[2a]), (ourselves[3a]), (ourself[3b]), (thyself[3b]), (yourselves[4b*])	se[1a], etc., (soi[2b])	sich[1a], etc.	sí[1a], etc.
send[1a], sent[1a], (despatch[6])	envoyer[1a], (expédier[3b]), (transmettre[4a])	senden[1b], schicken[1b], (zukommen[4a] lassen[1a]), (versenden[5a]), (entsenden[5b])	enviar[1a], mandar[1a], (remitir[3a]), (despachar[3b]), (transmitir[3b]), (expedir[5a])
separate[1b], (sever[5b])	séparer[1a]	trennen[1b], (scheiden[2a]), (ausscheiden[4b]), (sondern[4b]), (absondern[5a])	apartar[1a], separar[1b]
separate[1b], (apart[2a]), (aloof[6]), (asunder[6])	séparé (séparer[1a]) (séparément[6a])	getrennt (trennen[1b]), (auseinander[3a]), (voneinander[6a])	apartado (apartar[1a]), separado (separar[1b])
serve[1a], attend[1b]	servir[1a]	dienen[1a], (bedienen[2b]), (anrichten[5a]), (auftragen[5b])	servir[1a]
service[1b]	service[1a]	Dienst[1b], (Dienstpflicht[4b]), (Bedienung[5b])	servicio[1b]
settle[1b], (establish[2a])	disposer[1b], établir[1b]	bestimmen[1a], (festsetzen[2b])	establecer[1b], (asentar[3b]), (arraigar[6a])
several[1a]	plusieurs[1a]	mehrere[1a], (ein[1a] paar[2a])	varios (vario[1a])
shall[1a], will[1a], (I'll[2b]), (won't[2b]), (shalt[3a]), (we'll[3b]), (wilt[4a]), (you'll[4a]), ('twill[4b]), (they'll[6])	(ending on verb)	werden[1a]	(ending on verb)
she[1a], her[1a]	elle[1a], la[1a], lui[1a]	sie[1a]	ella[1*]
short[1a], (brief[2b])	court[1b], (bref[3a])	kurz[1a]	breve[1b], corto[1b]
(in) short[1a]	(en un) mot[1a], (bref [*adv.*][4a])	kurz[1a]	brevemente (breve[1b]), ([en] definitivo[2b]), ([en] concreto[5a])
should[1a], would[1a], (I'd[4b]), (wouldn't[4b]), (you'd[5b])	(ending on verb)	werden[1a]	(ending on verb)
show[1a] (*tr. vb.*), (manifest[4a]), (demonstrate[5b])	faire[1a] voir[1a], montrer[1a], (manifester[3a])	weisen[1b], zeigen[1a], (hinweisen[2a]), (nachweisen[2b])	mostrar[1a], demostrar[1b], manifestar[1b]
side[1a], (flank[5b])	côté[1a], (flanc[3a])	Seite[1a], (Flanke[5b])	lado[1a], (costado[5b]), (flanco[6b])
sight[1a], view[1b], (vision[3b])	vue (*n.*)[1a], spectacle[1b], (vision[3a])	Ansicht[1a], Anschauung[1b], Aussicht[1b], (Anblick[6a]), (Sicht[5b])	vista[1a], aspecto[1b], (visión[2a]), (espectáculo[2b]), (perspectiva[4a]), (panorama[4b])
simple[1b], plain[1a]	simple[1a]	einfach[1a], (schlicht[4b])	sencillo[1b], simple[1b]
simply (simple[1b]), (merely [mere[2a]])	simplement[1b], (purement[3b]), (bonnement[6a])	einfach[1a]	puramente (puro[1a])
since[1a] (time)	dès[1a], depuis[1b], (depuis que[3a])	seit[1a], (seitdem[2a]), (seither[6a])	desde[1a]
sister[1a]	sœur[1a]	Schwester[1b], (Geschwister[5a])	hermana (hermano[1a])
sit[1a], sat[1b] (be sitting)	être assis (asseoir[1b])	sitzen[1a]	sentar[1a]
sit[1a], sit[1a] down[1a], sat[1b]	s'asseoir[1b], (se rasseoir[3b])	Platz[1a] nehmen[1a], sich[1a] setzen[1a]	sentar[1a] se
so[1a], thus[1b], (accordingly[3b])	ainsi[1a]	so[1a], also[1a]	así[1a], tal[1a]

English	French	German	Spanish
so[1a] (then)	ainsi[1a], donc[1a]	nun[1a], so[1a]	luego[1a], (conque[6b])
so[1a] much[1a], as[1a] much[1a]	autant[1a], si[1a], tant[1a], (tellement[2a]), (d'autant[3a])	desto[1b], soweit[1b], sowohl[1b]	tanto[1a]
soldier[1a]	soldat[1b], (militaire [n.][4b])	Soldat[1b]	soldado[1b], (militar [n.][2a])
sometime[1a]	un[1a] jour[1a]	eines (ein[1a]) Tages (Tag[1a]), einst[1b], einmal[1a], (dereinst[6b])	algún[1a] día[1a]
son[1a]	fils[1a]	Sohn[1a]	hijo[1a]
soon[1a], (anon[5b])	bientôt[1a], sous[1a] peu[1a], (prochainement[6b])	bald[1a], sobald[1b], (demnächst[3a]), (in[1a] Kürze[5a]), (nächstens[6a])	a[1a] poco[1a], pronto[1a], (próximamente [próximo[2a]])
(no) sooner (soon[1a]) . . . . (than)	aussitôt[1b] . . . . aussitôt, (sitôt[3a] . . . . sitôt)	sobald[1b]	no[1a] bien[1a]
soul[1b]	âme[1a]	Seele[1a]	alma[1a], (ánima[4a])
speak[1a], spoke[1b], (utter[2a]), (spake[3b]), (spoken[4a])	parler[1a]	sprechen[1a]	hablar[1a]
spirit[1b]	esprit[1a]	Geist[1a]	ánimo[1b], espíritu[1a]
square[1b] (in town)	place[1a]	Platz[1a]	plaza[1b]
stand[1a], stood[1b] (*intr. vb.*)	être[1a], rester[1a] debout[1b]	stehen[1a], (dastehen[4b])	estar[1a] (de) pie[1a], poner[1a] (se) (de) pie, parar[1b] se
state[1a] (*n.*), condition[1b]	état[1a], situation[1b]	Zustand[1a], (Stadium[5a])	estado[1a], paso[1a], situación[1b], (trance[4b])
state[1a] (nation), (commonwealth[5b])	état[1a]	Staat[1a]	estado[1a]
state[1a], (declare[2a]), (maintain[2b]), (contend[4a]), (assert[4b]), (affirm[5a]), (testify[5b])	déclarer[1b], (affirmer[2a]), (professer[3b])	angeben[1b], behaupten[1b]	declarar[1b]
step[1a] (*n.*), (footstep[4b]), (stride[4b])	pas[1a]	Schritt[1b]	paso[1a]
still[1a], yet[1a] (time)	encore[1a], toujours[1a]	noch[1a]	aun, aún[1a], todavía[1a]
stop[1a] (*tr. vb.*), (cease[2b]), (halt[4a])	arrêter[1a], cesser[1a]	halten[1a], (stocken[5b])	detener[1a], cesar[1b], parar[1b], (atajar[4a])
story[1a], (tale[2a]), (chronicle[5a])	histoire[1a], (chronique[3b]), (conte[3b])	Geschichte[1a], (Erzählung[2a])	historia[1a], (cuento[2a]), (relato[4a]), (crónica[5a])
strange[1b], (odd[2b]), (peculiar[3a]), (queer[3b]), (singular[5b])	curieux[1b], étrange[1b], singulier[1b], (bizarre[2b]), (drôle [n.][4a]), (fantasque[6b]) (singulièrement[6a])	fremd[1a], (seltsam[2b]), (sonderbar[2b]), (wunderlich[3a]), (unheimlich[5b])	extraño[1b], raro[1b], (curioso[2a]), (singular[2a]), (peregrino[2b]), (pintoresco[3a]), (peculiar[3b])
street[1a], (St.[3a])	rue[1b]	Straße[1b]	calle[1a]
strong[1a], (mighty[2a]), (powerful[3b]), (potent[6])	fort[1a], puissant[1b], (robuste[4a]) (fortement[2b])	stark[1a], mächtig[1b], (gewaltig[2a]), (kräftig[2a])	fuerte[1a], poderoso[1b], (recio[2b]), (robusto[2b]), (esforzado[5a]), (potente[5b])
subject[1a], (topic[5b])	sujet[1b]	Gegenstand[1a], (Fach[3b]), (Materie[4a])	sujeto[1b], (tema[2b])
such[1a]	tel[1a]	solch[1a], derartig[1b], dergleichen[1b]	tal[1a]
sudden[1b]	soudain[1b], (subit[3b])	plötzlich[1b]	de[1a] pronto[1a], (repentino[3a]), (súbito[3a])

English	French	German	Spanish
suddenly (sudden[1b])	brusquement[1b], (tout à coup[2a]), (subitement[4a])	auf[1a] einmal[1a], plötzlich[1b]	de[1a] pronto[1a], (de[1a] repente[3a]), (repentinamente [repentino[3a]]) (súbitamente [súbito[3a]]), (de[1a] sobresalto[5b])
suffer[1b]	souffrir[1a]	leiden[1b], (erleiden[2b]), (ertragen[2b])	sufrir[1a], (padecer[2a])
sun[1a]	soleil[1a]	Sonne[1a]	sol[1a]
suppose[1b], (assume[3b])	supposer[1b]	meinen[1a], (vermuten[3a]), (vorstellen[3a]), (wähnen[5b])	suponer[1a]
sure[1a], certain[1a]	certain[1a], sûr[1b], (assuré[4a])	gewiß[1a], sicher[1a]	cierto[1a], seguro[1a]
(certainly[5a]*)	certainement[1b], (assurément[3b]), (parfaitement[6b]), (sûrement[3b])	freilich[1a], zwar[1a], (sicherlich[3a])	
table[1a]	table[1a]	Tisch[1b], (Tafel[3b])	mesa[1a]
take[1a], took[1b]	prendre[1a], reprendre[1a]	nehmen[1a], (mitnehmen[3a])	coger[1a], tomar[1a]
take[1a] away[1a], (remove[2a])	emporter[1a], éloigner[1b], enlever[1b], (écarter[2a]), (ôter[2a]), (emmener[2b]), (remporter[5a])	entfernen[1b], versetzen[1b], (beseitigen[2a]), (entziehen[2a]), (abnehmen[3a]), (räumen[7b]), (herausnehmen[6a]), (wegnehmen[6a]), (fortreißen[6b])	llevar[1a], quitar[1a], (arrebatar[2b])
take[1a] away[1a], separate[1b] (one thing from another)	éloigner[1b]	entfernen[1b]	alejar[1b]
talk[1a] (*vb.*), (converse[5a])	parler[1a], causer[1b], (s'entretenir[3b]), (converser[6a])	reden[1a], sprechen[1a], (sich[1a] unterhalten[2b])	hablar[1a], (charlar[4b]), (conversar[4b])
talk[1a] (*n.*), (conversation[3a]), (converse[5a])	conversation[1b], (entretien[2b]), (tête-à-tête[5b])	Rede[1a], (Gespräch[2a]), (Unterhaltung[3a]), (Besprechung[3b])	conversación[1b], (coloquio[4b]), (charla[6a])
tall[1b]	grand[1a]	groß[1a]	alto[1a]
teach[1b], (taught[2a]), (instruct[3a])	apprendre[1a] à[1a], (enseigner[2b]), (instruire[2b])	lehren[1a], (unterrichten[3a]), (beibringen[4b])	enseñar[1b], (instruir[3b])
teacher[1b], (tutor[5b]), (schoolmaster[6])	maître[1a], (maîtresse[2a]), (professeur[3a]), (instituteur[5a])	Lehrer[1b], (Lehrerin[5a])	maestro[1b], (profesor[3a]), (pedagogo[6a]), (dómine[6b])
tear[1b] (*n.*) (from eyes)	larme[1b], (pleurs[6a])	Träne[1b]	lágrima[1b], (llanto[2a])
tell[1a], told[1b], (relate[3a]), (recount[6])	dire[1a], raconter[1b], (conter[3a]), (retracer[6a])	erzählen[1b]	contar[1a], decir[1a], referir[1b], (relatar[4a]), (narrar[6b])
than[1a]	que (*conj.*)[1a]	als[1a]	que[1a]
thank[1a] (*vb.*)	remercier[1b]	danken[1b]	agradecer[1b]
that[1a], those[1a], (yon[4a]) (*adj.*)	ce[1a]	der[1a], jener[1a]	aquel[1a], ese[1a]
that[1a], those[1a] (*pron.*), one[1a]	cela[1a], celui(-ci, -là)[1a], ça[1b], celle(-ci, -là)[1a], ceux(-ci, -là)[1a], celles(-ci, -là)[1b]	derjenige[1a], etc., jener[1a], etc.	ése[1a], etc., eso[1a]
that[1a] (*conj.*), (lest[3a])	que[1a]	daß[1a]	que[1a]
the[1a]	le[1a]	der[1a]	el[1a]

English	French	German	Spanish
the[1a] (more, less) . . . . the[1a] (more, less)	plus[1a], moins[1a] . . . . plus[1a], moins[1a]	je[1a] . . . . desto[1b]	mientras[1a], más[1a] . . . . más[1a], etc.
their[1a]	leur[1a]	ihr[1a]	su[1*]
then[1a] (time)	alors[1a], ensuite[1a], puis[1a], lors[1b]	damals[1a], dann[1a], (sodann[2a]), (alsdann[2b])	entonces[1a]
there[1a] (place), (thence[3a]), (yonder[3a]), (thither[4b])	là[1a], y[1a], là-bas[1b]	da[1a], dahin[1a], dort[1a], hin[1a], (daselbst[2b]), (dorthin[3a]), (dortig[3a]), (drüben[5a])	allí[1a], allá[1a], (ahí[2a])
there[1a] is[1a], *there*[1a] are[1a]	voilà[1b]	da[1a] (ist, etc.)	hay (haber[1a]), he
there[1a] *is*[1a], there[1a] *are*[1a], (there's[5a])	il[1a] y[1a] a (avoir[1a])	es[1a] gibt (geben[1a])	hay (haber[1a])
therefore[1b], then[1a], (hence[2a]), (accordingly[3b])	donc[1a], (aussi[2a])	also[1a], daher[1a], darum[1a], deshalb[1a], (somit[2a]), (demnach[2b]), (deswegen[2b]), (mithin[4a]), (sonach[4b]), (infolgedessen[6b])	así[1a], luego[1a], por[1a] lo[1a] tanto[1a]
they[1a], them[1a], ('em[6])	ils[1a], elles[1a], eux[1a]	sie[1a]	ellos[1*]
thing[1a], object[1b]	chose[1a], objet[1a]	Ding[1a], Gegenstand[1a], (Objekt[4a])	cosa[1a], objeto[1a], (entidad[6b])
think[1a], thought[1a], (methinks[5b]), (methought[6])	penser[1a], songer[1a]	denken[1a], meinen[1a], (dünken[4a])	pensar[1a]
third[1a]	troisième[1b], (tiers[3b])	dritte[1a], (Drittel[3b])	tercero[1*], (tercio[6a])
this[1a], these[1a] (*adj.*)	ce[1a]	dies[1a]	este[1a]
this[1a], these[1a] (*pron.*), one[1a]	celui(-ci, -là)[1a], ceux(-ci, -là)[1a], celle(-ci, -là)[1a], celles(-ci, -là)[1b], ceci[1b]	dies[1a]	éste[1a]
thou[1b], thee[1b]	tu[1a]	du[1a]	tu[1*]
thought[1a] (*n.*)	pensée[1b]	Gedanke[1a], (Denken[4b])	pensamiento[1a]
three[1a]	trois[1a]	drei[1a]	tres[1*]
through[1a] (motion), (thro [thro'][5a])	par[1a], à travers[1b]	durch[1a], (hindurch[2a]), (wodurch[2a]), (hierdurch[3a])	por[1a], ([a] través[2a] [de])
through[1a] (agent), (thereby[4a]), (thro [thro'][5a])	par[1a], de[1a]	durch[1a], von[1a], dadurch[1a], (infolge[2a]), (hierdurch[3a]), (mittels[3a]), ([durch] Vermittelung[5b] [von])	por[1a], (mediante[4a]), (por[1a] conducto[5b] de[1a])
throw[1b], (cast[2a]), (threw[2a]), (toss[2b]), (pitch[3a]), (hurl[4a]), (fling[4b]), (flung[4b]), (chuck[6]), (thrown[6*])	jeter[1a], lancer[1b]	werfen[1a], (schleudern[5a])	arrojar[1a], echar[1a], lanzar[1b], tirar[1b], (despeñar[4b]) (from a cliff), (botar[6b])
till[1a], until[1a]	jusque[1a], jusqu'à[1a], (jusqu'à ce que[3b])	bis[1a], bis[1a] (*prep.*)	hasta[1a]
till[1a] now[1a], (hitherto[5a])	jusqu'à[1a] présent[1a]	bisher[1a], bisherig[1b]	hasta[1a] ahora[1a]
time[1a] (*n.*) (general)	temps[1a]	Zeit[1a], (Dienstzeit[3b]), (Arbeitszeit[6b])	tiempo[1a]
time[1a] (how many)	fois[1a]	Mal[1b]	vez[1a]
(what) time[1a] (is it), (o'clock[2a])	heure[1a]	Uhr[1b]	hora[1a]
(at the same) time[1a]	à[1a] la[1a] fois[1a], en[1a] même[1a] temps[1a]	zugleich[1a]	a[1a] la[1a] vez[1a]

English	French	German	Spanish
(at) times (time[1a]), now[1a] and[1a] then[1a]	(de) temps[1a] (en) temps[1a], (de) temps[1a] (à) autre[1a]	hin[1a] und[1a] wieder[1a], (dann[1a] und[1a] wann[2b]), (zeitweilig[6a]), (zeitweise[6b])	algunas (alguno[1a]) veces (vez[1a]), de[1a] vez[1a] en[1a] cuando[1a]
to[1a], (unto[2b])	à[1a]	dazu[1a], nach[1a], zu[1a], (hinzu[2a]), (hierzu[2b]), (heran[3a])	a[1a]
today(-)[1a]	aujourd'hui[1a]	heute[1a], heutig[1b], (heutzutage[4b])	hoy[1a]
together[1a]	ensemble[1a]	zusammen[1a], gleichzeitig[1b], (miteinander[3b]), (beisammen[4b]), (aneinander[5a])	junto[1a]
tongue[1b], (language[2a])	langue[1b]	Sprache[1a]	lengua[1a], (idioma[2a])
too[1a] (excess)	trop[1a]	zu[1a], (allzu[3a])	demasiado[1b], ([en] demasía[5a])
touch[1b] (*vb.*)	toucher[1a]	greifen[1b], (berühren[2a]), (rühren[2a]),(streifen[3b]), (anfassen[6b])	tocar[1a]
toward(s)[1b]	vers[1a], (envers[3a])	nach[1a]	hacia[1a]
(bring) toward(s)[1b] (put near)	approcher[1b]	nähern[1b]	acercar[1a], (aproximar[2b]), (arrimar[3b])
(go, come, move) toward(s)[1b], near[1a], (approach[2a])	approcher[1b], (s'approcher[2a])	sich[1a] nähern[1b], (heranziehen[4b]), (nahen[2b]), (antreten[3b]), (annähern[4b]), (herantreten[5a]), (herkommen[5b]), (herankommen[6a])	acercar[1a] se, (aproximar[2b] se), (allegar[5b] se)
tree[1a]	arbre[1b]	Baum[1b]	árbol[1b]
trouble[1b] (*n.*), (distress[3a])	peine[1a], difficulté[1b], (embarras[2b]), (détresse[3b])	Mühe[1b], (Beschwerde[3a])	pena[1a], (molestia[3b])
true[1a], (genuine[4b])	vrai[1a], (authentique[4b])	wahr[1a], treu[1b], (wahrhaft[3a]), (wahrhaftig[3b])	verdadero[1a], fiel[1b], (auténtico[5a]), (genuino[6a])
trust[1b], (confidence[3b])	confiance[1b]	Vertrauen[1b], (Zuversicht[4a]), (Zutrauen[5b])	confianza[1b]
truth[1b], (sooth[6])	vérité[1a]	Wahrheit[1a], (Richtigkeit[4b]), (Wahre[6a])	verdad[1a]
try[1a], (attempt[2a]), (tried[2a]), (endeavor[4a]), (essay[6])	essayer[1a], tenter[1b], (tâcher[2a])	versuchen[1b], (erproben[5b])	procurar[1a], tratar[1a], probar[1b], (intentar[2a]), (tentar[3a]), (dar[1a] un[1a] tiento[3b]), (ensayar[4a]), (atentar[7a])
turn[1a] (*vb.*), (revolve[6a])	tourner[1a], (circuler[4a])	wenden[1a], kehren[1b]	volver[1a], (revolver[2a]), (girar[3a])
(in) turn[1a]	(à –) tour[1a]	(an der) Reihe[1b]	(a –) vez[1a], ([por] turno[6b])
two[1a], (brace[4b]), (twain[6])	deux[1a]	zwei[1a]	dos[1]*
under[1a] (*prep.*), (beneath[2a]), (underneath[3b])	sous[1a], (au-dessous de[3a])	unter[1a], (darunter[2b])	debajo[1a] de
understand[1b], (perceive[3a]), (understood[3a]), (comprehend[4b]), (apprehend[6])	comprendre[1a], (percevoir[3a])	verstehen[1a], begreifen[1b], (vernehmen[2a]), (einsehen[3a]), (auffassen[3b])	comprender[1a], entender[1a]
unite[1b]	réunir[1b], (unir[2b])	vereinigen[1b], (vereinen[3b])	unir[1a], reunir[1b], (vincular[6b])

English	French	German	Spanish
use[1a](*vb.*), (employ[2a])	se[1a] servir[1a] (de), employer[1b], (utiliser[2b])	benutzen(+ü)[1b], verwenden[1b], (anwenden[2a]), (gebrauchen[3a]), (verwerten[5a]), (nutzen[5b]), (verarbeiten[6a])	emplear[1a], soler[1a], usar[1a], (utilizar[3a])
usual[1b], (ordinary[3a]), (customary[6])	ordinaire[1b], (habituel[2b]), (usuel[6a])	gewöhnlich[1a], (üblich[3a]), (gebräuchlich[5b]), (alltäglich[6b])	general[1a], (habitual[3b]), (usual[6a])
value[1b], worth[1b], (merit[3a])	valeur[1b], (mérite[3a])	Wert[1a], (Geltung[3a])	valor[1a], (mérito[2a]), (merecimiento[4b])
very[1a], (extremely[3b]*), (exceeding[5a])	très[1a], bien[1a], (extrêmement[2b]), (fort[4a]), (sensiblement[5b])	sehr[1a], (überaus[3b])	muy[1a]
voice[1a]	voix[1a]	Stimme[1a]	voz[1a]
wait[1a], (bide[6])	attendre[1a]	warten[1b]	esperar[1a], aguardar[1b]
wait[1a] for[1a], (await[2b])	attendre[1a]	erwarten[1a], (abwarten[3b])	esperar[1a], aguardar[1b]
walk[1a] (*vb.*), (stalk[4a])	aller[1a] à[1a] pied[1a], marcher[1a], promener[1b], (faire[1a] une[1a] promenade[2a]), (cheminer[5a])	zu[1a] Fuß[1a] gehen[1a], (spazieren[4b])	andar[1a], (pasear[2a]), (caminar[2b])
want[1a] (*vb.*), ([be] willing[2b])	vouloir[1a]	wollen[1a]	querer[1a]
war[1a], (warfare[6])	guerre[1b]	Krieg[1a]	guerra[1a]
watch[1a] (*vb.*), (observe[2a])	observer[1b], (veiller[2a]), (surveiller[2b]), (guetter[3b])	betrachten[1b], beobachten[1b], (zusehen[5b])	observar[1b], (velar[2a]), ([estar a la] mira[4a]), (vigilar[4a])
water[1a] (*n.*), *plu.*	eau[1b], *plu.*	Wasser[1a], (Wasserstraße[4b]), (Gewässer[6b])	agua[1a], *plu.*
way[1a], manner[1b]	façon[1a], manière[1a], moyen[1a], mode (*f.*)[1b], (guise[4b])	Art[1a], Weise[1a], (dergestalt[5a]), (Manier[5a])	forma[1a], manera[1a], modo[1a], (guisa[5b])
we[1a], us[1a], (let's[6])	nous[1a]	wir[1a], etc.	nosotros[1]*, etc.
wear[1b] (clothes), (worn[2b]), (wore[3a])	porter[1a]	tragen[1a]	llevar[1a], traer[1a]
well[1a] (*adv.*)	bien[1a]	gut[1a], wohl[1a]	bien[1a]
(be) well[1a] (health)	aller[1a] bien[1a], (se) porter[1a] bien[1a]	gut[1a] gehen[1a], wohl[1a] sein[1a]	estar[1a] bueno[1a]
what (*rel.* and *inter.*)[1a]	que[1a], quoi[1a]	was[1a]	que, qué[1a]
when[1a]	lorsque[1a], quand[1a], (alors que[3a])	als[1a], wie[1a], (wann[2b])	cuando, cuándo[1a]
where[1a], (whence[2b]), (wherever[3a]), (whither[3b])	où[1a]	wo[1a], (wohin[2a]), (woher[3b])	adonde[1a], donde, dónde[1a]
whether[1b]	si[1a], (soit . . . . soit[3b])	ob[1a]	si[1a]
which (*rel.* and *inter.*)[1a]	lequel[1a], que[1a], quel[1a], qui[1a]	der[1a], welch[1a]	cual, cuál[1a], que, qué[1a]
while[1a] (*conj.*)	tandis que[1a], pendant que[1b]	während[1a], indem[1a], indessen[1b], (solang[e][4a])	mientras[1a]
white[1a] (*adj.*)	blanc[1a]	weiß[1a]	blanco[1a]
who[1a], whom[1b] (*rel.* and *inter.*)	qui[1a]	der[1a], etc., wer[1a], etc.	que[1a], etc., quien[1a], etc.
whose[1b] (*rel.* and *inter.*)	dont[1a]	dessen (der[1a]), wessen (wer[1a])	cuyo (quien, quién[1a])
why[1a], (wherefore[4a])	pourquoi[1a]	warum[1a], (wozu[2b])	porqué[1a]
wife[1b], (mate[2b]), (wives[3b]), (spouse[5a]), (consort[6])	femme[1a], (épouse[4b])	Frau[1a], (Gattin[3a]), (Gemahlin[4a]), (Hausfrau[4b])	esposa (esposo[1a]), mujer[1a]

English	French	German	Spanish
will[1a] (e.g., free will)	volonté[1b]	Wille[1a]	voluntad[1a], (arbitrio[5a]), (albedrío[5b])
with[1a]	avec[1a]	damit[1a], mit[1a], (nebst[2a]), (hiermit[2b]), (womit[2b]), (samt[3b])	con[1a], conmigo[1a], consigo[1a], contigo[1a]
without[1a]	sans[1a], (sans que[2b])	ohne[1a]	sin[1a]
woman[1a], (women[2a])	femme[1a]	Frau[1a], Weib[1b], (Frauenzimmer[4a])	mujer[1a], (señá[5b] [vulgar])
wonder[1b] (e.g., I wonder whether . . . .)	se[1a] demander[1a], vouloir[1a] savoir[1a]	wissen[1a] mögen[1a]	desear[1a] saber[1a], preguntar[1a] (se)
word[1a]	mot[1a], parole[1a]	Wort[1a]	palabra[1a], (vocablo[4b])
work[1a] (*vb.*), labor[1b], (toil[2b]), (wrought[3a])	travailler[1a]	arbeiten[1b]	trabajar[1b], (labrar[3a]), (afanar[5a] se), (laborar[7a])
work[1a] (*n.*), labor[1b], (toil[2b])	travail[1a], (main d'œuvre[6b])	Arbeit[1a], (Anstellung[4a])	obra[1a], trabajo[1a], (labor[2a]), (faena[4a])
work[1a] (a work)	œuvre[1b], ouvrage[1b]	Werk[1a]	obra[1a], (labor[2a])
world[1a] (*n.*)	monde[1a]	Welt[1a], (All[6b])	mundo[1a]
(be) worth[1b], (worthy[2a]), (deserve[2b]), (merit[3a])	valoir[1a], (être) digne[1b]	gelten[1a], wert[1b] (sein)	digno[1a], merecer[1a], valer[1a]
write[1a], (written[2a]), (wrote[2b])	écrire[1a]	schreiben[1a], (niederschreiben[5b])	escribir[1a]
wrong[1b] (mistaken)	faux[1b]	falsch[1b], (unrichtig[3b]), (unrecht[6a]), (irrig[6b])	falso[1a], mal[1a]
year[1a]	an[1a], année[1a]	Jahr[1a], (Jahrgang[4b]), (jährig[4b]), (Lebensjahr[4b]), (zweijährig[6a]), (einjährig[6a]), (jahrelang[6b])	año[1a]
yes[1b], (yea[3b])	oui[1a], (si[3a])	ja[1a]	sí[1a]
yesterday[1b]	hier[1b]	gestern[1b], (gestrig[4a])	ayer[1a]
you[1a], (ye[2b])	vous[1a]	du[1a], ihr[1a], Sie[1a]	usted[1a]
young[1a], (junior[5a])	jeune[1a]	jung[1a]	joven[1a], mozo[1a]
your[1a]	votre, vos[1a]	euer[1a], Ihr[1a]	vuestro[1a]

SECTION 1.1. CONCEPTS 663 THROUGH 745

E F G S
1-1-1-2
1-2-1-1

Read: English, first thousand; French, first thousand; German, first thousand; Spanish, second thousand; *or* English, first thousand; French, second thousand; German, first thousand; Spanish, first thousand

English	French	German	Spanish
animal[1b]	animal[2b]	Tier[1b]	animal[1b]
around[1a] (*prep.*), about[1a]	autour de[1a]	um[1a], (rings[4a]), (ringsum[6b]) (*adv.*)	en[1a] torno[2a] de[1a], alrededor[2a] de[1a], (al[1a] derredor[5a] de[1a])
as[1a] long[1a] as[1a]	tant que[2b]	soweit[1b], (insofern[2b]), (sofern[3a]), (insoweit[5a])	tan, tanto[1a] como[1a]
beast[1b]	bête (*n.*)[1b]	Tier[1b]	bestia[2a], (fiera[3a]), (bicho[4a]), (res[6a])

English	French	German	Spanish
beat[1b], pound[1b], (thrash[5a]), (thump[5a]), (beaten[6])	battre[1a], frapper[1a], (rebattre[6a])	schlagen[1a]	batir[2a], (golpear[5a])
before[1a] (*conj.*)	avant que[2b]	ehe[1a], (bevor[2b])	antes[1a] que[1a]
break[1b], broken[1b], (broke[2b])	casser[2a]	brechen[1b]	romper[1a]
by[1a] and[1a] by[1a], later (late[1a]) on[1a], pretty[1a] soon[1a], (bye[5b] [and] bye), (presently[7*])	tantôt[2a], (tout à l'heure[4a])	später (spät[1a]), (nachher[2a])	pronto[1a]
circle[1b], set[1a] (of people)	milieu[1a], (cercle[2a]), (entourage[5b])	Kreis[1a], (Bekanntschaft[3b]), (Zirkel[5b])	círculo[2b], (cerco[3b]), (tertulia[3b])
country[1a] (fatherland)	patrie[2a]	Vaterland[1b], (Heimat[2a])	patria[1b]
course[1a], (drift[4a]), (tenor[6])	cours[1a], (parcours[6a])	Lauf[1b], (Verlauf[2b]), (Kurs[3b])	curso[2a], marcha[2b], (corrida[4b])
court[1b], yard[1b]	cour[1a], (basse-cour[5b])	Hof[1b]	corral[2b], patio[2b]
dear[1a], (costly[3a]), (expensive[4a])	cher[1a], (coûteux[5a])	teuer[1b], (kostspielig[5b])	caro[2b], (costoso[5b])
direct[1b] (*adv.*), straight[1b]	directement[2b], (droit [*adv.*][6b])	gerade[1a], direkt[1b], ([ohne] Umweg[5b]), (geradeaus[6b])	derecho[1a], (directo[2a]), (recto[2b])
distance[1b]	lointain[2a], distance[2b], (éloignement[6b])	Entfernung[1b], (Strecke[2b]), (Ferne[3a]), (Abstand[3b]), (Weite[5a])	distancia[1b], (trecho[4a])
divide[1b]	partager[2a], diviser[2b]	teilen[1b], (verteilen[2b]), (zerlegen[6b])	dividir[1b], (compartir[4b])
drive[1a] out[1a], (chase[2a])	chasser[2b]	treiben[1b]	echar[1a]
early[1a]	de[1a] bonne (bon[1a]) heure[1a], tôt[1b], (matinal[5b])	früh[1a], (frühzeitig[4b]), (zeitig[5a])	temprano[2a]
else[1b], (otherwise[3a])	autrement[2a], sinon[2a]	sonst[1a]	además[1a], sino[1a]
end[1a] (in), come[1a] (to)	aboutir[2a]	(zu —)werden[1a]	parar[1b] (en)
enjoy[1b] (*tr. vb.*), (revel[5a] in[1a])	jouir[2a]	genießen[1b], (erfreuen[2a]), (vergnügen[4a])	gozar[1a], (disfrutar[2b])
except[1b], but[1a]	sauf (*prep.*)[2b], (excepté [*prep.*][5b])	außer[1a]	menos[1a], (excepto[3b])
famous[1b], (prominent[4a]), (illustrious[5b]), (eminent[6])	fameux[2a], célèbre[2b], connu (*adj.*)[2b], illustre[2b], (éminent[4a])	bekannt[1a], (berühmt[2a]), (namhaft[5b])	famoso[1b], ilustre[1b], (célebre[2a]), (insigne[2b]), (eminente[3a])
fight[1b] (*n.*), (struggle[2a]), (contest[3b]), (strife[3b]), (combat[4a]), (conflict[4b]), (clash[5b]), (contention[6]), (discord[6]), (fray[6])	lutte[1b], (combat[2b]), (conflit[4a])	Kampf[1a], (Gefecht[2a]), (Bekämpfung[6a])	lucha[2a], conflicto[2b], (combate[3a]), (lid[4b]), (pelea[4b]), (riña[5b]), (discordia[6b])
figure[1b], number[1a]	chiffre[2a]	Nummer[1a], (Ziffer[4a])	número[1a], (cifra[3b]), (guarismo[6b])
fine[1a] (Amer.), (magnificent[3a])	magnifique[1b]	herrlich[1b], (wunderbar[2b])	magnífico[2a]
firm[1b] (*adj.*) (fixed), (stable[2b]), (steady[3a])	ferme (*adj.*)[2b], (fixe [*adj.*][3a])	fest[1a], sicher[1a], (feststehend[5b])	seguro[1a], fijo[1b], firme[1b]
firm[1b] (*adj.*) (character), (constant[2a]), (steady[3a]), (steadfast[5b])	constant[2b], ferme (*adj.*)[2b]	fest[1a], (beständig[2b]), (standhaft[6b])	firme[1b]
fix[1b], (determine[2b])	determiner[2b]	bestimmen[1b]	determinar[1b], (definir[3a])
following[1b] (*adj.*), (consequent[5a])	suivant[1b]	folgend[1a]	consiguiente[2b]

English	French	German	Spanish
forced (*adj.*) (force[1b])	forcé (*adj.*)[2b]	gezwungen (zwingen[1b])	obligado (obligar[1b]), (forzado [forzar[3b]])
fresh[1a]	frais (*adj.*)[2a]	frisch[1b]	fresco[1b]
general[1a] (*n.*)	général[2a]	General[1b], (Feldherr[3a])	general[1a]
good[1a] morning[1a], good[1a] day[1a], good[1a] evening[1a], (hello[5b])	bonjour[2a], (bonsoir[4b])	guten (gut[1a]) Tag[1a], (guten) Abend[1a], (guten) Morgen[1b]	buenos (buen[o][1a]) días (día[1a]), (buenas) tardes, (tarde [*n.*][1a]) (hola[3b])
government[1b]	gouvernement[2a], régime[2a]	Regierung[1a], (Staatsregierung[2a]), (Reichsregierung[6b])	gobierno[1b], (régimen[4a])
grow[1a] (increase in size)	croître[2b], grandir[2b], (grossir[4a])	wachsen[1b], (heranwachsen[6a])	crecer[1b]
hang[1b] (*tr. vb.*), (hung[2a]), (suspend[5a]), (dangle[6])	suspendre[2a], pendre[2b]	hängen[1b]	colgar[1b], (suspender[2a]), (ahorcar[4a]), (pender[4b])
height[1b], (altitude[6])	hauteur[2a], grandeur[2b]	Höhe[1a], Größe[1b]	altura[1b], (eminencia[5a])
help[1a] (*n.*), (aid[2a])	aide[1b], secours[1b], (renfort[6a])	Hilfe[1b], (Beistand[4a]), (Förderung[4b])	auxilio[2a], ayuda[2b], (socorro[3a])
his[1a] (*poss. pron.*)	sien[2a]	sein[1a], (seinige[3a])	suyo[1a]
increase[1b], (enlarge[4a]), (dilate[6]), (expand[6])	augmenter[2a], accroître[2b], (élargir[3a]), (agrandir[3b]), (amplifier[6b])	wachsen[1b], (vermehren[2a]), (weiten[3b]), (zunehmen[6b]), (vergrößern[4b]), (mehren[6a])	aumentar[1b], (ensanchar[3b]), (acrecentar[5a]), (ampliar[6a])
known[1a] (e.g., fact)	connu[2b]	bekannt[1a], (bekanntlich[2b]), (kund[5a]), (wohlbekannt[6b])	conocido (conocer[1a]), (notorio[4a]), (consabido[5b])
last[1a] (*vb.*)	durer[2a]	dauern[1b], währen[1b], (Bestand[3b] [haben])	durar[1b], (subsistir[5a])
live[1a], (lodge[2a]), (dwell[2b]), (dwelt[4a]), (reside[4a])	demeurer[1b], habiter[1b], (loger[3b]), (résider[4a])	wohnen[1b], (hausen[5b])	habitar[2a], (residir[3a]), (alojar[4a]), (morar[5b])
lord (L)[1b]	seigneur[2a], (châtelain[-e][4b])	Herr[1a]	señor[1a]
matter[1a] (*n.*)	matière[2a]	Stoff[1b]	materia[1b]
member[1b]	membre[1b]	Mitglied[1a], (Glied[2a])	miembro[2b]
mind[1a] (*n.*)	esprit[1a]	Sinn[1a]	mente[2b]
mine[1a] (*pron.*)	le[1a] mien[2a]	mein[1a], (meinige[3b])	mío[1a], el[1a] mío[1a]
miss (M)[1a] (title)	mademoiselle[2b]	Fräulein[1b], (Miß[5b])	señorita (señorito[1a])
move[1a] (*vb.*), (shift[3b]), (whisk[6])	remuer[2a], bouger[2b], (déplacer[3b]), (mouvoir[4a])	bewegen[1b], (rücken[2a])	mover[1a]
nation[1b]	nation[2a]	Nation[1b]	nación[1b]
(from) now[1a] (on), (henceforth[3a])	désormais[2a]	von[1a] nun[1a] an[1a]	(en) adelante[1b], desde[1a] ahora[1a], ([en lo] sucesivo[2b])
party[1b], (faction[6]), (sect[6])	parti[1b], (faction[6a]), (groupement[6a])	Partei[1b], (Anhang[5b])	partido[2a], (bando[3b]), (facción[4a]), (secta[6b])
picture[1a] (*n.*)	tableau[2a], image[2b]	Bild[1a]	cuadro[1b], (lámina[3b])
plan[1b] (*n.*), (scheme[4a]), (device[4b]), (schedule[6])	plan[1b], (dessein[3b])	Entwurf[1b], Plan[1b]	plan[2b]
pleasant[1b], (gracious[3a]), (agreeable[3b]), (delightful[3b]), (genial[4b]), (amiable[6])	aimable[2a], agréable[2a], gentil[2b], (plaisant[4b])	angenehm[1b], (gefällig[2a]), (erfreulich[3b]), (gemütlich[5b])	agradable[1b], (amable[2a]), (grato[2b]), (afable[3a]), (risueño[3a]), (simpático[3a]), (ameno[3b]), (gustoso[4a])
	(gentiment[4a]), (agréablement[6b])		

English	French	German	Spanish
present^{1a} (*adj.*), (current^{2b})	actuel^{2b}, présent (*adj.*)^{2b}	gegenwärtig^{1b}, jetzig^{1b}	presente^{1a}, (actual^{2a})
press^{1b} (*vb.*), (squeeze^{5a})	serrer^{1b}	drücken^{1b}, (dringen^{2a}), (drängen^{2a}), (pressen^{4b}), (zusammendrängen^{6a})	apretar^{2a}, (exprimir^{6a})
prince^{1b}	prince^{2a}	Fürst^{1a}, Prinz^{1b}, (Kronprinz^{3b})	príncipe^{1b}, (infante^{3b})
question^{1b} (something asked)	question^{1a}	Frage^{1a}	pregunta^{2a}
rather^{1b} (+*vb.*), (prefer^{2a})	préférer^{1b}	lieber (lieb^{1a}) (+*vb.*), (vorziehen^{4a})	preferir^{2a}
rest^{1a} (*n.*), (remainder^{3b}), (remnant^{4b})	reste^{1a}	übrig^{1a}, (Rest^{2b}), (übrige^{3b}), (Überrest^{6a})	resto^{2a}, (sobra^{3a}), (restante^{5a})
(in^{1a}) return^{1b}	en^{1a} revanche^{2b}	dafür^{1a}, dagegen^{1a}, ([als] Entschädigung^{3a}), ([als] Ersatz^{3a})	a^{1a} cambio^{1b}, (en^{1a} recompensa^{4a})
rule^{1b} (*n.*), direction^{1b}, (ordinance^{4b}), (regulation^{6})	direction^{2a}, règle^{2a}, règlement^{2b}	Maßregel^{1b}, Regel^{1b}, Vorschrift^{1b}, (Anordnung^{2a}), (Behörde^{2a}), (Regelung^{3a}), (Landgemeindeordnung^{3b}), (Anleitung^{5a}), (Arbeitsordnung^{5a}), (Regulierung^{5a}), (Reglement^{6a}), (Gewerbeordnung^{6b}), (Kreisordnung^{6b})	regla^{1b}, (máxima^{5b}), (ordenanza^{5b})
seize^{1b}, (grasp^{4a}), (grip^{4b}), (clutch^{5a})	saisir^{1a}, (ressaisir^{5a})	fassen^{1a}, ergreifen^{1b}, fangen^{1b}, greifen^{1b}, (erfassen^{3a}), (bemächtigen^{3b}), (erbeuten^{6b})	prender^{2a}, (apoderarse^{3a}), (asir^{3b}), (agarrar^{4a}), (empuñar^{4a}), (aferrar^{5a})
set^{1a} table^{1a}	mettre^{1a} couvert^{2a}	Tisch^{1b} decken^{1b}	poner^{1a} mesa^{1a}
shake^{1b} (hands)	donner^{1a}, serrer^{1b}	geben^{1a}, (schütteln^{3a})	estrechar^{2b}
(catch^{1b}) sight^{1a} (of^{1a}), (perceive^{3a})	apercevoir^{1a}	bemerken^{1b}, (absehen^{2a}), (erblicken^{2a}), (wahrnehmen^{3a}), (ersehen^{3b})	percibir^{2b}, (columbrar^{5a}), (vislumbrar^{5a})
sign^{1b}, mark^{1a}, (tick^{3b}), (token^{4b}), (badge^{6})	signe^{1a}, (marque^{2b}), (indice^{5a}), (insigne^{6b})	Zeichen^{1b}, (Merkmal^{5a})	seña^{2a}, señal^{2a}, (signo^{3a}), (marca^{4b})
step^{1a} (*vb.*), (tread^{2b}), (trod^{4a})	marcher^{1a}, (fouler^{4b})	treten^{1a}, (heraustreten^{6b})	pisar^{2a}
strike^{1b}, (hit^{2b}), (struck^{2b}), (smite^{4b}), (smote^{4b}), (spank^{5a}), (punch [P]^{5b}), (slap^{5b}), (smack^{6}), (smitten^{6})	battre^{1a}, frapper^{1a}, (cogner^{6b})	schlagen^{1a}, (stoßen^{2a})	batir^{2a}, pegar^{2a}, chocar^{2b}, (golpear^{5a}), (apalear^{6a})
supply^{1b}, (furnish^{2a}), (provide^{2a})	fournir^{1b}, (pourvoir^{3a}), (munir^{3b})	liefern^{1b}, (verschaffen^{2a}), (versehen^{2a}), (zuführen^{3b}), (versorgen^{5b})	proporcionar^{2a}, proveer^{2b}, (suplir^{3b}), (suministrar^{5b})
thanks (thank^{1a})	merci^{2a}, (remerciement^{6a})	Dank^{1b}	gracias (gracia^{1a})
train^{1a} (railroad)	train^{1b}	Zug^{1a}	tren^{2b}
turn^{1a} to^{1a}, (address^{2a}), (apply^{2a} to)	adresser^{2a}, s'adresser à^{2b}	sich^{1a} wenden^{1a} an^{1a}, (zuwenden^{3a}), (sich^{1a} anmelden^{5a})	dirigir^{1a} se^{1a}, (recurrir^{4b})

English	French	German	Spanish
use[1a] (*n.*), (employment[5b])	usage[2a], (emploi[3b]), (utilisation[4b])	Anwendung[1b], Gebrauch[1b], (Verwendung[2a]), (Benutzung[3b]), (Heranziehung[5a]), (Verwertung[5b])	uso[1b], (empleo[2b])
weak[1b], (feeble[3b]), (frail[3b]), (sickly[6])	faible[1b], (frêle[5a]), (grêle [*adj.*][6a]) (faiblement[5a])	schwach[1b]	débil[2a], flaco[2b], (flojo[3b]), (frágil[3b]), (deleznable[7a])
week[1a]	semaine[1a]	Woche[1b]	semana[2a]
wing[1b]	aile[2a]	Flügel[1b]	ala[1b]
within[1b], (indoors[6])	dedans[2b], (là-dedans[6a])	innerhalb[1b], (inne[n][2b]), (binnen[3b])	dentro[1a], (adentro[2b])
(piece of) work[1a], (task[2b]), (job[3a])	travail[1a], devoir[1b], (tâche[2b]), (besogne[2b])	Arbeit[1a], Aufgabe[1b]	labor[2a], (tarea[3a]), (faena[4a])
young[1a] lady[1b]	demoiselle[2b]	junge (jung[1a]) Dame[1b]	señorita (señorito[1a])

SECTION 1.2. CONCEPTS 746 THROUGH 783

E F G S
1–2–1–2
1–1–1–3
1–3–1–1

Read: English, first thousand; French, second thousand; German, first thousand; Spanish, second thousand; *or* English, first thousand; French, first thousand; German, first thousand; Spanish, third thousand; *or* English, first thousand; French, third thousand; German, first thousand; Spanish, first thousand

English	French	German	Spanish
answer[1a] (*n.*), reply[1b], (response[5b])	réponse[2a], (réplique[5a])	Antwort[1b], (Beantwortung[4b]), (Erwiderung[6b])	respuesta[2a], (contestación[3a])
army[1b]	armée[2a]	Armee[1a], Heer[1a], (Streitkraft[4b])	ejército[2a]
article[1b] (most meanings)	article[2a]	Artikel[1b]	artículo[2a]
bad[1a], (evil[2a]), (wicked[6b]), (vicious[5b]), (sinful[6])	mauvais[1a], (méchant[2a]), (vilain[3b]), (malveillant[7a])	schlecht[1b], (übel[2a])	infame[3a], villano[3b], (perverso[4b]), (malvado[5a]), (inicuo[6a]), (maligno[6a])
battle[1b]	bataille[2a], combat[2b]	Kampf[1a], Schlacht[1b]	batalla[2a], (combate[3a])
build[1a], building[1b], built[1b], (erect[4b]), (construct[3b])	construire[2a], bâtir[2b], (édifier[5b]), (reconstruire[6a])	aufstellen[1b], bauen[1b], (errichten[2a]), (erbauen[3a]), (konstruieren[3b]), (aufrichten[4b]), (aufbauen[5a])	construir[2a], (edificar[4a]), (erigir[6b])
(so) called (call[1a])	prétendu (*adj.* and *n.*)[3b], (soi-disant[6a])	sogenannt[1b]	supuesto (suponer[1a]), (presunto [presumir[2b]])
circle[1b], ring[1b]	cercle[2a], (anneau[4a]), (rond [*n.*][4a])	Kreis[1a], (Ring[2a]), (Zirkel[5b])	círculo[2b], (anillo[4b])
count[1b] (title), (earl[4b])	comte[2b]	Graf[1a]	conde[2a]
everything[1b]	tout (*indef. pron.*)[3a]	all[1a], (alledem[5b])	todo[1a]
fair[1a] (blond)	blond[2a]	hell[1a], (blond[6a])	rubio[2a]
fall[1a] (*n.*), (tumble[3a])	chute[2a], (tombée [*n.*][6a])	Fall[1a], (Sturz[6a])	caída[2a]
floor[1a]	parquet[3b], (plancher[4b])	Boden[1a]	suelo[1a]

English	French	German	Spanish
hurry[1b] (*intr. vb.*), rush[1b], (speed[2a]), (hasten[2b]), (sped[5a])	se[1a] presser[2a], s'empresser[2b], (se hâter[3a]), (se depêcher[4a])	sich[1a] eilen[1b]	apresurar[2b], apurar[2b] se[1a], (precipitar[3a]), (apremiar[5a])
lesson[1b]	leçon[2a]	Stunde[1a], Aufgabe[1b]	lección[2b]
loss[1b], (forfeit[5a])	perte[2a]	Verlust[1b]	pérdida[2b]
loud[1b] (*adj.*)	haut (*adj.*)[1a]	laut[1b]	ruidoso[3b]
(in like) manner[1b], (likewise[4b])	de[1a] même[1a], également[1b], (pareillement[5b])	ebenso[1a], (gleichfalls[2b])	asimismo[3a]
may (M)[1a] (month)	mai[2b]	Mai[1b]	mayo[2a]
(last) night[1a]	hier[1b] soir[1a]	gestern[1b] abend[1b]	anoche[3a]
O[1b], oh[1b], (ah[2b]), (ha[3a]), (ho[4b])	ah[3a], oh![3b]	ach[1b], (ei[4a]), (ha[4a]), (ah[4b]), (oh[6b])	o[1a], (ah[7b])
officer[1b]	officier[2a]	Offizier[1b]	oficial[2a]
page[1b] (of book)	page (*f.*)[2a]	Seite[1a]	página[2a]
point[1a] (*n.*)	pointe[2a]	Spitze[1b]	pico[2a], punta[2a]
race[1b] (speed) (*n.*)	course[2b]	Lauf[1b]	carrera[2a], (corrida[4b])
ready[1a]	prêt[1b]	bereit[1b], fertig[1b]	listo[3b]
rest[1a] (*n.*), (repose[3b])	repos[2a]	Ruhe[1b]	descanso[2a], reposo[2a]
row[1b] (*n.*), (rank[2a]), (file[3a])	rang[1b], (file[3a]), (rangée [*n.*][5a])	Reihe[1b]	fila[3b], (hilera[5a])
several[1a] times (time[1a]), again[1a] (and again)	(à plusieurs) reprises (reprise[3a])	immer[1a] wieder[1a], vielfach[1b], (mehrfach[3a]), (mannigfach[4b]), (mehrmals[5a])	(varias) veces (vez[1a])
slow[1b], (slack[6])	lent[2a]	langsam[1b]	lento[2a], (despacio[3b]), (tardo[5b])
	(doucement[1b]), (lentement[1b]), ([avec] lenteur[3b]), (posément[6a])		
sound[1a], fit[1b], (healthy[4a]), (hale[6])	sain[2b], (gaillard [*adj.*][3b])	gesund[1b]	sano[2a], robusto[2b], (lozano[5a])
sound[1a] (*n.*)	son[2b]	Ton[1b], (Klang[4a]), (Laut[4b]), (Schall[6b])	sonido[2a], (son[3a])
talk[1a], (speech[2a]), (lecture[4b]), (discourse[5a])	discours[2a], (conférence[3a]), (parler [*n.*][5a]), (causerie[5b]), (harangue[6a])	Rede[1a], (Vortrag[2b]), (Vorlesung[5b])	discurso[2a], (conferencia[3a]), (plática[5a])
thick[1b]	épais[2b]	dicht[1b], (dick[3b])	espeso[2a], grueso[2b]
trade[1b] (*n.*), (commerce[2b])	commerce[2a]	Handel[1b], Verkehr[1b], (Gewerbe[2b]), (Handelsverkehr[3b]), (Gewerbebetrieb[4b]), (Handeln[4b]), (Geschäftsbetrieb[6b])	comercio[2b]
village[1b], (hamlet[4b])	village[1b], (bourg[5b])	Dorf[1b], (Ortschaft[4a])	aldea[3a], (poblado[5a])
(as) well[1a] (as)	aussi bien que[3b]	sowohl[1b] . . . . als[1a] auch[1a]	tanto[1a] como[1a]
wonderful[1b], (marvelous[3b]), (wondrous[4a])	merveilleux[2a], (inouï[3b]), (prodigieux[3b]), (miraculeux[5a])	herrlich[1b], (wunderbar[2b]), (wundervoll[6a]), (wundersam[6b])	maravilloso[2b], (prodigioso[3a]), (estupendo[4b]), (portentoso[5b])
	(prodigieusement[4b]), (merveilleusement[7a])		

SECTION 1.3. CONCEPTS 784 THROUGH 805

E F G S
1–1–1–4
1–4–1–1
1–3–1–2
1–2–1–3

Read: English, first thousand; French, first thousand; German, first thousand; Spanish, fourth thousand; *or* English, first thousand; French, fourth thousand; German, first thousand; Spanish, first thousand; *or* English, first thousand; French, third thousand; German, first thousand; etc.

English	French	German	Spanish
bear[1a] (children)	mettre[1a] au[1a] monde[1a]	gebären[1b]	parir[4b]
beat[1b], (pulsate[6])	battre[1a], (palpiter[6a])	schlagen[1a]	palpitar[4a], (latir[5a]) palpitante[4b]
cares (care[1a])	souci[2a], ennui[2b], (préoccupation[4a])	Sorge[1b], (Besorgnis[6b])	preocupación[3a], (desvelo[5b])
catch[1b], (caught[2a])	attraper[4a]	fangen[1b]	coger[1a]
clock[1b]	horloge[3a], (pendule[4b])	Uhr[1a]	reloj[2b]
cloth[1b], (material[2a]), (stuff[2b]), (fabric[6])	étoffe[3b], (tissu[4b])	Stoff[1b], (Tuch[2b]), (Zeug[3a]), (Gewebe[4b])	material[2a], paño[2b], tela[2b]
demand[1b] (*n.*)	demande[2b]	Forderung[1b], (Verlangen[2b]), (Anforderung[3a])	demanda[3b]
grow[1a] (e.g., leaves)	pousser[3a]	wachsen[1b]	brotar[2b]
guide[1b] (*vb.*)	guider[3a]	führen[1a]	guiar[2a]
(take an) interest[1b] (in)	s'intéresser[3b]	Teil[1a] nehmen[1a]	interesar[2a] (se)
just[1a] (future time)	tout à l'heure[4a]	eben[1a], gleich[1a]	pronto[1a]
long[1a] ago[1b]	autrefois[1b], jadis[1b], (naguère[5b])	früher (früh[1a]), lange (lang[1a]) her[1a], vor[1a] langem (lang[1a]), (ehemals[5a])	antiguamente (antiguo[1a]), (antaño[1b])
myself[1b]	moi-même[4a]	selbst[1a], (ich) selber[1b]	yo[1a] mismo[1a]
old[1a] age[1a]	vieillesse[3b]	Alter[1b]	vejez[2b]
open[1a] (*adj.*), (frank[2b])	franc (*adj.*)[3a], (candide[5a]) franchement[3b], (hautement[5b])	offen[1b], (aufrichtig[2b])	franco[2a], (cándido[4a]), (ingenuo[5a]) (con[1a] franqueza[4a])
rising (rise[1b]) (*adj.*), growing (grow[1a])	naissant (naître[1a]), (croissant [croître[2b]])	werdend (werden[1a]), wachsend (wachsen[1b])	creciente[4b], (naciente[6b])
ship[1a], (vessel[2a])	navire[3b], vaisseau[3b], (galère[6a]), (nef[6a])	Schiff[1b]	barco[2b], (buque[3a]), (nave[3b]), (navío[5a]), (bajel[6a])
size[1b], (bulk[4a])	grandeur[2b]	Größe[1b]	tamaño[3a]
(stand) still[1a], (motionless[7])	immobile[2a]	fest[1a], still[1b]	inmóvil[3a]
top[1a], (crest[4b]), (peak[4b]), (summit[4b])	comble[3b], sommet[3b], (cime[4b]), (pic[5a]), (haut [*n.*][5b])	Spitze[1b]	cumbre[2a], (cima[3a]), (cresta[6b])
watch[1a] (to tell time)	montre[3b]	Uhr[1a]	reloj[2b]
yard[1b] (measure), (ft.[4a]), (meter[4a]), (yd.[5a])	mètre[2a]	Meter[1b]	metro[3a], vara[3a]

SECTION 1.4. CONCEPTS 806 THROUGH 1018

E F G S	*E F G S*
1–3–1–3	1–1–2–1
1–2–1–4	1–5–1–1
1–4–1–2	2–1–1–1

Read: English, first thousand; French, third thousand; German, first thousand; Spanish, third thousand; *or* English, first thousand; French, second thousand; German, first thousand; Spanish, fourth thousand; *or* English, first thousand; French, fourth thousand; etc.

English	French	German	Spanish
able[1b] (*adj.*), fit[1b], (capable[3b]), (apt[5a])	capable[1b]	tüchtig[2a], (fähig[3a]), (befähigt[5b])	capaz[1b], (adecuado[5b])
(in) addition[2b], (moreover[3b]), (besides[4b]), (withal[5a]), (furthermore[6])	d'ailleurs[1a], (en[1a] outre[2b])	außerdem[1b], übrigens[1b], (hierzu[2b]), (überdies[3b]), (als[1a] Ergänzung[4a]), (zudem[4a])	además[1a], por[1a] otra, (otro[1a]) parte[1a]
admit[2b], (confess[3a]), (acknowledge[4a])	reconnaître[1a], admettre[1b], avouer[1b], (confesser[5b])	anerkennen[1b], (bekennen[2b]), (gestehen[2b]), (zugeben[2b]), (einräumen[3b]), (zugestehen[3b])	admitir[1b], confesar[1b], reconocer[1b]
advice[2b], (counsel[3a])	conseil[1a], (avis[2a])	Rat[1b], (Beratung[2a]), (Ratschlag[6b])	consejo[1b]
arrive[1b]	arriver[1a]	ankommen[2a]	llegar[1a], (arribar[7a])
as[1a] (good) as[1a]	aussi . . . . que[5a], aussi[5a]	so[1a] . . . . wie[1a]	tan[1a] . . . . como[1a]
as[1a] it[1a] were[1a]	pour[1a] ainsi[1a] dire[1a]	gleichsam[2a], gewissermaßen[2b]	por[1a] decir[1a] lo[1a] así[1a]
assure[2b]	assurer[1a]	sichern[1b], versichern[1b], (bestätigen[2a])	asegurar[1b], (acreditar[4b])
back[1a] (*n.*), (rear[2b])	dos[1b], (derrière [*n.*][3b]), (reins[4b])	Rücken[2b]	espalda[1b], (lomo[4a])
bed[1a], (couch[3a]), (cot[4a])	lit[1b], (couche[3b])	Bett[2a]	cama[1b], (lecho[2a])
blow[1a] (*n.*), (thrust[3a])	coup[1a], (soufflet[5b])	Schlag[2b], (Streich[5a]), (Hieb[5b])	golpe[1b], (pedrada[6b]), (porrazo[6b])
blue[1a], (azure[6]), (indigo[6])	bleu[1a], (azur[6b])	blau[2b]	azul[1b]
born[1b] of[1a], (sprung[4a] from[1a])	issu (*adj.*)[5a], (né[6b])	entstanden (entstehen[1a])	nacido (nacer[1a])
bow[1b] (*vb.*), (greet[2a]), (salute[4a])	saluer[1b]	begrüßen[2b], grüßen[2b]	saludar[1b]
boy[1a], (lad[2a]), (youth[2a])	garçon[1b], (gamin[3a]), (adolescent[4b]), (gosse[6b])	Jüngling[2a], Knabe[2a], Junge[2b], (Bube[5b])	muchacho[1a], mozo[1b], (mancebo[4b]), (zagal[6a]), (adolescente[6b])
bread[1a]	pain[1b]	Brot[2b]	pan[1a]
bright[1b], (brilliant[4a])	clair[1a], (brillant[2a])	glänzend[2a], heiter[2a], hell[2a], (licht[5a]), (blank[6b])	claro[1a], (brillante[2a]), (luminoso[2b]), (luciente[6a])
broad[1a], wide[1a]	large[1a]	breit[2a]	ancho[1b]
burst[2a], (pop[5b]), (explode[8])	éclater[1b], (crever[3a])	brechen[1b], (zerbrechen[4b])	romper[1a], (estallar[2b]), (reventar[3a]), (explotar[3b])
business[1b] man[1a]	homme[1a] d'[1a]affaires (affaire[1a]), (commerçant[4a])	Kaufmann[2a], (Geschäftsmann[6a])	(hombre de) negocios (negocio[1b]), (comerciante[3a]), (negociante[6a])
buy[1a], (bought[2a]), (purchase[2a])	acheter[1b]	kaufen[2a], (erkaufen[5b]), (anschaffen[6b])	comprar[1b]

English	French	German	Spanish
call[1a] (*n.*), cry[1b], (halloo[6])	cri[1b]	Ruf[2a], (Zuruf[4a]), (Schrei[5b])	grito[1b]
call[1a] out[1a], (exclaim[2b])	s'écrier[1b], (se récrier[5b])	schreien[2b], (ausrufen[6a])	exclamar[1b]
century[2b]	siècle[1a]	Jahrhundert[1a]	siglo[1a]
chance[1b], (random[5a])	hasard[1b]	Zufall[2b]	suerte[1a], acaso[1b], (casualidad[3a])
(take) chances (chance[1b]), (risk[3b])	risquer[2a], (hasarder[7a])	Gefahr[1a] laufen[1b], (gefährden[4a])	aventurar[4a], arriesgar[4b]
change[1a] (*tr. vb.*), (alter[3b])	changer[1a], (modifier[2b]), (altérer[4a]), (évoluer[6b])	ändern[2a], verändern[2a], wechseln[2a], (wandeln[3a]), (abändern[5a])	cambiar[1b], (alterar[2a]), (mudar[2a]), (modificar[3a]), (trocar[3a])
clothes[1b], (attire[4b]), (apparel[5b]), (clothing[6*]), (wardrobe[6])	vêtement[1b]	Kleid(er)[2a], (Kleidung[4a]), (Gewand[4b])	ropa[1b], traje[1b], vestido[1b], (hábito[2b])
coast[1b], shore[1b]	côte[1b]	Küste[2b]	costa[1b], (litoral[5b])
collect[2b] (– money due)	toucher[1a]	erheben[1a]	cobrar[1b]
come[1a] forward[1b], (advance[2a])	avancer[1a]	hervortreten[2b]	adelantar[1b], (avanzar[2a])
come[1a] now[1a]! look[1a] here[1a]!	voyons![5b]	bitte! (bitten[1a])	¡vamos! (ir[1a])
common[1b]	commun[1b]	gemeinsam[2a], gemein[2b], gemeinschaftlich[2b]	común[1b]
common[1b] (person), (ordinary[3b])	commun[1b], ordinaire[1b]	gemein[2b]	común[1b]
consist[2b]	consister[2b]	bestehen[1a]	consistir[1b]
control[2b] (*vb.*), (have under –)	commander[1a] à[1a], (maîtriser[6b])	(in der) Hand[1a] (haben), (beherrschen[2b])	dominar[1b], (regular[2b])
cost[1b] (*vb.*)	coûter[1a]	kosten[2a]	costar[1b]
courage[2b], (bravery[5a]), (valor[5a])	courage[1b], valeur[1b], (bravoure[5a])	Mut[1b], (Tapferkeit[4b])	valor[1a], (coraje[4a]), (valentía[4b]), (fiereza[6a]), (bravura[6b])
court[1b] (law), (bar[2a])	tribunal[3b], (cour[1a] d'assises [assise[4b]])	Gericht[1b], (Gerichtshof[2b]), (Landgericht[5a]), (Amtsgericht[6a])	foro[3a], tribunal[3a]
cry[1b], cried[1b], (weep[2a]), (wept[6b]), (cries[4a])	pleurer[1a]	weinen[2a]	llorar[1a]
day[1a] before[1a], (eve[6a])	veille[1b]	(am) Tag[1a] vorher[1b], (Vorabend)	víspera[5b]
dead[1a], (decease[5b])	mort (*adj.*)[1b], (défunt[4b])	tot[2a], (Tote[3a]), (verstorben[4a]), (Verstorbene[6b])	muerto (morir[1a]), (difunto[2a])
defend[2b]	défendre[1b]	schützen[1b], (verteidigen[2b])	defender[1b]
degree[2a], grade[2b]	degré[1b]	Grad[1b], (Stufe[2b])	grado[1b]
deliver[2a]	remettre[1a], livrer[1b]	liefern[1b], (abgeben[2a]), (übergeben[2b]), (einreichen[4b]), (überliefern[6a]), (überbringen[6b])	entregar[1a], (consignar[4a])
difference[1b], (distinction[5b])	différence[1b], (distinction[5b]), (divergence[6b])	Unterschied[2a], (Verschiedenheit[3b]), (Differenz[4a]), (Ungleichheit[6a]), (Unterscheidung[6a])	diferencia[1b], (distinción[2b]), (desigualdad[4b])
disappear[2b], (vanish[3a])	disparaître[1b]	verschwinden[1b], (erlöschen[4a]), (schwinden[4b])	desaparecer[1b], (esfumar[6b] [se])
discover[1b], (detect[6])	découvrir[1a]	entdecken[2a]	descubrir[1a]

English	French	German	Spanish
draw[1a], (design[3a])	dessiner[3a]	zeichnen[1b]	dibujar[3a]
dream[1b] (*n.*)	rêve[1b], (cauchemar[4a]), (songe[4b])	Traum[2a]	sueño[1a], (ensueño[3a])
dress[1a], (garment[2b]), (gown[2b]), (robe[3a]), (frock [5a]), (costume[5b]), (toilet[5b])	robe[1b], (costume[2a]), (toilette[2a])	Kleid[2a], (Tracht[5b])	traje[1b], vestido[1b]
drink[1a], (drank[4b]), (drunk[4b])	boire[1b]	trinken[2a]	beber[1a], tomar[1a]
dry[1b] (*adj.*)	sec[1b] (sèchement[4b])	trocken[2b], (dürr[6b])	seco[1b], (enjuto[5b])
eat[1a], (ate[2b])	manger[1a]	essen[2b], (fressen[6a])	comer[1a]
effect[2a] (*n.*)	effet[1a]	Wirkung[1b], (Effekt[5a])	efecto[1a]
eight[1b]	huit[1a]	acht[2a]	ocho[1]*
event[2a], (circumstance[3a])	occasion[1a], circonstance[1b]	Umstand[1a]	circumstancia[1a]
everywhere[2b]	partout[1a]	überall[1b], (allenthalben[5a])	(en todas) partes (parte[1a])
exact[2a], (precise[6])	précis[1b], (exact[2b])	genau[1a]	preciso[1a], (exacto[2a]), (escrupuloso[3b]), (riguroso[3b])
	(exactement[2a]), (précisément[2a])		
example[2a], (specimen[6])	exemple[1a]	Beispiel[1a], (Muster[2b]), (Exempel[6b])	ejemplo[1a], (ejemplar[3a])
(for) example[2a], ([for] instance[3a])	(par) exemple[1a]	(zum) Beispiel[1a], (beispielsweise[4a])	(por) ejemplo[1a], (verbigracia[2b])
fair[1a] (*adj.*), just[1a]	droit[1a], juste[1a]	gerecht[2a], ehrlich[2b], (rechtlich[3a])	justo[1b], (justiciero[6a])
faith[2a]	foi[1b]	Glaube[1b]	fe[1a], (fervor[6a])
false[2b]	faux[1b]	falsch[1b]	falso[1b]
fault[2a]	faute[1b]	Schuld[1b]	falta[1b]
favor[1b] (*n.*), (boon[5b])	service[1a], faveur[1b]	Gnade[2a], Gunst[2a], (Gefälligkeit[6a]), (Anklang[6b])	favor[1a], merced[1b], servicio[1b]
fear[1a] (*n.*), (dread[2b]), (fright[2b]), (terror[2b])	crainte[1b], peur[1b], (terreur[2a]), (effroi[3a]), (épouvante[5a]), (appréhension[6b])	Furcht[2a], Angst[2b], Schrecken[2b], (Entsetzen[4b]), (Befürchtung[5a]), (Scheu[5b])	miedo[1b], temor[1b], (terror[2a]), (espanto[2b]), (susto[2b]), (recelo[3a]), (pavor[4b])
feed[1b], (fed[2b])	donner[1a] à[1a] manger[1a], (alimenter[5b])	zu[1a] essen[2b] geben[1a]	dar[1a] de[1a] comer[1a]
fill[1a]	remplir[1a], (emplir[3b])	füllen[2a], (ausfüllen[3b]), (anfüllen[6b])	llenar[1a], (henchir[3a]), (cuajar[5a])
fine[1a] (person), nice[1a]	brave[1b], (gentil[2b])	brav[2b], (nett[5a])	buen[1a]
finger[1b]	doigt[1a]	Finger[2b]	dedo[1b]
flower[1a] (*n.*)	fleur[1b]	Blume[2a]	flor[1a]
fortune[2a], (luck[3a])	chance[1b], fortune[1b], (veine[6b])	Glück[1a]	suerte[1a], fortuna[1b], (ventura[2a])
forward[1b] (*adv.*), (ahead[3b])	en[1a] avant[1a]	vorwärts[2b]	adelante[1b]
(in) front[1a] (*adv.*), (ahead[3b])	devant[1a], en[1a] avant[1a]	vorn[2b], (davor[4a]), (voran[4b])	delante[1a]
garden[1a]	jardin[1a]	Garten[2a]	jardín[1b], (huerta[2a] [truck])
gate[1b] (city –)	porte[1a]	Tor[2b]	puerta[1a]

English	French	German	Spanish
gentle[1b], (mild[2b]) (gently[3b])	doux[1a], (suave[6a])	mild[2b], (gelind[6a])	suave[1b], (manso[3b])
get[1a], (fetch[2b])	aller[1a] chercher[1a], (quérir[6a])	holen[2a]	conseguir[1b]
give[1a] up[1a], (renounce[5a])	renoncer[1b]	aufgeben[2b], (abtun[6a])	rendir[1b], (renunciar[2b])
go[1a] back[1a], return[1b]	retourner[1a], rentrer[1a]	zurückkehren[2a], (wiederkehren[4b])	retirar[1a] se[1a], volver[1a], (tornar[2a]), (retornar[6a])
go[1a] forward[1b], (advance[2a]), (go[1a] onward[3b])	avancer[1a]	vorwärts[2b] gehen[1a], (vordringen[4a]), (vorrücken[5a]), (vorschreiten[6a]), (weitergehen[6a])	ir[1a] adelante[1a], adelantar[1b], (avanzar[2a])
go[1a] out[1a]	sortir[1a]	ausgehen[2a], (hinausgehen[4a])	salir[1a]
golden[1b]	d'[1a]or[1a], en[1a] or[1a]	golden[2a]	de[1a] oro[1a], (dorado [dorar[3a]]), (áureo[5b])
grace[1b] (*n.*)	grâce[1a]	Reiz[2b], (Anstand[4b]), (Anmut[6a])	gracia[1a], (gentileza[4b]), (donaire[5a]), (garbo[6a]), (gallardía[5b])
grave[2a], earnest[2b], serious[2b]	grave[1a], sérieux[1a]	ernst[1b], (ernsthaft[3b]), (gewichtig[6a])	grave[1a], serio[1b], (de[1a] gravedad[2b]), (adusto[5b])
	(gravement[2b]), (sérieusement[2b]), (grièvement[6b])		
guess[1b] right[1a]	bien[1a] deviner[1b]	richtig[1a] raten[2b], (erraten[4b])	acertar[1b]
(on the other) hand[1a], side[1a]	(de l'autre) côté[1a], (d'autre) part[1a]	ander(er)seits[2b]	(por otra) parte[1a]
happiness[2b]	bonheur[1b], (félicité[5b])	Glück[1a]	dicha[1b], felicidad[1b]
hardly[2a]	guère[1b], (à peine[5b])	kaum[1a], (schwerlich[3b])	apenas[1a]
(of, from) here[1a], (local[3a])	d'[1a]ici[1a]	hiesig[2b]	de[1a] aquí[1a]
himself[1a] (intensive)	lui-même[5b]	(er) selber[1a], selbst[1a]	él[1*] mismo[1a]
history[2a]	histoire[1a]	Geschichte[1a]	historia[1a]
holy[2a]	saint[1b]	heilig[1b]	santo[1a], (sacro[4b])
human[2a] (*adj.*)	humain[1b]	menschlich[1b]	humano[1a]
hundred[1a]	cent[1a], (centaine[2a])	hundert[2a], (Hundert[4b])	cien[1*], ciento[1*], (centenar[5b])
idea[2a], (notion[3b])	idée[1a], (conception[3b]), (notion[4a])	Begriff[1b], Idee[1b], (Ahnung[3b]), (Einfall[4a])	idea[1a], (concepto[6a]), (noción[4a]), (concepción[5b])
imagine[2a], fancy[6a], (conceive[3b])	s'imaginer[1b], (concevoir[2a]), (se figurer[2b]), (imaginer[3a])	sich[1a] denken[1a], (vorstellen[3a]), (einbilden[5a])	figurar[1b], imaginar[1b], (concebir[2a])
impossible[2b]	impossible[1b]	unmöglich[1b]	imposible[1a], (imposibilitar[6a] [to make –])
inside[2a] (*n.*), (interior[4a])	intérieur[1a], (dedans[2b])	Innere[1b]	interior[1b]
inside[2a] (*adj.*), (interior[4a]), (inner[4b]), (inward[4b]), (internal[5b])	intérieur[1a]	innere[1a], innerhalb[1b], (innerlich[3b]), (inwendig[5b])	interior[1b], (adentro[2b]), (interno[3b])
		(inne[2b] [*adv.*])	
intend[2a]	compter[1a], ([avoir l']intention[2a])	sich[1a] vornehmen[1b], (beabsichtigen[2a]), (bezwecken[5a]), (vorsetzen[6a])	tener[1a] intención[1b]

English	French	German	Spanish
iron[1b] (*adj.*)	(de, en) fer[1b]	eisern[2b]	de[1a] hierro[1b], (férreo[4b])
keep[1a] from[1a], stop[1a], (prevent[2a]), (hinder[4a]), (foil[5b]), (thwart[6])	empêcher[1a], (contrarier[4b])	verhindern[2a], aufhalten[2b], hindern[2b], (abhalten[3a]), (anhalten[3a]), (wehren[4a]), (vorbeugen[5b])	impedir[1b]
kill[1a], (slain[3b]), (slaughter[4b]), (slay[4b]), (slew[5a])	tuer[1b], (assommer[6a]), (égorger[6a]), (massacrer[6a])	töten[2b], (erschlagen[5a]), (erlegen[6a])	matar[1a]
kiss[1b] (*vb.*)	embrasser[1b], (baiser [*vb.*][3a])	küssen[2b]	besar[1b]
landing (land[1a]) (stairs)	palier[4a]	Absatz[1b]	descanso[2a]
latter[2b]	celui(-ci, -là)[1a], celle(-ci, -là)[1a], ceux(-ci, -là)[1a], celles(-ci, -là)[1b], (ce) dernier[1a]	dies[1a], (letztere[3b])	éste[1a], último[1a]
letter[1a] (character)	lettre[1b]	Buchstabe[2b]	letra[1a]
liberty[2a], freedom[2a]	liberté [1b]	Freiheit[1b]	libertad[1a]
light[1a] (*adj.*) (in color, etc.)	clair[1b]	hell[2a]	claro[1a]
light[1a] (up[1a]), (lit[6])	éclairer[1b], (illuminer[4b])	leuchten[2a], (erleuchten[4a]), (beleuchten[4b])	encender[1b], (iluminar[2a]), (alumbrar[2b])
lip[1b]	lèvre[1b]	Lippe[2b]	labio[1b]
load[1b] (*n.*), (burden[3a])	fardeau[4a]	Last[1b], (Belastung[4a])	carga[2b]
long[1a] for[1a], (crave[4a]), (yearn[5a])	tarder[2a] (impersonal)	verlangen[1a], ([sich] sehnen[2b])	anhelar[4b], (ansiar[5a])
look[1a] out[1a], take[1a] care[1a], (beware[4b])	faire[1a] attention[1a], prendre[1a] garde[1b]	achten[2a], (Acht[4b] geben[1a])	tener[1a] cuidado[1a]
look[1a] out[1a]!, take[1a] care[1a]!, (beware[4b]!)	attention[1a]!, (gare![6b])	Achtung[2b]!, (Vorsicht[3a]!)	¡cuidado[1a]!
low[1a], lower[1b]	bas[1a], (inférieur[2a])	niedrig[2a]	bajo[1a], (inferior[2b])
make[1a] out[1a], (discern[4a]), (descry[6])	distinguer[1b], (discerner[4a])	erblicken[2a]	distinguir[1a], (divisar[4a]), (columbrar[5a])
march[1b] (*vb.*)	marcher[1a]	marschieren[2b]	marchar[1b]
master[1b] (*vb.*)	dominer[1b], (maîtriser[6b])	beherrschen[2b]	dominar[1b]
million[2a]	million[1b]	Million[1b]	millón[1*]
motion[2b], (movement[3a])	mouvement[1a]	Bewegung[1a], (Treiben[4b]), (Regung[5b])	movimiento[1a], (vaivén[4b])
news[2a], (tidings[5a])	nouvelle(-s) (*n.*)[1b]	Nachricht[1b], (Neue[2a])	noticias (noticia[1b]), (nueva[5a])
noble[2a] (birth and character)	noble[1b]	edel[1b]	noble[1a], (hidalgo[3a])
notice[1b] (*vb.*), (observe[2a])	remarquer[1b]	merken[2a], (gewahren[4b])	advertir[1a], notar[1b]
(give) notice[1b] (of), (advertise[5a]), (announce[5b]), (notify[5b])	annoncer[1b]	melden[2a], (anzeigen[3b]), (ankündigen[4b])	anunciar[1b], (notificar[6a]) (denunciar[6b])
observe[2a], behold[2a], gaze[2b] (at), (beheld[3b]), (contemplate[6])	observer[1b], (contempler[3a])	betrachten[1b], beobachten[1b]	contemplar[1b], notar[1b], observar[1b]
office[1b] (position)	situation[1b], (poste[2a]), (office[2b])	Amt[2b]	puesto[1a], cargo[1b], oficio[1b]
opinion[2a]	opinion[1b], (avis[2a])	Meinung[1a], (erachten[2b]), (Erachten[3a])	opinión[1b], (opinar[3b]) (have the opinion), (parecer[3a])

English	French	German	Spanish
opposite[2b] (*adv.*, *adj.*, and *prep.*)	en[1a] face[1a], (opposé [*adj.*][3a]), (vis-à-vis[3b])	gegenüber[1a], (angesichts[4b]), (gegenüberstehend[5a])	opuesto (oponer[1b]), (enfrente[3b])
(put in) order[1a], (regulate[5a])	ranger[1b], (classer[3a])	ordnen[2a], regeln[2b], (anordnen[3a]), (regulieren[5b])	arreglar[1b], ordenar[1b], (regular[2b]), (clasificar[6a])
outside[1b], (outdoor[s][6])	dehors[1a], hors[1b], (extérieur[2a])	außen[2b], (draußen[3b])	fuera[1a], (exterior[2b]), (afuera[4a])
(take) pains (pain[1b])	se[1a] donner[1a] la[1a] peine[1a], s'[1a]appliquer[1b]	sich[1a] Mühe[1b] geben[1a]	cuidar[1b](se), (afanar[5a][se]), (esmerarse[5b])
part[1a] (rôle)	part[1a], rôle[1b]	Rolle[2a]	papel[1a]
(on the) part[1a] (of)	de[1a] la[1a] part[1a] de[1a]	seitens[2a]	de[1a] parte[1a] de[1a]
(take) part[1a], (partake[5b])	prendre[1a] part[1a], (participer[5a])	beteiligen[2b], (teilnehmen[3b]), (mitmachen[6b])	tomar[1a] parte[1a], (participar[3b])
particular[6a] (*adj.*)	particulier[1b] (particulièrement[2a])	besondere[1a]	particular[1a]
pass[1a] (*vb.*), go[1a] past[1b]	passer[1a], dépasser[1b], (repasser[4a])	vorübergehen[2b]	pasar[1a]
past[1b], over[1a]	passé (passer[1a])	vorüber[2b], (vorbei[3a])	pasado[1b]
pleasure[1b]	plaisir[1a], (gré[2b]), (agrément[4a])	Genuß[2a], Lust[2a], Vergnügen[2a], (Gefallen[4b]), (Belieben[5b]), (Wohlgefallen[6a])	placer[1a], (agrado[3b]), (complacencia[5a])
point[1a] out[1a], (indicate[2b])	indiquer[1b], (désigner[2a]), (signaler[3a])	hinweisen[2a], nachweisen[2b], anweisen[2b], (andeuten[3a]), (anzeigen[3b])	indicar[1b], señalar[1b], (apuntar[2b])
position[2b], (situation[4a])	situation[1b], (position[2a])	Lage[1a], (Anstellung[4a]), (Situation[4a]), (Position[5b]), (Sachlage[5b])	situación[1b]
prepare[1b] (*tr. vb.*), get[1a] ready[1a]	préparer[1a]	bereiten[2a], vorbereiten[2b], (bahnen[6b]) (way)	preparar[1b], (prevenir[2b]), (aparejar[5a]), (apercibir[6a])
(for the) present[1a]	(pour le) moment[1a]	vorläufig[2b], (einstweilen[5a])	(por) ahora[1a]
present[1a] (*vb.*) (give)	offrir[1a], présenter[1a]	schenken[2a]	presentar[1a], (regalar[2a]), (obsequiar[4b])
profit[2b] (*vb.*), benefit[2b]	profiter[1b], (bénéficier[6b])	Vorteil[1b] ziehen[1a]	aprovechar[1b], (beneficiar[7a] [se])
pronounce[2b]	prononcer[1b]	aussprechen[1b]	pronunciar[1b]
proof[2b]	preuve[1b], (indice[5a])	Beweis[1b], (Nachweis[4b])	prueba[1b]
proper[1b], (suitable[4b])	(comme il) faut (falloir[1a]), (convenable[3b]) (proprement[3b])	gehörig[2b], (angemessen[3a]), (zutreffend [zutreffen[3b]]), (anständig[4b]), (ziemen[4b]), (zuständig[5b])	propio[1a], (conveniente[2b])
propose[2b], (suggest[3a])	proposer[1b], (suggérer[3b])	in[1a] Vorschlag[1b] bringen[1a], (vorlegen[2a]), (vorschlagen[2b]), (beantragen[3a])	proponer[1b], (sugerir[4a])
prove[1a], make[1a] (e.g., a point), (establish[2a])	constater[1b], établir[1b]	feststellen[2a], festsetzen[2b], (konstatieren[4a])	establecer[1b], probar[1b], (comprobar[5b])
public[1b] (*n.*)	public[1b]	Publikum[2a], (Öffentlichkeit[3b])	público[1a]
rare[2b], scarce[2a]	rare[1b]	selten[1b], (vereinzelt[5b])	raro[1b]
read[1a], sound[1a] (the paragraph –s well)	sonner[1b]	lauten[2a]	sonar[1b]

English	French	German	Spanish
really[2b], (truly[5b*]), (actually[6*]), (verily[6])	en[1a] vérité[1a], vraiment[1b], (réellement[2b])	wirklich[1a], (geradezu[2b]), (wahrhaftig[3b])	en[1a] verdad[1a], realmente (real[1a]), verdaderamente (verdadero[1a]), ([de] veras[2a]), (efectivamente [efectivo[3a]])
reason[1a], (judgment [ge][2b])	raison[1a], (jugement[2b])	Vernunft[2b]	razón[1a], juicio[1b]
recognize[2b]	reconnaître[1a]	erkennen[1a]	reconocer[1b]
represent[2a]	représenter[1b]	darstellen[1b], (vertreten[2a]), (repräsentieren[5b])	representar[1b]
return[1b] (*n.*)	retour[1b], (rentrée [*n.*][4b])	Rückzug[2b], (Rückkehr[3b])	vuelta[1b], (regreso[3b])
ring[1b], sound[1a], (knell[4a]), (rang[4a]), (peal[4b]), (rung[6])	sonner[1b]	klingen[2a], (tönen[5a]), (erschallen[6a]), (läuten[6b])	tocar[1a], sonar[1b], (tañer[6a]) (a bell)
sad[1b], (gloomy[4b]), (melancholy[5b]), (mournful[5b]), (sorrowful[5b]), (woeful[6])	triste[1b], (mélancolique[3b]), (chagrin [*adj.*][5b]), (lamentable[5b]), (plaintif[6b]) (tristement[3a])	traurig[2a], (wehmütig[6b])	triste[1a], (sombrío[3a]), (melancólico[3b]), (lloroso[5a])
science[2b]	science[1b]	Wissenschaft[1b], (Naturwissenschaft[5a])	ciencia[1a]
sell[1b], sold[1b]	vendre[1b]	verkaufen[2a]	vender[1b]
sense[2a]	sens[1a]	Sinn[1a]	sentido[1a]
sentence[2b], (phrase[4a])	phrase[1b]	Satz[1b], (Phrase[6b])	frase[1b]
seven[1b]	sept[1a]	sieben[2b]	siete[1*]
shade[1b] (*n.*)	ombre[1b]	Schatten[2b]	sombra[1a]
silver[1a] (*n.*)	argent[1a]	Silber[2a]	plata[1b]
sing[1a], (sang[2b]), (sung[3b])	chanter[1b]	singen[2a]	cantar[1a]
six[1a]	six[1a]	sechs[2a]	seis[1*]
sleep[1a] (*vb.*), ([be] asleep[2a]), (slept[3a]), (nap[4b])	dormir[1b]	schlafen[2a]	dormir[1a], (dormitar[6a])
smile[1b] (*vb.*)	sourire (*vb.*)[1b], (souriant[2b])	lächeln[2a]	sonreír[1b]
soft[1a] (not loud)	bas[1a], doux[1a]	leise[2a]	dulce[1a], suave[1b]
somebody[2b], (someone[3b])	quelqu'un[1a]	jemand[1b]	alguien[1a]
sometimes (sometime[1b])	parfois[1b], (quelquefois[2a])	manchmal[2a], zuweilen[2b], (bisweilen[4a]), (mitunter[4a])	(a) veces (vez[1a]), (algunas veces)
(in) spite[2a] (of), (despite[4b])	malgré[1a], ([en] dépit[3b] [de])	trotz[1b]	(a) pesar[1a] (de), (a[1a] despecho[3b] de[1a])
spread[1b], (expand[6])	étendre[1b]	verbreiten[2a], (ausbreiten[3b]), (breiten[3b])	tender[1b], (extender[3a]), (regar[4a]), (cundir[6a])
stone[1a], (pebble[5a])	pierre[1b], (caillou[5a])	Stein[2a]	piedra[1a]
stop[1a] (*intr. vb.*), (cease[2b]), (halt[4a])	s'arrêter[1a], cesser[1a], (stationner[6b])	aufhören[2b], (absetzen[5a])	detener[1a] se[1a], parar[1b] se[1a], (desistir[4a])
stream[1b] (*n.*)	courant[1b]	Strom[2a]	corriente[1b]
study[1b] (*vb.*)	étudier[1a]	studieren[2b]	estudiar[1b]
surprise[1b] (*vb.*)	surprendre[1b], (surpris[4a])	überraschen[2a]	sorprender[1b], (extrañar[2a])
sweet[1a] (*adj.*)	doux[1a], (sucré[4b])	süß[2a]	dulce[1a]
taste[1b] (*n.*), (flavor[4b]), (savor[6])	goût[1b], (saveur[5b])	Geschmack[2a]	gusto[1a], (sabor[3a])
ten[1a]	dix[1a], (dizaine[4a])	zehn[2a]	diez[1*]

English	French	German	Spanish
themselves[1b] (intensive)	eux-mêmes[5b]	(sie) selber[1a], selbst[1a]	ellos[1]* mismos (mismo[1a])
then[1a] (e.g., the then reigning . . . .)	(d')alors[1a]	damalig[2b]	entonces[1a]
thousand[1a]	mille[1a], (millier[2a]), (mil[4b])	tausend[2a], (Tausend[3b])	mil[1]*, (millar[6b])
tip[2a] (*n.*) (end)	bout[1a], (pointe[2a])	Spitze[1b]	cabo[1b], (punta[2a])
tomorrow (-)[1b]	demain[1b]	morgen[2a]	mañana[1a]
tone[2b] (*n.*)	ton (*n.*)[1b]	Ton[1b]	tono[1b]
tonight (-)[2b]	ce[1a] soir[1a]	heute[1a] abend[1b]	esta (este[1a]) noche[1a]
treat[2a] (*vb.*), handle[2a]	traiter[1b]	behandeln[1b]	tratar[1a]
trust[1b] (*vb.*)	avoir[1a] confiance[1b], confier[1b], (fier[6b]), (se fier[6b])	vertrauen[2b], (trauen[4a]), (zutrauen[6b])	tener[1a] confianza[1b], (confiar[2a]), (fiar[2a])
turn[1a] round[1a] (*intr. vb.*)	se[1a] retourner[1a]	umkehren[2b]	volver[1a] se[1a]
unless[2a]	à[1a] moins[1a] que[1a]	außer[1a] wenn[1a], wenn[1a] nicht[1a]	a[1a] menos[1a] que[1a]
upper[2a]	supérieur[1b]	höher (hoch[1a]), obere[1b]	superior[1b]
(be) used (use[1a]) (to), (wont[3b])	avoir[1a] l'[1a]habitude[1b], (habitué[3a]), (accoutumé [accoutumer[3b]] à)	gewöhnt (gewöhnen[2a])	acostumbrar[1b], tener[1a] costumbre[1b]
value[1b] (*vb.*)	estimer[1b], (apprécier[2b])	schätzen[2a]	estimar[1b], (preciar[3b])
visit[1a], (visitation[6])	visite[1b]	Besuch[2a]	visita[1b]
visit[1a] (*vb.*)	(rendre, faire) visite[1b] (à), (visiter[2a])	besuchen[2a]	visitar[1b]
wall[1a] (in a room)	mur[1b], (paroi[4b])	Wand[2a]	pared[1b], (muro[3a])
weather[1b]	temps[1a]	Wetter[2b], (Witterung[4b])	tiempo[1a], (bonanza[6a] [fine, good])
whenever[2b], (whene'er[4b])	lorsque[1a], (n'importe) quand[1a]	wenn[1a] immer[1a]	cuando[1a] quiera (querer[1a]) que[1a]
wind[1a] (*n.*)	vent[1b]	Wind[2b]	viento[1b]
window[1a], (casement[6])	fenêtre[1a]	Fenster[2a]	ventana[1b]
wine[2a]	vin[1b], (champagne[4b])	Wein[1b]	vino[1a], (champagne[6b])
winter[1a]	hiver[1b]	Winter[2b]	invierno[1b]
writing(s) (write[1a])	écrit (*n.*)[4a]	Schrift[1b], Werk[1a]	escrito[2b]
written (write[1a]) (in black and white)	(par) écrit (écrire[1a])	schriftlich[2b]	(por) escrito (escribir[1a])
(be) wrong[1b]	avoir[1a] tort[1b], (se tromper[4b])	unrecht[2b] haben[1a], sich[1a] irren[2b]	no[1a] tener[1a] razón[1a], engañar[1b] se[1a]
youth[2a] (time of life)	jeunesse[1b]	Jugend[1b]	juventud[1b], (mocedad[4a]) (youthfulness), (adolescencia[6b])

PART II

THE SECOND THOUSAND CONCEPTS

SECTION 1.5. CONCEPTS 1019 THROUGH 1137

E F G S	*E F G S*
1–1–2–2	1–5–1–2
1–2–2–1	1–3–1–4
2–1–1–2	1–4–1–3
2–2–1–1	1–1–1–6
1–2–1–5	1–6–1–1

Read: (*First column*) English, first thousand; French, first thousand; German, second thousand; Spanish, second thousand; *or* English, first thousand; French, second thousand; German, second thousand; Spanish, first thousand; *and so on for other alternatives in the first and succeeding columns*

English	French	German	Spanish
account[1b], report[1a]	récit[2a], (conte[3b])	Erzählung[2a]	relación[1a], (narración[4a])
advantage[2a], benefit[2b]	avantage[1b], (bénéfice[3a])	Vorteil[1b], Vorzug[1b]	beneficio[2b], provecho[2b], ventaja[2b]
author[2b] (originator)	auteur[2a]	Verfasser[1b], (Aussteller[4a]), (Urheber[4a])	autor[1b]
bank[1a] (river)	bord[1a], (rive[3a]), (rivage[4a]), (berge[5a])	Ufer[2a]	orilla[2a], ribera[2b]
beauty[1b]	beauté[2a]	Schönheit[2a]	belleza[1b], hermosura[1b], (primor[5a])
beyond[2b] (*prep.*)	(au) delà[2a] (de), outre[2b]	außer[1a], über[1a]	más[1a] allá[1a] (de), (allende[5a])
call[1a] upon[1a], (invoke[9])	invoquer[4b]	rufen[1a] (nach[1a], zu[1a], etc.)	invocar[3b]
car[1b], (carriage[2a])	voiture[1b]	Wagen[2b]	coche[2a]
change[1a] (*n.*)	changement[2a], (change[4a]), (variation[4a]), (modification[4b])	Änderung[2a], Veränderung[2a], (Abänderung[3b]), (Wandel[5a]), (Versetzung[6b]), (Wandlung[6b])	cambio[1b], (modificación[4b]), (mudanza[4b]), (variación[5a]), (alteración[5b])
chief[1b] (*n.*), head[1a]	chef[1b]	Haupt-[2a], Vorgesetzte[2b], (Chef[3b]), (Doge[4b]), (Häuptling[6a]), (Hauptperson[6a]), (Prinzipal[6a])	jefe[2a], (caudillo[4a])
command[1b] (*vb.*), order[1a], (bade[3a]), (ordain[4b]), (enjoin[6])	commander[2a], ordonner[2a]	befehlen[2a], Befehl[1b] erlassen[2b], gebieten[2b], vorschreiben[2b], (kommandieren[3a]), (beantragen[3a])	mandar[1a], ordenar[1b], (decretar[5a])
company[1a] (military)	compagnie[2a]	Kompanie[2a]	compañía[1b]
create[2b]	créer[1b]	schaffen[1a]	crear[2a]
danger[2a], (risk[3b]), (peril[4b])	danger[2a], (péril[3a])	Gefahr[1a]	peligro[1b], (riesgo[2a])
deserve[2b], earn[2a], (merit[3a]), (entitled [entitle[4a]])	mériter[2a]	verdienen[1b]	merecer[1a]

English	French	German	Spanish
destroy[1b], (ruin[2a]), (wreck[3a])	détruire[2a], ruiner[2b], (anéantir[4b]), (dévaster[6a])	zerstören[2a], vernichten[2b], (zerschlagen[6b])	deshacer[1b], destruir[1b], (arruinar[3a]), (aniquilar[4b]), (destrozar[4b]), (desbaratar[5a]), (desmoronar[6a])
doubt[1b] (*vb.*)	douter[2b]	zweifeln[2b], (bezweifeln[5a])	dudar[1b]
draw[1a] back[1a]	reculer[2a]	zurückziehen[2b]	echar[1a] (se) atrás[1b], (retroceder[3b])
drive[1a] back[1a]	refouler[5b]	zurück[1a] treiben[1b]	rechazar[2b]
ear[1a]	oreille[2a]	Ohr[2a]	oído[1b], (oreja[2b])
edge[1b], (border[2a]), (brim[4a]), (brink[5b]), (rim[5b]), (verge[6])	bord[1a], (lisière[5b])	Rand[2b]	canto[2a], orilla[2a], borde[2b]
eternal[2b], (everlasting[4a])	éternel[2a] (éternellement[4a])	ewig[1b]	eterno[1a]
examine[2b], (scan[6])	examiner[1b], (inspecter[4b])	betrachten[1b], (prüfen[2b]), (untersuchen[3a]), (besehen[6b])	examinar[2a], (escudriñar[6a]), (inspeccionar[6b]), (repasar[6b])
extreme[2b], (utmost[4a]), (excessive[5b])	extrême[2a], (outré [*adj.*][3b]), (excessif[4a])	äußerst (außere[1b]), (übermäßig[5a])	extremo[1b], (harto[2a]), (excesivo[3a]), ([en] demasía[5a]), (colmo[6b])
fall[1a] back[1a] again[1a], (subside[5])	retomber[2a]	zurück[1a] fallen[1a], (sinken[2a])	recaer[5b]
fate[2b], (doom[3b]), (destiny[5a])	destinée[2a], sort[2a], (destin[3b]), (lot[6b])	Bestimmung[1a], Schicksal[1b], (Los[3b])	sino[1a], suerte[1a], destino[1b], (hado[5a]), (fatalidad[5b])
feature[2b] (face)	trait[1b]	Zug[1a]	rasgo[2b], (facciónes [facción[4a]])
feeling[1b] (sensitiveness)	sensibilité[3b]	Gefühl[1a]	sensibilidad[4a]
fix[1b] (up) (Amer.), (arrange[2b])	arranger[2a], (ajuster[4b])	einrichten[2a], ordnen[2a], (reihen[5b])	arreglar[1b], (acomodar[2b]), (ajustar[2b]), (concertar[3b])
flow[1b] (*vb.*), stream[1b]	couler[2a], (ruisseler[4b])	fließen[2b], (strömen[3a])	correr[1a]
found[1a] (*vb. inf.*)	fonder[2a]	begründen[2a], gründen[2a], (stiften[4b]), (fundieren[5a])	fundar[1b]
front[1a] (*n.*), (fore[5a]) (e.g., of a building)	devant[2b], (façade[4a]), (devanture[6a])	Front[2b]	frente[1a], (faz[3a]), (fachada[5a]), (portada[5b])
fruit[1b]	fruit[2a]	Frucht[2a]	fruto[1b], (fruta[2b])
future[2a] (*n.*)	avenir[1b], (futur[2b])	Zukunft[1b]	futuro[2a], porvenir[2a]
game[1b] (play)	jeu[1b]	Spiel[2a]	juego[2a]
gather[1b], (collect[2b]), (assemble[3b]), (levy[6]), (muster[6])	recueillir[2a], (rassembler[3a]), (assembler[4a]), (amasser[7a])	sammeln[2a], versammeln[2a], (ansammeln[6b]), (zusammenziehen[6b])	recoger[1b], (amasar[5a])
gather[1b], (pluck[2b]), (glean[6])	recueillir[2a], cueillir[2b]	sammeln[2a]	recoger[1a], reunir[1b], (allegar[5b])
goodness[2b]	bonté[2b]	Güte[1b]	bondad[1b]
goods (good[1a]), (merchandise[4a]), (wares [ware[4a]])	marchandise[3b]	Ware[1b]	mercancía[4a]
green[1a] (*adj.*)	vert[2a]	grün[2a]	verde[1b]
guess[1b]	deviner[1b]	raten[2b]	adivinar[2b]
half[1a] hour[1a] (*n.*)	demi-heure[6b]	halbe (halb[1b]) Stunde[1a]	media (medio[1a]) hora[1a]
(to) half[1a] open[1a]	entr'ouvrir[3a]	halb[1b] öffnen[1b]	entreabrir[4b]
hall[1b]	salle[1b]	Saal[2b], (Halle[5b])	sala[2a], (salón[3a])
hat[1b], (bonnet[4a])	chapeau[1b]	Hut[2a]	sombrero[2a]

English	French	German	Spanish
health[1b]	santé[2a]	Gesundheit[2a]	salud[1b]
heat[1b] (*n.*), (warmth[4b])	chaleur[2a], (tiédeur[5b])	Wärme[2b], (Hitze[3a])	calor[1b]
hot[1a]	chaud[1b], (brûlant[4b])	heiß[2b]	caliente[2b], (cálido[4a])
ill[1b], sick[1b]	mal[1a], souffrant (souffrir[1a]), malade[1b]	krank[2b]	enfermo[2a], (doliente[5b])
island[1b], (isle[3a])	île[2b]	Insel[2a]	isla[1b]
itself[2a] (intensive)	même[1a], (soi[2b])	selbst[1a], selber[1b]	sí[1a], el[1a] mismo[1a]
judgment (ge)[2b] (decision)	jugement[2b]	Urteil[1b], (Gutachten[3a]), (Beurteilung[3b]), (Ermessen[5a])	juicio[1b]
knowledge[2a], (acquaintance[3a])	connaissance[2a]	Kenntnis[1b], (Erkenntnis[2a]), (Wissen[2b]), (Können[3a]), (Kunde[3a])	conocimiento[1b]
lack[2a] (*vb.*)	manquer[1b]	fehlen[1a], (entbehren[2b]), (gebrechen[4a]), (mangeln[4b])	carecer[2b]
(take[1a]) leave[1a]	(faire ses) adieux (adieu[2b]), ([prendre] congé[3b])	Abschied[2b] (nehmen)	despedir[1b] se[1a]
liking (like[1a]) (*n.*)	penchant[5b], (inclination[6a])	Neigung[1b]	afición[2b], (agrado[3a])
lock[2a] (*vb.*)	fermer[1a] à[1a] clef[2b]	schließen[1a], (verschließen[2b])	cerrar[1a]
loose[2a] (*vb.*), (loosen[6])	dégager[2a], détacher[2a], lâcher[2a], (relâcher[4b]), (dénouer[5a]), (délier[5b]), (détendre[5b])	lösen[1b]	soltar[1b], (desprender[2b]), (desatar[3a]), (despegar[5a]), (aflojar[6b])
maintain[2b] (keep up)	maintenir[2a]	erhalten[1a]	mantener[1b]
march[1b] (*n.*)	marche[1b]	Marsch[2b]	marcha[2b]
mean[1a], low[1a]	méchant[2a], (mesquin[5b])	gemein[2b]	bajo[1a], (ruin[4a]), (mezquino[4b])
middle[1b] (time)	milieu[1a]	Mitte[1b]	mediados[6b]
minister[2b]	ministre[2a]	Minister[1b], (Finanzminister[2a]), (Kriegsminister[5a]), (Handelsminister[6a]), (Kultusminister[6a]), (Ministerpräsident[6a])	ministro[1b], (consejero[5a])
minute[1b] (*n.*)	minute[1b]	Minute[2a]	minuto[2a]
(in a) moment[1b]	(en un) clin d'œil[6b]	(in einem) Augenblick[1a]	(en un abrir y cerrar de) ojos (ojo[1a])
mountain[1a]	montagne[2a], (mont[3b])	Berg[2a], (Gebirge[3a])	montaña[1b], monte[1b], (sierra[3a]), (cordillera[4b]) (range)
move[1a] (household)	déménager[5a]	beziehen[1b]	mudar[2a] se[1a]
move[1a], touch[1b] (emotionally)	toucher[1a], (émouvoir[2b]), (attendrir[3a]), (apitoyer[6a])	rühren[2a], (erschüttern[3a]), (erbarmen[6a])	conmover[2a], (enternecer[4b]), (emocionar[5b])
music[1b]	musique[2a]	Musik[2a]	música[1b]
neck[1b]	cou[2a], (nuque[5b])	Hals[2b]	cuello[1b], (pescuezo[4b])
now[1a] . . . . now, now[1a] . . . . then[1a]	tantôt[2a] . . . . tantôt	bald[1a] . . . . bald	ora[5b]
numerous[2b]	nombreux[1b]	zahlreich[1b]	numeroso[2a]

English	French	German	Spanish
order[1a] (*vb.*) (e.g., something to be delivered)	commander[2a]	bestellen[2b]	pedir[1a], ordenar[1b]
paint[1b] (*vb.*)	peindre[2a]	schildern[2a], malen[2b], (streichen[3b])	pintar[1b]
pen[1b] (for writing)	plume[2a]	Feder[2b]	pluma[1b]
pick[1a] up[1a] (e.g., from floor)	ramasser[2b]	aufheben[2b]	levantar[1a], recoger[1a], alzar[1b]
plant[1a] (*n.*)	plante[2b]	Pflanze[2b], (Gewächs[6b])	planta[1b], (mata[4b])
poet[2a], (bard[5a])	poète[2b]	Dichter[1a], (Poet[5b])	poeta[1a], (vate[5b])
position[2b] (in a difficult –), (plight[5b])	position[1a]	Lage[1a]	situación[1b], lance[2a]
present[1a] (*n.*) (time)	présent[2b]	Gegenwart[2a], (Neuzeit[6b])	presente[1a]
prize[2b] (*n.*)	prix[1a], (prime[5a]), (lot[6b])	Preis[1b], (Prämie[3a])	premio[2a], (galardón[5a])
property[2b], (estate[3a])	bien[2a], domaine[2a], propriété[2a]	Besitz[1b], Gut[1b], (Eigentum[9b])	bienes (bien[1b]), (hacienda[2a]), (propiedad[2a]), (heredad[5a])
province[2b]	région[2a], province[2b], (contrée[4b]), (diocèse[5a])	Provinz[1b], (Landschaft[3b]), (Landesteil[5a])	provincia[1b]
pure[1b] (blooded, language, etc.)	pur[1b]	rein[1a]	castizo[6a]
pursue[2b]	poursuivre[1b]	verfolgen[1b]	perseguir[2a]
(keep[1a]) quiet[1b]	(se) taire[2a]	schweigen[2a], (stillschweigen[4a])	callar[1a]
regard[2a] (*n.*) (consideration)	égard[2a]	Rücksicht[1b], (Hinsicht[3a]), (Beachtung[5a])	respeto (respe[c]to[1a]), (consideración[9b])
report[1b] (*vb.*)	rapporter[1b]	berichten[2a]	informar[2b]
result[2a] (*n.*), issue[2a], (consequence[3b])	résultat[1b], (conséquence[2a]), (issue[4a]), (dénouement[4b])	Folge[1a], (Resultat[2a]), (Ergebnis[2b])	consecuencia[2a], resultado[2a], (resulta[5b])
result[2a] (*vb.*), (ensue[5a])	résulter[2b], (s'ensuivre[7a])	erfolgen[1a], sich[1a] ergeben[1b], (hervorgehen[2a])	resultar[1b]
ride[1a] (horse), (rode[2b])	monter[1a] à[1a] cheval[1b]	reiten[2a]	montar[2a] a[1a] caballo[1a], (cabalgar[6a])
river[1a]	rivière[2b], (fleuve[3b])	Fluß[2a]	río[1a]
rose[1b] (*n.*)	rose[2a]	Rose[2b]	rosa[1b]
royal[2a], (regal[5b]), (kingly[5b])	royal[2b]	königlich[1b], (fürstlich[3b])	real[1a], (regio[4b])
run[1a] away[1a], (fled[3a]), (flee[3b])	fuir[2a], s'enfuir[2b], (se sauver[4a])	fliehen[9b], (flüchten[4b])	escapar[1a], huir[1a], (fugar[7a])
seldom[2b], rarely (rare[7b])	rarement[2b]	selten[1b]	rara (raro[1b]) vez[1a], raramente (raro[1b])
servant[2a], maid[2a]	domestique (*n.*)[2a], servante[2b], (bonne [*n.*][3b])	Mädchen[1b], (Magd[5b])	criada (criado[1a]), (sirviente[6a])
shoulder[1b] (*n.*)	épaule[1b]	Schulter[2b], (Achsel[6a])	hombro[2a]
silent[2a], (noiseless[6])	silencieux[2a]	still[1b], (schweigend [schweigen[2a]])	callado (+callar)[1a], (mudo[2b]), (silencioso[3a]), (taciturno[6a])
	(silencieusement[5a])		
sleep[1a] (*n.*), (nap[4b])	sommeil[2a]	Schlaf[2b]	sueño[1a], (siesta[4a])
so[1a] then[1a], now[1a] then[1a]	ainsi[1a]	so[1a], nun[1a]	conque[6b]
soft[1a] (in texture)	mou[2b], (mœlleux[6a]), (velouté[6b]) (mollement[6a])	sanft[2a], weich[2b], zart[2b]	suave[1b], (blando[2a]), (muelle[3b])

English	French	German	Spanish
spring[1a] (*vb.*), (jump[2a]), (leap[2a]), (hop[3a]), (sprang[3a]), (skip[3b]), (sprung[4a])	sauter[1b], (bondir[3a])	springen[2a]	saltar[2a]
star[1b]	étoile[2a], (astre[5b])	Stern[2a], (Gestirn[6b])	estrella[1b], (astro[3a]), (lucero[4b])
study[1b] (*n.*) (act)	étude[2a]	Studium[2a]	estudio[1b]
succeed[2a]	réussir[1b]	Erfolg[1b] haben[1a], gelingen[1b], (sich[1a] durchsetzen[4b]), (aufkommen[5a]), (glücken[5b])	tener[1a] buen[1a] éxito[2b]
success[2a]	succès[1b]	Erfolg[1b]	(buen) éxito[2b], (lucimiento[6b])
taste[1b] (*tr. vb.*)	goûter[2b]	kosten[2a], (schmecken[4b])	gustar[1a], (catar[5a]) (sample), (saborear[6b])
trouble[1b] (*vb.*), (disturb[3a]), (bother[4a]), (ruffle[5a]), (upset[5a]), (unsettle[d][6])	troubler[1b], (déranger[2a]), (ennuyer[3a]), (ahurir[5a])	stören[2a], (trüben[3a])	molestar[2a], (perturbar[4a]), (desconcertar[5a]), (incomodar[5a])
try[1a] hard[1a], (make[1a] an[1a] effort[2b]), (strive[3b]), (endeavor[4a]), (strove[5b])	faire[1a] des[1a] efforts (effort[1a]), (s'efforcer[2a])	sich[1a] bemühen[2b], (streben[3a]), (sich[1a] anstrengen[4b]), (anstreben[5a]), (bestreben[5a]), (erstreben[5b])	empeñar[2a] se[1a], (esforzarse[3b])
united (unite[1b])	uni[6b]	vereinigt (vereinigen[1a]), (einig[4a])	unido (unir[1a])
wealth[2a], (riches[4a])	richesse[2b], (biens[3a])	Besitz[1b], (Vermögen[2a]), (Reichtum[2b])	riqueza[1b], (caudal[2a]), (opulencia[6a])
weight[1b]	poids[2a]	Gewicht[2a]	peso[1b]
whatever[2a], (whatsoever[3b]), (whate'er[5a])	quelconque[2b], (quoi que[3b])	was[1a] . . . . auch[1a], was[1a] immer[1a]	cualquier(a)[1a]
whole[1a] (*n.*), (total[2a])	ensemble[1a], (total[2b]), (totalité[5b]), (tout [*n.*][6a])	Ganze[2a], (Gesamtheit[4b])	conjunto[2a], total[2a], (integridad[6a]), (totalidad[6b])
wise[1b], (politic[4a]), (sage[4b])	sage[2a]	klug[2b], (weise[4a])	sabio[1b]
wood[1a], (lumber[2b]), (timber[4a])	bois[1a]	Holz[2a]	madera[2b], (leña[3b]), (madero[6a])
wood[1a] (*adj.*), (wooden[2b])	(de, en) bois[1a]	(aus) Holz[2a], (hölzern[6b])	(de) madera[2b], (de) palo[2b]
worse[2a], worst[2b]	pire[2b], pis[2b]	schlechter, schlechteste (schlecht[1b]), (schlimmer, schlimmste [schlimm[2a]])	peor[1a]

SECTION 1.6. CONCEPTS 1138 THROUGH 1209

E F G S	*E F G S*
1–1–2–3	2–3–1–1
1–3–2–1	1–3–1–5
1–2–2–2	1–5–1–3
2–2–1–2	

Read: (*First column*) English, first thousand; French, first thousand; German, second thousand; Spanish, third thousand; *or* English, first thousand; French, third thousand; German, second thousand; Spanish, first thousand; *and so on for other alternatives in the first and succeeding columns*

English	French	German	Spanish
age^{1b}, grow^{1a} old^{1a}	vieillir^{3b}	alt^{1a} werden^{1a}	envejecer^{5a}
around^{1a} (*adv.*)	autour^{2b}	herum^{2b}, (umher^{3a})	alrededor^{2a}
(go to) bed^{1a}	se coucher^{2b}	zu^{1a} Bett^{2a} gehen^{1a}, (sich^{1a} niederlegen^{3a})	acostar^{7b} se^{1a}
beneath^{2a} (*adv.*), below^{2a}, (underneath^{3b})	dessous^{3a}, (au-dessous^{4b}), (en dessous^{6a})	unten^{1b}	debajo^{1b}
branch^{1b} (tree), (limb^{2b}), (bough^{3b}), (twig^{3b})	branche^{2a}, (rameau^{6b})	Zweig^{2a}, (Ast^{5b})	rama^{2a}
bride^{2b}, (bridal^{6})	mariée (marier^{7a})	junge (jung^{1a}) Frau^{1a}, (Braut^{3a})	novia (novio^{2a})
bringing (bring^{1a}) up^{1a}, (education^{6})	éducation^{2a}	Erziehung^{2b}	educación^{2a}, (cría^{4b})
building^{1b} (*n.*), (edifice^{5b})	bâtiment^{2b}, (édifice^{3b})	Bau^{2b}, Gebäude^{2b}, (Bauwerk^{4b}), (Bauten^{5a})	edificio^{2a}, fábrica^{2b}
burn^{1a} (*vb.*), (scorch^{5b})	brûler^{2a}	brennen^{2a}, (verbrennen^{4a})	arder^{2a}, consumir^{2a}, quemar^{2a}, (abrasar^{4a})
call^{1a} forth^{1b}, (summon^{3a})	évoquer^{3a}	hervorrufen^{2b}	llamar^{1a}, (evocar^{3b})
captain^{1b}	capitaine^{3a}	Hauptmann^{2a}, (Kapitän^{4b})	capitán^{2a}
(by) chance^{1b}, happen^{1b} (to)	(par) hasard^{1b}	zufällig^{2a}	(por) casualidad^{3a}
choice^{2a}, (selection^{6})	choix^{2a}	Wahl^{1b}, (Auswahl^{4b})	elección^{2b}, (selección^{6b})
club^{2b} (association)	cercle^{2a}, (club^{4a})	Verein^{1b}, (Klub^{6b})	círculo^{2b}, (casino^{6a})
compare^{2a}	comparer^{2b}	vergleichen^{1b}	comparar^{2a}
crossing (cross^{1a}), (passage^{3a})	passage^{1b}, (traversée^{5a}), (trajet^{5b})	Übergang^{2b}	pasaje^{3a}, (tránsito^{4b})
daily^{2b}	quotidien^{3a}, (journalier^{5a})	täglich^{1b}, (alltäglich^{6b})	diario^{1b}, (cotidiano^{6a})
disease^{2b}, (sickness^{3a}), (illness^{5b})	maladie^{2b}	Krankheit^{1b}, (Erkrankung^{6a})	enfermedad^{1a}, mal (*n.*)^{2a}, (dolencia^{3b}), (afección^{7b})
double^{1b}	double^{2a}	doppelt^{2a}	doble^{2a}
easily^{2b}, (readily^{4b})	facilement^{3a}, (aisément^{4a})	leicht^{1a}	fácilmente (fácil^{1a})
education^{2b}	éducation^{2a}	Bildung^{1b}, (Ausbildung^{2b})	educación^{2a}
exercise^{1b} (*vb.*), practice (se)^{1b}, (drill^{2b})	exercer^{2a}, (pratiquer^{3a})	üben^{2a}, ausüben^{2a}	ejercer^{2a}, (practicar^{3a}), (profesar^{3b}), (ejercitar^{4a})
experience^{2a} (*n.*)	expérience^{2a}	Erfahrung^{1b}, (Erlebnis^{5b})	experiencia^{2a}
feel^{1a} (with fingers)	tâter^{5b}	fühlen^{1a}, (rühren^{2a})	tentar^{3a}, (palpar^{5b})
feeling^{1b} (sensation)	sensation^{2b}	Empfindung^{2a}, (Empfinden^{6b})	sensación^{2a}
fight^{1b}, (fought^{2a}), (struggle^{2a}), (wrestle^{5b}), (scramble^{6})	combattre^{2a}, lutter^{2b}, (se battre^{3a})	kämpfen^{2a}, (streiten^{3b}), (fechten^{4b}), (ringen^{4b})	combatir^{2a}, luchar^{2a}, (pelear^{3b}), (lidiar^{4b}), (batallar^{6a})

English	French	German	Spanish
fly[1a] (*vb.*), (flew[2b]), (flies[3a])	s'envoler[3b], (voler[4a]), (voltiger[5b])	fliegen[2b]	volar[1b]
fourth[1b]	quatrième[3a]	vierte[2b]	cuarto[1a]
height[1b] (e.g., of career)	hauteur[2a]	Höhe[1a]	colmo[6b]
here[1a]!	tenez![3b]	sehen Sie!, siehst du! (sehen[1a])	ea[5a]
influence[2b] (*n.*)	influence[2b], (prestige[4a])	Einfluß[1b], (Einwirkung[3a])	influencia[2a], (influjo[4b])
judge[1b] (*n.*)	juge[2a]	Richter[2a], (Amtsrichter[6a])	juez[2a]
language[2a], speech[2a]	langage[2b], (parler [*n.*][5a])	Sprache[1a]	lenguaje[2b]
learned (learn[1a]) (*adj.*)	savant[3b], (lettré[5b]), (érudit[6b])	gelehrt[2b]	sabio[1b], (erudito[4a]), (docto[4b]), (letrado[5b])
limit[2a] (*vb.*), (confine[4a])	borner[2a], (limiter[4a]), (confiner[6b]), (restreindre[6b])	beschränken[1b], (einschränken[4a]), (begrenzen[4b])	limitar[2a], (confinar[7b])
mass[2a], pile[2a], heap[2b], (mound[4b]), (stack[6])	masse[2a], (tas[3a]), (amas[5a])	Masse[1b], (Haufe[3a])	masa[2a], (montón[3a]), (pila[4a]), (mole[6a])
meat[1b]	viande[3a]	Fleisch[2b]	carne[1a]
moon[1b]	lune[2b]	Mond[2b]	luna[2a]
north[1a]	nord[2a]	Norden[2b]	norte[2a], (aquilón[7b])
plain[1a] (*n.*)	plaine[2a]	Fläche[2b], (Ebene[4a])	llano[2b], (llanura[3a]), (pampa[6a]), (vega[6b])
possession[2b]	possession[2a]	Besitz[1b], (Besitzung[5b])	posesión[2a]
pound[1b] (*n.*), (lb.[4b])	livre (*f.*)[2a], (kilo[gramme][3b])	Pfund[2b], (Kilogramm[4a]), (Kilo[5b])	libra[2b], (gramo[4a]), (arroba[6b]), (kilogramo[6b])
prepare[1b] (*intr. vb.*), get[1a] ready[1a]	s'apprêter[3a]	(sich) bereiten[2a], (sich) vorbereiten[2b], ([sich] zurecht[5a] machen[1a])	preparar[1b] se[1a], (aderezar[4a] se[1a])
proud[1b]	fier[1b], (orgueilleux[6b]), (s'enorgueillir[7a]) (fièrement[5b])	stolz[2a], (trotzig[6a])	orgulloso[3a], (ufano[4a])
queen[1b]	reine[3a]	Königin[2a]	reina[1b]
quiet[1b], (silence[2a]), (calm[2b]), (lull[4a]), (soothe[5b]), (appease[6])	calmer[2a], (apaiser[3a])	beruhigen[2b]	calmar[2b], (sosegar[3b]), (tranquilizar[3b]), (aplacar[5a]), (serenarse[5a]) (*refl.*)
reading (read[1a]) (*n.*)	lecture[2b]	Lesung[2b], (Lektüre[5b]), (Lesen[6b])	lectura[2b]
relation[2b] (relationship)	rapport[1b], (relation[3a])	Verhältnis[1a]	relación[1a], (afinidad[5a])
religion[2b]	religion[2b]	Religion[1b], (Religionsunterricht[5a])	religión[2a]
round[1a] (*adj.*)	rond[2b]	rund[2b]	redondo[2b], (circular[3a]), (rotundo[6b])
run[1a] into[1a], (bump[6])	heurter[2a], (choquer[4b]), (buter[5b]), (se[1a] cogner[6b])	stoßen[2a]	chocar[2b], (topar[4b])
sacred[2b]	sacré[2a]	heilig[1b]	sagrado[2a], (sacro[4b])
severe[2b], (stern[3a]), (harsh[4a]), (strict[4a]), (grim[5a])	sévère[2b], (rigoureux[3b]), (austère[4a])	streng[1b]	severo[2a], (austero[4b]), (estricto[5b]), (exigente[6b])
	(durement[4a]), (sévèrement[4b]), (strictement[5a]), (rigoureusement[5b])		
shine[1b], (glow[2b]), (shone[3a]), (sparkle[3a]), (gleam[3b]), (glisten[5a])	briller[2b], (luire[3b])	glühen[2b], (glänzen[3a]), (strahlen[3b]), (blitzen[5b])	brillar[2a], lucir[2b], (resplandecer[4b]), (relucir[5b])

English	French	German	Spanish
shut[1b] out[1a], (bar[2a])	exclure[4b], (barrer[5b])	ausschließen[1b]	excluir[4a]
song[1b]	chant[2b], (chanson[3a])	Lied[2a], (Gesang[3a])	canto[2a], canción[2b], (cántico[5b])
(make a) speech[2a], deliver[2a] (an) address[2a]	(faire un) discours[2a]	(eine) Rede[1a] (halten)	pronunciar[1b] (un) discurso[2a]
spend[1b] (money), (spent[2a])	dépenser[2b]	anlegen[2a], (ausgeben[3b]), (auszahlen[6a])	gastar[2a]
storm[1b], (gale[4a]), (tempest[4a])	orage[2b], (tempête[3b])	Sturm[2a], (Gewitter[5b])	tempestad[2b], (tormenta[3a]), (temporal[3b]), (huracán[4a]), (borrasca[5a]), (vendaval[5a])
summer[1a]	été[2a]	Sommer[2a]	verano[2a], (estío[4b])
system[2a]	système[2a]	System[1b]	sistema[2a]
tax[2a] (*n.*), (tribute[4a])	impôt[3a], (contribution[4b]), (taxe[6a])	Steuer[1b], (Gebäudesteuer[2a]), (Gewerbesteuer[2a]), (Einkommensteuer[2b]), (Besteuerung[2b]), (Grundsteuer[3b]), (Abgabe[3b]), (Gebühr[4b]), (Steuerzahler[5b]), (Doppelbesteuerung[6a]), (Staatssteuer[6a]), (Betriebsteuer[6b]), (Gemeindeabgabe[6b]), (Kommunalsteuer[6b])	contribución[4b], tributo[4b]
thy[2a]	ton[3b]	dein[1a]	tu[1]*
tie[1b] (*vb.*), (bind[2a]), (bound[2a]), (gird[5a]), (girt[6])	lier[2a], (nouer[4a])	binden[2a], knüpfen[2b], (verknüpfen[4b])	atar[2a], (ligar[3b]), (amarrar[5a]), (anudar[5b])
tie[1b] (*n.*), (bond[3a])	lien[2b], (attache[6b])	Band[2b]	lazo[2a], (corbata[4a]), (vínculo[4b])
troop[2b]	troupe[2b]	Truppe[1a], (Truppenteil[4a])	tropa[2b]
union[2a], (confederacy[6])	union[2b], (alliance[5b])	Verbindung[1a], (Bund[2a]), (Vereinigung[2b]), (Bundesstaat[4b]), (Bündnis[4b]), (Union[6a])	unión[2a], (vínculo[4b]), (conjunción[5a]), (alianza[5b])
upon[1a] which[1a], (thereupon[4a]), (whereat[5a]), (whereupon[7])	là-dessus[3a]	worauf[2a]	sobre[1a] lo[1a] cual[1a]
(make) used (use[1a]) (to), (accustom[3a])	habituer[3a], accoutumer[3b]	gewöhnen[2a]	acostumbrar[1b], (habituar[5b])
walk[1a], (gait[5b])	démarche[3a]	Gang[2a]	andar[1a], paso[1a], (marcha[2b])
wild[1b], (fierce[2a]), (savage[2b]), (barbarous[5b])	sauvage[2b], (barbare[3b]), (féroce[3b]), (fauve[5a])	wild[2a], (gewaltsam[3b])	fiero[2a], (feroz[3b])
willingly (willing[2b])	volontiers[2b]	gern[1a]	(de buena) gana[2a]

SECTION 1.7. CONCEPTS 1210 THROUGH 1272

E F G S	*E F G S*	*E F G S*
1–1 –2–4	1–2–2–3	1–6–1–3
1–4 –2–1	1–3–2–2	2–2–1–3
1–1 –1–8*	1–2–1–7	2–3–1–2
1–8*–1–1	1–4–1–5	

Read: (*First column*) English, first thousand; French, first thousand; German, second thousand; Spanish, fourth thousand; *or* English, first thousand; French, fourth thousand; German, second thousand; Spanish, first thousand; *and so on for other alternatives in the first and succeeding columns*

English	French	German	Spanish
attack^{2b} (*n.*) (general), (assault^{4b})	attaque^{2b}, (assaut^{3a})	Angriff^{1b}	ataque^{3b}, (asalto^{5a}), (invasión^{5b})
August^{2a}, (Aug.^{6})	août^{3b}	August^{1b}	agosto^{2b}
base^{2a}, (basis^{4b})	base^{3a}	Grundlage^{1b}, (Basis^{4b}), (Hauptgrund^{4b}), (Ausgangspunkt^{5b}), (Fundament^{6b}), (Grundgedanke^{6b})	base^{2a}, (fundamento^{3a})
board^{1b}, (plank^{5a})	planche^{3a}	Tafel^{2b}, (Brett^{6a})	tabla^{2a}
border^{2a}, (boundary^{3b}), (frontier^{6})	limite^{2b}, (frontière^{3a})	Grenze^{1b}	frontera^{3b}, (ámbito^{4a})
bridge^{1b}	pont^{2b}	Brücke^{2b}	puente^{3a}
careful^{1b}	(prendre ses) précautions (précaution^{2b}) (soigneusement^{3b})	sorgfältig^{2b}, (mühsam^{4a}), (diplomatisch^{5a}), (sorgsam^{6a})	cuidadoso^{3a}, (solícito^{5a})
cent^{1b}, (penny^{2b}), (dime^{4b}), (nickel^{4b})	sou^{2a}, (centime^{3b})	Pfennig^{2b}, (Kopeke^{5b}), (Groschen^{6a})	céntimo^{3a}
claim^{2a} (*n.*)	prétention^{2b}	Anspruch^{1b}	pretensión^{3b}, (reclamación^{6b})
company^{1a}, (guest^{2a})	hôte^{3b}, convive^{3b}, (invité [*n.*]^{4b})	Gast^{2a}	huésped^{2b}
crown^{1b} (*n.*)	couronne^{3a}	Krone^{2b}	corona^{2a}, (diadema^{5a})
debt^{2a}	dette^{3a}	Schuld^{1b}	deuda^{2b}
draw^{1a} up^{1a} (water), (scoop^{6})	puiser^{4a}	entnehmen^{2b}, (schöpfen^{3b})	sacar^{1a}
empire^{2b}	empire^{3a}	Reich^{1a}	imperio^{2a}
enjoy^{1b} (oneself), (have a good time)	s'amuser^{3a}, (se^{1a} divertir^{5b})	sich^{1a} (gut^{1a}) unterhalten^{2b}	divertir^{2a} se^{1a}
even^{1a} (*adj.*) (number)	pair	gerade^{1a}	par^{1b}
except^{1b} (*vb.*)	excepter^{6a}	ausschließen^{1b}, (ausnehmen^{3b})	exceptuar^{3b}
exercise^{1b} (*n.*), practice(se)^{1b}	pratique^{2a}, exercice^{2b}	Praxis^{2b}, Übung^{2b}, (Ausübung^{3b})	ejercicio^{3a}, práctica^{3a}
free^{1a} (*vb.*), (deliver^{2a}), (release^{3b})	libérer^{4a}, affranchir^{4b}, délivrer^{4b}	befreien^{2a}, (erlösen^{5a}), (entledigen^{5b})	librar^{1b}, (libertar^{5a}), (emancipar^{6b})
frequent^{2a} (*adj.*)	fréquent^{3b}	häufig^{1b}	frecuente^{2a}
give^{1a} (oneself) up^{1a} (to)	s'abandonner^{4b}	sich^{1a} aufgeben^{2b}	abandonar^{1b} se^{1a}, entregar^{1a} se^{1a}
glass^{1b} (material)	verre^{1b}	Glas^{1b}	vidrio
gun^{2a}, (cannon^{3b}), (rifle^{5b})	fusil^{2b}, (canon^{3a})	Geschütz^{1b}, (Gewehr^{2b}), (Kanone^{3b}), (Muskete^{6a})	cañón^{3b}, (fusil^{4b}), (escopeta^{7a})

English	French	German	Spanish
herself[1a]	elle-même	sie[1a] selber[1a], selbst[1a]	ella[1]* misma[1a]
honor[1b] (*vb.*)	honorer[4a]	ehren[2a], verehren[2b]	honrar[1b]
keep[1a] back[1a], (retain[3b]), (withhold[6])	retenir[1a]	verhalten[2b], (zurückhalten[3a]), (beibehalten[4b])	retener[4b]
keep[1a] from[1a], (refrain[5a]), (forbear[5b]), (abstain[7])	s'abstenir[4a]	sich[1a] enthalten[1a]	abstenerse[5a]
kingdom[2a], (realm[3a])	royaume[3b]	Reich[1a], (Königreich[4a]), (Himmelreich[6a])	reino[2a]
kiss[1b] (*n.*)	baiser[3a]	Kuß[2b]	beso[2a]
length[1a]	longueur[4a]	Länge[2a]	largo[1a], (longitud[4b])
lie[1b] (here lies)	gésir[6a]	ruhen[1b]	yacer[3b]
load[1b] (*n.*), (cargo[4b])	charge[2a]	Last[1b], (Ladung[4a])	cargamento[7a]
market[1b]	marché[2a], (foire[5a])	Markt[1a]	mercado[7b], (feria[5a]), (lonja[6b])
mile[1a], (league[2b])	kilomètre[3a], lieue[3a], (mille[5a])	Meile[2a], (Kilometer[3b])	legua[1a], (kilómetro[3b]), (milla[7a])
nose[1b]	nez[2a]	Nase[2b]	nariz[3a]
notice[1b] (*n.*) (notice of something)	avis[2a]	Meldung[2b], (Notiz[3b]), (Bekanntmachung[4a])	aviso[3a], advertencia[3b], (anuncio[4a])
present[1a], gift[1b], (bounty[4b])	don[3a], cadeau[3b]	Gabe[2b], (Geschenk[3a])	regalo[2b], (don[7b]), (ofrenda[4b]), (dádiva[6b])
pressing (press[1b]), (urgent[6])	pressant (presser[2a]), (pressé[6b]), (urgent[6b])	dringend[1a]	imperioso[3b], urgente[3b], (imperativo[5a])
probable[2b], (likely[3a]), (apt[5a])	probable[3a], (vraisemblable[4a]), (probablement[2b])	wahrscheinlich[1b], (voraussichtlich[4a]), (vermutlich[5a])	probable[3a]
process[2b] (procedure)	procédé[2b]	Verfahren[1b], (Handlungsweise[5a])	procedimiento[3a]
pupil[2a]	élève[2b], (écolier[5b])	Schüler[1b], (Zögling[4b])	pupilo[3b], (alumno[4b]), (discípulo[5a]), (escolar[5a])
ringing (ring[1b]) (*adj.*) (sonorous)	sonore[3b]	klingend (klingen[2a])	sonoro[2b]
rock[1a] (*n.*)	rocher[3a], (roche[6a]), (roc[6b])	Fels[2b], (Gestein[6a])	peña[2b], roca[2b], (peñasco[4b])
safety[2b], (security[5b])	sécurité[3b], (sûreté[4a])	Sicherheit[1b]	seguridad[2a]
sharp[2a], (shrewd[5a])	malin[3b]	scharf[1b]	agudo[2b], (sagaz[6a])
shelter[2a] (*n.*), (lee [L][4b])	abri[2a]	Schutz[1b]	amparo[3a], (abrigo[4a])
(wrong[1b]) side[1a], (reverse[4b])	derrière (*n.*)[3b], (revers [*n.*][4b]), (inverse[6b]), (envers [*n.*])	umgekehrt (umkehren[6b])	revés[2b], (inverso[7a])
spring[1a] (water)	source[4b]	Quelle[2a]	fuente[1b], (manantial[4b])
start[1a] (*n.*) (of surprise, etc.)	sursaut[4a]	Satz[1b]	sobresalto[5b]
stay[1a] (*n.*), visit[1a], (sojourn[5b])	séjour[3a]	Aufenthalt[2b]	estancia[2b], (permanencia[5b])
step[1a] (of stair)	marche[1b]	Stufe[2a]	grada[4a], (escalón[6b])
(to be) subject[1b] (*adj.*) (to), ([to be] liable[6])	(être) sujet (*adj.*)[4b]	neigen[2a]	(estar) sujeto[1b]
take[1a] up[1a] (a subject), (embark[6] on)	aborder[2b], (entamer[4a])	aufnehmen[1b], (aufwerfen[5b])	abordar[7a]
tight[2b], (snug[4b])	serré[3b]	eng[1b]	apretado (apretar[2a]), muy[1a] ajustado (ajustar[2b])
trace[2a] (out) (*vb.*)	tracer[3a]	zeichnen[1b]	trazar[2b]

English	French	German	Spanish
understanding (*n.*) (understand[1b]) (comprehension)	entente[4b]	Auffassung[2a], Verstand[2a], Verständnis[2b]	entendido (entender[1a]), (entendimiento[2b]), (comprensión[4b])
valley[1b], (vale[3b]), (dale[5a]), (glen[5a]), (dell[6])	vallée[3a]	Tal[2b]	valle[2a]
wall[1a] (of city, garden, etc.)	muraille[2a], (enceinte [*n.*][5b])	Mauer[2b]	muro[3a], (tapia[4b]), (muralla[5b])
warm[1a] (*adj.*)	chaud[1b], (tiède[3b])	warm[2a]	tibio[4a]
wave[1b], (float[2b] [in air])	flotter[2b]	wehen[2a], schweben[2b]	flotar[3a]
(be in) way[1a]	gêner[2a]	stören[2a]	estorbar[3a]
wild[1b] (uncultivated)	sauvage[2b], (inculte[6b])	wild[2a]	salvaje[3a], (agreste[5b])
wonder[1b], (marvel[4a]), (miracle[4a])	merveille[3a], miracle[3a]	Wunder[2a]	maravilla[2a], milagro[2b], (prodigio[3a]), (portento[4a])

SECTION 1.8. CONCEPTS 1273 THROUGH 1393

E F G S	*E F G S*	*E F G S*
1–1–2–5	1–4–1–6	2–2–1–4
1–1–3–1	1–4–2–2	2–3–1–3
1–2–2–4	1–5–2–1	2–4–1–2
1–3–2–3	2–1–2–1	3–1–1–1

Read: (*First column*) English, first thousand; French, first thousand; German, second thousand; Spanish, fifth thousand; *or* English, first thousand; French, first thousand; German, third thousand; Spanish, first thousand; *and so on for other alternatives in the first and succeeding columns*

English	French	German	Spanish
absolute[2b]	absolu[2a] (*adj.*), (catégorique[4b]) absolument[1a]	unbedingt[2a], absolut[2b]	absoluto[1b]
account[1b], (reckoning [reckon[3b]])	compte[1a], (calcul[3a])	Berechnung[3a]	cuenta[1a], (cálculo[3b])
add[1a]	ajouter[1a]	hinzufügen[3a], (beifügen[5b]), (beigeben[6a])	añadir[1a], (agregar[2a]), (sumar[4a])
admit[2b] (let in)	recevoir[1a], accepter[1a], admettre[1b]	zulassen[2b], (einlassen[4a])	recibir[1a]
afterwards[2a]	après[1a], ensuite[1a]	nachher[2a], danach[2b], hierauf[2b], (darnach[3b]), (hernach[5a])	después[1a]
age[1b], (epoch[9])	époque[1b], âge[1b], (ère[4a])	Zeitalter[3b], (Epoche[4a])	época[1b], (era[6b])
anybody[3b], anyone[3b]	n'[1a]importe (importer[1b]) qui[1a], (venu [*n.*] [premier venu][6a])	irgend[1a] einer (ein[1a]), (irgend) jemand[1b]	quienquiera[1a], cualquiera[1a]
as[1a] much[1a]	autant[1a]	soviel[3a]	tan[1a], tanto[1a]
attempt[2a] (*n.*), trial[2b]	essai[3b], tentative[3b]	Versuch[1b], (Anlauf[5b])	ensayo[3b], (tentativa[6b])
attention[2b], (heed[3b])	attention[1a]	Aufmerksamkeit[2a], Achtung[2b], (Acht[4b])	atención[1b]
average[3a] (*adj.*)	moyen[1a]	mittlere[1b]	medio[1a], (promedio[7b])
avoid[2b], (shun[3b])	éviter[1b]	sich[1a] entziehen[2a], vermeiden[2a], (scheuen[3a]), (verhüten[4b]), (ausweichen[5a]), (meiden[5b])	evitar[1b]
bank[1a] (for money)	banque[4a]	Bank[2a], Reichsbank[2a], (Kasse[3b])	banco[2b]

English	French	German	Spanish
beauty[1b] (a –, belle)	belle (beau[1a])	Schöne[3b]	belleza[1b], (beldad[5b])
beyond[2b] (*adv.*)	plus[1a] loin[1a], (au[1a] delà[2a])	außerhalb[2b], (jenseits[3b])	más[1a] allá[1a], (allende[5a])
(be to) blame[2a], (be at) fault[2a], (guilty[3a])	coupable[2a]	(daran) Schuld[1b] (sein), (schuldig[2a]), (verschulden[6a])	culpable[4a], delincuente[4b]
bow[1b], (greeting[4b])	salut[2b]	Gruß[2a]	saludo[4a]
care[1a] about[1a], (be) concerned (concern[2b]) (about)	se soucier[5a]	sorgen[2a]	ocupar[1a] se[1a], (preocupar[2b] se[1a])
chair[1b], (armchair[9])	chaise[1b], fauteuil[1b]	Stuhl[3a], (Sessel[5b])	silla[1b], (butaca[5b]), (sillón[5b])
come[1a] back[1a], return[1b]	revenir[1a]	zurückkommen[3a], (wiederkommen[6b])	volver[1a], (regresar[2b]), (retornar[6a])
conscience[2b]	conscience[1b]	Gewissen[2b]	conciencia[1b]
consider[2a], (reflect[4a]), (ponder[6])	considérer[1b], réfléchir[1b], (envisager[2b])	bedenken[1a], (beachten[3b]), (berücksichtigen[3b]), (erwägen[6b]), (überlegen[5b]), (nachdenken[4a])	considerar[1a], (discurrir[2a]), (reflexionar[3b]), (ponderar[4a])
contrary[2b] (*n.*)	contraire[1b]	Gegenteil[7a]	contrario[1a]
(on the) contrary[2b]	(au) contraire[1b]	(im) Gegenteil[2a], ander(er)seits[2a], (hingegen[3a])	(al, por, el) contrario[1a]
cut[1a] (*vb.*), (shear[4a]), (clip[4b]), (hew[4b]), (slice[4b])	couper[1a], (tailler[3a]), (trancher[3b])	schneiden[3a], abschneiden[3b], (durchschneiden[5a])	cortar[1b]
dash[2a] (*vb.*), (dart[3a])	se[1a] précipiter[1b], (s'élancer[2b]), (se[1a] ruer[6b])	sich[1a] stürzen[2b]	lanzar[1b] se[1a]
direction[1b], (administration[5a]), (management[5b])	administration[2a], direction[2a], régime[2a]	Leitung[2a], Verwaltung[2a], (Direktion[5a])	administración[4a], régimen[4a], (manejo[5a]), (dominador[6b])
dish[2a] (of food)	plat[3a], (mets[5b])	Gericht[1b], (Platte[3a])	manjar[3b]
dispose[2b]	disposer[1b]	ordnen[2a]	disponer[1a]
do[1a] (over) again[1a]	refaire[4a]	wieder[1a] tun[1a]	rehacer[6b]
dream[1b] (*vb.*)	songer[1a], rêver[1b]	träumen[3a]	soñar[1b]
(make) easy[1b], (easier[4b])	faciliter[4a]	erleichtern[2b]	facilitar[2b], (allanar[5a])
effort[2b]	effort[1a]	Anstrengung[2b], (Bestrebung[3a]), (Streben[3a]), (Bestreben[3b]), (Bemühung[3b]), (Wirken[5a])	esfuerzo[1b]
entrance[2b], (entry[4a]), (gateway[6])	entrée[1b]	Eingang[2b], (Zugang[6b])	entrada[1b], (portal[3b]), (ingreso[5b])
error[2b], mistake[2a]	erreur[1b], faute[1b]	Irrtum[2b], (Versehen[5b])	error[1b], (equivocación[3b]), (yerro[4a]), (tropiezo[4b]), (desacierto[6a])
escape[1b] (*vb.*)	échapper[1b], (évader[5b]), (esquiver[6b])	entgehen[3a], umgehen[3a], (entfliehen[4b]), (entweichen[4b]), (entkommen[6b])	escapar[1b], (esquivar[7a])
excellent[2a]	excellent[1b]	ausgezeichnet (auszeichnen[2a]), vorzüglich[2a], trefflich[2b]	excelente[1b]
exist[3b]	exister[1a]	bestehen[1a], da[1a] sein[1a], vorhanden[1a] sein[1a], (befindlich[2b] sein[1a]), (existieren[3a])	existir[1a], (existente[5b])

English	French	German	Spanish
experience[2a] (*vb.*) (live through)	éprouver[1b], ([faire l']expérience[2a] [de])	erleben[2b]	sentir[1a], (experimentar[2a])
face[1a] (grimace)	grimace[4a]	Gesicht[1b]	mohín[6b], mueca[6b]
farmer[1b]	fermier[4a], (cultivateur[6a])	Bauer[2a], (Landwirt[4a]), (Landmann[5b])	labrador[2a], (agricultor[6a])
fault[2a], (defect[5a])	défaut[1b]	Fehler[2a]	falta[1a], (defecto[2a]), (tacha[5b])
fill[1a] (up[1a])	combler[2b]	füllen[2a]	colmar[4a], ([*p.p.*] relleno[5b])
fit[1b] up[1a], out[1a], (equip[5a]), (rig[6])	meubler[5a], (aménager[6a]), (équiper[7a])	einrichten[2a], (ausstatten[4a]), (ausrüsten[5a])	arreglar[1b]
forehead[2b], brow[2b]	front[1b]	Stirn[2b]	frente[1a]
further[2a] (*vb.*), (foster[5b]), (promote[6])	avancer[1a]	fördern[2a], (befördern[3a])	adelantar[1b], (fomentar[4a]), (impulsar[5a]), (promover[6a])
go[1a] round[1a], circle[1b] (round)	(faire le) tour (*m.*)[1a] (de), (contourner[6b])	umgehen[3a]	rodear[1b], (dar la) vuelta[1b]
grief[2b], sorrow[2a], (woe[3a]), (gloom[4a])	peine[1a], douleur[1b], (chagrin [*n.*][2a]), (deuil[3a])	Leid[2a], (Kummer[4a]), (Gram[5b]), (Leiden[5b])	dolor[1a], pesar[1a], pena[1a], (duelo[2b]), (pesadumbre[3a]), (congoja[4a]), (desconsuelo[5a]), (quebranto[5b])
group[2b], (brotherhood[6])	groupe[1b]	Gruppe[2b], (Schar[3a]), (Körperschaft[5b])	grupo[1b], (corro+corrillo[3a])
hand[1a] (*vb.*), pass[1a]	passer[1a]	überreichen[3b]	pasar[1a], (alargar[2b])
hurt[1b] (*tr. vb.*), (harm[2a]), (injure[3a]), (damage[3b])	faire[1a] mal[1a] à[1a], blesser[1b], (froisser[4a]), (nuire[4b])	schaden[3a], schädigen[3b], (beschädigen[5b])	herir[1b], (lastimar[4a]), (perjudicar[4b]), (agraviar[5b])
hurt[1b] (*intr. vb.*), (be[1a] sore[2b]), (ache[3b])	faire[1a] mal[1a]	weh[3b] tun[1b], (kränken[4a])	hacer[1a] daño[1b], (doler[2b])
import[3b] (*vb.*)	importer[1b]	einführen[1b]	importar[1a]
importance[2b]	importance[1b]	Gewicht[2a], Wichtigkeit[2b]	importancia[1b], (transcendencia[5b])
iron[1b] (*n.*)	fer[1b]	Eisen[3a]	hierro[1b], (plancha[5b]) (for ironing)
justice[2a], (equity[6])	justice[1b], (équité[5b])	Gerechtigkeit[2b]	justicia[1b]
laugh[1a] (*n.*)	rire[1a]	Lache[3b]	risa[1b]
leaning (lean[2a]), (tendency[5b])	tendance[4a], (inclination[6b])	Neigung[1b], (Tendenz[3b])	inclinación[2b], (tendencia[4a])
listen[1b], (hark[3b]), (hearken[5a])	écouter[1a]	anhören[3a], (horchen[4b]), (lauschen[5b]), (zuhören[6a])	escuchar[1a]
load[1b] (*vb.*), (burden[3a]), (lade[n][4a])	charger[1a]	laden[3a], beschweren[3b], (belasten[4b]), (beladen[6a]), (lasten[6b])	cargar[1b]
low[1a], (base[2a]), (vile[4a])	abject[5b]	niedrig[2a]	bajo[1a], (vil[2b]), (abyecto)
make[1a] up[1a], (constitute[5a])	constituer[1b]	ausmachen[3b]	constituir[1b]
man[1a] (of the) house[1a] (head of family)	maître[1a] (de) maison[1a], chef[1b] (de) famille[1a]	Hausherr[3b]	amo[1a] (de) casa[1a]
memory[2a], (remembrance[4b])	souvenir[1a], mémoire[1b]	Erinnerung[2a], (Gedächtnis[3a]), (Andenken[3b])	memoria[1a], recuerdo[1b]
modern[2b]	moderne[1b]	modern[2a]	moderno[1b]
(make) necessary[1b], (necessitate[8])	nécessiter[5a]	bedingen[2b]	necesitar[1a]
neighbor[1b]	voisin(-e)[1a]	Nachbar[3a]	vecino[1b]
(at) once[1a], ([at one] stroke[2b])	d'[1a]un[1a] (seul) coup[1a], (tout d'un coup[4b])	mit[1a] einem (ein[1a]) Schlag[2b]	de[1a] un[1a] tirón[5b]

English	French	German	Spanish
owe^{2a}	devoir^{1a}	schuldig^{2a} sein^{1a}, verdanken^{2b}, (schulden^{5a})	deber^{1a}
pace^{2b}, (gait^{5b})	pas^{1a}, (allure^{2b})	Gang^{2a}	paso^{1a}, (marcha^{2b})
parents (parent^{2a})	parents (parent^{1b})	Eltern^{2a}	padres (padre^{1a})
(for the most) part^{1a}, (chiefly^{6*})	(pour la) plupart^{1b}	meistens^{3a}, (größtenteils^{4a}), (zumeist^{5a})	principalmente (principal^{1a})
(take) possession^{2b} (of)	s'emparer^{3a}, ([s']approprier^{4b})	besetzen^{1b}, (sich^{1a} bemächtigen^{3b}), (aneignen^{5a})	apoderarse^{3a}, (apropiar^{5a} se^{1a})
(make) possible^{1b}, (enable^{4b})	rendre^{1a} possible^{1a}	ermöglichen^{3a}	hacer^{1a} posible^{1a}
presence^{2a}, (attendance^{5a})	présence^{1a}	Gegenwart^{2a}, (Anwesenheit^{4b})	presencia^{1b}, (asistencia^{6b})
present^{1a} (a person), (introduce^{3a})	présenter^{1a}	vorstellen^{3a}, (präsentieren^{5a})	presentar^{1a}
pretend^{3b} (to something)	prétendre^{1b}, (revendiquer^{6b})	Anspruch^{1b} machen^{1a}	pretender^{1b}
produce^{2a} (*vb.*)	produire^{1a}	hervorbringen^{2b}, (produzieren^{5b})	producir^{1a}
recall^{3b}, (remind^{4a})	rappeler^{1a}	erinnern^{1b}	recordar^{1a}
right^{1a}, (title^{2a})	droit^{1a}, titre^{1b}	Berechtigung^{3b}, (Behuf^{6b})	derecho^{1a}, título^{1b}
Roman^{2a}	romain^{3b}	römisch^{1b}, (Römer^{2b})	romano^{3a}
sake^{2b}	pour^{1a} (l'amour de)	(um) willen^{2b}, (behufs^{3b})	por^{1a}
saving (save^{1a}), (thrifty^{6}) (economical)	économique^{3a}	wirtschaftlich^{2a}, (rationell^{1b}), (sparsam^{6b})	económico^{3b}
scale^{2a} (*n.*)	échelle^{3b}	Maßstab^{1b}	escala^{3a}
scene^{2b}	scène^{1b}	Szene^{2b}, (Schauplatz^{5a})	escena^{1a}
secret^{2a} (*n.*)	secret (*n.*)^{1b}	Geheimnis^{2a}	secreto^{1a}
settle^{1b} (a dispute)	décider^{1b}, (régler^{2a})	erledigen^{3b}, (ausgleichen^{4a}), (beilegen^{4a})	componer^{1b}, (transigir^{4b})
shade^{1b}, (shadow^{2a})	ombrage^{5a}, pénombre^{6b}	Schatten^{2b}	sombra^{1a}, (penumbra^{5a})
shoot^{2a}, shot^{2a}	tirer^{1a}	schießen^{2b}, (beschießen^{6a}), (feuern^{6b})	tirar^{1b}, (disparar^{7a})
sit^{1a} up^{1a}, (stay^{1a} awake^{2a}) (e.g., all night)	veiller^{2a}	wachen^{2a}	desvelar^{4a} se^{1a}
(be) sorry^{2a}, (regret^{3b}), (rue^{6})	regretter^{1b}	bedauern^{2b}, (leid^{4a} tun^{1a})	sentir^{1a}
special^{2a}, particular^{2a}	particulier^{1b}, (spécial^{2a})	speziell^{2b}, (spezifisch^{5b}), (sonderlich^{6b})	especial^{1b}
spring^{1a} (of machine)	ressort^{3a}	Feder^{2b}	muelle^{3b}, (resorte^{5a})
start^{1a} (on a journey)	partir^{1a}	abgehen^{3a}, (abreisen^{5a})	partir^{1a}
state^{1a} (*adj.*)	(d')état^{1a}	staatlich^{3a}	(de) estado^{1a}
stock^{1b} (finance)	part^{1a}	Wertpapier^{3a}, Aktie^{3b}, (Effekten^{5a})	acción^{1a}
straight^{1b}, (erect^{2b}), (upright^{3a})	droit^{1a}	aufrecht^{3a}	derecho^{1a}, (recto^{2b}), (erguido [erguir^{3a}])
stranger^{2b}	étranger^{1a}, inconnu^{1b}	Fremde^{2b}	extraño^{1b}, (forastero^{5a})
suit^{1b} (law)	procès^{3b}, (procès-verbal^{6b})	Prozeß^{2a}	pleito^{3a}, (proceso^{4b})
support^{2a} (*vb.*), (sustain^{4a}), (uphold^{5b})	appuyer^{1b}, soutenir^{1a}	unterstützen^{2a}, stützen^{2b}, (bestärken^{6a})	sostener^{1b}, (sustentar^{3a}), (basar^{6b})

English	French	German	Spanish
surround[2b], (gird[5a]), (girt[6])	entourer[1b], (environner[5a])	umgeben[2a], (umringen[6b])	rodear[1b], (ceñir[2a]), (circundar[4b]), (cercar[4b])
take[1a] off[1a] (coat, etc.)	enlever[1b], (ôter[2a])	ablegen[3a], abnehmen[3a], (ausziehen[5a])	quitar[1a] se[1a]
tear[1b], (torn[3a]), (rip[3b]), (rend[4b]), (tore[4b])	déchirer[2a]	reißen[2a], (zerreißen[3a])	rasgar[4a], desgarrar[4b], despedazar[4b]
term[2a], period[2b]	terme[1b], (période[3a]), (durée[4a])	Dauer[2a], (Ablauf[3b])	término[1a], (período[3a]), (plazo[3a]), (duración[5a])
terrible[2a], awful[2b], dreadful[2b], (fearful[3a]), (horrible[3b]), (horrid[5a]), (dire[6]), (frightful[6])	terrible[1b], (affreux[2a]), (formidable[2b]), (horrible[2a]), (effroyable[3b]), (épouvantable[4a]), (funeste[4a]), (hideux[6a]) (terriblement[4b]), (horriblement[5a]), (affreusement[7a])	furchtbar[2b], schrecklich[2b], (entsetzlich[3a]), (fürchterlich[3a]), (abscheulich[5a]), (gräßlich[5a])	terrible[1b], (formidable[2a]), (horrible[2a]), (tremendo[2b]), (horrendo[3b]), (temible[4b]), (horroroso[5b]), (pavoroso[5b])
threaten[2b]	menacer[1b]	drohen[2a]	amenazar[1b], (amagar[6a])
title[2a]	titre[1b]	Titel[2b]	título[1b]
tongue[1b] (part of mouth)	langue[1b]	Zunge[3b]	lengua[1a]
travel[1b] (*vb.*)	voyager[3a]	reisen[2a]	viajar[3a]
tremble[2b], (shiver[3b]), (quiver[4b]), (quake[5b]), (shudder[6])	trembler[1b], (frémir[3a]), (frissonner[3a]), (grelotter[5b])	zittern[2b], (beben[5b]), (schaudern[6a])	temblar[1b], (trémulo[3a] [*adj.*]), (estremecer[3b] se[1a]), (tembloroso[4a] [*adj.*])
two[1a] times (time[1a]), (twicc[2a])	deux[1a] fois[1a]	zweimal[3b]	dos[1*] veces (vez[1a])
unhappy[2b], (discontent[ed][4a])	malheureux[1b], (mécontent[4a])	unglücklich[2a], (Unglückliche[4a]), (unzufrieden[5b]), (unselig[6b])	infeliz[1b], (desdichado[2b]), (desventurado[5b]), (aciago[6a]), (descontento[6a])
unknown[2b]	inconnu[1b]	unbekannt[2a]	desconocido[1b], (ignoto[6a])
(of no) use[1a], (useless[3b]), ([of no] avail[5b])	(ne) servir[1a] (à rien), (ne) – (de rien), inutile[1b]	(nichts) nützen[3a], (unnütz[4a] [sein]), (unbrauchbar[6a] [sein]), (nutzlos[6b] [sein])	inútil[1b]
(of same) value[1b], (equivalent[7])	équivalent[4a]	von[1a] gleichem (gleich[1a]) Wert[1a]	equivalente[6a]
vote[2b] (*vb.*), (poll[4b])	voter[2b]	wählen[1b], (stimmen[2a])	votar[4b]
while[1a] (*n.*), (awhile[3b])	instant[1a], moment[1a], temps[1a]	Weile[3b]	instante[1a], momento[1a], rato[1b]
wonder[1b] (*vb.*), (marvel[4a])	(s')étonner[1a]	(sich) wundern[3a]	admirar[1b] se[1a], (pasmar[6a])
work[1a] (of) art[1b]	objet[1a] d'[1a]art[1b], œuvre[1a] d'[1a]art[1b]	Kunstwerk[3b]	objeto[1a], obra[1a], (de arte)
worthy[2a]	digne[1b]	würdig[2a]	digno[1a], (acreedor[4a]), (meritorio[6b])
writing (*n.*) (write[1a])	écriture[3a]	Schreiben[2b], (Handschrift[3a])	escritura[3b]

SECTION 1.9. CONCEPTS 1394 THROUGH 1497

E F G S	*E F G S*	*E F G S*	*E F G S*
1–1–3–2	1–4–1–7	1–6–2–1	2–5–1–2
1–2–3–1	1–4–2–3	2–1–2–2	2–6–1–1
1–2–2–5	1–5–1–6	2–2–2–1	3–1–1–2
1–3–2–4	1–6–1–5	2–4–1–3	3–2–1–1

Read as before

English	French	German	Spanish
afternoon[1b]	après-midi[2a]	Nachmittag[3a], (nachmittags[6a])	tarde[1a]
alive[2a] (having life)	vivant[2a]	lebendig[2a]	vivo[1a], (viviente[4b])
anger[2a], (wrath[3b]), (indignation[4b]), (spleen[6])	colère[1b], (indignation[4b])	Zorn[2b], (Wut[3b]), (Unwille[5a]), (Empörung[6a]), (Erbitterung[6b]), (Ärger[7a])	cólera[2a], enojo[2a], ira[2a], indignación[2b], (enfado[4b]), (saña[5a])
author[2b], (writer[3b])	auteur[2a], (écrivain[3b]), (rédacteur[6a])	Schriftsteller[2b], (Autor[3b])	autor[1b], (escritor[2a]), (literato[3b]), (novelista[5b]), (dramaturgo[6b])
bargain[3b]	marché[2a]	Handel[1b]	trato[1b]
bend[2a], bent[2b]	se[1a] pencher[2a]	neigen[2a]	inclinar[1b] se[1a], (doblar[2a] se[1a])
(government) bill[1b]	projet[1b] (de) loi[1b]	Regierungsvorlage[3a]	proyecto[2b] (del) gobierno[1b]
bound[2a] (for)	(à) destination[5b] (de)	nach[1a]	destinado (destinar[2a])
bring[1a] up[1a] (child), (educate[6])	élever[1a]	erziehen[3a]	criar[2a], educar[2b], (dar[1a] crianza[4b])
capital[2b] (finance)	capital (*n.*)[6b]	Kapital[1b]	capital[1b]
charm[2a] (*n.*)	charme[2a], (attrait[4a])	Reiz[2b]	encanto[1b]
cheer[2a] (*n.*), (brightness[5a])	gaieté[2b]	Heiterkeit[2b]	alegría[1b]
cheerful[2b], gay[2a], merry[2a], (jolly[4b]), (cheery[6]), (jocund[6])	gai[2b]	froh[2a], heiter[2a], lustig[2b], (munter[3b])	alegre[1b], (festivo[6a])
	(gaîment [gaiement][3a])		
chest[2b], breast[2a], bosom[2b]	poitrine[2a], (sein[3a])	Brust[2a], (Busen[3b])	pecho[1a], (seno[2a]), (regazo[6a])
Christian[2b] (*n.*)	chrétien[2b]	Christ[2b]	cristiano[1b]
Christian[2b] (*adj.*)	chrétien[2b]	christlich[2a]	cristiano[1b]
clothe[1b], dress[1a], (array[4a]), (clad[4a]), (attire[4b])	habiller[2a], revêtir[2b], vêtir[2b]	sich[1a] anziehen[3a], kleiden[3a], (bekleiden[4b]), (antun[5a])	vestir[1a], (revestir[4a])
cloud[1b]	nuage[2b], (nuée[5b])	Wolke[3a]	nube[1b], (celaje[6a])
coal[1b]	charbon[4a]	Kohle[2b], (Steinkohle[6b])	carbón[3b]
coin[2b]	pièce[1a]	Münze[2b], (Silbermünze[6b])	moneda[2b]
cold[1a] (*n.*)	froid[2b], (froideur[5a])	Kälte[3b]	frío[1a]
commanding (command[1b]), (imperious[8])	impérieux[4a]	gebietend (gebieten[2b])	imperioso[3b]
cool[1b] (*adj.*)	frais[2a]	kühl[3b]	fresco[1b]
corner[1b]	coin[1b], (angle[3a])	Ecke[3b]	rincón[2a], (esquina[3a])
custom[2a], (wont[3b])	usage[2a], coutume[2b], mœurs[2b]	Sitte[2b], (Lebensweise[5a]), (Lebensart[6b])	costumbre[1b], (usanza[5a])

English	French	German	Spanish
deceive[2b], (beguile[5a])	tromper[2b], (décevoir[4a])	betrügen[2b], täuschen[2b]	engañar[1b], (engañoso[5a]) (deceiving)
devil[2b], (Satan[4b]), (fiend[5a])	diable[2a]	Teufel[2a]	demonio[1b], (diablo[2a]), (satánico[6a])
difficulty[3b]	difficulté[1b]	Schwierigkeit[1b], (Verwick[e]lung[6b])	dificultad[2a], inconveniente[2b]
dog[1b], (hound[4b]), (puppy[5b])	chien[2a]	Hund[3a]	perro[1b], (can[6b]), (galgo[6b])
dust[1b] (*n.*)	poussière[2b]	Staub[3a]	polvo[1b]
elate[2b]	exalter[4a]	erheben[1a], (anregen[3a])	entusiasmar[3b]
engage[2b], (enlist[6])	engager[1b], (recruter[6a])	verpflichten[2a]	empeñar[2a] (se), (contratar[5b])
(be) engaged (engage[2b]) (in), occupied (occupy[2a]) (with), (ply[5a])	s'occuper[2a]	betreiben[2b], (sich[1a] einlassen[4a] auf[1a]), (sich[1a] befassen[5b] mit[1a])	ocupar[1a] se[1a]
fat[1b], (stout[3a]), (plump[5a])	gros[1a], fort[1a], (gras[3a])	dick[3a], (fett[5a])	gordo[2b], grueso[2b]
feather[2a]	plume[2a]	Feder[2b]	pluma[1b], (plumaje[6a])
food[1a], (fare[2a]), (fodder[6])	manger[1a], (nourriture[4b]), (aliment[5a]), (denrée[5a])	Nahrung[3a], Speise[3a], (Lebensmittel[5a]), (Nahrungsmittel[5a]), (Kost[6b])	comida[2a], alimento[2b], (manjar[3b]), (vianda[5b]), (comestible[5b])
frighten[2b], (scare[3a]), (affright[5a]), (terrify[6])	effrayer[1b], (épouvanter[3a]), (effarer[3b]), (effaroucher[5a]), (terrifier[5b])	erschrecken[2b], (entsetzen[5a]), (schrecken[5b])	asustar[2b], espantar[2b], (aterrar[4b]), (horrorrizar[5b]), (atemorizar[6a]), (azorar[6a]), (arredrar[7a])
furious[3b], violent[3b]	furieux[2a], violent[2a] (violemment[3b])	heftig[1b], (ungestüm[6b])	violento[1b], (furioso[3a]), (sañudo[6a])
gain[1b] (*n.*)	gain[4b]	Gewinn[2a], (Erwerb[4a])	ganancia[3b]
give[1a] back[1a], return[1b], (repay[4b])	rendre[1a], (rembourser[5a])	wiedergeben[3b], (zurückgeben[5b])	devolver[2b]
give[1a] in[1a] charge[1b], (intrust[8])	confier[1b]	anvertrauen[3b], (betrauen[6a])	confiar[2a]
guide[1b] (*n.*)	guide[4b]	Führer[2a]	guía[3a]
honest[2a]	honnête[2a] (honnêtement[6a])	ehrlich[2b], (redlich[3b])	honrado (honrar[1b]), (honesto[3b])
intent[3b], (intention[4a])	intention[2a]	Absicht[1b]	intención[1b], (intento[2b]), (designio[4b])
interest[1b] (*tr. vb.*)	intéresser[1b]	interessieren[3a]	interesar[2a]
join[1b] (with), (allied[6]), (ally[7])	(s')allier[4a]	verbinden[1a]	aliarse[7b]
leg[1b]	jambe[1a]	Bein[3a]	pierna[2b], (pata[4a])
level[2a] (*n.*)	niveau[4a]	Höhe[1a]	nivel[3b]
longing (long[1a]), (yearning [yearn[5a]])	grande (grand[1a]) envie[1b], (aspiration[5a])	Sehnsucht[3a]	anhelo[2b]
look[1a] (mien)	mine[2b]	Miene[3a]	cara[1a], (gesto[2a])
look[1a] (*vb.*) (well, etc.)	(avoir[1a] –) mine[2b]	(–) aussehen[3a]	(–) cara[1a]
map[2a], (chart[5b])	carte[2a]	Karte[2b]	carta[1a], (plano[4a]), (mapa[5b])
march (M)[1b] (month)	mars[3b]	März[2a]	marzo[4b]
mourn[2b], (wail[4a]), (lament[4b]), (bewail[6])	pleurer[1a], (se lamenter[6b])	beklagen[2b], (jammern[5b])	lamentar[2b]
(as) much[1a] (as)	autant que[2b]	soviel[3a] wie[1a]	tanto[1a] como[1a]

English	French	German	Spanish
note[1b] (*n.*) (written)	billet[2b]	Note[3a], (Aufzeichnung[6a]), (Billett[6a])	nota[1b], (esquela[6b])
note[1b] (*vb.*)	noter[2b]	notieren[3b]	notar[1b]
object[1b], mind[1a]	opposer[2a], (objecter[5a]), (contester[6a])	widersprechen[3a], (einwenden[4b])	oponer[1b], (poner[1a] reparo[4a]), (hacer[1a] objeción[6b])
pair[1b], (couple[2b])	couple[2b], (paire[3a])	Paar[3a]	par[1b], (pareja[3a])
passing (pass[1a]) (*adj.*), (transient[6])	passager (*adj.*)[4b], (fuyant[6b])	vorübergehend (vorübergehen[2b]), (durchgehend [durch-gehen[5b]])	pasajero[3a], (efímero[5a]), (fugaz[6a])
past[1b] (*n.*)	passé[2a]	Vergangenheit[3a]	pasado[1b]
personal[3b]	personnel[1b] (personnellement[5b])	persönlich[1b], (subjektiv[6a])	personal[2a]
political[3b]	politique[2a]	politisch[1b]	político[1b]
president[2a]	président[2a]	Präsident[2a], Vorsitzende[2b]	presidente[1b]
press[1b] (*n.*)	presse[3a]	Presse[2b]	imprenta[4a], prensa[4b]
principle[3b]	principe[2a]	Grundsatz[1a], (Prinzip[2a])	principio[1a]
property[2b] (landed)	terres (terre)[1a], (propriété[2a]), (domaine[2b])	Grundbesitz[2b], (Habe[3b])	propiedad[2a]
put[1a] out[1a], (extinguish[6])	éteindre[1a]	ausmachen[3b], (löschen[5a])	apagar[2a], (extinguir[3a])
real[1b], (material[2a]) (*adj.*)	matériel[2b]	materiell[3a]	real[1a], (material[2a])
recover[2b] (get back again), (regain[4b])	retrouver[1a], (regagner[3a])	wieder[1a] erlangen[2a]	desempeñar[2b], recobrar[2b]
respect[2a] (*n.*)	respect[2a]	Achtung[2b], (Respekt[6a])	respe(c)to[1a]
rest[1a] on[1a] (to be based on)	fonder[2a] sur[1a]	beruhen[2a]	estribar[5a], (basar[6b])
return[1b], send[1a] back[1a]	retourner[1a], (renvoyer[2b])	wiedergeben[3b], (zurückgeben[5b])	devolver[2b]
(at the) same[1a] time[1a], (simultaneous[8])	simultané[5b] (simultanément[6a])	gleichzeitig[1b]	simultáneo[6a]
satisfy[2a], content[2a]	contenter[2a], satisfaire[2b], (satisfait[3a])	befriedigen[2a], sich[1a] bescheiden[2b], (sich[1a] begnügen[3a])	satisfacer[1b], (contentar[2b])
section[2b], (department[3a])	section[4a]	Abteilung[1b], (Sektion[5b])	sección[3a], (departamento[4a])
servant[2a] (man), (footman[6]) (*plu.*)	domestique (*n.*)[2a], serviteur[2b], (valet[4a]) (*plu.*)	Diener[2b], (Knecht[3a]), (Bediente[5a]) (*plu.*)	criado[1a], (servidor[2b]), (paje[3b]), (sirviente[6a]), (camarero[6b]), (servidumbre[4b])
shake[1b] (*tr. vb.*), (shook[2b]), (wag[4b])	agiter[1b], (secouer[2a]), (ébranler[3b]), (ballotter[7a])	schütteln[3a]	sacudir[2b], (estremecer[3b])
shut[1b] in [1a], up[1a], (enclose[3b]), (inclose[4b])	enfermer[2a], (enclos[5a])	einschließen[3a], (umschließen[5b])	encerrar[1b], (encierro[6a])
silence[2a] (*vb.*), (hush[3a])	faire[1a] taire[2a], (chut[5a])	schweigen[2a] machen[1a]	hacer[1a] callar[1a], (enmudecer[5a])
smile[1b] (*n.*)	sourire (*n.*)[1b]	Lächeln[3a]	sonrisa[2b]
solve[3b]	résoudre[2a]	lösen[1b], (auflösen[3a])	resolver[1b]
stand[1a] out[1a], ([be] conspicuous[6])	(se) détacher[2a], (ressortir[6a])	hervorragen[2a]	resaltar[5a]

English	French	German	Spanish
stir^{2a}, (excite^{3a}), (rouse^{4a}), (inflame^{5a}), (arouse^{5b})	agiter^{1b}, (exciter^{2b}), (passionner^{4b}), (enflammer^{6b})	erregen^{2a}, (anregen^{3a}), (empören^{4a}), (aufregen^{4b})	agitar^{2a}, excitar^{2b}, (alborotar^{3a}), (exaltar^{3a}), (inflamar^{4a}), (sublevar^{5a}), (estimular^{6a}), (enardecer^{6b}), (incitar^{6b})
struggle^{2a} (*n.*), (contest^{3b}), (conflict^{4b})	lutte^{1b}, (conflit^{4a}), (mêlée^{5a})	Streit^{2b}, (Konflikt^{5a})	lucha^{2a}, conflicto^{2b}, (contienda^{4b})
Sunday^{2a}, (Sabbath^{4a})	dimanche^{1b}	Sonntag^{2b}	domingo^{2b}
sweep^{2b}, (swept^{3b})	balayer^{4b}	kehren^{1b}	barrer^{3b}
take^{1a} back^{1a} (person)	ramener^{1b}, (reconduire^{4a})	zurückführen^{3a}	devolver^{2b}
test^{2b}, (examination^{3b})	épreuve^{2a}, examen^{2a}, (concours^{3a})	Prüfung^{2a}, Probe^{2b}, (Examen^{4a})	prueba^{1b}, (examen^{4a})
theatre(er)^{2b}	théâtre^{2a}	Theater^{2a}	teatro^{1b}
tired (tire [*vb.*]^{1b}), (weary^{2b})	fatigué^{2b}, las^{2b}	müde^{3b}	cansado (cansar^{1b}), (fatigado [fatigar^{2b}])
twelve^{1b}	douze^{1b}	zwölf^{3a}	doce^{2*}
twenty^{1b}, (score^{2b})	vingt^{1a}, (vingtaine^{4a})	zwanzig^{3a}	veinte^{2*}
uncle^{1b}	oncle^{2b}	Onkel^{3b}, (Oheim^{4a})	tío^{1a}
under^{1a} (*adj.*), (nether^{6})	de^{1a} dessous^{6b}	untere^{2a}	bajo^{1a}, debajo^{1a}
unfortunately^{3b}	malheureusement^{2b}	leider^{1b}	por^{1a} desgracia^{1b}, desgraciadamente (desgraciado^{1b})
(in) vain^{2a}	(en) vain^{2a}, (inutilement^{4a}), (vainement^{5b})	vergebens^{2b}, (vergeblich^{3a})	(en) vano^{1b}, inútilmente (inútil^{1b})
virtue^{2b}	vertu^{2a}	Tugend^{2a}	virtud^{1a}
wake^{2a} (*tr. vb.*), awake^{2a}, (woke^{4a}), (awaken^{4b}), (waken^{4b}), (awoke^{5a})	éveiller^{2a}, réveiller^{2a}	erwecken^{2b}, (wecken^{3a})	despertar^{1a}, (despierto^{3b})
wake^{2a} (*intr. vb.*), awake^{2a}, (woke^{4a}), (awaken^{4b}), (waken^{4b}), (awoke^{5a})	s'^{1a}éveiller^{2a}, (se réveiller^{3b})	wachen^{2a}, erwachen^{2b}	despertar^{1a} se^{1a}
well^{1a} (*n.*)	puits^{4b}	Quelle^{2a}, (Brunnen^{4b})	pozo^{3b}
west^{1b}, (westward^{4a})	ouest^{3a}	Westen^{2b}	occidente^{4b}, (oeste^{6a})
(become) white^{1a}, (make) white^{1a}, (bleach^{6}), (whiten^{7})	blanchir^{6a}	weiß^{1a} (werden), weiß (machen), (weißen^{2b})	blanquear^{5b}
yield^{2a} (*vb.*), (surrender^{4a})	céder^{2a}, (se rendre^{7a})	übergeben^{2b}, weichen^{2b}, (nachgeben^{4b})	rendir^{1b}, (ceder^{2a}), (capitular^{6a})

SECTION 2. CONCEPTS 1498 THROUGH 1607

E F G S	*E F G S*	*E F G S*	*E F G S*	*E F G S*
1–1–3–3	1–4 –2–4	2–1–2–3	2–4–1–4	3–2–1–2
1–2–2–6	1–5 –2–3	2–1–1–7	2–5–1–3	3–3–1–1
1–2–3–2	1–6 –2–2	2–2–2–2	2–6–1–2	2–3–2–1
1–3–3–1	1–8*–1–4	2–3–1–5	3–1–1–3	

Read as before

English	French	German	Spanish
advise^{2b}, (counsel^{3a})	conseiller^{2a}	raten^{2b}, (belehren^{3b}), (beraten^{5a})	aconsejar^{2a}
agony^{3b}, (anguish^{5b})	angoisse^{2a}, (agonie^{4b})	Schmerz^{1b}	angustia^{2a}, (angustiar^{4b}) (to inflict), (agonía^{5a})
alas^{3a}	hélas^{2a}	ach^{1b}, (weh^{3b})	ay^{2a}

English	French	German	Spanish
angel[2a]	ange[3a]	Engel[2b]	ángel[1b]
artist[3b]	artiste[2a]	Künstler[1b]	artista[2a]
aunt[2a]	tante[3b]	Tante[2b], (Tantchen[4a])	tía (tío[1a])
behind[1a] (*adv.*)	en arrière[3a], arrière (*adv.*)[3b]	hinten[3b]	atrás[1b], (en pos[4b])
bitter[2a]	amer[2a]	bitter[2b]	amargo[2a], (acerbo[6a]), (acre[7a])
bless[1b], (blessing[2b]), (blest[4b])	bénir[3b]	segnen[3a]	bendecir[1b], (santiguar[6a])
blind[1b] (*adj.*)	aveugle[3a]	blind[3a]	ciego[1b], (tuerto[5b]) (one eye)
car[1b] (railroad), (carriage[2a]), (coach[2b])	wagon[4a]	Wagen[2b]	carruaje[4b]
castle[2a]	château[2a], (bastille[6b])	Schloß[2a], (Burg[5a])	castillo[2b], (alcázar[5b])
celebrate[2b]	célébrer[3a]	feiern[2b]	celebrar[1b]
ceremony[3b]	cérémonie[3a], (formalité[6a])	Umstand[1a]	forma[1a], (gala[2b]), (etiqueta[4a]), (ceremonia[4b])
(take) chance[1b], ([run] risk[3b]), (venture[3b])	s'aventurer	wagen[1b]	aventurar[4a]
clear[1a], (lucid[9])	lucide	klar[1a]	lúcido[4b]
coat[1b]	manteau[2a]	Mantel[3b]	capa[2a], (saco[4a]), (capote[4b])
complain[2b], find[1a] fault[2a]	se plaindre[2a]	klagen[2b], sich[1a] beklagen[2b]	quejarse[2a]
conceive[3b]	concevoir[2a]	empfangen[1b]	concebir[2a]
content[2a] (*n.*)	contenu[4a]	Inhalt[1b]	contenido[4a]
convince[3b], persuade[3b] (passive)	convaincre[2a], persuader[2b], (être de la) conviction[2b]	überzeugen[1b], (der festen) Überzeugung[1b] (sein)	convencer[2a], (persuadir[3b])
(lose[1b]) courage[2b], (quail[6])	perdre[1a] courage[1b]	Mut[1b] verlieren[1a]	arredrar[7a](se), (intimidarse)
cross[1a] (*n.*)	croix[2b]	Kreuz[3a]	cruz[2b]
dangerous[2b], (perilous[5a])	dangereux[2a], (périlleux[6a])	gefährlich[2a]	peligroso[2a]
date[1b] (*n.*) (day)	date[2b]	Zeitpunkt[3a], (Datum[4b])	fecha[2b]
delay[2a] (*intr. vb.*), (linger[4a]), (tarry[5a])	tarder[2a]	(sich) aufhalten[2b], (verweilen[4a])	dilatar[2b], (retrasar[6a]), (retardar[7a])
delight[1b] (*vb.*)	enchanter[2a], réjouir[2a], ravir[2b]	entzücken[3b]	encantar[2b], (deleitar[4a])
describe[6a]	décrire[2b]	beschreiben[2b], (charakterisieren[5a])	describir[2a]
develop[3a]	développer[2a], (amplifier[6b])	entwickeln[1b], (entfalten[3b])	desarrollar[9b], (desenvolver[6a])
divine[2b]	divin[3a]	göttlich[2a]	divino[1b]
draw[1a] up[1a], (formulate[9])	dresser[1b], (formuler[4b])	entwerfen[3b], (formulieren[6b])	formular[3b]
east[1a], (Orient [o][5a]), (eastward[6])	est[5a], orient[5a]	Osten[2b]	oriente[3a], (este[7a])
egg[1a], (roe[6])	œuf[3a]	Ei[3a]	huevo[1b]
empty[2a] (*adj.*)	vide (*adj.*)[2a]	leer[2a]	vacío[2a]
event[2a], (incident[5b])	incident[2a], événement[2b]	Ereignis[2a], Vorgang[2b], (Begebenheit[4a]), (Vorfall[4a])	suceso[2a], (acontecimiento[3b]), (incidente[4a]), (ocurrencia[4a])
evil[2a], (wickedness[5a])	mal[1a], (méchanceté[5b])	Übel[2b], (Bosheit[5b])	maldad[3b], (perversidad[6a])

English	French	German	Spanish
exchange[2b] (*n.*)	échange[3a]	Wechsel[1b]	trueque[5a]
fancy[2a] (*n.*) (idle)	fantaisie[2b], (rêverie[3a]), (chimère[3b])	Phantasie[2a]	fantasía[2a], (quimera[4b])
fish[1b] (*n.*)	poisson[2b]	Fisch[3a]	pez[2b], (pescado[3b])
flame[2a]	flamme[2b]	Flamme[2a]	llama[2a]
flesh[2a]	chair[3a]	Fleisch[2b]	carne[1a]
forbid[2b], (forbidden[4b]), (prohibit[5a])	défendre[1b], (interdire[2a]), (défense[2b])	verbieten[2b], (untersagen[5a])	prohibir[3a]
former[1b] (e.g., times)	ancien[1a], (d')autrefois[1b]	ehemalig[3b]	previo[3a]
fortunate[3b], (lucky[4a])	heureux[1a], (chanceux)	glücklich[1a]	afortunado[3b], (venturoso[4a])
future[2a] (*adj.*)	futur[2b]	künftig[2a], (zukünftig[4b])	futuro[2a], (venidero[4b])
greatness[3b]	grandeur[2b]	Größe[1b]	grandeza[2a], (inmensidad[3a])
guard[1b] (*n.*), (keeper[4a]), (guardian[5b]), (watchman[6])	garde[1b], (gardien[ne][4a])	Wache[3a], (Wächter[6b])	guardia[3a], guarda[3b], (guardián[6b]), (vigilante[6b])
guard[1b] (*n.*) (military)	garde[1b]	Wache[3a], (Vorposten[4b]), (Patrouille[5a]), (Feldwache[6b])	guardia[3a], (centinela[4b])
harbor[2b], port[2a], (seaport[6])	port[2a]	Hafen[2a]	puerto[2a]
industry[2b]	industrie[2b]	Industrie[2b]	industria[2a]
information[3a]	renseignement[2b], (information[5a])	Mitteilung[1b], (Auskunft[3b]), (Bescheid[5a]), (Aufschluß[5b])	informe[2b], (información[5a])
insist[3b]	insister[2a]	bestehen[1a], (beharren[6a])	insistir[2b]
knee[1b]	genou[2a]	Knie[3a]	rodilla[2a], (hinojo[6b])
lie[1b] (*n.*), (falsehood[4b])	mensonge[3a]	Lüge[3b]	mentira[1b], (falsedad[4b]) (embuste[6a])
light[1a] (*n.*) (not artificial)	clarté[2b]	Klarheit[3b]	claridad[2a]
limb[2b] (member)	membre[1b]	Glied[2a]	miembro[3a]
locate[3a], situate[3b]	situer[2b]	legen[1a], gelegen (liegen[1a])	situar (+situado)[2a]
lover[2b], (swain[5a]), (beau[6])	amant[3b]	Geliebte[2b], (Liebhaber[4b]), (Liebende[5b])	amante[1b], (amador[5a]), (cortejo[6a])
machine[2a], engine[2b], (machinery[3b]), (motor[4a])	machine[2b], (mécanique[3a]), (moteur[4a]), (mécanisme[6b])	Maschine[2b]	máquina[2a]
match[2a] (sport)	match[6a]	Kampf[1a]	encuentro[2a], (desafío[3a])
material[2a] (*n.*)	matière[2a], (matériaux[6a])	Material[2a]	material[2a]
material[2a] (*adj.*)	matériel[2b]	körperlich[2b]	material[2a]
measure[1a] (*vb.*)	mesurer[2b]	messen[3b], (bemessen[5a])	medir[2a]
mercy[2b], pity[2a]	merci[2a], pitié[2a], (miséricorde[6b])	Gnade[2a]	misericordia[2b], (clemencia[5b])
minister[2b], (priest[3a]), (parson[4b]), (pastor[5a]), (preacher[5a]), (prelate[7]), (clergyman[7])	prêtre[2a], (curé[3b]), (clergé[5b]), (vicaire[5b]), (pasteur[6a]), (prélat[6a])	Pfarrer[2b], (Geistliche[3a]), (Priester[3b]), (Prediger[4b]), (Pastor[5a])	cura[2a], sacerdote[2a], (pastor[3a]), (clérigo[4a]), (canónigo[4b]), (eclesiástico[5b]), (capellán[6a]), (presbítero[6a]), (clerical[6b] [*adj.*])
model[2b], pattern[2b]	patron[2b], (modèle[3a])	Vorlage[2a], Muster[2b], (Modell[4a]), (Vorbild[4a])	modelo[2b], (patrón[3a])
national[2b]	national[2a]	national[2a], (vaterländisch[5a])	nacional[2a]
neglect[2b], (overlook[4b])	négliger[2b]	übersehen[2b], (versäumen[4a]), (vernachlässigen[5b])	descuidar[2b]

English	French	German	Spanish
northern[2b]	(du) nord[2a], (au) nord	nördlich[2a], (nordisch[6a])	norte[2a], (septentrional[6b])
owner[2b]	propriétaire[3a], (possesseur[6a])	Besitzer[2b], (Grundbesitzer[3a]), (Inhaber[3a]), (Eigentümer[4a]), (Gutsbesitzer[4a]), (Hausbesitzer[4a])	amo[1a], dueño[1a], (propietario[3b]), (poseedor[5b])
(be a) party[1b] (to), (confederate[6])	complice[4b]	beteiligt (beteiligen[2b])	cómplice[4b]
play[1a] (theatre), (performance[4b])	pièce[1a] (de théâtre), (représentation[4a])	Schauspiel[3a]	representación[3a]
post[1b] (*n.*), (mail[2a])	courrier[5a]	Post[2a]	correo[3b]
previous[3b]	antérieur[3b]	vorig[1b]	anterior[1b], (previo[3a])
prison[2b], (jail[5b])	prison[2b]	Gefängnis[2b], (Zuchthaus[5a])	carcél[2a], prisión[2b], (galera[5a]), (presidio[5a])
proceed[2a]	procéder[2b]	vorgehen[2a], (verfahren[3a]), (vorschreiten[6a])	proseguir[2a]
profit[2b] (*n.*)	profit[2b], (bénéfice[3a]), (utilité[5b])	Nutz[2a], Ertrag[2b]	beneficio[2b], (utilidad[3a])
railroad[2a], (railway[3b])	chemin[1a] de[1a] fer[1a]	Eisenbahn[2a]	ferrocarril[3a]
rain[1a] (*n.*), (rainfall[6])	pluie[2a]	Regen[3b]	lluvia[2b]
regular[2a]	régulier[2a] (régulièrement[4b])	regelmäßig[2a]	regular[2b]
reign[2b] (*vb.*)	règner[2b]	regieren[2b]	reinar[2a]
respect[2a] (*vb.*)	respecter[2b]	achten[2a]	respetar[2a]
ring[1b], (hoop[5b])	anneau[4a], (bague[6a])	Ring[2a]	anillo[4b], (sortija[6a])
roof[1b], (housetop[6])	toit[2a]	Dach[3b]	techo[2b], (tejado[4a]), (azotea[6a])
rule[1b], (sway[3a]), (dominion[4b]), (sovereignty[6])	domination[5a], (souveraineté[6a])	Herrschaft[2a]	dominio[3a], (dominador[6b]), (soberanía[6b])
sacrifice[2b] (*n.*)	sacrifice[2a]	Opfer[2a]	sacrificio[2a]
sand[1b]	sable[2a]	Sand[3b]	arena[2b]
savage[3b], (brutal[5b]), (barbarous[5b])	brutal[2b], sauvage[2b] (brutalement[6a])	roh[2b]	bárbaro[2b], (salvaje[3a]), (brutal[5b])
sentence[2b] (*n.*) (court)	condamnation[5b], (sentence[6b])	Urteil[1b]	sentencia[3b]
share[2a] (*n.*), portion[2b]	part[1a], (cote[3b]), (mise[3b]), (partage[4a]), (participation[4a]), (contribution[4b]), (portion[5b])	Anteil[2b], Teilnahme[1b], (Beteiligung[4b])	porción[3a], (contingente[5b]), (participación[6b])
skin[1b] (*n.*)	peau[2b]	Haut[3a]	piel[2a], (pellejo[4b])
snow[1b] (*n.*)	neige[2b]	Schnee[3b]	nieve[2b]
spent[2a] (*adj.*), (exhausted [exhaust[3b]])	épuisé (épuiser[2b])	erschöpft (erschöpfen[2b])	gastado (gastar[2a]), agotado (agotar[2b])
step[1a], (footstep[4b]), (footprint)	trace[2a]	Spur[2b]	pisada[6a]
stick[1b], (rod[2a]), (bat[3b]), (cane[3b]), (stake[3b])	bâton[2b], (canne[3a]), (baguette[5b])	Stab[3a], Stock[3b]	caña[2b], palo[2b], (vara[3a]), (bastón[4a]), (garrote[7a])
subject[1b] (*vb.*)	assujettir[6a], subordonner[6b]	unterwerfen[2a]	someter[2a], (subordinar[6b])
sum[2a] up[1a]	résumer[4a]	wiederholen[1b], (zusammenfassen[3a])	resumir[4a]

English	French	German	Spanish
supreme[3b]	suprême[2b]	höchst (hoch[1a])	sumo[2a], supremo[2a]
sword[2a]	épée[3b], (sabre[4b])	Schwert[2b], (Degen[4a]), (Säbel[6b])	espada[1b]
thin[1b], (gaunt[6])	mince[2a], maigre[2b]	dünn[3a]	flaco[2b], (magro[7b])
thorough[2b]	(à) fond[1a]	gründlich[2b], (intensiv[6a])	cabal[3b], minucioso[3b]
throat[2b]	gorge[2b]	Hals[2b]	garganta[2b]
treasure[2a] (*n.*)	trésor[2b]	Schatz[2a]	tesoro[2a]
trial[2b] (law)	procès[3b]	Prozeß[2a]	juicio[1b], (proceso[4b])
unusual[3b], (extraordinary[4b])	extraordinaire[2a], (inouï[3b]), (génial[6a])	außerordentlich[1b], (ungemein[3b]), (unerhört[5a]), (außergewöhnlich[6b])	extraordinario[2a], (inaudito[6a])
useful[2a]	utile[2a] (utilement[6a])	nützlich[2b], (brauchbar[4b]), (förderlich[5b])	útil[2a]
victory[2b]	victoire[2a]	Sieg[2a]	victoria[2b]
way[1a] out[1a] (exit)	sortie[2a], (issue[4a])	Ausgang[3a], (Ausweg[5b])	salida[2a]
working (work[1a]), (effective[7])	efficace[5a]	wirksam[2b]	eficaz[3a]
yellow[1b], (buff[6])	jaune[2b], (jaunir[5a])	gelb[3b]	amarillo[2b], (amarillento[6a])

SECTION 2.1. CONCEPTS 1608 THROUGH 1679

E F G S	*E F G S*	*E F G S*	*E F G S*	*E F G S*
1–1–3–4	1–4–2–5	1–8*–2–1	2–3–1–6	2–8*–1–1
1–2–3–3	1–4–3–1	2–1 –2–4	2–4–2–1	3–1 –1–4
1–3–2–6	1–5–1–8*	2–2 –2–3	2–4–1–5	3–2 –1–3
1–3–3–2	1–5–2–4	2–3 –2–2	2–6–1–3	3–3 –1–2

English	French	German	Spanish
actual[2b]	réel[2a], (effectif[4b]) (effectivement[4b])	tatsächlich[2a], (faktisch[6b])	efectivo[3a]
adopt[3b] (general)	adopter[2a]	annehmen[1a]	adoptar[3a]
April[2a]	avril[3a]	April[2a]	abril[2b]
attack[2b], (besiege[5a]), (assail[5b]), (beset[6])	attaquer[2a], (assiéger[4a]), (assaillir[5b])	angreifen[2a]	acometer[3a], atacar[3b], (asaltar[5b]), (embestir[5b]), (arremeter[6b])
ball[1a], (baseball[6])	boule[2b], (balle[3a]), (globe[6b]), (pelote[6b])	Kugel[3b], (Ball[5a])	bola[3a], (pelota[5a])
band[1b], (gang[5b])	bande[2a], (équipe[5a])	Schar[3a], (Bande[4a])	banda[3a], (cuadrilla[5b])
bar[2a], (obstacle[5b]), (barrier[5b])	embarras[2b], (barrière[3a]), (obstacle[3a])	Hindernis[2b]	obstáculo[3a], (barrera[5a]), (embarazo[6a])
bill[1b] (of) fare[2a]	menu (*n.*)[3a]	Karte[2b]	lista[2b] (de) platos (plato[2a]), (menú)
blessed (bless[1a]), (blest[4b])	bienheureux	selig[2b]	bendito[1b], (beato[5b]), (bienaventurado[6b])
(dead[1a]) body[1a], (corpse[5b])	cadavre[3a]	Leiche[3b], (Leichnam[5a])	cadáver[2b]
bold[2a], (brazen[6]), (presumptuous[6])	hardi[2b], (audacieux[3b])	unverschämt[2b]	audaz[3b], (arrogante[4b])
border[2a] (*vb.*) (on)	toucher[1a]	stoßen[2a] (an)	rayar[4a]
bottle[2a]	bouteille[2b], (flacon[4a])	Flasche[2b], (Ballon[5a])	botella[3a], frasco[3b]
brook[1b] (*n.*), (rill[4b])	ruisseau[3b]	Bach[3b]	arroya[2b]

English	French	German	Spanish
call[1a] together[1a], (summon[3a])	convoquer[4b]	berufen[2a], (zusammenberufen[6a])	convocar[5b]
car[1b], (trolley[5b] [Amer.]), (tram[15])	tramway[5a]	Wagen[2b]	tranvía[4b]
card[2a]	carte[2a]	Karte[2b]	tarjeta[3b]
chain[1b] (*n.*), (fetter[5b])	chaîne[3a]	Kette[3a], (Fessel[5a])	cadena[2a]
cheap[2b]	bon[1a] marché[2a]	billig[2a], (wohlfeil[6a])	barato[3a]
class[1b] (*vb.*) (classify)	classer[3a]	ordnen[2a]	clasificar[6a]
(live[1a]) coals (coal[1b])	braise[5a]	glühende (glühen[2b]) Kohle[2b], (Glut[4b])	brasa[4b], (ascua[7a])
comfortable[2b]	(à l')aise[2a], (confortable[4b]) (confortablement[7a])	bequem[2b], (behaglich[4b])	cómodo[3b]
council[2b]	concile[6b]	Rat[1b], (Kolleg[2b]), (Bundesrat[3b]), (Aufsichtsrat[5b]), (Staatsrat[6a])	junta[3b]
development[3b]	développement[2b], (évolution[4a])	Entwick(e)lung[1b], (Verbreitung[3b]), (Aufschwung[5a]), (Ausbreitung[6a]), (Entfaltung[6a]), (Ausbau[6a])	desarrollo[3b]
district[2b], (zone[3a]), (ward[3b]), (borough[6])	quartier[2a], (commune[7a]), (arrondissement[4a]), (canton[4b]), (zone[4b]), (district[5a]), (préfecture[5b])	Bezirk[2b], Gutsbezirk[6b], (Distrikt[6b]), (Regierungsbezirk[6b])	distrito[3b], zona[3b]
do[1a] without[1a], (dispense[5a] with)	se[1a] passer[1a] de[1a]	verzichten[3a]	prescindir[4a]
dry[1b] (*vb.*), (dried[4a]), (parch[6])	sécher[3b], (dessécher[4b])	trocknen[3a]	secar[2b]
election[3a]	élection[3b]	Wahl[1b], (Neuwahl[5b])	elección[3b]
emperor[3a], (czar[6])	empereur[3a]	Kaiser[1a], (Cäsar[5b]), (Zar[6a])	emperador[2b]
favor[1b] (*vb.*)	favoriser[3b]	begünstigen[3b]	favorecer[2a], (privilegiar[6a])
flat[2a], (apartment[4b] [Amer.])	appartement[2b]	Wohnung[2a]	aposento[6a], piso[3a]
go[1a] back[1a], (retreat[3b])	reculer[2a]	zurückgehen[3a], (zurücktreten[4b])	retroceder[3b]
grain[1b]	grain[3a]	Getreide[3a], Korn[3b]	grano[2b], (cereal[6b])
hero[2b]	héros[3a]	Held[2a]	héroe[2b]
include[2a]	renfermer[2b]	umfassen[2a]	incluir[3a]
knight[2a]	chevalier[4b]	Ritter[2b], (Edle[6b])	caballero[1a], (paladín[6b])
lace[2b] (*n.*)	dentelle[4a]	Spitze[1b]	encaje[5b]
lake[1b]	lac[3b]	See (*m.*)[3a]	lago[2b]
loose[2a] (*adj.*)	lâche[3a]	los[2a]	suelto[2a], (flojo[3b])
metal[2b]	métal[3b]	Metall[2b]	metal[2b]
noon[1b], (noonday[5b])	midi[2a]	Mittag[3a]	mediodía[3a]
persuade[3b], (induce[4b])	persuader[2b]	überzeugen[1b], (überreden[7a])	persuadir[3b], (inducir[4a])
praise[2a], (commend[3b])	louer[3a], (préconiser[4b])	loben[2a], (preisen[3a])	alabar[2b], (ensalzar[4a]), (elogiar[6b])
product[2b]	produit[3a]	Produkt[2b], (Erzeugnis[3a]), (Fabrikat[6a])	producto[2b]
profit[2b] (*n.*) (earned)	profit[2b], (gain[4b])	Verdienst[2a]	ganancia[3b]

English	French	German	Spanish
proportion[3a]	proportion[3a]	Verhältnis[1a]	proporción[2a]
protect[2a]	protéger[2a]	bewahren[2a], (beschützen[6a])	proteger[3a]
protection[3b]	couvert[2a], protection[2b]	Schutz[1b]	protección[3a]
punish[2b], (scourge[4b])	punir[3a], (châtier[6b]), (sévir[6b])	bestrafen[2b], (strafen[4a])	castigar[2a]
recommend[3b]	recommander[2b]	empfehlen[1b]	encomendar[3a], recomendar[3b], (encarecer[4a])
reign[2b] (*n.*)	règne[3a]	Regierung[1a]	reinado[6a]
relate[3a] (put in relationship)	mettre[1a] en[1a] rapport[1b], (se) rapporter[1b]	beziehen[1b]	relacionar[4a]
request[2b] (*n.*)	demande[2b], (requête[6a])	Bitte[2a]	ruego[3a], (petición[4a]), (súplica[6a])
salt[1b] (*n.*)	sel[4a]	Salz[3b]	sal[1b]
save[1a] (up[1a]), (hoard[6])	faire[1a] des[1a] économies (économie[2b]), (épargner[3b])	ersparen[3b], (sparen[4b])	ahorrar[3b], (economizar[6a])
scales (scale[2a]) (for weighing)	balance[4b]	Wage[2b]	peso[1b], (balanza[4b])
secret[2a] (*adj.* and *adv.*)	secret (*adj.*)[4b], (en[1a] cachette[5b]) (secrètement[6b])	geheim[2a], (heimlich[3a])	secreto[1a], (arcano[5b])
September[2a]	septembre[2b]	September[2a]	septiembre[3b]
(make) simple[1b], (simplify[9])	simplifier[5b]	einfach[1a] (machen), (vereinfachen)	simplificar
spring[1a], (springtime[6])	printemps[2b]	Frühjahr[3b], (Frühling[4a])	primavera[3a]
statement[3b], (contention[6])	déclaration[3a], (affirmation[5a]), (exposé [*n.*][6a])	Bestimmung[1a], Darstellung[1b], (Angabe[2a]), (Aufstellung[2b]), (Behauptung[2b]), (Ausspruch[3b]), (Aussage[5b]), (Darlegung[5b])	declaración[2b], (afirmación[3a]), (manifestación[3a])
stick[1b] (*intr. vb.*), (stuck[3b]), (glue[5b])	coller[3a]	haften[3a], (zusammenhalten[5a])	pegar[2a], (adherir[4a])
stir[2a] (a mixture)	agiter[1b], (remuer[2a])	rühren[2a]	remover[4a]
sugar[1b]	sucre[4b]	Zucker[3a]	azúcar[1b]
support[2a] (*n.*), (prop[6]), (strut[6])	appui[3b], (soutien[4b])	Unterstützung[2a], (Erhaltung[3a]), (Stütze[4b]), (Unterlage[5b]), (Anhalt[6b]), (Unterhalt[6a])	apoyo[2b], (sustento[4b])
temple[2b], (tabernacle[6])	temple[3b]	Tempel[2b]	templo[2a]
territory[3a], county[3a]	département[3a], territoire[3a]	Gebiet[1a]	territorio[2b], (jurisdicción[5b])
touch[1b] (act of touching)	toucher[1a], (tact[4b])	Berührung[3b]	toque[4a]
trace[2a] (*n.*) (vestige)	trace[2a]	Spur[2b]	indicio[3b], (traza[4a]), (vestigio[6a])
track[2a] (*n.*), (trail[3b])	trace[2a], (piste[4b]), (ornière[5b])	Spur[2b]	huella[3a], (rastro[6a])
yours[3b]	vôtre[3b], (tien [*poss. pron.*][4a])	Ihre (Ihr[1a]), (Ihrige[4b])	vuestro[2*], (tujo[3*])
yourself[2a]	vous-même	selbst[1a], Sie[1a] selber[1a]	usted[1a] mismo[1a]

SECTION 2.2. CONCEPTS 1680 THROUGH 1798

E F G S	*E F G S*	*E F G S*	*E F G S*	*E F G S*	*E F G S*
1–1–4–1	1–4–3–2	2–1–2–5	2–4–2–2	3–1–2–1	3–4–1–2
1–2–3–4	1–5–2–5	2–1–3–1	2–5–1–5	3–1–1–5	3–5–1–1
1–3–3–3	1–5–3–1	2–2–2–4	2–5–2–1	3–2–1–4	4–1–1–1
1–4–2–6	1–6–1–8*	2–3–2–3	2–6–1–4	3–3–1–3	

English	French	German	Spanish
above[1a] (mentioned)	(déjà) nommé (*adj.*)[5a], ([mentionner[6a]] plus[1a] haut[1a])	obig[3b]	dicho (decir[1a]), (susodicho [susodecir[5b]])
abroad[3b]	(à l')étranger[1a]	(im) Ausland[2b]	(en el) extranjero[1b]
admire[2b]	admirer[1b]	bewundern[3a]	admirar[1b]
advance[2a], (advancement[6])	avance[1b]	Fortschritt[2b], (Vormarsch[5b])	adelanto[5a]
(in) advance[2a], (beforehand[5b])	(d')avance[1b], (par) avance[1b]	voraus[2a]	(de) antemano[5a]
agree[2a], (chime[4a])	accorder[1b], convenir[1a], s'[1a] accorder[1b]	einverstanden[3a] sein[1a], übereinstimmen[3b], zustimmen[3b], (einig[4a] sein), (vereinbaren[5a]), (verabreden[5b]), (beitreten[6b])	acordar[1b], convenir[1b], (concurrir[3a]), (asentir[3b]), (avenir[4b])
allowed (allow[1b])	permis[5b]	zulässig[3b]	permitido (permitir[1a])
along[1a] (e.g., the river)	le[1a] long[1a] de[1a]	entlang[4b], längs[4b]	(a lo) largo[1a] (de)
application[3b]	application[4a]	Anwendung[1b]	aplicación[2b]
automobile[2b], (auto[5a])	auto(mobile)[3a]	Wagen[2b]	automóvil[3b], (auto[5a])
blossom[2a] (*n.*)	fleur[1b]	Blüte[3a]	flor[1a], (capullo[6b])
boast[2b] (*vb.*)	vanter[3b]	rühmen[2b]	ostentar[3a], (hacer[1a] alarde[4a])
break[1b] out[1a] (crying, etc.)	éclater[1b]	ausbrechen[4a]	romper[1a], (prorrumpir[6b])
bring[1a] before[1a] (e.g., judge)	amener[1b]	vorführen[4b]	traer[1a]
candle[2b], (taper[4b])	bougie[4b], (cierge[5a]), (chandelle[5b])	Licht[2b], (Kerze[6b])	vela[2a]
carrying (carry[1a]) out[1a], (execution[5b])	exécution[6a], (réalisation[4a])	Durchführung[3a]	ejecución[3b]
charge[1b] (*vb.*), (commission[3b])	charger[1a]	obliegen[4b] (passive), (beauftragen[5a])	encargar[1b]
citizen[2b]	citoyen[3b]	Bürger[2a], (Mitbürger[5a])	ciudadano[3a]
clean[1b] (*vb.*), (cleanse[4b]), (scour[5a]), (scrub[5a]), (purge[5b])	nettoyer[4a], (purifier[6a])	reinigen[3a]	limpiar[2b], (fregar[6a])
coat[1b], (overcoat[4b])	surtout[2b], (pardessus[3a])	Mantel[3b]	abrigo[4a], (gabán[5b])
commission[3b] (*n.*)	commission[3a]	Kommission[1a]	comisión[3a]
(to be) compared (compare[2a]), (comparable[11])	comparable[5a]	(zu) vergleichen[1b]	comparable[5b]
crowd[1b] (*vb.*)	encombrer[4b]	drängen[2a]	agolpar[6a]
darling[3b], beloved[3b], (sweetheart[6])	amour[1a], (trésor[2b]), (chéri[5b]), (bien-aimé [*n.*][6a])	Schatz[2a], (Liebste[6a])	amado (amar[1a]), amor[1a], querido[1b]
devote[3a]	(se) dévouer[5b], (dévoué[7a])	ergeben[1b]	dedicar[1b] (se), (devoto[3a])

English	French	German	Spanish
distinguish[3b]	distinguer[1b], (caractériser[4a])	unterscheiden[2a], auszeichnen[2a], (abweichen[3a])	distinguir[1a], (diferenciar[4b])
(*p.p.*)	(*p.p.*)	vornehm[2b]	(*p.p.*)
division[3a] (general and military)	division[3b]	Division[1b], (Kavalleriedivision[3b])	división[3b]
draft[3a] (of liquid), (draught[4a])	trait (*n.*)[1b]	Zug[1a]	trago[5a]
due[2a] (*adj.*)	dû (devoir[1a])	gebührend (gebühren[3b]), (fällig[5b])	debido (deber[1a])
effect[2a] (*vb.*)	effectuer[3b]	bewirken[2a]	efectuar[3a]
entrance[2b] (act), (entry[4a])	entrée[1b]	Eintritt[3a], (Einzug[6a])	entrada[1b]
everybody[2b], (everyone[4a])	tout[1a] le[1a] monde[1a], (tous[5b])	jedermann[3a]	todos (todo[1a]), todo[1a] el[1a] mundo[1a]
expose[3b]	exposer[1b]	aussetzen[2a], (herausstellen[4a])	exponer[1b], (expuesto[3b])
expression[4b], (utterance[5a])	expression[1b]	Ausdruck[1b], (Äußerung[2b])	expresión[1b]
fall[1a] (e.g., hair)	tomber[1a]	ausfallen[4a]	caer[1a]
favorable[3b]	favorable[2a], (avantageux[3b]), (propice[4a])	günstig[1b]	favorable[4a], propicio[4a], (provechoso[6a]), (ventajoso[6a])
finally [2a], ([in] conclusion[4b])	définitivement[4b], finalement[4b]	abschließend (abschließen[2a])	finalmente[2a]
foreign[2a]	étranger[1a], (exotique[6b])	ausländisch[3b], auswärtig[3b]	extranjero[1b], (forastero[5a]), (exótico[5b])
formerly[4b]*	autrefois[1b], jadis[1b], (naguère[5b])	früher (früh[1a]), (zuvor[2b]), (ehemals[5a])	antiguamente (antiguo[1a]), en[1a] tiempos (tiempo[1a]) pasados (pasado[1b]), anteriormente (anterior[1b])
free[1a] (*tr. vb.*), (rid[3a])	débarasser[4b]	befreien[2a]	desembarazar[6a]
front[1a] (*adj.*)	de[1a] devant (*n.*)[2b]	vordere[3a]	delantero[4a]
fully[3a]	abondamment[4b], (pleinement[5b])	völlig[1b]	plenamente (pleno[2b])
go[1a] down[1a], (descend[2b])	descendre[1a], (redescendre[3b])	hinunter[4b] gehen[1a], untergehen[4b]	bajar[1a], (descender[2a])
grave[2a] (*n.*), (tomb[3b])	tombe[3b], (tombeau[4a])	Grab[2a]	sepulcro[3a], sepultura[3a], tumba[3a]
gray (G)[1b], (*adj.*) (grey [G][3b])	gris[2a]	grau[3a]	cano (+cana)[4a] (hair), (gris[5b])
guilt[4a]	faute[1b], (crime[2a])	Schuld[1b]	culpa[1b]
habit[2b]	habitude[1b]	Gewohnheit[3a], (Lebensweise[5a])	costumbre[1b], (hábito[2b])
(on the one) hand[1a]	(d'un) côté[1a], (d'une) part[1a]	einerseits[4a]	(por una) parte[1a]
heat[1a] (*vb.*), warm[1a]	chauffer[3a], (réchauffer[4a]), (échauffer[4b])	erhitzen[3b], (erwärmen[4a])	calentar[3b], (acalorar[6a])
hole[1b]	trou[2b], (creux[3a])	Loch[3b]	agujero[4a], hoyo[4a]
(on) horseback[4a]	(à) cheval[1b]	(zu) Pferde (Pferd[1b])	(a) caballo[1a]
how[1a] much[1a]	combien[1b]	wieviel[4b]	cuanto, cuánto[1a]
import[3b] (*n.*), (meaning[5b]*)	portée[2b], (signification[4b])	Bedeutung[1b]	significación[4a], (acepción[7b] [words])
impression[4a]	impression[1b]	Eindruck[1b]	impresión[1b]

English	French	German	Spanish
impression[4a] (make an –), (impress[5a])	frapper[1a]	Eindruck[1b] machen[1a], (auffallen[2b]), (beeindrucken)	hacer[1a] impresión[1b]
January[2a], (Jan.[5b])	janvier[2b]	Januar[2a]	enero[4a]
joyful[2b], (joyous[5a])	joyeux[2a] (joyeusement[3b])	freudig[2b], fröhlich[2b]	gozoso[4b], (placentero[6a])
July[2a]	juillet[3a]	Juli[2a]	julio[3a]
lean[2a] (*vb.*)	appuyer[1b], (pencher[2a]), (s'incliner[3b]), (s'accouder[4b]), (adosser[5a])	lehnen[3a]	apoyar[1b] se, inclinar[1b] se
leave[1a] behind[1a]	laisser[1a]	zurücklassen[4a]	dejar[1a] atrás[1b]
lifting (lift[1a]) (*n.*), (elevation[5b])	élévation[5b]	Erhöhung[2b]	elevación[5a]
lord[1b] (title), (lordship[6])	monseigneur[5a], sire[5a]	Lord[3b]	señor[1a], (señoría[6b])
make[1a] out[1a], (decipher[10])	déchiffrer[6b]	lesen[1a], (deuten[3a])	descifrar
manage[2b]	ménager[7b], (administrer[6b])	regieren[2b], (vorstehen[4b]), (verwalten[5a])	administrar[4b]
mention[2a] (*vb.*)	mentionner[6a]	erwähnen[1b]	mencionar[4a]
merchant[2a], (trader[5a])	marchand[7b], (négociant[5a])	Kaufmann[2a], (Handelsmann[5b])	mercader[4a], (vendedor[6a])
middle[1b] ages (age[1b])	moyen[1a] âge[1b]	Mittelalter[4a]	edad[1a] media (medio[1a])
misfortune[4b], hardship[4b], (affliction[5b])	malheur[1b], (fatalité[6a])	Unglück[1b], (Unheil[5a])	desgracia[1b], (desdicha[3a]), (aflicción[3b]), (desventura[3b]), (infortunio[3b])
(make a) mistake[2a], (err[3b])	se tromper[4b]	sich[1a] irren[2b], versehen[2a]	equivocar[2b], (errar[4b])
mix[2a], (mingle[3b]), (blend[4b]), (compound[5b])	mêler[1b], (se mêler[3a]), (mélanger[5a])	mischen[3a], (vermischen[5b])	mezclar[1b], ([*p.p.*] mixto[5a])
mode[3b], (mood[4a])	mode (*m.*)[5a]	Form[1a]	modo[1a]
moving (move[1a]) (physical)	mouvant[6a]	(in) Bewegung[1a]	moviente
(at) night[1a]	(la) nuit[1a], (le) soir[1a]	nachts[4a]	de[1a] noche[1a]
now[1a] and[1a] then[1a]	(de) temps[1a] (en) temps, (de) temps[1a] (à autre)	mitunter[4a]	de[1a] cuando[1a] en[1a] cuando[1a]
obey[2a]	obéir[1b]	gehorchen[3b], (befolgen[4a])	obedecer[1b]
open[1a] (*intr. vb.*)	s'[1a]ouvrir[1a]	aufgehen[4a]	abrir[1a] (se)
ordinary[3a] (trite)	banal[4a]	gewöhnlich[1a]	vulgar[3b]
organ[2b] (anatomical)	organe[3b]	Organ[2a]	órgano[3a]
pardon[2b] (*vb.*), excuse[2b], (forgive[3a]), (remit[5b]), (absolve[6])	remettre[1a], (excuser[2a]), (pardonner[2a])	entschuldigen[3a], verzeihen[3a], vergeben[3b]	perdonar[1b], (disculpar[2b]), (excusar[2b]), (absolver[6b])
past[1b] (tense)	passé (*n.*)[2a]	Vergangenheit[3a]	pretérito[4b]
period[2b] (of time)	période[3a]	Frist[2b], Periode[2b], (Zeitraum[3b])	período[3a]
plenty[2a], (abundance[3b]), (fulness [full][5a])	abondance[4a], (ampleur[5b])	Fülle[2b], (Überfluß[6a])	caudal[2b], (abundancia[3a]), (copia[4b]), (plenitud[6a])
practical[3a]	pratique[3a]	praktisch[1b], (zweckmäßig[2b])	práctico[3a]
	(pratiquement[5b])		
pray[2a]	prier[1b]	beten[3a]	rogar[1b], (suplicar[2a]), (rezar[2b]), (orar[5b])

English	French	German	Spanish
put[1a] down[1a], (suppress[5b])	supprimer[2b], (réprimer[4a]), (rabattre[5a])	unterdrücken[3b], (ersticken[4b]), (dämpfen[6b])	reprimir[4a]
resign[3b] (oneself)	(se) résigner[3a], (s'abandonner[4b])	(sich) ergeben[1b]	resignarse[3a]
roll[1a], rock[1a]	balancer[2b], (se balancer[5b])	schwanken[3a], (rollen[4b])	mecer[4a], (balancear[6a])
scene[2b] (part of a play)	scène[1b]	Auftritt[3a]	escena[1a]
shake[1b] (head)	hocher[4a]	schütteln[3a]	sacudir[2b], (menear[3b])
sheet[2a] (of paper)	feuille[1b]	Bogen[3a]	hoja[1b], (pliego[4a]), (cuartilla[5a])
side[1a] (by side)	côte[1b] (à côte)	nebeneinander[4a]	juntos (junto[1a])
(on her) side[1a]	(de son) côté[1a], (de sa) part[1a]	ihrerseits[4a]	(de su) parte[1a]
(on his) side[1a]	(de son) côté[1a], (de sa) part[1a]	seinerseits[4b]	(de su) parte[1a]
(on their) side[1a]	(de leur) côté[1a]	ihrerseits[4a]	(de su) parte[1a]
silence[2a] (*n.*)	silence[1a]	Schweigen[3b]	silencio[1b]
simple[1b], (ingenuous[14])	simple[1a], (naïf[2b]) (naïvement[6a])	unbefangen[4b]	sencillo[1b]
sin[2b] (*n.*)	péché[5a]	Sünde[2a]	culpa[1b], pecado[1b]
slave[2a]	esclave[4b]	hörig (H)[2b], (Sklave[3a])	esclavo[2a], (siervo[5a])
south[1a], (southward[5b])	sud[3a], (midi[4a])	Süden[3a]	mediodía[3a], (sur[5b])
spend[1b] (time)	passer[1a]	verleben[4b], (verbringen[6b])	pasar[1a]
spot[1b] (*n.*), (stain[3a]), (blot[4a]), (speckle[5b]), (speck[6])	tache[3b]	Fleck[3b]	mancha[3a], (tacha[5b]), (mancilla[6b])
standard[2b] (*n.*) (norm)	mesure[1a], (régulateur[6b])	Maßgabe[3a], (Norm[6a])	medida[1b]
state[1a] (*vb.*) (pronounce)	préciser[2b], (énoncer[5b])	darlegen[3b], (vorbringen[4b])	precisar[4a], (plantear[6b])
stick[1b] (*tr. vb.*), (stuck[3b]), (glue[5b])	appliquer[1b], (coller[3a])	heften[4b], (kleben[6b])	aplicar[1b], (pegar[2a]), (adherir[4a])
superior[2b]	supérieur[1b]	überlegen (*adj.*)[3b]	superior[1b]
(make) sure[1a], (ascertain[7])	s'assurer[1a]	ermitteln[4a]	asegurar[1b] se
term[2a] (end of period)	terme[1b]	Termin[3b], (Kündigung[5b])	término[1a]
(every) time[1a]	chaque[1a] fois[1a]	jedesmal[4a]	cada[1a] vez[1a]
touch[1b] (*n.*), (contact[7])	contact[3a]	Berührung[3b]	contacto[3b], (tacto[5a])
unfortunate[3b]	malheureux[1b]	unglücklich[2a]	desgraciado[1b], infeliz[1b], (desdichado[2b])
unknown [2b] (to)	à l'insu de[5b]	ohne[1a] . . . . Wissen[2b]	sin[1a] saber[1a] lo[1a], sin[1a] noticia[1b] de[1a]
victim[3b]	victime[1b]	Opfer[2a]	víctima[1b]
wage[2b] (*n.*)	gage[4b]	Lohn[2a]	sueldo[2b], (paga[5b]), (jornal[6b])
warn[2b], (admonish[6])	prévenir[1b], (avertir[2a])	warnen[3b], (mahnen[4b]), (ermahnen[6a])	advertir[1a], (prevenir[2b])
(on the) way[1a]	chemin[1a] faisant (faire[1a]), en[1a] route[1a]	unterwegs[4b]	en[1a] camino[1a]
whoever[3b]	quiconque[5b]	wer[1a] immer[1a]	quienquiera[1a]
word[1a] for[1a] word, (literal[7])	mot[1a] à[1a] mot, (au) pied[1a] (de la) lettre[1b], (à la) lettre[1b]	wörtlich[4b]	palabra[1a] por[1a] palabra, (al) pie[1a] (de la) letra[1a]
worker[3b]	travailleur[3a]	Arbeiter[1a]	obrero[3a], trabajador[3a]
wound[2a] (*vb. inf.*)	blesser[1b]	verletzen[3a], verwunden[3b]	herir[1b]

SECTION 2.3. CONCEPTS 1799 THROUGH 1922

E F G S	*E F G S*	*E F G S*	*E F G S*	*E F G S*	*E F G S*	*E F G S*
1–1–3–6	1–3–3–4	1–6–2–5	2–2–3–1	2–5–1–6	3–1–2–2	3–5–1–2
1–1–4–2	1–4–3–3	1–6–3–1	2–2–2–5	2–5–2–2	3–2–2–1	4–2–1–1
1–2–3–5	1–4–2–7	2–1–2–6	2–3–2–4	2–6–1–5	3–3–1–4	
1–2–4–1	1–5–3–2	2–1–3–2	2–4–2–3	2–6–2–1	3–4–1–3	

English	French	German	Spanish
accident[3a], (mishap[6])	accident[1b], malheur[1b], (imprévu[4a])	Zufall[2b], (Unfall[3b]), (Unglücksfall[6b])	accidente[2b], (azar[5a])
act[1b], (deed[2a]), (instrument[3a])	acte[1b]	Akte[4b], Urkunde[4b]	instrumento[2a], (escritura[3b])
address[2a] (on letter)	adresse[2a]	Adresse[3b]	dirección[1b]
anxious[2b]	inquiet[1b], (préoccupé[3a]), (anxieux[3b]), (soucieux[5a]), (troublé[5b])	ängstlich[3a], (bang[4a])	inquieto[2a], (ansioso[4b]), (angustioso[6a])
(to make one's first) appearance[2b]	débuter[4b]	(zum ersten Mal) auftreten[2b]	estrenar[3b], (debutar[6b])
attack[6b] (*n.*), (assault[4b]) (individual)	attentat[6b]	Angriff[1b]	atentado[6b]
authority[2b]	autorité[2a]	Befugnis[3a], Autorität[3b], (Obrigkeit[6a])	autoridad[1b]
ball[1a], (bullet[5b])	balle[3a]	Kugel[3b]	bala[4b]
beam[2a], (rafter[6])	poutre[5a]	Baum[1b]	madero[6a]
(come, go) before[1a], (precede[6])	précéder[1b]	vorhergehen[4b], (vorangehen[6a])	preceder[2b]
belief[3b]	croyance[4a], (créance[5b])	Glaube[1b]	creencia[3b]
besides[4b] (*prep.*)	outre[2b]	außer[1a]	además[1a] de
(to go) between[1a], (mediate[19])	(être l')intermédiaire[3a], intervenir[3a]	vermitteln[3b] (zwischen)	mediar[3a], (intervenir[4a])
bird[1a], (birdie[6])	oiseau[2a]	Vogel[4a]	ave[1b], (pájaro[2a])
bits (bit[1a]), (fragment[5b])	débris[3b]	Übrige[3b], (Trümmer[4b])	fragmento[4a]
blessing[2b] (*n.*)	bénédiction[5b]	Segen[2b]	bendición[2b]
box[1a] (*n.*)	boîte[2b], caisse[6b], (carton[4a])	Kasten[4a], Kästchen[4a], (Schachtel[6b])	caja[1b]
break[1b] (in pieces)	briser[2a], rompre[2b]	zerbrechen[4b]	romper[1a], (quebrar[2b])
break[1b] out[1a] (e.g., war)	éclater[1b]	ausbrechen[4a]	estallar[1b]
burning (*n.*) (burn[1a])	incendie[4b]	Brand[3b]	incendio[3a]
canal[3a], channel[2b]	canal[4a]	Kanal[1b]	canal[3b]
capital[2b] (city)	capitale[2b]	Hauptstadt[3a]	capital[1b]
catch[1b] up[1a], (overtake[4a]), (overtook[6])	rejoindre[2a]	nachkommen[4a]	alcanzar[1a]
charming[2a]	charmant[1b], (ravissant[5a])	reizend[3b], (allerliebst[6b])	encantador[2a]
city[1a] (*adj.*)	municipal[3b]	städtisch[3b]	municipal[4a]
claim[2a] (*vb.*)	prétendre[1b], réclamer[1b], (revendiquer[6b])	beanspruchen[3b], (erheischen[5b])	reclamar[2b]
coffee[2a]	café[2a]	Kaffee[3a]	café[1b]
combine[3a]	combiner[3b]	verbinden[1a], (zusammensetzen[3a])	combinar[4a]
comfort[2a] (*n.*), (consolation[6]), (solace[6])	consolation[5a]	Trost[2b]	consuelo[2a]

English	French	German	Spanish
comfort[2a] (*vb.*), (console[8])	rassurer[1b], (consoler[2a]), (réconforter[5b])	trösten[3a]	consolar[2b]
command[1b] (*n.*) (military) (over forces)	commandement[4a]	Kommando[3a], Heeresleitung[3b], (Oberkommando[5b])	mando[3b]
commit[3b], (be) guilty[3a] (of)	commettre[2a]	begehen[2b]	cometer[1b]
companion[2a], (comrade[4a]), (playmate[4b])	camarade[2a], compagnon[2a], compagne[2b]	Genosse[3b], (Begleiter[4a]), (Gesell[4a]), (Gesellschafter[4a]), (Gefährte[5b])	compañero[1a], (camarada[4a])
conduct[2b] (*n.*)	conduite[2b], (tenue [*n.*][3a])	Verhalten[3a], (Aufführung[4a]), (Betragen[4a]), (Benehmen[5a]), (Handlungsweise[5a])	proceder[1b], (conducta[2a])
contract[3a] (*n.*), (convention[4a]), (agreement[4b]), (compact[5a]), (covenant[6])	convention[3a], (contrat[4b]), (pacte[6a])	Vertrag[1b], (Gesellschaftsvertrag[6b])	contrato[4b], pacto[4b], (alianza[5b])
cordial[3b], (hearty[4a]), (heartily[6])	cordial[4b]	herzlich[1b]	cordial[3b]
corner[1b], (nook[5b])	recoin[5a]	Ecke[3b]	rincón[2a]
cruel[2a]	cruel[2b] (cruellement[6a])	grausam[3b]	cruel[1b], (inhumano[5a])
December[2a]	décembre[3a]	Dezember[2a]	diciembre[4a]
delicate[3a]	délicat[2a], (fragile[4b])	zart[2b]	delicado[1b], (tenue[5a])
draft[3a] (of a bill), (draught[4a])	projet[1b] (de) loi[1b]	Gesetzentwurf[2a]	proyecto[2b] (de) ley[1a]
drive[1a] away[1a] (*tr. vb.*)	chasser[2a]	vertreiben[3a]	ahuyentar[5a]
duke[3b]	duc[4b]	Herzog[1b], (Großfürst[6a]), (Großherzog[6b])	duque[3a]
dwelling[3b], residence[3b], (abode[4a]), (habitation[6]), (lodging[6])	demeure[2a], (logis[3b]), (domicile[4b]), (gîte[4b]), (logement[4b]), (habitation[5a]), (résidence[5b])	Wohnung[2a], (Wohnhaus[6a]), (Wohnsitz[6a])	habitación[1b], (morada[3b]), (vivienda[3b]), (residencia[4a]), (domicilio[4b])
element[2b], (ingredient[6])	élément[2a], (facteur[3b])	Element[2a], Bestandteil[2b], (Faktor[3b])	elemento[1b], (factor[5a])
equal[1a] (*vb.*)	égaler[5b]	gleichen[3b]	igualar[2b], (equivaler[4a])
evidence[3b]	évidence[3a]	Beweis[1b]	evidencia[4b]
exceed[3a], (surpass[4b]), (outrun[6])	dépasser[1b]	überschreiten[2b], (übersteigen[4a]), (übertreffen[4a])	sobrar[2b], (exceder[4b])
fall[1a] (*n.*) (Amer.), (autumn[2b])	automne[3b]	Herbst[3b]	otoño[4a]
fame[2b], (renown[3b])	renom[6a], renommée[6b]	Ruhm[2b]	fama[1b], (celebridad[5b]), (nombradía[5b])
fellow[1b], (chap[7])	bonhomme[2b]	Kerl[4b], Bursche[4a]	sujeto[1b]
fifty[2a]	cinquante[1b], (cinquantaine[4b])	fünfzig[3b]	cincuenta[2*]
follow[1a], (succeed[2a])	succéder[2b]	nachfolgen[4a]	seguir[1a], suceder[1a]
following[1b] (*n.*), (escort[6])	suite[1a], (équipage[4b])	Gefolge[4a], (Begleitung[5a])	partido[2b], (acompañamiento[4b])
friendship[3a]	amitié[2a]	Freundschaft[2a]	amistad[1b]
glance[2b] (*vb.*), peep[2b]	entrevoir[2b]	flüchtig[2b] sehen[1a]	vislumbrar[5b], (atisbar[7a])

English	French	German	Spanish
glory[2a]	gloire[2a]	Herrlichkeit[3b]	gloria[1a]
grand[2a], (majestic[4b])	grandiose[4b], (majestueux[6b])	großartig[2b], (stattlich[4a])	majestuoso[3b], (grandioso[4a])
hunt[1b] (*vb.*)	chasser[2a]	jagen[3a]	cazar[5a]
(be) hurt[1b], (offended [offend[3a]])	(se) ressentir[3a], (se fâcher[4b])	beleidigt (beleidigen[3a])	resentirse[4b]
increase[1b] (*n.*)	augmentation[5a]	Vermehrung[3a], Steigerung[3b], (Zunahme[5b]), (Vergrößerung[6b])	aumento[2b]
interrupt[3b]	interrompre[2a]	unterbrechen[2b], (einstellen[3a]), (abbrechen[4a])	interrumpir[1b]
invite[2a]	inviter[1b]	auffordern[3b], (einladen[4a])	convidar[2a], invitar[2b]
(old) iron[1b], (scrap[4b])	ferraille[6b]	altes (alt[1a]) Eisen[3a]	hierro[1b] viejo[1a]
June[2a]	juin[3a]	Juni[2a]	junio[4a]
lead[1a] (*n.*) (metal)	plomb[3b]	Blei[3b]	plomo[4a]
leader[2a], (conductor[5a])	conducteur[3b]	Führer[2a], (Leiter[3b])	conductor[4a]
lovely[2a]	charmant[1b], (délicieux[2b])	lieblich[3a], (hold[4a])	encantador[2a], precioso[2a]
lower[1b] (*vb.*)	baisser[2a], abaisser[2b]	herunter[4a] lassen[1a], senken[4b], (erniedrigen[6a]), (herabsetzen[6a])	bajar[1a]
marry[2a], married[6b], (wed[3b])	épouser[1a], marier[2a], (se marier[3a])	heiraten[3a], verheiraten[3b], (vermählen[6a])	casar[1a], casar[1a] se[1a], (desposar[4a])
(go to) meet[1a]	(aller à) rencontre[1a]	entgegenkommen[4b]	salir[1a] al[1a] encuentro[2a]
moral[3a]	moral[2a]	moralisch[2b], sittlich[2a]	moral[1b]
moving (move[1a]) (*adj.*) (emotionally)	touchant[4b]	rührend (rühren[2a])	conmovedor[7a]
naughty[4b]	méchant[2a], (vilain[3b])	bös[1b]	malo (*adj.*)[1a], (travieso[4b])
necessity[3a]	nécessité[2a]	Notwendigkeit[2b], (Notfall[6a])	necesidad[1a], (precisión[3a])
(of) necessity[3a], (necessarily[1a])	forcément[5a]	notwendig[1a] (notwendigerweise)	forzosamente (forzoso[2b])
November[2a]	novembre[3a]	November[2a]	noviembre[4b]
opening (open[1a]), (vent[6])	ouverture[3a], (orifice[6a])	Öffnung[3a]	abertura[4a], (orificio[7b])
oppose[3a], resist[3b]	opposer[2a], résister[2a], (contrarier[4b])	entgegensetzen[2b], (widerstehen[3b]), (bekämpfen[3b]), (entgegentreten[3b]), (widerstreben[5b]), (entgegenstehen[6a]), (entgegenstellen[6a]), (widersetzen[6a])	oponer[1b], (resistir[2a]), (contrariar[4b])
original[3a], (primary[5b]), (primitive[7])	premier[1a], (primitif[3a]), (originaire[6b])	ursprünglich[2a]	original[2b], primitivo[2b]
palace[2a]	palais[2a]	Palast[3a]	palacio[1b], (mansión[4a])
park[2a]	parc[2b]	Anlage[2a], (Park[4b])	parque[5b]
particular[2a], (detail[4a])	détail[1b], particulier[1b]	Einzelheit[3b], (Detail[4b])	detalle[2b], (dato[3a]), (pormenor[6b])
passion[3a]	passion[2a]	Leidenschaft[2a]	pasión[1b]
plan[1a] (*vb.*)	projeter[3b]	entwerfen[3b], vorsehen[3b], (planen[5a])	proyectar[4a], (idear[5a])
pocket[2a]	poche[1b]	Tasche[3b]	bolsillo[2b], (faltriquera[5b])

English	French	German	Spanish
pot[2a]	pot[3a], vase[3a]	Gefäß[2b], (Topf[6b])	puchero[4a], (olla[5a]), (vasija[6b])
pour[2a]	verser[1b]	gießen[3b]	derramar[2a], verter[2b]
prayer[2a]	prière[2b], (oraison[6b])	Gebet[3a]	oración[1b], (plegaria[6a])
(be) present[1a], attend[1b]	assister à[2a]	anwesend[4b] sein[1a], beiwohnen[4b], (zugegen[6b] sein)	acudir[1b], asistir[1b], (presenciar[3b])
(crown[1b]) prince[1b]	héritier[3b] (du) trône[4b], (dauphin)	Kronprinz[3b]	infante[3b]
push[2a], (thrust[3a]), (shove[5a]) (*vb.*)	pousser[1a]	schieben[3a], vorschieben[3b], (vorrücken[5a])	empujar[2b]
rate[2a] (*vb.*), (estimate[3b])	évaluer[4a]	berechnen[2a], (anrechnen[6b])	calcular[3b], (calificar[4a])
ray[2b], beam[2a]	rayon[2a]	Strahl[3b]	rayo[1b]
refuse[2a] (*vb.*)	refuser[1a]	ablehnen[2b], (versagen[3a]), (verweigern[3b]), (weigern[4b]), (absprechen[6b])	rehusar[6b]
relation[2b], (relative[3a]), (kindred[4b]), (kin[6]), (kinsman[6])	parent[1b], (allié [*n.*][4a])	verwandt[3a], Verwandte[3b], (Angehörige[4b]), (Verwandtschaft[5a])	pariente[2b], (deudo[5a])
religious[3a]	religieux[2a], (fervent[6b])	religiös[2a], (gläubig[6a])	religioso[1b]
remark[3b] (*vb.*), (comment[6])	(faire une) remarque[3a] (sur), (commenter)	beobachten[1b], ([Bemerkung[2a]], [Anmerkung[5a]] machen[1a])	comentar[4b]
representative[3a], (agent[4b])	représentant[4a]	Abgeordnete[1a], (Stellvertreter[5b])	agente[3b], (representante[4a])
(give) rise[1a] to, (give) cause[1a] for (motivate)	motiver[6a]	begründen[2a], veranlassen[2a], hervorrufen[2b]	motivar[5a]
rob[2b], steal[2a], (stole[3a]), (stolen[4a])	dérober[2a], voler[2b], (cambrioler[6b])	rauben[3a], (berauben[4a]), (stehlen[4a])	robar[1b], (hurtar[4b])
roll[1a] (*tr. vb.*)	rouler[1b]	rollen[4b], (wälzen[5b])	rodar[2a]
room[1a] (living-, drawing-), (parlor[3a])	salon[1b]	Salon[4b]	sala[2a], (salón[3a])
scholar[3b]	savant[2b], (lettré [*n.*][3a]), (lettré [*adj.*][5b]), (érudit[6b])	Forscher[2b], (Gelehrte[4a])	hombre[1a] (de) letras (letra[1a]), (erudito[4a]), (letrado[5b])
second[1a] (*n.*)	seconde[2a]	Sekunde[4a]	segundo[1a]
(in the) second[1a] place[1a] (secondly)	(en) deuxième[2b] lieu[1a]	zweitens[4a]	(en) segundo[1*] lugar[1a]
sentence[2b] (*vb.*), (condemn[3b])	condamner[2a]	verurteilen[3b]	condenar[1b], (sentenciar[6a])
(divine[2b]) service[1b]	office[2b], (culte[3a])	Gottesdienst[3a]	oficio[1b], (culto[2a])
(be) sleepy[3b]	(avoir) sommeil[2a]	Schlaf[2b] (haben), (schläfern)	tener[1a] sueño[1a], (amodorrado)
social[3b]	social[2b]	sozial[2b], (gesellschaftlich[4a]), (gesellig[5a])	social[1b]
southern[2b]	(du, au) sud[3a], (méridional[5a])	südlich[2b]	meridional[4b], ([del] sur[5b]), (austral[7a])
subject[1b] (*n.*) (national)	sujet (*n.*)[1b]	Untertan[3b]	súbdito[6a]
substitute[3b], (replace[5b])	remplacer[1b], (substituer[3b]), (suppléer[5b])	ersetzen[2b]	substituir[2b], (reemplazar[3b])
tender[2a] (*adj.*)	tendre[2a] (tendrement[4b])	zärtlich[3a]	tierno[1b], (muelle[3b])

English	French	German	Spanish
thine[3a]	tien (*poss. pron.*)[4a]	dein[1a], etc.	tuyo[3*]
thirty[2a]	trente[1b], (trentaine[6b])	dreißig[3b]	treinta[2*]
throne[2b]	trône[4b]	Thron[2b]	trono[3a]
tooth[2b], teeth[2b]	dent[2a]	Zahn[3b]	diente[1b], (muela[6b])
tower[2a]	tour[2b]	Turm[3b]	torre[1b]
trunk[2a] (of tree)	tronc[4a]	Stamm[2b]	tronco[3a]
vain[2a] (*adj.*)	vain[2a], (vaniteux[6a])	eitel[3b]	vano[1b], (vanidoso[6b])
well[1a]!, come[1a] now[1a]!	eh bien![2a], (allons![3b])	na[4b]	como[1a]
wisdom[2a]	sagesse[3a]	Weisheit[2b], (Scharfsinn[6b])	sabiduría[4b]
wrap[2b] (*vb.*)	envelopper[2a]	einschlagen[3a], (verhüllen[5b]), (wickeln[7a])	envolver[1b]

SECTION 2.4. CONCEPTS 1923 THROUGH 2036

E F G S	*E F G S*	*E F G S*	*E F G S*	*E F G S*	*E F G S*
1–2–3–6	1–5–2–7	2–3–2–5	2–5–2–3	3–2–2–2	4–2–1–2
1–2–4–2	1–5–3–3	2–3–3–1	2–6–1–6	3–3–2–1	4–3–1–1
1–3–4–1	2–1–3–3	2–4–1–8*	2–6–2–2	3–4–1–4	
1–4–3–4	2–2–3–2	2–4–3–4	3–1–2–3	3–6–1–2	

English	French	German	Spanish
accent[4b] (*n.*) (stress)	accent[2b]	Ton[1b]	acento[2a]
angry[2a], (furious[3b]), (indignant[6]), (wroth[6])	en[1a] colère[1b], (fâché[3a]), (exaspéré [exaspérer[4b]]), (irrité[6b])	wütend (wüten[3b]), (zürnen[4b]), (zornig[5b]), (ärgerlich[6b])	enojado (enojar[3b]), (iracundo[4a]), (colérico[4b])
(get) angry[2a]	se[1a] mettre[1a] en[1a] colère[1b], (s'emporter[4b]), (se fâcher[4b])	wütend (wüten[3b]) werden[1a], (sich[1a] ärgern[4a])	enojarse[3b], (airarse[4a])
arm[1a] (*vb.*)	armer[2a]	bewaffnen[4a], rüsten[4b]	armar[2a]
arrangement[4b], (disposition[5a]), (disposal[6])	disposition[2a], (organisation[3b]), (arrangement[4a])	Einrichtung[1b], Ordnung[1b], (Anordnung[2a]), (Bearbeitung[4a]), (Disposition[4a]), (Einteilung[5b])	disposición[2a], (arreglo[3a]), (organización[4a])
bare[2a], (naked[3a])	nu[2a]	bar[3b], (nackt[5a])	desnudo[2b]
beaming (beam[2a]), (radiant[5a])	radieux[4b]	glänzend[2a]	radiante[4a]
bench[2b]	banc[2a]	Bank[3b]	banco[2b]
bend[2a], bent[2b], (curve[3b])	plier[2b], (courber[4a]), (fléchir[6a]), (ployer[6a])	beugen[3b], (biegen[5a]), (krümmen[5b])	doblar[6a], (encorvar[5a])
bow[1b], ([arch[2b]]) | [e.g., – and arrow])	arc[5b]	Bogen[3a]	arco[3a]
charm[2a] (*vb.*), (enchant[5a])	enchanter[2a], charmer[2b], (captiver[7a])	fesseln[3a], entzücken[3b], (bezaubern[6b])	encantar[2b], (fascinar[5b]), (prendar[5b]), (embelesar[6a])
civil[3a] (pertaining to citizen)	civil[2b]	bürgerlich[2a]	civil[2a], (ciudadano[3a])
complaint[3b]	plainte[2b], (réclamation[7a])	Klage[2a], (Klagen[3b])	queja[2a], (reclamación[6b])
consent[2a] (*vb.*), (comply[5b])	consentir[2a], (agréer[5b]), (acquiescer[6a])	zustimmen[3b]	consentir[2a]
consideration[3b] (thought), (reflection[4b])	réflexion[2a], (considération[3a])	Betrachtung[2a], Erwägung[2b], (Überlegung[4b]), (Nachdenken[5a])	consideración[2b], reflexión[2b]

English	French	German	Spanish
constant[2a]	constant[2b]	unverändert[3b], (ständig[5b]), (unausgesetzt[5b])	constante[2a], (invariable[5b])
correspond[4b] (to)	correspondre[3b]	entsprechen[1a], (analog[6a] sein)	corresponder[1b]
cousin[2a]	cousin[2a], (cousin germain[5b])	Vetter[3b], (Cousine[4b])	primo[2a]
crime[3a], (trespass[6])	crime[2a], (délit[5b]), (attentat[6b])	Verbrechen[2b]	crimen[2b], delito[2b], (atentado[5b])
damage[3b] (*n.*), (injury[4a])	dommage[3a], (dégât[4a]), (détriment[6a])	Schaden[2a], (Verletzung[4a]), (Regreß[6a]), (Schädigung[6a])	daño[1b], (mal [*n.*][2a]), (perjuicio[4a]), (avería[6b])
dance[1b] (*vb.*)	danser[2a]	tanzen[4a]	bailar[2a], (danzar[6b])
deny[2b]	nier[3a]	bestreiten[3a], leugnen[3a], (verneinen[5b])	negar[1a]
depend[2b]	dépendre[2b]	abhängig[3a] (sein), (abhängen[4a])	depender[2b], (atenerse[5b])
destine[4b]	destiner[2b]	bestimmen[1b]	destinar[2a]
dreaded (dread[2b])	redoutable[3a]	(zu) befürchten[3b]	temido (temer[1a]), (temible[4b])
drop[1a] (*n.*)	goutte[2b]	Tropfen[4a]	gota[2a]
eager[2b], (zealous[5b])	ardent[2b], (avide[4a]), (acharné [acharner[5b]]) (ardemment[5b])	eifrig[3a], ernstlich[3a], (begierig[6a])	ardiente[2a], (celoso[3a]), (ávido[5b]), (fervoroso[5b])
entertain[3a]	amuser[2a], (divertir[5b]), (régaler[5b])	unterhalten[2b]	divertir[2a], regalar[2a], entretener[2b]
even[1a], (smooth[2a]), (sleek[6])	ras[4b], (lisse[5b]), (uni[6b])	glatt[3a]	liso[4a], terso[4b]
exhaust[3b]	épuiser[2b], (exténuer[5b])	erschöpfen[2b]	agotar[2b], (agostar[7a])
experiment[4b] (*vb.*)	(faire des) expériences (expérience[2a])	versuchen[1b]	experimentar[2a]
false[2b], (faithless[6])	infidèle[6a]	falsch[1b]	infiel[6b]
February[2b]	février[4b]	Februar[2b]	febrero[4b]
(battle)field[1a]	champ[1a] (de) bataille[2a]	Schlachtfeld[4a]	campo[1a] (de) batalla[2a]
fool[2a], (dunce[6])	imbécile[2b], (sot[4a])	Narr[3a], Tor[3b], (Pinsel[6b])	necio[2a], tonto[2a], (bobo[4b]), (imbécil[4b])
frame[2a] (*n.*)	cadre[3a]	Rahmen[3b]	cuadro[1b], (marco[5a])
frightening (frighten[2b]) (*adj.*)	effrayant[6a]	furchtbar[2b]	espantoso[2b]
grandmother[2b], (grandma[4a])	grand'mère[3a], (aïeule [aïeul[4b]])	Großmutter[3a]	abuela (abuelo[1b])
grounds (ground[1a])	terrain[2a]	Terrain[4a], Gelände[4b]	terreno[2a]
hate[2a] (*n.*), (hatred[4a])	haine[2b]	Haß[3a]	odio[2a], (aborrecimiento[6a])
heel[2a] (on shoe)	talon[4a]	Absatz[1b]	tacón
humor[3a], (mood[4a])	humeur[2a]	Stimmung[2a], (Laune[3a])	humor[2b], (talante[6b])
hunt[1b] (*n.*)	chasse[2b]	Jagd[4b]	caza[2b]
hurry[1b] (*n.*), rush[1b], (haste[2a]), (speed[2a])	hâte[2b], (rapidité[4b]), (précipitation[6b]), (empressement[7a])	Eile[4b]	prisa[2a], (precipitación[5a]), (presteza[6b]), (urgencia[6b])
ice[1b]	glace[2a]	Eis[4a]	hielo[2b], helado (+helar)[2a] (to eat)
improve[2b] (*intr. vb.*)	(faire des) progrès[2a]	verbessern[3a]	mejorar[2a], (progresar[4a])
instruction[3a]	instruction[2a], enseignement[2b]	Unterricht[2a], (Belehrung[4b]), (Instruktion[4b])	enseñanza[2a], instrucción[2b]

English	French	German	Spanish
invent[3b]	inventer[2b]	erfinden[2b]	inventar[2b]
Italian[3a]	italien[2b]	italienisch[2a], (Italiener[5a])	italiano[2b]
keen[3b], (vivid[5b])	poignant[6b]	scharf[1b]	agudo[2b]
lap[2b] (knees)	genoux (genou[2a])	Schoß[3b]	falda[2a], (regazo[6a])
limit[2a] (*n.*)	limite[2b], (borne[3b])	Beschränkung[3a], Schranke[3b]	límite[2a], (ámbito[4a]), (confín[6a]), (lindero[6a]), (limitación[6b])
(old) man[1a], (hoary[6])	vieillard[3a]	Greis[4a]	viejo[1a], (anciano[2a])
mankind[3a], (humanity[5b])	humanité[2a]	Menschheit[2a], (Menschengeschlecht[5a])	humanidad[2a]
marriage[3a]	mariage[2a]	Ehe[2a]	matrimonio[2a], (casamiento[4a])
midnight[2a]	minuit[3a]	Mitternacht[3a]	media[1a] noche[1a]
military[3a]	militaire[2a]	militärisch[2b]	militar[2a]
modest[3a]	modeste[2b]	bescheiden[2b]	modesto[2b]
mystery[3a]	mystère[2a]	Geheimnis[2a]	misterio[2a]
nine[1b]	neuf[2a]	neun[4a]	nueve[2*]
number[1a] (digit)	numéro[3a]	Ziffer[4a]	número[1a]
observation[3b]	observation[2b]	Beobachtung[2a], (Wahrnehmung[4b])	observación[2a]
occupation[3b]	métier[2a], occupation[2b], (vocation[6a])	Beruf[2b], (Beschäftigung[3a]), (Handwerk[3a])	ocupación[2a], empleo[2b], (quehacer[5a]), (vocación[6a])
October[1a]	octobre[3a]	Oktober[2a]	octubre[5a]
operation[2b] (general)	opération[2b]	Operation[3a], (Handhabung[5a]), (Manöver[5b])	operación[2b]
overcome[3b] (e.g., difficulties)	surmonter[3b]	überwinden[2b], (überwältigen[4b]), (bewältigen[6b])	salvar[1b], vencer[1b]
peasant[3b]	paysan[1b], (campagnard[5b])	Bauer[2a]	campesino[3b], (labriego[4a]), (aldeano[5b])
pity[2a] (*n.*), (compassion[5b])	pitié[2a]	Menschenliebe[3b], (Erbarmen[6b])	piedad[2a], compasión[2b], misericordia[2b]
plant[1a] (*vb.*)	planter[2b]	pflanzen[4a]	sembrar[2a], (plantar[3a])
poetry[3b]	poésie[2b]	Dichtung[2b], Poesie[2b], (Dichtkunst[5a]), (Lyrik[6b])	poesía[7b]
policy[3b]	politique[2b]	Politik[2a]	política[2a]
precious[2b]	précieux[2a]	köstlich[3b]	precioso[2a], (preciado[3b])
pride[2a]	orgueuil[2a], (amour-propre[3b]), (fierté[4b])	Stolz[3b], (Hochmut[6b])	orgullo[2a], (soberbia[6a]), (altivez[3b])
print[2a] (*vb.*)	imprimer[2b]	drucken[3a]	imprimir+impreso[2a]
printed (print[2a]) matter[1a]	imprimé (imprimer[2b])	Drucksache[3b]	impresos (impreso +imprimir[2a])
prisoner[2a], (captive[4a]), (convict[6])	prisonnier[2b]	Gefangene[3a]	preso[2b], (cautivo[3a]), (prisionero[3b])
progress[3a] (*n.*)	progrès[2a]	Fortschritt[2b]	progreso[2b], (adelanto[5a])
prospect[3a]	perspective[4a]	Aussicht[1b], (Prospekt[6b])	perspectiva[4a]
provoke[3b]	provoquer[2a]	reizen[2a]	provocar[2b]
remark[3b] (*n.*), observation[3b], (comment[6])	observation[2b], propos[2b], (remarque[3a])	Bemerkung[2a], (Anmerkung[5a])	observación[2a], (comentario[4a])

English	French	German	Spanish
remarkable[3b], (notable[5a])	remarquable[2b], (notable[4a])	merkwürdig[2a], (bemerkenswert[6a])	notable[2a]
reveal[3a], (disclose[5a])	révéler[2a], (dévoiler[7a])	eröffnen[2a], (offenbaren[4a]), (enthüllen[6a])	revelar[2b], (divulgar[5b])
ruin[2a] (*n.*), (decay[3a]), (decline[3b])	ruine[2b]	Verderben[3b], (Ruin[4b])	ruina[2a], (estrago[5a]), (perdición[6a])
sale[2b]	vente[2b], (débit[6a])	Verkauf[3a], (Umsatz[6b])	venta[2a]
satisfaction[3b]	satisfaction[2a], (contentement[6b])	Befriedigung[2b], (Zufriedenheit[4a])	satisfacción[2b]
scatter[2a], (disperse[4b]), (litter[5b]), (strew[6])	répandre[2a], (disperser[4b]), (joncher[5b]), (éparpiller[6a]), (épars[4b])	zerstreuen[3a]	derramar[2a], esparcir[2a], (desparramar[4b]), (dispersar[7a]), (aventar[7a] [to the winds])
season[1b] (*n.*) (of year)	saison[2a]	Jahreszeit[4b]	estación[2b], (temporada[3b])
sign[1b] (*vb.*)	signer[2b]	unterschreiben[4b], unterzeichnen[4b]	firmar[2b], (subscribir[6a])
sin[2b] (*vb.*), (violate[4b]), (transgress[6])	pécher (*v.*)[6b]	sich[1a] vergehen[2a], (sündigen[6b])	pecar[2b]
smoke[1b] (*n.*)	fumée[2b]	Rauch[4b]	humo[2a]
station[1b] (railroad), (depot[5b] [Amer.])	gare[2a]	Bahnhof[4a]	estación[2b]
submit[3a] (oneself)	(se) soumettre[2a]	(sich) fügen[2a]	someter[2a] se
(to have) supper[2a], ([to] sup[6])	souper (*v.*)[5b]	(zu Abend) essen[2b]	cenar[3a]
surprise[1b], (amazement[5b]), (astonishment[5b])	surprise[2a], (étonnement[3a]), (éblouissement[6b])	Erstaunen[4a], Überraschung[4b], Verwunderung[4b]	sorpresa[2a], asombro[2b], (extrañeza[4b])
talent[3b]	talent[2b], (aptitude[4b])	Talent[2b], (Begabung[5a])	prenda[2a], talento[2a], (dote[4a]), (aptitud[5a])
(have a) taste[1b] (for), ([be] fond[2b] [of])	(être) amateur[3a] (de)	Vorliebe[4b] (haben[1a])	gustar[1a] de, (aficionado [aficionarse[3a]])
tend[3a], incline[3a], ([have] tendency[5b])	(avoir) tendance[4a], (penchant[5b])	Neigung[1b], (Tendenz[3b])	(tener) tendencia[4a]
thread[2a]	fil[2b]	Faden[3b]	hilo[2a], (hebra[5b])
tire[1b] (*vb.*), (weary[2b]), (fatigue[6])	fatiguer[3a], (lasser[4b]) (fatigant[5b])	ermüden[4b]	cansar[1b], (fatigar[2b])
trade[1b] (*vb.*)	(faire le) commerce[2a]	verkehren[3a]	negociar[6b]
transfer[3b] (*vb.*)	transporter[2b]	übertragen[2a], (überweisen[3a]), (übersenden[5a])	trasladar[2a], (transponer[4b])
traveler(ll)[2a], (passenger[3a])	voyageur[1b], (passager [*n.*][5a])	Reisende[3a]	pasajero[3a], viajero[3a]
trim[2a], deck[2b], (ornament[3a]), (adorn[4a]), (decorate[6])	orner[2b], parer[2b], (garnir[4b]), (décorer[5b]), (embellir[5b])	schmücken[3a], (zieren[5a]), (verzieren[6b])	adornar[2b], (aderezar[4a]), (ornar[5b]), (decorar[6a]), (agraciar[6b]), (asear[6b]), (engalanar[6b])
ugly[2b], (homely[5a] [Amer.])	laid[3b]	häßlich[3b]	feo[1b]
undertaking (*n.*) (undertake[3b]), (enterprise[5a])	entreprise[2b]	Unternehmen[2b], Unternehmung[2b]	empresa[2a]
walk[1a] (*n.*) (take a –)	promenade[2a]	Spaziergang[4b]	paseo[2a]
waste[1b], (desert[2a]), (wilderness[3a])	désert[2a]	Wüste[4b], (öde[5a]), (wüst[5b])	desierto[2a], (yermo[6b])

English	French	German	Spanish
water[1a] (*vb.*)	arroser[4a], (abreuver[6b])	gießen[3b]	regar[4a]
(grow[1a]) weak[1b]	(s')affaiblir[4a]	verfallen[3b]	desfallecer[4a]
western[2a]	(de l')ouest[3a], (occidental[4b])	westlich[2b]	occidental[5a]
(church[1a]) window[1a]	vitrail[5a]	Fenster[2a]	vidriera[7a]
what[1a](?!) (eh)	hein[3a]	na[4b]	¡qué[1a]!, ¡como[1a]!
witness[2b] (*n.*)	témoin[2b]	Zeuge[3a]	testigo[2a]
zeal[3b], (ardor[8])	ardeur[2b], (zèle[3b])	Eifer[2b]	celo[2b], (ardor[3a]), (ahinco[5b]), (fervor[6a])

PART III

THE THIRD THOUSAND CONCEPTS

SECTION 2.5. CONCEPTS 2037 THROUGH 2121

E F G S	*E F G S*	*E F G S*	*E F G S*	*E F G S*	*E F G S*
1–1–4–4	1–4–3–5	1–6–3–3	2–4–3–1	3–3–2–2	3–6–1–3
1–2–4–3	1–4–4–1	2–1–3–4	2–5–2–4	3–4–1–5	4–2–1–3
1–3–3–6	1–5–3–4	2–2–3–3	2–6–2–3	3–4–2–1	4–3–1–2
1–3–4–2	1–6–2–7	2–3–3–2	3–2–2–3	3–5–1–4	

English	French	German	Spanish
active^{3a}, (nimble^{5b}), (sprightly^{6}), (agile^{11})	alerte^{5a} (agile)	lebhaft^{1b}	ágil^{4b}
approve^{2b}	approuver^{2b}	billigen^{3a}, (genehmigen^{4b})	aprobar^{3a}
assign^{3b}	assigner^{4b}	erteilen^{2a}, (auferlegen^{3b}), (zuteilen^{5a}), (zuweisen^{5b})	fijar^{1b}, señalar^{1b}
band^{1b} (strip of cloth)	bande^{2a}	Band^{4a}	banda^{3a}, (faja^{4b}), (tira^{6b})
bell^{1b}	cloche^{3a}, (sonnette^{4b})	Glocke^{4a}	campana^{2a}, (timbre^{5a})
betray^{3b}	trahir^{2b}	verraten^{2b}	traicionar^{3b}
birth^{2a}	naissance^{2b}	Geburt^{3b}	nacimiento^{3b}, (parto^{4b})
brown^{1b}, (tan^{5a})	brun^{2b}	braun^{4a}	moreno^{3a}, pardo^{3a}
building^{1b}, (construction^{4a})	construction^{3a}	Konstruktion^{4a}	construcción^{2b}
(letter-, note-) case^{1a}, (wallet^{6})	portefeuille^{3b}	Tasche^{3b}	cartera^{6a}
chair^{1b} (university)	chaire^{4b}	Stuhl^{3a}	cátedra^{5b}
champion^{3b} (*n.*)	champion^{4b}	Meister^{1b}	campeón^{5b}
chapter^{3b}	chapitre^{3a}	Kapitel^{2a}	capítulo^{2a}
cheek^{2a}	joue^{2a}	Wange^{3b}	mejilla^{3a}
color^{1a} (*tr. vb.*), (dye^{4a})	colorer^{6a}	färben^{3b}	teñir^{3b}, (azular^{5b}) (blue), (colorear^{6b})
communication^{4b}	communication^{3a}	Mitteilung^{1b}	comunicación^{2b}
compass^{2b}, (area^{3a}), (tract^{4b})	ampleur^{5b}, (contenance^{6b})	Umfang^{2a}, Ausdehnung^{2b}, (Bereich^{4b})	ámbito^{4a}
confirm^{3b} (verify)	confirmer^{3a}, (vérifier^{4a})	bestätigen^{2a}	confirmar^{2b}
consideration^{3b}, (reference^{5a})	considération^{3a}	Betracht^{2a}, Betrachtung^{2a}, Erwägung^{2b}, (Berücksichtigung^{4a}), (Bedacht^{6a})	consideración^{2b}
continual^{3b}, (continuous^{4b})	continuel^{4a}, (incessant^{5a})	beständig^{2b}, (fortwährend^{3a}), (stetig^{3b}), (ununterbrochen^{4a}), (unaufhörlich^{4b}), (immerfort^{5a}), (unablässig^{6a}), (unaufhaltsam^{6b})	contínuo^{1b}, (incesante^{3b})
	constamment^{4a}, (continuellement^{5b})		

English	French	German	Spanish
convenient[3b]	commode (*adj.*)[3a]	bequem[2b]	conveniente[2b], (cómodo[3b])
cook[1b] (*vb.*), (bake[2a]), (roast[2b])	cuire[3a], (rôtir[6a])	kochen[4a]	cocer[2a], (asar[3a]), (guisar[4a]), (cocido[5b])
creature[2a]	créature[3a]	Geschöpf[3b]	criatura[2a]
decision[4a]	décision[2a]	Entscheidung[1b], (Entschluß[2a]), (Beschlußfassung[5b])	decisión[3a]
differ[3b]	différer[4b]	anderer[1a] Meinung[1a] (sein)	diferir[5a]
engaged (engage[2b]), (betrothed [betroth[6]])	fiancé(e)[4b]	Braut[3a], (Bräutigam[4b])	prometido (prometer)[1b], (novio[2a])
European[3b] (*adj.*)	européen[3b]	europäisch[2b]	europeo[2b]
evident[3b], (patent[5a])	évident[3a], (manifeste[6a])	offenbar[2a], (verständlich[4a]), (augenscheinlich[5b]), (merklich[5b]), (erklärlich[6b]), (unverkennbar[6b])	constar[2b] (to be), (evidente[4a]), (patente[4a])
	(évidemment[2a])		
exception[3b]	exception[3a]	Ausnahme[2a], (Abweichung[4a])	excepción[2b]
fine[1a] (*n.*)	amende[6b]	Geldstrafe[2b]	multa[7a]
(catch[1b] [on]) fire[1a]	prendre[1a] feu[1a]	sich[1a] entzünden[4a], (zünden[5b])	inflamar[4a] (se), (incendiar[6b] [se])
fish[1b] (*vb.*), (troll[6])	pêcher[4a], (faire la) pêche (*f.*)[4b]	Fische (Fisch[3a]) fangen[1b]	pescar[5a], pesca[5b]
flight[2b] (in air)	vol[3b], (volée [*n.*][4a])	Flucht[3a], (Flug[5b])	vuelo[2b]
flight[2b], (rout[6])	fuite[2a]	Flucht[3a]	fuga[3b], (huida[6a])
floor[1a], story[1a]	étage[2a]	Geschoß[4a], (Stockwerk[6a])	piso[3a]
gleam[3b] (*n.*), (glimmer[6])	lueur[3b]	Schein[2b], (Schimmer[6a])	claridad[2a], (destello[5a])
grateful[3a], (thankful[4a])	reconnaissant[4a]	dankbar[2b]	agradecido (agradecer[1b])
hate[2a], (abhor[4b]), (loathe[6])	détester[3a], haïr[3a]	hassen[3a], (abhold[5b] sein[1a])	aborrecer[2a], (odiar[3b])
hold[1a] (*n.*), (grasp[4a])	prise[2b]	Halt[4a]	presa[3a]
host[2b]	hôte[3b]	Wirt[3a]	huésped[2b]
hurry[1b] (*tr. vb.*), rush[1b], (hasten[2b]), (quicken[4a])	hâter[3b], (accélérer[4b]), (activer[5b])	beschleunigen[4b]	apresurar[2b], dar[1a] prisa[2b]
independent[3a]	indépendant[3b]	selbstandig[2a], (unabhängig[3a])	independiente[2b]
justify[3b], (warrant[4a])	justifier[2a], (motiver[6a])	berechtigen[2a], rechtfertigen[2b], (ermächtigen[6b])	justificar[2b]
lamp[2a]	lampe[2a]	Lampe[3b]	lámpara[3b], (candil[4b])
lion[1b]	lion[3b]	Löwe[4a]	león[2b]
majesty[3b]	majesté[4b]	Majestät[2a]	majestad[1b]
mayor[3a]	maire[3a]	Landrat[2b], (Gemeindevorsteher[3b]), (Bürgermeister[4a]), (Amtsvorsteher[6b]), (Gemeindevorstand[6a]), (Regierungskommissar[6a]), (Regierungspräsident[6a]), (Schulze[6a])	alcalde[2b], corregidor[2b]
(by) means (mean[1a]) (of)	moyennant[5a]	mittels[3a]	mediante[4a]
melt[2a], (thaw[5b]), (molten[6])	fondre[2b]	schmelzen[3b]	derretir[3b], (fundir[5a])
messenger[3a], (herald[5a])	commissionnaire[4b], (courrier[5a])	Bote[1b]	mensajero[5b], (nuncio[6a])

English	French	German	Spanish
method[3a]	méthode[2b], (tactique[5a])	Methode[2a], (Taktik[6a])	método[3a]
milk[1a]	lait[3a]	Milch[4b]	leche[2b]
monument[3a]	monument[3a]	Denkmal[2a]	monumento[2b]
oil[2a] (*n.*)	huile[3b]	Öl[3a]	aceite[2a]
patient[2b] (*n.*), (invalid[7])	malade[1b]	Kranke[3a], (Patient[6a])	paciente[4b], (doliente[5b])
payment[3b]	paiement[6b]	Zahlung[1b], (Bezahlung[5a])	pago[3a]
plate[2a] (*n.*)	assiette[3a]	Platte[3a], (Teller[6a])	plato[2a]
poem[3a]	poésie[2b], (poème[4a])	Gedicht[2a]	poema[3b], (soneto[5a])
population[3a]	population[3a]	Bevölkerung[2a]	población[2a]
prompt[2b], (punctual[6])	prompt[4b] (promptement[5a])	rechtzeitig[3a], (pünktlich[5b])	pronto[1a], (puntual[3a])
quarrel[2b] (*n.*), (brawl[6])	querelle[5a]	Streit[2b], (Streitigkeit[6a])	quimera[4b], (querella[5a]), (pendencia[5b]), (riña[5b])
quarter[1b] (of a town)	quartier[2a]	Quartier[4a], (Viertel[5b])	barrio[3a]
regard[2a] (*n.*), (esteem[3b])	égard[2a], (estime[3a])	Hochachtung[3b]	estimación[3b], (aprecio[4a])
renew[3a]	renouveler[3a]	erneue(r)n[2b]	renovar[2b]
rent[2a] (*n.*) (to pay)	loyer[6b]	Zins[2b]	alquiler[3b]
reward[3a] (*n.*)	récompense[3a]	Anerkennung[2b], (Belohnung[6a])	premio[2a], (recompensa[4a]), (galardón[5a])
series[4b]	série[2a]	Reihe[1b]	serie[3a]
shop[1b] (*n.*)	boutique[3b]	Laden[4b]	tienda[2a]
shower[2b] (*n.*)	averse[3b]	Guß[3b], (Schauer[7a])	lluvia[2b]
sincere[3a]	sincère[3a] (sincèrement[6a])	aufrichtig[2b]	sincero[2a]
speed[2a]	vitesse[2b], (rapidité[4b])	Geschwindigkeit[3b], (Schnelligkeit[4b])	rapidez[3a], ligereza[3b], (velocidad[4a]), (expedición[4b]), (prontitud[4b])
stairs (stair[2a])	escalier[2a], (perron[4a])	Treppe[3b]	escalera[3a]
steam[2a] (*n.*), (vapor[3a])	vapeur (*f.*)[3a]	Dampf[3a]	vapor[2a]
striking (*adj.*) (strike[1b])	saisissant (*adj.*)[6a], frappant (*adj.*)[6b]	auffallend (auffallen[2b]), (auffällig[6b])	sorprendente[7a]
style[2a]	style[3a]	Stil[3a]	estilo[2a]
sufficient[3a]	suffisant[3a] suffisamment[3b]	reichlich[2b]	suficiente[2a]
surprised (surprise[1b])	surpris[4a]	betroffen[4a]	sorprendido (sorprender[1b])
till[1a], (cultivate[3a]) (land)	cultiver[3a]	bearbeiten[4a]	cultivar[2b]
top[1a] (side)	dessus (*n.*)[4b]	Oberfläche[4a]	parte[1a] (lado[1a]) superior[1b]
tribe[2a]	tribu[5b]	Stamm[2b]	tribu[4b]
undertake[3b]	entreprendre[3a]	unternehmen[2a]	emprender[2a]
urge[2b] (*vb.*)	pousser[1a], (encourager[3a])	reizen[3a]	alentar[4a], (instar[6a])
wheat[1b], (buckwheat[6])	blé[3a]	Weizen[4b]	trigo[2b]
wheel[1b] (*n.*)	roue[3a]	Rad[4b]	rueda[2b]
workman(men)[4a], (laborer[5a])	ouvrier(-ère)[2a], (manœuvre[5b])	Arbeiter[1a], (Handwerker[2b])	trabajador[3a], (jornalero[5a]), (peón[6a])

SECTION 2.6. CONCEPTS 2122 THROUGH 2232

E F G S	*E F G S*	*E F G S*	*E F G S*	*E F G S*	*E F G S*	*E F G S*	*E F G S*
1–1–4–5	1–3–4–3	1–5 –4–1	2–2–3–4	2–5–3–1	3–2–2–4	3–5–1–5	4–3–1–3
1–1–5–1	1–4–3–6	1–6 –2–8*	2–3–3–3	2–6–2–4	3–3–2–3	3–6–1–4	4–5–1–1
1–2–3–8*	1–4–4–2	1–8*–2–6	2–4–3–2	3–1–2–5	3–4–2–2	4–1–2–1	5–1–1–1
1–2–4–4	1–5–3–5	2–1 –4–1	2–4–2–6	3–1–3–1	3–4–1–6	4–2–1–4	

English	French	German	Spanish
active[3a]	actif[3a]	tätig[2b], (aktiv[5b])	activo[3a]
ancient[2a], (antique[5b])	ancien[1a], (antique[3a])	antik[4b]	antiguo[1a], (anciano[2a]), (vetusto[5b]), (rancio[6a]), (añejo[7a])
apply[2a] (put on)	appliquer[1b]	auflegen[4b]	aplicar[1b]
assembly[3a], audience[3b], (congregation[5b])	assemblée[3a], congrès[3a], (assistance[4a]), (auditoire[5a])	Sammlung[2a], Versammlung[2a], Gemeindeversammlung[2b], (Generalversammlung[3a]), (Nationalversammlung[5a])	auditorio[3b], (concurrencia[4b]), (asamblea[5a])
balance[2b] (*n.*) (equilibrium)	équilibre[3b], (aplomb[5a])	Gleichgewicht[3a]	equilibrio[3b]
boat[1b], (canoe[4b]), (craft[5a]), (cutter[5b])	bateau[3a], barque[3b], (canot[6b])	Boot[4b], (Kahn[5a])	barca[3b], (lancha[4a]), (bote[4b])
bone[1b]	os[4b]	Knochen[4a]	hueso[2a]
brim[4a] (hat)	bord[1a]	Rand[2b]	ala[1b]
bring[1a] together[1a]	rapprocher[1b]	zusammenstellen[5b]	juntar[1b]
call[1a] back[1a]	rappeler[1a]	zurückrufen[5b]	llamar[1a], hacer[1a] volver[1a]
chariot[3b]	char[4b]	Wagen[2b]	carro[2a], (carruaje[4b])
church[1a] (*adj.*)	ecclésiastique[5b]	kirchlich[3a]	eclesiástico[5b]
clever[3b], (skilful[4a])	habile[3a], (adroit[4b]) (habilement[5b]), (adroitement[6b])	klug[2b], (schlau[5b]), (gescheit[7a])	diestro[1a], hábil[8a]
come[1a] (go[1a]) out[1a]	sortir[1a]	herauskommen[5a]	salir[1a]
compose[3b]	composer[1b], écrire[1a] (des vers)	dichten[3a], (verfassen[4b])	componer[1b]
conversation[2a]	conversation[1b], (entretien[2b])	Unterhaltung[3a]	conversación[1b]
country[1a] (*adj.*)	provincial[5a]	Land-[3a]	campestre[5b]
crack[2b] (*vb.*), (split[3b]), (cleave[4a]), (cleft[6])	craquer[4b], fendre[4b]	springen[1a]	hender[6b]
cry[1b] (*n.*)	cri[1b]	Geschrei[5a], Schrei[5b]	grito[1b]
current[2b] (*n.*)	courant[1b]	Strömung[4a]	corriente[1b]
decree[3b] (*n.*)	ordonnance[3b], (arrêté [*n.*][4a]), (décret[5a]), (édit[5b])	Verfügung[2a], (Erlaß[3a]), (Anzeige[3b]), (Verordnung[3b]), (Beschlußfassung[5b])	decreto[3b]
dense[3b]	dense[6a]	dicht[1b]	denso[4a]
depth[3a]	profondeur[2b]	Tiefe[2a], (Vertiefung[5b])	profundidad[4b]
detain[4b]	retenir[1a], (retarder[3b])	aufhalten[2b]	detener[1a], (retener[4b]), (retardar[7a])
dignity[3b]	dignité[3a]	Würde[2b]	dignidad[3a], (mesura[6b])
display[3a], (exhibition[5b])	exposition[3b], montre[3b], (exhibition[5b]), (étalage[6a])	Ausstellung[2b], (Weltausstellung[6a]), (Schau[6b])	exposición[3b]

English	French	German	Spanish
doctrine[4b]	doctrine[3a]	Lehre[1b]	doctrina[3a]
doubtful[3b], (uncertain[4b])	douteux[3b], indécis[3b], (équivoque[5a])	bedenklich[2b], (zweifelhaft[3a]), (fraglich[4a]), (unwahrscheinlich[6a])	dudoso[3b], (incierto[4b])
draw[1a] along[1a]	entraîner[1b]	hinziehen[5a]	tirar[1b]
edge[1b] (of knife)	fil[2b]	Schärfe[4b]	filo[4b]
enter[1b] (writing)	inscrire[2b]	eintragen[3b]	inscribir
escape[1b] (the memory)	échapper[1b]	entfallen[5a]	escapar[1b]
exchange[2b] (stock)	bourse[3b]	Börse[3a]	bolsa[3a]
existence[4b]	existence[1b]	Existenz[2b], (Dasein[3a]), (Sein[3a]), (Bestehen[6a])	existencia[1b]
expect[1b] (of a person)	attendre[1a] (de)	zumuten[5a]	esperar[1a]
experiment[4b] (*n.*)	expérience[2a], (essai[3b])	Versuch[1b], (Experiment[4b])	experimento[4b]
express[1b] (*adj.*), (deliberate[5b])	exprès (*adj.*)[3a]	absichtlich[4a], (vorsätzlich[6b])	expreso[3a], (deliberado [deliberar[5b]])
factory[3a]	usine[4a], (fabrique[5a])	Fabrik[2b], (Zuckerfabrik[6b])	fábrica[2b]
fail[2a]	manquer[1b], (faillir[3a]), (échouer[5b])	scheitern[4b]	dejar[1a], (malograr[4b] se[1a]), (fracasar[5b]), (fallar[7a])
fall[1a] (to pieces), (crumble[5a])	s'écrouler[4a], (crouler[5a]), (effondrer[5b]), (dégringoler[6a])	verfallen[3b], (zerfallen[4b]), (zusammenfallen[5b])	desmoronar[6a] (se)
farming (farm[1b])	culture[3a]	Wirtschaft[4a]	cultivo[3b], (labranza[6b])
fat[1b], (lard[4a]), (grease[5b])	gras[3a], (graisse[6a])	Fett[4b]	manteca[3a], (grasa[6b])
(for the) first[1a] time[1a]	(pour la) première (premier[1a]) fois[1a]	(zum) erstenmal[5b]	(por) primera (primero[1a]) vez[1a]
flag[2a], standard[2b], (banner[3b]), (ensign[6])	drapeau[3b], (pavillon[4a])	Fahne[3a], (Flagge[6a])	bandera[3a], (pabellón[4b]), (pendón[5b])
flow[1b] (*n.*), (tide[2b])	flux[6a]	Fluß[2a]	flujo
foreigner[4a]	étranger[1a]	Fremde[2b], (Ausländer[4b])	extranjero[1b]
fort[2b], (fortress[4b])	forteresse[5a]	Festung[3a], (Fort[4a]), (Befestigung[5a]), (Schanze[6a])	fuerte[1a], (fortaleza[3b])
free[1a] (of charge)	gratuit[5a]	umsonst[3b], (unentgeltlich[6b])	gratis[5b], (gratuito[7a])
Greek[3b]	grec[4a]	griechisch[2a], (Grieche[3b])	griego[2a]
hardy[3b], (rugged[5a]), (sturdy[5b]), (vigorous[6])	robuste[4a], vigoureux[4a]	kräftig[2a]	robusto[2b], (vigoroso[3a])
hill[1a], (ridge[3a]), (hillside[4a]), (knoll[6])	colline[3b], (coteau[5b]), (butte[6b])	Hügel[4a]	cerro[3b], (colina[6a]), (loma[6a]), (otero[6a])
holiday[2b]	jour[1a] (de) fête[1b]	Feier[4b], (Feiertag[6a])	(dia de) fiesta[1b]
hunter[2b]	chasseur[3a]	Jäger[3a]	cazador[3b]
impression[4a] (imprint)	empreinte[5b]	Eindruck[1b]	impresión[1b]
industry[2b], (application[3b]), (diligence[7])	application[4a], (assiduité[7a])	Fleiß[3a]	industria[2a], aplicación[2b], diligencia[2b]
institute[3b] (*n.*), (institution[4a])	institution[2b], (institut[3b])	Anstalt[2a], (Institut[3a]), (Institution[6b])	instituto[4a], institución[4b]
invention[3b]	invention[3a]	Erfindung[2a]	invención[3b]
judgment (ge)[2b] (insight)	jugement[2b]	Einsicht[3a]	criterio[4a]
knock[2a] (on door), (rap[5a]) (*vb.*)	frapper[1a], (taper[5a]), (cogner[6b])	klopfen[4a], (pochen[6a])	llamar[1a], tocar[1a]
leaf[5b] (of tree)	feuille[1b]	Blatt[1b]	hoja[1a]
lighted (light[1a])	éclairé[4b]	beleuchtet (beleuchten[4b])	alumbrado (alumbrar[2b])

English	French	German	Spanish
(as) little[1a] (as)	aussi peu que[5b]	ebensowenig[4a] wie[1a]	tan[1a] poco[1a] como[1a]
majority[3a], (bulk[4a])	majorité[3a]	Mehrzahl[2a], (Mehrheit[3a]), (Majorität[3b])	mayoría[3a]
meadow[2a], (mead[5a]), (lea[6])	pré[3b], (prairie[4a])	Au[3b], (Wiese[4b])	prado[3b], (pradera[4b])
mine[1a] (*n.*)	mine[3a]	Grube[4b], (Bergwerk[6b])	mina[3b]
namely[5b]	(c'est à) dire[1a]	nämlich[1a]	(es) decir[1a] . . . .
neat[3a]	net[1b], rangé (ranger[1b]), (propre[2b])	ordentlich[3a], (reinlich[6b])	arreglado (arreglar[1b]), limpio[1b], ordenado (ordenar[1b]), (aseado [asear[6b]])
noise[2a], (clamor[4b]), (din[5a]), (tumult[5a]), (clang[5b]), (clatter[5b]), (uproar[5b])	bruit[1a], (rumeur[4b]), (tapage[5a]), (clameur[5b]), (fracas[5b]), (tumulte[5b]), (brouhaha[7a])	Lärm[4a], (Geräusch[5a])	ruido[1b], (estruendo[3b]), (estrépito[4a]), (clamor[5a]), (algarabía[5b]), (alboroto[6a]), (tumulto[6a]), (bulla[6b]), (bullicio[6b]), (fragor[6b])
observing (observe[2a])	observateur[6a]	aufmerksam[2a]	observador[4b], (lince[6b])
(for my) part[1a], (on my) side[1a]	(pour ma) part[1a], (de mon) côté[1a]	meinerseits[5a]	(de mi) parte[1a]
pass[1a] (e.g., time), (elapse[8])	passer[1a], (s'écouler[3a])	verfließen[5a]	pasar[1a], (transcurrir[3b])
peer[2b], (nobleman[5b])	noble[1b], (seigneur[2a]), (gentilhomme[3b]), (hobereau[4b]), (pair [*n.*][6a])	Edelmann[4b], (Junker[6b])	noble[1a], (hidalgo[3a]), (aristócrata[6b])
professor[3a]	professeur[3a]	Professor[2a]	profesor[3a], (catedrático[5a])
progress[3a] (*vb.*)	(faire des) progrès[2a]	Fortschritte (Fortschritt[2b]) (machen), (fortschreiten[4a])	progresar[4a]
(in) proportion[3a], relatively (relative[3a])	relativement[4a]	verhältnismäßig[2b]	relativo[2a]
punishment[3a]	supplice[4a], (punition[6a])	Strafe[2a], (Züchtigung[5b]), (Bestrafung[6b])	castigo[2a]
put[1a] (off) (postpone)	remettre[1a], (différer[4b]), (ajourner[6b])	verschieben[4b]	diferir[5b], (aplazar[6a])
put[1a] (on) (e.g., hat)	mettre[1a], (coiffer[3b])	aufsetzen[5b]	poner[1a]
quarter[1b] (fractional)	quart[1b]	Viertel[5b]	cuarto[1a]
rank[3a] (*n.*)	grade[5b]	Rang[3a]	grado[1b], (rango)
realize[3b] (be cognisant of)	comprendre[1a], (se rendre[7a] compte[1a])	einsehen[3a]	dar[1a](se) cuenta[1a]
receipt[3b] (recipe)	recette[4a]	Vorschrift[1b]	receta[6b]
reckon[3b] (calculate)	calculer[3a]	berechnen[2a]	calcular[2b]
(not) recognize[2b] (a person)	(ne pas) reconnaître[1a], (méconnaître[4b])	verkennen[4a]	(no) reconocer[1b]
referring (refer[3b])	se rapportant (rapporter[1b])	bezüglich[2a]	referente[5b]
retreat[3b] (*n.*)	retraite[2a]	Rückzug[7b]	retiro[4a]
review[2b] (*n.*)	revue[3b]	Rundschau[3b], (Rückblick[6b])	revista[3a]
roll[1a] (*n.*)	rouleau	Rolle[2a]	rollo[6b]
root[2a] (*n.*)	racine[4a]	Wurzel[3a]	raíz[2b], (radical[3b])
run[1a] down[1a] (run out) (finish)	tirer[1a] (à sa fin), (s'[1a] épuiser[2b])	ablaufen[5a]	acabar[1a] se[1a], (agotar[2b] [se])
sacrifice[2b] (*vb.*)	sacrifier[3a]	opfern[3b], (aufopfern[5b])	sacrificar[3a]
saint[2b]	saint[1b]	Heilige[4a], (Sankt[6a])	santo[1a]
sending (send[1a]) (*n.*)	expédition[3a], (envoi[7a])	Expedition[4a]	despacho[3a], (transmisión[5b]), (envío[7a])

English	French	German	Spanish
shelter[2a] (*vb.*), (screen[4a])	abriter[3b]	hegen[3a], (unterbringen[5a])	abrigar[3a], amparar[3a], (refugiar[4b])
sigh[2a] (*vb.*)	soupirer[4a]	seufzen[3b]	suspirar[2a]
skirt[2a], (petticoat[5b])	jupe[4b]	Rock[3b]	falda[2a]
smoke[1b] (*vb.*)	fumer[3a]	rauchen[4b]	fumar[3a], (humear[5b])
snatch[3b]	arracher[1b], (happer[7a])	entreißen[3b], (auffangen[6a])	arrancar[1b], (arrebatar[2b])
splendid[2a]	splendide[4b]	prächtig[3a]	espléndido[2b]
spoil[2a], (decay[3a]), (corrupt[4b]), (rotten[5a]), (rot[5b]), (taint[5b])	gâter[3a], (abîmer[5a]), (décomposer[5a]), (pourrir[6a])	verderben[3a], verfallen[3b]	corromper[3b], descomponer[3b], (dañar[4a]), (podrir[4b]), (contaminar[6a])
spring[1a] (*n.*), (jump[2a]), (leap[2a])	bond[4b], (saut[6a])	Sprung[4b]	salto[2b], (brinco[6b])
stop[1a] (of tram, etc.)	station[2b], (arrêt[3a])	Station[3b]	parada
store[1b] (*n.*)	magasin[4a]	Laden[4b]	tienda[2a], (almacén[4a])
take[1a] away[1a], back[1a], (withdraw[3a]), (withdrew[5b])	reprendre[1a], retirer[1a]	zurücknehmen[5b], (abheben[6b])	sacar[1a], retirar[1b]
three[1a] times (time[1a]), (thrice[4a])	trois[1a] fois[1a]	dreifach[5a], dreimal[5a]	tres[1*] veces (vez[1a])
traffic[3b] (street)	circulation[5a]	Verkehr[1b]	circulación[5a]
treaty[4b]	traité[2b]	Vertrag[1b], (Handelsvertrag[5b])	tratado[4b]
twist[3b], (wring[5b])	tordre[3b]	drehen[2b], (schlingen[6b])	retorcer[3b]
unusual[3b]	peu[1a] commun[1b], peu[1a] courant[1b]	ungewöhnlich[3b], (ungewohnt[6b])	(no) común[1b], (poco) común, ([no] usual[6a])
various[2a]	divers[1b], (varié [varier[2b]])	mannigfaltig[4a], mannigfach[4b]	vario[1a], diverso[1b]
wash[1b] (*vb.*)	laver[4a]	waschen[4b]	lavar[2a]

SECTION 2.7. CONCEPTS 2233 THROUGH 2333

E F G S	*E F G S*	*E F G S*	*E F G S*	*E F G S*	*E F G S*	*E F G S*	*E F G S*
1–1–4–6	1–3–4–4	1–6–3–5	2–2–4–1	2–6–3–1	3–2–3–1	3–5–2–2	4–4–1–3
1–1–5–2	1–4–4–3	2–1–3–6	2–3–2–8*	3–1–2–6	3–3–2–4	3–6–1–5	5–2–1–1
1–2–4–5	1–5–3–6	2–1–4–2	2–3–3–4	3–1–3–2	3–4–1–7	4–1–2–2	
1–2–5–1	1–5–4–2	2–2–3–5	2–4–3–3	3–2–2–5	3–4–2–3	4–2–2–1	

English	French	German	Spanish
acquaintance[3a] (person)	connaissance[2a]	Bekannte[3b], Bekanntschaft[3b]	conocido (conocer[1a]), conocimiento[1b]
affirm[4b], assert[4b], (attest[6])	affirmer[2a]	bestätigen[2a]	afirmar[1b]
(be) ahead[3b] (of), (surpass[4b])	devancer[4a], (surpasser[6b])	übergehen[2a], (übertreffen[4a]), (zuvorkommen[6a])	destacar[3a] se, (sobresalir[4b]), (campear[5b]), (descollar[5b])
anger[2a] (*vb.*), make[1a] angry[2a], (vex[3a]), (enrage[6]), (irritate[7])	mettre[1a] en[1a] colère[1b], (indigner[3a]), (irriter[3b])	ärgern[4a], (erbittern[6a])	enfadar[2b], (indignar[3a]), (irritar[3b]), (enfurecer[5a])
animal[1b] (*adj.*)	animal[2b]	tierisch[5b]	animal[1b]
annual[3a], (yearly[5b])	annuel[4b]	jährlich[2a], (alljährlich[4b])	anual[3b]

English	French	German	Spanish
astonish[3b], amaze[3b]	étonner[1a], (émerveillé[5b])	erstaunen[3a], (verwundern[4a]), (staunen[5a])	asombrar[2a], (maravillar[5a])
attract[3b]	attirer[1b]	anziehen[3a]	atraer[2b]
beg[2a], (beseech[5b]), (entreat[5b]), (implore[5b])	supplier[2a], (implorer[4b])	beschwören[4b], (flehen[5a])	rogar[1b], (implorar[4a])
beginning[5b]*	commencement[2a], début[2a]	Anfang[1b], (Beginn[2b]), (Ansatz[6b])	principio[1a], (comienzo[4a])
bind[2a] (a book)	relier[3b]	binden[2a]	encuadernar
blind[1b] (*vb.*)	aveugler[4a]	blenden[4b]	cegar[3b]
board[1b] (food)	pension[2b]	Pension[4b]	pensión[5b]
breaking (break[1b]) up, (dissolution[7])	dissolution[6a]	Aufhebung[3b], Auflösung[3b]	disolución[5a]
breathe[2a], (out), (in), (snuff[5a])	respirer[2a], (exhaler[5a]), (aspirer[6b]), (humer[6b])	atmen[4a]	aspirar[1b], (respirar[2a]), (exhalar[3b])
cart[3a], (buggy[6])	cabriolet[5b], (carriole[6b])	Wagen[2b]	coche[2a]
chain[1b] (*vb.*)	enchaîner[6a]	fesseln[3a]	encadenar[5b]
clerk[2b], (salesman[6])	employé(-e)[3a], (vendeur[6a]), (commis [*n.*][6b])	Verkäufer[6b], (Handlungsgehilfe[6b])	dependiente[4b], (vendedor[6a])
climb[2a]	grimper[3b], (gravir[4a])	aufsteigen[3b], (besteigen[5a]), (ersteigen[5a])	trepar[4b], (escalar[6a])
collection[3b]	collection[3a], (recueil[6a]), (assemblage[5b])	Sammlung[2a], Versammlung[2a]	colección[4b]
communicate[5b]	communiquer[2a]	mitteilen[1b]	comunicar[1b], (participar[3b])
comparison[3b]	comparaison[4b]	Vergleich[2a], (Vergleichung[5a])	comparación[3a]
condemn[3b], (convict[6])	condamner[2a]	verurteilen[3b]	condenar[1b]
constitution[3b], (organization[5b])	constitution[3b]	Verfassung[2a]	constitución[4a]
copy[2a] (e.g., of a book)	exemplaire[4b]	Exemplar[3b], (Abschrift[5b])	ejemplar[3a]
correct[2a] (*vb.*)	corriger[4a], (rectifier[5a])	verbessern[3a]	corregir[3a], (escarmentar[4b]), (enmendar[5a]), (rectificar[5a])
corresponding (correspond[4b]) (*adj.*) (like)	correspondant[4b]	entsprechend[1b]	correspondiente[3a]
crop[2a], harvest[2a]	moisson[4b], (récolte[5b])	Ernte[3a]	cosecha[3a], (mies[6a])
cross[1a] (*tr. vb.*) (put crossways)	croiser[2a]	kreuzen[5b]	cruzar[1b], (terciar)
curious[3a]	curieux[1b]	wißbegierig[3b], (neugierig[5b])	curioso[2a]
dainty[4b]	délicat[2a]	zart[2b]	delicado[1b]
dedicate[4b], consecrate[4b]	consacrer[2b], (dévouer[5b])	widmen[2b], (weihen[4a])	dedicar[1b], (consagrar[2a])
defeat[3b], (vanquish[6])	vaincre[2b], (vaincu [*n.*][6a])	einnehmen[2a], (erobern[3a])	derrotar[5a], superar[5a]
delay[2a] (*tr.vb.*)	tarder[2a] (à), (retarder[3b]), (attarder[6a])	verzögern[4b]	tardar[1b], (dilatar[2b]), (atrasar[5a]), (retrasar[6a]), (retardar[7a])
deposit[3b] (*n.*), (depot[5b])	dépôt[3a]	Lager[2a]	depósito[4a]
dinner[1b]	dîner[1b]	Essen[5a]	comida[2a]
discharge[3b] (of gun)	coup[1a] de[1a] feu[1a]	Schuß[2a]	disparo[6b]
dismiss[3b], discharge[3b]	renvoyer[2b], (donner[1a] congé[3b]), (congédier[6a])	entlassen[3b]	despedir[1b]

English	French	German	Spanish
drag^{2b}	traîner^{2a}	schleppen^{4b}	arrastrar^{1b}
drink^{1a} (*n.*)	boisson^{5a}	Getränk^{4b}	bebida^{2b}
eastern^{3a}, (Oriental [o]^{6})	oriental^{4b}	östlich^{2b}, (orientalisch^{5a})	oriental^{3b}
exalt^{4b}, (glorify^{5b})	exalter^{4a}	erheben^{1a}	exaltar^{3a}
(the) faithful^{2a}	croyant (*n.*)^{6a}	Gläubige^{3a}	fieles (fiel^{1b})
faithful^{2a}, (trusty^{5b})	fidèle^{2a} (fidèlement^{5a})	getreu^{4a}	fiel^{1b}
(get) (grow) fat^{1b}	engraisser^{6b}	dick^{3a} (werden), zunehmen^{3b}	engordar^{5b}
fifth^{2a}	cinquième^{4b}	fünfte^{3b}	quinto^{3*}
flat^{2a} (*adj.*)	plat^{3b}	flach^{3b}, (platt^{6a})	plano^{4a}
furnace^{3b}	four^{4a}	Ofen^{2b}	horno^{3b}
game^{1b} (to shoot)	gibier^{5a}	Wild^{4a}	caza^{2b}
hasty^{4b}	précipité (précipiter^{1b})	flüchtig^{2b}, (hastig^{5b})	apresurado (apresurar^{2b}), (precipitado [precipitar^{3a}]), (presuroso^{5a})
inch^{1b}, (in.^{6})	pouce^{3b}, (centimètre^{4b})	Zentimeter^{4a}	centímetro^{4b}, palmo^{4b}
introduce^{3a} (e.g., a subject)	présenter^{1a}, (introduire^{2a})	einleiten^{3b}, (aufbringen^{4a})	introducir^{2a}
kindness^{2b}	bonté^{2b}, (complaisance^{5a}), (amabilité^{5b}), (bienveillance^{5b})	Gefalle(n)^{4b}, (Freundlichkeit^{5b})	bondad^{1b}, (benevolencia^{4a}), (amabilidad^{5b})
leave^{1a} (bequeath)	léguer^{5a}	hinterlassen^{3b}	legar^{6b}
(in) love^{1a}	amoureux^{2b}, (épris^{5b})	verliebt (verlieben^{5a})	enamorado^{1b}
(bad) luck^{3a}	fatalité^{6a}	Unglück^{1b}	fatalidad^{5b}
mad^{2a}, (crazy^{5a}), (madman^{6})	fou, folle (*adj.*)^{2a}, (insensé^{3b}), (fou [*n.*]^{3a}), (folle [*n.*]^{5a})	toll^{4a}	loco^{1a}, (rabioso^{4a}), (frenético^{5a}), (insano^{5b})
mass^{2a} (religious)	messe^{2b}	Messe^{4b}	misa^{1b}
miserable^{3b}, wretched^{3b}	misérable^{2a}, (pitoyable^{5a})	elend^{3b}	miserable^{1a}, (mísero^{3a})
misery^{3b}	misère^{2a}	Elend^{3a}	miseria^{1b}
mouth^{1b} (of river)	embouchure^{5b}	Mündung^{3b}	ría^{6b}
(spend^{1b}) night^{1a}	passer^{1a} la^{1a} nuit^{1a}	(die) Nacht^{1a} zubringen^{4a}	trasnochar^{6a}
oven^{3b}	four^{4a}	Ofen^{2b}	horno^{3b}
overcome^{3b} (emotionally), (upset^{5a})	bouleverser^{2b}	(aus der) Fassung^{2b} (bringen)	embargar^{5a}
pale^{2b}, (ghastly^{6}), (wan^{6})	pâle^{1b}, (livide^{5a}), (blême^{5b}), ([être d'une] paleur^{6a} . . . .)	bleich^{4b}, (blaß^{5a}), (farblos^{6a})	pálido^{2b}, (descolorido^{5a}), (lívido^{5b})
perish^{3a}	périr^{4a}	vergehen^{2a}	perecer^{3a}, (sucumbir^{4b})
pledge^{3b} (*vb.*), (warrant^{4a}), (guarantee^{5b})	garantir^{4a}	versprechen^{1b}, (garantieren), (zusichern)	garantizar^{7a}
pond^{2b}	étang^{3b}	Lache^{3b}	laguna^{4a}, (charco^{6b})
porch^{2b}, (portal^{6})	portail^{4b}, (porche^{6b})	Tor^{3b}, (Pforte^{4b})	portal^{3b}, (atrio^{7a})
possibility^{4b}	possibilité^{4a}	Möglichkeit^{1b}	posibilidad^{3b}
potato^{2a}	pomme^{3b} de^{1a} terre^{1a}	Kartoffel^{3b}	patata^{4b}
praise^{2a} (*n.*)	éloge^{4a}	Lob^{3a}	alabanza^{3a}, elogio^{3b}
(on) principle^{3b}	(par) principe^{2a}	prinzipiell^{3b}, (grundsätzlich^{5a})	(en) principio^{1a}

English	French	German	Spanish
print[2a] (*n.*)	gravure[4b]	Stich[3b], (Holzschnitt[4b]), (Kupferstich[6b])	lámina[3b], (grabado[4b])
promise[1b] (*n.*)	promesse[4a]	Versprechen[4b]	promesa[3a]
quality[2a]	qualité[2a]	Qualität[4a]	c(u)alidad[1b]
raw[3a]	cru (*adj.*)[5a]	roh[2b]	crudo[2b]
recent[3a]	récent[2b]	neulich[3b]	reciente[1b]
recover[2b] (health)	(se) remettre[1a]	erholen[4a]	reponer[2b] (se), (sanar[6b])
relieve[3a]	décharger[4a], soulager[4a]	erleichtern[2b]	aliviar[3b], (desahogar[4b])
reproach[3b], (censure[5b]), (rebuke[5b]), (reproof[6])	reproche[2b]	Vorwurf[2a], (Tadel[5a])	censura[5a], reproche[5a]
reserve[3a] (*vb.*)	réserver[1b]	vorbehalten[3b], (zurücklegen[4a])	reservar[2b]
restless[3b]	inquiet[1b], (sans[1a] repos[2a])	unruhig[3b], (rastlos[5b])	inquieto[2a]
restore[2b] (put back)	remettre[1a], (rétablir[3b]), (restaurer[4a])	erstatten[4b]	reponer[2b], (restablecer[4a]), (restituir[4b]), (restaurar[6b])
reverence[3b] (*vb.*)	vénérer[4a]	verehren[2b]	venerar[3b]
salary[3a]	salaire[5b]	Lohn[2a]	sueldo[1b]
sample[3b]	échantillon[5a]	Muster[2b]	muestra[2b]
seed[1b]	grain[3a], (graine[5b])	Same(n)[4b], (Saat[6b])	simiente[4b], (semilla[5a])
set[1a] (on) fire[1a], (kindle[4b])	allumer[2a], (embraser[5a]), (enflammer[6b]), (incendier[6b])	anzünden[5a], (anstecken[6a])	encender[1b], (incendiar[6b])
settlement[3a], (agreement[4b])	accord[1b], (arrangement[4a])	Feststellung[3a], (Ausgleich[5a]), (Erledigung[5a]), (Ausgleichung[6b])	acuerdo[2a], (arreglo[3a])
source[3a], (origin[4b])	origine[2a], source[2b]	Entstehung[3b], Ursprung[3b]	fuente[1b], origen[1b]
stem[3a], (stalk[4a])	tige[3b]	Stamm[2b]	tallo[4b]
suit[1b] (clothes)	costume[2a], habit[2a], (complet [*n.*][5a])	Anzug[5a]	traje[1b]
summon[3a]	sommer[5b]	bestellen[2b]	requerir[2b], (intimar[4b])
swear[3b] (take oath), (sworn[4a]), (swore[5b])	jurer[2a], ([faire] serment[6b]), (prêter[2a] serment[3b])	schwören[3a], (Eid[4a] ablegen[3a])	jurar[1b]
Thursday[2b]	jeudi[2b]	Donnerstag[3b]	jueves[5a]
valuable[2b]	(de grande) valeur[1b], (précieux[2a])	kostbar[3a], wertvoll[3a]	valioso[6a]
verse[3a]	vers[3b], (couplet[5b])	Vers[3b]	verso[1b], (estrofa[6a]), (décima[6b])
wander[2a], (roam[3b]), (rove[4a]), (stroll[6])	errer[4a], rôder[4a]	wandern[3b], (durchziehen[5b])	vagar[6b], (errar[4b])
weigh[2a]	peser[2a]	wiegen[4a]	pesar[1a]
wit[2a], (humor[3a])	esprit[1a]	Humor[4a]	ingenio[2a]

SECTION 2.8. CONCEPTS 2334 THROUGH 2420

E F G S	*E F G S*	*E F G S*	*E F G S*	*E F G S*	*E F G S*	*E F G S*
1–2–5–2	1–4–4–4	2–1–4–3	2–4–2–8*	2–6 –3–2	3–3–3–1	3–5–2–3
1–3–4–5	1–5–3–7	2–2–3–6	2–4–3–4	2–8*–2–4	3–3–2–5	3–6–1–6
1–3–5–1	1–6–3–6	2–2–4–2	2–5–2–7	3–1 –3–3	3–4–2–4	4–2–2–2
1–4–3–8*	1–6–4–2	2–3–4–1	2–6–2–6	3–2 –3–2	3–4–1–8*	4–3–2–1
						4–4–1–4

English	French	German	Spanish
admiration[3b]	admiration[2a]	Bewunderung[3b]	admiración[2a]
agreed (agree[2a])	entendu[2a]	einverstanden[3a], (vertragsmäßig[5b])	acorde[6a]
agriculture[3a]	agriculture[4a]	Landwirtschaft[2b]	agricultura[4a]
appeal[3a], (make – to)	(avoir) recours[4a](à)	(sich) berufen[2a]	apelar[4a]
arrival[3b]	arrivée[2a], (venue [*n.*][3b])	Ankunft[3a], (Kommen[6b])	llegada[2b], (venida[4b])
assemble[3b]	rassembler[3a], (assembler[4a])	zusammensetzen[3a]	reunir[1b]
assume[3b] (take over)	assumer[4a]	übernehmen[1b]	asumir
attentive[4b]	attentif[2b] (attentivement[6a])	aufmerksam[2a]	atento[2a]
back[1a] (*adj.*), (hind[3a])	arrière[3b]	hintere[5a]	(de) atrás[1b], (posterior[4b])
backward[3b], (backwards[6]*)	(en) arrière[3a]	rückwärts[3b]	(de) espaldas (espalda[1b]), hacia[1a] atrás[1b]
basket[1b]	panier[3b], (corbeille[5b])	Korb[4b]	cesto[5b], (cesta[6a])
birthday[2b]	anniversaire	Geburtstag[1b]	cumpleaños
blame[2a], (reproach[3b]), (censure[5b]), (reprove[6])	blâmer[4a]	tadeln[3b]	culpar[4b], (achacar[5b]), (censurar[6a]), (tachar[6a])
breath[2a]	souffle[2a], (haleine[4a])	Atem[4b], (Hauch[5a])	aliento[2a], (soplo[3b]), (hálito[4b])
camp[2a] (*n.*)	camp[5a]	Lager[2a], (Biwak[5b])	aduar[7a] (nomad)
(in) cash[3b]	comptant (compter[1a])	bar[3b]	(al) contado[3b]
clap[3a], (applaud[5b])	applaudir[2b], (acclamer[5b])	Beifall[3a] geben[1a]	aplaudir[2b], (aclamar[6b])
coming (come[1a]) before[1a] (preceding)	précédent[4a]	vorhergehend (vorhergehen[4b])	precedente[4b]
commercial[3b]	commercial[4a], commerçant[4a]	kaufmännisch[2b], (geschäftlich[4b])	comercial[4a], (mercantil[6a])
consent[2a] (*n.*)	consentement[6b]	Zustimmung[2b], (Einwilligung[5a])	consentimiento[6b]
convention[4a], (meeting [*n.*][6]*)	réunion[2a], séance[2b]	Sitzung[2a], (Zusammenkunft[5a])	reunión[2a]
cream[2a] (of) crop[2a] (best)	prémices	(das) Beste[2b]	primicia[4b]
cut[1a] off[1a] (curtail)	retrancher[5a]	abschneiden[3b], (verringern[5b])	mermar[7a]
defense[3a]	défense[2b]	Verteidigung[3a], (Abwehr[6b])	defensa[2a]
delicious[3b]	délicieux[2b]	köstlich[3b]	delicioso[2b], (sabroso[3a])
demonstrate[5b]	démontrer[3a]	beweisen[1b]	demostrar[1b]
despair[3a] (*vb.*)	désespérer[2b]	verzweifeln[3b]	desesperar[2a]
desperate[3b], (hopeless[4b])	désespéré (désespérer[2b])	verzweifelt (verzweifeln[3b])	desesperado (desesperar[2a])
director[4b], (boss[6]), (manager[6])	directeur[2b], (administrateur[5a]), (gérant[6a]), (intendant[6b])	Arbeitgeber[2b], (Direktor[3a]), (Unternehmer[4a]), (Verwalter[4a]), (Vorstand[4b])	director[2b], (administrador[5a]), (mayordomo[6b])

English	French	German	Spanish
dispute[3a] (*vb.*)	disputer[2a]	bestreiten[3a]	disputar[2b]
(take) down[1a] (e.g., from wall)	décrocher[6b]	abnehmen[3a]	descolgar[6a]
fashion[2a], style[2a], (mode[3b])	mode (*f.*)[1b]	Mode[4b]	moda[3a]
fell[1a] (*vb. infin.*), (knock[2a] down)	terrasser[6b]	niederschlagen[4b]	derribar[2b], (atropellar[3b]), (tumbar[6b]), (derrumbar[7a])
foolish[2b], (silly[4a])	bête[2b], (sot[4a]), (niais[5a]), (badaud[5b]) (sottement[6b])	töricht[4a]	tonto[2a], (bobo[4b]), (majadero[5a]), (fatuo[6a])
fountain[2b]	fontaine[3a]	Brunnen[4b]	fuente[1b]
(make) fun[2a] (of), mock[2b], (scoff[5b]), (chaff[5a])	se moquer[2b](de), (se ficher[6b]), ([se] railler[6a])	spotten[4b]	burlar[2a], (escarnecer[5b]), (burlón[5b])
function[4b] (*vb.*)	fonctionner[4a]	gehen[1a]	funcionar[4b]
fury[3b], rage[3a], (madness[4b]), (frenzy[6])	rage[2b], (délire[3b]), (fureur[3b]), (furie[5b])	Wut[3b], (Wahnsinn[5b])	furor[2b], (furia[3a]), (rabia[3a])
gas[3a]	gaz[4a]	Gas[2b]	gas[4b]
genius[3b]	génie[2b]	Genie[3b], (Genius[5b])	genio[2a]
(put on) hat[1b]	coiffer[3b]	Hut[2a] aufsetzen[5b]	tocar[1a] (se)
hide[1b] (fact), (disguise[3b])	dissimuler[2b], (feindre[3b]), (déguiser[4a])	verhehlen[5b]	disimular[2b], (encubrir[3b])
horseman[3b], (rider[4a])	cavalier[3a]	Reiter[3a]	caballero[1a], (jinete[4b])
(be) hungry[2a]	(avoir) faim[3a]	Hunger[4b] (haben)	(tener) hambre[1b], (hambriento[3b])
immediate[2a]	immédiat[3a], (momentané[6b])	sofortig[4b], (unverzüglich[6b])	inmediato[1b], (instantáneo[4b]), (momentáneo[6b])
	(immédiatement[2a]), (instantanément[6a]), (momentanément[7a])		
innocent[3a], (guiltless[5a]), (blameless[6])	innocent[2b]	unschuldig[3a]	inocente[2a]
key[2a]	clef[2b]	Schlüssel[illegible]	llave[2a]
kitchen[2a]	cuisine[2b]	Küche[4a]	cocina[2b]
Latin[3a]	latin[6b]	lateinisch[3b]	latino[2b], (latín[3b])
league[2b] (union)	ligue[6b]	Bund[2a]	liga[6a]
lock[2a] (*n.*) (on door)	serrure[4b]	Schloß[2a]	cerradura, cerrojo
meanwhile[4b], (in the) meantime[4b]	en attendant[6b]	inzwischen[2a], (unterdessen[4a]), ([in der] Zwischenzeit[6b])	mientras[1a] tanto[1a], (entretanto[3a])
mirror[3a]	glace[2a], (miroir[4a])	Spiegel[3a]	espejo[2a]
(give) notice[1b] (to)	donner[1a] congé[3b]	kündigen[5a]	despedir[1b]
offend[3a]	offenser[3b], (fâcher[5a])	beleidigen[3a], (verstoßen[6b])	ofender[1b], (desagradar[4a])
official[3a] (*adj.*)	officiel[2b]	amtlich[3a], (offiziell[4b]), (dienstlich[6a])	oficial[2a]
official[3a] (*n.*)	fonctionnaire[3b]	Beamte[2a]	funcionario[5b]
parliament[3b]	parlement[3b]	Reichstag[2a], (Parlament[3b])	parlamento[5b]
patience[3a]	patience[2b]	Geduld[3a]	paciencia[2a]
powder[3a], (gunpowder[6])	poudre[3b]	Pulver[3b]	polvo[1b], (pólvora[6b])

English	French	German	Spanish
publish^{3a}	publier^{2b}	veröffentlichen^{3a}, herausgeben^{3b}	publicar^{2a}
pull^{1b} down^{1a}, (demolish^{10})	démolir^{4b}	niederlegen^{3a}	demoler
recently (recent^{3a})	récemment^{3a}	neulich^{3b}, (kürzlich^{4a})	poco^{1a} ha, recién^{1b}, recientemente (reciente^{1b})
reproach^{3b}, (rebuke^{5b}), (reprove^{6})	reprocher^{1b}	verweisen^{3b}, (vorwerfen^{6a})	reprender^{3b}
republic^{3b}	république^{2b}	Republik^{3b}	república^{2a}
resist^{3b}, (withstand^{5a})	résister^{2a}	widerstehen^{3b}, (widerstreben^{5b})	resistir^{2a}
revenge^{3a}, (vengeance^{4a})	revanche^{2b}, (vengeance^{5b})	Rache^{3b}	venganza^{2a}
sigh^{2a} (*n.*)	soupir^{2b}	Seufzer^{4a}	suspiro^{2b}
slant^{4b}, (tilt^{6})	incliner^{3b}	neigen^{2a}	inclinar^{1b}
slip^{2a}, (slide^{3a}), (glide^{3b})	glisser^{2a}	gleiten^{4b}, (entfallen^{5a})	deslizar^{2b}, (escurrir^{4a}), (resbalar^{4a})
smell^{2a} (*n.*), (odor^{3b})	odeur^{2a}, (senteur^{4a})	Geruch^{4a}	olor^{2a}, (olfato^{7a})
solemn^{3b}	solennel^{2b} (solennellement^{4a})	feierlich^{3a}, (festlich^{5b})	solemne^{2b}
splendor^{3b} (brilliance)	splendeur^{5a}	Glanz^{2b}	esplendor^{3a}
steep^{2b} (*adj.*)	rapide^{1b}, (raide^{3b}), (abrupt^{5a})	steil^{4a}, (schroff^{5b})	pendiente^{3a}, (pino^{4a})
surface^{2b}	surface^{2b}, (superficie^{7a})	Oberfläche^{4a}	superficie^{2b}
suspect^{3b}, ([have] suspicion^{5b})	soupçonner^{2b}, ([se] méfier^{4a})	(im) Verdacht^{3b} (haben)	sospechar^{2a}, ([tener] malicia^{3a}), (desconfiar^{4b})
sympathy^{3b}	sympathie^{2b}, (sentiments [sentiment^{1b}] sympathiques [sympathique^{4a}])	Mitleid^{3b}, (Sympathie^{4b})	simpatía^{2b}
throughout^{2b}	complètement^{2a}	durchweg^{4b}	(al) través^{2a} (de) . . . .
transform^{4b}, convert^{4b}	transformer^{2a}, (convertir^{3b})	verwandeln^{2a}, (umwandeln^{5b})	transformar^{2b}, (modular^{6b})
treatment^{3b}	traitement^{4b}	Behandlung^{2a}	tratamiento^{4a}
vacant^{3b}	vacant^{6b}	frei^{1a}	vacante^{6b}
vast^{2b}, (extensive^{5a})	vaste^{1b}	weitgehend^{4a}, (weitläufig^{5b})	amplio^{3a}, extenso^{3a}, vasto^{3a}
vote^{2b} (*n.*)	vote^{6a}	Abstimmung^{3b}	voto^{2a}
wear^{1b} (out), (worn^{2b}) (e.g., clothes)	user^{2b}	verbrauchen^{5b}, (ausnutzen^{6a})	gastar^{2b}
wool^{2a}, (of) wool^{2a}, (woolen^{4b}), (yarn^{5b})	laine^{2b}, (de) laine^{2b}	Wolle^{4b}, (aus) Wolle^{4b}	lana^{2b}, (de) lana^{2b}
worry^{3b} (*n.*)	inquiétude^{2a}, (anxiété^{4a}), (émoi^{6a})	Unruhe^{3a}	afán^{2a}, ansia^{2b}, inquietud^{2b}, (zozobra^{3b}), (ansiedad^{4a})
wound^{2a} (*n.*)	blessure^{2b}	Wunde^{4a}	herida^{2a}

SECTION 2.9. CONCEPTS 2421 THROUGH 2527

E F G S	*E F G S*	*E F G S*	*E F G S*	*E F G S*	*E F G S*
1-1-5-4	1-5-3-8*	2-2-4-3	3-2-3-3	3-4-3-1	4-8*-1-1
1-2-5-3	1-5-4-4	2-3-4-2	3-3-2-6	3-5-1-8*	5-1 -1-4
1-3-5-2	1-6-4-3	2-4-4-1	3-3-3-2	4-2-2-3	5-2 -1-3
1-4-5-1	2-1-4-4	2-4-3-5	3-4-2-5	4-3-2-2	5-3 -1-2

English	French	German	Spanish
absent[3a] (mind)	absent[3b], (distrait[6a]) (distraitement[6a])	zerstreut (zerstreuen[3a])	distraído (distraer[2b])
adversary[5b]	adversaire[2b]	Gegner[1b]	adversario[3b]
agent[4b]	agent[2a], (facteur[3b])	Vertreter[2a], Anwalt[2b], (Agent[3b]), (Kommissionär[3b])	agente[3b], (casero[6b])
amount[1b] (to), (sum)	revenir[1a]	belaufen[5a]	sumar[4a]
(too) bad[1a]	dommage[3a], (regrettable[6b])	schade[5a]	lástima[2a]
bloody[3b]	sanglant[2b]	blutig[3a]	sangriento[2b]
blow[1a] (*vb.*), (blew[3a])	souffler[2a]	blasen[5a]	soplar[3a]
brilliant[4a]	éclatant[3a]	glänzend[2a]	brillante[2a], luminoso[2b], (resplandeciente[3b])
burst[7a] (of laughter)	éclat[1b]	Ausbruch[4a]	carcajada[4a]
bursting (burst[2a]), (explosion[8])	éclat[1b], (explosion[5a])	Ausbruch[4a], (Explosion[7a])	explosión[4a]
catholic (C)[4b]	catholique[3a]	katholisch[2b], (Katholik[5b])	católico[1b]
change[1a] (conversion)	change[4a], transformation[4a], (conversion[7a])	Umwandlung[5a], (Umgestaltung[6b])	cambio[1b], (mudanza[4b]), (transformación[5a])
charity[3a]	charité[3b]	Menschenliebe[3b]	caridad[2a], (beneficencia[7a])
charter[4b]	charte	Brief[1a]	carta[1a], (patente[4a]), (cédula[6a])
clear[1a] (up) (get lighter)	éclaircir[5a]	aufklären[4a], erhellen[4b]	aclarar[4b], despejar[4b], (esclarecer[5b])
clearly (clear[1a])	clairement[4b], ouvertement[4b], (manifestement[6a])	augenscheinlich[5b]	claramente (claro[1a]), (manificstamente [manifiesto[4a]])
coarse[3a] (person), (vulgar[5b])	vulgaire[3b], (grossier[4b])	grob[3b]	ordinario[2a], vulgar[2b], (grosero[3a])
colony[2b]	colonie[2b]	Kolonie[4a]	colonia[3a]
column[3a] (military)	colonne[3a]	Kolonne[3a]	columna[2a]
community[4b] (of individuals)	commune[3a]	Gemeinde[1a], (Landgemeinde[3b]), (Kommune[4a])	comunidad[6a]
congress[2b]	congrès[3a]	Kongreß[4a]	congreso[2b]
connection[3b], (association[4b])	association[3a], (liaison[4a])	Zusammenhang[2a], (Umgang[3a])	enlace[6a]
conquer[2b]	conquérir[3a]	besiegen[4a], siegen[4a]	conquistar[2b]
cover[1a], (lid[4a])	couvercle[6a]	Deckel[4a], (Klappe[6a])	cubierta[3b]
credit[3a] (*n.*)	crédit[3b]	Kredit[3a], (Haben[5a])	crédito[2b]
crown[1b] (*vb.*)	couronner[3b]	krönen[5a]	coronar[2b]
cure[2b] (*vb.*), (heal[3a])	guérir[3a]	heilen[4a]	curar[2b], (sanar[6b])
(make) curious[3a]	intriguer[5a]	beschäftigen[1b]	intrigar

English	French	German	Spanish
cut^{1a} (off), (isolated [isolate^{6}])	isolé^{2b} (isolément^{4b})	vereinzelt^{5b}	aislado (aislar^{3a}), (retirado^{4b})
darkness^{2a}, (gloom^{4a})	obscurité^{3a}, (ténèbres^{4b})	Dunkelheit^{4a}, Finsternis^{4a}, Dunkel^{4b}	obscuridad^{2a}, (tiniebla^{3a})
debate^{3b}, (discuss^{4a}), (argue^{5b})	discuter^{2a}, (débattre^{4a})	erörtern^{3b}, (verhandeln^{4a})	discutir^{3b}, (argüir^{6b})
demand^{1b} (supply and –)	demande^{2b}	Nachfrage^{5a}	demanda^{3b}
disappoint^{3b}	décevoir^{4a}	täuschen^{2b}, (enttäuschen)	desengañar^{5a}
discussion^{5b}	discussion^{2a}	Verhandlung^{1b}, (Diskussion^{3b}), (Abhandlung^{4b}), (Auseinandersetzung^{6a})	discusión^{3a}
domestic^{3a} (pertaining to house)	domestique^{2a}	häuslich^{3b}	doméstico^{3b}
dumb^{3a}, (mute^{4a})	muet^{3b}	stumm^{3b}	mudo^{2b}
duty^{1b} (custom)	douane^{5b}	Zoll^{3a}	aduana
eleven^{2b}	onze^{2b}	elf^{4b}	once^{3*}
essential^{5b}, vital^{5b}	indispensable^{2b}, (essentiel^{3a}) (essentiellement^{5b})	wesentlich^{1a}, (unentbehrlich^{3b}), (unerläßlich^{5b})	esencial^{3a}, indispensable^{3a}, (vital^{4a}), (imprescindible^{5b})
exalted (exalt^{4b}), sublime^{4b}	sublime^{3a}, (relevé^{4b})	erhaben^{2b}	sublime^{2b}, (exaltado [exaltar^{3a}]), (excelso^{6a})
excuse^{2b} (*n.*)	excuse^{2b}	Entschuldigung^{4b}	excusa^{3b}, (disculpa^{4a})
explanation^{5b}	explication^{3b}	Erklärung^{1b}, (Aufklärung^{4a}), (Auslegung^{5b}), (Deutung^{6a})	explicación^{2b}
fasten^{2b}, (attach^{3b})	attacher^{1b}	anknüpfen^{4b}	trabar^{4a}
fellow^{1b} worker^{3b}, associate^{3b}	collègue^{3a}, confrère^{3b}, (collaborateur^{4b}), (adjoint^{6b})	Kollege^{2b}, (Bundesgenosse^{5a}), (Mitarbeiter^{5b})	colega^{6a}
final^{2a}	décisif^{3a}, définitif^{3a}, final^{3a}	definitiv^{4b}, endgültig^{4b}	final^{2a}
fit^{1b} (*vb.*), (adapt^{7})	adapter^{3b}, (ajuster^{4b})	anpassen^{5a}	ajustar^{2b}, (adaptar^{4b})
float^{2b} (in water), (drift^{4a})	flotter^{2b}, (flottant^{6a})	schwimmen^{4a}	flotar^{3a}, (flotante^{6a}) (*adj.*)
forty^{2a}	quarante^{2a}, (quarantaine^{6a})	vierzig^{4b}	cuarenta^{3*}
(have) fun^{2a}	(s')amuser^{3a}, (se) distraire^{3b}, ([se] divertir^{5b})	Spaß^{4a} (haben), (sich) vergnügen^{4a}	divertir^{2a} (se)
funny^{3a}	drôle^{2b}, (comique^{3b})	komisch^{3b}	cómico^{3a}
grass^{1b}	herbe^{2a}	Gras^{5a}	hierba^{3b}, (yerba^{5b})
heir^{3b}	héritier^{3b}	Erbe^{3a}	heredero^{2b}
hers^{5a}	(le) sien^{2a}	ihre (ihr^{1a})	suyo^{3*}
household^{3a}	ménage^{2b}	Haushalt^{3b}, (Hauswesen^{4a}), (Wirtschaft^{4a})	establecimiento^{3a}
included (include^{2a})	compris^{4a}	einschließlich^{4b}	comprendido (comprender^{1a}), (incluso [incluir^{3a}])
instrument^{3a}	instrument^{3a}, (ustensile^{6a})	Instrument^{3b}, (Gerät^{5b})	instrumento^{2a}
joke^{3b} (*n.*), (jest^{4b})	plaisanterie^{3b}	Witz^{3a}, (Scherz^{4a}), (Spaß^{4a})	broma^{2b}, (chiste^{3b}), (chasco^{4b}), (chanza^{6a})

English	French	German	Spanish
knife[2a], (knives[6])	couteau[2b]	Messer[4b]	cuchillo[3a], (cuchilla[7a])
leave[1a] (of absence)	permission[3a], congé[3b]	Urlaub[5b]	licencia[2b], (permiso[3a])
liberal[4a]	libéral[3b]	nationalliberal[2a], (liberal[4b]), (Nationalliberale[4a]), (freisinnig[5a])	liberal[2b]
list[1b] (*n.*), (catalog[ue][5b])	liste[3a]	Liste[5a], Verzeichnis[5b]	lista[2b], (catálogo[5a])
literature[4b]	littérature[3a]	Literatur[2a]	literatura[2b]
(make[1a]) mad[2a], (crazy[5a]), (craze[5b])	rendre[1a] fou[2a], (affoler[3a]), (enrager[5a])	toll[4a] machen[1a]	trastornar[3a], (enloquecer[4b]), (enajenar[6a])
make[1a] (up for), (make amends [amend[4b]] for), (redress[6])	réparer[3a], (restituer[5b])	büßen[5a]	reparar[2a]
mamma[3a]	maman[2a]	Mama[3b]	mamá[3b]
(good) manners (manner[1b])	politesse[2b]	Höflichkeit[5b]	cortesía[3a], (corrección[4b]), (urbanidad[5b])
manufacture[3b] (*n.*)	fabrication[4b]	Herstellung[3a], (Fabrikation[4b]), (Erzeugung[5b])	fabricación[5a]
miracle[4a]	miracle[3a]	Wunder[2a]	milagro[2b]
mortal[2b], (fatal[3b]), (deadly[4a])	fatal[3a], mortel[3b] (fatalement[6a])	tödlich[4b], (verderblich[5a]), (verhängnisvoll[5a])	mortal[2a], fatal[3b]
murmur[2a] (*vb.*), (mutter[4b])	murmurer[3a], (grogner[5a])	murmeln[4b]	murmurar[2a]
neighborhood[3a], (vicinity[6]), (surroundings[8])	voisinage[3a], (alentours [les][5a])	Umgebung[3a], (Nachbarschaft[5b]), (Umgegend[6a])	alrededores[2a], (proximidad[4a]), (inmediación[4b]), (vecindad[4b]), (vecindario[6a]), (cercanía[6b])
novel[4b] (*n.*)	roman[3a]	Roman[2b], (Novelle[4b])	novela[2b]
office[1b] (place), (bureau[3b])	bureau[2a], cabinet[2a]	Bureau[5a]	despacho[3a], (oficina[4a])
path[1b], (lane[6a]), (pathway[6])	allée[2b], sentier[2b]	Pfad[5a]	senda[3b], sendero[3b]
pause[3b] (*n.*)	cesse[3b], (arrêt[3a])	Pause[3b]	pausa[3a]
peaceful[3b], pacific[3b], (peaceable[6])	paisible[3a], (pacifique[4b]) (paisiblement[4a])	friedlich[3a], (ungestört[6a])	pacífico[2b], (apacible[3a])
pearl[2b]	perle[3b]	Perle[4b]	perla[2b]
pious[4b], (devout[6])	pieux[3a], (dévot[4b]), (pratiquant [*adj.*][5b])	fromm[2b]	piadoso[2b], (devoto[6a]), (pío[6a])
pledge[3b] (*n.*), (guarantee[5a])	garantie (*n.*)[4a], gage[4b]	Deckung[2b], (Garantie[4a]), (Sicherung[4b]), (Bürgschaft[6a]), (Pfand[6a])	abono[5a], garantía[5a]
princess[3a]	princesse[4b]	Fürstin[3a], Prinzessin[3b]	princesa (príncipe[1b])
profession[4b] (occupational)	profession[3b]	Beruf[2b]	profesión[2b]
provided (provide[2a]) (that)	pourvu que[3b]	vorausgesetzt[4b] (daß)	provisto (proveer[2b]) (que)
question[1b] (*vb.*)	interroger[2a], (questionner[4a])	befragen[5b]	interrogar[3b]
(get) rid[3a] (of)	(se) débarasser[3a]	(sich) befreien[2a]	desembarazar[6a] (se)

English	French	German	Spanish
ring^{1b}, (echo^{2b}), (resound^{5a})	retentir^{2b}, (résonner^{4b})	ertönen^{5b}	resonar^{3a}, (retumbar^{5a}), (repercutir^{6b})
ripe^{2b}, (mature^{4a}), (mellow^{5a})	mûr(-e)^{2b}	reif^{4a}	(en) sazón^{3a}, (maduro^{4b})
rock^{1a} (*vb.*)	bercer^{5a}	wiegen^{4a}	mecer^{4a}
sailor^{2b}, (seamen^{5b}), (marine^{6})	marin^{3b}, (matelot^{5b})	Schiffer^{4a}	marinero^{2b}, (marino^{3a})
saying (say^{1a}), saw^{1a}	proverbe^{6b}	Spruch^{4b}	refrán^{3b}
scorn^{3a} (*vb.*), despise^{3a}	mépriser^{3b}, (dédaigner^{5a})	verachten^{3b}, (verschmähen^{5a})	despreciar^{2a}, (desdeñar^{3b}), (desairar^{5b})
shade^{1b}, (hue^{5a}), (tint^{6})	nuance^{2b}, (teinte^{4a})	Färbung^{5b}	matiz^{3a}, (tinte^{6a})
silk^{1b} (*n.*)	soie^{3a}	Seide^{5a}	seda^{2b}
stable^{2b} (*adj.*), (motionless^{7})	immobile^{2a}	stet^{4a}, (unbeweglich^{6a})	inmóvil^{3a}, (estable)
stale^{4b} (e.g., bread)	rassis	alt^{1a}	duro^{1a}
stature^{5a}	taille^{1b}	Gestalt^{1b}	estatura^{4a}, (talla^{7a})
strip^{2a} (*n.*)	bande^{2a}	Strich^{4b}, (Streifen^{6b})	cinta^{3b}, (faja^{4b}), (tira^{6b})
suspect^{3b} (have a presentiment)	se douter^{3a} (de)	ahnen^{2b}	recelar^{6a}, (barruntar^{7a})
use^{1a} (up), (consume^{4a})	consommer^{3a}	verbrauchen^{5b}	consumir^{2a}
virgin^{3b} (*n.*)	vierge^{3a}	Jungfrau^{3b}	virgen^{2a}
visible^{4b}	visible^{2b} (visiblement^{6a})	sichtbar^{2b}, (bemerkbar^{5b}), (sichtlich^{6b})	visible^{3b}
volume^{3a} (book)	volume^{3a}	Band^{3a}	volumen^{2b}, (tomo^{4a})
vulgar^{5b}	vulgaire^{3b}	gemein^{1a}	vulgar^{2b}
wave^{1b} (*n.*), (roller^{5a}), (billow^{5a}), (ripple^{5a}), (surge^{6})	flot^{3a}, vague^{3a}	Welle^{5a}	ola^{2b}, (onda^{3a}), (oleaje^{6b})
weakness^{3a}, (frailty^{6}), (infirmity^{6})	faiblesse^{2b}	Schwäche^{3a}, (Schwachheit^{6b})	flaqueza^{3b}, (debilidad^{4a})
wet^{2a} (*adj.*)	mouillé (mouiller^{2b})	naß^{4b}	mojado (mojar^{3a})
wet^{2a} (*vb.*)	mouiller^{2b}	naß^{4b} machen^{1a}	mojar^{3a}
(to be) willing^{2b}, (fain^{6})	vouloir^{1a} bien^{1a}	willig^{4a} (sein), (bereitwillig^{6b})	(ser) (estar) gustoso^{4a}

SECTION 3. CONCEPTS 2528 THROUGH 2650

E F G S	*E F G S*	*E F G S*	*E F G S*	*E F G S*	*E F G S*	*E F G S*	*E F G S*	*E F G S*
1–1–5–5	1–4–4–6	1–8*–3–6	2–3–4–3	2–5 –4–1	3–1–4–1	3–5–2–5	4–2 –2–4	5–2–1–4
1–1–6–1	1–4–5–2	2–1 –4–5	2–4–3–6	2–6 –3–4	3–2–3–4	3–6–1–8*	4–3 –2–3	5–3–1–3
1–2–5–4	1–5–4–5	2–1 –5–1	2–4–4–2	2–8*–3–2	3–3–3–3	3–6–2–4	4–4 –2–2	5–4–1–2
1–3–5–3	1–6–4–4	2–2 –4–4	2–5–3–5	3–1 –3–5	3–4–3–2	4–1–3–1	4–8*–1–2	5–5–1–1
							5–1 –2–1	6–1–1–1

English	French	German	Spanish
(be) absorbed (absorb^{5b}) (in work, etc.)	absorber^{2b}	(in) Anspruch^{1b} (nehmen), (vertiefen^{5a})	absorto^{4a}, (embeber^{6b},
advantage^{2a} (to have the –) (in height, etc.)	dépasser^{1b}	übertreffen^{4a}	aventajar^{5a}
air^{1a} (*n.*), (tune^{3a}), (melody^{4b})	air^{1a}	Melodie^{5b}	melodía^{5b}, (tonada^{6b})

English	French	German	Spanish
air[1a] (*adj.*)	aérien[4a]	Luft-[4a]	aéreo[6b]
(fit of) anger[2a]	accès[3a] (de) colère[1b]	Ausbruch[4a] von[1a] Wut[3b]	arranque[3b], (arrebato[5b])
apparent[4b]	apparent[3b]	scheinbar[2b], (anscheinend[4b])	aparente[3a]
appearance[2b] (coming into view)	apparition[3b]	Erscheinen[4b]	aparición[3a]
(be) ashamed[2b]	(avoir) honte[3a], (être) honteux[3a]	sich[1a] schämen[4a]	avergonzado (avergonzar[3a])
associate[3b] (*vb.*)	(s')associer[2a], (fréquenter[4b])	verkehren[3a]	asociar[4b]
audience[3b] (member of), (spectator[6])	spectateur[3b]	Zuschauer[3a], (Anwesende[6a])	espectador[3b], (circunstante[4a])
bag[1b], (sack[2b]), (pouch[6])	sac[2a], (bourse[3b])	Sack[5b], (Beutel[6b])	saco[4a], maleta[4b], (alforja[5a] [saddle-])
ball[1a] (dance)	bal[4a]	Ball[5a]	baile[2b]
basin[3b] (of river)	bassin[5a]	Bett[2a]	cuenca[5b], (cauce[6b])
bloom[2b] (*vb.*), blossom[2a]	fleurir[3a], (s')épanouir[3b]	blühen[4a]	florecer[3a]
(on) board[1b], (aboard[4b])	(à) bord[1a]	(an) Bord[5a]	(a) bordo[5b]
breakfast[1b] (*n.*)	déjeuner (*n.*)[2a]	Frühstück[5b]	desayuno[4b]
burst[2a] (out laughing)	éclater[1b]	anschlagen[5b]	echar[1a] (se), romper[1a] (a reír)
capacity[3b]	capacité[3b], (contenance[6b])	Gehalt[3a]	capacidad[3b]
carriage[2a], (bearing[8])	tournure[5a], pose[5b]	Haltung[3a]	porte[5a]
cave[1b], (cavern[6])	cave[3a]	Höhle[4b]	cueva[3b], (caverna[5b])
characteristic[5b] (*n.*), attribute[5b]	caractéristique[4b], (attribut[6a]), (propre [*n.*][6a])	Eigenschaft[1b], (Grundzug[3a]), (Eigentümlichkeit[4a]), (Eigenart[5b])	rasgo[2b], (atributo[5a]), (característica[5b])
charge[1b] (a price)	demander[1a]	anrechnen[6b]	cobrar[1b]
class[1b], (group[2b])	catégorie[6b]	Kategorie[5a]	categoría[3b]
cleaning (*n.*) (clean[1b])	nettoyage[6b]	Reinigung[4b]	limpieza[4a]
committee[3b]	comité[3a]	Kreisausschuß[3b], (Ausschuß[4a]), (Kommittee[5b])	comisión[3a], junta[3b]
conclusion[4b]	conclusion[3b]	Abschluß[2b]	conclusión[3a]
conference[4b]	conférence[3a]	Beratung[2a], (Unterredung[4b]), (Konferenz[5a]), (Unterhandlung[5b])	conferencia[3a], (consulta[6b])
consult[3b], (confer[4a]), (commune[6])	consulter[3a]	besprechen[7a]	consultar[3a]
copper[2b]	cuivre[2b]	Kupfer[4b]	cobre[4b]
creep[2b], (crept[3b]), (crawl[3b])	ramper[5a]	schleichen[4a], (kriechen[6a])	arrastrar[1b] se
crush[2b]	écraser[2b], (broyer[4b])	zerbrechen[4b], (zerschlagen[6b])	abrumar[4b], aplastar[4b], machacar[4b]
dealing[5a], (negotiation[7])	négociation[5a]	Verhandlung[1b]	trato[1b], (negociación[7b])
debate[3b], argument[3b]	argument[3a], (différend[5b]), (débat[6a])	Erörterung[3a], (Debatte[4a])	argumento[3b], (debate[6b])
decree[3b] (*vb.*)	arrêter[1a]	verfügen[3a]	decretar[5a]
demand[1b], (requirement[6]), (requisite[6])	exigence[5b]	Erfordernis[4a]	exigencia[5a]

English	French	German	Spanish
despair[3a] (*n.*)	désespoir[3a]	Verzweiflung[3a]	desesperación[3b]
discovery[3b]	découverte[3b]	Entdeckung[3a]	descubrimiento[3b]
display[3a] (*vb.*), (exhibit[4b])	étaler[3b]	ausstellen[3b], (aufweisen[4a])	desplegar[3a], (exhibir[5a])
disposed (dispose[2b]) (well – or ill –)	disposé (disposer[1a])	gesinnt[5b]	dispuesto (disponer[1a])
draft[3a] (sketch), (draught[4a])	brouillon[6b]	Entwurf[1b]	borrador
drinking (drink[1a]) (act of)	boire[1b]	Trinken[6b]	beber[1a]
elect[2a]	élire[4a], (élu[6a])	erwählen[4b]	elegir[2a]
electric[3a], (electrical[6])	électrique[3b]	elektrisch[3b]	eléctrico[3a]
embrace[3a] (*vb.*)	embrasser[1b]	umarmen[4a]	abrazar[1b]
endless[3b]	interminable[6b]	unendlich[2a], (endlos[6b])	interminable[4a]
errand[4a]	commission[3a]	Auftrag[2a]	recado[3b], (embajada[5b])
exclusively (exclusive[4b])	exclusivement[4a]	ausschließlich[2a]	exclusivamente (exclusivo[2b])
extol[5b]	préconiser[4b]	erheben[1a], (preisen[3a])	alabar[2b], (ensalzar[4a])
flatter[3a]	flatter[3a]	schmeicheln[3b]	halagar[3a], (adular[7a]), lisonjero[3b] (flattering)
fleet[2b] (*n.*)	flotte[6b]	Flotte[3b]	escuadra[4a], (armada[6b]), (flota[6b])
flow[1a] into[1a] (crowd, produce, river)	affluer	strömen[3a]	afluir[6b]
get[1a] up[1a] (rise[1b]) early[1a]	se lever[6a] tôt[1a], (de bonne heure)	früh[1a] aufstehen[4b]	madrugar[4a]
glow[2b], (luster[re][4b]), (brightness[5a])	brillant[2a]	Glut[4b]	fulgor[4b]
(with one's own) hand[1a]	(de sa propre) main[1a]	eigenhändig[6b]	(de propia) mano[1a]
(learn by) heart[1a]	(par) cœur[1a]	auswendig[6b]	(de) memoria[1a]
hell[3b]	enfer[4a]	Hölle[3b]	infierno[2a]
henceforth[3a]	dès[1a] maintenant[1a]	fortan[4b]	(de) ahora[1a] (en) adelante[1b]
hollow[2a] (*adj.*)	creux[3a]	hohl[4a]	hueco[3a]
(get) ill[1b]	(tomber) malade[1b]	erkranken[5b]	enfermar[5b], (adolecer[6b])
impose[4a]	imposer[1b]	auferlegen[3b]	imponer (+impuesto)[1b]
(well) informed (inform[2b])	(au) courant[1a], (s'y) connaître[1a]	geläufig[6b] (sein)	(al) corriente[1b]
(person) interested (interest[1b]), (concerned [concern[2b]])	intéressé (*n.*)[4a]	Interessent[5b]	interesado (interesar[2a])
invest[5a] (money)	placer[1b]	anlegen[2a]	colocar[1a] (dinero)
lawful[5b], legal[5b], (legitimate[7])	légitime[3a]	gesetzlich[1b], (gerichtlich[4b]), (gültig[4b]), (rechtmäßig[6b])	legítimo[3a], (legal[4b]), (lícito[4b])
lawyer[3b]	avocat[3a], (avoué [*n.*][6b])	Jurist[3b], (Advokat[5b])	abogado[3b]
(tell) lie[1b]	mentir[4a]	lügen[5a]	mentir[2a]
lunch[3b] (*vb.*)	déjeuner[3b]	zu[1a] Mittag[3a] essen[2b]	almorzar[3b]
magazine[4b]	revue[3b]	Zeitschrift[2b], (Wochenblatt[6b])	revista[3a]
manufacture[2b] (*vb.*)	fabriquer[3b]	anfertigen[4a], fertigen[4a], (verfertigen[6a])	fabricar[3b], (elaborar[6b])

English	French	German	Spanish
message[2a], (communication[4b])	communication[3a], (message[6b])	Botschaft[4b]	recado[3b]
mill[1b]	moulin[4a]	Mühle[5b]	molino[2b]
moderate[3a] (*adj.*)	modéré (modérer[3b])	mäßig[3a], (gemäßigt[6b])	moderado (moderar[3b]), (mediano[4a])
nail[2a] (*n.*), (tack[6])	clou[3b]	Nagel[4a]	clavo[3b]
nightly[6]	chaque[1a] nuit[1a], (toutes les nuits)	jede (jeder[1a]) Nacht[1a]	cada[1a] noche[1a], (todas las noches)
nought[5a]	néant[5a]	nichts[1a]	nada[1a]
object[1b] (grammatical)	complément[6b]	Objekt[4a]	complemento[4b]
opposition[4b]	opposition[3b]	Widerspruch[2a], Widerstand[2a], (Opposition[5a])	oposición[3b]
outlet[4b]	débouché	Absatz[1b]	salida[2a], (desembocadura)
outstretched (outstretch[6]) (arms)	(à bras) ouverts (ouvert[1b])	offen[1b]	(con brazos) abiertos (abrir[1a])
painter[3b]	peintre[3a]	Maler[3a]	pintor[3b]
performance[4b] (fulfilment)	exécution[3a]	Leistung[2a], (Durchführung[3a])	ejecución[3b]
post[1b] (*adj.*), (postal[5b])	postal[5b]	Post-[4b]	postal[5a]
post[1b] (*n.*), (pole[2a])	poteau[4b]	Stange[5a]	palo[2b], (estaca[5b])
(Great [great[1a]]) Power (power[1a])	puissance[1b]	Großmacht[6a]	poder[1b], (potencia[2b])
preach[2b]	prêcher[4a]	predigen[4a]	predicar[2b]
preparation[3b]	préparation[2a], (préparatifs [préparatif[4b]]), (apprêt[6b])	Vorbereitung[3a], (Bereitung[6b])	preparación[4a], (preparativo[5a]), (adobo[7b]) (of food)
preserve[2a] (*vb.*)	conserver[1b], (préserver[5b])	aufbewahren[4a], (verwahren[6a])	preservar[5a], (conserva[6a])
private[2a], privy[2b]	particulier[1b], (privé[3b])	privat[5b]	particular[1b], (privado [privar[2a]])
put[1a] over[1a], lay[1a] on[1a] (top)	superposer[5b]	auflegen[4b]	sobreponer[5a]
reader[4b] (person)	lecteur(-trice)[4b]	Leser[2a]	lector[2a]
reason[1a] (*vb.*)	raisonner[4b]	urteilen[4a]	razonar[6a]
register[3a] (*vb.*), (enroll[6])	enregistrer[3b]	eintragen[3b], (verzeichnen[4b]), (anmelden[5a])	registrar[3b]
retire[2b] (*intr. vb.*), (withdraw[3a])	se[1a] retirer[1a], (se replier[4a])	abtreten[5b], (zurückweichen[6b])	retirar[1a] se
rough[2a] (to touch)	rude[2a] (rudement[4a])	rauh[4a]	áspero[4a]
Russia(n)[3a]	russe[5b]	russisch[2a], (Russe[5b])	ruso[5b]
sail[1a] (*vb.*), (embark[6])	embarquer[3a]	an[1a] Bord[5a] gehen[1a]	embarcar[3a]
sea[1a] (*adj.*)	maritime[5b]	See-[4b]	marítimo[5a]
sheep[1b], (ram[4a]), (ewe[4b])	mouton[3a]	Schaf[5b]	carnero[3b], oveja[3b]
shipping (ship[1a])	navigation[5b]	Schiffahrt[4b], (Binnenschiffahrt[6b])	marina[5a], navegación[5a]
skill[3a], (craft[5a]), (prowess[6])	adresse[2a]	Geschick[3a], (Geschicklichkeit[4b]), (Fertigkeit[5b]), (Gewandtheit[6b])	tino[4a], maña[4b], (destreza[5b])

English	French	German	Spanish
somewhere[3b], (anywhere[4b])	quelque[1a] part[1a]	irgendwo[4b]	en[1a] alguna (algún[1a]) parte[1a]
spare[2a] (in reserve)	(de, en) réserve[3a]	in[1a] Vorrat[4a]	(de) sobra[3a]
spite[2a] (*n.*)	rancune[3b]	Trotz[4a]	rencor[3b]
stage[3a] (theatre)	scène[1b]	Bühne[3a]	escenario[5a], (tablado[6b])
standard[2b] (*adj.*)	(d')étalon	maßgebend[3a]	tipo[2a]
statesman[3b]	(homme d')État (état[1a])	Staatsmann[4a]	(hombre de) Estado (estado[1a])
(of) stone[1a]	(de, en) pierre[1b]	steinern[6a]	(de) piedra[1a]
strike[1b] (*n.*) (stopping work)	grève[4a]	Streik[4b], (Ausstand[6a])	huelga[6b]
subtle[5b]	subtil[4a]	fein[1b]	sutil[2b]
successive[5b]	successif[4b] (successivement[3b])	einander[1a] folgend[1a]	sucesivo[2b]
supply[1b] later (late[1a])	fournir[1b] plus tard	nachliefern[5a]	suministrar[5b] posteriormente (posterior[4b])
swing[2b] (*vb.*), (sway[3a])	balancer[2b], (osciller[6a])	schwingen[4b]	mecer[4a]
temperature[3b]	température[3a]	Temperatur[3a]	temperatura[3a]
tool[2b], (implement[5a])	outil[4b]	Werkzeug[3b]	herramienta[6a]
torrent[4b]	torrent[2b]	Strom[2b], (Guß[3b])	torrente[4b], (raudal[5a])
turn[1a], (revolution[4a])	tour (*m.*)[1a], (révolution[2a])	Drehung[6b]	vuelta[1b], (giro[2b]), (revolución[2b])
turn[1a] away[1a]	détourner[2a], (dévier[5a])	abwenden[5b]	desviar[4b]
upstairs[5b]	en[1a] haut (*n.*)[5b]	oben[1a]	arriba[1b]
(for) want[1a] of	(à) défaut[1b] de, (faute de[3b])	mangels[6a]	(a) falta[1a] de
want[1a] (*n.*), (scarcity[8])	défaut[1b], (manque[3b])	Ermangelung[6b]	falta[1a], (escasez[4b])
widow[3b]	veuve[4a]	Witwe[3a]	viuda (viudo[2a])
workmanship[6]	travail[1a], art[1b] (de) travailler[1a]	Arbeit[1a]	(el) trabajo[1a]
(make) worse[2a], (aggravate[6])	aggraver[5a]	erschweren[3b]	agraviar[5b]

SECTION 3.1. CONCEPTS 2651 THROUGH 2739

E F G S	*E F G S*	*E F G S*	*E F G S*	*E F G S*	*E F G S*	*E F G S*	*E F G S*	*E F G S*
1–1–5–6	1–4–5–3	1–8*–4–3	2–4 –4–3	3–1–4–2	3–5–3–2	4–2–2–5	4–5 –2–2	5–1–2–2
1–1–6–2	1–5–5–2	2–2 –4–5	2–5 –3–6	3–2–4–1	3–6–2–5	4–2–3–1	4–6 –1–5	5–2–2–1
1–2–6–1	1–5–4–6	2–2 –5–1	2–5 –4–2	3–3–3–4	3–6–3–1	4–3–2–4	4–6 –2–1	5–3–1–4
1–3–5–4	1–6–4–5	2–3 –4–4	2–8*–3–3	3–4–3–3	4–1–3–2	4–4–2–3	4–8*–1–3	5–4–1–3
								6–1–1–2

English	French	German	Spanish
accused (accuse[3b]) (*n.*)	accusé[5b], (inculpé[6a])	Angeklagte[3a]	acusado (acusar[2b])
addition[2b] (not mathematical)	addition[5b], (accroissement[6a])	Zusatz[3a], (Anschluß[4a]), (Zuschlag[5a]), (Beilage[6a])	añadidura[6a]
admirable[5b]	admirable[1b] (admirablement[4b])	vortrefflich[2b], wunderbar[2b]	admirable[2a]

English	French	German	Spanish
agreement[4b] (state)	accord[1b], (entente[4b])	Übereinstimmung[3a], (Verständigung[4b]), (Vereinbarung[5a]), (Einverständnis[5b]), (Abkommen[6a]), (Abrede[6a]), (Verabredung[6b])	acuerdo[2a], (solidaridad[6a])
aside[3a]	(à l')écart[2b]	seitwärts[4a], (beiseite)	(a un) lado[1a]
attract[3b], (entice[4b]), (allure[5b]), (lure[5b])	attirer[1b], tenter[1b], (séduire[4b]), (captiver[7a])	locken[4a]	atraer[2b], (cautivar[4b]), (seducir[4b])
avenue[2b]	allée[2b], (avenue[3a]), (boulevard[3b])	Chaußee[4b]	avenida[5b]
battery[4b] (military)	batterie[6a]	Batterie[1b]	batería[5b]
blind[1b], (shutter[6])	volet[5a]	Laden[4b]	celosía[6b]
boil[2a] (*vb.*)	bouillir[5a]	kochen[4a]	hervir[2a]
bury[2a]	enterrer[4a], (enfouir[7a])	begraben[4a]	enterrar[3b], (sepultar[4a])
cheat[4a]	tricher[6b]	betrügen[2b]	engañar[1b], ([hacer] trampa[7a])
clasp[3a], (hug[5b])	serrer[1b], (étreindre[4a]), (resserrer[5b])	umarmen[1a], (klammern[6b] [an])	estrechar[2b], (abarcar[4a])
confound[4b], confuse[4b]	confondre[2a], rendre[1a] confus[2a], (déconcerter[3b])	verwirren[3b]	confundir[1b], corrido (correr[1a])
contrast[4b] (*n.*)	contraste[3b]	Gegensatz[2a], (Kontrast[6b])	contraste[4b]
cut[1a] (off), (isolate[6])	isoler[4a]	absondern[5a], (isolieren[6a])	aislar[3a]
dance[1b] (*n.*)	danse[5a]	Tanz[5a]	baile[2b], (danza[4a]), (jota[6b]), (tango[6b]), ([baile] flamenco[6a])
den[3a]	repaire[6b]	Bau[2b], (Höhle[4b])	guarida[5a]
departure[5b]	départ[1b]	Abschied[2b], (Abzug[6a]), (Abreise[4b]), (Auszug[5b]), (Fortgang[5a]), (Abgang[6b]), (Abmarsch[6b])	partida[2a], salida[2a], (ida[6a])
description[3b]	description[4a]	Schilderung[3a], Beschreibung[3b], (Charakteristik[6a])	descripción[3b]
design[3a] (*n.*)	dessin[3a]	Zeichnung[3a]	designio[4b]
dine[2b]	dîner[2a]	speisen[5a]	comer[1a]
dominion[4b] (possession, title)	empire[3a]	Herrschaft[2a]	señorío[4b]
drive[1a] back[1a], (push[2a]), (repel[7])	repousser[1b]	zurückdrängen[6a]	rechazar[2b]
earthly[3b]	terrestre[5a]	irdisch[3a], (zeitlich[6a])	terreno[2a], (terrestre[6b])
employee[4b]	employé(-e)[3a]	Beamte[2a], (Handlungsgehilfe[5b])	empleado[4a]
encounter[3b] (*n.*) (friendly)	rencontre[1b]	Treffen[4b], (Zusammenkunft[5a])	encuentro[2a]
envy[3a] (*n.*)	envie[1b]	Neid[4b]	envidia[2b]
etc.[4b]	etc.	(und so) weiter (weit[1a])	etcétera[3b]
expedition[4a], campaign[4b], (crusade[8])	campagne[1a], (expédition[3a])	Feldzug[3a]	campaña[2a], (expedición[4b]), (cruzada[5b])
failure[5a]	échec[3b]	Fall[1a]	fracaso[4a]
fun[2a], (chaff[5a]), (mockery[6])	raillerie[5a], (moquerie[6b])	Spott[4b]	burla[2a]

English	French	German	Spanish
governor[2a], (ruler[3a])	gouverneur[4a]	Herrscher[4a], (Statthalter[5a]), (Gouverneur[6b])	gobernador[3a], (gobernante[5a])
handle[2a] (*n.*)	poignée[3b], (manche [*m.*][5a]), (anse[6b])	Heft[4a], (Griff[5b])	puño[4b], (mango[6b])
harmony[3b], (accord[4a])	accord[1b], (harmonie[4b])	Harmonie[4b], (Einklang[5a])	armonía[2b], (harmonía[6b])
(state of) health[1b]	(état de) santé[2a]	Befinden[6b]	(estado de) salud[1b]
illustrious[5b]	illustre[2b]	berühmt[2a]	ilustre[1b]
Indian[1b]	indien, hindou	indisch[4b]	indio[3a], (indiano[5a])
indoors[6]	(à la) maison[1a], (dedans[2b])	(im) Hause (Haus[1a])	adentro[2b], bajo[1a] techo[2b]
inspire[4b]	inspirer[2a]	begeistern[3b], (einflößen[5b])	inspirar[1b], (infundir[3b])
jewel[3a], (jewelry[4b])	bijou[4a], (joyau[6a])	Schmuck[3b]	alhaja[3b], (dije[6a]), (pedrería[6a])
lend[3a], (lent[4b])	prêter[2a]	leihen[4b]	prestar[1b]
look[1a] (over), (review[2b])	revoir[1b], (repasser[4a])	durchgehen[5b]	repasar[6b]
male[3b]	mâle[5a]	männlich[3b]	varón[2a], (macho[5a])
manifest[4a] (*vb.*)	manifester[6a]	ausdrücken[2b]	manifestar[1b]
martyr[4b]	martyr[3b]	Opfer[2a]	mártir[4a]
minute[1b] (*adj.*)	minutieux[4a], (menu[6a])	umständlich[5b]	minucioso[3b]
mist[3a], (fog[4a])	brouillard[3b], brume[3b]	Nebel[3a]	niebla[4a], (bruma[5a])
morning[1a] (*adj.*)	matinal[5b]	Morgen-[4a]	matinal[6a]
mould[4a] (*n.*) (form)	moule	Form[1a]	molde[3b]
mourning (mourn[2b])	deuil[3a]	Trauer[4b]	luto[4a]
mutual[4b]	réciproque[5a]	gegenseitig[2b], (beiderseitig[5a]), (untereinander[5b])	mutuo[2b], (recíproco[6a])
nail[2a] (finger)	ongle[4b]	Nagel[4a]	uña[3b]
net[2b] (*n.*)	filet[4a], (réseau[6a])	Netz[4a]	red[3a], (malla[5b])
oak[1b]	chêne[3b]	Eiche[5b]	encina[4b], (roble[6a])
overthrow[4a]	renverser[2a]	stürzen[2b]	volcar[5a]
performance[4b] (theatre)	représentation[4a]	Vorstellung[2a]	representación[3a]
pierce[3b]	percer[2b], (trouer[4b])	durchbrechen[4b], (durchbohren[6a]), (durchschlagen[6b])	atravesar[1b], (calar[3a]), (agujerear[6a])
poison[3a] (*n.*)	poison[4b], (venin[6b])	Gift[3b]	veneno[3b]
prophet[3a]	prophète[4b]	Prophet[3b]	profeta[3b]
proposition[5b]	proposition[3a]	Antrag[1a]	proposición[4a], (propuesta[6a])
reality[5b]	réalité[2a]	Wirklichkeit[2a]	realidad[1b]
reel[3b], (stagger[4a]), (totter[6])	chanceler[4b], vaciller[4b], (osciller[6a])	schwanken[3a]	vacilar[3a]
refer[3b] (to), (allude[7])	(faire) allusion[3a] (à)	verweisen[3b]	aludir[4b], (referente[5b])
renounce[4b]	renoncer[1b], (abdiquer[7a])	verzichten[3a], (entsagen[4a]), (Verzicht[5b] leisten[1b])	renunciar[2b]
required (require[1b]), (compulsory[8])	obligatoire[5b]	obligatorisch[5a], (verbindlich[6a])	forzoso[2b], (obligatorio[7a])
ribbon[2b], (tape[6])	ruban[4a]	Band[4a]	cinta[3b]
run[1a] through[1a]	parcourir[2a]	durchlaufen[6a]	recorrer[1b]

English	French	German	Spanish
settle[1b] (down), (alight[5b])	(se) poser[1a]	niederlassen[5a]	posar[6a] se
soften[4b]	attendrir[3a]	weich[2b] machen[1a]	ablandar[4a], suavizar[4b]
speaker[3b], (orator[6])	orateur[4a]	Redner[3a], Vorredner[3a], (Referent[4b])	orador[3b]
staff[3b] (military)	état-major[6a]	Generalstab[3a]	estado[1a] mayor[1a]
stamp[2a] (*n.*)	timbre[4a]	Stempel[4a], (Gepräge[6b])	sello[3a], estampa[3b], (timbre[5a])
(gold) standard[2b]	étalon (or)	Goldwährung[3b]	patrón[3a] oro[1a]
steel[2a]	acier[4b]	Stahl[4b]	acero[3a]
stop[1a] up[1a] (obstruct)	obstruer[6a], boucher (*vb.*)[6b]	hemmen[4a]	tupir[5a]
stray[3b] (*vb.*)	égarer[3b]	verfahren[3a], (verlaufen[5a])	extraviar[4b]
student[2b]	étudiant[4a]	Student[4b]	estudiante[3b]
succession[5b]	succession[4b]	Folge[1a]	sucesión[3b]
summing (sum[2a]) (up) (*n.*), (summary[9])	résumé[4b], (sommaire[5b])	Wiederholung[4b]	resumen[3b], (compendio[6b])
testimony[4b]	témoignage[4a]	Zeugnis[7a]	testimonio[3a]
text[3b]	texte[3a]	Text[3a], (Wortlaut[5a])	texto[4b]
torment[3b] (*vb.*), (harrow[6])	tourmenter[4a], (harasser[6b])	quälen[3b], (plagen[6a])	atormentar[3b]
train[1a] (military) (of baggage)	train[1b]	Train[6a]	tren[1b]
triumph[3b] (*n.*)	triomphe[2b]	Triumph[4a]	triunfo[1b]
uniform[3a] (*adj.*)	uniforme[3b]	einheitlich[3b]	uniforme[4a]
whisper[2a] (*vb.*)	chuchoter[5b]	flüstern[4a]	murmurar[2a], (susurrar[6b])
will[1a] (*n.*), (testament [T][7])	testament[6a]	Testament[4a]	testamento[5b]
wrong[1a] (*n.*), (injury[4a])	tort[1b]	Unrecht[5a]	sinrazón[6b]

SECTION 3.2. CONCEPTS 2740 THROUGH 2846

E F G S	*E F G S*	*E F G S*	*E F G S*	*E F G S*	*E F G S*	*E F G S*	*E F G S*
1–1–6–3	1–6–5–2	2–3–4–5	2–5–4–3	3–2–4–2	3–5–3–3	4–3–2–5	5–1–2–3
1–2–6–2	2–1–5–3	2–3–5–1	2–6–3–6	3–3–3–5	3–6–3–2	4–3–3–1	5–2–2–2
1–3–6–1	2–2–4–6	2–4–3–8*	3–1–4–3	3–3–4–1	4–1–3–3	4–4–2–4	5–6–1–2
1–4–5–4	2–2–5–2	2–4–4–4	3–2–3–6	3–4–3–4	4–2–3–2	4–5–[illegible]	6–2–1–2

English	French	German	Spanish
ability[4b], (faculty[5a])	adresse[2a], faculté[2b], (habileté[4a]), (aptitude[4b])	Fähigkeit[3a], (Veranlagung[5a])	facultad[2a], habilidad[2b], (acierto[3b]), (aptitud[5a])
absence[3b]	absence[3b]	Abwesenheit[4b]	ausencia[2a]
affect[3a]	affecter[2b], (impressionner[4b])	einwirken[4a]	afectar[2b], (impresionar[5a])
aim[2b] (*vb.*) (point gun)	viser[2b], (pointer[5a]), (braquer[6a])	zielen[5b]	apuntar[2b]
arrow[2b], (shaft[4a])	flèche[4a]	Pfeil[4a]	flecha[4a], (dardo[5b]), (saeta[6a])
artificial[4b]	artificiel[4b], (factice[6b])	künstlich[2b]	artificial[4b], (postizo[6b])
(on the) average[3a]	(en) moyenne[3b]	(im) Durchschnitt[4a], durchschnittlich[4a]	medio[1a], (media[3b]), (promedio[7b])
balance[2b] (*vb.*)	balancer[2b], (équilibrer[5a])	ausgleichen[4a], (Bilanz[6b] ziehen[1a])	balancear[6a]
bead[3b]	perle[3b]	Perle[4b]	cuenta[1a]

English	French	German	Spanish
beard[2b]	barbe[2b]	Bart[5b]	barba[2a]
blame[2a] (*n.*)	critique (*f.*)[3b]	Tadel[5a]	culpa[1b], (censura[5a])
care[1a], charge[1b], (supervision[9])	surveillance[4a], (vigilance[6a])	Aufsicht[5a]	vigilancia[4b]
carry[1a] (back)	reporter[3b]	zurückbringen[6b]*	(volver a) llevar[1a]
chamber[2a] (of) commerce[2b]	chambre[1a] (de) commerce[2a]	Handelskammer[5b]	cámara[2b] (de) comercio[2b]
chant[5a] (*vb.*)	chanter[1b]	singen[2a]	entonar[3b]
check[2a] (*n.*)	contrôle[4b]	Kontrolle[3b]	control
check[2a], control[2b], (restrain[3b]), (curb[4b])	réprimer[4a]	hemmen[4a]	reprimir[4a]
civil[3a], polite[3b], (gallant[4a])	poli[2b], (galant[4b]) (poliment[4a])	höflich[4b]	galán[2a], (cortés[3b]), (galante[5a]), (urbano[6a])
confused (confuse[4b])	confus[2a]	verwirrt[3b]	confuso[2a]
confusion[3b]	trouble[2a], (confusion[6a])	Verwirrung[4b]	confusión[2a], (turbación[5a]), (trastorno[5b])
contest[3b] (*vb.*)	contester[6a]	bestreiten[3a]	luchar[2a], (discutir[3b])
contribute[5b]	contribuer[2b], (concourir[5b])	beitragen[2b], (spenden[5b])	contribuir[2a]
cool[1b] (*n.*)	fraîcheur[3a]	Frische[6b]	fresco[1b], (frescura[3a])
copy[2a] (*n.*) (reproduction)	copie[4a]	Abbildung[4a], (Abdruck[5a]), (Abschrift[5b]), (Kopie[5b]), (Nachbildung[6a])	copia[4b]
copy[2a] (*vb.*), (imitate[4b]), (ape[6])	imiter[2a]	nachahmen[5b], (nachmachen[6a])	imitar[2a], (copiar[3b]), (remedar[6a])
crew[2b] (ship)	équipage[4b]	Mannschaft[3a], (Besatzung[4b])	tripulación, dotación
defy[3b], (challenge[6])	défier[3a]	auffordern[3b]	desafiar[5a]
deprive[5b]	priver[2b]	entziehen[2a]	privar (+privado)[2a]
dip[3a], plunge[3a] (*tr. vb.*)	plonger[2a]	tauchen[4a]	hundir[2a]
draw[1a] up[1a] (e.g., document)	rédiger[4a]	aufsetzen[5b]	redactar[4b]
ease[2b], comfort[2a]	aise[2a], (aisance[4b])	Bequemlichkeit[5b], (Behagen[6b])	comodidad[2b]
embarrass[5b]	embarrasser[2a], gêner[2a], (déconcerter[3b])	verlegen[2b] machen[1a], ([in] Verlegenheit[3a] setzen[1a])	turbar[2a], ([poner en] apuro[3b]), (desconcertar[5a])
emotion[5b] (e.g., speak with –)	émoi[6a]	Bewegung[1a], (Bewegtheit)	emoción[2a]
(real) estate[3a]	immeuble[4a]	Grundstück[3a]	finca[4a]
farm[1a], (plantation[5a]), (grange[6])	ferme (*n.*)[2a]	Gehöft[6a]	hacienda[2a], (heredad[5a]), (cortijo[6a]), (predio[6b])
fifteen[2a]	quinze[1a], (quinzaine[6a])	fünfzehn[5a]	quince[3]*
flood[2b] (*n.*)	déluge[6a], inondation[6b]	Flut[3b]	diluvio[6b]
flour[2a]	farine[5b]	Mehl[4a]	harina[3a]
follower[4b], (attendant[5a]), (disciple[8])	partisan[4a], adhérent[4b], (disciple[5b])	Jünger[2b], (Anhänger[3b])	partidario[4a], (discípulo[5a])
folly[3a]	folie[2a]	Torheit[4a]	locura[2a], (desatino[3b]), (temeridad[4a]), (tontería[4a]), (extravagancia[5b]), (sandez[6b])
ghost[2b], (phantom[6])	esprit[1a], (apparition[3b]), (fantôme[4a])	Gespenst[5a]	fantasma[3b], (espectro[5a])

English	French	German	Spanish
grandfather[3a], (grandpa[4b])	grand-père[3b], (aïeul[4b])	Großvater[4b]	abuelo[1b]
heap[2b] (up), (hoard[6]), (stack[6])	entasser[4b], (accumuler[5a]), (amasser[7a])	häufen[4b]	colmar[4a], amontonar[4b], (acumular[6a])
hearth[3b], (fireplace[6])	cheminée[2a], foyer[2a]	Herd[4b], (Kamin[5b])	hogar[2a]
hotel[3a]	hôtel[1b]	Hotel[4b]	hotel[3b], (fonda[5a])
hunger[3a]	faim[3a]	Hunger[4b]	hambre[1b]
ideal[4a] (*adj.* and *n.*)	idéal[2b]	ideal[3b], Ideal[3a]	ideal[2a]
individual[3a] (*n.*)	individu[2a]	Individuum[4b]	individuo[2a]
industrious[4a], diligent[4b]	appliqué (appliquer[1b]), (laborieux[5a]), (assidu[7a])	fleißig[3a]	trabajador[3a], (laborioso[4b]), (diligente[5a]), (hacendoso[5b]), (asiduo[7a])
influence[2b] (*vb.*), (sway[3a])	influencer[5a]	einwirken[4a]	influir[3a]
inhabitant[4b], (tenant[5a]), (resident[5b])	habitant[2b], (locataire[6a])	Bewohner[3a], Einwohner[3a]	habitante[2b], (morador[4b]), (residente[5a])
install[5b]	installer[1b]	einrichten[2a], anbringen[2b]	instalar[3b]
instance[3a]	instance[4b]	Instanz[3b]	instancia[4a]
instinct[4b]	instinct[2a]	Trieb[4b]	instinto[2b]
interesting[5b]*	intéressant[2a]	interessant[2a]	interesante[2a]
intimate[5b] (*adj.*)	intime[2a]	innig[2a]	íntimo[2a]
invitation[3a]	invitation[4b]	Aufforderung[3b], (Einladung[4b])	convite[4b], (invitación[7a])
land[1a] (*vb.*) (go ashore)	débarquer[4a]	landen[5a]	desembarcar[4a]
landscape[4b]	paysage[2b]	Landschaft[3b]	paisaje[4b]
(commercial[3b]) law[1a]	loi[1b] commerciale (commercial[4a])	Handelsrecht[3b]	ley[1a] comercial[4a], (ley[1a] mercantil[6a])
lighting (light[1a])	éclairage[6a]	Beleuchtung[5a]	alumbrado (alumbrar[2a])
major[4a] (*n.*)	commandant[3b]	Major[2a]	comandante[5b]
mark[1a] (*vb.*) (characterize)	caractériser[4a]	kennzeichnen[5b]	caracterizar[4a]
meal[2a] (repast)	repas[2a]	Mahlzeit[5b], (Mahl[6a])	comida[2a]
moonlight[4b]	clair[1a] (de) lune[2b]	Mondschein[3b]	luz[1a] (de la) luna[2a]
native[2a] (*adj.*)	indigène[4a], (natal[5b])	inländisch[4a], einheimisch[4b], heimisch[4b], (eingeboren[5a]), (angeboren[6a])	indígena[4b], natal[4b], (criollo[5b]), (patrio[5a]), (nativo[6b])
nod[1b] (*vb.*)	incliner[3b], (hocher[4a])	nicken[5b]	inclinar[1b]
nourish[4b]	nourrir[2a]	nähren[3a], (ernähren[5b])	alimentar[2b], (nutrir[4b])
obedient[4b]	obéissant (obéir[1b]), (docile[4b]), (soumis [*adj.*][5b]) (docilement[6b])	gehorsam[3b]	dócil[3b], (obediente[5a]), (sumiso[5b])
painful[4b], (grievous[5a])	pénible[2a], (douloureux[3a]) (péniblement[4b]), (douloureusement[5a])	schmerzlich[3a], (peinlich[4a])	doloroso[2b], (penoso[3a])
painting[5b]*, (portrait[9])	portrait[2b], (peinture[3b])	Gemälde[2b], Fresko[2b], (Malerei[4a]), (Porträt[5a]), (Bildnis[6b])	retrato[2a], pintura[2b], (retratar[4b]) (make –)
passenger[3a]	passager (*n.*)[5a]	Reisende[3a]	pasajero[3a]
persecute[5b]	persécuter[6b]	verfolgen[1b]	perseguir[2a]
phenomenon[6]	phénomène[2b]	Erscheinung[1b]	fenómeno[2b]
pipe[2a], (tube[4a])	tuyau[4b], (tube[5a])	Röhre[4a]	tubo[4b]

English	French	German	Spanish
prevail[3a]	prévaloir[4b]	überwiegen[3b], (vorwiegen[5b]), (obwalten[6a])	predominar[4b], (prevalecer[5a])
purchase[2a] (*n.*)	achat[4b], (acquisition[5b])	Kauf[4a], (Ankauf[5b]), (Einkauf[6b])	compra[4a]
race[1b] (ethnic)	race[2a]	Rasse[6a]	raza[2a], (casta[3a]), (linaje[3b]), (estirpe[6a])
rage[3a] (*vb.*) (war, disease, etc.)	sévir[6b]	wüten[3b]	reinar[2a], (imperar[4b])
reception[4b]	accueil[3a], (réception[4b])	Aufnahme[2b], (Empfang[3a])	acogida[5a], (recibimiento[6b])
reform[4b] (*n.*)	réforme[4a]	Reform[2b], (Steuerreform[4b]), (Neuerung[5b]), (Erneuerung[6a]), (Reformation[6a])	reforma[4b]
reject[4b], (spurn[5b])	rejeter[2b]	verwerfen[3b], zurückweisen[3b], (abweisen[4a])	rechazar[2b], (desechar[4a])
rejoice[2a]	réjouir[2a]	jubeln[5b], (jauchzen[6b])	alegrar[2a] (se), (regocijar[5a] [se])
reputation[4b], (repute[6])	réputation[3a]	Ruf[2a]	reputación[5b]
reserve[3a] (*n.*) (character)	réserve[3a]	Reserve[3a], (Zurückhaltung[6b])	reserva[5a]
resolution[4b]	résolution[2b]	Resolution[3b], (Entschließung[5b]), (Kommissionsbeschluß[5b])	resolución[2a], empeño[2b], (determinación[4a])
revolution[4a]	révolution[2a]	Revolution[3a]	revolución[2b]
rub[2b], (chafe[6])	frotter[3a]	reiben[4b]	frotar[5b], (restregar[6a])
shed[2a], (hut[3a]), (cabin[3b])	case[5a], hutte[5a], (cabane[6b])	Hütte[4a]	barraca[3b], (cabaña[4a]), (choza[5a])
shock[2b] (sensibilities)	scandaliser[4b]	ärgern[4a]	escandalizar[4b]
shoe[1b]	soulier[2b], (sabot[3b]), (chaussure[4b])	Schuh[6a]	zapato[2b], (calzado[6a])
sink[2a], (sank[4a]), (sunk[4a]), (founder[4b])	enfoncer[2a], (s'affaisser[5a]), (effondrer[5b]), (sombrer[6b])	versinken[5a], (versenken[6b])	hundir[2a], (sumergir[4a])
solid[3a], (compact[5a])	solide[2a], (massif [*adj.*][4a]) (solidement[5b])	solid[4a], (derb[6a])	sólido[2b], (macizo[4b])
spear[3a], (lance[4a])	trait (*n.*)[1b]	Lanze[4a]	lanza[3a], (pica[6b])
stiff[2b]	raide[3b]	starr[4a], (steif[5b])	rígido[5a]
sunshine[2b], (sunlight[4b])	lumière[1a] (du) soleil[1a], (clarté[2b] [du] soleil[1a])	Sonnenschein[5a]	luz[1a] solar[3a]
temporary[4b]	provisoire[5b] (provisoirement[6a])	vorläufig[2b]	temporal[3b]
tendency[5b]	tendance[4a], (penchant[5b])	Neigung[1b], (Tendenz[3b])	tendencia[4a]
theme[4b] (paper)	composition[3a], (mémoire [*m.*][4b])	Aufsatz[3a]	memoria[1a]
time[1a] (music)	mesure[1a]	Takt[6a]	compás[3a]
transport[3b], (transportation[4b])	transport[2b]	Transport[3b], (Beförderung[4a])	transporte[6b]
(pay) tribute[4a] (to)	honorer[4a]	ehren[2a]	tributar[4a]
trick[2b] (*n.*)	tour (*m.*)[1a], (niche[5a])	List[5a], Kunststück[5b]	artificio[3b], (maña[4b]), (argucia[7a])
vice[3a]	vice (*n.*)[2b]	Laster[4a]	vicio[2a]

English	French	German	Spanish
wand[3b]	baguette[5b]	Stab[3a]	vara[3a]
worry[3b], fret[3a]	inquiéter[2a], (préoccuper[6a]), ([se faire de la] bile[6a])	beunruhigen[4a], kümmern[4a]	preocupar[2b], (inquietar[5a])
wrong[1b], (misdeed[14])	méfait[6b]	Unrecht[5a]	mal (*n.*)[2a], (sinrazón[6b])

SECTION 3.3. CONCEPTS 2847 THROUGH 2950

E F G S	*E F G S*	*E F G S*	*E F G S*	*E F G S*	*E F G S*	*E F G S*	*E F G S*	*E F G S*	*E F G S*
1-1-5-8*	1-5 -5-4	2-2-4-7	2-4-4-5	3-1-4-4	3-4-3-5	3-8*-2-5	4-3-3-2	5-1-1-8*	5-5 -1-4
1-1-6-4	1-6 -5-3	2-2-5-3	2-4-5-1	3-2-4-3	3-4-4-1	4-1 -2-8*	4-4-2-5	5-2-2-3	5-8*-1-1
1-3-5-6	1-8*-4-5	2-3-4-6	2-5-3-8*	3-3-3-6	3-5-2-8*	4-1 -3-4	4-4-3-1	5-3-2-2	6-3 -1-2
1-3-6-2	1-8*-5-1	2-3-5-2	2-6-4-3	3-3-4-2	3-6-3-3	4-2 -3-3	4-6-2-3	5-4-3-1	

English	French	German	Spanish
activity[6]	activité[3a]	Tätigkeit[1b]	actividad[2b]
agricultural[4b]	agricole[4b]	landwirtschaftlich[2b]	agrícola[5a]
(first) appearance[2b]	début[2a]	(erstes) Auftreten[4a]	debut[7b]
ash(es)[3b]	cendre[3b]	Asche[4b]	ceniza[2b], (ceniciento[6a]) (*adj.*)
bishop[4b]	évêque[3a]	Bischof[3b]	obispo[2b]
borrow[3a]	emprunter[4b]	Anleihe[4a] aufnehmen[1b], leihen[4b]	tomar[1a] prestado (prestar[1b])
brain[3a]	cerveau[3a], cervelle[3a]	Gehirn[4a]	cerebro[2a], (seso[4a])
camp[2a] (*vb.*), (encamp[6])	camper[5a]	lagern[3b]	acampar
carve[3b] (general)	découper[3a]	schneiden[3a]	recortar[6b], (trinchar[7b])
chances (chance[1b]), (probability[7])	probabilité	Wahrscheinlichkeit[4a]	probabilidad[5b]
cherish[5a]	chérir	(mit) Liebe[1a] behandeln[1b]	querer[1a], estimar[1b]
childhood[4a], (infancy[6])	enfance[2b]	Kindheit[3b]	infancia[6b], (niñez[4a])
chimney[2b]	cheminée[2a]	Kamin[5b]	chimenea[3b]
Christ[3b], (Jesus[5b])	Christ[5a]	Christus[2a], Jesus[2b]	Cristo, Jesús
circular[4a] (*adj.*)	circulaire[6b]	rund[2b]	circular[6a], (rotundo[6b])
column[3a], (pillar[4a])	colonne[3b], (pilier[4b])	Säule[4a]	columna[2a]
conquest[3b]	conquête[3a]	Eroberung[4b]	conquista[2a]
conscious[4b] (of), sensible[4b] (of), (aware[5b] [of])	sensible[2b]	empfindlich[3b]	sensible[3a]
considerable[4a]	considérable[3a]	beträchtlich[3b]	considerable[3b]
copy[2a] (*n.*), (imitation[8])	imitation[6b]	Nachahmung[4a]	imitación[3b]
country[1a] house[1a] (establishment)	maison[1a] (de) campagne[1a], (villa[5b])	Villa[6b]	quinta[4a]
date[1b] (*vb.*)	dater[3b]	datieren[5b]	datar[6a], (fechar[7a])
decline[3b], (lessen[5b]), (abate[6]), (dwindle[6]), (ebb[6])	atténuer[4b], (amoindrir[7a])	vermindern[4a], (ermäßigen[6b])	reducir[1b], (disminuir[2b]), (rebajar[5b]), (declinar[6a])
discuss[4a]	discuter[2a]	besprechen[3a], (bereden[5b])	discutir[3b]
distribute[5a]	distribuer[3b], (répartir[4a])	verteilen[2b]	repartir[2a], (distribuir[3b])
ear[1a] (hearing)	ouïe	Gehör[5a]	oído[1b]
ease[2b] (*n.*) (facility)	facilité[3b], (aisance[4b])	Leichtigkeit[5a]	facilidad[2b], (soltura[5a])

English	French	German	Spanish
(full of) energy[4b], (energetic[8])	énergique[3b] (énergiquement[5b])	energisch[3a]	enérgico[2b]
enlarge[4a], (dilate[6]), (expand[6])	élargir[3a], (amplifier[5b])	weiten[3b]	dilatar[2b], (ensanchar[3b]), (ampliar[6a])
excess[4a], extra[4a]	excès[2b], (surplus[4a])	Überschuß[3a]	exceso[3a], sobra[3a], (demasía[5a])
expectation[4b]	prévision[4a]	Erwartung[3a], Ahnung[3b]	esperanza[1a], (previsión[6a])
expense[2b]	frais (*n.*)[2a], dépense[2a], (dépens[5b])	Aufwand[5a], Auslage[5b], (Unkosten[6a])	gasto[3a], (coste[7b])
faint[2a] (*vb.*)	s'évanouir[3b]	ohnmächtig[5a] (werden), ([in] Ohnmacht[6a] [fallen])	desvanecer[2b], (desmayar[3a])
familiar[2b], (intimate[5b])	familier[2b] (familièrement[6b])	befreundet[5b], vertraulich[5b]	familiar[3a]
female[3a] (*adj.*)	féminin[6a]	weiblich[3a]	femenino[3b], hembra[3b]
fever[2b]	fièvre[2b]	Fieber[5a]	fiebre[3a], (calentura[4b])
flash[2a] (of) lightning[3a]	éclair[3b]	Blitz[4b]	relámpago[2b]
freeze[2b], frozen[2b]	glacer[3a], (geler[4b])	erstarren[5b]	helar[2a]
furnish[2a] (room, house)	garni[4b], (meubler[5a])	ausstatten[4a], (möblieren)	amueblar[5b]
globe[3a]	globe[6b]	Kugel[3b]	globo[3b]
globe[3a] (earth), sphere[3b], (orb[5a])	globe[6b]	Kugel[3b]	globo[3b], orbe[3b]
graceful[4a]	gracieux[3b]	zierlich[3b], (anmutig[4a])	gracioso[2a], gentil[2b], (gallardo[3a])
gratitude[4a]	reconnaissance[2b], (gratitude[4b])	Dankbarkeit[3b]	agradecimiento[3a], gratitud[3a], (reconocimiento[4a])
historic[5b]	historique[2b]	historisch[2a], (geschichtlich[3a])	histórico[3b]
imperial[4a]	impérial[6b]	kaiserlich[2a]	imperial[3b]
institute[3b] (*vb.*)	instituer[5a]	einrichten[2a]	instituir
insurance[5b], assurance[5b]	assurance[4a]	Versicherung[2a], (Lebensversicherung[6a])	seguro[1a], (aseguro)
kindly[2a]	aimable[2a], (bienveillant[6a])	gemütlich[5b]	bondadoso[3b]
link[3b] (in chain)	chaînon	Glied[2a]	eslabón[5a]
literary[5b]	littéraire[3a]	literarisch[2b]	literario[2b]
loaf[4b] (bread)	pain[1b]	Brot[2b]	bollo, hogaza
lonely[4b], solitary[4a], (lonesome[5a]), (forlorn[5b])	solitaire[3b]	einsam[3a]	solitario[2b]
(full of) meaning[5b]*, (significant[7])	expressif[5a], significatif[5a]	bedeutend[1b], (bedeutsam[5a])	expresivo[4a], (significativo[6a])
melting (melt[2a]) (of metals)	fonte[5b]	Guß[3b]	fundición
monarch[3b]	monarque[6a]	Monarch[3b]	monarca[3a]
Monday[2a]	lundi[4b]	Montag[4a]	lunes[5b]
murder[3a] (*n.*)	meurtre[3b], (assassinat[5b])	Mord[3b]	homicidio[6b]
nest[1b]	nid[3b]	Nest[6a]	nido[2b]
night[1a] (*adj.*)	nocturne[6b]	nächtlich[5b]	nocturno[3b]
one[1a] after[1a] (the) other[1a], (in[1a] succession[5b])	successivement[3b]	hintereinander[6a]	sucesivo[2b], (sucesivamente)
overcome[3b] (to be)	subjugué	unterliegen[2b]	subyugado (subyugar[5b])

English	French	German	Spanish
pale[2b] (*vb.*)	pâlir[3a]	bleich[4b] werden[1a], (blaß[5a] werden[1a])	palidecer[6b]
pane[4b]	vitre[2b], (carreau[4a])	Scheibe[3b]	vidrio[3a]
paragraph[5b]	paragraphe	Paragraph[1a], Absatz[1b], (Abschnitt[2b])	aparte[1a], (párrafo[3b])
permission[4b]	permission[3a]	Erlaubnis[3a], Zulassung[3b], (Bewilligung[5a])	licencia[2b], (permiso[3a])
philosopher[4b]	philosophe[3b]	Philosoph[3b], (Denker[6b])	filósofo[2b]
philosophy[4a]	philosophie[3a]	Philosophie[3a], (Weltanschauung[6a])	filosofía[2b]
pointed (point[1a])	aigu[3a], (pointu[4b])	gespitzt (spitzen[6a])	agudo[2b], (puntiagudo[6a])
pope (P)[3b]	pape[3b]	Papst[3a]	papa[6b]
porter[4b], (carrier[5a]), (bearer[5b])	facteur[3b], porteur[3b], (commissionnaire[4b])	Träger[3b]	mozo[1b] (de) cuerda[2b], (portador[5b])
post-office[5b]	poste[2a]	Post[2a]	casa[1a] (de) correos (correo[3b]), (posta[6b])
preference[6]	préférence[3b]	Vorzug[1b]	afición[2b], (preferencia[3b])
problem[3a]	problème[2b]	Problem[4a]	problema[3a]
prudent[4b], (cautious[6])	prudent[3a]	vorsichtig[3b]	prudente[2b], (cuerdo[4a]), (cauto[6a]), (cauteloso[6b]), (juicioso[6b])
	(prudemment[6a])		
queer[illegible] person[1a]	original[3a]	Original[4a]	original[7b]
receipt[6b] (receiving)	réception[4b]	Empfang[3a]	recibo[5a]
receipts (receipt[3b]) (e.g., for expenditures)	recettes (recette[4a])	Einnahme[3a]	recibo[5a]
relief[3a]	soulagement[6a]	Erleichterung[3a], (Befreiung[4a]), (Entlastung[5a]), (Ablösung[6a])	alivio[3b], (desahogo[4b])
robe[3a] (e.g., hermit's)	robe[1b]	Gewand[4b]	túnica[4a]
rope[2b], string[2b], (cord[3b]), (cable[4b])	corde[3a], (cordon[4a]), (câble[5b])	Schnur[5b], (Strick[6a])	cuerda[2b], (cable[5b]), (cordón[6a]), (cordel[7a])
rural[3b], (rustic[4b])	rustique[6a]	ländlich[3a]	rústico[3a], (rural[6b])
schoolroom[5a]	salle[1b] (de) classe[1b]	Klasse[1b]	aula
scorn[3a] (*n.*), (contempt[4b]), (disdain[4b])	mépris[3a], (dédain[5a])	Verachtung[4a], (Hohn[6b])	desdén[2b], desprecio[2b]
sex[4b]	sexe[6a]	Geschlecht[2a]	sexo[3a]
shame[2a] (*n.*)	honte[3a]	Scham[5b]	vergüenza[2a], (desvergüenza[5b]), (sonrojo[6b])
shed[2a] (*vb.*) (e.g., tree)	(se) dépouiller[3a]	ausfallen[4a], (abfallen[5b])	deshojar[6a] (se)
silk[1b] (*adj.*), (silken[6])	(de) soie[3a]	seiden[6a]	(de) seda[2b]
slight[2a], (slender[3b])	mince[2a], (élancé[6a]), (grêle [*adj.*][6a])	schlank[5a]	delgado[3a], (esbelto[5b])
sore[2b] (*n.*)	plaie[4a]	Wunde[4a]	llaga[5b]
spiritual[4b]	spirituel[2b]	geistlich[3a]	espiritual[3a]
stove[3a]	fourneau[5a], poêle (*m.*)[5a]	Ofen[2b]	estufa
stride[4b] (*vb.*)	marcher[1a] (à grand pas), (enjamber[5b])	schreiten[2a]	tranquear
take[1a] off[1a] (clothes), (undress[7])	déshabiller[6a]	ausziehen[5a]	desnudar[3b] (se)
theory[5b]	théorie[2b]	Theorie[2b]	teoría[3b]

English	French	German	Spanish
thirst[3a]	soif[3b]	Durst[4a]	sed[2b]
(home[1a] [native[2a]]) town[1a]	ville[1a] natale (natal[5b])	Vaterstadt[5b]	ciudad[1a] (pueblo[1a]) natal[4b]
university[3a]	université[6b]	Universität[3a]	universidad[3b]
unjust[3b]	injuste[3b]	ungerecht[4a], (unrecht[6b])	injusto[2b]
vanity[3b]	vanité[3a], amour-propre[3b]	Eitelkeit[4a]	vanidad[2a]
wash[1b] (*n.*) (clothes), (laundry[5b])	linge[3a]	Wäsche[6a]	lavado (lavar[2a])
welcome[2a] (*adj.*)	bienvenu[5a]	willkommen[3a]	bienvenido
wind[1a] (*vb.*)	rouler[1b], ([s']enrouler[6a])	winden[5b]	enrollar
wounded[2a]	blessé[4a]	Verwundete[5b]	herido (herir+herido[1b])
youthful[4b]	jeune[1a]	jugendlich[3a]	juvenil[4a]

SECTION 3.4. CONCEPTS 2951 THROUGH 3047

E F G S	*E F G S*	*E F G S*	*E F G S*	*E F G S*	*E F G S*	*E F G S*	*E F G S*	*E F G S*	*E F G S*
1-1-6-5	1-4-6-2	1-8*-4-6	2-4-5-2	2-8*-4-2	3-4-4-2	3-8*-2-6	4-4-3-2	5-1-3-1	5-5-2-1
1-2-6-4	1-5-5-5	2-1 -6-1	2-4-4-6	3-1 -5-1	3-4-3-6	4-1 -4-1	4-5-2-5	5-2-2-4	5-6-1-4
1-3-6-3	1-6-4-8*	2-2 -5-4	2-5-4-5	3-2 -4-4	3-5-3-5	4-2 -3-4	4-6-2-4	5-3-2-3	6-1-2-1
1-4-5-6	1-6-5-4	2-3 -5-3	2-6-4-4	3-3 -4-3	3-6-3-4	4-3 -3-3	5-1-2-5	5-4-2-2	

English	French	German	Spanish
(of own) accord[4a], (fain[6]), (voluntary[6])	volontaire[2a], (spontané[5a]) (volontairement[6a])	freiwillig[3a]	voluntario[4a]
across[1a] (athwart)	en travers[4a]	quer[6b] über[1a]	(de) través[2a]
aisle[5b]	passage[1b], (allée[2b])	Gang[2a]	pasillo[5b], (crujía), (pasadizo)
angle[4b]	angle[3a]	Winkel[3b]	ángulo[3b]
artistic[5b]	artistique[4b], (esthétique[6b])	künstlerisch[2b], (ästhetisch[4b])	artístico[2b]
basis[4a] (hypothesis)	hypothèse[5a], (supposition[6a])	Voraussetzung[2b], (Hypothese[6b])	suposición[5a], (hipótesis[7a])
beget[5b]	engendrer[4b]	erzeugen[2a], (zeugen[3b])	engendrar[2b]
benefit[2b] (*n.*)	bienfait[4b]	Wohltat[5a]	beneficio[2b], provecho[2b]
bridle[3b], rein[3b]	bride[6b]	Zügel[3b]	rienda[4a], freno[4b]
carry[1a] away[1a] (by passion)	passionner[4b]	fortreißen[6b]	apasionar (+apasionado -a -mente)[2b]
clay[2b]	argile[6b]	Ton[4b]	barro[4a]
comrade[4a]	camarade[2a]	Kamerad[3a]	camarada[4a]
converse[4b] (*vb.*)	converser[6a]	unterhalten[2b]	conversar[4b]
cottage[2b], (cot[4a])	chaumière[5b]	Hütte[4a]	choza[5a]
cow[1b], (heifer[5b])	vache[4a]	Kuh[6b]	vaca[2b]
crack[2b] (*n.*)	fente[5a]	Sprung[4b]	quiebra[5a], grieta[5b], (raja[7b])
creation[4b]	création[3b]	Schöpfung[3a], (Schaffen[6a])	creación[3a]
damp[3b], (moist[4a])	humide[3b]	feucht[4a]	húmedo[3a]
disgrace[3b], (dishonor[5a]) (*n.*)	déshonneur[6b]	Schande[3b], (Schmach[5a])	afrenta[4a], (baldón[7a])

English	French	German	Spanish
downward(s)[3b]	(de) haut[1a] (en) bas (*adj.*)[1a], ([en] descendant[5a])	abwärts[5b]	hacia[1a] abajo[1b]
dozen[2a]	douzaine[3b]	Dutzend[5b]	docena[3a]
fairy[2b] tale[2a], (fable[4a])	conte[3b] (de) fée[4b], (fable[5a])	Märchen[4a]	cuento[2a] (de) hadas (hada[6b])
farewell[2b], (good-by[3b])	(au) revoir[1b], (adieu[2b])	(auf) Wiedersehen[6a]	(hasta la) vista[1a], (hasta la) luego[1a], adiós[1b]
favorite[2b]	favori (*adj.*)[6a], favori(-te) (*n.*)[6b]	Liebling[4b]	favorito[4b], predilecto[4b]
festival[4b], (celebration[5b]), (jubilee[6])	fête[1b]	Feier[4b]	fiesta[1b]
fist[3b]	poing[2b]	Faust[4b]	puño[4b]
fluid[4b] (*n.*)	liquide[4a], (fluide[5b])	Flüssigkeit[3a]	líquido[2a]
fourteen[3b]	quatorze[3a]	vierzehn[4a]	catorce[3]*
freeing (free[1a]), (emancipation[9])	émancipation	Befreiung[4a]	emancipación[6b]
generation[3b]	génération[3a]	Generation[4b]	generación[3a]
gospel[4b]	évangile[6a]	Evangelium[2b]	evangelio[4b]
grant[1b] (*n.*)	concession[4b]	Gewährung[5b]	concesión[6b]
graze[3b], (skim[4b] [over]) (just touch)	effleurer[5a], frôler[5b]	streifen[3b]	rozar[5a]
grieve[3a] (*tr. vb.*), (afflict[4b])	affliger[4a], attrister[4a], (fâcher[5a]), (navrer[5a]), (peiner[7a])	betrüben[4a], (bekümmern[5a])	afligir[2a], (quebrantar[6b]), (entristecer[4b]), (apenar[7a])
(city, town) hall[1b]	hôtel[1b] (de) ville[1a], (mairie[5a])	Rathaus[6b]	ayuntamiento[5a]
headquarters[5b]	quartier[2a] général[1b]	Hauptquartier[2b]	cuartel[4a] general[1a]
hearty[4a] (fellow), (lusty[5b])	gaillard (*adj.*)[3b]	munter[3b]	cordial[3b]
House (house[1a]) of[1a] Representatives (representative[3a]), (House of Commons)	Chambre (chambre[1a]) (des) Députés (député[3b])	Abgeordnetenhaus[4b], (Burgerschaft[6b]), (Volksvertretung[6b])	Cámara (cámara[2b]) (de) Representantes (representante[4a])
innocence[4b]	innocence[4a]	Unschuld[3b]	inocencia[2b]
insult[4a] (*vb.*)	insulter[4b], (injurier[6a])	beleidigen[3a]	insultar[2b], (afrentar[6b])
keeping (keep[1a]) up[1a] (*n.*) (maintenance)	entretien[2b], (maintien[6b])	Aufrechterhaltung[6a]	conservación[4b]
(give the) lie[1b] (to), (refute[7])	démentir[5b]	widerlegen[5a]	desmentir[5a]
lieutenant[4b]	lieutenant[2b]	Leutnant[3b]	teniente[4b]
liquid[3b] (*adj.*), (fluid[4b])	liquide[4a], (fluide[5b])	flüssig[4a]	líquido[2a], (flúido[6b])
(the) living (live[1a])	vivant[2a]	Lebende[6a]	viviente[4b]
medicine[2b]	médecine[3a]	Medizin[5b], (Arznei[6a])	medicina[3a]
ministry[5b]	ministère[2b]	Ministerium[2b]	ministerio[4b]
neighbor[1b] (fellow-being)	autrui[6a], (prochain [*n.*][7a])	Nächste[5b]	prójimo[4b]
nowhere[6]	nulle (nul[1a]) part[1a]	nirgends[2b]	(en) ninguna (ninguno[1a]) parte[1a]
obstacle[5a]	obstacle[3a]	Hindernis[2b]	obstáculo[3a], (embarazo[6a])
outward(s)[4a], (outer[6]), (external[8])	extérieur[2a]	äußerlich[3a]	externo[4b]
papa[3a], (pa[6])	papa[2b]	Papa[4a]	papá[4b]
parish[5b]	paroisse[6a]	Gemeinde[1a]	parroquia[4a]

English	French	German	Spanish
partner[3b]	associé (associer[2a]), (partenaire[6a])	Aktionär[4a], Gesellschafter[4a], Beteiligte[4a], (Anteilseigner[6a])	socio[4a]
perfection[4b]	perfection[4a]	Vollendung[3b], (Vollkommenheit[5a]), (Vervollkommnung[6a])	perfección[2b], (remate[5b])
ply[5a] (go to and fro regularly)	(faire le) service[1a]	verkehren[3a]	ir[1a] (y) venir[1a]
pool[3b] (water)	mare[6a]	Lache[3b]	estanque[4a]
practice(se)[1b], trade[1b], (custom[2a]) (clientele)	pratique[2b], (clientèle[5b])	Kundschaft[6a]	parroquia[4a], (parroquiano[5b])
pressure[4b]	pression[3b]	Zwang[3b]	presión[3a]
prey[3a], (quarry[5a])	proie[3b]	Beute[4b]	presa[3a]
produce[2a], yield[2a] (the field yields –)	produire[1a]	hergeben[6b]	producir[1a], rendir[1b]
pursuit[4b]	poursuite[2b]	Verfolgung[3a]	persecución[4b]
rate[2a] (of speed)	vitesse[2b]	Tempo[5b]	velocidad[4a]
reasonable[4a], sensible[4b]	logique[2b], raisonnable[2b], (sensé[6b]), (judicieux[6b])	vernünftig[3a], verständig[3a]	lógico[4a], racional[4b], (razonable[5a])
reed[3b]	roseau[5b]	Rohr[3b]	junco[5a]
regret[3b] (*n.*)	regret[1b]	Bedauern[5b]	pesar[1a]
(get) ripe[2b], (ripen[4a]), (mature[4a]), (mellow[5a])	mûrir[6a]	reifen[4b]	madurar[4a]
risk[3b] (*n.*)	risque[4a]	Risiko[4b]	riesgo[2a]
senate[3a]	sénat[4b]	Senat[3b]	senado[6a]
send[1a] forth[1b], (emit[8])	émettre[4b]	(in) Umlauf[5b] (setzen)	emitir[6b]
separation[4b], (parting[6*])	séparation[3b]	Trennung[3a], (Scheidung[6a])	separación[3b]
shame[2a] (*vb.*)	(faire) honte[3a] à	beschämen[5b]	avergonzar[3a]
shell[2a] (explosive)	bombe[5b], (obus[6b])	Granate[4a], (Schrapnell[6b])	bomba[5a]
shooting (*n.*) (shoot[2a])	tir	Schießen[4b]	tiro[2b], (disparo[6b])
show[1a] (through), ([be] transparent[7])	(être) transparent[5a]	durchsichtig[5a] (sein)	traslucir[5b] (se)
sign[1b] (over shop)	enseigne[6b]	Schild[4b]	rótulo
sojourn[5b] (*vb.*)	séjourner[5b]	(sich) aufhalten[2b], (weilen[4b])	pasar[1a] (unos) dias (dia[1a])
solicit[4b]	solliciter[4a]	erbitten[3b]	solicitar[2a]
somewhere[3b] else[1a], (elsewhere[4a])	ailleurs[1a]	anderweit[5b], (anderwärts[6a]), (anderswo[6b])	(en alguna otra) parte[1a]
spare[2a] (*vb.*)	faire[1a] grâce[1a], (épargner[3b])	verschonen[6b]	perdonar[1b]
square[1b] (*adj.*), (sq.[6])	carré[3b]	viereckig[6b]	cuadrado[3a]
staff[3b] (of people)	personnel[1b]	Personal[5a]	cuerpo[1a], (personal[2a])
stay[1a] away[1a], (absent[3a] [oneself])	rester[1a] absent[3b]	ausbleiben[6a]	permanecer[1b] ausente[3a]
strengthen[4b], (fortify[6])	fortifier[5a], (affermir[6a]), (consolider[6b])	verstärken[2b], (stärken[3b]), (bestärken[6a])	consolidar[5b], reforzar[5b]
successful[3a]	(avoir du) succès[1b], heureux[1a]	erfolgreich[5a]	feliz[1a], (afortunado[3b])

English	French	German	Spanish
summit[4b]	sommet[3b], (cime[4b]), (haut [n.][5b])	Gipfel[3b]	cima[3a]
tent[2a]	tente[4b]	Zelt[5a]	tienda[2a]
tide[2b]	marée	Flut[3b]	marea[6b]
(put in) tune[3a] (with)	assortir, harmoniser	stimmen[2a]	armonizar[6a]
unfold[4b]	dérouler[3b], (déployer[4a]), (déplier[6a])	entfalten[3b]	desenvolver[3a], desplegar[3a]
veil[3b] (*n.*)	voile (*m.*)[3a]	Schleier[4b]	velo[3b], (mantilla[5a])
warning (warn[2b])	avertissement[3b]	Warnung[5a], Mahnung[5b]	aviso[3a], (amonestación[6a])
waver[4a], hesitate[4b], (falter[6])	hésiter[1b], (vaciller[4b]), (branler[6a])	zögern[4a], (wanken[5a])	dudar[1b], (vacilar[3a]), (titubear[5b])
web[3b]	tissu[4b]	Gewebe[4b]	tejido (tejer[2b]), (red[3a]), (malla[5b])
wedding[4b]	noce[4a]	Hochzeit[3a], (Heirat[4a])	boda[2a], (nupcias[6b])
width[3a], breadth[3b]	largeur[5a], large (*n.*)[5b]	Breite[6a]	latitud[5a], (anchura[6a])
wrapping (wrap[2b]), (envelope[4a])	enveloppe[3a]	Hülle[5a]	cubierta[3b]

PART IV

THE FOURTH THOUSAND CONCEPTS

SECTION 3.5. CONCEPTS 3048 THROUGH 3138

EFGS	*EFGS*	*EFGS*	*EFGS*	*EFGS*	*EFGS*	*EFGS*	*EFGS*	*EFGS*	*EFGS*
1–3–6–4	2–1–6–2	2–4–4–7	2–6 –4–5	3–1–5–2	3–3–4–4	4–1–4–2	4–4–3–3	5–1–3–2	5–4–2–3
1–4–6–3	2–2–5–5	2–4–5–3	2–6 –5–1	3–2–4–5	3–4–4–3	4–2–3–5	4–5–2–6	5–2–2–5	5–5–1–6
1–5–5–6	2–2–6–1	2–5–5–2	2–8*–4–3	3–2–5–1	3–5–3–6	4–2–4–1	4–6–2–5	5–2–3–1	5–6–1–5
1–5–6–2	2–3–5–4	2–5–4–6	3–1 –4–6	3–3–3–8*	3–5–4–2	4–3–3–4	4–6–3–1	5–3–2–4	6–4–1–3
									6–6–1–1

English	French	German	Spanish
abuse[3b] (*n.*)	abus[3b]	Mißbrauch[4b]	abuso[4b]
affection[3b]	affection[2b], (attachement[6b])	Anhänglichkeit[5b], Zuneigung[5b]	afecto[1b]
alarm[2b] (*vb.*), (startle[4b])	alarmer[6a]	beunruhigen[4b]	alarmar[5a]
altar[3b], (shrine[4b])	autel[5a]	Altar[4a]	altar[2b], (ara[5b])
amuse[4a]	amuser[2a], (distraire[3b]), (amusant[3a])	zerstreuen[3a]	recrear[5a]
animate[5b] (*vb.*)	animer[2b]	beleben[3a], (beseelen[5a])	animar[1b]
apple[1a]	pomme[3b]	Apfel[6a]	manzana[4b]
bar[2a] (metal or wood)	barre[4a], (barreau[5b])	Stange[5a]	barra[3b], (palanca[6a])
bill[1b] (poster)	affiche[5b]	Zettel[5b]	cartel[6a]
burden[3a] (*vb.*), (overwhelm[5b])	charger[1b], (accabler[3a])	belasten[4b]	agobiar[6a]
burst[2a] (into tears)	fondre[2b] (en larmes)	ergießen[6a]	romper[1a], echar[1a] (se)
butter[1b]	beurre[4b]	Butter[6a]	mantequilla,(+manteca)[3a]
cabinet[4b]	cabinet[2a]	Kabinett[3a]	gabinete[5a]
celestial[4b], heavenly[4a]	céleste[4a]	himmlisch[3a]	celeste[3a], (celestial[4a])
ceremony[3b], (rite[5b])	cérémonie[3a]	Feier[4b]	ceremonia[4b]
confidence[3b] (disclosure)	confidence[3b]	Eröffnung[3b]	confidencia
contrary[2b] (to)	contrairement[6a]	zuwider[5b]	contrariamente (contrario[1a])
corporation[5b]	corporation[5a]	Gesellschaft[1a], (Aktiengesellschaft[2b])	corporación[6a]
correspondence[4b] (similarity)	correspondance[4a]	Übereinstimmung[3a]	correspondencia[3a]
curse[2b] (*n.*)	malédiction	Fluch[4a]	maldición[3a]
dawn[2a] (*n.*)	point[1a] (du) jour[1a], (aurore[3b]), (aube[4a])	Dämmerung[6a]	aurora[2b], (amanecer[3a]), (alba[3a]), (madrugada[4b]), (albor[5b]), (alborada[6a])
definite[5b], (concrete[6])	défini (*adj.*)[6a]	bestimmt[1a]	concreto[5a]
desirable[4b]	désirable[6a]	wünschenswert[3b]	(de) desear[1a] se
diffuse[5b]	répandre[2a]	verbreiten[2a]	difundir[5a]
dull[3a], (stupid[4b])	bête (*adj.*)[2b], (stupide[3b]), (hébété[5b]), (idiot[5b])	dumm[4a], (stumpf[6b])	estúpido[5a], insensato[5a], (lerdo[6b])
(not) envy[3a]	(ne pas) envier[5b]	gönnen[4a]	(no) envidiar[2b]

English	French	German	Spanish
excel[4b]	exceller[6a]	hervorragen[2a]	descollar[5b]
exchange[2b] (*vb.*)	échanger[2a]	vertauschen[6b]	cambiar[1b], (canjear)
feast[2a], (banquet[3b])	banquet[4a], (festin[5a])	Essen[5a]	banquete[3a], (festín[5a])
friendly[2a]	amical[5a] (amicalement[6a])	freundschaftlich[4a]	amistoso[6a]
fugitive[5a] (*adj.*)	passager (*adj.*)[4b], (fuyant[6b])	flüchtig[2b]	pasajero[3a], (fugitivo[4b]), (fugaz[6a])
hostile[5b]	hostile[5a]	feindlich[1b], (feindselig[6b])	hostil[6b]
humble[3a], (meek[4a]), (lowly[6])	humble[2b] (humblement[5b])	demütig[5b]	humilde[1b], (sumiso[5b])
identical[6]	identique[4b]	vollkommen[1b] gleich[1a]	idéntico[3a]
image[3a]	image[2b]	Gleichnis[5b]	imagen[1b]
improve[2b] (*tr. vb.*)	améliorer[5a], perfectionner[5b]	bessern[5b]	mejorar[2a], (perfeccionar[5a])
infinite[3b]	infini[2a] (infiniment[3a])	unermeßlich[5b]	infinito[1b]
inhabit[4b]	habiter[1b]	bewohnen[4a]	habitar[2a]
inquiry[5b], (investigation[6])	recherche[2b], (enquête[3a]), (investigation[6b])	Untersuchung[2a], (Forschung[3b]), (Ermittelung[5a])	investigación[5a]
Jew[4a]	juif[6a]	Jude[2a]	judío[5a]
-s	-s	(Judentum[5a])	-s
lantern[4b]	lanterne[3b]	Lampe[3b]	linterna[4a], farol[4b]
library[2b]	bibliothèque[3a]	Bibliothek[5a]	biblioteca[4a]
magic[3a] (*n.*)	pouvoir[2a] magique[5a]	Zauber[4b]	poder[1b] mágico[2b]
magnificent[3a], (gorgeous[4b])	magnifique[1b], (superbe[2b])	prachtvoll[5a]	magnífico[2a], (augusto[3b]), (vistoso[4b]), (pomposo[5b])
maintain[2b], (affirm[4b]), (profess[5a]), (allege[5b])	affirmer[2a], maintenir[2a]	bejahen[6b]	mantener[1b], (alegar[4a])
maker[3a], (manufacturer[5b])	industriel[2b], (fabricant[6b])	Fabrikant[4a], (Industrielle[6b])	fabricante[5a], industrial[5a]
mechanic[4a] (*adj.*), (mechanical[6])	mécanique[3a]	mechanisch[3b]	mecánico[4a]
mistress[2b] (*f.* of master)	maîtresse[2a]	Herrin[6b]	señora (señor[1a])
murder [3a] (*vb.*)	assassiner[4a], (assommer[6a])	ermorden[4a], (morden[6b])	asesinar[3b]
mysterious[4b]	mystérieux[1b]	geheimnisvoll[4b], (rätselhaft[6b])	misterioso[2a]
nerve[4a]	nerf[4a]	Nerv[2b]	nervio[3a]
oppression[4b]	oppression[6b]	Druck[2a]	opresión[5a]
oration[6]	oraison[6b]	Rede[1a]	oración[1b]
organization[5b]	organisation[3b], organisme[3b]	Betrieb[2a], Organisation[2b], (Verband[3a]), (Schulverband[5a]), (Zweckverband[6a]), (Geschäftsbetrieb[6b])	organización[4a], (organismo[5b])
pack[2a] (*vb.*)	(faire la) malle[4b]	packen[4a]	(hacer el) baúl[7a]
pasture[2b]	herbage[6a]	Wiese[4b]	pasto[5a]
peer[2b], (stare[3b]), (glare[4a])	fixer[1b]	starren[6a]	clavar[2a] (la mirada)
post[1b] bill[1b]	afficher[5b]	Zettel[5b] anschlagen[5b]	fijar[1b] carteles (cartel[6a])
prescribe[4a]	prescrire[5b]	vorschreiben[2b]	prescribir[6b]
proclaim[3a], (announce[5b])	proclamer[4a]	verkünden[4a]	proclamar[3a], (pregonar[5a])

English	French	German	Spanish
project[4b] (*n.*)	projet[1b]	Projekt[4a]	proyecto[2b]
quaint[5a]	bizarre[2b]	wunderlich[3a]	(agradablemente) raro[1b]
realize[3b] (literally)	réaliser[1b]	verwirklichen[5b]	realizar[2a]
reduce[3a], (decrease[4a]), (diminish[5a])	réduire[1b], (abattre[2a]), (diminuer[2b]), (amoindrir[7a])	abfallen[5b], (nachlassen[6b])	disminuir[2b], (menguar[3b])
representation[5b]	représentation[4a]	Gemeindevertretung[2b], (Vertretung[3b])	representación[3a]
sadness[4b]	tristesse[2a]	Trauer[4b]	tristeza[1b]
sail[1a] (*n.*)	voile (*f.*)[5a]	Segel[6b]	vela[2a]
Saturday[2b]	samedi[3a]	Sonnabend[5a]	sábado[4a]
shield[3a] (*n.*)	écu[4b]	Schild[4b]	escudo[3b]
shift[3b] (of workmen)	équipe[5a]	Schicht[3a]	turno[6b]
shock[2b] (*n.*)	choc[3a]	Anstoß[5a]	choque[4a]
(put on) shoes (shoe[1b])	(se) chausser[4b]	Schuhe (Schuh[6a]) anziehen[3a]	calzar[3b]
slip[2a] (of paper)	fiche (*n.*)[5b]	Zettel[5b]	trozo[2b]
smell[2a] (*vb.*), (scent[4b]), (smelt[6])	sentir[1a], (flairer[5a])	riechen[6b]	oler[2b]
solution[5b]	solution[3a]	Lösung[2b], (Auflösung[3b])	solución[4a]
spoils (spoil[2a]), (booty[7])	butin	Beute[4b]	despojo[3a], (botín[6a])
sting[3a], (stung[6]) (insect)	piquer[2b]	stechen[5b]	picar[1b]
substance[3b]	substance[5a]	Substanz[4a]	substancia[2b]
swallow[2a] (*vb.*)	avaler[4b]	verschlingen[5b]	tragar[3b]
tailor[2b]	tailleur[4a]	Schneider[5b]	sastre[3b]
tax[2a] (*vb.*)	taxer[6b]	besteuern[5b]	cobrar[1b] impuestos (imponer+impuesto[1b])
tip[2a] over[1a], (overturn[5a]), (upset[5a]), (spill[5b])	renverser[2a]	überfallen[5a]	volcar[5a], (tumbar[6b]), (voltear[7a])
torment[3b] (*n.*)	tourment[5b]	Qual[4a]	tormento[2b]
torture[4a] (*vb.*)	torturer[4b]	quälen[3b]	atormentar[3b]
undone[6] (figurative) (done for)	fichu (*adj.*)[6b]	ab[1a], aus[1a]	deshecho (deshacer[1b])
unexpected[4b]	inattendu[3a], (imprévu[4a])	unerwartet[3b]	inesperado[4a], (de) improviso[4b], (imprevisto[7a])
union[2a] (bringing together)	rapprochement[5b]	Annäherung[5b]	reunión[2a], unión[2a]
warp[5b] (*vb.*)	jouer[1a], (gauchir)	verderben[3a], verwerfen[3b]	torcer[2a] (se)
warrior[3a], (fighter[6])	combattant[4b], (guerrier[5a])	Krieger[4b], (Kämpfer[6a])	guerrero[3b]
welfare[4a]	bien-être[4a]	Heil[3a], Wohl[3a]	bienestar[3a]
wire[2b], (telegram[4b])	dépêche[4a], (télégramme[5a])	Telegramm[5a], Depesche[5b]	despacho[3a], (telegrama[5b])

SECTION 3.6. CONCEPTS 3139 THROUGH 3236

E F G S	*E F G S*	*E F G S*	*E F G S*	*E F G S*	*E F G S*	*E F G S*	*E F G S*	*E F G S*	*E F G S*
1-3-6-5	1-6 -5-6	2-2-6-2	2-6 -4-6	3-3 -4-5	3-5-3-7	4-3-3-5	4-6 -3-2	5-3 -2-5	6-2-2-2
1-3-7-1	1-8*-4-8*	2-3-5-5	2-8*-4-4	3-3 -5-1	3-5-4-3	4-3-4-1	4-8*-1-8*	5-4 -2-4	6-3-1-5
1-4-5-8*	2-1 -5-7	2-4-5-4	3-1 -5-3	3-4 -4-4	4-1-3-7	4-4-2-8*	5-1 -3-3	5-5 -2-3	6-5-1-3
1-4-6-4	2-1 -6-3	2-5-4-7	3-2 -4-6	3-4 -3-8*	4-1-4-3	4-5-3-3	5-2 -2-6	5-8*-1-4	
1-5-6-3	2-2 -5-6	2-5-5-3	3-2 -5-2	3-8*-3-4	4-2-4-2	4-6-2-6	5-2 -3-2	6-2 -1-6	

English	French	German	Spanish
adventure[3b]	aventure[2a]	Abenteuer[5a]	aventura[2a]
ample[3b]	ample[5a]	hinlänglich[4a]	amplio[3a]
appreciate[4b]	apprécier[2b]	würdigen[4b]	apreciar[2b]
approach[2a] (*n.*)	abord[2a], (accès[3a]), (approche[3b])	Annäherung[5b]	acceso[6a]
attitude[5b]	attitude[2a]	Haltung[3a]	actitud[2a]
barrel[3a]	tonne[5a], tonneau[5a], (barrique[6a])	Tonne[3a], (Faß[4b])	barril[7a]
benefit[2b] (*tr. vb.*)	(faire du) bien[1a], (bénéficier[6b])	wohltun[5b]	beneficiar[7a]
breath[2a], breathing (breathe[2a])	respiration[5a]	Atem[4b], (Atmen)	respiración[7a]
case[1a] (spectacle, etc.)	étui[6b]	Hülle[5a]	estuche[6b]
contemporary[6] (*adj.*)	contemporain[3a]	gleichzeitig[1b]	contemporáneo[5a]
customer[3b]	client[3a]	Kommittent[4a]	cliente[5a]
decisive[6]	décisif[3a]	bestimmt[1a]	decisivo[5b]
defeat[3b], (rout[6]) (*n.*)	défaite (*n.*)[4a], (déroute[6a])	Niederlage[4a]	derrota[4b], (rota[5a]) (vencimiento[6a])
demonstration[6]	démonstration[5b]	Beweis[1b]	demostración[3b]
desk[2a]	bureau[2a], (pupitre[5b])	Schreibtisch[5b]	escritorio[6a]
(in) detail[4a]	(en) détail[1a]	ausführlich[3a], (umständlich[5b])	detalladamente (detallar[7a])
diamond[2a]	diamant[4a]	Diamant[5a]	diamante[4a]
distract[5b]	détourner[2a], (distraire[3b])	zerstreuen[3a]	distraer[2b]
ditch[6a] (irrigation)	fossé[3b]	Graben[4b]	acequia[5b]
draft[3a] (draw up) (*vb.*)	élaborer	entwerfen[3b]	redactar[4b]
edition[5b]	édition[4b]	Ausgabe[2a], Auflage[2b]	edición[4b]
elegant[4b]	élégant[2b]	elegant[4b]	elegante[2b]
energy[4b]	énergie[2a]	Energie[4a], (Arbeitskraft[5b])	energía[2a]
enthusiasm[5b]	enthousiasme[2a]	Begeisterung[3a]	entusiasmo[2a]
exquisite[5b]	exquis[2b]	köstlich[3b], (ausgesucht [aussuchen[5b]])	exquisito[2b], (primoroso[5b])
fare[2a], rates (rate[2a])	tarif[6a]	Tarif[4b]	tarifa[6b]
fiery[3b]	ardent[2b], (brûlant [*adj.*][4b])	feurig[4a]	ardoroso[6a], brioso[6a]
Friday[2a]	vendredi[4a]	Freitag[5b]	viernes[4a]
function[4b] (*n.*)	fonction[2b]	Funktion[4b]	función[2a]
gem[2b], precious[2b] stone[1a]	pierre[1b] précieuse (précieux[2a])	Edelstein[6b]	piedra[1a] preciosa (precioso[2a]), joya[2b], (pedrería[6a])
glitter[3a], sparkle[3a], twinkle[3b], (glisten[5a])	briller[2b], (étinceler)	schimmern[5a], (funkeln[6a])	brillar[2a], (resplandecer[4b])
group[2b] (*vb.*)	grouper[3b]	zusammenstellen[5b]	agrupar[5b]

English	French	German	Spanish
grouping (group[2b])	groupement[6a]	Zusammenstellung[4b]	agrupación[6b]
gush[4b], (jet[5a])	jet[3b], (effusion[6a])	Guß[3b]	efusión[5a], chorro[5b]
hallow[5a], (sanctify[6])	consacrer[2b]	heiligen[3b]	consagrar[2a], (santificar)
horn[2a], (trumpet[3a]), (bugle[4b])	trompe[3b]	Horn[5b]	trompa[5a], trompeta[5a], clarín[5b]
imprison[4b]	emprisonner[6a]	(ins) Gefängnis[2b] setzen[1a]	aprisionar[6b]
improvement[4b]	réforme[4a]	Verbesserung[2b], (Besserung[4a])	mejora
income[4b], (revenue[5b])	rente[2b], (revenu [n.][4a])	Einkommen[4a]	renta[2b]
incur[5b]	encourir	(auf sich) ziehen[1a]	incurrir[4b]
independence[4a]	indépendance[2b]	Selbständigkeit[4b], (Unabhängigkeit[5a])	independencia[2b]
inferior[4a]	inférieur[2a]	nachstehen[4b] (to be –), (untergeordnet[5a])	inferior[2b]
intelligent[5b]	intelligent[2b]	verständig[3a], (gescheit[7a])	inteligente[2b]
kick[2b] (*n.*)	coup[1a] (de) pied[1a]	Tritt[5a]	patada[7a]
learning (learn[1a]) (*n.*)	érudition[5b]	Gelehrsamkeit[6b]	saber (*n.*)[3b], (sabiduría[4b]), (erudición[6a])
line[1a] up[1a]	aligner[4a]	ausrichten[5b]	alinear
linen[2b], (canvas[3b])	toile[2a], (linge[3a])	Leinwand[6a]	tela[2b] (de) hilo[2a], (lienzo[3a])
linger[4a], (tarry[5a]), (lag[5b]), (loiter[6])	s'attarder[6b]	(sich) aufhalten[2b]	retrasar[6a] (se)
loyalty[5b], allegiance[5b]	loyauté[5a], (fidélité[6a])	Treue[2b]	fidelidad[3b], (lealtad[4a])
mental[6]	mental[5b] (mentalement[6b])	geistig[1b]	mental[3a]
mention[2a] (*n.*)	mention	Erwähnung[4b]	mención[4b]
morals (moral[3a]), (morality[8])	morale (*n.*)[3a], (moralité[4a])	Moral[5a], (Sittlichkeit[6a])	moral[1b], (moralidad[5b])
(so) much[1a] (the) more[1a], all[1a] (the) more[1a]	d'autant plus[3a]	umsomehr[7a]	tanto[1a] (más)
musical[3a] (person)	musicien[4a]	musikalisch[4a]	músico[4b]
navy[3a]	marine[3a]	Marine[4b]	marina[5a]
(bank) note[1b]	billet[2b] (de) banque[4a]	Banknote[6b]	billete[4a] (de) banco[2b]
ocean[1b]	océan[5a]	Ozean[6a]	océano[3a]
offer[1b] (*n.*)	offre[3b]	Angebot[6b]	ofrecimiento[5b], (oferta[6b])
operate[5b]	opérer[3a]	betreiben[2b]	operar[5b]
(surgical) operation[2b]	opération[2b]	Eingriff[6b]	operación[2b]
overcoat[4b]	pardessus[3a]	Mantel[3b]	gabán[5b]
pardon[2b] (*n.*), (forgiveness[5b])	pardon[2a]	Vergebung[6a], Verzeihung[6a]	perdón[2a], (indulto[6a])
peculiar[3a] (to)	propre[1a], particulier[1b]	eigenartig[5a]	peculiar[3b]
perplex[4b], puzzle[4b]	embrouiller[5a]	verwirren[3b]	aturdir[3b], (embrollar[5b])
personage[6]	personnage[2a]	Persönlichkeit[2b]	personaje[2a]
pipe[2a] (to smoke)	pipe[2b]	Pfeife[5b]	pipa[6a]
prick[3b] (*n.*)	piqûre[5b]	Stich[3b]	pinchazo[7b]
prolong[4a], (lengthen[5b])	prolonger[2a], (allonger[3b]), (éterniser[6a])	verlängern[4b]	prolongar[2b]
range[2a], (extent[4a]), (tract[4b]), (span[5a])	portée[2b], (étendue[3a])	Tragweite[6a]	extensión[2a], (alcance[3a]), (dimensión[4b]), (anchura[6a])
rebel[3b], (revolt[4b])	révolter[3a]	(sich) empören[4a]	rebelarse[5b]

English	French	German	Spanish
regiment[6]	régiment[2b]	Regiment[1b]	regimiento[6a]
remedy[3a] (*n.*)	remède[3b]	Abhilfe[5b]	remedio[1b], (cura[2a])
remit[5b]	remettre[1a]	überweisen[3a]	remitir[3a]
resource[5b]	ressource[2a]	Hilfsmittel[3a]	recurso[2b]
ridiculous[5b]	ridicule[2a], (grotesque[4b]), (burlesque[6a])	lächerlich[3b]	ridículo[2a]
secretary[3b]	secrétaire[2b]	Sekretär[5a]	secretario[2b], (secretaría[6b])
slope[2b]	pente[2b], (talus[4b]), (inclinaison[6b])	Abfall[6a], Abhang[6a], Hang[6a]	inclinación[2b], (pendiente[3a]), (cuesta[4b]), (ladera[6b])
(be) slow[1b] (e.g., watch)	retarder[3b]	nachgehen[6a]	atrasar[5a]
solitude[4a]	solitude[2b]	Einsamkeit[4b]	soledad[2a]
sow[2b] (*vb.*)	semer[2b]	säen[6a]	sembrar[2b], (sembrado[6a])
splendor[3b], (magnificence[6])	éclat[1b], (splendeur[5a])	Pracht[5a]	esplendor[3a], (brillo[4a]), (magnificencia[6a])
spur[4a], (impulse[6])	impulsion[6b]	Trieb[3b], (Drang[4a]), (Stoß[4b]), (Anstoß[5a]), (Antrieb[6a])	impulso[2a]
squeeze[5a] (e.g., water out of something)	presser[2a]	ausdrucken[2b]	exprimir[6a]
stage[3a] (e.g., in a journey)	traite[4a], (étape[5a])	Station[3b]	etapa
stately[4b], (dignify [ied][5b])	(plein de) dignité[3a]	stattlich[4a]	grave[1a], (respetable[3a]), (augusto[3b])
statue[3a]	statue[2a], (statuette[6b])	Statue[5b]	estatua[2a]
stripe[4a], (streak[6])	bande[2a], (galon[5b])	Strich[4b], (Streifen[6b])	lista[2b], (raya[3b]), (tira[6b])
substantial[4b]	substantiel	wesentlich[1a]	su(b)stancial
swim[2a], (swam[6])	nager	schwimmen[4a]	nadar[4a]
theirs[4b]*	(le) leur[1a]	ihrige[4a]	suyo[3]*
thunder[2b]	tonnerre[5a]	Donner[5b]	trueno[3a]
vary[3a]	varier[2b], (différer[4b])	abwechseln[5a]	variar[2a]
vein[3a]	veine[3b]	Ader[5a]	vaso[1b], (vena[3a])
violence[3b]	violence[2a], (véhémence[4b])	Heftigkeit[5a]	violencia[2a]
wax[3a] (*n.*)	cire[5a]	Wachs[4b]	cera[3b]
work[1a] together[1a] (collaborate)	collaborer	mitwirken[4b]	colaborar
worship[3a] (*n.*)	adoration[5b], (vénération[6b])	Verehrung[4a], (Andacht[5b])	veneración[3b], (adoración[5b])
worship[3a], (adore[4b])	adorer[3a]	anbeten[5b]	adorar[1b], (idolatrar[5a])

SECTION 3.7. CONCEPTS 3237 THROUGH 3323

E F G S	*E F G S*	*E F G S*	*E F G S*	*E F G S*	*E F G S*	*E F G S*	*E F G S*	*E F G S*	*E F G S*
1–3–6–6	1–8*–6–1	2–3–5–6	2–5 –5–4	3–2–5–3	3–4–4–5	4–1–3–8*	4–3–4–2	4–5–3–4	5–3–3–2
1–4–6–5	2–1 –6–4	2–3–6–2	2–6 –5–3	3–3–4–6	3–5–3–8*	4–1–4–4	4–4–3–5	4–6–3–3	5–4–2–5
1–5–6–4	2–2 –6–3	2–4–5–5	2–8*–4–5	3–3–5–2	3–6–4–3	4–2–4–3	4–5–2–8*	5–2–3–3	5–5–2–4
									6–2–2–3

English	French	German	Spanish
absurd[5b]	absurde[3b]	lächerlich[3b]	absurdo[2b]
acid[5b] (*n.*)	acide[4b]	Säure[2b], (Schwefelsäure[4a]), (Salpetersäure[5a]), (Salzsäure[6a])	ácido[5b]
ambition[3b]	ambition[2b]	Ehrgeiz[5a]	ambición[3a]

English	French	German	Spanish
apparatus[6]	appareil[2b]	Apparat[2b]	aparato[3a]
applause[5a], hurrah[5a]	bravo[3b], (applaudissement[5b])	Beifall[3a], bravo[3a], (Hurra[6b])	aplauso[2b], (viva[6b])
attribute[5b], (impute[6])	attribuer[3a]	zuschreiben[3b]	atribuir[2b], (imputar[6b])
authorize[6]	autoriser[2b]	berechtigen[2a], (ermächtigen[6b]) (befugt[4b])	autorizar[3a]
bathe[3a]	baigner[3a]	baden[5b]	bañar[2a]
bite[2a] (*vb.*), (nibble[6]), (nip[6])	mordre[3a]	beißen[6a]	morder[2b], (hincar[5a] el diente)
bliss[4a], rapture[4b], (ecstasy[6])	transport[2b], (ivresse[3a]), (délire[3b]), (félicité[5b])	Seligkeit[4a], (Wonne[5b]), (Glückseligkeit[6a])	delirio[3a], (embeleso[6a]), (éxtasis[6a])
button[2b] (*n.*)	bouton[3b]	Knopf[5b]	botón[6a]
cattle[2a]	bétail[6b]	Vieh[5b]	ganado[3a]
ceiling[4b]	plafond[3b]	Decke[4b]	techo[2b]
chest[2b] (box)	coffre[6b]	Kiste[5b]	arca[3b]
china[2b]	porcelaine[5b]	Porzellan[5b]	porcelana[4b]
choir[4b] (loft)	chœur[3b]	Chor[4b]	coro[2b]
choke[4a] (*intr. vb.*), (stifle[6]), (strangle[6])	étouffer[2b], (suffoquer[4b])	ersticken[4b]	sofocar[3b]
comedy[4b]	comédie[3a]	Komödie[4b], (Lustspiel[5b])	comedia[2a], (sainete[5b])
correction[5b]	correction[5b]	Verbesserung[2b], (Korrektur[4b])	corrección[4b]
crooked[4b]	de[1a] travers[3b]	schräg[4a], (schief[5b])	torcido (torcer[2a])
culture[5b], (civilization[6])	civilisation[2b], (culture[3a])	Kultur[3b]	civilización[3a], cultura[3a]
deck[2b] (*n.*) (ship)	pont[2b]	Deck[6b]	cubierta[3b]
deny[2b], (disown[9])	méconnaître[4b], (renier[5b])	verleugnen[5b]	renegar[5b]
device[4b] (technical)	appareil[2b]	Vorrichtung[4b]	aparato[3a]
distribution[4b]	distribution[5a]	Verteilung[3a]	reparto[4a], distribución[4b]
drain[2b], empty[2a]	vider[3a], (dessécher[4b])	leeren[6b]	agotar[2b], (escurrir[4a]), (disocupar[4b])
drama[5b]	drame[3a], (l'art) dramatique[3b]	Drama[3b]	drama[2a]
employer[6]	patron[2b]	Arbeitgeber[2b]	patrón[3a]
employment[5b]	emploi[3b]	Beschäftigung[3a]	empleo[2b]
fancy[2a], (whim[10])	caprice[3b], (frivolité[6a])	Grille[6b]	capricho[2b], (quimera[4b]), (antojo[5a])
(in the) first[1a] (place), firstly (first[1a])	premièrement	erstlich[6b]	(en primer) lugar[1a], primeramente (primero[1a])
fortunately (fortunate[3b]), (happily[4a])	heureusement[2a]	glücklicherweise[5b]	afortunadamente (afortunado[3b])
genuine[4b]	authentique[4b]	wahrhaft[3a], wahrhaftig[3b]	auténtico[5a], (genuino[6a])
gruff[5a]	rude[2a], brusque[2b]	grob[3b], (rauh[4a])	brusco[3b]
hinder[4a]	empêcher[1a], (gêner[2a])	abhalten[3a]	entorpecer
hint[4b], (intimate[5b])	insinuer[5b]	andeuten[3a]	insinuar[4a], intimar[4b]
horn[2a]	corne[5a]	Horn[5b]	cuerno[4a]
idle[2b]	oisif[6b]	müßig[5a]	ocioso[3b]
introduction[5b] (book, etc.)	introduction[5b]	Einführung[2a], (Einleitung[4a]), (Anleitung[5a]), (Vorrede[6a])	introducción[4b], (preámbulo[5b]), (prólogo[6b])

English	French	German	Spanish
invisible[4b]	invisible[2b], (imperceptible[4a])	unsichtbar[4a]	invisible[3b]
lavish[5b] (*adj.*)	prodigue[5b]	reichlich[2b]	pródigo[4a]
luxury[3a]	luxe[2b]	Luxus[5b]	lujo[3a]
mansion[4a]	hôtel[1b] particulier[1b], (château[2a])	Herrenhaus[4b]	mansión[4a]
mortal[2b] (susceptible to death)	mortel[3b]	sterblich[6a]	mortal[2a]
native[2a] (*n.*)	naturel[1a], (nationaux [national[2a]]), (indigène[4a])	Eingeborene[6a]	indígena[4b]
nephew[4a]	neveu[4a]	Neffe[4b]	sobrino[1b]
nobility[5b] (the –)	noblesse[3a], (aristocratie[4b])	Adel[3a]	nobleza[2b], (hidalguía[6b])
occasional[4b]	(de) temps[1a] (en temps)	gelegentlich[3a]	ocasional
organize[4b], (contrive[6])	organiser[2a]	organisieren[4b], (veranstalten[5a])	organizar[3b]
passionate[5b]	passionné[3b]	leidenschaftlich[3a], (feurig[4a])	apasionado (apasionar[2b])
photograph[5b]	photographie[4a]	Aufnahme[2b], (Photographie[5a])	fotografía[5a]
plane[4b] (mathematical)	plan[1b]	Ebene[4a]	plano[4a]
plume[4a]	panache[5a]	Feder[2b]	penacho
police[4a] (*n.*)	police[2b]	Polizei[4b]	alguacil[3b], (policía[4b])
precept[6]	précepte[6b]	Regel[1b], Vorschrift[1b]	precepto[3b]
privilege[3b]	privilège[3a], (prérogative[7a])	Privileg(ium)[5a], (Vorrecht[6a])	privilegio[2b], (prerrogativa[7a])
project[4b], (jut[6])	dépasser[1b], (projeter[3b]), (saillir[7a])	ragen[4b]	sobresalir[4b]
prudence[5b], (caution[6])	précaution[2b], (prudence[3a])	Vorsicht[3a], (Klugheit[4a])	prudencia[3a], (precaución[4a]), (cautela[6a]), (recato[6a])
questioning (question[1b]) (formal)	interpellation[5a]	Anfrage[5a]	interpelación, interrogatorio
rage[3a], (rave[5a]), (fume[6])	s'emporter[4b]	rasen[4a], stürmen[4a], (toben[5b]), (brausen[6a])	rabiar[5a], (delirar[6b])
relative[3a] (*adj.*), (comparative[5b])	relatif[3b]	relativ[5a]	relativo[2a]
repair[2a], (mend[3a]), (patch[4a]), (darn[6])	réparer[3a], (raccommoder[6b])	wiederherstellen[6a]	reparar[2a], compuesto[2b], (remendar[5b]), (restaurar[6b]), (compostura[5b])
respective[4b]	respectif[6b]	respektiv[3a], (jeweilig[6b]) (beziehungsweise[2b])	respectivo[3a]
robber[3a]	bandit[4a], brigand[4a]	Räuber[4b]	bandolero[5b], (bandido[6a])
satisfactory[5b]	satisfaisant[4b]	befriedigend (befriedigen[2a])	satisfactorio[5a]
savings (save[1a])	épargne[4b]	Ersparnis[6a]	ahorro[5b] (*pl.*)
sermon[4b]	sermon[6a]	Predigt[3b]	sermón[3b]
shell[2a]	coquille[6b]	Schale[5a]	concha[3b]
shepherd[2b]	berger[6a], pâtre[6a], (bergère[7a])	Hirt[5a]	pastor[3a], (zagal[6a])
sixth[2b]	sixième	sechste[4a]	sexto[5*]

English	French	German	Spanish
(be) sore[2b]	(avoir) mal[1a]	wund[6a] (sein[1a])	dolorido[4a]
sovereign[4b]	souverain[3a]	Herrscher[4a]	soberano[2a]
sprinkle[3b], spray[3b]	arroser[4a]	sprengen[4b]	rociar[5b]
steamer[3b], (steamship[6]), (steamboat[6])	vapeur (*m.*)[6a], paquebot[6b]	Dampfer[4a]	buque[3a] (de) vapor[2a]
stomach[4a]	estomac[3a]	Magen[4b]	estómago[2b]
straw[2a]	paille[2b]	Stroh[6b]	paja[3b]
strip[2a] (*tr. vb.*)	dépouiller[3a]	entblößen[6a]	despojar[2b], (desnudar[3b]), (deshojar[6a]) (leaves)
substitute[3b] (*n.*)	substitut[5b]	Ersatz[3a]	substituto
supply[1b] (– and demand)	offre[3b]	Angebot[6b]	oferta[6b]
suppress[5b]	supprimer[2b]	unterdrücken[3b], (verdrängen[4b]), (dämpfen[6b])	suprimir[3a]
thief[3a], (thieve[s][5a])	voleur[3a]	Dieb[5a]	ladrón[2a]
(be) thirsty[4b]	(avoir) soif[3b]	Durst[4a] (haben)	(tener) sed[2b], (sediento[6b])
ton[3a]	tonne[5a], tonneau[5a]	Tonne[3a], Zentner[3b]	tonelada
tradition[4a]	tradition[2a]	Überlieferung[4a], Tradition[4b]	tradición[3b]
Tuesday[2b]	mardi[4a]	Dienstag[5b]	martes[5b]
white[1a] (*n.*)	blancheur[5a]	Weiß [6b]	blancura[4b]
wreath[3a], (garland[4a])	couronne[3a]	Kranz[4b]	guirnalda[6b]

SECTION 3.8. CONCEPTS 3324 THROUGH 3422

E F G S	*E F G S*	*E F G S*	*E F G S*	*E F G S*	*E F G S*	*E F G S*	*E F G S*	*E F G S*	*E F G S*
1–4 –6–6	2–2–6–4	2–5 –5–5	3–1–5–5	3–4–5–2	3–8*–4–2	4–5–3–5	5–3–3–3	5–6–1–8*	6–3–2–3
1–5 –6–5	2–3–6–3	2–5 –6–1	3–1–6–1	3–5–4–5	4–3 –4–3	4–6–2–8*	5–4–2–6	5–6–2–4	6–4–1–6
1–6 –6–4	2–4–5–6	2–6 –5–4	3–2–4–8*	3–5–5–1	4–4 –3–6	4–6–3–4	5–4–3–2	6–1–2–5	6–4–2–2
1–8*–5–6	2–4–6–2	2–8*–5–2	3–3–5–3	3–6–4–4	4–4 –4–2	5–1–4–1	5–5–2–5	6–1–3–1	6–5–1–5
									8–1–1–1

English	French	German	Spanish
acceptance[5b]	acceptation[6b]	Annahme[1b], (Genehmigung[3a]), (Akzept[5b])	aceptación
accommodate[5b]	accommoder[4b], approprier[4b]	einstellen[3a], (anpassen[5a])	acomodar[2b], ajustar[2b]
adjoining (adjoin[5a])	voisin[1a]	benachbart[4a]	vecino[1b]
adoption[5b]	adoption[6b]	Annahme[1b]	adopción
antiquity[5b]	antiquité[3b]	Altertum[3a]	antigüedad[3b]
appeal[3a] (*n.*)	appel[2a], (recours[4a])	Berufung[4a]	apelación
artillery[6]	artillerie[4b]	Artillerie[1b], (Korpsartillerie[5b])	artillería[6a]
avenge[5b]	venger[4a]	rächen[3b]	vengar[2b]
bestowing (bestow[3b])	don[3a]	Erteilung[5b]	don (gift)[3b], (donación)
blank[3a] (void) (*adj.*)	en[1a] blanc[1a]	blank[6b]	en[1a] blanco[1a]
boot[2b]	botte[3a], (bottine[6b])	Stiefel[6a]	bota[3b], (botín[6a])
break[1b] (*n.*) (rupture)	rupture[4b]	Bruch[6a]	ruptura[6b]
buyer[5b]	acheteur[4b]	Käufer[2b]	comprador[6b]

English	French	German	Spanish
cap[1b]	casquette[4b], (képi[5a])	Mütze[6b]	gorra[6a], gorro[6b], montera[6b]
casual[5b]	éventuel[6a]	zufällig[2a]	casual[4b]
cellar[3a]	cave[3a]	Keller[5a]	cueva[3b], (bodega[5a])
(– in the) chair[1b], (chairman[5b])	présidence[5b]	Vorsitz[6a]	presidencia[5a]
characteristic[5b] (*adj.*)	caractéristique[4b]	eigentümlich[2a], (charakteristisch[4a])	característico[6a], típico[6a]
check[2a] (*vb.*)	vérifier[4a], (contrôler[5a])	kontrollieren[6b]	verificar[2b], (comprobar[5b])
classic[4b] (*adj.*)	classique[3b]	klassisch[4a]	clásico[3a]
clerk[2b] (who writes)	greffier[6a], clerc[6b]	Schreiber[5a]	escribano[4a]
cock[2a], (rooster[5b])	coq[4a]	Hahn[6a]	gallo[2b]
college[2a]	collège[3a]	Seminar[6b]	colegio[3a]
community[4b] (e.g., of interests)	communauté[4b]	Gemeinschaft[3b]	comunidad[6a]
competition[5b]	concurrence[3b]	Konkurrenz[3b]	concurso[6b], (competencia[5b])
composition[4b]	composition[3a]	Zusammensetzung[4a], (Komposition[5a])	composición[3b]
contemplation[5b]	contemplation[6a]	Betrachtung[2a]	contemplación[4a]
convent[5a]	couvent[3b], (cloître[4b]), (communauté[4b]), (monastère[5a])	Kloster[3b]	convento[3a], (monasterio[6a])
corps[8]	corps[1a]	Korps (C)[1a], (Garde[3a]), (Gardekorps[3a])	cuerpo[1a]
cotton[2a], (gingham[6])	coton[6b]	Baumwolle[5b]	algodón[4a]
criticism[6]	critique (*f*)[3b]	Kritik[2b]	crítica[3b]
curtain[2a]	rideau[2a], (portière[4a])	Vorhang[6a]	cortina[4b], (telón[5a]) (theatre)
delay[2a] (*n.*)	retard[2a], (délai[3b])	Verschiebung[6b], Verzögerung[6b]	tardanza[4b]
devour[4a], (gobble[6])	dévorer[3b], (engloutir[7a])	verzehren[4a], (verschlingen[5b])	devorar[3a], (engullir[6a])
discharge[3b] (dismissal)	congé[6b], (renvoi[5b])	Entlassung[5b]	despedida[3b]
division[3a] (act of dividing)	division[3b]	Teilung[5b]	división[3b]
draft[3a] (on bank)	traite[4a]	Tratte[5b]	giro[2b]
enjoyment[6]	jouissance[4b]	Genuß[2a]	goce[2b]
establishment[5b] (act of establishing)	établissement[3a], (fondation[5b])	Begründung[3a], (Errichtung[4a]), (Gründung[4b]), (Festsetzung[5a]), (Etablissement[5b])	establecimiento[3a]
estimate[3b] (*n.*)	appréciation[6a]	Schätzung[4b], (Einschätzung[6a]), (Würdigung[6a])	presupuesto[4a], (apreciación[5a])
(New Year's) Eve[3a]	(la) veille[1b] (du jour de l'an)	Sylvester[5a] (-abend)	víspera[5b] (de Año Nuevo)
explore[4b]	explorer[6a]	untersuchen[3a]	explorar[4b]
face[1a] (*vb.*) (stand up to)	braver[5b], (affronter[7a])	entgegenstehen[6a]	arrostrar[5a]
fancied (fancy[2a]), (imaginary[6])	imaginaire[4a]	eingebildet (einbilden[5a])	imaginario[6a]
fertile[4a], fruitful[4b]	fécond[4a], (fertile[5b])	fruchtbar[4a]	fecundo[2b], (fértil[4b]), (productivo[6a])
foster[5b]	protéger[2a]	hegen[3a]	fomentar[4a]

English	French	German	Spanish
freight^{3a}	chargement	Fracht^{4a}	carga^{2b}
glorious^{2b}	glorieux^{4a}	glorreich^{6b}	glorioso^{2a}
gravity^{6}, (seriousness^{10})	sérieux^{1a}, (gravité^{3a})	Ernst^{2a}	seriedad^{5b}
hover^{5a}	se balancer^{5b}, voltiger^{5b} (au-dessus de . . . .)	schweben^{2b}	cerner^{5b} se
immortal^{3a}	immortel^{3b}	unsterblich^{5b}	inmortal^{3a}
individual^{3a} (*adj.*)	individuel^{5a}	individuell^{4b}	individual^{5b}
invade^{4a}	envahir^{3a}, ([faire une] invasion^{5b})	einfallen^{4a}	invadir^{3a}
laughter^{3a}	rire^{1a}	Gelächter^{6a}	risa^{1b}
layer^{5a}	assise (*n.*)^{4b}	Schicht^{3a}	capa^{2a}, (camada)
lazy^{2b}	paresseux^{4b}	faul^{6a}	perezoso^{2b}, (holgazán^{6a})
leather^{2a}	cuir^{3b}	Leder^{6a}	cuero^{3a}
life^{1a} (animation)	vivacité^{5b}	Lebhaftigkeit^{6a}	animación^{5a}, (viveza^{6a})
lighten^{4a}	alléger^{6b}	erleichtern^{2b}	aligerar
local^{3a}	local (*adj.*)^{3a}	lokal^{5a}, örtlich^{5a}	local^{3b}
(be in the) majority^{3a}	(avoir la) majorité^{3a}	(im) Übergewicht^{5b}	(estar en) mayoría^{3a}
manly^{4b}, (masculine^{5b})	mâle^{5a}	männlich^{3b}	viril^{5a}, varonil^{5b}
marble^{2b}	marbre^{3a}	Marmor^{6a}	mármol^{3a}
moderation^{6} (temperateness)	sobriété^{5a}	Maß^{1b}, (Mäßigung^{6b})	moderación^{5b}, (sobriedad^{7a})
needle^{2b}	aiguille^{3b}	Nadel^{6a}	aguja^{3a}
negro^{3a}	nègre^{5b}	Neger^{5a}	negro^{1a}
offense^{3a}, (insult^{4a})	injure^{3b}, (affront^{6b}), (insulte^{7a})	Beleidigung^{5a}	agravio^{3b}, (afrenta^{4a}), (injuria^{4a}), (insulto^{4b}), (ofensa^{4b}), (denuesto^{6b})
offering (offer^{1b})	offrande^{6b}	Angebot^{6b}	ofrenda^{4b}
ox(en)^{2a}	bœuf^{3a}	Ochse^{6b}	buey^{3a}
paradise^{3a}	paradis^{3b}	Paradies^{5a}	paraíso^{3a}
(be) patient^{2b}	(avoir de la) patience^{2b}, (patient^{5a})	geduldig^{6a} (sein), gedulden^{6b}	paciente^{4b}
persist^{5b}	persister^{3b}, (persévérer^{5b}), (s'obstiner^{6b})	verbleiben^{3a}, (beharren^{6a})	obstinarse^{3a}, (porfiar^{4b}), (persistir^{6a})
positive^{4b}	positif^{3a}	positiv^{4a}	positivo^{3b}
purse^{2b}	bourse^{3b}	Beutel^{6b}	bolsa^{3a}
rate^{2a} (of interest)	taux	Prozentsatz^{5a}, (Zinsfuß^{6a})	tipo^{2a} (de) interés^{1b}
record^{2a} (*n.*), (register^{3a})	dossier^{4b}, registre^{4b}	Archiv^{5a}, Protokoll^{5a}, (Register^{6a})	registro^{6b}
reliable^{6}	digne^{1b} (de) confiance^{1b}	zuverlässig^{3b}	digno^{1a} (de) confianza^{1b}
reward^{3a} (*vb.*), (recompense^{4b})	récompenser^{6b}	lohnen^{4a}, belohnen^{4b}	recompensar^{4b}, (premiar^{5a})
rumor^{4b}	rumeur^{4b}	Gerücht^{4a}	rumor^{2a}
saddle^{2b} (*n.*)	selle^{5a}	Sattel^{6a}	silla^{1b}
see^{1a} (in) advance^{2a}, (foresee^{5b})	prévoir^{2a}	voraussehen^{6a}	prever^{4a}
shirt^{2b}	chemise^{3a}	Hemd^{6b}	camisa^{3a}
slap^{5b}, (smack^{6}) (*n.*)	soufflet^{5b}	Schlag^{2b}	bofetada^{5b}, palmada^{5b}, (bofetón^{6a})
snake^{3b}, (serpent^{4a})	serpent^{6b}	Schlange^{4b}	serpiente^{4b}, (culebra^{5b}), (sierpe^{6b})

English	French	German	Spanish
sober^{3a}, moderate^{3a}, temperate^{3b}	sobre^{6b}	nüchtern^{4b}	sobrio^{4b}
stable^{2b} (*n.*)	écurie^{5a}	Stall^{5b}	establo^{5a}
successor^{5b}	successeur^{3b}	Nachfolger^{3b}, (Folgende^{4b})	sucesor^{3b}
translate^{4b}	traduire^{3a}	übersetzen^{4a}	traducir^{3a}
trimming (trim^{2a}), (ornament^{3a}), (decoration^{4b})	décor^{3b}, (décoration^{5b}), (ornement^{5b}), (parure^{6a})	Verzierung^{6a}	adorno^{3a}, decoración^{3b}, (guarnición^{5b}), (aliño^{6b})
undergo^{5b}	subir^{1b}	(sich) unterziehen^{4b}	pasar^{1a}, sufrir^{1a}
unity^{5b}	unité^{3b}	Einheit^{3a}	unidad^{3a}
universal^{3a}	universel^{3a}	allseitig^{5a}	universal^{3a}
unpleasant^{5b}, disagreeable^{5b}	fâcheux^{3a}, (désagréable^{4b})	unangenehm^{3a}, (verdrießlich^{5a})	desagradable^{3b}
upright^{3a}, (righteous^{5a})	juste^{1a}	rechtschaffen^{6a}	justo^{1b}
variety^{3a}	variété^{3b}	Mannigfaltigkeit^{5a}	variedad^{7a}
vexing (vex^{7a}), (annoying [annoy^{5b}]), (troublesome^{6b})	importun^{6a}	lästig^{4a}, (beschwerlich^{6a}), (ärgerlich^{6b})	molesto^{4a}, importuno^{4b}, (fastidioso^{5b})
victor^{4a}	vainqueur^{6b}	Sieger^{4a}	vencedor^{3a}
vivid^{5b}	imagé^{4a}	lebendig^{2a}	gráfico^{6b}
wave^{1b} (*n.*) (undulation)	ondulation	Welle^{5a}	ondulación^{6b}

SECTION 3.9. CONCEPTS 3423 THROUGH 3515

E F G S	*E F G S*	*E F G S*	*E F G S*	*E F G S*	*E F G S*	*E F G S*	*E F G S*
2–1–6–6	2–5–6–2	3–2–6–1	3–5–4–6	4–3–4–4	4–6–3–5	5–2–4–1	5–5 –3–2
2–2–6–5	2–6–5–5	3–3–4–8*	3–5–5–2	4–4–3–7	4–6–4–1	5–3–2–8*	5–8*–2–3
2–3–6–4	3–1–5–6	3–3–5–4	4–2–5–1	4–4–4–3	5–1–4–2	5–3–3–4	6–1 –2–6
2–4–6–3	3–1–6–2	3–4–5–3	4–3–3–8*	4–5–3–6	5–2–3–5	5–4–3–3	6–3 –2–4
							6–5 –2–2

English	French	German	Spanish
abolish^{5b}	abolir^{3b}	vernichten^{6b}	abolir
accent^{4b} (*vb.*)	accentuer^{4b}	betonen^{3a}	acentuar^{7b}
actor^{4b}	acteur^{4b}, (comédien^{5b}), (actrice^{6a})	Schauspieler^{4b}	actor^{3a}, (protagonista^{6b})
ambassador^{4b}	ambassadeur^{6b}	Gesandte^{3b}	embajador
ass^{3b}, (donkey^{4a})	âne^{4a}	Esel^{5a}	burro + borrico^{3a}, asno^{3b}, (pollino^{6b}), (jumento^{7a})
assistance^{4a} (collaboration)	collaboration^{5a}	Mitwirkung^{3b}	colaboración^{6a}
bath^{3a}	bain^{4a}	Bad^{5a}	baño^{3a}
beach^{2b}, (strand^{5a})	grève^{4a}, rivage^{4a}, (plage^{5a})	Strand^{6a}	playa^{3a}
beer^{4b}, (ale^{6})	bière^{3b}	Bier^{3b}	cerveza
(from the) beginning^{5b}*	dès^{1a} (le) commencement^{2a}	(von) vornherein^{4a}	(desde un) principio^{1a}
(make) bitter^{2a}	rendre^{1a} amer^{2a}	erbittern^{6a}	amargar^{5a}
brood^{4a}, (meditate^{5b})	méditer^{4a}	sinnen^{4a}	meditar^{3a}
cab^{6}, hack^{6}	fiacre^{5a}	Wagen^{2b}	coche^{2a} ([de] alquiler^{3b})
chapel^{3a}	chapelle^{3a}	Kapelle^{5b}	capilla^{4a}
circuit^{4b}	circuit^{6a}	Umgebung^{3a}	derredor^{5a}

English	French	German	Spanish
colonel[6]	colonel[3b]	Oberst[2b]	coronel[4a]
correspondence[4b] (writing)	correspondance[4a]	Korrespondenz[4a], (Briefwechsel[5a])	correspondencia[3a]
countless[5b], (innumerable[6]), (myriad[6])	innombrable[4b]	zahllos[3a], (unzählig[4a])	innumerable[3a]
cure[2b] (*n.*)	cure[5a]	Erholung[6a], Kur[6a]	cura[2a]
dazzle[4b]	éblouir[3b], (éblouissant[4b])	blenden[4b]	deslumbrar[4a]
deceit[5b], fraud[5b]	déception[5b]	Betrug[3b], Täuschung[3b]	engaño[2a]
dew[2b]	rosée[5b]	Tau[6b]	sereno[2a], (rocío[6a])
disaster[5b], (calamity[6]), (catastrophe[8])	catastrophe[3a], désastre[3b], sinistre[3b]	Unfall[3b], (Katastrophe[4b]), (Unheil[5a])	calamidad[4a], catástrofe[4a], desastre[4a]
discretion[6]	discrétion[3b]	Vernunft[2b], (Einsicht[3a])	discreción[4b]
dismal[4b], gloomy[4b], (dreary[5b])	morne[3b], (funèbre[4a]), (lugubre[4a]), (ténébreux[6b])	düster[4a], trüb[4a]	lúgubre[4b], (fúnebre[6a]), (tétrico[6b])
dissolve[3b]	dissoudre[3b]	zersetzen[5b]	disolver[4a]
distinction[5b]	distinction[5b]	Ehrung[3b], (Auszeichnung[5b])	distinción[2b]
ditch[3a], pit[3a], (trench[5a])	fossé[3b]	Graben[4b]	fosa, zanja
drove[2b] (*n.*) (group of animals, etc.), flock[2b], herd[2b], (swarm[3b])	troupeau[3b], (volée [*n.*][4a]) (birds), (nuée[5b]), (essaim[6a])	Herde[6b]	bandada[4a] (birds), rebaño[4b], (enjambre[5b])
dull[3a] (unpolished)	mat (*adj.*)[5a], terne (*adj.*)[5a]	matt[4a]	mate[6b]
empty[2a] (river)	(se) jeter[1a]	(sich) ergießen[6a]	desembocar[6a]
encounter[3b] (*n.*) (military)	rencontre[1b]	Aktion[6b], Zusammenstoß[6a]	encuentro[2a]
ending[4b] (e.g., of a session)	dissolution[6a]	Aufhebung[3b]	disolución[5a], terminación[5b]
envy[3a] (*vb.*)	envier[5b]	beneiden[5b]	envidiar[2b]
eternity[4b]	éternité[5a]	Ewigkeit[3b]	eternidad[6a]
fan[2b] (*n.*)	éventail[6b]	Fächer[5a]	abanico[5a]
fiction[6]	roman[3a]	Dichtung[2b]	ficción[4b]
fostering (foster[5b]) (*n.*)	protection[2b]	Pflege[3b]	fomento[5b]
glove[2b], (mitten[5a])	gant[4b]	Handschuh[6b]	guante[3b]
handle[2a], (wield[6])	manier[4b], (manœuvrer[5a])	handhaben[6a]	manejar[3b], (esgrimir[6a])
harsh[4a] (to touch, etc.)	âpre[3a]	rauh[4a]	áspero[4a]
hive[4a] (bee)	ruche[6b]	Stock[3b]	colmena[5b]
honey[2a]	miel[5a]	Honig[6b]	miel[2b]
imagination[3b]	imagination[2a]	Einbildung[6b]	imaginación[1b]
imperfect[4b], (defective[6])	défectueux[6b]	mangelhaft[4b], (dürftig[5a])	pobre[1a], (imperfecto[3b]), (falto[5a])
inheritance[4b]	héritage[4a]	Erbschaft[4b], (Nachlaß[5a])	herencia[3a], (patrimonio[4b])
inland[5a]	intérieur[1a]	Inland[4b]	tierra[1a] adentro[2b]
invert[6]	retourner[1a]	umkehren[2b]	invertir[6a]
involve[4b]	impliquer[4b], (brouiller[5b])	verwickeln[4a], (befangen[6a])	enredar[3a], (implicar[4b])
kneel[4a]	s'agenouiller[3b]	knien[4b]	arrodillarse[4a], (hincar[5a] [la] rodilla[2a]), (poner[1a] [se] [de] hinojos [hinojo[6b]])
legend[5b]	légende[3a]	Sage[3a]	leyenda[4a]
likeness[4b]	ressemblance[3b]	Ähnlichkeit[4a]	semejanza[4a]
loyal[4a]	loyal[4b] (loyalement[6b])	getreu[4a]	leal[3a]

English	French	German	Spanish
margin^{5a}	marge	Rand^{2b}	margen^{3a}
mixture^{4a}	mélange^{3a}	Mischung^{4b}, (Gemenge^{6a}), (Gemisch^{6b})	mezcla^{4a}
movable (move)^{5b}	mobile^{3b}	beweglich^{3b}, (mobil^{6b})	móvil^{4b}, (movible^{5b})
normal^{4b}	normal^{3a}	normal^{4a}	normal^{4a}
ours^{3a}	nôtre^{3a}	unsrige^{5b}	nuestro^{4*}
overtake^{4a}, (overtook^{6})	rejoindre^{2a}, (rattrapper^{4a})	einholen^{5b}	alcanzar^{1a}
pensive^{4b}, thoughtful^{4b}	rêveur^{4a}, (pensif^{5a})	(sinnen^{4a}), (besonnen^{6a})	pensativo^{3a}, (reflexivo^{5b})
periodical^{6} (*n.* and *adj.*)	périodique^{5a}	Zeitschrift^{2b}, (periodisch)	periódico^{2a}
personality^{6}	personnalité^{3b}	Persönlichkeit^{2b}, (Individualität^{5b})	personalidad^{4a}
pig^{2a}, (hog^{3b}), (pork^{4a}), (swine^{5a})	cochon^{4a}, (porc^{5b}), (sanglier^{5b})	Schwein^{6b}	puerco^{3b}, (cerdo^{4b}), (cochino^{6a})
planet^{4b}	planète^{4b}	Planet^{4b}	planeta^{3a}
plot^{3a}, (conspiracy^{5b})	complot^{5b}	Anschlag^{4b}, (Verschwörung^{6b})	intriga^{6a}
poetic^{5b}	poétique^{4a}	poetisch^{3a}, dichterisch^{3b}	poético^{3b}
production^{4b}	production^{4a}	Produktion^{4a}, (Erzeugung^{5b}), (Gewinnung^{6a})	producción^{3a}
recite^{4b}	réciter^{3a}, (déclamer^{5b})	vortragen^{4a}	recitar^{4a}
refuge^{3b}, (haven^{5b})	asile^{3b}, (refuge^{6a})	Zuflucht^{5a}	asilo^{4a}, (refugio^{5a})
(take) refuge^{3b}	se réfugier^{3b}	Zuflucht^{5a} finden^{1a}, Zuflucht^{5a} suchen^{1a}	refugiarse^{4b}
relieve^{4a} (someone of a duty)	relever^{1a}	ablösen^{5b}	relevar^{6b}
respectful^{5b}	respectueux^{4b}	hochachtungsvoll^{3b}, (hochachtend^{6a}), (achtungsvoll^{6b})	respetuoso^{3b}
(priest's) robe^{3a}	soutane^{5a}	Gewand^{4b}	sotano^{6b}
salvation^{5b}	salut^{3b}	Rettung^{3b}	salvación^{4b}
scientific^{6}	scientifique^{4a}	wissenschaftlich^{2a}, (naturwissenschaftlich^{6a})	científico^{3a}
secretary^{3b} (of) state^{1a}	ministre^{6a} (des Affaires) étrangères (étranger^{1b})	Staatssekretär^{6a}	ministro^{1b} (de Estado)
shipment^{4b}, (despatch^{6})	expédition^{3a}, (envoi^{7a})	Sendung^{4a}	expedición^{4b}, (envío^{7a})
sketch^{5b} (*n.*)	dessin^{3a}, (esquisse^{6a})	Aufsatz^{7a}, (Skizze^{6a}), (Riß^{6b})	dibujo^{4a}
(go to) sleep^{1a}	s'endormir^{2b}, (s'assoupir^{6b}), (se rendormir^{6b})	einschlafen	dormir^{1a} (se), (adormecer^{4a} [se])
sly^{4a}, (furtive^{9})	furtif^{6a}	heimlich^{3a}	furtivo^{5b}
spin^{3a}, (spun^{6a})	filer^{2b}	spinnen^{5b}	hilar^{5b}
stamp^{2a} (*vb.*) (e.g., a paper)	timbrer^{6b}	ausprägen^{5b}, prägen^{5b}, (abdrucken^{6b})	estampar^{5b}
steer^{3b} (*vb.*)	diriger^{1a}, (gouverner^{4b})	steuern^{6a}	gobernar^{2a}, (navegar^{4a})
swell^{2b}, (swollen^{6})	gonfler^{3b}, (enfler^{6a})	schwellen^{6b}	hinchar^{4a}
team^{2b}	attelage	Joch^{5a}, (Gespann)	tronco^{3a} (horses), (equipo^{7b})
tobacco^{3a}	tabac^{3b}	Tabak^{5a}	tabaco^{4a}
torture^{4a} (*n.*)	supplice^{4a}, (torture^{5a}), (tourment^{5b})	Qual^{4a}	martirio^{3a}, (suplicio^{5b})

English	French	German	Spanish
transport[3b], (convey[4b])	transporter[2b]	übersenden[5a], versenden[5a]	transportar[5a], (acarrear[6a])
trifle[3b] (*n.*)	petitesse[6a]	Kleinigkeit[4b]	friolera[5a], pequeñez[5b]
unequal[5b], (uneven[6])	inégal[4a]	ungleich[3a]	desigual[3a]
victorious[4a]	vainqueur[3b]	siegreich[4a]	victorioso[4b]
want[1a] (privation)	privation[6b]	Entbehrung[6b]	privación[5a]
whistle[2a] (*n.*)	sifflet[5a]	Pfeife[5b]	silbido[6a]

SECTION 4. CONCEPTS 3516 THROUGH 3601

E F G S	*E F G S*	*E F G S*	*E F G S*	*E F G S*	*E F G S*	*E F G S*	*E F G S*	*E F G S*
1–3–8*–1	1–8*–5–8*	2–4–6–4	3–2–5–6	3–4 –5–4	3–8*–4–4	4–4 –4–4	4–8*–3–4	5–5–3–3
1–4–6 –8*	2–2 –6–6	2–5–6–3	3–2–6–2	3–5 –5–3	4–2 –5–2	4–5 –3–7	5–1 –4–3	6–3–2–5
1–4–7 –4	2–2 –7–2	2–6–5–6	3–3–5–5	3–6 –4–6	4–3 –4–5	4–5 –4–3	5–2 –4–2	6–3–3–1
1–5–6 –7	2–3 –6–5	2–6–6–2	3–3–6–1	3–6 –5–2	4–3 –5–1	4–6 –4–2	5–4 –2–8*	6–5–2–3
1–6–6 –6	2–4 –5–8*	3–1–6–3	3–4–4–8*	3–8*–3–8*	4–4 –3–8*	4–8*–2–8*	5–4 –3–4	6–6–1–9

English	French	German	Spanish
accuse[3b]	accuser[2b]	anklagen[6b], beschuldigen[6b]	acusar[2b]
attractive[4a], enticing (entice[4b]), (alluring [allure[5b]])	séduisant[5b]	lockend (locken[4a])	atractivo[3a], seductor[3b], (halagüeño[5a]), (tentador[6b])
baron[5b]	baron[4b]	Freiherr[2b], (Baron[3a]), (Baronin[6b])	barón
beggar[3a]	gueux[5a], mendiant[5b]	Bettler[5b]	mendigo[3b]
blank[3a] book[1a]	cahier[4a]	Heft[4a]	cuaderno
blanket[4b]	couverture[3a] (de lit)	Decke[4b]	manta[5a]
block[2a] up[1a]	encombrer[4b]	sperren[5a]	obstruir
blush[3b] (*vb.*)	rougir[2b]	erröten[5b]	ruborizar[6b] (se)
bore[2b] (*n.*) (tedium)	ennui[2b], (cauchemar[4a])	Langeweile[6a]	hastío[6b]
bundle[3b], package[3a], parcel[3a]	paquet[2b], (ballot[4b]), (fagot[6a]) (wood)	Ballen[6b], (Paket)	bulto[2b], (fardo[6a]), (lío[6b]), (paquete[6b])
career[4b]	carrière[2b]	Laufbahn[5b]	carrera[2a]
catching (catch[1b]), (contagious[8])	contagieux[5b]	ansteckend (anstecken[6a])	contagioso[7a]
choir[4b] (people)	maîtrise[6a]	Chor[4b]	coro[2b]
climate[3a], (clime[5a])	climat[6b]	Klima[5a]	clima[2b]
conception[6] (physical)	conception[3b]	Auffassung[2a]	concepción[5b]
conscious[4b]	conscient	(bei) Bewußtsein[2a]	consciente
copy[2a] (make a copy)	copier[5a]	abschreiben[6a], abbilden[6b]	copiar[3b]
correspond[4b] (writing)	correspondre[3b]	(in) Briefwechsel[5a] (stehen)	corresponder[1b]
cunning[3a], (craft[5a])	ruse[4b], (artifice)	List[5a]	ardid[4b]
day[1a] before[1a] yesterday[1b]	avant-hier[4a]	vorgestern[6a]	anteayer
(in) debt[2a]	(être) débiteur[6a]	verschulden[6a]	(en) deuda[2b]
decent[5b], (respectable[6])	(comme il) faut (falloir[1a]), (convenable[3b]), (respectable[4a])	anständig[4b], (schicklich[6b])	respetable[3a], decente[3b]
defiance[4b]	défi[5a]	Trotz[4a]	desafío[3a]
divorce[4b] (*vb.*)	divorcer	scheiden[2a]	divorciar

English	French	German	Spanish
(become[1a]) dumb[3a]	devenir[1a] muet[3b]	verstummen[5a]	enmudecer[5a]
Dutch[3a]	hollandais	niederländisch[4a], (holländisch[6a])	holandés[4b]
fold[2a] (*vb.*)	plier[2b]	falten[7a]	doblar[2a], (plegar[4a])
formation[5b]	formation[4b]	Gestaltung[3a], (Gebilde[5a])	formación[4a]
(man of) genius[4a]	(homme de) génie[2b]	Genius[5b]	genio[2a]
giant[2a] (*n.*)	colosse[6b], géant[6b]	Riese[6a]	gigante[2b]
green[1a] (*n.*) (verdure)	verdure[4b]	Grün(e)[7a]	verdura[4b], (verdor[6a])
grievous[5a], (lamentable[8])	lamentable[5b], (regrettable[6b])	schmerzlich[3a], (verdrießlich[5a])	lamentable[3a]
(do) hair[1a]	coiffer[3b]	frisieren	tocar[1a] (sc)
honorable[3a]	honorable[4b]	ehrenvoll[5b], (rühmlich[6b])	honroso[4a]
horizon[4b]	horizon[2a]	Horizont[5a]	horizonte[2b]
imitate[4b]	imiter[2a]	nachahmen[5b]	imitar[2a]
inflict[5b]	infliger[5a]	auferlegen[3b]	inferir[3b]
insignificant[5b]	insignifiant[5a]	unbedeutend[3a], (unerheblich[6a])	insignificante[5b]
inspiration[5b]	inspiration[5a]	Anregung[3a]	inspiración[3a]
intelligence[4a]	intelligence[2a]	Intelligenz[5b]	inteligencia[2a]
intensity[6]	intensité[5a]	Stärke[2b]	intensidad[3b]
(of the same) kind[1a], (homogeneous[14])	homogène[6b]	gleichartig[6a]	homogéneo[6b]
legal[5b] (juristic)	légal[4b], (judiciaire[6b])	juristisch[3a]	legal[4b]
magistrate[4b]	magistrat[3b]	Magistrat[4b], (Amtmann[5a])	magistrado[5a]
mature[4a], (adult[9])	adulte	erwachsen[3a]	maduro[4b], (adulto)
motive[3b]	motif[3a], mobile[3b]	Beweggrund[6b]	motivo[1b], (móvil[4b])
museum[4a]	musée[4b]	Museum[4a]	museo[4b]
obligation[5b]	obligation[2b]	Verbindlichkeit[4b]	obligación[2a], empeño[2b]
patron[4a], (protector[6])	patron[2b], (protecteur[5a])	Patron[5b]	protector[2b], (patrón[3a]), (padrino[4a])
perfume[4a], scent[4b], (fragrance[5b])	odeur[2a], parfum[2b]	Duft[5a]	perfume[2b], (aroma[4a]), (fragancia[5b])
petition[4b]	pétition	Petition[3b], (Gesuch[5b])	petición[4a]
physical[5b]	physique[2b]	physisch[4a]	físico[illegible]
pin[2a] (*n.*)	épingle[4a]	Nadel[6a]	alfiler[4b]
placing (place[1a]) (localization)	placement[4b]	Lokalisierung[6b]	localización
platter[6]	plat (*n.*)[3a]	Platte[3a]	fuente[1b]
poverty[3b]	pauvreté[6a]	Armut[5a]	pobreza[2b]
presume[4a] (presuppose)	présumer[6b]	voraussetzen[4a]	presumir[2b]
pretense(ce)[5b], (pretext[10])	prétexte[2a]	Vorwand[4b]	pretexto[2b]
put[1a] (to) sleep[1a]	endormir[3a]	einschläfern	hacer[1a] dormir[1a]
quote[4b], (cite[6])	citer[2b], ([faire une] citation[5b])	zitieren[5b]	citar[2a]
rebel[3b] (*n.*)	rebelle[5a], (mutin[6b])	Rebell[5b]	rebelde[3b]
relish[6] (*vb.*), savor[6]	savourer[6a]	genießen[1b]	saborear[6b]
remedy[3a] (*vb.*)	remédier[5b]	abhelfen[5b]	remediar[3a]

English	French	German	Spanish
resolute[4b]	résolu (*adj.*)[3b] (résolument[5b])	entschlossen[5b]	resuelto (resolver[1b])
rocking (rock[1a])	balancement	Schwankung[5b]	balanceo
scold[3b]	gronder[2b]	schelten[6a]	reñir[2a]
seal[2b] (*n.*)	sceau[5b], (cachet[6b])	Siegel[6a]	sello[3a]
sharp[2a] (taste), (tart[6] [*adj.*])	piquant (*adj.*)[3b], (acide[4b]), (âcre[6a])	herb[6a], (pikant)	picante[5a]
sixty[3a]	soixante[1b]	sechzig[6b]	sesenta[3]*
slice[4b] (*n.*)	tranche[4b]	Scheibe[3b]	tajada, rebanada
stormy[3a], (tempestuous[6])	(d')orage[2b]	stürmisch[5a]	turbulento[6b]
suspicion[5b]	soupçon[4a]	Verdacht[3b]	sospecha[4a]
swamp[4a], (bog[5a]), (marsh[5a])	marais[5a]	Marsch[3b]	pantano[7a]
tax[2a] rate[2a]	tarif[6a] (d')impôt[3a]	Steuersatz[5a]	tarifa[6b] (de impuesto)
tempt[3a]	tenter[1b]	anfechten[6b]	tentar[3a]
theme[4b] (topic)	thème[6b]	Thema[4b]	tema[2b]
tin[3a] (metal)	étain[6b]	Zinn[4b]	lata[6b]
transfer[3b] (*n.*) (money)	transfert	Überweisung[3a]	remesa
trembling (tremble[2b]) (*n.*)	tremblement[4b]	Zittern[6b]	temblor[4a]
twist[3b], (twine[4a]) (*vb.*), (coil[5b]), (wreathe[6])	(s')enrouler[6a]	verschlingen[5b]	torcer[2a]
uncertain[4b]	incertain[4a], (précaire[5a]), (hasardeux[6a])	unsicher[4b], (ungewiß[6a])	incierto[4b], (inseguro[6a])
vague[5b]	vague[2a], (indécis[3b]) (vaguement[4b])	dumpf[4b], (unbestimmt[5a]), (ungewiß[6a])	vago[2a], (indeciso[6b])
vigor[3b]	vigueur[5a], fermeté[5b]	Lebenskraft[5b]	brío[3a], vigor[3a], (lozanía[5b])
vine[2b]	vigne[3a]	Rebe[6b]	parra[5b]
whirl[3b] (*n.*)	tourbillon[6a]	Wirbel[5b]	giro[2b], (remolino[7a])
wrestle[5b]	lutter[2b]	ringen[4b]	luchar[2a]

SECTION 4.1. CONCEPTS 3602 THROUGH 3692

E F G S	E F G S	E F G S	E F G S	E F G S	E F G S	E F G S	E F G S	E F G S	E F G S
1–1–8*–4	1–6 –6–7	2–3 –6–6	2–8*–6–1	3–4–5–5	3–8*–4–5	4–3–5–2	4–6–4–3	5–4–3–5	6–3 –3–2
1–2–8*–3	1–6 –7–3	2–4 –6–5	3–1 –6–4	3–5–4–8*	4–1 –4–8*	4–4–4–5	5–1–4–4	5–4–4–1	6–4 –2–5
1–4–8*–1	1–8*–6–5	2–6 –6–3	3–2 –6–3	3–5–5–4	4–2 –5–3	4–5–3–8*	5–2–4–3	5–5–2–8*	6–5 –2–4
1–5–7 –4	2–3 –7–2	2–8*–5–5	3–3 –6–2	3–6–4–7	4–3 –4–6	4–5–4–4*	5–3–3–6	5–5–3–4	6–6 –2–3
							5–3–4–2	5–6–3–3	6–8*–2–1

English	French	German	Spanish
abyss[5b]	abîme[3b], (gouffre[4b])	Abgrund[4b]	abismo[2b]
amends (amend[4b])	réparation[3a], (compensation[6a])	Buße[5b]	satisfacción[2b]
anywhere[4b]	(n'importe) où[1a]	irgendwo[4b]	dondequiera, doquiera
atmosphere[5b]	atmosphère[3a]	Atmosphäre[4b]	ambiente[2b], (atmósfera[3a])
Austria(n)[5b]	autrichien[5b]	österreichisch[2a]	austriaco
banish[3b], (exile[4b])	exiler[5a], (bannir[6a])	verbannen[5b], (bannen[6a])	desterrar[4a]
bee[1b]	abeille[6b]	Biene[7a]	abeja[3b]
beef[3b]	bœuf[3a]	Ochse[6b]	vaca[2b], (res[6a])

English	French	German	Spanish
brighten[4b] (*intr. vb.*)	s'éclaircir[5a]	erleuchten[4a]	aclarar[4b]
candidate[4a]	candidat[4a]	Kandidat[4b]	pretendiente[5b]
cat[2a], (pussy[3b]), (kitty [K][4b]), (kitten[5a]), (puss[6])	chat[3a]	Katze[7a]	gato[2b]
compliment[5b] (*n.*)	compliment[3a], (galanterie[5a])	Empfehlung[4b], (Kompliment[6a])	cumplimiento[2b], (elogio[3b]), (galantería[5b]), (parabién[6a]), (requiebro[6b])
concert[4a]	concert[3a]	Konzert[5a]	concierto[2b]
conqueror[4a]	conquérant[5b]	Sieger[4a], (Eroberer)	conquistador[4a]
consequently (consequent[5a])	(par) conséquent[3a]	folglich[4b], (infolgedessen[6b])	(por) consiguiente[2b]
couch[3a], (sofa[5b])	canapé[4b], (divan[6b])	Sofa[5b]	sofá[5a], (diván[6b])
countenance[4a]	physionomie[3a]	Antlitz[4a]	fisonomía[6a]
covet[5b]	convoiter[5a]	begehren[3b]	codiciar[4b]
creditor[5b]	créancier[5a]	Gläubiger[3a]	acreedor[4a]
criminal[5b] (*adj.*)	criminel[3b]	strafbar[4b]	criminal[2b], (reo[4a])
deliberate[5b] (*vb.*)	délibérer[4b]	erwägen[3b], überlegen[3b]	deliberar[5b]
denounce[6b]	dénoncer[3b]	anzeigen[3b]	denunciar[6b]
dim[3a] (*adj.*), cloudy[3b], (obscure[5a]), (dusky[6]), (misty[6])	sombre[1b], (obscur[2a]), (indécis[3b])	unklar[6a]	lóbrego[4b], (indefinido[5b])
eagle[2b]	aigle[6b]	Adler[6a]	águila[3a]
eighth[3a]	huitième[5a]	achte[5b]	octavo[4*]
emerge[5b]	surgir[3a]	auftauchen[4b]	surgir[2b]
eminently (eminent[6])	éminemment[6b]	hervorragend (hervorragen[2a])	eminentemente (eminente[3a])
excursion[5b]	excursion[6b]	Fahrt[3a], Partie[3b], (Wanderung[5a]), (Ausflug)	excursión[3b]
expansion[6]	expansion[5b]	Ausdehnung[2b], (Ausbreitung[6a])	expansión[4b]
extra[4a], (additional[5b])	(en) plus[1a], (supplémentaire[6b])	(zur) Ergänzung[4a]	extra
faint[2a] (*n.*)	évanouissement[6b]	Ohnmacht[6a]	desmayo[3b]
feminine[5b]	féminin[6a]	weiblich[3a]	femenino[3b]
financial[5b]	financier[3b]	finanziell[6a]	financiero[6b]
flourish[3b] (*vb.*), (prosper[4a]), (thrive[4a])	prospérer	gedeihen[4a]	medrar[5a], (prosperar[6a])
go[1a] along[1a] (e.g., a river)	longer[4b]	entlanglaufen	ir[1a] (a lo) largo[1a] de
goblet[6a]	coupe[3b]	Becher[3b]	copa[2a], (cáliz[5a])
grapes (grape[2a])	raisin[4a]	Traube[6b]	uva[5a] (*pl.*)
harry (H)[2a] (*vb.*)	harasser[6b]	plagen[6a]	acosar[3b]
hint[4b] (*n.*)	allusion[3a]	Wink[4b], (Andeutung[5a])	insinuación[6b]
inconvenience[6]	inconvénient[3a]	Übelstand[3b]	inconveniente[2b], (incomodidad[6a])
indulge[6] (in)	s'adonner	sich[1a] ergehen[2b]	gozar[1a] (de)
insensible[6] (unconscious of)	insensible[4a]	nicht[1a] bewußt[2b]	insensible[5a]
jealous[3b]	jaloux[2b]	eifersüchtig[6b]	celoso[3a]
lasting (last[1a]), (durable[6])	durable[6b]	dauerhaft[6a]	duradero[7a]

English	French	German	Spanish
madness^{4b}, (frenzy^{6})	folie^{2a}, (délire^{3b})	Wahnsinn^{5a}	manía^{3b}, (extravío^{6b}), (frenesí^{7a})
magnify^{5a}	grossir^{4a}	vergrößern^{4b}	aumentar^{1b}
make^{1a} (up for) (compensate)	(faire) compensation^{6a}	entschädigen^{6a}	compensar^{7a}
mission^{4b}	mission^{2b}	Mission^{5b}	misión^{3a}
monster^{4b}	monstre^{3a}	Ungeheuer^{5a}	monstruo^{2b}
mother^{1a} (*adj.*), (maternal^{7})	maternel^{5b}	mütterlich^{7a}, (Mutter-)	maternal^{4b}, (materno^{7a})
murderer^{4b}	assassin^{4a}, meurtrier (*n.*)^{4b}	Mörder^{4a}	asesino^{5a}, (homicida^{6a})
niece^{5b}	nièce^{4a}	Nichte^{4a}	sobrina (sobrino^{1b})
original^{3a} (an – idea)	original^{3a}	originell^{6b}	original^{2b}
polish (P)^{3b} (Polish)	polonais^{5a}	polnisch^{4a}	polaco
popular^{3b}	populaire^{2a}	populär^{6b}	popular^{3a}
procession^{4b}, (parade^{5a})	cortège^{3a}, (procession^{4b}), (parade^{6a})	Aufmarsch^{4a}, (Aufzug^{6a}), (Parade^{6b})	cortejo^{6a}, procesión^{6a}
profitable^{5a} (advantageous)	avantageux^{3b}	vorteilhaft^{3b}	productivo^{6a}, provechoso^{6a}, ventajoso^{6a}
protest^{4b} (*n.*)	protestation^{6a}	Protest^{4a}, (Einwendung^{5a})	protesta^{3a}
provision^{3b}	provision^{4a}	Provision^{5b}	provisión^{5a}
(out of) reach^{1a}, (inaccessible^{11})	(hors de) portée^{2b}, ([hors d']atteinte^{3a})	unerreichbar	(fuera de) alcance^{3a}, (inaccesible^{6b})
refrain^{5a} (from doing)	s'abstenir^{4a}	unterlassen^{3a}	abstenerse^{5a}
remorse^{5b}, (repentance^{6})	remords^{2b}	Reue^{4b}	remordimiento^{3a}, (arrepentimiento^{6a})
residence^{3b} (general and special)	résidence^{5b}	Residenz^{5b}	residencia^{4a}
restraint^{4b}	contrainte^{3a}	Einschränkung^{4b}	limitación^{6b}
reverence^{3b}, (awe^{4a})	révérence^{5a}	Ehrfurcht^{5a}	reverencia^{4b}
satisfied (satisfy^{2a}) (hunger)	rassasié	satt^{6a}	satisfecho (satisfacer^{1b}), (saciado [saciar^{5b}])
(take off) shoes (shoe^{1b})	déchausser	Schuhe (Schuh^{6a}) ausziehen^{5a}	descalzar^{5b}
side^{1a} (*adj.*), (lateral^{7})	(de) côté^{1a}	seitlich	lateral^{4b}
signature^{5b}	signature^{3b}	Unterschrift^{4a}	firma^{2b}
slab^{6}	plaque^{4b}, (dalle^{5a})	Tafel^{2b}	plancha^{5b}, (losa^{6a})
spread^{1b} (*n.*), (diffusion^{11})	diffusion	Zerstreuung^{6a}	difusión^{5a}
statute^{5b}	statut^{5a}	Statut^{3b}, (Städteordnung^{6a}), (Ortsstatut^{6b})	fuero^{4a}, (estatuto^{6b})
strain^{3a} (*n.*), (tension^{11})	tension^{6b}	Spannung^{4b}	tensión^{7b}
stubborn^{4a}, (obstinate^{5b}), (wilful^{6})	obstiné^{6a}, têtu^{6a}	hartnäckig^{4b}	obstinado (+obstinarse)^{3a}, (terco^{4b})
stuff^{2b} (*vb.*), (pad^{5a}), (cram^{6})	bourrer^{3b}	anfüllen^{6b}	cebar^{6a}
subsequent^{5b}	suivant^{1b}	nachträglich^{4a}	ulterior^{4b}
superfluous^{5b}	superflu^{5b}	überflüssig^{3b}	prolijo^{4a}
tail^{1b} (animal)	queue^{2b}	Schwanz	cola^{3b}, (rabo^{5a})
take^{1a} (out), (suppress^{5b})	supprimer^{2b}	ausmerzen	suprimir^{3a}
tavern^{4b}	café^{2a}, (cabaret^{4b}), (brasserie^{6a})	Wirtshaus^{5a}	taberna^{3a}

English	French	German	Spanish
tea[2a]	thé	Tee[5b]	té (*n.*)[5a]
tenth[3a]	dixième[5b]	zehnte[5b]	décimo[4*]
testify[5b], (attest[6])	témoigner[3a], attester[3b]	zeugen[3b], (bezeugen[4a])	atestiguar[6b]
thunderbolt[5b]	foudre[4a]	Blitz[4b]	rayo[1b], (centella[4b])
tinkle[5b] (*vb.*)	tinter[5a]	klingen[2a]	tintinear
tuck[4b] (sewing) (*vb.*)	plisser[5a]	einschlagen[3a]	(hacer) alforzas
unable[4b], (incapable[7])	incapable[2a]	unfähig[5b]	incapaz[3b]
upright[3a], (vertical[6])	vertical	senkrecht[4b]	vertical[5b]
vex[3a], (bother[4a]), (gall[5a]), (annoy[5b])	ennuyer[3a], (agacer[4a]), (contrarier[4b]), (impatienter[4a])	belästigen[6b], plagen[6a], verdrießen[6b]	molestar[2a], (enojar[3b]), (contrariar[4b]), (fastidiar[5a]), (mortificar[5a])
virgin[3b] (*adj.*) (e.g., ground, etc.)	vierge[3a]	unberührt[6b]	virgen[2a]
witty[5b]	spirituel[2b]	geistreich[4b], (geistvoll[6a]), (witzig[6a])	ingenioso[3a], (donoso[5b])

SECTION 4.2. CONCEPTS 3693 THROUGH 3782

E F G S	*E F G S*	*E F G S*	*E F G S*	*E F G S*	*E F G S*	*E F G S*	*E F G S*	*E F G S*	*E F G S*
1-2-8*-4	1-8*-6-6	2-6-6-4	3-4-5-6	3-8*-4-6	4-4-4-6	5-1-5-1	5-4-4-2	6-1-4-1	7-1-3-1
1-3-8*-3	2-2-6-6*	2-8*-5-6	3-4-6-2	4-1-6-1	4-4-5-2	5-2-4-4	5-5-3-5	6-3-3-6	7-4-2-2
1-4-7-6	2-4-6-6	3-1-6-5	3-5-5-5	4-2-4-8*	4-5-4-5	5-3-3-7	5-5-4-1	6-5-3-1	8-2-1-4
1-5-8*-1	2-5-6-5	3-2-6-4	3-5-6-1	4-2-5-4	4-6-3-8*	5-3-4-3	5-6-2-8*	6-6-2-4	
1-6-6-8*	2-6-5-8*	3-3-6-3	3-6-5-4	4-3-5-3	4-6-4-4	5-4-3-6	5-6-3-4	6-8*-2-2	

English	French	German	Spanish
abundant[3b], (plentiful[5a])	abondant[4a]	unerschöpflich[6b], massenhaft[6b]	abundante[2b], (abundar[3b]), (copioso[5b])
anyhow[6]	(n'importe) comment[1a]	irgendwie[4b]	(de todos) modos (modo[1a])
argument[3b]	argument[3a]	Argument[6a]	argumento[3b]
aspire[5b]	aspirer à[5b]	trachten[4b]	aspirar[1b]
background[7]	fond[1a]	Hintergrund[3b]	fondo[1a]
blow[1a] nose[1b]	moucher[5a]	schneuzen	sonar[1b]
book[1a] shop[1b]	librairie	Buchhandlung[6b]	librería[6a]
bowl[2a] (*n.*)	écuelle[6b]	Schale[6a]	escudilla
brand[6b] (of goods)	marque[2b]	Marke[6a]	marca[4b]
British[2b]	britannique[6a]	britisch[6b]	británico[4b]
carpet[3b], rug[3a]	tapis[4a]	Teppich[6a]	alfombra[4a]
chop[3a], (mince[6])	hacher[5b]	hauen[6a]	picar[1b]
Christmas[1b]	noël	Weihnacht[6a]	navidad[6b]
colored (*adj.*)[4a*]	coloré[4a]	bunt[4a], (farbig[5a])	coloreado (colorear[6b])
conviction[8] (feeling)	conviction[2b]	Überzeugung[1b]	convicción[4b]
corporal[6]	brigadier[5b]	Unteroffizier[3a], (Wachtmeister[6b])	cabo[1b]
damn[5a]	damner[5b]	verdammen[4b]	condenar[1b]
deplore[7]	déplorer[4b]	beklagen[2b]	lamentar[2b], (deplorar[7a])
destruction[3a]	destruction[5b]	Verfall[5a], Vernichtung[5a], Zerstörung[5a]	destrucción[5a]
device[4b], (motto[7])	devise[4a]	Spruch[4b]	divisa[6b], lema[6b], mote[6b]

English	French	German	Spanish
dirty[3b], foul[3a], (filthy[6]), (unclean[6])	sale[3b]	schmutzig[6a], unrein[6a]	sucio[3a], (asqueroso[7a])
dive[4b]	plonger[2a]	tauchen[4a]	bucear
double[1b] (*vb.*)	doubler[4a], (redoubler[5b])	verdoppeln[7a]	duplicar[6a]
elevation[5b]	élévation[5b]	Erhebung[3a], (Hebung[5a])	elevación[5a]
even[1a] (off), (level[2a] [off]), (grade[2b])	aplanir[6b], (niveler)	ebnen[6b]	nivelar
excitement[5b]	agitation[3b], (excitation[6a])	Aufregung[4b], Erregung[4b], (Aufsehen[5b])	agitación[3b], (alborozo[7a])
exclusive[4b]	exclusif[4b]	alleinig[5b]	exclusivo[2b]
expert[4b] (*n.*)	expert[5a]	Sachverständige[4a], (Kenner[5b])	experto[5b], (conocedor[6a]), (perito[6b])
feeding (feed[1b]) (action)	alimentation[6b]	Ernährung[6a], (Fütterung)	alimentación, nutrición
fly[1a] (*n.*)	mouche[3b]	Fliege	mosca[3a]
fork[2b] (table)	fourchette[5a]	Gabel[6a]	tenedor[5a]
foundation[3a], (establishment[5b])	fondation[5b]	Stiftung[5b], (Stift[6a])	fundación[5b]
gallery[4a]	galerie[2b]	Galerie[5a]	galería[4b]
glasses (glass[1b]), (spectacles [spectacle[4a]])	lunette[3b], (lorgnon[6b])	Brille	lentes (lente[3b]), (anteojo[4a]), (gafas[7a])
growth[3a] (amount)	cru (*n.*)[4b], (accroissement[6a])	Wachstum[5a]	crecimiento[6a]
head[1a] dress[1a], hair[1a] dressing (dress[1a])	coiffure[5b]	Frisur, Kopfputz	tocado (tocar[1a])
headlong[5a], (impetuous[7])	impétueux[5b]	mit[1a] Begeisterung[3a]	impetuoso[5a]
hook[2b] (*n.*)	crochet[4b]	Haken[6a]	garabato[6a]
imperfect[4b] (incomplete)	incomplet[3b]	unvollkommen[5b]	imperfecto[3b]
incidents (incident[5b])	incident[2a], (péripétie[6a])	Vorfall[4a]	incidente[4a]
indebted[6]	(être) redevable	verdanken[2b]	(en) deuda[2b]
indignation[4b]	indignation[4b]	Unwille[5a], (Empörung[6a])	indignación[2b]
inn[3b]	auberge[3a]	Gasthof[6b]	posada[3b], (fonda[5a]), (mesón[7a])
interpret[5b]	interpréter[6a]	deuten[3a], (auslegen[6a])	interpretar[4b]
jealousy[4a]	jalousie[4a]	Eifersucht[5a]	celos (celo[2b])
jewel[3a]	bijou[4a], (joyau[6a])	Edelstein[6b]	joya[2b], (alhaja[3b])
journal[5b] (diary)	journal[1b]	Archiv[5a], Tagebuch[5b]	diario[1b]
lamentation[5b]	plainte[2b]	Jammer[4b]	lamento[4a], (plañido)
lay[1a] (person)	laïque[6b]	Laie[6a]	laico, lego
lime[4a] (mineral)	chaux[6a]	Kalk[3a]	cal
luminous[7]	lumineux[4a]	leuchtend (leuchten[2a])	luminoso[2b]
make[1a] believe[1a], (pretend[3b]), (feign[4a])	faire[1a] semblant[5a]	vorgeben	pretender[1b], (fingir[2a]), (simular)
manifest[4a] (*adj.*)	manifeste[6a]	ersichtlich[4b]	manifiesto[4a]
marshal[5a] (*n.*)	maréchal[3a]	Marschall[3b], (Feldmarschall[6b])	mariscal[7a]
merciful[6]	clément[6a]	gnädig[2a]	compasivo[4a], (misericordioso[6a])
moderate[3a] (*vb.*)	modérer[3b]	ermäßigen[6b]	moderar[3b]
pencil[2b]	crayon[4b]	Stift[6a]	lápiz[6a]
permanent[4a], everlasting[4a], perpetual[4a]	permanent[3b], (perpétuel[4a])	ständig[5b]	perpetuo[3a], permanente[3b], (perenne[5a])

English	French	German	Spanish
persecution[5b]	persécution[6a]	Verfolgung[3a]	persecución[4b]
prejudice[5b], (bias[6])	préjugé (*n.*)[4a]	Vorurteil[3b], (Vorliebe[4b])	prejuicio[6b]
program[5b]	programme[2b]	Programm[4a], Tagesordnung[4b]	programa[4b]
rain[1a] (*vb.*)	pleuvoir[3b]	regnen	llover[3a]
(little[1a]) rascal[5a], (imp[11])	morveux[6b], polisson[6b]	Teufel[2a], (Teufelchen)	granujilla, truhán
registering (register[3a]), (registration[9])	enregistration	Eintragung[4b], (Anmeldung[5b])	registro[6b]
relation[2b], ([family] relationship[8])	parenté	Verwandtschaft[5a]	parentesco[6a]
rigor[5b], (severity[6])	rigueur[4a], sévérité[4b]	Strenge[4a], Schärfe[4b]	rigor[2a], (severidad[3b]), (inclemencia[5b]), (austeridad[7a])
(have) roots (root[2a]) (in), (be rooted in)	enraciné (dans)	wurzeln[5b]	arraigado (arraigar[6a])
(make) rounds (round[1a]) (military)	ronde[2b]	Runde	ronda[4b]
rule[1b] (*vb.*) (draw lines)	régler[2a]	linieren	rayar[4a]
sap[4a]	sève[5a]	Saft[4b]	savia[5a]
school[1a] system[2a]	système[2a] scolaire[5b]	Schulwesen[6a]	sistema[2a] escolar[5a]
scientist[6]	(homme de) science[1b]	Naturforscher[4b]	(hombre de) ciencia[1a]
shatter[4b]	fracasser[6a]	zerbrechen[4b]	estrellar[4b]
shy[4b], (bashful[5b])	farouche[3a], timide[3b] (timidement[4b])	scheu[5a], schüchtern[5b]	tímido[3a], (vergonzoso[4a]), (esquivo[6a])
skillful[4a] (dexterous)	habile[3a], (adroit[4b])	geschickt[5b]	diestro[3a], (artificioso[5b])
sly[4a]	malin[3b]	schlau[5b]	astuto[3b], (malicioso[5a]), (socarrón[5a]), (artificioso[5b]), (cuco[6a])
staff[3b] (university)	conseil[1a], (faculté[2b])	Kollegium[6b]	claustro[5a]
temper[3a], (disposition[5a])	disposition[2a], (tempérament[3b])	Temperament[6b]	temperamento[4a], (talante[6b])
threshold[5b]	seuil[2b]	Schwelle[4b]	umbral[4b]
thunder[2b] (*vb.*)	tonner[5b]	donnern[6b]	tronar[5a]
ticket[3a]	billet[2b], (bulletin[6a])	Billett[6a]	billete[4a]
triumph[3b] (*vb.*)	triompher[4a]	triumphieren[6a]	triunfar[2a]
twenty[1b] five[1a]	vingt-cinq[2b]	fünfundzwanzig	veinticinco[4*]
tyrant[4a]	tyran[4a]	Tyrann[5a]	tirano[2a], (déspota[6a])
unit[6]	unité[3b]	Einheit[3a]	unidad[3a]
university[3a] (*adj.*)	universitaire[6a]	akademisch[5b]	académico[4b]
unnecessary[5b], needless[5b]	(pas, peu) nécessaire[1a], inutile[1a]	unnötig[5a], (entbehrlich[6b])	(no es) necesario[1a], inútil[1b]
waste[1b] (*vb.*)	dissiper[3a]	verschwenden	disipar[3b], (malograr[4b])
wire[2b] (metal)	fil[2b] (de fer, cuivre, etc.)	Draht[6b]	alambre
worthless[4a]	sans[1a] valeur[1b]	wertlos[6a]	sin[1a] valor[1a]

SECTION 4.3. CONCEPTS 3783 THROUGH 3859

E F G S	*E F G S*	*E F G S*	*E F G S*	*E F G S*	*E F G S*	*E F G S*	*E F G S*	*E F G S*	*E F G S*
1–1–8*–6	1–5–8*–2	2–3–6–8*	3–3–5–8*	3–5 –6–2	4–2–6–1	4–6 –4–5	5–2–4–5	5–5–4–2	6–6–2–5
1–3–8*–4	1–6–8*–1	2–3–7–4	3–3–6–4	3–6 –5–5	4–4–5–3	4–8*–4–3	5–3–4–4	5–6–3–5	7–3–1–8*
1–4–8*–3	2–1–8*–2	2–5–6–6	3–4–6–3	3–8*–5–3	4–5–4–6	5–1 –5–2	5–4–4–3	6–2–3–5	7–3–2–4
1–5–7 –6	2–2–8*–1	3–2–6–5	3–5–5–6	4–1 –6–2	4–5–5–2	5–2 –5–1	5–5–3–6	6–4–3–3	7–4–2–3

English	French	German	Spanish
abuse[3b] (*vb.*)	abuser[3b]	mißbrauchen[6a]	abusar[4a], maltratar[4b]
academy[5b]	académie[4a]	Akademie[4a]	academia[3b]
affectionate[5b]	affectueux[5a], (câlin[6a])	liebevoll[4b]	amoroso[2a], cariñoso[2b], (expresivo[4a]), (afectuoso[4b])
amen[5b]	ainsi[1a] soit[5b] il[1a]	Amen[3b]	amén[6b]
Arabia(n)[4b]	arabe[5a]	arabisch[4b]	árabe[6a]
audience[3b] (member of –), (hearer[6])	auditeur[5a]	Zuhörer[5a]	oyente[6a]
beckon[5b]	faire[1a] signe[1a]	winken[5a]	(llamar con) señas (seña[2a])
blaze[2b] (*vb.*)	flamber[3b]	flammen[6a]	llamear
bow[1b] (prow)	avant[1a]	Bug	proa[6a]
breakfast[1b] (*vb.*)	déjeuner (*vb.*)[3b]	frühstücken	desayunarse[4b]
clear[1a] (table)	desservir[6a]	abräumen	quitar[1a] (la mesa), (alzar los manteles)
coat[1b] (of suit)	veste[5b], veston[5b]	Jacke	americana (americano[2a])
combination[3b]	combinaison[3a]	Kombination[6b]	combinación[4a]
condense[5b]	concentrer[4b], (condenser[6a])	konzentrieren[4a], (zusammendrängen[6a])	condensar[3b], (comprimir[5b])
confession[5b], admission[5b]	aveu[3b], (confession[4b]), (admission[6b])	Bekenntnis[4b], (Geständnis[5b]), (Konfession[5b])	confesión[4a]
contract[3a] (*vb.*) (literally)	contracter[4a], (rétrécir[5a])	zusammenziehen[6b]	contraer[3a]
contradiction[7]	contradiction[3b]	Widerspruch[2a]	contradicción[4a]
cook[1b] (*n.*)	cuisinière[4a]	Koch, Köchin	cocinero[3a]
cool[1b] (*vb.*), (chill[3a])	refroidir[3b]	kühlen	enfriar[4b]
costume[5b]	costume[2a]	Tracht[5b]	traje[1b]
courteous[5a]	galant[4b], (courtois[6b])	höflich[4b], (ritterlich[6b])	cortés[3b], (cortesano[4b]), (caballeresco[6a]), (urbano[6a])
cradle[3b], (crib[6])	berceau[4a]	Wiege[6b]	cuna[3b]
cup[1b], (mug[6])	tasse[3a]	Tasse	taza[4a], (jícara[6a])
day[1a] after[1a] tomorrow[1b]	après-demain[6a]	übermorgen	pasado[1b] mañana[1a]
decay[3a], decline[3b] (*n.*)	décadence[6b], déclin[6b]	Verfall[5a], Vergehen[5a], Abnahme[5b]	decadencia[5b]
decidedly[7]	décidément[3a]	entschieden (entscheiden[1a])	decididamente
disastrous[6]	funeste[4a], (désastreux)	entsetzlich[3a]	funesto[3b], (desastroso[5b])
dispute[3a] (*n.*), (controversy[6])	dispute[3b], (polémique[6b])	Auseinandersetzung[6a]	disputa[4b]
double[1b] (effort), (redouble[8])	redoubler[5b]	verdoppeln[7a]	redoblar[6b]
drown[2a]	noyer[2b]	ertränken, ertrinken	ahogar[1b], (anegar[4a])
drum[2b]	tambour[5b]	Trommel[6a]	tambor[6a]

English	French	German	Spanish
eighteen[2b]	dix-huit[3b]	achtzehn[7a]	dieciocho[4]*
emotion[5b]	émotion[1b], (attendrissement[5a])	Rührung[5b]	emoción[2a]
endow[5b]	doter[3b], (douer[4b])	ausstatten[4a], (ausrüsten[5a])	dotar[4a]
expel[5a]	expulser[3b], (reléguer[6b])	vertreiben[3a]	expulsar
expire[4b] (e.g., a certain time)	expirer[4b]	verfließen[5a]	expirar[3b]
(of) genius[3b]	génial[6a]	genial[5a]	genial[5b]
gesture[5b]	geste[1b]	Gebärde[5a]	gesto[2a], ademán[2b]
Hebrew[6] (*adj.*)	juif[6a]	jüdisch[2b]	judío[5a]
helper[5b], (assistant[6])	auxiliaire[4b], (adjoint[6b])	Gehilfe[4a], (Adjutant[6a])	auxiliar[3a]
impatient[4b]	impatient[4a]	ungeduldig[5a]	impaciente[3b]
infamous[7]	infâme[4b]	gemein[2b]	infame[3a]
injurious[5b]	nuisible[5a]	schädlich[3b], (nachteilig[4a])	nocivo[6b], perjudicial[6b]
interview[5a] (*n.*)	entretien[2b], (interview[5b])	Unterredung[4b]	entrevista[5b]
joke[3b] (*vb.*), (jest[4b])	plaisanter[3a]	scherzen[5a]	bromear, embromar, chancear
juice[4a]	jus	Saft[4b]	jugo[3b]
lawn[2b] (grass)	pelouse[3b], (gazon[6a])	Rasen[6b]	césped
liquor[4b], (gin[6])	alcool[4a], liqueur[4a], (eau-de-vie[5a]), (absinthe[5a]), (rhum[6a])	Alkohol[5a], Branntwein[5a], Spiritus[5a]	licor[3b], (alcohol[4a]), (aguardiente[5b])
mistrust[5b] (*n.*)	défiance[6a], méfiance[6b]	Mißtrauen[3b]	desconfianza[5b]
novelty[4b]	nouveauté[5a]	Neuigkeit[5b]	novedad[2b]
pension[5b] (money)	pension[2b]	Pension[4b], Rente[4b]	pensión[5b]
people[1a] (*vb.*), (populate[12])	peupler[4b]	bevölkern	poblar[3a]
projecting (project[4b]), (salient[13])	saillant[6b]	vorstehend (vorstehen[4b])	saliente[5a]
providence[4a]	providence[4b]	Vorsehung[5b]	providencia[3b]
rapt[6]	transporté (transporter[2b])	begeistert (begeistern[3b])	transportado (transportar[5a]), (rapto)
reflect[4a] (e.g., in a glass)	réfléchir[1b], (refléter[4b])	spiegeln[6a], zurückwerfen[6a]	reflejar[2b]
repent[3b]	se repentir[5a]	bereuen[6a]	arrepentirse[2b]
reproduce[6]	reproduire[4a]	wiedergeben[3b]	reproducir[3a]
(place of) residence[3b]	(lieu de) séjour[3a], (résidence[5b])	Wohnort[6b]	domicilio[4b]
responsible[5b]	responsable[3b]	verantwortlich[4b]	responsable[4b]
roll[1a] (of carriage, thunder, etc.)	roulement[5b]	Rollen	(el) rodar[2a], (redoble)
romantic[5b]	romantique[4b], (romanesque[5b])	romantisch[4a]	romántico[3a]
(make the) rounds (round[1a])	(faire une) tournée[3b]	bereisen	(hacer la) ronda[4b]
rude[2b], rough[2a], (unpolished) (person), (crude[6])	commun[1b], (vulgaire[3b])	ungeschliffen	rudo[2b], (tosco[3a]), (agreste[5b])
singer[4a]	chanteur[4b]	Sänger[5a]	cantor[3b]
sole[2b] (*n.*) (foot)	plante[2b]	Sohle	planta[1b]
soothe[5b]	adoucir[4a], (alléger[6b])	mildern[4a]	aliviar[3b], tranquilizar[3b]
start[1a] toward(s)[1b] (bend one's steps)	(s')acheminer[5b]	(sich) aufmachen	encaminar[2b] (se)

English	French	German	Spanish
subdue^{3b}, (quell^{6})	soumettre^{2a}, (dompter^{6b})	bezwingen^{6b}	subyugar^{5b}
sunbeam^{4b}	rayon^{2a} (de soleil)	Sonnenstrahl^{6b}	rayo^{1b} (de sol)
supreme^{3b} court^{1b}	cour de cassation	Reichsgericht^{5a}	tribunal^{3a} supremo^{2a}
suspect^{4a} (*adj.*), (suspicious^{6})	suspect^{6a}	verdächtig^{4b}	sospechoso^{5b}, (receloso^{6a})
thorn^{3a}, (briar^{4a})	épine^{4b}	Dorn^{6b}	espina^{3b}, (abrojo^{5a})
thumb^{3b} (*n.*)	pouce^{3b}	Daumen^{5a}	pulgar
treason^{4b}, (treachery^{6})	trahison^{4b}	Verrat^{5a}	traición^{3a}
twilight^{3b}, (dusk^{6})	crépuscule^{4b}	Dämmerung^{6a}	anochecer^{3b}, crepúsculo^{3b}
Wednesday^{2b}	mercredi^{3b}	Mittwoch^{6a}	miércoles

SECTION 4.4. CONCEPTS 3860 THROUGH 3952

E F G S	*E F G S*	*E F G S*	*E F G S*	*E F G S*	*E F G S*	*E F G S*	*E F G S*	*E F G S*	*E F G S*
1–2–8*–6	2–1–8*–3	2–6 –6–6	3–4 –6–4	4–1–6–3	4–5 –5–3	5–3–4–5	5–6 –4–2	6–5 –3–3	7–6–1–6
1–3–8*–5	2–2–8*–2	2–8*–5–8*	3–5 –6–3	4–2–6–2	4–8*–3–8*	5–4–3–8*	5–8*–3–4	6–6 –2–6	8–2–2–2
1–4–8*–4	2–3–8*–1	2–8*–6–4	3–6 –6–2	4–3–5–5	4–8*–4–4	5–4–4–4	6–2 –3–6	6–8*–2–4	
1–5–8*–3	2–3–7 –5	3–3 –6–5	3–8*–4–8*	4–4–4–8*	5–2 –4–6	5–5–4–3	6–4 –2–8*	7–1 –2–7	
1–6–8*–2	2–4–6 –8*	3–4 –5–8*	3–8*–5–4	4–4–5–4	5–2 –5–2	5–6–3–6	6–4 –3–4	7–5 –2–3	

English	French	German	Spanish
acre^{2b}	hectare^{4b}	Hektar^{6b}	hectárea, fanega
Africa(n)^{2b} (*adj.*)	africain	afrikanisch^{6b}	africano^{4a}
alleged (allege^{5b})	allégué	angeblich^{3b}	alegado (alegar^{4a})
armor^{3a}	armure	Rüstung^{4b}	armadura
assurance^{5b}, (certainty^{7})	certitude^{2b}, (assurance^{4a})	Gewißheit^{4a}	certeza^{6b}
baby^{1b}, (babe^{4a})	bébé^{6b}	Säugling	criatura^{2a}
bedroom^{4a}	chambre^{1a} (à) coucher^{1b}	Schlafzimmer^{6a}	alcoba^{3b}, (dormitorio^{6b})
clamor^{4b}, (din^{5a})	clameur^{5b}	Geschrei^{5a}	estruendo^{3b}, (clamor^{5a}), (fragor^{6b})
collar^{2b}	col^{3a}, collier^{3b}, (collet^{4b})	Kragen	cuello^{1b}
commander^{4b}	commandant^{3b}	Kommandeur^{5a}, (Kommandant^{6a}), (Befehlshaber^{6b})	comandante^{5b}
conservative^{6}	conservateur	konservativ^{2b}, (Konservative^{6a})	conservador^{4a}
continent^{3a} (*n.*)	continent^{6b}	Weltteil^{6b}	continente^{2b}
contribution^{6}	contribution^{4b}	Beitrag^{3a}	contribución^{4b}
creator^{5b}	créateur^{5a}	Schöpfer^{4b}	creador^{3a}
decline^{3b} (*n.*) (person)	déchéance^{6a}	Sturz^{6a}	ruina^{2a}
delivery^{4b}, surrender^{4a}	remise^{4b}	Übergabe^{4b}	entrega
disappointment^{4b}	déception^{5b}	Verdruß^{5a}, (Enttäuschung^{6a})	desengaño^{3a}, (contrariedad^{4b}), (contratiempo^{6b})
disturbance^{5b}	désordre^{3a}, agitation^{3b}	Störung^{4a}	perturbación^{5a}, (alboroto^{6a})
(make) dizzy^{6}	étourdir^{5b}	verwirren^{3b}	aturdir^{3b}
dove^{3a}, (pigeon^{4b})	pigeon^{5a}, (colombe^{7a})	Taube^{6a}	paloma^{3a}, (pichón^{6b}), (tórtola^{6b})
driver^{4a}	cocher^{3b}, conducteur^{3b}, (chauffeur^{5b})	Kutscher^{5b}	cochero^{5a}, (mayoral^{6b})

English	French	German	Spanish
droop[3b]	(se) flétrir[4b], ([se] faner[5b])	zusammenfallen[5b], (verwelken)	languidecer
emphasize[7]	appuyer[1b] (sur), (accentuer[4b])	hervorheben[2a]	acentuar[7b]
enforce[5b]	(faire) exécuter[2a]	erzwingen[5b]	ejecutar[2a]
entangle[6], snarl[6]	embrouiller[5a]	verwirren[3b]	enredar[3a], (embrollar[5b]), (enmarañar[6a])
extension[5a]	extension[6a]	Erweiterung[4a], (Verlängerung[5a]), (Anbau[6b])	extensión[2a]
fable[4a]	fable[5a]	Fabel[5b]	fábula[3b]
fast[1a] (*n.*)	jeûne[3a]	Fasten	ayuno[5a]
fold[2a] (*n.*)	pli[3a], (repli[6a])	Falte[7a]	pliegue[5b], doblez[5b]
foundation[3a] (of a building)	fondation[5b]	Fundament[6b]	cimiento[3a]
full[1a] (river, carrying much water)	abondant[4a]	wasserreich	caudaloso[4b]
furniture[7b]	meuble[2a], (mobilier[4a]), (ameublement[6b])	Möbel	muebles (mueble[2b])
ground[1a] floor[1a]	rez-de-chaussée[5b]	Erdgeschoß	piso[3a] bajo[1a]
hire[2b], rent[2a]	louer[3b]	mieten[7a]	alquilar[5b]
horror[4a], (outrage[5])	horreur[2a]	Greuel[6b]	horror[2a]
inevitable[5b]	inévitable[4a]	unvermeidlich[4a]	inevitable[4b]
inquiry[5b], interrogation[5b]	demande[2b], (interrogation[5b])	Anfrage[5a], Nachfrage[5a], (Erkundigung[6b])	pregunta[2a]
insect[3a], (bug[5a] [Amer.])	insecte[4b]	Insekt[6b]	insecto[4a]
insert[5b]	introduire[2a]	einlegen[4b], (einrücken[5b]), (einfügen[6b])	insertar[6b]
knot[3b] (*n.*)	nœud[5a]	Knoten[6a]	nudo[3b]
manifold[5b]	multiple[4b]	mannigfaltig[4a]	múltiple[4b]
medal[5b]	médaille[4a]	Orden[4b]	medalla[4b]
memorial[4b]	– commémoratif	Gedächtnis[3a]	– conmemorativo
minor[7]	mineur[6a]	minder[1b]	menor[6a]
moisture[4b]	humidité[4a]	Nässe[5a], Feuchtigkeit[5b]	humedad[4a]
nervous[4b]	ému[2a], nerveux[2a], (énervé [énerver[3b]])	nervös[6b]	nervioso[2b]
objection[5b]	objection[4a]	Einwand[4b]	reparo[4a], (objeción[6b])
omit[4b]	laisser[1a] (de) côté[1a]	auslassen[6b]	suprimir[3a], (omitir[5a])
opening (open[1a]) (first performance)	début[2a]	Debut	estreno[6b]
pass[1a], (permit[2a])	passe[5b]	Paß	permiso[3a], (pase[7b]), (salvoconducto)
polish[3b] (*vb.*)	cirer[4b], (polir[5a])	putzen[6b]	pulir[4a]
politics[8]	politique (*n.*)[2b]	Politik[2a]	política[2a]
pomp[4a]	pompe[5b]	Pracht[5a]	aparato[3a], (pompa[4a]), (solemnidad[5a])
printing (print[2a]) office[1b], (printing) business[1b]	imprimerie	Druckerei[6a]	imprenta[4a]
prosperity[4b]	prospérité[4a]	Wohlstand[5a], (Gedeihen[6a])	prosperidad[4b]
protest[4b] (*vb.*)	protester[2b], (se récrier[5b])	protestieren[6a]	protestar[2a]
Protestant (p)[6]	protestant[4a]	evangelisch[2b], (Protestant[4b]), (protestantisch[4a])	protestante

English	French	German	Spanish
purify[5b]	purifier[6a]	reinigen[3a], (klären[6b])	purificar[6b]
refuse[2a] (*n.*)	ordure[6b]	Abfall[6a]	basura[6a]
regulate[5a]	règler[2a]	regulieren[5b]	regular[2b]
republican (R)[4b]	républicain[3b]	republikanisch[5b]	republicano[5a]
restore[2b] (to youth)	rajeunir[4b]	verjüngen[6a]	rejuvenecer
revolt[4b] (*n.*), (rebellion[5b])	révolte[4b]	Aufruhr[5a]	revuelta[4b], rebelión[4b]
rub[2a] out[1a], (erase[9])	effacer[2a]	ausradieren	borrar[2b]
search[2a] (*n.*), (quest[5b])	recherche[2b]	Suche	busca[2b]
sensitive[6]	sensible[2b], (sensitif)	empfindlich[3b]	sensitivo[6b]
sheath[5b] (*n.*)	fourreau[4b]	Hülse[3b], (Scheide[6a])	vaina
similar[3b]	analogue[4b], conforme[4b], correspondant[4b]	gleichartig[6a]	análogo[4a]
slander[5b] (*vb.*)	calomnier	beleidigen[3a]	calumniar[4b]
slow[1b] down[1a], up[1a], (slacken[7])	ralentir[6a]	verlangsamen	reducir[1b] (la) marcha[2b], (acortar[6a] [la] marcha[2b]), (acortar[6a] [el] paso[1a])
sour[4b]	aigre[4a]	sauer[4b]	agrio
spark[3b]	étincelle	Funke[5a]	chispa[4a]
spell[2b] (*n.*)	enchantement[6a]	Bann[6b]	hechizo[6a]
sphere[3b]	sphère[6b]	Sphäre[6b]	esfera[2b]
spot[1b] (*vb.*)	tacher[6b]	beflecken	manchar[2b]
square[1b] (geometrical), (sq.[6])	carré[5a]	Quadrat	cuadrado[3a]
stocking[2b], (hose[4b])	bas[1b]	Strumpf	media[3b]
stroke[2b] (*vb.*), (pet[4a]), (caress[6])	caresser[2b]	streicheln	acariciar[2b]
temptation[4b]	tentation	Versuchung[4a], (Anfechtung[6b])	tentación[4a]
tenderness[5b]	tendresse[2b]	Zärtlichkeit[5b]	ternura[2b]
thrill[4a] (*vb.*)	tressaillir[5a], vibrer[5b], (palpiter[6a])	beben[5b]	estremecer[3b] se
tragedy[4b]	tragédie[4b]	Tragödie[5b]	tragedia[4a]
transition[6]	transition[6a]	Übergang[2b]	transición[6b]
troublesome[5b]	ennuyeux[4a], (importun[6a])	lästig[4a], (beschwerlich[6a])	importuno[4b]
unconscious[4b]	inconscient[4a]	unbewußt[5a]	inconsciente[4b]
under[1a] side[1a]	dessous (*n.*)[6b]	Kehrseite	parte[1a] inferior[2b]
uniform[3a] (*n.*), (livery[5b])	uniforme (*n.*)[4a], (tunique[6a])	Uniform[6a]	uniforme[4a]
van[4b] (military)	avant-garde	Avantgarde[3b]	vanguardia
vibrate[7]	vibrer[5b]	zittern[2b]	vibrar[3a], (vibrante[6b])
waist[2b]	taille[1b]	Hüfte(n)	talle[3a], (cintura[4b])
waking (wake[2a]) (*n.*)	réveil[3b]	Erwachen	despertar[1a]
wretched[3b], (disconsolate[9])	désolé (désoler[3a]), (inconsolable)	trostlos[6b]	desolado (desolar[5a]), (desconsolado)
yoke[3b] (*n.*)	joug	Joch[5a]	yugo[4a]

SECTION 4.5. CONCEPTS 3953 THROUGH 4013

E F G S	*E F G S*	*E F G S*	*E F G S*	*E F G S*	*E F G S*	*E F G S*	*E F G S*	*E F G S*	*E F G S*
1–3–8*–6	1–6–8*–3	2–8*–6–5	3–8*–5–5	4–3–6–2	4–8*–4–5	5–4–4–5	5–6 –4–3	6–4 –3–5	7–5–1–8*
1–4–8*–5	2–2–8*–3	3–2 –7–3	3–8*–6–1	4–4–5–5	5–1 –5–4	5–4–5–1	5–8*–3–5	6–5 –3–4	7–6–2–3
1–5–8*–4	2–3–8*–2	3–4 –6–5	4–2 –5–7	4–5–4–8*	5–2 –5–3	5–5–3–8*	6–2 –4–3	6–8*–2–5	8–4–1–5
1–6–7 –7	2–4–8*–1	3–5 –5–8*	4–2 –6–3	4–6–4–7	5–3 –5–2	5–5–4–4	6–3 –4–2	6–8*–3–1	

English	French	German	Spanish
adjust[5b]	adapter[3b], (ajuster[4b])	anpassen[5a], berichtigen[5a]	ajustar[2b], (adaptar[4b])
advertisement[6]	annonce[5b]	Anzeige[3b]	anuncio[4a]
amendment[4b]	amendement	Ergänzung[4a]	enmienda[5b]
ancestor[4a], (forefather[6])	ancêtre[4a], aïeul[4b]	Vorfahr[5a], (Ahne[6a])	antecesor[5a], antepasado[5a], (ascendiente[7a])
appointment[4b] (to meet), engagement[4b]	rendez-vous[3a]	Verabredung[6b]	cita[2b]
appointment[4b] (to something)	nomination[4b]	Ernennung[5b]	nombramiento[5a]
bag[1b] (suitcase), (valise[16])	valise[5b]	Reisetasche, Koffer	saco[4a] (de viaje), maleta[4b], (valija)
bay[1b] (*n.*) (water)	baie[4a], (anse[6b])	Bucht	bahía[5a]
bear[1a] (*n.*)	ours[6b]	Bär[7a]	oso[7b]
blade[2b] (e.g., of knife)	lame[4a]	Klinge	hoja[1b]
brass[2b]	cuivre[2b]	Messing	bronce[3b]
candy[2b], (goody[6])	bonbon[4a]	Süßigkeiten	dulce[1a]
capture[3b] (*n.*)	prise[2b]	Fang[7a]	presa[3a]
central[2b]	central[2b]	zentral	central[3b]
Chinese[5a] (*adj.*)	chinois[5b]	chinesisch[4b]	chino[4b]
criminal[5b] (*n.*)	criminel[3b], (malfaiteur[5a]), (scélérat[6a])	Verbrecher[5b]	criminal[2b]
(grow) dark[1a], (darken[4b])	s'assombrir[6a]	dunkeln	obscurecer[3b]
declaration[6] (customs)	déclaration[3a]	Deklaration[4b]	declaración[7b]
dish[7a] (container)	plat (*n.*)[3a], (écuelle[6b]), (vaisselle[6b]) (dishes)	Geschirr	plato[2a]
duly[6]	dûment	angemessen[3a]	debidamente (debido+deber[1a])
dying[3b] (*adj.*)	mourant (*adj.*)[4a]	sterbend[6b]	moribundo[5a]
echo[2b] (*n.*)	écho[3a]	Echo	eco[2b]
evolution[8]	évolution[4a]	Entwick(e)lung[1b], (Entfaltung[6a])	evolución[5a]
exaggerate[6]	exagérer[2b]	übertreiben[4a]	exagerar[3b], (extremar[4a])
gap[4a], (breach[6])	brèche[6a]	Lücke[4a]	brecha[7a]
gild[4a]	dorer[2b]	vergolden[6b]	dorar[3a]
gush[4b] (*vb.*), (spout[6])	jaillir[3a]	ergießen[6a]	brotar[2b], (manar[6b])
handkerchief[2b]	mouchoir[2b]	Taschentuch	pañuelo[3b]
howl[3a], (growl[5a]) (*vb.*)	hurler[4a]	heulen[6b]	latir[5a] (dog)
import[3b], (importation[9])	importation[5b]	Einfuhr[5b]	importación
knave[4a], wretch[4a], (rascal[5a]), (rogue[5a]), (villain[5a])	vilain[3b], (bandit[4a]), (brigand[4a]), (canaille[4a]), (drôle [*n.*][4a]), (scélérat[6a])	Schurke[6a], Schelm[6b]	pícaro[2b], (villano[3b]), (golfo[4a]), (malvado[5a]), (bribón[5b]), (bandido[6a]), (bellaco[6b]), (pillo[6b])
lunch[3b] (*n.*), (luncheon[6])	déjeuner (*n.*)[2a]	Gabelfrühstück	almuerzo[3b]

English	French	German	Spanish
mask[4b] (*n.*)	masque[4b]	Maske[5b]	máscara[5b]
mischief[3b]	espièglerie	Unheil[5a]	travesura[5b]
opera[4a]	opéra[5a]	Oper[4a]	ópera
organic[6]	organique[5b]	organisch[3a]	orgánico[4b]
outline[5a] (*vb.*), sketch[5b]	ébaucher[5b]	entwerfen[3b], (skizzieren)	esbozar
overcome[3b], (overpower[7])	subjuguer	hinreißen[5b]	subyugar[5b]
partial[5b] (biassed)	prévenu	einseitig[3b]	parcial[5b]
peninsula[4b]	péninsule	Halbinsel[4a]	península[5b]
petty[5a], (trivial[6])	petit[1a], (mesquin[5b])	kleinlich[5b]	mezquino[4b]
poise[6]	savoir-faire	Fassung[2b]	aplomo[5b]
presence[2a] (of mind)	sang-froid[4a]	Geistesgegenwart	sangre[1a] fría (frío[1a])
presentation[7]	présentation[6a]	Vorstellung[2a]	presentación[3b]
professional[6]	professionel[4b]	gewerblich[3b]	profesional[5a]
Prussia(n)[7] (*adj.*)	prussien[5a]	preußisch[1a]	prusiano
recommendation[5b]	recommendation[6b]	Empfehlung[4b]	recomendación[3b]
respite[7]	relâche[6a]	Frist[2b]	pausa[3a], (respiro)
scanty[5b], (scant[6])	peu[1a] abondant[4a]	knapp[5b]	escaso[1b]
season[1b], (flavor[4b])	assaisonner[6b]	würzen	sazonar[3b]
seventh[3a]	septième	siebente[5a]	séptimo[5]*
shallow[3b], (superficial[9])	superficiel	oberflächlich[5a]	superficial[5a]
shelf[4b]	rayon[2a], (planche[3a])	Bord[5a]	estante[7a]
signal[4a] (*n.*)	signal[3a]	Signal[6b]	señal[2a]
slumber[3a] (*vb.*)	sommeiller	schlummern[6b]	dormir[1a], (dormitar[6a]) (lightly)
sowing (*n.*) (sow[2b])	semailles	Saat[6b], (Säen)	siembra[5b]
spread[1b] (butter) (*vb.*)	étaler[3b]	schmieren	untar[6a]
subtract[5b]	soustraire[4b]	abziehen[4a]	deducir[5a], restar[5a], sustraer[5b], (descontar[6a])
suffering (*n.*)[5b]*	souffrance[2b]	Leiden[5b]	sufrimiento[3b], (padecimiento[5b])
usurp[6]	usurper	(an sich) reißen[2a]	usurpar[5b]
wait[1a] (*n.*)	attente[4a]	Warten	espera[5b]

PART V

THE FIFTH THOUSAND CONCEPTS

SECTION 4.6. CONCEPTS 4014 THROUGH 4106

E F G S	*E F G S*	*E F G S*	*E F G S*	*E F G S*	*E F G S*	*E F G S*	*E F G S*	*E F G S*	*E F G S*
1–4–8*–6	2–3–8*–3	2–8*–6 –6	3–5 –6–5	4–2–5–8*	4–5 –6–1	5–1–5–5	5–5 –4–5	6–2–3–8*	6–8*–2–6
1–5–8*–5	2–4–8*–2	3–1 –8*–1	3–6 –6–4	4–3–6–3	4–6 –4–8*	5–3–5–3	5–6 –3–8*	6–3–4–3	6–8*–3–2
1–6–8*–4	2–5–8*–1	3–2 –6 –8*	3–8*–5–6	4–4–5–6	4–6 –5–4	5–4–4–6	5–6 –4–4	6–4–4–2	7–3 –3–3
2–2–8*–4	2–6–6 –8*	3–3 –6 –7	3–8*–6–2	4–4–6–2	4–8*–4–6	5–4–5–2	5–8*–4–2	6–6–2–8*	7–6 –1–8*
									7–8*–1–6

English	French	German	Spanish
accusation[5b]	accusation[4b]	Anklage[4b]	acusación[6a]
add[1a] up[1a]	additionner[6b]	zusammenzählen	sumar[4a]
alley[5a]	passage[1b]	Gasse[5a]	calleja[5a]
ankle[4a]	cheville[6a]	Enkel[4b]	tobillo
bars (bar[7a]), (grating [grate[4a]])	grille[3b]	Gitter	reja[3b], (verja[5b])
beating[6b] (heart)	battement	Schlag[2b]	latido[6a]
beg[7a] (literally)	mendier[5b]	betteln	pedir[1a]
bible (B)[4b], (scripture[5b])	bible[6a]	Bibel[4a]	Biblia
bore[2b] (tire)	ennuyer[3a], (embêter[4a])	langweilen	aburrir[3a]
box[1a] (theatre)	loge[5b]	Loge	palco[5b]
brave[1b] (*vb.*)	braver[5b], (affronter[7a])	trotzen	arrostrar[5a]
brush[2a] (paint)	pinceau, brosse	Pinsel[6b]	pincel[6b]
cathedral[4b]	cathédrale[3b]	Dom[6a]	catedral[3a]
cell[3a] (organic)	cellule[3b]	Zelle[6a]	célula[7b]
changing (change[1a]), (unsettle[d][6])	variable[5b]	veränderlich	variable[5a]
charity[3a] societies (society[2b])	sociétés (société[1b]) (de) bienfaisance[6a]	Gesamtarmenverbände[6b]	sociedades (sociedad[1b]) benéficas (benéfico[4a])
cheer[2a] (up) (*tr. vb.*)	égayer[5a]	aufmuntern	animar[1b], (alentar[4a])
childish[5b]	enfantin[3b], ([être de l']enfantillage[6a]), (puéril[6b])	kindisch[5b]	infantil[3b], (pueril[4a])
cliff[3a], (bluff[5a]), (crag[6])	falaise[6b]	Abhang[6a]	risco[5a], (precipicio[7a])
cowardly[5b]	lâche[3a]	feig[5b]	cobarde[3a], medroso[3b]
crystal[4a] (*n.*)	cristal[4a]	Kristall[6a]	cristal[2a]
curse[2b] (*vb.*), (accursed[5a])	maudit (*adj.*)[4a], (maudire[6a])	verfluchen	maldecir[2a]
curve[3b] (*n.*)	courbe[5b]	Krümmung[6b]	curva[5a]
daylight[3b]	jour[1a]	Tageslicht	luz[1a] (diurna), luz[1a] (de día)
discontent(ed)[4a]	mécontent[4a]	unzufrieden[5b]	descontento[6a]
disgust[5b] (*n.*)	dégoût[4b]	Widerwille[5b], (Abscheu[6a])	disgusto[2a], (asco[6a]), (hastío[6b])
(side) dish[2a]	entremets[6a]	Einlage[6b]	entremés
dramatic[7]	dramatique[3b]	dramatisch[3b]	dramático[3b]

English	French	German	Spanish
empress[6]	impératrice	Kaiserin[3b]	emperatriz (emperador[2b])
entertainment[5a] (treat)	fête[1b]	Essen[5a]	agasajo[5b]
equality[5b]	égalité[3b]	Gleichheit[5a]	igualdad[3a]
excessive[5b]	outré (*adj.*)[3b], (excessif[4a])	übermäßig[5a]	excesivo[3a]
exploration[5b]	exploration[6b]	Forschung[3b]	exploración
funds (fund[4b])	fonds[5a]	Fonds[6a]	fondos (fondo[1a])
groom[5b] (Amer.), (bridegroom[6])	(nouveau) marié	Bräutigam[4b]	novio[2a]
grudge[5b] (*n.*)	rancune[3b], (ressentiment[5a])	Unwille[5a]	rencor[3b]
homage[5b]	hommage[3b]	Huldigung[5b]	homenaje[3b]
ignoble[6]	ignoble[6a]	niedrig[2a]	innoble
ignorance[4a]	ignorance[4a]	Unwissenheit[6b]	ignorancia[2b]
indicative[7]	indicatif	Zeichen[1b] (für)	indicativo[6a]
initial[7]	initial[6b]	erste[1a], (Anfangs-)	inicial
injustice[5b]	injustice[3b]	Ungerechtigkeit[5a], Unrecht[5a]	injusticia[3a]
investigate[5b]	approfondir[6b]	forschen[4b]	inquirir[4b], (indagar[6a]), (investigar[6a])
jerk[6] (*vb.*)	(donner une) secousse[4a], ([donner des coups] saccadés [saccadé[5a]])	zucken[4a]	sacudir[2b]
kernel[6]	noyau	Kern[3b]	grano[2b]
lame[3a] (*vb.*), (cripple[4b])	estropier	lähmen[5b]	estropear[6a]
leadership[6]	direction[2a], conduite[2b]	Führung[3a]	jefatura
legislation[6]	législation	Gesetzgebung[2a]	legislación[6a]
license[4b]	concession[4b], (autorisation[5b])	Konzession[6a]	licencia[2b]
muse[3b] (*n.*)	muse[6a]	Muse[6a]	musa[4a]
nail[2a] (*vb.*)	clouer[4b]	nageln	clavar[2a]
oath[6] (e.g., take an –)	serment[3b]	Eid[4a]	juramento[3a]
picturesque[5b]	pittoresque[3b]	malerisch[5b]	pintoresco[3a]
pink[2b] (*adj.*), (rosy[4a])	rose[2a]	rosa	rosado[4a], (sonrosado[6b])
pity[2a] (*vb.*)	(avoir de la) pitié[2a], plaindre[2b]	bemitleiden	compadecer[4a]
plague[3b], (pestilence[6])	peste[6a]	Seuche[6a]	peste[4b], (plaga[6a])
pole[2a] (N. and S.)	pôle	Pol[6b]	polo[6b]
police[4a] department[3a]	gendarmerie[6a]	Polizei[4b]	comisaría
policy[3b] (life insurance)	police[2b]	Police[6b]	póliza
preliminary[6]	préliminaire[6b], préalable[6b]	vorläufig[2b]	preliminar
publication[5b]	publication[5a]	Veröffentlichung[4b], Verlag[4b], (Publikation[6b])	publicación[5a]
quit[2b]	quitte[5a]	quitt	libre[1a]
reasoning (reason[1a])	raisonnement[5a]	Gedankengang	razonamiento[5a], (raciocinio[6a])
reconcile[4a] (things)	concilier[4a], (réconcilier[5a])	vereinbaren[5a]	conciliar[6a], reconciliar[6b]
removal[7] (taking away)	enlèvement[6b]	Entfernung[1b]	remoción, deposición
riddle[4a]	rébus, devinette	Rätsel[4a]	enigma[6a]
riot[4b]	troubles (trouble [*n.*][2a]), (désordre[3a]), (émeute[6b])	Aufruhr[5a], Aufstand[5r]	motín

English	French	German	Spanish
run[1a] (into) (a street into another)	déboucher[4b]	münden	desembocar[6a]
rustle[4b] (*vb.*)	bruire	rauschen[4a]	susurrar[6b]
school[1a] (*adj.*)	scolaire[5b]	Schul-	escolar[5a]
scroll[6]	rouleau	Rolle[2a]	rollo[6b] (de papel), (pergamino)
smart[3a] (dashing person)	chic[5a]	keck[6a]	bizarro[5a], (apuesto[7a])
soap[3a]	savon[6a]	Seife[6b]	jabón[4b]
spoil[2a] (child)	gâter[3a]	verziehen	mimar[3b]
straighten[5b] (up)	redresser[3b], (se redresser[4a])	ausrichten[5b]	enderezar[3b]
supper[2a]	souper (*n.*)[4a]	Abendessen	cena[2b]
surpass[4b]	surpasser[6b]	übertreffen[4a]	sobrepasar
tap[3a] (*vb.*), (pat[3b])	taper[5a]	pochen[6a]	golpear[5a]
theatre[2b] (*adj.*)	(de) théâtre[2a], (théâtral)	Theater-	teatral[4b]
threat[5a]	menace[3b]	Drohung[5b]	amenaza[3b]
timid[4a]	timide[3b]	furchtsam[6b]	tímido[3a], temeroso[3b]
toe[3a]	doigt[1a] de[1a] pied[1a]	Zehe	dedo[1b] (del) pie[1a]
trade[1b] (*adj.*)	syndical[6a]	Handels- und Gewerbe-	comercial[4a], (mercantil[6a])
triumphant[5b]	triomphant[5a]	siegreich[4a]	triunfante[6b], triunfal[5b]
trot[3b] (*n.*)	trot	Trab[6b]	trote[6a]
twenty[1b] two [1a]	vingt-deux[5a]	zweiundzwanzig	veintidós[5]*
uncomfortable[5b]	(peu) confortable[4b], (incommode[6a])	unbequem[5a]	inconveniente[2b], (incómodo[5a])
unwillingly (unwilling[5b])	à contre-cœur	ungern[4b]	(a) disgusto[2a]
voter[5b]	électeur[5a]	Wähler[4b]	vocal[5b]
weave[3a], (woven[4b]), (wove[5b])	tisser	einschießen[6a], weben[6a]	tejer[2b]
whistle[2a] (*vb.*)	siffler[3a], (siffloter[5a])	pfeifen	silbar[3a]
wholesome[4a], (healthful[6]), (sanitary[6])	salutaire[6b]	heilsam[5a]	saludable[4b]
worldly[5a] (mundane)	mondain[4b]	weltlich[4a]	mundano[6a]

SECTION 4.7. CONCEPTS 4107 THROUGH 4180

E F G S	*E F G S*	*E F G S*	*E F G S*	*E F G S*	*E F G S*	*E F G S*	*E F G S*	*E F G S*
1-3-8*-8*	2-2-8*-5	3-1-8*-2	3-4 -6-7	4-3-6-4	4-5 -6-2	5-4-4-7	6-4-3-7	6-6 -3-5
1-4-8*-7	2-3-8*-4	3-2-8*-1	3-6 -6-5	4-4-5-7	4-6 -5-5	5-4-5-3	6-4-4-3	6-8*-2-7
1-5-8*-6	2-4-8*-3	3-3-6 -8*	3-8* 6 3	4-4-6-3	4-8*-5-3	6-2-5-1	6-5-3-6	7-5 -2-6
1-6-8*-5	2-5-8*-2	3-3-7 -4	4-2 -6-5	4-5-5-6	5-3 -5-4	6-3-4-4	6-5-4-2	7-8*-2-3

English	French	German	Spanish
accidental[6]	fortuit	zufällig[2a]	accidental[7a]
Arab[6]	arabe[5a]	Araber[3b]	árabe[6a]
attorney[5a]	procureur[4b]	Rechtsanwalt[4a], Verteidiger[4b]	procurador[7a]
belt[2b], (sash[4a]), (girdle[4b])	ceinture[3a]	Gürtel	faja[4b], (cinto), (cinturón)
boldness[5b], (daring[6])	audace[3b], (aplomb[5a]), (hardiesse[6a])	Kühnheit[5b]	atrevimiento[4a], audacia[4a], (osadía[6b])
breed[3b], (bred[4a])	élever[1a]	züchten	criar[2a]

English	French	German	Spanish
cake[1b]	gâteau[6b]	Kuchen	torta[5b], (melindre[6b]), (pastel[6b])
cheese[2b]	fromage[4b]	Käse	queso[3b]
conjecture[6]	supposition[6a]	Vermutung[3b]	suposición[5a]
continuation[7]	continuation	Fortsetzung[2a]	continuación[3b]
corrupt[4b] (*vb.*)	corrompre	verführen[5b]	corromper[3b]
(fellow[1b]) countryman[6], (compatriot[13])	compatriote[3b]	Landsmann[4a]	paisano[4b], (compatriota[5a])
courtesy[5a]	courtoisie[4b]	Höflichkeit[5b]	cortesía[3a], (obsequio[4a]), (finura[5b]), (galantería[5b])
cross[1a] (out)	rayer[5a]	durchstreichen	tachar[6a]
cut[1a], (mow[6])	faucher[6b]	mähen	segar[5b]
dam[4a] (*n.*)	barrage	Wall[5b], (Damm[6a])	presa[3a] (de) agua[1a]
decrease[4a], (reduction[5b])	réduction[5b]	Abnahme[5b], Verminderung[5b]	mengua[6a]
duchess[6]	duchesse[4b]	Herzogin[4b]	duquesa (duque[3a])
engagement[4b] (to do something)	engagement[3b]	Verabredung[6b]	compromiso[4a]
fantastic[5b]	fantastique[4a]	phantastisch[5a]	fantástico[3a]
fisherman[4b], (fisher[6])	pêcheur[4a]	Fischer[6b]	pescador[3b]
flood[2b] (*vb.*)	inonder[4a], (submerger[6a])	überschwemmen	inundar[3a]
frequent[2a] (*vb.*)	fréquenter[4b]	frequentieren	frecuentar[3b]
gallop[3b] (*n.*)	galop[3b]	Galopp[6a]	galope
gather[1b] (sewing)	froncer[6b]	kräuseln	fruncir[5a]
generous[3a]	généreux[2b]	großzügig	generoso[1b]
grandson[6], (granddaughter[12])	petit-fils[5a], (petite-fille[6a])	Enkel[4b]	nieto[2b]
hateful[5b], (odious[6])	odieux[3b], (détestable[5a])	verhaßt[5b]	odioso[4a], detestable[4b]
haughty[4a]	hautain[5a], (orgueilleux[6b])	hochmütig[6a], übermütig[6a], (im) Übermut[6a]	soberbio[2a], (altivo[3a]), (orgulloso[3a]), (arrogante[4b]), (altanero[5a])
head[1a] (of bed)	chevet[6a]	Kopfende	cabecera[5a]
hen[2a]	poule[5b]	Henne	gallina (gallo[2b])
herb[4a]	herbe[2a]	Kraut[6b]	yerba[5b]
illusion[6]	illusion[2b]	Wahn[5a]	ilusión[1b]
indifference[6]	indifférence[4a]	Gleichgültigkeit[4a]	indiferencia[3a], (desvío[5a])
ingenious[5b]	ingénieux[4b]	genial[5a]	ingenioso[3a]
maker[3a]	fabricant[6b]	Produzent[6a], (Hersteller)	fabricante[5a]
making (make[1a]) (e.g., of clothes)	confection[6a]	Konfektion	hechura[5a], confección[5b]
miner[5b]	mineur[4b]	Bergmann[4b], (Bergarbeiter[6b])	minero[7a]
modesty[5b]	modestie[4a], (pudeur[5a])	Scham[5b], (Bescheidenheit[6a])	modestia[3b], (pudor[4b])
monk[5a], friar[5b]	moine[4b], (capucin[5a])	Mönch[5b]	fraile[3a], monje[3a]
monstrous[4a]	monstrueux[3b]	unnatürlich[6a]	monstruoso[4a], grotesco[4b]
neglect[2b] (*n.*)	négligence[5b]	Vernachlässigung	descuido[2b]
ninth[3a]	neuvième[6a]	neunte[6a]	noveno[5*]
opening (open[1a]) (e.g., of a meeting)	ouverture[3a]	Eröffnung	apertura

English	French	German	Spanish
ounce[3b], (oz.[4b])	once	Gramm[6a]	onza[3b], (gramo[4a])
piano[4a]	piano[2b]	Klavier[6b]	piano[5a]
prosperous[3b]	prospère[6b]	segensreich[6a]	próspero[5b]
purity[5a]	pureté[4a], (candeur[5a])	Reinheit[5a]	pureza[3b]
quart[3b], (pint[4a]), (qt.[5a]), (gallon[5b]), (pt.[6])	litre[4a]	Liter[6b]	litro[7a], cuartillo[7b]
rally[7] (*vb.*)	rallier[5b]	versammeln[2a]	rehacer[6b] (se)
recess[3b] (time)	trêve[6b]	Zwischenzeit[6b]	intermedio[5a], tregua[5a]
reconcile[4a] (persons)	réconcilier[5a]	versöhnen[5a], (Versöhnung[6b])	reconciliar[6b]
redeem[4b]	racheter[5b]	einlösen[6b]	desempeñar[2b], (redimir[5b])
restaurant[4b]	restaurant[4b]	Lokal[5b]	restaurant[7b]
rice[3a]	riz[6b]	Reis[6a]	arroz[5a]
roar[2a], (bellow[4b])	hurler[4a]	brüllen	rugir[3b], (bramar[4a])
salt[1b] (*vb.*)	saler[6a]	salzen	salar[5a]
severity[6]	sévérité[4b]	Strenge[4a]	severidad[3b]
sew[2a]	coudre[4b]	nähen	coser[3a]
shameful[5b]	honteux[3a], (scandaleux[6b])	schändlich[5b]	vergonzoso[4a], (escandaloso[6a])
sharpen[4a]	aiguiser[6b]	schleifen[5b], (spitzen[6a])	afilar[5b], aguzar[5b]
shiver[3b] (*n.*), (shudder[6])	frisson[3b], (frémissement[5b])	Schauer[7a]	temblor[4a], (estremecimiento[7a])
shrill[4a]	criard[5a]	grell[6b]	agudo[2b], (penetrante[7a])
sweat[4a] (*n.*)	sueur[4a]	Schweiß[6a]	sudor[3a]
technical[6]	technique[4b]	technisch[3a]	técnico[7b]
twenty[1b] four[1a]	vingt-quatre[6b]	vierundzwanzig	veinticuatro[5*]
twenty[1b] six[1a]	vingt-six[6a]	sechsundzwanzig	veintiseis[5*]
unworthy[5b]	indigne[4b]	unwürdig[5a]	indigno[3a]
vault[4a]	voûte[3a]	Gewölbe[6a]	bóveda[4b]
wagon[2a], (cart[3a])	charrette[5a], (chariot[6b])	Fuhrwerk	carro[2a], (galera[5a]), (carreta[5b])
wipe[2b]	essuyer[2b]	wischen	enjugar[5a]
wolf[2a], (wolves[5b])	loup[3b]	Wolf	lobo[4a]
working (work[1a]) (action)	exploitation[4b]	Auswertung, Ausbeutung	explotación[7b]
worm[2b]	ver[4b]	Wurm	gusano[3b]

SECTION 4.8. CONCEPTS 4181 THROUGH 4281

E F G S	*E F G S*	*E F G S*	*E F G S*	*E F G S*	*E F G S*	*E F G S*	*E F G S*	*E F G S*	*E F G S*
1-8*-8*-4	2-5 -8*-3	3-2 -8*-2	4-4-6-4	4-8*-4-8*	5-3-5-5	5-6 -4-6	6-4 -4-4	6-8*-3-4	7-6-2-6
2-2 -8*-6	2-6 -8*-2	3-3 -8*-1	4-5-5-7	4-8*-5-4	5-4-5-4	5-8*-3-8*	6-5 -4-3	7-3 -3-5	8-3-2-5
2-3 -8*-5	2-8*-6 -8*	3-6 -6 -6	4-5-6-3	5-1 -6-3	5-5-4-7	5-8*-4-4	6-6 -3-6	7-4 -2-8*	8-4-1-8*
2-4 -8*-4	3-1 -8*-3	3-8*-5 -8*	4-6-5-6	5-2 -6-2	5-5-5-3	6-3 -4-5	6-6 -4-2	7-4 -3-4	8-4-2-4
						6-3 -5-1	6-8*-2-8*	7-5 -3-3	9-4-1-4

English	French	German	Spanish
alternately (alternate[5b])	alternativement[5b]	abwechselnd (abwechseln[5a])	alternativo[3b], (alternado [alternar[6a]])
aspiration[7]	aspiration[5a]	Sehnsucht[3a], Streben[3a]	aspiración[3b]
(without) authority[2b], (illicit[15])	illicite	unberechtigt[6a]	ilícito

English	French	German	Spanish
bleak^{6}	morne^{3b}	öde^{5a}	triste^{1a}, (sombrío^{3a})
bud^{2b} (*n.*)	bouton^{3b}	Knospe	yema^{5a}, (botón^{6a}), (capullo^{6b})
budget^{7}	budget^{4b}	Etat^{3a}	presupuesto^{4a}
bunch^{3a}, cluster^{3b}, (bouquet^{6})	bouquet^{2b}	Strauß	ramo^{2b}, (racimo^{5b})
cake^{1b} (of) soap^{3a}	pain^{1b} (de) savon^{6a}	Stück^{1a} Seife^{6b}	pastilla^{6b} (de) jabón^{4b}
check^{2a}, (cheque^{12})	chèque	Check^{6b}	cheque
chicken^{2a}, (chick^{3b})	poulet^{4b}, (poule^{5b})	Huhn, Kücken	pollo^{4b}
cloak^{2b}, (cape^{3a}), (mantle^{3b})	pèlerine^{6a}	Pellerine	capa^{2a}, manto^{2b}
clump^{8} (trees, etc.)	massif (*n.*)^{4a}	Gruppe^{2b}	macizo^{4b}
code^{7}	code^{3b}	Gesetzbuch^{3a}, Handelsgesetzbuch^{3a}, (Zivilprozeßordnung^{4b}), (Strafgesetzbuch^{5b})	código^{5b}
comet^{6}	comète	Komet^{3b}	cometa^{4b}
community^{4b} (*adj.*)	communal	kommunal^{4a}	comunal
concentrate^{6}	concentrer^{4b}	konzentrieren^{4a}	concentrar^{4b}, reconcentrar^{4b}
contemporary^{6} (*n.*)	contemporain^{3a}	Zeitgenosse^{4b}	contemporáneo^{5a}
corn^{1a} (Amer.)	maïs	Mais	maíz^{4a}
cruelty^{4b}	barbarie^{5a}, (cruauté)	Grausamkeit^{6b}	crueldad^{3a}, (barbarie^{5a})
curiosity^{5a}	curiosité^{2a}	Neugier^{6b}, Neugierde^{6b}	curiosidad^{2a}
curl^{2b} (*vb.*)	boucler^{4b}, (friser^{6a})	kräuseln	rizar^{4a}
deaf^{3b}	sourd^{2b}	taub	sordo^{2a}
dealer^{4b}	vendeur^{6a}	Händler^{5a}	vendedor^{6a}
debtor^{6}	débiteur^{6a}	Schuldner^{3a}, (Bezogene^{5b})	deudor^{6a}
delivery^{4b} (of goods)	livraison	Lieferung^{4a}	entrega
detachment^{8} (troops)	détachement^{4b}	Abteilung^{1b}	destacamento
dig^{2b}, (dug^{3b}), (scoop^{6})	creuser^{2b}, fouiller^{2b}	graben	cavar^{6a}
disadvantage^{6}	désavantage	Nachteil^{2a}	desventaja
discipline^{5a}	discipline	Disziplin^{4b}, (Zucht^{5b})	disciplina^{4a}
discontent^{4a} (*n.*)	mécontentement^{6a}	Unzufriedenheit^{5b}	descontento^{6a}
disobey^{5a}	désobéir	(nicht) gehorchen^{3b}, (ungehorsam sein)	desobedecer
(put in) disorder^{5b}	(mettre en) désordre^{3a}	durcheinander^{5a} (bringen), (in) Unordnung^{6a} (bringen)	desordenar^{5a}
(make) drunk^{4b}	griser^{4a}, (enivrer^{6b})	berauschen^{6b}, (trunken machen)	embriagar^{4a}
Easter^{4a}	pâques^{6b}	Ostern^{5b}	pascua^{6b}
encourage^{3a}	encourager^{3a}	ermutigen	animar^{1b}, (alentar^{4a})
engineer^{4a}	ingénieur^{5b}	Ingenieur^{6a}	ingeniero^{3a}
exceptionally (exceptional^{5b})	exceptionnellement^{6b}	ausnahmsweise^{4b}	excepcionalmente (excepcional^{6b})
fence^{2a}	barrière^{3a}, (clôture^{5a})	Zaun	valla^{5b}
fervor^{7}	ferveur^{6b}	Eifer^{2b}	fervor^{6a}
goddess^{4a}	déesse	Göttin^{5b}	diosa^{4a}
grease^{5b} (*n.*)	graisse^{6a}	Fett^{4b}	grasa^{6b}

English	French	German	Spanish
greedy[4a]	avide[4a]	begierig[6a]	insaciable[4b], (ávido[5b])
hammer[2b] (*n.*)	marteau[4b]	Hammer	martillo[4a]
harvest[2a] (*vb.*), (reap[3b])	(faire la) récolte[5b]	ernten	(hacer la) cosecha[3a]
hay[2a]	foin[5b]	Heu	paja[3b]
heathen[4a]	païen[5b]	Heide[5a]	pagano[7a]
highness[6] (title)	excellence[3a]	Hoheit[4a]	alteza[5b]
inaugurate[8]	inaugurer[3b]	eröffnen[2a]	inaugurar[5a]
international[7]	international[3b]	international[3a]	internacional[5a]
inventor[5b]	inventeur[5a]	Erfinder[4b]	inventor[7a]
investment[7]	placement[4b]	Anlage[2a]	inversión
kettle[3a]	bouillotte	Kessel[5b]	marmita
leisure[5a]	loisir[3b]	Muße[5b]	ocio[5a]
lock[2a] (sluice)	écluse	Schleuse[6a]	esclusa
log[2b]	bûche[5a]	Kloben	tronco[3a]
lust[4b] (*n.*)	cupidité	Begierde[5a]	codicia[4b]
malice[5a]	malice[5a]	Bosheit[5b]	malicia[3a]
metal[2b] (*adj.*)	métallique[4b]	metallisch	metálico[4b]
metropolis[6]	métropole[6a]	Hauptstadt[3a]	metrópoli[6b]
mockery[6]	moquerie[6b]	Spott[4b]	burla[2a]
mud[6b], (mire[5a])	boue[4b]	Schlamm	barro[4a], lodo[4a]
multiple[9] (*adj.*)	multiple (*adj.*)[4b]	vielfach[1b]	múltiple[4b]
murmur[2a] (*n.*)	murmure[3b]	Gemurmel, Getuschel	cuchicheo[5a], murmullo[5b]
musician[4b]	musicien[4a]	Musiker[6b]	músico[4b]
negative[5b] (*adj.*)	négatif[5b]	verneinend (verneinen[5b])	negativo[3b]
oar[4b]	rame	Ruder[5b]	remo[4b]
oath[6] (blasphemy)	juron[5b]	Fluch[4a]	juramento[3a], (blasfemia[4b])
organism[6]	organisme[6b]	Organismus[4a]	organismo[5b]
outline[5a] (*n.*)	contour[5a], silhouette[5a]	Umriß[5b]	contorno[3a], (silueta[6a])
overwhelm[5b]	accabler[3a]	niederdrücken[5a]	arrollar[5a]
passage[3a], (corridor[7])	passage[1b], (couloir[3a]), (corridor[3b])	Flur	corredor[3b], (pasillo[5b])
pastime[4b], (entertainment[5a]), (amusement[5b])	distraction[4a], (amusement[6a]), (récréation[6a])	Zerstreuung[6a]	distracción[4a], diversión[4a], pasatiempo[4b], (recreo[5a]), (entretenimiento[6a])
paternal[6]	paternel[4a]	väterlich[4a]	paternal[4a], (paterno[5a])
patriotic[5b]	patriote[4a]	patriotisch[5b]	patriótico[4b]
pigeon[4b]	pigeon[5a]	Taube[6a]	paloma[3a], (pichón[6b])
rabbit[2b]	lapin[4b]	Kaninchen	conejo[4a]
reference[5a]	référence	Berufung[4a], (Hinweis[5b])	referencia[4a]
robbery[5b]	vol[3a]	Raub[5a], (Diebstahl[6b])	robo[5a], (rapiña[6b])
savior (S)[5a]	sauveur	Heiland[4b], (Erlöser[5a])	salvador[4b]
seduce[5b]	séduire[4b]	verleiten[5a], verführen[5b]	seducir[4b]
senior[6]	aîné[3a]	Älteste[5b]	mayor[1a]
share[2a] holder[4b]	actionnaire	Aktionär[4a], (Anteilseigner[6a])	accionista
shorten[5b]	abréger[5a]	verkürzen[5b]	encoger[3b], (abreviar[4b]), (acortar[6a])
siege[5b]	siège[1b]	Belagerung[6a]	cerco[3b]

English	French	German	Spanish
slander^{5b} (*n.*)	calomnie^{5a}	Beleidigung^{5a}	calumnia^{3b}
spacious^{5a}, (capacious^{6})	vaste^{1b}, (ample^{5a})	geräumig^{6b}	amplio^{3a}
spoon^{2b}, (teaspoon^{6})	cuiller(-ère)^{4a}	Löffel	cuchara^{4a}
studious^{6}	studieux	fleißig^{2a}	estudioso
swing^{2b} (*n.*) (motion)	balancement	Schwung^{6b}	balanceo
temple^{2b} (head)	tempe^{4a}	Schläfe	sien^{4b}
(legal^{5b}) tender^{2a}, (currency^{6})	monnaie^{3a} légale (légal^{4b})	Zahlungsmittel^{5b}	moneda^{2b} legal^{4b}
thoughtless^{5b}	étourdi (*adj.*)^{5b}, (distrait^{6a})	leichtsinnig^{5a}, (im) Leichtsinn^{5b}	aturdido (aturdir^{3b})
type^{3a} (*n.*)	type^{2a}	Typ	tipo^{2a}
unseen^{4a}	inaperçu^{5a}	unbemerkt^{5a}	inadvertido^{7a}
urge^{2b} on^{1a}, whip^{2b} up (horse)	exciter^{2b} (un cheval)	antreiben, anspornen	arrear^{6b}
vegetable^{2b}	légume^{4b}, (végétal^{5a})	Gemüse	legumbre^{4a}, vegetal^{4a}, (hortalizas^{5b})
vehement^{6}	véhément	energisch^{3a}	vehemente^{4b}
virtuous^{4a}	vertueux^{5b}	tugendhaft^{6a}	virtuoso^{3b}
weaken^{5b} (make weak)	affaiblir^{4a}, (faiblir^{5a})	schwächen^{5a}, verdünnen^{5b}	debilitar^{4b}
whip^{2b} (*vb.*), (lash^{5a})	fouetter^{4b}	peitschen	azotar^{4b}
whip^{2b} (*n.*), (lash^{5a})	fouet^{5a}	Peitsche	azote^{3b}, (látigo^{5b})

SECTION 4.9. CONCEPTS 4282 THROUGH 4377

E F G S	*E F G S*	*E F G S*	*E F G S*	*E F G S*	*E F G S*	*E F G S*	*E F G S*	*E F G S*
1–5 –8*–8*	2–5–8*–4	3–8*–6–5	4–5 –6–4	5–2–6–3	5–4–5–5	5–6 –4–7	6–2–5–3	6–5 –3–8*
1–8*–8*–5	2–6–8*–3	4–3 –7–2	4–6 –5–7	5–3–5–6	5–5–5–4	5–8*–4–5	6–3–5–2	6–6 –3–7
2–3 –8*–6	3–1–8*–4	4–4 –6–5	4–8*–5–5	5–3–6–2	5–5–4–8*	6–1 –4–8*	6–4–4–5	6–8*–3–5
2–4 –8*–5	3–3–8*–2	4–5 –5–8*	4–8*–6–1	5–4–6–1	5–6–5–3	6–1 –5–4	6–4–5–1	7–5 –3–4
								8–6 –2–3

English	French	German	Spanish
access^{5b}	accès^{3a}	Zutritt^{5b}	acceso^{6a}
aggravate^{6}	aggraver^{5a}	erschweren^{3b}	agravar
alarm^{2b} (*n.*)	alerte^{5a}	Alarm	alarma^{4a}
amend^{4b} (*vb.*)	amender	berichtigen^{5a}	enmendar^{5a}
awkward^{5b}	maladroit^{3a}, (gauche [*awkward*]^{5a}), ([d'une grande] maladresse^{6a})	ungeschickt^{6b}	torpe^{2b}
axis^{5b}, (axle^{6})	axe^{5b}	Achse^{5b}	eje^{4b}
bark^{2a} (of tree)	écorce^{5a}	Rinde	corteza^{4b}, (cáscara^{5b})
berry^{2b}	grain^{3a}, (baie^{4a}), (graine^{5b})	Beere	mora^{6b} (black –)
boundless^{4b}	illimité^{6b}	unbeschränkt^{5b}	ilimitado^{7a}
box^{1a} (tree)	buis^{5b}	Buchs	boj
bush^{2a}	buisson^{5a}	Gebüsch	mata^{4b}
butt^{6} (*n.*) (end)	bout^{1a}	Kolben^{4b}	culata
chat^{5b} (*vb.*)	bavarder^{5b}	plaudern^{5b}	charlar^{4b}
chemical^{7} (*adj.*)	chimique^{5a}	chemisch^{3a}	químico^{4a}
coach^{2b} (e.g., and four)	carrosse^{5b}	Gefährt	carruaje^{4b}
consul^{6}	consul^{6b}	Konsul^{3b}	cónsul^{7b}

English	French	German	Spanish
cool[1b] (*vb.*) (refresh)	rafraîchir	erfrischen	refrescar[5a]
curl[2b] (*n.*)	boucle[4a]	Locke	rizo[5a]
currency[6]	monnaie[3a] (du pays)	Valuta[5b], Zahlungsmittel[5b], (Währung[6a])	moneda[2b]
cylinder[5b]	cylindre	Zylinder[4a], (Walze[5b])	cilindro[5a]
depose[6]	déposer[1b]	absetzen[5a]	deponer[4b], (destronar[6b])
depress[6]	abattre[2a], (déprimer)	niederdrücken[5a]	abatir[3a]
deputy[5b], delegate[5b]	député[2b]	Delegierte[6a], Deputierte[6b], Bevollmächtigte[6a]	diputado[3b], (delegado[4a]), (comisario[6b])
dining (dine[2b]) room[1a]	salle à manger[6b], réfectoire[6b]	Eßzimmer	comedor[3b]
divinity[5b]	divinité	Gottheit[4a]	divinidad[5b]
doll[2b], (dolly [D][5a])	poupée[5a]	Puppe	muñeca[4a]
extensive[5a]	répandu[6a]	umfangreich[5a]	extenso[3a]
fade[2b], (wither[3b]), (wilt[4a])	flétrir[4b], (faner[5b])	verwelken	marchitar[5a], mustio[5a], marchito[5b]
fast[1a] (*vb.*)	jeûner	fasten	ayunar[5b]
finding (find[1a]) (something found)	trouvaille	Fund	hallazgo[5b]
flap[5a] (of table)	battant (*n.*)[4b]	Klappe[6a]	hoja[1b] (de la mesa)
fox[2a]	renard[5a]	Fuchs	zorro[4b]
fraction[5a]	fraction[6b]	Fraktion[4b]	fracción[4b]
garrison[6]	garnison[4b]	Besatzung[4b], (Garnison[5b])	presidio[5a], guarnición[5b]
goat[2a], kid[2b]	chèvre[6b]	Ziege	cabra[3a]
grumble[5a] (*vb.*)	grogner[5a]	jammern[5b]	gruñir[4a]
heel[2a] (on foot)	talon[4a]	Ferse	talón[5b]
helmet[4b]	casque[5a]	Helm[6a]	casco[4a]
hospitality[6]	hospitalité[5b]	Gastfreundschaft[3a]	hospitalidad
instinctive[6]	instinctif[4b] (instinctivement[5a])	unwillkürlich[4a]	instintivo[5a]
interval[5a]	intervalle[3a]	Zwischenraum[5b]	intervalo[6b]
lamb[2a]	brebis[6a]	Lamm	cordero[3a]
lily[3a]	lis	Lilie[6b]	azucena[5b], (lirio[6a])
marble[2b] (game)	bille[6b]	Marmel	bola[3a]
mob[5b]	canaille[4a]	Pöbel[5b]	canalla[5a], turba[5a], (plebe[6a])
nomination[5b]	nomination[4b]	Ernennung[5b]	nombramiento[5a]
note[1b] book[1a] (small)	carnet[5b]	Taschenbuch	cuaderno, carnet
nucleus[6]	noyau	Kern[3b]	núcleo[5b]
orange[2a] blossom[2a]	(fleur d')oranger[5b]	Orangenblüte	azahar[4b]
Orient (o)[5a] (*vb.*)	s'orienter[5b]	sich[1a] erkundigen[4b]	orientarse
pan[2b]	casserole[5b], (poêle [*f.*][6a])	Pfanne	cazuela[4a], (cacerola[5b])
parallel[4b] (*adj.*)	parallèle[5a]	parallel[6b]	paralelo[4b]
pastor[5a]	pasteur[6a]	Pastor[5a]	pastor[3a]
pay[1a] off[1a], settle[1b] up[1a]	liquider[5b]	ausbezahlen	liquidar
piety[5b]	piété[3b]	Frömmigkeit[6a]	piedad[2a], (devoción[3a])
pine[2b] (*n.*)	pin[5a]	Tanne	pino[4a]

English	French	German	Spanish
preceding (precede[6])	précédent[4a]	vorhergehend (vorhergehen[4b])	precursor[5a]
preceding (precede[6]) year[1a]	année[1a] précédente (précédent[4a])	Vorjahr[5b]	año[1a] anterior[1b], ([año] precedente[4b])
proverb[5b]	proverbe[6b]	Sprichwort[5b]	refrán[3b]
purple[2b] (royal)	pourpre[4b]	Purpur	púrpura[5b], cárdeno[5b]
radiance[8]	rayonnement[6a]	Glanz[2b]	esplendor[3a], (radiancia)
rash[4b], (reckless[7])	téméraire	übereilt (übereilen[6b])	atrevido (+atreverse)[1a], (temerario[4a])
receipt[3b] (for payment)	reçu	Quittung[6a]	recibo[5a]
reverend[4b]	révérend	ehrwürdig[5a]	reverendo[5b]
ringing (ring[1b]) (*n.*) (bell)	sonnerie[5a]	Geläute	tañido, timbrazo, campaneo
round[1a] (off) (e.g., edge), make[1a] round[1a]	arrondir[5a]	abrunden	redondear
select[2b] (people)	élite[5a]	erlesen	selecto[4b], (granado[5b])
shade[1b] (*vb.*)	ombrager[5b]	schatten	sombrear
sheet[2a] (bed)	drap[3b]	Bettuch	sábana[6b]
(sea) sickness[3a]	mal[1a] de[1a] mer[1b]	Seekrankheit	mareo[4a]
sink[2a] (under a burden), (succumb[14])	succomber[5b]	zusammenbrechen	sucumbir[4b]
skin[1b] (*vb.*), (flay[11])	écorcher	schinden	desollar[5a]
snow[1b] (*vb.*)	neiger	schneien	nevar[5b]
soil[1b], (dirty[3b]) (*vb.*)	salir[5b]	beschmutzen	ensuciar
spring[1a] (*adj.*) (season)	printanier[5b]	Frühlings-	primaveral
squadron[6]	escadron	Eskadron[3b], (Schwadron[4b])	escuadrón[5a]
(make) stiff[2b], (stiffen[8])	raidir[4a]	versteifen	(hacer) rígido[5a]
strain[3a], (sift[4b])	passer[1a]	sieben	colar[4a], filtrar[4b], (cerner[5b])
survey[4a] (*n.*), (inspection[7])	inspection[5a]	Übersicht[5a], (Überblick[6b])	inspección
syllable[5a]	syllabe[5b]	Silbe[5b]	sílaba[4b]
telegraph[4a] (*n.*)	télégraphe[4b]	Telegraph[6b]	telégrafo[5a]
tell[1a] (in) advance[2a], (prophesy[5a]), (foretold[6]), (predict[7])	prédire[4b]	voraussagen	augurar[5a]
temper[3a] (*vb.*) (steel)	tremper[3a]	härten, tempern	templar[2b]
tragic[6]	tragique[3a]	tragisch[5a]	trágico[2b]
traitor[4a]	traître[3b]	Verräter[7a]	traidor[2b]
tramp[4a], (rover[5a])	gueux[5a], vagabond[5a]	Wanderer[6a]	vagabundo[4b]
treat[2a] (give a treat to)	régaler[5b]	traktieren	obsequio[4a]
turn[1a] (up), (hem[4a]), (tuck[4b] [up])	retrousser[5a]	schürzen	remangar
ungrateful[5b]	ingrat[3b]	undankbar[6b]	ingrato[2b]
vow[3a] (*n.*)	vœu[3a]	Gelübde	voto[2a]
wandering (wander[2a]), (errant[13])	errant[5a]	Fahrende	errante[4b], (andante[5a])
(lay) waste[1b], (ravage[8])	ravager[5a]	verheeren, verwüsten	asolar, devastar
wings (wing[1b]) (in theatre)	coulisse[5b]	Kulisse	bastidores
womb[6]	matrice	Schoß[3b]	matriz[5a]
working (work[1a]) (out)	élaboration[5b]	Ausarbeitung	elaboración
world[1a] (*adj.*)	mondial[5b]	Welt-	mundial

SECTION 5. CONCEPTS 4378 THROUGH 4477

E F G S	*E F G S*	*E F G S*	*E F G S*	*E F G S*	*E F G S*	*E F G S*	*E F G S*	*E F G S*	*E F G S*
1–6 –8*–8*	2–5 –8*–5	3–3 –8*–3	4–1–8*–1	4–6 –5–8*	5–3–6–3	5–6–4–8*	6–4 –4–6	6–8*–4–2	7–8*–2–6
1–8*–8*–6	2–6 –8*–4	3–5 –8*–1	4–2–6 –8*	4–8*–5–6	5–4–5–6	6–1–6–1	6–5 –4–5	7–4 –3–6	7–8*–3–2
2–2 –8*–8*	2–8*–8*–2	3–6 –6 –8*	4–4–6 –6	5–2 –5–8*	5–4–6–2	6–2–4–8*	6–6 –4–4	7–6 –2–8*	8–3 –3–3
2–4 –8*–6	3–1 –8*–5	3–8*–6 –6	4–5–6 –5	5–2 –6–4	5–5–5–5	6–3–5–3	6–8*–3–6	7–6 –3–4	8–4 –2–6

English	French	German	Spanish
absent[3a]	absent[3b]	abwesend	ausente[3a]
appetite[3b]	appétit[3a]	Appetit	apetito[3a]
apple[1a] tree[1a]	pommier[6b]	Apfelbaum	manzano
assurance[5b], security[5b]	assurance[4a]	Gewähr[6a]	seguridad[2a]
astonishing[5b]	étonnant[3b]	erstaunlich[6a]	asombroso[3b]
ax(e)[2b], (hatchet[5a])	hache[5a]	Axt	hacha[5b]
banker[5b]	banquier[4b]	Bankier[5b]	banquero[6a]
battalion[8]	bataillon[4b]	Bataillon[2a], Armeekorps[2b]	batallón[6a]
bent[2b] (*adj.*), arched (arch[2b]), (stooped [back of person] [stoop[3a]])	voûté[2b]	gewölbt	arqueado, abombado
bleed[4a]	saigner[6a]	bluten[5b]	sangrar
bleeding (bleed[4a]) (*adj.*)	saignant (*adj.*)[6a]	blutend (bluten[5b])	sangrante
bore[2b], drill[2b] (*vb.*)	percer[2b], (trouer[4b])	bohren	taladrar
brick[2a]	brique[4b]	Ziegel	ladrillo[6a]
cape[3a] (headland)	cap[5b]	Kap	cabo[1b]
cling[5a], (clung[6])	(s')accrocher[2b], (se cramponner)	(sich) klammern[6b]	adherir[4a] (se)
commissioner[4b]	commissaire[4a]	Kommissar[6a], Regierungskommissar[6a]	comisionado[6b]
conservation[7], (preservation[8])	conservation[6b]	Erhaltung[3a]	conservación[4b], (preservación)
consign[7]	consigner[6b]	überweisen[3a]	consignar[4a]
corn[1a] (on toe)	cor	Hühnerauge	callo[6a]
coward[3b]	lâche[3a]	Feigling	cobarde[3a]
critical[7]	critique	kritisch[3b]	crítico[2b]
cube[5a]	cube[6a]	Würfel[4b]	cubo
deepen[5b]	creuser[2b], (foncer[4a]), (approfondir[6b])	vertiefen[5a]	profundizar
democrat[5b]	démocratique[5b]	demokratisch[5b]	democrático[5a]
devotion[5a]	dévouement[3b]	Hingebung[6a]	devoción[3a]
dictate[5a]	dicter[4b]	diktieren[6a]	dictar[2b]
dislike[5b] (*n.*)	aversion[5a], répugnance[5b]	Abneigung[5b]	repugnancia[5a]
disorder[5b], mess[5b]	désordre[3a], (désarroi[6b])	Unordnung[6a]	desorden[3a]
dragon[3b]	dragon[6a]	Drache[6b]	dragón
duck[2b]	canard[5b]	Ente	pato[5a]
elephant[4a]	éléphant	Elefant[5a]	elefante[6b]
enrich[5a]	enrichir[3b]	bereichern[6a]	enriquecer[3a]
extract[5b] (*vb.*)	extraire[5b]	ausziehen[5a]	extraer[5a]
fairy[2b]	fée[4b]	Fee	hada[6b]
fan[2b] (up) (e.g., fire)	activer[5b]	anfachen	avivar[5a]

English	French	German	Spanish
felt[1b] (material)	feutre[6a]	Filz	fieltro
frost[2a]	givre	Frost	helada (helar[2a])
fur[2a]	fourrure	Pelz	piel[2a]
graze[3b] (e.g., flock)	paître	weiden[6b]	pacer[6b]
grind[2b] (teeth)	grincer[5a]	knirschen	crujir[5a] (los dientes)
groan[3a] (*vb.*), (moan[4a])	gémir[3b]	stöhnen	gemir[3a]
gulf[2b]	golfe[6b]	Meerbusen	golfo[4a]
heating (heat[1b])	chauffage[6b]	Heizung	calefacción
helpless[4a]	impuissant[5a]	hilflos[6b]	desvalido[5a], (impotente[6a])
highland[4b]	terre[1a] haute (haut[1a])	Hochland	tierra[1a] (de) altura[1b]
(do) homage[5b] (to)	(rendre) hommage[3b] (à)	huldigen[6a]	rendir[1b] homenaje[3b]
hospital[3a]	hôpital[3a]	Krankenhaus	hospital[3b]
humble[3a] (*vb.*)	humilier[3b]	demütigen	humillar[3a]
ignorant[3b]	ignorant[3a]	unwissend	ignorante[3a]
impartial[6]	objectif[4b], (impartial[6b])	sachlich[4a], objektiv[4b]	imparcial[6a]
imprisonment[6]	emprisonnement	Gefängnisstrafe[4a], (Haft[6b])	prisión[2b]
indication[8]	indication[3b], (indice[5a])	Anzeige[3b]	indicación[3b]
indirect[6]	indirect[6a]	indirekt[4a]	indirecto[4a]
involved (involve[4a])	compliqué[4b]	kompliziert[6a]	intrincado[6b]
irregular[4b]	anormal[5a]	unnatürlich[6a]	irregular[5b]
jury[5b]	jury[6b]	Geschworene[4b]	jurado
knot[3b] (hair)	chignon	Knoten[6a]	moño[6a]
ladder[3a]	échelle[3b]	Leiter (*f.*)	escala[3a]
landing (land[1a]) (from ship, etc.)	débarquement[6b]	Ausschiffung	desembarco
manager[6]	administrateur[5a]	Verwalter[4a]	administrador[5a]
melancholy[5b] (*n.*)	mélancolie[3a]	Wehmut[6b]	melancolía[3b]
melancholy[5b] (*adj.*)	mélancolique[3b]	wehmütig[6b]	melancólico[3b]
mouse[2a], (mice[4a])	souris (*f.*)[6a]	Maus	ratón[4a]
nonsense[5a]	bêtise[3b], (sottise[4b])	Dummheit[6b], Unsinn[6b]	disparate[3b], (tontería[4a]), (necedad[5a]), (despropósito[6a]), (estupidez[6a])
orange[2a] tree[1a]	oranger[5b]	Orange(nbaum)	naranjo[5a]
pathetic[7]	pathétique[6b]	rührend (rühren[2a])	patético
police[4a] (*adj.*)	(de) police[2b]	polizeilich[6b]	policiaco
prohibition[6]	défense[2b]	Verbot[4b]	prohibición
radical[6]	radical[3a]	radikal[5b]	radical[3b]
reform[4b] (*vb.*)	réformer[4b]	reformieren[6b]	reformar[6a]
repay[4b]	rendre[1a], (rembourser[5a])	rückzahlen	pagar[1a], (reembolsar)
revolutionary[6]	révolutionnaire[3b]	revolutionär[5b]	revolucionario[3b]
rib[3a]	côte[1b]	Rippe	costilla[5a]
ripple[5a] (*vb.*)	onduler[5a]	wogen[5a]	ondular[5b]
rival[3b] (*n.*)	rival[3a], (concurrent[5b])	Mitbewerber	rival[3b]
row[1b] (*vb.*)	ramer	rudern	bogar[6b]
rubber[3a]	caoutchouc[6a]	Kautschuk[6a]	goma, caucho
sinister[8]	sinistre[3b]	finster[3a]	siniestro[3b]

English	French	German	Spanish
skin[1b] (*vb.*) (scrape)	écorcher	schaben	descarnar[6a]
soup[3a]	soupe[3b]	Suppe	sopa[3a]
stimulus[7]	stimulant	Reiz[2b]	estímulo[6b]
sumptuous[5b]	somptueux[5a]	üppig[5a]	suntuoso[5a]
superintendent[5b]	gérant[6a]	Verwalter[4a]	superintendente
swallow[2a] (bird)	hirondelle[4b]	Schwalbe	golondrina[6b]
swarm[3b] (*vb.*)	grouiller[6b]	schwärmen[6a]	enjambrar
torch[4b]	flambeau[5a], torche[5b]	Fackel[6b]	antorcha[5a]
tough[6]	dur[1b]	zäh[6b]	duro[1a]
translation[7]	version[4b], (traduction[5b])	Übersetzung[3b], (Übertragung[4a])	traducción[6a], versión[6a]
trivial[6]	trivial	unbedeutend[3a]	fútil[6b]
trunk[2a] (to pack)	malle[4b]	Koffer	cofre[6b], (baúl[7a])
Turkish[5a], Turk[5b]	turc[4a]	türkisch[5a]	turco[6a]
unanimous[6]	unanime[4a]	einstimmig[4b]	unánime[6a]
uneasiness[7]	malaise[4a]	Unruhe[3a]	malestar[6b]
vegetable[2b] (*adj.*)	potager[6a]	Gemüse-	vegetal[4a]
vehicle[6]	véhicule[5b]	Fahrzeug[4a]	vehículo[5a]
villain[5a]	vilain[3b]	Schurke[6a]	villano[3b], (malvado[5a])
vomit[7] (*vb.*)	vomir	(sich) übergeben[2b]	vomitar[6a]
water[1a] (*adj.*)	aquatique	Wasser-	acuático[6a]
(stopping [stop[1a]] of) work[1a]	chômage[6b]	Arbeitsunterbrechung	paro
working (work[1a]) (*n.*) (functioning)	fonctionnement[6b]	Funktionieren	funcionamiento

SECTION 5.1. CONCEPTS 4478 THROUGH 4543

E F G S	*E F G S*	*E F G S*	*E F G S*	*E F G S*	*E F G S*	*E F G S*	*E F G S*	*E F G S*
2–3–8*–8*	2–8*–8*–3	3–5–8*–2	4–4–6–7	5–1–6–6	5–4–6–3	5–8*–4–7	6–4–5–3	7–3–4–4
2–4–8*–7	3–2–8*–5	3–6–8*–1	4–4–7–3	5–2–6–5	5–5–5–6	5–8*–5–3	6–6–4–5	7–6–4–1
2–5–8*–6	3–3–8*–4	3–8*–6–7	4–5–6–6	5–3–6–4	5–5–6–2	6–3–5–4	6–8*–3–7	8–6–3–1
2–6–8*–5	3–4–8*–3	4–2–8*–1	4–5–7–2	5–4–5–7	5–6–6–1	6–4–4–7	6–8*–4–3	

English	French	German	Spanish
abominable[5b]	abominable[5a]	abscheulich[5a]	abominable[6b]
almighty[5a]	tout[1a] puissant[1b]	allmächtig[6b]	omnipotente[6b]
bark[2a] (*vb.*)	aboyer[6a]	bellen	ladrar[6a]
border[2a], (hem[4a]) (put a – on)	border[3b]	umranden	(tomar el) ruedo, (hacer el) ruedo
cardinal[5b] (*n.*)	cardinal (*n.*)[5a]	Kardinal[5b]	cardenal[6a]
cigar[5b]	cigare[3b]	Zigarre[6a]	cigarro[4a]
clash[5b] (*n.*) (physical)	choc[3a]	Zusammenstoß[6a]	choque[4a]
confederacy[6]	fédération[4b]	Bundesstaat[4b]	federación[7a], confederación[7b]
confident[5a]	confident[6b]	getrost[6a]	cierto[1a], seguro[1a], (confiado [confiar[2a]])
confirmation[5b]	confirmation	Bestätigung[4b]	confirmación[7a]
contrast[4b] (*vb.*)	contraster[5b]	abheben[6b]	contrastar[6a]
cream[2a]	crème[5b]	Sahne	nata[6b]

English	French	German	Spanish
critic[5a]	critique (*m.*)[5a]	Kritiker[6a]	crítico[2b]
cunning[3a] (quality)	adresse[2a], (ruse[4b])	Verschlagenheit	astucia[5a], sutileza[5b]
descent[5a]	descente[4b]	Niedergang[5b]	descenso[7a]
despatch[6] (*n.*)	dépêche[4a]	Depesche[5b]	despacho[3a]
document[5b]	document[4a]	Dokument[6b], Schriftstück[6b]	documento[3a]
elbow[3b]	coude[3a]	Ellbogen	codo[4a]
eloquence[5a]	éloquence[3b]	Beredsamkeit[6a]	elocuencia[4b]
emphasis[6]	emphase[6b]	Nachdruck[4a], (nachdrücklich[6a])	énfasis[5b]
enclosed (enclose[3b]) (e.g., in letter)	ci-inclus, ci-joint	einliegend[6b]	adjunto[7a]
entry[4a], item[4b]	article[2a]	Eintrag	entrada[1b], (partida[2a])
excellence[6] (superiority)	excellence[3a]	Exzellenz[5a]	excelencia[4a]
export[5b] (*n.*)	exportation[5a]	Export[5a], (Ausfuhr[6a])	exportación[6b]
extremity[5b]	extrémité[2b]	Äußerste[6b]	extremidad[5b]
famine[3b]	famine[6b]	Hungersnot	hambre[1b]
formal[6]	cérémonieux	förmlich[4a], formell[4b]	formal[3a], ([de] etiqueta[4a])
fowl[3a], (poultry[4a])	volaille[5b]	Geflügel	(aves de) corral[2b]
frail[3b]	fragile[4b], (frêle[5a])	zerbrechlich	frágil[3b]
frame[2a] (*vb.*)	encadrer[3b]	rahmen	enmarcar, encuadrar
grind[2b]	moudre	mahlen	moler[3a]
hoof[3a]	sabot[3b]	Huf	casco[4a]
ink[3a]	encre[4a]	Tinte	tinta[3a]
lately[7]*	dernièrement[6b]	kürzlich[4a]	últimamente (último[1a])
laurel[4b]	laurier[4b]	Lorbeer[7a]	laurel[3a], (lauro[5b])
limit[2a], (confine[4a]), (particularize[16])	confiner[6b]	spezifizieren	concretar[5b]
medical[5b]	médical[5b]	medizinisch[6a], ärztlich[6b]	médico[2a]
meditation[6]	méditation[3b]	Nachdenken[5a]	meditación[4b]
multiply[3a]	multiplier[4b]	vervielfältigen	multiplicar[3a]
nut[2a]	noix[6a]	Nuß	nuez[5b]
palm[3a] (of hand)	paume[5a]	Handfläche	palma[2b]
paw[3b] (*n.*)	patte[3b]	Pfote	pata[4a]
pie[2a] (meat)	pâté[5b]	Pastete	pastel[6b]
plate[2a] (*vb.*)	plaquer[6b]	plattieren	platear[5b]
plead[3b]	plaider[5a]	plaidieren	suplicar[2a]
poison[3a] (*vb.*)	empoisonner[3b]	vergiften	envenenar[4b]
procedure[8]	procédure[6a]	Vorgehen[3b]	proceder[1b]
publication[6] (of the) general[1a] staff[3b]	Revue (revue[3b]) (de l')état-major[6a]	Generalstabswerk[4b]	publicación[5a] (del) estado[1a]
responsibility[7]	responsabilité[3a]	Haftung[4a], (Verantwortlichkeit[5a]), (Verantwortung[5a])	responsabilidad[4a]
saucy[6]	insolent[4b]	frech[5b]	impertinente[3b], (insolente[4a])
scornful[6], contemptuous[6]	méprisant (mépriser[3b]), (dédaigneux[4b])	verächtlich[5a]	desdeñoso[4b]
seventy[2a]	soixante-dix[6b]	siebzig	setenta[5]*

English	French	German	Spanish
sinner[5a]	pécheur	Sünder[5a]	pecador[3a]
sleeve[3b]	manche (*f.*)[3b]	Ärmel	manga[4a]
sport[2a] (*n.*)	sport[3b]	Sport	deporte
spy[2b] (*vb.*)	épier[5a]	spähen	espiar[6a], acechar[6b]
structure[6]	structure[6a]	Zusammensetzung[4a]	estructura[5a]
suffrage[6] (right to vote)	suffrage	Stimmrecht[3a], (Wahlrecht[4a])	sufragio[7a]
suggestion[5b]	suggestion[5b]	Andeutung[5a]	sugestión[6b]
thickness[4b]	épaisseur[5a]	Dicke[7a]	grueso[2b], (espesor[7a])
tights (tight[2b])	maillot[6a]	Trikot	mallas (malla[5b])
toy[2a], (plaything[5a])	jouet	Spielzeug	juguete[3b]
trap[2b] (*n.*), (snare[4b])	piège[4a], (trappe[6b])	Falle	trampa[7a]
venerable[6]	vénérable[4a]	ehrwürdig[5a]	venerable[3b]
vineyard[5b]	vigne[3a]	Weinberg[6a]	viña[4a]
visitor[4a]	visiteur[4b]	Besucher[6b]	visitante[7a]

SECTION 5.2. CONCEPTS 4544 THROUGH 4621

E F G S	*E F G S*	*E F G S*	*E F G S*	*E F G S*	*E F G S*	*E F G S*	*E F G S*
2-4 -8*-8*	2-8*-8*-4	3-6 -8*-2	4-4 -6-8*	5-3 6 5	5-5 -0-3	6-4-4-8*	6-8*-3-8*
2-5 -8*-7	3-3 -8*-5	3-8*-6 -8*	4-4 -7-4	5-4-5-8*	5-6 -5-6	6-4-5-4	6-8*-4-4
2-6 -8*-6	3-4 -8* 4	4-2 -8*-2	4-8*-5-8*	5 4-6-4	5-8*-4-8*	6-5 4 7	7-4 -3-8*
2-8*-7 -8*	3-5 8*-3	4 3 -8*-1	4-8*-6-4	5 5-5-7	5-8*-5-4	6-5 5-3	7-8*-3-4
						6-6 4-6	8-4 -3-4

English	French	German	Spanish
abound[5b]	abonder[5a]	Überfluß[6a] (haben)	abundar[3b]
allied[6]	allié (allier[4a])	verbündet[4b]	aliado
anchor[3b]	ancre	Anker[6b]	ancla
audience [3b] (have – with)	audience[4b]	Audienz	audiencia[4a]
block[2a] (*n.*)	bloc[4a]	Block	bloque
(can be) borne[3b], (bearable)	supportable	erträglich[6b]	soportable
bower[3b], (arbor[6])	charmille	Laube[6b]	glorieta
breeze[3a], (zephyr[9])	brise[4b]	Brise	brisa[4a], (aura[5a]), (céfiro[6b])
butterfly[3b]	papillon[4b]	Schmetterling	mariposa[4a]
buzz[3b], hum[3b] (*vb.*)	bourdonner[4b]	summen	zumbar[4b]
careless[3b], (thoughtless[5b])	négligent[6a]	unvorsichtig	descuidado[2b]
complement[6]	complet	Ergänzung[4a]	complemento[4b]
convert[4b] (*vb.*)	convertir[3b]	bekehren	convertir[1b]
countryman[6]	campagnard[5b]	Landmann[5b]	campesino[3b]
deliverance[5a]	délivrance	Befreiung[4a], (Erlösung[6b])	liberación
dependent[7] (*adj.*)	dépendant	abhängig[3a]	dependiente[4b]
desirous[5b]	désireux[5a]	begierig[6a]	deseoso[3b]
draft[3a] (military)	enrôlement	Einziehung[6b]	cuota
dull[3a], (blunt[4b]) (*adj.*)	émoussé	stumpf[6b]	boto, embotado, romo
embrace[3a], (hug[5b]) (*n.*)	étreinte[6a]	Umarmung	abrazo[2b]
falling (fall[1a]) due[2a] (*n.*)	échéance[6b]	Fälligkeit	vencimiento[6a]

English	French	German	Spanish
foliage[5b]	feuillage[3b]	Laub[6b]	follaje[5a], ramaje[5b]
fuel[3b]	combustible	Brennmaterial[6b]	combustible
fundamental[6]	fondamental[4a]	Grund-[5b]	fundamental[4a]
germ[5b]	germe	Keim[5a]	germen[4b]
grasp[4a] (convulsively)	crisper[4a]	klammern[6b]	crispar
gross[4a] (measure)	grosse	Gros[5b]	gruesa
heroic[4b]	heroïque[2b]	heldenhaft	heroico[2b]
holidays (holiday[2b]), (vacation[3b])	vacances[4a]	Ferien	vacaciones
illustrate[5a]	illustrer[5a]	illustrieren[6b]	ilustrar[3a]
inscription[6]	inscription[5a]	Inschrift[4b]	inscripción[7a]
interpose[6]	interposer	einlegen[4b]	interponer[4b]
kite[4b]	cerf-volant	Drache[6b]	cometa[4b]
knoll[6]	butte[6b]	Hügel[4a]	otero[6a]
label[5b], (tag[6] [Amer.])	étiquette	Zettel[5b], (Etikette)	etiqueta[4a], (letrero[6a])
lawn[2b] (cloth), (muslin[6])	mousseline[6a]	Musselin	gasa[6b]
legislature[5b]	législature	Landtag[4b]	legislatura
lung[4b]	poumon[4b]	Lunge[6b]	pulmón
mar[5a], (deform[6]) (mutilate)	mutiler[4a]	entstellen[6b]	afear[4b], (menoscabar[6a])
match[2a] (to light)	allumette[6a]	Streichholz	fósforo[6a]
mechanically (mechanical[7])	machinalement[4a]	mechanisch[3b]	mecánicamente, maquinalmente
muddy[6]	boueux	trüb[4a]	turbio[4a]
muzzle[5b] (of an animal)	museau[6b]	Maul[5b]	hocico[6b]
naval[6]	naval[6a]	See-[4b]	naval[6b]
orange[2a]	orange	Apfelsine	naranja[4a]
orchard[2b]	verger	Obstgarten	huerto[4b]
patent[5a] (*n.*)	brevet	Patent[5a]	patente[4a], (cédula[6a])
patriot[5b]	patriote[4a]	Patriot[6b]	patriota[4b]
peel[5a], (husk[6]), (pare[6])	peler	schälen[5b]	pelar[4b]
perseverance[6]	persévérance	Konsequenz[3b], (Ausdauer[6a])	perseverancia
philosophical[8]	philosophique[4a]	philosophisch[3b]	filosófico[4a]
pillow[3a]	oreiller[4b]	Kissen	almohada[4a]
rat[2b]	rat[4a]	Ratte	rata
refresh[5a] (in spirit)	ranimer[5b]	erquicken[5b]	reanimar[7a]
relief[3a] (raised)	(en) relief[3b]	Relief	relieve[5a]
revive[4b] (*intr. vb.*)	ressuciter[4a], revivre[4b]	auferstehen[7a]	resucitar[4a]
rose[1b] bush[2a]	rosier[6a]	Rosenstrauch	rosal[6a]
rude[2b] (impolite)	impoli[5a]	ungeschliffen	descortés[7a]
rust[3b] (*n.*)	rouille	Rost[6b]	moho, orín
scale[2a] (*vb.*)	escalader[6b]	erklettern	escalar[6a]
seal[2b] (*vb.*)	sceller	siegeln	sellar[4a]
senator[4b]	sénateur[4b]	Senator[6a]	senador
shrink[5a]	rétrécir[5a]	einlaufen[6a]	encoger[3b]
sixteen[3b]	seize[3b]	sechzehn	dieciseis[5]*
sole[2b] (on shoe)	semelle[4b]	Sohle	suela

English	French	German	Spanish
stall^{3b}, (booth^{5a})	baraque^{5b}	Bude	barraca^{3b}
sulphur^{6}	soufre	Schwefel^{3a}	azufre
sweetness^{4b}	douceur^{2a}	Süße	dulzura^{2a}
tedious^{5a}, (tiresome^{6})	ennuyeux^{4a}, (embêtant^{6b})	langweilig^{5b}	aburrido
thigh^{4a}	cuisse^{4b}	Schenkel^{6a}	muslo
thirteen^{3a}	treize^{3a}	dreizehn	trece^{5*}
tip^{2a}, (fee^{4a})	pourboire^{6b}	Trinkgeld	propina^{6b}
velvet^{3a}	velours^{3a}	Samt	terciopelo^{5a}
violet^{3a} (flower)	violette^{3a}	Veilchen	violeta^{5a}
void^{4a}, (vacancy^{6})	vide (*n.*)^{2b}	Leere	vacío^{2a}
vow^{3a} (*vb.*)	vouer^{6b}	geloben	(hacer) votos (voto^{2a})
ward^{3b} (*n.*) (person)	pupille^{5b}	Mündel	pupilo^{3b}
witch^{3a}	sorcier(-ère)^{4b}	Hexe	bruja^{4a}

SECTION 5.3. CONCEPTS 4022 THROUGH 4707

E F G S	*E F G S*	*E F G S*	*E F G S*	*E F G S*	*E F G S*	*E F G S*	*E F G S*
2-5 -8*-8*	3-4 -8*-5	4-4 -8*-1	5-5-5-8*	5-8*-5-5	6-3-6-2	6-6 -5-3	7-5 -3-8*
2-6 -8*-7	3-5 -8*-4	4-8*-6 -5	5-5-6-4	6-1 -6-4	6-4-5-5	6-8*-1-5	7-5 -4-4
2-8*-8*-5	3-6 -5-3	5-3 -6 -6	5-6-5-7	6-2 -5-7	6-5-4-8*	7-2 -5-3	7-8*-3-5
3-3 -8*-6	3-8*-8*-1	5-4 -6 -5	5-6-6-3	6-3 -5-6	6-5-5-4	7-3 -5-2	8-8*-2-5
					6-6-4-7	7-4 -4-5	9-6 -2-3

English	French	German	Spanish
abolition^{7}	abolition^{5b}	Beseitigung^{3b}	abolición
accomplishment^{6}	atteinte^{3a}	Erreichung^{5a}	adquisición^{6a}
accuracy^{7}	justesse^{5b}	Richtigkeit^{4b}	exactitud^{4a}
acid^{5b} (*adj.*)	aigre^{4a}, acide^{4b}	herb^{6a}	ácido^{5b}, (acre^{7a})
artisan^{8}	artisan	Handwerker^{7b}	artífice^{5b}
bandage^{7}	pansement	Verband^{3a}	venda^{5b}
bankrupt^{7} (*n.*) (person)	banqueroutier	Gemeinschuldner^{3b}	(en) quiebra^{5a}
barren^{3b}	stérile^{6b}	unfruchtbar	estéril^{3b}, (yermo^{6b})
blade^{2b} (grass)	brin^{5b}	Halm	brizna
boiling (boil^{2a}) (*n.*)	ébullition^{5b}	Kochen	ebullición
buffet^{5b}, (dresser^{6}) (sideboard)	buffet^{5a}	Servante^{5b}	aparador
cask^{7}	tonneau^{5a}	Tonne^{6a}, (Faß^{4b})	tonel, cuba
cavalry^{9}	cavalerie^{6b}	Kavallerie^{2a}, (Kavalleriedivision^{3b}), (Reiterei^{5b})	caballería^{3a}
choice^{2a} (*adj.*)	recherché (*adj.*)^{5a}, (enlevé [*adj.*]^{7a})	erlesen	escogido
choke^{4a}, (strangle^{6}) (*tr. vb.*)	étrangler^{4a}	strangulieren	ahogar^{1b}, (estrangular)
cleanliness^{6}	propreté^{5a}	Reinheit^{5a}	aseo^{4a}
coffin^{5b}	cercueil^{6b}	Sarg^{5a}	ataúd^{7a}
complex^{7} (*adj.*)	complexe^{5a}	zusammengesetzt (zusammensetzen^{3a})	complejo
compromise^{6} (*vb.*)	compromettre^{3a}	Kompromiß^{6a} (schließen)	comprometer^{2b}

English	French	German	Spanish
conceit[5b]	amour-propre[3b]	Einbildung[6b]	presunción[6a], vanagloria[6a]
congratulation[6]	félicitation[6a]	Glückwunsch[5a]	enhorabuena[3b], (albricias[6b]), (felicitación[6b])
contradict[7]	contredire[5b]	widersprechen[3a]	contradecir
cricket[4b] (insect)	grillon	Grille[6b]	grillo[5a]
crow[2b] (*n.*), (raven[3b])	corbeau	Rabe	cuervo[5a]
descendant[6]	descendant[5a]	Nachkomme[5b]	descendiente[4a]
dull[3a] (*vb.*) (numb)	engourdir[5b]	abstumpfen	adormecer[4a]
dull[3a] (*vb.*) (tarnish)	ternir[5a]	anlaufen, beschlagen	empañar[4a]
eighty[3b]	quatre-vingts[4a]	achtzig	ochenta[5*]
eminence[7]	éminence	(hohe) Rang[3a]	eminencia[5a]
entrance[2b] hall[1b]	antichambre[5b]	Vorzimmer	antecámara, recibidor
equipment[5b], (outfit[6])	équipement[6b]	Ausstattung[5b], (Ausrüstung[6a])	equipo[7b]
exclamation[6]	exclamation[4b]	Geschrei[5a]	exclamación[5b], (interjección[6b])
failure[5a] (bankruptcy)	banqueroute	Konkurs[5a]	quiebra[5a]
finance[6]	finance[3a]	Finanz[6a]	hacienda[2a]
flat[2a] (*adj.*) (taste)	fade[5b]	fade, schal	soso
foam[3b] (*n.*)	écume[6a], mousse (*f.*)[6a]	Schaum	espuma[3a]
formula[7]	formule[3a]	Formel[5b], (Formular[6b])	fórmula[2b]
goodwill[6]	bienveillance[5b]	Wohlwollen[5a]	benevolencia[4a]
goose[2a], (geese[4b])	oie[5a]	Gans	ganso
groan[3a] (*n.*), (moan[4a])	gémissement[5a]	Stöhnen	gemido[4a], (quejido[6b])
hail[2b] (*n.*)	grêle[5b]	Hagel	granizo
harmonious[6]	harmonieux[5a]	harmonisch[5b]	armonioso[4b], (armónico[5a])
harness[3a] (*vb.*), yoke[3b]	atteler[4a]	anspannen	ensillar[5b]
heath[5a]	bruyère[6a]	Heide[5a]	matorral[7a]
hood[3b]	bonnet[3b]	Kappe, Kapuze	gorro[6b]
humane[6]	humain[1b], (bienfaisant[4b])	(mit) Menschlichkeit[6b]	bienhechor[4a]
impatience[7]	impatience[2b]	Ungeduld[5a]	impaciencia[3b]
index[6] (*n.*)	(table des) matières (matière[2a])	Tabelle[5b]	índice[7a]
indulge[6] (*tr. vb.*)	(avoir de l')indulgence[5b] (pour)	(jemandem etwas) nachsehen[4b]	gratificar
intense[6]	intense[3b]	intensiv[6a]	intenso[2b]
intolerable[7], (unbearable[12])	insupportable[4a], intolérable[4a]	unerträglich[4b]	intolerable[5b], (insufrible[6b])
legal[5b] information[3a]	renseignements (renseignement[2b]) légaux (légal[4b])	Rechtsbelehrung[6b]	información[5a] legal[4b]
loan[6] (*n.*)	emprunt[4b]	Darlehen[5b]	préstamo[5b]
lock[2a] (of hair)	mèche[5b]	Locke	mechón
peel[5a], (husk[6]) (*n.*)	pelure	Schale[5a]	cáscara[5b]
plea[6]	requête[6a]	Gesuch[5b]	ruego[3a], (petición[4a])
plow[3a], (plough[4b]) (*n.*)	charrue[5b]	Pflug	arado[4a]
prose[5b]	prose[6a]	Prosa[6a]	prosa[3a]
pump[3a] (*n.*)	pompe[4b]	Pumpe	bomba[5a]

English	French	German	Spanish
pupil[2a] (eye)	prunelle[5a]	Pupille	pupila
rag[3a], (tatter[6])	lambeau[5a], (haillon[6b])	Lumpen	trapo[4b], (harapo[7a])
rail[2b] (for vehicle)	rail[5b]	Schiene	rail, riel
reduction[5b]	réduction[5b]	Ermäßigung[5b], (Herabsetzung[6a])	reducción
repetition[6]	répétition	Wiederholung[4b]	repetición[5b]
resort[3b] (*vb.*)	recourir[5a]	zurückgreifen	recurrir[4b]
roar[2a] (*n.*)	rugissement	Brüllen	rugido[5b]
ruddy[6] (healthy complexion)	vermeil	blühend[4a]	lozano[5a]
sanctuary[5a]	sanctuaire	Heiligtum[5b]	santuario[5b]
scratch[3a] (*vb.*)	gratter[4b]	kratzen	rascar[5a], escarbar[5b] (chicken)
session[5b]	session[5a]	Session[6a]	sesión[4b]
social[7b] democracy[6]	démocratie[5b] sociale (social[2b])	Sozialdemokratie[4a]	social democracia
solemnity[6]	solennité[4b]	Weihe[5a]	solemnidad[5a]
speculation[7]	spéculation[5b]	Spekulation[3b]	especulación
spelling (spell[2b]), (orthography[15])	orthographe[6b]	Rechtschreibung	ortografía[7b]
sport[2a] (*adj.*)	sportif[5a]	sportlich	deportivo
(editorial[7]) staff[3b]	rédaction[4b]	Redaktion[4b]	redacción[5a]
starve[3a]	affamer[5a]	aushungern	desfallecer[4a] (de hambre)
strait[3b] (*n.*)	détroit	Enge	estrecho[1b]
sunset[3b]	coucher (*n.*)[4b] (du soleil)	Sonnenuntergang	puesta[5b] (del sol), ocaso[5a]
syrup[6]	sirop[6a]	Saft[4b], (Sorghum[5b])	almíbar[7a]
telegraph[4a] (*adj.*)	télégraphique	telegraphisch[6a]	telegráfico[5b]
telephone[3a], (phone[5a])	téléphone[4a]	Fernsprecher	teléfono[5b]
ticket[3a] window[1a]	guichet[6b]	Schalter	reja[3b] (de taquilla), (ventanilla)
unheard[6] (of)	inouï[3b]	unerhört[5a]	inaudito[6a]
virgin[3b] (*adj.*), (virginal[12])	vierge[3a]	jungfräulich	virginal[6a]
weed[2b] (*n.*)	mauvaise herbe	Unkraut	maleza[5a]

SECTION 5.4. CONCEPTS 4708 THROUGH 4780

E F G S	*E F G S*	*E F G S*	*E F G S*	*E F G S*	*E F G S*	*E F G S*	*E F G S*	*E F G S*
2-6 -8*-8*	3-4 -8*-6	4-1-8*-5	4-6 -6 -8*	5 4-6-6	5-8*-5-6	6-5 -5-5	7-1-6-1	7-6 -4-4
2-8*-8*-6	3-5 -8*-5	4-3-8*-3	4-8*-6 -6	5-5-6-5	6-2 -6-4	6-6 -4-8*	7-3-4-7	7-8*-3-6
3-2 -8*-8*	3-6 -8*-4	4-4-7 -6	5-1 -8*-1	5-6-5-8*	6-3 -6-3	6-6 -5-4	7-3-5-3	8-6 -2-8*
3-3 -8*-7	3-8*-8*-2	4-4-8*-2	5-2 -6 -8*	5-6-6-4	6-4 -6-2	6-8*-4-6	7-5-4-5	8-6 -3-4
								10-4 -2-2

English	French	German	Spanish
abandon[4a] (*n.*)	abandon[3b]	Hingabe, Rückhaltlosigkeit	abandono[3a]
admission[5b] (concession)	concession[4b], (admission[6b])	Zugeständnis[6a]	concesión[6b]
alternate[5b] (*vb.*)	alterner	abwechseln[5a]	alternar[6a]
apostle[8]	apôtre[6b]	Apostel[3a]	apóstol[4a]
apron[3b]	tablier[4b]	Schürze	delantal[6b]

English	French	German	Spanish
arbitrary[7]	arbitraire	willkürlich[3b]	arbitrario[6b]
associate[3b] (e.g., professor)	adjoint[6b]	Adjunkt	asociado (asociar[4b]), (adjunto[7a])
aware[5b] (knowingly)	(en) connaissance[2a] (de cause), (sciemment)	wissentlich[6b]	consciente(mente)
backward[3b] (*adj.*)	arriéré[5b]	rückständig	tardo[5b]
beads (bead[3b]) (rosary)	chapelet[6a]	Rosenkranz	rosario[4a]
bean[2b]	haricot	Bohne	haba[6a], judía[6b], lenteja[6b]
binding (bind[2a]) (of book)	reliure[6a]	Einband	encuadernación
bull[3a]	taureau	Stier	toro[2b]
buzz[3b], hum[3b] (*n.*)	bourdonnement[5a]	Summen	zumbido[5a]
charitable[6]	bienveillant[6a], charitable[6b]	wohltätig[5a]	benévolo[4b]
chin[4a]	menton[4a]	Kinn	barba[2a]
chocolate[4a]	chocolat[4a]	Schokolade	chocolate[2b]
circulation[6]	circulation[5a]	Umlauf[5b]	circulación[5a]
colt[3a]	poulain[6a]	Füllen	potro[4b]
countess[10]	comtesse[4a]	Gräfin[2b]	condesa (conde[2a])
crowded (*adj.*)[7]* (with people)	rempli (remplir[1a]), plein[1a], (bondé)	massenhaft[6b]	lleno[1a], (abarrotado)
deity (D)[6]	déité	Gottheit[4a]	deidad[6b]
delicacy[6]	délicatesse[3a], finesse[3b]	Feinheit[6a]	delicadeza[3b], (fineza[5a])
disk[8], (disc[9])	disque[6b]	Scheibe[3b]	disco[4b]
dock[4a], (pier[6])	quai[3a]	Dock, Pier, Quai, Kaje	muelle[3b]
dye[4a] (*n.*)	teinture	Farbstoff[6a]	tinte[6a]
efficacy[7], (efficiency[9])	efficacité	Wirksamkeit[3b], (Tüchtigkeit[6b])	eficacia[6a]
Egyptian[5b]	égyptien	ägyptisch[5a]	egipcio[6a]
enthusiastic[5b]	enthousiaste[6a]	schwärmend (schwärmen[6a]) (für)	entusiasto[4a]
exceptional[5b]	exceptionnel[4a]	außergewöhnlich[6b]	excepcional[6b]
extract[5b] (*n.*)	extrait (*n.*)[6a]	Auszug[5b]	extracto
firmness[7] (of character), stability[7]	fermeté[5b]	Festigkeit[4b]	firmeza[5b]
funeral[3a] (procession)	convoi[3b] funèbre[4a]	Leichenzug	funeral[6b]
hardness[7]	dureté[6b]	Härte[4a]	dureza[4a]
hedge[3a]	haie[2b]	Hecke	seto
hiss[4a] (*vb.*)	siffler[3a]	zischen	silbar[3a]
humility[5b], (meekness[6])	humilité[6b]	Demut[6a]	humildad[4a], (mansedumbre[6a])
incredible[6]	incroyable[5a]	unglaublich[5a]	increíble[5a], (inverosímil[6a])
invasion[6]	invasion[5b]	Besetzung[5a]	invasión[5b]
involuntary[6]	involontaire[6b] (involontairement[5b])	unwillkürlich[4a]	involuntario
irresistible[7]	irrésistible[3b]	unwiderstehlich[5b], (unüberwindlich[6b])	irresistible[3a]
irritation[8] (physical)	irritation[6a]	Reiz[2b]	irritación
jar[3a], (urn[4b]), (vase[6])	vase (*m.*)[3a]	Krug	jarra[7a]
knit[3a]	tricotter	stricken	tejer[2b]
loop[4b]	boucle[4a]	Schleife	lazo[2a]

English	French	German	Spanish
lowland[5b]	terre[1a] basse (bas[1a])	Flachland	tierra[1a] baja (bajo[1a])
luggage[5b]	bagage(s)[5a]	Gepäck[6b]	equipaje[5a]
martial[6], warlike[6]	martial	kriegerisch[4a]	bélico[6a]
mask[4b] (*vb.*)	masquer[3a]	maskieren	disfrazar[3b]
merciless[6], pitiless[6]	impitoyable[4b]	rücksichtslos[6a]	sin[1a] piedad[2a], (desalmado[5b])
observer[7]	observateur[6a]	Beobachter[4b]	observador[4b]
oral[7], (verbal[9])	verbal	mündlich[3a], (wörtlich[4b])	verbal[6a]
parade[5a]	parade[6a]	Parade[6b]	alarde[4a]
pea[3a]	pois[5a]	Erbse	garbanzo[5b] (chick-pea), (guisante[7b])
perfume[4a] (*vb.*), scent[4b]	parfumer[3b], (embaumer[5b])	parfümieren	perfumar[3b]
plot[3a] (*vb.*), (conspire[6])	conjurer[4a]	verschwören	conjurar[6a], conspirar[6a]
plow[3a] (*vb.*) (e.g., ship –s through waves)	fendre[4b]	pflügen	surcar[6b]
quench[3b] (thirst)	étancher	stillen	apagar[2a], (saciar[5b])
reflection[4b] (in glass, etc.)	reflet[6a]	Spiegelung	reflejo[3a]
resistance[6], (endurance[7])	résistance[3a]	Ausdauer[6a]	resistencia[3a]
roast[2b] (*n.*)	rôti (*n.*)[6a]	Braten	asado
(behind the) scene[2b]	(à la) cantonade[6a]	(hinter d.) Kulissen	tras bastidores
shoot[2a], (sprout[6]) (*n.*)	pousse (*n.*)[6b]	Schößling, Sproß	brote, retoño
simplicity[4b] (of nature)	simplicité[3a], (naïveté[6a])	Einfalt	sencillez[3a], (ingenuidad[6a])
soften[4b] (a blow), (deaden[12] [a sound])	amortir[6a]	dämpfen[6b]	amortiguar
sole[2b] (*vb.*)	ressemeler[6a]	besohlen	(poner, echar) suela (al) calzado[6a]
spy[2b] (*n.*)	espion[6a]	Spion	espía
telescope[7]	lunette[3b] (d')approche[3b]	Fernrohr[4b]	telescopio[7a]
umbrella[4b]	parapluie[4b]	Schirm[7a]	paraguas[6b]
universe[6]	univers[3a]	All[6b]	universo[3b]
void[4a] (*adj.*)	nul[1b], (vide[2a])	nichtig	nulo[5b]
windmill[4b]	moulin[4a] (à vent)	Windmühle	molino[2b] (de viento)
wrinkle[4a] (*n.*)	ride[4a]	Falte[7a]	arruga[6a]

SECTION 5.5. CONCEPTS 4781 THROUGH 4828

E F G S	*E F G S*	*E F G S*	*E F G S*	*E F G S*	*E F G S*
2-8*-8*-7	3-8*-8*-3	4-5-7-6	5-4-6-7	6-3-6-4	7-1-4-7
3-4-8*-7	4-1-8*-6	4-5-8*-2	5-5-6-6	6-5-5-6	7-5-4-6
3-5-8*-6	4-3-8*-4	5-1-8*-2	5-6-6-5	6-8*-4-7	7-6-4-5
3-6-8*-5	4-4-8*-3	5-2-8*-1	6-2-6-5	7-2-6-1	8-2-4-5
					8-4-4-3

English	French	German	Spanish
baptism[6]	baptême[5a]	Taufe[5a]	bautismo[6b], (bautizo[7a])
barn[2a]	grange	Scheune	pajar[7b], (granero)
blush[3b] (*n.*)	rougeur	Röte	rubor[3b]
bolt[3a] (metal)	verrou[4a]	Riegel	tornillo[7b]
broom[3b] (to sweep)	balai[6b]	Besen	escoba[5b]
cage[3b]	cage[5a]	Käfig	jaula[6b]
carpenter[3a]	menuisier[6b], (charpentier[7a])	Zimmermann	carpintero[5b]

English	French	German	Spanish
chestnut^{3b} (*n.*)	marron (*n.*)^{5b}	Kastanie	castaña^{6b}
detachment^{8}, unconcern^{8}	détachement^{4b}	Gleichgültigkeit^{4a}	indiferencia^{3a}, (despego)
displease^{4b}	déplaire^{3a}	mißfallen	desagradar^{4a}, disgustar^{4a}
distracted (distract^{5b}), (frantic^{7})	éperdu^{6a}	bestürzt^{6b}	frenético^{5a}
drunk^{4b} (*adj.*)	ivre^{4a}	(be)trunken	borracho^{3b}, (ebrio^{7a})
fiber^{5a}	fibre^{6a}	Faser^{6b}	fibra^{5b}
firmness^{7} (physical), stability^{7}	fixité^{6b}	Festigkeit^{4b}	fijeza^{5b}
flowery^{4b}	fleuri (fleurir^{3a})	blumig	florido^{4a}
fragrant^{4b}	parfumé (parfumer^{3b}), (odoriférant)	duftig	oloroso^{4b}
frown^{3b} (*vb.*)	froncer^{6b}	(Stirn) runzeln	fruncir^{5a} (el) ceño^{3b}, arrugar^{5b} (el) ceño
gentleness^{6}	douceur^{2a}	Milde^{6b}	suavidad^{5a}
guardian^{5b} (of a child)	tuteur^{4b}	Vormund^{6a}	tutor^{7a}
industrial^{8}	industriel^{2b}	industriell^{4b}	industrial^{5a}
interpretation^{6}	interprétation^{5a}	Auslegung^{5b}	version^{6a}, interpretación^{6b}
laboratory^{7}	laboratoire^{6a}	Werkstatt^{4b}	laboratorio^{5b}
(be) lame^{3a} (*adj.*), (limp^{5b})	(être) boiteux, boiter	lahm (sein)	(estar) cojo^{3a}
location^{4b}	situation^{1b}	Örtlichkeit	localidad^{6a}
locomotive^{5b}	locomotive^{5a}	Lokomotive^{6b}	locomotora^{6a}
mirth^{3b}, (glee^{5a})	allégresse^{6a}	Frohsinn	júbilo^{5a}
napkin^{3b}	serviette^{4a}	Serviette	servilleta^{7b}
nationality^{7}	nationalité^{5b}	Nationalität^{4a}	nacionalidad^{6a}
orchestra^{5b}	orchestre^{5b}	Orchester^{6b}	orquesta^{6b}
overflow^{4a} (*vb.*)	déborder^{3b}	überlaufen	rebosar^{4a}, desbordar^{4b}
palm^{3a} tree^{1a}	palmier^{6a}	Palme	palmera^{5a}
pear^{3a}	poire^{5a}	Birne	pera^{6b}
politician^{7}	politique (*n.*)^{2b}, (politicien)	Politiker^{6a}	político^{1b} (*n.*)
precipice^{7}	précipice^{4b}	Abgrund^{4b}	precipicio^{7a}
refine^{3b}	policer^{6a}, raffiné^{6b}	verfeinern	refinar^{5a}
revelation^{6}	révélation^{3a}	Offenbarung^{6a}	revelación^{4a}
revolve^{5a}	tourner^{1a}, (circuler^{4a})	herumlaufen	revolver^{2a}, (girar^{3a})
sauce^{4a}, (gravy^{6})	sauce^{5a}	Tunke	salsa^{2b}, (caldo^{4a})
scrap^{4b} (paper, cloth, etc.)	chiffon^{5b}	Fetzen	trozo^{2b}
screen^{4a} (*n.*)	écran^{5b}	Schirm^{7a}	pantalla^{6b}
sidewalk^{4a} (Amer.), pavement^{4b} (Eng.)	trottoir^{3b}	Bürgersteig	acera^{4a}
socket^{6} (of eye)	orbite	Höhle^{4b}	órbita^{7a}
stumble^{4b}	trébucher^{5b}	stolpern	tropezar^{2a}
trot^{3b} (*vb.*)	trotter^{5b}	trotteln	trotar^{6a}
undo^{5a}, (undone^{6})	défaire^{2b}	rückgängig (machen)	deshacer^{1b}
uneasy^{5a}	inquiet^{1b}, (gêné [gêner^{2a}]), ([être à la] gêne^{3b})	geniert	inquieto^{2a}
violet^{3a} (color)	mauve^{6b}	violett	violeta^{5a}
workshop^{8}	atelier^{4a}	Werkstatt^{4b}	taller^{3a}

SECTION 5.6. CONCEPTS 4829 THROUGH 4913

E F G S	*E F G S*	*E F G S*	*E F G S*	*E F G S*	*E F G S*	*E F G S*
2-8*-8*-8*	4-3-8*-5	4-6- 8*-2	5-4 -6-8*	6-4-5-8*	6-8*-4-8*	8-3 -4-5
3-4 -8*-8*	4-4-8*-4	4-8*-6 -8*	5-8*-5-8*	6-4-6-4	6-8*-5-4	8-6 -3-6
3-6 -8*-6	4-5-7 -7	5-1 -8*-3	5-8*-6-4	6-6-5-6	7-8*-3-8*	9-8*-1-8*
3-8*-8*-4	4-5-8*-3	5-2 -8*-2	6-3 -6-5	6-6-6-2	7-8*-4-4	10-8*-1-4

English	French	German	Spanish
ammunition[6]	munitions	Munition[4a]	municiones
astounded (astound[8]), (stupefied [stupefy[11]])	stupéfait[3b]	betroffen[4a]	atónito[5b]
besiege[5a]	assiéger[4a]	belagern[6b]	asediar
blacksmith[3a]	forgeron[4b]	Schmied	herrero
brake[3b]	frein	Bremse	freno[4b]
brush[2a] (*n.*) (instrument)	brosse	Bürste	brocha, cepillo
bubble[2a]	bulle	Blase	pompa[4a]
butcher[3a]	boucher (*n.*)[6a]	Schlachter	carnicero[6a]
carve[3b] (art)	sculpter[4b], (sculpté[6a])	schnitzen	esculpir, tallar
chancellor[6]	chancelier	Reichskanzler[4a] (Kanzler[5b])	canciller
cherry[2b]	cerise	Kirsche	cereza
chime[4a] (*n.*)	carillon[6b]	Glockenspiel	juego[2a] (de campanas)
closet[3b], (cupboard[5a])	armoire[4a]	Schrank	armario, alacena
corruption[6]	corruption[6b]	Mißstand[5a]	corrupción[6a]
crash[4a] (*n.*)	fracas[5b]	Krach	estruendo[3b], (choque[4a])
cushion[3b]	coussin[4a]	Kissen	cojín, almohadón
dagger[6]	dague	Dolch[5b]	puñal[4a], (daga[6b])
decade[6]	décennie	Jahrzehnt[4a]	década
desolate[4b] (*vb.*)	désoler[3a]	verheeren	desolar[5a]
dimension[6]	dimension[4b]	Dimension[6a]	dimensión[4b]
disgrace[6b] (*vb.*), (dishonor[5a]), (degrade[6])	avilir[6a], (déshonorer)	entehren	deshonrar[6a]
dividend[6]	dividende	Dividende[4b]	dividendo
drug[3b] store[1b]	pharmacie[6b]	Drogerie	botica[6a]
elector[7] (title)	électeur	Kurfürst[3b]	elector
electricity[6]	électricité[4a]	Elektrizität[6a]	electricidad[4b]
envelope[4a] (for letter)	enveloppe[3a], pli[3a]	Umschlag	sobre[5a]
excellence[6], refinement[6]	excellence[3a], (raffinement[5b])	Feinheit[6a]	refinamiento[5b]
exile[4b] (person banished)	proscrit[4b]	Verbannte	desterrado (desterrar[4a])
expert[4b] (*adj.*)	ferré[3b]	beschlagen	experto[5b], (perito[6b])
frog[3a]	grenouille	Frosch	rana[4b]
fugitive[5a] (*n.*)	fugitif	Flüchtling[6b]	fugitivo[4b]
(bear) grudge[5b]	(en) vouloir[1a] (à), ([garder] [de la] rancune[3b], [du] ressentiment[5a])	verargen	guardar[1a] rencor[3b]
handful[4b]	poignée[3b]	Handvoll	puñado[5a], manojo[5b]
hare[3b]	lièvre	Hase	liebre[4b]
helm[5a]	gouvernail	Ruder[5b]	caña[2b] (del) timón, rueda[2b] (del) timón

English	French	German	Spanish
helpful[5b]	utile[2a], (secourable)	hilfreich	útil[2a], (provechoso[6a])
historian[6]	historien[4a]	Historiker[6b]	historiador[4a]
imposing (impose[4a])	imposant (*adj.*)[4b]	eindrucksvoll	imponente[4b]
infantry[9]	infanterie	Infanterie[1b]	infantería
ingenuity[6]	ingéniosité[6a]	Scharfsinn[6b]	ingenio[2a]
ivory[3b]	ivoire	Elfenbein	marfil[4b]
jaw[3a]	mâchoire[4b]	Kiefer	quijada
mast[3a]	mât[6b]	Mast	mástil[6b]
monarchy[6]	monarchie	Monarchie[4a]	monarquía
monkey[4a], (ape[6])	singe[4a]	Affe	mono[4a]
muscle[5b]	muscle[4b]	Muskel[6a]	músculo
nourishment[6]	nourriture[4b]	Verpflegung[5a], (Ernährung[6a])	nutrición
onion[4a]	oignon[5a]	Zwiebel	cebolla[3b]
orphan[4a]	orphelin[4a]	Waise	huérfano[4a]
owl[2b]	hibou	Eule	buho, lechuza
oxygen[7]	oxygène	Sauerstoff[3a]	oxígeno
pail[3a], (bucket[4a])	seau	Eimer	balde[4a]
perch[3b] (*vb.*)	se percher[6b]	hocken	posar[6a] (se), (encaramar [se])
Persian[5a]	perse, persan	persisch[5b]	persa
pitcher[4a], (jug[7])	pot[3a]	Krug	cántaro[5a], jarro[5a]
porter[4b] (of a building)	concierge[3a]	Hauswart	portero[5a]
promotion[6] (fostering)	avancement	Beförderung[4a]	adelantamiento
proximity[10]	proximité	Nähe[1b]	proximidad[4a]
psalm[5b]	psaume	Psalm[5b]	salmo
robin[2b]	rouge-gorge	Rotkehlchen	petirrojo
rye[4b]	seigle	Roggen[6a]	centeno
scrape[3b]	gratter[4b]	kratzen	raspar
secular[7]	temporel	weltlich[4a]	secular[4b]
sensual[8]	sensuel[6a]	sinnlich[3b]	sensual[6a]
shave[4b] (*vb.*)	raser[3b]	rasieren	afeitar[5b]
silvery[6]	argentin	silbern[4a]	plateado
soar[5a]	(s')élever[1a]	(sich) aufschwingen	remontar[3a]
soda[6] (bicarbonate)	soude	Natron[4b]	bicarbonato
spectacle[4a] (great sight)	féerie[6b]	Feerie, Zauberstück	espectáculo[2b]
stain[3a] (with blood)	tacher (*spot*)[6b] (de sang)	(mit Blut) beflecken	ensangrentar[6b]
sway[3a] (the body)	se dandiner[6b]	watscheln	balancear[6a] (se)
symbol[4b]	symbole[5a]	Symbol	símbolo[3b]
tame[3a] (*vb.*)	dompter[6b]	zähmen	domar[6a]
tangle[7] (*n.*)	embrouillement	Verwirrung[4b]	enredo[4b]
thrill[4a] (*n.*), (shudder[6])	tressaillement[5b]	Schauer[7a]	estremecimiento[7a]
thumb[3b] (turn over pages)	feuilleter[4b]	blättern	hojear
toast[4b] (*vb.*), toast[4b] (*n.*)	griller[5a]	rösten	tostar[3b], (tostada[6a] [*n.*])
treasury[4b]	trésorerie	Staatskasse[6b]	tesorería
trousers[4a]	pantalon[4a]	Hose(n)	calzón[4b], (pantalón[5a])
turkey[3a]	dindon	Puter	pavo[4b]

English	French	German	Spanish
typewriter[5b]	machine[2b] à[1a] écrire[1a]	Schreibmaschine	máquina[2a] (de) escribir[1a], (máquina dactilográfica)
tyranny[4b]	tyrannie[5a]	Tyrannei	tiranía[3b], (despotismo[5b])
unsteady[8], (unstable[11])	instable[6a]	schwankend (schwanken[3a])	inseguro[6a]
weariness[5b], (fatigue[6])	fatigue[1b], (lassitude[6a])	Überdruß	cansancio[3a], fatiga[3a]
willow[3b] (*n.*), willow[3b] (tree)	osier[6b], saule[6a]	Weide	mimbre[6a]

SECTION 5.7. CONCEPTS 4914 THROUGH 4974

E F G S	*E F G S*	*E F G S*	*E F G S*	*E F G S*	*E F G S*
3–5 –8*–8*	4–3–8*–6	5–1–8*–4	5–8*–6–5	6–5 –5–8*	7–3 –5–6
3–6 –8*–7	4–4–8*–5	5–2–8*–3	6–2 –6–7	6–5 –6–4	7–4 –5–5
3–8*–8*–5	4–5–8*–4	5–3–8*–2	6–3 –6–6	6–6 –5–7	7–5 –5–4
4–2 –8*–7	4–6–8*–3	5–5–6 –8*	6–4 –6–5	6–8*–5–5	7–8*–4–5
				7–2 –6–3	8–4 –4–5

English	French	German	Spanish
absorb[5b]	absorber[2b]	aufsaugen	absorber[6b]
alight[5b] (person)	descendre[1a]	aussteigen	apearse[4b]
architect[6]	architecte[4b]	Architekt[6b]	arquitecto[5a]
barbarous[5b]	barbare[3b]	barbarisch	bárbaro[2b]
bitterness[5b]	amertume[3b], (âpreté[6b])	Bitterkeit	amargura[2a]
blast[3a], (gust[6]) (of wind)	rafale	Bö	ráfaga[5b]
bruise[4a] (*vb.*)	froisser[4a], (meurtrir[5a])	schürfen	golpear[5a]
brute[4b] (*n.*)	bourreau[6a], brute[6b]	(brutale) Mensch	bruto[3a]
burial[4a]	enterrement[5a]	Beerdigung	entierro[4b]
captivity[5b], (bondage[6])	captivité	Gefangenschaft[6b]	cautiverio[5b]
compromise[6] (*n.*)	compromis[5a]	Kompromiß[6a]	compromiso[4a]
contend[4a], (compete[8])	concourir[5b]	bewerben	competir[4a], (contender[6b])
cough[4a] (*vb.*)	tousser[5a]	husten	toser[4b]
courtier[4b]	courtisan[5b]	Höfling	cortesano[4b]
dairy[6b]	laiterie[5b]	Molkerei	lechería
discreet[5b]	discret[3b] (discrètement[5b])	diskret	discreto[2a]
elm[3b]	orme	Ulme	álamo[5b]
envious[5a]	jaloux[2b]	neidisch	envidioso[3b]
episode[6]	épisode[4a]	Vorfall[4a]	episodio[5b]
equity[6]	équité[5b]	Billigkeit[5b]	equidad
essence[5b]	essence[3b]	Essenz	esencia[2b], (médula[6a])
fertilizer[6]	engrais	Kali[5b], (Salpeter[6b])	abono[5a], (fertilizante)
filthy[6]	sale[3b]	unrein[6a]	inmundo[6b]
flutter[3a], (flit[5a])	voltiger[5b]	flattern, huschen	revolotear
foam[3b] (*vb.*)	écumer[6a]	schäumen	espumar[7a]
forge[4b] (*vb.*) (metal)	forger[5a]	schmieden	forjar[4b], (fraguar[6b])
grate[4a], (squeak[5a]) (*vb.*)	grincer[5a]	knarren	rechinar[4a]
gutter[5b] (street)	ruisseau[3b]	Gosse	arroyo[2b] (de la calle)
ham[4a]	jambon[6b]	Schinken	jamón[3b]
haunt[3b]	hanter[5b]	heimsuchen	rondar

English	French	German	Spanish
howl[3a] (*n.*), (bellow[4b])	hurlement	Geheul	aullido[5b]
independent[3a] person[1a] (financially)	rentier[5b]	Rentner	rentista
infer[7]	conclure[2a], (déduire)	folgern[6b]	inferir[3b]
inherit[4a]	hériter[6a]	erben	heredar[3a]
initiative[7]	initiative[5a]	Initiative[5b]	iniciativo[4a]
loin[4b] (on person)	reins[4b]	Lende	riñones (riñón[5a])
mould[4a] (*vb.*), (knead[8])	pétrir[4b]	kneten	amasar[5a]
nostril[4a]	narine[6b]	Nüster	nariz[3a]
offensive[6] (*adj.*)	injurieux[6a]	offensiv[5b]	ofensivo[7a]
olive[3a] tree[1a]	olivier	Olive	olivo[5b]
pant[3a], (gasp[6]) (*vb.*)	haleter[5a]	keuchen	jadear
paralyze(se)[7]	paralyser[4b]	lähmen[5b]	paralizar[5b]
pavement[4b] (Amer.)	pavé (*n.*)[3a]	Pflaster	pavimento[6a]
penance[6]	pénitence	Buße[5b]	penitencia[5b]
plow[3a], (plough[4b]) (*vb.*) (agricultural)	labourer	pflügen	arar[5a]
postage[4b]	port[2a] (de lettre), (affranchissement)	Porto	franqueo[7b]
prank[6]	espièglerie	Streich[5a]	travesura[5b]
pyramid[6]	pyramide[5b]	Pyramide[6b]	pirámide[4b]
rainy[4a]	(de) pluie[2a], (pluvieux)	regnerisch	lluvioso[7a]
refusal[7]	refus[3b]	Ablehnung[5a]	negativa[6a]
scout[4b], (runner[5a])	coureur[6a]	Läufer	corredor[3b]
selfish[4a]	égoïste[4a], (par, avec) égoïsme[4b]	selbstisch	egoísta[5a]
shift[3b] (change of place)	déplacement[5b]	Umstellung, Umzug	desplazamiento
slipper[3b]	pantoufle[6b]	Pantoffel	babucha[7b]
stump[3a] (of tree)	souche[5a]	Stumpf	tocón
sultan[7]	sultan	Sultan[4b]	sultán[5b]
tradesman[6]	marchand[2b]	Gewerbetreibende[6a]	tendero[7a]
transparent[7]	transparent[5a]	durchsichtig[5a]	transparente[4b], (diáfano[5a])
vest[3a] (Amer.), (waistcoat[8])	gilet[5b]	Weste	chaleco
weekly[5b]	hebdomadaire[5b]	wöchentlich[6a]	semanario
wrinkle[4a] (*vb.*)	froisser[4a], (rider[5a])	runzeln	arrugar[5b]

PART VI

THE SIXTH THOUSAND CONCEPTS

SECTION 5.8. CONCEPTS 4975 THROUGH 5080

E F G S	*E F G S*	*E F G S*	*E F G S*	*E F G S*	*E F G S*	*E F G S*
3–6 –8*–8*	4–4 –8*–6	5–2–8*–4	5–6 –6 –8*	6–5 –6–5	6–8*–6–2	7–6 –4–8*
3–8*–8*–6	4–5 –8*–5	5–3–8*–3	5–8*–6 –6	6–6 –5–8*	7–2 –6–4	7–8*–4–6
4–2 –8*–8*	4–6 –8*–4	5–4–8*–2	6–1 –8*–1	6–6 –6–4	7–3 –6–3	8–2 –4–8*
4–3 –8*–7	4–8*–8*–2	5–5–7 –5	6–4 –6 –6	6–8*–5–6	7–5 –5–5	8–8*–3–6
						10–6 –1–8*

English	French	German	Spanish
ambitious[4b] (be – for)	ambitieux[4b]	ehrgeizig	ambicioso[6b], (ambicionar[7a])
apprenticeship[10]	apprentissage[6a]	Lehre[1b]	aprendizaje
blackboard[4a]	tableau[2a] noir[1a]	Wandtafel	pizarra
bob[3b] (mane, etc.) (*vb.*)	rogner	stutzen	recortar[6b]
boiler[6]	chaudière[6b]	Kessel[5b]	caldera
bond[3a] (commercial)	bon	Kaution	bono[6a]
brood[4a] (*n.*)	engeance[6a] (pejorative), (couvée)	Brut	cría[4b]
butcher[3a] shop[1b]	boucherie[6a]	Metzgerei, Schlachterei	carnicería
cable[4b]	câble[5b]	Kabel	cable[5b]
calendar[5b]	calendrier[6a]	Kalender[6b]	calendario
calf[4a], (calves[6]) (animal)	veau[5a]	Kalb	ternera[5b], (becerro[7a])
cedar[3b]	cèdre	Zeder	cedro[6b]
certificate[5b]	certificat	Coupon[6b], Dokument[6b]	certificado[6a]
cloudy[3b], (misty[6])	nuageux	bewölkt	nublado[6b]
consecration[6]	consécration	Weihe[5a]	consagración[6a]
crisis[7]	crise[2b]	Krisis[6b]	crisis[4b]
crumb[4b]	miette[6b]	Krume	miga[4a]
crust[4a]	croûte[6b]	Kruste	corteza[4b]
deer[3a], (hart[5a]), (stag[6])	cerf	Reh	ciervo[6a]
discharge[3b], (volley[6])	décharge, salve	Salve	descarga[6a], salva[6b]
discourage[4a]	décourager[3b]	entmutigen	desalentar[7a]
disguise[3b] (*n.*)	déguisement[6b]	Tarnung, Verkleidung	disfraz
drug[3b]	drogue[6b]	Droge	droga
(get) drunk[4b] (*intr. vb.*)	s'enivrer[6a]	(sich) betrinken	embriagar[4a] se
drunken[5b] revel[5a]	débauche[5b]	Ausschweifung[7a]	orgía[5b]
enmity[6], (hostility[7])	hostilité[4b]	Feindschaft[6b]	hostilidad[6b]
exploit[5b] (*vb.*)	exploiter[3a]	ausbeuten	explotar[3b]
farce[6]	farce (*n.*)[6b]	Posse[6b]	farsa[4b]
filial[7]	filial	kindlich[4a]	filial[6a]
flourish[3b] (*n.*) (trumpets)	fanfare[6b]	Fanfare, Trompetenstoß	charanga
fringe[4b]	frange	Franse	borde[2b]

English	French	German	Spanish
frivolous[7]	frivole[6a]	leichtsinnig[5a]	frívolo[4b]
gardener[4a]	jardinier[3b]	Gärtner	jardinero[7a]
grate[4a], (creak[7]) (e.g., door)	grincer[5a]	kreischen	crujir[5a]
harmless[5a]	inoffensif[6a]	harmlos[6a], unschädlich[6b]	inofensivo
hawk[3b]	épervier, faucon	Habicht	halcón[6b], (falcón)
heroine[6]	héroïne	Heldin[6a]	heroína (héroe[2b])
hymn[4a]	cantique[5a], hymne[5a]	Choral	himno[5a]
idiot[5a]	imbécile[2b], (idiot[5b])	Idiot, Dummkopf	idiota[4b], imbécil[4b]
indulgence[6]	indulgence[4a]	Nachsicht[6a]	indulgencia[6b]
innkeeper[8]	aubergiste	Wirt[3a]	ventero[6a]
isthmus[3b]	isthme	Isthmus	istmo[6b]
joint[3a] (anatomical)	joint, jointure, articulation	Gelenk	coyuntura[6b], (articulación[7a])
lark[3a] (bird)	alouette[6b]	Lerche	alondra
legion[4b]	légion[5a]	Legion	legión[5a]
legitimate[7] (child)	légitime[3a]	ehelich[6a]	legítimo[3a]
liable[6] (– to do)	capable[1b]	imstande	capaz[1b]
manuscript[6]	manuscrit	Manuskript[5a]	manuscrito[6a]
mariner[5a]	marin[3b]	Seemann	marino[3a]
mat[3b] (straw)	paillasson	Matte	estera[6a]
moderation[6] (diminution)	modération[5a]	Mäßigung[6b]	moderación[5b]
monthly[5b]*	mensuel	monatlich[6a]	mensual[6b]
moor (M)[4a] (*adj.*)	mauresque	maurisch	moro[2b], (morisco[6b])
moss[3b]	mousse (*f.*)[6a]	Moos	musgo
musical[3a] (composition, etc.)	musical	Musik-	musical[6a]
mutton[5b]	mouton[3a]	Schafs-	carnero[3b]
nameless[6]	sans[1a] nom[1a]	namenlos	sin[1a] nombre[1a]
ninety[3b]	quatre-vingt-dix	neunzig	noventa[6]*
noisy[5b], (boisterous[6])	bruyant[3b]	lärmend	ruidoso[3b], (fragoso[6a])
nursery[6]	chambre[1a] (d') enfants (enfant[1a])	Kinderstube	cuarto[1a] (de los) niños (niño[1a])
olive[3a]	olive	Olive	oliva[6a], aceituna[6b]
oppress[4a]	opprimer	bedrücken	oprimir[2b]
output[7]	rendement[6a]	Leistungsfähigkeit[4b]	rendimiento
outrageous[7], (atrocious[14])	atroce[5a]	gräßlich[5a]	atroz[5a]
Parisian[8] (*adj.*)	parisien[2b]	parisisch[4a]	parisién, parisiense
peach[3a]	pêche (*f.*)[6b]	Pfirsich	melocotón
(do) penance[6]	(faire) pénitence	büßen[5a]	penar[6a]
pestilence[6]	peste[6a]	Seuche[6a]	peste[4b], (pestilencia)
pilgrim[4a]	pélerin	Pilger	peregrino[2b]
platform[4a]	tribune[4b]	Tribüne	tribuna[6a]
poisoning (poison[3a])	empoisonnement[6b]	Vergiftung	envenenamiento
policeman[5b], (constable[6]), (sheriff[6])	gendarme[3b], (policier[6a])	Polizist	alguacil[3b], (policía[4b])
precision[7]	précision[3a], (exactitude[5a]), (justesse[5b])	Genauigkeit[6a]	precisión[3a], (exactitud[4a])

English	French	German	Spanish
publisher[6]	éditeur	Verleger[5a], Herausgeber[5b], (Buchhändler[6b])	editor[6b]
puff[3a] (praise) (*n.*)	réclame[6a]	Puff, Reklame	reclamo
rainbow[3b]	arc-en-ciel	Regenbogen	iris[6b]
recall[3b] (*n.*)	rappel[6a]	Widerruf	revocación
(have) recess[3b]	vaquer[6b]	Ferien (haben)	(estar de) receso
ruffle[5a] (hair)	ébouriffer[6b]	(in) Unordnung[6a] (bringen)	desgreñar
rust[3b] (*vb.*)	rouiller[6a]	rosten	enmohecer
satin[4b] (*n.*)	satin[6b]	Satin	raso[4b]
sausage[5b]	saucisse	Wurst[6a]	chorizo[6b]
scandal[5b]	scandale[4b]	Skandal	escándalo[2b]
screw[5a] (*n.*)	vis	Schraube[6a]	rosca[6b], (tornillo[7b])
spade[3b], (shovel[4b])	pelle[6a]	Schaufel	pala
specific[6]	spécifique	spezifisch[5b]	específico[6b]
spur[4a] (on boot)	éperon[6a]	Spore	espuola[4b]
steeple[4b], spire[4b]	clocher[4a]	Kirchturm	campanario[6b]
strawberry[3b]	fraise[6a]	Erdbeere	fresa
sullen[4a]	maussade[5a]	verstimmt	mohino[5b]
sunrise[3b]	lever (*n.*)[4a] (du soleil)	Sonnenaufgang	salida[2a] (del sol)
survey[4a], (inspect[6])	inspecter[4b]	übersehen, inspizieren	inspeccionar[6b]
survive[5a]	survivre[6a]	überleben[6a]	sobrevivir
suspension[8] (tension)	suspension[5b]	Spannung[4b]	suspensión[5a]
swan[3b]	cygne	Schwan	cisne[6a]
sweat[4a] (*vb.*)	suer[5a]	schwitzen	sudar[3a]
tapestry[6]	tapisserie[4b]	Teppich[6a], (Gobelin)	tapiz[6a], (tapicería)
tiger[4b]	tigre[6b]	Tiger	tigre[4b]
tile[4a]	carreau[4a]	Fliese	losa[6a]
triple[7]	triple[4b]	dreifach[5a]	triple[6a]
turf[5a], sod[6a]	gazon[6a]	Rasen[6b]	césped
twin[7a]	jumeau(-elle)	Zwilling	gemelo[6b]
vexation[6]	chagrin (*n.*)[2a], ennui[2b]	Ärger[7a]	enfado[4b], (irritación)
wink[7b] (*vb.*)	cligner[6b] (de l'œil)	zwinkern	pestañear
wretched[3b]	déplorable[6a]	jämmerlich	deplorable
yawn[4b] (*vb.*), (gape[6])	bâiller[5a]	gähnen	bostezar[5a]

SECTION 5.9. CONCEPTS 5081 THROUGH 5124

E F G S	*E F G S*	*E F G S*	*E F G S*	*E F G S*
3–7 –8*–8*	4–5 –8*–6	5–3–8*–2	6–1 –8*–2	10–5–2–6
3–8*–8*–7	4–6 –8*–5	5–4–8*–3	6–6 –6 –5	10–6–2–5
4–3 –8*–8*	4–8*–8*–3	5–5–8*–2	6–8*–6 –3	11–2–2–5
4–4 –8*–7	5–1 –8*–6	5–6–8*–1	9–5 –3 –6	11–4–2–3

English	French	German	Spanish
arbiter[10]	arbitre[5b]	Richter[2a]	árbitro[6b]
architecture[6]	architecture[6a]	Baukunst[6a]	arquitectura[5a]
arid[10]	aride[6b]	trocken[2b]	árido[5a], (yermo[6b])
ballad[6]	ballade	Ballade[6b]	copla[3a]

English	French	German	Spanish
beak[5a]	bec[5b]	Schnabel	pico[2a]
bourgeois[11]	bourgeois[2a]	Bürger[2a]	burgués[5b]
cabbage[4b]	chou[6a]	Kohl	col[5a]
confer[4a], (award[6])	conférer[5b]	zuerkennen	conferir[6a]
continuance[6], (continuation[7])	continuation	Fortdauer[6a]	continuación[3b], (prolongación[6b])
convenience[5a]	convenance[4b]	Annehmlichkeit	conveniencia[3b]
creek[4a]	baie[4a]	Bucht	ensenada[7b]
dispense[5a] (give out)	dispenser[4a]	verabreichen	dispensar[3a]
drunken[5b] (person)	ivrogne[4b]	Trunkenbold	borracho[3b], (beodo[7a])
embroider[5b]	broder[3b]	sticken	bordar[4a]
exploit[5b], feat[5a]	exploit[4b]	Heldentat	hazaña[3a], (proeza[5a])
fir[4b]	sapin[3b]	Tanne	abeto
forge[4b] (*n.*)	forge[5a]	Schmiede	fragua[6a]
gorge[6] (*n.*)	défilé	Schlucht[6b]	cañón[3b], (barranco[4b])
graduate[4a] (*vb.*)	. . . .	absolvieren	graduar[3b]
grin[4b] (*vb.*) (with a jeer)	ricaner[6b]	grinsen	sonreír[1b] burlonamente (burlón[5b])
harness[3a] (*n.*)	harnais	Geschirr	aparejo[7b]
idol[4b]	idole	Abgott	ídolo[3b]
meddle[5a], (interfere[6])	intervenir[3a]	einmischen	intervenir[4a], (entremeterse)
pepper[4a]	poivre	Pfeffer	pimienta[3b], (pimiento[5b])
pertaining (pertain[6])	appartenant (appartenir[1b])	zugehörig	relativo[2a], (perteneciente[4a])
pistol[4a]	revolver[4b], (pistolet[5a])	Pistole	pistola[7a]
preside[5b]	présider[3a]	vorsitzen	presidir[4a]
prestige[11]	prestige[4a]	Ruf[2a]	prestigio[3b]
rocky[4a]	couvert[2a] (de) rochers (rocher[3a]), (rocheux)	felsig	rocoso
scepter(re)[4b]	sceptre	Szepter	cetro[3a]
scruple[5b]	scrupule[3a]	Skrupel	escrúpulo[4a]
sincerity[5b]	sincérité[4a]	Aufrichtigkeit	sinceridad[3b]
slaughter[4b] (*n.*)	massacre[5b]	Totschlag	matanza[6b]
snap[3a] (e.g., dog) (and seize)	happer[7a]	schnappen	pegar[2a] una dentellada
soak[5b]	tremper[3a]	durchnässen	empapar[4b]
sob[5a] (*n.*)	sanglot[3b]	Schluchzer	sollozo[4a]
spit[4b] (*vb.*)	cracher[5a]	speien	escupir[6b]
switch[5b] (hair)	faux[1b] cheveu(x)[1b]	(falsche) Zopf	postizo[6b]
tease[5b]	taquiner[6b]	necken	tomar[1a] (el) pelo[1b], (molestar[2a])
theoretical[9], (theoretically)	théoriquement[5b]	theoretisch[3b]	teórico[6a]
thrash[5a] (agricultural)	battre[1a]	dreschen	trillar[6a]
trample[4a]	piétiner	trampeln	hollar[3b]
unit[6] (military), (contingent[14])	contingent	Kontingent[6b]	unidad[3a], (contingente[5b])
writ[4b]	mandat[5a]	Mandat	mandamiento[6b]

SECTION 6. CONCEPTS 5125 THROUGH 5210

E F G S	*E F G S*	*E F G S*	*E F G S*	*E F G S*	*E F G S*
3-8*-8*-8*	4-8*-8*-4	5-5 -8*-3	6-2-8*-2	6-8*-5-8*	7-5 -6-3
4-4 -8*-8*	5-1 -8*-7	5-6 -8*-2	6-3-8*-1	6-8*-6-4	7-6 -5-6
4-5 -8*-7	5-3 -8*-5	5-8*-6 -8*	6-4-6 -8*	7-3 -6-5	8-8*-4-4
4-6 -8*-6	5-4 -8*-4	6-1 -8*-3	6-6-6 -6	7-5 -5-7	9-4 -3-8*

English	French	German	Spanish
adequate[7]	suffisant[3a]	sachgemäß[6a]	adecuado[5b]
alms[5a]	aumône[5b]	Almosen	limosna[3a]
ant[4a]	fourmi	Ameise	hormiga[4b]
attraction[5b]	attraction[5a]	Anziehen	atracción[3b]
baker[4a]	boulanger[4b]	Bäcker	panadero
baptize[7]	baptiser[5b]	taufen[5a]	bautizar[7a]
barge[6]	chaland, péniche	Kahn[6a]	barcaza
braid[4b] (*n.*) (hair, etc.)	natte	Zopf	trenza[4b]
bribe[5b] (*vb.*)	acheter[1b]	bestechen	sobornar[7a]
bulb[5b]	oignon[5a]	Zwiebel	cebolla[3b], (bulbo)
bushel[3a], (bu.[6]), (peck[3b])	boisseau	Scheffel	fanega
capture[3b] (*vb.*)	capturer	kapern	capturar
cavalier[6]	cavalier[3a]	Kavalier	caballero[1a]
cemetery[5b], (churchyard[6])	cimetière[5b]	Friedhof	cementerio[5a]
chatter[4a] (teeth) (*vb.*)	claquer[4a]	klappern	castañetear (los dientes)
comb[4a] (*vb.*)	peigner	kämmen	peinar[4a]
combustion[6]	combustion	Verbrennung[5b]	combustión
cuff[4a]	manchette	Manschette	puño[4b]
dependence[7]	dépendance[5a]	Abhängigkeit[6a]	dependencia[3b]
determination[6]	détermination	Entschlossenheit[6b]	determinación[4a]
dirt[6b]	saleté	Schmutz	mugre, suciedad
disgust[5b] (*vb.*), (sicken[6])	dégoûter[4a], (écœurer[7a])	anekeln	disgustar[4a], repugnar[4a]
earthquake[4b]	tremblement[4b] (de terre)	Erdbeben	temblor de tierra, terremoto
eighteenth[6]	dix-huitième[6a]	achtzehnte[6b]	décimoctavo[6*]
elf[5a], (sprite[6])	lutin	Theaterkobold[6a]	duende
ether[6]	éther	Äther[6a]	éter[4b]
exile[4b], (banishment[6b])	exil[4a]	Verbannung	destierro
fashionable[6]	(à la) mode[1b], (chic[5a])	modisch	(a la) moda[3a]
fife[6]	fifre	Pfeife[5b], (Flöte)	flautín
furrow[5a]	sillon[3b], (ornière[5b])	Furche	surco[5b]
gorge[6] (*vb.*)	se gorger	fressen[6a]	hartar[4b]
greedy[4a] (pejorative)	gourmand[6a]	gierig	codicioso[6a], voraz[6a]
hello[5b]	hé[5b], (holà[6a])	hallo	hola[3b]
hydrogen[6]	hydrogène	Wasserstoff[5a]	hidrógeno
icy[4b], (frosty[5a])	glacial[6b]	eisig	glacial[6a]
immortality[5b]	immortalité	Unsterblichkeit[6b]	inmortalidad
liver[4b] (anatomical)	foie[4b]	Leber	hígado
mistrust[5b] (*vb.*)	(se) méfier[4a]	mißtrauen	desconfiar[4b]
misunderstanding (misunderstand[6])	malentendu	Mißverständnis[5a]	malentendido

English	French	German	Spanish
mule[4a]	mule	Maulesel	mula[4a]
nap[4b] (sleep) (*n.*)	somme	Schlummer	siesta[4a]
needy[7]	dépourvu[6b]	dürftig[5a]	menesteroso[6b]
oat[3a]	avoine	Hafer	avena
obedience[4a]	obéissance	Gehorsam	obediencia[4b]
obscure[5a] (*vb.*)	obscurcir[5a]	verdunkeln	obscurecer[3b]
peg[5a] (for hat, etc.)	patère	Haken[6a]	clavija, gancho (de ropa)
pinch[4a] (*vb.*)	pincer[4a]	kneifen	pellizcar
plane[4b] tree[1a]	platane[6b]	Platane	plátano[6a]
plateau[5a]	plateau[3b]	Plateau	meseta[5a]
player[5b]	joueur[4b]	Spieler	jugador[4b], (tocador[6b])
playground[6]	terrain[2a]	Spielplatz	campo[1a] (de) juegos (juego[2a])
plum[3a]	prune	Pflaume	ciruela
poisonous[6]	vénéneux, venimeux	giftig[5a]	venenoso
predecessor[6]	prédécesseur	Vorgänger[5a]	predecesor
pudding[3b]	pouding	Pudding	pudín
pulse[4a]	pouls	Puls	pulso[4b]
ragged[4b]	(en) haillons (haillon[6b]), (déguenillé)	zerlumpt	desastrado[6b]
rattle[3b] (child's)	hochet	Klapper	sonajero
receiver[6]	receveur, récipient	Empfänger[5b]	receptor
rhyme[3b]	rime	Reim	rima
salad[5b]	salade[4a]	Salat	ensalada[4b]
sandy[3b]	sablonneux	sandig	arenoso
serene[5a]	serein (*adj.*)[6a]	abgeklärt	sereno[2a]
seventeen[4b]	dix-sept[6a]	siebzehn	diecisiete[6]*
sinew[5a]	tendon	Sehne[6b]	tendón
skate[3b] (*vb.*)	patiner	Schlittschuh (laufen)	patinar
skull[5a]	crâne[4a]	Schädel	casco[4a], (cráneo[5b]), (calavera[6a])
sparrow[3a]	moineau	Spatz, Sperling	gorrión
spice[3b]	épice	Gewürz	especia
spider[4a]	araignée	Spinne	araña[4a]
spontaneous[7]	spontané[5a] (spontanément[6a])	(aus eignem) Antrieb[6a]	espontáneo[3b]
squire[4a] (*n.*) (equerry)	écuyer	Knappe	escudero[4b]
squirrel[3a]	écureuil	Eichhörnchen	ardilla
stammer[5b]	balbutier[4a], (bégayer[5b]), (ânonner[6a])	stottern	balbucear[4b]
stony[5a]	pierreux	steinern[6a], (steinig)	pétreo, pedregoso
submission[6]	soumission	Unterwerfung[6b]	sumisión[4a]
suck[4b]	sucer[6b]	saugen	mamar[6b], (chupar[7a])
sunny[3b]	ensoleillé	sonnig	soleado
(in) suspense[8]	(en) suspens	(in) Spannung[4b]	suspenso[4a]
thatch[7]	chaume[5b]	Stroh[6b], (Dachstroh)	paja[3b] (de) techo[2b]
thicket[4b]	buisson[5a]	Dickicht	matorral[7a]

English	French	German	Spanish
treacherous[5a], (faithless[6])	traître[3b], (perfide[5a])	verräterisch	alevoso[5a], perfido[5a], (aleve[6a])
unaware[5b]	(au) dépourvu[6b]	unversehens	(de) sorpresa[2a], ([de] imprevisto[7a])
unfavorable[9]	peu[1a] propice[4a]	ungünstig[3a]	desfavorable
wireless[6]	sans[1a] fil[2b]	drahtlos	sin[1a] hilos (hilo[2a])
zinc[6]	zinc[4b]	Zink[6b]	cinc

SECTION 6. 1. CONCEPTS 5211 THROUGH 5272

E F G S	*E F G S*	*E F G S*	*E F G S*	*E F G S*
4–5 –8*–8*	5–3 –8*–6	5–8*–8*–1	6–8*–6–5	8–3 –6–2
4–6 –8*–7	5–4 –8*–5	6–1 –8*–4	7–5 –5–8*	8–5 –4–8*
4–8*–8*–5	5–5 –8*–4	6–2 –8*–3	7–6 –6–3	8–5 –5–4
5–1 –8*–8*	5–8*–8*–1	6–3 –8*–2	8–3 –5–6	11–8*–1–5

English	French	German	Spanish
(under) arrest[4a]	(en état d')arrestation[5b]	(in) Arrest	arrestado, detenido
bacon[4a]	lard fumé	Speck	tocino[5a]
balloon[7]	ballon[6b]	Ballon[6a]	globo[3b]
barber[5a], (hair[1a] dresser[6])	coiffeur[6b]	Haarschneider	barbero[3b]
barley[4a]	orge	Graupen	cebada[5a]
bust[5a]	buste[4a]	Büste	busto[5b]
claw[5a] (*n.*)	serre[4b], (griffe[6a])	Klaue	garra[5a]
cod[4b]	morue[6b]	Kabeljau	bacalao[7a]
colonist[4b], settler[4a], (colonial[5b])	colon	Kolonist, Siedler	colono[5a]
concrete[6] (*adj.*)	concret	real[6a]	concreto[5a]
consistent[8]	conséquent[3a]	konsequent[6b]	consiguiente[2b]
drawer[4a]	tiroir[5b]	Schublade	gaveta, cajón
drawers (drawer[4a]) (chest of –)	commode (*n.*)[5a]	Kommode	cómoda
dungeon[4b]	cachot[5b]	Verließ	calabozo
dusty[4b]	poussiéreux[5b]	staubig	polvoriento
dwarf[4b] (*n.*)	nain	Zwerg	enano[5a]
editor[8]	rédacteur[5a]	Redakteur[5a]	redactor[4b]
focus[6] (*n.*)	foyer[2a]	Brennpunkt	foco[3b]
founder[4b] (*n.*)	fondateur[5b]	Gründer	fundador
friction[6]	friction	Reibung[6a]	roce[5b]
frock[5a] coat[1b]	redingote[4b]	Überrock, Gehrock	levita[5a], casaca[5b]
gnaw[5a]	ronger[5a]	nagen	roer[4a]
graduate[4a] (*n.*) (from university)	bachelier	Bakkalaurius	bachiller[5a], licenciado[5b]
grammar[5a]	grammaire[6b]	Grammatik	gramática[3a]
harden[4b]	endurcir[6b]	härten	endurecer[7a]
harp[4a]	harpe	Harfe	arpa[5b]
hopelessly (hopeless[4b])	désespérément[5b]	hoffnungslos	desesperadamente
imminent[7]	imminent[5a]	bevorstehend[5a]	inminente
incense[4a]	encens	Weihrauch	incienso[5a]

English	French	German	Spanish
intellectual^{6}	intellectuel^{3a}	intellektuell	intelectual^{2b}
jacket^{5a}	pourpoint^{5b}, veste^{5b}	Jacke	saco^{4a}
jelly^{4a}, (jam^{8})	confiture^{5b}, (gelée)	Gelée	jalea
lemon^{4a}	citron	Zitrone	limón^{5a}
liar^{5a}	menteur(-se)^{5b}	Lügner	embustero^{4b}, (mentiroso^{5b})
miller^{4a}	meunier	Müller	molinero^{5b}
mineral^{4b} (*adj.*)	minéral	mineralisch	mineral^{5a}
nightingale^{4b}	rossignol	Nachtigall	ruiseñor^{5b}
oversight^{8}	oubli^{3b}	Versehen^{5b}	imprevisión^{6a}, inadvertencia^{6a}
pansy (P)^{5a} (flower)	pensée	Stiefmütterchen	pensamiento^{1a}
paste^{5b} (*n.*)	pâte^{4a}	Paste	pasta^{5a}
pumpkin^{4b}	citrouille	Kürbis	calabaza^{5b}
quack^{5a} (*vb.*) (duck)	crier^{1b}	quaken	graznar
raving (rave^{5a}) (*n.*)	délire^{3b}	Faseln	desvarío^{6a}
rehearse^{6}	répéter^{1a}	proben	ensayar^{4a}
relic^{5b} (religious)	relique^{5a}	Reliquie	reliquia^{4a}
ruffle^{5a} (*n.*)	volant (*n.*)^{4b}	Volant	volante^{5b}
scarf^{4a}	écharpe^{5a}	Schärpe	bufanda
shady^{4b}, (shadowy^{6})	ombragé (ombrager^{5b})	schattig	umbroso
shrub^{4a}	buisson^{5a}	Busch	arbusto
sip^{5a} (*vb.*)	boire^{1b} (à petits coups)	schlürfen	tomar^{1a} a sorbos
slippery^{4a}	glissant (*adj.*)^{5b}	schlüpferig	resbaladizo, resbaloso
sob^{5a} (*vb.*)	sangloter^{4a}	schluchzen	sollozar^{5a}
socialist^{8}	socialiste^{3a}	Sozialdemokrat^{5b}, (sozialdemokratisch^{4a})	socialista^{6b}
statistics^{8}	statistique^{5a}	Statistik^{4a}, statistisch^{4b}	estadísticas
stitch^{4a} (knitted)	maille^{5b}	Masche	puntada
tank^{4b}, (cistern^{6})	réservoir^{5a}	Behälter, Tank	cisterna, tanque
thesis^{11}	thèse	Satz^{1b}, (These)	tesis^{5b}
unkind^{5b}	peu^{1a} charitable^{6b}	unfreundlich	poco^{1a} bondadoso^{3b}
violin^{5a}, (fiddle^{6})	violon^{4b}	Geige	violín^{5b}
wedge^{5a} (*n.*)	coin^{1b}	Keil	cuña
wring^{5b} (out)	tordre^{3b} (e.g., linge)	wringen	exprimir^{6a}
wrist^{5b}	poignet^{5b}	Handgelenk	muñeca^{4a}

SECTION 6.2. CONCEPTS 5273 THROUGH 5348

E F G S	*E F G S*	*E F G S*	*E F G S*	*E F G S*	*E F G S*
4–6 –8*–8*	5–5–8*–5	6–3 –8*–3	7–2–6–8*	7–8*–5–6	10–4–3–6
4–8*–8*–6	5–6–8*–4	6–4 –8*–2	7–4–6–6	7–8*–6–2	10–5–3–5
5–2 –8*–8*	6–1–8*–5	6–6 –6 –8*	7–5–6–5	8–3 –6–3	10–6–2–8*
5–4 –8*–6	6–2–8*–4	6–8*–6 –6	7–6–5–8*	8–6 –4–8*	

English	French	German	Spanish
appendix^{7} (book)	appendice	Anhang^{5b}	apéndice^{6a}
archbishop^{7}	archevêque^{5b}	Erzbischof^{6a}	arzobispo^{5b}
assumption^{7} (taking over)	adoption^{6b}	Übernahme^{5a}	adopción
bachelor^{6}	garçon^{1b}	Junggeselle	soltero^{5a}

English	French	German	Spanish
bald[6]	chauve	kahl[6b]	calvo[6b]
banana[4b]	banane	Banane	plátano[6a]
behead[6]	couper[1a] (la tête), (décapiter)	enthaupten	degollar[5a]
belly[6]	ventre[3a]	Bauch	vientre[3b], (panza[5b])
blunt[4b] (*vb.*)	émousser	abstumpfen	embotar[6a]
bridal[6]	(de) noces (noce[4a]), (de mariée)	bräutlich	(de) matrimonio[2a]
brigade[10]	brigade[6a]	Brigade[2a]	brigada
bronze[6]	bronze[3b]	Bronze	bronce[3b]
caress[6] (*n.*)	caresse[4b]	Liebkosung	caricia[2b], (mimo[6b])
chalk[4b]	craie[6b]	Kreide	tiza
chaste[5b]	chaste[5b]	keusch	casto[5b]
Christianity[10]	christianisme[4b]	Christentum[3a]	cristianismo[6b]
circus[5a]	cirque[4b]	Zirkus	circo[6b]
coldness[10]	froideur[5a]	Kälte[3b]	frialdad[5b]
colonial[6b]	colonial[4a]	kolonial	colonial[6a]
comb[4a] (on bird)	crête	Kamm	cresta[6b]
complicate[7]	compliquer[2b], (compliqué[4b])	komplizieren[6a]	complicar
congratulate[5b]	féliciter[4b]	beglückwünschen	felicitar[6a]
constable[6]	garde[1b] champêtre	Vogt[6b]	guardia[3a] rural[6b]
correspondent[7]	correspondant[4b]	Korrespondent[6b]	corresponsal[6a]
cough[4a] (*n.*)	toux[6b]	Husten	tos
crab[4b]	crabe	Krabbe, Krebs	cangrejo[6b]
Cuba(n)[4a] (*adj.*)	cubain	kubanisch	cubano[6a]
cuckoo[4b]	coucou	Kuckuck	cuco[6a], (cuchillo)
demonstration[6] (public – against something)	manifestation[3b]	Kundgebung	manifestación[3b]
diameter[7]	diamètre	Durchmesser[6a]	diámetro[6a]
diet[5b]	régime[2a]	Diät	dieta
digest[6]	digérer[6b]	verarbeiten[6a]	digerir
din[5a] (*vb.*)	abasourdir[4b], (étourdir[5b])	betäuben	atronar[6a]
disgusting (disgust[5b])	dégoûtant[6a]	eklig	repugnante[4a]
dome[4b]	dôme	Kuppel	cúpula[6b]
dough[6]	pâte[4a]	Teig	masa[2a]
(musical[3a]) drama[5b]	opéra[5a] comique[3b]	Operette	zarzuela[5a]
drawers (drawer[4a]) (clothing)	chausse[6b]	Hose(n)	calzoncillos, pantaloncillos
drowsy[4a] (to become –)	s'assoupir[6b]	schläfrig (sein)	adormilarse, ([estar] soñoliento)
economic[8]	économique[3a]	ökonomisch[6b]	económico[3b]
economy[6] (both senses)	économie[2b]	Ökonomie	economía[4a]
fairyland[5b]	(pays de) fées (fée[4b])	Märchenland	(país de las) hadas (hada[6b])
forge[4b] (falsify)	contrefaire	fälschen	falsear[6b]
gentry[7]	bourgeoisie, gentry	Gentry[6b]	clase[1b] acomodada (acomodar[2b])
geography[4b]	géographie	Geographie	geografía[6b]
grasshopper[4a]	sauterelle	Heuschrecke	cigarra

English	French	German	Spanish
housekeeper[6], housewife[6]	ménagère[4b]	Haushälterin	ama (amo[1a]) (de) llaves (llave[2a])
lick[4a]	lécher[6b]	lecken	lamer
logic[6]	logique[2b]	Logik	lógica[4b]
lump[4b]	motte	Klumpen	terrón[6a]
morsel[6]	morceau[1b]	Bissen	bocado[5a]
moulding (mould[4a]) (architectural)	moulure	Leiste	moldura[6a]
mute[4a] (*n.*) (music)	sourdine[6b]	Dämpfer	sordina
oblique[8], (slanting[10*])	oblique[6a]	schräg[4a]	oblicuo, soslayado
oyster[4a]	huître	Auster	ostra[6a]
pantry[5a]	office[2b]	Speisekammer	despensa
pave[4b]	paver[6b]	pflastern	pavimentar
platform[4a] (dais)	estrade	Podium	dosel[6a], (plataforma)
prairie[5b]	terre[1a] inculte[6b]	Prärie	pradera[4b], (pampa[6a])
rake[4b] (*n.*)	râteau[6b]	Harke, Rechen	rastrillo
scar[4b] (*n.*)	cicatrice	Narbe	cicatriz[6a]
shapeless[6]	informe[4b]	formlos	informe[2b]
shoemaker[4a], (cobbler[5a])	cordonnier	Schuster	zapatero[6b]
slavery[5a]	servitude[6b], (esclavage)	Sklaverei	esclavitud[4b]
sprout[6] (*vb.*)	germer[4a]	sprießen	brotar[2b]
strap[4b] (*n.*)	courroie, lavière	Riemen	correa[6a]
surpassing (surpass[4b]), (transcendental)	transcendant(al)	transzendental	transcendental[6b]
tablet[4b] (viz., cough drop)	pastelle	Pastille	pastilla[6b]
towel[4b]	torchon[6b]	Handtuch	to(b)alla
tub[4a]	cuve[6a], (baquet)	Wanne	cuba, tonel
vigil[6]	veille[1b]	Nachtwache	vigilia[5a]
(make) void[4a]	annuler	annullieren	anular[6b]
waterfall[5a], (cascade[6]), (cataract[6])	cascade[5b]	Wasserfall	cascada[5b], (catarata[7a])
whirlwind[5a]	tourbillon[6a]	Wirbelsturm	torbellino[4a]
wizard[5a]	sorcier(-ère)[4b]	Hexer	hechicero[6a], mago[6b], adivino[6b]
yawn[4b] (*n.*)	bâillement	Gähnen	bostezo[6a]

SECTION 6.3. CONCEPTS 5349 THROUGH 5394

E F G S	*E F G S*	*E F G S*	*E F G S*	*E F G S*
4–8*–8*–7	5–6 –8*–5	6–3 –8*–4	7–5–6–6	9–5 –5–2
5–3 –8*–8*	5–8*–8*–3	6–4 –8*–3	7–6–6–5	9–8*–3–7
5–4 –8*–7	6–1 –8*–6	6–5 –8*–2	8–4–6–3	10–4 –4–3
5–5 –8*–6	6–2 –8*–5	6–8*–6 –7	8–6–5–5	11–4 –3–3

English	French	German	Spanish
acquisition[7]	acquisition[5b]	Beschaffung[6a], Erlangung[6b], Erwerbung[6b]	adquisición[6a]
admiral[5a]	amiral[4b]	Admiral	almirante[7a]
admonish[6], (exhort[8])	exhorter	ermahnen[6a]	amonestar[7a], exhortar[7a]

English	French	German	Spanish
(in) anguish[5b], agonizing (agonize[12])	angoissant[6a]	(in) Todesangst	(en) agonía[5a]
ark[5a]	arche	Arche	arca[3b]
attic[5b]	mansarde[3b], (grenier[5a])	Estrich	ático, desván
bet[6] (*vb.*)	parier[4b]	wetten	apostar[3b], (apuesta[5b])
bodily[6], corporal[6]	corporel	leiblich[6a]	corporal[7a], corpóreo[7b]
Christendom[9]	chrétienté	Christentum[3a]	cristiandad[7a]
congeal[9]	figer[5b]	erstarren[5b]	helar[2a], (congelar)
counter[5a] (in a shop)	comptoir[5a]	Tresen	mostrador[6a]
embassy[7]	ambassade[6a]	Gesandtschaft[6b]	embajada[5b]
exaltation[11]	exaltation[4a]	Erhebung[3a]	exaltación[3b]
eyebrow[6]	sourcil[3b]	Braue	ceja[4b]
fearless[5b]	intrépide[6b]	furchtlos	intrépido[5a]
flax[4b]	lin	Flachs	lino[7a]
fry[5a]	frire	braten	freír[3a]
heretic[7]	hérétique[6b]	Ketzer[6b]	hereje[5b]
hoe[4b] (*n.*)	houe	Hacke	azadón[7a]
index[6] finger[1b]	index	Zeigefinger[6b]	índice[7a]
interruption[8]	interruption[6b]	Unterbrechung[5b]	interrupción[5a]
lavish[5b] (*vb.*)	prodiguer[5b]	verschwenden	prodigar[6a]
legislator[8]	législateur[6a]	Gesetzgeber[5b]	legislador[6a]
mason[6a]	maçon[5b]	Maurer	albañil[6a]
militia[6]	milice	Landwehr[6a]	milicia[7a]
(have) misgiving[8], (forebode[10])	pressentir[4b]	voraussehen[6a]	presentir[3b]
mole[5a] (on body)	grain[3a] de[1a] beauté[2a]	Leberfleck	lunar
nineteen[4a]	dix-neuf	neunzehn	diez y nueve[7]*, (diecinueve)
nun[5b]	nonne	Nonne	monja (monje[3a])
pamphlet[7]	brochure[6a]	Broschüre[6b], Prospekt[6b]	folleto[5a]
picnic[4b]	pique-nique	Picknick	merienda[7a] campestre[5b]
productive[7], (creative[11])	producteur[5a]	schöpferisch[6a]	productivo[6a]
profane[5b] (*adj.*)	profane[6b]	profan	profano[5b]
protector[6]	protecteur[5a]	Beschützer	protector[2b]
retail[6] (*vb.*)	vendre[1b] (au) détail[1b], (débiter[5a])	verhökern	vender[1b] (al, por) menor[6a]
selfishness[8]	égoïsme[4b]	Selbstsucht[6b]	egoísmo[6b]
suburb[5b]	faubourg[4a]	Vorort	arrabal[7a]
superiority[10]	supériorité[4a]	Überlegenheit[4b], (Übermacht[5a] [military])	superioridad[3b]
superstition[5a]	superstition[5b]	Aberglaube	superstición[6b]
tributary[4a]	tributaire	Zufluß	afluente[7b]
twelfth[4b]	douzième	zwölfte	duodécimo[7]*, (décimo segundo)
upset[5a] (*n.*)	bouleversement[6a]	Umsturz	trastorno[5b]
valve[6]	clapet	Klappe[6a]	válvula[7b]
vinegar[5a]	vinaigre	Essig	vinagre[3b]
waft[6] (*n.*)	souffle[2a]	Wehen	emanación[5a]
walnut[5b]	noix[6a]	Walnuß	nuez[5b]

SECTION 6.4. CONCEPTS 5395 THROUGH 5477

E F G S	*E F G S*	*E F G S*	*E F G S*	*E F G S*
4–8*–8*–8*	5–8*–8*–4	6–6 –8*–2	7–5 –6–7	8–8*–4–8*
5–4 –8*–8*	6–3 –8*–5	6–8*–6 –8*	7–8*–5–8*	9–4 –5–4
5–5 –8*–7	6–4 –8*–4	7–3 –8*–1	8–4 –5–8*	
5–6 –8*–6	6–5 –8*–3	7–4 –6 –8*	8–4 –6–4	

English	French	German	Spanish
agency[5b] (place and office)	agence[6b]	Agentur	agencia[6b]
ally[7] (*n.*)	allié (*n.*)[4a]	Verbündete[6a]	aliado
astronomer[7]	astronome	Astronom[5b]	astrónomo
babble[4b], chatter[4a] (*vb.*)	babiller	babbeln	parlotear
balm[5a]	baume	Balsam	bálsamo[4b]
beating[6] (*n.*) (pommeling)	volée (*n.*)[4a] (de coups)	Prügel	paliza[4a]
bicycle[4a]	bicyclette	Fahrrad	bicicleta
birch[4b]	bouleau	Birke	abedul
bowel[4b]	intestin	Eingeweide	intestino
breeches[6]	culotte[4b]	Kniehose(n)	calzón[4b]
builder[4a]	constructeur	Erbauer	constructor
camel[4b]	chameau	Kamel	camello
cement[4a] (*n.*)	ciment	Zement	cemento
chemist[7]	chimiste	Chemiker[6a]	químico[4a]
clover[4b]	trèfle	Klee	trébol
cluck[4b] (*vb.*)	glousser	glucken	cacarear
complexion[5b]	teint	Gesichtsfarbe	tez[4a]
conscientious[8]	consciencieux	gewissenhaft[4a]	meticuloso
crouch[5b]	accroupir[4a]	hocken	agachar, agazapar
deign[6]	daigner[4b]	geruhen	dignarse[4a]
dial[6] (clock)	cadran[6b]	Zifferblatt	esfera[2b]
dismay[4a] (*vb.*)	consterner	bestürzen	consternar
dizzy[6] (feel –)	(avoir) vertige[4a], (vertigineux[5b])	schwindlig	tener[1a] vértigo[4a], (mareado [marear[6a]])
drip[4a]	dégoutter	tröpfeln	gotear
ebb[6] (tide)	marée descendante, reflux	Ebbe[6b]	bajamar, reflujo
eloquent[6]	éloquent[5a]	beredt	elocuente[3a]
engrave[6]	graver[5a]	gravieren	grabar[3b]
fermentation[7]	fermentation	Gärung[5a]	fermentación
fern[4b]	fougère	Farn	helecho
fifteenth[5b]	quinzième[6b]	fünfzehnte	décimo quinto[6*]
fig[4b]	figue	Feige	higo
flank[5b] (*vb.*)	flanquer[4b]	flankieren	flanquear
fleece[4b]	toison	Vlies	vellocino, vellón
flexible[6]	souple[4b]	biegsam	flexible[4b]
ford[4a] (*n.*)	gué	Furt	vado
frying (fry[5a]) pan[2b]	poêle (*f.*)[6a]	Pfanne	sartén[6a]
gall[5a] (*n.*) (anatomical)	fiel	Galle	hiel[4b]
generosity[6]	générosité[5b]	Weitherzigkeit	generosidad[3b]
ghastly[6]	hagard[6b]	grausig	espantoso[2b], pálido[2b]

English	French	German	Spanish
glacier[6]	glacier	Gletscher[6a]	glaciar
grocer[4a]	épicier	Kolonialwarenhändler	bodegonero, especiero
hideous[6]	hideux[6a]	greulich	horrible[2a], espantoso[2b], (horrendo[3b])
hip[4a]	hanche	Hüfte(n)	cadera
honesty[6]	honnêteté[4b]	Ehrlichkeit	honradez[4a], (honestidad[6b])
incomparable[9], unique[9]	incomparable[4a]	unvergleichlich[5b]	incomparable[4a]
linden[6]	tilleul	Linde[6a]	tilo
(of) lowly[6] (birth)	(de) basse (bas[1a]) extraction[5b]	(von) niederer (nieder[1b]) Herkunft	(de) humilde[1b] cuna[3b]
mane[5a]	crinière	Mähne	melena[4a]
maple[4b]	érable	Ahorn	arce
masterpiece[7]	chef-d'œuvre[3b]	Meisterstück	obra[1a] maestra (maestro[1b])
mew[4a]	miauler	miauen	maullar, mayar
necklace[6]	collier[3b]	Halsband	collar[5b]
necktie[6]	cravate[4a]	Krawatte, Schlips	corbata[4a]
nymph[5a]	nymphe	Nymphe	ninfa[4b]
pavilion[6]	pavillon[4a]	Pavillon	pabellón[4b]
peacock[5a]	paon	Pfau	pavo[4b] real[1a]
prune[4b]	pruneau	Zwetsch(g)e	ciruela pasa
raisin[5b]	raisin[4a] sec[1b]	Rosine	pasa
rampart[8]	rempart[4a]	Wall[5b]	baluarte
ration[6]	ration	Quotisierung[6a]	racionamiento
realization[8]	réalisation[4a]	Verwirklichung[6b]	realización[4b]
rebellious[6]	rebelle[5a]	aufrührerisch	rebelde[3b]
recruit[6] (*n.*)	recrue	Rekrut[6b]	recluta
regent[8]	régente	Regentin[4b]	regente
romance (R)[6] (*adj.*)	roman (*adj.*)[5a]	romanisch	romance[3a]
seam[4b]	couture	Naht	costura
sergeant[7]	sergent[5a]	Wachtmeister[6b], (Feldwebel)	sargento[7b]
stool[4a]	tabouret	Schemel	banqueta, poyo, taburete
submission[6], (resignation[7])	résignation[5b]	Ergebung	resignación[3b]
Swiss[5a]	suisse[6a]	schweizerisch	suizo[6b]
tar[4b]	goudron	Teer	brea
temperance[5a]	sobriété[5a]	Mäßigkeit	sobriedad[7a], (temperanza)
thistle[4b]	chardon	Distel	cardo
tomato[5a]	tomate	Tomate	tomate[4a]
tongs[5a]	tenailles (tenaille[6b])	Zange	tenazas (tenaza[6b])
tunnel[5b]	tunnel[6a]	Tunnel	túnel[6b]
tufted (tuft[6]), (bushy[11])	touffu[6b]	buschig	espeso[2a], (frondoso[4b])
turtle[4b]	tortue	Schildkröte	tortuga
unfit[5a]	impropre[6b]	unpassend	impropio[6b]
wanton[4b] (*adj.*)	déréglé	leichtfertig	desenfrenado
watchful[4b]	(en) éveil, vigilant	wachsam	alerto
wigwam[4b]	wigwam	Wigwam	jacal (del) Indio
zero[5a]	zéro[6b]	Null	cero[6b]

SECTION 6.5. CONCEPTS 5478 THROUGH 5538

E F G S	*E F G S*	*E F G S*	*E F G S*	*E F G S*
5–5 –8*–8*	6–2–8*–7	6–6 –8*–3	7–8*–6–5	9–8*–4–5
5–6 –8*–7	6–3–8*–6	6–8*–8*–1	8–5 –6–4	10–1 –5–4
5–8*–8*–5	6–4–8*–5	7–3 –8*–2	8–8*–5–5	11–5 –3–4
6–1 –8*–8*	6–5–8*–4	7–5 –6 –8*	9–4 –5–5	

English	French	German	Spanish
abbot[6]	abbé[2b]	Abt	abate[7a]
abstract[7] (*adj.*)	abstrait	abstrakt[6a]	abstracto[5b]
analyze[6]	analyser[5a]	analysieren	analizar[4b]
bang[6] (a door)	claquer[4a]	schletzen	golpear[5a]
(regulations [regulation[6]] for) bankruptcy[9]	(lois concernant la) banqueroute	Konkursordnung[4b]	leyes (ley[1a]) (de) quiebra[5a]
benign[9]	bienfaisant[4b]	wohltätig[5a]	benigno[5a]
bracelet[5a]	bracelet[6a]	Armband	pulsera[7b]
constitutional[7]	constitutionnel	konstitutionell[6a]	constitucional[5b]
coral[5a]	corail	Koralle	coral[5a]
cork[5b] (stopper)	bouchon[5b]	Kork	tapón
crackle[5b] (*vb.*)	pétiller	knistern	crujir[5a]
crisp[5b]	croustillant	knusperig	crespo[5b]
crumbling (crumble[5a]) (caving in)	effondrement[5b]	Einsturz	derrumbe
crutch[5b]	béquille	Krücke	muleta[5b]
defile[6] (*vb.*)	défiler[3b]	defilieren, vorbeimarschieren	desfilar[6a]
dialog(ue)[6]	dialogue[6a]	Dialog	diálogo[3a]
embroidery[5b]	broderie	Stickerei	bordado[5b]
executive[5b] (*adj.*)	exécutif	Exekutiv-	ejecutivo[5a]
federal[5b]	fédéral	Bundes-	federal[5b]
fickle[6]	capricieux[6a]	unbeständig	caprichoso[3b]
flint[5b]	silex	Feuerstein	pedernal[5a]
flute[5b]	flûte	Flöte	flauta[5b]
foreground[10]	premier[1a] plan (*n.*)[1b], (devant [*n.*][2b])	Vordergrund[5a]	primer[1a] plano[4a]
forgetfulness[7], (oblivion[8])	oubli[3b]	Vergessen	olvido[2b]
geographical[8]	géographique	geographisch[5a]	geográfico[5a]
glade[6]	clairière	Lichtung	claro[1a], (raso[4b])
grope[6]	tâtonner[6b]	tasten	tentar[3a], andar[1a] (a) tientas[3b]
hinge[5b] (*n.*)	gond[5b]	Angel	gozne
hoarse[6]	rauque[6b]	heiser	ronco[3b]
horizontal[6]	horizontal[4b]	wagerecht	horizontal[5b]
idleness[5a]	oisivité	Müßiggang	ocio[5a]
impious[6]	impie[6b]	ruchlos	impío[3b]
lawless[6]	illégal	gesetzlos	fuera[1a] (de) ley[1a], (ilegal)
liable[6] (to something)	susceptible[3b]	imstande	susceptible[6a] (de)
lyric[8] (*adj.*), (lyrical[11])	lyrique[5b]	lyrisch[6a]	lírico[4a]
manual[7] (textbook)	manuel	Lehrbuch[6a]	manual[5b]

English	French	German	Spanish
matron[6]	femme[1a] (d'un certain âge)	Matrone	matrona
miser[6]	avare[4a]	Geizhals	avaro[5a]
parrot[5b]	perroquet	Papagei	loro[5a]
patriotism[6]	patriotisme[6b]	Vaterlandsliebe	patriotismo[3b]
plaster[5b]	plâtre[5b]	Gips	yeso
plunder[5a] (*vb.*)	piller[5b], (saccager[6b])	plündern	saquear
pretense(ce)[5b], (dissimulation[13])	dissimulation	Verstellung	disímulo[5b]
profane[5b] (*vb.*)	profaner	herabziehen	profanar[5b]
quell[6]	rabattre[5a]	stillen	reprimir[4a]
rebellion[5b] (state)	rébellion	Widerspenstigkeit	rebeldía[5b]
restoration[7]	restauration[5b]	wiederherstellen[6a], (Wiederherstellung)	retraso
ruinous[8]	ruineux	verderblich[5a]	ruinoso[5b]
scissors[5a]	ciseaux	Scheere	tijera[5b]
sling[5b] (*n.*)	fronde	Schleuder	honda[5b]
southwest[5a]	sud-ouest[5b]	Südwesten	suroeste
stab[5a] (*n.*)	(coup de) poignard	Dolchstoß	puñalada[5b], (estocada[6b])
stricken[5a] (with an illness)	atteint (*adj.*)[5b]	befallen	atacado
tenant[5a] (*n.*)	occupant[5b], (locataire[6a])	Pächter	inquilino
uncertainty[8]	incertitude	Unsicherheit[5b]	incertidumbre[5b]
unquestionable[11]	incontestable[5a]	zweifellos[3b]	indiscutible[4a]
verb[6]	verbe	Zeitwort	verbo[1b]
vicious[5b]	vicieux	lasterhaft	vicioso[5b]
windy[6]	(de) vent[1b], (venteux)	windig	avendavalado, ventoso
winner[6]	gagnant (gagner[1a])	Gewinner	ganador
wintry[6]	(d')hiver[1b]	wintrig	invernal

SECTION 6.6. CONCEPTS 5539 THROUGH 5600

E F G S	*E F G S*	*E F G S*	*E F G S*
5–6 –8*–8*	6–4 –8*–6	7–2–8*–4	8 6 5 8*
5–8*–8*–6	6 5 –8*–5	7–4–8*–2	9–6–4–8*
6–2 –8*–8*	6 6 –8*–4	7–6–6 –8*	13–1–3–1
6–3 –8*–7	6–8*–8*–2	8–4–6 –6	13 6 1 4

English	French	German	Spanish
airy[5a]	aéré	luftig	airoso[6a]
amber[5b]	ambre[6b]	Bernstein	ámbar
anecdote[6]	anecdote[4b]	Anekdote	anécdota[6b]
annex[7] (*n.*)	annexe[6b]	Anbau[6b]	anexo
apprentice[8]	apprenti[6b]	Lehrling[5a]	aprendiz
approval[6]	approbation[6b]	Beistimmung	aprobación[4b]
chaos[6]	chaos[4b]	Chaos	caos[6b]
civilize[6]	civiliser[5a]	kultivieren	civilizar[5a], (civilizador[6b])
clause[5a]	clause	Klausel	cláusula[6b]
confidential[8]	confidentiel[6b]	vertraulich[5b]	confidencial

English	French	German	Spanish
contractor[9]	entrepreneur[6b]	Unternehmer[4a], Kontrahent[4b]	contratista
cork[5b] (material)	liège[6a]	Kork	corcho
delegate[5b] (*vb.*)	déléguer[6a]	beordern	delegar
denial[8]	dénégation[6a]	Ablehnung[5a]	denegación
desolation[5b]	désolation	Öde	desolación[6a]
druggist[7], (apothecary[10])	pharmacien[6b]	Apotheker[6b]	droguero
eaves[6]	(bord du) toit[2a]	Traufe	alero
elastic[5b] (*adj.*)	élastique	elastisch	elástico[6b]
flattery[5b]	flatterie	Schmeichelei	lisonja[6b], (adulación[7a])
fretful[6]	irritable	reizbar	inquieto[2a], (irritado [irritar[3b]])
frolic[5a] (*vb.*)	gambader	ausgelassen (sein)	retozar[6b]
gallows[5a]	potence	Galgen	horca[6a]
gossip[6] (tales)	racontar[5b], (commérage)	Klatsch	murmuración[5b]
headache[6]	migraine[5b]	Kopfweh	jaqueca[5a]
hermit[5b]	ermite	Einsiedler	ermitaño[6a]
holiness[6]	sainteté[6b]	Heiligkeit	santidad[4a]
Hungarian[8]	hongrois[6a]	ungarisch[5b]	húngaro
integral[13]	intégral[6b]	wesentlich[1a]	íntegro[4b], (integral)
interpreter[6]	interprète[6a]	Ausleger	intérprete[4a]
leafy[7]	couvert[2a] (de) feuilles (feuille[1b])	belaubt	frondoso[4b]
leak[6] (*n.*)	fuite[2a]	Leck	gotera
lighthouse[6]	phare[6b]	Leuchtturm	faro[4b]
luxurious[6]	luxueux[6b]	prunkvoll	lujoso[4b]
mercury (M)[5b]	mercure	Quecksilber	mercurio[6a]
penetrate[13]	pénétrer[1b]	durchdringen[3a], eindringen[3a]	penetrar[1b]
pitiful[6]	pitoyable[5a], (piteux[6b])	bemitleidenswert	lastimoso[5b], (lastimero[6b])
posterity[5b]	postérité	Nachwelt	posteridad[6a]
prophecy[5a]	prophétie	Prophezeiung	profecía[6b]
prostrate[6] (*vb.*)	prosterner[6b]	sich hinwerfen	postrar[4a] (se), (prosternar [se])
rave[5a], ([be] delirious[11])	délirer	phantasieren	delirar[6b]
reaction[8]	réaction[4a]	Reaktion[6b]	reacción[6b]
recoil[6]	reculer[2a]	zurückfahren	recular
refinement[6]	raffinement[5b]	Verfeinerung	refinamiento[5b]
refrain[5a] (*n.*)	refrain[6b]	Kehrreim	estribillo
rusty[5b]	rouillé (rouiller[6a])	rostig	enmohecido
secondary[6]	secondaire[5a]	sekundär	secundario[5b]
sentimental[7]	sentimental[4b]	empfindsam	sentimental[2b]
sheaf[6] (grain)	gerbe[6b]	Garbe	haz[4a]
shroud[5b] (*n.*)	linceul	Leilach	mortaja[6b]
snowy[6]	couvert[2a] (de) neige[2b]	schneebedeckt	nevado
spindle[5b]	broche[6a]	Spindel	carretel, huso
splash[5b] (*vb.*)	éclabousser	spritzen	salpicar[6a]
sponge[5a] (*n.*)	éponge[6b]	Schwamm	esponja

English	French	German	Spanish
stroll[6] (*vb.*)	flâner	schlendern	pasear[2a] (se)
technique[9]	technique (*n.*)[6b]	Technik[4b]	técnica
thermometer[5b]	thermomètre	Thermometer	termómetro[6a]
toad[5a]	crapaud	Kröte	sapo[6a]
tray[6]	plateau[3b]	Tablett	bandeja[7a]
truck[5a]	camion[6b]	Lastwagen	camión
underground[5a]	souterrain[6a]	unterirdisch	subterráneo
vassal[6] (e.g., feudal)	vassal[6b]	Vasall	vasallo[4a]
warble[5a] (*n.*)	gazouillement	Triller	gorjeo[6b]

SECTION 6.7. CONCEPTS 5601 THROUGH 5635

E F G S	*E F G S*	*E F G S*
5–8*–8*–7	6–6 –8*–5	7–6–8*–1
6–3 –8*–8*	6–8*–8*–3	8–2–8*–1
6–4 –8*–7	7–4 –8*–3	8–3–6 –8*
6–5 –8*–6	7–5 –8*–2	10–5–5 –2
		11–3–4 –4

English	French	German	Spanish
afloat[6]	(à) flot[3a]	flott	a flote
anniversary[5b]	anniversaire	Jahrestag	aniversario[7a]
Argentine[6]	argentin	argentinisch	argentino[3a]
badge[6] (metal)	insigne[6b]	Plakette	placa[5b]
biscuit[6], cracker[6] (Amer.)	biscuit[6a]	Keks	bizcocho[5b]
blackbird[5b]	merle	Amsel	mirlo[7b]
clove[5b]	girofle	Nelke	clavo[3b] (de) especia[7a]
communion[6]	communion[5b]	Abendmahl, Kommunion	comunión[6a]
cooperative[8] (*n.*)	association[3a], (coopérative)	Konsumverein[6b]	cooperativa
dessert[7]	dessert[4b]	Nachtisch	postre[3b]
encouragement[7]	encouragement[5b]	Ermutigung	aliento[6a]
eyelid[6]	paupière[4a]	Lid	párpado[7a]
fitness[7] (appropriateness)	à-propos (*n.*)[6a]	Eignung	(a) propósito[1a]
Gothic[6]	gothique[6a]	gotisch	gótico[5b]
incomprehensible[11]	incompréhensible[3b]	unbegreiflich[1b], (unverständlich[6b])	incomprehensible[4b]
infernal[6]	infernal	höllisch	infernal[3b]
ivy[5a]	lierre	Efeu	hiedra[7a]
magnet[6]	aimant (*n.*)[5b]	Magnet	imán[6b]
mathematics[6]	mathématiques (mathématique[6a])	Mathematik	matemáticas[5b]
mattress[6]	matelas[6b]	Matratze	colchón[5b]
mountainous[5a]	montagneux	gebirgig	montañoso[7b]
outrage[6]	attentat[6b], (outrage)	Beschimpfung	atropello[5b]
pilgrimage[6]	pélerinage[6a]	Pilgerzug	peregrinación[5b]
plus[8]	plus[2a]	plus	más[1a]
Portuguese[6]	portugais	portugiesisch	portugués[3a]
progressive[6]	progressif[5b] (progressivement[6b])	fortschrittlich	progresivo[6a]

English	French	German	Spanish
sanction[7], penalty[7]	sanction[6a]	Sanktion	pena[1a], (sanción)
skeleton[6]	squelette[6b]	Knochengerüst	esqueleto[5b]
snore[6]	ronfler[5b]	schnarchen	roncar[6a]
terrace[6]	terrasse[3a]	Terrasse	terraza
Teutonic[10], (Germanic[17])	germanique[5b]	germanisch[5b]	alemán[2b]
turnip[5b]	navet	Runkelrübe	nabo[7a]
unload[7]	décharger[4a]	entladen	descargar[3a]
unspeakable[6]	indicible[5b]	unsäglich	indecible[6a]
volcano[6]	volcan	Vulkan	volcán[3a]

SECTION 6.8. CONCEPTS 5636 THROUGH 5752

E F G S	*E F G S*	*E F G S*	*E F G S*
5–8*–8*–8*	6–8*–8*–4	8–8*–5–8*	10–4 –4–8*
6–4 –8*–8*	7–3 –8*–5	8–8*–6–4	10–5 –5–3
6–5 –8*–7	7–4 –8*–4	9–4 –5–8*	10–8*–3–8*
6–6 –8*–6	7–8*–6 –8*	10–2 –6–2	10–8*–4–4
			11–2 –5–2

English	French	German	Spanish
accommodations (accommodation[6])	installation[4a]	Einstellung	acomodo, alojamiento
acorn[5b]	gland	Eichel	bellota
anticipate[6]	anticiper	vorwegnehmen	anticipar[4a]
arctic[5b]	arctique	arktisch	ártico
aristocratic[6]	aristocratique[6a]	aristokratisch	aristocrático[6a]
asset[10]	actif (*n.*)[5a]	Haben[5a]	activo[3a]
athletic[5b]	athlétique	turnerisch	atlético
bait[5a]	appât	Köder	cebo
beet[5b]	betterave	Rübe	remolacha
beetle[5b]	scarabée	Käfer	escarabajo
betroth[6]	fiancer	verloben	desposar[4a]
blasphemy[6]	blasphème	Lästerung	blasfemia[4b]
bleat[5a] (*vb.*)	bêler	blöken	balar
blindness[5b]	aveuglement	Blindheit	ceguera
blouse[6]	blouse[4a]	Bluse	blusa
buckle[6] (*n.*)	boucle[4a]	Schnalle	hebilla
burr[5b] (vegetal)	bouton de pompier	Klette	cadillo, erizo
carbon[7] dioxide[8]	acide carbonique	Kohlensäure[5b]	dióxido de carbono
chew[6], (ruminate[9])	ruminer[6a], mâcher[6b]	kauen	mascar[6a]
chirp[5a] (*vb.*)	pépier	piepen	gorjear
croak[5a] (*vb.*)	coasser	quaken	graznar
currant[6]	groseille[4b]	Johannisbeere	grosella
Danish[8]	danois	dänisch[5a]	danés
defender[10]	défenseur	Verteidiger[4b]	defensor[4b]
dipper[6]	cuiller(-ère)[4a] (à) pot[3a]	Kochlöffel	cucharón
dissemble[11]	dissimuler[2b]	verhehlen[5b]	disimular[2b]
dukedom[8]	duché	Herzogtum[6a]	ducado[4b]
embody[6]	incarner	verkörpern	encarnar[4b]

English	French	German	Spanish
enamel[6]	émail[6b]	Emaille	esmalte[6a]
ennoble[6]	ennoblir[6a]	adeln	ennoblecer[6a]
enumerate[7]	énumérer[4b]	aufzählen	enumerar[4a]
fellowship[5a]	camaraderie	Kameradschaft	camaradería
ferry[5a]	bac	Fähre	barca de transbordo
fertilize[6]	féconder	düngen	fecundar[4a]
(bull[3a]) fighter[6]	toréador	Stierkämpfer	torero[4b]
film[5b]	pellicule	Film, Häutchen	película
flake[5a] (*n.*)	écaille	Flocke	escama
football[5b]	football	Fußball	fútbol
gasoline(ene)[5b] (for car)	essence	Benzin	gasolina
ginger[5b]	gingembre	Ingwer	jengibre
godmother[6]	marraine	Patin	comadre[4b], (madrina[6b])
gossip[6] (person)	bavard[6a]	Schwatzbase	hablador[6a]
granite[6b]	granit	Granit	granito
gravel[5b]	gravier	Kies	arenillas
gum[5b] (of teeth)	gencive	Gaumen	encía
hardware[5b]	quincaillerie	Metallwaren	ferretería, quincallería
harlot[6]	prostituée	Dirne	zorra (zorro[4b])
hatch[5a] (*vb.*)	couver	brüten	empollar
herring[7]	hareng	Hering[6b]	arenque
hostess[7]	hôtesse	Wirtin[6a]	anfitriona
hypocrite[6]	hypocrite	Heuchler	hipócrita[4a]
illustration[6]	illustration[5b]	Illustration	ilustración[7a]
inert[7]	inerte[3b]	träg	inerte[5b]
inseparable[6]	inséparable[5b]	unzertrennlich	inseparable[7a]
intimacy[7], (familiarity[9])	intimité[4a]	Vertrautheit	familiaridad[4b], intimidad[4b]
Japanese[5a]	japonais	japanisch	japonés
languish[6a]	languir	schmachten	languidecer
latch[5a] (*n.*)	loquet	Bolzen	aldab(ill)a, picaporte
ledge[5b] (rock)	rebord	Riff	reborde
lemonade[5a]	limonade	Limonade	limonada
lining[5a]	doublure	Futter	forro
locust[6]	cigale[6a]	Lokust	langosta[6b]
manger[5b]	mangeoire	Krippe	pesebre
manhood[5a]	virilité	Männlichkeit	hombría, virilidad
Mexican[6]	mexicain	mexikanisch	mejicano[4a]
moisten[6]	humecter	anfeuchten	humedecer[4b]
monotonous[7]	monotone[3b]	eintönig	monótono[5a]
moth[5b]	mite	Motte	polilla
neigh[5b] (*vb.*)	hennir	wiehern	relinchar
northwest[5a]	nord-ouest	Nordwesten	noroeste
offender[6]	délinquant	Missetäter	delincuente[4b]
oracle[5a]	oracle	Orakel	oráculo
originality[9]	originalité[4a]	Eigenart[5b], (Originalität)	originalidad
patriarch[8]	patriarche	Patriarch[5a]	patriarca

English	French	German	Spanish
pickle[5b] (*n.*)	cornichon	Essiggurke	encurtido
pill[5a]	pilule	Pille	píldora
pilot[6]	pilote[6b]	Lotse	piloto[6b]
pioneer[5b]	pionnier	Pionier	explorador
polar[6]	polaire[6b]	Polar-	polar[6b]
pronoun[6]	pronom	Pronomen	pronombre[4b]
pulpit[6]	chaire[4b], tribune[4b]	Kanzel	púlpito
quilt[5a], comforter[5b] (Amer.)	édredon	Steppdecke	colcha, edredón
ransom[5b]	rançon	Lösegeld	rescate
rectangle[5b]	rectangle	Rechteck	rectángulo
refreshment[5b]	rafraîchissement	Erfrischung	refresco, refrigerio
reindeer[5b]	renne	Rentier	reno
revision[10]	révision	Revision[3b]	revisión
sandwich[5b]	sandwich	Butterbrot	emparedado
scalp[5b] (*n.*)	cuir[3b] chevelu	Kopfhaut, Skalp	cuero[3a] cabelludo
sculpture[6]	sculpture[6a]	Skulptur	escultura[6a]
slate[5a]	ardoise	Schiefer	pizarra
sled[5b]	luge	Schlitten	trineo
sledge[5a], sleigh[5a]	traîneau	Schlitten	trineo
snail[6]	escargot, limaçon	Schnecke	caracol[4a]
sock[5b]	chaussette	Socken	calcetín
soluble[7]	soluble	löslich[6b]	soluble
spangle[5a]	paillette	Flitter	lentejuela
steak[5b]	bifteck	Beefsteak	bifteque, loncha (de carne)
stork[5b]	cigogne	Storch	cigueña
Swedish[8]	suédois	schwedisch[5a]	sueco
tennis[6]	tennis[4b]	Tennis	tenis
thwart[6]	contrarier[4b]	durchkreuzen	frustrar
tickle[5a] (*vb.*)	chatouiller	kitzeln	cosquillear, (hacer) cosquillas
tortoise[5a]	tortue	Schildkröte	carey, tortuga
treble[7]	aigu[3a]	Violin-	tiple[5a]
trophy[5b]	trophée	Trophäe	trofeo
trough[6]	auge	Trog	pila[4a]
trout[5a]	truite	Forelle	trucha
tuft[6]	touffe[4b]	Büschel	mechón
varnish[6] (*vb.*)	vernir[4a]	lackieren	barnizar
violation[10]	violation[4a]	Verletzung[4a]	violación
wardrobe[6]	armoire[4a]	Schrank	armario, ropero
waterproof[7]	imperméable	wasserdicht[6b]	impermeable
wig[5a]	perruque	Perücke	peluca
wren[5a]	roitelet	Zaunkönig	abadejo, reyezuelo
wrench[5a] (*n.*) (sprain)	foulure	Verrenkung	torcedura
zest[10]	élan[2b]	Schwung[6b]	entusiasmo[2a], (deleite[3b])

SECTION 6.9. CONCEPTS 5753 THROUGH 5801

E F G S	*E F G S*	*E F G S*	*E F G S*
6–5 –8*–8*	7–4–8*–5	8–5–6–8*	10–5 –4–8*
6–6 –8*–7	7–5–8*–4	8–6–6–7	12–8*–2–5
6–8*–8*–5	7–6–8*–3	9–3–6–6	
7–3 –8*–6	8–3–8*–2	9–5–5–8*	

English	French	German	Spanish
abbey[6]	abbaye[5b]	Abtei	abadía
accessible[10]	accessible[5a]	zugänglich[4a]	accesible
adverse[6]	adverse	widrig	adverso[5b]
almond[6]	amande	Mandel	almendra[5b]
avarice[6]	avarice	Geiz	avaricia[5b]
bristle[6] (*vb.*)	se hérisser	sträuben	erizar[5b]
brotherly[6], fraternal[6]	fraternel	brüderlich	fraternal[5b]
carter[6]	charretier	Kärrner	carretero[5b]
clergy[8]	clergé[5b]	Geistlichkeit[6b]	clero
coo[6] (*vb.*) (*n.*)	roucouler, roucoulement	girren, Girren	arrullar[5b], arrullo[5b]
dancer[6]	danseuse[6b]	Tänzerin	bailarina (bailarín[7a])
democracy[6]	démocratie[5b]	Demokratie	democracia
disarm[7]	désarmer[4b]	entwaffnen	desarmar[5b]
distil[6]	distiller	destillieren	destilar[5b]
emerald[6]	émeraude	Smaragd	esmeralda[5a]
feverish[7] (literally)	fiévreux[5a]	fieberhaft	febril[4a]
garage[6]	garage	Garage	cochera (cochero[5a])
grocery[6]	épicerie	Kolonialwarenhandlung	bodega[5a]
hopeful[6], (optimistic[16])	optimiste[5b]	hoffnungsvoll	optimista
hypocrisy[6]	hypocrisie	Heuchelei	hipocresía[5a]
inspector[6]	inspecteur[5a]	Inspektor	inspector
insufficient[9]	insuffisant[3b]	ungenügend[6a]	insuficiente[6a]
itch[6] (*n.*), (irritation[8])	démangeaison	Jucken	pique[5b]
kerosene[6]	pétrole[5a]	Petroleum	petróleo
lyre[6]	lyre	Leier	lira[5b]
marquis[8]	marquis[3a], (marquise[6a])	Marquis	marqués[2b]
melon[6]	melon	Melone	melón[5a]
millionaire[6]	millionnaire	Millionär	millonario[5b]
mystic[7]	mystique[5b]	mystisch	místico[4a]
partridge[6]	perdrix	Rebhuhn	perdiz[5a]
petroleum[6]	pétrole[5a]	Petroleum	petróleo
pirate[6]	pirate	Seeräuber	pirata[5b]
prism[6]	prisme	Prisma	prisma[5a]
privy[6] councilor[12]	conseiller	Geheimrat[2a]	consejero[5a]
ranch[6]	ranche	Ranch	rancho[5b]
renewal[8]	renouvellement[6a]	Erneuerung[6a]	renovación[7a]
reproduction[6]	reproduction	Wiedergabe	reproducción[5b]
righteousness[6]	droiture[6b]	Rechtlichkeit	rectitud[7a]
satire[6]	satire	Satire	sátira[5a]

English	French	German	Spanish
savory[7] (*adj.*)	savoureux[6a]	schmackhaft	sabroso[3a]
shipwreck[6] (*n.*), (*vb.*), shipwrecked (shipwreck[6]) man	naufrage, faire naufrage, naufragé	Schiffbruch, stranden, Gestrandete	naufragio[5a], (naufragar[7a]), náufrago[5a]
sickle[6]	faucille	Sichel	hoz[5a]
sloth[7], (indolence[12])	paresse[5a]	Faulheit	pereza[4a], (indolencia[6a])
susceptible[7]	susceptible[3b]	empfänglich	susceptible[6a]
systematic[9]	méthodique[5b], (systématique[6a])	systematisch[5b]	metódico, sistemático
tourist[8]	touriste[5b]	Wanderer[6a], (Tourist)	turista
tropic[6] (*n.*), (*adj.*)	tropique, tropical	Tropen, tropisch	trópico[5b], tropical[5b]
unfinished[7], (incomplete[9])	incomplet[3b]	unvollständig	incompleto[6a]
unhealthy[8]	malsain[5a]	ungesund[6b]	malsano

SECTION 7. CONCEPTS 5802 THROUGH 5861

E F G S	*E F G S*	*E F G S*
6–6 –8*–8*	7–5–8*–5	8–6 –6–8*
6–8*–8*–6	7–6–8*–4	8–8*–6–6
7–4 –8*–6	8–4–8*–2	9–8*–5–6
		11–2 –4–8*

English	French	German	Spanish
admirer[6]	admirateur	Bewunderer	admirador[6a]
adversity[6]	adversité	Widrigkeit	adversidad[6b]
anoint[6]	oindre	salben	untar[6a], (ungir[7a])
atonement[9]	expiation	Buße[5b]	expiación[6b]
atrocity[8]	atrocité	Greuel[6b]	atrocidad[6b]
beech[6]	hêtre[6a]	Buche	haya
brew[6] (*vb.*)	brasser	brauen	elaborar[6b]
caravan[6]	caravane[6b]	Karawane	caravana
chancellor[6] (university)	recteur	Rektor	rector[6a]
cider[6]	cidre	Most	sidra[6a]
cocoanut (coco)[6]	noix de coco	Kokusnuß	coco[6a]
consumer[8]	consommateur[6b]	Konsument[6a]	consumidor
crêpe[6], (crape[10])	crêpe (*crape*)[6b]	Krepp	crespón
cypress[6]	cyprès	Zypresse	ciprés[6b]
dean[6]	doyen[6a]	Dekan	deán, decano
definition[7]	définition[5b]	Definition	definición[5a]
discord[6]	discorde	Zwietracht	discordia[6b]
duel[8]	duel[4b]	Duell, Zweikampf	duelo[2b], (desafío[3a])
eclipse[6] (*vb.*)	éclipser	verfinstern	eclipsar[6a]
ethereal[6]	éthéré	ätherisch	etéreo[6b]
falcon[6]	faucon	Falke	halcón[6b]
fathom[6] (*vb.*)	approfondir[6b]	ergründen	sondear
flirt[6] (*n.*)	coquette	Flirt	coqueta[6a]
garter[6]	jarretière	Strumpfband	liga[6a]
hack[6], (nag[13])	rosse	Gaul	rocín[6b]
hemisphere[6]	hémisphère	Halbkugel	hemisferio[6b]

English	French	German	Spanish
honeycomb[6]	gâteau de miel	Wabe	panal[6b]
hygiene[7]	hygiène[5b]	Hygiene	higiene[5b]
ingratitude[7]	ingratitude[6b]	Undankbarkeit	ingratitud[4a]
iris[6] (of eye)	iris	Iris	iris[6b]
jostle[6]	bousculer[6a]	herumwerfen	empellar, rempujar
manure[6], muck[6]	fumier	Dünger, Dung	estiércol[6b]
maze[6]	labyrinthe	Irrgarten	laberinto[6b]
memorable[7]	mémorable[5a]	denkwürdig	memorable[5b]
multiplication[6]	multiplication	Vervielfältigung	multiplicación[6b]
nestle[6]	se nicher	einnisten	anidar[6b]
oasis[6]	oasis	Oase	oasis[6b]
ointment[6]	onguent	Salbung	ungüento[6a]
omission[6]	omission	Auslassung	omisión[6b]
pancake[6]	crêpe	Pfannkuchen	tortilla[6b]
parliamentary[11]	parlementaire[2b]	parlamentarisch[4a]	parlamentario
particle[6]	particule	Partikel	partícula[6b]
peddler[6]	forain[6a]	Hausierer	buhonero
prize[2b] fighter[6], (boxer[13])	boxeur[6b]	Boxer	boxeador
pronunciation[6]	prononciation	Aussprache	pronunciación[6b]
propagate[6]	propager	fortpflanzen	propagar[6b]
ruffian[6]	scélérat[6a], (malotru)	Raufbold	rufián
saucer[6]	soucoupe[6a]	Untertasse	platillo
servile[6]	servile[6b]	diensteifrig	servil
siren[7]	sirène[5b]	Sirene	sirena[5a]
spine[7], (backbone[8])	épine[4b] (dorsale)	Rückgrat	espinazo[6a]
stirrup[6]	étrier	Steigbügel	estribo[6b]
subordinate[8], (subaltern[16])	subordonné	Untergebene[6b]	subordinado (subordinar[6b])
tassel[6]	gland	Quaste	borla[6b]
(fortune[2a]) teller[6]	bohémienne, diseuse de bonne aventure, tireuse de cartes	Wahrsager	adivino[6b]
triangle[6]	triangle	Dreieck	triángulo[6a]
turret[6]	tourelle[6a]	Türmchen	torrecilla
twitter[6] (*n.*)	gazouillement	Zwitschern	gorjeo[6b]
unmoved[7]	impassible[5a]	ungerührt	impasible[5b]
viper[6]	vipère	Viper	víbora[6a]

SECTION 7.1. CONCEPTS 5862 THROUGH 5881

E F G S	*E F G S*	*E F G S*
6–8*–8*–7	7–4–8*–7	8–1–8*–6
6–7 –8*–8*	7–5–8*–6	10–4–5 –7
7–8*–8*–3	7–6–8*–5	

English	French	German	Spanish
adjective[7]	adjectif	Adjektiv	adjetivo[3a]
analysis[7]	analyse[4b]	Analyse	análisis[7a]
articulate[7] (*vb.*)	articuler[5b]	artikulieren	articular[6b]
bastard[6]	bâtard, (enfant naturel)	Bastard	bastardo[7a]

English	French	German	Spanish
celery[6]	céleri	Sellerie	apio[7b]
clam[6]	palourde	Miesmuschel	almeja[7a]
concentration[7]	concentration[6b]	Konzentration	recogimiento[5a]
constancy[7]	constance	Beständigkeit	constancia[3a]
fabulous[7]	fabuleux[6a]	fabelhaft	fabuloso[5a]
horseshoe[8]	fer[1b] (à) cheval[1b]	Hufeisen	herradura[6b]
impossibility[10]	impossibilité[4b]	Unmöglichkeit[5a]	imposibilidad[7a]
lettuce[6]	laitue	Salat	lechuga[7a]
ostrich[6]	autruche	Strauß	avestruz[7a]
pore[6]	pore	Pore	poro[7b]
(joint[3a]) responsibility[7]	solidarité[5a]	Solidarität, Zusammengehörigkeit	solidaridad[6a]
scaffold[7]	échafaud[5b]	Gerüst	horca[6a], (cadalso[7a])
thrush[6]	grive	Drossel	tordo[7a]
twentieth[6]	vingtième	zwanzigste	vigésimo[7]*
wade[6]	patauger[7a]	waten	vadear
whale[6]	baleine	Wal(fisch)	ballena[7a]

SECTION 7.2. CONCEPTS 5882 THROUGH 5986

E F G S	*E F G S*	*E F G S*	*E F G S*
6–8*–8*–8*	7–4 –8*–8*	8–4 –8*–4	10–8*–5–4
7–8*–8*–4	8–5 –8*–3	9–4 –6– 8*	10–8*–4–8*
7–6 –8*–6	8–8*–6 –8*	9–8*–5– 8*	

English	French	German	Spanish
alderman[6]	alderman	Ratsherr	concejal
anvil[6]	enclume	Amboß	yunque
applicant[9]	candidat[4a]	Antragsteller[6a]	candidato
arrogance[7]	arrogance	Arroganz	arrogancia[4b]
ascent[7], (ascension[11])	ascension[6a]	Aufstieg	ascensión[6a], (ascenso)
assimilate[7]	assimiler[6b]	assimilieren	asimilar[6b]
atom[7]	atome	Atom	átomo[4b]
bamboo[6]	bambou	Bambus	bambú
barefoot[7]	nu-pied	barfuß	descalzo[4b]
blacken[7]	noircir[4a]	schwärzen	ennegrecer
blister[6]	ampoule	Blase	ampolla
bramble[6]	ronce	Brombeere	zarza
bran[6]	son	Kleie	afrecho, salvado
buffalo[6]	bison	Büffel	búfalo
canary[7]	serin	Kanarienvogel	canario[4b]
cashier[6]	caissier	Kassierer	cajero
caterpillar[6]	chenille	Raupe	oruga
caw[6]	croasser	krächzen	graznar
chisel[6] (*n.*)	burin (metal), ciseau (wood)	Meißel, Stemmeisen	escoplo, formón, gubia, (wood); cincel (art)
chivalry[6]	chevalerie	Ritterlichkeit	caballerosidad
coincide[10]	coincider	zusammentreffen[5a]	coincidir[4b]
complication[9]	complication[4b]	Verwick(e)lung[6b]	complicación

English	French	German	Spanish
cone[6]	cône	Kegel	cono
consonant[7]	consonne	Mitlaut	consonante[4b]
consumption[6] (using)	consomption, consummation	Verbrauch	consumación
coping[10] stone[1a]	corniche	Schlußstein[4b]	(piedra de) albardilla
(engineer[4a]) corps[8]	génie[5b]	Pioniere	(cuerpo de) ingenieros (ingeniero[3a])
deliverer[7], (liberator[16])	libérateur	Befreier	libertador[4b]
delta[6]	delta	Delta	delta
dimple[6]	fossette	Grübchen	hoyuelo
elementary[7]	élémentaire	elementar	elemental[4a]
eleventh[6]	onzième	elfte	onceno, undécimo
equator[6]	équateur	Gleicher	ecuador
feeder[6]	mangeur	Esser	alimentador
fervent[7]	fervent[6b]	inbrünstig	ferviente[6b]
flannel[6]	flanelle	Flanell	franela
frankness[8]	franchise[5b]	Offenheit	candor[3b]
gingerbread[6]	pain d'épice	Honigkuchen	pan de especias
giver[6]	donateur	Geber, Stifter	dador
groove[6]	rainure	Rinne	ranura
gymnasium[6]	gymnase	Turnhalle	gimnasio
hedgehog[6]	hérisson	Igel	erizo
heroism[8]	héroïsme[5a]	Heldentum	heroísmo[3b]
holly[6]	houx	Stechpalme	acebo
hospitable[6]	hospitalier	gastlich	hospitalario
improper[7]	impropre[6b]	ungehörig	impropio[6b]
indescribable[8]	indescriptible	unbeschreiblich[6b]	indescriptible
instructive[9]	instructif	lehrreich[5a]	instructivo
justification[8]	justification	Rechtfertigung[6b]	justificación
lisp[6]	zézayer	lispeln	cecear
lute[6]	luth	Laute	laúd
mahogany[6]	acajou	Mahagoni	caoba
mechanism[7]	mécanisme[6b]	Mechanismus	mecanismo[6b]
meridian[6]	méridien	Längengrad	meridiano
meteor[6]	météore	Meteor	meteoro
milky[6]	lacté, laiteux	milchig	lácteo, lechoso
minstrel[6]	troubadour	Spielmann	juglar, trovador
mint[6] (plant)	menthe	Minze	menta
missionary[6]	missionnaire	Missionar	misionero
miter(re)[6]	mitre	Mitra	mitra
momentary[7]	momentané[6b]	Augenblicks-, momentan	momentáneo[6b]
mortgage[6]	hypothèque	Hypothek	hipoteca
mosquito[7]	moustique	Mücke	mosquito[4b]
mower[6] (man)	faucheur	Mäher	guadañador
muff[6] (*n.*)	manchon	Muff	manguito
myrtle[6]	myrte	Myrte	mirto

English	French	German	Spanish
navigable[6]	navigable	schiffbar	navegable
obstinacy[7]	entêtement	Hartnäckigkeit	porfía[4a], (obstinación[6a])
paddle[6] (*vb.*)	pagayer	paddeln	remar
petal[6]	pétale	Blütenblatt	pétalo
piper[6]	(joueur de) cornemuse	Pfeifer	flautista
planter[6]	planteur	Pflanzer	sembrador
poppy[6]	pavot	Mohn	adormidera, amapola
postscript[6]	post-scriptum	Nachschrift	pos(t)data
qualify[8]	qualifier[4a]	qualifizieren	calificar[4a]
radiator[6]	radiateur	Heizkörper	radiador
razor[6]	rasoir	Rasierapparat, Rasiermesser	navaja
retort[8] (chemical)	cornue	Retorte[6a]	retorta
rhetoric[7]	rhétorique	Rhetorik	retórica[4b]
rheumatism[7]	rhumatisme[4a]	Rheumatismus	reuma, reumatismo
saber(re)[9]	sabre[4b]	Säbel[6b]	sable
salmon[6]	saumon	Salm	salmón
sieve[6]	crible, tamis	Sieb	cedazo, cernedera, criba, tamiz
stave[6] (on barrel)	douve	Daube	duela
sweater[6]	chandail	Sweater	zamarreta (tejida de lana)
theological[8]	théologique	theologisch[6b]	teológico
thimble[6]	dé	Fingerhut	dedal
tick[3b] tock[6]	tic-tac	Ticktack	tic-tac
tire (*n.*)[6]	pneu	Reifen	(p)neumático
tonnage[6]	tonnage	Tonnage	tonelaje
treasurer[6]	trésorier	Schatzmeister	tesorero
unreasonable[6]	déraisonnable	unvernünftig	irrazonable
untiring[9], (indefatigable[15])	infatigable	unermüdlich[5b]	incansable, infatigable
unwelcome[6]	indésirable	unwillkommen	malvenido
valentine[6]	lettre de valentin	. . . .	San Valentín
vegetation[7]	végétation	Vegetation	vegetación[4b]
veteran[6]	vétéran	Veteran	veterano
wasp[6]	guêpe	Wespe	avispa
watery[6]	aqueux	wässerig	acuoso
weaver[6]	tisserand	Weber	tejedor
woodman[6]	bûcheron	Holzhacker	leñador
woodpecker[6]	pivert	Specht	picamaderos, picaposte
yew[6]	if	Eibe	tejo
zigzag[6]	zigzag	Zickzack	zigzag
zoological[6]	zoologique	zoologisch	zoológico

PART VII

THE FIRST HALF OF THE SEVENTH THOUSAND CONCEPTS

SECTION 7.3. CONCEPTS 5987 THROUGH 6018

E F G S	*E F G S*	*E F G S*
7–5 –8*–8*	8–4–8*–5	9–8*–6–5
7–6 –8*–7	8–5–8*–4	10–4 –6–5
7–8*–8*–5	8–6–8*–3	10–5 –6–4
8–3 –8*–6	9–1–8*–4	10–6 –6–3

English	French	German	Spanish
bankruptcy[9]	banqueroute	Zahlungseinstellung[6a]	quiebra[5a]
(procedure[8] in) bankruptcy[9]	(procédure pour la) banqueroute	Konkursverfahren[6b]	proceso[4b] (de) quiebra[5a]
Bohemian[7] (in taste)	bohème	Bohème	bohemio[5a]
(become) breathless[7] (from emotion)	(devenir) oppressé	benommen (werden)	embargar[5a]
caste[8]	caste[6a]	Kaste	casta[3a]
conjunction[7] (literal and grammatical)	conjonction	Konjunktion	conjunción[5a]
drunkenness[8]	ivresse[3a]	Trunkenheit	embriaguez[6a]
emigrant[8]	émigré (*n.*)[5a]	Auswanderer	emigrante[4b]
extravagant[7] (fantastic)	extravagant[5b]	extravagant	extravagante
flatten[10]	aplatir[5b]	ebnen[6b]	aplastar[4b], (aplanar)
hangman[10]	bourreau[6a]	Henker[6b]	verdugo[3a]
hereditary[7]	héréditaire[5a]	erblich	hereditario
hesitation[8]	hésitation[3a]	Zögern	vacilación[6b]
insistence[10]	insistance[5b]	Bestehen[6a]	insistencia[4b]
intact[10]	intact[4a]	unberührt[6b]	intacto[5b]
invincible[6]	invincible[5a]	unbesiegbar	invencible[4b]
irrigation[7]	irrigation	Bewässerung	riego[5a]
kidney[7]	rein, rognon	Niere	riñón[5a]
manual[7] (*adj.*)	manuel	Hand-	manual[5b]
martyrdom[8]	martyre[6a]	Marter, Märtyrertum	martirio[3a]
monopoly[7]	monopole[5a]	Monopol	monopolio
noun[9]	nom[1a]	Hauptwort	substantivo[4a]
panic[7]	panique (*adj.* and *n.*)[6a]	Panik	pánico[7a]
passive[7]	passif	passiv	pasivo[5a]
pedestal[7]	piédestal	Fuß(gestell)	pedestal[5a]
populous[7]	populeux	bevölkert	populoso[5b]
preface[7], (prolog[ue][8])	préface	Vorwort	preámbulo[5b], (prólogo[6b])
prevention[7]	prévention	Vermeidung	prevención[5a]
resignation[7] (act)	démission[5b]	Abdankung	dimisión, renuncia
scythe[7]	faux (*n.*)[5a]	Sense	guadaña
subsist[8]	subsister[4a]	fortbestehen	subsistir[5a]
usher[7] (*n.*)	huissier[5a]	Türsteher	accomodador, ujier

SECTION 7.4. CONCEPTS 6019 THROUGH 6055

E F G S	E F G S	E F G S
7–6 –8*–8*	8–8*–8*–2	9–4–8*–2
7–8*–8*–6	8–5 –8*–5	9–3–8*–3
8–6 –8*–4	8–4 –8*–6	10–6–6 –4
		11–2–6 –4

English	French	German	Spanish
annex[7] (*vb.*)	annexer[6b]	(sich) einverleiben	anexionar
balcony[9]	balcon[4a]	Balkon	balcón[2a]
bayonet[7]	baïonnette[6a]	Seitengewehr	bayoneta
confessor[8]	confesseur[6b]	Beichtvater	confesor[4b]
contraction[7] (shrinking)	contraction, rétrécissement	Einlaufen	contracción[6b]
cucumber[7]	concombre	Gurke	pepino[6b]
degenerate[7]	dégénérer[6b]	ausarten	degenerar
devilish[7]	diabolique	teuflisch	diabólico[6a], endiablado[6a], satánico[6a]
dictionary[7]	dictionnaire[6a]	Wörterbuch	diccionario
digestion[7]	digestion[6a]	Verdauung	digestión
eliminate[7]	éliminer[6b]	ausmerzen	eliminar
gypsy[8]	bohémien	Zigeuner	gitano[2a]
heresy[7]	hérésie[6b]	Häresie, Ketzerei	herejía
(in a) huddle[7]	pêle-mêle[6b]	Durcheinander	apelotonado
incurable[7]	incurable	unheilbar	incurable[6a]
inequality[10]	inégalité[6a]	Ungleichheit[6a]	desigualidad[4b]
insolence[8]	insolence[6a]	Frechheit	insolencia[4b]
intruder[7]	intrus	Eindringling	intruso[6b]
languid[7]	languide	sehnlich	lánguido[6b]
logical[11]	logique[2b]	logisch[6a]	lógico[4a]
magnetic[7]	magnétique	magnetisch	magnético[6a]
maximum[8]	maximum[5a]	Höchstmaß	máximo[5a]
minimum[8]	minimum[6b]	Mindestmaß	mínimo[4a]
misgiving[8], (presentiment[12])	pressentiment[4a]	Vorahnung	presentimiento[6b]
mustache[9]	moustache[3a]	Schnurrbart	bigote[3b]
naturalist[7]	naturaliste	Naturwissenschaftler	naturalista[6a]
opportune[8]	opportun	gelegen	oportuno[2b]
parchment[7]	parchemin[6a]	Pergament	pergamino
playful[8]	joueur[4b]	spielerisch	juguetón[6a]
popularity[7]	popularité	Beliebtheit	popularidad[6a]
proclamation[7]	proclamation[6b]	Ausruf(en)	proclama, proclamación
reef[7]	écueil[6b]	Klippe	escollo
reptile[7]	reptile	Reptil	reptil[6a], lagarto[6a]
sculptor[7]	sculpteur	Bildhauer	escultor[6a]
shawl[7]	châle[6a]	Schal	chal
superstitious[7]	superstitieux	abergläubisch	supersticioso[6b]
unruly[7]	indomptable	widerspenstig	indómito[6b]

SECTION 7.5. CONCEPTS 6056 THROUGH 6062

E F G S	*E F G S*	*E F G S*
8–6–8*–5	10–6–6–5	11–3–6–4
8–5–8*–6	10–5–6–6	11–5–5–6
		12–4–5–3

English	French	German	Spanish
anarchy[8]	anarchie[6a]	Anarchie	anarquía[5a]
distort[8]	fausser[5a]	verzerren	falsear[6b]
elegance[11]	élégance[3b]	Feinheit[6a]	elegancia[4a]
identity[11]	identité[5a]	Gleichheit[5a]	identidad[6b]
impure[10]	impur[6a]	unrein[6a]	impuro[5b]
lightness[12]	légèreté[4a]	Leichtigkeit[5a]	ligereza[3b]
propaganda[10]	propagande[5b]	Agitation[6a]	propaganda[6b]

SECTION 7.6. CONCEPTS 6063 THROUGH 6079

E F G S	*E F G S*	*E F G S*
8–6–8*–6	8–4–8*–8*	9–8*–6–8*
8–5–8*–7	9–4–8*–4	11–8*–4–8*
8–8*–8*–4	9–6–8*–3	12–4–5–4

English	French	German	Spanish
analogy[8]	analogie[6b]	Entsprechung	analogía[6b]
diplomatic[12]	diplomatique[4a]	diplomatisch[5a]	diplomático[4a]
dowry[9]	dot[4a]	Mitgift	dote[4a]
emigrate[8]	émigrer[6a]	auswandern	emigrar[6b]
gout[9]	goutte[6b]	Gicht	gota[2a]
hundredth[8]	centième[5a]	hundertste	centésimo[7*]
infamy[8]	infamie	Gemeinheit	infamia[4a], (oprobio[6a])
morbid[9]	morbide	krankhaft[6b]	morboso
navigator[8]	navigateur	Seefahrer	navegante[4b]
neutral[8]	neutre[4b]	neutral	neutral
plastic[9]	plastique	plastisch[6a]	plástico
public[1b] trustee[8]	notaire[4a]	Notar	notario
reinforcement[11]	renforcement	Verstärkung[4b]	refuerzo
spiral[8] (*n.*)	spirale[6b]	Spirale	espiral[6a]
strategy[11]	stratégie	Strategie[4a]	estrategia
vibration[8]	vibration	Vibration	vibración[4a]
walker[8]	promeneur[4a]	Spaziergänger	caminante, paseante

SECTION 7.7. CONCEPTS 6080 THROUGH 6103

E F G S	*E F G S*	*E F G S*
8–8*–8*–5	9–5–8*–4	11–8*–6–1
8–5–8*–8*	9–6–8*–3	13–5–3–8*
8–6–8*–7	10–5–6–8*	

English	French	German	Spanish
aggressive[8]	agressif	agressiv	agresivo[5b]
alcoholic[8]	alcoolique[5b]	alkoholisch	alcohólico
(half[1a]) caste[8]	métis, mulâtre	Mestize, Mulatte	mestizo[5b], (mulato[6a])

English	French	German	Spanish
chastity[8]	chasteté	Keuschheit	castidad[5a]
cigarette[9]	cigarette[5a]	Zigarette	cigarro[4a], (cigarrillo)
conspirator[8]	conspirateur[5b], (conjuré [n.][6a])	Verschworene	conjurado, conspirador
emigration[9]	émigration[6a]	Auswanderung	emigración[3b]
entrails[8]	entrailles	Eingeweide	tripa[5a]
evacuate[13]	évacuer[5a]	räumen[3b]	evacuar
exaggeration[10]	exagération[5b]	Übertreibung[6a]	exageración
executor[8]	exécuteur[5b]	-vollstrecker (e.g., Testamentsvollstrecker)	ejecutor
experimental[8]	expérimental[6a]	experimental, experimentell	experimental[7a]
ferment[8] (*vb.*)	fermenter[5b]	gären	fermentar
imaginative[8]	imaginatif	phantasiereich	imaginativo[5a]
implacable[9]	implacable[5b]	unerbittlich	implacable[4a]
infallible[8]	infaillible	unfehlbar	infalible[5b]
miniature[8]	miniature[5a]	Miniatur	miniatura
minority[8]	minorité[5b]	Minderheit	minoría
reliability[11]	confiance	Zuverlässigkeit[6b]	confianza[1b]
routine[8]	routine[6a]	Routine	rutina[7a]
sixteenth[8]	seizième[6a]	sechzehnte	décimo sexto[7*]
suppliant[8]	suppliant[5a]	bittfällig	suplicante
symptom[8]	symptome[6b]	Symptom	síntoma[7a]
toleration[8]	tolérance	Duldung	tolerancia[5b]

SECTION 7.8. CONCEPTS 6104 THROUGH 6136

E F G S	*E F G S*	*E F G S*
8–6 –8*–8*	9–4–8*–6	12–6–4–8*
8–8*–8*–6	10–6–6 –8*	15–6–1–8*
9–6 –8*–4	11–6–6 –4	

English	French	German	Spanish
adventurer[9]	aventurier[6b]	Abenteurer	aventurero[4a]
aggression[15]	agression[6a]	Angriff[1b]	agresión
chemistry[8]	chimie[6b]	Chemie	química
coincidence[8]	coïncidence[6a]	Zusammentreffen	coincidencia
conciliation[10]	conciliation[6b]	Versöhnung[6b]	conciliación
daze[8] (*n.*)	étourdissement[6b]	Betäubung	alelamiento, atontamiento, aturdimiento
density[8]	densité	Dichte	densidad[6b]
dishonest[8]	malhonnête[6b]	unredlich	deshonesto
dreg[8]	lie[6a]	Hefe	heces
dynasty[8]	dynastie	Dynastie	dinastía[6b]
exemption[12]	exemption[6a]	Befreiung[4a], (Erlassung)	exención
feudal[8]	féodal[6b]	feudal, Leh(e)ns-	feudal
fierceness[8], (ferocity[9])	férocité	Grimmigkeit	ferocidad[6a]
flea[8]	puce	Floh	pulga[6b]

English	French	German	Spanish
geranium[8]	géranium[6b]	Geranie	geranio
hairy[8]	velu[6a]	behaart	peludo, velludo
harshness[9]	âpreté[6b]	Rauheit	aspereza[4b]
imperceptible[9]	imperceptible[4a], (insaisissable[6b])	unmerklich	imperceptible[6a]
maturity[8]	maturité[6a]	Reife	madurez
monumental[8]	monumental[6a]	monumental	monumental
nightmare[9]	cauchemar[4a]	Albdruck	pesadilla[6a]
opaque[8]	opaque	undurchsichtig	opaco[6b]
optic[8]	optique	optisch	óptico[6b]
papal[8] bull[3a]	bulle	Bulle	bula[6b]
participation[8] (e.g., in crime)	complicité[6a]	Mitverantwortlichkeit	complicidad
pastry[8]	pâtisserie[6b]	Gebäck	pastelería
premature[8]	prématuré[6b]	vorschnell	prematuro
publicity[8]	publicité[6b]	Reklame	publicidad
rivalry[8]	rivalité	Nebenbuhlerschaft	rivalidad[6b]
smallpox[8]	petite vérole	Blattern	viruela[6a]
snowflake[8]	flocon	Schneeflocke	copo[6a]
stepmother[8]	belle-mère[6a]	Stiefmutter	madrastra
traditional[11]	traditionnel[6a]	überliefert[6a]	tradicional[4b]

SECTION 7.9. CONCEPTS 6137 THROUGH 6148

E F G S	*E F G S*
9–3–8*–8*	9–4–8*–7
9–6–8*–5	10–3–8*–4
9–5–8*–6	11–5–6 –6

English	French	German	Spanish
accessory[9]	accessoire[5b]	zugehörig	accesorio
album[9]	album[6b]	Album	álbum[5b]
barrack(s)[10]	caserne[5b]	Kaserne	cuarteles (cuartel[4a])
formality[9]	formalité[6a]	Formsache	formalidad[6b]
humiliation[9]	humiliation[5b]	Demütigung	humillación[6a]
improbable[11]	invraisemblable[5b]	unwahrscheinlich[6a]	inverosímil[6a]
novelist[8]	romancier[6a]	Romanschriftsteller	novelista[5b]
precocious[9]	précoce[5b]	frühreif	precoz[6b]
preferable[9]	préférable[6a]	vorzuziehen	preferente[5b], preferible[5b]
provincial[9]	provincial[5a]	Provinzler	provinciano[6b]
react[9]	réagir[4a]	reagieren	reaccionar[7a]
rhythm[9]	rythme[6a]	Rhythmus	ritmo[5a]

SECTION 8. CONCEPTS 6149 THROUGH 6159

E F G S	*E F G S*	*E F G S*
9–5 –8*–7	9–4 –8*–8*	12–2 –6–6
9–8*–8*–4	10–8*–6 –8*	13–8*–3–8*
9–6 –8*–6	12–5 –6 –3	

English	French	German	Spanish
abstraction[9]	abstraction[5b]	Abstraktion	abstracción[7a]
cinnamon[9]	cannelle	Zimt	canela[4a]
guitar[9]	guitare	Guitarre	guitarra[4a]
paleness[9]	pâleur[6a]	Blässe	palidez[6b]
Pharisee[10]	pharisien	Pharisäer[6a]	fariseo
physics[12]	physique[2b]	physikalisch[6b], (Physik)	física[6b]
regularity[9]	régularité[5a]	Regelmäßigkeit	regularidad[7a]
sardine[9]	sardine	Sardine	sardina[4b]
strategic[13]	stratégique	strategisch[3a]	estratégico
tenacious[12]	tenace[5b]	zäh[6a]	tenaz[3b]
underline[9]	souligner[4a]	unterstreichen	subrayar

SECTION 8.1. CONCEPTS 6160 THROUGH 6175

E F G S
9–5 –8*–8*
9–8*–8*–5
13–3 –5 –6

English	French	German	Spanish
aeroplane (air)[9]	avion[5b]	Flugzeug	aeroplano, avión
bagpipe[9]	cornemuse	Dudelsack	gaita[5b]
bus[9], (omnibus[12])	omnibus[5b]	Omnibus	ómnibus
citadel[9]	citadelle[5b]	Zitadelle	ciudadela
detour[13]	détour[3a]	Umweg[5b]	rodeo[6a]
enslave[9]	(réduire à) l'esclavage	knechten	esclavizar[5b], (avasallar[7a])
indulgent[9]	indulgent[5a]	nachgiebig	indulgente
inestimable[9]	inestimable	unschätzbar	inestimable[5a]
irresolute[9]	irrésolu[5a]	unentschlossen	irresoluto
monotony[9]	monotonie[5b]	Eintönigkeit	monotonía
palate[9] (of mouth)	palais	Gaumen	paladar[5a]
parsley[9]	persil	Petersilie	perejil[5a]
preposition[9]	préposition	Präposition	preposición[5a]
revival[9], (renaissance [R][11])	renaissance[5a]	Renaissance, Wiederherstellung	renacimiento
sexton[9]	sacristain	Küster	sacristán[5b]
submarine[9]	sous-marin[5b]	Unterseeboot, unterseeisch	submarino

SECTION 8.2. CONCEPTS 6176 THROUGH 6194

E F G S	E F G S
9–6 –8*–8*	11–4 –8*–2
9–8*–8*–6	11–6 –6 –8*
11–3 –8*–3	11–8*–6 –6

English	French	German	Spanish
apostolic[9]	apostolique	apostolisch	apostólico[6a]
atheist[9]	athée	Atheist	ateo[6b]
athlete[9]	athlète[6a]	Athlet	atleta
Celtic[9]	celtique[6a]	keltisch	celta, céltico
chess[9]	échecs[6a]	Schach	ajedrez
contagion[9]	contagion	Ansteckung	contagio[6b]
distaff[9]	quenouille	Rocken	rueca[6b]
dupe[11] (*n.*)	dupe[4a]	Dumme	tonto[2a], (incauto[7a])
governess[9]	gouvernante[6a]	Gouvernante	aya, institutriz
hostage[9]	otage[6b]	Geisel	rehén
imposition[9]	imposition	Zumutung	imposición[6a]
influential[11]	influent[6b]	einflußreich[6b]	influyente
irony[11]	ironie[3a]	Ironie	ironía[3a]
isolation[9]	isolement	Abgeschlossenheit	aislamiento[6a]
laudable[11]	louable	löblich[6b]	laudable[6b], meritorio[6b]
slang[9]	argot[6b]	Mundart	caló, jerga
stretcher[9]	brancard[6b]	Bahre	angarilla, camilla
stupidity[11]	stupidité	Dummheit[6b]	estupidez[6a]
trinket[9]	bibelot[6a]	Nippsache(n)	chuchería, fruslería

SECTION 8.3. CONCEPTS 6195 THROUGH 6200

E F G S
10–8*–8*–3
10–5 –8*–6
10–6 –8*–5
14–6 –4 –5

English	French	German	Spanish
antecedent[10]	antécédent	Vorausgehende	antecedente[3b]
disappearance[10]	disparition[5b]	Verschwinden	desaparición[6a]
dogma[10]	dogme[6a]	Dogma	dogma[6b]
indiscreet[10]	indiscret[5a]	taktlos	indiscreto[6b]
mathematical[10]	mathématique[6a]	mathematisch	matemático[6b]
solidity[14]	solidité[6a]	Festigkeit[4b]	solidez[5b]

SECTION 8.4. CONCEPTS 6201 THROUGH 6216

E F G S	E F G S	E F G S
10–8*–8*–4	10–5 –8*–7	11–4 –8*–4
10–6 –8*–6	11–8*–6 –8*	12–8*–5 –8*
10–4 –8*–8*	11–3 –8*–5	12–6 –6 –6
		13–8*–4 –8*

English	French	German	Spanish
carnation[10]	œillet	Nelke	clavel[4b]
distillation[11]	distillation	Destillation[6a]	destilación
distillery[12]	distillerie	Brennerei[5b]	destilería

English	French	German	Spanish
dressmaker^{10}	couturière^{6b}	Schneiderin	modista^{6b}
electoral^{10}	électoral^{6b}	Wahl-	electoral^{6b}
intervention^{11}	intervention^{3a}	Dazwischenkunft	intervención^{5a}
phase^{10}	phase^{4b}	Phase	fase
plaintiff^{12}	plaignant	Kläger^{5b}, (Klägerin^{6b})	demandante
rabbi^{13}	rabbin	Rabbiner^{4b}	rabino
reëlection^{12}	réélection	Neuwahl^{5b}	reelección
suicide^{12}	suicide^{6b}	Selbstmord^{6b}	suicidio^{6a}
supernatural^{10}	surnaturel^{4b}	übernatürlich	sobrenatural
suppression^{10}	suppression^{4a}	Unterdrückung	supresión
timidity^{11}	timidité^{4a}	Schüchternheit	timidez^{4b}
trumpeter^{11}	trompette (*m.*)	Trompeter^{6b}	trompetero
viscount^{10}	vicomte^{5b}	Vicomte	vizconde^{7b}

SECTION 8.5. CONCEPTS 6217 THROUGH 6224

E F G S
10–8*–8*–5
10–5 –8*–8*
11–4 –8*–5
12–6 –6 –7

English	French	German	Spanish
affirmative^{10}	affirmatif	beipflichtend	afirmativo^{5b}
boarder^{10}	pensionnaire^{5b}	Kostgänger	pensionado
curly^{10} (kinky)	crépu	kraus	crespo^{5b}
delegation^{10}	délégation^{5a}	Abordnung	delegación
fad^{12}	engouement^{6b}	Grille^{6b}	boga^{7a}
ironical^{11}	ironique^{4a}	ironisch	irónico^{5a}
psychology^{10}	psychologie	Psychologie	psicología^{5a}
tournament^{10}	tournoi^{5a}	Turnier	torneo

SECTION 8.6. CONCEPTS 6225 THROUGH 6244

E F G S	*E F G S*	*E F G S*
10–8*–8*–6	11–5–8*–5	14–8*–4–6
10–6 –8*–8*	11–4–8*–6	16–1 –5–1
11–6 –8*–4	12–6–6 –8*	

English	French	German	Spanish
aberration^{14}	aberration	Abweichung^{4a}	aberración^{6b}
biography^{10}	biographie	Biographie	biografía^{6b}
cardboard^{10}	carton	Pappe	cartón^{6a}
dragoon^{12}	dragon^{6a}	Dragoner^{6a}	dragón
fairness^{16}	justice^{1b}	Billigkeit^{5b}	justicia^{1b}
godfather^{11}	parrain^{6a}	Pate	padrino^{4a}, (compadre^{5a})
greediness^{11}, (greed^{16})	avidité^{6b}	Geiz	codicia^{4b}
hysterical^{10}	hystérique	hysterisch	histérico^{6b}
installation^{12} (e.g., collection of machinery, etc.)	outillage^{6b}	Ausrüstung^{6a}	instalación

English	French	German	Spanish
languor[10]	langueur[6b]	Mattigkeit	languidez
moralist[11]	moraliste[5b]	Moralist	moralista[5b]
nickname[10]	surnom	Spitzname	apodo[6b], mote[6b]
oratory[10]	art oratoire	Redekunst	oratoria[6b]
subsidy[12]	subvention[6b]	Zuschuß[6b]	subvención
synthetic[10]	synthétique	synthetisch	sintético[6b]
thyme[10]	thym	Thymian	tomillo[6a]
unconquered[10]	invaincu	unbesiegt	invicto[6b]
unselfish[11]	désintéressé[4b]	uneigennützig	desinteresado[6b]
viceroy[10]	vice-roi	Vizekönig	virrey[6a]
voluptuous[11]	voluptueux[5b]	wollüstig	voluptuoso[5a]

SECTION 8.7. CONCEPTS 6245 THROUGH 6248

E F G S
11–5–8*–6
11–4–8*–7
13–6–6 –5

English	French	German	Spanish
impotence[11], (inability[12]), (incapacity[12])	impuissance[6b], (incapacité[6b])	Impotenz, Unfähigkeit	impotencia[6a]
inexhaustible[13]	inépuisable[6a]	unerschöpflich[6b]	inagotable[5a]
inexplicable[11]	inexplicable[4b]	unerklärlich	inexplicable[7a]
profile[11]	profil[6b]	Profil	perfil[5b]

SECTION 8.8. CONCEPTS 6249 THROUGH 6257

E F G S	*E F G S*
11–6 –8*–6	13–6 –6–6
12–4 –8*–4	14–8*–4–8*
12–8*–6 –8*	

English	French	German	Spanish
aesthetic[11]	esthétique[6b]	ästhetisch	estética[6b]
chlorine[14]	chlore	Chlor[4a]	cloro
impregnate[10]	imprégner[4b]	imprägnieren	impregnar[4a]
judicial[13] (pertaining to court)	judiciaire[6b]	richterlich[6b]	judicial[6a]
millennium[14]	millénaire	Jahrtausend[4b]	milenario
sarcasm[11]	sarcasme[6a]	Sarkasmus	sarcasmo[6a]
semicircle[12]	demi-cercle	Halbkreis[6b]	semicírculo
specialty[11]	spécialité[6b]	Spezialität	especialidad[6b]
validity[12]	validité	Gültigkeit[6a]	validez

SECTION 8.9. CONCEPTS 6258 THROUGH 6265

E	F	G	S
11	8*	8*	5
11	5	8*	8*
12	5	8*	4
17	4	4	1

English	French	German	Spanish
avenger[11]	vengeur	Rächer	vengador[5a]
customhouse[11] officer[1b]	douanier[5a]	Zollbeamte, Zöllner	aduanero
improvise[12]	improviser[5a]	improvisieren	improvisar[4b]
inkwell[11]	encrier	Tintenfaß	tintero[5a]
setting[17] (*n.*) (of sun, etc.)	coucher (*n.*)[4b]	Untergang[4a]	fondo[1a]
specify[11]	spécifier	spezifizieren	especificar[5b]
unchangeable[11], (immutable[12])	immuable, inaltérable	unveränderlich	inmutable[5a]
woodwork[11]	boiserie[5b]	Täfelung	entablado, maderamen

SECTION 9. CONCEPTS 6266 THROUGH 6284

E	F	G	S
11	8*	8*	6
11	6	8*	8*
12	6	8*	4
12	4	8*	6
13	8*	6	6
14	8*	5	6
16	6	3	8*

English	French	German	Spanish
accusative[11]	accusatif	Akkusativ	acusativo[6b]
adverb[11]	adverbe	Adverb	adverbio[6b]
Belgian[12] (*adj.*)	belge[4b], (flamand[6b])	belgisch	belga[6b]
bookseller[13]	libraire	Buchhändler[6b]	librero[6b]
brutality[11]	brutalité[6b]	Roheit	brutalidad
cartridge[11]	cartouche[6b]	Patrone	cartucho
expulsion[11]	expulsion	Austreibung	expulsión[6a]
idealism[11]	idéalisme	Idealismus	idealismo[6b]
indiscretion[12], (imprudence[15])	imprudence[6a], indiscrétion[6a]	Taktlosigkeit	imprudencia[4b]
innate[14]	inné	eingeboren[5a]	innato[6b]
insurgent[11] (*n.*)	insurgé (*n.*)[6b]	Ausfständische	insurgente, insurrecto
islander[11]	insulaire[6a]	Insulaner	insular, isleño
Jesuit[11]	jésuite	Jesuit	jesuíta[6a]
multiplicity[14]	multiplicité	Mannigfaltigkeit[5a]	multiplicidad[6b]
obelisk[11]	obélisque	Obelisk	obelisco[6b]
ostentation[11]	ostentation	Gepränge	ostentación[6a]
pigeonhole[16]	casier[6b]	Fach[3b]	encasillado
realist[11]	réaliste	Realist	realista[6b]
upstart[11]	parvenu(-e) (*n.*)[6b]	Emporkömmling	advenedizo

SECTION 9.1. CONCEPTS 6285 THROUGH 6287

E F G S
12–8*–8*–3
12–5 –8*–6
13–2 –8*–5

English	French	German	Spanish
affected[13]	affecté (affecter[2b]), (maniéré[4b])	affektiert	artificioso[5b]
garlic[12]	ail	Knoblauch	ajo[3b]
table-cloth[12]	nappe[5a]	Tischtuch	mantel[6a]

SECTION 9.2. CONCEPTS 6288 THROUGH 6296

E F G S	*E F G S*
12–4 –8*–8*	13–4 –8*–4
12–6 –8*–6	17–8*–2 –8*
13–8*–6 –8*	18–2 –4 –2

English	French	German	Spanish
administrative[12]	administratif[6a]	Verwaltungs-	administrativo[6a]
aggressor[13]	agresseur	Angreifer[6b]	agresor
billion[12]	milliard[4a]	Milliarde	mil millones
neatness[13]	netteté[4b]	Sauberkeit	esmero[4a], limpieza[4a]
sceptic[12] (*adj.*)	sceptique[4b]	skeptisch, ungläubig	escéptico
shorthand[17], stenography[17]	sténographie	Stenographie[2b]	taquigrafía
sortie[18] (military)	sortie[2a]	Ausfall[4a]	salida[2a]
stupor[12]	stupeur[4a]	Betäubung	estupefacción, estupor
undecided[12]	(être dans l')indécision[6b]	unentschieden	indeciso[6b]

SECTION 9.3. CONCEPTS 6297 THROUGH 6308

E F G S	*E F G S*
12–8*–8*–5	13–6–8*–3
12–5 –8*–8*	15–1–6 –8*
12–6 –8* 7	

English	French	German	Spanish
cipher[12] (*vb.*)	chiffrer	chiffrieren	cifrar[5a]
ermine[12]	hermine	Hermelin	armiño[6b]
expansive[12]	expansif[6b]	expansiv	expansivo
frivolity[13]	frivolité[6a]	Leichtsinnigkeit	ligereza[3b], (devaneo[5a]), (liviandad[6a])
generalize[12]	généraliser[6b]	verallgemeinern	generalizar[7a]
geometric[12]	géométrique[6a]	geometrisch	geométrico[7a]
inexpressible[12], ineffable[12]	indicible	unsäglich	inefable[5a], (indecible[6a])
penetration[12]	pénétration	Durchdringung	penetración[5a]
predisposed (predispose[15])	disposer[1a] (d')avance[1b], (prédisposer)	veranlagt[6b]	predispuesto
psychological[12]	psychologique	psychologisch	psicológico[5b]
stiffness[12], (rigidity[14])	raideur	Starre	rigidez[5b]
syndicate[12]	syndicat[5a]	Syndikat	sindicado

SECTION 9.4. CONCEPTS 6309 THROUGH 6323

E F G S
12–6 –8*–8*
12–8*–8*–6
14–6 –6 –8*
15–6 –5 –8*

English	French	German	Spanish
arcade[14]	arcade[6a]	Laube[6b], (Laubengang)	arcada
armpit[12]	aisselle[6a]	Achselhöhle	axila
barrenness[12], (sterility[17])	stérilité	Unfruchtbarkeit	esterilidad[6b]
candidacy[12]	candidature[6a]	Kandidatur	candidatura
crater[12]	cratère	Krater	cráter[6b]
diplomacy[12]	diplomatie	Diplomatie	diplomacia[6b]
estuary[12]	estuaire	Förde	ría[6b]
hussar[15]	hussard[6a]	Husar[5a]	húsar
impertinence[12]	impertinence[6b]	Frechheit, Unverfrorenheit	impertinencia
intuition[12]	intuition[6a]	Eingebung	intuición
mobility[14]	mobilité[6b]	Beweglichkeit[6b]	flexibilidad
phoenix[12]	phénix	Phönix	fénix[6b]
superhuman[12]	surhumain	übermenschlich	sobrehumano[6b]
trellis[12]	espalier[6b]	Spalier	enrejado
volt[12]	volt[6b]	Volt	voltio

SECTION 9.5. CONCEPT 6324

E F G S
14–8*–6–7

English	French	German	Spanish
attorney-general[14]	procureur général	Staatsanwalt[6a]	procurador[7a] general[1a]

SECTION 9.6. CONCEPTS 6325 THROUGH 6336

E F G S
13–8*–8*–4
13–6 –8*–6
13–5 –8*–7

E F G S
14–8*–6–8*
15–8*–6–4
17–4 –4–8*
17–8*–3–8*

English	French	German	Spanish
anonymous[13]	anonyme	anonym	anónimo[4b]
archipelago[13]	archipel	Archipel	archipielgo[4b]
bodice[13]	corsage[6b]	Mieder	jubón[6b]
collective[13]	collectif[5b]	kollektiv	colectivo[7a]
composer[14]	compositeur	Komponist[6b]	compositor
conjugal[14]	conjugal	ehelich[6a]	conyugal
infinity[13]	infinité	Endlosigkeit	infinidad[4a]
jurisprudence[14]	jurisprudence	Rechtspflege[6b]	jurisprudencia

English	French	German	Spanish
pedant[13]	pédant[6a]	Pedant	pedante[6a]
setting[17] (*adj.*)	couchant[4b]	untergehend (untergehen[4b])	poniente
(in) shorthand[17] (stenographically)	sténographique	stenographisch[3b]	taquigráficamente
thinker[15]	penseur	Denker[6b]	pensador[4b]

SECTION 9.7. CONCEPTS 6337 THROUGH 6343

E F G S
13–5 –8*–8*
13–8*–8*–5
14–4 –8*–5
15–8*–6 –5
19–5 –2 –8*

English	French	German	Spanish
biblical[13]	biblique	biblisch	bíblico[5b]
contradictory[15]	contradictoire	widersprechend[6b]	contradictorio[5a]
dreamer[14]	rêveur[4a]	Träumer	soñador[5b]
flexibility[13]	souplesse[5b]	Schmiegsamkeit	flexibilidad
optimism[13]	optimisme[5a]	Optimismus	optimismo
proscribe[13]	proscrire	ächten	proscribir[5b]
reconstitute[19]	reconstituer[5a]	erneue(r)n[2b]	reconstituir, reconstruir

SECTION 9.8. CONCEPTS 6344 THROUGH 6351

E F G S	*E F G S*
13–8*–8*–6	16–8*–5–6
13–6 –8*–8*	17–8*–4–6
14–5 –8*–5	

English	French	German	Spanish
applicable[13]	applicable	anwendbar	aplicable[6a], extensivo[6b]
brushwood[14]	broussaille[5a]	Unterholz	maleza[5a]
idyll[13]	idylle	Idyll	idilio[6a]
Mussulman[13]	musulman[6b]	Muselman	musulmán
Peruvian[13] (*adj.*)	péruvien	peruanisch	peruano[6b]
refractory[13]	réfractaire[6b]	widerspenstig	reacio, refractario
urgency[17]	urgence	Eile[4b]	urgencia[6b]
vice-president[16]	vice-président	Vizepräsident[5b]	vicepresidente[6a]

SECTION 9.9. CONCEPTS 6352 THROUGH 6354

E F G S
14–8*–8*–3
14–6 –8*–5
14–5 –8*–6

English	French	German	Spanish
impetuosity[14]	impétuosité	Ungestüm	ímpetu[3a]
incompatible[14]	incompatible[6b]	unvereinbar	incompatible[5b]
irreparable[14]	irréparable[5a]	unheilbar	irremediable[6a]

SECTION 10. CONCEPTS 6355 THROUGH 6364

E F G S
14–6 –8*–6
14–8*–8*–4
15–4 –8*–4
15–8*–6 –8*

English	French	German	Spanish
buttock[14]	fesse[6b]	Hinterbacke	anca[6a], (nalga)
confessional[15]	confessionnel	konfessionell[6a]	confesionario
fanaticism[14]	fanatisme[6a]	Fanatismus	fanatismo[6b]
generality[14]	généralité[6b]	Allgemeine	generalidad[6a]
imprudent[15]	imprudent[4a]	unvorsichtig	imprudente[4a]
jessamine[14], (jasmine[15])	jasmin	Jasmin	jazmín[4b]
participant[15], (participator)	participant	Teilnehmer[6a]	participante, participe
promptitude[15]	promptitude[4b]	Promptheit	prontitud[4b]
royalist[14]	royaliste[6a]	Königstreue, Royalist	realista[6b]
talkative[14], loquacious[14]	bavard[6a]	redselig	parlero[6a]

SECTION 10.1. CONCEPTS 6365 THROUGH 6372

E F G S
14–5 –8*–8*
14–8*–8*–5
15–4 –8*–5

English	French	German	Spanish
estimable[14]	estimable[5b]	schätzbar	estimable
flagrant[14]	flagrant[5b]	offenkundig	flagrante
halo[14]	auréole	Heiligenschein	aureola[5b]
insufficiency[14]	insuffisance[5b]	Mangelhaftigkeit	insuficiencia
insuperable[14]	insurmontable	unübersteigbar	insuperable[5b]
irruption[14]	irruption[5b]	Einbruch	irrupción
patriarchal[14]	patriarcal	patriarchisch	patriarcal[5b]
sulk[15]	bouder[4b]	schmollen	(estar) mohino[5b]

SECTION 10.2. CONCEPTS 6373 THROUGH 6384

E F G S
14 –6 –8*–8*
14 –8*–8*–6
15 –4 –8*–6
21*–8*–1 –6

English	French	German	Spanish
explanatory[14]	explicatif	erklärend	explicativo[6a]
guillotine[14]	guillotine[6b]	Guillotine	guillotina
inertia[14]	inertie	Trägheit	inercia[6a]
intimidate[14]	intimider[6a]	einschüchtern	intimidar

English	French	German	Spanish
intonation[14]	intonation[6a]	Anstimmen	entonación
parishioner[14]	paroissien[6b]	Gemeindemitglied	feligrés
participle[14]	participe	Partizip	participio[6b]
roguish[15], knavish[15]	coquin[4b]	boshaft	picaresco[6b]
snuffle[14], (snivel[17]) (*vb.*)	renifler[6a]	schnüffeln	gimotear, lloriquear
spontaneity[14]	spontanéité	Spontaneität	espontaneidad[6a]
ugliness[14]	laideur[6a]	Häßlichkeit	fealdad
undefinable	indéfinissable	(nicht zu) bestimmen[1b]	indefinible[6b]

SECTION 10.3. CONCEPT 6385

E F G S
16–5–8* 2

English	French	German	Spanish
widower[10]	veuf[5b]	Witwer	viudo[2a]

SECTION 10.4. CONCEPTS 6386 THROUGH 6389

E F G S
15–4 –8*–8*
16–4 –8*–4
18–8*–5 –4

English	French	German	Spanish
crossroads (crossroad[15])	carrefour[4a]	Scheideweg	encrucijada
decanter[15]	carafe[4b]	Karaffe	garrafa
journalist[16]	journaliste[4a]	Journalist	periodista[4a]
romanticism[18]	romantisme	Romantik[5a]	romanticismo[4b]

SECTION 10.5. CONCEPTS 6390 THROUGH 6397

E F G S
15–5 –8*–8*
15–8*–8*–5
15–6 –8*–7
16–3 –8*–6

English	French	German	Spanish
cohesion[15]	cohésion[5b]	Kohäsion	cohesión
crossroad[15]	(rue de) traverse[5b]	Querstraße	(calle) transversal
discouragement[15]	découragement	Entmutigung	desaliento[5b]
mediocrity[15]	médiocrité[5a]	Mittelmässigkeit	medianía, mediocridad
monosyllable[15]	monosyllabe	einsilbig	monosilabo[5b]
prosaic[15]	prosaïque	prosaisch	prosaico[5a]
slowness[16]	lenteur[3b]	Langsamkeit	lentitud[6b]
substitution[15]	substitution[6b]	Ersetzung	substitución[7a]

SECTION 10.6. CONCEPTS 6398 THROUGH 6402

E	F	G	S
15	-8*	-8*	-6
15	-6	-8*	-8*
21*	-6	-2	-8*

English	French	German	Spanish
centennial[15] (*adj.*)	centenaire	hundertjährig	centenario[6a]
embargo[15]	embargo	Sperre	embargo[6b]
milkman[15]	laitier[6a]	Milchmann	lechero
nonentity[15]	nullité[6a]	Null	nulidad
set-up (*n.*)	mise en scène[6b]	Szene[2b], (Szenerie)	montaje

SECTION 10.8. CONCEPTS 6403 THROUGH 6406

E	F	G	S
17	-8*	-6	-8*
18	-8*	-5	-8*
21*	-4	-3	-8*

English	French	German	Spanish
bimetallism[18]	bimétalisme	Doppelwährung[5b]	bimetalismo
coat-tail	pan[4b]	Schoß[3b]	faldón
debatable[17]	discutable	streitig[6b]	discutible
(self) starter[17]	démarreur	Selbsteintritt[6b]	arranque[3b] automático

SECTION 10.9. CONCEPTS 6407 THROUGH 6410

E	F	G	S
16	-5	-8*	-8*
16	-8*	-8*	-5
17	-3	-8*	-6
19	-8*	-5	-5

English	French	German	Spanish
abnegation[19]	abnégation	Ablehnung[5a]	abnegación[5a]
optimistic[16], (optimist[17])	optimiste[5b]	Optimist, optimistisch	optimista
passerby[17]	passant (*n.*)[3b]	Passant, Vorbeigehende	transeunte[6b]
unforgettable[16]	inoubliable	unvergeßlich	inolvidable[5a]

SECTION 11. CONCEPTS 6411 THROUGH 6418

E	F	G	S
16	-6	-8*	-8*
16	-8*	-8*	-6
17	-6	-8*	-4
19	-5	-6	-5
21*	-8*	-3	-6

English	French	German	Spanish
brother-in-law[19]	beau-frère[5b]	Schwager[6a]	cuñado[5a]
father-in-law[17]	beau-père[6b]	Schwiegervater	suegro[4b]
hindquarters (horse)	croupe	Kreuz[3a]	ancas (anca[6a])

English	French	German	Spanish
mawkish[16]	doucereux[6b], mielleux[6b]	empfindsam	almibarado, meloso
monolog(ue)[16]	monologue	Monolog	monólogo[6b]
organizer[16]	organisateur	Organisator	organizador[6b]
phosphorus	phosphore	Phosphor[3a]	fósforo[6a]
protégé[16]	protégé (*n.*)[6a]	Schützling	protegido

SECTION 11.2 CONCEPTS 6419 THROUGH 6420

E F G S
18–8*–6–8*

English	French	German	Spanish
autonomy[18]	autonomie	Selbstverwaltung[6b]	autonomía
indorsement[18]	endos(sement)	Indossament[6a]	endoso

SECTION 11.3 CONCEPTS 6421 THROUGH 6423

E F G S
17–5–8*–8*
18–3–8*–6

English	French	German	Spanish
cinema[17]	cinéma[5b]	Kinematograph, Kino	cine, cinematógrafo
epicure[17]	gourmet[5a]	Feinschmecker	epicúreo, sibarita
mediocre[18]	médiocre[3a]	mittelmäßig	mediocre[6b]

SECTION 11.4. CONCEPTS 6424 THROUGH 6430

E F G S
17–6 –8*–8*
17–8*–8* 6

English	French	German	Spanish
(hen[2a]) coop[17]	poulailler[6b]	Hühnerstall	gallinero
enviable[17]	enviable	beneidenswert	envidiable[6a]
fatherhood[17], (paternity[18])	paternité	Vaterschaft	paternidad[6b]
idealist[17]	idéaliste	Idealist	idealista[6b]
immorality[17]	immoralité	Unsittlichkeit	inmoralidad[6a]
mobilize[17]	mobiliser[6a]	mobilisieren	movilizar
sheepish[17]	penaud[6a]	beschämt	avergonzado, cortado

SECTION 11.5. CONCEPTS 6431 THROUGH 6433

E F G S
18 –5–8*–6
18 –6–8*–5
21*–4–6 –3

English	French	German	Spanish
dryness[18]	sécheresse[5b]	Trockenheit	sequedad[6b]
egoism	égoïsme[4b]	Selbstsucht[6b]	egoísmo[3b]
poacher[18]	braconnier[6b]	Wilddieb, Wilderer	cazador[3b] furtivo[5b]

SECTION 11.7. CONCEPTS 6434 THROUGH 6436

E F G S
18 –5–8*–8*
19 –5–8*–4
21*–5–5 –8*

English	French	German	Spanish
banister[18] (railing)	rampe[5a]	Geländer	baranda, barandilla
son-in-law[19]	gendre[5a]	Schwiegersohn	yerno[4a]
tactical	tactique[5a]	taktisch[5b]	táctico

SECTION 12. CONCEPTS 6437 THROUGH 6439

E F G S
21*–4 –6–8*
21*–8*–5–8*

English	French	German	Spanish
county-head	préfet[4b]	Regierungspräsident[6a]	prefecto
insurer	assureur	Versicherer[5a]	asegurador
mobilization	mobilisation	Mobilmachung[5b]	movilización

SECTION 12.1. CONCEPT 6440

E F G S
21*–1–8*–4

English	French	German	Spanish
naturalness	naturel[1a]	Natürlichkeit	naturalidad[4a]

SECTION 12.2. CONCEPTS 6441 THROUGH 6445

E F G S
19 –6 –8*–8*
19 –8*–8*–6
21*–8*–6 –6
21*–4 –8*–2

English	French	German	Spanish
conciseness	concision	Genauigkeit[6a]	concisión[6b]
gesticulate[19]	gesticuler[6b]	gestikulieren	gesticular
immoral[19]	immoral	unsittlich	inmoral[6a]
unbutton[19]	déboutonner	aufknöpfen	desabrochar[6a]
work-yard	chantier[4b]	Bauplatz	patio[2b] (de) trabajo[1a]

SECTION 12.4. CONCEPTS 6446 THOUGH 6449

E F G S
20 –6 –8*–6
21*–8*–6 –8*

English	French	German	Spanish
accepter, drawee	accepteur, tiré	Akzeptant[6a]	(el) girado, (el) librado
arbitrariness	arbitraire	Willkür[6b]	arbitrariedad
Calvary[20]	calvaire[6b]	Kalvarienberg	calvario[6b]
nationalization	nationalisation	Verstaatlichung[6a]	nacionalización

SECTION 12.5. CONCEPT 6450

E F G S
20–8*–8*–5

English	French	German	Spanish
muleteer[20]	muletier	Mauleseltreiber	arriero[6a]

SECTION 12.6. CONCEPT 6451

E F G S
21*–4–8*–6

English	French	German	Spanish
journalistic	(de) journaliste[4a]	journalistisch	periodístico[6b]

SECTION 12.7. CONCEPT 6452

E F G S
21*–8*–8*–3

English	French	German	Spanish
mother-of-pearl	nacre	Perlmutter	nácar[3b]

SECTION 12.8. CONCEPT 6453

E F G S
21*–4–8*–8*

English	French	German	Spanish
unpublished	inédit[4b]	unveröffentlicht	inédito

SECTION 12.9. CONCEPTS 6454 THROUGH 6459

E F G S
21*–5 –8*–8*
21*–8*–8*–5

English	French	German	Spanish
cross-examination	interrogatoire[5a]	Kreuzverhör	interrogatorio
immobility	immobilité[5a]	Reglosigkeit	inmovilidad
interlocutor	interlocuteur	Gesprächspartner	interlocutor[5b]
seduction	séduction[5b]	Verführung	seducción
spoonful	cuillerée	Löffel	cucharada[5b]
wet-nurse	nourrice	Amme	nodriza[5b]

SECTION 13. CONCEPTS 6460 THROUGH 6473

E F G S
21*–8*–8*–6
21*–6 –8*–8*

English	French	German	Spanish
bondsman	caution	Bürge	fiador[6a]
catholicism	catholicisme[6a]	Katholizismus	catolicismo
communicative	communicatif	mitteilsam	comunicativo[6b]
echelon (*vb.*) (military)	échelonner[6b]	staffeln	escalonar
flower-bed	parterre[6b]	Beet	cuadro de flores
greengrocer	fruitier[6b]	Gemüsehändler, Kohlhöker	frutero
late-comer, (belated[11])	retardataire[6b]	Nachzügler	retrasado
riding-school	manège[6a]	Reitschule	escuela[1b] de equitación, picadero
shirt-front	plastron[6b]	Hemd(en)brust	pechera
(use) thou-form	tutoyer[6a]	duzen	tutear
three-colored, tricolor	tricolore[6b]	dreifarbig, Trikolore	tricolor
vituperation	vitupération	Schmähung	vituperio[6a]
watercolor	aquarelle[6a]	Aquarell	acuarela
zouave	zouave[6a]	Zuawe	zuavo

INDEXES

INDEX TO ENGLISH WORDS IN THE LIST

After an indexed word, everything inclosed in parentheses or italicized is explanatory material; everything neither inclosed in parentheses nor italicized, and followed by a section number on the same line, indicates the word in the text under which the indexed word is to be found. For example: "bad[1a]" is to be found in Section 1.; as a synonym of "evil," in Section 1.2; in the phrase "bad luck," listed under "luck" in Section 2.7; in the phrase "too bad," listed under "bad" in Section 2.9.

A

	Section
affliction[5b]	
misfortune	2.2
afford[3b]	
grant	1.
affright(ed)[5a]	
afraid	1.
frighten	1.9
afloat[6]	6.7
afraid[1b]	
(be –)	1.
African[2b]	4.4
after[1a]	1.
one – the other	3.3
day – tomorrow	4.3
afternoon[1b]	1.9
afterwards[2a]	1.8
again[1a]	1.
begin –	1.
– (and again)	
several times	1.2
say –	1.
against[1a]	1.
age[1b]	
(years old)	1.
old –	1.3
vb.	1.6
(epoch)	1.8
middle -s	2.2
aged[6]	
old	1.
agency[5b]	6.4
agent[4b]	2.9
representative	2.3
aggravate[6]	4.9
(make) worse	3.
aggression[15]	7.8
aggressive[8]	7.7
aggressor[13]	9.2
ago[1b]	1.
long –	1.3
agony[3b]	2.
agree[2a]	2.2
-d	2.8
agreeable[3b]	
pleasant	1.1
agreement[4b]	
contract	2.3
settlement	2.7
(state)	3.1
agriculture[3a]	2.8
agricultural[4b]	3.3
ah[2a]	
O	1.2
ahead[3b]	
forward	1.4
front	1.4
(be – of)	2.7
aid[2a]	
vb. help	1.
n. help	1.1
ail[6]	
matter	1.
aim[2b]	
n. purpose	1.
(point gun)	3.2
air[1a]	
n. (to breathe)	1.
n. (tune)	3.
adj.	3.
airy[5a]	6.6
aisle[5b]	3.4
alarm[2b]	
vb.	3.5
n.	4.9
alas[3a]	2.

	Section
album[9]	7.9
alcoholic[8]	7.7
alderman[6]	7.2
ale[6]	
beer	3.9
alight[5b]	
settle	3.1
(person)	5.7
alike[2b]	
like (*adj.*)	1.
alive[2a]	
be –	
live	1.
(having life)	1.9
all[1a]	
adv.	1.
above –	1.
(not at all)	1.
– right	1.
– the more	
much	3.6
allege[5b]	
maintain	3.5
-d	4.4
allegiance[5b]	
loyalty	3.6
alley[5a]	4.6
allied[6]	5.2
join	1.9
allow[1b]	1.
-ed	2.2
allude[7]	
refer	3.1
allure[5b]	
attract	3.1
alluring	
attractive	4.
ally[7]	
n.	6.4
vb. join	1.9
almighty[5a]	5.1
almond[6]	6.9
almost[1a]	1.
alms[5a]	6.
aloft[6]	
above (*adv.*)	1.
alone[1a]	1.
along[1a]	
– the river	2.2
draw –	2.6
go –	4.1
aloof[6]	
separate	1.
aloud[3a]	
(out) loud	1.
already[1b]	1.
also[1a]	1.
altar[3b]	3.5
alter[3b]	
tr. vb. change	1.4
alternate[5b]	
-ly	4.8
vb.	5.4
although[1b]	1.
altitude[6]	
height	1.1
altogether[3b]	
all	1.
always[1a]	1.
am[1a]	
be	1.
amaze[3b]	
astonish	2.7
amazement[5b]	
surprise	2.4
ambassador[4b]	3.9

	Section
amber[5b]	6.6
ambition[3b]	3.7
ambitious[4b]	
(be – for)	5.8
amen[5b]	4.3
amend[4b]	4.9
make -s for	
make up for	2.9
-s	4.1
amendment[4b]	4.5
American[1b]	
English	1.
amiable[6]	
pleasant	1.1
amid[5a]	
among	1.
ammunition[6]	5.6
among[1a]	1.
amongst[6]	
among	1.
amount[1b]	
n.	1.
– to	2.9
ample[3b]	3.6
amuse[4a]	3.5
amusement[5b]	
pastime	4.8
an[1a]	
a	1.
analogy[8]	7.6
analysis[7]	7.1
analyze[6]	6.5
anarchy[8]	7.5
ancestor[4a]	4.5
anchor[3b]	5.2
ancient[2a]	2.6
and[1a]	1.
now – then	
(at) time(s)	1.
anecdote[6]	6.6
angel[2a]	2.
anger[2a]	
n.	1.9
vb.	2.7
(fit of –)	3.
angle[4b]	3.4
angry[2a]	2.4
(get –)	2.4
make –	
anger	2.7
anguish[5b]	
agony	2.
(in –)	6.3
animal[1b]	
n.	1.1
adj.	2.7
animate[5b]	3.5
ankle[4a]	4.6
annex[7]	
n.	6.6
vb.	7.4
anniversary[5b]	6.7
announce[5b]	
(give) notice	1.4
proclaim	3.5
annoy[5b]	
-ing	
vexing	3.8
vex	4.1
annual[3a]	2.7
anoint[6]	7.
anon[5b]	
soon	1.
anonymous[13]	9.6

	Section
another[1a]	1.
one –	
each other	1.
-'s	1.
answer[1a]	
vb.	1.
n.	1.2
ant[4a]	6.
antecedent[10]	8.3
anticipate[6]	6.8
antique[5b]	
ancient	2.6
antiquity[5b]	3.8
anvil[6]	7.2
anxious[2b]	2.3
any[1a]	1.
(whatever)	1.
in – case	
case	1.
anybody[3b]	1.8
anyhow[6]	4.2
case	1.
anyone[3b]	
anybody	1.8
anything[1b]	1.
anyway[4b]	
case	1.
anywhere[4b]	4.1
somewhere	3.
apart[2a]	
separate	1.
apartment[5a]	
flat	2.1
ape[6]	
copy	3.2
monkey	5.6
apiece[5a]	
each	1.
apostle[8]	5.4
apostolic[9]	8.2
apparatus[6]	3.7
apparel[5b]	
clothes	1.4
apparent[4b]	3.
appeal[3a]	
vb.	2.8
n.	3.8
appear[1b]	
(come into view)	1.
(seem)	1.
appearance[2b]	
looks	1.
(make one's first –)	2.3
(coming into view)	3.
(first)	3.3
appease[6]	
quiet	1.6
appendix[7]	
(book)	6.2
appetite[3b]	5.
applaud[5b]	
clap	2.8
applause[5a]	3.7
apple[1a]	3.5
– tree	5.
applicable[13]	9.8
applicant[9]	7.2
application[3b]	2.2
industry	2.6
apply[2a]	
– to	
turn to	1.1
(put on)	2.6
appoint[2a]	
name	1.

B

Section

babble[4b] . . . 6.4
babe[4a]
  baby . . . 4.4
baby[1b] . . . 4.4
bachelor[6] . . . 6.2
back[1a]
  (in – of) . . . 1.
  (be –) . . . 1.
  n. . . . 1.4
  go – . . . 1.4
  draw – . . . 1.5
  drive – . . . 1.5
  fall – again . . . 1.5
  come – . . . 1.8
  give – . . . 1.9
  send –
    return . . . 1.9
  take – (person) . . . 1.9
  go – (retreat) . . . 2.1
  call – . . . 2.6
  take – (thing) . . . 2.6
  adj. . . . 2.8
  drive – (repel) . . . 3.1
  carry – . . . 3.2
background[7] . . . 4.2
backward[3b]
  (backwards) . . . 2.8
  adj. . . . 5.4
backwards[6]*
  backward . . . 2.8
bacon[4a] . . . 6.1
bad[1a] . . . 1.
  (evil) . . . 1.2
  – luck
    luck . . . 2.7
  (too –) . . . 2.9
bade[3a]
  ask . . . 1.
  command . . . 1.5
badge[6]
  sign: . . . 1.1
  (metal) . . . 6.7
bag[1b] . . . 3.
  (suitcase) . . . 4.5
bagpipe[9] . . . 8.1
bait[5a] . . . 6.8
bake[2a]
  cook . . . 2.5
baker[4a] . . . 6.
balance[2b]
  (equilibrium) . . . 2.6
  vb. . . . 3.2
balcony[9] . . . 7.4
bald[6] . . . 6.2
ball[1a] . . . 2.1
  (bullet) . . . 2.3
  (dance) . . . 3.
ballad[6] . . . 5.9
balloon[7] . . . 6.1
balm[5a] . . . 6.4
bamboo[6] . . . 7.2
banana[4b] . . . 6.2
band[1b]
  (of people) . . . 2.1
  (strip of cloth) . . . 2.5
bandage[7] . . . 5.3
bang[6] . . . 6.5
banish[3b] . . . 4.1
banishment[5b]
  exile . . . 6.
banister[18] . . . 11.7
bank[1a]
  (of river) . . . 1.5
  (for money) . . . 1.8
banker[5b] . . . 5.

Section

bankrupt[7] *n.* . . . 5.3
bankruptcy[9] . . . 7.3
  (regulations for –) . . . 6.5
  (procedure in –) . . . 7.3
banner[3b]
  flag . . . 2.6
banquet[3b]
  feast . . . 3.5
baptism[6] . . . 5.5
baptize[7] . . . 6.
bar[2a]
  court (law) . . . 1.4
  vb. shut out . . . 1.6
  (obstacle) . . . 2.1
  (metal or wood) . . . 3.5
  -s (grating) . . . 4.6
barbarous[5b] . . . 5.7
  wild . . . 1.6
  savage . . . 2.
barber[5a] . . . 6.1
bard[5a]
  poet . . . 1.5
bare[2a] . . . 2.4
barefoot[7] . . . 7.2
bargain[3b] . . . 1.9
barge[6] . . . 6.
bark[2a]
  (of tree) . . . 4.9
  vb. . . . 5.1
barley[4a] . . . 6.1
barn[2a] . . . 5.5
baron[5b] . . . 4.
barrack(s)[10] . . . 7.9
barrel[3a] . . . 3.6
barren[3b] . . . 5.3
barrenness[12] . . . 9.4
barrier[5b]
  bar . . . 2.1
base[2a]
  n. . . . 1.7
  adj. low . . . 1.8
baseball[6]
  ball . . . 2.1
bashful[5b]
  shy . . . 4.2
basin[3b] . . . 3.
basis[4b]
  base . . . 1.7
  (hypothesis) . . . 3.4
basket[1b] . . . 2.8
bastard[6] . . . 7.1
bat[3b]
  stick . . . 2.
bath[3a] . . . 3.9
bathe[3a] . . . 3.7
battalion[8] . . . 5.
battery[4b] . . . 3.1
battle[1b] . . . 1.2
  -field
    field . . . 2.4
bay[1b] . . . 4.5
bayonet[7] . . . 7.4
be[1a] . . . 1.
beach[2b] . . . 3.9
bead[3b] . . . 3.2
  -s . . . 5.4
beak[5a] . . . 5.9
beam[2a]
  (rafter) . . . 2.3
  ray . . . 2.3
  -ing . . . 2.4
bean[2b] . . . 5.4

Section

bear[1a]
  vb. (stand) . . . 1.
  (children) . . . 1.3
  n. . . . 4.5
beard[2b] . . . 3.2
bearer[5b]
  porter . . . 3.3
beast[1b] . . . 1.1
beat[1b]
  (in a game) . . . 1.
  (pound) . . . 1.1
  (pulsate) . . . 1.3
beaten[6]
  beat . . . 1.1
beating[6]*
  (heart) . . . 4.6
  n. . . . 6.4
beau[6]
  lover . . . 2.
beauteous[6]
  beautiful . . . 1.
beautiful[1a] . . . 1.
beauty[1b] . . . 1.5
  (belle) . . . 1.8
became[2a]
  become . . . 1.
because[1a] . . . 1.
  – of . . . 1.
beckon[5b] . . . 4.3
become[1a] . . . 1.
  – white
    white . . . 1.9
  – dumb
    dumb . . . 4.
bed[1a] . . . 1.4
  (go to –) . . . 1.6
bedroom[4a] . . . 4.4
bee[1b] . . . 4.1
beech[6] . . . 7.
beef[3b] . . . 4.1
been[1a]
  be . . . 1.
beer[4b] . . . 3.9
beet[5b] . . . 6.8
beetle[5b] . . . 6.8
befall[4a]
  happen . . . 1.
before[1a]
  (place) . . . 1.
  (time) . . . 1.
  conj. . . . 1.1
  day – . . . 1.4
  bring – . . . 2.2
  (come –, go –) . . . 2.3
  day – yesterday . . . 4.
  coming – . . . 2.8
beforehand[5b]
  advance . . . 2.2
beg[2a]
  ask . . . 1.
  (beseech) . . . 2.7
  (literally) . . . 4.6
began[1b]
  begin . . . 1.
beget[5b] . . . 3.4
beggar[3a] . . . 4.
begin[1a] . . . 1.
  – again . . . 1.
beginning[5b]* . . . 2.7
  begin . . . 1.
  (from the –) . . . 3.9
beguile[5a]
  deceive . . . 1.9
begun[2b]
  begin . . . 1.

Section

behalf[4a]
  in – of
    for . . . 1.
behave[4a]
  act . . . 1.
behead[6] . . . 6.2
beheld[3b]
  observe . . . 1.4
behind[1a]
  back . . . 1.
  adv. . . . 2.
  leave – . . . 2.2
behold[2a]
  observe . . . 1.4
being[1a]
  n. . . . 1.
  be . . . 1.
Belgian[12] . . . 9.
belief[3b] . . . 2.3
believe[1a] . . . 1.
  make – . . . 4.2
bell[1b] . . . 2.5
bellow[4b]
  vb. roar . . . 4.7
  n. howl . . . 5.7
belly[6] . . . 6.2
belong[1b] . . . 1.
beloved[3b]
  darling . . . 2.2
below[2a]
  adv. beneath . . . 1.6
belt[2b] . . . 4.7
beneath[2a]
  prep. under . . . 1.
  adv. . . . 1.6
bench[2b] . . . 2.4
bend[2a]
  vb. . . . 1.9
  vb. (curve) . . . 2.4
benefit[2b]
  vb. profit . . . 1.4
  advantage . . . 1.5
  n. . . . 3.4
  tr. vb. . . . 3.6
benign[9] . . . 6.5
bent[2b]
  bend . . . 1.9
  bend (curve) . . . 2.4
  adj. . . . 5.
berry[2b] . . . 4.9
beseech[5b]
  beg . . . 2.7
beset[6]
  attack . . . 2.1
beside[1b] . . . 1.
besides[4b]
  addition . . . 1.4
  prep. . . . 2.3
besiege[5a] . . . 5.6
  attack . . . 2.1
best[1a] . . . 1.
bestow[3b]
  grant . . . 1.
  -ing . . . 3.8
bet[6] . . . 6.3
betray[3b] . . . 2.5
betroth[6] . . . 6.8
  -ed
    engage . . . 2.5
better[1a] . . . 1.
between[1a] . . . 1.
  (go –) . . . 2.3
bewail[6]
  mourn . . . 1.9
beware[4b]
  look out . . . 1.4

	Section
brisk[5a]	
fast	1.
bristle[6]	6.9
British[2b]	4.2
English	1.
Briton[6]	
English	1.
broad[1b]	1.4
broke[2b]	
break	1.1
broken[1b]	
break	1.1
bronze[6]	6.2
brood[4a]	
(meditate)	3.9
n.	5.8
brook[1b]	2.1
broom[3b]	5.5
brother[1a]	1.
brotherhood[6]	
group	1.8
brother-in-law[19]	11.
brotherly[6]	6.9
brought[1a]	
bring	1.
brow[2b]	
forehead	1.8
brown (B)[1b]	2.5
bruise[4a] *vb.*	5.7
brush[2a]	
(paint)	4.6
n.	5.6
brushwood[14]	9.8
brutal[5b]	
savage	2.
brutality[11]	9.
brute[4b]	5.7
bu.[6]	
bushel	6.
bubble[3a]	5.6
bucket[4a]	
pail	5.6
buckle[6]	6.8
buckwheat[6]	
wheat	2.5
bud[2b] *n.*	4.8
budget[7]	4.8
buff[6]	
yellow	2.
buffalo[6]	7.2
buffet[5b]	5.3
bug[5a]	
insect	4.4
buggy[6]	
cart	2.7
bugle[4b]	
horn	3.6
build[1a]	1.2
builder[4a]	6.4
building[1b]	
build	1.2
(edifice)	1.6
(construction)	2.5
built[1b]	
build	1.2
bulb[5b]	6.
bulk[4a]	
size	1.3
majority	2.6
bull[3a]	5.4
– fighter	
fighter	6.8
papal –	7.8

	Section
bullet[5b]	
ball	2.3
bump[6]	
run into	1.6
bunch[3a]	4.8
bundle[3b]	4.
burden[3a]	
n. load	1.4
vb. load	1.8
vb.	3.5
bureau[3b]	
office	2.9
burial[4a]	5.7
burn[1a]	1.6
-ing (*n.*)	2.3
burr[5b]	6.8
burst[2a]	
(explode)	1.4
(of laughter)	2.9
-ing	2.9
(out laughing)	3.
(into tears)	3.5
bury[2a]	3.1
bus[9]	8.1
bush[2a]	4.9
rose –	5.2
bushel[3a]	6.
busily[6]	
busy	1.
business[1b]	1.
– man	1.4
printing –	4.4
bust[5a]	6.1
busy[1b]	1.
but[1a]	1.
except	1.1
butcher[3a]	5.6
– shop	5.8
butt[6]	4.9
butter[1b]	3.5
butterfly[3b]	5.2
buttock[14]	10.
button[2b]	3.7
buy[1a]	1.4
buyer[5b]	3.8
buzz[3b]	
vb.	5.2
n.	5.4
by[1a]	
(instrument-agent)	1.
(according to)	1.
– and –	1.1
bye[5b]	
by	1.1

C

	Section
cab[6]	3.9
cabbage[4b]	5.9
cabin[3b]	
shed	3.2
cabinet[4b]	3.5
cable[4b]	5.8
rope	3.3
cage[3b]	5.5
cake[1b]	4.7
– of soap	4.8
calamity[6]	
disaster	3.9
calendar[5b]	5.8
calf[4a]	5.8

	Section
call[1a]	
vb.	1.
-ed (so called)	1.2
n.	1.4
– out	1.4
– upon (invoke)	1.5
– forth	1.6
– together	2.1
– back	2.6
calm[2b]	
adj. quiet	1.
n. quiet	1.
vb. quiet	1.6
Calvary[20]	12.4
calves[6]	
calf	5.8
came[1a]	
come	1.
camel[4b]	6.4
camp[2a]	
n.	2.8
vb.	3.3
campaign[4b]	
expedition	3.1
can[1a]	
able	1.
canal[3a]	2.3
canary[7]	7.2
candidacy[12]	9.4
candidate[4a]	4.1
candle[2b]	2.2
candy[2b]	4.5
cane[3b]	
stick	2.
cannon[3b]	
gun	1.7
cannot[1b]	
able	1.
canoe[4b]	
boat	2.6
canst[3a]	
able	1.
can't[2b]	
able	1.
canvas[3b]	
linen	3.6
cap[1b]	3.8
capable[3b]	
able	1.4
capacious[6]	
spacious	4.8
capacity[3b]	3.
cape[3a]	
cloak	4.8
(headland)	5.
capital[2b]	
(finance)	1.9
(city)	2.3
captain[1b]	1.6
captive[4a]	
prisoner	2.4
captivity[5b]	5.7
capture[3b]	
n.	4.5
vb.	6.
car[1b]	
(carriage)	1.5
(railroad)	2.
(tram)	2.1
caravan[6]	7.
carbon[7]	
– dioxide	6.8
card[2a]	2.1
cardboard[10]	8.6
cardinal[5b] *n.*	5.1

	Section
care[1a]	
n. (solicitude)	1.
(take – of)	1.
– for	
like	1.
not –	
(all the) same	1.
-s	1.3
take –!	
look out!	1.4
take –	
look out	1.4
– about	1.8
(charge)	3.2
career[4b]	4.
careful[1b]	1.7
careless[3b]	5.2
caress[6]	
stroke	4.4
n.	6.2
cargo[4b]	
load	1.7
carnation[10]	8.4
carpenter[3a]	5.5
carpet[3b]	4.2
carriage[2a]	
car (railroad)	2.
(bearing)	3.
carrier[5a]	
porter	3.3
carry[1a]	1.
– out, – through	1.
-ing out (execution)	2.2
– back	3.2
– away	3.4
cart[3a]	
(buggy)	2.7
wagon	4.7
carter[6]	6.9
cartridge[11]	9.
carve[3b]	
(general)	3.3
(art)	5.6
cascade[6]	
waterfall	6.2
case[1a]	1.
(in any –)	1.
(letter –, note –)	2.5
(spectacle, etc.)	3.6
casement[6]	
window	1.4
cash[3b]	2.8
cashier[6]	7.2
cask[7]	5.3
cast[2a]	
throw	1.
caste[8]	7.3
(half –)	7.7
castle[2a]	2.
casual[5b]	3.8
cat[2a]	4.1
catalog(ue)[5b]	
list	2.9
cataract[6]	
waterfall	6.2
catch[1b]	
– sight of	
sight	1.1
vb.	1.3
– up	2.3
– fire	
fire	2.5
-ing	4.
caterpillar[6]	7.2
cathedral[4b]	4.6
catholic (C)[4b]	2.9
catholicism	13.

Section

- cling[5a] 5.
- clip[4b]
  - cut 1.8
- cloak[2b] 4.8
- clock[1b] 1.3
- close[1a]
  - *vb.* 1.
  - *adj.* near 1.
- closet[3b] 5.6
- cloth[1b] 1.3
- clothe[1b] 1.9
- clothes[1b] 1.4
  - take off – 3.3
- clothing[6]*
  - clothes 1.4
- cloud[1b] 1.9
- cloudy[3b] 5.8
  - dim 4.1
- clove[5b] 6.7
- clover[4b] 6.4
- club[2b] (association) 1.6
- cluck[4b] 6.4
- clump[8] (trees, etc.) 4.8
- clung[6]
  - cling 5.
- cluster[3b]
  - bunch 4.8
- clutch[5a]
  - seize 1.1
- coach[2b]
  - car (railroad) 2.
  - – (e.g., and four) 4.9
- coal[1b] 1.9
  - (live coals) 2.1
- coarse[3a] 2.9
- coast[1b] *n.* 1.4
- coat[1b] 2.
  - (overcoat) 2.2
  - – (of suit) 4.3
  - frock – 6.1
- coat-tail 10.8
- cobbler[5a]
  - shoemaker 6.2
- cock[2a] 3.8
- cocoanut (coco)[6] 7.
- cod[4b] 6.1
- code[7] 4.8
- coffee[2a] 2.3
- coffin[5b] 5.3
- cohesion[15] 10.5
- coil[5b]
  - *vb.* twist 4.
- coin[2b] 1.9
- coincide[10] 7.2
- coincidence[8] 7.8
- cold[1a]
  - *adj.* 1.
  - *n.* 1.9
- coldness[10] 6.2
- collar[2b] 4.4
- collect[2b]
  - – money due 1.4
  - gather 1.5
- collection[3b] 2.7
- collective[13] 9.6
- college[2a] 3.8
- colonel[6] 3.9
- colonial[5b] 6.2
  - colonist 6.1
- colonist[4b] 6.1
- colony[2b] 2.9

Section

- color[1a]
  - *n.* 1.
  - *tr. vb.* 2.5
- colored *adj.*[4a]* 4.2
- colt[3a] 5.4
- column[3a] 3.3
  - (military) 2.9
- comb[4a]
  - *vb.* 6.
  - (on bird) 6.2
- combat[4a]
  - *n.* fight 1.1
- combination[3b] 4.3
- combine[3a] 2.3
- combustion[6] 6.
- come[1a] 1.
  - – from 1.
  - – to
    - end in 1.1
  - – forward 1.4
  - – now! (look here!) 1.4
  - – back 1.8
  - – before
    - before 2.3
  - – now!
    - well 2.3
  - – out 2.6
  - coming before 2.8
- comedy[4b] 3.7
- comely[6]
  - pretty 1.
- comet[6] 4.8
- comfort[2a]
  - *n.* 2.3
  - *vb.* 2.3
  - ease 3.2
- comfortable[2b] 2.1
- comforter[5b]
  - quilt 6.8
- coming[1b]
  - come 1.
- command[1b]
  - *n.* order 1.
  - *vb.* 1.5
  - -ing (imperious) 1.9
  - *n.* (military, over forces) 2.3
- commander[4b] 4.4
- commandment[6]
  - order 1.
- commence[3b]
  - begin 1.
- commend[3b]
  - praise 2.1
- comment[6]
  - *vb.* remark 2.3
  - *n.* remark 2.4
- commerce[2b]
  - trade 1.2
  - chamber of – 3.2
- commercial[3b] 2.8
  - – law
    - law 3.2
- commission[3b]
  - *n.* 2.2
  - *vb.* charge 2.2
- commissioner[4b] 5.
- commit[3b] 2.3
- committee[3b] 3.
- common[1b] 1.4
  - – (person) 1.4
- commonwealth[5b]
  - state 1.
- commune[6]
  - consult 3.
- communicate[5b] 2.7

Section

- communication[4b] 2.5
  - message 3.
- communicative 13.
- communion[6] 6.7
- community[4b]
  - (of individuals) 2.9
  - (e.g., of interests) 3.8
  - *adj.* 4.8
- compact[5a]
  - contract 2.3
  - solid 3.2
- companion[2a] 2.3
- company[1a]
  - (business) 1.
  - (social) 1.
  - (military) 1.5
  - (guest) 1.7
- comparative[5b]
  - relative 3.7
- compare[2a] 1.6
  - (be -d) 2.2
- comparison[3b] 2.7
- compass[2b] (area) 2.5
- compassion[5b]
  - pity 2.4
- compel[3a]
  - force 1.
- competition[5b] 3.8
- complain[2b] 2.
- complaint[3b] 2.4
- complement[6] 5.2
- complete[1b]
  - *adj.* 1.
  - *tr. vb.* 1.
- completely[6]*
  - all 1.
- complex[7] 5.3
- complexion[5b] 6.4
- complicate[7] 6.2
- complication[9] 7.2
- compliment[5b] 4.1
- comply[5b]
  - consent 2.4
- compose[3b] 2.6
- composer[14] 9.6
- composition[4b] 3.8
- compound[5b]
  - mix 2.2
- comprehend[4b]
  - understand 1.
- compromise[6]
  - *n.* 5.7
  - *vb.* 5.3
- comrade[4a] 3.4
  - companion 2.3
- conceal[3b]
  - hide 1.
- conceit[5b] 5.3
- conceive[3b]
  - imagine 1.4
  - (literal) 2.
- concentrate[6] 4.8
- concentration[7] 7.1
- conception[6] 4.
- concern[2b]
  - matter 1.
  - interest 1.
  - *vb.* have to do with 1.
  - be -ed about
    - care 1.8
  - person -ed
    - interested 3.
- concerning[4a]
  - about 1.
  - as for 1.

Section

- concert[4a] 4.1
- conciliation[10] 7.8
- conciseness 12.2
- conclude[3a]
  - complete 1.
- conclusion[4b] 3.
  - end 1.
  - in –
    - finally 2.2
- concrete[6]
  - definite 3.5
  - *adj.* 6.1
- condemn[3b] 2.7
  - sentence 2.3
- condense[5b] 4.3
- condition[1b] 1.
  - state 1.
- conduct[2b]
  - lead 1.
  - *n.* 2.3
- conductor[5a]
  - leader 2.3
- cone[6] 7.2
- confederacy[6] 5.1
  - union 1.6
- confederate[6]
  - party 2.
- confer[4a]
  - grant 1.
  - consult 3.
  - (award) 5.9
- conference[4b] 3.
- confess[3a]
  - admit 1.4
- confession[5b] 4.3
- confessional[15] 10.
- confessor[8] 7.4
- confidence[3b]
  - trust 1.
  - (disclosure) 3.5
- confident[5a] 5.1
- confidential[8] 6.6
- confine[4a]
  - *vb.* limit 1.6
  - *vb.* limit (in meaning) 5.1
- confirm[3b]
  - (verify) 2.5
- confirmation[5b] 5.1
- conflict[4a]
  - *n.* fight 1.1
  - *n.* struggle 1.9
- confound[4b] 3.1
- confuse[4b]
  - confound 3.1
  - -d 3.2
- confusion[3b] 3.2
- congeal[9] 6.3
- congratulate[5b] 6.2
- congratulation[6] 5.3
- congregation[5b]
  - assembly 2.6
- congress[2b] 2.9
- conjecture[6] 4.7
- conjugal[14] 9.6
- conjunction[7] 7.3
- connect[2a]
  - join 1.
- connection[3b] 2.9
- conquer[2b] 2.9
- conqueror[4a] 4.1
- conquest[3b] 3.3
- conscience[2b] 1.8
- conscientious[8] 6.4

Section
cream[2a] 5.1
  – of crop 2.8
create[2b] 1.5
creation[4b] 3.4
creator[5b] 4.4
creature[2a] 2.5
credit[3a] *n.* 2.9
creditor[5b] 4.1
creek[4a] 5.9
creep[2b] 3.
crêpe[6] 7.
crept[3b]
  creep 3.
crest[4b]
  top 1.3
crew[2b] 3.2
crib[6]
  cradle 4.3
cricket[4b] 5.3
cried[1b]
  cry 1.
  cry (weep) 1.4
cries[4a]
  cry 1.
  cry 1.4
crime[3a] 2.4
criminal[5b]
  adj. 4.1
  n. 4.5
crimson[4b]
  red 1.
cripple[4b]
  lame 4.6
crisis[7] 5.8
crisp[5b] 6.5
critic[5a] 5.1
critical[7] 5.
criticism[6] 3.8
croak[5a] 6.8
crooked[4b] 3.7
crop[2a] 2.7
  cream of – 2.8
cross[1a]
  vb. 1.
  -ing (passage) 1.6
  n. 2.
  tr. vb. (put crossways) 2.7
  – out 4.7
cross-examination 12.9
crossroad[15] 10.5
  -s 10.4
crouch[5b] 6.4
crow[2b] *n.* 5.3
crowd[1b]
  n. 1.
  vb. 2.2
crowded *adj.*[7]* 5.4
crown[1b]
  n. 1.7
  – prince
    prince 2.3
  vb. 2.9
crude[6]
  rude 4.3
cruel[2a] 2.3
cruelty[4b] 4.8
crumb[4b] 5.8
crumble[5a]
  fall 2.6
  crumbling (caving in) 6.5
crusade[8]
  expedition 3.1
crush[2b] 3.
crust[4a] 5.8

Section
crutch[5b] 6.5
cry[1b]
  vb. (shout) 1.
  n. call 1.4
  vb. (weep) 1.4
  n. 2.6
crystal[4a] *n.* 4.6
Cuba(n)[4a] *adj.* 6.2
cube[5a] 5.
cuckoo[4b] 6.2
cucumber[7] 7.4
cuff[4a] 6.
cultivate[3a]
  till 2.5
culture[5b] 3.7
cunning[3a] 4.
  (quality) 5.1
cup[1b] 4.3
cupboard[5a]
  closet 5.6
curb[4b]
  check 3.2
cure[2b]
  vb. 2.9
  n. 3.9
curiosity[5a] 4.8
curious[3a] 2.7
  (make –) 2.9
curl[2b]
  vb. 4.8
  n. 4.9
curly[10] 8.5
currant[6] 6.8
currency[6] 4.9
current[2b]
  present 1.1
  n. 2.6
curse[2b]
  n. 3.5
  vb. 4.6
curtain[2a] 3.8
curve[3b]
  vb. bend 2.4
  n. 4.6
cushion[3b] 5.6
custom[2a] 1.9
  practice 3.4
customary[6]
  usual 1.
customer[3b] 3.6
customhouse[11]
  – officer 8.9
cut[1a]
  vb. (shear) 1.8
  – off (curtail) 2.8
  – off (isolated) 2.9
  – off (*vb.*) 3.1
  vb. (mow) 4.7
cutter[5b]
  boat 2.6
cylinder[5b] 4.9
cypress[6] 7.
czar[6]
  emperor 2.1

D

dagger[6] 5.6
daily[2b] 1.6
dainty[4b] 2.7
dairy[3b] 5.7
dale[5a]
  valley 1.7
dam[4a] 4.7

Section
damage[3b]
  tr. vb. hurt 1.8
  n. 2.4
dame[3b]
  lady 1.
damn[5a] 4.2
damp[3b] 3.4
damsel[5a]
  girl 1.
dance[1b]
  vb. 2.4
  n. 3.1
dancer[6] 6.9
danger[2a] 1.5
dangerous[2b] 2.
dangle[6]
  hang 1.1
Danish[8] 6.8
dare[1b] 1.
daring[6]
  dare 1.
  boldness 4.7
dark[1a]
  adj. 1.
  (grow –) 4.5
darken[4b]
  dark 4.5
darkness[2a] 2.9
darling[3b] 2.2
darn[6]
  repair 3.7
dart[3a]
  vb. dash 1.8
dash[2a] *vb.* 1.8
date[1b]
  n. (day) 2.
  vb. 3.3
daughter[1b] 1.
dawn[2a] 3.5
day[1a] 1.
  (the – after) 1.
  good – 1.1
  – before 1.4
  – before yesterday 4.
  – after tomorrow 4.3
daylight[3b] 4.6
daytime[5b]
  day 1.
daze[8] 7.8
dazzle[4b] 3.9
dead[1a] 1.4
  – body
    body 2.1
deadly[4a]
  mortal 2.9
deaf[3b] 4.8
deal[1b]
  a great –
    much 1.
dealer[4b] 4.8
dealing[5a] *n.* 3.
dean[6] 7.
dear[1a]
  (in affection) 1.
  (costly) 1.1
death[1a] 1.
debatable[17] 10.8
debate[3b]
  vb. 2.9
  n. 3.
debt[2a] 1.7
  (in –) 4.
debtor[6] 4.8

Section
decade[6] 5.6
decanter[15] 10.4
decay[3a]
  ruin 2.4
  spoil 2.6
  n. 4.3
decease[5b]
  die 1.
  dead 1.4
deceit[5b] 3.9
deceive[2b] 1.9
December[2a] 2.3
decent[5b] 4.
decide[1b] 1.
decidedly[7] 4.3
decision[4a] 2.5
decisive[6] 3.6
deck[2b]
  vb. trim 2.4
  n. (ship) 3.7
declaration[6] 4.5
declare[2a]
  state 1.
decline[3b]
  ruin 2.4
  (lessen) 3.3
  n. decay 4.3
  (person) 4.4
decorate[6]
  trim 2.4
decoration[4b]
  trimming 3.8
decrease[4a]
  reduce 3.5
  n. 4.7
decree[3b]
  n. 2.6
  vb. 3.
dedicate[4b] 2.7
deed[2a]
  act 1.
  act (document) 2.3
deem[3b]
  decide 1.
deep[1a] 1.
deepen[5b] 5.
deer[3a] 5.8
defeat[3b]
  vb. 2.7
  n. 3.6
defect[5a]
  fault 1.8
defective[6]
  imperfect 3.9
defend[2b] 1.4
defender[10] 6.8
defense[3a] 2.8
defiance[4b] 4.
defile[6] 6.5
definite[5b] 3.5
definition[7] 7.
deform[6]
  mar 5.2
defy[3b] 3.2
degenerate[7] 7.4
degrade[6]
  disgrace 5.6
degree[2a]
  by -s
    little by little 1.
  (grade) 1.4
deign[6] 6.4
deity (D)[6] 5.4

Section
dissolve[3b] 3.9
distaff[9] 8.2
distance[1b] 1.1
distant[2a]
  far 1.
distil[6] 6.9
distillation[11] 8.4
distillery[12] 8.4
distinct[3a]
  clear 1.
distinction[5b] 3.9
  difference 1.4
distinguish[3b] 2.2
distort[8] 7.5
distract[5b] 3.6
  -ed 5.5
distress[3a]
  trouble 1.
distribute[5a] 3.3
distribution[4b] 3.7
district[2b] 2.1
disturb[3a]
  trouble 1.5
disturbance[5b] 4.4
ditch[3a]
  (irrigation) 3.6
  (trench) 3.9
dive[4b] 4.2
divide[1b] 1.1
dividend[6] 5.6
divine[2b] 2.
  – service
    service 2.3
divinity[5b] 4.9
division[3a]
  (general and military) 2.2
  (act of dividing) 3.8
divorce[4b] *vb.* 4.
dizzy[6]
  (make –) 4.4
  (feel –) 6.4
do[1a] 1.
  (auxiliary) 1.
  have to – with 1.
  – over again 1.8
  – without 2.1
  – hair
    hair 4.
dock[4a] 5.4
doctor[1b] 1.
doctrine[4b] 2.6
document[5b] 5.1
does[1a]
  do 1.
doesn't[3b]
  do 1.
dog[1b] 1.9
dogma[10] 8.3
doings[3b]
  act 1.
doll[2b] 4.9
dollar[2a]
  pound 1.
dolly (D)[5a]
  doll 4.9
dome[4b] 6.2
domestic[3a] 2.9
dominion[4b]
  rule 2.
  (possession, title) 3.1
done[1a]
  do 1.
donkey[4a]
  ass 3.9

Section
don't[1b]
  do 1.
doom[3b]
  fate 1.5
door[1a] 1.
dost[4a]
  do 1.
dot[2b]
  point 1.
doth[3a]
  do 1.
double[1b] 1.6
  vb. 4.2
  vb. (effort) 4.3
doubt[1b]
  n. 1.
  (without –) 1.
  vb. 1.5
doubtful[3b] 2.6
doubtless[4a]
  doubt 1.
dough[6] 6.2
dove[3a] 4.4
down[1a]
  adv. 1.
  sit – 1.
  go – 2.2
  put – 2.2
  run – 2.6
  pull – 2.8
  take – 2.8
  knock –
    fell 2.8
  settle – 3.1
  slow – 4.4
downward(s)[3b] 3.4
dowry[9] 7.6
dozen[2a] 3.4
Dr.[5b]
  doctor 1.
draft[3a]
  (of liquid) 2.2
  (of a bill) 2.3
  n. (sketch) 3.
  (draw up) 3.6
  (on a bank) 3.8
  (military) 5.2
drag[2b]
  pull 1.
  vb. 2.7
dragon[3b] 5.
dragoon[12] 8.6
drain[2b] 3.7
drama[5b] 3.7
  (musical –) 6.2
dramatic[7] 4.6
drank[4b]
  drink 1.4
draught[4a]
  draft (of liquid) 2.2
  draft (of a bill) 2.3
  draft (sketch) 3.
draw[1a]
  pull 1.
  vb. (design) 1.4
  – back 1.5
  – up (water) 1.7
  – up (formulate) 2.
  – along 2.6
  – up (e.g., document) 3.2
drawer[4a] 6.1
  -s (chest of -s) 6.1
  -s (clothing) 6.2
drawn[4b]
  pull 1.
dread[2b]
  afraid 1.
  n. fear 1.4
  -ed 2.4

Section
dreadful[2b]
  terrible 1.8
dream[1b]
  n. 1.4
  vb. 1.8
dreamer[14] 9.7
dreary[5b]
  dismal 3.9
dreg[8] 7.8
dress[1a]
  n. 1.4
  clothe 1.9
  head – 4.2
dresser[6]
  buffet 5.3
  hair –
    barber 6.1
dressmaker[10] 8.4
drew[2b]
  pull 1.
dried[4a]
  dry 2.1
drift[4a]
  course 1.1
  float 2.9
drill[2b]
  exercise 1.6
  bore 5.
drink[1a]
  vb. 1.4
  n. 2.7
  -ing 3.
drip[4a] 6.4
drive[1a]
  intr. vb. 1.
  (car, etc.) 1.
  (horse) 1.
  (force) 1.
  – out 1.1
  – back 1.5
  – away (*tr. vb.*) 2.3
  – back (repel) 3.1
driver[4a] 4.4
droop[3b] 4.4
drop[1a]
  tr. vb. 1.
  n. 2.4
drove[2b]
  drive *intr. vb.* 1.
  drive (car) 1.
  drive (horse) 1.
  n. 3.9
drown[2a] 4.3
drowsy[4a] 6.2
drug[3b] 5.8
  – store 5.6
druggist[7] 6.6
drum[2b] 4.3
drunk[4b]
  drink 1.4
  (make –) 4.8
  adj. 5.5
  (get –) 5.8
drunken[5b]
  – revel 5.8
  (person) 5.9
drunkenness[8] 7.3
dry[1b]
  adj. 1.4
  vb. 2.1
dryness[18] 11.5
duchess[6] 4.7
duck[2b] 5.
due[2a] 2.2
  falling – 5.2
duel[8] 7.

Section
dug[3b]
  dig 4.8
duke[3b] 2.3
dukedom[8] 6.8
dull[3a]
  (stupid) 3.5
  (unpolished) 3.9
  adj. (blunt) 5.2
  vb. (numb) 5.3
  vb. (tarnish) 5.3
duly[6] 4.5
dumb[3a] 2.9
  (become –) 4.
dunce[6]
  fool 2.4
dungeon[4b] 6.1
dupe[11] *n.* 8.2
durable[6]
  last 4.1
during[1a] 1.
dusk[6]
  twilight 4.3
dusky[6]
  dim 4.1
dust[1b] 1.9
dusty[4b] 6.1
Dutch[3a] 4.
duty[1b]
  (obligation) 1.
  (custom) 2.9
dwarf[4b] 6.1
dwell[2b]
  live 1.1
dwelling[3b] *n.* 2.3
dwelt[4a]
  live 1.1
dwindle[6]
  decline 3.8
dye[4a]
  tr. vb. color 2.5
  n. 5.4
dying[3b] 4.5
dynasty[8] 7.8

E

each[1a]
  adj. 1.
  pron. 1.
  – other 1.
eager[2b] 2.4
eagle[2b] 4.1
ear[1a] 1.5
  (hearing) 3.3
earl[4b]
  count 1.2
early[1a] 1.1
  get up – 3.
earn[2a]
  gain 1.
  deserve 1.5
earnest[2b]
  grave 1.4
earth[1a] 1.
earthly[3b] 3.1
earthquake[4b] 6.
ease[2b]
  n. (comfort) 3.2
  (facility) 3.3
easier[4b]
  easy 1.
  (make) easy 1.8
easily[2b] 1.6
east[1a] 2.
Easter[4a] 4.8

Section
establish[2a]
settle 1.
– a point
prove 1.4
establishment[5b]
(act of establishing) 3.8
foundation 4.2
estate[3a]
property 1.5
(real –) 3.2
esteem[3b]
n. regard 2.5
estimable[14] 10.1
estimate[3b]
rate 2.3
n. 3.8
estuary[12] 9.4
etc.[4b] 3.1
eternal[2b] 1.5
eternity[4b] 3.9
ether[6] 6.
ethereal[6] 7.
European[3b] *adj.* 2.5
evacuate[13] 7.7
eve (E)[3a]
day 1.4
(New Year's –) 3.8
even[1a]
adv. 1.
adj. (number) 1.7
adj. (smooth) 2.4
– off 4.2
evening[1b] 1.
good – 1.1
event[2a]
(circumstance) 1.4
(incident) 2.
ever[1a] 1.
always 1.
everlasting[4a]
eternal 1.5
permanent 4.2
evermore[5b]
always 1.
every[1a] 1.
– time
time 2.2
everybody[2b] 2.2
everyone[4a]
everybody 2.2
everything[1b] 1.2
everywhere[2b] 1.4
evidence[3b] 2.3
evident[3b] 2.5
evil[2a]
bad 1.2
n. 2.
evolution[8] 4.5
ewe[4b]
sheep 3.
exact[2a]
vb. demand 1.
adj. 1.4
exaggerate[6] 4.5
exaggeration[10] 7.7
exalt[4b] 2.7
-ed 2.9
exaltation[11] 6.3
examination[3b]
test 1.9
examine[2b] 1.5
example[2a] 1.4
(for –) 1.4
exceed[3a] 2.3
exceeding[5a]
very 1.

Section
excel[4b] 3.5
excellence[6] 5.6
(superiority) 5.1
excellent[2a] 1.8
except[1b] 1.1
vb. 1.7
exception[3b] 2.5
exceptional[5b] 5.4
-ly 4.8
excess[4a] 3.3
excessive[5b] 4.6
extreme 1.5
exchange[2b]
n. 2.
(stock) 2.6
vb. 3.5
excite[3a]
stir 1.9
excitement[5b] 4.2
exclaim[2b]
call (out) 1.4
exclamation[6] 5.3
exclusive[4b] 4.2
-ly 3.
excursion[5b] 4.1
excuse[2b]
vb. pardon 2.2
n. 2.9
execute[4a]
carry out 1.
execution[5b]
carrying out 2.2
executive[5b] *adj.* 6.5
executor[8] 7.7
exempt[6]
free 1.
exemption[12] 7.8
exercise[1b]
vb. 1.6
n. 1.7
exhaust[3b] 2.4
-ed
spent 2.
exhibit[4b]
display 3.
exhibition[5b]
display 2.6
exile[4b]
banish 4.1
(person) 5.6
(banishment) 6.
exist[3b] 1.8
existence[4b] 2.6
expand[6]
extend 1.
increase 1.1
spread 1.4
enlarge 3.3
expansion[6] 4.1
expansive[12] 9.3
expect[1b] 1.
– of a person 2.6
expectation[4b] 3.3
expedition[4a] 3.1
expel[5b] 4.3
expense[2b] 3.3
expensive[4a]
dear 1.1
experience[2a]
n. 1.6
vb. 1.8
experiment[4b]
vb. 2.4
n. 2.6
experimental[8] 7.7

Section
expert[4b]
n. 4.2
adj. 5.6
expire[4b]
die 1.
(e.g., a certain time) 4.3
explain[2a]
account for 1.
explanation[5b] 2.9
explanatory[14] 10.2
exploit[5b]
vb. 5.8
n. 5.9
exploration[5b] 4.6
explore[4b] 3.8
export[5b] (*n.*) 5.1
expose[3b] 2.2
express[1b]
vb. 1.
adj. 2.6
expression[4b] 2.2
expulsion[11] 9.
exquisite[5b] 3.6
extend[1b] 1.
extension[5a] 4.4
extensive[5a] 4.9
vast 2.8
extent[4a]
range 3.6
extinguish[6]
put out 1.9
extol[5b] 3.
extra[4a] 4.1
excess 3.3
extract[5b]
vb. 5.
n. 5.4
extraordinary[4b]
unusual 2.
extravagant[7] 7.3
extreme[2b] 1.5
extremely[3b]*
very 1.
extremity[5b] 5.1
eye[1a] *n.* 1.
eyebrow[6] 6.3
eyelid[6] 6.7

F

fable[4a] 4.4
fairy tale 3.4
fabric[6]
cloth 1.3
fabulous[7] 7.1
face[1a]
n. 1.
(grimace) 1.8
vb. 3.8
fact[1b] 1.
(in –) 1.
faction[6]
party 1.1
factory[3a] 2.6
faculty[5a]
ability 3.2
fad[12] 8.5
fade[2b] 4.9
fail[2a] 2.6
failure[5a] 3.1
(bankruptcy) 5.3

Section
fain[6]
willing 2.
accord 3.
faint[2a]
vb. 3.
n. 4.
fair[1a]
(blond) 1.
(just) 1.
fairness[16] 8.
fairy[2b] 5.
– tale 3.
fairyland[5b] 6.
faith[2a] 1.
faithful[2a] 2.
(the –) 2.
faithless[6]
false 2.
treacherous 6.
falcon[6] 7.
fall[1a]
vb. 1.
n. (tumble) 1.
– back again 1.
vb. (e.g., hair) 2.
n. (autumn) 2.
– to pieces 2.
-ing due 5.
fallen[3b]
fall 1.
false[2b] 1.
(faithless) 2.
falsehood[4b]
lie 2.
falter[6]
waver 3.
fame[2b] 2.
familiar[2b] 3.
family[1a] 1.
famine[3b] 5.
famous[1b] 1.
fan[2b]
n. 3.
– up (e.g., fire) 5.
fanaticism[14] 10.
fancy[2a]
imagine 1.4
n. (idle) 2.
(whim) 3.7
fancied 3.8
fantastic[5b] 4.7
far[1a] 1.
farce[6] 5.8
fare[2a]
food 1.9
bill of – 2.1
(rates) 3.6
farewell[2b] 3.4
farm[1b] 3.2
-ing 2.6
farmer[1b] 1.8
far-off[6]
far 1.
farther[2a]
far 1.
farthest[5a]
far 1.
fashion[2a] 2.8
fashionable[6] 6.
fast[1a]
adj. 1.
n. 4.4
vb. 4.9
fasten[2b] 2.9
join 1.

Section

fond[2b]
be – of
like .... 1.
be – of
(have a) taste for .. 2.4
food[1a] 1.9
fool[2a] 2.4
foolish[2b] 2.8
foot[1a] (part of body) ... 1.
football[5b] 6.8
footman[6]
servant 1.9
footstep[4b]
step (stride) .... 1.
step (footprint) .... 2.
for[1a]
as – .... 1.
conj. because .... 1.
care – .... 1.
prep. (in behalf of) ... 1.
prep. (in favor of) .... 1.
wait – .... 1.
forbear[5b]
keep from 1.7
forbid[2b] .... 2.
forbidden[4b]
forbid .... 2.
force[1b]
vb. .... 1.
n. .... 1.
-d 1.1
ford (F)[4a] 6.4
fore[5a]
front 1.5
forefather[6]
ancestor 4.5
foreground[10] 6.5
forehead[2b] 1.8
foreign[2a] 2.2
foreigner[4a] 2.6
foremost[4b]
chief .... 1.
first .... 1.
forenoon[4a]
morning .... 1.
foresee[5b]
see 3.8
forest[1b] .... 1.
foretold[6]
tell 4.9
forever[3b]
always .... 1.
forfeit[5a]
loss 1.2
forge[4b]
vb. (metal) 5.7
n. 5.9
(falsify) 6.2
forget[1b] .... 1.
forgetfulness[7] 6.5
forgive[3a]
pardon 2.2
forgiveness[5b]
pardon 3.6
forgot[2b]
forget .... 1.
forgotten[2b]
forget .... 1.
fork[2b] 4.2
forlorn[5b]
lonely 3.3
form[1a]
figure .... 1.
vb. .... 1.
formal[6] 5.1
formality[9] 7.9

Section

formation[5b] .... 4.
former[1b]
(opposite of latter) ... 1.
(e.g., times) .... 2.
formerly[4b*] 2.2
formula[7] 5.3
forsake[3b]
leave .... 1.
fort[2b] 2.6
forth[1b] .... 1.
call – 1.6
send – 3.4
forthwith[5b]
(at) once .... 1.
fortify[6]
strengthen 3.4
fortress[4b]
fort 2.6
fortunate[3b] .... 2.
-ly 3.7
fortune[2a]
(luck) 1.4
– teller
teller .... 7.
forty[2a] 2.9
forward[1b]
come – 1.4
adv. 1.4
go – 1.4
foster[5b]
further 1.8
vb. 3.8
-ing (*n.*) 3.9
fought[2a]
fight 1.6
foul[3a]
dirty 4.2
found[1a]
find .... 1.
vb. infin. 1.5
foundation[3a] 4.2
(of a building) 4.4
founder[4b]
sink 3.2
n. 6.1
fountain[2b] 2.8
four[1a] .... 1.
twenty – 4.7
fourteen[3b] 3.4
fourth[1b] 1.6
fowl[3a] 5.1
fox[2a] 4.9
fraction[5a] 4.9
fragment[5b]
piece .... 1.
bit 2.3
fragrance[5b]
perfume .... 4.
fragrant[4b] 5.5
frail[3b] 5.1
weak 1.1
frailty[6]
weakness 2.9
frame[2a]
n. 2.4
vb. 5.1
frank (F)[2b]
adj. open 1.3
frankness[8] 7.2
frantic[7]
distracted 5.5
fraternal[6]
brotherly 6.9
fraud[5b]
deceit 3.9
fray[6]
fight 1.1

Section

free[1a]
adj. .... 1.
(deliver) 1.7
(rid) 2.2
(of charge) 2.6
-ing (*n.*) 3.4
freedom[2a]
liberty 1.4
freeman[5b]
free .... 1.
freeze[2b] 3.3
freight[3a] 3.8
French[1b] .... 1.
Frenchman[6]
French .... 1.
frenzy[6]
fury 2.8
madness 4.1
frequent[2a]
-ly
often .... 1.
adj. 1.7
vb. 4.7
fresh[1a] 1.1
fret[3a]
worry 3.2
fretful[6] 6.6
friar[5b]
monk 4.7
friction[6] 6.1
Friday[2a] 3.6
friend[1a] .... 1.
friendly[2a] 3.5
friendship[3a] 2.3
fright[2b]
fear 1.4
frighten[2b] 1.9
-ing (*adj.*) 2.4
frightful[6]
terrible 1.8
fringe[4b] 5.8
frivolity[13] 9.3
frivolous[7] 5.8
fro[4b]
from .... 1.
frock[5a]
dress 1.4
– coat 6.1
frog[3a] 5.6
frolic[5a] 6.6
from[1a] .... 1.
come – .... 1.
– now on
now 1.1
front[1a]
in – of
before .... 1.
(in –) (*adv.*) 1.4
n. (e.g., of building) .. 1.5
adj. 2.2
frontier[6]
border 1.7
frost[2a] .... 5.
frosty[5a]
icy .... 6.
frown[3b] 5.5
frozen[2b]
freeze 3.3
fruit[1b] 1.5
fruitful[4b]
fertile 3.8
fry[5a] 6.3
-ing pan 6.4
ft.[4a]
yard 1.3
fuel[3b] 5.2

Section

fugitive[5a]
adj. .... 3.
n. .... 5.
fulfil(l)[4a]
carry out .... 1.
full[1a] .... 1.
– of life
life .... 1.
– of energy
energy .... 3.
(river, carrying much water) .... 4.
fully[3a] .... 2.
all .... 1.
fulness (full)[5a]
plenty .... 2.
fume[6]
rage .... 3.
fun[2a] .... 3.
(make – of) .... 2.
(have –) .... 2.
function[4b]
vb. 2.8
n. 3.6
fund[4b] .... 4.
fundamental[6] 5.2
funeral[3a] 5.4
funny[3a] .... 2.
fur[2a] .... 5.
furious[3b] 1.9
angry 2.4
furnace[3b] 2.7
furnish[2a]
supply 1.1
(room, house) 3.3
furniture[2b] 4.4
furrow[5a] .... 6.
further[2a] *vb.* 1.8
furthermore[6]
addition 1.4
fury[3b] 2.8
future[2a]
n. 1.5
adj. .... 2.

G

gain[1b]
vb. .... 1.
n. 1.9
gait[5b]
walk 1.6
pace 1.8
gale[4a]
storm 1.6
gall[5a]
vex 4.1
n. (anatomical) 6.4
gallant[4a]
(be) brave .... 1.
civil 3.2
gallery[4a] 4.2
gallon[5b]
quart 4.7
gallop[3b] *n.* 4.7
gallows[5a] 6.6
game[1b]
(play) 1.5
(to shoot) 2.7
gang[5b]
band 2.1
gap[4a] 4.5
gape[6]
yawn 5.8
garage[6] 6.9
garden[1a] 1.4

Section

- gravy^{6}
  - sauce 5.5
- gray (G)^{1b} 2.2
- graze^{3b}
  - (just touch) 3.4
  - (e.g., flock) 5.
- grease^{5b}
  - *n.* fat 2.6
  - *n.* 4.8
- great^{1a} 1.
  - (a – man) 1.
  - Great Power
    - Power 3.
- greatness^{3b} 2.
- greediness^{11} 8.6
- greedy^{4a} 4.8
  - (pejorative) 6.
- Greek^{3b} 2.6
- green (G)^{1a}
  - *adj.* 1.5
  - *n.* 4.
- greengrocer 13.
- greet^{2a}
  - bow 1.4
- greeting^{4b}
  - bow 1.8
- grew^{1b}
  - become 1.
- grey (G)^{3b}
  - gray 2.2
- grief^{2b} 1.8
- grieve^{3a} *tr. vb.* 3.4
- grievous^{5a} 4.
  - painful 3.2
- grim^{5a}
  - severe 1.6
- grin^{4b} 5.9
- grind^{2b} 5.1
  - (teeth) 5.
- grip^{4b}
  - seize 1.1
- groan^{3a}
  - *vb.* 5.
  - *n.* 5.3
- grocer^{4a} 6.4
- grocery^{6} 6.9
- groom^{5b} 4.6
- groove^{6} 7.2
- grope^{6} 6.5
- gross^{4a} (measure) 5.2
- ground^{1a}
  - *n.* 1.
  - -s 2.4
  - – floor 4.4
- group^{2b}
  - *n.* 1.8
  - class 3.
  - *vb.* 3.6
  - -ing 3.6
- grove^{2b}
  - forest 1.
- grow^{1a}
  - become 1.
  - (increase in size) 1.1
  - (e.g., leaves) 1.3
  - -ing
    - rising 1.3
  - – old
    - age 1.6
  - – fat
    - fat 2.7
  - – dark
    - dark 4.5
- growl^{5a}
  - howl 4.5
- growth^{3a} (amount) 4.2

Section

- grudge^{5b} 4.6
  - (bear –) 5.6
- gruff^{5a} 3.7
- grumble^{5a} 4.9
- guarantee^{5b}
  - *vb.* pledge 2.7
  - *n.* pledge 2.9
- guard^{1b}
  - *vb.* 1.
  - *n.* (watchman) 2.
  - *n.* (military) 2.
- guardian^{5b}
  - guard 2.
  - (of a child) 5.5
- guess^{1b} 1.5
  - – right 1.4
- guest^{2a}
  - company 1.7
- guide^{1b}
  - *vb.* 1.3
  - *n.* 1.9
- guillotine^{14} 10.2
- guilt^{4a} 2.2
- guiltless^{5a}
  - innocent 2.8
- guilty^{3a}
  - blame 1.8
  - be – of
    - commit 2.3
- guinea^{6}
  - pound 1.
- guitar^{9} 8.
- gulf^{2b} 5.
- gum^{5b} 6.8
- gun^{2a} 1.7
- gunpowder^{6}
  - powder 2.8
- gush^{4b}
  - *n.* 3.6
  - *vb.* 4.5
- gust^{6}
  - blast 5.7
- gutter^{5b} 5.7
- gymnasium^{6} 7.2
- gypsy^{8} 7.4

H

- ha^{3a}
  - O 1.2
- habit^{2b} 2.2
- habitation^{6}
  - dwelling 2.3
- hack^{6}
  - cab 3.9
  - (nag) 7.
- had^{1a}
  - have 1.
- hadst^{4a}
  - have 1.
- hail^{2b} 5.3
- hair^{1a} 1.
  - (do –) 4.
  - – dressing
    - head 4.2
  - – dresser
    - barber 6.1
- hairy^{8} 7.8
- hale^{6}
  - sound 1.2
- half^{1a}
  - *n.* 1.
  - *adj.* 1.
  - – hour 1.5
  - – open 1.5

Section

- half^{1a}—*continued*
  - – caste
    - caste 7.7
- hall^{1b} 1.5
  - (city –) 3.4
  - entrance 5.3
- halloo^{6}
  - call 1.4
- hallow^{5a} 3.6
- halo^{14} 10.1
- halt^{4a}
  - *tr. vb.* stop 1.
  - *intr. vb.* stop 1.4
- ham^{4a} 5.7
- hamlet (H)^{4b}
  - village 1.2
- hammer^{2b} 4.8
- hand^{1a}
  - *n.* 1.
  - (on the other –) 1.4
  - *vb.* 1.8
  - (on the one –) 2.2
  - (with one's own –) 3.
- handful^{4b} 5.6
- handkerchief^{2b} 4.5
- handle^{2a}
  - *vb.* treat 1.4
  - *n.* 3.1
  - *vb.* (wield) 3.9
- handsome^{2b}
  - beautiful 1.
- hang^{1b} *tr. vb.* 1.1
- hangman^{10} 7.3
- haply^{6}
  - perhaps 1.
- happen^{1b} 1.
  - – to . . . .
    - chance 1.6
- happily^{4a}
  - fortunate 3.7
- happiness^{2b} 1.4
- happy^{1a}
  - glad 1.
- harbor^{2b} 2.
- hard^{1a}
  - (difficult) 1.
  - (not soft) 1.
  - try – 1.5
- harden^{4b} 6.1
- hardly^{2a} 1.4
- hardness^{7} 5.4
- hardship^{4b}
  - misfortune 2.2
- hardware^{5b} 6.8
- hardy^{3b} 2.6
- hare^{3b} 5.6
- hark^{3b}
  - listen 1.8
- harlot^{6} 6.8
- harm^{2a}
  - *tr. vb.* hurt 1.8
- harmless^{5a} 5.8
- harmonious^{6} 5.3
- harmony^{3b} 3.1
- harness^{3a}
  - *vb.* 5.3
  - *n.* 5.9
- harp^{4a} 6.1
- harrow^{6}
  - torment 3.1
- harry (H)^{2a} 1.4
- harsh^{4a}
  - severe 1.6
  - (to touch) 3.9
- harshness^{9} 7.8

Section

- hart^{5a}
  - deer 5.8
- harvest^{2a}
  - crop 2.7
  - *vb.* 4.8
- has^{1a}
  - have 1.
- hasn't^{6}
  - have 1.
- hast^{3b}
  - have 1.
- haste^{2a}
  - hurry 2.4
- hasten^{2b}
  - *intr. vb.* hurry 1.2
  - *tr. vb.* hurry 2.5
- hastily^{5a}
  - fast 1.
- hasty^{4b} 2.7
  - fast 1.
- hat^{1b} 1.5
  - (put on –) 2.8
- hatch^{5a} 6.8
- hatchet^{5a}
  - ax 5.
- hate^{2a}
  - *n.* 2.4
  - *vb.* 2.5
- hateful^{5b} 4.7
- hath^{4a}
  - have 1.
- hatred^{4a}
  - hate 2.4
- haughty^{4a} 4.7
- haul^{5a}
  - pull 1.
- haunt^{3b} 5.7
- have^{1a} 1.
  - – to
    - must 1.
  - – to do with 1.
- haven^{5b}
  - refuge 3.9
- hawk^{3b} 5.8
- hay^{2a} 4.8
- he^{1a} 1.
- head^{1a}
  - (part of body) 1.
  - *adj.* chief 1.
  - *n.* chief 1.5
  - – dress 4.2
  - (of bed) 4.7
- headache^{6} 6.6
- headlong^{5a} 4.2
- headquarters^{5b} 3.4
- heal^{3a}
  - cure 2.9
- health^{1b} 1.5
  - (state of –) 3.1
- healthful^{6}
  - wholesome 4.6
- healthy^{4a}
  - sound 1.2
- heap^{2b}
  - mass 1.6
  - – up 3.2
- hear^{1a} 1.
- heard^{1b}
  - hear 1.
- hearer^{6}
  - audience 4.3
- hearken^{5a}
  - listen 1.8
- heart^{1a} 1.
  - (learn by –) 3.

Section
hurl[4a]
  throw 1.
hurrah[5a]
  applause 3.7
hurry[1b]
  intr. vb. 1.2
  n. 2.4
  tr. vb. 2.5
hurt[1b]
  intr. vb. 1.8
  tr. vb. 1.8
  (be –) (offended) 2.3
husband[1b] 1.
hush[3a]
  quiet (*n.*) 1.
  vb. silence 1.9
husk[6]
  vb. peel 5.2
  n. peel 5.3
hussar[15] 9.4
hut[3a]
  shed 3.2
hydrogen[6] 6.
hygiene[7] 7.
hymn[4a] 5.8
hypocrisy[6] 6.9
hypocrite[6] 6.8
hysterical[10] 8.6

I

I[1a] 1.
ice[1b] 2.4
icy[4b] 6.
I'd[4b]
  should 1.
idea[2a] 1.4
ideal[4a] (*n.* and *adj.*) 3.2
idealism[11] 9.
idealist[17] 11.4
identical[6] 3.5
identity[11] 7.5
idiot[5a] 5.8
idle[2b] 3.7
idleness[5a] 6.5
idol[4b] 5.9
idyll[13] 9.8
if[1a] 1.
ignoble[6] 4.6
ignorance[4a] 4.6
ignorant[3b] 5.
  be – of
    (not) know 1.
ill[1b] 1.5
  (get –) 3.
I'll[2b]
  shall 1.
illness[5b]
  disease 1.6
illusion[6] 4.7
illustrate[5a] 5.2
illustration[6] 6.8
illustrious[5b] 3.1
  famous 1.1
I'm[2b]
  be 1.
image[3a] 3.5
imaginary[6]
  fancy 3.8
imagination[3b] 3.9
imaginative[8] 7.7
imagine[2a] 1.4

Section
imitate[4b] 4.
  copy 3.2
immediate[2a] 2.8
  -ly
    once 1.
immense[3b]
  great 1.
imminent[7] 6.1
immobility 12.9
immoral[19] 12.2
immorality[17] 11.4
immortal[3a] 3.8
immortality[5b] 6.
impart[4b]
  (let) know 1.
impartial[6] 5.
impatience[7] 5.3
impatient[4b] 4.3
imperceptible[9] 7.8
imperfect[4b]
  (defective) 3.9
  (incomplete) 4.2
imperial[4a] 3.3
impertinence[12] 9.4
impetuosity[14] 9.9
impetuous[7]
  headlong 4.2
impious[6] 6.5
implacable[9] 7.7
implement[5a]
  tool 3.
implore[5b]
  beg 2.7
import[3b]
  vb. 1.8
  n. (meaning) 2.2
  (importation) 4.5
importance[2b] 1.8
important[1b] 1.
impose[4a] 3.
  imposing 5.6
imposition[9] 8.2
impossibility[10] 7.1
impossible[2b] 1.4
impotence[11] 8.7
impregnate[12] 8.8
impress[5a]
  impression 2.2
impression[4a] 2.2
  (make an –) 2.2
  (imprint) 2.6
imprison[4b] 3.6
imprisonment[6] 5.
improbable[11] 7.9
improper[7] 7.2
improve[2b]
  intr. vb. 2.4
  tr. vb. 3.5
improvement[4b] 3.6
improvise[12] 8.9
imprudent[15] 10.
impulse[6]
  spur 3.6
impure[10] 7.5
impute[6]
  attribute 3.7
in[1a] 1.
  – no way
    (not at) all 1.
  shut – 1.9
  – love
    love 2.7
  – succession
    one 3.3

Section
in.[6]
  inch 2.7
inaugurate[8] 4.8
incapable[7]
  unable 4.1
incense[4a] 6.1
inch[1b] 2.7
incident[5b]
  event 2.
  -s 4.2
incline[3a]
  tend 2.4
inclose[4b]
  shut in 1.9
include[2a] 2.1
  -d 2.9
income[4b] 3.6
incomparable[9] 6.4
incompatible[14] 9.9
incomprehensible[11] 6.7
inconvenience[6] 4.1
increase[1b]
  vb. 1.1
  n. 2.3
incredible[6] 5.4
incur[5b] 3.6
incurable[7] 7.4
indebted[6] 4.2
indeed[1b] 1.
independence[4a] 3.6
independent[3a] 2.5
  – person 5.7
indescribable[8] 7.2
index[6]
  n. 5.3
  – finger 6.3
Indian[1b] 3.1
  English 1.
indicate[2b]
  point 1.4
indication[8] 5.
indicative[7] 4.6
indifference[6] 4.7
indifferent[6]
  (all the) same 1.
indignant[6]
  angry 2.4
indignation[4b] 4.2
  anger 1.9
indigo[6]
  blue 1.4
indirect[6] 5.
indiscreet[10] 8.3
indiscretion[12] 9.
individual[3a]
  n. 3.2
  adj. 3.8
indoors[6] 3.1
  within 1.1
indorsement[18] 11.2
induce[4b]
  persuade 2.1
indulge[6]
  – in 4.1
  tr. vb. 5.3
indulgence[6] 5.8
indulgent[9] 8.1
industrial[8] 5.5
industrious[4a] 3.2
industry[2b] 2.
  (application) 2.6
inequality[10] 7.4
inert[7] 6.8

Section
inertia[14] 10.2
inestimable[9] 8.1
inevitable[5b] 4.4
inexhaustible[13] 8.7
inexplicable[11] 8.7
inexpressible[12] 9.3
infallible[8] 7.7
infamous[7] 4.3
infamy[8] 7.6
infancy[6]
  childhood 3.3
infant[3b]
  child 1.
infantry[9] 5.6
infer[7] 5.7
inferior[4a] 3.6
infernal[6] 6.7
infinite[3b] 3.5
infinity[13] 9.6
infirmity[6]
  weakness 2.9
inflame[5a]
  stir 1.9
inflict[5b] 4.
influence[2b]
  n. 1.6
  vb. 3.2
influential[11] 8.2
inform[2b]
  (let) know 1.
  (well -ed) 3.
information[3a] 2.
  legal – 5.3
ingenious[5b] 4.7
ingenuity[6] 5.6
ingratitude[7] 7.
ingredient[6]
  element 2.3
inhabit[4b] 3.5
inhabitant[4b] 3.2
inherit[4a] 5.7
inheritance[4b] 3.9
initial[7] 4.6
initiative[7] 5.7
injure[3a]
  hurt 1.8
injurious[5b] 4.3
injury[4a]
  damage 2.4
  wrong (*n.*) 3.1
injustice[5b] 4.6
ink[3a] 5.1
inkwell[11] 8.9
inland[5a] 3.9
inn[3b] 4.2
innate[14] 9.
inner[4b]
  inside 1.4
innkeeper[8] 5.8
innocence[4b] 3.4
innocent[3a] 2.8
innumerable[6]
  countless 3.9
inquire[3a]
  ask (a question) 1.
inquiry[5b]
  (investigation) 3.5
  (interrogation) 4.4
inscription[6] 5.2
insect[3a] 4.4

Section

kind[1a]
  n. ... 1.
  adj. ... 1.
  (of the same –) ... 4.
kindle[4b]
  set on fire ... 2.7
kindly[2a] ... 3.3
kindness[2b] ... 2.7
kindred[4b]
  relation ... 2.3
king[1a] ... 1.
kingdom[2a] ... 1.7
kingly[5b]
  royal ... 1.5
kinsman[6]
  relation ... 2.3
kiss[1b]
  vb. ... 1.4
  n. ... 1.7
kitchen[2a] ... 2.8
kite[4b] ... 5.2
kitten[5a]
  cat ... 4.1
kitty (K)[4b]
  cat ... 4.1
knave[4a] ... 4.5
knee[1b] ... 2.
kneel[4a] ... 3.9
knell[4a]
  ring ... 1.4
knew[1b]
  know ... 1.
knife[2a] ... 2.9
knight[2a] ... 2.1
knit[3a] ... 5.4
knives[6]
  knife ... 2.9
knock[2a]
  (on door) ... 2.6
  – down
    fell ... 2.8
knoll[6] ... 5.2
  hill ... 2.6
knot[3b] ... 4.4
  (hair) ... 5.
know[1a] ... 1.
  (have knowledge of) ... 1.
  (let –) ... 1.
  (not –) ... 1.
knowledge[2a] ... 1.5
known[1a]
  know ... 1.
  (e.g., fact) ... 1.1

L

label[5b] ... 5.2
labor[1b]
  n. work ... 1.
  vb. work ... 1.
laboratory[7] ... 5.5
laborer[5a]
  workman ... 2.5
lace[2b] ... 2.1
lack[2a] *vb.* ... 1.5
lad[2a]
  boy ... 1.4
ladder[3a] ... 5.
lade(n)[4a]
  load ... 1.8
ladies[2b]
  lady ... 1.
lady[1b] ... 1.
  young – ... 1.1

Section

lag[5b]
  linger ... 3.6
laid[1b]
  lay ... 1.
lain[6]
  lie ... 1.
lake[1b] ... 2.1
lamb[2a] ... 4.9
lame[3a]
  vb. ... 4.6
  adj. ... 5.5
lament[4b]
  mourn ... 1.9
lamentation[5b] ... 4.2
lamp[2a] ... 2.5
lance[4a]
  spear ... 3.2
land[1a]
  n. (not sea) ... 1.
  -ing (stairs) ... 1.4
  vb. (go ashore) ... 3.2
  -ing (from ship) ... 5.
landscape[4b] ... 3.2
lane[3a]
  path ... 2.9
language[2a]
  tongue ... 1.
  (speech) ... 1.6
languid[7] ... 7.4
languish[5a] ... 6.8
languor[10] ... 8.6
lantern[4b] ... 3.5
lap[2b] (knees) ... 2.4
lard[4a]
  fat ... 2.6
large[1a]
  big ... 1.
lark[3a] ... 5.8
lash[5a]
  vb. whip ... 4.8
  n. whip ... 4.8
lass[5b]
  girl ... 1.
last[1a]
  adj. ... 1.
  (at –) ... 1.
  vb. ... 1.1
  – night
    night ... 1.2
  -ing ... 4.1
latch[5a] *n.* ... 6.8
late[1a] ... 1.
  -r on
    by and by ... 1.1
  supply -r ... 3.
late-comer ... 13.
lately[7]* ... 5.1
lateral[7]
  side ... 4.1
Latin[3a] ... 2.8
latter[2b] ... 1.4
laudable[11] ... 8.2
laugh[1a]
  vb. ... 1.
  n. ... 1.8
laughter[3a] ... 3.8
launch[5a]
  begin ... 1.
laundry[5b]
  wash ... 3.3
laurel[4b] ... 5.1
lavish[5b]
  adj. ... 3.7
  vb. ... 6.3
law[1a] ... 1.
  commercial – ... 3.2

Section

lawful[5b] ... 3.
lawless[6] ... 6.5
lawn[2b]
  (grass) ... 4.3
  (cloth) ... 5.2
lawyer[3b] ... 3.
lay[1a]
  vb. infin. ... 1.
  lie ... 1.
  – on (top)
    put ... 3.
  (person) ... 4.2
  – waste
    waste ... 4.9
layer[5a] ... 3.8
lazy[2b] ... 3.8
lb.[4b]
  pound ... 1.6
lea[6]
  meadow ... 2.6
lead[1a]
  vb. ... 1.
  n. (metal) ... 2.3
leader[2a] ... 2.3
leadership[6] ... 4.6
leaf[5b] (of tree) ... 2.6
leafy[7] ... 6.6
league[2b]
  mile ... 1.7
  (union) ... 2.8
leak[6] ... 6.6
lean[2a]
  -ing ... 1.8
  vb. ... 2.2
leap[2a]
  vb. spring ... 1.5
  n. spring ... 2.6
learn[1a] ... 1.
  -ed (*adj.*) ... 1.6
  -ing (*n.*) ... 3.6
least[1b] ... 1.
  (at –) ... 1.
leather[2a] ... 3.8
leave[1a]
  (abandon) ... 1.
  go away ... 1.
  (quit) ... 1.
  (take –) ... 1.5
  – behind ... 2.2
  (bequeath) ... 2.7
  (of absence) ... 2.9
lecture[4b]
  talk ... 1.2
led[1b]
  lead ... 1.
ledge[5b] ... 6.8
lee (L)[4b]
  shelter ... 1.7
left[1a]
  (*adj.* and *adv.*) ... 1.
  vb. leave (quit) ... 1.
  vb. leave (abandon) ... 1.
leg[1b] ... 1.9
legal[5b]
  lawful ... 3.
  (juristic) ... 4.
  – tender
    tender ... 4.8
  – information ... 5.3
legend[5b] ... 3.9
legion[4b] ... 5.8
legislation[6] ... 4.6
legislator[8] ... 6.3
legislature[5b] ... 5.2
legitimate[7]
  lawful ... 3.
  (child) ... 5.8
leisure[5a] ... 4.8

Section

lemon[4a] ... 6.1
lemonade[5a] ... 6.8
lend[3a] ... 3.1
length[1a] ... 1.7
lengthen[5b]
  prolong ... 3.6
lent (L)[4b]
  lend ... 3.1
less[1a] ... 1.
lessen[5b]
  decline ... 3.3
lesser[6]
  less ... 1.
lesson[1b] ... 1.2
lest[3a]
  that (*conj.*) ... 1.
let[1a]
  allow ... 1.
let's[6]
  allow ... 1.
  we ... 1.
letter[1a]
  (epistle) ... 1.
  (character) ... 1.4
lettuce[6] ... 7.1
level[2a]
  n. ... 1.9
  – off
    even ... 4.2
levy[6]
  gather ... 1.5
liable[6]
  subject to ... 1.7
  (– to do something) ... 5.8
  (to something) ... 6.5
liar[5a] ... 6.1
liberal[4a] ... 2.9
liberty[2a] ... 1.4
library[2b] ... 3.5
license[4b] ... 4.6
lick[4a] ... 6.2
lid[4a]
  cover ... 2.9
lie[1b]
  vb. (position) ... 1.
  (here -s) ... 1.7
  n. ... 2.
  (tell –) ... 3.
  (give the – to) ... 3.4
lieutenant[4b] ... 3.4
life[1a] ... 1.
  (full of –) ... 1.
  (animation) ... 3.8
lift[1b]
  vb. ... 1.
  -ing (*n.*) (elevation) ... 2.2
light[1a]
  n. ... 1.
  adj. (weight) ... 1.
  adj. (in color) ... 1.4
  – up (*vb.*) ... 1.4
  n. (not artificial) ... 2.
  -ed ... 2.6
  -ing ... 3.2
lighten[4a] ... 3.8
lighthouse[6] ... 6.6
lightness[12] ... 7.5
lightning[3a]
  flash ... 3.3
like[1a]
  as ... 1.
  adj. ... 1.
  vb. ... 1.
  (look –) ... 1.
  in – manner
    manner ... 1.2
  liking (*n.*) ... 1.5

Section
mansion[4a] 3.7
mantle[3b]
cloak 4.8
manual[7]
(textbook) 6.5
adj. 7.3
manufacture[2b]
n. 2.9
vb. 3.
manufacturer[5b]
maker 3.5
manure[6] 7.
manuscript[6] 5.8
many[1a] 1.
map[2a] 1.9
maple[4b] 6.4
mar[5a] 5.2
marble[2b] 3.8
(game) 4.9
march (M)[1b]
vb. 1.4
n. 1.5
(March) 1.9
mare[4b]
horse 1.
margin[5a] 3.9
marine[6]
sailor 2.9
mariner[5a] 5.8
mark[1a]
vb. 1.
n. sign 1.1
vb. (characterize) 3.2
market[1b] 1.7
marquis[8] 6.9
marriage[3a] 2.4
married[2b]
marry 2.3
marry[2a] 2.3
marsh[5a]
swamp 4.
marshal[5a] 4.2
martial[6] 5.4
martyr[4b] 3.1
martyrdom[8] 7.3
marvel[4a]
n. wonder 1.7
vb. wonder 1.8
marvelous[3b]
wonderful 1.2
masculine[5b]
manly 3.8
mask[4b]
n. 4.5
vb. 5.4
mason[5a] 6.3
mass[2a]
n. 1.6
(religious) 2.7
massy[6]
big 1.
mast[3a] 5.6
master[1b]
n. 1.
vb. 1.4
masterpiece[7] 6.4
mat[3b]
(straw) 5.8
match[2a]
(sport) 2.
(to light) 5.2
mate[2b]
husband 1.
wife 1.

Section
material[2a]
cloth 1.3
adj. real 1.9
n. 2.
adj. 2.
maternal[7]
mother 4.1
mathematical[10] 8.3
mathematics[6] 6.7
matron[6] 6.5
matter[1a]
n. (affair) 1.
(what's the –) 1.
(neg.) 1.
n. (substance) 1.1
printed – 2.4
mattress[6] 6.7
mature[4a]
ripe 2.9
(get) ripe 3.4
(adult) 4.
maturity[8] 7.8
mawkish[16] 11.
maximum[8] 7.4
may (M)[1a]
vb. 1.
(May) 1.2
maybe[4a]
perhaps 1.
mayor[3a] 2.5
mayst[6]
may 1.
maze[6] 7.
me[1a]
I 1.
mead[5a]
meadow 2.6
meadow[2a] 2.6
meal[2a] (repast) 3.2
mean[1a]
-s (*n.*) 1.
vb. 1.
(low) 1.5
(by -s of) 2.5
meaning[5b]*
import 2.2
(full of –) 3.3
meant[2b]
mean 1.
meantime[4b]
meanwhile 2.8
meanwhile[4b] 2.8
measure[1a]
n. 1.
vb. 2.
measurement[5b]
measure 1.
meat[1b] 1.6
mechanic[4a] 3.5
mechanical[6]
mechanic 3.5
-ly 5.2
mechanism[7] 7.2
medal[5b] 4.4
meddle[5a] 5.9
medical[5b] 5.1
medicine[2b] 3.4
mediocre[18] 11.3
mediocrity[15] 10.5
meditate[5b]
brood 3.9
meditation[6] 5.1
medium[4b]
means 1.
meek[4a]
humble 3.5

Section
meekness[6]
humility 5.4
meet[1a]
vb. 1.
(go to –) 2.3
meeting *n.*[6]*
convention 2.8
melancholy[5b]
sad 1.4
n. 5.
adj. 5.
mellow[5a]
ripe 2.9
(get) ripe 3.4
melody[4b]
air 3.
melon[6] 6.9
melt[2a] 2.5
-ing (of metals) 3.3
member[1b] 1.1
memorable[7] 7.
memorial[4b] 4.4
memory[2a] 1.8
men[1a]
man 1.
mend[3a]
repair 3.7
mental[6] 3.6
mention[2a]
vb. 2.2
n. 3.6
merchandise[4a]
goods 1.5
merchant[2a] 2.2
merciful[6] 4.2
merciless[6] 5.4
mercury (M)[5b] 6.6
mercy[2b] 2.
mere[2a]
only (*adj.*) 1.
-ly
simply 1.
meridian[6] 7.2
merit[3a]
n. value 1.
vb. (be) worth 1.
vb. deserve 1.5
merry[2a]
cheerful 1.9
mess[5b]
disorder 5.
message[2a] 3.
messenger[3a] 2.5
met[1b]
meet 1.
metal[2b]
n. 2.1
adj. 4.8
meteor[6] 7.2
meter[4a]
yard 1.3
methinks[5b]
think 1.
method[3a] 2.5
methought[6]
think 1.
metropolis[6] 4.8
mew[4a] 6.4
Mexican[6] 6.8
mice[4a]
mouse 5.
mid[4a]
among 1.

Section
middle[1b]
center 1.
(time) 1.5
– ages 2.2
midnight[2a] 2.4
midst[3a]
among 1.
might[1a]
n. power 1.
vb. may 1.
mighty[2a]
strong 1.
mild[2b]
gentle 1.4
mile[1a] 1.7
military[3a] 2.4
militia[6] 6.3
milk[1a] 2.5
milkman[15] 10.6
milky[6] 7.2
mill[1b] 3.
millennium[14] 8.8
miller[4a] 6.1
million[2a] 1.4
millionaire[6] 6.9
mince[6]
chop 4.2
mind[1a]
vb. (take) care (of) 1.
n. 1.1
vb. object 1.9
presence of – 4.5
mine[1a]
pron. 1.1
n. 2.6
miner[5b] 4.7
mineral[4b] 6.1
mingle[3b]
mix 2.2
miniature[8] 7.7
minimum[8] 7.4
minister[2b] 1.5
(clergyman) 2.
ministry[5b] 3.4
minor[7] 4.4
minority[8] 7.7
minstrel[6] 7.2
mint[6] 7.2
minute[1b]
n. 1.5
adj. 3.1
miracle[4a] 2.9
wonder 1.7
mire[5a]
mud 4.8
mirror[3a] 2.8
mirth[3b] 5.5
mischief[3b] 4.5
miser[6] 6.5
miserable[3b] 2.7
misery[3b] 2.7
misfortune[4b] 2.2
misgiving[8] 7.4
(have –) 6.3
mishap[6]
accident 2.3
miss (M)[1a]
vb. 1.
(Miss) 1.1
mission[4b] 4.1
missionary[6] 7.2

N

Section

neither[1b]
adv. 1.
conj. 1.
– one 1.

nephew[4a] 3.7

nerve[4a] 3.5

nervous[4b] 4.4

nest[1b] 3.3

nestle[6] 7.

net[2b] *n.* 3.1

nether[6]
under 1.9

neutral[8] 7.6

never[1a] 1.

nevertheless[4a]
however 1.

new[1a] 1.
(New Year's) Eve 3.8

news[2a] 1.4

newspaper[2b]
paper 1.

next[1a] 1.

nibble[6]
bite 3.7

nice[1b] (person)
fine 1.4

nickel[4b]
cent 1.7

nickname[10] 8.6

niece[5b] 4.1

nigh[4a]
adj. and *adv.* near 1.
prep. near 1.

night[1a] 1.
(last –) 1.2
(at –) 2.2
(spend –) 2.7
adj. 3.3

nightingale[4b] 6.1

nightly[6] 3.

nightmare[9] 7.8

nimble[5b]
active 2.5

nine[1b] 2.4

nineteen[4a] 6.3

ninety[3b] 5.8

ninth[3a] 4.7

nip[6]
bite 3.7

no[1a]
adv. 1.
adj. 1.
– longer, – more 1.
– one 1.
in – way (not at) all 1.

nobility[5b] 3.7

noble[2a] *adj.* 1.4

nobleman[5b]
peer 2.6

nobody[2b]
no one 1.

nod[2b] 3.2

noise[2a] 2.6

noiseless[6]
silent 1.5

noisy[5b] 5.8

nomination[5b] 4.9

none[1b] 1.

nonenity[15] 10.6

nonsense[5a] 5.

Section

nook[5b]
corner 2.3

noon[1b] 2.1

noonday[5b]
noon 2.1

nor[1b]
neither .... nor 1.
adv. neither 1.

normal[4b] 3.9

north[1a] 1.6

northern[2b] 2.

northwest[5a] 6.8

nose[1b] 1.7
blow – 4.2

nostril[4a] 5.7

not[1a] 1.

notable[5a]
remarkable 2.4

note[1b]
n. (written) 1.9
vb. 1.9
(bank –) 3.6
– book 4.9

nothing[1a] 1.

notice[1b]
vb. 1.4
(give – of) 1.4
n. – of something 1.7
(give – to) 2.8

notify[5b]
(let) know 1.
(give) notice (of) 1.4

notion[3b]
idea 1.4

notwithstanding[5b]
however 1.

nought[5a] 3.
nothing 1.

noun[9] 7.3

nourish[4b] 3.2

nourishment[6] 5.6

novel[4b] 2.9

novelist[9] 7.9

novelty[4b] 4.3

November[2a] 2.3

now[1a]
adv. 1.
conj. 1.
till – 1.
– and then
(at) times 1.
(from – on) 1.1
now .... now 1.5
now .... then 1.5
– then
so 1.5
come –!, look here! 1.4
– and then 2.2
come –!
well 2.3

nowhere[6] 3.4

nucleus[6] 4.9

number[1a]
n. (quantity) 1.
figure 1.1
(digit) 2.4

numerous[2b] 1.5

nun[5b] 6.3

nurse[2a]
(take) care (of) 1.

nursery[6] 5.8

nut[2a] 5.1

nymph[5a] 6.4

O

Section

O[1b] 1.2

oak[1b] 3.1

oar[4b] 4.8

oasis[6] 7.

oat[3a] 6.

oath[6]
(take an –) 4.6
(blasphemy) 4.8

obedience[4a] 6.

obedient[4b] 3.2

obelisk[11] 9.

obey[2a] 2.2

object[1b]
thing 1.
vb. 1.9
(grammatical) 3.

objection[5b] 4.4

obligation[5b] 4.

oblige[2b]
force (*vb.*) 1.

oblique[8] 6.2

obscure[5a]
dim (*adj.*) 4.1
vb. 6.

observation[3b] 2.4
remark 2.4

observe[2a] 1.4
notice 1.4
watch 1.
observing 2.6

observer[7] 5.4

obstacle[5b] 3.4
bar 2.1

obstinacy[7] 7.2

obstinate[5b]
stubborn 4.1

obtain[2a]
get 1.

occasion[2a]
chance 1.

occasional[4b] 3.7

occupation[3b] 2.4

occupy[2a]
occupied with
engaged 1.9

occur[2b]
happen 1.

ocean[1b] 3.6

o'clock[2a]
(what) time (is it) 1.

October[2a] 2.4

odd[2b]
strange 1.

odious[6]
hateful 4.7

odor[3b]
smell 2.8

o'er[3a]
prep. above 1.

of[1a] 1.

off[1a]
away 1.
right –
(at) once 1.
take – (coat, etc.) 1.8
put – (postpone) 2.6
cut – (curtail) 2.8
cut – (isolated) 2.9
vb. cut – 3.1
take – clothes 3.3
(take –) shoes 4.1
even –, level – 4.2
pay – 4.9

Section

offend[3a] 2.8
-ed
hurt 2.3

offender[6] 6.8

offense[3a] 3.8

offensive[6] 5.7

offer[1b]
vb. 1.
n. 3.6
-ing 3.8

office[1b]
(position) 1.4
(place) 2.9
printing – 4.4

officer[1b] 1.2
customhouse – 8.9

official[3a]
adj. 2.8
n. 2.8

offspring[5b]
child 1.

oft[3b]
often 1.

often[1a] 1.

oh[1b]
O 1.2

oil[2a] *n.* 2.5

ointment[6] 7.

old[1a] 1.
– age 1.3
grow –
age 1.6
– iron
iron 2.3
– man
man 2.4

olive[3a] 5.8
– tree 5.7

omission[6] 7.

omit[4b] 4.4

on[1a] 1.
– the way
way 2.2
put – (e.g., hat) 2.6
– board
board 3.
lay – (top)
put 3.
urge – 4.8

once[1a]
(one time + once upon a time) 1.
(at –) (immediately) 1.
(at –) (at one stroke) 1.8

one[1a]
indef. pron. 1.
(numeral) 1.
each other 1.
no – 1.
that (*pron.*) 1.
this (*pron.*) 1.
– after the other 3.3

onion[4a] 5.6

only[1a]
adv. 1.
adj. 1.

onward[3b]
go forward 1.4

opaque[8] 7.8

open[1a]
vb. 1.
adj. 1.3
(to) half – 1.5
intr. vb. 2.2
-ing (*n.*) (vent) 2.3
-ing (first performance) 4.4
-ing (*n.*) (e.g., of a meeting) 4.7

	Section
past[1b]—*continued*	
n.	1.9
(tense)	2.2
paste[5b] *n.*	6.1
pastime[4b]	4.8
pastor[5a]	4.9
minister	2.
pastry[8]	7.8
pasture[2b]	3.5
pat[3b]	
tap	4.6
patch[3a]	
repair	3.7
patent[5a]	
evident	2.5
n.	5.2
paternal[6]	4.8
path[1b]	2.9
pathetic[7]	5.
pathway[6]	
path	2.9
patience[3a]	2.8
patient[2b]	
n.	2.5
(be –)	3.8
patriarch[8]	6.8
patriarchal[14]	10.1
patriot[5b]	5.2
patriotic[5b]	4.8
patriotism[6]	6.5
patron[4a]	4.
pattern[2b]	
model	2.
pause[3b]	2.9
pave[4b]	6.2
pavement[4b]	
sidewalk (Amer.)	5.5
(Amer.)	5.7
pavilion[6]	6.4
paw[3b] *n.*	5.1
pay[1a]	1.
– off	4.9
payment[3b]	2.5
pea[3a]	5.4
peace[1b]	1.
peaceable[6]	
peaceful	2.9
peaceful[3b]	2.9
peach[3a]	5.8
peacock[5a]	6.4
peak[4b]	
top	1.3
peal[4b]	
ring	1.4
pear[3a]	5.5
pearl[2b]	2.9
peasant[3b]	2.4
pebble[5a]	
stone	1.4
peck[3b]	
bushel	6.
peculiar[3a]	
strange	1.
(be –)	3.6
pedant[13]	9.6
peddler[6]	7.
pedestal[7]	7.3
peel[5a]	
vb.	5.2
n.	5.3
peep[2b]	
look (*n.*)	1.
vb. glance	2.3
peer[2b]	
n.	2.6
vb.	3.5
peg[5a]	6.
pen[1b] (for writing)	1.5
penalty[7]	
sanction	6.7
penance[6]	5.7
(do –)	5.8
pencil[2b]	4.2
penetrate[13]	6.6
penetration[12]	9.3
peninsula[4b]	4.5
penny[2b]	
cent	1.7
pension[5b]	4.3
pensive[4b]	3.9
people[1a]	
(race)	1.
(persons)	1.
(common)	1.
vb.	4.3
pepper[4a]	5.9
per[2b]	
by (as –)	1.
perceive[3a]	
understand	1.
catch sight	1.1
percent (per cent)[7]	
interest	1.
perch[3b]	5.6
perchance[5b]	
perhaps	1.
perfect[1b] *adj.*	1.
perfection[4b]	3.4
perform[2b]	
carry out	1.
performance[4b]	
play	2.
(fulfilment)	3.
(theatre)	3.1
perfume[4a]	
n.	4.
vb.	5.4
perhaps[1b]	1.
peril[4b]	
danger	1.5
perilous[5a]	
dangerous	2.
period[2b]	
term	1.8
(of time)	2.2
periodical[6] (*n.* and *adj.*).	3.9
perish[3a]	2.7
permanent[4a]	4.2
permission[4b]	3.3
permit[2a]	
allow	1.
pass	4.4
perpetual[4a]	
permanent	4.2
perplex[4b]	3.6
persecute[5b]	3.2
persecution[5b]	4.2
perseverance[6]	5.2
Persia(n)[5a]	5.6
persist[5b]	3.8
person[1a]	1.
queer –	3.3
independent –	5.7
personage[6]	3.6
personal[3b]	1.9
personality[6]	3.9
persuade[3b]	
convince	2.
(induce)	2.1
pertain[6]	
belong	1.
-ing	5.9
Peruvian[13]	9.8
pestilence[6]	5.8
plague	4.6
pet[4a]	
stroke	4.4
petal[6]	7.2
petition[4b]	4.
petroleum[6]	6.9
petticoat[5b]	
skirt	2.6
petty[5a]	4.5
phantom[6]	
ghost	3.2
Pharisee[10]	8.
phase[10]	8.4
phenomenon[6]	3.2
philosopher[4b]	3.3
philosophical[8]	5.2
philosophy[4a]	3.3
phoenix[12]	9.4
phone[5a]	
telephone	5.3
phosphorus	11.
photograph[5b]	3.7
phrase[4a]	
sentence	1.4
physical[5b]	4.
physician[3a]	
doctor	1.
physics[12]	8.
piano[4a]	4.7
pick[1b]	
choose	1.
– up (e.g., from floor)	1.5
pickle[5b]	6.8
picnic[4b]	6.3
picture[1a] *n.*	1.1
picturesque[5b]	4.6
pie[2a] (meat)	5.1
piece[1a]	
n.	1.
– of work	
work	1.1
fall to -s	2.6
pier[6]	
dock	5.4
pierce[3b]	3.1
piety[5b]	4.9
pig[2a]	3.9
pigeon[4b]	4.8
dove	4.4
pigeonhole[16]	9.
pile[2a]	
mass	1.6
pilgrim[4a]	5.8
pilgrimage[6]	6.7
pill[5a]	6.8
pillar[4a]	
column	3.3
pillow[3a]	5.2
pilot[6]	6.8
pin[2a]	4.
pinch[4a] *vb.*	6.
pine[2b]	4.9
pink[2b]	4.6
pint[4a]	
quart	4.7
pioneer[5b]	6.8
pious[4b]	2.9
pipe[2a]	3.2
(to smoke)	3.6
piper[6]	7.2
pirate[6]	6.9
pistol[4a]	5.9
pit[3a]	
ditch	3.9
pitch[3a]	
vb. throw	1.
pitcher[4a]	5.6
pitiful[6]	6.6
pitiless[6]	
merciless	5.4
pity[2a]	
mercy	2.
n. (compassion)	2.4
vb.	4.6
place[1a]	
n.	1.
vb.	1.
(take –)	1.
placing	4.
in the second –	
second	2.3
plague[3b]	4.6
plain[1a]	
clear	1.
simple	1.
n.	1.6
plaintiff[12]	8.4
plan[1b]	
n.	1.1
vb.	2.3
plane[4b]	3.7
– tree	6.
planet[4b]	3.9
plank[5a]	
board	1.7
plant[1a]	
n.	1.5
vb.	2.4
plantation[5a]	
farm	3.2
planter[6]	7.2
plaster[5b]	6.5
plastic[9]	7.6
plate[2a]	
n.	2.5
vb.	5.1
plateau[5a]	6.
platform[4a]	5.8
(dais)	6.2
platter[6]	4.
play[1a]	
vb.	1.
(theatre)	2.
player[5b]	6.
playful[8]	7.4
playground[6]	6.
playmate[4b]	
companion	2.3
plaything[5a]	
toy	5.1
plea[6]	5.3
plead[3b]	5.1
pleasant[1b]	1.1
please[1a]	1.
pleasure[1b]	1.4
pledge[3b]	
vb.	2.7
n.	2.9
plentiful[5a]	
abundant	4.2

Section
professional[6] 4.5
professor[3a] 2.6
profile[11] 8.7
profit[2b]
  vb. 1.4
  n. 2.
  n. (earned) 2.1
profitable[5a] 4.1
profound[5a]
  deep 1.
program[5b] 4.2
progress[3a]
  n. 2.4
  vb. 2.6
progressive[6] 6.7
prohibit[5a]
  forbid 2.
prohibition[6] 5.
project[4b]
  n. 3.5
  vb. 3.7
  -ing 4.3
prolong[4a] 3.6
prominent[4a]
  famous 1.1
promise[1b]
  vb. 1.
  n. 2.7
promote[6]
  further 1.8
promotion[6] (fostering) 5.6
prompt[2b] 2.5
promptitude[15] 10.
pronoun[6] 6.8
pronounce[2b] 1.4
pronunciation[6] 7.
proof[2b] 1.4
prop[6]
  n. support 2.1
propaganda[10] 7.5
propagate[6] 7.
proper[1b] 1.4
property[2b] 1.5
  (landed) 1.9
prophecy[5a] 6.6
prophesy[5a]
  tell 4.9
prophet[3a] 3.1
proportion[3a] 2.1
  (in –) 2.6
propose[2b] 1.4
proposition[5b] 3.1
prosaic[13] 10.5
proscribe[13] 9.7
prose[5b] 5.3
prospect[3a] 2.4
prosper[4a]
  flourish 4.1
prosperity[4b] 4.4
prosperous[3b] 4.7
prostrate[6] 6.6
protect[2a] 2.1
protection[3b] 2.1
protector[6] 6.3
  patron 4.
protégé[16] 11.
protest[4b]
  n. 4.1
  vb. 4.4
Protestant (p)[6] 4.4
proud[1b] 1.6
prove[1b] 1.
  – a point 1.4

Section
proverb[5b] 4.9
provide[2a]
  supply 1.1
  -d that 2.9
providence[4a] 4.3
province[2b] 1.5
provincial[9] 7.9
provision[3b] 4.1
provoke[3b] 2.4
prowess[6]
  skill 3.
proximity[10] 5.6
prudence[5b] 3.7
prudent[4b] 3.3
prune[4b] 6.4
Prussia(n)[7] 4.5
psalm[5b] 5.6
psychological[12] 9.3
psychology[10] 8.5
pt.[6]
  quart 4.7
public[1b]
  adj. 1.
  n. 1.4
  – trustee 7.6
publication[5b] 4.6
  – of the general staff 5.1
publicity[8] 7.8
publish[3a] 2.8
publisher[6] 5.8
pudding[3b] 6.
puff[3a] 5.8
pull[1b]
  vb. 1.
  – down 2.8
pulpit[6] 6.8
pulsate[6]
  beat 1.3
pulse[4a] 6.
pump[3a] 5.3
pumpkin[4b] 6.1
punch (P)[5b]
  strike 1.1
punctual[6]
  prompt 2.5
punish[2b] 2.1
punishment[3a] 2.6
pupil[2a] 1.7
  (eye) 5.3
puppy[5b]
  dog 1.9
purchase[2a]
  buy 1.4
  n. 3.2
pure[1b] 1.
  (blooded, etc.) 1.5
purge[5b]
  clean 2.2
purify[5b] 4.4
purity[5a] 4.7
purple[2b] 4.9
purpose[1b] 1.
purse[2b] 3.8
pursue[2b] 1.5
pursuit[4b] 3.4
push[2a]
  vb. 2.3
  drive 3.1
puss[6]
  cat 4.1
pussy[3b]
  cat 4.1

Section
put[1a]
  place 1.
  – out (extinguish) 1.9
  – down (suppress) 2.2
  – off (postpone) 2.6
  – on (e.g., hat) 2.6
  – on hat
    hat 2.8
  – over 3.
  – on shoes
    shoes 3.5
  – to sleep 4.
puzzle[4b]
  perplex 3.6
pyramid[6] 5.7

Q

qt.[5a]
  quart 4.7
quack[5a]
  vb. (duck) 6.1
quail[6]
  (lose) courage 2.
quaint[5a] 3.5
quake[5b]
  tremble 1.8
qualify[8] 7.2
quality[2a] 2.7
quantity[2a]
  amount 1.
quarrel[2b] *n.* 2.5
quarry[5a]
  prey 3.4
quart[3b] 4.7
quarter[1b]
  (of town) 2.5
  (fractional) 2.6
queen[1b] 1.6
queer[3b]
  strange 1.
  (person) 3.3
quell[6] 6.5
  subdue 4.3
quench[3b] 5.4
quest[5b]
  search 4.4
question[1b]
  matter 1.
  (be a – of) 1.
  n. (something asked) 1.1
  vb. 2.9
  -ing (formal) 3.7
quick[1a]
  fast 1.
quicken[4a]
  tr. vb. hurry 2.5
quiet[1b]
  adj. 1.
  n. 1.
  (keep –) 1.5
  vb. 1.6
quilt[5a] 6.8
quit[2b] 4.6
  vb. leave 1.
quite[1b]
  all (*adv.*) 1.
  pretty (moderately) 1.
quiver[4b]
  tremble 1.8
quote[4b] 4.
quoth[5b]
  say 1.

R

rabbi[13] 8.4
rabbit[2b] 4.8

Section
race[1b]
  n. (speed) 1.2
  (ethnic) 3.2
rack[3a]
  extend 1.
radiance[8] 4.9
radiant[5a]
  beaming 2.4
radiator[6] 7.2
radical[6] 5.
rafter[6]
  beam 2.3
rag[3a] 5.3
rage[3a]
  fury 2.8
  vb. (war, disease, etc.) 3.2
  (rave) 3.7
ragged[4b] 6.
rail[2b] 5.3
railroad[2a] 2.
railway[3b]
  railroad 2.
rain[1a]
  n. 2.
  vb. 4.2
rainbow[3b] 5.8
rainfall[6]
  rain 2.
rainy[4a] 5.7
raise[1a]
  lift 1.
raisin[5b] 6.4
rake[4b] *n.* 6.2
rally[7] *vb.* 4.7
ram[4a]
  sheep 3.
rampart[8] 6.4
ran[1b]
  run 1.
ranch[6] 6.9
random[5a]
  chance 1.4
rang[4a]
  ring 1.4
range[2a] 3.6
rank[2a]
  row 1.2
  n. 2.6
ransom[5b] 6.8
rap[5a]
  knock (on door) 2.
rapid[1b]
  fast 1.
rapt[6] 4.3
rapture[4b]
  bliss 3.
rare[2b] 1.
  -ly
    seldom 1.
rascal[5a]
  (little –) 4.
  knave 4.
rash[4b] 4.
rat[2b] 5.
rate[2a]
  vb. 2.
  (of speed) 3.
  -s
    fare 3.
  – of interest 3.
  tax – 4.
rather[1b] 1.
  pretty 1.
  (prefer) 1.
ration[6] 6.

	Section
require[1b]	
need	1.
-d	3.1
requirement[6]	
demand	3.
requisite[6]	
demand	3.
rescue[3b]	
save	1.
resemble[4a]	
(look) like	1.
reserve[3a]	
vb.	2.7
n. (character)	3.2
reside[4a]	
live	1.1
residence[3b]	
dwelling	2.3
(general and special)	4.1
(place of –)	4.3
resident[5b]	
inhabitant	3.2
resign[3b] (oneself)	2.2
resignation[7]	
submission	6.4
(act)	7.3
resist[2b]	2.8
oppose	2.3
resistance[6]	5.4
resolute[4b]	4.
resolution[4b]	3.2
resolve[3a]	
decide	1.
resort[3b]	5.3
resound[5a]	
ring	2.9
resource[5b]	3.6
respect[2a]	
n.	1.9
vb.	2.
respectable[6]	
decent	4.
respectful[5b]	3.9
respective[4b]	3.7
respite[7]	4.5
respond[5a]	
answer	1.
response[5b]	
answer	1.2
responsibility[7]	5.1
(joint –)	7.1
responsible[5b]	4.3
rest[1a]	
vb.	1.
n. (remainder)	1.1
n. (repose)	1.2
– on (be based on)	1.9
restaurant[4b]	4.7
restless[3b]	2.7
restoration[7]	6.5
restore[2b]	2.7
(to youth)	4.4
restrain[3b]	
check	3.2
restraint[4b]	4.1
result[2a]	
n.	1.5
vb.	1.5
resume[4a]	
begin again	1.
retail[6]	6.3
retain[3b]	
keep back	1.7
retire[2b]	3.
retort[8] (chemical)	7.2

	Section
retreat[3b]	
go back	2.1
n.	2.6
return[1b]	
(in –)	1.1
n.	1.4
go back	1.4
come back	1.8
give back	1.9
(send back)	1.9
reveal[3a]	2.4
revel[5a]	
– in	
enjoy	1.1
drunken –	5.8
revelation[6]	5.5
revenge[3a]	2.8
revenue[5b]	
income	3.6
reverence[3b]	
vb.	2.7
n.	4.1
reverend[4b]	4.9
reverse[4b]	
(wrong) side	1.7
review[2b]	
n.	2.6
look over	3.1
revision[10]	6.8
revival[9]	8.1
revive[4b]	5.2
revolt[4b]	4.4
rebel	3.6
revolution[4a]	3.2
turn	3.
revolutionary[6]	5.
revolve[5a]	5.5
turn	1.
reward[3a]	
n.	2.5
vb.	3.8
rhetoric[7]	7.2
rheumatism[7]	7.2
rhyme[3b]	6.
rhythm[9]	7.9
rib[3a]	5.
ribbon[2b]	3.1
rice[3a]	4.7
rich[1a]	1.
riches[4a]	
wealth	1.5
rid[3a]	
(get – of)	2.9
tr. vb. free	2.2
riddle[4a]	4.6
ride[1a]	
drive	1.
(horse)	1.5
rider[4a]	
horseman	2.8
ridge[3a]	
hill	2.6
ridiculous[5b]	3.6
riding-school	13.
rifle[5b]	
gun	1.7
rig[6]	
fit up	1.8
right[1a]	
all –	1.
(correct)	1.
– hand	1.
(be –)	1.
– off	
(at) once	1.
guess –	1.4
n. (title)	1.8

	Section
righteous[5a]	
upright	3.8
righteousness[6]	6.9
rigor[5b]	4.2
rill[4b]	
brook	2.1
rim[5b]	
edge	1.5
ring[1b]	
circle	1.2
vb. (sound)	1.4
-ing (*adj.*) (sonorous)	1.7
n. (hoop)	2.
vb. (echo)	2.9
-ing (*n.*)	4.9
riot[4b]	4.6
rip[3b]	
tear	1.8
ripe[2b]	2.9
(get –)	3.4
ripen[4a]	
ripe	3.4
ripple[5a]	
n. wave	2.9
vb.	5.
rise[1b]	
rising (*adj.*)	1.3
(give – to)	2.3
– early	
get up	3.
risk[3b]	
vb. (take) chances	1.4
danger	1.5
run –	
chance	2.
n.	3.4
rite[5b]	
ceremony	3.5
rival[3b] *n.*	5.
rivalry[8]	7.8
river[1a]	1.5
road[1a]	1.
roam[3b]	
wander	2.7
roar[2a]	
vb.	4.7
n.	5.3
roast[2b]	
vb. cook	2.5
n.	5.4
rob[2b]	
vb.	2.3
robber[3a]	3.7
robbery[5b]	4.8
robe[3a]	
dress	1.4
(e.g., hermit's)	3.3
(priest's –)	3.9
robin[2b]	5.6
rock[1a]	
n.	1.7
vb. roll	2.2
vb.	2.9
-ing	4.
rocky[4a]	5.9
rod[2a]	
stick	2.
rode[2b]	
drive	1.
ride (horse)	1.5
roe[6]	
egg	2.
rogue[5a]	
knave	4.5
roguish[15]	10.2

	Section
roll[1a]	
vb. (rock)	2.2
tr. vb.	2.3
n.	2.6
(of carriage, thunder, etc.)	4.3
roller[5a]	
wave	2.9
Roman[2a]	1.8
romance (R)[6]	6.4
romantic[5b]	4.3
romanticism[18]	10.4
roof[1b]	2.
room[1a]	
(in a house)	1.
(space)	1.
living –, drawing –	2.3
dining –	4.9
rooster[5b]	
cock	3.8
root[2a]	2.6
(have -s in)	4.2
rope[2b]	3.3
rose (R)[1b]	
n.	1.5
– bush	5.2
rosy[4a]	
pink	4.6
rot[5b]	
spoil	2.6
rotten[5a]	
spoil	2.6
rough[2a]	
(to touch)	3.
rude	4.3
round[1a]	
intr. vb. turn –	1.4
adj.	1.6
go –	1.8
(make -s) (military)	4.2
(make a –) (the rounds)	4.3
– off (e.g., edge)	4.9
rouse[4a]	
stir	1.9
rout[6]	
flight	2.5
defeat	3.6
route[3a]	
road	1.
routine[8]	7.7
rove[4a]	
wander	2.7
rover[5a]	
tramp	4.9
row[1b]	
n.	1.2
vb.	5.
royal[2a]	1.5
royalist[14]	10.
rub[2b]	3.2
– out	4.4
rubber[3a]	5.
ruby[5b]	
red	1.
ruddy[6]	
red	1.
(healthy complexion)	5.3
rude[2b]	
(unpolished) (person)	4.3
(impolite)	5.2
rue[6]	
(be) sorry	1.8
ruffian[6]	7.
ruffle[5a]	
trouble	1.5
n.	6.1
(hair)	5.8

	Section
selfishness[8]	6.3
selfsame[5a]	
same	1.
sell[1b]	1.4
semicircle[12]	8.8
senate[3a]	3.4
senator[4b]	5.2
send[1a]	1.
– back	
return	1.9
-ing (*n.*)	2.6
– forth	3.4
senior[6]	4.8
old	1.
sense[2a]	1.4
sensible[4b]	
– of	
conscious (of)	3.3
reasonable	3.4
sensitive[6]	4.4
sensual[8]	5.6
sent[1a]	
send	1.
sentence[2b]	
(phrase)	1.4
vb.	2.3
n. (court)	2.
sentiment[5b]	
feeling	1.
sentimental[7]	6.6
separate[1b]	
vb.	1.
adj.	1.
take away	1.
separation[4b]	3.4
September[2a]	2.1
serene[5a]	6.
quiet	1.
sergeant[7]	6.4
series[4b]	2.5
serious[2b]	
grave	1.4
sermon[4b]	3.7
serpent[4a]	
snake	3.8
servant[2a]	1.5
(man)	1.9
serve[1a]	1.
service[1b]	1.
(divine –)	2.3
servile[6]	7.
session[5b]	5.3
set[1a]	
vb. place	1.
circle (of people)	1.1
– table	1.1
– on fire	2.7
setting[17]	
n.	8.9
adj.	9.6
settle[1b]	
(establish)	1.
(a dispute)	1.8
– down	3.1
– up	
pay	4.9
settlement[3a]	2.7
settler[4a]	
colonist	6.1
set-up *n.*	10.6
seven[1b]	1.4
seventeen[4b]	6.
seventh[3a]	4.5
seventy[2a]	5.1
sever[5b]	
separate	1.
several[1a]	1.
– times	1.2
severe[2b]	1.6
severity[6]	4.7
rigor	4.2
sew[2a]	4.7
sex[4b]	3.3
sexton[9]	8.1
shade[1b]	
n.	1.4
n. (shadow)	1.8
n. (hue)	2.9
vb.	4.9
shadow[2a]	
shade	1.8
shadowy[6]	
shady	6.1
shady[4b]	6.1
shaft[4a]	
arrow	3.2
shake[1b]	
(hands)	1.1
tr. vb.	1.9
(e.g., head)	2.2
shall[1a]	1.
shallow[3b]	4.5
shalt[3a]	
shall	1.
shame[2a]	
n.	3.3
vb.	3.4
shameful[5b]	4.7
shape[1b]	
figure	1.
shapeless[6]	6.2
share[2a]	
n.	2.
– holder	4.8
sharp[2a]	
(shrewd)	1.7
(taste)	4.
sharpen[4a]	4.7
shatter[4b]	4.2
shave[4b]	5.6
shawl[7]	7.4
she[1a]	1.
sheaf[6]	6.6
shear[4a]	
cut	1.8
sheath[5b]	4.4
shed[2a]	
(hut)	3.2
vb. (e.g., tree)	3.3
sheep[1b]	3.
sheepish[17]	11.4
sheet[2a]	
(of paper)	2.2
(bed)	4.9
shelf[4b]	4.5
shell[2a]	
n.	3.7
(explosive)	3.4
shelter[2a]	
n.	1.7
vb.	2.6
shepherd[2b]	3.7
sheriff[6]	
policeman	5.8
shield[3a]	3.5
shift[3b]	
move	1.1
(of workmen)	3.5
(change of place)	5.7
shine[1b]	1.6
ship[1a]	
n.	1.3
shipping	3.
shipment[4b]	3.9
shipwreck[6]	
n. and *vb.*	6.9
-ed man	6.9
shirt[2b]	3.8
shirt-front	13.
shiver[3b]	
tremble	1.8
n.	4.7
shock[2b]	
(sensibilities)	3.2
n.	3.5
shoe[1b]	
n.	3.2
(put on -s)	3.5
(take off -s)	4.1
shoemaker[4a]	6.2
shone[3a]	
shine	1.6
shook[2b]	
shake	1.9
shoot[2a]	1.8
-ing (*n.*)	3.4
n.	5.4
shop[1b]	
n.	2.5
book -	4.2
butcher –	5.8
shore[1b]	
coast	1.4
short[1a]	1.
(in –)	1.
shorten[5b]	4.8
shorthand[17]	9.2
(in –)	9.6
shot[2a]	
shoot	1.8
should[1a]	1.
shoulder[1b] *n.*	1.5
shout[1b]	
cry	1.
shove[5a]	
vb. push	2.3
shovel[4b]	
spade	5.8
show[1a]	
tr. vb.	1.
– through	3.4
shower[2b]	
n.	2.5
shrewd[5a]	
sharp	1.7
shriek[3b]	
cry	1.
shrill[4a]	4.7
shrine[4b]	
altar	3.5
shrink[5a]	5.2
shroud[5b]	6.6
shrub[4a]	6.1
shudder[6]	
tremble	1.8
n. shiver	4.7
thrill	5.6
shun[3b]	
avoid	1.8
shut[1b]	
close	1.
– out	1.6
– in (enclose)	1.9
shutter[6]	
blind	3.1
shy[4b]	4.2
sick[1b]	
ill	1.5
sicken[6]	
disgust	6.
sickle[6]	6.9
sickly[6]	
weak	1.1
sickness[3a]	
disease	1.6
(sea –)	4.9
side[1a]	
n.	1.
on the other –	
hand	1.4
(wrong –)	1.7
– by –	2.2
(on her –)	2.2
(on his –)	2.2
(on their –)	2.2
on my –	
part	2.6
adj.	4.1
under –	4.4
– dish	
dish	4.6
sidewalk[4a]	5.5
siege[5b]	4.8
sieve[6]	7.2
sift[4b]	
strain	4.9
sigh[2a]	
n.	2.8
vb.	2.6
sight[1a]	
n. (view)	1.
(catch – of)	1.1
sign[1b]	
n.	1.1
vb.	2.4
(over shop)	3.4
signal[4a] *n.*	4.5
signature[5b]	4.1
significant[7]	
(full of) meaning	3.3
signify[5b]	
mean	1.
silence[2a]	
vb. quiet	1.6
vb.	1.9
n.	2.2
silent[2a]	1.5
silk[1b]	
n.	2.9
adj.	3.3
silken[6]	
silk	3.3
silly[4a]	
foolish	2.8
silver[1a]	
n.	1.4
silvery[6]	5.6
similar[3b]	4.4
simple[1b]	
(plain)	1.
simply (merely)	1.
(make –)	2.1
(ingenuous)	2.2
simplicity[4b]	5.4
sin[2b]	
n.	2.2
vb.	2.4
since[1a]	
as	1.
(time)	1.
sincere[3a]	2.5
sincerity[5b]	5.9

Section

span[5a]
extend 1.
range 3.6
spangle[5a] 6.8
Spaniard[4b]
French 1.
Spanish[2a]
French 1.
spank[5a]
strike 1.1
spare[2a]
(in reserve) 3.
vb. 3.4
spark[3b] 4.4
sparkle[3a]
shine 1.6
glitter 3.6
sparrow[3a] 6.
speak[1a] 1.
speaker[3b] 3.1
spear[3a] 3.2
special[2a] 1.8
specially[6]
above all 1.
specialty[11] 8.8
specific[6] 5.8
specify[11] 8.9
specimen[6]
example 1.4
speck[6]
spot 2.2
speckle[5b]
spot 2.2
spectacle[4a]
(great sight) 5.6
-s
glasses 4.2
spectator[6]
audience 3.
speculation[7] 5.3
sped[5a]
hurry 1.2
speech[2a]
talk 1.2
language 1.6
(make a –) 1.6
speed[2a]
intr. vb. hurry 1.2
n. hurry 2.4
n. 2.5
speedy[4b]
fast 1.
spell[2b] 4.4
-ing (*n.*) 5.3
spend[1b] 1.6
– time 2.2
– night
night 2.7
spent[2a]
spend 1.6
adj. (exhausted) 2.
sphere[3b] 4.4
globe 3.3
spice[3b] 6.
spider[4a] 6.
spill[5b]
tip 3.5
spin[3a] 3.9
spindle[5b] 6.6
spine[7] 7.
spiral[8] *n.* 7.6
spire[4b]
steeple 5.8
spirit[1b] 1.
spiritual[4b] 3.3
spit[4b] *vb.* 5.9

Section

spite[2a]
(in – of) 1.4
n. 3.
splash[5b] 6.6
spleen[6]
anger 1.9
splendid[2a] 2.6
splendor[3b]
(brilliance) 2.8
(magnificence) 3.6
split[3b]
vb. crack 2.6
spoil[2a] 2.6
-s (booty) 3.5
(a child) 4.6
spoke[1b]
speak 1.
spoken[4a]
speak 1.
sponge[5a] *n.* 6.6
spontaneity[14] 10.2
spontaneous[7] 6.
spoon[2b] 4.8
spoonful 12.9
sport[2a]
n. 5.1
adj. 5.3
spot[1b]
n. 2.2
vb. 4.4
spouse[5a]
husband 1.
wife 1.
spout[6]
gush 4.5
sprang[3a]
spring 1.5
spray[3b]
sprinkle 3.7
spread[1b]
vb. (expand) 1.4
n. (diffusion) 4.1
vb. (butter) 4.5
sprightly[6]
active 2.5
spring[1a]
vb. 1.5
n. (water) 1.7
n. (of machine) 1.8
n. (season) 2.1
n. (jump) 2.6
adj. 4.9
springtime[6]
spring 2.1
sprinkle[3b] 3.7
sprite[6]
elf 6.
sprout[6]
n. shoot 5.4
vb. 6.2
sprung[4a]
– from
born 1.4
spring 1.5
spun[5a]
spin 3.9
spur[4a]
(impulse) 3.6
(on boot) 5.8
spurn[5b]
reject 3.2
spy[2b]
vb. 5.1
n. 5.4
sq.[6]
adj. square 3.4
square (geometrical) 4.4
squadron[6] 4.9

Section

square[1b]
n. (in town) 1.
adj. 3.4
(geometrical) 4.4
squeak[5a]
vb. grate 5.7
squeeze[5a]
press 1.1
(e.g., water out of something) 3.6
squire[4a] 6.
squirrel[3a] 6.
St.[3a]
street 1.
stab[5a] 6.5
stability[7]
firmness 5.4
stable[2b]
firm 1.1
adj. 2.9
n. 3.8
stack[6]
mass 1.6
heap up 3.2
staff[3b]
(military) 3.1
(of people) 3.4
(university) 4.2
publication of the general – 5.1
(editorial –) 5.3
stag[6]
deer 5.8
stage[3a]
(theatre) 3.
(e.g., in a journey) 3.6
stagger[4a]
reel 3.1
stain[3a]
n. spot 2.2
(with blood) 5.6
stair[2a]
-s 2.5
stake[3b]
stick 2.
stale[4b] (e.g., bread) 2.9
stalk[4a]
walk 1.
stem 2.7
stall[3b] 5.2
stammer[5b] 6.
stamp[2a]
n. 3.1
vb. 3.9
stand[1a]
bear 1.
intr. vb. 1.
– out 1.9
standard[2b]
n. (norm) 2.2
flag 2.6
adj. 3.
(gold –) 3.1
star[1b] 1.5
stare[3b]
peer 3.5
start[1a]
begin 1.
n. (of surprise) 1.7
– on a journey 1.8
– towards 4.3
starter[17]
self – 10.8
startle[4b]
alarm 3.5
starve[3a] 5.3
state[1a]
n. (condition) 1.

Section

state[1a]—*continued*
n. (nation) 1.
vb. (declare) 1.
adj. 1.8
vb. (pronounce) 2.2
– of health
health 3.1
secretary of – 3.9
stately[4b] 3.6
statement[3b] 2.1
statesman[3b] 3.
station[1b] (railroad) 2.4
statistics[8] 6.1
statue[3a] 3.6
stature[5a] 2.9
statute[5b] 4.1
law 1.
stave[6] 7.2
stay[1a]
remain 1.
n. (sojourn) 1.7
– awake
sit up 1.8
– away 3.4
stead[5a]
place (*n.*) 1.
steadfast[5b]
firm 1.1
steady[3a]
firm (fixed) 1.1
firm (character) 1.1
steak[5b] 6.8
steal[2a]
rob 2.3
steam[2a] *n.* 2.5
steamboat[6]
steamer 3.7
steamer[3b] 3.7
steamship[6]
steamer 3.7
steed[4b]
horse 1.
steel[2a] 3.1
steep[2b] *adj.* 2.8
steeple[4b] 5.8
steer[3b] 3.9
stem[3a] *n.* 2.7
step[1a]
n. (stride) 1.
vb. 1.1
(of stair) 1.7
(footprint) 2.
stepmother[8] 7.8
stern[3a]
severe 1.6
stick[1b]
n. 2.
intr. vb. 2.1
tr. vb. 2.2
stiff[2b] 3.2
make – 4.9
stiffness[12] 9.3
stifle[6]
choke 3.7
still[1a]
however 1.
adj. quiet 1.
(time) 1.
(stand –) 1.3
stillness[5a]
quiet 1.
stimulus[7] 5.
sting[3a] 3.5
stir[2a]
vb. 1.9
vb. (a mixture) 2.1
stirrup[6] 7.

Section

swamp[4a] . . . 4.
swan[3b] . . . 5.8
swarm[3b]
  drove . . . 3.9
  vb. . . . 5.
sway[3a]
  rule . . . 2.
  swing . . . 3.
  influence . . . 3.2
  (the body) . . . 5.6
swear[3b] *vb.* (take oath) . . . 2.7
sweat[4a]
  n. . . . 4.7
  vb. . . . 5.8
sweater[6] . . . 7.2
Swedish[8] . . . 6.8
sweep[2b] . . . 1.9
sweet[1a] *adj.* . . . 1.4
sweetheart[6]
  darling . . . 2.2
sweetness[4b] . . . 5.2
swell[2b] . . . 3.9
swept[3b]
  sweep . . . 1.9
swift[2a]
  fast . . . 1.
swim[2a] . . . 3.6
swine[5a]
  pig . . . 3.9
swing[2b]
  vb. . . . 3.
  n. . . . 4.8
Swiss[5a] . . . 6.4
switch[5b] . . . 5.9
swollen[6]
  swell . . . 3.9
sword[2a] . . . 2.
swore[5b]
  swear . . . 2.7
sworn[4a]
  swear . . . 2.7
syllable[5a] . . . 4.9
symbol[4b] . . . 5.6
sympathy[3b] . . . 2.8
symptom[8] . . . 7.7
syndicate[12] . . . 9.3
synthetic[10] . . . 8.6
syrup[6] . . . 5.3
system[2a] . . . 1.6
  school – . . . 4.2
systematic[9] . . . 6.9

T

tabernacle[6]
  temple . . . 2.1
table[1a] . . . 1.
  set – . . . 1.1
table-cloth[12] . . . 9.1
tablet[4b] . . . 6.2
tack[6]
  nail . . . 3.
tactical . . . 11.7
tag[6]
  label . . . 5.2
tail[1b] (animal) . . . 4.1
tailor[2b] . . . 3.5
taint[5b]
  spoil . . . 2.6
take[1a] . . . 1.
  – care of
    care . . . 1.
  – away (remove) . . . 1.
  – away (separate) . . . 1.

Section

take[1a]—*continued*
  – place
    place . . . 1.
  – care
    look out . . . 1.4
  – care!
    look out! . . . 1.4
  – leave
    leave . . . 1.5
  – up (a subject) . . . 1.7
  – off (coat, etc.) . . . 1.8
  – back . . . 1.9
  – away (withdraw) . . . 2.6
  – down
    down . . . 2.8
  – off clothes . . . 3.3
  – off shoes
    shoes . . . 4.1
  – refuge
    refuge . . . 3.9
  – out . . . 4.1
tale[2a]
  story . . . 1.
  fairy – . . . 3.4
talent[3b] . . . 2.4
talk[1a]
  vb. . . . 1.
  n. (conversation) . . . 1.
  n. (lecture) . . . 1.2
talkative[14] . . . 10.
tall[1b] . . . 1.
tame[3a] . . . 5.6
tan[5a]
  brown . . . 2.5
tangle[7] . . . 5.6
tank[4b] . . . 6.1
tap[3a] . . . 4.6
tape[6]
  ribbon . . . 3.1
taper[4b]
  candle . . . 2.2
tapestry[6] . . . 5.8
tar[4b] . . . 6.4
tardy[4b]
  late . . . 1.
tarry[5a]
  delay . . . 2.
  linger . . . 3.6
tart[6]
  sharp . . . 4.
task[2b]
  work . . . 1.1
tassel[6] . . . 7.
taste[1b]
  n. . . . 1.4
  tr. vb. . . . 1.5
  (have a – for) . . . 2.4
tatter[6]
  rag . . . 5.3
taught[2a]
  teach . . . 1.
tavern[4b] . . . 4.1
tax[2a]
  n. . . . 1.6
  vb. . . . 3.5
  – rate . . . 4.
tea[2a] . . . 4.1
teach[1b] . . . 1.
teacher[1b] . . . 1.
team[2b] . . . 3.9
tear[1b]
  n. (from eyes) . . . 1.
  vb. . . . 1.8
tease[5b] . . . 5.9
teaspoon[6]
  spoon . . . 4.8
technical[6] . . . 4.7
technique[9] . . . 6.6

Section

tedious[5a] . . . 5.2
teeth[2b]
  tooth . . . 2.3
telegram[4b]
  wire . . . 3.5
telegraph[4a]
  n. . . . 4.9
  adj. . . . 5.3
telephone[3a] . . . 5.3
telescope[7] . . . 5.4
tell[1a] . . . 1.
  – in advance . . . 4.9
teller[6]
  fortune – . . . 7.
temper[3a]
  n. . . . 4.2
  vb. (steel) . . . 4.9
temperance[5a] . . . 6.4
temperate[3b]
  sober . . . 3.8
temperature[3b] . . . 3.
tempest[4a]
  storm . . . 1.6
tempestuous[6]
  stormy . . . 4.
temple[2b] . . . 2.1
  (head) . . . 4.8
temporary[4b] . . . 3.2
tempt[3a] . . . 4.
temptation[4b] . . . 4.4
ten[1a] . . . 1.4
tenacious[12] . . . 8.
tenant[5a]
  inhabitant . . . 3.2
  n. . . . 6.5
tend[3a] (incline) . . . 2.4
tendency[5b] . . . 3.2
  leaning . . . 1.8
  have –
    tend . . . 2.4
tender[2a]
  adj. . . . 2.3
  (legal –) . . . 4.8
tenderness[5b] . . . 4.4
tennis[6] . . . 6.8
tenor[6]
  course . . . 1.1
tent[2a] . . . 3.4
tenth[3a] . . . 4.1
term[2a]
  (period) . . . 1.8
  (end of period) . . . 2.2
terrace[6] . . . 6.7
terrible[2a] . . . 1.8
terrify[6]
  frighten . . . 1.9
territory[3a] . . . 2.1
terror[2b]
  fear . . . 1.4
test[2b] . . . 1.9
testament (T)[7]
  will . . . 3.1
testify[5b] . . . 4.1
  state . . . 1.
testimony[4b] . . . 3.1
Teutonic[10] . . . 6.7
text[3b] . . . 3.1
than[1a] . . . 1.
thank[1a]
  vb. . . . 1.
  -s . . . 1.1
thankful[4a]
  grateful . . . 2.5

Section

that[1a]
  adj. . . . 1.
  pron. . . . 1.
  conj. . . . 1.
  conj. (in) order . . . 1.
  provided – . . . 2.9
thatch[7] . . . 6.
thaw[5b]
  melt . . . 2.5
the[1a] . . . 1.
  – (more, etc.) . . . –
    (more, etc.) . . . 1.
theatre(er)[2b]
  n. . . . 1.9
  adj. . . . 4.6
thee[1b]
  thou . . . 1.
their[1a] . . . 1.
  on – side
    side . . . 2.2
theirs[4b]* . . . 3.6
them[1a]
  they . . . 1.
theme[4b]
  (paper) . . . 3.2
  (topic) . . . 4.
themselves[1b]
  self . . . 1.
  (intensive) . . . 1.4
then[1a]
  (time) . . . 1.
  conj. therefore . . . 1.
  now and –
    (at) times . . . 1.
  – (e.g., the – reign-
    ing . . . .) . . . 1.4
  now . . . – . . . 1.5
  so – . . . 1.5
  now and – . . . 2.2
thence[3a]
  there . . . 1.
theological[8] . . . 7.2
theoretical[9] . . . 5.9
theory[5b] . . . 3.3
there[1a]
  (place) . . . 1.
  there is . . . 1.
  there *is* . . . 1.
  across . . . 1.
thereby[4a]
  through . . . 1.
therefor[6]
  for . . . 1.
therefore[1b] . . . 1.
therein[6]
  in . . . 1.
thereof[3b]
  of . . . 1.
thereon[4b]
  on . . . 1.
there's[5a]
  there *is* . . . 1.
thereupon[4a]
  upon which . . . 1.6
thermometer[5b] . . . 6.6
these[1a]
  adj. this . . . 1.
  pron. this . . . 1.
thesis[11] . . . 6.1
they[1a]
  pers. pron. . . . 1.
  indef. pron. one . . . 1.
they'll[6]
  shall . . . 1.
thick[1b] . . . 1.2
thicket[4b] . . . 6.
thickness[4b] . . . 5.1

Section

- transportation[4b]
  - transport 3.2
- trap[2b] *n.* 5.1
- travel[1b] *vb.* 1.8
- traveler(ll)[2a] 2.4
- traverse[5b]
  - cross 1.
- tray[6] 6.6
- treacherous[5a] 6.
- treachery[6]
  - treason 4.3
- tread[2b]
  - step 1.1
- treason[4b] 4.3
- treasure[2a] 2.
- treasurer[6] 7.2
- treasury[4b] 5.6
- treat[2a]
  - *vb.* (handle) 1.4
  - (give a treat to) 4.9
- treatment[3b] 2.8
- treaty[4b] 2.6
- treble[7] 6.8
- tree[1a] 1.
  - apple – 5.
  - orange – 5.
  - palm – 5.5
  - olive – 5.7
  - plane – 6.
- trellis[12] 9.4
- tremble[2b] 1.8
  - trembling (*n.*) 4.
- tremendous[5a]
  - great 1.
- trench[5a]
  - ditch 3.9
- trespass[6]
  - crime 2.4
- trial[2b]
  - attempt 1.8
  - (law) 2.
- triangle[6] 7.
- tribe[2a] 2.5
- tributary[4a] 6.3
- tribute[4a]
  - tax 1.6
  - (pay – to) 3.2
- trick[2b] *n.* 3.2
- tried[2a]
  - try 1.
- trifle[3b] 3.9
- trim[2a]
  - *vb.* 2.4
  - trimming (*n.*) 3.8
- trinket[9] 8.2
- trip[1b]
  - journey 1.
- triple[7] 5.8
- triumph[3b]
  - *n.* 3.1
  - *vb.* 4.2
- triumphant[5b] 4.6
- trivial[6] 5.
  - petty 4.5
- trod[4a]
  - step 1.1
- troll[6]
  - *vb.* fish 2.5
- trolley[5b]
  - car 2.1
- troop[2b] 1.6
- trophy[5b] 6.8
- tropic[6] 6.9
- trot[3b]
  - *n.* 4.6
  - *vb.* 5.5
- trouble[1b]
  - *n.* 1.
  - *vb.* (bother) 1.5
- troublesome[5b] 4.4
  - vexing 3.8
- trough[6] 6.8
- trousers[4a] 5.6
- trout[5a] 6.8
- truck[5a] 6.6
- true[1a] 1.
- truly[5b]*
  - really 1.4
- trumpet[3a]
  - horn 3.6
- trumpeter[11] 8.4
- trunk[2a]
  - (of tree) 2.3
  - (to pack) 5.
- trust[1b]
  - *n.* 1.
  - *vb.* 1.4
- trustee[8]
  - public – 7.6
- trusty[5b]
  - faithful 2.7
- truth[1b] 1.
- try[1a] 1.
  - – hard 1.5
- tub[4a] 6.2
- tube[4a]
  - pipe 3.2
- tuck[4b]
  - (sewing) 4.1
  - – up
    - turn 4.9
- Tuesday[2b] 3.7
- tuft[6] 6.8
  - -ed 6.4
- tug[4b]
  - pull 1.
- tumble[3a]
  - *vb.* fall 1.
  - *n.* fall 1.2
- tumult[5a]
  - noise 2.6
- tune[3a]
  - air 3.
  - (put in – with) 3.4
- tunnel[5b] 6.4
- turf[5a] 5.8
- Turk[5b]
  - Turkish 5.
- turkey (T)[3a] 5.6
- Turkish[5a] 5.
- turn[1a]
  - *vb.* 1.
  - (in –) 1.
  - – to 1.1
  - – round (*intr. vb.*) 1.4
  - *n.* (revolution) 3.
  - – away 3.
  - – up 4.9
- turnip[5b] 6.7
- turret[6] 7.
- turtle[4b] 6.4
- tutor[5b]
  - teacher 1.
- twain[6]
  - two 1.
- 'twas[3b]
  - be 1.
- twelfth[4b] 6.3
- twelve[1b] 1.9
- twentieth[6] 7.1
- twenty[1b] 1.9
  - – five 4.2
  - – two 4.6
  - – four 4.7
  - – six 4.7
- 'twere[4b]
  - be 1.
- twice[2a]
  - two 1.8
- twig[3b]
  - branch 1.6
- twilight[3b] 4.3
- 'twill[4b]
  - shall 1.
- twin[3a] 5.8
- twine[4a]
  - *vb.* twist 4.
- twinkle[3b]
  - glitter 3.6
- twist[3b]
  - (wring) 2.6
  - *vb.* (twine) 4.
- twitter[6] *n.* 7.
- two[1a] 1.
  - – times 1.8
  - twenty – 4.6
- type[3a] *n.* 4.8
- typewriter[5b] 5.6
- tyranny[4b] 5.6
- tyrant[4a] 4.2

U

- ugliness[14] 10.2
- ugly[2b] 2.4
- umbrella[4b] 5.4
- unable[4b] 4.1
- unanimous[6] 5.
- unaware[5b] 6.
- unbound[6]
  - free 1.
- unbutton[19] 12.2
- uncertain[4b] 4.
  - doubtful 2.6
- uncertainty[8] 6.5
- unchangeable[11] 8.9
- uncle[1b] 1.9
- unclean[6]
  - dirty 4.2
- uncomfortable[5b] 4.6
- unconquered[10] 8.6
- unconscious[4b] 4.4
- uncover[5a]
  - open 1.
- undecided[12] 9.2
- undefinable 10.2
- under[1a]
  - *prep.* 1.
  - *adj.* 1.9
  - – side 4.4
- undergo[5b] 3.8
  - bear 1.
- underground[5a] 6.6
- underline[9] 8.
- underneath[3b]
  - *prep.* under 1.
  - *adv.* beneath 1.6
- understand[1b] 1.
  - -ing 1.7
- understood[3a]
  - understand 1.
- undertake[3b] 2.5
  - undertaking 2.4
- undisturbed[6]
  - quiet 1.
- undo[5a] 5.5
- undone[6]
  - (figurative) 3.5
  - undo 5.5
- undress[7]
  - take off clothes 3.3
- uneasiness[7] 5.
- uneasy[5a] 5.5
- unequal[5b] 3.9
- uneven[6]
  - unequal 3.9
- unexpected[4b] 3.5
- unfavorable[9] 6.
- unfinished[7] 6.9
- unfit[5a] 6.4
- unfold[4b] 3.4
- unforgettable[16] 10.9
- unfortunate[3b] 2.2
  - -ly 1.9
- ungrateful[5b] 4.9
- unhappy[2b] 1.8
- unhealthy[8] 6.9
- unheard[6]
  - – of 5.3
- uniform[3a]
  - *adj.* 3.1
  - *n.* 4.4
- union[2a]
  - (confederacy) 1.6
  - (bringing together) 3.5
- unit[6] 4.2
  - (military) 5.9
- unite[1b] 1.
  - -d 1.5
- unity[5b] 3.8
- universal[3a] 3.8
- universe[6] 5.4
- university[3a]
  - *n.* 3.3
  - *adj.* 4.2
- unjust[3b] 3.3
- unkind[5b] 6.1
- unknown[2b] 1.8
  - – to 2.2
- unless[2a] 1.4
- unlike[4b]
  - different 1.
- unload[7] 6.7
- unlock[6]
  - open 1.
- unmoved[7] 7.
- unnecessary[5b] 4.2
- unpleasant[5b] 3.8
- unpublished 12.8
- unquestionable[11] 6.5
- unreasonable[6] 7.2
- unruly[7] 7.4
- unseen[4a] 4.8
- unselfish[11] 8.6
- unsettle(d)[6]
  - trouble (*vb.*) 1.5
  - changing 4.6
- unspeakable[6] 6.7
- unsteady[8] 5.6
- until[1a]
  - till 1.
- untiring[9] 7.2
- unto[2b]
  - to 1.

Section

warfare[6]
war ... 1.
warlike[6]
martial ... 5.4
warm[1a]
adj. ... 1.7
vb. heat ... 2.2
warmth[4b]
heat ... 1.5
warn[2b] ... 2.2
-ing ... 3.4
warp[5b] ... 3.5
warrant[4a]
vb. justify ... 2.5
vb. pledge ... 2.7
warrior[3a] ... 3.5
was[1a]
be ... 1.
wash[1b]
vb. ... 2.6
n. ... 3.3
wasn't[5a]
be ... 1.
wasp[6] ... 7.2
wast[4b]
be ... 1.
waste[1b]
(desert) ... 2.4
vb. ... 4.2
(lay –) ... 4.9
watch[1a]
vb. ... 1.
n. (to tell time) ... 1.3
watchful[4b] ... 6.4
watchman[6]
guard ... 2.
water[1a]
n. ... 1.
vb. ... 2.4
adj. ... 5.
watercolor ... 13.
waterfall[5a] ... 6.2
waterproof[7] ... 6.8
watery[6] ... 7.2
wave[1b]
vb. ... 1.7
n. (surge) ... 2.9
n. (undulation) ... 3.8
waver[4a] ... 3.4
wax[3a] ... 3.6
way[1a]
(manner) ... 1.
in no –
(not at) all ... 1.
road ... 1.
(be in –) ... 1.7
– out ... 2.
(on the –) ... 2.2
we[1a] ... 1.
weak[1b] ... 1.1
(grow –) ... 2.4
weaken[5b] ... 4.8
weakness[3a] ... 2.9
wealth[2a]
(riches) ... 1.5
wealthy[3b]
rich ... 1.
weapon[3a]
arm ... 1.
wear[1b]
vb. ... 1.
– out ... 2.8
weariness[5b] ... 5.6
weary[2b]
adj. tired ... 1.9
vb. tire ... 2.4
weather[1b] ... 1.4

Section

weave[3a] ... 4.6
weaver[6] ... 7.2
web[3b] ... 3.4
wed[3b]
marry ... 2.3
wedding[4b] ... 3.4
wedge[5a] ... 6.1
Wednesday[2b] ... 4.3
wee[3a]
little ... 1.
weed[2b] *n.* ... 5.3
week[1a] ... 1.1
weekly[5b] ... 5.7
weep[2a]
cry ... 1.4
weigh[2a] ... 2.7
weight[1b] ... 1.5
welcome[2a] *adj.* ... 3.3
welfare[4a] ... 3.5
well[1a]
adv. ... 1.
(be –) (health) ... 1.
(as – as) ... 1.2
n. ... 1.9
–! ... 2.3
– informed
informed ... 3.
we'll[3b]
shall ... 1.
went[1a]
go ... 1.
wept[3b]
cry ... 1.4
were[1a]
be ... 1.
as it – ... 1.4
wert[4b]
be ... 1.
west[1b] ... 1.9
western[2a] ... 2.4
westward[4a]
west ... 1.9
wet[2a]
adj. ... 2.9
vb. ... 2.9
wet-nurse ... 12.9
whale[6] ... 7.1
what[1a]
rel. and *inter. pron.* ... 1.
– (?!) ... 2.4
whate'er[5a]
whatever ... 1.5
whatever[2a] ... 1.5
whatsoever[3b]
whatever ... 1.5
wheat[1b] ... 2.5
wheel[1b] *n.* ... 2.5
when[1a] ... 1.
whence[2b]
where ... 1.
whene'er[4b]
whenever ... 1.4
whenever[2b] ... 1.4
where[1a] ... 1.
whereat[5a]
upon which ... 1.6
whereby[4b]
by ... 1.
wherefore[4a]
why ... 1.
wherein[4a]
in ... 1.
whereof[6]
of ... 1.

Section

whereon[6]
on ... 1.
whereupon[7]
upon which ... 1.6
wherever[3a]
where ... 1.
whether[1b] ... 1.
which[1a]
rel. and *inter. pron.* ... 1.
upon – ... 1.6
while[1a]
conj. ... 1.
n. ... 1.8
whip[2b]
n. ... 4.8
vb. ... 4.8
– up
urge ... 4.8
whirl[3b] ... 4.
whirlwind[5a] ... 6.2
whisk[6]
move ... 1.1
whisper[2a] *vb.* ... 3.1
whistle[2a]
n. ... 3.9
vb. ... 4.6
white[1a]
adj. ... 1.
(become –, make –) ... 1.9
n. ... 3.7
whiten[7]
white ... 1.9
whither[3b]
where ... 1.
who[1a] *rel.* and *inter. pron.* 1.
whoever[3b] ... 2.2
whole[1a]
complete ... 1.
n. ... 1.5
wholesome[4a] ... 4.6
wholly[4b]
all ... 1.
whom[1b]
who ... 1.
whose[1b] ... 1.
why[1a] ... 1.
wicked[2b]
bad ... 1.2
wickedness[5a]
evil ... 2.
wide[1a]
broad ... 1.4
widow[3b] ... 3.
widower[16] ... 10.3
width[3a] ... 3.4
wield[6]
handle ... 3.9
wife[1b] ... 1.
wig[5a] ... 6.8
wigwam[4b] ... 6.4
wild[1b]
(savage) ... 1.6
(uncultivated) ... 1.7
wilderness[3a]
waste ... 2.4
wilful[6]
stubborn ... 4.1
will (W)[1a]
shall ... 1.
n. (e.g., free will) ... 1.
n. (testament) ... 3.1
willing[2b]
be –
want ... 1.
-ly ... 1.6
(be –) ... 2.9

Section

willow[3b] ... 5.6
wilt[4a]
shall ... 1.
fade ... 4.9
win[1b]
beat ... 1.
gain ... 1.
wind[1a]
n. ... 1.4
vb. ... 3.3
windmill[4b] ... 5.4
window[1a] ... 1.4
(church –) ... 2.4
ticket – ... 5.3
windy[6] ... 6.5
wine[2a] ... 1.4
wing[1b] ... 1.1
-s (in theatre) ... 4.9
wink[3b] *vb.* ... 5.8
winner[6] ... 6.5
winter[1a] ... 1.4
wintry[6] ... 6.5
wipe[2b] ... 4.7
wire[2b]
(telegram) ... 3.5
(metal) ... 4.2
wireless[6] ... 6.
wisdom[2a] ... 2.3
wise[1b] ... 1.5
wish[1a]
n. desire ... 1.
vb. desire ... 1.
wit[2a] ... 2.7
witch[3a] ... 5.2
with[1a] ... 1.
withal[5a]
addition ... 1.4
withdraw[3a]
take away ... 2.6
retire ... 3.
withdrew[5b]
take away ... 2.6
wither[3b]
fade ... 4.9
withhold[6]
keep back ... 1.7
within[1b] ... 1.1
without[1a] ... 1.
– doubt
doubt ... 1.
do – ... 2.1
withstand[5a]
resist ... 2.8
witness[2b] *n.* ... 2.4
witty[5b] ... 4.1
wives[3b]
wife ... 1.
wizard[5a] ... 6.2
woe[3a]
grief ... 1.8
woeful[6]
sad ... 1.4
woke[4a]
tr. vb. wake ... 1.9
intr. vb. wake ... 1.9
wolf[2a] ... 4.7
wolves[5b]
wolf ... 4.7
woman[1a] ... 1.
womb[6] ... 4.9
women[2a]
woman ... 1.
won[2a]
gain ... 1.

INDEX TO FRENCH WORDS IN THE LIST

After a French word or phrase the first English word not inclosed in parentheses and followed by a section number indicates the position of the entry in which the French word will be found.

A

Section

aller (s'en)[2a]
go away . . . 1.
allez![5a]
indeed . . . 1.
alliance[5b]
union . . . 1.6
allié (*n.*)[4a]
relation . . . 2.3
ally . . . 6.4
allier[4a]
s'–, join with . . . 1.9
allié, allied . . . 5.2
allonger[3b]
prolong . . . 3.6
allons![3b]
well, come now! . . . 2.3
allouer[6b]
grant . . . 1.
allumer[2a]
set (on) fire . . . 2.7
allumette[6a]
match . . . 5.2
allure[2b]
pace . . . 1.8
allusion[3a]
faire –, refer to . . . 3.1
hint . . . 4.1
alors[1a]
then . . . 1.
d'–, (the) then(. . . .) . . 1.4
alors que[3a]
when . . . 1.
alouette[6b]
lark . . . 5.8
altérer[4a]
change . . . 1.4
alternativement[5b]
alternately . . . 4.8
alterner
alternate . . . 5.4
amabilité[5b]
kindness . . . 2.7
amande
almond . . . 6.9
amant[3b]
lover . . . 2.
amas[5a]
mass . . . 1.6
amasser[7a]
gather (collect) . . . 1.5
heap up . . . 3.2
amateur[3a]
être – de
(have a) taste for 2.4
ambassade[6a]
embassy . . . 6.3
ambassadeur[3b]
ambassador . . . 3.9
ambitieux[4b]
ambitious . . . 5.8
ambition[2b]
ambition . . . 3.7
ambre[6b]
amber . . . 6.6
âme[1a]
nature (character) . . 1.
soul . . . 1.
améliorer[5a]
improve . . . 3.5
aménager[6a]
fit up . . . 1.8
amende[6b]
fine . . . 2.5
amendement
amendment . . . 4.5
amender
amend . . . 4.9

Section

amener[1b]
bring . . . 1.
lead . . . 1.
bring before . . . 2.2
amer[2a]
bitter . . . 2.
rendre –, (make) bitter 3.9
américain[2b]
French . . . 1.
amertume[3b]
bitterness . . . 5.7
ameublement[6b]
furniture . . . 4.4
ami[1a]
friend . . . 1.
amical[5a]
friendly . . . 3.5
amicalement[6a]
friendly . . . 3.5
amiral[4b]
admiral . . . 6.3
amitié[2a]
friendship . . . 2.3
amoindrir[7a]
decline . . . 3.3
reduce . . . 3.5
amortir[6a]
soften . . . 5.4
amour[1a]
love . . . 1.
darling . . . 2.2
amoureux[2b]
(in) love . . . 2.7
amour-propre[3b]
pride . . . 2.4
vanity . . . 3.3
conceit . . . 5.3
ample[5a]
ample . . . 3.6
spacious . . . 4.8
ampleur[5b]
plenty . . . 2.2
compass . . . 2.5
amplifier[5b]
increase . . . 1.1
develop . . . 2.
enlarge . . . 3.3
ampoule
blister . . . 7.2
amusant[3a]
amuse . . . 3.5
amusement[6a]
pastime . . . 4.8
amuser[2a]
entertain . . . 2.4
amuse . . . 3.5
amuser (s')[3a]
enjoy oneself . . . 1.7
(have) fun . . . 2.9
an[1a]
year . . . 1.
veille du jour de l'–
(New Year's) Eve 3.8
analogie[6b]
analogy . . . 7.6
analogue[4b]
similar . . . 4.4
analyse[4b]
analysis . . . 7.1
analyser[5a]
analyse . . . 6.5
anarchie[6a]
anarchy . . . 7.5
ancêtre[4a]
ancestor . . . 4.5
ancien[1a]
old . . . 1.
former . . . 2.
ancient . . . 2.6

Section

ancre
anchor . . . 5.2
âne[4a]
ass . . . 3.9
anéantir[4b]
destroy . . . 1.5
anecdote[4b]
anecdote . . . 6.6
ange[3a]
angel . . . 2.
anglais[1b]
French . . . 1.
angle[3a]
corner . . . 1.9
angle . . . 3.4
angoissant[6a]
(in) anguish . . . 6.3
angoisse[2a]
agony . . . 2.
animal[2b]
animal . . . 1.1
animal (*adj.*) . . . 2.7
animer[2b]
animé, (full of) life . . . 1.
animate . . . 3.5
anneau[4a]
circle . . . 1.2
ring . . . 2.
année[1a]
year . . . 1.
– précédente
preceding year . . . 4.9
annexe[6b]
annex . . . 6.6
annexer[6b]
annex . . . 7.4
anniversaire
birthday . . . 2.8
anniversary . . . 6.7
annonce[5b]
advertisement . . . 4.5
annoncer[1b]
(give) notice of . . . 1.4
annuel[4b]
annual . . . 2.7
annuler.
void . . . 6.2
ânonner[6a]
stammer . . . 6.
anonyme
anonymous . . . 9.6
anormal[5a]
irregular . . . 5.
anse[6b]
handle . . . 3.1
bay (water) . . . 4.5
antécédent
antecedent . . . 8.3
antérieur[3b]
previous . . . 2.
antichambre[5b]
entrance hall . . . 5.3
anticiper
anticipate . . . 6.8
antique[3a]
ancient . . . 2.6
antiquité[3b]
antiquity . . . 3.8
anxiété[4a]
worry . . . 2.8
anxieux[3b]
anxious . . . 2.3
août[3b]
August . . . 1.7
apaiser[3a]
quiet . . . 1.6
apercevoir[1a]
(catch) sight of . . . 1.1

Section

apitoyer[6a]
move . . . 1.5
aplanir[6b]
even off . . . 4.2
aplatir[5b]
flatten . . . 7.3
aplomb[5a]
balance . . . 2.6
boldness . . . 4.7
apostolique
apostolic . . . 8.2
apôtre[6b]
apostle . . . 5.4
apparaître[1a]
appear (loom) . . . 1.
appareil[2b]
apparatus . . . 3.7
device (technical) . . 3.7
apparence[2a]
looks . . . 1.
apparent[3b]
apparent . . . 3.
apparition[3b]
appearance . . . 3.
ghost . . . 3.2
appartement[2b]
flat (apartment) . . . 2.1
appartenir[1b]
belong . . . 1.
appartenant
pertaining . . . 5.9
appât
bait . . . 6.8
appel[2a]
appeal . . . 3.8
appeler[1a]
call . . . 1.
s' –, (what is your)
name . . . 1.
appendice
appendix . . . 6.2
appétit[3a]
appetite . . . 5.
applaudir[2b]
clap . . . 2.8
applaudissement[5b]
applause . . . 3.7
applicable
applicable . . . 9.8
application[4a]
application . . . 2.2
industry . . . 2.6
appliquer[1b]
s'–, (take) pains . . . 1.4
stick (*tr. vb.*) . . . 2.2
apply . . . 2.6
appliqué, industrious . 3.2
apporter[1a]
bring . . . 1.
appréciation[6a]
estimate . . . 3.8
apprécier[2b]
value . . . 1.4
appreciate . . . 3.6
appréhension[6b]
fear . . . 1.4
apprendre[1a]
learn . . . 1.
– à, teach . . . 1.
apprenti[6b]
apprentice . . . 6.6
apprentissage[6a]
apprenticeship . . . 5.8
apprêt[6b]
preparation . . . 3.
apprêter (s')[3a]
prepare . . . 1.6
approbation[6b]
approval . . . 6.6

Section

- attacher[1b]
  - join ... 1.
  - fasten ... 2.9
- attaque[2b]
  - attack ... 1.7
- attaquer[2a]
  - attack ... 2.1
- attarder[6a]
  - delay ... 2.7
- attarder (s')[6b]
  - linger ... 3.6
- atteindre[1b]
  - reach ... 1.
- atteint[5b]
  - stricken ... 6.5
- atteinte[3a]
  - hors d'–,
    - (out of) reach ... 4.1
    - accomplishment ... 5.3
- attelage
  - team ... 3.9
- atteler[4a]
  - harness ... 5.3
- attendant (en)[3b]
  - meanwhile ... 2.8
- attendre[1a]
  - expect ... 1.
  - wait ... 1.
  - wait for ... 1.
  - – de, expect ... 2.6
- attendre (s')[4b]
  - count on ... 1.
- attendre à (s')[3a]
  - expect ... 1.
- attendrir[3a]
  - move ... 1.5
  - soften ... 3.1
- attendrissement[5a]
  - feeling ... 1.
  - emotion ... 4.3
- attentat[6b]
  - attack ... 2.3
  - crime ... 2.4
  - outrage ... 6.7
- attente[4a]
  - wait ... 4.5
- attentif[2b]
  - attentive ... 2.8
- attention[1a]
  - faire –, look out ... 1.4
  - –!, look out! ... 1.4
  - attention ... 1.8
- attentivement[6a]
  - attentive ... 2.8
- atténuer[4b]
  - decline ... 3.3
- attester[3b]
  - testify ... 4.1
- attirer[1b]
  - pull ... 1.
  - attract ... 2.7
  - attract (entice) ... 3.1
- attitude[2a]
  - attitude ... 3.6
- attraction[5a]
  - attraction ... 6.
- attrait[4a]
  - charm ... 1.9
- attraper[4a]
  - catch ... 1.3
- attribuer[3a]
  - attribute ... 3.7
- attribut[6a]
  - characteristic ... 3.
- attrister[4a]
  - grieve ... 3.4
- aube[4a]
  - dawn ... 3.5

Section

- auberge[3a]
  - inn ... 4.2
- aubergiste
  - innkeeper ... 5.8
- aucun[1a]
  - no (*adj.*) ... 1.
  - none ... 1.
- aucunement[5a]
  - (not at) all ... 1.
- audace[3b]
  - boldness ... 4.7
- audacieux[3b]
  - bold ... 2.1
- au-dessous[4b]
  - beneath ... 1.6
- au-dessous de[3a]
  - under ... 1.
- au-dessus[5a]
  - above (*adv.*) ... 1.
- au-dessus de[1b]
  - above (*prep.*) ... 1.
- audience[4b]
  - audience ... 5.2
- auditeur[5a]
  - audience ... 4.3
- auditoire[5a]
  - assembly ... 2.6
- auge
  - trough ... 6.8
- augmentation[5a]
  - increase ... 2.3
- augmenter[2a]
  - increase ... 1.1
- aujourd'hui[1a]
  - today ... 1.
- aumône[5b]
  - alms ... 6.
- auparavant[2b]
  - before (time) ... 1.
- auprès[2b]
  - near (*adv.*) ... 1.
- auprès de[1b]
  - beside ... 1.
  - near (*prep.*) ... 1.
- auréole
  - halo ... 10.1
- aurore[3b]
  - dawn ... 3.5
- aussi (*also*)[1a]
  - also ... 1.
- aussi (*therefore*)[2a]
  - therefore ... 1.
- aussi (*as*)[5a]
  - as (good) as ... 1.4
- aussi bien (= car)[6a]
  - because ... 1.
- aussi bien que (= de même que)[3b]
  - (as) well as ... 1.2
- aussi peu que[5b]
  - (as) little as ... 2.6
- aussi .... que (*as .... as*)[5a]
  - as (good) as ... 1.4
- aussitôt[1b]
  - (at) once ... 1.
  - (no) sooner ... 1.
- aussitôt que[5a]
  - as soon as ... 1.
- austère[4a]
  - severe ... 1.6
- autant[1a]
  - so much, as much ... 1.
- autant que[2b]
  - (as) much as ... 1.9
- autant (d')[3a]
  - so much ... 1.
- autant que (d')[5a]
  - as (since) ... 1.

Section

- autant plus (d')[3a]
  - (so) much the more ... 3.6
- autel[5a]
  - altar ... 3.5
- auteur[2a]
  - author (originator) ... 1.5
  - author (writer) ... 1.9
- authentique[4b]
  - true ... 1.
  - genuine ... 3.7
- auto(mobile)[3a]
  - automobile ... 2.2
- automne[3b]
  - fall ... 2.3
- autonomie
  - autonomy ... 11.2
- autorisation[5b]
  - license ... 4.6
- autoriser[2b]
  - authorize ... 3.7
- autorité[2a]
  - authority ... 2.3
- autour[2b]
  - around (*adv.*) ... 1.6
- autour de[1a]
  - around ... 1.1
- autre[1a]
  - de l'– côté, (be) across ... 1.
  - un –, another ... 1.
  - d'un –, another's ... 1.
  - l'un et l'–, both ... 1.
  - different ... 1.
  - l'un l'–, each other ... 1.
  - other ... 1.
  - l'un ou l'–, either (one) ... 1.
  - ni l'un ni l'– neither (one) ... 1.
  - de temps à –, (at) times ... 1.
  - d'– part (on the other) hand ... 1.4
  - de temps à – now and then ... 2.2
- autrefois[1b]
  - long ago ... 1.3
  - d'–, former ... 2.
  - formerly ... 2.2
- autrement[2a]
  - else ... 1.1
- autrichien[5b]
  - Austrian ... 4.1
- autruche
  - ostrich ... 7.1
- autrui[6a]
  - d'–, another's ... 1.
  - other ... 1.
  - neighbor ... 3.4
- auxiliaire[4b]
  - helper ... 4.3
- avaler[4b]
  - swallow ... 3.5
- avance[1b]
  - advance ... 2.2
  - d'–, par – (in) advance ... 2.2
  - disposer d'– predisposed ... 9.3
- avancement
  - promotion ... 5.6
- avancer[1a]
  - come forward ... 1.4
  - go forward ... 1.4
  - further ... 1.8
- avant[1a]
  - – tout, above all ... 1.
  - before (time) ... 1.
  - en –, forth ... 1.
  - en –, forward ... 1.4
  - en –, (in) front ... 1.4
  - bow ... 4.3

Section

- avant de[1b]
  - before (time) ... 1.
- avant que[2b]
  - before ... 1.1
- avantageux[3b]
  - favorable ... 2.2
  - profitable ... 4.1
- avantage[1b]
  - advantage ... 1.5
- avant-garde
  - van ... 4.4
- avant-hier[4a]
  - day before yesterday ... 4.
- avare[4a]
  - miser ... 6.5
- avarice
  - avarice ... 6.9
- avec[1a]
  - with ... 1.
- avenir[1b]
  - future ... 1.5
- aventure[2a]
  - adventure ... 3.6
- aventurer (s')
  - (take) chance ... 2.
- aventurier[6b]
  - adventurer ... 7.8
- avenue[3a]
  - avenue ... 3.1
- averse[3b]
  - shower ... 2.5
- aversion[5a]
  - dislike ... 5.
- avertir[2a]
  - (let) know ... 1.
  - warn ... 2.2
- avertissement[3b]
  - warning ... 3.4
- aveu[3b]
  - confession ... 4.3
- aveugle[3a]
  - blind ... 2.
- aveuglement
  - blindness ... 6.8
- aveugler[4a]
  - blind ... 2.7
- avide[4a]
  - eager ... 2.4
  - greedy ... 4.8
- avidité[6b]
  - greediness ... 8.6
- avilir[6a]
  - disgrace ... 5.6
- avion[5b]
  - aeroplane ... 8.1
- avis[2a]
  - advice ... 1.4
  - opinion ... 1.4
  - notice ... 1.7
- aviser[2a]
  - (let) know ... 1.
- aviser de (s')[5a]
  - decide ... 1.
- avocat[3a]
  - lawyer ... 3.
- avoine
  - oat ... 6.
- avoir[1a]
  - il y a, ago ... 1.
  - have ... 1.
  - (what's the) matter ... 1.
  - il y a, there *is* ... 1.
- avoué (*n.*)[6b]
  - lawyer ... 3.
- avouer[1b]
  - admit ... 1.4
- avril[3a]
  - April ... 2.1

Section

bière[3b]
beer ... 3.9

bifteck
steak ... 6.8

bijou[4a]
jewel (jewelry) ... 3.1
jewel ... 4.2

bile[6a]
se faire de la –, worry. 3.2

bille[6b]
marble ... 4.9

billet[2b]
note (written) ... 1.9
– de banque
(bank) note ... 3.6
ticket ... 4.2

bimétalisme
bimetallism ... 10.8

biographie
biography ... 8.6

biscuit[6a]
biscuit ... 6.7

bison
buffalo ... 7.2

bizarre[2b]
strange ... 1.
quaint ... 3.5

blâmer[4a]
blame ... 2.8

blanc[1a]
white ... 1.
en –, blank ... 3.8

blancheur[5a]
white ... 3.7

blanchir[6a]
(become) white ... 1.9

blasphème
blasphemy ... 6.8

blé[3a]
wheat ... 2.5

blême[5b]
pale ... 2.7

blessé[4a]
wounded ... 3.3

blesser[1b]
hurt (*tr. vb.*) ... 1.8
wound ... 2.2

blessure[2b]
wound ... 2.8

bleu[1a]
blue ... 1.4

bloc[4a]
block ... 5.2

blond[2a]
fair ... 1.2

blouse[4a]
blouse ... 6.8

bœuf[3a]
ox ... 3.8
beef ... 4.1

bohème
Bohemian ... 7.3

bohémien
gypsy ... 7.4
-ne, (fortune) teller ... 7.

boire[1b]
drink ... 1.4
drinking ... 3.
– à petits coups, sip ... 6.1

bois[1a]
forest ... 1.
wood (lumber) ... 1.5
de, en –, wood (*adj.*) ... 1.5

boiserie[5b]
woodwork ... 8.9

boisseau
bushel ... 6.

Section

boisson[5a]
drink ... 2.7

boîte[2b]
box ... 2.3

boiteux
lame ... 5.5

bombe[5b]
shell (explosive) ... 3.4

bon[1a]
good ... 1.
kind ... 1.
– cœur, kind ... 1.
de -ne heure, early ... 1.1
– marché, cheap ... 2.1
se lever de -ne heure
get up early ... 3.

bon (*n.*)
bond ... 5.8

bonbon[4a]
candy ... 4.5

bond[4b]
spring ... 2.6

bondir[3a]
spring ... 1.5

bonheur[1b]
happiness ... 1.4

bonhomme[2b]
fellow ... 2.3

bonjour[2a]
good morning ... 1.1

bonne (*n.*)[3b]
servant ... 1.5

bonnement[6a]
simply ... 1.

bonnet[3b]
hood ... 5.3

bonsoir[4b]
good morning ... 1.1

bonté[2b]
goodness ... 1.5
kindness ... 2.7

bord[1a]
edge ... 1.5
bank ... 1.5
brim ... 2.6
à –, (on) board ... 3.
– du toit, eaves ... 6.6

border[3b]
border ... 5.1

borne[3b]
limit ... 2.4

borner[2a]
limit ... 1.6

botte[3a]
boot ... 3.8

bottine[6b]
boot ... 3.8

bouche[1b]
mouth ... 1.

boucher (*n.*)[6a]
butcher ... 5.6

boucher (*vb.*)[6b]
stop up ... 3.1

boucherie[6a]
butcher shop ... 5.8

bouchon[5b]
cork ... 6.5

boucle[4a]
curl ... 4.9
loop ... 5.4
buckle ... 6.8

boucler[4b]
curl ... 4.8

bouder[4b]
sulk ... 10.1

boue[4b]
mud ... 4.8

boueux
muddy ... 5.2

Section

bouger[2b]
move ... 1.1

bougie[4b]
candle ... 2.2

bouillir[5a]
boil ... 3.1

bouillotte
kettle ... 4.8

boulanger[4b]
baker ... 6.

boule[2b]
ball ... 2.1

bouleau
birch ... 6.4

boulevard[3b]
avenue ... 3.1

bouleversement[6a]
upset ... 6.3

bouleverser[2b]
overcome ... 2.7

bouquet[2b]
bunch ... 4.8

bourdonnement[5a]
buzz ... 5.4

bourdonner[4b]
buzz ... 5.2

bourg[5b]
village ... 1.2

bourgeois[2a]
bourgeois ... 5.9

bourgeoisie
gentry ... 6.2

bourreau[6a]
brute ... 5.7
hangman ... 7.3

bourrer[3b]
stuff ... 4.1

bourse[3b]
exchange (stock) ... 2.6
bag ... 3.
purse ... 3.8

bousculer[6a]
jostle ... 7.

bout[1a]
end ... 1.
tip ... 1.4
butt ... 4.9

bouteille[2b]
bottle ... 2.1

boutique[3b]
shop ... 2.5

bouton[3b]
button ... 3.7
bud ... 4.8

bouton de pompier
burr ... 6.8

boxeur[6b]
prize fighter ... 7.

bracelet[6a]
bracelet ... 6.5

braconnier[6b]
poacher ... 11.5

braise[5a]
coals ... 2.1

brancard[6b]
stretcher ... 8.2

branche[2a]
branch ... 1.6

branler[6a]
waver ... 3.4

braquer[6a]
aim ... 3.2

bras[1a]
arm (part of body) ... 1.
à – ouverts
outstretched ... 3.

brasser
brew ... 7.

Section

brasserie[6a]
tavern ... 4.1

brave[1b]
(be) brave ... 1.
good ... 1.
fine ... 1.4

bravement[5a]
(be) brave ... 1.

braver[5b]
face ... 3.8
brave ... 4.6

bravo[3b]
applause ... 3.7

bravoure[5a]
courage ... 1.4

brebis[6a]
lamb ... 4.9

brèche[6a]
gap ... 4.5

bref (*adj.*)[3a]
short ... 1.

bref (*adv.*)[4a]
(in) short ... 1.

breton[6a]
English ... 1.

brevet
patent ... 5.2

bribe[6b]
piece ... 1.

bride[6b]
bridle ... 3.4

brigade[6a]
brigade ... 6.2

brigadier[5b]
corporal ... 4.2

brigand[4a]
robber ... 3.7
knave ... 4.5

brillant[2a]
bright ... 1.4
glow ... 3.

briller[2b]
shine ... 1.6
glitter ... 3.6

brin[5b]
blade ... 5.3

brique[4b]
brick ... 5.

brise[4b]
breeze ... 5.2

briser[2a]
break (in pieces) ... 2.3

britannique[6a]
British ... 4.2

broche[6a]
spindle ... 6.6

brochure[6a]
pamphlet ... 6.3

broder[3b]
embroider ... 5.9

broderie
embroidery ... 6.5

bronze[3b]
bronze ... 6.2

brosse
brush (paint) ... 4.6
brush ... 5.6

brouhaha[7a]
noise ... 2.6

brouillard[3b]
mist ... 3.1

brouiller[5b]
involve ... 3.9

brouillon[6b]
draft ... 3.

broussaille[5a]
brushwood ... 9.8

Section

causer (*cause*)[1b]
cause ... 1.
causer (*chat*)[1b]
talk ... 1.
causerie[5b]
talk ... 1.2
caution
bondsman ... 13.
cavalerie[6b]
cavalry ... 5.3
cavalier[3a]
horseman ... 2.8
cavalier ... 6.
cave[3a]
cave ... 3.
cellar ... 3.8
ce, cet, cette, ces[1a]
that (*adj.*) ... 1.
this (*adj.*) ... 1.
ceci[1b]
this (*pron.*) ... 1.
céder[2a]
yield ... 1.9
cèdre
cedar ... 5.8
ceinture[3a]
belt ... 4.7
cela[1a]
that (*pron.*) ... 1.
célèbre[2b]
famous ... 1.1
célébrer[3a]
celebrate ... 2.
céleri
celery ... 7.1
céleste[4a]
celestial ... 3.5
celle(-ci, -là)[1a]
former ... 1.
that (*pron.*) ... 1.
this (*pron.*) ... 1.
latter ... 1.4
celles(-ci, -là)[1b]
former ... 1.
that (*pron.*) ... 1.
this (*pron.*) ... 1.
latter ... 1.4
celui(-ci, -là)[1a]
former ... 1.
that (*pron.*) ... 1.
this (*pron.*) ... 1.
latter ... 1.4
cellule[3b]
cell ... 4.6
celtique[6a]
Celtic ... 8.2
cendre[3b]
ash(es) ... 3.3
cent[1a]
pour –
interest (percent) 1.
hundred ... 1.4
centaine[2a]
hundred ... 1.4
centenaire
centennial ... 10.6
centième[5a]
hundredth ... 7.6
centime[3b]
cent ... 1.7
centimètre[4b]
inch ... 2.7
central[2b]
central ... 4.5
centre[2a]
center ... 1.
cependant[1a]
however ... 1.

Section

cercle[2a]
circle (set of people) 1.1
circle (ring) ... 1.2
club ... 1.6
cercueil[6b]
coffin ... 5.3
cérémonie[3a]
ceremony ... 2.
ceremony (rite) ... 3.5
cérémonieux
formal ... 5.1
cerf
deer ... 5.8
cerf-volant
kite ... 5.2
cerise
cherry ... 5.6
certes[2a]
indeed ... 1.
certain[1a]
sure ... 1.
femme d'un – âge
matron ... 6.5
certainement[1b]
sure ... 1.
certificat
certificate ... 5.8
certitude[2b]
assurance ... 4.4
cerveau[3a]
brain ... 3.3
cervelle[3a]
brain ... 3.3
cesse[2b]
pause ... 2.9
cesser[1a]
stop (*tr. vb.*) ... 1.
stop (*intr. vb.*) ... 1.4
ceux(-ci, -là)[1a]
former ... 1.
that (*pron.*) ... 1.
this (*pron.*) ... 1.
latter ... 1.4
chacun[1a]
each (*pron.*) ... 1.
chagrin (*n.*)[2a]
grief ... 1.8
vexation ... 5.8
chagrin (*adj.*)[5b]
sad ... 1.4
chaîne[3a]
chain ... 2.1
chaînon
link ... 3.3
chair[3a]
flesh ... 2.
chaire[4b]
chair (university) .. 2.5
pulpit ... 6.8
chaise[1b]
chair ... 1.8
chaland
barge ... 6.
châle[6a]
shawl ... 7.4
chaleur[2a]
heat ... 1.5
chambre[1a]
room (chamber) ... 1.
– de commerce
chamber of commerce ... 3.2
Chambre des Députés
House of Representatives ... 3.4
– à coucher, bedroom. 4.4
– d'enfants, nursery .. 5.8
chameau
camel ... 6.4

Section

champ[1b]
field ... 1.
– de bataille
(battle) field ... 2.4
champagne (*wine*)[4b]
wine ... 1.4
champêtre
garde –, constable ... 6.2
champion[4b]
champion ... 2.5
chance[1b]
chance ... 1.
fortune ... 1.4
chanceler[4b]
reel ... 3.1
chancelier
chancellor ... 5.6
chandail
sweater ... 7.2
chandelle[5b]
candle ... 2.2
change[4a]
change ... 1.5
change (conversion) 2.9
changement[2a]
change ... 1.5
changer[1a]
change ... 1.4
chanson[3a]
song ... 1.6
chant[2b]
song ... 1.6
chanter[1b]
sing ... 1.4
chant ... 3.2
chanteur[4b]
singer ... 4.3
chantier[4b]
work-yard ... 12.2
chaos[4b]
chaos ... 6.6
chapeau[1b]
hat ... 1.5
chapelet[6a]
beads ... 5.4
chapelle[3a]
chapel ... 3.9
chapitre[3a]
chapter ... 2.5
chaque[1a]
each (*adj.*) ... 1.
every ... 1.
– fois, (every) time ... 2.2
char[4b]
chariot ... 2.6
charbon[4a]
coal ... 1.9
chardon
thistle ... 6.4
charge[2a]
load ... 1.7
chargement
freight ... 3.8
charger[1a]
load ... 1.8
charge ... 2.2
burden ... 3.5
chariot[6b]
wagon ... 4.7
charitable[6b]
charitable ... 5.4
peu –, unkind ... 6.1
charité[3b]
charity ... 2.9
charmant[1b]
charming ... 2.3
lovely ... 2.3
charme[2a]
charm ... 1.9

Section

charmer[2b]
charm ... 2.4
charmille
bower ... 5.2
charpentier[7a]
carpenter ... 5.5
charretier
carter ... 6.9
charrette[5a]
wagon ... 4.7
charrue[5b]
plow ... 5.3
charte
charter ... 2.9
chasse[2b]
hunt ... 2.4
chasser[2a]
drive out ... 1.1
drive away ... 2.3
hunt ... 2.3
chasseur[3a]
hunter ... 2.6
chaste[5b]
chaste ... 6.2
chasteté
chastity ... 7.7
chat(-te)[3a]
cat ... 4.1
château[2a]
castle ... 2.
mansion ... 3.7
châtelain(-e)[4b]
lady ... 1.
lord ... 1.1
châtier[6b]
punish ... 2.1
chatouiller
tickle ... 6.8
chaud[1b]
hot ... 1.5
warm ... 1.7
chaudière[6b]
boiler ... 5.8
chauffage[6b]
heating ... 5.
chauffer[3a]
heat ... 2.2
chauffeur[5b]
driver ... 4.4
chaume[5b]
thatch ... 6.
chaumière[5b]
cottage ... 3.4
chausse[6b]
drawers (clothing) .. 6.2
chaussée[5b]
road ... 1.
chausser[4b]
se –, (put on) shoes ... 3.5
chaussette
sock ... 6.8
chaussure[4b]
shoe ... 3.2
chauve
bald ... 6.2
chaux[6a]
lime ... 4.2
chef[1b]
chief (*adj.*) ... 1.
chief (*n.*) ... 1.5
– de famille
man of the house 1.8
chef-d'œuvre[3b]
masterpiece ... 6.4
chemin[1a]
road ... 1.
– de fer, railroad ... 2.
– faisant, (on the) way 2.2

Section

collection[3a]
  collection ... 2.7
collège[3a]
  college ... 3.8
collègue[3a]
  fellow worker ... 2.9
coller[3a]
  stick (*intr. vb.*) ... 2.1
  stick (*tr. vb.*) ... 2.2
collet[4b]
  collar ... 4.4
collier[3b]
  collar ... 4.4
  necklace ... 6.4
colline[3b]
  hill ... 2.6
colombe[7a]
  dove ... 4.4
colon
  colonist ... 6.1
colonel[3b]
  colonel ... 3.9
colonial[4a]
  colonial ... 6.2
colonie[2b]
  colony ... 2.9
colonne[3a]
  column (military) ... 2.9
  column (pillar) ... 3.3
coloré[4a]
  colored ... 4.2
colorer[6a]
  color ... 2.5
colossal[5b]
  great (huge) ... 1.
colosse[6b]
  giant ... 4.
combat[2b]
  fight ... 1.1
  battle ... 1.2
combattant[4b]
  warrior ... 3.5
combattre[2a]
  fight ... 1.6
combien[1b]
  how much ... 2.2
combinaison[3a]
  combination ... 4.3
combiner[3b]
  combine ... 2.3
comble[3b]
  top ... 1.3
combler[2b]
  fill ... 1.8
combustible
  fuel ... 5.2
combustion
  combustion ... 6.
comédie[3a]
  comedy ... 3.7
comédien[5b]
  actor ... 3.9
comète
  comet ... 4.8
comique[3b]
  funny ... 2.9
  opéra –
    (musical) drama ... 6.2
comité[3a]
  committee ... 3.
commandant[3b]
  major ... 3.2
  commander ... 4.4
commande[4b]
  order ... 1.
commandement[4a]
  order ... 1.
  command ... 2.3

Section

commander[2a]
  – à, control ... 1.4
  command ... 1.5
  order ... 1.5
comme[1a]
  as (*prep.*) ... 1.
  as (*conj.*) ... 1.
  – il faut, proper ... 1.4
  – il faut, decent ... 4.
commémoratif
  memorial ... 4.4
commencement[2a]
  beginning ... 2.7
  dès le –
    (from the) beginning ... 3.9
commencer[1a]
  begin ... 1.
comment[1a]
  how ... 1.
  n'importe –, anyhow 4.2
commerçant[4a]
  business ... 1.4
  commercial ... 2.8
commerce[2a]
  trade ... 1.2
  faire le –, trade ... 2.4
  chambre de –
    chamber of commerce ... 3.2
commercial[4a]
  commercial ... 2.8
  loi -e
    (commercial) law 3.2
commettre[2a]
  commit ... 2.3
commis (*n.*)[6b]
  clerk ... 2.7
commissaire[4a]
  commissioner ... 5.
commission[3a]
  commission ... 2.2
  errand ... 3.
commissionnaire[4b]
  messenger ... 2.5
  porter ... 3.3
commode (*n.*)[5a]
  (chest of) drawers .. 6.1
commode (*adj.*)[3a]
  convenient ... 2.5
commun[1b]
  common ... 1.4
  common (person) ... 1.4
  peu –, unusual ... 2.6
  rude ... 4.3
communal
  community ... 4.8
communauté[4b]
  convent ... 3.8
  community ... 3.8
commune (*n.*)[3a]
  district ... 2.1
  community ... 2.9
communicatif
  communicative ... 13.
communication[3a]
  communication ... 2.5
  message ... 3.
communion[5b]
  communion ... 6.7
communiquer[2a]
  communicate ... 2.7
compagne[2b]
  companion ... 2.3
compagnie[2a]
  company (business) 1.
  company (military) 1.5
compagnon[2a]
  companion ... 2.3

Section

comparable[5a]
  (to be) compared ... 2.2
comparaison[4b]
  comparison ... 2.7
comparaître[7a]
  appear (loom) ... 1.
comparer[2b]
  compare ... 1.6
compatriote[3b]
  (fellow) countryman 4.7
compensation[6a]
  faire –, make up for 4.1
    amends ... 4.1
complaire[6b]
  please ... 1.
complaisance[5a]
  kindness ... 2.7
complaisant[6b]
  kind ... 1.
complément[6b]
  object ... 3.
complet (*n.*)[5a]
  suit ... 2.7
complet (*adj.*)[1b]
  complete ... 1.
complet
  complement ... 5.2
complètement[2a]
  all ... 1.
  throughout ... 2.8
compléter[3a]
  complete ... 1.
complexe[5a]
  complex ... 5.3
complication[4b]
  complication ... 7.2
complice[4b]
  party to ... 2.
complicité[6a]
  participation ... 7.8
compliment[3a]
  compliment ... 4.1
compliqué[4b]
  involved ... 5.
  complicate ... 6.2
compliquer[2b]
  complicate ... 6.2
complot[5b]
  plot ... 3.9
comporter[3a]
  se –, act (behave) ... 1.
composer[1b]
  compose ... 2.6
compositeur
  composer ... 9.6
composition[3a]
  theme (paper) ... 3.2
  composition ... 3.8
comprendre[1a]
  understand ... 1.
  realize ... 2.6
compris (*including*)[4a]
  included ... 2.9
compromettre[3a]
  compromise ... 5.3
compromis[5a]
  compromise ... 5.7
compte[1a]
  account ... 1.
  account (reckoning) 1.8
  (in) cash ... 2.8
compter[1a]
  count ... 1.
  – sur, count on ... 1.
  intend ... 1.4
  comptant, (in) cash .. 2.8
comptoir[5a]
  counter ... 6.3

Section

comte[2b]
  count ... 1.2
comtesse[4a]
  countess ... 5.4
concéder[6a]
  grant ... 1.
concentration[6b]
  concentration ... 7.1
concentrer[4b]
  condense ... 4.3
  concentrate ... 4.8
conception[3b]
  idea ... 1.4
  conception ... 4.
concerner[2b]
  have (to do with) .. 1.
concert[3a]
  concert ... 4.1
concession[4b]
  grant ... 3.4
  license ... 4.6
  admission ... 5.4
concevoir[2a]
  imagine ... 1.4
  conceive ... 2.
concierge[3a]
  porter ... 5.6
concile[6b]
  council ... 2.1
conciliation[6b]
  conciliation ... 7.8
concilier[4a]
  reconcile ... 4.6
concision
  conciseness ... 12.2
conclure[2a]
  complete ... 1.
  infer ... 5.7
conclusion[3b]
  end ... 1.
  conclusion ... 3.
concombre
  cucumber ... 7.4
concourir[5b]
  contribute ... 3.2
  contend ... 5.7
concours[3a]
  test ... 1.9
concret
  concrete ... 6.1
concurrence[3b]
  competition ... 3.8
concurrent[5b]
  rival ... 5.
condamnation[5b]
  sentence ... 2.
condamner[2a]
  sentence ... 2.3
  condemn ... 2.7
condenser[6a]
  condense ... 4.3
condition[1b]
  condition ... 1.
conducteur[3b]
  leader ... 2.3
  driver ... 4.4
conduire[1a]
  se –, act (behave) ... 1.
  drive (car) ... 1.
  drive (horse) ... 1.
  lead ... 1.
conduite[2b]
  conduct ... 2.3
  leadership ... 4.6
cône
  cone ... 7.2
confection[6a]
  making (e.g., of clothes) ... 4.7

	Section
conviction[2b]	
être de la –, convince	2.
conviction	4.2
convive[3b]	
company	1.7
convoi[3b]	
funeral (procession)	5.4
convoiter[5a]	
covet	4.1
convoquer[4b]	
call together	2.1
copie[4a]	
copy	3.2
copier[5a]	
copy	4.
coq[4a]	
cock	3.8
coquette	
flirt	7.
coquille[6b]	
shell	3.7
coquin[4b]	
roguish	10.2
cor	
corn	5.
corail	
coral	6.5
corbeau	
crow	5.3
corbeille[5b]	
basket	2.8
corde[3a]	
rope	3.3
cordial[4b]	
cordial	2.3
cordon[4a]	
rope	3.3
cordonnier	
shoemaker	6.2
corne[5a]	
horn	3.7
cornemuse	
joueur de –, piper	7.2
bagpipe	8.1
cornichon	
pickle	6.8
corniche	
coping stone	7.2
cornue	
retort	7.2
corporation[5a]	
corporation	3.5
corporel	
bodily	6.3
corps[1a]	
body	1.
corps	3.8
correct[5a]	
right (correct)	1.
correctement[6a]	
right (correct)	1.
correction[5b]	
correction	3.7
correspondance[4a]	
correspondence (similarity)	3.5
correspondence	3.9
correspondant[4b]	
corresponding	2.7
similar	4.4
correspondent	6.2
correspondre[3b]	
correspond to	2.4
correspond	4.
corridor[3b]	
passage	4.8
corriger[4a]	
correct	2.7
corrompre	
corrupt	4.7
corruption[6b]	
corruption	5.6
corsage[6b]	
bodice	9.6
cortège[3a]	
procession	4.1
costume[2a]	
dress	1.4
suit	2.7
costume	4.3
cote[3b]	
share	2.
côte[1b]	
coast	1.4
rib	5.
– à –, side by side	2.2
côté[1a]	
de l'autre –, across	1.
à – de, beside	1.
side	1.
de l'autre – (on the other) hand	1.4
d'un – (on the one) hand	2.2
de son –, (on her) side	2.2
de son –, (on his) side	2.2
de leur – (on their) side	2.2
de mon – (for my) part	2.6
de –, side (*adj.*)	4.1
laisser de –, omit	4.4
coteau[5b]	
hill	2.6
coton[6b]	
cotton	3.8
cou[2a]	
neck	1.5
couchant[4b]	
setting	9.6
couche[3b]	
bed	1.4
coucher (*n.*)[4b]	
– du soleil, sunset	5.3
setting	8.9
coucher (*vb.*)[1b]	
lay	1.
être couché, lie	1.
chambre à –, bedroom	4.4
coucher (se)[2b]	
(go to) bed	1.6
coucou	
cuckoo	6.2
coude[3a]	
elbow	5.1
coudre[4b]	
sew	4.7
couler[2a]	
flow	1.5
couleur[1b]	
color	1.
coulisse[5b]	
wing	4.9
couloir[3a]	
passage	4.8
coup[1a]	
– d'œil, look	1.
blow	1.4
d'un seul –, (at) once	1.8
– de feu discharge (of gun)	2.7
– de pied, kick	3.6
boire à petits -s, sip	6.1
volée de -s, beating	6.4
– de poignard, stab	6.5
coupable[2a]	
(be to) blame	1.8
coupe[3b]	
goblet	4.1
couper[1a]	
cut	1.8
– la tête, behead	6.2
couple[2b]	
pair	1.9
couplet[5b]	
verse	2.7
cour[1a]	
court (royal)	1.
faire –, court	1.
court (yard)	1.1
– d'assises, court	1.4
cour de cassation	
supreme court	4.3
courage[1b]	
avoir du –, (be) brave	1.
courage	1.4
perdre –, (lose) courage	2.
courageusement[5b]	
(be) brave	1.
courageux[4a]	
(be) brave	1.
courant[1b]	
stream	1.4
peu –, unusual	2.6
current	2.6
au –, (well) informed	3.
courbe[5b]	
curve	4.6
courber[4a]	
bend	2.4
coureur[6a]	
scout	5.7
courir[1a]	
run	1.
couronne[3a]	
crown	1.7
wreath	3.7
couronner[3b]	
crown	2.9
courrier[5a]	
post	2.
messenger	2.5
courroie	
strap	6.2
cours[1b]	
course	1.1
course[2b]	
race	1.2
court[1b]	
short	1.
courtisan[5b]	
courtier	5.7
courtiser[6b]	
court	1.
courtois[6b]	
courteous	4.3
courtoisie[4b]	
courtesy	4.7
cousin[2a]	
cousin	2.4
cousin germain[5b]	
cousin	2.4
coussin[4a]	
cushion	5.6
couteau[2b]	
knife	2.9
coûter[1a]	
cost	1.4
coûteux[5a]	
dear	1.1
coutume[2b]	
custom	1.9
couture	
seam	6.4
couturière[6b]	
dressmaker	8.4
couvée	
brood	5.8
couvent[3b]	
convent	3.8
couver	
hatch	6.8
couvercle[6a]	
cover	2.9
couvert[2a]	
set	1.1
protection	2.1
– de rochers, rocky	5.9
– de feuilles, leafy	6.6
– de neige, snowy	6.6
couverture[3a]	
– (de lit), blanket	4.
couvrir[1b]	
cover	1.
crabe	
crab	6.2
cracher[5a]	
spit	5.9
craie[6b]	
chalk	6.2
craindre[1a]	
afraid	1.
crainte[1b]	
fear	1.4
cramponner (se)	
cling	5.
crâne (*n.*)[4a]	
skull	6.
crapaud	
toad	6.6
craquer[4b]	
crack	2.6
cratère	
crater	9.4
cravate[4a]	
necktie	6.4
crayon[4b]	
pencil	4.2
créance[5b]	
belief	2.3
créancier[5a]	
creditor	4.1
créateur[5a]	
creator	4.4
création[3b]	
creation	3.4
créature[3a]	
creature	2.5
crédit[3b]	
credit	2.9
créer[1b]	
create	1.5
crème[5b]	
cream	5.1
crêpe (*crape*)[6b]	
crêpe	7.
crêpe	
pancake	7.
crépu	
curly	8.5
crépuscule[4b]	
twilight	4.3
crête	
comb	6.2
creuser[2b]	
dig	4.8
deepen	5.

Section

- défaite (*n.*)[4a]
  - defeat . . . 3.6
- défaut[1b]
  - fault . . . 1.8
  - à – de, (for) want of . . 3.
  - want (scarcity) . . . 3.
- défectueux[6b]
  - imperfect . . . 3.9
- défendre[1b]
  - defend . . . 1.4
  - forbid . . . 2.
- défense[2b]
  - forbid . . . 2.
  - defense . . . 2.8
  - prohibition . . . 5.
- défenseur
  - defender . . . 6.8
- défi[5a]
  - defiance . . . 4.
- défiance[6a]
  - mistrust . . . 4.3
- défier[3a]
  - defy . . . 3.2
- défilé
  - gorge . . . 5.9
- défiler[3b]
  - defile . . . 6.5
- défini (*adj.*)[6a]
  - definite . . . 3.5
- définir[3b]
  - name (appoint) . . . 1.
- définitif[3a]
  - final . . . 2.9
- définition[5b]
  - definition . . . 7.
- définitivement[4b]
  - finally . . . 2.2
- défunt[4b]
  - dead . . . 1.4
- dégager[2a]
  - loose . . . 1.5
- dégât[4a]
  - damage . . . 2.4
- dégénérer[6b]
  - degenerate . . . 7.4
- dégoût[4b]
  - disgust . . . 4.6
- dégoûtant[6a]
  - disgusting . . . 6.2
- dégoûter[4a]
  - disgust . . . 6.
- dégoutter
  - drip . . . 6.4
- degré[1b]
  - degree . . . 1.4
- dégringoler[6a]
  - fall . . . 1.
  - fall to pieces . . . 2.6
- déguisement[6b]
  - disguise . . . 5.8
- déguiser[4a]
  - hide . . . 2.8
- dehors[1a]
  - out . . . 1.
  - outside . . . 1.4
- déité
  - deity (D) . . . 5.4
- déjà[1a]
  - already . . . 1.
  - – nommé, above . . . 2.2
- déjeuner (*n.*)[2a]
  - breakfast . . . 3.
  - lunch . . . 4.5
- déjeuner (*vb.*)[3b]
  - lunch . . . 3.
  - breakfast . . . 4.3
- delà[2a]
  - au – de, beyond (*prep.*) 1.5
  - au –, beyond (*adv.*) . . . 1.8
- délai[3b]
  - delay . . . 3.8
- délaisser[4a]
  - leave (desert) . . . 1.
- délégation[5a]
  - delegation . . . 8.5
- déléguer[6a]
  - delegate . . . 6.6
- délibérer[4b]
  - deliberate . . . 4.1
- délicat[2a]
  - delicate . . . 2.3
  - dainty . . . 2.7
- délicatesse[3a]
  - delicacy . . . 5.4
- délicieux[2b]
  - lovely . . . 2.3
  - delicious . . . 2.8
- délier[5b]
  - loose . . . 1.5
- délinquant
  - offender . . . 6.8
- délire[3b]
  - fury . . . 2.8
  - bliss . . . 3.7
  - madness . . . 4.1
  - raving . . . 6.1
- délirer
  - rave . . . 6.6
- délit[5b]
  - crime . . . 2.4
- délivrance
  - deliverance . . . 5.2
- délivrer[4b]
  - free . . . 1.7
- delta
  - delta . . . 7.2
- déluge[6a]
  - flood . . . 3.2
- demain[1b]
  - tomorrow . . . 1.4
  - après –
    - day after tomorrow . . . 4.3
- demande[2b]
  - demand . . . 1.3
  - request . . . 2.1
  - demand (supply and demand) . . . 2.9
  - inquiry . . . 4.4
- demander[1a]
  - ask . . . 1.
  - se –, wonder . . . 1.
  - charge . . . 3.
- démangeaison
  - itch . . . 6.9
- démarche[3a]
  - walk . . . 1.6
- démarreur
  - (self) starter . . . 10.8
- déménager[5a]
  - move . . . 1.5
- démentir[5b]
  - (give the) lie . . . 3.4
- demeure[2a]
  - dwelling . . . 2.3
- demeurer[1b]
  - live . . . 1.1
- demi[1a]
  - half . . . 1.
- demi-cercle
  - semicircle . . . 8.8
- demi-heure[6b]
  - half-hour . . . 1.5
- démission[5b]
  - resignation . . . 7.3
- démocratie[5b]
  - – sociale
    - social democracy . 5.3
  - democracy . . . 6.9
- démocratique[5b]
  - democrat . . . 5.
- demoiselle[2b]
  - young lady . . . 1.1
- démolir[4b]
  - pull down . . . 2.8
- démonstration[5b]
  - demonstration . . . 3.6
- démontrer[3a]
  - demonstrate . . . 2.8
- dénégation[6a]
  - denial . . . 6.6
- dénoncer[3b]
  - denounce . . . 4.1
- dénouement[4b]
  - result . . . 1.5
- dénouer[5a]
  - loose . . . 1.5
- denrée[5a]
  - food . . . 1.9
- dense[6a]
  - dense . . . 2.6
- densité
  - density . . . 7.8
- dent[2a]
  - tooth . . . 2.3
- dentelle[4a]
  - lace . . . 2.1
- départ[1b]
  - departure . . . 3.1
- département[3a]
  - territory . . . 2.1
- départir[6a]
  - grant . . . 1.
- dépasser[1b]
  - pass . . . 1.4
  - exceed . . . 2.3
  - (have the) advantage . . . 3.
  - project . . . 3.7
- dépêche[4a]
  - wire . . . 3.5
  - despatch . . . 5.1
- dépêcher (se)[4a]
  - hurry . . . 1.2
- dépendance[5a]
  - dependence . . . 6.
- dépendant
  - dependent . . . 5.2
- dépendre[2b]
  - depend . . . 2.4
- dépens[5b]
  - expense . . . 3.3
- dépense[2a]
  - expense . . . 3.3
- dépenser[2b]
  - spend (money) . . . 1.6
- dépit[3b]
  - spite . . . 1.4
- déplacement[5b]
  - shift . . . 5.7
- déplacer[3b]
  - move . . . 1.1
- déplaire[3a]
  - displease . . . 5.5
- déplier[6a]
  - unfold . . . 3.4
- déplorable[6a]
  - wretched . . . 5.8
- déplorer[4b]
  - deplore . . . 4.2
- déployer[4a]
  - unfold . . . 3.4
- déposer[1b]
  - place . . . 1.
  - depose . . . 4.9
- dépôt[3a]
  - deposit . . . 2.7
- dépouiller[3a]
  - se –, shed . . . 3.3
  - strip . . . 3.7
- dépourvu[6b]
  - needy . . . 6.
  - au –, unaware . . . 6.
- depuis[1a]
  - since . . . 1.
- depuis que[3a]
  - since . . . 1.
- député[2b]
  - Chambre des Députés
    - House of Representatives . . . 3.4
  - deputy . . . 4.9
- déraisonnable
  - unreasonable . . . 7.2
- déranger[2a]
  - trouble . . . 1.5
- déréglé
  - wanton . . . 6.4
- dernier[1a]
  - last . . . 1.
  - ce –, latter . . . 1.4
- dernièrement[6b]
  - lately . . . 5.1
- dérober[2a]
  - rob . . . 2.3
- dérouler[3b]
  - unfold . . . 3.4
- déroute[6a]
  - defeat . . . 3.6
- derrière (*n.*)[3b]
  - back . . . 1.4
  - (wrong) side . . . 1.7
- derrière (*prep.*)[1a]
  - back . . . 1.
- dès[1a]
  - since . . . 1.
  - – maintenant
    - henceforth . . . 3.
  - – le commencement
    - (from the) beginning . . . 3.9
- dès que[1b]
  - as soon as . . . 1.
- désagréable[4b]
  - unpleasant . . . 3.8
- désarmer[4b]
  - disarm . . . 6.9
- désarroi[6b]
  - disorder . . . 5.
- désastre[3b]
  - disaster . . . 3.9
- désavantage
  - disadvantage . . . 4.8
- descendant[5a]
  - en –, downward . . . 3.4
  - descendant . . . 5.3
- descendre[1a]
  - go down . . . 2.2
  - alight . . . 5.7
- descente[4b]
  - descent . . . 5.1
- description[4a]
  - description . . . 3.1
- désert[2a]
  - waste . . . 2.4
- déserter[4b]
  - leave (desert) . . . 1.
- désespérément[5b]
  - hopelessly . . . 6.1

Section

dissoudre[3b]
dissolve 3.9
distance[2a]
distance 1.1
distant[5a]
far .... 1.
distillation
distillation 8.4
distiller
distil 6.9
distillerie
distillery 8.4
distinct[3a]
clear .... 1.
distinction[5b]
difference 1.4
distinction 3.9
distinguer[1b]
make out 1.4
distinguish 2.2
distraction[4a]
pastime 4.8
distraire[3b]
se –, (have) fun 2.9
amuse 3.5
distract 3.6
distrait[6a]
absent (mind) 2.9
thoughtless 4.8
distraitement[6a]
absent (mind) 2.9
distribuer[3b]
distribute 3.3
distribution[5a]
distribution 3.7
district[5a]
district 2.1
dit (*adj.*)[6a]
say .... 1.
divan[6b]
couch 4.1
divergence[6b]
difference 1.4
divers[1b]
different .... 1.
various 2.6
divertir[5b]
se –, enjoy 1.7
entertain 2.4
se –, (have) fun 2.9
dividende
dividend 5.6
divin[3a]
divine .... 2.
divinité
divinity 4.9
diviser[2b]
divide 1.1
division[3b]
division (general and military) 2.2
division (act of dividing) 3.8
divorcer
divorce .... 4.
dix[1a]
ten 1.4
dix-huit[3b]
eighteen 4.3
dix-huitième[6a]
eighteenth .... 6.
dixième[5b]
tenth 4.1
dix-neuf
nineteen 6.3
dix-sept[6a]
seventeen .... 6.
dizaine[4a]
ten 1.4

Section

docile[4b]
obedient 3.2
docilement[6b]
obedient 3.2
docteur[2b]
doctor .... 1.
doctrine[3a]
doctrine 2.6
document[4a]
document 5.1
dogme[5a]
dogma 8.3
doigt[1b]
finger 1.4
– de pied, toe 4.6
domaine[2a]
property 1.5
property (landed) .. 1.9
dôme
dome 6.2
domestique (*n.*)[2a]
servant (maid) 1.5
servant (man) 1.9
domestique (*adj.*)
domestic (pertaining to house) .... †2.9
domicile[4b]
dwelling 2.3
domination[5a]
rule .... 2.
dominer[1b]
rule .... 1.
master 1.4
dommage[3a]
damage 2.4
(too) bad 2.9
dompter[6b]
subdue 4.3
tame 5.6
don[3a]
present 1.7
bestowing 3.8
donateur
giver 7.2
donc[1a]
so .... 1.
therefore .... 1.
donner[1a]
give .... 1.
shake 1.1
– à manger, feed 1.4
se – la peine (take) pains 1.4
– congé, dismiss 2.7
– congé (give) notice (to) 2.8
– une secousse, – des coups saccadés jerk 4.6
dont[1a]
whose .... 1.
dorer[2b]..
gild 4.5
dormir[1b]
sleep 1.4
dos[1b]
back 1.4
dossier[4b]
record 3.8
dot[4a]
dowry 7.6
doter[3b]
endow 4.3
douane[5b]
duty 2.9
douanier[5a]
custom house officer 8.9
double[2a]
double 1.6

Section

doubler[4a]
double 4.2
doublure
lining 6.8
doucement[1b]
slow 1.2
doucereux[6b]
mawkish .... 11.
douceur[2a]
sweetness 5.2
gentleness 5.5
douer[4b]
endow 4.3
douleur[1b]
pain .... 1.
grief 1.8
douloureusement[5a]
painful 3.2
douloureux[3a]
painful 3.2
doute[1a]
doubt .... 1.
sans – (without) doubt .. 1.
douter[2b]
doubt 1.5
douter (se)[3a]
– de, suspect 2.9
douteux[3b]
doubtful 2.6
douve
stave 7.2
doux[1a]
gentle 1.4
soft 1.4
sweet 1.4
douzaine[3a]
dozen 3.4
douze[1b]
twelve 1.9
douzième
twelfth 6.3
doyen[6a]
dean .... 7.
dragon[6a]
dragon .... 5.
dragoon 8.6
dramatique[3b]
l'art –, drama 3.7
dramatic 4.6
drame[3a]
drama 3.7
drap[3b]
sheet 4.9
drapeau[3b]
flag 2.6
draper[6b]
cover .... 1.
dresser[1b]
lift .... 1.
draw up (formulate) 2.
drogue[6b]
drug 5.8
droit (*n.*)[1a]
right 1.8
droit (*adj.*)[1a]
direct .... 1.
right (correct) .... 1.
right (hand) .... 1.
fair 1.4
straight 1.8
droit (*adv.*)[6b]
direct 1.1
droiture[6b]
righteousness 6.9
drôle (*adj.*)[2b]
strange .... 1.
funny 2.9

Section

drôle (*n.*)[4a]
knave 4.5
duc[4b]
duke 2.3
duché
dukedom 6.8
duchesse[4b]
duchess 4.7
duel[4b]
duel .... 7.
dûment
duly 4.5
dupe[4a]
dupe 8.2
dur[1b]
hard (not soft) .... 1.
tough .... 5.
durable[6b]
lasting 4.1
durant (*prep.*)[2a]
during .... 1.
durée[4a]
term 1.8
durement[4a]
severe 1.6
durer[2a]
last 1.1
dureté[6b]
hardness 5.4
dynastie
dynasty 7.8

E

eau[1b]
water .... 1.
eau-de-vie[5a]
liquor 4.3
ébaucher[5b]
outline 4.5
éblouir[3b]
dazzle 3.9
éblouissant[4b]
dazzle 3.9
éblouissement[6b]
surprise 2.4
ébouriffer[6b]
ruffle 5.8
ébranler[3b]
shake 1.9
ébullition[5b]
boiling 5.3
écaille
flake 6.8
écart[2b]
à l' –, aside 3.1
écarter[2a]
take away .... 1.
ecclésiastique[5b]
church 2.6
échafaud[5b]
scaffold 7.1
échange[3a]
exchange .... 2.
échanger[2a]
exchange 3.5
échantillon[5a]
sample 2.7
échapper[1b]
escape 1.8
escape (the memory) 2.6
écharpe[5a]
scarf 6.1
échauffer[4b]
heat 2.2

Section

émeute[6b]
riot 4.6

émigration[6a]
emigration 7.7

émigré (*n.*)[5a]
emigrant 7.3

émigrer[6a]
emigrate 7.6

éminemment[6b]
eminently 4.1

éminence
eminence 5.3

éminent[4a]
famous 1.1

emmener[2b]
bring .... 1.
take away .... 1.

émoi[6a]
worry 2.8
emotion 3.2

émotion[1b]
feeling .... 1.
emotion 4.3

émousser
blunt 6.2
émoussé
dull 5.2

émouvoir[2b]
move 1.5

emparer de (s')[3a]
(take) possession (of) 1.8

empêcher[1a]
keep from 1.4
hinder 3.7

empereur[3a]
emperor 2.1

emphase[6b]
emphasis 5.1

empire[3a]
empire 1.7
dominion 3.1

emplir[3b]
fill 1.4

emploi[3b]
use 1.1
employment 3.7

employé(-e) (*n.*)[3a]
clerk 2.7
employee 3.1

employer[1b]
use .... 1.

empoisonnement[6b]
poisoning 5.8

empoisonner[3b]
poison 5.1

emporter[1a]
take away .... 1.

emporter (s')[4b]
(get) angry 2.4
rage 3.7

empreinte[5b]
impression 2.6

empressement[7a]
hurry 2.4

empresser (s')[2b]
hurry 1.2

emprisonnement
imprisonment .... 5.

emprisonner[6a]
imprison 3.6

emprunt[4b]
loan 5.3

emprunter[4b]
borrow 3.3

ému (*adj.*)[2a]
nervous 4.4

Section

en (*prep.*)[1a]
in .... 1.

en (*pron.*)[1a]
any (some) .... 1.
of .... 1.

encadrer[3b]
frame 5.1

enceinte (*n.*)[5b]
wall 1.7

encens
incense 6.1

enchaîner[6a]
chain 2.7

enchantement[6a]
spell 4.4

enchanter[2a]
delight .... 2.
charm 2.4

enclos[5a]
shut in, up 1.9

enclume
anvil 7.2

encombrer[4b]
crowd (*vb.*) 2.2
block up .... 4.

encore[1a]
again .... 1.
still .... 1.

encouragement[5b]
encouragement 6.7

encourager[3a]
urge 2.5
encourage 4.8

encourir
incur 3.6

encre[4a]
ink 5.1

encrier
inkwell 8.9

en dessous[6a]
beneath 1.6

endormir[3a]
put to sleep .... 4.

endormir (s')[2b]
(go to) sleep 3.9

endos(sement)
indorsement 11.2

endroit[1b]
place .... 1.

endurcir[6b]
harden 6.1

énergie[2a]
energy 3.6

énergique[3b]
(full of) energy 3.3

énergiquement[5b]
(full of) energy 3.3

énerver[3b]
énervé, nervous 4.4

enfance[2b]
childhood 3.3

enfant[1a]
child .... 1.
chambre d'-s, nursery . 5.8

enfantillage[6a]
childish 4.6

enfantin[3b]
childish 4.6

enfer[4a]
hell .... 3.

enfermer[2a]
shut in, up 1.9

enfin[1a]
(at) last .... 1.

Section

enflammer[6b]
stir 1.9
set (on) fire 2.7

enfler[6a]
swell 3.9

enfoncer[2a]
sink 3.2

enfouir[7a]
bury 3.1

enfuir (s')[2b]
run away 1.5

engagement[3b]
engagement 4.7

engager[1b]
engage 1.9

engeance[6a]
brood 5.8

engendrer[4b]
beget 3.4

engloutir[7a]
devour 3.8

engouement[6b]
fad 8.5

engourdir[5b]
dull 5.3

engrais
fertilizer 5.7

engraisser[6b]
(get, grow) fat 2.7

enivrer[6b]
(make) drunk 4.8

enivrer (s')[6a]
(get) drunk 5.8

enjamber[5b]
stride 3.3

enlevé (*adj.*)[7a]
choice 5.3

enlèvement[6b]
removal 4.6

enlever[1b]
take away .... 1.
take off 1.8

ennemi[1a]
enemy .... 1.

ennoblir[6a]
ennoble 6.8

ennui[2b]
care 1.3
bore .... 4.
vexation 5.8

ennuyer[3a]
trouble 1.5
vex 4.1
bore 4.6

ennuyeux[4a]
troublesome 4.4
tedious 5.2

énoncer[5b]
state 2.2

enorgueillir (s')[7a]
(be) proud (of) 1.6

énorme[1b]
great (huge) .... 1.

enquête[3a]
inquiry 3.5

enraciné
– dans, (have) roots in 4.2

enrager[5a]
(make) mad 2.9

enregistration
registering 4.2

enregistrer[3b]
register .... 3.

enrichir[3b]
enrich .... 5.

enrôlement
draft 5.2

Section

enrouler (s')[6a]
wind 3.3
twist .... 4.

enseigne[6b]
sign 3.4

enseignement[2b]
instruction 2.4

enseigner[2b]
teach .... 1.

ensemble[1a]
together .... 1.
whole 1.5

ensoleillé
sunny .... 6.

ensuite[1a]
then .... 1.
afterwards 1.8

ensuivre (s')[7a]
follow .... 1.
result 1.5

entamer[4a]
take up 1.7

entasser[4b]
heap up 3.2

entendre[1a]
hear .... 1.

entendu (*adj.*)[2a]
bien –, (of) course .... 1.
agreed 2.8

entente[4b]
understanding 1.7
agreement 3.1

enterrement[5a]
burial 5.7

enterrer[4a]
bury 3.1

entêtement
obstinacy 7.2

enthousiasme[2a]
enthusiasm 3.6

enthousiaste[6a]
enthusiastic 5.4

entier[1a]
complete .... 1.

entièrement[2b]
all .... 1.

entourage[5b]
circle 1.1

entourer[1b]
surround 1.8

entrailles
entrails 7.7

entraîner[1b]
draw along 2.6

entre[1a]
among .... 1.
between .... 1.

entrée[1b]
entrance (place) 1.8
entrance (act) 2.2

entremets[6a]
(side) dish 4.6

entreprendre[3a]
undertake 2.5

entrepreneur[6b]
contractor 6.6

entreprise[2b]
undertaking 2.4

entrer[1a]
enter .... 1.

entretenir (s')[3b]
talk .... 1.

entretien[2b]
talk .... 1.
conversation 2.6
keeping up 3.4
interview 4.3

Section

étourdissement[6b]
daze ... 7.8
étrange[1b]
strange ... 1.
étranger[1a]
stranger ... 1.8
à l'–, abroad ... 2.2
foreign ... 2.2
foreigner ... 2.6
étrangler[4a]
choke ... 5.3
être (*vb.*)[1a]
be ... 1.
être (*n.*)[1b]
being ... 1.
étreindre[4a]
clasp ... 3.1
étreinte[6a]
embrace ... 5.2
étrier
stirrup ... 7.
étroit[1b]
narrow ... 1.
étroitement[4b]
narrow ... 1.
étude[2a]
study ... 1.5
étudiant[4a]
student ... 3.1
étudier[1b]
study ... 1.4
étui[6b]
case ... 3.6
européen[3b]
European ... 2.5
eux[1a]
they ... 1.
eux-mêmes[5b]
themselves ... 1.4
évacuer[5a]
evacuate ... 7.7
évader[5b]
escape ... 1.8
évaluer[4a]
rate ... 2.3
évangile[6a]
gospel ... 3.4
évanouir (s')[3b]
faint ... 3.3
évanouissement[6b]
faint ... 4.1
éveil
en –, watchful ... 6.4
éveiller[2a]
wake (*tr. vb.*) ... 1.9
s'–, wake (*intr. vb.*) ... 1.9
événement[1b]
event ... †2.
éventail[6b]
fan ... 3.9
éventuel[6a]
casual ... 3.8
évêque[3a]
bishop ... 3.3
évidemment[2a]
evident ... 2.5
évidence[3a]
evidence ... 2.3
évident[3a]
evident ... 2.5
éviter[1b]
avoid ... 1.8
évoluer[6a]
change ... 1.4
évolution[4a]
development ... 2.1
evolution ... 4.5

Section

évoquer[3a]
call forth ... 1.6
exact[2b]
exact ... 1.4
exactement[2a]
exact ... 1.4
exactitude[5a]
precision ... 5.8
exagération[5b]
exaggeration ... 7.7
exagérer[2b]
exaggerate ... 4.5
exaltation[4a]
exaltation ... 6.3
exalter[4a]
elate ... 1.9
exalt ... 2.7
examen[2a]
test ... 1.9
examiner[1b]
examine ... 1.5
exaspérer[4b]
exaspéré, angry ... 2.4
excellence[3a]
highness ... 4.8
excellence (superiority) ... 5.1
excellence (refinement) ... 5.6
excellent[1b]
excellent ... 1.8
exceller[6a]
excel ... 3.5
excepté (*prep.*)[5b]
except ... 1.1
excepter[6a]
except ... 1.7
exception[3a]
exception ... 2.5
exceptionnel[4a]
exceptional ... 5.4
exceptionnellement[6b]
exceptionally ... 4.8
excès[2b]
excess ... 3.3
excessif[4a]
extreme ... 1.5
excessive ... 4.6
excitation[6a]
excitement ... 4.2
exciter[2b]
stir ... 1.9
urge on ... 4.8
exclamation[4b]
exclamation ... 5.3
exclure[4a]
shut out ... 1.6
exclusif[4b]
exclusive ... 4.2
exclusivement[4a]
exclusively ... 3.
excursion[6b]
excursion ... 4.1
excuse[2b]
excuse ... 2.9
excuser[2a]
pardon ... 2.2
exécuter[2a]
carry out ... 1.
faire –, enforce ... 4.4
exécuteur[5b]
executor ... 7.7
exécutif
executive ... 6.5
exécution[3a]
carrying out ... 2.2
performance ... 3.

Section

exemplaire (*n.*)[4b]
copy ... 2.7
exemple[1a]
example ... 1.4
par –, (for) example ... 1.4
exemption[6a]
exemption ... 7.8
exercer[2a]
exercise ... 1.6
exercice[2b]
exercise ... 1.7
exhaler[5a]
breathe ... 2.7
exhibition[5b]
display ... 2.6
exhorter
admonish ... 6.3
exigence[5b]
demand ... 3.
exiger[2a]
demand ... 1.
exil[4a]
exile ... 6.
exiler[5a]
banish ... 4.1
existence[1b]
existence ... 2.6
exister[1a]
exist ... 1.8
exotique[6b]
foreign ... 2.2
expansif[5b]
expansive ... 9.3
expansion[5b]
expansion ... 4.1
expédier[3b]
send ... 1.
expédition[3a]
sending ... 2.6
expedition ... 3.1
shipment ... 3.9
expérience[2a]
experience ... 1.6
faire l'–, experience ... 1.8
faire des -s, experiment 2.4
experiment ... 2.6
expérimental[6a]
experimental ... 7.7
expert[5a]
expert (*n.*) ... 4.2
expiation
atonement ... 7.
expirer[4b]
expire ... 4.3
explicatif
explanatory ... 10.2
explication[3b]
explanation ... 2.9
expliquer[1a]
account for ... 1.
exploit[4b]
exploit ... 5.9
exploitation[4b]
working ... 4.7
exploiter[3a]
exploit ... 5.8
exploration[6b]
exploration ... 4.6
explorer[6a]
explore ... 3.8
explosion[5a]
bursting ... 2.9
exportation[5a]
export ... 5.1
exposé (*n.*)[6a]
statement ... 2.1

Section

exposer[1b]
expose ... 2.2
exposition[3b]
display ... 2.6
exprès (*adj.*)[3a]
express ... 2.6
expressif[5a]
(full of) meaning ... 3.3
expression[1b]
expression ... 2.2
exprimer[1b]
express ... 1.
expulser[3b]
expel ... 4.3
expulsion
expulsion ... 9.
exquis[2b]
exquisite ... 3.6
extension[6a]
extension ... 4.4
exténuer[5b]
exhaust ... 2.4
extérieur[2a]
outside ... 1.4
outward(s) ... 3.4
extraction[5b]
de basse – (of) lowly birth ... 6.4
extraire[5b]
extract ... 5.
extrait (*n.*)[6a]
extract ... 5.4
extraordinaire[2a]
unusual ... 2.
extravagant[5b]
extravagant ... 7.3
extrême[2a]
extreme ... 1.5
extrêmement[2b]
very ... 1.
extrémité[2b]
extremity ... 5.1

F

fable[5a]
fairy tale ... 3.4
fable ... 4.4
fabricant[6b]
maker (manufacturer) ... 3.5
maker ... 4.7
fabrication[4b]
manufacture ... 2.9
fabrique[5a]
factory ... 2.6
fabriquer[3b]
manufacture ... 3.
fabuleux[6a]
fabulous ... 7.1
façade[4a]
front ... 1.5
face[1a]
en –, across ... 1.
face ... 1.
en –, opposite ... 1.4
fâché[3a]
angry ... 2.4
fâcher[5a]
offend ... 2.8
grieve ... 3.4
fâcher (se)[4b]
(be) hurt ... 2.3
(get) angry ... 2.4
fâcheux[3a]
unpleasant ... 3.8
facile[1b]
easy ... 1.

Section

figue
fig . . . 6.4
figure[1a]
face . . . 1.
figurer[6b]
be . . . 1.
figurer (se)[2b]
imagine . . . 1.4
fil[2b]
thread . . . 2.4
edge (of knife) . . . 2.6
– de fer, cuivre, etc.
wire . . . 4.2
sans –, wireless . . . 6.
file[3a]
row . . . 1.2
filer[2b]
spin . . . 3.9
filet[4a]
net . . . 3.1
filial
filial . . . 5.8
fille[1a]
daughter . . . 1.
jeune –, girl . . . 1.
fillette[5b]
girl . . . 1.
fils[1a]
son . . . 1.
fin (*n.*)[1a]
end . . . 1.
tirer à sa –, run down 2.6
fin (*adj.*)[1b]
fine . . . 1.
final[3a]
final . . . 2.9
finalement[4b]
(at) last . . . 1.
finally . . . 2.2
finance[3a]
finance . . . 5.3
financier[3b]
financial . . . 4.1
finesse[3b]
delicacy . . . 5.4
fini (*adj.*)[3b]
end . . . 1.
finir[1a]
end . . . 1.
fixe (*adj.*)[3a]
fix . . . 1.
firm (fixed) . . . 1.1
fixer[1b]
fix . . . 1.
peer . . . 3.5
fixité[6b]
firmness (physical) . 5.5
flacon[4a]
bottle . . . 2.1
flairer[5a]
smell . . . 3.5
flagrant[5b]
flagrant . . . 10.1
flamand[6b]
Belgian . . . 9.
flambeau[5a]
torch . . . 5.
flamber[3b]
blaze . . . 4.3
flamme[2b]
flame . . . 2.
flanc[3a]
side . . . 1.
flanelle
flannel . . . 7.2
flâner
stroll . . . 6.6
flanquer[4b]
flank . . . 6.4

Section

flatter[3a]
flatter . . . 3.
flatterie
flattery . . . 6.6
flèche[4a]
arrow . . . 3.2
fléchir[6a]
bend . . . 2.4
flétrir[4b]
se –, droop . . . 4.4
fade . . . 4.9
fleur[1b]
flower . . . 1.4
blossom . . . 2.2
– d'oranger
orange blossom . . 4.9
fleurir[3a]
blossom . . . 3.
fleuri, flowery . . . 5.5
fleuve[3b]
river . . . 1.5
flocon
snowflake . . . 7.8
flot[3a]
wave . . . 2.9
à –, afloat . . . 6.7
flottant[6a]
float . . . 2.9
flotte[6b]
fleet . . . 3.
flotter[2b]
wave . . . 1.7
float . . . 2.9
fluide[5b]
fluid . . . 3.4
liquid . . . 3.4
flûte
flute . . . 6.5
flux[6a]
flow . . . 2.6
foi[1b]
faith . . . 1.4
foie[4b]
liver . . . 6.
foin[5b]
hay . . . 4.8
foire[5a]
market . . . 1.7
fois[1a]
encore une –, again . . . 1.
une –, once . . . 1.
time (how many) . . 1.
à la –, (at same) time . . 1.
deux –, two times 1.8
chaque –, every time . 2.2
pour la première –
(for the) first time 2.6
folie[2a]
folly . . . 3.2
madness . . . 4.1
folle (*n.*)[5a]
mad . . . 2.7
foncer[4a]
deepen . . . 5.
fonction[2b]
function . . . 3.6
fonctionnaire[3b]
official . . . 2.8
fonctionnement[6b]
working . . . 5.
fonctionner[4a]
function . . . 2.8
fond[1a]
bottom . . . 1.
à –, thorough . . . 2.
background . . . 4.2
fondamental[4a]
fundamental . . . 5.2
fondateur[5b]
founder . . . 6.1

Section

fondation[5b]
establishment . . . 3.8
foundation . . . 4.2
foundation (of a
building) . . . 4.4
fonder[2a]
found . . . 1.5
– sur, rest on . . . 1.9
fondre[2b]
melt . . . 2.5
– en larmes
burst into tears . . 3.5
fonds[5a]
funds . . . 4.6
fontaine[3a]
fountain . . . 2.8
fonte[5b]
melting . . . 3.3
football
football . . . 6.8
forain[6a]
peddler . . . 7.
force (*n.*)[1a]
force . . . 1.
forcé (*adj.*)[2b]
forced . . . 1.1
forcément[5a]
(of) necessity . . . 2.3
forcer[1b]
force . . . 1.
forêt[2a]
forest . . . 1.
forge[5a]
forge . . . 5.9
forger[5a]
forge . . . 5.7
forgeron[4b]
blacksmith . . . 5.6
formalité[5a]
ceremony . . . 2.
formality . . . 7.9
formation[4b]
formation . . . 4.
forme[1a]
figure . . . 1.
former[1a]
form . . . 1.
formidable[2b]
terrible . . . 1.8
formule[3a]
formula . . . 5.3
formuler[4b]
draw up . . . 2.
fort (*adj.*)[1a]
strong . . . 1.
fat . . . 1.9
fort (*adv.*)[4a]
very . . . 1.
fortement[2b]
strong . . . 1.
forteresse[5a]
fort . . . 2.6
fortifier[5a]
strengthen . . . 3.4
fortuit
accidental . . . 4.7
fortune[1b]
fortune . . . 1.4
fossé[3b]
ditch (irrigation) . . . 3.6
ditch . . . 3.9
fossette
dimple . . . 7.2
fou (*n.*)[3a]
mad . . . 2.7
fou, folle (*adj.*)[2a]
mad . . . 2.7
rendre –, (make) mad 2.9

Section

foudre[4a]
thunderbolt . . . 4.1
fouet[5a]
whip . . . 4.8
fouetter[4b]
whip . . . 4.8
fougère
fern . . . 6.4
fouiller[2b]
dig . . . 4.8
foule[1b]
crowd . . . 1.
fouler[4b]
step . . . 1.1
foulure
wrench . . . 6.8
four[4a]
furnace . . . 2.7
oven . . . 2.7
fourchette[5a]
fork . . . 4.2
fourmi
ant . . . 6.
fourneau[5a]
stove . . . 3.3
fournir[1b]
supply . . . 1.1
– plus tard
supply later . . . 3.
fourreau[4b]
sheath . . . 4.4
fourrer[4b]
place . . . 1.
fourrure
fur . . . 5.
foyer[2a]
hearth . . . 3.2
focus . . . 6.1
fracas[5b]
noise . . . 2.6
crash . . . 5.6
fracasser[6a]
shatter . . . 4.2
fraction[6b]
fraction . . . 4.9
fragile[4b]
delicate . . . 2.3
frail . . . 5.1
fraîcheur[3a]
cool . . . 3.2
frais (*adj.*)[2a]
fresh . . . 1.1
frais (*n.*)[2a]
price . . . 1.
cool . . . 1.9
expense . . . 3.3
fraise[6a]
strawberry . . . 5.8
franc (*n.*)[1b]
pound . . . 1.
franc (*adj.*)[3a]
open . . . 1.3
français (*adj.*)[1a]
English . . . 1.
Français (*n.*)[5a]
English . . . 1.
franchement[3b]
open . . . 1.3
franchir[2a]
cross . . . 1.
franchise[5b]
frankness . . . 7.2
frange
fringe . . . 5.8
frappant (*adj.*)[6b]
striking . . . 2.5

Section

glace[2a]
- ice 2.4
- mirror 2.8

glacer[3a]
- freeze 3.3

glacial[6b]
- icy 6.

glacier
- glacier 6.4

gland
- acorn 6.8
- tassel 7.

glissant (*adj.*)[5b]
- slippery 6.1

glisser[2a]
- slip 2.8

globe[6b]
- ball 2.1
- globe 3.3
- globe (earth) 3.3

gloire[2a]
- glory 2.3

glorieux[4a]
- glorious 3.8

glousser
- cluck 6.4

golfe[6b]
- gulf 5.

gond[5b]
- hinge 6.5

gonfler[3b]
- swell 3.9

gorge[2b]
- throat 2.

gorger (se)
- gorge 6.

gosse[6b]
- boy 1.4

gothique[6a]
- Gothic 6.7

goudron
- tar 6.4

gouffre[4b]
- abyss 4.1

gourmand[6a]
- greedy 6.

gourmet[5a]
- epicure 11.3

goût[1b]
- taste 1.4

goûter[2b]
- taste 1.5

goutte (*drop*)[2b]
- drop 2.4

goutte (*gout*)[6b]
- gout 7.6

gouvernail
- helm 5.6

gouvernante[6a]
- governess 8.2

gouvernement[2a]
- government 1.1

gouverner[4b]
- rule 1.
- steer 3.9

gouverneur[4a]
- governor 3.1

grâce[1a]
- grace 1.4
- faire –, spare 3.4

gracieux[3b]
- graceful 3.3

grade[5b]
- rank 2.6

grain[3a]
- grain 2.1
- seed 2.7

Section

grain[3a]—*continued*
- berry 4.9
- – de beauté, mole 6.3

graine[5b]
- seed 2.7
- berry 4.9

graisse[6a]
- fat 2.6
- grease 4.8

grammaire[6b]
- grammar 6.1

grand[1a]
- big 1.
- great (huge) 1.
- great (a great man) 1.
- tall 1.
- -e envie, longing 1.9
- de -e valeur, valuable 2.7
- marcher à -s pas, stride 3.3

grand'chose[6a]
- much 1.

grandeur[2b]
- height 1.1
- size 1.3
- greatness 2.

grandiose[4b]
- grand 2.3

grandir[2b]
- grow 1.1

grand'mère[3a]
- grandmother 2.4

grand-père[3b]
- grandfather 3.2

grange
- barn 5.5

granit
- granite 6.8

gras[3a]
- fat (stout) 1.9
- fat 2.6

gratitude[4b]
- gratitude 3.3

gratter[4b]
- scratch 5.3
- scrape 5.6

gratuit[5a]
- free (of charge) 2.6

grave[1a]
- grave 1.4

gravement[2b]
- grave 1.4

graver[5a]
- engrave 6.4

gravier
- gravel 6.8

gravir[4a]
- climb 2.7

gravité[3a]
- gravity 3.8

gravure[4b]
- print 2.7

gré[2b]
- pleasure 1.4

grec[4a]
- Greek 2.6

greffier[6a]
- clerk (who writes) 3.8

grêle (*n.*)[5b]
- hail 5.3

grêle (*adj.*)[6a]
- weak 1.1
- slight 3.3

grelotter[5b]
- tremble 1.8

grenier[5a]
- attic 6.3

grenouille
- frog 5.6

Section

grève[4a]
- strike 3.
- beach 3.9

grièvement[6b]
- grave 1.4

griffe[6a]
- claw 6.1

grille[3b]
- bar 4.6

griller[5a]
- toast 5.6

grillon
- cricket 5.3

grimace[4a]
- face 1.8

grimper[3b]
- climb 2.7

grincer[5a]
- grind (teeth) 5.
- grate (squeak) 5.7
- grate (creak) (e.g., door) 5.8

gris (*gray*)[2a]
- gray 2.2

griser[4a]
- (make) drunk 4.8

grive
- thrush 7.1

grogner[5a]
- murmur 2.9
- grumble 4.9

gronder[2b]
- scold 4.

gros[1a]
- big 1.
- fat 1.9

groseille[4b]
- currant 6.8

grosse
- gross 5.2

grossier[4b]
- coarse 2.9

grossir[4a]
- grow 1.1
- magnify 4.1

grotesque[4b]
- ridiculous 3.6

grouiller[6b]
- swarm 5.

groupe[1b]
- group 1.8

groupement[6a]
- party 1.1
- grouping 3.6

grouper[3b]
- group 3.6

gué
- ford 6.4

guêpe
- wasp 7.2

guère[1a]
- hardly 1.4

guérir[3a]
- cure 2.9

guerre[1b]
- war 1.

guerrier[5a]
- warrior 3.5

guetter[3b]
- watch 1.

gueule[6a]
- mouth 1.

gueux[5a]
- beggar 4.
- tramp 4.9

guichet[6b]
- ticket window 5.3

Section

guide[4b]
- guide 1.9

guider[3a]
- guide 1.3

guillotine[6b]
- guillotine 10.2

guise[4b]
- way 1.

guitare
- guitar 8.

gymnase
- gymnasium 7.2

H

habile[3a]
- clever 2.6
- skilful 4.2

habilement[5b]
- clever 2.6

habileté[4a]
- ability 3.2

habiller[2a]
- clothe 1.9

habit[2a]
- suit 2.7

habitant[2b]
- inhabitant 3.2

habitation[5a]
- dwelling 2.3

habiter[1b]
- live 1.1
- inhabit 3.5

habitude[1b]
- d'–, (in) general 1.
- avoir l'–, (be) used 1.4
- habit 2.2

habitué (*adj.*)[3a]
- (be) used 1.4

habituel[2b]
- usual 1.

habituellement[5a]
- (in) general 1.

habituer[3a]
- (make) used (to) 1.6

hache[5a]
- ax(e) 5.

hacher[5b]
- chop 4.2

hagard[6b]
- ghastly 6.4

haie[2b]
- hedge 5.4

haillon[6b]
- rag 5.3
- en -s, ragged 6.

haine[2b]
- hate 2.4

haïr[3a]
- hate 2.5

haleine[4a]
- breath 2.8

haleter[5a]
- pant 5.7

hanche
- hip 6.4

hanter[5b]
- haunt 5.7

happer[7a]
- snap 5.9

harangue[6a]
- talk 1.2

harasser[6b]
- torment 3.1
- harry 4.1

I

Section

idée[1a]
idea 1.4
identique[4b]
identical 3.5
identité[5a]
identity 7.5
idiot[5b]
dull 3.5
idiot 5.8
idole
idol 5.9
idylle
idyll 9.8
if
yew 7.2
ignoble[6a]
ignoble 4.6
ignorance[4a]
ignorance 4.6
ignorant[3a]
ignorant 5.
ignorer[1b]
(not) know 1.
il(s)[1a]
he 1.
it 1.
they 1.
ainsi soit-il, amen 4.3
île[2b]
island 1.5
illégal
lawless 6.5
illicite
(without) authority 4.8
illimité[6b]
boundless 4.9
illuminer[4b]
light 1.4
illusion[2b]
illusion 4.7
illustration[5b]
illustration 6.8
illustre[2b]
famous 1.1
illustrious 3.1
illustrer[5a]
illustrate 5.2
image[2b]
picture 1.1
image 3.5
imagé[4a]
vivid 3.8
imaginaire[4a]
fancied 3.8
imaginatif
imaginative 7.7
imagination[2a]
imagination 3.9
imaginer[3a]
imagine 1.4
imaginer (s')[1b]
imagine 1.4
imbécile[2b]
fool 2.4
idiot 5.8
imitation[6b]
copy 3.3
imiter[2a]
copy 3.2
imitate 4.
immédiat[3a]
immediate 2.8
immédiatement[2a]
(at) once 1.
immediate 2.8
immense[1b]
great (huge) 1.

Section

immeuble[4a]
(real) estate 3.2
imminent[5a]
imminent 6.1
immobile[2a]
still 1.3
stable 2.9
immobilité[5a]
immobility 12.9
immoral
immoral 12.2
immoralité
immorality 11.4
immortalité
immortality 6.
immortel[3b]
immortal 3.8
immuable
unchangeable 8.9
impartial[6b]
impartial 5.
impassible[5a]
unmoved 7.
impatience[2b]
impatience 5.3
impatient[4a]
impatient 4.3
impatienter[4a]
vex 4.1
impératrice
empress 4.6
imperceptible[4a]
invisible 3.7
imperceptible 7.8
impérial[6b]
imperial 3.3
impérieux[4a]
commanding 1.9
imperméable
waterproof 6.8
impertinence[6b]
impertinence 9.4
impétueux[5b]
headlong 4.2
impétuosité
impetuosity 9.9
impie[6b]
impious 6.5
impitoyable[4b]
merciless 5.4
implacable[5b]
implacable 7.7
impliquer[4b]
involve 3.9
implorer[4b]
beg 2.7
impoli[5a]
rude 5.2
importance[1b]
importance 1.8
important[1b]
important 1.
importation[5b]
import 4.5
importer[1b]
n'importe
any (whatever) 1.
matter (neg.) 1.
n'importe quand
whenever 1.4
n'importe qui
anybody 1.8
import 1.8
n'importe où
anywhere 4.1
n'importe comment
anyhow 4.2

Section

importun[6a]
vexing 3.8
troublesome 4.4
imposant (*adj.*)[4b]
imposing 5.6
imposer[1b]
impose 3.
imposition
imposition 8.2
impossible[1b]
impossible 1.4
impossibilité[4b]
impossibility 7.1
impôt[3a]
tax 1.6
tarif d'–, tax rate 4.
imprégner[4b]
impregnate 8.8
impression[1b]
impression 2.2
impressionner[4b]
affect 3.2
imprévu[4a]
accident 2.3
unexpected 3.5
imprimer[2b]
print 2.4
imprimé
printed matter 2.4
imprimerie
printing office 4.4
impropre[6b]
unfit 6.4
improper 7.2
improviser[5a]
improvise 8.9
imprudence[6a]
indiscretion 9.
imprudent[4a]
imprudent 10.
impuissance[5b]
impotence 8.7
impuissant[5a]
helpless 5.
impulsion[6b]
spur 3.6
impur[6a]
impure 7.5
inaperçu[5a]
unseen 4.8
inattendu[3a]
unexpected 3.5
inaugurer[3b]
inaugurate 4.8
incapable[2a]
unable 4.1
incapacité[6b]
impotence 8.7
incarner
embody 6.8
incendie[4b]
fire 1.
burning 2.3
incendier[6b]
set (on) fire 2.7
incertain[4a]
uncertain 4.
incertitude
uncertainty 6.5
incessant[5a]
continual 2.5
incident[2a]
event 2.
incident 4.2
inclinaison[6b]
slope 3.6

Section

inclination[6b]
liking 1.5
leaning 1.8
incliner[3b]
slant 2.8
nod 3.2
incliner (s')[3b]
lean 2.2
incommode[6a]
uncomfortable 4.6
incomparable[4a]
incomparable 6.4
incompatible[6b]
incompatible 9.9
incomplet[3b]
imperfect 4.2
unfinished 6.9
incompréhensible[3b]
incomprehensible 6.7
inconnu[1b]
stranger 1.8
unknown 1.8
inconscient[4a]
unconscious 4.4
incontestable[5a]
unquestionable 6.5
inconvénient[3a]
inconvenience 4.1
incroyable[5a]
incredible 5.4
inculpé[6a]
accused 3.1
inculte[6b]
wild 1.7
terre –, prairie 6.2
incurable
incurable 7.4
indécis[3b]
doubtful 2.6
vague 4.
dim 4.1
indécision[6b]
être dans l' –
undecided 9.2
indéfinissable
undefinable 10.2
indépendance[2b]
independence 3.6
indépendant[3b]
independent 2.5
indescriptible
indescribable 7.2
indésirable
unwelcome 7.2
index
index finger 6.3
indicatif
indicative 4.6
indication[3b]
indication 5.
indice[5a]
sign 1.1
proof 1.4
indication 5.
indicible[5b]
unspeakable 6.7
inexpressible 9.3
indien
Indian 3.1
indifférence[4a]
indifference 4.7
indifférent[2b]
(all the) same 1.
indigène[4a]
native (*adj.*) 3.2
native (*n.*) 3.7
indignation[4b]
anger 1.9
indignation 4.2

Section

intervention[3a]
intervention ... 8.4
interview[5b]
interview ... 4.3
intestin
bowel ... 6.4
intime[2a]
intimate ... 3.2
intimider[6a]
intimidate ... 10.2
intimité[4a]
intimacy ... 6.8
intituler[4b]
(give) name to ... 1.
intolérable[4a]
intolerable ... 5.3
intonation[6a]
intonation ... 10.2
intrépide[6b]
(be) brave ... 1.
fearless ... 6.3
intriguer[5a]
(make) curious ... 2.9
introduction[5b]
introduction (book, etc.) ... 3.7
introduire[2a]
introduce ... 2.7
insert ... 4.4
intrus
intruder ... 7.4
intuition[6a]
intuition ... 9.4
inutile[1b]
(of no) use ... 1.8
unnecessary ... 4.2
inutilement[4a]
(in) vain ... 1.9
invaincu
unconquered ... 8.6
invasion[5b]
faire une –, invade ... 3.8
invasion ... 5.4
inventer[2b]
invent ... 2.4
inventeur[5a]
inventor ... 4.8
invention[3a]
invention ... 2.6
inverse[5b]
(wrong) side ... 1.7
investigation[6b]
inquiry ... 3.5
invincible[5a]
invincible ... 7.3
invisible[2b]
invisible ... 3.7
invitation[4b]
invitation ... 3.2
invité (*n.*)[4b]
company ... 1.7
inviter[1b]
invite ... 2.3
involontaire[6b]
involuntary ... 5.3
involontairement[5b]
involuntary ... 5.3
invoquer[4b]
call upon ... 1.5
invraisemblable[5b]
improbable ... 7.9
iris
iris ... 7.
ironie[3a]
irony ... 8.2
ironique[4a]
ironical ... 8.5

Section

irréparable[5a]
irreparable ... 9.9
irrésistible[3b]
irresistible ... 5.4
irrésolu[5a]
irresolute ... 8.1
irrigation
irrigation ... 7.3
irritable
fretful ... 6.6
irritation[6a]
irritation (physical) 5.4
irrité[6b]
angry ... 2.4
irriter[3b]
anger ... 2.7
irruption[5b]
irruption ... 10.1
isolé[2b]
cut off ... 2.9
isolément[4b]
cut off ... 2.9
isolement
isolation ... 8.2
isoler[4a]
cut off ... 3.1
issu (*adj.*)[5a]
born (of) ... 1.4
issue (*n.*)[4a]
result ... 1.5
way out ... 2.
isthme
isthmus ... 5.8
italien[2b]
Italian ... 2.4
ivoire
ivory ... 5.6
ivre[4a]
drunk ... 5.5
ivresse[3a]
bliss ... 3.7
drunkenness ... 7.3
ivrogne[4b]
drunken (person) ... 5.9

J

jadis[1b]
once ... 1.
long ago ... 1.3
formerly ... 2.2
jaillir[3a]
gush ... 4.5
jalousie[4a]
jealousy ... 4.2
jaloux[2b]
jealous ... 4.1
envious ... 5.7
jamais[1a]
ever ... 1.
never ... 1.
jambe[1a]
leg ... 1.9
jambon[6b]
ham ... 5.7
janvier[2b]
January ... 2.2
japonais
Japanese ... 6.8
jardin[1b]
garden ... 1.4
jardinier[3b]
gardener ... 5.8
jarretière
garter ... 7.
jasmin
jessamine ... 10.

Section

jaune[2b]
yellow ... 2.
jaunir[5a]
yellow ... 2.
je[1a]
I ... 1.
jésuite
Jesuit ... 9.
jet[3b]
gush ... 3.6
jeter[1a]
throw ... 1.
se –, empty ... 3.9
jeu[1b]
game ... 1.5
jeudi[2b]
Thursday ... 2.7
jeune[1a]
– fille, girl ... 1.
young ... 1.
youthful ... 3.3
jeûne[3a]
fast ... 4.4
jeûner
fast ... 4.9
jeunesse[1b]
youth ... 1.4
joie[1b]
delight ... 1.
joindre[2a]
join ... 1.
joint
joint ... 5.8
jointure
joint ... 5.8
joli[1a]
pretty (comely) ... 1.
joliment[4b]
pretty (comely) ... 1.
joncher[5b]
scatter ... 2.4
joue[2a]
cheek ... 2.5
jouer[1a]
play ... 1.
warp ... 3.5
jouet
toy ... 5.1
joueur[4b]
player ... 6.
– de cornemuse, piper. 7.2
playful ... 7.4
joug
yoke ... 4.4
jouir[2a]
enjoy ... 1.1
jouissance[4b]
enjoyment ... 3.8
jour[1a]
day ... 1.
un –, sometime ... 1.
– de fête, holiday ... 2.6
point du –, dawn ... 3.5
la veille du – de l'an (New Year's) Eve 3.8
daylight ... 4.6
journal[1b]
paper (newspaper) ... 1.
journal (diary) ... 4.2
journalier[5a]
daily ... 1.6
journaliste[4a]
journalist ... 10.4
de –, journalistic ... 12.6
journée[1b]
day ... 1.

Section

joyau[6a]
jewel (jewelry) ... 3.1
jewel ... 4.2
joyeusement[3b]
joyful ... 2.2
joyeux[2a]
joyful ... 2.2
judiciaire[6b]
legal ... 4.
judicial ... 8.8
judicieux[6b]
reasonable ... 3.4
juge[2a]
judge ... 1.6
jugement[2b]
reason ... 1.4
judgment (decision) 1.5
judgment (insight). 2.6
juger[1b]
judge ... 1.
juif[6a]
Jew ... 3.5
-s, Jew ... 3.5
Hebrew ... 4.3
juillet[3a]
July ... 2.2
juin[3a]
June ... 2.3
jumeau(-elle)
twin ... 5.8
jument[5a]
horse ... 1.
jupe[4b]
skirt ... 2.6
jurer[2a]
swear ... 2.7
jurisprudence
jurisprudence ... 9.6
juron[5b]
oath ... 4.8
jury[6b]
jury ... 5.
jus
juice ... 4.3
jusqu'à[1a]
till ... 1.
– présent, till now ... 1.
jusqu'à ce que[3b]
till ... 1.
jusque[1a]
till ... 1.
juste[1a]
right (correct) ... 1.
fair ... 1.4
upright ... 3.8
justement[2a]
just ... 1.
justesse[5b]
accuracy ... 5.3
precision ... 5.8
justice[1b]
justice ... 1.8
fairness ... 8.6
justification
justification ... 7.2
justifier[3a]
justify ... 2.5

K

képi[5a]
cap ... 3.8
kilo(gramme)[3b]
pound ... 1.6
kilomètre[3a]
mile ... 1.7

L

Section

loin[1a]
- away . . . 1.
- far . . . 1.
- plus –, beyond . . . 1.8

lointain[2a]
- far . . . 1.
- distance . . . 1.1

loisir[3b]
- leisure . . . 4.8

long[1a]
- long (*adj.*) . . . 1.
- le – de, along . . . 2.2

longer[4b]
- go along . . . 4.1

longtemps[1a]
- long (time) . . . 1.

longueur[4a]
- length . . . 1.7

loquet
- latch . . . 6.8

lorgnon[6b]
- glasses . . . 4.2

lors[1b]
- then . . . 1.

lorsque[1a]
- when . . . 1.
- whenever . . . 1.4

lot[6b]
- fate . . . 1.5
- prize . . . 1.5

louable
- laudable . . . 8.2

louer (*praise*)[3a]
- praise . . . 2.1

louer (*rent*)[3b]
- hire . . . 4.4

loup[3b]
- wolf . . . 4.7

lourd[1b]
- heavy . . . 1.

lourdement[5b]
- heavy . . . 1.

loyal[4b]
- loyal . . . 3.9

loyalement[6b]
- loyal . . . 3.9

loyauté[5a]
- loyalty . . . 3.6

loyer[6b]
- rent . . . 2.5

lucide
- clear . . . 2.

lueur[3b]
- gleam . . . 2.5

luge
- sled . . . 6.8

lugubre[4a]
- dismal . . . 3.9

lui (*pron.*)[1a]
- he . . . 1.
- she . . . 1.

lui-même[5b]
- himself . . . 1.4

luire[3b]
- shine . . . 1.6

lumière[1b]
- light . . . 1.
- – du soleil, sunshine . . 3.2

lumineux[4a]
- luminous . . . 4.2

lundi[4b]
- Monday . . . 3.3

lune[2b]
- moon . . . 1.6
- clair de –, moonlight . . 3.2

lunette[3b]
- glasses . . . 4.2
- – d'approche, telescope 5.4

Section

luth
- lute . . . 7.2

lutin
- elf . . . 6.

lutte[1b]
- fight . . . 1.1
- struggle . . . 1.9

lutter[2b]
- fight . . . 1.6
- wrestle . . . 4.

luxe[2b]
- luxury . . . 3.7

luxueux[6b]
- luxurious . . . 6.6

lycée[5a]
- school . . . 1.

lyre
- lyre . . . 6.9

lyrique[5b]
- lyric . . . 6.5

M

mâcher[6b]
- chew . . . 6.8

machinalement[4a]
- mechanically . . . 5.2

machine[2b]
- machine . . . 2.
- – à écrire, typewriter . . 5.6

mâchoire[4b]
- jaw . . . 5.6

maçon[5b]
- mason . . . 6.3

madame[1b]
- Mrs. . . . 1.

mademoiselle[2b]
- miss . . . 1.1

magasin[4a]
- store . . . 2.6

magique[5a]
- pouvoir –, magic . . . 3.5

magistrat[3b]
- magistrate . . . 4.

magnétique
- magnetic . . . 7.4

magnifique[1b]
- fine . . . 1.1
- magnificent . . . 3.5

mai[2b]
- May . . . 1.2

maigre[2b]
- thin . . . 2.

maille[5b]
- stitch . . . 6.1

maillot[6a]
- tights . . . 5.1

main[1a]
- hand . . . 1.
- de sa propre – (with one's own) hand . . . 3.

main-d'œuvre[6b]
- work . . . 1.

maintenant[1a]
- now (at present) . . . 1.
- dès –, henceforth . . . 3.

maintenir[2a]
- maintain (keep up) . 1.5
- maintain (affirm) . . . 3.5

maintien[6b]
- keeping up . . . 3.4

maire[3a]
- mayor . . . 2.5

mairie[5a]
- (city) hall . . . 3.4

Section

mais[1a]
- but . . . 1.

maïs
- corn . . . 4.8

maison[1a]
- à la –, (at) home . . . 1.
- house . . . 1.
- à la –, indoors . . . 3.1
- – de campagne, country house . . . 3.3

maître[1a]
- master . . . 1.
- teacher . . . 1.
- – de maison man of the house . 1.8

maîtresse[2a]
- teacher . . . 1.
- mistress (*f.* of master) . . . 3.5

maîtrise[6a]
- choir . . . 4.

maîtriser[6b]
- control . . . 1.4
- master . . . 1.4

majesté[4b]
- majesty . . . 2.5

majestueux[6b]
- grand . . . 2.3

majeur[4a]
- chief . . . 1.

majorité[3a]
- majority . . . 2.6
- avoir – (be in the) majority . . . 3.8

mal (*adv.*)[1a]
- bad . . . 1.
- ill . . . 1.5

mal (*n.*)[1a]
- faire – à, hurt (*tr. vb.*) 1.8
- faire –, hurt (*intr. vb.*) 1.8
- evil . . . 2.
- avoir –, (be) sore . . . 3.7
- – de mer, sickness . . . 4.9

malade[1b]
- ill . . . 1.5
- patient . . . 2.5
- tomber –, (get) ill . . . 3.

maladie[2b]
- disease . . . 1.6

maladresse[6a]
- d'une grande – awkward . . . 4.9

maladroit[3a]
- awkward . . . 4.9

malaise[4a]
- uneasiness . . . 5.

mâle[5a]
- male . . . 3.1
- manly . . . 3.8

malédiction
- curse . . . 3.5

malentendu
- misunderstanding . . 6.

malfaiteur[5a]
- criminal . . . 4.5

malgré[1a]
- (in) spite of . . . 1.4

malheur[1b]
- misfortune . . . 2.2
- accident . . . 2.3

malheureusement[2b]
- unfortunately . . . 1.9

malheureux[1b]
- unhappy . . . 1.8
- unfortunate . . . 2.2

malhonnête[6b]
- dishonest . . . 7.8

malice[5a]
- malice . . . 4.8

Section

malin[3b]
- sharp . . . 1.7
- sly . . . 4.2

malle[4b]
- faire la –, pack . . . 3.5
- trunk . . . 5.

malsain[5a]
- unhealthy . . . 6.9

malveillant[7a]
- bad . . . 1.2

maman[2a]
- mamma . . . 2.9

manche (*m.*)[5a]
- handle . . . 3.1

manche (*f.*)[3b]
- sleeve . . . 5.1

manchette
- cuff . . . 6.

manchon
- muff . . . 7.2

mandat[5a]
- writ . . . 5.9

mander[5a]
- (let) know . . . 1.

manège[6a]
- riding-school . . . 13.

mangeoire
- manger . . . 6.8

manger[1a]
- eat . . . 1.4
- donner à –, feed . . . 1.4
- food . . . 1.9

mangeur
- feeder . . . 7.2

manier[4b]
- handle . . . 3.9

manière[1a]
- way . . . 1.

maniéré[4b]
- affected . . . 9.1

manifestation[3b]
- demonstration . . . 6.2

manifeste[6a]
- evident . . . 2.5
- manifest . . . 4.2

manifestement[6a]
- clearly . . . 2.9

manifester[3a]
- show . . . 1.
- manifest . . . †3.1

manœuvre[5b]
- workman . . . 2.5

manœuvrer[5a]
- handle . . . 3.9

manque[3b]
- want . . . 3.

manqué[5b]
- miss . . . 1.

manquer[1b]
- miss . . . 1.
- lack . . . 1.5
- fail . . . 2.6

mansarde[3b]
- attic . . . 6.3

manteau[2a]
- coat . . . 2.

manuel
- manual (textbook) . 6.5
- manual (*adj.*) . . . 7.3

manuscrit
- manuscript . . . 5.8

marais[5a]
- swamp . . . 4.

marbre[3a]
- marble . . . 3.8

marchand[2b]
- merchant . . . 2.2
- tradesman . . . 5.7

Section

méthodique[5b]
  systematic . . . 6.9
métier[2a]
  occupation . . . 2.4
métis
  (half) caste . . . 7.7
mètre[2a]
  yard . . . 1.3
métropole[6a]
  metropolis . . . 4.8
mets[5b]
  dish . . . 1.8
mettre[1a]
  place . . . 1.
  – couvert, set (table) . 1.1
  – au monde, bear . . . 1.3
  – en rapport, relate . . . 2.1
  se – en colère
  (get) angry . . . 2.4
  put on . . . 2.6
  – en colère, anger . . . 2.7
  – en désordre
  (put in) disorder . 4.8
mettre à (se)[1b]
  begin . . . 1.
meuble[2a]
  furniture . . . 4.4
meubler[5a]
  fit up . . . 1.8
  furnish . . . 3.3
meunier
  miller . . . 6.1
meurtre[3b]
  murder . . . 3.3
meurtrier (*n.*)[4b]
  murderer . . . 4.1
meurtrir[5a]
  bruise . . . 5.7
mexicain
  Mexican . . . 6.8
miauler
  mew . . . 6.4
midi (*noon*)[2a]
  noon . . . 2.1
midi (*south*)[4a]
  south . . . 2.2
miel[5a]
  honey . . . 3.9
mielleux[6b]
  mawkish . . . 11.
mien (*poss. pron.* and *adj.*)[2a]
  mine . . . 1.1
miette[6b]
  crumb . . . 5.8
mieux[1a]
  best . . . 1.
  better . . . 1.
mignon[4a]
  little . . . 1.
migraine[5b]
  headache . . . 6.6
mil (*numeral*)[4b]
  thousand . . . 1.4
milice
  militia . . . 6.3
milieu[1a]
  center . . . 1.
  circle (set of people) 1.
  middle . . . 1.5
militaire (*adj.*)[2a]
  military . . . 2.4
militaire (*n.*)[4b]
  soldier . . . 1.
mille (*thousand*)[1a]
  thousand . . . 1.4
mille (*mile*)[5a]
  mile . . . 1.7
millénaire
  millennium . . . 8.8

Section

milliard[4a]
  billion . . . 9.2
millier[2a]
  thousand . . . 1.4
million[1b]
  million . . . 1.4
millionnaire
  millionaire . . . 6.9
mince[2a]
  thin . . . 2.
  slight . . . 3.3
mine (*mine*)[3a]
  mine (*n.*) . . . 2.6
mine (*bearing, appearance*)[2b]
  looks . . . 1.
  look (*n.*) . . . 1.9
  avoir . . . . –, look (*vb.*) 1.9
minéral
  mineral . . . 6.1
mineur (*minor*)[6a]
  minor . . . 4.4
mineur (*miner*)[4b]
  miner . . . 4.7
miniature[5a]
  miniature . . . 7.7
minimum[6b]
  minimum . . . 7.4
ministère[2b]
  ministry . . . 3.4
ministre[2a]
  minister . . . 1.5
  – des affaires étrangères
  secretary of state 3.9
minorité[5b]
  minority . . . 7.7
minuit[3a]
  midnight . . . 2.4
minuscule[6a]
  little . . . 1.
minute[1b]
  minute . . . 1.5
minutieux[4a]
  minute . . . 3.1
miracle[3a]
  wonder . . . 1.7
  miracle . . . 2.9
miraculeux[5a]
  wonderful . . . 1.2
miroir[4a]
  mirror . . . 2.8
mise[3b]
  share . . . 2.
mise en scène[6b]
  set-up . . . 10.6
misérable[2a]
  miserable . . . 2.7
misère[2a]
  misery . . . 2.7
miséricorde[6b]
  mercy . . . 2.
mission[2b]
  mission . . . 4.1
missionnaire
  missionary . . . 7.2
mite
  moth . . . 6.8
mitre
  miter . . . 7.2
mobile[3b]
  movable . . . 3.9
  motive . . . 4.
mobilier[4a]
  furniture . . . 4.4
mobilisation
  mobilization . . . 12.

Section

mobiliser[6a]
  mobilize . . . 11.4
mobilité[6b]
  mobility . . . 9.4
mode (*f.*)[1b]
  way . . . 1.
  fashion . . . 2.8
  à la –, fashionable . . . 6.
mode (*m.*)[5a]
  mode . . . 2.2
modèle[3a]
  model . . . 2.
modération[5a]
  moderation (diminution) . . . 5.8
modérer[3b]
  modéré, moderate . . . 3.
  moderate . . . 4.2
moderne[1b]
  modern . . . 1.8
modeste[2b]
  modest . . . 2.4
modestie[4a]
  modesty . . . 4.7
modification[4b]
  change . . . 1.5
modifier[2b]
  change . . . 1.4
moelleux[6a]
  soft . . . 1.5
mœurs[2b]
  custom . . . 1.9
moi[1a]
  I . . . 1.
moi-même[4a]
  myself . . . 1.3
moindre[1b]
  least . . . 1.
moine[4b]
  monk . . . 4.7
moineau
  sparrow . . . 6.
moins[1a]
  le –, least . . . 1.
  au –, (at) least . . . 1.
  less . . . 1.
  – . . . . –, the . . . . the 1.
  à – que, unless . . . 1.4
mois[1a]
  month . . . 1.
moisson[4b]
  crop . . . 2.7
moitié[1b]
  half . . . 1.
mollement[6a]
  soft . . . 1.5
moment[1a]
  moment . . . 1.
  pour le –
  (for the) present 1.4
  (a) while . . . 1.8
momentané[6b]
  immediate . . . 2.8
  momentary . . . 7.2
momentanément[7a]
  immediate . . . 2.8
mon, ma, mes[1a]
  my . . . 1.
monarchie
  monarchy . . . 5.6
monarque[6a]
  monarch . . . 3.3
monastère[5a]
  convent . . . 3.8
mondain[4b]
  worldly . . . 4.6
monde (*society, people*)[1a]
  company (social) . . . 1.
  people (persons) . . . 1.
  tout le –, everybody . . 2.2

Section

monde (*world*)[1a]
  world . . . 1.
  mettre au –, bear . . . 1.3
mondial[5b]
  world . . . 4.9
monnaie[3a]
  – légale, (legal) tender 4.8
  – (du pays), currency . 4.9
monologue
  monologue . . . 11.
monopole[5a]
  monopoly . . . 7.3
monosyllabe
  monosyllable . . . 10.5
monotone[3b]
  monotonous . . . 6.8
monotonie[5b]
  monotony . . . 8.1
monseigneur[5a]
  lord . . . 2.2
monsieur[1a]
  gentleman . . . 1.
  Mr. . . . 1.
monstre[3a]
  monster . . . 4.1
monstrueux[3b]
  monstrous . . . 4.7
mont[3b]
  mountain . . . 1.5
montagne[2a]
  mountain . . . 1.5
montagneux
  mountainous . . . 6.7
montant (*n.*)[6a]
  amount . . . 1.
monter[1a]
  go up . . . 1.
  – à cheval, ride (horse) 1.5
montre[3b]
  watch . . . 1.3
  display . . . 2.6
montrer[1a]
  show . . . 1.
monument[3a]
  monument . . . 2.5
monumental[6a]
  monumental . . . 7.8
moquer (se)[2b]
  – de, (make) fun (of) . . 2.8
moquerie[6b]
  fun . . . 3.1
  mockery . . . 4.8
moral (*adj.*)[2a]
  moral . . . 2.3
morale (*n.*)[3a]
  morals . . . 3.6
moraliste[5b]
  moralist . . . 8.6
moralité[4a]
  morals . . . 3.6
morbide
  morbid . . . 7.6
morceau[1b]
  piece . . . 1.
  morsel . . . 6.2
mordre[3a]
  bite . . . 3.7
morne[3b]
  dismal . . . 3.9
  bleak . . . 4.8
mort (*n.*)[1a]
  death . . . 1.
mort (*adj.*)[1b]
  dead . . . 1.4
mortel[3b]
  mortal . . . 2.9
  mortal (susceptible to death) . . . 3.7

Section

noircir[4a]
blacken 7.2
noix[6a]
nut 5.1
walnut 6.3
noix de coco
cocoanut .... 7.
nom[1a]
name .... 1.
sans –, nameless 5.8
noun 7.3
nombre[1a]
number .... 1.
nombreux[1b]
numerous 1.5
nomination[4b]
appointment (to . . . .) 4.5
nomination 4.9
nommé (*adj.*)[5a]
name (appoint) .... 1.
déjà –, above 2.2
nommer[1b]
(give) name (to) .... 1.
name (appoint) .... 1.
non[1a]
– plus, neither (*adv.*) .... 1.
no .... 1.
nonne
nun 6.3
nord[2a]
north 1.6
du –, au –, northern .... 2.
nord-ouest
northwest 6.8
normal[3a]
normal 3.9
notable[4a]
remarkable 2.4
notaire[4a]
public trustee 7.6
notamment[3a]
above all .... 1.
note[2b]
account .... 1.
noter[2b]
note (*vb.*) 1.9
notion[4a]
idea 1.4
notre, nos (*poss. adj.*)[1a]
our .... 1.
nôtre (*poss. pron.*)[3a]
ours 3.9
nouer[4a]
tie 1.6
nourrice
wet-nurse 12.9
nourrir[2a]
nourish 3.2
nourriture[4b]
food 1.9
nourishment 5.6
nous[1a]
we .... 1.
nouveau[1a]
de –, again .... 1.
new .... 1.
nouveauté[5a]
novelty 4.3
nouvelle(-s) (*n.*)[1b]
news 1.4
novembre[3a]
November 2.3
noyau
kernel 4.6
nucleus 4.9
noyer[2b]
drown 4.3
nu[2a]
bare 2.4

Section

nuage[2b]
cloud 1.9
nuageux
cloudy 5.8
nuance[2b]
shade 2.9
nuée[5b]
cloud 1.9
drove 3.9
nuire[4b]
hurt (*tr. vb.*) 1.8
nuisible[5a]
injurious 4.3
nuit[1a]
night .... 1.
la –, (at) night 2.2
passer la – (spend) night 2.7
chaque –, toutes les -s nightly .... 3.
nul[1b]
no (*adj.*) .... 1.
none .... 1.
nulle part, nowhere 3.4
void 5.4
nullement[2b]
(not at) all .... 1.
nullité[6a]
nonentity 10.6
numéro[3a]
number 2.4
nu-pied
barefoot 7.2
nuque[5b]
neck 1.5
nymphe
nymph 6.4

O

oasis
oasis .... 7.
obéir[1b]
obey 2.2
obéissant, obedient 3.2
obéissance
obedience .... 6.
obélisque
obelisk .... 9.
objecter[5a]
object 1.9
objectif[4b]
purpose .... 1.
impartial .... 5.
objection[4a]
objection 4.4
objet[1a]
thing .... 1.
– d'art, work of art 1.8
obligation[2b]
obligation .... 4.
obligatoire[5b]
required 3.1
obliger[1a]
force .... 1.
oblique[6a]
oblique 6.2
obscur[2a]
dark .... 1.
dim 4.1
obscurcir[5a]
obscure .... 6.
obscurité[3a]
darkness 2.9
observateur[6a]
observing 2.6
observer 5.4

Section

observation[2b]
observation 2.4
remark 2.4
observer[1b]
watch .... 1.
observe 1.4
obstacle[3a]
bar 2.1
obstacle 3.4
obstiné[6a]
stubborn 4.1
obstiner (s')[6b]
persist 3.8
obstruer[6a]
stop up 3.1
obtenir[1b]
get (obtain) .... 1.
obus[6b]
shell (explosive) 3.4
occasion[1a]
chance .... 1.
event 1.4
occidental[4b]
western 2.4
occupant[5b]
tenant 6.5
occupation[2b]
occupation 2.4
occuper[1a]
busy .... 1.
occuper (s')[2a]
busy .... 1.
(be) engaged 1.9
océan[5a]
ocean 3.6
octobre[3a]
October 2.4
octroyer[6b]
grant .... 1.
odeur[2a]
smell 2.8
perfume .... 4.
odieux[3b]
hateful 4.7
œil (yeux)[1a]
eye .... 1.
coup d'œil, look .... 1.
cligner de l'œil, wink 5.8
œillet
carnation 8.4
œuf[3a]
egg .... 2.
œuvre[1b]
work .... 1.
– d'art, work of art 1.8
offenser[3b]
offend 2.8
office[2b]
office 1.4
(divine) service 2.3
pantry 6.2
officiel[2b]
official 2.8
officier[2a]
officer 1.2
offrande[6b]
offering 3.8
offre[3b]
offer 3.6
supply 3.7
offrir[1a]
offer .... 1.
present 1.4
oh![3b]
O 1.2
oie[5a]
goose 5.3

Section

oignon[5a]
onion 5.6
bulb .... 6.
oindre
anoint .... 7.
oiseau[2a]
bird 2.3
oisif[6b]
idle 3.7
oisiveté
idleness 6.5
olive
olive 5.8
olivier
olive tree 5.7
ombrage[5a]
shade 1.8
ombrager[5b]
shade 4.9
ombragé, shady 6.1
ombre[1b]
shade 1.4
omission
omission .... 7.
omnibus[5b]
bus 8.1
on[1a]
one (*indef. pron.*) .... 1.
once
ounce 4.7
oncle[2b]
uncle 1.9
ondulation
wave 3.8
onduler[5a]
ripple .... 5.
ongle[4b]
nail (finger) 3.1
onguent
ointment .... 7.
onze[2b]
eleven 2.9
onzième
eleventh 7.2
opaque
opaque 7.8
opéra[5a]
opera 4.5
– comique (musical) drama 6.2
opération[2b]
operation (general) 2.4
operation (surgical) 3.6
opérer[3a]
operate 3.6
opinion[1b]
opinion 1.4
opportun
opportune 7.4
opposé (*adj.*)[3a]
opposite 1.4
opposer[2a]
object 1.9
oppose 2.3
opposition[3b]
opposition .... 3.
oppressé
breathless 7.3
oppression[6b]
oppression 3.5
opprimer
oppress 5.8
optimisme[5a]
optimism 9.7
optimiste[5b]
hopeful 6.9
optimistic 10.9

P

Section

parenté
relation 4.2
parer[2b]
trim 2.4
paresse[5a]
sloth 6.9
paresseux[4b]
lazy 3.8
parfait[1b]
perfect . . . . 1.
parfaitement[1b]
perfect . . . . 1.
parfaitement (*certainly*)[3b]
sure . . . . 1.
parfois[1b]
sometimes 1.4
parfum[2b]
perfume . . . . 4.
parfumer[3b]
perfume 5.4
parfumé, fragrant 5.5
parier[4b]
bet 6.3
parisien[2b]
Parisian 5.8
parlement[3b]
parliament 2.8
parlementaire[2b]
parliamentary . . . . . 7.
parler (*vb.*)[1a]
speak . . . . 1.
talk . . . . 1.
parler (*n.*)[5a]
talk 1.2
language 1.6
parmi[1a]
among . . . . 1.
paroi[4b]
wall 1.4
paroisse[6a]
parish 3.4
paroissien[6b]
parishioner 10.2
parole[1a]
word . . . . 1.
parquet[3b]
floor 1.2
parrain[6a]
godfather 8.6
part (*f.*)[1a]
faire –, (let) know . . . . 1.
part (*n.*) . . . . 1.
d'autre –
(on the other) hand 1.4
part (rôle) 1.4
de la – de
(on the) part 1.4
prendre –, (take) part . 1.4
stock 1.8
share . . . . 2.
d'une –
(on the one) hand 2.2
de sa –, (on her) side . 2.2
de sa –, (on his) side . . 2.2
pour ma –
(for my) part 2.6
quelque –, somewhere 3.
nulle –, nowhere 3.4
partage[4a]
share . . . . 2.
partager[2a]
divide 1.1
partenaire[6a]
partner 3.4
parterre[6b]
flower-bed . . . . 13.
parti[1b]
part (*n.*) . . . . 1.
party 1.1

Section

participation[4a]
share . . . . 2.
participant
participant . . . . 10.
participe
participle 10.2
participer[5a]
(take) part 1.4
particule
particle . . . . 7.
particulier[1b]
particular 1.4
special 1.8
particular (detail) . . 2.3
private . . . . 3.
peculiar (to) 3.6
hôtel –, mansion 3.7
particulièrement[2a]
particular 1.4
partie[1a]
part (*n.*) . . . . 1.
en –, (in) part . . . . 1.
partir (*depart*)[1a]
parti, away . . . . 1.
go away . . . . 1.
start 1.8
partisan[4a]
follower 3.2
partout[1a]
everywhere 1.4
parure[6a]
trimming 3.8
parvenir[1b]
reach . . . . 1.
parvenu(-e) (*n.*)[6b]
upstart . . . . 9.
pas (*n.*)[1a]
step . . . . 1.
pace 1.8
marcher à grands –
stride 3.3
pas (*neg. adv.*)[1a]
– du tout, (not at) all. 1.
ne . . . . –, not . . . . 1.
– nécessaire
unnecessary 4.2
passage[1b]
crossing 1.6
aisle 3.4
alley 4.6
passage 4.8
passager (*adj.*)[4b]
passing 1.9
fugitive 3.5
passager (*n.*)[5a]
traveler 2.4
passenger 3.2
passant (*n.*)[3b]
passerby 10.9
passe[5b]
pass (permit) 4.4
passé (*n.*)[2a]
past 1.9
past (tense) 2.2
passer[1a]
se –, happen . . . . 1.
pass 1.4
passé, past 1.4
hand 1.8
se – de, do without . . . 2.1
spend 2.2
pass (e.g., time) 2.6
– la nuit, (spend) night 2.7
strain 4.9
passif
passive 7.3
passion[2a]
passion 2.3
passionné[3b]
passionate 3.7

Section

passionner[4b]
stir 1.9
carry away 3.4
pastelle
tablet 6.2
pasteur[6a]
minister . . . . 2.
pastor 4.9
patauger[7a]
wade 7.1
pâte[4a]
paste 6.1
dough 6.2
pâté[5b]
pie 5.1
patère
peg . . . . 6.
paternel[4a]
paternal 4.8
paternité
fatherhood 11.4
pathétique[6b]
pathetic . . . . 5.
patience[2b]
patience 2.8
avoir de la –
(be) patient 3.8
patient (*adj.*)[5a]
(be) patient 3.8
patiner
skate . . . . 6.
pâtisserie[6b]
pastry 7.8
pâtre[6a]
shepherd 3.7
patriarcal
patriarchal 10.1
patriarche
patriarch 6.8
patrie[2a]
country 1.1
patriote[4a]
patriotic 4.8
patriot 5.2
patriotisme[6b]
patriotism 6.5
patron[2b]
model . . . . 2.
employer 3.7
patron . . . . 4.
patte[3b]
paw 5.1
paume[5a]
palm 5.1
paupière[4a]
eyelid 6.7
pauvre[1a]
poor . . . . 1.
pauvreté[6a]
poverty . . . . 4.
pavé (*n.*)[3a]
pavement 5.7
paver[6b]
pave 6.2
pavillon[4a]
flag 2.6
pavilion 6.4
pavot
poppy 7.2
payer[1a]
pay . . . . 1.
pays[1a]
country (geographical) . . . . 1.
– de fées, fairyland . . . 6.2
paysage[2b]
landscape 3.2
paysan[1b]
peasant 2.4

Section

peau[2b]
skin . . . . 2.
pêche (*f.*) (*peach*)[6b]
peach 5.8
pêche (*f.*) (*fishing*)[4b]
faire la –, fish 2.5
péché (*m.*)[5a]
sin 2.2
pécher (*vb.*)[6b]
sin 2.4
pêcher (*vb.*) (*fish*)[4a]
fish 2.5
pêcheur (*fisherman*)[4a]
fisherman 4.7
pécheur
sinner 5.1
pédant[6a]
pedant 9.6
peigner
comb . . . . 6.
peindre[2a]
paint 1.5
peine (*n.*)[1a]
pain . . . . 1.
trouble . . . . 1.
se donner la –
(take) pains 1.4
grief 1.8
peine (à)[5b]
hardly 1.4
peiner[7a]
grieve 3.4
peintre[3a]
painter . . . . 3.
peinture[3b]
painting 3.2
pêle-mêle[6b]
(in a) huddle 7.4
peler
peel 5.2
pélerin
pilgrim 5.8
pélerinage[6a]
pilgrimage 6.7
pélerine[6a]
cloak 4.8
pelle[6a]
spade 5.8
pellicule
film 6.8
pelote[6b]
ball 2.1
pelouse[3b]
lawn 4.3
pelure
peel 5.3
penaud[6a]
sheepish 11.4
penchant[5b]
liking 1.5
avoir –, tend 2.4
tendency 3.2
pencher[2a]
se –, bend 1.9
lean 2.2
pendant (*prep.*)[1a]
during . . . . 1.
pendant que[1b]
while . . . . 1.
pendre[2b]
hang 1.1
pendule[4b]
clock 1.3
pénétration
penetration 9.3
pénétrer[1b]
enter . . . . 1.
penetrate 6.6
pénible[2a]
painful 3.2

Section

plaignant
plaintiff ... 8.4
plaindre[2b]
pity ... 4.6
plaindre (se)[2a]
complain ... 2.
plaine[2a]
plain ... 1.6
plainte[2b]
complaint ... 2.4
lamentation ... 4.2
plaintif[6b]
sad ... 1.4
plaire[1a]
plaise à Dieu
God grant ... 1.
please ... 1.
plaisant[4b]
pleasant ... 1.1
plaisanter[3a]
joke ... 4.3
plaisanterie[3b]
joke ... 2.9
plaisir[1a]
faire –, please ... 1.
pleasure ... 1.4
plan (*n.*)[1b]
plan ... 1.1
plane (mathematical) ... 3.7
premier –, foreground ... 6.5
planche[3a]
board ... 1.7
shelf ... 4.5
plancher[4b]
floor ... 1.2
planète[4b]
planet ... 3.9
plante[2b]
plant ... 1.5
sole ... 4.3
planter[2b]
plant ... 2.4
planteur
planter ... 7.2
plaque[4b]
slab ... 4.1
plaquer[6b]
plate ... 5.1
plastique
plastic ... 7.6
plastron[6b]
shirt-front ... 13.
plat (*adj.*)[3b]
flat ... 2.7
plat (*n.*)[3a]
dish (of food) ... 1.8
platter ... 4.
dish (container) ... 4.5
platane[6b]
plane tree ... 6.
plateau[3b]
plateau ... 6.
tray ... 6.6
plâtre[5b]
plaster ... 6.5
plein[1a]
full ... 1.
– de dignité, stately ... 3.6
crowded ... 5.4
pleinement[5b]
all ... 1.
fully ... 2.2
pleurer[1a]
cry ... 1.4
mourn ... 1.9
pleurs[6a]
tear ... 1.

Section

pleuvoir[3b]
rain ... 4.2
pli[3a]
fold ... 4.4
envelope ... 5.6
plier[2b]
bend ... 2.4
fold ... 4.
plisser[5a]
tuck ... 4.1
plomb[3b]
lead ... 2.3
plonger[2a]
dip ... 3.2
dive ... 4.2
ployer[6a]
bend ... 2.4
pluie[2a]
rain ... 2.
de –, rainy ... 5.7
plume[2a]
pen ... 1.5
feather ... 1.9
plupart[1b]
most ... 1.
pour la –, (most) part 1.8
plus (*adv.*)[1a]
more ... 1.
le –, most ... 1.
non –, neither (*adv.*) ... 1.
ne . . . . –, no longer ... 1.
– . . . . –, the . . . . the 1.
– loin, beyond ... 1.8
en –, extra ... 4.1
plus (*plus*)[2a]
plus ... 6.7
plusieurs[1a]
(a) few ... 1.
several ... 1.
à – reprises
several times ... 1.2
plutôt[1b]
rather ... 1.
pneu
tire ... 7.2
poche[1b]
pocket ... 2.3
poêle (*m.*)[5a]
stove ... 3.3
poêle (*f.*)[6a]
pan ... 4.9
frying pan ... 6.4
poème[4a]
poem ... 2.5
poésie[2b]
poetry ... 2.4
poem ... 2.5
poète[2b]
poet ... 1.5
poétique[4a]
poetic ... 3.9
poids[2a]
weight ... 1.5
poignant[6b]
keen ... 2.4
poignard
coup de –, stab ... 6.5
poignée[3b]
handle ... 3.1
handful ... 5.6
poignet[5b]
wrist ... 6.1
poil[4b]
hair ... 1.
poing[2b]
fist ... 3.4
point (*n.*)[1a]
être sur le – de
(be) about to ... 1.
point (dot) ... 1.

Section

point (*n.*)[1a]—*continued*
– de vue, point of view 1.
– du jour, dawn ... 3.5
point (*neg. adv.*)[1a]
ne . . . . –, none ... 1.
pointe[2a]
point ... 1.2
tip ... 1.4
pointer[5a]
aim ... 3.2
pointu[4b]
pointed ... 3.3
poire[5a]
pear ... 5.5
pois[5a]
pea ... 5.4
poison[4b]
poison ... 3.1
poisson[2b]
fish ... 2.
poitrine[2a]
chest ... 1.9
poivre
pepper ... 5.9
polaire[6b]
polar ... 6.8
pôle
pole ... 4.6
polémique[6b]
dispute ... 4.3
poli (*adj.*)[2b]
civil ... 3.2
police[2b]
police ... 3.7
policy ... 4.6
de –, police ... 5.
policer[6a]
refine ... 5.5
policier[6a]
policeman ... 5.8
poliment[4a]
civil ... 3.2
polir[5a]
polish ... 4.4
polisson[6b]
(little) rascal ... 4.2
politesse[2b]
(good) manners ... 2.9
politique (*n.*)[2b]
policy ... 2.4
politics ... 4.4
politician ... 5.5
politique (*adj.*)[2a]
political ... 1.9
polonais[5a]
Polish ... 4.1
pomme[3b]
– de terre, potato ... 2.7
apple ... 3.5
pommier[6b]
apple tree ... 5.
pompe (*pomp*)[5b]
pomp ... 4.4
pompe (*pump*)[4b]
pump ... 5.3
pont[2b]
bridge ... 1.7
deck (of a ship) ... 3.7
populaire[2a]
popular ... 4.1
popularité
popularity ... 7.4
population[3a]
population ... 2.5
populeux
populous ... 7.3
porc[5b]
pig ... 3.9

Section

porcelaine[5b]
china ... 3.7
porche[6b]
porch ... 2.7
pore
pore ... 7.1
port[2a]
harbor ... 2.
– (de lettre), postage ... 5.7
portail[4b]
porch ... 2.7
porte[1a]
door ... 1.
gate ... 1.4
portée[2b]
import ... 2.2
range ... 3.6
hors de –
(out of) reach ... 4.1
portefeuille[3b]
case ... 2.5
porter[1a]
carry ... 1.
wear ... 1.
se – bien, (be) well ... 1.
porteur[3b]
porter ... 3.3
portière[4a]
curtain ... 3.8
portion[5b]
share ... 2.
portrait[2b]
painting ... 3.2
portugais
Portuguese ... 6.7
pose[5b]
carriage ... 3.
posément[6a]
slow ... 1.2
poser[1a]
place ... 1.
se –, settle down ... 3.1
positif[3a]
positive ... 3.8
position[2a]
place ... 1.
position (situation) ... 1.4
position (plight) ... 1.5
posséder[1b]
own ... 1.
possesseur[6a]
owner ... 2.
possession[2a]
possession ... 1.6
possibilité[4a]
possibility ... 2.7
possible[1a]
possible ... 1.
rendre –
(make) possible ... 1.8
postal[5b]
post ... 3.
poste[2a]
office ... 1.4
post-office ... 3.3
postérité
posterity ... 6.6
post-scriptum
postscript ... 7.2
pot[3a]
pot ... 2.3
pitcher ... 5.6
cuiller à –, dipper ... 6.8
potager[6a]
vegetable ... 5.
poteau[4b]
post ... 3.

Section

prix[1a]
- price 1.
- prize 1.5

probabilité
- chances 3.3

probable[3a]
- probable 1.7

probablement[2b]
- probable 1.7

problème[2b]
- problem 3.3

procédé[2b]
- process 1.7

procéder[2b]
- proceed 2.

procédure[6a]
- procedure 5.1
- – pour la banqueroute (procedure in) bankruptcy 7.3

procès[3b]
- suit 1.8
- trial (law) 2.

procession[4b]
- procession 4.1

procès-verbal[6b]
- suit 1.8

prochain (*adj.*)[1b]
- next 1.

prochain (*n.*)[7a]
- neighbor 3.4

prochainement[6b]
- soon 1.

proche[3a]
- near (*adj.*) 1.

proclamation[6b]
- proclamation 7.4

proclamer[4a]
- proclaim 3.5

procurer[3a]
- get (obtain) 1.

procureur[4b]
- attorney 4.7

procureur général
- attorney-general 9.5

prodigieusement[4b]
- wonderful 1.2

prodigieux[3b]
- wonderful 1.2

prodigue[5b]
- lavish 3.7

prodiguer[5b]
- lavish 6.3

producteur[5a]
- productive 6.3

production[4a]
- production 3.9

produire[1a]
- produce 1.8
- produce (yield) 3.4

produit (*n.*)[3a]
- product 2.1

profane[6b]
- profane 6.3

profaner
- profane 6.5

professer[3b]
- state 1.

professeur[3a]
- teacher 1.
- professor 2.6

profession[3b]
- profession 2.9

professionnel[4b]
- professional 4.5

profil[6b]
- profile 8.7

Section

profit[2b]
- profit 2.
- profit (earned) 2.1

profiter[1b]
- profit 1.4

profond[1a]
- deep 1.

profondément[2b]
- deep 1.

profondeur[2b]
- depth 2.6

programme[2b]
- program 4.2

progrès[2a]
- faire des –, improve 2.4
- progress (*n.*) 2.4
- faire des –, progress 2.6

progressif[5b]
- progressive 6.7

progressivement[6b]
- progressive 6.7

proie[3b]
- prey 3.4

projet[1b]
- – de loi, bill 1.9
- – de loi, draft (of bill) 2.3
- project 3.5

projeter[3b]
- plan 2.3
- project 3.7

prolonger[2a]
- prolong 3.6

promenade[2a]
- faire une –, walk 1.
- walk 2.4

promener[1b]
- se – en voiture drive (*intr. vb.*) 1.
- walk 1.

promeneur[4a]
- walker 7.6

promesse[4a]
- promise 2.7

promettre[1b]
- promise 1.

prompt[4b]
- prompt 2.5

promptement[5a]
- prompt 2.5

promptitude[4b]
- promptitude 10.

pronom
- pronoun 6.8

prononcer[1b]
- pronounce 1.4

prononciation
- pronunciation 7.

propagande[5b]
- propaganda 7.5

propager
- propagate 7.

prophète[4b]
- prophet 3.1

prophétie
- prophecy 6.6

propice[4a]
- favorable 2.2
- peu –, unfavorable 6.

proportion[3a]
- proportion 2.1

propos[2b]
- remark 2.4

propos de (à)[3a]
- as for 1.

proposer[1b]
- propose 1.4

proposition[3a]
- proposition 3.1

Section

propre (*own*)[1a]
- own 1.
- de sa – main (with own) hand 3.
- peculiar 3.6

propre (*clean*)[2b]
- clean 1.
- neat 2.6

propre (*n.*)[6a]
- characteristic 3.

proprement[3b]
- proper 1.4

propreté[5a]
- cleanliness 5.3

propriétaire[3a]
- owner 2.

propriété[2a]
- property 1.5
- property (landed) 1.9

prosaïque
- prosaic 10.5

proscrire
- proscribe 9.7

proscrit[4b]
- exile 5.6

prose[6a]
- prose 5.3

prospère[6b]
- prosperous 4.7

prospérer
- flourish 4.1

prospérité[4a]
- prosperity 4.4

prosterner[6b]
- prostrate 6.6

prostituée
- harlot 6.8

protecteur[5a]
- patron 4.
- protector 6.3

protection[2b]
- protection 2.1
- fostering 3.9

protégé (*n.*)[6a]
- protégé 11.

protéger[2a]
- protect 2.1
- foster 3.8

protestant[4a]
- Protestant 4.4

protestation[6a]
- protest 4.1

protester[2b]
- protest 4.4

prouver[1b]
- prove 1.

provenir[4a]
- come from 1.

proverbe[6b]
- saying 2.9
- proverb 4.9

providence[4b]
- providence 4.3

province[2b]
- province 1.5

provincial[5a]
- country (*adj.*) 2.6
- provincial 7.9

provision[4a]
- provision 4.1

provisoire[5b]
- temporary 3.2

provisoirement[6a]
- temporary 3.2

provoquer[2a]
- provoke 2.4

proximité
- proximity 5.6

Section

prudemment[6a]
- prudent 3.3

prudence[3a]
- prudence 3.7

prudent[3a]
- prudent 3.3

prune
- plum 6.

pruneau
- prune 6.4

prunelle[5a]
- pupil 5.3

prussien[5a]
- Prussian 4.5

psaume
- psalm 5.6

psychologie
- psychology 8.5

psychologique
- psychological 9.3

public[1b]
- public (*adj.*) 1.
- public (*n.*) 1.4

publication[5a]
- publication 4.6

publicité[6b]
- publicity 7.8

publier[2b]
- publish 2.8

puce
- flea 7.8

pudeur[5a]
- modesty 4.7

puéril[6b]
- childish 4.6

puis[1a]
- then 1.

puiser[4a]
- draw up 1.7

puisque[1a]
- as (since) 1.

puissance[1b]
- power 1.
- (Great) Power 3.

puissant[1b]
- strong 1.
- tout –, almighty 5.1

puits[4b]
- well 1.9

punir[3a]
- punish 2.1

punition[6a]
- punishment 2.6

pupille[5b]
- ward 5.2

pupitre[5b]
- desk 3.6

pur[1b]
- pure 1.
- pure (blooded, etc.) 1.5

purement[3b]
- simply 1.

pureté[4a]
- purity 4.7

purifier[6a]
- clean 2.2
- purify 4.4

pyramide[5b]
- pyramid 5.7

Q

quai[3a]
- dock 5.4

qualifier[4a]
- qualify 7.2

qualité[2a]
- nature (character) 1.
- quality 2.7

Section

receveur
- receiver 6.

recevoir[1a]
- get (receive) 1.
- admit 1.8

réchauffer[4a]
- heat 2.2

recherche[2b]
- inquiry 3.5
- search 4.4

recherché (*adj.*)[5a]
- choice 5.3

rechercher[2b]
- look for 1.

récipient
- receiver 6.

réciproque[5a]
- mutual 3.1

récit[2a]
- account 1.5

réciter[3a]
- recite 3.9

réclamation[7a]
- complaint 2.4

réclame[6a]
- puff 5.8

réclamer[1b]
- demand 1.
- claim 2.3

recoin[5a]
- corner 2.3

récolte[5b]
- crop 2.7
- faire la –, harvest 4.8

recommandation[6b]
- recommendation 4.5

recommander[2b]
- recommend 2.1

recommencer[1b]
- begin again 1.

récompense[3a]
- reward 2.5

récompenser[6b]
- reward 3.8

réconcilier[5a]
- reconcile (things) 4.6
- reconcile (persons) 4.7

reconduire[4a]
- take back 1.9

réconforter[5b]
- comfort 2.3

reconnaissance[2b]
- gratitude 3.3

reconnaissant[4a]
- grateful 2.5

reconnaître[1a]
- admit 1.4
- recognize 1.4
- ne pas – (not) recognize 2.6

reconstituer[5a]
- reconstitute 9.7

reconstruire[6a]
- build 1.2

recourir[5a]
- resort 5.3

recours[4a]
- avoir – à, appeal 2.8
- appeal 3.8

recouvrir[2a]
- cover 1.

récréation[6a]
- pastime 4.8

récrier (se)[5b]
- call out 1.4
- protest 4.4

recrue
- recruit 6.4

Section

recruter[6a]
- engage 1.9

rectangle
- rectangle 6.8

recteur
- chancellor 7.

rectifier[5a]
- correct 2.7

reçu
- receipt 4.9

recueil[5a]
- collection 2.7

recueillir[2a]
- gather (collect) 1.5
- gather (glean) 1.5

reculer[2a]
- draw back 1.5
- go back 2.1
- recoil 6.6

rédacteur[5a]
- author 1.9
- editor 6.1

rédaction[4b]
- (editorial) staff 5.3

redescendre[3b]
- go down 2.2

redevable
- indebted 4.2

redevenir[2b]
- become 1.

rédiger[4a]
- draw up 3.2

redingote[4b]
- frock coat 6.1

redire[3b]
- say again 1.

redoubler[5b]
- double 4.2
- double (effort) 4.3

redoutable[3a]
- dreaded 2.4

redouter[2a]
- (be) afraid 1.

redresser[3b]
- straighten (up) 4.6

redresser (se)[4a]
- straighten (up) 4.6

réduction[5b]
- decrease 4.7
- reduction 5.3

réduire[1b]
- reduce 3.5

réel[2a]
- real 1.
- actual 2.1

réélection
- reëlection 8.4

réellement[2b]
- really 1.4

refaire[4a]
- do over again 1.8

réfectoire[6b]
- dining room 4.9

référence
- reference 4.8

refermer[3a]
- close 1.

réfléchir[1b]
- consider 1.8
- reflect 4.3

reflet[3a]
- reflection 5.4

refléter[4b]
- reflect 4.3

réflexion[2a]
- consideration 2.4

Section

reflux
- ebb 6.4

réforme[4a]
- reform 3.2
- improvement 3.6

réformer[4b]
- reform 5.

refouler[5b]
- drive back 1.5

réfractaire[6b]
- refractory 9.8

refrain[6b]
- refrain 6.6

refroidir[3b]
- cool 4.3

refuge[6a]
- refuge 3.9

réfugier (se)[3b]
- (take) refuge 3.9

refus[3b]
- refusal 5.7

refuser[1a]
- refuse 2.3

regagner[3a]
- recover 1.9

régaler[5b]
- entertain 2.4
- treat 4.9

regard[1a]
- look 1.

regarder[1a]
- have to do with 1.
- look at 1.

régente
- regent 6.4

régime[2a]
- government 1.1
- direction 1.8
- diet 6.2

régiment[2b]
- regiment 3.6

région[2a]
- province 1.5

régir[6a]
- rule 1.

registration
- registering 4.2

registre[4b]
- record 3.8

règle (*rule*)[2a]
- rule 1.1

règlement[2b]
- rule 1.1

régler[2a]
- settle 1.8
- rule 4.2
- regulate 4.4

règne[3a]
- reign 2.1

régner[2b]
- reign 2.

regret[1b]
- regret 3.4

regrettable[6b]
- (too) bad 2.9
- grievous 4.

regretter[1b]
- (be) sorry 1.8

régularité[5a]
- regularity 8.

régulateur[6b]
- standard 2.2

régulier[2a]
- regular 2.

régulièrement[3b]
- regular 2.

rein
- kidney 7.3

Section

reine[3a]
- queen 1.6

reins (*pl.*)[4b]
- back 1.4
- loin 5.7

rejeter[5b]
- reject 3.2

rejoindre[2a]
- catch up 2.3
- overtake 3.9

réjouir[2a]
- delight 2.
- rejoice 3.2

relâche[6a]
- respite 4.5

relâcher[4b]
- loose 1.5

relatif[3b]
- relative 3.7

relation[3a]
- relation 1.6

relativement[4a]
- (in) proportion 2.6

reléguer[6b]
- expel 4.3

relevé[4b]
- exalted 2.9

relever[1a]
- lift 1.
- relieve 3.9

relief[3b]
- en –, relief 5.2

relier[3b]
- bind (a book) 2.7

religieux[2a]
- religious 2.3

religion[2b]
- religion 1.6

relique[5a]
- relic 6.1

relire[5a]
- read 1.

reliure[6a]
- binding 5.4

remarquable[2b]
- remarkable 2.4

remarque[3a]
- faire une –, remark 2.3
- remark 2.4

remarquer[1b]
- notice 1.4

rembourser[5a]
- give back 1.9
- repay 5.

remède[3b]
- remedy 3.6

remédier[5b]
- remedy 4.

remerciement[6a]
- thanks 1.1

remercier[1b]
- thank 1.

remettre[1a]
- deliver 1.4
- pardon 2.2
- put off 2.6
- se –, recover 2.7
- restore 2.7
- remit 3.6

remise[4b]
- delivery 4.4

remonter[1a]
- go up 1.

remords[2b]
- remorse 4.1

rempart[4a]
- rampart 6.4

Section

retrancher[5a]
- cut off 2.8

rétrécir[5a]
- contract 4.3
- shrink 5.2

retrousser[5a]
- turn up 4.9

retrouver[1a]
- find 1.
- recover 1.9

réunion[2a]
- convention 2.8

réunir[1b]
- unite 1.

réussir[1b]
- succeed 1.5

revanche[2b]
- en –, (in) return 1.1
- revenge 2.8

rêve[1b]
- dream 1.4

réveil[3b]
- waking 4.4

réveiller[2a]
- wake (*tr. vb.*) 1.9

réveiller (se)[3b]
- wake (*intr. vb.*) 1.9

révélation[3a]
- revelation 5.5

révéler[2a]
- reveal 2.4

revendiquer[6b]
- pretend 1.8
- claim 2.3

revenir[1a]
- come back 1.8
- amount to 2.9

revenu (*n.*)[4a]
- income 3.6

rêver[1b]
- dream 1.8

révérence[5a]
- reverence 4.1

révérend
- reverend 4.9

rêverie[3a]
- fancy 2.

revers (*n.*)[4b]
- (wrong) side 1.7

revêtir[2b]
- clothe 1.9

rêveur[4a]
- pensive 3.9
- dreamer 9.7

révision
- revision 6.8

revivre[4b]
- revive 5.2

revoir[1b]
- see 1.
- look over 3.1
- au –, farewell 3.4

révolte[4b]
- revolt 4.4

révolter[3a]
- rebel 3.6

révolution[2a]
- turn 3.
- revolution 3.2

révolutionnaire[3b]
- revolutionary 5.

revolver[4b]
- pistol 5.9

revue[3b]
- review 2.6
- magazine 3.
- Revue de l'état-major publication of the general staff 5.1

Section

rez-de-chaussée[5b]
- ground floor 4.4

rhétorique
- rhetoric 7.2

rhum[6a]
- liquor 4.3

rhumatisme[4a]
- rheumatism 7.2

ricaner[6b]
- grin 5.9

riche[1a]
- rich 1.

richesse[2b]
- wealth 1.5

ride[4a]
- wrinkle 5.4

rideau[2a]
- curtain 3.8

rider[5a]
- wrinkle 5.7

ridicule[2a]
- ridiculous 3.6

rien[1a]
- nothing 1.
- ne servir à, de – (of no) use 1.8

rigoureusement[5b]
- severe 1.6

rigoureux[3b]
- severe 1.6

rigueur[4a]
- rigor 4.2

rime
- rhyme 6.

riposter[6b]
- answer 1.

rire[1a]
- laugh (*vb.*) 1.
- laugh (*n.*) 1.8
- laughter 3.8

risque[4a]
- risk 3.4

risquer[2a]
- (take) chances 1.4

rivage[4a]
- bank 1.5
- beach 3.9

rival[3a]
- rival 5.

rivalité
- rivalry 7.8

rive[3a]
- bank 1.5

rivière[2b]
- river 1.5

riz[6b]
- rice 4.7

robe[1b]
- dress 1.4
- robe (e.g., hermit's) 3.3

robuste[4a]
- strong 1.
- hardy 2.6

roc[6b]
- rock 1.7

roche[6a]
- rock 1.7

rocher[3a]
- rock 1.7
- couvert de -s, rocky 5.9

rôder[4a]
- wander 2.7

rogner
- bob 5.8

rognon
- kidney 7.3

Section

roi[1b]
- king 1.

roitelet
- wren 6.8

rôle[1b]
- part (rôle) 1.4

romain[3b]
- Roman 1.8

roman (*n.*)[3a]
- novel 2.9
- fiction 3.9

roman (*adj.*)[5a]
- romance 6.4

romancier[6a]
- novelist 7.9

romanesque[5b]
- romantic 4.3

romantique[4b]
- romantic 4.3

romantisme
- romanticism 10.4

rompre[2b]
- break (in pieces) 2.3

ronce
- bramble 7.2

rond (*adj.*)[2b]
- round 1.6

rond (*n.*)[4a]
- circle 1.2

ronde[2b]
- part (of country) 1.
- (make) rounds 4.2

ronfler[5b]
- snore 6.7

ronger[5a]
- gnaw 6.1

rose[2a]
- rose (*n.*) 1.5
- pink (*adj.*) 4.6

roseau[5b]
- reed 3.4

rosée[5b]
- dew 3.9

rosier[6a]
- rose bush 5.2

rosse
- hack 7.

rossignol
- nightingale 6.1

rôti (*n.*)[6a]
- roast 5.4

rôtir[6a]
- cook 2.5

roucoulement
- coo 6.9

roucouler
- coo 6.9

roue[3a]
- wheel 2.5

rouge[1a]
- red 1.

rouge-gorge
- robin 5.6

rougeâtre[6a]
- red 1.

rougeur
- blush 5.5

rougir[2b]
- blush 4.

rouille
- rust 5.2

rouiller[6a]
- rust 5.8
- rouillé, rusty 6.6

rouleau
- roll 2.6
- scroll 4.6

Section

roulement[5b]
- roll 4.3

rouler[1b]
- roll 2.3
- wind 3.3

route[1a]
- road 1.
- en –, (on the) way 2.2

routine[6a]
- routine 7.7

rouvrir[5a]
- open 1.

roux[4a]
- red 1.

royal[2b]
- royal 1.5

royaliste[6a]
- royalist 10.

royaume[3b]
- kingdom 1.7

ruban[4a]
- ribbon 3.1

ruche[6b]
- hive 3.9

rude[2a]
- rough 3.
- gruff 3.7

rudement[4a]
- rough 3.

rue[1b]
- street 1.
- – de traverse crossroad 10.5

ruer[6b]
- se –, dash 1.8

rugissement
- roar 5.3

ruine[2b]
- ruin 2.4

ruiner[2b]
- destroy 1.5

ruineux
- ruinous 6.5

ruisseau[3b]
- brook 2.1
- gutter 5.7

ruisseler[4b]
- flow 1.5

rumeur[4b]
- noise 2.6
- rumor 3.8

ruminer[6a]
- chew 6.8

rupture[4b]
- break 3.8

ruse[4b]
- cunning (craft) 4.
- cunning (quality) 5.1

russe[5b]
- Russian 3.

rustique[6a]
- rural 3.3

rythme[6a]
- rhythm 7.9

S

sable[2a]
- sand 2.

sablonneux
- sandy 6.

sabot[3b]
- shoe 3.2
- hoof 5.1

sabre[4b]
- sword 2.
- saber 7.2

	Section
sensibilité[3b]	
feeling	1.5
sensible[2b]	
conscious of	3.3
sensitive	4.4
sensiblement[5b]	
very	1.
sensuel[6a]	
sensual	5.6
sentence[6b]	
sentence	2.
senteur[4a]	
smell	2.8
sentier[2b]	
path	2.9
sentiment[1b]	
feeling	1.
-s sympathiques sympathy	2.8
sentimental[4b]	
sentimental	6.6
sentir[1a]	
feel	1.
smell	3.5
séparation[3b]	
separation	3.4
séparément[6a]	
separate	1.
séparer[1a]	
separate	1.
séparé, separate	1.
sept[1a]	
seven	1.4
septembre[2b]	
September	2.1
septième	
seventh	4.5
serein (*adj.*)[6a]	
quiet	1.
serene	6.
sérénité[6a]	
quiet	1.
sergent[5a]	
sergeant	6.4
série[2a]	
series	2.5
sérieusement[2b]	
grave	1.4
sérieux[1a]	
grave	1.4
gravity	3.8
serin	
canary	7.2
serment[3b]	
faire, prêter –, swear	2.7
oath	4.6
sermon[6a]	
sermon	3.7
serpent[6b]	
snake	3.8
serre[4b]	
claw	6.1
serré[3b]	
tight	1.7
serrer[1b]	
press	1.1
shake	1.1
clasp	3.1
serrure[4b]	
lock	2.8
servante[2b]	
servant	1.5
service[1a]	
service	1.
favor	1.4
faire le –, ply	3.4
serviette (*napkin*)[4a]	
napkin	5.5
servile[6b]	
servile	7.
servir[1a]	
serve	1.
se – de, use	1.
ne – à rien, de rien (of no) use	1.8
serviteur[2b]	
servant	1.9
servitude[6b]	
slavery	6.2
session[5a]	
session	5.3
seuil[2b]	
threshold	4.2
seul[1a]	
alone	1.
only (*adj.*)	1.
seulement[1a]	
only (*adv.*)	1.
sève[5a]	
sap	4.2
sévère[2b]	
severe	1.6
sévèrement[4b]	
severe	1.6
sévérité[4b]	
rigor	4.2
severity	4.7
sévir[6b]	
punish	2.1
rage	3.2
sexe[6a]	
sex	3.3
si (*so*)[1a]	
so much	1.
si (*if*)[1a]	
if	1.
whether	1.
si (*yes*)[3a]	
yes	1.
siècle[1a]	
century	1.4
siège[1b]	
seat	1.
siege	4.8
sien (*poss. pron.*)[2a]	
his	1.1
hers	2.9
siffler[3a]	
whistle	4.6
hiss	5.4
sifflet[5a]	
whistle	3.9
siffloter[5a]	
whistle	4.6
signal[3a]	
signal	4.5
signaler[3a]	
point out	1.4
signature[3b]	
signature	4.1
signe[1a]	
sign	1.1
faire –, beckon	4.3
signer[2b]	
sign	2.4
significatif[5a]	
(full of) meaning	3.3
signification[4b]	
import (meaning)	2.2
signifier[2a]	
mean	1.
silence[1a]	
silence	2.2
silencieusement[5a]	
silent	1.5
silencieux[2a]	
silent	1.5
silex	
flint	6.5
silhouette[5a]	
outline	4.8
sillon[3b]	
furrow	6.
simple[1a]	
only (*adj.*)	1.
simple	1.
simple (ingenuous)	2.2
simplement[1b]	
simply	1.
simplicité[3a]	
simplicity	5.4
simplifier[5b]	
(make) simple	2.1
simultané[5b]	
(at the) same time	1.9
simultanément[6a]	
(at the) same time	1.9
sincère[3a]	
sincere	2.5
sincèrement[6a]	
sincere	2.5
sincérité[4a]	
sincerity	5.9
singe[4a]	
monkey	5.6
singulier[1b]	
strange	1.
singulièrement[6a]	
strange	1.
sinistre[3b]	
disaster	3.9
sinister	5.
sinon[2a]	
else	1.1
sire[5a]	
lord	2.2
sirène[5b]	
siren	7.
sirop[6a]	
syrup	5.3
site[4b]	
place	1.
sitôt[3a]	
– . . . . –, (no) sooner	1.
situation[1b]	
state (condition)	1.
office	1.4
position	1.4
location	5.5
situer[2b]	
locate	2.
six[1a]	
six	1.4
sixième	
sixth	3.7
sobre[6b]	
sober	3.8
sobriété[5a]	
moderation	3.8
temperance	6.4
social[2b]	
social	2.3
démocratie -e social democracy	5.3
socialiste[3a]	
socialist	6.1
société[1b]	
company (business)	1.
company (social)	1.
-s de bienfaisance charity societies	4.6
sœur[1a]	
sister	1.
soi[2b]	
self	1.
itself	1.5
soi-disant[6a]	
(so) called	1.2
soie[3a]	
silk	2.9
de –, silk	3.3
soif[3b]	
thirst	3.3
avoir –, (be) thirsty	3.7
soigner[2a]	
(take) care	1.
soigneusement[3b]	
careful	1.7
soin[1b]	
care	1.
prendre –, (take) care	1.
soir[1a]	
evening	1.
hier –, (last) night	1.2
ce –, tonight	1.4
le –, (at) night	2.2
soirée[2a]	
evening	1.
soit (*so be it*)[5b]	
ainsi – il, amen	4.3
soit . . . . soit (*whether . . . . or*)[3b]	
whether	1.
soixante[1b]	
sixty	4.
soixante-dix[6b]	
seventy	5.1
sol[1b]	
earth	1.
ground	1.
soldat[1b]	
soldier	1.
soleil[1a]	
sun	1.
lumière, clarté du – sunshine	3.2
rayon de –, sunbeam	4.3
coucher du –, sunset	5.3
lever du –, sunrise	5.8
solennel[2b]	
solemn	2.8
solennellement[4a]	
solemn	2.8
solennité[4b]	
solemnity	5.3
solidarité[5a]	
(joint) responsibility	7.1
solide[2a]	
solid	3.2
solidement[5b]	
solid	3.2
solidité[6a]	
force	1.
solidity	8.3
solitaire[3b]	
lonely	3.3
solitude[2b]	
solitude	3.6
solliciter[4a]	
ask (a question)	1.
solicit	3.4
sollicitude[6a]	
care	1.
soluble	
soluble	6.8
solution[3a]	
solution	3.5
sombre[1b]	
dark	1.
dim	4.1
sombrer[6b]	
sink	3.2

Section

succession[4b]
  succession ... 3.1

successivement[3b]
  little by little ... 1.
  successive ... 3.
  one after the other. 3.3

succomber[5b]
  sink ... 4.9

sucer[6b]
  suck ... 6.

sucre[4b]
  sugar ... 2.1

sucré[4b]
  sweet ... 1.4

sud[3a]
  south ... 2.2
  du, au –, southern ... 2.3

sud-ouest[5b]
  southwest ... 6.5

suédois
  Swedish ... 6.8

suer[5a]
  sweat ... 5.8

sueur[4a]
  sweat ... 4.7

suffire[1a]
  (be) enough ... 1.

suffisamment[3b]
  sufficient ... 2.5

suffisant[3a]
  sufficient ... 2.5
  adequate ... 6.

suffoquer[4b]
  choke ... 3.7

suffrage
  suffrage ... 5.1

suggérer[3b]
  propose ... 1.4

suggestion[5b]
  suggestion ... 5.1

suicide[6b]
  suicide ... 8.4

suisse[6a]
  Swiss ... 6.4

suite[1a]
  following ... 2.3

suivant[1b]
  by (according to) ... 1.
  next ... 1.
  following ... 1.1
  subsequent ... 4.1

suivre[1a]
  follow ... 1.

sujet (*n.*)[1b]
  subject (topic) ... 1.
  subject (national) .. 2.3

sujet (*adj.*)[4b]
  être –, (be) subject ... 1.7

sultan
  sultan ... 5.7

superbe[2b]
  magnificent ... 3.5

superficie[7a]
  surface ... 2.8

superficiel
  shallow ... 4.5

superflu[5b]
  superfluous ... 4.1

supérieur[1b]
  – à, above (*prep.*) ... 1.
  above (*adv.*) ... 1.
  higher ... 1.
  upper ... 1.4
  superior ... 2.2

supériorité[4a]
  superiority ... 6.3

superposer[5b]
  put over ... 3.

Section

superstitieux
  superstitious ... 7.4

superstition[5b]
  superstition ... 6.3

suppléer[5b]
  substitute ... 2.3

supplémentaire[6b]
  extra ... 4.1

suppliant[5a]
  suppliant ... 7.7

supplice[4a]
  punishment ... 2.6
  torture ... 3.9

supplier[2a]
  beg ... 2.7

supportable
  (can be) borne ... 5.2

supporter[1a]
  bear ... 1.

supposer[1b]
  suppose ... 1.

supposition[6a]
  basis ... 3.4
  conjecture ... 4.7

suppression[4a]
  suppression ... 8.4

supprimer[2b]
  put down ... 2.2
  suppress ... 3.7
  take out ... 4.1

suprême[2b]
  supreme ... 2.

sur[1a]
  on ... 1.

sûr[1b]
  bien –, (of) course ... 1.
  safe ... 1.
  sure ... 1.

sûrement[3b]
  sure ... 1.

sûreté[4a]
  safety ... 1.7

surface[2b]
  surface ... 2.8

surgir[3a]
  emerge ... 4.1

surhumain
  superhuman ... 9.4

surmonter[3b]
  overcome ... 2.4

surnaturel[4b]
  supernatural ... 8.4

surnom
  nickname ... 8.6

surpasser[6b]
  (be) ahead (of) ... 2.7
  surpass ... 4.6

surplus[4a]
  excess ... 3.3

surprendre[1b]
  surprise ... 1.4

surpris[4a]
  surprise ... 1.4
  surprised ... 2.5

surprise[2a]
  surprise ... 2.4

sursaut[4a]
  start ... 1.7

surtout (*adv.*)[1a]
  above all ... 1.

surtout (*n.*)[2b]
  overcoat ... 2.2

surveillance[4a]
  care ... 3.2

surveiller[2b]
  watch ... 1.

survenir[4a]
  happen ... 1.

Section

survivre[6a]
  survive ... 5.8

susceptible[3b]
  liable ... 6.5
  susceptible ... 6.9

suspect[6a]
  suspect ... 4.3

suspendre[2a]
  hang ... 1.1

suspens
  en –, (in) suspense ... 6.

suspension[5b]
  suspension (tension) 5.8

syllabe[5b]
  syllable ... 4.9

symbole[5a]
  symbol ... 5.6

sympathie[2b]
  avoir de la – pour, like 1.
  sympathy ... 2.8

sympathique[4a]
  sentiments -s
  sympathy ... 2.8

symptôme[6b]
  symptom ... 7.7

syndical[6a]
  trade ... 4.6

syndicat[5a]
  syndicate ... 9.3

synthétique
  synthetic ... 8.6

systématique[6a]
  systematic ... 6.9

système[2a]
  system ... 1.6
  – scolaire
  school system ... 4.2

T

tabac[3b]
  tobacco ... 3.9

table[1a]
  table ... 1.
  – des matières, index .. 5.3

tableau[2a]
  picture ... 1.1
  – noir, blackboard ... 5.8

tablier[4b]
  apron ... 5.4

tabouret
  stool ... 6.4

tache (*spot*)[3b]
  spot ... 2.2

tâche (*task*)[2b]
  (piece of) work ... 1.1

tâcher (*try*)[2a]
  try ... 1.

tacher (*spot*)[6b]
  spot ... 4.4
  stain ... 5.6

tact[4b]
  touch ... 2.1

tactique[5a]
  method ... 2.5
  tactical ... 11.7

taille[1b]
  figure ... 1.
  stature ... 2.9
  waist ... 4.4

tailler[3a]
  cut ... 1.8

tailleur[4a]
  tailor ... 3.5

taire[2a]
  se –, (keep) quiet ... 1.5
  faire –, silence (*vb.*) ... 1.9

Section

talent[2b]
  talent ... 2.4

talon[4a]
  heel (on shoe) ... 2.4
  heel (on foot) ... 4.9

talus[4b]
  slope ... 3.6

tambour[5b]
  drum ... 4.3

tamis
  sieve ... 7.2

tandis que[1a]
  while ... 1.

tant[1a]
  so much ... 1.

tant que[2b]
  as long as ... 1.1

tante[3b]
  aunt ... 2.

tantôt[2a]
  by and by ... 1.1
  – . . . . –,
  now . . . . now ... 1.5

tapage[5a]
  noise ... 2.6

taper[5a]
  knock (on door) ... 2.6
  tap ... 4.6

tapis[2a]
  carpet ... 4.2

tapisserie[4b]
  tapestry ... 5.8

taquiner[6b]
  tease ... 5.9

tard[1a]
  late ... 1.
  fournir plus –
  supply later ... 3.

tarder[2a]
  long for ... 1.4
  delay (*intr. vb.*) ... 2.
  – à, delay (*tr. vb.*) ... 2.7

tardif[4a]
  late ... 1.

tarif[6a]
  fare ... 3.6
  – d'impôt, tax rate ... 4.

tas[3a]
  mass ... 1.6

tasse[3a]
  cup ... 4.3

tâter[5b]
  feel (with fingers) ... 1.6

tâtonner[6b]
  grope ... 6.5

taureau
  bull ... 5.4

taux
  rate ... 3.8

taxe[6a]
  tax ... 1.6

taxer[6b]
  tax ... 3.5

technique (*adj.*)[4b]
  technical ... 4.7

technique (*n.*)[6b]
  technique ... 6.6

teint
  complexion ... 6.4

teinte[4a]
  shade ... 2.9

teinture
  dye ... 5.4

tel[1a]
  such ... 1.

télégramme[5a]
  wire ... 3.5

Section

tourmenter[4a]
torment ... 3.1

tournée[3b]
faire une –
(make the) rounds 4.3

tourner[1a]
turn ... 1.
revolve ... 5.5

tournoi[5a]
tournament ... 8.5

tournure[5a]
carriage ... 3.

tous (*pron.*)[5b]
– les deux, both ... 1.
everybody ... 2.2

tousser[5a]
cough ... 5.7

tout (*adj.*)[1a]
avant –, above all ... 1.
pas du –, (not at) all ... 1.
en – cas, (in any) case 1.
every ... 1.
– le monde, everybody 2.2
-es les nuits, nightly ... 3.

tout (*adv.*)[1a]
all ... 1.
complete ... 1.
– puissant, almighty ... 5.1

tout (*n.*)[6a]
whole ... 1.5

tout (*indef. pron.*)[3a]
everything ... 1.2

tout à coup[2a]
suddenly ... 1.

tout à fait[1b]
all ... 1.

tout à l'heure[4a]
by and by ... 1.1
just ... 1.3

tout de même[4b]
however ... 1.

tout de suite[1b]
(at) once ... 1.

tout d'un coup[4b]
(at) once ... 1.8

toutefois[2a]
however ... 1.

toux[6b]
cough ... 6.2

trace[2a]
step ... 2.
trace ... 2.1
track ... 2.1

tracer[3a]
trace ... 1.7

tradition[2a]
tradition ... 3.7

traditionnel[6a]
traditional ... 7.8

traduction[5b]
translation ... 5.

traduire[3a]
translate ... 3.8

tragédie[4b]
tragedy ... 4.4

tragique[3a]
tragic ... 4.9

trahir[2b]
betray ... 2.5

trahison[4b]
treason ... 4.3

train[1b]
train ... 1.1
train (military) ... 3.1

traîneau
sledge ... 6.8

traîner[2a]
drag ... 2.7

Section

trait (*n.*)[1b]
feature ... 1.5
draft ... 2.2
spear ... 3.2

traite[4a]
stage ... 3.6
draft ... 3.8

traité[2b]
treaty ... 2.6

traitement[4b]
treatment ... 2.8

traiter[1b]
treat ... 1.4

traître[3b]
traitor ... 4.9
treacherous ... 6.

trajet[5b]
crossing ... 1.6

tramway[5a]
car (trolley) ... 2.1

tranche[4b]
slice ... 4.

trancher[3b]
cut ... 1.8

tranquille[1b]
quiet ... 1.

tranquillement[3b]
quiet ... 1.

tranquillité[4a]
quiet ... 1.

transcendant(al)
surpassing ... 6.2

transfert
transfer ... 4.

transformation[4a]
change ... 2.9

transformer[2a]
transform ... 2.8

transition[6a]
transition ... 4.4

transmettre[4a]
send ... 1.

transparent[5a]
être –, show through ... 3.4
transparent ... 5.7

transport[2b]
transport ... 3.2
bliss ... 3.7

transporter[2b]
transfer ... 2.4
transport ... 3.9
transporté, rapt ... 4.3

trappe[6b]
trap ... 5.1

travail[1a]
work ... 1.
(piece of) work ... 1.1
workmanship ... 3.

travailler[1a]
work ... 1.
art de –, workmanship 3.

travailleur[3a]
worker ... 2.2

travers (à)[1b]
through (motion) ... 1.

travers (*n.*)[3b]
de –, crooked ... 3.7

travers (en)[4a]
across ... 3.4

traverse[5b]
rue de –, crossroad ... 10.5

traversée[5a]
crossing ... 1.6

traverser[1a]
cross ... 1.

trébucher[5b]
stumble ... 5.5

trèfle
clover ... 6.4

Section

treize[3a]
thirteen ... 5.2

tremblement[4b]
trembling ... 4.
– de terre, earthquake 6.

trembler[1b]
tremble ... 1.8

tremper[3a]
temper ... 4.9
soak ... 5.9

trentaine[6b]
thirty ... 2.3

trente[1b]
thirty ... 2.3

très[1a]
very ... 1.

trésor[2b]
treasure ... 2.
darling ... 2.2

trésorerie
treasury ... 5.6

trésorier
treasurer ... 7.2

tressaillement[5b]
thrill ... 5.6

tressaillir[5a]
thrill ... 4.4

trêve[6b]
recess ... 4.7

triangle
triangle ... 7.

tribu[5b]
tribe ... 2.5

tribunal[3b]
court ... 1.4

tribune[4b]
platform ... 5.8
pulpit ... 6.8

tributaire
tributary ... 6.3

tricher[6b]
cheat ... 3.1

tricolore[6b]
three-colored ... 13.

tricotter
knit ... 5.4

triomphant[5a]
triumphant ... 4.6

triomphe[2b]
triumph ... 3.1

triompher[4a]
triumph ... 4.2

triple[4b]
triple ... 5.8

triste[1b]
sad ... 1.4

tristement[3a]
sad ... 1.4

tristesse[2a]
sadness ... 3.5

trivial
trivial ... 5.

trois[1a]
three ... 1.
– fois, three times ... 2.6

troisième[1b]
third ... 1.

trompe[3b]
horn ... 3.6

tromper[2b]
deceive ... 1.9

tromper (se)[4b]
(be) wrong ... 1.4
(make a) mistake ... 2.2

trompette (*m.*)
trumpeter ... 8.4

tronc[4a]
trunk ... 2.3

Section

trône[4b]
héritier du –
(crown) prince ... 2.3
throne ... 2.3

trop[1a]
too ... 1.

trophée
trophy ... 6.8

tropical
tropic ... 6.9

tropique
tropic ... 6.9

trot
trot ... 4.6

trotter[5b]
trot ... 5.5

trottoir[3b]
sidewalk ... 5.5

trou[2b]
hole ... 2.2

troubadour
minstrel ... 7.2

trouble (*n.*)[2a]
confusion ... 3.2
riot ... 4.6

troublé[5b]
anxious ... 2.3

troubler[1b]
trouble ... 1.5

trouer[4b]
pierce ... 3.1
bore ... 5.

troupe[2b]
troop ... 1.6

troupeau[3b]
drove ... 3.9

trouvaille
finding ... 4.9

trouver[1a]
se –, be ... 1.
find ... 1.

truite
trout ... 6.8

tu, te, toi[1a]
thou ... 1.

tube[5a]
pipe ... 3.2

tuer[1b]
kill ... 1.4

tumulte[5b]
noise ... 2.6

tunique[6a]
uniform ... 4.4

tunnel[6a]
tunnel ... 6.4

turc[4a]
Turkish ... 5.

tuteur[4b]
guardian (of a child) 5.5

tutoyer[6a]
(use) thou-form ... 13.

tuyau[4b]
pipe ... 3.2

type[2a]
type ... 4.8

tyran[4a]
tyrant ... 4.2

tyrannie[5a]
tyranny ... 5.6

U

un (*art.*)[1a]
a ... 1.

un (*numeral*)[1a]
l'– et l'autre, both ... 1.
l'– l'autre, each other. 1.
-e fois, once ... 1.

V

Section

victoire[2a]
victory . . . 2.
vide (*adj.*)[2a]
empty . . . 2.
void . . . 5.4
vide (*n.*)[2b]
void . . . 5.2
vider[3a]
drain . . . 3.7
vie[1a]
life . . . 1.
vieil (*adj.*)[2a]
old . . . 1.
vieillard[3a]
(old) man . . . 2.4
vieille (*adj.* and *n.*)[1b]
old . . . 1.
vieillesse[3b]
old age . . . 1.3
vieillir[3b]
age . . . 1.6
vierge[3a]
girl . . . 1.
virgin (*n.*) . . . 2.9
virgin (*adj.*) (soil) . . 4.1
virgin (*adj.*) . . . 5.3
vieux (*adj.* and *n.*)[1a]
old . . . 1.
vif[1b]
fast . . . 1.
(full of) life . . . 1.
vigilance[6a]
care . . . 3.2
vigilant
watchful . . . 6.4
vigne[3a]
vine . . . 4.
vineyard . . . 5.1
vigoureux[4a]
hardy . . . 2.6
vigueur[5a]
force . . . 1.
vigor . . . 4.
vilain[3b]
bad . . . 1.2
naughty . . . 2.3
knave . . . 4.5
villain . . . 5.
villa[5b]
country house . . . 3.3
village[1b]
village . . . 1.2
ville[1a]
city . . . 1.
– natale, (home) town 3.3
hôtel de –, (city) hall . . 3.4
vin[1b]
wine . . . 1.4
vinaigre
vinegar . . . 6.3
vingt[1a]
twenty . . . 1.9
vingtaine[4a]
twenty . . . 1.9
vingt-cinq[2b]
twenty-five . . . 4.2
vingt-deux[5a]
twenty-two . . . 4.6
vingtième
twentieth . . . 7.1
vingt-quatre[6b]
twenty-four . . . 4.7
vingt-six[6a]
twenty-six . . . 4.7

Section

violation[4a]
violation . . . 6.8
violemment[3b]
furious . . . 1.9
violence[2a]
violence . . . 3.6
violent[2a]
furious . . . 1.9
violette[3a]
violet . . . 5.2
violon[4b]
violin . . . 6.1
vipère
viper . . . 7.
virilité
manhood . . . 6.8
vis
screw . . . 5.8
visage[1a]
face . . . 1.
vis-à-vis[3b]
(be) across . . . 1.
opposite . . . 1.4
viser[2b]
aim . . . 3.2
visible[2b]
visible . . . 2.9
visiblement[6a]
visible . . . 2.9
vision[3a]
sight . . . 1.
visite[1b]
visit . . . 1.4
rendre –, visit (*vb.*) . . . 1.4
visiter[2a]
visit (*vb.*) . . . 1.4
visiteur[4b]
visitor . . . 5.1
vite[1a]
fast . . . 1.
vitesse[2b]
speed . . . 2.5
rate (of speed) . . . 3.4
vitrail[5a]
(church) window . . . 2.4
vitre[2b]
pane . . . 3.3
vitupération
vituperation . . . 13.
vivacité[5b]
life . . . 3.8
vivant (*adj.*)[2a]
(full of) life . . . 1.
alive . . . 1.9
(the) living . . . 3.4
vivement[2b]
fast . . . 1.
vivre[1a]
live . . . 1.
vocation[6a]
occupation . . . 2.4
vœu[3a]
vow . . . 4.9
voici[1a]
here . . . 1.
voie[1b]
road . . . 1.
voilà[1b]
there is . . . 1.
voile (*m.*)[3a]
veil . . . 3.4
voile (*f.*)[5a]
sail . . . 3.5

Section

voiler[5a]
hide . . . 1.
voir[1a]
see . . . 1.
faire –, show . . . 1.
voire[4b]
even . . . 1.
voisin(-e)[1a]
near (*adj.*) . . . 1.
neighbor . . . 1.8
adjoining . . . 3.8
voisinage[3a]
neighborhood . . . 2.9
voiture[1b]
aller, se promener en –
drive (*intr. vb.*) . . . 1.
car . . . 1.5
voix[1a]
voice . . . 1.
à haute –, (out) loud . 1.
vol (*flight*)[3b]
flight (in air) . . . 2.5
vol (*theft*)[3a]
robbery . . . 4.8
volaille[5b]
fowl . . . 5.1
volant (*n.*)[4b]
ruffle . . . 6.1
volcan
volcano . . . 6.7
volée (*n.*)[4a]
flight (in air) . . . 2.5
drove . . . 3.9
– de coups, beating . . . 6.4
voler (*fly*)[4a]
fly . . . 1.6
voler (*steal*)[2b]
rob . . . 2.3
volet[5a]
blind . . . 3.1
voleur[3a]
thief . . . 3.7
volontaire[2a]
(of own) accord . . . 3.4
volontairement[6a]
(of own) accord . . . 3.4
volonté[1b]
will . . . 1.
volontiers[2b]
willingly . . . 1.6
volt[6b]
volt . . . 9.4
voltiger[5b]
fly . . . 1.6
– au-dessus de, hover . . 3.8
flutter . . . 5.7
volume[3a]
volume . . . 2.9
voluptueux[5b]
voluptuous . . . 8.6
vomir
vomit . . . 5.
vote[6a]
vote . . . 2.8
voter[2b]
vote . . . 1.8
votre, vos (*poss. adj.*)[1a]
your . . . 1.
vôtre (*poss. pron.*)[3b]
yours . . . 2.1
vouer[6b]
vow . . . 5.2

Section

vouloir[1a]
desire . . . 1.
– dire, mean . . . 1.
want . . . 1.
– savoir, wonder . . . 1.
– bien, (be) willing . . . 2.9
en – à, (bear) grudge . 5.6
vous[1a]
you . . . 1.
vous-même
yourself . . . 2.1
voûte[3a]
vault . . . 4.7
vouté[2b]
bent . . . 5.
voyage[1b]
journey . . . 1.
voyager[3a]
travel . . . 1.8
voyageur[1b]
traveler . . . 2.4
voyons![5b]
come now! . . . 1.4
vrai[1a]
real . . . 1.
true . . . 1.
vraiment[1b]
really . . . 1.4
vraisemblable[4a]
probable . . . 1.7
vue (*n.*)[1a]
point de –
point of view . . . 1.
sight . . . 1.
vulgaire[3b]
coarse . . . 2.9
vulgar . . . 2.9
rude . . . 4.3

W

wagon[4a]
car . . . 2.
wigwam
wigwam . . . 6.4

Y

y[1a]
il – a, ago . . . 1.
there . . . 1.
il – a, there *is* . . . 1.
s'– connaître
(well) informed . . 3.

Z

zèle[3b]
zeal . . . 2.4
zéro[6b]
zero . . . 6.4
zézayer
lisp . . . 7.2
zigzag
zigzag . . . 7.2
zinc[4b]
zinc . . . 6.
zone[4b]
district . . . 2.1
zoologique
zoological . . . 7.2
zouave[6a]
zouave . . . 13.

INDEX TO GERMAN WORDS IN THE LIST

(Read as directed for Index to French Words)

A

Section

ächten
proscribe ... 9.7
Achtung[2b]
–!, look out! ... 1.4
attention ... 1.8
respect ... 1.9
achtungsvoll[6b]
respectful ... 3.9
achtzehn[7a]
eighteen ... 4.3
achtzehnte[6b]
eighteenth ... 6.
achtzig
eighty ... 5.3
Acker[5a]
field ... 1.
Adel[3a]
nobility ... 3.7
adeln
ennoble ... 6.8
Ader[5a]
vein ... 3.6
Adjektiv
adjective ... 7.1
Adjunkt
associate ... 5.4
Adjutant[6a]
helper ... 4.3
Adler[6a]
eagle ... 4.1
Admiral
admiral ... 6.3
Adresse[3b]
address ... 2.3
Adverb
adverb ... 9.
Advokat[5b]
lawyer ... 3.
Affe
monkey ... 5.6
affektiert
affected ... 9.1
afrikanisch[6b]
African ... 4.4
Agent[3b]
agent ... 2.9
Agentur
agency ... 6.4
Agitation[6a]
propaganda ... 7.5
agressiv
aggressive ... 7.7
ägyptisch[5a]
Egyptian ... 5.4
ah[4a]
O ... 1.2
Ahne[6a]
ancestor ... 4.5
ahnen[2b]
suspect ... 2.9
ähnlich[1a]
like ... 1.
– sein, (look) like ... 1.
Ähnlichkeit[4a]
likeness ... 3.9
Ahnung[3b]
idea ... 1.4
expectation ... 3.3
Ahorn
maple ... 6.4
Akademie[4a]
academy ... 4.3
akademisch[5b]
university ... 4.2
Akkusativ
accusative ... 9.

Section

Akt[3b]
act (*n.*) ... 1.
Akte[4b]
act ... 2.3
Aktie[3b]
stock ... 1.8
Aktiengesellschaft[2b]
corporation ... 3.5
Aktion[6b]
encounter ... 3.9
Aktionär[4a]
partner ... 3.4
share holder ... 4.8
aktiv[5b]
active ... 2.6
Akzept[5b]
acceptance ... 3.8
Akzeptant[6a]
accepter ... 12.4
akzeptieren[4b]
accept ... 1.
Alarm
alarm ... 4.9
Albdruck
nightmare ... 7.8
Album
album ... 7.9
Alkohol[5a]
liquor ... 4.3
alkoholisch
alcoholic ... 7.7
all[1a]
all ... 1.
every ... 1.
everything ... 1.2
All[6b]
world ... 1.
universe ... 5.4
alledem[5b]
everything ... 1.2
allein[1a]
alone ... 1.
alleinig[5b]
exclusive ... 4.2
allemal[4b]
always ... 1.
allenfalls[5a]
perhaps ... 1.
allenthalben[5a]
everywhere ... 1.4
allerdings[1a]
indeed ... 1.
allerhand[6a]
kind ... 1.
allerhöchst[6b]
high ... 1.
allerlei[3a]
kind ... 1.
allerliebst[6b]
charming ... 2.3
allezeit[5b]
always ... 1.
allgemein[1a]
general ... 1.
im -en, (in) general ... 1.
Allgemeine
generality ... 10.
alljährlich[4b]
annual ... 2.7
allmächtig[6b]
almighty ... 5.1
allmählich[1b]
little by little ... 1.
allseitig[5a]
universal ... 3.8
alltäglich[6b]
usual ... 1.
daily ... 1.6

Section

allzu[3a]
too ... 1.
Almosen
alms ... 6.
als[1a]
as (e.g., I was walking) ... 1.
than ... 1.
when ... 1.
sowohl . . . . – auch
(as) well (as) ... 1.2
– Ergänzung
(in) addition ... 1.4
als(o)bald[3a]
(at) once ... 1.
alsdann[2b]
then ... 1.
also[1a]
so (thus) ... 1.
therefore ... 1.
alt[1a]
old ... 1.
– werden, age ... 1.6
-es Eisen, (old) iron ... 2.3
stale ... 2.9
Altar[4a]
altar ... 3.5
Alter[1b]
age ... 1.
old age ... 1.3
Altertum[3a]
antiquity ... 3.8
Älteste[5b]
senior ... 4.8
Amboß
anvil ... 7.2
Ameise
ant ... 6.
Amen[3b]
amen ... 4.3
amerikanisch[3b]
French ... 1.
Amme
wet-nurse ... 12.9
Amsel
blackbird ... 6.7
Amt[2b]
office ... 1.4
amtlich[3a]
official ... 2.8
Amtmann[5a]
magistrate ... 4.
Amtsgericht[6a]
court ... 1.4
Amtsrichter[6a]
judge ... 1.6
Amtsvorsteher[6b]
mayor ... 2.5
an[1a]
at ... 1.
von nun –, (from) now ... 1.1
analog[6a]
– sein, correspond ... 2.4
analysieren
analyze ... 6.5
Analyse
analysis ... 7.1
Anarchie
anarchy ... 7.5
Anbau[6b]
extension ... 4.4
annex ... 6.6
anbelangt[6a]
was . . . . –, as for ... 1.
anbeten[5b]
worship ... 3.6
anbetrifft[5a]
was . . . . –
about (concerning) ... 1.

Section

anbieten[3b]
offer ... 1.
Anblick[2a]
sight ... 1.
anbringen[2b]
install ... 3.2
Andacht[5b]
worship ... 3.6
Andenken[3b]
memory ... 1.8
andere[1a]
another ... 1.
eines -n, another's ... 1.
der eine oder der –
either (one) ... 1.
weder der eine noch der –
neither (one) ... 1.
other ... 1.
=r Meinung sein,
differ ... 2.5
ander(er)seits[2a]
(on the other) hand ... 1.4
(on the) contrary ... 1.8
ändern[2a]
change ... 1.4
anders[1a]
different ... 1.
anderswo[6b]
somewhere else ... 3.4
Änderung[2a]
change ... 1.5
anderwärts[6a]
somewhere else ... 3.4
anderweit[5b]
somewhere else ... 3.4
anderweitig[5a]
other ... 1.
andeuten[3a]
point out ... 1.4
hint ... 3.7
Andeutung[5a]
hint ... 4.1
suggestion ... 5.1
aneignen[5a]
(take) possession (of) ... 1.8
aneinander[5a]
together ... 1.
Anekdote
anecdote ... 6.6
anekeln
disgust ... 6.
anerkennen[1b]
admit ... 1.4
Anerkennung[2b]
reward ... 2.5
anfachen
fan up ... 5.
Anfang[1b]
am –, (at) first ... 1.
beginning ... 2.7
anfangen[1a]*
begin ... 1.
anfänglich[4b]
(at) first ... 1.
anfangs[2b]
(at) first ... 1.
anfassen[6b]
touch ... 1.
anfechten[6b]
tempt ... 4.
Anfechtung[6b]
temptation ... 4.4
anfertigen[4a]
manufacture ... 3.
anfeuchten
moisten ... 6.8
Anforderung[3a]
demand ... 1.3

Section

Apfelsine
orange . . . 5.2
Apostel[3a]
apostle . . . 5.4
apostolisch
apostolic . . . 8.2
Apotheker[6b]
druggist . . . 6.6
Apparat[2b]
apparatus . . . 3.7
Appetit
appetite . . . 5.
April[2a]
April . . . 2.1
Aquarell
watercolor . . . 13.
Araber[3b]
Arab . . . 4.7
arabisch[4b]
Arabian . . . 4.3
Arbeit[1a]
work (labor) . . . 1.
(piece of) work . . . 1.1
workmanship . . . 3.
arbeiten[1b]
work . . . 1.
Arbeiter[1a]
worker . . . 2.2
workman . . . 2.5
Arbeitgeber[2b]
director . . . 2.8
employer . . . 3.7
Arbeitskraft[5b]
energy . . . 3.6
Arbeitsordnung[5a]
rule . . . 1.1
Arbeitsunterbrechung
(stopping of) work . 5.
Arbeitszeit[6b]
time (general) . . . 1.
Arche
ark . . . 6.3
Archipel
archipelago . . . 9.6
Architekt[6b]
architect . . . 5.7
Archiv[5a]
record . . . 3.8
journal . . . 4.2
arg[4a]
bad . . . 1.
argentinisch
Argentine . . . 6.7
Ärger[7a]
anger . . . 1.9
vexation . . . 5.8
ärgerlich[6b]
angry . . . 2.4
vexing . . . 3.8
ärgern[4a]
sich –, (get) angry . . . 2.4
anger . . . 2.7
shock . . . 3.2
Argument[6a]
argument . . . 4.2
aristokratisch
aristocratic . . . 6.8
arktisch
arctic . . . 6.8
Arm[1a]
arm (part of body) . 1.
arm[1a]
poor . . . 1.
Armband
bracelet . . . 6.5
Armee[1a]
army . . . 1.2

Section

Armeekorps[2b]
battalion . . . 5.
Ärmel
sleeve . . . 5.1
Armut[5a]
poverty . . . 4.
Arrest
in –, (under) arrest . . . 6.1
Arroganz
arrogance . . . 7.2
Art[1a]
kind . . . 1.
way . . . 1.
artig[5a]
good . . . 1.
Artikel[1b]
article . . . 1.2
artikulieren
articulate . . . 7.1
Artillerie[1b]
artillery . . . 3.8
Arznei[6a]
medicine . . . 3.4
Arzt[2a]
doctor . . . 1.
ärztlich[6b]
medical . . . 5.1
Asche[4b]
ash(es) . . . 3.3
assimilieren
assimilate . . . 7.2
Ast[5b]
branch . . . 1.6
ästhetisch[4b]
artistic . . . 3.4
aesthetic . . . 8.8
Astronom[5b]
astronomer . . . 6.4
Atem[4b]
breath . . . 2.8
breathing . . . 3.6
Atheist
atheist . . . 8.2
Äther[6a]
air . . . 1.
ether . . . 6.
ätherisch
ethereal . . . 7.
Athlet
athlete . . . 8.2
atmen[4a]
breathe . . . 2.7
Atmosphäre[4b]
atmosphere . . . 4.1
Atom
atom . . . 7.2
Au[3b]
meadow . . . 2.6
auch[1a]
also . . . 1.
wenn –, although . . . 1.
– nicht, neither (*adv.*) . 1.
sowohl . . . . als –
(as) well (as) 1.2
was . . . . –, whatever 1.5
Audienz
audience . . . 5.2
auf[1a]
on . . . 1.
– einmal, suddenly . . . 1.
– Wiedersehen
farewell . . . 3.4
– sich ziehen, incur . . . 3.6
aufbauen[5a]
build . . . 1.2
aufbewahren[4a]
preserve . . . 3.

Section

aufbrechen[5b]
go away . . . 1.
aufbringen[4a]
introduce . . . 2.7
Aufenthalt[2b]
stay . . . 1.7
auferlegen[3b]
assign . . . 2.5
impose . . . 3.
inflict . . . 4.
auferstehen[7a]
revive . . . 5.2
auffahren[6b]
drive (*intr. vb.*) . . . . 1.
auffallen[2b]
(make an) impression . . . 2.2
-d, striking . . . 2.5
auffällig[6b]
striking . . . 2.5
auffangen[6a]
snatch . . . 2.6
auffassen[3b]
understand . . . 1.
Auffassung[2a]
understanding . . . 1.7
conception . . . 4.
auffinden[4b]
find . . . 1.
auffordern[3b]
invite . . . 2.3
defy . . . 3.2
Aufforderung[3b]
invitation . . . 3.2
aufführen[2b]
sich –, act (behave) . . 1.
Aufführung[4a]
conduct . . . 2.3
Aufgabe[1b]
work . . . 1.1
lesson . . . 1.2
aufgeben[2b]
leave (desert) . . . 1.
give up . . . 1.4
sich –
give (oneself) up 1.7
aufgehen[4a]
open . . . 2.2
aufhalten[2b]
keep from . . . 1.4
sich –, delay . . . 2.
detain . . . 2.6
sich –, sojourn . . . 3.4
sich –, linger . . . 3.6
aufheben[2b]
pick up . . . 1.5
Aufhebung[3b]
breaking up . . . 2.7
ending . . . 3.9
aufhören[2b]
stop . . . 1.4
aufklären[4a]
clear up . . . 2.9
Aufklärung[4a]
explanation . . . 2.9
aufknöpfen
unbutton . . . 12.2
aufkommen[5a]
succeed . . . 1.5
Auflage[2b]
edition . . . 3.6
auflegen[4b]
apply . . . 2.6
put over . . . 3.
auflösen[3a]
solve . . . 1.9

Section

Auflösung[3b]
breaking up . . . 2.7
solution . . . 3.5
aufmachen
sich –, start . . . 4.3
Aufmarsch[4a]
procession . . . 4.1
aufmerksam[2a]
observing . . . 2.6
attentive . . . 2.8
Aufmerksamkeit[2a]
attention . . . 1.8
aufmuntern
cheer (up) . . . 4.6
Aufnahme[2b]
reception . . . 3.2
photograph . . . 3.7
aufnehmen[1b]
take up . . . 1.7
Anleihe –, borrow 3.3
aufopfern[5b]
sacrifice . . . 2.6
aufrecht[3a]
straight . . . 1.8
Aufrechterhaltung[6a]
keeping up . . . 3.4
aufregen[4b]
stir . . . 1.9
Aufregung[4b]
excitement . . . 4.2
aufrichten[4b]
build . . . 1.2
aufrichtig[2b]
open . . . 1.3
sincere . . . 2.5
Aufrichtigkeit
sincerity . . . 5.9
Aufruhr[5a]
revolt . . . 4.4
riot . . . 4.6
aufrührerisch
rebellious . . . 6.4
Aufsatz[3a]
theme . . . 3.2
sketch . . . 3.9
aufsaugen
absorb . . . 5.7
aufschlagen[5b]
open . . . 1.
Aufschluß[5b]
information . . . 2.
aufschwingen
sich –, soar . . . 5.6
Aufschwung[5a]
development . . . 2.1
Aufsehen[5b]
excitement . . . 4.2
aufsetzen[5b]
put on . . . 2.6
Hut –, (put on) hat . . 2.8
draw up . . . 3.2
Aufsicht[5a]
care (solicitude) . . . . 1.
care (charge) 3.2
Aufsichtsrat[5b]
council . . . 2.1
Aufstand[5a]
riot . . . 4.6
Aufständische
insurgent . . . 9.
aufstehen[4b]
früh –, get up early . . . 3.
aufsteigen[3b]
climb . . . 2.7
aufstellen[1b]
build . . . 1.2

Section

auswandern
  emigrate . . . 7.6

Auswanderung
  emigration . . . 7.7

auswärtig[3b]
  foreign . . . 2.2

Ausweg[5b]
  way out . . . 2.

ausweichen[5a]
  avoid . . . 1.8

auswendig[6b]
  (learn by) heart . . . 3.

Auswertung
  working . . . 4.7

auszahlen[6a]
  spend . . . 1.6

auszeichnen[2a]
 ausgezeichnet
   excellent . . . 1.8
  distinguish . . . 2.2

Auszeichnung[5b]
  distinction . . . 3.9

ausziehen[5a]
  take off . . . 1.8
  take off clothes . . . 3.3
 Schuhe –
   (take off) shoes . . 4.1
  extract . . . 5.

Auszug[5b]
  departure . . . 3.1
  extract . . . 5.4

Autor[3b]
  author . . . 1.9

Autorität[3b]
  authority . . . 2.3

Avantgarde[3b]
  van . . . 4.4

Axt
  ax . . . 5.

B

babbeln
  babble . . . 6.4

Bach[3b]
  brook . . . 2.1

Bäcker
  baker . . . 6.

Bad[5a]
  bath . . . 3.9

baden[5b]
  bathe . . . 3.7

Bahn[1b]
  road . . . 1.

bahnen[6b]
  prepare . . . 1.4

Bahnhof[4a]
  station . . . 2.4

Bahre
  stretcher . . . 8.2

Bakkalaurius
  graduate (*n.*) . . . 6.1

bald[1a]
  soon . . . 1.
 – . . . . –
   now . . . . now . . 1.5

baldig[4b]
  near . . . 1.

Balkon
  balcony . . . 7.4

Ball[5a]
  ball (baseball) . . . 2.1
  ball (dance) . . . 3.

Ballade[6b]
  ballad . . . 5.9

Ballen[6b]
  bundle . . . 4.

Section

Ballon[6a]
  bottle . . . 2.1
  balloon . . . 6.1

Balsam
  balm . . . 6.4

Bambus
  bamboo . . . 7.2

Banane
  banana . . . 6.2

Band[2b]
  tie . . . 1.6

Band[3a]
  volume . . . 2.9

Band[4a]
  band (strip of cloth) 2.5
  ribbon . . . 3.1

Bande[4a]
  band (of people) . . . 2.1

bang[4a]
  anxious . . . 2.3

Bank[2a]
  bank . . . 1.8

Bank[3b]
  bench . . . 2.4

Bankier[5b]
  banker . . . 5.

Banknote[6b]
  (bank) note . . . 3.6

Bann[6b]
  spell . . . 4.4

bannen[6a]
  banish . . . 4.1

bar[3b]
  bare . . . 2.4
  (in) cash . . . 2.8

Bär[7a]
  bear . . . 4.5

barbarisch
  barbarous . . . 5.7

barfuß
  barefoot . . . 7.2

Baron[3a]
  baron . . . 4.

Baronin[6b]
  baron . . . 4.

Bart[5b]
  beard . . . 3.2

Basis[4b]
  base . . . 1.7

Bastard
  bastard . . . 7.1

Bataillon[2a]
  battalion . . . 5.

Batterie[1b]
  battery . . . 3.1

Bau[2b]
  building . . . 1.6
  den . . . 3.1

Bauch
  belly . . . 6.2

bauen[1b]
  build . . . 1.2

Bauer[2a]
  farmer . . . 1.8
  peasant . . . 2.4

Baukunst[6a]
  architecture . . . 5.9

Baum[1b]
  tree . . . 1.
  beam . . . 2.3

Baumwolle[5b]
  cotton . . . 3.8

Bauplatz
  work-yard . . . 12.2

Bauten[5a]
  building . . . 1.6

Section

Bauwerk[4b]
  building . . . 1.6

beabsichtigen[2a]
  intend . . . 1.4

beachten[3b]
  consider . . . 1.8

Beachtung[5a]
  regard . . . 1.5

Beamte[2a]
  official . . . 2.8
  employee . . . 3.1

beanspruchen[3b]
  claim . . . 2.3

beantragen[3a]
  propose . . . 1.4
  command . . . 1.5

beantworten[3a]
  answer . . . 1.

Beantwortung[4b]
  answer . . . 1.2

bearbeiten[4a]
  till . . . 2.5

Bearbeitung[4a]
  arrangement . . . 2.4

beauftragen[5a]
  charge . . . 2.2

beben[5b]
  tremble . . . 1.8
  thrill . . . 4.4

Becher[3b]
  goblet . . . 4.1

Bedacht[6a]
  consideration . . . 2.5

Bedarf[3a]
  need . . . 1.

bedauern[2b]
  (be) sorry . . . 1.8

Bedauern[5b]
  regret . . . 3.4

bedecken[2a]
  cover . . . 1.

bedenken[2a]
  consider . . . 1.8

Bedenken[2a]
  doubt . . . 1.

bedenklich[2b]
  doubtful . . . 2.6

bedeuten[1b]
  mean . . . 1.

bedeutend[1b]
  (full of) meaning . . . 3.3

bedeutsam[5a]
  (full of) meaning . . . 3.3

Bedeutung[1b]
  import . . . 2.2

bedienen[2b]
  serve . . . 1.

Bediente[5a]
  servant . . . 1.9

Bedienung[5b]
  service . . . 1.

bedingen[2b]
  (make) necessary . . . 1.8

Bedingung[1b]
  condition . . . 1.

bedrücken
  oppress . . . 5.8

bedürfen[2a]
  need . . . 1.

Beefsteak
  steak . . . 6.8

beeindrucken
  (make an) impression 2.2

Beerdigung
  burial . . . 5.7

Section

Beere
  berry . . . 4.9

Beet
  flower-bed . . . 13.

befähigt[5b]
  able . . . 1.4

befallen
  stricken . . . 6.5

befangen[6a]
  involve . . . 3.9

befassen[5b]
 sich – mit
   (be) engaged (in) 1.9

Befehl[1b]
  order . . . 1.
  – erlassen, command . . 1.5

befehlen[2a]
  command . . . 1.5

Befehlshaber[6b]
  commander . . . 4.4

befestigen[2a]
  fix . . . 1.

Befestigung[5a]
  fort . . . 2.6

befinden[1a]
  judge . . . 1.

Befinden[6b]
  (state of) health . . . 3.1

befindlich[2b]
  – sein, exist . . . 1.8

beflecken
  spot . . . 4.4
  stain . . . 5.6

befolgen[4a]
  obey . . . 2.2

befördern[3a]
  further . . . 1.8

Beförderung[4a]
  transport . . . 3.2
  promotion . . . 5.6

befragen[5b]
  question . . . 2.9

befreien[2a]
  free (deliver) . . . 1.7
  free (rid) . . . 2.2
 sich –, (get) rid (of) . . . 2.9

Befreier
  deliverer . . . 7.2

Befreiung[4a]
  relief . . . 3.3
  freeing . . . 3.4
  deliverance . . . 5.2
  exemption . . . 7.8

befreundet[5b]
  familiar . . . 3.3

befriedigen[2a]
  satisfy . . . 1.9
  -d, satisfactory . . . 3.7

Befriedigung[2b]
  satisfaction . . . 2.4

Befugnis[3a]
  authority . . . 2.3

befugt[4b]
  authorize . . . 3.7

befürchten[3b]
  (be) afraid . . . 1.
 zu –, dreaded . . . 2.4

Befürchtung[5a]
  fear . . . 1.4

Begabung[5a]
  talent . . . 2.4

begeben[2a]
 sich –, happen . . . 1.

Begebenheit[4a]
  event . . . 2.

begegnen[1b]
  meet . . . 1.

Section

- berauschen[6b]
  - (make) drunk 4.8
- berechnen[2a]
  - rate 2.3
  - reckon 2.6
- Berechnung[3a]
  - account 1.8
- berechtigen[2a]
  - justify 2.5
  - authorize 3.7
- Berechtigung[3b]
  - right 1.8
- bereden[5b]
  - discuss 3.3
- Beredsamkeit[6a]
  - eloquence 5.1
- beredt
  - eloquent 6.4
- Bereich[4b]
  - compass 2.5
- bereichern[6a]
  - enrich 5.
- bereisen
  - (make the) rounds 4.3
- bereit[1b]
  - ready 1.2
- bereiten[2a]
  - prepare 1.4
  - sich –, prepare 1.6
- bereits[1a]
  - already 1.
- Bereitung[6b]
  - preparation 3.
- bereitwillig[6b]
  - (be) willing 2.9
- bereuen[6a]
  - repent 4.3
- Berg[2a]
  - mountain 1.5
- Bergarbeiter[6b]
  - miner 4.7
- bergen[4a]
  - hide 1.
- Bergmann[4b]
  - miner 4.7
- Bergwerk[6b]
  - mine 2.6
- Bericht[1b]
  - report 1.
- berichten[2a]
  - report 1.5
- berichtigen[5a]
  - adjust 4.5
  - amend 4.9
- Bernstein
  - amber 6.6
- berücksichtigen[3b]
  - consider 1.8
- Berücksichtigung[4a]
  - consideration 2.5
- Beruf[2b]
  - occupation 2.4
  - profession 2.9
- berufen[2a]
  - call together 2.1
  - sich –, appeal 2.8
- Berufsgenossenschaft[6b]
  - company (social) 1.
- Berufung[4a]
  - appeal 3.8
  - reference 4.8
- beruhen[2a]
  - rest on 1.9
- beruhigen[2b]
  - quiet 1.6
- berühmt[2a]
  - famous 1.1
  - illustrious 3.1
- berühren[2a]
  - touch 1.
- Berührung[3b]
  - touch (act of touching) 2.1
  - touch (contact) 2.2
- besagen[5a]
  - mean 1.
- Besatzung[4b]
  - crew 3.2
  - garrison 4.9
- beschädigen[5b]
  - hurt (*tr. vb.*) 1.8
- beschaffen[3b]
  - get (obtain) 1.
- Beschaffenheit[3a]
  - nature (character) 1.
- Beschaffung[6a]
  - acquisition 6.3
- beschäftigen[1b]
  - beschäftigt, busy 1.
  - (make) curious 2.9
- Beschäftigung[3a]
  - occupation 2.4
  - employment 3.7
- beschämen[5b]
  - shame 3.4
- beschämt
  - sheepish 11.4
- Bescheid[5a]
  - information 2.
- bescheiden[2b]
  - sich –, satisfy 1.9
- bescheiden[3b]
  - modest 2.4
- Bescheidenheit[6a]
  - modesty 4.7
- beschießen[6a]
  - shoot 1.8
- Beschimpfung
  - outrage 6.7
- beschlagen
  - dull (tarnish) 5.3
  - expert 5.6
- beschleunigen[4b]
  - hurry 2.5
- beschließen[1b]
  - decide 1.
- Beschluß[1b]
  - zum –, (at) last 1.
- Beschlußfassung[5b]
  - decision 2.5
  - decree 2.6
- beschmutzen
  - soil 4.9
- beschränken[1b]
  - limit 1.6
- Beschränkung[3a]
  - limit 2.4
- beschreiben[2b]
  - describe 2.
- Beschreibung[3b]
  - description 3.1
- beschuldigen[6b]
  - accuse 4.
- beschützen[6a]
  - protect 2.1
- Beschützer
  - protector 6.3
- Beschwerde[3a]
  - trouble 1.
- beschweren[3b]
  - load 1.8
- beschwerlich[6a]
  - vexing 3.8
  - troublesome 4.4
- beschwören[4b]
  - beg 2.7
- beseelen[5a]
  - animate 3.5
- besehen[6b]
  - examine 1.5
- beseitigen[2a]
  - take away 1.
- Beseitigung[3b]
  - abolition 5.3
- Besen
  - broom 5.5
- besetzen[1b]
  - (take) possession 1.8
- Besetzung[5a]
  - invasion 5.4
- besiegen[4a]
  - conquer 2.9
- besinnen[3b]
  - remember 1.
- Besitz[1b]
  - property 1.5
  - wealth 1.5
  - possession 1.6
- besitzen[1b]
  - own 1.
- Besitzer[2b]
  - owner 2.
- Besitzung[5b]
  - possession 1.6
- besohlen
  - sole 5.4
- besondere[1a]
  - particular 1.4
- besonders[1a]
  - above all 1.
- besonnen[6a]
  - pensive 3.9
- besorgen[2a]
  - (take) care 1.
- Besorgnis[3b]
  - care 1.
  - cares 1.3
- besprechen[3a]
  - consult 3.
  - discuss 3.3
- Besprechung[3b]
  - talk 1.
- besser[1a]
  - better 1.
- bessern[5b]
  - improve 3.5
- Besserung[4a]
  - improvement 3.6
- Bestand[3b]
  - – haben, last 1.1
- beständig[2b]
  - firm (character) 1.1
  - continual 2.5
- Beständigkeit
  - constancy 7.1
- Bestandteil[2b]
  - element 2.3
- bestärken[6a]
  - support 1.8
  - strengthen 3.4
- bestätigen[2a]
  - assure 1.4
  - confirm 2.5
  - affirm 2.7
- Bestätigung[4b]
  - confirmation 5.1
- beste[1a]
  - best 1.
- Beste[2b]
  - best 1.
  - das –, cream of crop 2.8
- bestechen
  - bribe 6.
- bestehen[1a]
  - consist 1.4
  - exist 1.8
  - insist 2.
- Bestehen[6a]
  - existence 2.6
  - insistence 7.3
- besteigen[5a]
  - climb 2.7
- bestellen[2b]
  - order 1.5
  - summon 2.7
- Bestellung[5a]
  - order 1.
- bestens[6a]
  - best 1.
- besteuern[5b]
  - tax 3.5
- Besteuerung[2b]
  - tax 1.6
- bestimmen[1b]
  - decide 1.
  - name (appoint) 1.
  - settle 1.
  - fix 1.1
  - destine 2.4
  - nicht zu –, undefinable 10.2
- bestimmt[1a]
  - definite 3.5
  - decisive 3.6
- Bestimmung[1a]
  - fate 1.5
  - statement 2.1
- bestrafen[2b]
  - punish 2.1
- Bestrafung[6b]
  - punishment 2.6
- Bestreben[3b]
  - effort 1.8
- bestreben[5a]
  - try hard 1.5
- Bestrebung[3a]
  - effort 1.8
- bestreiten[3a]
  - deny 2.4
  - dispute 2.8
  - contest 3.2
- bestürzen
  - dismay 6.4
- bestürzt[6b]
  - distracted 5.5
- Besuch[2a]
  - visit 1.4
- besuchen[2a]
  - visit 1.4
- Besucher[6b]
  - visitor 5.1
- betäuben
  - din 6.2
- Betäubung
  - daze 7.8
  - stupor 9.2
- beteiligen[2b]
  - (take) part 1.4
  - beteiligt, (be a) party 2.
- Beteiligte[4a]
  - partner 3.4
- Beteiligung[4b]
  - share 2.
- beten[3a]
  - pray 2.2
- betonen[3a]
  - accent 3.9
- Betracht[2a]
  - consideration 2.5
- betrachten[1b]
  - watch 1.
  - observe 1.4
  - examine 1.5

Section

Block
block ... 5.2

blöken
bleat ... 6.8

blond[6a]
fair ... 1.2

bloß[1a]
only ... 1.
pure ... 1.

blühen[4a]
bloom ... 3.

blühend[4a]
ruddy ... 5.3

Blume[2a]
flower ... 1.4

blumig
flowery ... 5.5

Bluse
blouse ... 6.8

Blut[1b]
blood ... 1.

Blüte[3a]
blossom ... 2.2

bluten[5b]
bleed ... 5.
-d, bleeding ... 5.

blutig[3a]
bloody ... 2.9

Blüttenblatt
petal ... 7.2

Bö
blast ... 5.7

Boden[1a]
bottom ... 1.
earth ... 1.
ground ... 1.
floor ... 1.2

Bogen[3a]
sheet ... 2.2
bow (arch) ... 2.4
bow (and arrow) ... 2.4

Bohème
Bohemian ... 7.3

böhmisch[5b]
English ... 1.

Bohne
bean ... 5.4

bohren
bore ... 5.

Bolzen
latch ... 6.8

Boot[5a]
boat ... 2.6

Bord[5a]
an –, (on) board ... 3.
an – gehen, sail ... 3.
shelf ... 4.5

Börse[3a]
exchange ... 2.6

bös[1b]
naughty ... 2.3

boshaft
roguish ... 10.2

Bosheit[5b]
evil ... 2.
malice ... 4.8

Bote[4a]
messenger ... 2.5

Botschaft[4b]
message ... 3.

Boxer
prize fighter ... 7.

Brand[3b]
fire ... 1.
burning ... 2.3

Branntwein[5a]
liquor ... 4.3

Section

Braten
roast ... 5.4

braten
fry ... 6.3

brauchbar[4b]
useful ... 2.

brauchen[1a]
need ... 1.

Braue
eyebrow ... 6.3

brauen
brew ... 7.

braun[4a]
brown ... 2.5

brausen[6a]
rage ... 3.7

Braut[3a]
bride ... 1.6
engaged ... 2.5

Bräutigam[4b]
engaged ... 2.5
groom ... 4.6

bräutlich
bridal ... 6.2

brav[2b]
– sein, (be) brave ... 1.
fine ... 1.4

bravo[3a]
applause ... 3.7

brechen[1b]
break ... 1.1
burst ... 1.4

breit[2a]
broad ... 1.4

Breite[3a]
width ... 3.4

breiten[3b]
spread ... 1.4

Bremse
brake ... 5.6

brennen[2a]
burn ... 1.6

Brennerei[5b]
distillery ... 8.4

Brennmaterial[6b]
fuel ... 5.2

Brennpunkt
focus ... 6.1

Brett[6a]
board ... 1.7

Brief[1a]
letter ... 1.
charter ... 2.9

Briefwechsel[5a]
correspondence ... 3.9
in – stehen
correspond ... 4.

Brigade[2a]
brigade ... 6.2

Brille
glasses ... 4.2

bringen[1a]
bring ... 1.
carry ... 1.
zur Ausführung –, in Erfüllung –
carry out ... 1.
in Vorschlag –
propose ... 1.
aus der Fassung –
overcome ... 2.7
in Unordnung –
(put in) disorder. 4.8

Brise
breeze ... 5.2

britisch[6b]
British ... 4.2

Section

Brombeere
bramble ... 7.2

Bronze
bronze ... 6.2

Broschüre[6b]
pamphlet ... 6.3

Brot[2b]
bread ... 1.4
loaf ... 3.3

Bruch[6a]
break ... 3.8

Brücke[2b]
bridge ... 1.7

Bruder[1a]
brother ... 1.

brüderlich
brotherly ... 6.9

brüllen
roar ... 4.7

Brüllen
roar ... 5.3

Brunnen[4b]
well ... 1.9
fountain ... 2.8

Brust[2a]
chest ... 1.9

Brut
brood ... 5.8

brutal
-e Mensch, brute ... 5.7

brüten
hatch ... 6.8

Bube[5b]
boy ... 1.4

Buch[1a]
book ... 1.

Buche
beech ... 7.

Buchhändler[6b]
publisher ... 5.8
bookseller ... 9.

Buchhandlung[6b]
book shop ... 4.2

Buchs
box ... 4.9

Buchstabe[2b]
letter ... 1.4

Bucht
bay ... 4.5
creek ... 5.9

Bude
stall ... 5.2

Büffel
buffalo ... 7.2

Bug
bow ... 4.3

Bühne[3a]
stage ... 3.

Bulle
papal bull ... 7.8

Bund[2a]
union ... 1.6
league ... 2.8

Bundes-
federal ... 6.5

Bundesgenosse[5a]
fellow worker ... 2.9

Bundesrat[3b]
council ... 2.1

Bundesstaat[4b]
union ... 1.6
confederacy ... 5.1

Bündnis[4b]
union ... 1.6

bunt[4a]
colored ... 4.2

Section

Bureau[5a]
office ... 2.9

Burg[5a]
castle ... 2.

Bürge
bondsman ... 13.

Bürger[2a]
citizen ... 2.2
bourgeois ... 5.9

bürgerlich[2a]
civil ... 2.4

Bürgermeister[4a]
mayor ... 2.5

Bürgerschaft[6b]
House of Representatives ... 3.4

Bürgersteig
sidewalk ... 5.5

Bürgschaft[6a]
pledge ... 2.9

Bursche[4a]
fellow ... 2.3

Bürste
brush ... 5.6

Busch
shrub ... 6.1

Büschel
tuft ... 6.8

buschig
tufted ... 6.4

Busen[3b]
chest ... 1.9

Buße[5b]
amends ... 4.1
penance ... 5.7
atonement ... 7.

büßen[5a]
make up for ... 2.9
(do) penance ... 5.8

Büste
bust ... 6.1

Butter[6a]
butter ... 3.5

Butterbrot
sandwich ... 6.8

C

Cäsar[5b]
emperor ... 2.1

Chaos
chaos ... 6.6

Charakter[1b]
character ... 1.

charakterisieren[5a]
describe ... 2.

Charakteristik[6a]
description ... 3.1

charakteristisch[4a]
characteristic ... 3.8

Chaußee[4b]
road ... 1.
avenue ... 3.1

Check[6b]
check ... 4.8

Chef[3b]
chief ... 1.5

Chemie
chemistry ... 7.8

Chemiker[6a]
chemist ... 6.4

chemisch[3a]
chemical ... 4.9

chiffrieren
cipher ... 9.3

Section

Dichte
density 7.8
dichten[3a]
compose 2.6
Dichter[1a]
poet 1.5
dichterisch[3b]
poetic 3.9
Dichtkunst[5a]
poetry 2.4
Dichtung[2b]
poetry 2.4
fiction 3.9
dick[3b]
thick 1.2
fat 1.9
– werden, (get) fat ... 2.7
Dicke[7a]
thickness 5.1
Dickicht
thicket .... 6.
Dieb[5a]
thief 3.7
Diebstahl[6b]
robbery 4.8
dienen[1a]
serve .... 1.
Diener[2b]
servant 1.9
Dienst[1b]
service .... 1.
Dienstag[5b]
Tuesday 3.7
diensteifrig
servile .... 7.
dienstlich[6a]
official 2.8
Dienstpflicht[4b]
service .... 1.
Dienstzeit[3b]
time (general) ..... 1.
dies[1a]
this (*adj.*) .... 1.
this (*pron.*) .... 1.
latter 1.4
diesmal[2b]
now .... 1.
Differenz[4a]
difference 1.4
diktieren[6a]
dictate .... 5.
Dimension[6a]
dimension 5.6
Ding[1a]
thing .... 1.
Diplomatie
diplomacy 9.4
diplomatisch[5a]
careful 1.7
diplomatic 7.6
direkt[1b]
direct (*adj.*) .... 1.
direct (*adv.*) 1.1
Direktion[5a]
direction 1.8
Direktor[3a]
director 2.8
dirigieren[6a]
lead .... 1.
Dirne
harlot 6.8
diskret
discreet 5.7
Diskussion[3b]
discussion 2.9
Disposition[4a]
arrangement 2.4

Section

Distel
thistle 6.4
Distrikt[6b]
district 2.1
Disziplin[4b]
discipline 4.8
Dividende[4b]
interest (percent) .. 1.
dividend 5.6
Division[1b]
division 2.2
doch[1a]
however .... 1.
Dock
dock 5.4
Doge[4b]
chief 1.5
Dogma
dogma 8.3
Doktor[1a]
doctor .... 1.
Dokument[6b]
document 5.1
certificate 5.8
Dolch[5b]
dagger 5.6
Dolchstoß
stab 6.5
Dollar[5b]
pound .... 1.
Dom[6a]
cathedral 4.6
Donner[5b]
thunder 3.6
donnern[6b]
thunder 4.2
Donnerstag[3b]
Thursday 2.7
Doppelbesteuerung[6a]
tax 1.6
doppelt[2a]
double 1.6
Doppelwährung[5b]
bimetallism 10.8
Dorf[1b]
village 1.2
Dorn[6b]
thorn 4.3
dort[1a]
there .... 1.
dorthin[3a]
there .... 1.
dortig[3a]
there .... 1.
Drache[6b]
dragon .... 5.
kite 5.2
Dragoner[6a]
dragoon 8.6
Draht[6b]
wire 4.2
drahtlos
wireless .... 6.
Drama[3b]
drama 3.7
dramatisch[3b]
dramatic 4.6
Drang[4a]
spur 3.6
drängen[2a]
press 1.1
crowd 2.2
draußen[3b]
outside 1.4
drehen[2b]
twist 2.6

Section

Drehung[6b]
turn .... 3.
drei[1a]
three .... 1.
Dreieck
triangle .... 7.
dreifach[5a]
three times 2.6
triple 5.8
dreifarbig
three-colored ...... 13.
dreimal[5a]
three times 2.6
dreißig[3b]
thirty 2.3
dreizehn
thirteen 5.2
dreschen
thrash 5.9
dringen[2a]
press 1.1
dringend[2a]
pressing 1.7
dritte[1a]
third .... 1.
Drittel[3b]
third .... 1.
Droge
drug 5.8
Drogerie
drug store 5.6
drohen[2a]
threaten 1.8
Drohung[5b]
threat 4.6
Drossel
thrush 7.1
drüben[5a]
(be) across .... 1.
there .... 1.
Druck[2a]
oppression 3.5
drücken[1b]
press 1.1
drucken[3a]
print 2.4
Druckerei[6a]
printing office 4.4
Drucksache[3b]
printed matter 2.4
du[1a]
thou .... 1.
you .... 1.
siehst –!, here! 1.6
Dudelsack
bagpipe 8.1
Duell
duel .... 7.
Duft[5a]
perfume .... 4.
duftig
fragrant 5.5
dulden[3b]
bear .... 1.
Duldung
toleration 7.7
dumm[4a]
dull 3.5
Dumme
dupe 8.2
Dummheit[6b]
nonsense .... 5.
stupidity 8.2
dumpf[4b]
vague .... 4.
düngen
fertilize 6.8

Section

Dünger
manure .... 7.
dunkel[1b]
dark .... 1.
Dunkel[4b]
darkness 2.9
Dunkelheit[4a]
darkness 2.9
dunkeln
(grow) dark 4.5
dünken[4a]
think .... 1.
dünn[3a]
thin .... 2.
durch[1a]
by (agent) .... 1.
through (motion) ... 1.
through (agent) .... 1.
durchaus[1a]
all .... 1.
durchbohren[6a]
pierce 3.1
durchbrechen[4b]
pierce 3.1
durchdringen[3a]
penetrate 6.6
Durchdringung
penetration 9.3
durcheinander[5a]
– bringen
(put in) disorder 4.8
Durcheinander
(in a) huddle 7.4
durchführen[2b]
carry out .... 1.
Durchführung[3a]
carrying out 2.2
performance .... 3.
durchgehen[5b]
-d, passing 1.9
look over 3.1
durchkreuzen
thwart 6.8
durchlaufen[6a]
run through 3.1
durchmachen[6a]
bear .... 1.
Durchmesser[5a]
diameter 6.2
durchnässen
soak 5.9
durchschlagen[6b]
pierce 3.1
durchschneiden[5a]
cut 1.8
Durchschnitt[4a]
im –
(on the) average 3.2
durchschnittlich[4a]
(on the) average ... 3.2
durchsetzen[4b]
sich –, succeed 1.5
durchsichtig[5a]
– sein, show through .. 3.4
transparent 5.7
durchstreichen
cross out 4.7
durchweg[4b]
throughout 2.8
durchziehen[5b]
wander 2.7
dürfen[1a]
may .... 1.
dürftig[5a]
imperfect 3.9
needy .... 6.

Section

einlösen[6b]
redeem 4.7
einmal[1a]
once 1.
sometime 1.
auf –, suddenly 1.
einmalig[6a]
only 1.
einmischen
meddle 5.9
Einnahme[3a]
receipt 3.3
einnehmen[2a]
defeat 2.7
einnisten
nestle 7.
einräumen[3b]
admit 1.4
einreichen[4b]
deliver 1.4
einrichten[2a]
fix (up) 1.5
fit up 1.8
install 3.2
institute 3.3
Einrichtung[1b]
arrangement 2.4
einrücken[5b]
insert 4.4
einsam[3a]
lonely 3.3
Einsamkeit[4b]
solitude 3.6
Einschätzung[6a]
estimate 3.8
einschließen[6a]
weave 4.6
einschlafen
(go to) sleep 3.9
einschläfern
put to sleep 4.
einschlagen[3a]
wrap 2.3
tuck 4.1
einschließen[3a]
shut in 1.9
einschließlich[4b]
included 2.9
einschränken[4a]
limit 1.6
Einschränkung[4b]
restraint 4.1
einschüchtern
intimidate 10.2
einsehen[3a]
understand 1.
realize 2.6
einseitig[3b]
partial 4.5
einsetzen[3b]
begin 1.
Einsicht[3a]
judgment 2.6
discretion 3.9
Einsiedler
hermit 6.6
einsilbig
monosyllable 10.5
einst[1b]
once 1.
sometime 1.
einstellen[3a]
interrupt 2.3
accommodate 3.8
Einstellung
accommodations 6.8
einstimmig[4b]
unanimous 5.

Section

Einsturz
crumbling 6.5
einstweilen[5a]
(for the) present 1.4
Einteilung[5b]
arrangement 2.4
eintönig
monotonous 6.8
Eintönigkeit
monotony 8.1
Eintrag
entry 5.1
eintragen[3b]
enter 2.6
register 3.
Eintragung[4b]
registering 4.2
eintreffen[2a]
happen 1.
eintreten[1a]
enter 1.
Eintritt[3a]
entrance 2.2
einverleiben
sich –, annex 7.4
einverstanden[3a]
– sein, agree 2.2
agreed 2.8
Einverständnis[5b]
agreement 3.1
Einwand[4b]
objection 4.4
einwenden[4b]
object 1.9
Einwendung[5a]
protest 4.1
Einwilligung[5a]
consent 2.8
einwirken[4a]
affect 3.2
influence 3.2
Einwirkung[3a]
influence 1.6
Einwohner[3a]
inhabitant 3.2
Einzelheit[3b]
particular 2.3
einzeln[1a]
only 1.
einziehen[3b]
enter 1.
Einziehung[6b]
draft 5.2
einzig[1a]
only 1.
Einzug[6a]
entrance 2.2
Eis[4a]
ice 2.4
Eisen[3a]
iron 1.8
altes –, (old) iron 2.3
Eisenbahn[2a]
railroad 2.
eisern[2b]
iron 1.4
eisig
icy 6.
eitel[3b]
vain 2.3
Eitelkeit[4a]
vanity 3.3
eklig
disgusting 6.2
elastisch
elastic 6.6

Section

Elefant[5a]
elephant 5.
elegant[4b]
elegant 3.6
elektrisch[3b]
electric 3.
Elektrizität[6a]
electricity 5.6
Element[2a]
element 2.3
elementar
elementary 7.2
Elend[3a]
misery 2.7
elend[3b]
miserable 2.7
elf[4b]
eleven 2.9
Elfenbein
ivory 5.6
elfte
eleventh 7.2
Ellbogen
elbow 5.1
Eltern[2a]
parents 1.8
Emaille
enamel 6.8
Empfang[3a]
reception 3.2
receipt 3.3
empfangen[1b]
get (receive) 1.
get (obtain) 1.
conceive 2.
Empfänger[5b]
receiver 6.
empfänglich
susceptible 6.9
empfehlen[1b]
recommend 2.1
Empfehlung[4b]
compliment 4.1
recommendation 4.5
empfinden[1b]
feel 1.
Empfinden[6b]
feeling 1.6
empfindlich[3b]
conscious 3.3
sensitive 4.4
empfindsam
sentimental 6.6
mawkish 11.
Empfindung[2a]
feeling 1.6
empor[3a]
go up 1.
empören[4a]
stir 1.9
sich –, rebel 3.6
Emporkömmling
upstart 9.
Empörung[6a]
anger 1.9
indignation 4.2
Ende[1a]
end 1.
enden[3a]
end 1.
endgültig[4b]
final 2.9
endigen[5a]
end 1.
endlich[1a]
(at) last 1.

Section

endlos[6b]
endless 3.
Endlosigkeit
infinity 9.6
Energie[4a]
energy 3.6
energisch[3a]
(full of) energy 3.3
vehement 4.8
eng[1b]
narrow 1.
tight 1.7
Enge
strait 5.3
Engel[2b]
angel 2.
Engländer[4b]
French 1.
englisch[1b]
English 1.
Enkel[4b]
ankle 4.6
grandson 4.7
enorm[5a]
great (huge) 1.
entbehren[2b]
lack 1.5
entbehrlich[6b]
unnecessary 4.2
Entbehrung[6b]
want 3.9
entblößen[6a]
strip 3.7
entdecken[2a]
discover 1.4
Entdeckung[3a]
discovery 3.
Ente
duck 5.
entehren
disgrace 5.6
entfallen[5a]
escape 2.6
slip 2.8
entfalten[3b]
develop 2.
unfold 3.4
Entfaltung[6a]
development 2.1
evolution 4.5
entfernen[1b]
go away 1.
take away 1.
Entfernung[1b]
distance 1.1
removal 4.6
entfliehen[4b]
escape 1.8
entgegen[1b]
against 1.
entgegenkommen[4b]
(go to) meet 2.3
entgegensehen[5b]
expect 1.
entgegensetzen[2b]
oppose 2.3
entgegenstehen[6a]
oppose 2.3
face 3.8
entgegenstellen[6a]
oppose 2.3
entgegentreten[3b]
oppose 2.3
entgegnen[4b]
answer 1.
entgehen[3a]
escape 1.8

Section

Erlassung
- exemption 7.8

erlauben[1b]
- allow 1.

Erlaubnis[3a]
- permission 3.3

erläutern[5b]
- account for 1.

erleben[2b]
- experience 1.8

Erlebnis[5b]
- experience 1.6

erledigen[3b]
- settle 1.8

Erledigung[5a]
- settlement 2.7

erlegen[6a]
- kill 1.4

erleichtern[2b]
- (make) easy 1.8
- relieve 2.7
- lighten 3.8

Erleichterung[3a]
- relief 3.3

erleiden[2b]
- suffer 1.

erlesen
- select 4.9
- choice 5.3

erleuchten[4a]
- light (up) 1.4
- brighten 4.1

erlöschen[4a]
- disappear 1.4

erlösen[5a]
- free 1.7

Erlöser[5a]
- savior 4.8

Erlösung[6b]
- deliverance 5.2

ermächtigen[6b]
- justify 2.5
- authorize 3.7

ermahnen[6a]
- warn 2.2
- admonish 6.3

Ermangelung[6b]
- want 3.

ermäßigen[6b]
- decline 3.3
- moderate 4.2

Ermäßigung[5b]
- reduction 5.3

Ermessen[5a]
- judgment 1.5

ermitteln[4a]
- (make) sure 2.2

Ermittelung[5a]
- inquiry 3.5

ermöglichen[3a]
- (make) possible 1.8

ermorden[4a]
- murder 3.5

ermüden[4b]
- tire 2.4

ermutigen
- encourage 4.8

Ermutigung
- encouragement 6.7

ernähren[5b]
- nourish 3.2

Ernährung[6a]
- feeding 4.2
- nourishment 5.6

ernennen[2b]
- name (appoint) 1.

Section

Ernennung[5b]
- appointment (to something) 4.5
- nomination 4.9

erneuern[2b]
- renew 2.5
- reconstitute 9.7

Erneuerung[6a]
- reform 3.2
- renewal 6.9

erniedrigen[6a]
- lower 2.3

ernst[1b]
- grave 1.4

Ernst[2a]
- gravity 3.8

ernsthaft[3b]
- grave 1.4

ernstlich[3a]
- eager 2.4

Ernte[3a]
- crop 2.7

ernten
- harvest 4.8

Eroberer
- conqueror 4.1

erobern[3a]
- defeat 2.7

Eroberung[4b]
- conquest 3.3

eröffnen[2a]
- reveal 2.4
- inaugurate 4.8

Eröffnung[3b]
- opening 4.7
- confidence 3.5

erörtern[3b]
- debate 2.9

Erörterung[3a]
- debate 3.

erproben[5b]
- try 1.

erquicken[5b]
- refresh 5.2

erraten[4b]
- guess right 1.4

erregen[2a]
- stir 1.9

Erregung[4b]
- excitement 4.2

erreichen[1a]
- reach 1.

Erreichung[5a]
- accomplishment 5.3

errichten[2a]
- build 1.2

Errichtung[4a]
- establishment 3.8

erringen[3a]
- gain 1.

erröten[5b]
- blush 4.

Ersatz[3a]
- als –, (in) return 1.1
- substitute 3.7

erschallen[6a]
- ring 1.4

erscheinen[1a]
- appear (loom) 1.

Erscheinen[4b]
- appearance 3.

Erscheinung[1b]
- looks 1.
- phenomenon 3.2

erschlagen[5a]
- kill 1.4

Section

erschließen[5b]
- open 1.

erschöpfen[2b]
- erschöpft, spent 2.
- exhaust 2.4

erschrecken[2b]
- frighten 1.9

erschüttern[3a]
- move 1.5

erschweren[3b]
- (make) worse 3.
- aggravate 4.9

ersehen[3b]
- (catch) sight (of) 1.1

ersetzen[2b]
- substitute 2.3

Ersetzung
- substitution 10.5

ersichtlich[4b]
- manifest 4.2

ersparen[3b]
- save (up) 2.1

Ersparnis[6a]
- savings 3.7

erstarren[5b]
- freeze 3.3
- congeal 6.3

erstatten[4b]
- restore 2.7

erstaunen[3a]
- astonish 2.7

Erstaunen[4a]
- surprise 2.4

erstaunlich[6a]
- astonishing 5.

erst[1a]
- only 1.

erste[1a]
- first 1.
- zum -n Mal auftreten (make one's first) appearance 2.3
- initial 4.6

erstehen[6b]
- come from 1.

ersteigen[5a]
- climb 2.7

erstenmal[5b]
- zum – (for the) first time 2.6

erstens[6a]
- (at) first 1.

ersticken[4b]
- put down 2.2
- choke 3.7

erstlich[6b]
- (in the) first (place) 3.7

erstreben[5b]
- try hard 1.5

erstrecken[3a]
- extend 1.

ersuchen[3a]
- ask (a favor) 1.

erteilen[2a]
- assign 2.5

Erteilung[5b]
- bestowing 3.8

ertönen[5b]
- ring 2.9

Ertrag[2b]
- profit 2.

ertragen[2b]
- suffer 1.

erträglich[6b]
- (can be) borne 5.2

ertränken
- drown 4.3

Section

ertrinken
- drown 4.3

erwachen[2b]
- wake (*intr. vb.*) 1.9

Erwachen
- waking 4.4

erwachsen[3a]
- mature 4.

erwägen[3b]
- consider 1.8
- deliberate 4.1

Erwägung[2b]
- consideration 2.4
- consideration (reference) 2.5

erwählen[4b]
- choose 1.
- elect 3.

erwähnen[1b]
- mention 2.2

Erwähnung[4b]
- mention 3.6

erwärmen[4a]
- heat 2.2

erwarten[1a]
- expect 1.
- wait for 1.

Erwartung[3a]
- expectation 3.3

erwecken[2b]
- wake (*tr. vb.*) 1.9

erweisen[1b]
- prove 1.

erweitern[3a]
- extend 1.

Erweiterung[4a]
- extension 4.4

Erwerb[4a]
- gain 1.9

erwerben[1b]
- gain 1.

Erwerbung[6b]
- acquisition 6.3

erwidern[1b]
- answer 1.

Erwiderung[6b]
- answer 1.2

erwünschen[3b]
- desire 1.

erzählen[1b]
- tell 1.

Erzählung[2a]
- story 1.
- account 1.5

Erzbischof[6a]
- archbishop 6.2

erzeugen[2a]
- beget 3.4

Erzeugnis[3a]
- product 2.1

Erzeugung[5b]
- manufacture (*n.*) 2.9
- production 3.9

erziehen[3a]
- bring up 1.9

Erziehung[2b]
- bringing up 1.6

erzielen[2a]
- carry out 1.

erzwingen[5b]
- force 1.
- enforce 4.4

es[1a]
- it 1.
- – gibt, there *is* 1.

Esel[5a]
- ass 3.9

	Section
Fertigkeit[5b]	
skill	3.
Fessel[5a]	
chain	2.1
fesseln[3a]	
charm	2.4
chain	2.7
fest[1a]	
– machen, fix	1.
firm (fixed)	1.1
firm (character)	1.1
still	1.3
Fest[1b]	
party	1.
festhalten[2a]	
hold	1.
Festigkeit[4b]	
firmness	5.4
firmness (physical)	5.5
solidity	8.3
festlich[5b]	
solemn	2.8
festsetzen[2b]	
settle	1.
prove	1.4
Festsetzung[5a]	
establishment	3.8
feststehend[5b]	
firm (fixed)	1.1
feststellen[2a]	
prove	1.4
Feststellung[3a]	
settlement	2.7
Festung[3a]	
fort	2.6
Fett[4b]	
fat	2.6
grease	4.8
fett[5a]	
fat	1.9
Fetzen	
scrap	5.5
feucht[4a]	
damp	3.4
Feuchtigkeit[5b]	
moisture	4.4
feudal	
feudal	7.8
Feuer[1b]	
fire	1.
feuern[6b]	
shoot	1.8
Feuerstein	
flint	6.5
feurig[4a]	
fiery	3.6
passionate	3.7
Fieber[5a]	
fever	3.3
fieberhaft	
feverish	6.9
Figur[1b]	
figure	1.
Film	
film	6.8
Filz	
felt	5.
Finanz[6a]	
finance	5.3
finanziell[3a]	
financial	4.1
Finanzminister[2a]	
minister	1.5
finden[1a]	
find	1.
Finger[2b]	
finger	1.4

	Section
Fingerhut	
thimble	7.2
finster[3a]	
dark	1.
sinister	5.
Finsternis[4a]	
darkness	2.9
Firma[2a]	
company (business)	1.
Fisch[3a]	
fish	2.
-e fangen, fish	2.5
Fischer[6b]	
fisherman	4.7
fixieren[6a]	
fix	1.
flach[3b]	
flat	2.7
Fläche[2b]	
plain	1.6
Flachland	
lowland	5.4
Flachs	
flax	6.3
Flagge[6a]	
flag	2.6
Flamme[2a]	
flame	2.
flammen[6a]	
blaze	4.3
Flanell	
flannel	7.2
Flanke[3b]	
side	1.
flankieren	
flank	6.4
Flasche[2b]	
bottle	2.1
flattern	
flutter	5.7
Fleck[3b]	
spot	2.2
flehen[5a]	
beg	2.7
Fleisch[2b]	
meat	1.6
flesh	2.
Fleiß[3a]	
industry	2.6
fleißig[2a]	
industrious	3.2
studious	4.8
Fliege	
fly	4.2
fliegen[2b]	
fly	1.6
fliehen[2b]	
run away	1.5
Fliese	
tile	5.8
fließen[2b]	
flow	1.5
Flirt	
flirt	7.
Flitter	
spangle	6.8
Flocke	
flake	6.8
Floh	
flea	7.8
Flöte	
flute	6.5
flott	
afloat	6.7
Flotte[3b]	
fleet	3.

	Section
Fluch[4a]	
curse	3.5
oath	4.8
Flucht[3a]	
flight (in air)	2.5
flight (rout)	2.5
flüchten[4b]	
run away	1.5
flüchtig[2b]	
– sehen, glance	2.3
hasty	2.7
fugitive	3.5
Flüchtling[6b]	
fugitive	5.6
Flug[5b]	
flight (in air)	2.5
Flügel[1b]	
wing	1.1
Flugzeug	
aeroplane (air)	8.1
Flur	
passage	4.8
Fluß[2a]	
river	1.5
flow	2.6
flüssig[4a]	
liquid	3.4
Flüssigkeit[3a]	
fluid	3.4
flüstern[4a]	
whisper	3.1
Flut[3b]	
flood	3.2
tide	3.4
Folge[1a]	
result	1.5
succession	3.1
folgen[1a]	
follow	1.
folgend[1a]	
next	1.
following	1.1
einander –	
successive	3.
Folgende[4b]	
successor	3.8
folgern[6b]	
infer	5.7
folglich[4b]	
consequently	4.1
Fonds[6a]	
funds	4.6
Förde	
estuary	9.4
förderlich[5b]	
useful	2.
fordern[1b]	
demand	1.
fördern[2a]	
further	1.8
Forderung[1b]	
demand	1.3
Förderung[4b]	
help	1.1
Forelle	
trout	6.8
Form[1a]	
figure	1.
mode	2.2
mould	3.1
Formel[5b]	
formula	5.3
formell[4b]	
formal	5.1
formen[5a]	
form	1.
formieren[6a]	
form	1.

	Section
förmlich[4a]	
formal	5.1
formlos	
shapeless	6.2
Formsache	
formality	7.9
Formular[6b]	
formula	5.3
formulieren[6b]	
draw up	2.
forschen[4b]	
investigate	4.6
Forscher[2b]	
scholar	2.3
Forschung[3b]	
inquiry	3.5
exploration	4.6
fort[1a]	
away	1.
Fort[4a]	
fort	2.6
fortan[4b]	
henceforth	3.
fortbestehen	
subsist	7.3
Fortdauer[6a]	
continuance	5.9
fortdauern[4b]	
continue	1.
fortfahren[4a]	
continue	1.
go away	1.
fortführen[5b]	
continue	1.
Fortgang[5a]	
departure	3.1
fortgehen[5b]	
go away	1.
fortpflanzen	
propagate	7.
fortreißen[6b]	
take away	1.
carry away	3.4
fortschreiten[4a]	
progress	2.6
Fortschritt[2b]	
advance	2.2
progress	2.4
– machen, progress	2.6
fortschrittlich	
progressive	6.7
fortsetzen[2a]	
continue	1.
Fortsetzung[2a]	
continuation	4.7
fortwährend[3a]	
continual	2.5
Fracht[4a]	
freight	3.8
Frage[1a]	
question	1.1
fragen[1a]	
ask (a question)	1.
fraglich[4a]	
doubtful	2.6
Fraktion[4b]	
fraction	4.9
Franken[4b]	
pound	1.
Franse	
fringe	5.8
Franzose[2a]	
French	1.
französisch[1a]	
French	1.

Section

Gebäudesteuer[2a]
tax 1.6

geben[1a]
give . . . . 1.
Gott gebe
God grant. . . . . . . 1.
es gibt, there *is* . . . . . . 1.
shake (hands) 1.1
zu essen –, feed 1.4
sich Mühe –
(take) pains 1.4
Beifall –, clap 2.8

Geber
giver 7.2

Gebet[3a]
prayer 2.3

Gebiet[1a]
territory 2.1

gebieten[2b]
command 1.5
-d, commanding 1.9

Gebilde[5a]
formation . . . . 4.

Gebirge[3a]
mountain 1.5

gebirgig
mountainous 6.7

Gebot[2b]
order . . . . 1.

Gebrauch[1b]
use 1.1

gebrauchen[3a]
use . . . . 1.

gebräuchlich[5b]
usual . . . . 1.

gebrechen[4a]
lack 1.5

Gebühr[4b]
tax 1.6

gebühren[3b]
-d, due 2.2

Geburt[3b]
birth 2.5

Geburtstag[1b]
birthday 2.8

Gebüsch
bush 4.9

Gedächtnis[3a]
memory 1.8

Gedächtnis-
memorial 4.4

Gedanke[1a]
thought . . . . 1.

Gedankengang
reasoning 4.6

gedeihen[4a]
flourish 4.1

Gedeihen[6a]
prosperity 4.4

gedenken[2b]
remember . . . . 1.

Gedicht[2a]
poem 2.5

Geduld[3a]
patience 2.8

gedulden[6b]
(be) patient 3.8

geduldig[6a]
– sein, (be) patient . . . 3.8

Gefahr[1a]
danger 1.5
– laufen, (take) chances 1.4

gefährden[4a]
(take) chances 1.4

gefährlich[2a]
dangerous . . . . 2.

Section

Gefährt
coach 4.9

Gefährte[5b]
companion 2.3

gefallen[2a]
please . . . . 1.

Gefallen[4b]
pleasure 1.4
kindness 2.7

gefällig[2a]
pleasant 1.1

Gefälligkeit[6a]
favor 1.4

Gefangene[3a]
prisoner 2.4

Gefangenschaft[6b]
captivity 5.7

Gefängnis[2b]
prison . . . . 2.
ins – setzen, imprison . 3.6

Gefängnisstrafe[4a]
imprisonment . . . . . . 5.

Gefäß[2b]
pot 2.3

Gefecht[2a]
fight 1.1

Geflügel
fowl 5.1

Gefolge[4a]
following 2.3

Gefühl[1a]
feeling (sentiment) . 1.
feeling (sensitive-
ness) 1.5

gegen[1a]
against . . . . 1.

Gegend[1b]
part (of country) . . . 1.

Gegensatz[2a]
contrast 3.1

gegenseitig[2b]
mutual 3.1

Gegenstand[1a]
subject . . . . 1.
thing . . . . 1.

Gegenteil[2a]
contrary 1.8
im –
(on the) contrary 1.8

gegenüber[1a]
(be) across . . . . 1.
opposite 1.4

gegenüberstehend[5a]
opposite 1.4

Gegenwart[2a]
present 1.5
presence 1.8

gegenwärtig[1b]
present 1.1

Gegner[1b]
adversary 2.9

Gehalt[3a]
capacity . . . . 3.

geheim[2a]
secret 2.1

Geheimnis[2a]
secret 1.8
mystery 2.4

geheimnisvoll[4b]
mysterious 3.5

Geheimrat[2a]
privy councilor 6.9

gehen[1a]
über . . . . –, cross . . . . 1.
hinüber –, cross . . . . . . 1.
go . . . . 1.
mit –, go with . . . . 1.
zu Fuß –, walk . . . . 1.

Section

gehen[1a]—*continued*
gut –, (be) well . . . . . . 1.
vorwärts –, go forward 1.4
zu Bett –, (go to) bed . 1.6
hinunter –, go down . . 2.2
function 2.8
an Bord –, sail . . . . 3.

Geheul
howl 5.7

Gehilfe[4a]
helper 4.3

Gehirn[4a]
brain 3.3

Gehöft[6a]
farm 3.2

Gehölz[6b]
forest . . . . 1.

Gehör[5a]
ear 3.3

gehorchen[3b]
obey 2.2
nicht –, disobey 4.8

gehören[1b]
belong . . . . 1.

gehörig[2b]
proper 1.4

gehorsam[3b]
obedient 3.2

Gehorsam
obedience . . . . 6.

Gehrock
frock coat 6.1

Geige
violin 6.1

Geisel
hostage 8.2

Geist[1a]
spirit . . . . 1.

Geistesgegenwart
presence of mind . . . 4.5

geistig[1b]
mental 3.6

geistlich[3a]
spiritual 3.3

Geistliche[3a]
minister . . . . 2.

Geistlichkeit[6b]
clergy 6.9

geistreich[4b]
witty 4.1

geistvoll[6a]
witty 4.1

Geiz
avarice 6.9
greediness 8.6

Geizhals
miser 6.5

Gelächter[6a]
laughter 3.8

Gelände[4b]
ground 2.4

Geländer
banister 11.7

gelangen[1a]
reach . . . . 1.

geläufig[6b]
– sein, (well) informed 3.

Geläute
ringing 4.9

gelb[3b]
yellow . . . . 2.

Geld[1a]
money . . . . 1.

Geldstrafe[2b]
fine 2.5

Gelée
jelly 6.1

Section

gelegen
opportune 7.4

Gelegenheit[1a]
chance . . . . 1.

gelegentlich[3a]
occasional 3.7

Gelehrsamkeit[6b]
learning 3.6

gelehrt[2b]
learned 1.6

Gelehrte[4a]
scholar 2.3

Gelenk
joint 5.8

Geliebte[2b]
lover . . . . 2.

gelind[6a]
gentle 1.4

gelingen[1b]
succeed 1.5

geloben
vow 5.2

gelten[1a]
(be) worth . . . . 1.

Geltung[3a]
value . . . . 1.

Gelübde
vow 4.9

Gemach[4b]
room (chamber) . . . . 1.

Gemahl[4a]
husband . . . . 1.

Gemahlin[4a]
wife . . . . 1.

Gemälde[2b]
painting 3.2

gemäß[2b]
by (according to) . . . 1.

gemäßigt[6b]
moderate . . . . 3.

gemein[2b]
common 1.4
common (person) . . . 1.4
mean 1.5
vulgar 2.9
infamous 4.3

Gemeinde[1a]
community 2.9
parish 3.4

Gemeindeabgabe[6b]
tax 1.6

Gemeindemitglied
parishioner 10.2

Gemeindeversammlung[2b]
assembly 2.6

Gemeindevertretung[2b]
representation 3.5

Gemeindevorstand[6a]
mayor 2.5

Gemeindevorsteher[3b]
mayor 2.5

Gemeinheit
infamy 7.6

gemeinsam[2a]
common 1.4

Gemeinschaft[3b]
community 3.8

gemeinschaftlich[2b]
common 1.4

Gemeinschuldner[3b]
bankrupt 5.3

Gemenge[6a]
mixture 3.9

Gemisch[6b]
mixture 3.9

Gemurmel
murmur 4.8

	Section
Gewässer[6b]	
water	1.
Gewebe[4b]	
cloth	1.3
web	3.4
Gewehr[2b]	
arm (weapon)	1.
gun	1.7
Gewerbe[2b]	
trade	1.2
Gewerbe-	
Handels- und –, trade	4.6
Gewerbebetrieb[4b]	
trade	1.2
Gewerbeordnung[6b]	
rule	1.1
Gewerbesteuer[2a]	
tax	1.6
Gewerbetreibende[6a]	
tradesman	5.7
gewerblich[3b]	
professional	4.5
Gewicht[2a]	
weight	1.5
importance	1.8
gewichtig[6a]	
important	1.
grave	1.4
Gewinn[2a]	
gain	1.9
gewinnen[1a]	
beat	1.
gain	1.
Gewinner	
winner	6.5
Gewinnung[6a]	
production	3.9
gewiß[1a]	
(of) course	1.
sure	1.
Gewissen[2b]	
conscience	1.8
gewissenhaft[4a]	
conscientious	6.4
gewissermaßen[2b]	
as it were	1.4
Gewißheit[4a]	
assurance	4.4
Gewitter[5b]	
storm	1.6
gewöhnen[2a]	
gewöhnt	
(be) used (to)	1.4
(make) used (to)	1.6
Gewohnheit[3a]	
habit	2.2
gewöhnlich[1a]	
(in) general	1.
usual	1.
ordinary	2.2
Gewölbe[5b]	
vault	4.7
gewölbt	
bent	5.
Gewürz	
spice	6.
Gicht	
gout	7.6
gierig	
greedy	

	Section
Gipfel[3b]	
summit	3.4
Gips	
plaster	6.5
girren	
coo	6.9
Girren	
coo	6.9
Gitter	
bar	4.6
Glanz[2b]	
splendor	2.8
radiance	4.9
glänzen[3a]	
shine	1.6
glänzend[2a]	
bright	1.4
beaming	2.4
brilliant	2.9
Glas[1b]	
glass (drinking)	1.
glass (material)	1.7
glatt[3a]	
even	2.4
Glaube[1b]	
faith	1.4
belief	2.3
glauben[1a]	
believe	1.
gläubig[6a]	
religious	2.3
Gläubige[6a]	
(the) faithful	†2.7
Gläubiger[3a]	
creditor	4.1
gleich[1a]	
as (like)	1.
equal	1.
like	1.
matter (neg.)	1.
same	1.
just	1.3
von -em Wert	
(of same) value	1.8
vollkommen –	
identical	3.5
gleichartig[6a]	
(of the same) kind	4.
similar	4.4
gleichen[3b]	
like	1.
equal	2.3
Gleicher	
equator	7.2
gleichfalls[2b]	
also	1.
(in like) manner	1.2
Gleichgewicht[3a]	
balance	2.6
gleichgültig[2b]	
(all the) same	1.
Gleichgültigkeit[4a]	
indifference	4.7
detachment	5.5
Gleichheit[5a]	
equality	
identity	
gleichmäßig[2b]	
equal	
Gleichnis	

	Section
gleichzeitig[1b]	
together	1.
(at the) same time	1.9
contemporary	3.6
gleiten[4b]	
slip	2.8
Gletscher[6a]	
glacier	6.4
Glied[2a]	
member	1.1
limb	2.
link	3.3
Glocke[4a]	
bell	2.5
Glockenspiel	
chime	5.6
glorreich[6b]	
glorious	3.8
Glück[1a]	
fortune	1.4
happiness	1.4
glücken[5b]	
succeed	1.5
glucken	
cluck	6.4
glücklich[1a]	
glad	1.
fortunate	2.
glücklicherweise[5b]	
fortunately	3.7
Glückseligkeit[6a]	
bliss	3.7
Glückwunsch[5a]	
congratulation	5.3
glühen[2b]	
shine	1.6
-de Kohle, (live) coals	2.1
Glut[4b]	
(live) coals	2.1
glow	3.
Gnade[2a]	
favor	1.4
mercy	2.
gnädig[2a]	
kind	1.
merciful	4.2
Gold[1b]	
gold	1.
golden[2a]	
golden	1.4
Goldwährung[3b]	
(gold) standard	3.1
gönnen[4a]	
(not) envy	3.5
Gosse	
gutter	5.7
gothisch	
Gothic	6.7
Gott[1a]	
God	1.
– gebe, God grant	1.
ach –!, Heavens!	1.
Gottesdienst[3a]	
(divine) service	
Gottheit[4a]	
divinity	
deity (D)	
ess	

	Section
Graben[4b]	
ditch (irrigation)	3.6
ditch (trench)	3.9
graben	
dig	4.8
Grad[1b]	
degree	1.4
Graf[1a]	
count	1.2
Gräfin[2b]	
countess	5.4
Gram[5b]	
grief	1.8
Gramm[6a]	
ounce	4.7
Grammatik	
grammar	6.1
Granate[4a]	
shell	3.4
Granit	
granite	6.8
Gras[5a]	
grass	2.9
gräßlich[5a]	
terrible	1.8
outrageous	5.8
grau[3a]	
gray	2.2
Graupen	
barley	6.1
grausam[3b]	
cruel	2.3
Grausamkeit[6b]	
cruelty	4.8
grausig	
ghastly	6.4
gravieren	
engrave	6.4
greifen[1b]	
touch	1.
seize	1.1
Greis[4a]	
(old) man	2.4
grell[6b]	
shrill	4.7
Grenze[1b]	
border	1.7
Greuel[6b]	
horror	4.4
atrocity	7.
greulich	
hideous	6.4
Grieche[3b]	
Greek	2.6
griechisch[2a]	
Greek	2.6
Griff[5b]	
handle	3.1
Grille[6b]	
fancy	3.7
cricket	5.3
fad	8.5
Grimmigkeit	
fierceness	7.8
	5.9

Section

hauen[6a]
chop 4.2
Haufe[3a]
mass 1.6
häufen[4b]
heap up 3.2
häufig[1b]
often 1.
frequent 1.7
Haupt[2a]
head 1.
Haupt-[2a]
chief (*adj.*) 1.
chief (*n.*) 1.5
Hauptaufgabe[5b]
chief 1.
Hauptgrund[4b]
chief 1.
base 1.7
Häuptling[6a]
chief 1.5
Hauptmann[2a]
captain 1.6
Hauptperson[6a]
chief 1.5
Hauptquartier[2b]
headquarters 3.4
Hauptsache[2a]
chief 1.
hauptsächlich[1b]
above all 1.
chief 1.
Hauptstadt[3a]
capital 2.3
metropolis 4.8
Hauptwort
noun 7.3
Haus[1a]
zu -e, (at) home 1.
nach -e, (at) home 1.
house 1.
im -e, indoors 3.1
Hausbesitzer[4a]
owner 2.
hausen[5a]
live 1.1
Hausfrau[4b]
wife 1.
Hausfreund[5b]
friend 1.
Haushalt[3b]
household 2.9
Haushälterin
housekeeper 6.2
Hausherr[3b]
man of the house 1.8
Hausierer
peddler 7.
häuslich[3b]
domestic 2.9
Haustür[3b]
door 1.
Hauswart
porter 5.6
Hauswesen[4a]
household 2.9
Haut[3a]
skin 2.
Häutchen
film 6.8
heben[1b]
lift 1.
Hebung[5a]
elevation 4.2
Hecke
hedge 5.4
Heer[1a]
army 1.2

Section

Heeresleitung[3b]
command 2.3
Hefe
dreg 7.8
Heft[4a]
handle 3.1
blank book 4.
heften[4b]
stick 2.2
heftig[1b]
furious 1.9
Heftigkeit[5a]
violence 3.6
hegen[3a]
shelter 2.6
foster 3.8
Heide[5a]
heathen 4.8
heath 5.3
Heil[3a]
welfare 3.5
Heiland[4b]
savior 4.8
heilen[4a]
cure 2.9
heilig[1b]
holy 1.4
sacred 1.6
Heilige[4a]
saint 2.6
heiligen[3b]
hallow 3.6
Heiligenschein
halo 10.1
Heiligkeit
holiness 6.6
Heiligtum[5b]
sanctuary 5.3
heilsam[5a]
wholesome 4.6
heim[5a]
(at) home 1.
Heimat[2a]
country 1.1
heimisch[4b]
native 3.2
heimlich[3a]
secret 2.1
sly 3.9
heimsuchen
haunt 5.7
Heirat[4a]
wedding 3.4
heiraten[3a]
marry 2.3
heiser
hoarse 6.5
heiß[2b]
hot 1.5
heißen[1a]
mean 1.
(what is your) name 1.
heiter[2a]
bright 1.4
cheerful 1.9
Heiterkeit[2b]
cheer 1.9
Heizkörper
radiator 7.2
Heizung
heating 5.
Hektar[6b]
acre 4.4
Held[2a]
hero 2.1
heldenhaft
heroic 5.2

Section

Heldentat
exploit 5.9
Heldentum
heroism 7.2
Heldin[6a]
heroine 5.8
helfen[1b]
help 1.
hell[2a]
fair 1.2
bright 1.4
light 1.4
Helm[6a]
helmet 4.9
Hemd[6b]
shirt 3.8
Hemd(en)brust
shirt-front 13.
hemmen[4a]
stop up 3.1
check 3.2
Henker[6b]
hangman 7.3
Henne
hen 4.7
her[1a]
here 1.
lange –, long ago 1.3
herab[2b]
down 1.
herabsetzen[6a]
lower 2.3
Herabsetzung[6a]
reduction 5.3
herabziehen
profane 6.5
heran[3a]
to 1.
herankommen[6a]
(go) toward(s) 1.
herantreten[5a]
(go) toward(s) 1.
heranwachsen[6a]
grow 1.1
heranziehen[2b]
(go) toward(s) 1.
Heranziehung[5a]
use 1.1
herauf[5a]
on 1.
heraus[1b]
out 1.
herausgeben[3b]
publish 2.8
Herausgeber[5b]
publisher 5.8
herauskommen[5a]
come out 2.6
herausnehmen[6a]
take away 1.
herausstellen[4a]
expose 2.2
heraustreten[6b]
step 1.1
herb[6a]
sharp (taste) 4.
acid 5.3
herbei[3b]
near 1.
herbeiführen[2a]
cause 1.
Herbst[3b]
fall 2.3
Herd[4b]
hearth 3.2
Herde[6b]
drove 3.9

Section

herein[3a]
– kommen, enter 1.
into 1.
hergeben[6b]
produce 3.4
Hering[6b]
herring 6.8
herkommen[5b]
(go) toward(s) 1.
Herkunft
von niederer –
(of) lowly (birth) 6.4
herleiten[6b]
lead 1.
Hermelin
ermine 9.3
hernach[5a]
afterwards 1.8
Herr[1a]
gentleman 1.
Mr. 1.
lord 1.1
Herrenhaus[4b]
mansion 3.7
Herrin[6b]
mistress 3.5
herrlich[1b]
fine 1.1
wonderful 1.2
Herrlichkeit[3b]
glory 2.3
Herrschaft[2a]
rule 2.
dominion 3.1
herrschen[1b]
rule 1.
Herrscher[4a]
governor 3.1
sovereign 3.7
herrühren[5a]
come from 1.
herstellen[1b]
place (put) 1.
Hersteller
maker 4.7
Herstellung[3a]
manufacture 2.9
herüber[5a]
(be) across 1.
herum[2b]
around 1.6
herumlaufen
revolve 5.5
herumwerfen
jostle 7.
herunter[4a]
down 1.
– lassen, lower 2.3
hervor[1b]
forth 1.
hervorbringen[2b]
produce 1.8
hervorgehen[2a]
result 1.5
hervorheben[2a]
emphasize 4.4
hervorragen[2a]
stand out 1.9
excel 3.5
-d, eminently 4.1
hervorrufen[2b]
call forth 1.6
(give) rise to 2.3
hervortreten[2b]
come forward 1.4
Herz[1a]
heart 1.

Section

Hund[3a]
dog 1.9
hundert[2a]
hundred 1.4
Hundert[4b]
hundred 1.4
hundertjährig
centennial 10.6
hundertste
hundredth 7.6
Hunger[4b]
– haben
(be) hungry 2.8
hunger 3.2
Hungersnot
famine 5.1
Hurra[6b]
applause 3.7
Husar[5a]
hussar 9.4
huschen
flutter 5.7
husten
cough 5.7
Husten
cough 6.2
Hut[2a]
hat 1.5
– aufsetzen
(put on) hat 2.8
hüten[3b]
guard .... 1.
Hütte[4a]
shed 3.2
cottage 3.4
Hygiene
hygiene .... 7.
Hypothek
mortgage 7.2
Hypothese[6b]
basis 3.4
hysterisch
hysterical 8.6

I

ich[1a]
I .... 1.
– selbst, selber, myself 1.3
Ideal[3a]
ideal 3.2
ideal[3b]
ideal 3.2
Idealismus
idealism .... 9.
Idealist
idealist 11.4
Idee[1b]
idea 1.4
Idiot
idiot 5.8
Idyll
idyll 9.8
Igel
hedgehog 7.2
ihr (*pers. pron.*)[1a]
you .... 1.
ihr (*poss. pron. sing.*)[1a]
her .... 1.
-e, hers 2.9
ihr (*poss. pron. pl.*)[1a]
their .... 1.
Ihr[1a]
your .... 1.
-e, yours 2.1
ihrerseits[4a]
(on her) side 2.2
(on their) side 2.2

Section

ihrige[4a]
theirs 3.6
Ihrige[4b]
yours 2.1
Illustration
illustration 6.8
illustrieren[6b]
illustrate 5.2
immer[1a]
always .... 1.
wenn –, whenever 1.4
was –, whatever 1.5
wer –, whoever 2.2
– wieder, several times 1.2
immerfort[5a]
continual 2.5
immerhin[2b]
(in any) case ...... 1.
Impotenz
impotence 8.7
imprägnieren
impregnate 8.8
improvisieren
improvise 8.9
imstande
liable (to do) 5.8
liable (to something) 6.5
in[1a]
in .... 1.
inbrünstig
fervent 7.2
indem[1a]
as (e.g., I was walking) .... 1.
while .... 1.
indes[2a]
however .... 1.
indessen[1b]
while .... 1.
indirekt[4a]
indirect .... 5.
indisch[4b]
Indian 3.1
Individualität[5b]
personality 3.9
individuell[4b]
individual 3.8
Individuum[4b]
individual 3.2
Indossament[6a]
indorsement 11.2
Industrie[2b]
industry .... 2.
industriell[4b]
industrial 5.5
Industrielle[6b]
maker 3.5
Infanterie[1b]
infantry 5.6
infolge[2a]
because of .... 1.
through (agent) .... 1.
infolgedessen[6b]
therefore .... 1.
consequently 4.1
Ingenieur[6a]
engineer 4.8
Ingwer
ginger 6.8
Inhaber[3a]
owner .... 2.
Inhalt[1b]
content .... 2.
Initiative[5b]
initiative 5.7
Inland[4b]
inland 3.9

Section

inländisch[4a]
native 3.2
inmitten[5a]
among .... 1.
inne[2b]
within 1.1
inside 1.4
innere[1a]
inside 1.4
Innere[1b]
inside 1.4
innerhalb[1b]
within 1.1
inside 1.4
innerlich[3b]
inside 1.4
innig[2a]
intimate 3.2
insbesondere[1b]
above all .... 1.
Inschrift[4b]
inscription 5.2
Insekt[6b]
insect 4.4
Insel[2a]
island 1.5
insofern[2b]
as long as 1.1
insoweit[5a]
as long as 1.1
Inspektor
inspector 6.9
inspizieren
survey 5.8
Instanz[3b]
instance 3.2
Institut[3a]
institute 2.6
Institution[6b]
institute 2.6
Instruktion[4b]
instruction 2.4
Instrument[3b]
instrument 2.9
Insulaner
islander .... 9.
intellektuell
intellectual 6.1
Intelligenz[5b]
intelligence .... 4.
intensiv[6a]
thorough .... 2.
intense 5.3
interessant[2a]
interesting 3.2
Interesse[1a]
interest (concern) .. 1.
-n, interest (percent) .. 1.
Interessent[5b]
interested .... 3.
interessieren[3a]
interest 1.9
international[3a]
international 4.8
inwendig[5b]
inside 1.4
inzwischen[2a]
meanwhile 2.8
irdisch[3a]
earthly 3.1
irgend[1a]
any (whatever) .... 1.
– einer, – jemand
anybody 1.8
irgendwie[4b]
anyhow 4.2

Section

irgendwo[4b]
somewhere .... 3.
anywhere 4.1
Iris
iris .... 7.
Ironie
irony 8.2
ironisch
ironical 8.5
irren[2b]
sich –, (be) wrong 1.4
sich –
(make a) mistake 2.2
Irrgarten
maze .... 7.
irrig[6b]
wrong .... 1.
Irrtum[2b]
error 1.8
isolieren[6a]
cut off 3.1
Isthmus
isthmus 5.8
Italiener[5a]
Italian 2.4
italienisch[2a]
Italian 2.4

J

ja[1a]
indeed .... 1.
yes .... 1.
Jacke
coat 4.3
jacket 6.1
Jagd[4b]
hunt 2.4
jagen[3a]
hunt 2.3
Jäger[3a]
hunter 2.6
Jahr[1a]
year .... 1.
jahrelang[6b]
year .... 1.
Jahrestag
anniversary 6.7
Jahreszeit[4b]
season 2.4
Jahrgang[4b]
year .... 1.
Jahrhundert[1a]
century 1.4
jährig[4b]
year .... 1.
jährlich[2a]
annual 2.7
Jahrtausend[4b]
millennium 8.8
Jahrzehnt[4a]
decade 5.6
Jammer[4b]
lamentation 4.2
jämmerlich
wretched 5.8
jammern[5b]
mourn 1.9
grumble 4.9
Januar[2a]
January 2.2
japanisch
Japanese 6.8
Jasmin
jessamine .... 10.
jauchzen[6b]
rejoice 3.2

Section

Kern[3b]
- kernel ... 4.6
- nucleus ... 4.9

Kerze[6b]
- candle ... 2.2

Kessel[5b]
- kettle ... 4.8
- boiler ... 5.8

Kette[3a]
- chain ... 2.1

Ketzer[6b]
- heretic ... 6.3

Ketzerei
- heresy ... 7.4

keuchen
- pant ... 5.7

keusch
- chaste ... 6.2

Keuschheit
- chastity ... 7.7

Kiefer
- jaw ... 5.6

Kies
- gravel ... 6.8

Kilo[5b]
- pound ... 1.6

Kilogramm[4a]
- pound ... 1.6

Kilometer[3b]
- mile ... 1.7

Kind[1a]
- child ... 1.

Kinderstube
- nursery ... 5.8

Kindheit[3b]
- childhood ... 3.3

kindisch[5b]
- childish ... 4.6

kindlich[4a]
- filial ... 5.8

Kinematograph
- cinema ... 11.3

Kinn
- chin ... 5.4

Kino
- cinema ... 11.3

Kirche[1b]
- church ... 1.

kirchlich[3a]
- church ... 2.6

Kirchturm
- steeple ... 5.8

Kirsche
- cherry ... 5.6

Kissen
- pillow ... 5.2
- cushion ... 5.6

Kiste[5b]
- chest ... 3.7

kitzeln
- tickle ... 6.8

Klage[2a]
- complaint ... 2.4

klagen[2b]
- complain ... 2.

Klagen[3b]
- complaint ... 2.4

Kläger[5a]
- plaintiff ... 8.4

Klägerin[6b]
- plaintiff ... 8.4

klammern[6b]
- – an, clasp ... 3.1
- sich –, cling ... 5.
- grasp ... 5.2

Klang[4a]
- sound ... 1.2

Klappe[6a]
- cover ... 2.9
- flap ... 4.9
- valve ... 6.3

Klapper
- rattle ... 6.

klappern
- chatter ... 6.

klar[1a]
- clear ... 1.
- clear (lucid) ... 2.

klären[6b]
- purify ... 4.4

Klarheit[3b]
- light ... 2.

Klasse[1b]
- class ... 1.
- schoolroom ... 3.3

klassisch[4a]
- classic ... 3.8

Klatsch
- gossip ... 6.6

Klaue
- claw ... 6.1

Klausel
- clause ... 6.6

Klavier[6b]
- piano ... 4.7

kleben[6b]
- stick ... 2.2

Klee
- clover ... 6.4

Kleid[2a]
- -er, clothes ... 1.4
- dress ... 1.4

kleiden[3a]
- clothe ... 1.9

Kleidung[4a]
- clothes ... 1.4

Kleie
- bran ... 7.2

klein[1a]
- little (small) ... 1.

Kleine[1a]
- child ... 1.

Kleinigkeit[4b]
- trifle ... 3.9

kleinlich[5b]
- petty ... 4.5

Klette
- burr ... 6.8

Klima[5a]
- climate ... 4.

Klinge
- blade ... 4.5

klingen[2a]
- ring ... 1.4
- -d, ringing ... 1.7
- tinkle ... 4.1

Klippe
- reef ... 7.4

Kloben
- log ... 4.8

klopfen[4a]
- knock ... 2.6

Kloster[3b]
- convent ... 3.8

Klub[6b]
- club ... 1.6

klug[2b]
- wise ... 1.5
- clever ... 2.6

Klugheit[4a]
- prudence ... 3.7

Klumpen
- lump ... 6.2

Knabe[2a]
- boy ... 1.4

knapp[5b]
- scanty ... 4.5

Knappe
- squire ... 6.

knarren
- grate ... 5.7

Knecht[3a]
- servant ... 1.9

knechten
- enslave ... 8.1

kneifen
- pinch ... 6.

kneten
- mould ... 5.7

Knie[3a]
- knee ... 2.

Kniehose
- breeches ... 6.4

knien[4b]
- kneel ... 3.9

knirschen
- grind (teeth) ... 5.

knistern
- crackle ... 6.5

Knoblauch
- garlic ... 9.1

Knochen[4a]
- bone ... 2.6

Knochengerüst
- skeleton ... 6.7

Knopf[5b]
- button ... 3.7

Knospe
- bud ... 4.8

Knoten[6a]
- knot ... 4.4
- knot (hair) ... 5.

knüpfen[2b]
- tie ... 1.6

knusperig
- crisp ... 6.5

Koch
- cook ... 4.3

kochen[4a]
- cook ... 2.5
- boil ... 3.1

Kochen
- boiling ... 5.3

Köchin
- cook ... 4.3

Kochlöffel
- dipper ... 6.8

Köder
- bait ... 6.8

Koffer
- bag ... 4.5
- trunk ... 5.

Kohäsion
- cohesion ... 10.5

Kohl
- cabbage ... 5.9

Kohle[2b]
- coal ... 1.9
- glühende – (live) coals ... 2.1

Kohlensäure[5b]
- carbon dioxide ... 6.8

Kokusnuß
- cocoanut ... 7.

Kolben[4b]
- butt ... 4.9

Kolleg[2b]
- council ... 2.1

Kollege[2b]
- fellow worker ... 2.9

Kollegium[6b]
- staff ... 4.2

kollektiv
- collective ... 9.6

kolonial
- colonial ... 6.2

Kolonialwarenhändler
- grocer ... 6.4

Kolonialwarenhandlung
- grocery ... 6.9

Kolonie[4a]
- colony ... 2.9

Kolonist
- colonist ... 6.1

Kolonne[3a]
- column ... 2.9

kolossal[5a]
- great (huge) ... 1.

Kombination[6b]
- combination ... 4.3

Komet[3b]
- comet ... 4.8

komisch[3b]
- funny ... 2.9

Kommandant[6a]
- commander ... 4.4

Kommandeur[5a]
- commander ... 4.4

kommandieren[3a]
- command ... 1.5

Kommando[3a]
- command ... 2.3

kommen[1a]
- zum Vorschein – appear (loom) ... 1.
- come ... 1.
- come from ... 1.
- herein –, enter ... 1.

Kommen[6b]
- arrival ... 2.8

Kommissar[6a]
- commissioner ... 5.

Kommission[1a]
- commission ... 2.2

Kommissionär[3b]
- agent ... 2.9

Kommissionsbeschluß[5b]
- resolution ... 3.2

Kommittee[5b]
- committee ... 3.

Kommittent[4a]
- customer ... 3.6

Kommode
- drawer ... 6.1

kommunal[4a]
- community ... 4.8

Kommunalsteuer[6b]
- tax ... 1.6

Kommune[4a]
- community ... 2.9

Kommunion
- communion ... 6.7

Komödie[4b]
- comedy ... 3.7

Kompagnie[2a]
- company (business) ... 1.
- company (military) ... 1.5

Kompliment[6a]
- compliment ... 4.1

komplizieren[6a]
- kompliziert, involved ... 5.
- complicate ... 6.2

Komponist[6b]
- composer ... 9.6

Section

Kündigung[5b]
- term . . . 2.2

Kundschaft[6a]
- practice . . . 3.4

künftig[2a]
- future . . . 2.

Kunst[1a]
- art . . . 1.

Künstler[1b]
- artist . . . 2.

künstlerisch[2b]
- artistic . . . 3.4

künstlich[2b]
- artificial . . . 3.2

Kunststück[5b]
- trick . . . 3.2

Kunstwerk[3b]
- work of art . . . 1.8

Kupfer[4b]
- copper . . . 3.

Kupferstich[6b]
- print . . . 2.7

Kuppel
- dome . . . 6.2

Kur[6a]
- cure . . . 3.9

Kürbis
- pumpkin . . . 6.1

Kurfürst[3b]
- elector . . . 5.6

Kurs[3b]
- course . . . 1.1

kurz[1a]
- short . . . 1.
- (in) short . . . 1.

Kürze[5a]
- in –, soon . . . 1.

kürzlich[4a]
- recently . . . 2.8
- lately . . . 5.1

Kuß[2b]
- kiss . . . 1.7

küssen[2b]
- kiss . . . 1.4

Küste[2b]
- coast . . . 1.4

Küster
- sexton . . . 8.1

Kutscher[5b]
- driver . . . 4.4

L

Lache[3b]
- laugh . . . 1.8
- pond . . . 2.7
- pool . . . 3.4

lachen[1b]
- laugh . . . 1.

lächeln[2a]
- smile . . . 1.4

Lächeln[3a]
- smile . . . 1.9

lächerlich[3b]
- ridiculous . . . 3.6
- absurd . . . 3.7

lackieren
- varnish . . . 6.8

laden[3a]
- load . . . 1.8

Laden[4b]
- shop . . . 2.5
- store . . . 2.6
- blind . . . 3.1

Ladung[4a]
- load . . . 1.7

Section

Lage[1a]
- position (situation) . . . 1.4
- position (plight) . . . 1.5

Lager[2a]
- deposit . . . 2.7
- camp . . . 2.8

lagern[3b]
- lay . . . 1.
- camp . . . 3.3

lahm
- lame . . . 5.5

lähmen[5b]
- lame . . . 4.6
- paralyze . . . 5.7

Laie[6a]
- lay (person) . . . 4.2

Lamm
- lamb . . . 4.9

Lampe[3b]
- lamp . . . 2.5
- lantern . . . 3.5

Land[1a]
- country (geographical) . . . 1.
- country (not town) . . . 1.
- land . . . 1.

Land-[3a]
- country (*adj.*) . . . 2.6

landen[5a]
- land . . . 3.2

Landesteil[5a]
- province . . . 1.5

Landgemeinde[3b]
- community . . . 2.9

Landgemeindeordnung[3b]
- rule . . . 1.1

Landgericht[5a]
- court . . . 1.4

ländlich[3a]
- rural . . . 3.3

Landmann[5b]
- farmer . . . 1.8
- countryman . . . 5.2

Landrat[2b]
- mayor . . . 2.5

Landrecht[5a]
- law . . . 1.

Landschaft[3b]
- province . . . 1.5
- landscape . . . 8.2

Landsmann[4a]
- countryman . . . 4.7

Landtag[4b]
- legislature . . . 5.2

Landwehr[6a]
- militia . . . 6.3

Landwirt[4a]
- farmer . . . 1.8

Landwirtschaft[2b]
- agriculture . . . 2.8

landwirtschaftlich[2b]
- agricultural . . . 3.3

lang[1a]
- long (*adj.*) . . . 1.
- long (*adv.*) . . . 1.
- längst, long (*adv.*) . . . 1.
- -e her, vor -em long ago . . . 1.3

Länge[2a]
- length . . . 1.7

langen[1b]
- (be) enough . . . 1.
- extend . . . 1.

Längengrad
- meridian . . . 7.2

Langeweile[6a]
- bore . . . 4.

Section

langjährig[6b]
- long (*adv.*) . . . 1.

längs[4b]
- along . . . 2.2

langsam[1b]
- slow . . . 1.2

Langsamkeit
- slowness . . . 10.5

langweilen
- bore . . . 4.6

langweilig[5b]
- tedious . . . 5.2

Lanze[4a]
- spear . . . 3.2

Lärm[4a]
- noise . . . 2.6

lärmend
- noisy . . . 5.8

lassen[1a]
- allow . . . 1.
- cause . . . 1.
- fallen –, drop . . . 1.
- wissen –, (let) know . . . 1.
- leave (quit) . . . 1.
- zukommen –, send . . . 1.
- herunter –, lower . . . 2.3

Last[1b]
- load . . . 1.4
- load (cargo) . . . 1.7

lasten[6b]
- load . . . 1.8

Laster[4a]
- vice . . . 3.2

lasterhaft
- vicious . . . 6.5

Lästerung
- blasphemy . . . 6.8

lästig[4a]
- vexing . . . 3.8
- troublesome . . . 4.4

Lastwagen
- truck . . . 6.6

lateinisch[3b]
- Latin . . . 2.8

Laub[6b]
- foliage . . . 5.2

Laube[6b]
- bower . . . 5.2
- arcade . . . 9.4

Laubengang
- arcade . . . 9.4

Lauf[1b]
- course . . . 1.1
- race . . . 1.2

Laufbahn[5b]
- career . . . 4.

laufen[1b]
- run . . . 1.
- Gefahr – (take) chances . . . 1.4
- Schlittschuh –, skate . . . 6.

Läufer
- scout . . . 5.7

Laune[3a]
- humor . . . 2.4

lauschen[5b]
- listen . . . 1.8

laut[1b]
- (out) loud . . . 1.
- loud (*adj.*) . . . 1.2

Laut[4b]
- sound . . . 1.2

Laute
- lute . . . 7.2

lauten[2a]
- read . . . 1.4

läuten[6b]
- ring . . . 1.4

Section

lauter[3a]
- only . . . 1.

leben[1a]
- live . . . 1.

Leben[1a]
- life . . . 1.

Lebende[6a]
- (the) living . . . 3.4

lebendig[2a]
- (full of) life . . . 1.
- alive . . . 1.9
- vivid . . . 3.8

Lebensart[6b]
- custom . . . 1.9

Lebensjahr[4b]
- year . . . 1.

Lebenskraft[5b]
- vigor . . . 4.

Lebensmittel[5a]
- food . . . 1.9

Lebensversicherung[6a]
- insurance . . . 3.3

Lebensweise[5a]
- custom . . . 1.9
- habit . . . 2.2

Leber
- liver . . . 6.

Leberfleck
- mole . . . 6.3

lebhaft[1b]
- (full of) life . . . 1.
- active . . . 2.5

Lebhaftigkeit[6a]
- life . . . 3.8

Leck
- leak . . . 6.6

lecken
- lick . . . 6.2

Leder[6a]
- leather . . . 3.8

lediglich[1b]
- only . . . 1.

leer[2a]
- empty . . . 2.

Leere
- void . . . 5.2

leeren[6b]
- drain . . . 3.7

legen[1a]
- lay . . . 1.
- place . . . 1.
- locate . . . 2.

Legion
- legion . . . 5.8

lehnen[3a]
- lean . . . 2.2

Leh(e)ns-
- feudal . . . 7.8

Lehranstalt[6a]
- school . . . 1.

Lehrbuch[6a]
- manual . . . 6.5

Lehre[1b]
- doctrine . . . 2.6
- apprenticeship . . . 5.8

lehren[1b]
- teach . . . 1.

Lehrer[1b]
- teacher . . . 1.

Lehrerin[5a]
- teacher . . . 1.

Lehrling[5a]
- apprentice . . . 6.6

lehrreich[5a]
- instructive . . . 7.2

Leib[2a]
- body . . . 1.

Section

Madame[4a]
Mrs. ... 1.

Mädchen[1b]
junges –, girl ... 1.
servant ... 1.5

Magd[5b]
servant ... 1.5

Magen[4b]
stomach ... 3.7

Magistrat[4b]
magistrate ... 4.

Magnet
magnet ... 6.7

magnetisch
magnetic ... 7.4

Mahagonie
mahogany ... 7.2

mähen
cut ... 4.7

Mäher
mower ... 7.2

Mahl[6a]
meal ... 3.2

mahlen
grind ... 5.1

Mahlzeit[5b]
meal ... 3.2

Mähne
mane ... 6.4

mahnen[4b]
warn ... 2.2

Mahnung[5b]
warning ... 3.4

Mai[1b]
May ... 1.2

Mais
corn ... 4.8

Majestät[2a]
majesty ... 2.5

Major[2a]
major ... 3.2

Majorität[3b]
majority ... 2.6

mal[2b]
even ... 1.
indeed ... 1.

Mal[1b]
time (how many) ... 1.

malen[2b]
paint ... 1.5

Maler[3a]
painter ... 3.

Malerei[4a]
painting ... 3.2

malerisch[5b]
picturesque ... 4.6

Mama[3b]
mamma ... 2.9

man[1a]
one (*indef. pron.*) ... 1.

manch[1a]
many ... 1.

mancherlei[3a]
different ... 1.

manchmal[2a]
sometimes ... 1.4

Mandat
writ ... 5.9

Mandel
almond ... 6.9

Mangel[1b]
need ... 1.

mangelhaft[4a]
imperfect ... 3.9

Mangelhaftigkeit
insufficiency ... 10.1

Section

mangeln[4b]
lack ... 1.5

mangels[6a]
(for) want of ... 3.

Manier[5a]
way ... 1.

Mann[1a]
husband ... 1.
man ... 1.

mannigfach[4b]
several times ... 1.2
various ... 2.6

mannigfaltig[4a]
various ... 2.6
manifold ... 4.4

Mannigfaltigkeit[5a]
variety ... 3.8
multiplicity ... 9.

männlich[3b]
male ... 3.1
manly ... 3.8

Männlichkeit
manhood ... 6.8

Mannschaft[3a]
crew ... 3.2

Manöver[5b]
operation ... 2.4

Manschette
cuff ... 6.

Mantel[3b]
coat ... 2.
coat (overcoat) ... 2.2
overcoat ... 3.6

Manuskript[5a]
manuscript ... 5.8

Märchen[4a]
fairy tale ... 3.4

Märchenland
fairyland ... 6.2

Marine[4b]
navy ... 3.6

Mark[1a]
pound ... 1.

Marke[6a]
brand ... 4.2

Markt[2a]
market ... 1.7

Marmel
marble ... 4.9

Marmor[6a]
marble ... 3.8

Marquis
marquis ... 6.9

Marsch (*m.*)[2b]
march ... 1.5

Marsch (*f.*)[3b]
swamp ... 4.

Marschall[3b]
marshal ... 4.2

marschieren[2b]
march ... 1.4

Marter
martyrdom ... 7.3

Märtyrertum
martyrdom ... 7.3

März[2a]
March ... 1.9

Masche
stitch ... 6.1

Maschine[2b]
machine ... 2.

Maske[5b]
mask ... 4.5

maskieren
mask ... 5.4

Maß[1b]
measure ... 1.
moderation ... 3.8

Section

Masse[1b]
crowd ... 1.
mass ... 1.6

massenhaft[6b]
abundant ... 4.2
crowded ... 5.4

Maßgabe[3a]
standard ... 2.2

maßgebend[3a]
standard ... 3.

mäßig[3a]
moderate ... 3.

Mäßigkeit
temperance ... 6.4

Mäßigung[6b]
moderation (temperateness) ... 3.8
moderation (diminution) ... 5.8

Maßnahme[5a]
measure ... 1.

Maßregel[1b]
rule ... 1.1

Maßstab[1b]
scale ... 1.8

Mast
mast ... 5.6

Material[2a]
material ... 2.

Materie[4a]
subject ... 1.

materiell[3a]
real ... 1.9

Mathematik
mathematics ... 6.7

mathematisch
mathematical ... 8.3

Matratze
mattress ... 6.7

Matrone
matron ... 6.5

matt[4a]
dull ... 3.9

Matte
mat ... 5.8

Mattigkeit
languor ... 8.6

Mauer[2b]
wall ... 1.7

Maul[5b]
mouth ... 1.
muzzle ... 5.2

Maulesel
mule ... 6.

Mauleseltreiber
muleteer ... 12.5

Maurer
mason ... 6.3

maurisch
Moor ... 5.8

Maus
mouse ... 5.

mechanisch[3b]
mechanic ... 3.5
mechanically ... 5.2

Mechanismus
mechanism ... 7.2

Medizin[5b]
medicine ... 3.4

medizinisch[6a]
medical ... 5.1

Meer[1b]
sea ... 1.

Meerbusen
gulf ... 5.

Mehl[4a]
flour ... 3.2

Section

mehr[1a]
more ... 1.
nicht –, no longer ... 1.

mehren[6a]
increase ... 1.1

mehrere[1a]
several ... 1.

mehrfach[3a]
several times ... 1.2

Mehrheit[3a]
majority ... 2.6

mehrmals[5a]
several times ... 1.2

Mehrzahl[2a]
majority ... 2.6

meiden[5b]
avoid ... 1.8

Meile[2a]
mile ... 1.7

mein[1a]
my ... 1.
mine ... 1.1

meinen[1a]
mean ... 1.
suppose ... 1.
think ... 1.

meinerseits[5a]
(on my) side ... 2.6

meinig[3b]
mine ... 1.1

Meinung[1a]
opinion ... 1.4
anderer – sein, differ ... 2.5

Meißel
chisel ... 7.2

meist[1a]
most ... 1.

Meiste[6a]
most ... 1.

meistens[3a]
(for the most) part ... 1.8

Meister[1b]
master ... 1.
champion ... 2.5

Meisterstück
masterpiece ... 6.4

melden[2a]
(give) notice (of) ... 1.4

Meldung[2b]
notice ... 1.7

Melodie[5b]
air ... 3.

Melone
melon ... 6.9

Menge[1b]
amount ... 1.
crowd ... 1.

Mensch[1a]
man ... 1.
person ... 1.
brutale –, brute ... 5.7

Menschengeschlecht[5a]
mankind ... 2.4

Menschenleben[3a]
life ... 1.

Menschenliebe[3b]
pity ... 2.4
charity ... 2.9

Menschheit[2a]
mankind ... 2.4

menschlich[1b]
human ... 1.4

Menschlichkeit[6b]
mit –, humane ... 5.3

merken[2a]
notice ... 1.4

Section

Münze[2b]
coin . . . 1.9
murmeln[4b]
murmur . . . 2.9
Muse[6a]
muse . . . 4.6
Muselman
Mussulman . . . 9.8
Museum[4a]
museum . . . 4.
Musik[2a]
music . . . 1.5
Musik-
musical . . . 5.8
musikalisch[4a]
musical . . . 3.6
Musiker[6b]
musician . . . 4.8
Muskel[6a]
muscle . . . 5.6
Muskete[6a]
gun . . . 1.7
Muße[5b]
leisure . . . 4.8
Musselin
lawn . . . 5.2
müssen[1a]
must . . . 1.
müßig[5a]
idle . . . 3.7
Müßiggang
idleness . . . 6.5
Muster[2b]
example . . . 1.4
model . . . 2.
sample . . . 2.7
Mut[1b]
– haben, (be) brave . . . 1.
courage . . . 1.4
– verlieren
(lose) courage . . . 2.
mutig[4b]
(be) brave . . . 1.
Mutter[1a]
mother . . . 1.
mütterlich[7a]
mother . . . 4.1
Mütze[6b]
cap . . . 3.8
Myrte
myrtle . . . 7.2
mystisch
mystic . . . 6.9

N

na[4b]
well! . . . 2.3
what! . . . 2.4
nach[1a]
after . . . 1.
by (according to) . . . 1.
– Hause, (at) home . . . 1.
to . . . 1.
toward(s) . . . 1.
bound (for) . . . 1.9
nachahmen[5b]
copy . . . 3.2
imitate . . . 4.
Nachahmung[4a]
copy . . . 3.3
Nachbar[3a]
neighbor . . . 1.8
Nachbarschaft[5b]
neighborhood . . . 2.9
Nachbildung[6a]
copy . . . 3.2
nachdem[1a]
after . . . 1.

nachdenken[4a]
consider . . . 1.8
Nachdenken[5a]
consideration . . . 2.4
meditation . . . 5.1
Nachdruck[4a]
emphasis . . . 5.1
nachdrücklich[6a]
emphasis . . . 5.1
nachfolgen[4a]
follow . . . 2.3
Nachfolger[3b]
successor . . . 3.8
Nachfrage[5a]
demand . . . 2.9
inquiry . . . 4.4
nachgeben[4b]
yield . . . 1.9
nachgehen[6a]
follow . . . 1.
(be) slow . . . 3.6
nachgiebig
indulgent . . . 8.1
nachher[2a]
by and by . . . 1.1
afterwards . . . 1.8
Nachkomme[5b]
descendant . . . 5.3
nachkommen[4a]
catch up . . . 2.3
Nachlaß[5a]
inheritance . . . 3.9
nachlassen[6b]
reduce . . . 3.5
nachliefern[5a]
supply later . . . 3.
nachmachen[6a]
copy . . . 3.2
Nachmittag[3a]
afternoon . . . 1.9
nachmittags[6a]
afternoon . . . 1.9
Nachricht[1b]
news . . . 1.4
Nachschrift
postscript . . . 7.2
nachsehen[4b]
(take) care . . . 1.
look for . . . 1.
jemandem etwas –
indulge . . . 5.3
Nachsicht[6a]
indulgence . . . 5.8
Nächste[5b]
neighbor . . . 3.4
nachstehen[4b]
(be) inferior . . . 3.6
nächstens[6a]
soon . . . 1.
Nacht[1a]
night . . . 1.
die – zubringen
(spend) night . . . 2.7
jede –, nightly . . . 3.
Nachteil[2a]
disadvantage . . . 4.8
nachteilig[4a]
injurious . . . 4.3
Nachtigall
nightingale . . . 6.1
Nachtisch
dessert . . . 6.7
nächtlich[5b]
night . . . 3.3
nachträglich[4a]
subsequent . . . 4.1
nachts[4a]
(at) night . . . 2.2

Nachtwache
vigil . . . 6.2
Nachweis[4b]
proof . . . 1.4
nachweisen[2b]
show . . . 1.
point out . . . 1.4
Nachwelt
posterity . . . 6.6
Nachzügler
late-comer . . . 13.
nackt[5a]
bare . . . 2.4
Nadel[6a]
needle . . . 3.8
pin . . . 4.
Nagel[4a]
nail (tack) . . . 3.
nail (finger) . . . 3.1
nageln
nail . . . 4.6
nagen
gnaw . . . 6.1
nah[1a]
nächst, beside . . . 1.
der nächste Tag
(the) day (after) . 1.
near (*adj.* and *adv.*) . 1.
nächst, next . . . 1.
Nähe[1b]
in der –, near . . . 1.
proximity . . . 5.6
nahen[2b]
(go) toward(s) . . . 1.
nähen
sew . . . 4.7
nähern[1b]
(bring) toward(s) . . . 1.
sich –, (go) toward(s) . 1.
nahezu[4b]
almost . . . 1.
nähren[3a]
nourish . . . 3.2
Nahrung[3a]
food . . . 1.9
Nahrungsmittel[5a]
food . . . 1.9
Naht
seam . . . 6.4
Name[1a]
name . . . 1.
namenlos
nameless . . . 5.8
namentlich[1a]
above all . . . 1.
namhaft[5b]
famous . . . 1.1
nämlich[1a]
(of) course . . . 1.
namely . . . 2.6
nämliche[3b]
same . . . 1.
Narbe
scar . . . 6.2
Narr[3a]
fool . . . 2.4
Nase[2b]
nose . . . 1.7
naß[4b]
wet . . . 2.9
– machen, wet . . . 2.9
Nässe[5a]
moisture . . . 4.4
Nation[1b]
nation . . . 1.1
national[2a]
national . . . 2.

Nationalität[4a]
nationality . . . 5.5
nationalliberal[2a]
liberal . . . 2.9
Nationalliberale[4a]
liberal . . . 2.9
Nationalversammlung[5a]
assembly . . . 2.6
Natron[4b]
soda . . . 5.6
Natur[a]
nature . . . 1.
Naturforscher[4b]
scientist . . . 4.2
naturgemäß[2b]
natural . . . 1.
Naturgesetz[6a]
law . . . 1.
natürlich[1a]
(of) course . . . 1.
natural . . . 1.
Natürlichkeit
naturalness . . . 12.1
Naturwissenschaft[5a]
science . . . 1.4
Naturwissenschaftler
naturalist . . . 7.4
naturwissenschaftlich[6a]
scientific . . . 3.9
Nebel[3a]
mist . . . 3.1
neben[1a]
beside . . . 1.
near (*adj.* and *adv.*) 1.
near (*prep.*) . . . 1.
nebenbei[3b]
near (*adj.* and *adv.*) . 1.
Nebenbuhlerschaft
rivalry . . . 7.8
nebeneinander[4a]
side by side . . . 2.2
Nebenzimmer[6b]
room (chamber) . . . 1.
nebst[2a]
with . . . 1.
necken
tease . . . 5.9
Neffe[4b]
nephew . . . 3.7
Neger[5a]
negro . . . 3.8
nehmen[1a]
in Angriff –, begin . . . 1.
in Anspruch –, demand 1.
Platz –, sit (sit down) 1.
take . . . 1.
Teil –
(take an) interest 1.3
Abschied –
(take) leave . . . 1.5
in Anspruch –
(be) absorbed . . . 3.
Neid[4b]
envy . . . 3.1
neidisch
envious . . . 5.7
neigen[2a]
(be) subject . . . 1.7
bend . . . 1.9
slant . . . 2.8
Neigung[1b]
liking . . . 1.5
leaning . . . 1.8
tend . . . 2.4
tendency . . . 3.2
nein[1a]
no . . . 1.

Section

Ökonomie
economy 6.2
ökonomisch[6b]
economic 6.2
Oktober[2a]
October 2.4
Öl[3a]
oil 2.5
Olive
olive tree 5.7
olive 5.8
Omnibus
bus 8.1
Onkel[3b]
uncle 1.9
Oper[4a]
opera 4.5
Operation[3a]
operation 2.4
Operette
(musical) drama ... 6.2
Opfer[2a]
sacrifice .... 2.
victim 2.2
martyr 3.1
opfern[3b]
sacrifice 2.6
Opposition[5a]
opposition .... 3.
Optimismus
optimism 9.7
Optimist
optimistic 10.9
optimistisch
optimistic 10.9
optisch
optic 7.8
Orakel
oracle 6.8
Orange(nbaum)
orange tree .... 5.
Orangenblüte
orange blossom 4.9
Orchester[6b]
orchestra 5.5
Orden[4b]
medal 4.4
ordentlich[3a]
neat 2.6
ordnen[2a]
(put in) order 1.4
fix 1.5
dispose 1.8
class 2.1
Ordnung[1b]
arrangement 2.4
Ordre[4b]
order .... 1.
Organ[2a]
organ 2.2
Organisation[2b]
organization 3.5
Organisator
organizer .... 11.
organisch[3a]
organic 4.5
organisieren[4b]
organize 3.7
Organismus[4a]
organism 4.8
orientalisch[5a]
eastern 2.7
Original[4a]
queer person 3.3
Originalität
originality 6.8

Section

originell[6b]
original 4.1
Ort[1a]
place .... 1.
örtlich[5a]
local 3.8
Örtlichkeit
location 5.5
Ortschaft[4a]
place .... 1.
village 1.2
Ortsstatut[6b]
statute 4.1
Osten[2b]
east .... 2.
Ostern[5b]
Easter 4.8
österreichisch[2a]
Austrian 4.1
östlich[2b]
eastern 2.7
Ozean[6a]
ocean 3.6

P

paar[2a]
ein –, (a) few .... 1.
ein –, several .... 1.
Paar[3a]
pair 1.9
Pächter
tenant 6.5
packen[4a]
pack 3.5
paddeln
paddle 7.2
Palast[3a]
palace 2.3
Palme
palm tree 5.5
Panik
panic 7.3
Pantoffel
slipper 5.7
Papa[4a]
papa 3.4
Papagei
parrot 6.5
Papier[1b]
paper .... 1.
Pappe
cardboard 8.6
Papst[3a]
pope 3.3
Parade[6b]
procession 4.1
parade 5.4
Paradies[5a]
paradise 3.8
Paragraph[1a]
paragraph 3.3
parallel[6b]
parallel 4.9
parfümieren
perfume 5.4
parisisch[4a]
Parisian 5.8
Park[4b]
park 2.3
Parlament[3b]
parliament 2.8
parlamentarisch[4a]
parliamentary ..... 7.
Partei[1b]
party 1.1

Section

Partie[3b]
excursion 4.1
Partikel
particle .... 7.
Partizip
participle 10.2
Paß
pass 4.4
Passant
passerby 10.9
passen[2a]
fit .... 1.
passieren[3a]
happen .... 1.
passiv
passive 7.3
Paste
paste 6.1
Pastete
pie 5.1
Pastille
tablet 6.2
Pastor[5a]
minister .... 2.
pastor 4.9
Pate
godfather 8.6
Patent[5a]
patent 5.2
Patient[6a]
patient 2.5
Patin
godmother 6.8
Patriarch[5a]
patriarch 6.8
patriarchisch
patriarchal 10.1
Patriot[6b]
patriot 5.2
patriotisch[5b]
patriotic 4.8
Patron[5b]
patron .... 4.
Patrone
cartridge .... 9.
Patrouille[5a]
guard (military) ... 2.
Pause[3b]
pause 2.9
Pavillon
pavilion 6.4
Pedant
pedant 9.6
peinlich[4a]
painful 3.2
Peitsche
whip (*n.*) 4.8
peitschen
whip (*vb.*) 4.8
Pellerine
cloak 4.8
Pelz
fur .... 5.
Pension[4b]
board 2.7
pension 4.3
per[2b]
by (agent) .... 1.
Pergament
parchment 7.4
Periode[2b]
period 2.2
periodisch
periodical 3.9
Perle[4b]
pearl 2.9
bead 3.2

Section

Perlmutter
mother-of-pearl 12.7
persisch[5b]
Persian 5.6
Person[1a]
person .... 1.
Personal[5a]
staff 3.4
persönlich[1b]
personal 1.9
Persönlichkeit[2b]
personage 3.6
personality 3.9
peruanisch
Peruvian 9.8
Perücke
wig 6.8
Petersilie
parsley 8.1
Petition[3b]
petition .... 4.
Petroleum
kerosene 6.9
petroleum 6.9
Pfad[5a]
path 2.9
Pfand[6a]
pledge 2.9
Pfanne
pan 4.9
frying pan 6.4
Pfannkuchen
pancake .... 7.
Pfarrer[2b]
minister .... 2.
Pfau
peacock 6.4
Pfeffer
pepper 5.9
Pfeife[5b]
pipe 3.6
whistle 3.9
fife .... 6.
pfeifen
whistle 4.6
Pfeifer
piper 7.2
Pfeil[4a]
arrow 3.2
Pfennig[2b]
cent 1.7
Pferd[1b]
horse .... 1.
zu -e, horseback 2.2
Pfirsich
peach 5.8
Pflanze[2b]
plant 1.5
pflanzen[4a]
plant 2.4
Pflanzer
planter 7.2
Pflaster
pavement 5.7
pflastern
pave 6.2
Pflaume
plum .... 6.
Pflege[3b]
care .... 1.
fostering 3.9
pflegen[1b]
(take) care .... 1.
Pflicht[1b]
duty .... 1.
Pflug
plow 5.3

Section

- Puff
  - puff 5.8
- Puls
  - pulse 6.
- Pulver[3b]
  - powder 2.8
- Pumpe
  - pump 5.3
- Punkt[1a]
  - point 1.
- pünktlich[5b]
  - prompt 2.5
- Pupille
  - pupil (eye) 5.3
- Puppe
  - doll 4.9
- Purpur
  - purple 4.9
- Puter
  - turkey 5.6
- putzen[6b]
  - polish 4.4
- Pyramide[6b]
  - pyramid 5.7

Q

- Quadrat
  - square 4.4
- Quai
  - dock 5.4
- quaken
  - quack 6.1
  - croak 6.8
- Qual[4a]
  - torment 3.5
  - torture 3.9
- quälen[3b]
  - torment 3.1
  - torture 3.5
- qualifizieren
  - qualify 7.2
- Qualität[4a]
  - quality 2.7
- Quantität[4a]
  - amount 1.
- Quantum[6a]
  - amount 1.
- Quartier[4a]
  - quarter (of town) 2.5
- Quaste
  - tassel 7.
- Quecksilber
  - mercury 6.6
- Quelle[2a]
  - spring 1.7
  - well 1.9
- quer[6b]
  - – über, across 3.4
- Querstraße
  - crossroad 10.5
- quitt
  - quit 4.6
- Quittung[6a]
  - receipt 4.9
- Quotisierung[6a]
  - ration 6.4

R

- Rabbiner[4b]
  - rabbi 8.4
- Rabe
  - crow 5.3
- Rache[3b]
  - revenge 2.8
- rächen[3b]
  - avenge 3.8
- Rächer
  - avenger 8.9
- Rad[4b]
  - wheel 2.5
- radikal[5b]
  - radical 5.
- ragen[4b]
  - project 3.7
- Rahmen[3b]
  - frame 2.4
- rahmen
  - frame 5.1
- Ranch
  - ranch 6.9
- Rand[2b]
  - edge 1.5
  - brim 2.6
  - margin 3.9
- Rang[3a]
  - rank 2.6
  - hohe –, eminence 5.3
- rasch[1b]
  - fast 1.
- rasen[4a]
  - rage 3.7
- Rasen[6b]
  - lawn 4.3
  - turf 5.8
- Rasierapparat
  - razor 7.2
- rasieren
  - shave 5.6
- Rasiermesser
  - razor 7.2
- Rasse[6a]
  - race 3.2
- rastlos[5b]
  - restless 2.7
- Rat[1b]
  - advice 1.4
  - council 2.1
- raten[2b]
  - richtig –, guess right 1.4
  - guess 1.5
  - advise 2.
- Rathaus[6b]
  - (city) hall 3.4
- rationell[4b]
  - saving 1.8
- Ratschlag[6b]
  - advice 1.4
- Rätsel[4a]
  - riddle 4.6
- rätselhaft[6b]
  - mysterious 3.5
- Ratsherr
  - alderman 7.2
- Ratte
  - rat 5.2
- Raub[5a]
  - robbery 4.8
- rauben[3a]
  - rob 2.3
- Räuber[4b]
  - robber 3.7
- Rauch[4b]
  - smoke 2.4
- rauchen[4b]
  - smoke 2.6
- Raufbold
  - ruffian 7.
- rauh[4a]
  - rough 3.
  - gruff 3.7
  - harsh 3.9
- Rauheit
  - harshness 7.8
- Raum[1b]
  - place 1.
  - room (space) 1.
- räumen[3b]
  - take away 1.
  - evacuate 7.7
- Raupe
  - caterpillar 7.2
- rauschen[4a]
  - rustle 4.6
- reagieren
  - react 7.9
- Reaktion[6b]
  - reaction 6.6
- real[6a]
  - concrete 6.1
- Realist
  - realist 9.
- Rebe[6b]
  - vine 4.
- Rebell[5b]
  - rebel 4.
- Rebhuhn
  - partridge 6.9
- Rechen
  - rake 6.2
- Rechenschaft[5a]
  - account 1.
- rechnen[1b]
  - count 1.
  - – auf, count on 1.
- Rechnung[1b]
  - account 1.
- recht[1a]
  - right (correct) 1.
  - right (hand) 1.
- Recht[1a]
  - – haben, (be) right 1.
- Rechteck
  - rectangle 6.8
- rechtfertigen[2b]
  - justify 2.5
- Rechtfertigung[6b]
  - justification 7.2
- rechtlich[3a]
  - fair 1.4
- Rechtlichkeit
  - righteousness 6.9
- rechtmäßig[6b]
  - lawful 3.
- Rechtsanwalt[4a]
  - attorney 4.7
- Rechtsbelehrung[6b]
  - legal information 5.3
- rechtschaffen[6a]
  - upright 3.8
- Rechtschreibung
  - spelling 5.3
- Rechtspflege[6b]
  - jurisprudence 9.6
- rechtzeitig[3a]
  - prompt 2.5
- Redakteur[5a]
  - editor 6.1
- Redaktion[4b]
  - (editorial) staff 5.3
- Rede[1a]
  - talk (conversation) 1.
  - talk (lecture) 1.2
  - (make a) speech 1.6
  - oration 3.5
- Redekunst
  - oratory 8.6
- reden[1a]
  - talk 1.
- redlich[3b]
  - honest 1.9
- Redner[3a]
  - speaker 3.1
- redselig
  - talkative 10.
- Referent[4b]
  - speaker 3.1
- Reform[2b]
  - reform 3.2
- Reformation[6a]
  - reform 3.2
- reformieren[6b]
  - reform 5.
- rege[3b]
  - (full of) life 1.
- Regel[1b]
  - rule 1.1
  - precept 3.7
- regelmäßig[2a]
  - regular 2.
- Regelmäßigkeit
  - regularity 8.
- regeln[2b]
  - (put in) order 1.4
- Regelung[3a]
  - rule 1.1
- Regen[3b]
  - rain 2.
- Regenbogen
  - rainbow 5.8
- Regentin[4b]
  - regent 6.4
- regieren[2b]
  - reign 2.
  - manage 2.2
- Regierung[1a]
  - government 1.1
  - reign 2.1
- Regierungsbezirk[6b]
  - district 2.1
- Regierungskommissar[6a]
  - mayor 2.5
  - commissioner 5.
- Regierungspräsident[6a]
  - mayor 2.5
  - county head 12.
- Regierungsvorlage[3a]
  - (government) bill 1.9
- Regiment[1b]
  - regiment 3.6
- Register[6a]
  - record 3.8
- Reglement[6a]
  - rule 1.1
- Reglosigkeit
  - immobility 12.9
- regnen
  - rain 4.2
- regnerisch
  - rainy 5.7
- Regress[6a]
  - damage 2.4
- regulieren[5b]
  - (put in) order 1.4
  - regulate 4.4
- Regulierung[5a]
  - rule 1.1
- Regung[5b]
  - motion 1.4
- Reh
  - deer 5.8
- reiben[4b]
  - rub 3.2
- Reibung[6a]
  - friction 6.1

	Section
rückwärts[3b]	
backward	2.8
rückzahlen	
repay	5.
Rückzug[2b]	
return	1.4
retreat	2.6
Ruder[5b]	
oar	4.8
helm	5.6
rudern	
row	5.
Ruf[2a]	
call	1.4
reputation	3.2
prestige	5.9
rufen[1a]	
call	1.
cry	1.
– nach, zu, etc. call upon	1.5
Ruhe[1b]	
quiet	1.
rest	1.2
ruhen[1b]	
rest	1.
lie	1.7
ruhig[1b]	
quiet	1.
Ruhm[2b]	
fame	2.3
rühmen[2b]	
boast	2.2
rühmlich[6b]	
honorable	4.
rühren[2a]	
touch	1.
move	1.5
feel	1.6
stir	2.1
-d, moving	2.3
-d, pathetic	5.
Rührung[5b]	
feeling	1.
emotion	4.3
Ruin[4b]	
ruin	2.4
rund[2b]	
round	1.6
circular	3.3
Runde	
(make) rounds	4.2
Rundschau[3b]	
review	2.6
Runkelrübe	
turnip	6.7
runzeln	
frown	5.5
wrinkle	5.7
Russe[5b]	
Russian	3.
russisch[2a]	
Russian	3.
rüsten[4b]	
arm	2.4
Rüstung[4b]	
armor	4.4

S

	Section
Saal[2b]	
hall	1.5
Saat[6b]	
seed	2.7
sowing	4.5
Säbel[6b]	
sword	2.
saber	7.2

	Section
Sache[1a]	
matter	1.
sachgemäß[6a]	
adequate	6.
Sachlage[5b]	
position	1.4
sachlich[4a]	
impartial	5.
sächsisch[3b]	
English	1.
Sachverständige[4a]	
expert	4.2
Sack[5b]	
bag	3.
säen[6a]	
sow	3.6
Saft[4b]	
sap	4.2
juice	4.3
syrup	5.3
Sage[3a]	
legend	3.9
sagen[1a]	
say	1.
Sahne	
cream	5.1
Salat	
salad	6.
lettuce	7.1
salben	
anoint	7.
Salbung	
ointment	7.
Salm	
salmon	7.2
Salon[4b]	
room	2.3
Salpeter[6b]	
fertilizer	5.7
Salpetersäure[5a]	
acid	3.7
Salve	
discharge	5.8
Salz[3b]	
salt	2.1
salzen	
salt	4.7
Salzsäure[6a]	
acid	3.7
Samen[4b]	
seed	2.7
sammeln[2a]	
gather (collect)	1.5
gather (pluck)	1.5
Sammlung[2a]	
assembly	2.6
collection	2.7
samt[3b]	
with	1.
Samt	
velvet	5.2
sämtlich[1b]	
complete	1.
Sand[3b]	
sand	2.
sandig	
sandy	6.
sanft[2a]	
soft	1.5
Sänger[5a]	
singer	4.3
Sankt[6a]	
saint	2.6
Sanktion	
sanction	6.7
Sardine	
sardine	8.

	Section
Sarg[5a]	
coffin	5.3
Sarkasmus	
sarcasm	8.8
Satin	
satin	5.8
Satire	
satire	6.9
satt[6a]	
satisfied	4.1
Sattel[6a]	
saddle	3.8
Satz[1b]	
sentence	1.4
start	1.7
thesis	6.1
sauber[4b]	
clean	1.
Sauberkeit	
neatness	9.2
sauer[4b]	
sour	4.4
Sauerstoff[3a]	
oxygen	5.6
saugen	
suck	6.
Säugling	
baby	4.4
Säule[4a]	
column	3.3
Säure[2b]	
acid	3.7
schaben	
skin	5.
Schach	
chess	8.2
Schachtel[6b]	
box	2.3
schade[5a]	
(too) bad	2.9
Schädel	
skull	6.
Schaden[2a]	
damage	2.4
schaden[3a]	
hurt (*tr. vb.*)	1.8
schädigen[3b]	
hurt (*tr. vb.*)	1.8
Schädigung[6a]	
damage	2.4
schädlich[3b]	
injurious	4.3
Schaf[5b]	
sheep	3.
schaffen[1a]	
busy	1.
create	1.5
Schaffen[6a]	
creation	3.4
Schafs-	
mutton	5.8
schal	
flat	5.3
Schal	
shawl	7.4
Schale[5a]	
shell	3.7
bowl	4.2
peel	5.3
schälen[5b]	
peel	5.2
Schall[6b]	
sound	1.2
Schalter	
ticket window	5.3
Scham[5b]	
shame	3.3
modesty	4.7

	Section
schämen[4a]	
sich –, (be) ashamed	3.
Schande[3b]	
disgrace	3.4
schändlich[5b]	
shameful	4.7
Schanze[6a]	
fort	2.6
Schar[3a]	
group	1.8
band	2.1
scharf[1b]	
sharp	1.7
keen	2.4
Schärfe[4b]	
edge	2.6
rigor	4.2
Scharfsinn[6b]	
wisdom	2.3
ingenuity	5.6
Schärpe	
scarf	6.1
Schatten[2b]	
shade	1.4
shade (shadow)	1.8
schatten	
shade	4.9
schattig	
shady	6.1
Schatz[2a]	
treasure	2.
darling	2.2
schätzbar	
estimable	10.1
schätzen[2a]	
value	1.4
Schatzmeister	
treasurer	7.2
Schätzung[4b]	
estimate	3.8
Schau[6b]	
display	2.6
schaudern[6a]	
tremble	1.8
schauen[2a]	
look at	1.
Schauer[7a]	
shower	2.5
shiver	4.7
thrill	5.6
Schaufel	
spade	5.8
Schaum	
foam	5.3
schäumen	
foam	5.7
Schauplatz[5a]	
scene	1.8
Schauspiel[3a]	
play	2.
Schauspieler[4b]	
actor	3.9
Scheere	
scissors	6.5
Scheffel	
bushel	6.
Scheibe[3b]	
pane	3.3
slice	4.
disk	5.4
Scheide[6a]	
sheath	4.4
scheiden[2a]	
separate	1.
divorce	4.
Scheideweg	
crossroads	10.4

	Section
Schoß[3b]	
lap	2.4
womb	4.9
coat-tail	10.8
Schößling	
shoot	5.4
schräg[4a]	
crooked	3.7
oblique	6.2
Schrank	
closet	5.6
wardrobe	6.8
Schranke[3b]	
limit	2.4
Schrapnell[6b]	
shell	3.4
Schraube[6a]	
screw	5.8
Schrecken[2b]	
fear	1.4
schrecken[5b]	
frighten	1.9
schrecklich[2b]	
terrible	1.8
Schrei[5b]	
call	1.4
cry	2.6
schreiben[1a]	
write	1.
Schreiben[2b]	
writing	1.8
Schreiber[5a]	
clerk	3.8
Schreibmaschine	
typewriter	5.6
Schreibtisch[5b]	
desk	3.6
schreien[2b]	
cry	1.
call out	1.4
schreiten[2a]	
go	1.
stride	3.3
Schrift[1b]	
writing	1.4
schriftlich[2b]	
written	1.4
Schriftsteller[2b]	
author	1.9
Schriftstück[6b]	
document	5.1
Schritt[1b]	
step	1.
schroff[5b]	
steep	2.8
Schublade	
drawer	6.1
schüchtern[5b]	
shy	4.2
Schüchternheit	
timidity	8.4
Schuh[6a]	
shoe	3.2
-e anziehen	
(put on) shoes	3.5
-e ausziehen	
(take off) shoes	4.1
Schul-	
school	4.6
Schuld[1b]	
fault	1.4
debt	1.7
daran – sein	
(be to) blame	1.8
guilt	2.2
schulden[5a]	
owe	1.8

	Section
schuldig[2a]	
(be to) blame	1.8
– sein, owe	1.8
Schuldigkeit[6a]	
duty	1.
Schuldner[3a]	
debtor	4.8
Schule[1b]	
school	1.
Schüler[1b]	
pupil	1.7
Schulter[2b]	
shoulder	1.5
Schulverband[5a]	
organization	3.5
Schulwesen[6a]	
school system	4.2
Schulze[6a]	
mayor	2.5
schürfen	
bruise	5.7
Schurke[6a]	
knave	4.5
villain	5.
Schürze	
apron	5.4
schürzen	
turn up	4.9
Schuß[2a]	
discharge	2.7
Schuster	
shoemaker	6.2
schütteln[3a]	
shake (hands)	1.1
shake (*tr. vb.*)	1.9
shake (head)	2.2
Schutz[1b]	
shelter	1.7
protection	2.1
schützen[1b]	
guard	1.
defend	1.4
Schützling	
protégé	11.
schwach[1b]	
weak	1.1
Schwäche[3a]	
weakness	2.9
schwächen[5a]	
weaken	4.8
Schwachheit[6b]	
weakness	2.9
Schwadron[4b]	
squadron	4.9
Schwager[6a]	
brother-in-law	11.
Schwalbe	
swallow	5.
Schwamm	
sponge	6.6
Schwan	
swan	5.8
schwanken[3a]	
roll	2.2
reel	3.1
-d, unsteady	5.6
Schwankung[5b]	
rocking	4.
Schwanz	
tail	4.1
schwärmen[6a]	
swarm	5.
-d, enthusiastic	5.4
schwarz[1b]	
black	1.
schwärzen	
blacken	7.2

	Section
Schwatzbase	
gossip	6.8
schweben[2b]	
wave	1.7
hover	3.8
schwedisch[5a]	
Swedish	6.8
Schwefel[3a]	
sulphur	5.2
Schwefelsäure[4a]	
acid	3.7
schweigen[2a]	
(keep) quiet	1.5
-d, silent	1.5
– machen, silence	1.9
Schweigen[3b]	
silence	2.2
Schwein[6b]	
pig	3.9
Schweiß[6a]	
sweat	4.7
schweizerisch	
Swiss	6.4
Schwelle[4b]	
threshold	4.2
schwellen[6b]	
swell	3.9
schwer[1a]	
hard (difficult)	1.
heavy	1.
schwerlich[3b]	
hardly	1.4
Schwert[2b]	
sword	2.
Schwester[1b]	
sister	1.
Schwiegersohn	
son-in-law	11.7
Schwiegervater	
father-in-law	11.
schwierig[2a]	
hard (difficult)	1.
Schwierigkeit[1b]	
difficulty	1.9
schwimmen[4a]	
float	2.9
swim	3.6
schwinden[4b]	
disappear	1.4
schwindlig	
dizzy	6.4
schwingen[4b]	
swing	3.
schwitzen	
sweat	5.8
schwören[3a]	
swear	2.7
Schwung[6b]	
swing	4.8
zest	6.8
sechs[2a]	
six	1.4
sechste[4a]	
sixth	3.7
sechsundzwanzig	
twenty-six	4.7
sechzehn	
sixteen	5.2
sechzehnte	
sixteenth	7.7
sechzig[6b]	
sixty	4.
See (*f.*)[3a]	
sea	1.
See (*m.*)[3a]	
lake	2.1

	Section
See-[4b]	
sea	3.
naval	5.2
Seefahrer	
navigator	7.6
Seekrankheit	
(sea) sickness	4.9
Seele[1a]	
soul	1.
Seemann	
mariner	5.8
Seeräuber	
pirate	6.9
Segel[6b]	
sail	3.5
Segen[2b]	
blessing	2.3
segensreich[6a]	
prosperous	4.7
segnen[3a]	
bless	2.
sehen[1a]	
see	1.
– Sie!, siehst Du!	
here!	1.6
flüchtig –, glance	2.3
Sehne[6b]	
sinew	6.
sehnen[2b]	
sich –, long for	1.4
sehnlich	
languid	7.4
Sehnsucht[3a]	
longing	1.9
aspiration	4.8
sehr[1a]	
very	1.
Seide[5a]	
silk	2.9
seiden[6a]	
silk	3.3
Seife[6b]	
soap	4.6
Stück –, cake of soap	4.8
sein (*adj.* and *pron.*)[1a]	
his	1.
its	1.
his (*poss. pron.*)	1.1
sein (*vb.*)[1a]	
be	1.
da ist, *there* is	1.
da –, exist	1.8
Sein[3a]	
existence	2.6
seinerseits[4b]	
(on his) side	2.2
seinige[3a]	
his	1.1
seit[1a]	
since	1.
seitdem[2a]	
since	1.
Seite[1a]	
side	1.
page	1.2
Seitengewehr	
bayonet	7.4
seitens[2a]	
(on the) part (of)	1.4
seither[6a]	
since	1.
seitlich	
side	4.1
seitwärts[4a]	
aside	3.1
Sekretär[5a]	
secretary	3.6

Section

Sorte[3b]
kind .... 1.
soviel[3a]
as much as 1.8
– wie, (as) much (as) . 1.9
soweit[1b]
so much .... 1.
as long as 1.1
sowie[1a]
(in) order (to) .... 1.
sowohl[1b]
so much .... 1.
– . . . . als auch
(as) well (as) 1.2
sozial[2b]
social 2.3
Sozialdemokrat[5b]
socialist 6.1
Sozialdemokratie[4a]
social democracy ... 5.3
sozialdemokratisch[4a]
socialist 6.1
spähen
spy 5.1
Spalier
trellis 9.4
spanisch[3a]
French .... 1.
spannen[3b]
extend .... 1.
Spannung[4b]
strain 4.1
suspension 5.8
in –, (in) suspense ... 6.
sparen[4b]
save (up) 2.1
sparsam[6b]
saving 1.8
Spaß[4a]
– haben, (have) fun .. 2.9
joke 2.9
spät[1a]
late .... 1.
-er, by and by 1.1
spätestens[6a]
late .... 1.
Spatz
sparrow .... 6.
spazieren[4b]
walk .... 1.
Spaziergang[4b]
walk 2.4
Spaziergänger
walker 7.6
Specht
woodpecker 7.2
Speck
bacon 6.1
speien
spit 5.9
Speise[3a]
food 1.9
Speisekammer
pantry 6.2
speisen[5a]
dine 3.1
Spekulation[3b]
speculation 5.3
spenden[5b]
contribute 3.2
Sperling
sparrow .... 6.
Sperre
embargo 10.6
sperren[5a]
block up .... 4.
Spezialität
specialty 8.8

Section

speziell[2b]
above all .... 1.
special 1.8
spezifisch[5b]
special 1.8
specific 5.8
spezifizieren
limit 5.1
specify 8.9
Sphäre[6b]
sphere 4.4
Spiegel[3a]
mirror 2.8
spiegeln[6a]
reflect 4.3
Spiegelung
reflection 5.4
Spiel[2a]
game 1.5
spielen[1b]
play .... 1.
Spieler
player .... 6.
spielerisch
playful 7.4
Spielmann
minstrel 7.2
Spielplatz
playground .... 6.
Spielzeug
toy 5.1
Spindel
spindle 6.6
Spinne
spider .... 6.
spinnen[5b]
spin 3.9
Spion
spy 5.4
Spirale
spiral 7.6
Spiritus[5a]
liquor 4.3
Spitze[1b]
point 1.2
top 1.3
tip 1.4
lace 2.1
spitzen[6a]
gespitzt, pointed 3.3
sharpen 4.7
Spitzname
nickname 8.6
Spontaneität
spontaneity 10.2
Spore
spur 5.8
Sport
sport 5.1
sportlich
sport 5.3
Spott[4b]
fun 3.1
mockery 4.8
spotten[4b]
(make) fun (of) 2.8
Sprache[1a]
tongue .... 1.
language 1.6
sprechen[1a]
speak .... 1.
talk .... 1.
sprengen[4b]
sprinkle 3.7
Sprichwort[5b]
proverb 4.9
sprießen
sprout 6.2

Section

springen[2a]
spring 1.5
crack 2.6
spritzen
splash 6.6
Sproß
shoot 5.4
Spruch[4b]
saying 2.9
device 4.2
Sprung[4b]
spring 2.6
crack 3.4
Spur[2b]
step .... 2.
trace 2.1
track 2.1
spüren[5b]
feel .... 1.
Staat[1a]
state (nation) .... 1.
staatlich[3a]
state 1.8
Staatsanwalt[6a]
attorney-general ... 9.5
Staatskasse[6b]
treasury 5.6
Staatsmann[4a]
statesman .... 3.
Staatsrat[6a]
council 2.1
Staatsregierung[2a]
government 1.1
Staatssekretär[6a]
secretary of state ... 3.9
Staatssteuer[6a]
tax 1.6
Stab[3a]
stick .... 2.
wand 3.2
Stadium[5a]
state (condition) ... 1.
Stadt[1a]
city .... 1.
Städtchen[5a]
city .... 1.
Städteordnung[6a]
statute 4.1
städtisch[3b]
city 2.3
staffeln
echelon .... 13.
Stahl[4b]
steel 3.1
Stall[5b]
stable 3.8
Stamm[2b]
trunk (of tree) 2.3
tribe 2.5
stem 2.7
stammen[3a]
come from .... 1.
Stand[1a]
place .... 1.
standhaft[6b]
firm (character) 1.1
ständig[5b]
constant 2.4
permanent 4.2
Standpunkt[2a]
point of view .... 1.
Stange[5a]
post .... 3.
bar 3.5
stark[1a]
strong .... 1.

Section

Stärke[2b]
force .... 1.
intensity .... 4.
stärken[3b]
strengthen 3.4
starr[4a]
stiff 3.2
Starre
stiffness 9.3
starren[6a]
peer 3.5
Station[3b]
stop 2.6
stage 3.6
Statistik[4a]
statistics 6.1
statistisch[4b]
statistics 6.1
statt[1a]
instead .... 1.
Statt[6b]
place .... 1.
Stätte[4a]
place .... 1.
stattfinden[1b]
(take) place .... 1.
Statthalter[5a]
governor 3.1
stattlich[4a]
grand 2.3
stately 3.6
Statue[5b]
statue 3.6
Statut[3b]
statute 4.1
Staub[3a]
dust 1.9
staubig
dusty 6.1
staunen[5a]
astonish 2.7
stechen[5b]
sting 3.5
Stechpalme
holly 7.2
stecken[2a]
place .... 1.
stehen[1a]
stand .... 1.
in Briefwechsel –
correspond .... 4.
stehlen[4a]
rob 2.3
steif[5b]
stiff 3.2
Steigbügel
stirrup .... 7.
steigen[1b]
go up .... 1.
steigern[2a]
lift .... 1.
Steigerung[3b]
increase 2.3
steil[4a]
steep 2.8
Stein[2a]
stone 1.4
steinern[6a]
(of) stone .... 3.
stony .... 6.
Steinkohle[6b]
coal 1.9
Stelle[1a]
place .... 1.
stellen[1a]
anheim –, allow .... 1.
place .... 1.

Section

Symbol
symbol 5.6
Sympathie[4b]
sympathy 2.8
sympathisch[5b]
like . . . . 1.
Symptom
symptom 7.7
Syndikat
syndicate 9.3
synthetisch
synthetic 8.6
System[1b]
system 1.6
systematisch[5b]
systematic 6.9
Szene[2b]
scene 1.8
set-up 10.6
Szenerie
set-up 10.6
Szepter
scepter 5.9

T

Tabak[5a]
tobacco 3.9
Tabelle[5b]
index 5.3
Tablett
tray 6.6
Tadel[5a]
reproach 2.7
blame 3.2
tadeln[3b]
blame 2.8
Tafel[2b]
table . . . . 1.
board 1.7
slab 4.1
Täfelung
woodwork 8.9
Tag[1a]
day . . . . 1.
der nächste –
day after . . . . 1.
eines -es
sometime . . . . 1.
guten –, good morning 1.1
am – vorher
day before 1.4
Tagebuch[5b]
journal 4.2
Tageslicht
daylight 4.6
Tagesordnung[4b]
program 4.2
täglich[1b]
daily 1.6
Takt[6a]
time (music) 3.2
Taktik[6a]
method 2.5
taktisch[5b]
tactical 11.7
taktlos
indiscreet 8.3
Taktlosigkeit
indiscretion . . . . 9.
Tal[2b]
valley 1.7
Talent[2b]
talent 2.4
Taler[2b]
pound . . . . 1.
Tank
tank 6.1

Section

Tanne
pine 4.9
fir 5.9
Tantchen[4a]
aunt . . . . 2.
Tante[2b]
aunt . . . . 2.
Tanz[5a]
dance 3.1
tanzen[4a]
dance 2.4
Tänzerin
dancer 6.9
tapfer[3a]
(be) brave . . . . 1.
Tapferkeit[4b]
courage 1.4
Tarif[4b]
fare 3.6
Tarnung
disguise 5.8
Tasche[3b]
pocket 2.3
case 2.5
Taschenbuch
note book 4.9
Taschentuch
handkerchief 4.5
Tasse
cup 4.3
tasten
grope 6.5
Tat[1a]
act . . . . 1.
in der –, (in) fact . . . . 1.
tätig[2b]
active 2.6
Tätigkeit[1b]
activity 3.3
Tatsache[1b]
fact . . . . 1.
tatsächlich[2a]
real . . . . 1.
actual 2.1
Tau[6b]
dew 3.9
taub
deaf 4.8
Taube[6a]
dove 4.4
pigeon 4.8
tauchen[4a]
dip 3.2
dive 4.2
Taufe[5a]
baptism 5.5
taufen[5a]
baptize . . . . 6.
taugen[6a]
fit . . . . 1.
täuschen[2b]
deceive 1.9
disappoint 2.9
Täuschung[3b]
deceit 3.9
tausend[2a]
thousand 1.4
Tausend[3b]
thousand 1.4
Technik[4b]
technique 6.6
technisch[3a]
technical 4.7
Tee[5b]
tea 4.1
Teer
tar 6.4

Section

Teig
dough 6.2
Teil[1a]
part . . . . 1.
– nehmen
(take an) interest 1.3
teilen[1b]
divide 1.1
Teilnahme[2b]
share . . . . 2.
teilnehmen[3b]
(take) part 1.4
Teilnehmer[6a]
participant . . . . 10.
teils[1b]
(in) part . . . . 1.
Teilung[5b]
division 3.8
teilweise[2b]
(in) part . . . . 1.
Telegramm[5a]
wire 3.5
Telegraph[6b]
telegraph 4.9
telegraphisch[6a]
telegraph 5.3
Teller[6a]
plate 2.5
Tempel[2b]
temple 2.1
Temperament[6b]
temper 4.2
Temperatur[3a]
temperature . . . . 3.
tempern
temper 4.9
Tempo[5b]
rate 3.4
Tendenz[3b]
leaning 1.8
tend 2.4
tendency 3.2
Tennis
tennis 6.8
Teppich[6a]
carpet 4.2
tapestry 5.8
Termin[3b]
term 2.2
Termingeschäft[5a]
business . . . . 1.
Terminhandel[3a]
business . . . . 1.
Terrain[4a]
grounds 2.4
Terrasse
terrace 6.7
Testament[4a]
will 3.1
teuer[1b]
dear (in affection) . . 1.
dear (costly) 1.1
Teufel[2a]
der –!, Heavens! . . . . . 1.
devil 1.9
rascal 4.2
teuflisch
devilish 7.4
Text[3a]
text 3.1
Theater[2a]
theatre 1.9
Theater-
theatre 4.6
Theaterkobold[6a]
elf . . . . 6.

Section

Thema[4b]
theme . . . . 4.
theologisch[6b]
theological 7.2
theoretisch[3b]
theoretical 5.9
Theorie[2b]
theory 3.3
Thermometer
thermometer 6.6
Thron[2b]
throne 2.3
Thymian
thyme 8.6
Ticktack
tick tock 7.2
tief[1a]
deep . . . . 1.
Tiefe[2a]
depth 2.6
Tier[1b]
animal 1.1
beast 1.1
tierisch[5b]
animal 2.7
Tiger
tiger 5.8
Tinte
ink 5.1
Tintenfaß
inkwell 8.9
Tisch[1b]
table . . . . 1.
– decken, set table . . . 1.1
Tischtuch
table-cloth 9.1
Titel[2b]
title 1.8
toben[5b]
rage 3.7
Tochter[1b]
daughter . . . . 1.
Tod[1a]
death . . . . 1.
Todesangst
in –, (in) anguish 6.3
tödlich[4b]
mortal 2.9
toll[4a]
mad 2.7
– machen, (make) mad 2.9
Tomate
tomato 6.4
Ton (*tone*)[1b]
sound 1.2
tone 1.4
accent 2.4
Ton (*clay*)[4b]
clay 3.4
tönen[5a]
ring 1.4
Tonnage
tonnage 7.2
Tonne[3a]
barrel 3.6
ton 3.7
cask 5.3
Topf[6b]
pot 2.3
Tor (*m.*)[3b]
fool 2.4
Tor (*neutr.*)[3b]
gate 1.4
porch 2.7
Torheit[4a]
folly 3.2

Section

übermäßig[5a]
extreme ... 1.5
excessive ... 4.6
übermenschlich
superhuman ... 9.4
übermorgen
day after tomorrow ... 4.3
Übermut[6a]
im –, haughty ... 4.7
übermütig[6b]
haughty ... 4.7
Übernahme[6a]
assumption ... 6.2
übernatürlich
supernatural ... 8.4
übernehmen[1b]
assume ... 2.8
überraschen[2a]
surprise ... 1.4
Überraschung[4b]
surprise ... 2.4
überreden[7a]
persuade ... 2.1
überreichen[3b]
hand ... 1.8
Überrest[6a]
rest ... 1.1
Überrock
frock coat ... 6.1
überschreiten[2b]
exceed ... 2.3
Überschuß[3a]
excess ... 3.3
überschwemmen
flood ... 4.7
übersehen[2b]
neglect ... 2.
übersehen
survey ... 5.8
übersenden[5a]
transfer ... 2.4
transport ... 3.9
übersetzen[4a]
translate ... 3.8
Übersetzung[3b]
translation ... 5.
Übersicht[5a]
survey ... 4.9
übersteigen[4a]
exceed ... 2.3
übertragen[2a]
transfer ... 2.4
Übertragung[4a]
translation ... 5.
übertreffen[4a]
exceed ... 2.3
(be) ahead (of) ... 2.7
(have the) advantage ... 3.
surpass ... 4.6
übertreiben[4a]
exaggerate ... 4.5
Übertreibung[6a]
exaggeration ... 7.7
überwältigen[4b]
overcome ... 2.4
überweisen[2a]
transfer ... 2.4
remit ... 3.6
consign ... 5.
Überweisung[3a]
transfer ... 4.
überwiegen[3b]
prevail ... 3.2
überwinden[2b]
overcome ... 2.4

Section

überzeugen[1b]
convince ... 2.
persuade ... 2.1
Überzeugung[1b]
der festen – sein
convince ... 2.
conviction ... 4.2
überziehen[4a]
cover ... 1.
üblich[3a]
usual ... 1.
übrig[1a]
rest ... 1.1
Übrige[3b]
rest ... 1.1
bits ... 2.3
übrigens[1b]
(in) addition ... 1.4
Übung[2b]
exercise ... 1.7
Ufer[2a]
bank ... 1.5
Uhr[1a]
time (o'clock) ... 1.
clock ... 1.3
watch ... 1.3
Ulme
elm ... 5.7
um[1a]
– . . . . zu
(in) order (to) ... 1.
around ... 1.1
– . . . . willen
sake ... 1.8
umarmen[4a]
embrace ... 3.
clasp ... 3.1
Umarmung
embrace ... 5.2
Umfang[2a]
compass ... 2.5
umfangreich[5a]
extensive ... 4.9
umfassen[2a]
include ... 2.1
Umgang[3a]
connection ... 2.9
umgeben[2a]
surround ... 1.8
Umgebung[3a]
neighborhood ... 2.9
circuit ... 3.9
Umgegend[6a]
neighborhood ... 2.9
umgehen[3a]
escape ... 1.8
go round ... 1.8
Umgestaltung[6b]
change ... 2.9
umher[3a]
around ... 1.6
umkehren[2b]
turn round ... 1.4
umgekehrt
(wrong) side ... 1.7
invert ... 3.9
Umlauf[5b]
in – setzen
send forth ... 3.4
circulation ... 5.4
umranden
border ... 5.1
umringen[6b]
surround ... 1.8
Umriß[5b]
outline ... 4.8
Umsatz[6b]
sale ... 2.4

Section

Umschlag
envelope ... 5.6
umschließen[5b]
shut in ... 1.9
umsehen[6a]
look at ... 1.
umsomehr[7a]
(so) much ... 3.6
umsonst[3b]
free (of charge) ... 2.6
Umstand[1a]
condition ... 1.
event ... 1.4
ceremony ... 2.
umständlich[5b]
minute ... 3.1
(in) detail ... 3.6
Umstellung
shift ... 5.7
Umsturz
upset ... 6.3
umwandeln[5b]
transform ... 2.8
Umwandlung[5a]
change ... 2.9
Umweg[5b]
ohne –, direct ... 1.1
detour ... 8.1
Umzug
shift ... 5.7
unabhängig[3a]
independent ... 2.5
Unabhängigkeit[5a]
independence ... 3.6
unablässig[6a]
continual ... 2.5
unangenehm[3a]
unpleasant ... 3.8
unaufhaltsam[6b]
continual ... 2.5
unaufhörlich[4b]
continual ... 2.5
unausgesetzt[5b]
constant ... 2.4
unbedeutend[3a]
insignificant ... 4.
trivial ... 5.
unbedingt[2a]
absolute ... 1.8
unbefangen[4b]
simple ... 2.2
unbegreiflich[4b]
incomprehensible ... 6.7
unbekannt[2a]
unknown ... 1.8
unbemerkt[5a]
unseen ... 4.8
unbequem[5a]
uncomfortable ... 4.6
unberechtigt[6a]
(without) authority ... 4.8
unberührt[6b]
virgin ... 4.1
intact ... 7.3
unbeschränkt[5b]
boundless ... 4.9
unbeschreiblich[6b]
indescribable ... 7.2
unbesiegbar
invincible ... 7.3
unbesiegt
unconquered ... 8.6
unbeständig
fickle ... 6.5
unbestimmt[5a]
vague ... 4.

Section

unbeweglich[6a]
stable ... 2.9
unbewußt[5a]
unconscious ... 4.4
unbrauchbar[6a]
– sein, (of no) use ... 1.8
und[1a]
and ... 1.
– so weiter, etc. ... 3.1
undankbar[6b]
ungrateful ... 4.9
Undankbarkeit
ingratitude ... 7.
undurchsichtig
opaque ... 7.8
uneigennützig
unselfish ... 8.6
unendlich[2a]
endless ... 3.
unentbehrlich[3b]
essential ... 2.9
unentgeltlich[6b]
free (of charge) ... 2.6
unentschieden
undecided ... 9.2
unentschlossen
irresolute ... 8.1
unerbittlich
implacable ... 7.7
unerheblich[6a]
insignificant ... 4.
unerhört[5a]
unusual ... 2.
unheard of ... 5.3
unerklärlich
inexplicable ... 8.7
unerläßlich[5b]
essential ... 2.9
unermeßlich[5b]
infinite ... 3.5
unermüdlich[5b]
untiring ... 7.2
unerreichbar
(out of) reach ... 4.1
unerschöpflich[6b]
abundant ... 4.2
inexhaustible ... 8.7
unerträglich[4b]
intolerable ... 5.3
unerwartet[3b]
unexpected ... 3.5
unfähig[5b]
unable ... 4.1
Unfähigkeit
impotence ... 8.7
Unfall[3b]
accident ... 2.3
disaster ... 3.9
unfehlbar
infallible ... 7.7
unfreundlich
unkind ... 6.1
unfruchtbar
barren ... 5.3
Unfruchtbarkeit
barrenness ... 9.4
ungarisch[5b]
Hungarian ... 6.6
ungeachtet[4b]
however ... 1.
Ungeduld[5a]
impatience ... 5.3
ungeduldig[5a]
impatient ... 4.3
ungefähr[2a]
about (approximately) ... 1.
almost ... 1.

Section

unverzüglich[6b]
- (at) once ... 1.
- immediate ... 2.8

unvollkommen[5b]
- imperfect ... 4.2

unvollständig
- unfinished ... 6.9

unvorsichtig
- careless ... 5.2
- imprudent ... 10.

unwahrscheinlich[6a]
- doubtful ... 2.6
- improbable ... 7.9

unwiderstehlich[5b]
- irresistible ... 5.4

Unwille[5a]
- anger ... 1.9
- indignation ... 4.2
- grudge ... 4.6

unwillkommen
- unwelcome ... 7.2

unwillkürlich[4a]
- instinctive ... 4.9
- involuntary ... 5.4

unwissend
- ignorant ... 5.

Unwissenheit[6b]
- ignorance ... 4.6

unwürdig[5a]
- unworthy ... 4.7

unzählig[4a]
- countless ... 3.9

unzertrennlich
- inseparable ... 6.8

unzufrieden[5b]
- unhappy ... 1.8
- discontent(ed) ... 4.6

Unzufriedenheit[5b]
- discontent ... 4.8

unzweifelhaft[3b]
- (without) doubt ... 1.

üppig[5a]
- sumptuous ... 5.

uralt[5a]
- old ... 1.

Urheber[4a]
- author ... 1.5

Urkunde[4b]
- act ... 2.3

Urlaub[5b]
- leave ... 2.9

Ursache[1b]
- cause ... 1.
- reason ... 1.

Ursprung[3b]
- source ... 2.7

ursprünglich[2a]
- original ... 2.3

Urteil[1b]
- judgment ... 1.5
- sentence ... 2.

urteilen[4a]
- judge ... 1.
- reason ... 3.

V

Valuta[5b]
- currency ... 4.9

Vasall
- vassal ... 6.6

Vater[1a]
- father ... 1.

Vaterland[1b]
- country ... 1.1

vaterländisch[5a]
- national ... 2.

Section

Vaterlandsliebe
- patriotism ... 6.5

väterlich[4a]
- paternal ... 4.8

Vaterschaft
- fatherhood ... 11.4

Vaterstadt[5b]
- (home) town ... 3.3

Vegetation
- vegetation ... 7.2

Veilchen
- violet ... 5.2

verabreden[5b]
- agree ... 2.2

Verabredung[6b]
- agreement ... 3.1
- appointment (to meet) ... 4.5
- engagement ... 4.7

verabreichen
- dispense ... 5.9

verachten[3b]
- scorn ... 2.9

verächtlich[5a]
- scornful ... 5.1

Verachtung[4a]
- scorn ... 3.3

verallgemeinern
- generalize ... 9.3

veränderlich
- changing ... 4.6

verändern[2a]
- change ... 1.4

Veränderung[2a]
- change ... 1.5

veranlagt[6b]
- predisposed ... 9.3

Veranlagung[5a]
- ability ... 3.2

veranlassen[2a]
- cause ... 1.
- (give) rise to ... 2.3

Veranlassung[2b]
- cause ... 1.

veranstalten[5a]
- organize ... 3.7

verantwortlich[4b]
- responsible ... 4.3

Verantwortlichkeit[5a]
- responsibility ... 5.1

Verantwortung[5a]
- responsibility ... 5.1

verarbeiten[6a]
- use ... 1.
- digest ... 6.2

verargen
- (bear) grudge ... 5.6

Verband[3a]
- organization ... 3.5
- bandage ... 5.3

verbannen[5b]
- banish ... 4.1

Verbannte
- exile ... 5.6

Verbannung
- exile ... 6.

verbergen[1b]
- hide ... 1.

verbessern[3a]
- improve ... 2.4
- correct ... 2.7

Verbesserung[2b]
- improvement ... 3.6
- correction ... 3.7

verbieten[2b]
- forbid ... 2.

Section

verbinden[1a]
- join ... 1.
- join (with) ... 1.9
- combine ... 2.3

verbindlich[6a]
- required ... 3.1

Verbindlichkeit[4b]
- obligation ... 4.

Verbindung[1a]
- union ... 1.6

verbleiben[3a]
- persist ... 3.8

Verbot[4b]
- prohibition ... 5.

Verbrauch
- consumption ... 7.2

verbrauchen[5b]
- wear out ... 2.8
- use up ... 2.9

Verbrechen[2b]
- crime ... 2.4

Verbrecher[5b]
- criminal ... 4.5

verbreiten[2a]
- spread ... 1.4
- diffuse ... 3.5

Verbreitung[3b]
- development ... 2.1

verbrennen[4a]
- burn ... 1.6

Verbrennung[5b]
- combustion ... 6.

verbringen[6b]
- spend ... 2.2

verbündet[4b]
- allied ... 5.2

Verbündete[6a]
- ally ... 6.4

Verdacht[3b]
- im – haben, suspect ... 2.8
- suspicion ... 4.

verdächtig[4b]
- suspect ... 4.3

verdammen[4b]
- damn ... 4.2

verdanken[2b]
- owe ... 1.8
- indebted ... 4.2

Verdauung
- digestion ... 7.4

verdecken[6a]
- hide ... 1.

verderben[3a]
- spoil ... 2.6
- warp ... 3.5

Verderben[3b]
- ruin ... 2.4

verderblich[5a]
- mortal ... 2.9
- ruinous ... 6.5

verdienen[1b]
- gain ... 1.
- deserve ... 1.5

Verdienst[2a]
- profit ... 2.1

verdoppeln[7a]
- double ... 4.2
- double (effort) ... 4.3

verdrängen[4b]
- suppress ... 3.7

verdrießen[6b]
- vex ... 4.1

verdrießlich[5a]
- unpleasant ... 3.8
- grievous ... 4.

Verdruß[5a]
- disappointment ... 4.4

Section

verdunkeln
- obscure ... 6.

verdünnen[5b]
- weaken ... 4.8

verehren[2b]
- honor ... 1.7
- reverence ... 2.7

Verehrung[4a]
- worship ... 3.6

Verein[1b]
- company (social) ... 1.
- club ... 1.6

vereinbaren[5a]
- agree ... 2.2
- reconcile ... 4.6

Vereinbarung[5a]
- agreement ... 3.1

vereinen[3b]
- unite ... 1.

vereinigen[1b]
- unite ... 1.
- vereinigt, united ... 1.5

Vereinigung[2b]
- union ... 1.6

vereinzelt[5b]
- rare ... 1.4
- cut off ... 2.9

Verfahren[1b]
- process ... 1.7

verfahren[3a]
- proceed ... 2.
- stray ... 3.1

Verfall[5a]
- destruction ... 4.2
- decay ... 4.3

verfallen[3b]
- (grow) weak ... 2.4
- fall to pieces ... 2.6
- spoil ... 2.6

verfassen[4b]
- compose ... 2.6

Verfasser[1b]
- author ... 1.5

Verfassung[2a]
- constitution ... 2.7

verfehlen[4a]
- miss ... 1.

verfeinern
- refine ... 5.5

Verfeinerung
- refinement ... 6.6

verfertigen[6a]
- manufacture ... 3.

verfinstern
- eclipse ... 7.

verfließen[5a]
- pass ... 2.6
- expire ... 4.3

verfluchen
- curse ... 4.6

verfolgen[1b]
- pursue ... 1.5
- persecute ... 3.2

Verfolgung[3a]
- pursuit ... 3.4
- persecution ... 4.2

verfügen[3a]
- decree ... 3.

Verfügung[2a]
- decree ... 2.6

verführen[5b]
- corrupt ... 4.7
- seduce ... 4.8

Verführung
- seduction ... 12.9

Vergangenheit[3a]
- past ... 1.9
- past (tense) ... 2.2

Section

Versicherer[5a]
insurer ... 12.
versichern[1b]
assure ... 1.4
Versicherung[2a]
insurance ... 3.3
versinken[5a]
sink ... 3.2
versöhnen[5a]
reconcile ... 4.7
Versöhnung[6b]
reconcile ... 4.7
conciliation ... 7.8
versorgen[5b]
supply ... 1.1
versprechen[1b]
promise ... 1.
pledge ... 2.7
Versprechen[4b]
promise ... 2.7
Verstaatlichung[6a]
nationalization ... 12.4
Verstand[2a]
understanding ... 1.7
verständig[3a]
reasonable ... 3.4
intelligent ... 3.6
Verständigung[4b]
agreement ... 3.1
verständlich[4a]
evident ... 2.5
Verständnis[2b]
understanding ... 1.7
verstärken[2b]
strengthen ... 3.4
Verstärkung[4b]
reinforcement ... 7.6
verstecken[5a]
hide ... 1.
verstehen[1a]
understand ... 1.
versteifen
(make) stiff ... 4.9
Verstellung
pretense ... 6.5
verstimmt
sullen ... 5.8
verstorben[4a]
dead ... 1.4
Verstorbene[6b]
dead ... 1.4
verstoßen[6b]
offend ... 2.8
verstummen[5a]
(become) dumb ... 4.
Versuch[1b]
attempt ... 1.8
experiment ... 2.6
versuchen[1b]
try ... 1.
experiment ... 2.4
Versuchung[4a]
temptation ... 4.4
vertauschen[6b]
exchange ... 3.5
verteidigen[2b]
defend ... 1.4
Verteidiger[4b]
attorney ... 4.7
defender ... 6.8
Verteidigung[3a]
defense ... 2.8
verteilen[2b]
divide ... 1.1
distribute ... 3.3
Verteilung[3a]
distribution ... 3.7

Section

vertiefen[5a]
vertieft, absorbed ... 3.
deepen ... 5.
Vertiefung[5b]
depth ... 2.6
Vertrag[1b]
contract ... 2.3
treaty ... 2.6
vertragen[4b]
bear ... 1.
vertragsmäßig[5b]
agreed ... 2.8
Vertrauen[1b]
trust ... 1.
vertrauen[2b]
– auf, count on ... 1.
trust ... 1.4
vertraulich[5b]
familiar ... 3.3
confidential ... 6.6
Vertrautheit
intimacy ... 6.8
vertreiben[3a]
drive away ... 2.3
expel ... 4.3
vertreten[2a]
represent ... 1.4
Vertreter[2a]
agent ... 2.9
Vertretung[3b]
representation ... 3.5
verursachen[3a]
cause ... 1.
verurteilen[3b]
sentence ... 2.3
condemn ... 2.7
vervielfältigen
multiply ... 5.1
Vervielfältigung
multiplication ... 7.
Vervollkommnung[6a]
perfection ... 3.4
verwahren[6a]
preserve ... 3.
verwalten[5a]
manage ... 2.2
Verwalter[4a]
director ... 2.8
superintendent ... 5.
manager ... 5.
Verwaltung[2a]
direction ... 1.8
Verwaltungs-
administrative ... 9.2
verwandeln[2a]
transform ... 2.8
Verwandtschaft[5a]
relation (relative) ... 2.3
relation (family relationship) ... 4.2
verwandt[3a]
relation ... 2.3
Verwandte[3b]
relation ... 2.3
verweigern[3b]
refuse ... 2.3
verweilen[4a]
delay ... 2.
verweisen[3b]
reproach ... 2.8
refer (to) ... 3.1
verwelken
fade ... 4.9
verwenden[1b]
use ... 1.
Verwendung[2a]
use ... 1.1

Section

verwerfen[3b]
reject ... 3.2
warp ... 3.5
verwerten[5a]
use ... 1.
Verwertung[5b]
use ... 1.1
verwickeln[4a]
involve ... 3.9
Verwick(e)lung[6b]
difficulty ... 1.9
complication ... 7.2
verwirklichen[5b]
realize ... 3.5
Verwirklichung[6b]
realization ... 6.4
verwirren[3b]
confound ... 3.1
verwirrt, confused ... 3.2
perplex ... 3.6
(make) dizzy ... 4.4
entangle ... 4.4
Verwirrung[4b]
confusion ... 3.2
tangle ... 5.6
verwunden[3b]
wound ... 2.2
verwundern[4a]
astonish ... 2.7
Verwunderung[4b]
surprise ... 2.4
Verwundete[5b]
wounded ... 3.3
verwüsten
waste ... 4.9
verzehren[4a]
devour ... 3.8
verzeichnen[4b]
register ... 3.
Verzeichnis[5b]
list ... 2.9
verzeihen[3a]
pardon ... 2.2
Verzeihung[6a]
pardon ... 3.6
verzerren
distort ... 7.5
Verzicht[5b]
– leisten, renounce ... 3.1
verzichten[3a]
do without ... 2.1
renounce ... 3.1
verziehen
spoil ... 4.6
verzieren[6b]
trim ... 2.4
Verzierung[6a]
trimming ... 3.8
verzögern[4b]
delay ... 2.7
Verzögerung[6b]
delay ... 3.8
verzweifeln[3b]
despair ... 2.8
verzweifelt
desperate ... 2.8
Verzweiflung[3a]
despair ... 3.
Veteran
veteran ... 7.2
Vetter[3b]
cousin ... 2.4
Vibration
vibration ... 7.6
Vicomte
viscount ... 8.4
Vieh[5b]
cattle ... 3.7

Section

viel[1a]
-e, many ... 1.
much ... 1.
vielfach[1b]
several times ... 1.2
multiple ... 4.8
vielleicht[1a]
perhaps ... 1.
vielmehr[1b]
rather ... 1.
vier[1b]
four ... 1.
viereckig[6b]
square ... 3.4
vierte[2b]
fourth ... 1.6
Viertel[5b]
quarter (of town) ... 2.5
quarter ... 2.6
vierundzwanzig
twenty-four ... 4.7
vierzehn[4a]
fourteen ... 3.4
vierzig[4b]
forty ... 2.9
Villa[6b]
country house ... 3.3
violett
violet (color) ... 5.5
Violin-
treble ... 6.8
Viper
viper ... 7.
Vizekönig
viceroy ... 8.6
Vizepräsident[5b]
vice-president ... 9.8
Vlies
fleece ... 6.4
Vogel[4a]
bird ... 2.3
Vogt[6b]
constable ... 6.2
Volant
ruffle ... 6.1
Volk[1a]
people (race) ... 1.
people (common) ... 1.
Volksschule[4a]
school ... 1.
Volksvertretung[6b]
House of Representatives ... 3.4
voll[1a]
full ... 1.
vollbringen[4b]
carry out ... 1.
vollenden[1b]
complete ... 1.
vollends[4a]
all ... 1.
Vollendung[3b]
perfection ... 3.4
völlig[1b]
complete ... 1.
fully ... 2.2
vollkommen[1b]
complete ... 1.
perfect ... 1.
– gleich, identical ... 3.5
Vollkommenheit[5a]
perfection ... 3.4
vollständig[1b]
complete ... 1.
-vollstrecker (e.g., Testaments-)
executor ... 7.7

W

Section

Wagen[2b]
- car (carriage) 1.5
- car (railroad) 2.
- car (tram) 2.1
- automobile 2.2
- chariot 2.6
- cart 2.7
- cab 3.9

wagerecht
- horizontal 6.5

Wahl[1b]
- choice 1.6
- election 2.1

Wahl-
- electoral 8.4

wählen[1b]
- choose 1.
- vote 1.8

Wähler[4b]
- voter 4.6

Wahlrecht[4a]
- suffrage 5.1

Wahn[5a]
- illusion 4.7

wähnen[5b]
- suppose 1.

Wahnsinn[5b]
- fury 2.8
- madness 4.1

wahr[1a]
- true 1.

Wahre[6a]
- truth 1.

währen[1b]
- last 1.1

während[1a]
- during 1.
- while 1.

wahrhaft[3a]
- true 1.
- genuine 3.7

wahrhaftig[3b]
- true 1.
- really 1.4
- genuine 3.7

Wahrheit[1a]
- truth 1.

wahrlich[3a]
- indeed 1.

wahrnehmen[3a]
- (catch) sight of 1.1

Wahrnehmung[4b]
- observation 2.4

Wahrsager
- (fortune) teller 7.

wahrscheinlich[1b]
- probable 1.7

Wahrscheinlichkeit[4a]
- chances 3.3

Währung[6a]
- currency 4.9

Waise
- orphan 5.6

Wal(fisch)
- whale 7.1

Wald[1b]
- forest 1.

Waldung[6a]
- forest 1.

Wall[5b]
- dam 4.7
- rampart 6.4

Walnuß
- walnut 6.3

walten[3b]
- rule 1.

Walze[5b]
- cylinder 4.9

wälzen[5b]
- roll 2.3

Wand[2a]
- wall 1.4

Wandel[5a]
- change 1.5

wandeln[3a]
- change 1.4

Wanderer[6a]
- tramp 4.9
- tourist 6.9

wandern[3b]
- wander 2.7

Wanderung[5a]
- excursion 4.1

Wandlung[6b]
- change 1.5

Wandtafel
- blackboard 5.8

Wange[3b]
- cheek 2.5

wanken[5a]
- waver 3.4

wann[2b]
- dann und – (at) times 1.
- when 1.

Wanne
- tub 6.2

Ware[1b]
- goods 1.5

warm[2a]
- warm 1.7

Wärme[2b]
- heat 1.5

warnen[3b]
- warn 2.2

Warnung[5a]
- warning 3.4

warten[1b]
- wait 1.

Warten
- wait 4.5

warum[1a]
- why 1.

was[1a]
- what 1.
- – . . . . auch, – immer whatever 1.5

Wäsche[6a]
- wash 3.3

waschen[4b]
- wash 2.6

Wasser[1a]
- water 1.

Wasser-
- water 5.

wasserdicht[6b]
- waterproof 6.8

Wasserfall
- waterfall 6.2

wässerig
- watery 7.2

wasserreich
- full 4.4

Wasserstoff[5a]
- hydrogen 6.

Wasserstraße[4b]
- water 1.

waten
- wade 7.1

watscheln
- sway 5.6

weben[6a]
- weave 4.6

Weber
- weaver 7.2

Wechsel[1b]
- exchange 2.

wechseln[2a]
- change 1.4

wecken[3a]
- wake (*tr. vb.*) 1.9

weder[1b]
- – . . . . noch neither . . . . nor 1.
- – der eine noch der andere neither (one) 1.

weg[2a]
- away 1.

Weg[1a]
- road 1.

wegen[1a]
- because of 1.

wegnehmen[6a]
- take away 1.

weh[3b]
- – tun, hurt (*intr. vb.*) 1.8
- alas 2.

wehen[2a]
- wave 1.7

Wehen
- waft 6.3

Wehmut[6b]
- melancholy (*n.*) 5.

wehmütig[6b]
- sad 1.4
- melancholy (*adj.*) 5.

wehren[4a]
- keep from 1.4

Weib[1b]
- woman 1.

weiblich[3a]
- female 3.3
- feminine 4.1

weich[2b]
- soft 1.5
- – machen, soften 3.1

weichen[2b]
- yield 1.9

Weide
- willow 5.6

weiden[6b]
- graze 5.

weigern[4b]
- refuse 2.3

Weihe[5a]
- solemnity 5.3
- consecration 5.8

weihen[4a]
- dedicate 2.7

Weihnacht[6a]
- Christmas 4.2

Weihrauch
- incense 6.1

weil[1a]
- because 1.

weilen[4b]
- sojourn 3.4

Weile[3b]
- while 1.8

Wein[1b]
- wine 1.4

Weinberg[6a]
- vineyard 5.1

weinen[2a]
- cry 1.4

Weise[1a]
- way 1.

weise[4a]
- wise 1.5

weisen[1b]
- direct 1.
- show 1.

Weisheit[2b]
- wisdom 2.3

weiß[1a]
- white 1.
- – werden, – machen (become, make) white 1.9

Weiß[6b]
- white 3.7

weißen[2b]
- (become) white 1.9

Weisung[5a]
- order 1.

weit[1a]
- far 1.
- und so -er, etc. 3.1

Weite[5a]
- distance 1.1

weiten[3b]
- increase 1.1
- enlarge 3.3

weitergehen[6a]
- go forward 1.4

weiterhin[6a]
- far 1.

weitgehend[4a]
- vast 2.8

Weitherzigkeit
- generosity 6.4

weithin[6b]
- far 1.

weitläufig[5b]
- vast 2.8

Weizen[4b]
- wheat 2.5

welch(-e)[1a]
- any (some) 1.
- which 1.

Welle[5a]
- wave (surge) 2.9
- wave (undulation) 3.8

Welt[1a]
- world 1.

Welt-
- world 4.9

Weltanschauung[6a]
- philosophy 3.3

Weltausstellung[6a]
- display 2.6

weltlich[4a]
- worldly 4.6
- secular 5.6

Weltteil[6b]
- continent 4.4

wenden[1a]
- turn 1.
- sich – an, turn to 1.1

wenig[1a]
- -e, (a) few 1.
- -ste, least 1.
- -er, less 1.
- little (*n.*) 1.

wenigstens[1a]
- (at) least 1.

wenn[1a]
- – auch, although 1.
- if 1.
- außer –, – nicht, unless 1.4
- – immer, whenever 1.4

wenngleich[5a]
- although 1.

wer[1a]
- who 1.
- wessen, whose 1.
- – immer, whoever 2.2

werben[5a]
- court 1.

Section

Wohnsitz[6a]
dwelling . . . 2.3

Wohnung[2a]
flat . . . 2.1
dwelling . . . 2.3

Wolf
wolf . . . 4.7

Wolke[3a]
cloud . . . 1.9

Wolle[4b]
wool . . . 2.8
aus –, wool . . . 2.8

wollen[1a]
want . . . 1.

wollüstig
voluptuous . . . 8.6

womit[2b]
with . . . 1.

womöglich[5b]
perhaps . . . 1.

wonach[3b]
after . . . 1.

Wonne[5b]
bliss . . . 3.7

woran[4a]
at . . . 1.

worauf[2a]
on . . . 1.
upon which . . . 1.6

woraus[4b]
from . . . 1.

worin[2a]
in . . . 1.

Wort[1a]
word . . . 1.

Wörterbuch
dictionary . . . 7.4

Wortlaut[5a]
text . . . 3.1

wörtlich[4b]
word for word . . . 2.2
oral . . . 5.4

worüber[4b]
above (*prep.*) . . . 1.

wovon[3a]
of . . . 1.

wozu[2b]
why . . . 1.

wringen
wring . . . 6.1

wund[6b]
– sein, (be) sore . . . 3.7

Wunde[4a]
wound . . . 2.8
sore . . . 3.3

Wunder[2a]
wonder . . . 1.7
miracle . . . 2.9

wunderbar[2b]
fine . . . 1.1
wonderful . . . 1.2
admirable . . . 3.1

wunderlich[3a]
strange . . . 1.
quaint . . . 3.5

wundern[3a]
sich –, wonder . . . 1.8

wundersam[6b]
wonderful . . . 1.2

wundervoll[6a]
wonderful . . . 1.2

Wunsch[1a]
desire . . . 1.

wünschen[1a]
desire . . . 1.

wünschenswert[3b]
desirable . . . 3.5

Section

Würde[2b]
dignity . . . 2.6

würdig[2a]
worthy . . . 1.8

würdigen[4b]
appreciate . . . 3.6

Würdigung[6a]
estimate . . . 3.8

Würfel[4b]
cube . . . 5.

Wurm
worm . . . 4.7

Wurst[6a]
sausage . . . 5.8

würtembergish[6a]
English . . . 1.

Wurzel[3a]
root . . . 2.6

wurzeln[5b]
(have) roots (in) . . . 4.2

würzen
season . . . 4.5

wüst[5b]
waste . . . 2.4

Wüste[4b]
waste . . . 2.4

Wut[3b]
anger . . . 1.9
fury . . . 2.8
Ausbruch von –
(fit of) anger . . . 3.

wüten[3b]
-d, angry . . . 2.4
-d werden
(get) angry . . . 2.4
rage . . . 3.2

Z

zäh[6b]
tough . . . 5.
tenacious . . . 8.

Zahl[1a]
number . . . 1.

zahlen[1b]
pay . . . 1.

zählen[2a]
count . . . 1.

zahllos[3a]
countless . . . 3.9

zahlreich[1b]
numerous . . . 1.5

Zahlung[1b]
payment . . . 2.5

Zahlungseinstellung[6a]
bankruptcy . . . 7.3

Zahlungsmittel[5b]
(legal) tender . . . 4.8
currency . . . 4.9

zähmen
tame . . . 5.6

Zahn[3b]
tooth . . . 2.3

Zange
tongs . . . 6.4

Zar[6a]
emperor . . . 2.1

zart[2b]
soft . . . 1.5
delicate . . . 2.3
dainty . . . 2.7

zärtlich[3a]
tender . . . 2.3

Zärtlichkeit[5b]
tenderness . . . 4.4

Zauber[4b]
magic . . . 3.5

Section

Zaun
fence . . . 4.8

Zaunkönig
wren . . . 6.8

Zeche[5b]
account . . . 1.

Zeder
cedar . . . 5.8

Zehe
toe . . . 4.6

zehn[2a]
ten . . . 1.4

zehnte[5b]
tenth . . . 4.1

Zeichen[1b]
sign . . . 1.1
– für, indicative . . . 4.6

zeichnen[1b]
mark . . . 1.
draw . . . 1.4
trace . . . 1.7

Zeichnung[3a]
design . . . 3.1

Zeigefinger[6b]
index finger . . . 6.3

zeigen[1a]
show . . . 1.

Zeile[2b]
line . . . 1.

Zeit[1a]
time (general) . . . 1.

Zeitalter[3b]
age . . . 1.8

Zeitgenosse[4b]
contemporary . . . 4.8

zeitig[5a]
early . . . 1.1

zeitlich[6a]
earthly . . . 3.1

Zeitpunkt[3a]
date . . . 2.

Zeitraum[3b]
period . . . 2.2

Zeitschrift[2b]
magazine . . . 3.
periodical . . . 3.9

Zeitung[1b]
paper (newspaper) . 1.

zeitweilig[6a]
(at) times . . . 1.

zeitweise[6b]
(at) times . . . 1.

Zeitwort
verb . . . 6.5

Zelle[6a]
cell . . . 4.6

Zelt[5a]
tent . . . 3.4

Zement
cement . . . 6.4

Zentimeter[4a]
inch . . . 2.7

Zentner[3b]
ton . . . 3.7

zentral
central . . . 4.5

Zentrum[3a]
center . . . 1.

zerbrechen[4b]
burst . . . 1.4
break (in pieces) . . . 2.3
crush . . . 3.
shatter . . . 4.2

zerbrechlich
frail . . . 5.1

zerfallen[4b]
fall to pieces . . . 2.6

Section

zerlegen[6b]
divide . . . 1.1

zerlumpt
ragged . . . 6.

zerreißen[3a]
tear . . . 1.8

zerschlagen[6b]
destroy . . . 1.5
crush . . . 3.

zersetzen[5b]
dissolve . . . 3.9

zerstören[2a]
destroy . . . 1.5

Zerstörung[5a]
destruction . . . 4.2

zerstreuen[3a]
scatter . . . 2.4
zerstreut, absent . . . 2.9
amuse . . . 3.5
distract . . . 3.6

Zerstreuung[6a]
spread . . . 4.1
pastime . . . 4.8

Zettel[5b]
bill . . . 3.5
– anschlagen
post bill . . . 3.5
slip . . . 3.5
label . . . 5.2

Zeug[3a]
cloth . . . 1.3

Zeuge[3a]
witness . . . 2.4

zeugen[3b]
beget . . . 3.4
testify . . . 4.1

Zeugnis[2a]
testimony . . . 3.1

Zickzack
zigzag . . . 7.2

Ziege
goat . . . 4.9

Ziegel
brick . . . 5.

ziehen[1a]
pull . . . 1.
Vorteil –, profit . . . 1.4
Bilanz –, balance . . . 3.2
auf sich –, incur . . . 3.6

Ziel[1a]
purpose . . . 1.

zielen[5b]
aim . . . 3.2

ziemen[4b]
proper . . . 1.4

ziemlich[1b]
pretty (moderately) 1.

zieren[5a]
trim . . . 2.4

zierlich[3b]
graceful . . . 3.3

Ziffer[4a]
figure . . . 1.1
number . . . 2.4

Zifferblatt
dial . . . 6.4

Zigarette
cigarette . . . 7.7

Zigarre[6a]
cigar . . . 5.1

Zigeuner
gypsy . . . 7.4

Zimmer[1b]
room (chamber) . . . 1.

Zimmermann
carpenter . . . 5.5

Zimt
cinnamon . . . 8.

Section

zusetzen[6a]
lose .... 1.

zusichern
pledge 2.7

Zustand[1a]
condition .... 1.
state (condition) ... 1.

zuständig[5b]
proper 1.4

zustehen[3b]
belong .... 1.

zustimmen[3b]
agree 2.2
consent 2.4

Zustimmung[2b]
consent 2.8

zuteilen[5a]
assign 2.5

Zutrauen[5b]
trust .... 1.

zutrauen[6b]
trust 1.4

zutreffen[3b]
-d, proper 1.4

Zutritt[5b]
access 4.9

zuverlässig[3b]
reliable 3.8

Zuverlässigkeit[6b]
reliability 7.7

Zuversicht[4a]
trust .... 1.

Section

zuvor[2b]
formerly 2.2

zuvörderst[5b]
(at) first .... 1.

zuvorkommen[6a]
(be) ahead (of) 2.7

zuweilen[2b]
sometimes 1.4

zuweisen[5b]
assign 2.5

zuwenden[3a]
turn to 1.1

zuwider[5b]
contrary 3.5

zuziehen[5b]
pull .... 1.

Zwang[3b]
ohne –, free .... 1.
pressure 3.4

zwanzig[3a]
twenty 1.9

zwanzigste
twentieth 7.1

zwar[1a]
indeed .... 1.
sure .... 1.

Zweck[1a]
purpose .... 1.

zweckmäßig[2b]
practical 2.2

Zweckverband[6a]
organization 3.5

Section

zwei[1a]
two .... 1.

zweierlei[6b]
different .... 1.

Zweifel[1b]
doubt .... 1.
ohne –
(without) doubt .. 1.

zweifelhaft[3a]
doubtful 2.6

zweifellos[3b]
(without) doubt .... 1.
unquestionable 6.5

zweifeln[2b]
doubt 1.5

Zweig[2a]
branch 1.6

zweijährig[6a]
year .... 1.

Zweikampf
duel .... 7.

zweimal[3b]
two times 1.8

zweite[1a]
second .... 1.

zweitens[4a]
(in the) second place 2.3

zweiundzwanzig
twenty-two 4.6

Zwerg
dwarf 6.1

Section

Zwetch(g)e
prune 6.4

Zwiebel
onion 5.6
bulb .... 6.

Zwietracht
discord .... 7.

Zwilling
twin 5.8

zwingen[1b]
force .... 1.
gezwungen, forced 1.1

zwinkern
wink 5.8

zwischen[1a]
among .... 1.
between .... 1.

Zwischenraum[5b]
interval 4.9

Zwischenzeit[6b]
in der –, meanwhile .. 2.8
recess 4.7

Zwitschern
twitter .... 7.

zwölf[3a]
twelve 1.9

zwölfte
twelfth 6.3

Zylinder[4a]
cylinder 4.9

Zypresse
cypress .... 7.

INDEX TO SPANISH WORDS IN THE LIST

(Read as directed for Index to French Words)

A

Section

a[1a]
  at . . . . 1.
  to . . . . 1.
abadejo
  wren 6.8
abadía
  abbey 6.9
abajo[1b]
  down . . . . 1.
  hacia –, downward(s) . 3.4
abandonar[1b]
  leave (desert) . . . . . . 1.
  -se
    give (oneself) up (to) 1.7
abandono[3a]
  abandon 5.4
abanico[5a]
  fan 3.9
abarcar[4a]
  clasp 3.1
abate[7a]
  abbot 6.5
abatir[3a]
  depress 4.9
abedul
  birch 6.4
abeja[3b]
  bee 4.1
aberración[6b]
  aberration 8.6
abertura[4a]
  opening (*n.*) 2.3
abeto
  fir 5.9
abismo[2b]
  abyss 4.1
ablandar[4a]
  soften 3.1
abnegación[5a]
  abnegation 10.9
abogado[3b]
  lawyer . . . . 3.
abolición
  abolition 5.3
abolir
  abolish 3.9
abombado
  bent . . . . 5.
abominable[6b]
  abominable 5.1
abonar[3a]
  pay . . . . 1.
abono[5a]
  pledge (*n.*) 2.9
  fertilizer 5.7
abordar[7a]
  take up 1.7
aborrecer[2a]
  hate 2.5
aborrecimiento[6a]
  hate (*n.*) 2.4
abrasar[4a]
  burn (*vb.*) 1.6

Section

abrazar[1b]
  embrace (*vb.*) . . . . . . 3.
abrazo[2b]
  embrace 5.2
abreviar[4b]
  shorten 4.8
abrigar[3a]
  shelter (*vb.*) 2.6
abrigo[4a]
  shelter (*n.*) 1.7
  coat 2.2
abril[2b]
  April 2.1
abrir[1a]
  open . . . . 1.
  -se, open (*intr. vb.*) . . . 2.2
  con brazos abiertos
    outstretched arms 3.
abrojo[5a]
  thorn 4.3
abrumar[4b]
  crush . . . . 3.
absoluto[1b]
  absolute 1.8
absolver[6b]
  pardon (*vb.*) 2.2
absorber[3b]
  absorb 5.7
absorto[4a]
  absorb . . . . 3.
abstenerse[5a]
  keep from 1.7
  refrain 4.1
abstracción
  abstraction . . . . 8.
abstracto[6b]
  abstract 6.5
absurdo[2b]
  absurd 3.7
abuelo[1b]
  abuela, grandmother . 2.4
  grandfather 3.2
abundancia[3a]
  plenty 2.2
abundante[2b]
  abundant 4.2
abundar[3b]
  abundant 4.2
  abound 5.2
aburrido
  tedious 5.2
aburrir[3a]
  bore 4.6
abusar[4a]
  abuse 4.3
abuso[4b]
  abuse 3.5
abyecto
  low 1.8
acá[1a]
  here . . . . 1.
acabar[1a]
  end . . . . 1.
  – de, just . . . . 1.
  -se, run down 2.6

Section

academia[3b]
  academy 4.3
académico[4b]
  university 4.2
acaecer[5a]
  happen . . . . 1.
acalorar[6a]
  heat (*vb.*) 2.2
acampar
  camp (*vb.*) 3.3
acariciar[2b]
  stroke 4.4
acarrear[6a]
  transport 3.9
acaso[1b]
  chance 1.4
accesible
  accessible 6.9
acceso[6a]
  approach 3.6
  access 4.9
accesorio
  accessory 7.9
accidental[7a]
  accidental 4.7
accidente[7b]
  accident 2.3
acción[1a]
  act (*n.*) . . . . 1.
  stock 1.8
accionista
  share holder 4.8
acebo
  holly 7.2
acechar[6b]
  spy 5.1
aceite[4a]
  oil (*n.*) 2.5
aceituna[6b]
  olive 5.8
acento[2a]
  accent (*n.*) 2.4
acentuar[7b]
  accent (*vb.*) 3.9
  emphasize 4.4
acepción[7b]
  import (*n.*) 2.2
aceptación
  acceptance 3.8
aceptar[1b]
  accept . . . . 1.
acequia[5b]
  ditch 3.6
acera[4a]
  sidewalk 5.5
acerbo[6a]
  bitter . . . . 2.
acerca[2a]
  as for . . . . 1.
acercar[1a]
  (bring) toward(s) . . . 1.
  -se, (go) toward(s) . . . 1.
acertar[1b]
  guess right 1.4

Section

acero[3a]
  steel 3.1
aciago[6a]
  unhappy 1.8
ácido[5b]
  acid (*n.*) 3.7
  acid (*adj.*) 5.3
acierto[3b]
  ability 3.2
aclamar[6b]
  clap 2.8
aclarar[4b]
  clear up 2.9
  brighten 4.1
acoger[2b]
  get (receive) . . . . 1.
acogida[5a]
  reception 3.2
acometer[3a]
  attack 2.1
acomodador
  usher 7.3
acomodar[2b]
  fix (up) 1.5
  accommodate 3.8
  clase acomodada
    gentry 6.2
acomodo
  accommodation 6.8
acompañamiento[4b]
  following (*n.*) 2.3
acompañar[1a]
  go with . . . . 1.
aconsejar[2a]
  advise . . . . 2.
acontecer[3a]
  happen . . . . 1.
acontecimiento[3b]
  event . . . . 2.
acordar[1b]
  agree 2.2
acorde[6a]
  agreed 2.8
acortar[6a]
  – la marcha, – el paso
    slow down 4.4
  shorten 4.8
acosar[3b]
  harry 4.1
acostar[2b]
  -se, (go to) bed 1.6
acostumbrar[1b]
  (be) used (to) 1.4
  (make) used (to) . . . 1.6
acre[7a]
  bitter . . . . 2.
  acid 5.3
acrecentar[5a]
  increase 1.1
acreditar[4b]
  assure 1.4
acreedor[4a]
  worthy 1.8
  creditor 4.1
actitud[2a]
  attitude 3.6

Section
actividad[2b]
activity 3.3
activo[3a]
active 2.6
asset 6.8
acto[1a]
act (*n.*) .... 1.
actor + actriz[3a]
actor 3.9
actual[2a]
present (*adj.*) 1.1
actualidad[5b]
en la –
now (at present) . 1.
actuar[4b]
act (take action) ... 1.
acuarela
water-color .... 13.
acuático[6a]
water .... 5.
acudir[1b]
(be) present 2.3
acuerdo[2a]
de –, by (according to) 1.
settlement 2.7
agreement 3.1
acumular[6a]
heap up 3.2
acuoso
watery 7.2
acusación[6a]
accusation 4.6
acusar[2b]
acusado, accused 3.1
accuse .... 4.
acusativo[6b]
accusative .... 9.
achacar[5b]
blame 2.8
achaque[5a]
matter .... 1.
adaptar[4b]
fit (*vb.*) 2.9
adjust 4.5
adecuado[5b]
able 1.4
adequate .... 6.
adelantamiento
promotion 5.6
adelantar[1b]
come forward 1.4
go forward 1.4
further (*vb.*) 1.8
adelante[1b]
forth .... 1.
en –, (from) now on .. 1.1
forward 1.4
ir –, go forward 1.4
de ahora en –
henceforth .... 3.
adelanto[5a]
advance (*n.*) 2.2
progress 2.4
ademán[2b]
gesture 4.3
además[1a]
also .... 1.
else 1.1
(in) addition 1.4
– de, besides 2.3
adentro[2b]
within 1.1
inside (*adj.*) 1.4
indoors 3.1
tierra –, inland 3.9
aderezar[4a]
-se, prepare 1.6
trim 2.4

Section
adherir[4a]
stick (*intr. vb.*) 2.1
stick (*tr. vb.*) 2.2
-se, cling .... 5.
adiós[1b]
farewell 3.4
adivinar[2b]
guess 1.5
adivino[6b]
wizard 6.2
(fortune) teller .... 7.
adjetivo[3a]
adjective 7.1
adjunto[7a]
enclosed 5.1
associate 5.4
administración[4a]
direction 1.8
administrador[5a]
director 2.8
manager .... 5.
administrar[4b]
manage 2.2
administrativo[6a]
administrative 9.2
admirable[2a]
admirable 3.1
admiración[2a]
admiration 2.8
admirador[6a]
admirer .... 7.
admirar[1b]
-se, wonder (*vb.*) 1.8
admire 2.2
admitir[1b]
get (receive) .... 1.
admit 1.4
adobo[7b]
preparation .... 3.
adolecer[6b]
(get) ill .... 3.
adolescencia[6b]
youth 1.4
adolescente[6b]
boy 1.4
adonde[1a]
where .... 1.
adopción
adoption 3.8
assumption 6.2
adoptar[3a]
adopt 2.1
adoración[5b]
worship (*n.*) 3.6
adorar[1b]
worship (adore) 3.6
adormecer[4a]
-se, (go to) sleep 3.9
dull 5.7
adormidera
poppy 7.2
adormilarse
drowsy 6.2
adornar[2b]
trim 2.4
adorno[3a]
trimming 3.8
adquirir[1b]
get (obtain) .... 1.
adquisición[6a]
accomplishment 5.3
acquisition 6.3
aduana
duty (custom) 2.9
aduanero
custom house officer 8.9
aduar[7a]
camp 2.8

Section
adulación[7a]
flattery 6.6
adular[7a]
flatter .... 3.
adulto
mature .... 4.
adusto[5b]
grave 1.4
advenedizo
upstart .... 9.
adverbio[6b]
adverb .... 9.
adversario[3b]
adversary 2.9
adversidad[6b]
adversity .... 7.
adverso[5b]
adverse 6.9
advertencia[3b]
notice (*n.*) 1.7
advertir[1a]
(let) know .... 1.
notice (*vb.*) 1.4
warn 2.2
aéreo[6b]
air (*adj.*) .... 3.
aeroplano
aeroplane 8.1
afable[3a]
pleasant 1.1
afán[2a]
worry 2.8
afanar[5a]
-se, work (*vb.*) .... 1.
-se, (take) pains 1.4
afear[4b]
mar 5.2
afección[7b]
disease 1.6
afectar[2b]
affect 3.2
afecto[1b]
affection 3.5
afectuoso[4b]
affectionate 4.3
afeitar[5b]
shave 5.6
aferrar[5a]
seize 1.1
afianzar[6b]
fix .... 1.
afición[2b]
liking (*n.*) 1.5
preference 3.3
aficionarse[3a]
aficionado
(have a) taste (for) 2.4
afilar[5b]
sharpen 4.7
afinidad[5a]
relationship 1.6
afirmación[3a]
statement 2.1
afirmar[1b]
fix .... 1.
affirm 2.7
afirmativo[5b]
affirmative 8.5
aflicción[3b]
misfortune 2.2
afligir[2a]
grieve 3.4
aflojar[6b]
loose (*vb.*) 1.5
afluir[6b]
flow into .... 3.

Section
afortunado[3b]
fortunate .... 2.
successful 3.4
afortunadamente
fortunately 3.7
afrenta[4a]
disgrace 3.4
offense 3.8
afrentar[6b]
insult 3.4
africano[4a]
African 4.4
afluente
tributary 6.3
afrecho
bran 7.2
afuera[4a]
out .... 1.
outside 1.4
agachar
crouch 6.4
agarrar[4a]
seize 1.1
agasajo[5b]
entertainment 4.6
agazapar
crouch 6.4
agencia[6b]
agency 6.4
agente[3b]
representative 2.3
agent 2.9
ágil[4b]
active 2.5
agitación[3b]
excitement 4.2
agitar[2a]
stir 1.9
agobiar[6a]
burden 3.5
agolpar[6a]
crowd (*vb.*) 2.2
agonía[5a]
agony .... 2.
en –, (in) anguish 6.3
agostar[7a]
exhaust 2.4
agosto[2b]
August 1.7
agotar[2b]
agotado, spent (*adj.*) . 2.
exhaust 2.4
-se, run down 2.6
drain 3.7
agraciar[6b]
trim 2.4
agradable[1b]
pleasant 1.1
-mente raro
quaint 3.5
agradar[2a]
please .... 1.
agradecer[1b]
thank .... 1.
agradecido, grateful .. 2.5
agradecimiento[3a]
gratitude 3.3
agrado[3b]
pleasure 1.4
liking (*n.*) 1.5
agravar
aggravate 4.9
agraviar[5b]
hurt (*tr. vb.*) 1.8
(make) worse .... 3.
agravio[3b]
offense 3.8

Section

alternar[6a]
alternado
alternately 4.8
alternate 5.4
alternativo[3b]
alternately 4.8
alteza[5b]
highness 4.8
altivez[3b]
pride 2.4
altivo[3a]
haughty 4.7
alto[1a]
high 1.
(out) loud 1.
tall 1.
altura[1b]
height 1.1
tierra de –, highland 5.
aludir[4b]
refer (to) 3.1
alumbrar[2a]
light (up) 1.4
alumbrado, lighted 2.6
alumbrado, lighting 3.2
alumno[4b]
pupil 1.7
alzar[1b]
lift 1.
pick up 1.5
– los manteles
clear (table) 4.3
allá[1a]
there 1.
más – de
beyond (*prep.*) 1.5
más –, beyond (*adv.*) 1.8
allanar[5a]
(make) easy 1.8
allegar[5b]
-se, (go) toward(s) 1.
gather (glean) 1.5
allende[5a]
beyond (*prep.*) 1.5
beyond (*adv.*) 1.8
allí[1a]
there 1.
amabilidad[5b]
kindness 2.7
amable[2a]
pleasant 1.1
amador[5a]
lover 2.
amagar[6a]
threaten 1.8
amanecer[3a]
dawn 3.5
amante[1b]
lover 2.
amapola
poppy 7.2
amar[1a]
love 1.
amado, darling 2.2
amargar[5a]
(make) bitter 3.9
amargo[2a]
bitter 2.
amargura[2a]
bitterness 5.7
amarillento[6a]
yellow 2.
amarillo[2b]
yellow 2.
amarrar[5a]
tie (*vb.*) 1.6
amasar[5a]
gather (collect) 1.5
mould 5.7

Section

ámbar
amber 6.6
ambición[3a]
ambition 3.7
ambicionar[7a]
(be) ambitious 5.8
ambicioso[6b]
ambitious 5.8
ambiente[2b]
atmosphere 4.1
ámbito[4a]
border 1.7
limit 2.4
compass 2.5
ambos[1a]
both 1.
amén[6b]
amen 4.3
amenaza[3b]
threat 4.6
amenazar[1b]
threaten 1.8
ameno[3b]
pleasant 1.1
americano[2a]
French 1.
americana
coat (of suit) 4.3
amigo[1a]
friend 1.
amistad[1b]
friendship 2.3
amistoso[6a]
friendly 3.5
amo[1a]
master (*n.*) 1.
– de casa
man of the house 1.8
owner 2.
ama de llaves
housekeeper 6.2
amonestación[6a]
warning 3.4
amonestar[7a]
admonish 6.3
amontonar[4b]
heap up 3.2
amor[1a]
love 1.
darling 2.2
amoroso[2a]
affectionate 4.3
amortiguar
soften 5.4
amparar[3a]
shelter (*vb.*) 2.6
amparo[3a]
shelter (*n.*) 1.7
ampliar[6a]
increase 1.1
enlarge 3.3
amplio[3a]
vast 2.8
ample 3.6
spacious 4.8
ampolla
blister 7.2
amueblar[5b]
furnish 3.3
análisis[7a]
analysis 7.1
analizar[4b]
analyze 6.5
analogía[6b]
analogy 7.6
análogo[4a]
similar 4.4

Section

anarquía[5a]
anarchy 7.5
anca[6a]
buttock 10.
-s
hindquarters
(horse) 11.
anciano[2a]
(old) man 2.4
ancient 2.6
ancho[1b]
broad 1.4
anchura[6a]
width 3.4
range 3.6
ancla
anchor 5.2
andaluz[3a]
English 1.
andante[5a]
wander 4.9
andar[1a]
walk (*vb.*) 1.
walk (gait) 1.6
– a tientas, grope 6.5
anécdota[6b]
anecdote 6.6
anegar[4a]
drown 4.3
anexionar
annex 7.4
anexo
annex 6.6
anfitriona
hostess 6.8
angarilla
stretcher 8.2
ángel[1b]
angel 2.
angosto[4a]
narrow 1.
ángulo[3b]
angle 3.4
angustia[2a]
agony 2.
angustiar[4b]
agony 2.
angustioso[6a]
anxious 2.3
anhelar[4b]
long for 1.4
anhelo[2b]
longing 1.9
anidar[6b]
nestle 7.
anillo[4b]
circle 1.2
ring (*n.*) 2.
ánima[4a]
soul 1.
animación[5a]
life 3.8
animal[1b]
animal 1.1
animal (*adj.*) 2.7
animar[1b]
animate 3.5
cheer (up) 4.6
encourage 4.8
ánimo[1b]
spirit 1.
animoso[6a]
(be) brave 1.
aniquilar[4b]
destroy 1.5
aniversario
anniversary 6.7

Section

anoche[3a]
(last) night 1.2
anochecer[3b]
twilight 4.3
anónimo[4b]
anonymous 9.6
ansia[2b]
worry 2.8
ansiar[5a]
long for 1.4
ansiedad[4a]
worry 2.8
ansioso[4b]
anxious 2.3
antaño[4b]
long ago 1.3
ante[5a]
– todo, above all 1.
before (in front of) 1.
anteayer
day before yesterday 4.
antecámara
entrance hall 5.3
antecedente[3b]
antecedent 8.3
antecesor[5a]
ancestor 4.5
antemano[5a]
de –, (in) advance 2.2
anteojo[4a]
glasses 4.2
antepasado[5a]
ancestor 4.5
anteponer[5b]
place (*vb.*) 1.
anterior[1b]
-mente, before (time) 1.
previous 2.
-mente, formerly 2.2
año –, preceding year 4.9
antes[1a]
before (time) 1.
rather 1.
– que, before (*conj.*) 1.1
anticipar[4a]
anticipate 6.8
antigüedad[3b]
antiquity 3.8
antiguo[1a]
old 1.
antiguamente
long ago 1.3
antiguamente
formerly 2.2
ancient 2.6
antojar(se)[3b]
desire (*vb.*) 1.
antojo[5a]
fancy 3.7
antorcha[5a]
torch 5.
anual[3b]
annual 2.7
anudar[5b]
tie (*vb.*) 1.6
anular[6b]
(make) void 6.2
anunciar[1b]
(give) notice 1.4
anuncio[4a]
notice (*n.*) 1.7
advertisement 4.5
añadidura[6a]
addition 3.1
añadir[1a]
join 1.
add 1.8

Section

arremeter[6b]
attack 2.1
arrepentimiento[6a]
remorse 4.1
arrepentirse[2b]
repent 4.3
arrestado
(under) arrest 6.1
arriba[1a]
– de, above (*prep.*) 1.
above (*adv.*) 1.
upstairs 3.
arribar[7a]
arrive 1.4
arriero[5a]
muleteer 12.5
arriesgar[4b]
chance 1.4
arrimar[3b]
(bring) toward(s) 1.
arroba[6b]
pound (*n.*) 1.6
arrodillarse[4a]
kneel 3.9
arrogancia[4b]
arrogance 7.2
arrogante[4b]
bold 2.1
haughty 4.7
arrojar[1b]
throw 1.
arrollar[5a]
overwhelm 4.8
arrostrar[5a]
face 3.8
brave 4.6
arroyo[2b]
brook (*n.*) 2.1
– de la calle, gutter 5.7
arroz[5a]
rice 4.7
arruga[6a]
wrinkle 5.4
arrugar[5b]
– el ceno, frown 5.5
wrinkle 5.7
arruinar[3a]
destroy 1.5
arrullar[6b]
coo 6.9
arrullo[5b]
coo 6.9
arte[1a]
art 1.
ártico
arctic 6.8
articulación
joint 5.8
articular[6b]
articulate 7.1
artículo[2a]
article 1.2
artífice[5b]
artisan 5.3
artificial[4b]
artificial 3.2
artificio[3b]
trick (*n.*) 3.2
artificioso[5b]
skilful 4.2
sly 4.2
affected 9.1
artillería[6a]
artillery 3.8
artista[2a]
artist 2.
artístico[2b]
artistic 3.4

Section

arzobispo[5b]
archbishop 6.2
asado
roast 5.4
asaltar[5b]
attack 2.1
asalto[5a]
attack (*n.*) 1.7
asamblea[5a]
assembly 2.6
asar[3a]
cook (*vb.*) 2.5
asaz[4b]
pretty (moderately) 1.
ascender[3b]
go up 1.
ascendiente[7a]
ancestor 4.5
ascensión[6a]
ascent 7.2
asco[6a]
disgust 4.6
ascua[7a]
(live) coals 2.1
asear[6b]
trim 2.4
aseado, neat 2.6
asediar
besiege 5.6
asegurador
insurer 12.
asegurar[1b]
fix 1.
assure 1.4
-se, (make) sure 2.2
asentar[3b]
settle 1.
asentir[4b]
agree 2.2
aseo[4a]
cleanliness 5.3
asesinar[3b]
murder 3.5
asesino[5a]
murderer 4.1
así[1a]
so 1.
therefore 1.
asiduo[7a]
industrious 3.2
asiento[2a]
seat 1.
asilo[4a]
refuge 3.9
asimilar[6b]
assimilate 7.2
asimismo[3a]
(in like) manner 1.2
asir[3b]
grasp 1.1
asistencia[6b]
presence 1.8
asistir[1b]
(be) present 2.3
asno[3b]
ass 3.9
asociación[5a]
company (business) 1.
company (social) 1.
asociar[4b]
associate 3.
asociado
associate (e.g., professor) 5.4
asolar
(lay) waste 4.9
asomar[1b]
appear (loom) 1.

Section

asombrar[2a]
astonish 2.7
asombro[2b]
surprise (*n.*) 2.4
asombroso[3b]
astonishing 5.
aspecto[1b]
sight 1.
aspereza[4b]
harshness 7.8
áspero[4a]
rough 3.
harsh 3.9
aspiración[3b]
aspiration 4.8
aspirar[1b]
breathe 2.7
aspire 4.2
asqueroso[7a]
dirty 4.2
astro[3a]
star 1.5
astrónomo
astronomer 6.4
astucia[5a]
cunning 5.1
asturiano[6b]
English 1.
astuto[3b]
sly 4.2
asumir
assume 2.8
asunto[1b]
business 1.
matter 1.
asustar[2b]
frighten 1.9
atacado
stricken 6.5
atacar[3b]
attack 2.1
atajar[4a]
stop 1.
ataque[3b]
attack 1.7
atar[2a]
tie (*vb.*) 1.6
ataúd
coffin 5.3
atemorizar[6a]
frighten 1.9
atención[1b]
en – a, as for 1.
attention 1.8
atender[1b]
(take) care 1.
ateo[6b]
atheist 8.2
atenerse[5b]
depend 2.4
atentado[5b]
attack (*n.*) 2.3
crime 2.4
atentar[7a]
try 1.
atento[2a]
attentive 2.8
aterrar[4b]
frighten 1.9
atestiguar[6b]
testify 4.1
ático
attic 6.3
atisbar[7a]
glance (*vb.*) 2.3
atleta
athlete 8.2

Section

atlético
athletic 6.8
atmósfera[3a]
atmosphere 4.1
átomo[4b]
atom 7.2
atónito[5b]
astounded 5.6
atormentar[3b]
torment 3.1
torture 3.5
atracción[3b]
attraction 6.
atractivo[3a]
attractive 4.
atraer[2b]
attract 2.7
attract (entice) 3.1
atrás[1b]
echarse –
draw back 1.5
behind (*adv.*) 2.
de –, back (*adj.*) 2.8
hacia –, backward 2.8
atrasar[5a]
delay (*vb.*) 2.7
(be) slow 3.6
atravesar[1b]
cross 1.
pierce 3.1
atreverse + atrevido[1a]
dare 1.
rash 4.9
atrevimiento[4a]
boldness 4.7
atribuir[2b]
attribute 3.7
atributo[5a]
characteristic 3.
atrio[7a]
porch 2.7
atrocidad[6b]
atrocity 7.
atronar[6a]
din 6.2
atropellar[3b]
fell 2.8
atropello[5b]
outrage 6.7
atroz[5a]
outrageous 5.8
aturdir[3b]
perplex 3.6
(make) dizzy 4.4
thoughtless 4.8
audacia[4a]
boldness 4.7
audaz[3b]
bold 2.1
audiencia[4a]
audience 5.2
auditorio[3b]
assembly 2.6
augurar[5a]
tell in advance 4.9
augusto[3b]
magnificent 3.5
stately 3.6
aula
schoolroom 3.3
aullido[5b]
howl 5.7
aumentar[1b]
increase 1.1
magnify 4.1
aumento[2b]
increase (*n.*) 2.3

Section

bastón[4a]
stick (*n.*) .... 2.
basura[6a]
refuse 4.4
batalla[2a]
battle 1.2
batallar[6a]
fight (*vb.*) 1.6
batallón[6a]
battalion .... 5.
batería[5b]
battery 3.1
batir[2a]
beat 1.1
strike (*vb.*) 1.1
baúl[7a]
hacer el –
pack (*vb.*) 3.5
trunk .... 5.
bautismo[6b]
baptism 5.5
bautizar
baptize .... 6.
bautizo[7a]
baptism 5.5
bayoneta
bayonet 7.4
beato[5b]
blessed 2.1
beber[1a]
drink (*vb.*) 1.4
drinking .... 3.
bebida[2b]
drink (*n.*) 2.7
becerro[7a]
calf 5.8
beldad[5b]
beauty 1.8
belga[6b]
Belgian .... 9.
bélico[6a]
martial 5.4
bellaco[6b]
knave 4.5
belleza[1b]
beauty 1.5
(a) beauty 1.8
bello[1a]
beautiful .... 1.
bellota
acorn 6.8
bendecir + bendito[1b]
bless .... 2.
blessed 2.1
bendición[2b]
blessing (*n.*) 2.3
beneficencia[7a]
charity 2.9
beneficiar(se)[7a]
profit (*vb.*) 1.4
benefit 3.6
beneficio[2b]
advantage 1.5
profit .... 2.
benefit 3.4
benéfico[4a]
kind .... 1.
benevolencia[4a]
kindness 2.7
goodwill 5.3
benévolo[4b]
kind .... 1.
charitable 5.4
benigno[5a]
benign 6.5
beodo[7a]
drunken 5.9

Section

besar[1b]
kiss (*vb.*) 1.4
beso[2a]
kiss (*n.*) 1.7
bestia[2a]
beast 1.1
Biblia
bible 4.6
bíblico[5b]
biblical 9.7
biblioteca[4a]
library 3.5
bicarbonato
soda 5.6
bicho[4a]
beast 1.1
bicicleta
bicycle 6.4
bien (*adv.*)[1a]
all right .... 1.
no –
(no) sooner (than) 1.
well .... 1.
bien (*n.*)[1b]
-es, property 1.5
bienaventurado[6b]
blessed 2.1
bienestar[3a]
welfare 3.5
bienhechor[4a]
humane 5.3
bienvenido
welcome 3.3
bifteque
steak 6.8
bigote[3b]
mustache 7.4
billete[4a]
– de banco
(bank) note 3.6
ticket 4.2
bimetalismo
bimetallism 10.8
biografía[6b]
biography 8.6
bizarro[5a]
smart 4.6
bizcocho[5b]
biscuit 6.7
blanco[1a]
white .... 1.
en –, blank 3.8
blancura[4b]
white 3.7
blando[2a]
soft 1.5
blanquear[5b]
(become) white 1.9
blasfemia[4b]
oath 4.8
blasphemy 6.8
bloque
block 5.2
blusa
blouse 6.8
bobo[5a]
fool 2.4
foolish 2.8
boca[1a]
mouth .... 1.
bocado[5a]
morsel 6.2
boda[2a]
wedding 3.4
bodega[5a]
cellar 3.8
grocery 6.9

Section

bodegonero
grocer 6.4
bofetada[5b]
slap 3.8
bofetón[6a]
slap 3.8
boga[7a]
fad 8.5
bogar[6b]
row .... 5.
bohemio[5a]
Bohemian 7.3
boj
box 4.9
bola[3a]
ball 2.1
-s, marble (game) 4.9
bolsa[3a]
exchange 2.6
purse 3.8
bolsillo[2b]
pocket 2.3
bollo
loaf 3.3
bomba[5a]
shell 3.4
pump 5.3
bonanza[6a]
weather 1.4
bondad[1b]
goodness 1.5
kindness 2.7
bondadoso[3b]
kind .... 1.
kindly 3.3
poco –, unkind 6.1
bonito (*adj.*)[1a]
pretty (comely) .... 1.
bono[6a]
bond 5.8
bordado[5b]
embroidery 6.5
bordar[4a]
embroider 5.9
borde[2b]
edge 1.5
fringe 5.8
bordo[5b]
a –, (on) board .... 3.
borla[6b]
tassel .... 7.
borracho[3b]
drunk (*adj.*) 5.5
drunken (person) 5.9
borrador
draft .... 3.
borrar[2b]
rub out 4.4
borrasca[5a]
storm 1.6
bosque[2a]
forest .... 1.
bostezar[5a]
yawn 5.8
bostezo[6a]
yawn 6.2
bota[3b]
boot 3.8
botar[6b]
throw .... 1.
bote[4b]
boat 2.6
botella[3a]
bottle 2.1
botica[6a]
drug store 5.6

Section

botín[6a]
spoils 3.5
boot 3.8
boto
dull 5.2
botón[6a]
button 3.7
bud 4.8
bóveda[4b]
vault 4.7
boxeador
prize fighter .... 7.
bramar[4a]
roar 4.7
brasa[4b]
(live) coals 2.1
bravo[2a]
(be) brave .... 1.
bravura[6b]
courage 1.4
brazo[1a]
arm (part of body) 1.
brea[7b]
tar 6.4
brecha[7a]
gap 4.5
breve[1b]
short .... 1.
-mente, (in) short .... 1.
bribón[5b]
knave 4.5
brigada
brigade 6.2
brillante[2a]
bright 1.4
brilliant 2.9
brillar[2a]
shine 1.6
glitter 3.6
brillo[4a]
splendor 3.6
brinco[6b]
spring (*n.*) 2.6
brindar[3a]
offer .... 1.
brío[3a]
vigor .... 4.
brioso[6a]
fiery 3.6
brisa[4a]
breeze 5.2
británico[4b]
British 4.2
brizna
blade 5.3
brocha
brush 5.6
broma[2b]
joke (*n.*) 2.9
bromear
joke (*vb.*) 4.3
bronce[3b]
brass 4.5
bronze 6.2
brotar[2b]
grow 1.3
gush 4.5
sprout 6.2
brote
shoot 5.4
bruja[4a]
witch 5.2
bruma[5a]
mist 3.1
brusco[3b]
gruff 3.7

Section

candidato
applicant 7.2
candidatura
candidacy 9.4
cándido[4a]
open (*adj.*) 1.3
candil[4b]
lamp 2.5
candor[3b]
frankness 7.2
canela[4a]
cinnamon .... 8.
cangrejo[6b]
crab 6.2
canjear
exchange (*vb.*) 3.5
cano + cana[4a]
hair .... 1.
gray 2.2
canónigo[4b]
minister .... 2.
cansancio[3a]
weariness 5.6
cansar[1b]
cansado, tired 1.9
tire (*vb.*) 2.4
cantar[1a]
sing 1.4
cántaro[5a]
pitcher 5.6
cántico[5b]
song 1.6
cantidad[1b]
amount .... 1.
canto[2a]
edge 1.5
song 1.6
cantor[3b]
singer 4.3
caña[2b]
stick (*n.*) .... 2.
– del timón, helm 5.6
cañón[3b]
gun 1.7
gorge 5.9
caoba
mahogany 7.2
caos[6b]
chaos 6.6
capa[2a]
coat .... 2.
layer 3.8
cloak 4.8
capacidad[3b]
capacity .... 3.
capaz[1b]
able 1.4
liable 5.8
capellán[6a]
minister .... 2.
capilla[4a]
chapel 3.9
capital[1b]
capital (finance) 1.9
capital (city) 2.3
capitán[2a]
captain 1.6
capitular[6a]
yield 1.9
capítulo[2a]
chapter 2.5
capote[5a]
coat .... 2.
capricho[2b]
fancy 3.7
caprichoso[3b]
fickle 6.5

capturar
capture .... 6.
capullo[6b]
blossom (*n.*) 2.2
bud 4.8
cara[1a]
face .... 1.
look 1.9
.... cara
look (well, etc.) 1.9
caracol[4a]
snail 6.8
carácter[1b]
character .... 1.
nature (character) .... 1.
característica[5b]
characteristic .... 3.
característico[6a]
characteristic 3.8
caracterizar[4a]
mark 3.2
caramba[5a]
Heavens! .... 1.
caravana
caravan .... 7.
carbón[3b]
coal 1.9
carbono
dióxido de –
carbon dioxide 6.8
carcajada[4a]
burst (of laughter) 2.9
cárcel[2a]
prison .... 2.
cardenal[6a]
cardinal 5.1
cárdeno[5b]
purple 4.9
cardo
thistle 6.4
carecer[2b]
lack (*vb.*) 1.5
carey
tortoise 6.8
carga[2b]
load (burden) 1.4
freight 3.8
cargamento[7a]
load (*n.*) 1.7
cargar[1b]
carry .... 1.
load (*vb.*) 1.8
cargo[1b]
office 1.4
caricia[2b]
caress 6.2
caridad[2a]
charity 2.9
cariño[1b]
love .... 1.
cariñoso[2b]
affectionate 4.3
carne[1a]
meat 1.6
flesh .... 2.
loncha de –, steak 6.8
carnero[3b]
sheep .... 3.
mutton 5.8
carnet
note book 4.9
carnicería
butcher shop 5.8
carnicero[6a]
butcher 5.6
caro[2b]
dear (in affection) .... 1.
dear (costly) 1.1

carpintero[5b]
carpenter 5.5
carrera[2a]
race (*n.*) 1.2
career .... 4.
carreta[5b]
wagon 4.7
carretel
spindle 6.6
carretera[3b]
road .... 1.
carretero[5b]
carter 6.9
carro[2a]
chariot 2.6
wagon 4.7
carruaje[4b]
car .... 2.
chariot 2.6
coach 4.9
carta[1a]
letter .... 1.
map 1.9
charter 2.9
cartel[6a]
bill 3.5
fijar -es, post bill 3.5
cartera[6a]
(letter) case 2.5
cartón[6a]
cardboard 8.6
cartucho
cartridge .... 9.
casa[1a]
en –, (at) home .... 1.
house .... 1.
amo de –
man of the house 1.8
– de correos
post-office 3.3
casaca[5b]
frock coat 6.1
casamiento[4a]
marriage 2.4
casar[1a]
marry 2.3
-se, marry 2.3
cascada[5b]
waterfall 6.2
cáscara[5b]
bark 4.9
peel 5.3
casco[4a]
helmet 4.9
hoof 5.1
skull .... 6.
casero[6b]
agent 2.9
casi[1a]
almost .... 1.
casino[6a]
club 1.6
caso[1a]
case .... 1.
en todo –, en
cualquier –
(in any) case .... 1.
casta[3a]
race 3.2
caste 7.3
castaña[6b]
chestnut 5.5
castañetear
chatter .... 6.
castellano[1b]
English .... 1.
castidad[5a]
chastity 7.7

castigar[2a]
punish 2.1
castigo[2a]
punishment 2.6
castillo[2b]
castle .... 2.
castizo[6a]
pure 1.5
casto[5b]
chaste 6.2
casual[4b]
casual 3.8
casualidad[3a]
chance 1.4
por –, (by) chance 1.6
catalán[4b]
English .... 1.
catálogo[5a]
list (*n.*) 2.9
catar[5a]
taste (*vb.*) 1.5
catástrofe[4a]
disaster 3.9
cátedra[5b]
chair 2.5
catedral[3a]
cathedral 4.6
catedrático[5a]
professor 2.6
categoría[3b]
class .... 3.
catolicismo
catholicism .... 13.
católico[2b]
catholic 2.9
catorce[3*]
fourteen 3.4
cauce[6b]
basin .... 3.
caucho
rubber .... 5.
caudal[2b]
wealth 1.5
plenty 2.2
caudaloso[4b]
full (river) 4.4
caudillo[4a]
chief (*n.*) 1.5
causa[1a]
a – de, because .... 1.
cause .... 1.
causar[1b]
cause (*vb.*) .... 1.
cautela[6a]
care .... 1.
prudence 3.7
cauteloso[6b]
prudent 3.3
cautivar[4b]
attract 3.1
cautiverio[5b]
captivity 5.7
cautivo[3a]
prisoner 2.4
cauto[6a]
prudent 3.3
cavar[6a]
dig 4.8
caverna[5b]
cave .... 3.
caza[2b]
hunt (*n.*) 2.4
game (*n.*) 2.7
cazador[3b]
hunter 2.6
– furtivo, poacher 11.5

Section

clavija
peg ... 6.
clavo[3b]
nail ... 3.
– de especia, clove ... 6.7
clemencia[5b]
mercy ... 2.
clerical[6b]
minister ... 2.
clérigo[4a]
minister ... 2.
clero
clergy ... 6.9
cliente[5a]
customer ... 3.6
clima[2b]
climate ... 4.
cloro
chlorine ... 8.8
cobarde[3a]
cowardly ... 4.6
coward ... 5.
cobrar[1b]
get (receive) ... 1.
collect ... 1.4
charge (*vb.*) ... 3.
– impuestos, tax ... 3.5
cobre[4b]
copper ... 3.
cocer[2a]
cook (*vb.*) ... 2.5
cocido[5b]
cook (*vb.*) ... 2.5
cocina[2b]
kitchen ... 2.8
cocinero[3a]
cook ... 4.3
coco[6a]
cocoanut ... 7.
coche[2a]
car ... 1.5
cart ... 2.7
– de alquiler, cab ... 3.9
cochero[5a]
driver ... 4.4
cochera, garage ... 6.9
cochino[6a]
pig ... 3.9
codicia[4b]
lust ... 4.8
greediness ... 8.6
codiciar[4b]
covet ... 4.1
codicioso[6a]
greedy ... 6.
código[5b]
law ... 1.
code ... 4.8
codo[4a]
elbow ... 5.1
cofre[6b]
trunk ... 5.
coger[1a]
take ... 1.
catch ... 1.3
cohesión
cohesion ... 10.5
coincidencia
coincidence ... 7.8
coincidir[4b]
coincide ... 7.2
cojín
cushion ... 5.6
cojo[3a]
lame ... 5.5
col[5a]
cabbage ... 5.9

Section

cola[3b]
tail ... 4.1
colaboración[6a]
assistance ... 3.9
colaborar
work together ... 3.6
colar[4a]
strain ... 4.9
colcha
quilt ... 6.8
colchón[5b]
mattress ... 6.7
colección[4b]
collection ... 2.7
colectivo[7a]
collective ... 9.6
colega[6a]
fellow worker ... 2.9
colegio[3a]
college ... 3.8
cólera[2a]
anger ... 1.9
colérico[4b]
angry ... 2.4
colgar[1b]
hang ... 1.1
colina[6a]
hill ... 2.6
colmar[4a]
fill (up) ... 1.8
heap up ... 3.2
colmena[5b]
hive ... 3.9
colmo[6b]
extreme ... 1.5
height (of career) ... 1.6
colocación[3b]
place ... 1.
colocar[1a]
place (*vb.*) ... 1.
– dinero, invest ... 3.
colonia[3a]
colony ... 2.9
colonial[6a]
colonial ... 6.2
colono[5a]
colonist ... 6.1
coloquio[4b]
talk (*n.*) ... 1.
color[1a]
color ... 1.
colorado[3b]
red ... 1.
colorear[6b]
color (*vb.*) ... 2.5
coloreado
colored ... 4.2
colorido[6a]
color ... 1.
colosal[3b]
great (huge) ... 1.
columbrar[5a]
(catch) sight of ... 1.1
make out ... 1.4
columna[2a]
column (military) ... 2.9
column (pillar) ... 3.3
collar[5b]
necklace ... 6.4
comadre[4b]
godmother ... 6.8
comandante[5b]
major ... 3.2
commander ... 4.4
comarca[3a]
part (of country) ... 1.

Section

combate[3a]
fight ... 1.1
battle ... 1.2
combatir[2a]
fight (*vb.*) ... 1.6
combinación[4a]
combination ... 4.3
combinar[4a]
combine ... 2.3
combustible
fuel ... 5.2
combustión
combustion ... 6.
comedia[2a]
comedy ... 3.7
comedor[3b]
dining room ... 4.9
comentar[4b]
remark (*vb.*) ... 2.3
comentario[4a]
remark (*n.*) ... 2.4
comenzar[1a]
begin ... 1.
comer[1a]
eat ... 1.4
dar de –, feed ... 1.4
dine ... 3.1
comercial[4a]
commercial ... 2.8
ley –
(commercial) law 3.2
trade ... 4.6
comerciante[3a]
business man ... 1.4
comercio[2b]
trade (*n.*) ... 1.2
cámara de –
chamber of commerce ... 3.2
comestible[5b]
food ... 1.9
cometa[4b]
comet ... 4.8
kite ... 5.2
cometer[1b]
commit ... 2.3
cómico[3a]
funny ... 2.9
comida[2a]
food ... 1.9
dinner ... 2.7
meal ... 3.2
comienzo[4a]
beginning ... 2.7
comisaría
police department ... 4.6
comisario[6b]
deputy ... 4.9
comisión[3a]
commission ... 2.2
committee ... 3.
comisionado[6b]
commissioner ... 5.
como, cómo[1a]
about (approximately) ... 1.
as (like) ... 1.
how ... 1.
well! ... 2.3
¡–!, what! ... 2.4
comodidad[2b]
ease ... 3.2
cómoda
drawer ... 6.1
cómodo[3b]
comfortable ... 2.1
convenient ... 2.5

Section

compadecer[4a]
pity ... 4.6
compadre[5a]
godfather ... 8.6
compañero[1a]
companion ... 2.3
compañía[1b]
company (business) 1.
company (social) ... 1.
company (military) 1 5
comparable[5b]
(to be) compared ... 2.2
comparación[3a]
comparison ... 2.7
comparar[2a]
compare ... 1.6
comparecer[5b]
appear (loom) ... 1.
compartir[4b]
divide ... 1.1
compás[3a]
measure ... 1.
time ... 3.2
compasión[2b]
pity ... 2.4
compasivo[4a]
merciful ... 4.2
compatriota[5a]
(fellow) countryman 4.7
compendio[6b]
summing up ... 3.1
compensar[7a]
make up for ... 4.1
competencia[5b]
competition ... 3.8
competir[4a]
contend ... 5.7
complacencia[5a]
pleasure ... 1.4
complacer[2a]
please ... 1.
complejo
complex ... 5.3
complemento[4b]
object (grammatical) 3.
complement ... 5.2
completar[3b]
complete ... 1.
completo[1a]
completamente, all ... 1.
complete ... 1.
complicación
complication ... 7.2
complicar
complicate ... 6.2
cómplice[4b]
(be a) party (to) ... 2.
complicidad
participation (e.g., in a crime) ... 7.8
componer[1b]
settle ... 1.8
compose ... 2.6
composición[3b]
composition ... 3.8
compositor
composer ... 9.6
compostura[5b]
repair (*n.*) ... 3.7
compra[4a]
purchase ... 3.2
comprador[6b]
buyer ... 3.8
comprar[1b]
buy ... 1.4
comprender[1a]
understand ... 1.
comprendido, included 2.9

Section

contado[3b]
al –, (in) cash 2.8
contagio[6b]
contagion 8.2
contagioso[7a]
catching .... 4.
contaminar[6a]
spoil 2.6
contar[1a]
count (*vb.*) .... 1.
– con, count on ...... 1.
tell .... 1.
contemplación[4a]
contemplation 3.8
contemplar[1b]
observe 1.4
contemporáneo[5a]
contemporary (*adj.*) 3.6
contemporary (*n.*) .. 4.8
contender[6b]
contend 5.7
contener[1b]
contain .... 1.
contenido[4a]
content (*n.*) .... 2.
contentar[2b]
satisfy 1.9
contento[1b]
glad .... 1.
contestación[3a]
answer (*n.*) 1.2
contestar[1a]
answer .... 1.
contienda[4b]
struggle 1.9
contigo[1a]
with .... 1.
contiguo[6a]
near (*adj.* and *adv.*). 1.
continente[2b]
continent 4.4
contingente[5b]
share .... 2.
unit (military) 5.9
continuación[3b]
continuation 4.7
continuance 5.9
continuar[1b]
continue .... 1.
continuo[1b]
continual 2.5
contorno[3a]
part (of country) ... 1.
outline 4.8
contra[1a]
against .... 1.
contracción[6b]
contraction 7.4
contradecir
contradict 5.3
contradicción[4a]
contradiction 4.3
contradictorio[5a]
contradictory 9.7
contraer[3a]
contract 4.3
contrariar[4b]
oppose 2.3
vex 4.1
contrariedad[4b]
disappointment 4.4
contrario[1a]
contrary (*n.*) 1.8
al, por el –
(on the) contrary 1.8
contrariamente
contrary (to) 3.5

Section

contrastar[6a]
contrast 5.1
contraste[4b]
contrast 3.1
contratar[5b]
engage 1.9
contratiempo[6b]
disappointment 4.4
contratista
contractor 6.6
contrato[4b]
contract (*n.*) 2.3
contribución[4b]
tax 1.6
contribution 4.4
contribuir[2a]
contribute 3.2
control
check (*n.*) 3.2
convencer[2a]
convince .... 2.
conveniencia[3b]
convenience 5.9
conveniente[2b]
proper 1.4
convenient 2.5
convenir[1b]
fit .... 1.
agree 2.2
convento[3a]
convent 3.8
conversación[1b]
talk (*n.*) .... 1.
conversation 2.6
conversar[4b]
talk .... 1.
converse 3.4
convertir[1b]
convert 5.2
convicción[4b]
conviction 4.2
convidar[2a]
invite 2.3
convite[4b]
invitation 3.2
convocar[5b]
call together 2.1
conyugal
conjugal 9.6
cooperativa
cooperative 6.7
copa[2a]
goblet 4.1
copia[4b]
plenty 2.2
copy (reproduction) 3.2
copiar[3b]
copy (imitate) 3.2
(make a) copy ..... 4.
copioso[5b]
abundant 4.2
copla[3a]
ballad 5.9
copo[6a]
snowflake 7.8
coqueta[6a]
flirt .... 7.
coraje[4a]
courage 1.4
coral[5a]
coral 6.5
corazón[1a]
heart .... 1.
corbata[4a]
tie 1.6
necktie 6.4

Section

corcho
cork 6.6
cordel[7a]
rope 3.3
cordero[3a]
lamb 4.9
cordial[3b]
cordial 2.3
hearty 3.4
cordillera[4b]
mountain 1.5
cordón[6a]
rope 3.3
coro[2b]
choir (loft) 3.7
choir (people) ...... 4.
corona[2a]
crown (*n.*) 1.7
coronar[2b]
crown (*vb.*) 2.9
coronel[4a]
colonel 3.9
corporación[6a]
corporation 3.5
corporal[7a]
bodily 6.3
corpulento[6b]
big .... 1.
corral[2b]
court 1.1
aves de –, fowl 5.1
correa[6a]
strap 6.2
corrección[4b]
(good) manners 2.9
correction 3.7
correcto[3b]
right (correct) ..... 1.
corredor[3b]
passage 4.8
scout 5.7
corregidor[2b]
mayor 2.5
corregir[3a]
correct (*vb.*) 2.7
correo[3b]
post .... 2.
casa de -s, post-office. 3.3
correr + corrido[1a]
run .... 1.
flow (*vb.*) 1.5
confound 3.1
correspondencia[3a]
correspondence (similarity) 3.5
correspondence (writing) 3.9
corresponder[1b]
correspond (to) 2.4
correspond .... 4.
correspondiente[3a]
corresponding 2.7
corresponsal[6a]
correspondent 6.2
corrida[4b]
course 1.1
race (*n.*) 1.2
corriente[1b]
stream 1.4
current 2.6
al –, (well) informed .. 3.
corro + corrillo[3a]
group 1.8
corromper[3b]
spoil 2.6
corrupt 4.7
corrupción[6a]
corruption 5.6

Section

cortado
sheepish 11.4
cortar[1a]
cut (*vb.*) 1.8
corte[1b]
court .... 1.
hacer la –
court (woo) ..... 1.
cortejar[7a]
court (woo) .... 1.
cortejo[6a]
lover .... 2.
procession 4.1
cortés[3b]
civil 3.2
courteous 4.3
cortesano[4b]
courteous 4.3
courtier 5.7
cortesía[3a]
(good) manners 2.9
courtesy 4.7
corteza[4b]
bar, ... 4.9
crust 5.8
cortijo[6a]
farm 3.2
cortina[4b]
curtain 3.8
corto[1b]
short .... 1.
cosa[1a]
alguna –, anything ... 1.
matter .... 1.
thing .... 1.
cosecha[3a]
crop 2.7
hacer –, harvest 4.8
coser[3a]
sew 4.7
cosquillear
tickle 6.8
cosquillas
hacer –, tickle 6.8
costa[1b]
coast 1.4
costado[5b]
side .... 1.
costar[1b]
cost (*vb.*) 1.4
coste[7a]
expense 3.3
costilla[5a]
rib .... 5.
costoso[5b]
dear 1.1
costumbre[1b]
tener –, (be) used (to). 1.4
custom 1.9
habit 2.2
costura
seam 6.4
cotidiano[6a]
daily 1.6
coyuntura[6b]
joint 5.8
cráneo[5b]
skull .... 6.
cráter[6b]
crater 9.4
creación[3a]
creation 3.4
creador + criador[3a]
creator 4.4
crear[2a]
create 1.5
crecer[1b]
grow 1.1

CII

Section
chillar[5b]
cry (*vb.*) . . . . 1.
chimenea[3b]
chimney 3.3
chino[4b]
Chinese 4.5
chispa[4a]
spark 4.4
chiste[3b]
joke 2.9
chocar[2b]
strike (*vb.*) 1.1
run into 1.6
chocolate[2b]
chocolate 5.4
choque[4a]
shock 3.5
clash 5.1
crash 5.6
chorizo[6b]
sausage 5.8
chorro[5b]
gush 3.6
choza[5a]
shed 3.2
cottage 3.4
chuchería
trinket 8.2
chupar[7a]
suck . . . . 6.

D

dable[6b]
possible . . . . 1.
dactilográfica
máquina –
typewriter 5.6
dádiva[6b]
present 1.7
dador
giver 7.2
daga[6b]
dagger 5.6
dama[1b]
lady . . . . 1.
danés
Danish 6.8
danza[4a]
dance 3.1
danzar[6b]
dance (*vb.*) 2.4
dañar[4a]
spoil 2.6
daño[1b]
hacer –, hurt (*intr. vb.*) 1.8
damage (*n.*) 2.4
dar[1a]
give . . . . 1.
– crianza
bring up (child) . . 1.9
dardo[5b]
arrow 3.2
datar[6a]
date 3.3
dato[3a]
particular 2.3
de[1a]
about (concerning) . 1.
from . . . . 1.
of . . . . 1.
deán
dean . . . . 7.
debajo[1b]
– de, under (*prep.*) . . . 1.
beneath 1.6
under (*adj.*) 1.9

Section
debate[6b]
debate . . . . 3.
deber + debido[1a]
must . . . . 1.
ought . . . . 1.
owe 1.8
due (*adj.*) 2.2
debidamente, duly . . . 4.5
deber (*n.*)[1b]
duty . . . . 1.
débil[2a]
weak 1.1
debilidad[4a]
weakness 2.9
debilitar[4b]
weaken 4.8
debut[7b]
(first) appearance . . 3.3
debutar[6b]
(make one's first)
appearance 2.3
década
decade 5.6
decadencia[5b]
decay 4.3
decano
dean . . . . 7.
decente[3b]
decent . . . . 4.
decididamente
decidedly 4.3
decidir[1b]
decide . . . . 1.
-se, decide . . . . 1.
décima[6b]
verse 2.7
décimo[4]*
tenth 4.1
décimoctavo[6]*
eighteenth . . . . 6.
décimo quinto[6]*
fifteenth 6.4
décimo sexto[7]*
sixteenth 7.7
decir[1a]
querer –, mean (*vb.*) . . 1.
say . . . . 1.
tell . . . . 1.
por – lo así
as it were 1.4
dicho
above (mentioned) 2.2
es –, namely 2.6
decisión[3a]
decision 2.5
decisivo[5b]
decisive 3.6
declaración[2b]
statement 2.1
declaration 4.5
declarar[1b]
state (*vb.*) . . . . 1.
declinar[6a]
decline 3.3
decoración[3b]
trimming 3.8
decorar[6a]
trim 2.4
decoro[3a]
honor . . . . 1.
decretar[5a]
command (*vb.*) 1.5
decree . . . . 3.
decreto[3b]
decree (*n.*) 2.6
dedal
thimble 7.2

Section
dedicar[1b]
-se, devote (*vb.*) 2.2
dedicate 2.7
dedo[1b]
finger 1.4
– del pie, toe 4.6
deducir[5a]
subtract 4.5
defecto[2a]
fault 1.8
defender[1b]
defend 1.4
defensa[2a]
defense 2.8
defensor[4b]
defender 6.8
definición[5a]
definition . . . . 7.
definir[3a]
fix 1.1
definitivo[2b]
en –, (in) short . . . . . 1.
degenerar
degenerate 7.4
degollar[5a]
behead 6.2
deidad[6b]
deity 5.4
dejar[1a]
allow . . . . 1.
leave (quit) . . . . 1.
– atrás
leave behind 2.2
fail 2.6
del[1a]
of . . . . 1.
delantal[6b]
apron 5.4
delante[1a]
– de, before (in front of) 1.
(in) front 1.4
delantero[4a]
first . . . . 1.
front (*adj.*) 2.2
delegación
delegation 8.5
delegado[4a]
deputy 4.9
delegar
delegate 6.6
deleitar[4a]
delight (*vb.*) . . . . 2.
deleite[3b]
delight . . . . 1.
zest 6.8
deleznable[7a]
weak 1.1
delgado[3a]
slight 3.3
deliberar[5b]
deliberado
express (*adj.*) 2.6
deliberate 4.1
delicadeza[3b]
delicacy 5.4
delicado[1b]
delicate 2.3
dainty 2.7
delicia[3a]
delight . . . . 1.
delicioso[2b]
delicious 2.8
delincuente[4b]
(be to) blame 1.8
offender 6.8
delirar[6b]
rage 3.7
rave 6.6

Section
delirio[3a]
bliss 3.7
delito[2b]
crime 2.4
demanda[3b]
demand (*n.*) 1.3
(supply and) demand 2.9
demandante
plaintiff 8.4
demandar[3b]
demand . . . . 1.
demás[1a]
other . . . . 1.
demasía[5a]
en –, too . . . . 1.
en –, extreme 1.5
excess 3.3
demasiado[1b]
too . . . . 1.
democracia
democracy 6.9
democrático[5a]
democrat . . . . 5.
demoler
pull down 2.8
demonio[1b]
devil 1.9
demostración[3b]
demonstration 3.6
demostrar[1b]
show . . . . 1.
demonstrate 2.8
denegación
denial 6.6
denominar[4a]
(give) name (to) . . . 1.
denotar[6b]
express (*vb.*) . . . . 1.
densidad[6b]
density 7.8
denso[4a]
dense 2.6
dentellada
pegar una –
snap 5.9
dentro[1a]
into . . . . 1.
within 1.1
denuesto[6b]
offense 3.8
denunciar[6b]
(give) notice (of) . . . 1.4
denounce 4.1
deparar[6a]
grant (*vb.*) . . . . 1.
departamento[4a]
section 1.9
dependencia[3b]
dependence . . . . 6.
depender[2b]
– de, count on . . . . . . 1.
depend 2.4
dependiente[4b]
clerk 2.7
dependent 5.2
deplorable
wretched 5.8
deplorar[7a]
deplore 4.2
deponer[4b]
depose 4.9
deporte
sport 5.1
deportivo
sport 5.3
deposición
removal 4.6

Section

despecho[3b]
a – de, (in) spite (of) 1.4
despedazar[4b]
tear (*vb.*) 1.8
despedida[3b]
discharge 3.8
despedir[1b]
-se, (take) leave 1.5
dismiss 2.7
(give) notice (to) 2.8
despegar[5a]
loose (*vb.*) 1.5
despejar[4b]
clear up 2.9
despensa
pantry 6.2
despeñar[4b]
throw 1.
despertar[1a]
wake (*tr. vb.*) 1.9
-se, wake (*intr. vb.*) 1.9
waking 4.4
despierto[3b]
wake (*tr. vb.*) 1.9
desplazamiento
shift 5.7
desplegar[3a]
display (*vb.*) 3.
unfold 3.4
desplomar[4b]
fall (*vb.*) 1.
despojar[2b]
strip 3.7
despojo[3a]
spoils 3.5
desposar[4a]
marry 2.3
betroth 6.8
déspota[6a]
tyrant 4.2
despotismo[5b]
tyranny 5.6
despreciar[2a]
scorn (*vb.*) 2.9
desprecio[2b]
scorn 3.3
desprender[2b]
loose (*vb.*) 1.5
despropósito[6a]
nonsense 5.
después[1a]
after 1.
afterwards 1.8
despuntar[5b]
appear (loom) 1.
destacamento
detachment (of troops) 4.8
destacar[3a]
-se, (be) ahead (of) 2.7
destello[5a]
gleam (*n.*) 2.5
desterrar[4a]
banish 4.1
desterrado
exile 5.6
destierro
exile 6.
destilación
distillation 8.4
destilar[5b]
distil 6.9
destilería
distillery 8.4
destinar[2a]
destinado, bound for 1.9
destine 2.4

Section

destino[1b]
fate 1.5
destreza[5b]
skill 3.
destronar[6b]
depose 4.9
destrozar[4b]
destroy 1.5
destrucción[5a]
destruction 4.2
destruir[1b]
destroy 1.5
desvalido[5a]
helpless 5.
desván
attic 6.3
desvanecer[2b]
faint 3.3
desvarío[6a]
raving 6.1
desvelar[4a]
-se, sit up 1.8
desvelo[5b]
cares 1.3
desventaja
disadvantage 4.8
desventura[3b]
misfortune 2.2
desventurado[5b]
unhappy 1.8
desvergüenza[5b]
shame 3.3
desviar[4b]
turn away 3.
desvío[5a]
indifference 4.7
detallar[7a]
detalladamente (in) detail 3.6
detalle[2b]
particular 2.3
detener[1a]
stop 1.
-se, stop 1.4
detain 2.6
detenido
(under) arrest 6.1
determinación[4a]
resolution 3.2
determination 6.
determinar[1b]
fix 1.1
detestable[4b]
hateful 4.7
detrás[1b]
after 1.
back of 1.
deuda[2b]
debt 1.7
en –, (in) debt 4.
en –, indebted 4.2
deudo[5a]
relation 2.3
deudor[6a]
debtor 4.8
devaneo[5a]
frivolity 9.3
devastar
(lay) waste 4.9
devoción[3a]
piety 4.9
devotion 5.
devolver[2b]
give back 1.9
return 1.9
take back 1.9
devorar[3a]
devour 3.8

Section

devoto[3a]
devote 2.2
pious 2.9
día[1a]
day 1.
el – siguiente (the) day (after) 1.
algún –, sometime 1.
– de fiesta, holiday 2.6
luz de –, daylight 4.6
diablo[2a]
devil 1.9
diabólico[6a]
devilish 7.4
diadema[5a]
crown (*n.*) 1.7
diáfano[5a]
transparent 5.7
diálogo[3a]
dialog(ue) 6.5
diamante[4a]
diamond 3.6
diámetro[6a]
diameter 6.2
diantre[5b]
Heavens! 1.
diario[1b]
paper 1.
daily 1.6
journal 4.2
dibujar[3a]
draw 1.4
dibujo[4a]
sketch 3.9
diccionario
dictionary 7.4
diciembre[4a]
December 2.3
dictar[2b]
dictate 5.
dicha[1b]
happiness 1.4
dichoso[2a]
glad 1.
diecinueve[7]*
nineteen 6.3
dieciocho[4]*
eighteen 4.3
diecisiete[6]*
seventeen 6.
dieciseis[5]*
sixteen 5.2
diente[1b]
tooth 2.3
hincar el –, bite 3.7
diestro + diestra[3a]
right (hand) 1.
clever 2.6
skilful 4.2
dieta
diet 6.2
diez[1]*
ten 1.4
diferencia[1b]
difference 1.4
diferenciar[4b]
distinguish 2.2
diferente[1b]
different 1.
diferir[5a]
differ 2.5
put off 2.6
difícil[1b]
hard (difficult) 1.
dificultad[2a]
difficulty 1.9
difundir[5a]
diffuse 3.5

Section

difunto[2a]
dead 1.4
difusión[5a]
spread 4.1
digerir
digest 6.2
digestión
digestion 7.4
dignarse[4a]
deign 6.4
dignidad[3a]
dignity 2.6
digno[1a]
(be) worth 1.
worthy 1.8
– de confianza reliable 3.8
dije[6a]
jewel 3.1
dilatar[2b]
delay (*intr. vb.*) 2.
delay (*tr. vb.*) 2.7
enlarge 3.3
diligencia[2b]
industry 2.6
diligente[5a]
industrious 3.2
diluvio[6b]
flood 3.2
dimensión[4b]
range 3.6
dimension 5.6
diminuto[6b]
little 1.
dimisión
resignation 7.3
dinastía[6b]
dynasty 7.8
dinero[1a]
money 1.
dios[1a]
God 1.
Dios quiera, Dios permita God grant 1.
¡ – !, Heavens! 1.
diosa[4a]
goddess 4.8
dióxido
– de carbono carbon dioxide 6.8
diplomacia[6b]
diplomacy 9.4
diplomático[4a]
diplomatic 7.6
diputado[3b]
deputy 4.9
dirección[1b]
direction 1.
address 2.3
directo[2a]
direct (*adj.*) 1.
direct (*adv.*) 1.1
director[2b]
director 2.8
dirigir[1a]
direct (*vb.*) 1.
-se, turn to 1.1
disciplina[4a]
discipline 4.8
discípulo[5a]
pupil 1.7
follower 3.2
disco[4b]
disk 5.4

E

Section

ebullición
- boiling 5.3

eclesiástico[5b]
- minister 2.
- church (*adj.*) 2.6

eclipsar[6a]
- eclipse 7.

eco[2b]
- echo 4.5

economía[4a]
- economy 6.2

económico[3b]
- saving 1.8
- economic 6.2

economizar[6a]
- save (up) 2.1

ecuador
- equator 7.2

echar[1a]
- drive (force) 1.
- lay 1.
- -se, lie (*vb.*) 1.
- – de menos, miss 1.
- throw 1.
- drive out 1.1
- -se atrás, draw back 1.5
- -se
  - burst (out laughing) 3.
- -se, burst 3.5

edad[1a]
- age 1.
- – media, middle ages 2.2

edición[4b]
- edition 3.6

edificar[4a]
- build 1.2

edificio[2a]
- building (*n.*) 1.6

editor[6b]
- publisher 5.8

edredón
- quilt 6.8

educación[2a]
- bringing up 1.6
- education 1.6

educar[2b]
- bring up (child) 1.9

efectivo[3a]
- efectivamente, really 1.4
- actual 2.1

efecto[1a]
- en –, (in) fact 1.
- en –, indeed 1.
- effect 1.4

efectuar[3a]
- effect (*vb.*) 2.2

eficacia[6a]
- efficacy 5.4

eficaz[3a]
- working 2.

efímero[5a]
- passing 1.9

efusión[5a]
- gush 3.6

egipcio[6a]
- Egyptian 5.4

egoísmo[3b]
- selfishness 6.3
- egoism 11.5

egoísta[5a]
- selfish 5.7

eje[4b]
- axis 4.9

ejecución[3b]
- carrying out 2.2
- performance 3.

Section

ejecutar[2a]
- carry out 1.
- enforce 4.4

ejecutivo[5a]
- executive 6.5

ejecutor
- executor 7.7

ejemplar[3a]
- example 1.4
- copy 2.7

ejemplo[1a]
- example 1.4
- por –, (for) example 1.4

ejercer[2a]
- exercise (*vb.*) 1.6

ejercicio[3a]
- exercise (*n.*) 1.7

ejercitar[4a]
- exercise 1.6

ejército[2a]
- army 1.2

el, él[1a]
- he 1.
- the 1.
- – mismo, himself 1.4
- – mismo, itself 1.5

elaboración
- working out 4.9

elaborar[6b]
- manufacture 3.
- brew 7.

elástico[6b]
- elastic 6.6

elección[2b]
- choice 1.6
- election 2.1

elector
- elector 5.6

electoral[6b]
- electoral 8.4

electricidad[4b]
- electricity 5.6

eléctrico[3a]
- electric 3.

elefante[6b]
- elephant 5.

elegancia[4a]
- elegance 7.5

elegante[2b]
- elegant 3.6

elegir[2a]
- elect 3.

elemental[4a]
- elementary 7.2

elemento[1b]
- element 2.3

elevación[5a]
- lifting (*n.*) 2.2
- elevation 4.2

elevar[1b]
- lift 1.

eliminar
- eliminate 7.4

elocuencia[4b]
- eloquence 5.1

elocuente[3a]
- eloquent 6.4

elogiar[6a]
- praise 2.1

elogio[3b]
- praise 2.7
- compliment 4.1

ella[1]*
- she 1.
- – misma, herself 1.7

ellos[1]*
- they 1.
- – mismos, themselves 1.4

Section

emanación[5a]
- waft 6.3

emanar[5a]
- come from 1.

emancipación[6b]
- freeing 3.4

emancipar[6b]
- free (*vb.*) 1.7

embajada[5b]
- errand 3.
- embassy 6.3

embajador
- ambassador 3.9

embarazo[6a]
- bar 2.1
- obstacle 3.4

embarcar[3a]
- sail (*vb.*) 3.

embargar[5a]
- overcome 2.7
- (become) breathless 7.3

embargo[6b]
- sin –, however 1.
- embargo 10.6

embeber[6b]
- absorbed 3.

embelesar[6a]
- charm (*vb.*) 2.4

embeleso[6a]
- bliss 3.7

embestir[5b]
- attack 2.1

embotado
- dull 5.2

embotar[6a]
- blunt 6.2

embozado[5b]
- hide 1.

embriagar[4a]
- (make) drunk 4.8
- -se, (get) drunk 5.8

embriaguez[6a]
- drunkenness 7.3

embrollar[5b]
- perplex 3.6
- entangle 4.4

embromar
- joke (*vb.*) 4.3

embuste[6a]
- lie (*n.*) 2.

embustero[4b]
- liar 6.1

emigración[3b]
- emigration 7.7

emigrante[4b]
- emigrant 7.3

emigrar[6b]
- emigrate 7.6

eminencia[5a]
- height 1.1
- eminence 5.3

eminente[3a]
- famous 1.1
- -mente, eminently 4.1

emitir[6b]
- send forth 3.4

emoción[2a]
- feeling 1.
- emotion (e.g., speak with emotion) 3.2
- emotion 4.3

emocionar[5b]
- move 1.5

empañar[4a]
- dull 5.3

empapar[4b]
- soak 5.9

Section

emparedado
- sandwich 6.8

empellar
- jostle 7.

empeñar[2a]
- -se, try hard 1.5
- -se, engage 1.9

empeño[2b]
- resolution 3.2
- obligation 4.

emperador[2b]
- emperor 2.1
- emperatriz
  - empress 4.6

empero[5b]
- however 1.

empezar[1a]
- begin 1.

empinar[6a]
- lift 1.

empleado[4a]
- employee 3.1

emplear[1a]
- use 1.

empleo[2b]
- use (*n.*) 1.1
- occupation 2.4
- employment 3.7

empollar
- hatch 6.8

emprender[2a]
- undertake 2.5

empresa[2a]
- undertaking (*n.*) 2.4

empujar[2b]
- push 2.3

empuñar[4a]
- seize 1.1

en[1a]
- at 1.
- in 1.
- into 1.
- – vano, (in) vain 1.9

enajenar[6a]
- (make) mad 2.9

enamorar + enamorado[1b]
- court (woo) 1.
- (in) love 2.7

enano[5a]
- dwarf 6.1

enardecer[6b]
- stir 1.9

encadenar[5b]
- chain (*vb.*) 2.7

encajar[6b]
- fit (*vb.*) 1.

encaje[5b]
- lace (*n.*) 2.1

encaminar[2b]
- -se, start toward(s) 4.3

encantador[2a]
- charming (*adj.*) 2.3
- lovely 2.3

encantar[2b]
- delight (*vb.*) 2.
- charm (*vb.*) 2.4

encanto[1b]
- charm (*n.*) 1.9

encaramarse
- perch 5.6

encarecer[4a]
- recommend 2.1

encargar[1b]
- charge 2.2

encargo[2b]
- order (*n.*) 1.

encarnado[4a]
- red 1.

Section

equivocar[2b]
(make a) mistake... 2.2
era[6b]
age... 1.8
erguir[3a]
erguido, straight... 1.8
erigir[6b]
lift... 1.
build... 1.2
erizar[5b]
bristle... 6.9
erizo
burr... 6.8
hedgehog... 7.2
ermitaño[6a]
hermit... 6.6
errante[4b]
wander... 4.9
errar[4b]
(make a) mistake... 2.2
wander... 2.7
error[1b]
error... 1.8
erudición[6a]
learning... 3.6
erudito[4a]
learned... 1.6
scholar... 2.3
esbelto[5b]
slight... 3.3
esbozar
outline (*vb.*)... 4.5
escala[3a]
scale (*n.*)... 1.8
ladder... 5.
escalar[6a]
climb... 2.7
scale... 5.2
escalera[3a]
stairs... 2.5
escalón[6b]
step... 1.7
escalonar
echelon... 13.
escama
flake... 6.8
escandalizar[4b]
shock... 3.2
escándalo[2b]
scandal... 5.8
escandaloso[6a]
shameful... 4.7
escapar[1b]
run away... 1.5
escape (*vb.*)... 1.8
escape (the memory) 2.6
escarabajo
beetle... 6.8
escarbar[5b]
scratch... 5.3
escarmentar[4b]
correct (*vb.*)... 2.7
escarnecer[5b]
(make) fun (of)... 2.8
escasez[4b]
want (*n.*)... 3.
escaso[1b]
scanty... 4.5
escena[1a]
scene... 1.8
scene (of a play)... 2.2
escenario[5a]
stage... 3.
escéptico
sceptic... 9.2
esclarecer[5b]
clear up... 2.9

Section

esclavitud[4b]
slavery... 6.2
esclavizar[5b]
enslave... 8.1
esclavo[2a]
slave... 2.2
esclusa
lock... 4.8
escoba[5b]
broom... 5.5
escoger[1b]
choose... 1.
escogido
choice... 5.3
escolar[5a]
pupil... 1.7
sistema –
school system... 4.2
school... 4.6
escollo
reef... 7.4
esconder[1b]
hide... 1.
escopeta[7a]
gun... 1.7
escoplo
chisel (wood)... 7.2
escribano[4a]
clerk... 3.8
escribir[1a]
write... 1.
por escrito
written... 1.4
máquina de –
typewriter... 5.6
escrito[2b]
writing(s)... 1.4
escritor[2a]
author... 1.9
escritorio[6a]
desk... 3.6
escritura[3b]
writing (*n.*)... 1.8
act (document)... 2.3
escrúpulo[4a]
scruple... 5.9
escrupuloso[3b]
exact... 1.4
escuadra[4a]
fleet (*n.*)... 3.
escuadrón[5a]
squadron... 4.9
escuchar[1a]
listen... 1.8
escudero[4b]
squire... 6.
escudilla
bowl... 4.2
escudo[3b]
shield... 3.5
escudriñar[6a]
examine... 1.5
escuela[1b]
school... 1.
– secundaria, school... 1.
– de equitación
riding-school... 13.
esculpir
carve... 5.6
escultor[6a]
sculptor... 7.4
escultura[6a]
sculpture... 6.8
escupir[6b]
spit... 5.9
escurrir[4a]
slip... 2.8
drain... 3.7

Section

ese, ése[1a]
that (*adj.*)... 1.
that (*pron.*)... 1.
esencia[2b]
essence... 5.7
esencial[3a]
essential... 2.9
esfera[2b]
sphere... 4.4
dial... 6.4
esforzado[5a]
strong... 1.
esforzarse[3b]
try hard... 1.5
esfuerzo[1b]
effort... 1.8
esfumar[6a]
-se, disappear... 1.4
esgrimir[6a]
handle... 3.9
eslabón[5a]
link... 3.3
esmalte[6a]
enamel... 6.8
esmeralda[5a]
emerald... 6.9
esmerarse[5b]
(take) pains... 1.4
esmero[4a]
care... 1.
neatness... 9.2
eso[1a]
nada de –, (not at) all. 1.
that (*pron.*)... 1.
espacio[1a]
room (space)... 1.
espada[1b]
sword... 2.
espalda[1b]
back (*n.*)... 1.4
de -s, backward... 2.8
espantar[2b]
frighten... 1.9
espanto[2b]
fear (*n.*)... 1.4
espantoso[2b]
frightening... 2.4
ghastly... 6.4
hideous... 6.4
español[1a]
English... 1.
esparcir[2a]
scatter... 2.4
especia[7a]
spice... 6.
clavo de –, clove... 6.7
especial[1b]
-mente, above all... 1.
special... 1.8
especialidad[6b]
specialty... 8.8
especie[1b]
kind... 1.
especiero
grocer... 6.4
especificar[5b]
specify... 8.9
específico[6b]
specific... 5.8
espectáculo[2b]
sight... 1.
spectacle... 5.6
espectador[3b]
audience... 3.
espectro[5a]
ghost... 3.2

Section

especulación
speculation... 5.3
espejo[2a]
mirror... 2.8
espera[5b]
wait... 4.5
esperanza[1a]
hope (*n.*)... 1.
expectation... 3.3
esperar[1a]
expect... 1.
hope (*vb.*)... 1.
wait... 1.
wait (for)... 1.
expect (of a person) 2.6
espeso[2a]
thick... 1.2
tufted... 6.4
espesor
thickness... 5.1
espía
spy... 5.4
espiar[6a]
spy... 5.1
espina[3b]
thorn... 4.3
espinazo[6a]
spine... 7.
espiral[6a]
spiral... 7.6
espíritu[1a]
spirit... 1.
espiritual[3a]
spiritual... 3.3
espléndido[2b]
splendid... 2.6
esplendor[3a]
splendor... 2.8
splendor (magnificence)... 3.6
radiance... 4.9
esponja
sponge... 6.6
espontaneidad[6a]
spontaneity... 10.2
espontáneo[3b]
spontaneous... 6.
esposo[1a]
husband... 1.
esposa, wife... 1.
espuela[4b]
spur... 5.8
espuma[3a]
foam... 5.3
espumar[7a]
foam... 5.7
esquela[6b]
note (*n.*)... 1.9
esqueleto[5b]
skeleton... 6.7
esquina[3a]
corner... 1.9
esquivar[7a]
escape (*vb.*)... 1.8
esquivo[6a]
shy... 4.2
establecer[1b]
settle... 1.
prove... 1.4
establecimiento[3a]
household... 2.9
establishment... 3.8
establo[5a]
stable... 3.8
estaca[5b]
post (*n.*)... 3.

Section

exploración
exploration........ 4.6

explorador
pioneer........... 6.8

explorar[4b]
explore............ 3.8

explosión[4a]
bursting.......... 2.9

explotación[7b]
working........... 4.7

explotar[3b]
burst............. 1.4
exploit............ 5.8

exponer[1b]
expose............ 2.2

exportación[6b]
export............ 5.1

exposición[3b]
display............ 2.6

expresar[1b]
express (*vb.*)....... 1.

expresión[1b]
expression......... 2.2

expresivo[4a]
(full of) meaning... 3.3
affectionate....... 4.3

expreso[3a]
express (*adj.*)...... 2.6

exprimir[6a]
press (*vb.*)......... 1.1
squeeze........... 3.6
wring............. 6.1

expuesto[3b]
expose............ 2.2

expulsar
expel............. 4.3

expulsión[6a]
expulsion.......... 9.

exquisito[2b]
exquisite.......... 3.6

éxtasis[6a]
bliss.............. 3.7

extender[1b]
extend............ 1.
spread............ 1.4

extensión[2a]
range............. 3.6
extension.......... 4.4

extensivo[6b]
applicable......... 9.8

extenso[3a]
vast.............. 2.8
extensive.......... 4.9

exterior[2b]
outside........... 1.4

externo[4b]
outward(s)........ 3.4

extinguir[3a]
put out........... 1.9

extra
extra............. 4.1

extracto
extract............ 5.4

extraer[5a]
extract............ 5.

extranjero[1b]
en el –, abroad...... 2.2
foreign............ 2.2
foreigner.......... 2.6

extrañar[2a]
surprise (*vb.*)....... 1.4

extrañeza[4b]
surprise (*n.*)....... 2.4

extraño[1b]
strange........... 1.
stranger........... 1.8

Section

extraordinario[2a]
unusual........... 2.

extravagancia[5b]
folly.............. 3.2

extravagante
extravagant....... 7.3

extraviar[4b]
stray............. 3.1

extravío[6b]
madness.......... 4.1

extremar[4a]
exaggerate........ 4.5

extremidad[5b]
extremity......... 5.1

extremo[1b]
extreme........... 1.5

F

fábrica[2b]
building (*n.*)....... 1.6
factory........... 2.6

fabricación[5a]
manufacture....... 2.9

fabricante[5a]
maker (manufacturer)...... 3.5
maker............ 4.7

fabricar[3b]
manufacture....... 3.

fábula[3b]
fable............. 4.4

fabuloso[5a]
fabulous.......... 7.1

facción[4a]
party............. 1.1
-es, feature....... 1.5

fácil[1b]
easy.............. 1.
-mente, easily........ 1.6

facilidad[2b]
ease.............. 3.3

facilitar[2b]
(make) easy....... 1.8

factor[5a]
element........... 2.3

factura[6b]
account........... 1.

facultad[2a]
ability............ 3.2

fachada[5a]
front (*n.*).......... 1.5

faena[4a]
work (*n.*).......... 1.
(piece of) work..... 1.1

faja[4b]
band.............. 2.5
strip (*n.*).......... 2.9
belt.............. 4.7

falda[2a]
lap............... 2.4
skirt.............. 2.6

faldón
coat-tail.......... 10.8

falsear[6b]
forge............. 6.2
distort............ 7.5

falsedad[4b]
lie (*n.*)............ 2.

falso[1b]
wrong (*adj.*)....... 1.
false.............. 1.4

falta[1a]
hacer –, need (*vb.*).... 1.
fault.............. 1.4
fault (defect)...... 1.8
a – de, (for) want of 3.
want (*n.*).......... 3.

Section

faltar[1a]
miss.............. 1.

fallar[7a]
fail............... 2.6

fallecer[3b]
die (*vb.*)........... 1.

falto[5a]
imperfect......... 3.9

faltriquera[5b]
pocket............ 2.3

fama[1b]
fame............. 2.3

familia[1a]
family............ 1.

familiar[3a]
familiar........... 3.3

familiaridad[4b]
intimacy.......... 6.8

famoso[1b]
famous........... 1.1

fanatismo[6b]
fanaticism......... 10.

fanega
acre.............. 4.4
bushel............ 6.

fantasía[2a]
fancy (*n.*)......... 2.

fantasma[3b]
ghost............. 3.2

fantástico[3a]
fantastic.......... 4.7

fardo[6a]
bundle............ 4.

fariseo
Pharisee.......... 8.

faro[4b]
lighthouse......... 6.6

farol[4b]
lantern............ 3.5

farsa[4b]
farce............. 5.8

fascinar[5b]
charm (*vb.*)........ 2.4

fase
phase............. 8.4

fastidiar[5a]
vex............... 4.1

fastidioso[5b]
vexing............ 3.8

fatal[2b]
mortal............ 2.9

fatalidad[5b]
fate.............. 1.5
(bad) luck........ 2.7

fatiga[3a]
weariness......... 5.6

fatigar[2b]
fatigado, tired....... 1.9
tire (*vb.*).......... 2.4

fatuo[6a]
foolish............ 2.8

favor[1a]
a – de
for (in favor of).. 1.
favor (*n.*)......... 1.4

favorable[4a]
favorable......... 2.2

favorecer[2a]
favor (*vb.*)......... 2.1

favorito[4b]
favorite........... 3.4

faz[3a]
face.............. 1.
front (*n.*)......... 1.5

fe[1a]
faith.............. 1.4

Section

fealdad
ugliness........... 10.2

febrero[4b]
February.......... 2.4

febril[4a]
feverish........... 6.9

fecundar[4a]
fertilize........... 6.8

fecundo[2b]
fertile............. 3.8

fecha[2b]
date (*n.*).......... 2.

fechar[7a]
date (*vb.*).......... 3.3

federación[7a]
confederacy....... 5.1

federal[5b]
federal............ 6.5

felicidad[1b]
happiness......... 1.4

felicitación[6b]
congratulation..... 5.3

felicitar[6a]
congratulate..... 6.2

feligrés
parishioner........ 10.2

feliz[1a]
glad.............. 1.
successful......... 3.4

femenino[3b]
female............ 3.3
feminine.......... 4.1

fenecer[6a]
die (*vb.*)........... 1.

fénix[6b]
phoenix........... 9.4

fenómeno[2b]
phenomenon....... 3.2

feo[1b]
ugly.............. 2.4

feria[5a]
market............ 1.7

fermentación
fermentation....... 6.4

fermentar
ferment........... 7.7

ferocidad[6a]
fierceness......... 7.8

feroz[3b]
wild.............. 1.6

férreo[4b]
iron (*adj.*)......... 1.4

ferretería
hardware.......... 6.8

ferrocarril[3a]
railroad........... 2.

fértil[4b]
fertile............. 3.8

ferviente[6b]
fervent............ 7.2

fervor[6a]
faith.............. 1.4
zeal.............. 2.4
fervor............. 4.8

fervoroso[5b]
eager............. 2.4

festín[5a]
feast.............. 3.5

festivo[6a]
cheerful........... 1.9

feudal
feudal............ 7.8

fiador[6a]
bondsman......... 13.

fiar[2a]
trust (*vb.*)......... 1.4

Section

frutero
greengrocer .... 13.
fruto[1b]
fruit 1.5
fuego[1a]
fire .... 1.
fuente[1b]
spring 1.7
source 2.7
fountain 2.8
platter .... 4.
fuera[1a]
away .... 1.
out .... 1.
outside 1.4
– de alcance
(out of) reach 4.1
– de ley, lawless 6.5
fuero[4a]
statute 4.1
fuerte[1a]
strong .... 1.
fort 2.6
fuerza[1a]
force .... 1.
power .... 1.
fuga[3b]
flight (rout) 2.5
fugar[7a]
run away 1.5
fugaz[6a]
passing 1.9
fugitive 3.5
fugitivo[4b]
fugitive (*adj.*) 3.5
fugitive (*n.*) 5.6
fulgor[4b]
glow .... 3.
fumar[3a]
smoke (*vb.*) 2.6
función[2a]
function 3.6
funcionamiento
working .... 5.
funcionar[4b]
function (*vb.*) 2.8
funcionario[5b]
official (*n.*) 2.8
fundación[5b]
foundation 4.2
fundador
founder 6.1
fundamental[4a]
fundamental 5.2
fundamento[3a]
base 1.7
fundar[1b]
found 1.5
fundición
melting 3.3
fundir[5a]
melt 2.5
fúnebre[6a]
dismal 3.9
funeral[6b]
funeral 5.4
funesto[3b]
disastrous 4.3
furia[3a]
fury 2.8
furioso[3a]
furious 1.9
furor[2b]
fury 2.8
furtivo[5b]
sly 3.9
cazador –, poacher 11.5

Section

fusil[4b]
gun 1.7
fútbol
football 6.8
fútil[6b]
trivial .... 5.
futuro[2a]
future (*n.*) 1.5
future (*adj.*) .... 2.

G

gabacho[5b]
French .... 1.
gabán[5b]
coat 2.2
overcoat 3.6
gabinete[5a]
cabinet 3.5
gaceta[6b]
paper (newspaper) .... 1.
gafas[7a]
glasses 4.2
gaita[5b]
bagpipe 8.1
gala[2b]
ceremony .... 2.
galán[2a]
civil 3.2
galante[5a]
civil 3.2
galantería[5b]
compliment 4.1
courtesy 4.7
galardón[5a]
prize (*n.*) 1.5
reward (*n.*) 2.5
galera[5a]
prison .... 2.
wagon 4.7
galería[4b]
gallery 4.2
galgo[6b]
dog 1.9
galope
gallop 4.7
gallardía[5b]
grace 1.4
gallardo[3a]
graceful 3.3
gallego[3a]
English .... 1.
gallinero
(hen) coop 11.4
gallo[2b]
cock 3.8
gallina, hen 4.7
gana[2a]
tener –, desire (*vb.*) .... 1.
de buena –, willingly 1.6
ganado[3a]
cattle 3.7
ganador
winner 6.5
ganancia[3b]
gain (*n.*) 1.9
profit (*n.*) 2.1
ganar[1a]
beat (in game) .... 1.
gain .... 1.
gancho
peg .... 6.
ganso
goose 5.3
garabato[6a]
hook 4.2

Section

garantía[5a]
pledge (*n.*) 2.9
garantizar[7a]
pledge (*vb.*) 2.7
garbanzo[5b]
pea 5.4
garbo[5a]
grace 1.4
garganta[2b]
throat .... 2.
garra[5a]
claw 6.1
garrafa
decanter 10.4
garrote[7a]
stick (*n.*) .... 2.
gas[4b]
gas 2.8
gasa[6b]
lawn 5.2
gasolina
gasoline 6.8
gastar[2a]
spend 1.6
gastado, spent (*adj.*) .... 2.
wear out 2.8
gasto[3a]
expense 3.3
gato[2b]
cat 4.1
gaveta
drawer 6.1
gemelo[6b]
twin 5.8
gemido[4a]
groan 5.3
gemir[3a]
groan .... 5.
generación[3a]
generation 3.4
general[1a]
general (*adj.*) .... 1.
en, por lo –
(in) general .... 1.
usual .... 1.
general (*n.*) 1.1
cuartel –
headquarters 3.4
procurador –
attorney-general 9.5
generalidad[6a]
generality .... 10.
generalizar[7a]
generalize 9.3
género[1b]
kind .... 1.
generosidad[3b]
generosity 6.4
generoso[1b]
generous 4.7
genial[5b]
(of) genius 4.3
genio[2a]
nature (character) .... 1.
genius 2.8
(man of) genius .... 4.
gente[1a]
crowd .... 1.
people (folk) .... 1.
gentil[2b]
graceful 3.3
gentileza[4b]
grace 1.4
genuino[6a]
true .... 1.
genuine 3.7
geografía[6b]
geography 6.2

Section

geográfico[5a]
geographical 6.5
geométrico[7a]
geometric 9.3
geranio
geranium 7.8
germen[4b]
germ 5.2
gesticular
gesticulate 12.2
gesto[2a]
look 1.9
gesture 4.3
gigante[2b]
giant .... 4.
gigantesco[3b]
great (huge) .... 1.
gimnasio
gymnasium 7.2
gimotear
snuffle 10.2
girado (el)
accepter 12.4
girar[3a]
turn (*vb.*) .... 1.
revolve 5.5
giro[2b]
turn (*n.*) .... 3.
draft 3.8
whirl .... 4.
gitano[2a]
gypsy 7.4
glacial[6a]
icy .... 6.
glaciar
glacier 6.4
globo[3b]
globe 3.3
globe (earth) 3.3
balloon 6.1
gloria[1a]
glory 2.3
glorieta
bower 5.2
glorioso[2a]
glorious 3.8
gobernador[3a]
governor 3.1
gobernante[5a]
governor 3.1
gobernar[2a]
rule (*vb.*) .... 1.
steer 3.9
gobierno[1b]
government 1.1
goce[2b]
enjoyment 3.8
golfo[4a]
knave 4.5
gulf .... 5.
golondrina[6b]
swallow .... 5.
golpe[1b]
blow 1.4
golpear[5a]
beat 1.1
strike 1.1
tap 4.6
bruise 5.7
bang 6.5
goma
rubber .... 5.
gordo[2b]
fat 1.9
gorjear
chirp 6.8

Section

helar + helado[2a]
- ice 2.4
- freeze 3.3
- frost 5.
- congeal 6.3

helecho
- fern 6.4

hembra[3b]
- female 3.3

hemisferio[6b]
- hemisphere 7.

henchir[3a]
- fill 1.4

hender[6b]
- crack (*vb.*) 2.6

heredad[5a]
- property 1.5
- farm 3.2

heredar[3a]
- inherit 5.7

heredero[2b]
- heir 2.9

hereditario
- hereditary 7.3

hereje[5b]
- heretic 6.3

herejía
- heresy 7.4

herencia[3a]
- inheritance 3.9

herida[2a]
- wound 2.8

herir + herido[1b]
- hurt (*tr. vb.*) 1.8
- wound (*vb.*) 2.2
- wounded 3.3

hermano[1a]
- brother 1.
- hermana, sister 1.

hermoso[1a]
- beautiful 1.

hermosura[1b]
- beauty 1.5

héroe[2b]
- hero 2.1
- heroína, heroine 5.8

heroico[2b]
- heroic 5.2

heroísmo[3b]
- heroism 7.2

herradura[6b]
- horseshoe 7.1

herramienta[6a]
- tool 3.

herrero
- blacksmith 5.6

hervir[2a]
- boil (*vb.*) 3.1

hidalgo[3a]
- noble 1.4
- peer 2.6

hidalguía[6b]
- nobility 3.7

hiedra[7a]
- ivy 6.7

hidrógeno
- hydrogen 6.

hiel[4b]
- gall 6.4

hielo[2b]
- ice 2.4

hierba[3b]
- grass 2.9

hierro[1b]
- de –, iron (*adj.*) 1.4
- iron (*n.*) 1.8
- – viejo, (old) iron 2.3

Section

hígado
- liver 6.

higiene[5b]
- hygiene 7.

higo
- fig 6.4

hijo[1a]
- hija, daughter 1.
- son 1.

hilar[5b]
- spin 3.9

hilera[5a]
- row (*n.*) 1.2

hilo[2a]
- thread 2.4
- tela de –, linen 3.6
- sin -s, wireless 6.

himno[5a]
- hymn 5.8

hincar[5a]
- – el diente, bite 3.7
- – la rodilla, kneel 3.9

hinchar[4a]
- swell 3.9

hinojo[6b]
- knee 2.
- ponerse de -s, kneel 3.9

hipocresía[5a]
- hypocrisy 6.9

hipócrita[4a]
- hypocrite 6.8

hipoteca
- mortgage 7.2

hipótesis[7a]
- basis 3.4

hispanoamericano[5a]
- French 1.

histérico[6b]
- hysterical 8.6

historia[1a]
- story 1.
- history 1.4

historiador[4a]
- historian 5.6

histórico[3b]
- historic 3.3

hocico[6b]
- muzzle 5.2

hogar[2a]
- hearth 3.2

hogaza
- loaf 3.3

hoguera[4a]
- fire 1.

hoja[1b]
- sheet 2.2
- leaf 2.6
- blade 4.5
- flap (of table) 4.9

hojear
- thumb 5.6

hola[3b]
- good morning 1.1
- hello 6.

holandés[4b]
- Dutch 4.

holgar[4b]
- rest (*vb.*) 1.

holgazán[6a]
- lazy 3.8

hollar[3b]
- trample 5.9

hombre[1a]
- man 1.
- – de negocios business man 1.4
- – de letras, scholar 2.3
- – de Estado, statesman 3.
- – de ciencia, scientist 4.2

Section

hombría
- manhood 6.8

hombro[2a]
- shoulder (*n.*) 1.5

homenaje[3b]
- homage 4.6
- rendir –, (do) homage 5.

homicida[6a]
- murderer 4.1

homicidio[6b]
- murder 3.3

homogéneo[6b]
- (of the same) kind 4.

honda[5b]
- sling 6.5

hondo[2a]
- deep 1.

honestidad[6b]
- honesty 6.4

honesto[3b]
- honest 1.9

honor[1a]
- honor (*n.*) 1.

honra[2a]
- honor (*n.*) 1.

honradez[4a]
- honesty 6.4

honrar + honrado[1b]
- honor (*vb.*) 1.7
- honest 1.9

honroso[4a]
- honorable 4.

hora[1a]
- hour 1.
- (what) time (is it) 1.
- media –, half hour 1.5

horca[6a]
- gallows 6.6
- scaffold 7.1

horizontal[5b]
- horizontal 6.5

horizonte[2b]
- horizon 4.

hormiga[4b]
- ant 6.

horno[3b]
- furnace 2.7
- oven 2.7

horrendo[3b]
- terrible 1.8
- hideous 6.4

horrible[2a]
- terrible 1.8
- hideous 6.4

horror[2a]
- horror 4.4

horrorizar[5b]
- frighten 1.9

horroroso[5b]
- terrible 1.8

hortalizas[5b]
- vegetable 4.8

hospital[3b]
- hospital 5.

hospitalario
- hospitable 7.2

hospitalidad
- hospitality 4.9

hostil[6b]
- hostile 3.5

hostilidad[6b]
- enmity 5.8

hotel[3b]
- house 1.
- hotel 3.2

hoy[1a]
- today 1.

Section

hoyo[4a]
- hole 2.2

hoyuelo
- dimple 7.2

hoz[5a]
- sickle 6.9

hueco[3a]
- hollow (*adj.*) 3.

huelga[6b]
- strike (*n.*) 3.

huella[3a]
- track (*n.*) 2.1

huérfano[4a]
- orphan 5.6

huerta[2a]
- garden 1.4

huerto[4b]
- orchard 5.2

hueso[2a]
- bone 2.6

huésped[2b]
- company 1.7
- host 2.5

huevo[1b]
- egg 2.

huida[6a]
- flight (rout) 2.5

huir[1a]
- run away 1.5

humanidad[2a]
- mankind 2.4

humano[1a]
- human 1.4

humear[5b]
- smoke (*vb.*) 2.6

humedad[4a]
- moisture 4.4

humedecer[4b]
- moisten 6.8

húmedo[3a]
- damp 3.4

humildad[4a]
- humility 5.4

humilde[1b]
- humble 3.5
- de – cuna (of) lowly (birth) 6.4

humillación[6a]
- humiliation 7.9

humillar[3a]
- humble 5.

humo[2a]
- smoke (*n.*) 2.4

humor[2b]
- humor 2.4

hundir[2a]
- dip 3.2
- sink 3.2

húngaro
- Hungarian 6.6

huracán[4a]
- storm 1.6

hurtar[4b]
- rob 2.3

húsar
- hussar 9.4

huso
- spindle 6.6

I

ida[6a]
- departure 3.1

idea[1a]
- idea 1.4

ideal[2a]
- ideal 3.2

Section

- indiferencia[3a]
  - indifference 4.7
  - detachment 5.5
- indiferente[2a]
  - (all the) same 1.
- indígena[4b]
  - native (*adj.*) 3.2
  - native (*n.*) 3.7
- indignación[2b]
  - anger 1.9
  - indignation 4.2
- indignar[3a]
  - anger (*vb.*) 2.7
- indigno[3a]
  - unworthy 4 7
- indio[3a]
  - Indian 3.1
- indirecto[4a]
  - indirect 5.
- indiscreto[6b]
  - indiscreet 8.3
- indiscutible[4a]
  - unquestionable 6.5
- indispensable[3a]
  - essential 2.9
- individual[5b]
  - individual 3.8
- individuo[2a]
  - individual 3.2
- índole[3a]
  - nature (character) 1.
- indolencia[6a]
  - sloth 6.9
- indómito[6b]
  - unruly 7.4
- inducir[4a]
  - persuade 2.1
- indudable[3a]
  - (without) doubt 1.
- indulgencia[6b]
  - indulgence 5.8
- indulgente
  - indulgent 8.1
- indulto[6a]
  - pardon 3.6
- industria[2a]
  - industry 2.
  - industry (application) 2.6
- industrial[5a]
  - maker 3.5
  - industrial 5.5
- inédito
  - unpublished 12.8
- inefable[5a]
  - inexpressible 9.3
- inercia[6a]
  - inertia 10.2
- inerte[6b]
  - inert 6.8
- inesperado[4a]
  - unexpected 3.5
- inestimable[5a]
  - inestimable 8.1
- inevitable[4b]
  - inevitable 4.4
- inexplicable[7a]
  - inexplicable 8.7
- infalible[5b]
  - infallible 7.7
- infame[3a]
  - bad 1.2
  - infamous 4.3
- infamia[4a]
  - infamy 7.6
- infancia[3b]
  - childhood 3.3
- infante[3b]
  - prince 1.1
  - (crown) prince 2.3
- infantería
  - infantry 5.6
- infantil[3b]
  - childish 4.6
- infatigable
  - untiring 7.2
- infeliz[1b]
  - unhappy 1.8
  - unfortunate 2.2
- inferior[2b]
  - low 1.4
  - inferior 3.6
  - parte –, under side 4.4
- inferir[3b]
  - inflict 4.
  - infer 5.7
- infernal[3b]
  - infernal 6.7
- infiel[6b]
  - false 2.4
- infierno[2a]
  - hell 3.
- infinidad[4a]
  - infinity 9.6
- infinito[1b]
  - infinite 3.5
- inflamar[4a]
  - stir 1.9
  - -se, (catch on) fire 2.5
- influencia[2a]
  - influence 1.6
- influir[3a]
  - influence 3.2
- influjo[4b]
  - influence 1.6
- influyente
  - influential 8.2
- información[5a]
  - information 2.
  - – legal
    - legal information 5.3
- informar[2b]
  - (let) know 1.
  - report (*vb.*) 1.5
- informe[2b]
  - report 1.
  - information 2.
  - shapeless 6.2
- infortunio[3b]
  - misfortune 2.2
- infundir[3b]
  - inspire 3.1
- ingeniero[3a]
  - engineer 4.8
  - cuerpo de -s
    - (engineer) corps 7.2
- ingenio[2a]
  - wit 2.7
  - ingenuity 5.6
- ingenioso[3a]
  - witty 4.1
  - ingenious 4.7
- ingenuidad[6a]
  - simplicity 5.4
- ingenuo[5a]
  - open (*adj.*) 1.3
- inglés[1b]
  - French 1.
- ingratitud[4a]
  - ingratitude 7.
- ingrato[2b]
  - ungrateful 4.9
- ingreso[5b]
  - entrance 1.8
- inhumano[5a]
  - cruel 2.3
- inicial
  - initial 4.6
- iniciar[3b]
  - begin 1.
- iniciativo[4a]
  - initiative 5.7
- inicuo[6a]
  - bad 1.2
- injuria[4a]
  - offense 3.8
- injusticia[3a]
  - injustice 4.6
- injusto[2b]
  - unjust 3.3
- inmediación[4b]
  - neighborhood 2.9
- inmediato[1b]
  - next 1.
  - (at) once 1.
  - immediate 2.8
- inmensidad[3a]
  - greatness 2.
- inmenso[1b]
  - great (huge) 1.
- inminente
  - imminent 6.1
- inmoral[6a]
  - immoral 12.2
- inmoralidad[6a]
  - immorality 11.4
- inmortal[3a]
  - immortal 3.8
- inmortalidad
  - immortality 6.
- inmóvil[3a]
  - (stand) still 1.3
  - stable (*adj.*) 2.9
- inmovilidad
  - immobility 12.9
- inmundo[6b]
  - filthy 5.7
- inmutable[5a]
  - unchangeable 8.9
- innato[6b]
  - innate 9.
- innoble
  - ignoble 4.6
- innumerable[3a]
  - countless 3.9
- inocencia[2b]
  - innocence 3.4
- inocente[2a]
  - innocent 2.8
- inofensivo
  - harmless 5.8
- inolvidable[5a]
  - unforgettable 10.9
- inquietar[5a]
  - worry 3.2
- inquieto[2a]
  - anxious 2.3
  - restless 2.7
  - uneasy 5.5
  - fretful 6.6
- inquietud[2b]
  - worry 2.8
- inquilino
  - tenant 6.5
- inquirir[4b]
  - ask (question) 1.
  - investigate 4.6
- insaciable[4b]
  - greedy 4.8
- insano[5b]
  - mad 2.7
- inscribir
  - enter (writing) 2.6
- inscripción[7a]
  - inscription 5.2
- insecto[4a]
  - insect 4.4
- inseguro[6a]
  - uncertain 4.
  - unsteady 5.6
- insensato[5a]
  - dull 3.5
- insensible[5a]
  - insensible 4.1
- inseparable[7a]
  - inseparable 6.8
- insertar[6b]
  - insert 4.4
- insigne[2b]
  - famous 1.1
- insignificante[3b]
  - insignificant 4.
- insinuación[6b]
  - hint 4.1
- insinuar[4a]
  - hint 3.7
- insistencia[4b]
  - insistence 7.3
- insistir[2b]
  - insist 2.
- insolencia[4b]
  - insolence 7.4
- insolente[4a]
  - saucy 5.1
- inspección
  - survey 4.9
- inspeccionar[6b]
  - examine 1.5
  - survey 5.8
- inspector
  - inspector 6.9
- inspiración[3a]
  - inspiration 4.
- inspirar[1b]
  - inspire 3.1
- instalación
  - installation 8.6
- instalar[3b]
  - install 3.2
- instancia[4a]
  - instance 3.2
- instantáneo[4b]
  - immediate 2.8
- instante[1a]
  - al –, (at) once 1.
  - while (*n.*) 1.8
- instar[6a]
  - urge (*vb.*) 2.5
- instintivo[5a]
  - instinctive 4.9
- instinto[2b]
  - instinct 3.2
- institución[4b]
  - institute (*n.*) 2.6
- instituir
  - institute 3.3
- instituto[4a]
  - institute (*n.*) 2.6
- institutriz
  - governess 8.2
- instrucción[2b]
  - instruction 2.4
- instructivo
  - instructive 7.2
- instruir[3b]
  - teach 1.

Section

jueves[5a]
- Thursday . . . 2.7

juez[2a]
- judge . . . 1.6

jugador[4b]
- player . . . 6.

jugar[1b]
- play (*vb.*) . . . 1.

juglar
- minstrel . . . 7.2

jugo[3b]
- juice . . . 4.3

juguete[3b]
- toy . . . 5.1

juguetón[6a]
- playful . . . 7.4

juicio[1b]
- reason . . . 1.4
- judgment . . . 1.5
- trial . . . 2.

juicioso[6b]
- prudent . . . 3.3

julio[3a]
- July . . . 2.2

jumento[7a]
- ass . . . 3.9

junco[5a]
- reed . . . 3.4

junio[4a]
- June . . . 2.3

junta[3b]
- council . . . 2.1
- committee . . . 3.

juntar[1b]
- join . . . 1.
- bring together . . . 2.6

junto[1a]
- – a, beside . . . 1.
- near (*adj.* and *adv.*) . 1.
- together . . . 1.
- -s, side by side . . . 2.2

jurado
- jury . . . 5.

juramento[3a]
- oath . . . 4.6
- oath (blasphemy) . . 4.8

jurar[1b]
- swear . . . 2.7

jurisdicción[5b]
- territory . . . 2.1

jurisprudencia
- jurisprudence . . . 9.6

justicia[1b]
- justice . . . 1.8
- fairness . . . 8.6

justiciero[6a]
- fair (*adj.*) . . . 1.4

justificación
- justification . . . 7.2

justificar[2b]
- justify . . . 2.5

justo[1b]
- right (correct) . . . 1.
- fair (*adj.*) . . . 1.4
- upright . . . 3.8

juvenil[4a]
- youthful . . . 3.3

juventud[1b]
- youth . . . 1.4

juzgar[1b]
- judge (*vb.*) . . . 1.

K

kilogramo[6b]
- pound (*n.*) . . . 1.6

kilómetro[3b]
- mile . . . 1.7

L

Section

laberinto[6b]
- maze . . . 7.

labio[1b]
- lip . . . 1.4

labor[2a]
- work (*n.*) . . . 1.
- (a) work . . . 1.
- (piece of) work . . . 1.1

laborar[7a]
- work (*vb.*) . . . 1.

laboratorio[5b]
- laboratory . . . 5.5

laborioso[4b]
- industrious . . . 3.2

labrador[2a]
- farmer . . . 1.8

labranza[6b]
- farming . . . 2.6

labrar[3a]
- work (*vb.*) . . . 1.

labriego[4a]
- peasant . . . 2.4

lácteo
- milky . . . 7.2

ladera[6b]
- slope . . . 3.6

lado[1a]
- al otro –
  - (be) across . . . 1.
- al – de, beside . . . 1.
- side . . . 1.
- – superior
  - top (side) . . . 2.6
- a un –, aside . . . 3.1

ladrar[5a]
- bark . . . 5.1

ladrillo[6a]
- brick . . . 5.

ladrón[2a]
- thief . . . 3.7

lagarto[6a]
- reptile . . . 7.4

lago[2b]
- lake . . . 2.1

lágrima[1b]
- tear (*n.*) . . . 1.

laguna[4a]
- pond . . . 2.7

laico
- lay (*adj.*) . . . 4.2

lamentable[3a]
- grievous . . . 4.

lamentar[2b]
- mourn . . . 1.9
- deplore . . . 4.2

lamento[4a]
- lamentation . . . 4.2

lamer
- lick . . . 6.2

lámina[3b]
- picture (*n.*) . . . 1.1
- print (*n.*) . . . 2.7

lámpara[3b]
- lamp . . . 2.5

lana[2b]
- wool . . . 2.8
- de –, wool . . . 2.8

lance[2a]
- position . . . 1.5

lancha[4a]
- boat . . . 2.6

langosta[6b]
- locust . . . 6.8

languidecer
- droop . . . 4.4
- languish . . . 6.8

Section

languidez
- languor . . . 8.6

lánguido[6b]
- languid . . . 7.4

lanza[3a]
- spear . . . 3.2

lanzar[1b]
- throw . . . 1.
- -se, dash (*vb.*) . . . 1.8

lápiz[6a]
- pencil . . . 4.2

largo[1a]
- long (*adj.*) . . . 1.
- length . . . 1.7
- a lo – de, along . . . 2.2
- ir a lo – de, go along . . 4.1

lástima[2a]
- (too) bad . . . 2.9

lastimar[4a]
- hurt (*tr. vb.*) . . . 1.8

lastimero[6b]
- pitiful . . . 6.6

lastimoso[6b]
- pitiful . . . 6.6

lata[6b]
- tin . . . 4.

lateral[4b]
- side . . . 4.1

latido[6a]
- beating . . . 4.6

látigo[5b]
- whip . . . 4.8

latín[3b]
- Latin . . . 2.8

latino[2b]
- Latin . . . 2.8

latir[5a]
- beat . . . 1.3
- howl (dog) . . . 4.5

latitud[5a]
- width . . . 3.4

laúd
- lute . . . 7.2

laudable[6b]
- laudable . . . 8.2

laurel[3a]
- laurel . . . 5.1

lauro[5b]
- laurel . . . 5.1

lavar[2a]
- wash (*vb.*) . . . 2.6
- lavado, wash (*n.*) . . . 3.3

lazo[2a]
- tie (*n.*) . . . 1.6
- loop . . . 5.4

leal[3a]
- loyal . . . 3.9

lealtad[4a]
- loyalty . . . 3.6

lección[2b]
- lesson . . . 1.2

lector[2a]
- reader (person) . . . 3.

lectura[2b]
- reading (*n.*) . . . 1.6

leche[2b]
- milk . . . 2.5

lechería
- dairy . . . 5.7

lechero
- milkman . . . 10.6

lechoso
- milky . . . 7.2

lecho[2a]
- bed . . . 1.4

Section

lechuga[7a]
- lettuce . . . 7.1

leer[1a]
- read . . . 1.

legal[4b]
- lawful . . . 3.
- legal . . . 4.
- moneda –
  - (legal) tender . . . 4.8
- información –
  - legal information . 5.3

legar[6b]
- leave . . . 2.7

legión[5a]
- legion . . . 5.8

legislación[6a]
- legislation . . . 4.6

legislador[5a]
- legislator . . . 6.3

legislatura
- legislature . . . 5.2

legítimo[3a]
- lawful . . . 3.
- legitimate . . . 5.8

legua[2a]
- a –, far . . . 1.
- mile . . . 1.7

legumbre[4a]
- vegetable . . . 4.8

lejano[2a]
- far . . . 1.

lejos[1a]
- away . . . 1.
- far . . . 1.

lema[6b]
- device . . . 4.2

lengua[1a]
- tongue (language) . . 1.
- tongue (part of mouth) . . . 1.8

lenguaje[2b]
- language . . . 1.6

lente[3b]
- -s, glasses . . . 4.2

lenteja[6b]
- bean . . . 5.4

lentejuela
- spangle . . . 6.8

lentitud[6b]
- slowness . . . 10.5

lento[2a]
- slow . . . 1.2

leña[3b]
- wood . . . 1.5

leñador
- woodman . . . 7.2

león[2b]
- lion . . . 2.5

lerdo[6b]
- dull . . . 3.5

letra[1a]
- letter . . . 1.4
- al pie de la –
  - word for word . . . 2.2
- hombre de -s, scholar . 2.3

letrado[5b]
- learned . . . 1.6
- scholar . . . 2.3

letrero[6a]
- label . . . 5.2

levantar[1a]
- lift . . . 1.
- pick up . . . 1.5

leva[2a]
- light (*adj.*) . . . 1.

levita[5a]
- frock coat . . . 6.1

LL

Section

llover[3a]
rain . . . 4.2
lluvia[2b]
rain (*n.*) . . . 2.
shower (*n.*) . . . 2.5
lluvioso[7a]
rainy . . . 5.7

M

macizo[4b]
solid . . . 3.2
clump . . . 4.8
machacar[4b]
crush . . . 3.
macho[5a]
male . . . 3.1
madera[2b]
wood . . . 1.5
de –, wood (*adj.*) . . . 1.5
madero[6a]
wood . . . 1.5
beam . . . 2.3
madrasta
step-mother . . . 7.8
madre[1a]
mother . . . 1.
madrileño[4a]
English . . . 1.
madrina[6b]
godmother . . . 6.8
madrugada[4b]
dawn . . . 3.5
madrugar[4a]
get up early . . . 3.
madurar[4a]
(get) ripe . . . 3.4
madurez
maturity . . . 7.8
maduro[4b]
ripe . . . 2.9
mature . . . 4.
maestro[1b]
teacher . . . 1.
obra maestra
masterpiece . . . 6.4
mágico[2b]
poder –, magic . . . 3.5
magnético[6a]
magnetic . . . 7.4
magistrado[5a]
magistrate . . . 4.
magnificencia[6a]
splendor . . . 3.6
magnífico[2a]
fine . . . 1.1
magnificent . . . 3.5
magnitud[6b]
amount . . . 1.
mago[6b]
wizard . . . 6.2
magro[7b]
thin . . . 2.
maíz[4a]
corn . . . 4.8
majadero[5a]
foolish . . . 2.8
majestad[1b]
majesty . . . 2.5
majestuoso[3b]
grand . . . 2.3
mal(o) (*adj.* and *adv.*)[1a]
bad . . . 1.
wrong (*adj.*) . . . 1.
naughty . . . 2.3
mal (*n.*)[2a]
disease . . . 1.6
damage (*n.*) . . . 2.4
wrong . . . 3.2

Section

maldad[3b]
evil (*n.*) . . . 2.
maldecir + maldito[2a]
curse . . . 4.6
maldición[3a]
curse . . . 3.5
malentendido
misunderstanding . . . 6.
malestar[6b]
uneasiness . . . 5.
maleta[4b]
bag . . . 3.
bag (suitcase) . . . 4.5
maleza[5a]
weed . . . 5.3
brushwood . . . 9.8
malicia[3a]
tener –
suspect (*vb.*) . . . 2.8
malice . . . 4.8
malicioso[5a]
sly . . . 4.2
maligno[6a]
bad . . . 1.2
malograr[4b]
-se, fail . . . 2.6
waste . . . 4.2
malsano
unhealthy . . . 6.9
maltratar[4b]
abuse . . . 4.3
malvado[5a]
bad . . . 1.2
knave . . . 4.5
villain . . . 5.
malvenido
unwelcome . . . 7.2
malla[5b]
net . . . 3.1
web . . . 3.4
-s, tights . . . 5.1
mamá[3b]
mamma . . . 2.9
mamar[6b]
suck . . . 6.
manantial[4b]
spring . . . 1.7
manar[6b]
gush . . . 4.5
mancebo[4b]
boy . . . 1.4
mancilla[6b]
spot . . . 2.2
mancha[3a]
spot . . . 2.2
manchar[2b]
spot . . . 4.4
manchego[6b]
English . . . 1.
mandamiento[6b]
order . . . 1.
writ . . . 5.9
mandar[1a]
send . . . 1.
command (*vb.*) . . . 1.5
mandato[4a]
order . . . 1.
mando[3b]
command (*n.*) . . . 2.3
manejar[3b]
drive (car, etc.) . . . 1.
handle . . . 3.9
manejo[5a]
direction . . . 1.8
manera[1a]
de ninguna –
(not at) all . . . 1.
way . . . 1.

Section

manga[4a]
sleeve . . . 5.1
mango[6b]
handle . . . 3.1
manguito
muff . . . 7.2
manía[3b]
madness . . . 4.1
manifestación[3b]
statement . . . 2.1
demonstration . . . 6.2
manifestar[1b]
show (*vb.*) . . . 1.
manifest . . . 3.1
manifiesto[4a]
manifiestamente
clearly . . . 2.9
manifest . . . 4.2
manjar[3b]
dish . . . 1.8
food . . . 1.9
mano[1a]
hand (*n.*) . . . 1.
de propia –
(with one's own)
hand . . . 3.
manojo[5b]
handful . . . 5.6
mansedumbre[6a]
humility . . . 5.4
mansión[4a]
palace . . . 2.3
mansion . . . 3.7
manso[3b]
gentle . . . 1.4
manta[5a]
blanket . . . 4.
manteca, mantequilla[3a]
fat . . . 2.6
butter . . . 3.5
mantel[6a]
table-cloth . . . 9.1
alzar los -es
clear (table) . . . 4.3
mantener[1b]
maintain (keep up) . . . 1.5
maintain (affirm) . . . 3.5
mantilla[5a]
veil . . . 3.4
manto[2b]
cloak . . . 4.8
manual[5b]
manual (textbook) . . . 6.5
manual (*adj.*) . . . 7.3
manuscrito[6a]
manuscript . . . 5.8
manzana[4b]
apple . . . 3.5
manzano
apple tree . . . 5.
maña[4b]
skill . . . 3.
trick . . . 3.2
mañana[1a]
morning . . . 1.
tomorrow . . . 1.4
pasado –
day after to-
morrow . . . 4.3
mapa[5b]
map . . . 1.9
máquina[2a]
machine . . . 2.
– de escribir
typewriter . . . 5.6
maquinalmente
mechanically . . . 5.2
mar[1a]
sea . . . 1.

Section

maravedí[6b]
pound . . . 1.
maravilla[2a]
wonder (*n.*) . . . 1.7
maravillar[5a]
astonish . . . 2.7
maravilloso[2b]
wonderful . . . 1.2
marca[4b]
sign (*n.*) . . . 1.1
brand . . . 4.2
marcar[2a]
mark (*vb.*) . . . 1.
marco[5a]
frame (*n.*) . . . 2.4
marcha[2b]
course . . . 1.1
march . . . 1.5
walk . . . 1.6
pace (*n.*) . . . 1.8
reducir la –, acortar
la –
slow down . . . 4.4
marchar[1b]
-se, go away . . . 1.
march (*vb.*) . . . 1.4
marchitar[5a]
fade . . . 4.9
marchito[5b]
fade . . . 4.9
marea[6b]
tide . . . 3.4
marear[6a]
mareado, dizzy . . . 6.4
mareo[4a]
(sea) sickness . . . 4.9
marfil[4b]
ivory . . . 5.6
margen[3a]
margin . . . 3.9
marido[1a]
husband . . . 1.
marina[5a]
shipping . . . 3.
navy . . . 3.6
marinero[2b]
sailor . . . 2.9
marino[3a]
sailor . . . 2.9
mariner . . . 5.8
mariposa[4a]
butterfly . . . 5.2
mariscal[7a]
marshal . . . 4.2
marítimo[5a]
sea (*adj.*) . . . 3.
marmita
kettle . . . 4.8
mármol[3a]
marble . . . 3.8
marqués[2b]
marquis . . . 6.9
martes[5b]
Tuesday . . . 3.7
martillo[4a]
hammer . . . 4.8
mártir[4a]
martyr . . . 3.1
martirio[3a]
torture . . . 3.9
martyrdom . . . 7.3
marzo[4b]
March . . . 1.9
mas, más[1a]
but . . . 1.
more . . . 1.
lo –, most . . . 1.

Section

mi, mí[1a]
my .... 1.
miedo[1b]
tener –, (be) afraid .... 1.
fear 1.4
miel[2b]
honey 3.9
miembro[2b]
member 1.1
limb .... †2.
mientras[1a]
the . . . . the .... 1.
while .... 1.
– tanto, meanwhile 2.8
miércoles
Wednesday 4.3
mies[6a]
crop 2.7
miga[4a]
crumb 5.8
mil[1]*
thousand 1.4
milagro[2b]
wonder (*n.*) 1.7
miracle 2.9
milenario
millennium 8.8
milicia[7a]
militia 6.3
militar[2a]
soldier .... 1.
military 2.4
mil millones
billion 9.2
milla[7a]
mile 1.7
millar[6b]
thousand 1.4
millón[1]*
million 1.4
millonario[5b]
millionaire 6.9
mimar[3b]
spoil 4.6
mimbre[6a]
willow 5.6
mimo[6b]
caress 6.2
mina[3b]
mine 2.6
mineral[5a]
mineral 6.1
minero[7a]
miner 4.7
miniatura
miniature 7.7
mínimo[4a]
minimum 7.4
ministerio[4b]
ministry 3.4
ministro[1b]
minister 1.5
– de Estado
secretary of state 3.9
minoría
minority 7.7
minucioso[3b]
thorough .... 2.
minute 3.1
minuto[2a]
minute (*n.*) 1.5
mío[1a]
mine 1.1
mira[4a]
estar a la –
watch (*vb.*) .... 1.

Section

mirada[1b]
look (*n.*) .... 1.
clavar la –, peer 3.5
miramiento[6b]
care .... 1.
mirar (*vb.*)[1a]
look at .... 1.
mirar (*n.*)[5b]
look .... 1.
mirlo[7b]
blackbird 6.7
mirto
myrtle 7.2
misa[1b]
mass 2.7
miserable[1b]
miserable 2.7
miseria[1b]
misery 2.7
misericordia[2b]
mercy .... 2.
pity (*n.*) 2.4
misericordioso[6a]
merciful 4.2
mísero[3a]
miserable 2.7
misión[3a]
mission 4.1
misionero
missionary 7.2
mismo[1a]
ahora –, ya –, (at) once 1.
same .... 1.
yo –, myself 1.3
él –, himself 1.4
ellos -s, themselves 1.4
el –, itself 1.5
ella misma, herself 1.7
usted –, yourself 2.1
misterio[2a]
mystery 2.4
misterioso[2a]
mysterious 3.5
místico[4a]
mystic 6.9
mitad[1b]
half (*n.*) .... 1.
mitra
mitre 7.2
mixto[5a]
mix 2.2
mocedad[4a]
youth 1.4
moda[3a]
fashion 2.8
a la –, fashionable .... 6.
modelo[2b]
model .... 2.
moderación[5b]
moderation (temperateness) 3.8
moderation (diminution) 5.8
moderar + moderado[3b]
moderate (*adj.*) .... 3.
moderate (*vb.*) 4.2
moderno[1b]
modern 1.8
modestia[3b]
modesty 4.7
modesto[2b]
modest 2.4
modificación[4b]
change (*n.*) 1.5
modificar[3a]
change (*vb.*) 1.4
modista[6b]
dressmaker 8.4

Section

modo[1a]
de ningún –
(not at) all .... 1.
de todos -s
(in any) case .... 1.
way .... 1.
mode 2.2
de todos -s, anyhow 4.2
modular[6b]
transform 2.8
mohín[6b]
face 1.8
mohino[5b]
sullen 5.8
estar –, sulk 10.1
moho
rust 5.2
mojar[3a]
mojado, wet (*adj.*) 2.9
wet (*vb.*) 2.9
molde[3b]
mould 3.1
moldura[6a]
moulding 6.2
mole[6a]
mass 1.6
moler[3a]
grind 5.1
molestar[2a]
trouble (*vb.*) 1.5
vex 4.1
tease 5.9
molestia[3b]
trouble .... 1.
molesto[4a]
vexing 3.8
molinero[5b]
miller 6.1
molino[2b]
mill .... 3.
– de viento, windmill 5.4
momentáneo[6b]
immediate 2.8
momentary 7.2
momento[1a]
moment .... 1.
while (*n.*) 1.8
monarca[3a]
monarch 3.3
monarquía
monarchy 5.6
monasterio[5a]
convent 3.8
moneda[2b]
coin 1.9
– legal
(legal) tender 4.8
currency 4.9
monje[3a]
monk 4.7
monja, nun 6.3
mono[4a]
monkey 5.6
monólogo[6b]
monologue .... 11.
monopolio
monopoly 7.3
monosílabo[5b]
monosyllable 10.5
monotonía
monotony 8.1
monótono[5a]
monotonous 6.8
monstruo[2b]
monster 4.1
monstruoso[4a]
monstrous 4.7

Section

montaje
set-up (*n.*) 10.6
montaña[1b]
mountain 1.5
montañoso[7b]
mountainous 6.7
montar[2a]
– a caballo
ride (horse) 1.5
monte[1b]
forest .... 1.
mountain 1.5
montera[6b]
cap 3.8
montón[3a]
mass 1.6
monumental
monumental 7.8
monumento[2b]
monument 2.5
moño[6a]
knot .... 5.
mora[6b]
berry 4.9
morada[3b]
dwelling 2.3
morador[4b]
inhabitant 3.2
moral[1b]
moral 2.3
morals 3.6
moralidad[5b]
morals 3.6
moralista[5b]
moralist 8.6
morar[5b]
live 1.1
morboso
morbid 7.6
morder[2b]
bite 3.7
moreno[3a]
brown 2.5
moribundo[5a]
dying 4.5
morir[1a]
die (*vb.*) .... 1.
muerto, dead 1.4
morisco[6b]
Moor 5.8
moro[2b]
Moor 5.8
mortaja[6b]
shroud 6.6
mortal[2a]
mortal (deadly) 2.9
mortal (susceptible to death) 3.7
mortificar[5a]
vex 4.1
mosca[3a]
fly 4.2
mosquito[4b]
mosquito 7.2
mostrador[6a]
counter 6.3
mostrar[1a]
show (*vb.*) .... 1.
mote[6b]
device 4.2
nickname 8.6
motín
riot 4.6
motivar[5a]
cause (*vb.*) .... 1.
(give) rise 2.3

	Section
noción[4a]	
idea	1.4
nocivo[6b]	
injurious	4.3
nocturno[3b]	
night	3.3
noche[1a]	
night	1.
esta –, tonight	1.4
de –, (at) night	2.2
media –, midnight	2.4
cada –, todas las -s nightly	3.
nodriza[5b]	
wet-nurse	12.9
nombradía[5b]	
fame	2.3
nombramiento[5a]	
appointment (to something)	4.5
nomination	4.9
nombrar[1b]	
(give) name (to)	1.
name (appoint)	1.
nombre[1a]	
name (*n.*)	1.
sin –, nameless	5.8
normal[4a]	
normal	3.9
noroeste	
northwest	6.8
norte[2a]	
north	1.6
northern	2.
nosotros[1]*	
we	1.
nota[1b]	
note (*n.*)	1.9
notable[2a]	
remarkable	2.4
notar[1b]	
notice (*vb.*)	1.4
observe	1.4
note (*vb.*)	1.9
notario	
public trustee	7.6
noticia[1b]	
-s, news	1.4
sin – de, unknown	2.2
notificar[6a]	
(let) know	1.
(give) notice (of)	1.4
notorio[4a]	
known	1.1
novedad[2b]	
novelty	4.3
novela[2b]	
novel (*n.*)	2.9
novelista[5b]	
author	1.9
novelist	7.9
noveno[5]*	
ninth	4.7
noventa[6]*	
ninety	5.8
noviembre[4b]	
November	2.3
novio[2a]	
novia, bride	1.6
engaged	2.5
groom	4.6
nube[1b]	
cloud	1.9
nublado[6b]	
cloudy	5.8
núcleo[5b]	
nucleus	4.9
nudo[3b]	
knot	4.4
nuestro (*adj.*)[1]*	
our	1.
nuestro (*pron.*)[4]*	
ours	3.9
nueva[5a]	
news	1.4
nueve[2]*	
nine	2.4
nuevo[1a]	
de –, again	1.
new	1.
víspera de Año Nuevo (New Year's) Eve	3.8
nuez[5b]	
nut	5.1
walnut	6.3
nulidad	
nonentity	10.6
nulo[5b]	
void	5.4
número[1a]	
number (quantity)	1.
figure	1.1
number (digit)	2.4
numeroso[2a]	
numerous	1.5
nunca[1a]	
ever	1.
never	1.
nuncio[6a]	
messenger	2.5
nupcias[6b]	
wedding	3.4
nutrición	
feeding	4.2
nourishment	5.6
nutrir[4b]	
nourish	3.2

O

	Section
o[1a]	
either (*conj.*)	1.
el uno – el otro either (one)	1.
or	1.
¡o!, O	1.2
oasis[6b]	
oasis	7.
obedecer[1b]	
obey	2.2
obediencia[4b]	
obedience	6.
obediente[5a]	
obedient	3.2
obelisco[6b]	
obelisk	9.
obispo[2b]	
bishop	3.3
objeción[6b]	
hacer –, object (*vb.*)	1.9
objection	4.4
objetivo[4b]	
purpose	1.
objeto[1a]	
thing	1.
– de arte work of art	1.8
oblicuo	
oblique	6.2
obligación[2a]	
obligation	4.
obligar[1a]	
force	1.
obligado forced (*adj.*)	1.1
obligatorio[7a]	
required	3.1
obra[1a]	
work (*n.*)	1.
(a) work	1.
– de arte work of art	1.8
– maestra masterpiece	6.4
obrar[2b]	
act (take action)	1.
obrero[3a]	
worker	2.2
obscurecer[3b]	
(grow) dark	4.5
obscure	6.
obscuridad[2a]	
darkness	2.9
obscuro[1a]	
dark	1.
obsequiar[4b]	
present (*vb.*)	1.4
obsequio[4a]	
courtesy	4.7
treat	4.9
observación[2a]	
observation	2.4
remark (*n.*)	2.4
observador[4b]	
observing (*adj.*)	2.6
observer	5.4
observar[1b]	
watch (*vb.*)	1.
observe	1.4
obstáculo[3a]	
bar	2.1
obstacle	3.4
obstante[2b]	
no –, however	1.
obstinación[6a]	
obstinacy	7.2
obstinarse + **obstinado**[3a]	
persist	3.8
stubborn	4.1
obstruir	
block up	4.
obtener[2a]	
get (obtain)	1.
ocasión[1a]	
chance	1.
ocasional	
occasional	3.7
ocasionar[2b]	
cause (*vb.*)	1.
ocaso[5a]	
sunset	5.3
occidental[5a]	
western	2.4
occidente[4b]	
west	1.9
océano[3a]	
ocean	3.6
ocio[5a]	
leisure	4.8
idleness	6.5
ocioso[3b]	
idle	3.7
octavo[4]*	
eighth	4.1
octubre[5a]	
October	2.4
ocultar[2a]	
hide	1.
oculto[2a]	
hide	1.
ocupación[2a]	
occupation	2.4
ocupar[1a]	
ocupado, busy	1.
-se, care about	1.8
-se, (be) engaged	1.9
ocurrencia[4a]	
event	2.
ocurrir[1b]	
happen	1.
(take) place	1.
ochenta[5]*	
eighty	5.3
ocho[1]*	
eight	1.4
odiar[3b]	
hate	2.5
odio[2a]	
hate (*n.*)	2.4
odioso[4a]	
hateful	4.7
oeste[6a]	
west	1.9
ofender[1b]	
offend	2.8
ofensa[4b]	
offense	3.8
ofensivo[7a]	
offensive	5.7
oferta[6b]	
offer	3.6
supply	3.7
oficial[2a]	
officer	1.2
official (*adj.*)	2.8
oficina[4a]	
office	2.9
oficio[1b]	
office	1.4
(divine) service	2.3
ofrecer[1a]	
offer	1.
ofrecimiento[5b]	
offer	3.6
ofrenda[4b]	
present	1.7
offering	3.8
oído[1b]	
ear	1.5
ear (hearing)	3.3
oír[1a]	
hear	1.
ojalá[4b]	
God grant	1.
ojeada[6b]	
look	1.
ojo[1a]	
eye	1.
en un abrir y cerrar de -s (in a) moment	1.5
ola[2b]	
wave (*n.*)	2.9
oleaje[6b]	
wave (*n.*)	2.9
oler[2b]	
smell	3.5
olfato[7a]	
smell (*n.*)	2.8
oliva[6a]	
olive	5.8
olivo[5b]	
olive tree	5.7
olor[2a]	
smell (*n.*)	2.8
oloroso[4b]	
fragrant	5.5
olvidar[1a]	
forget	1.

Section

panorama[4b]
sight ... 1.
pantalón[5a]
trousers ... 5.6
pantaloncillos
drawers ... 6.2
pantalla[6b]
screen ... 5.5
pantano[7a]
swamp ... 4.
panza[5b]
belly ... 6.2
paño[2b]
cloth ... 1.3
pañuelo[3b]
handkerchief ... 4.5
papa[6b]
pope ... 3.3
papá[4b]
papa ... 3.4
papel[1a]
paper ... 1.
part ... 1.4
rollo de –, scroll ... 4.6
paquete[6b]
bundle ... 4.
par[1b]
even (*adj.*) ... 1.7
pair ... 1.9
para[1a]
estar –
(be) about (to) ... 1.
for (in behalf of) ... 1.
(in) order (to) ... 1.
parabién[6a]
compliment ... 4.1
parada
stop (*n.*) ... 2.6
paraguas[6b]
umbrella ... 5.4
paraíso[3a]
paradise ... 3.8
paraje[3a]
place ... 1.
paralelo[4b]
parallel ... 4.9
paralizar[5b]
paralyze ... 5.7
parar[1b]
-se, stand ... 1.
stop (*tr. vb.*) ... 1.
– en, end (in) ... 1.1
-se, stop (*intr. vb.*) ... 1.4
parcial[5b]
-mente, (in) part ... 1.
partial ... 4.5
pardo[3a]
brown ... 2.5
parecer (*vb.*)[1a]
appear (look) ... 1.
-se, (look) like ... 1.
parecer (*n.*)[3a]
looks ... 1.
opinion ... 1.4
pared[1b]
wall ... 1.4
pareja[3a]
pair ... 1.9
parentesco[6a]
relation ... 4.2
pariente[2b]
relation ... 2.3
parir[4b]
bear (children) ... 1.3
parisien
Parisian ... 5.8
parisiense
Parisian ... 5.8

Section

parlamentario
parliamentary ... 7.
parlamento[5b]
parliament ... 2.8
parlero[6a]
talkative ... 10.
parlotear
babble ... 6.4
paro
(stopping of) work. 5.
párpado[7a]
eyelid ... 6.7
parque[5b]
park ... 2.3
parra[5b]
vine ... 4.
párrafo[3b]
paragraph ... 3.3
parroquia[4a]
parish ... 3.4
practice ... 3.4
parroquiano[5b]
practice ... 3.4
parte[1a]
part ... 1.
en –, (in) part ... 1.
por otra –
(in) addition ... 1.4
en todas -s
everywhere ... 1.4
por otra –
(on the other) hand ... 1.4
de – de
(on the) part (of) 1.4
tomar –, (take) part .. 1.4
por una –
(on the one) hand 2.2
de su –, (on her) side . 2.2
de su –, (on his) side . . 2.2
de su –, (on their) side 2.2
– superior, top ... 2.5
de mi –, (for my) part 2.6
en alguna –
somewhere ... 3.
en ninguna –
nowhere ... 3.4
en alguna otra –
somewhere else .. 3.4
– inferior, under side. 4.4
participación[6b]
share ... 2.
participante
participant ... 10.
participar[3b]
(take) part ... 1.4
communicate ... 2.7
partícipe
participant ... 10.
participio[6b]
participle ... 10.2
partícula[6b]
particle ... 7.
particular[1b]
particular ... 1.4
private ... 3.
partida[2a]
departure ... 3.1
entry ... 5.1
partidario[4a]
follower ... 3.2
partido[2a]
party ... 1.1
following (*n.*) ... 2.3
partir[1a]
go away ... 1.
start ... 1.8
parto[4b]
birth ... 2.5

Section

párvulo[6a]
child ... 1.
pasa
ciruela –, prune ... 6.4
raisin ... 6.4
pasado[1b]
past (over) ... 1.4
past (*n.*) ... 1.9
en tiempos -s
formerly ... 2.2
– mañana
day after tomorrow ... 4.3
pasaje[3a]
journey ... 1.
crossing ... 1.6
pasajero[3a]
passing ... 1.9
traveler ... 2.4
passenger ... 3.2
fugitive ... 3.5
pasar[1a]
qué pasa
(what's the) matter ... 1.
pass (*vb.*) ... 1.4
hand (*vb.*) ... 1.8
spend ... 2.2
pass (e.g., time) ... 2.6
– unos días, sojourn .. 3.4
undergo ... 3.8
pasatiempo[4b]
pastime ... 4.8
pascua[6b]
Easter ... 4.8
pase[7b]
pass ... 4.4
paseante
walker ... 7.6
pasear[2a]
walk ... 1.
-se, stroll ... 6.6
paseo[2a]
walk (*n.*) ... 2.4
pasillo[5b]
aisle ... 3.4
passage ... 4.8
pasión[1b]
passion ... 2.3
pasivo[5a]
passive ... 7.3
pasmar[6a]
wonder (*vb.*) ... 1.8
paso[1a]
state (condition) ... 1.
step ... 1.
walk ... 1.6
pace (*n.*) ... 1.8
acortar el –
slow down ... 4.4
pasta[5a]
paste ... 6.1
pastel[6b]
cake ... 4.7
pie ... 5.1
pastelería
pastry ... 7.8
pastilla[6b]
– de jabón
cake of soap ... 4.8
tablet ... 6.2
pasto[5a]
pasture ... 3.5
pastor[3a]
minister ... 2.
shepherd ... 3.7
pastor ... 4.9
pata[4a]
leg ... 1.9
paw ... 5.1

Section

patada[7a]
kick ... 3.6
patata[4b]
potato ... 2.7
patente[4a]
evident ... 2.5
charter ... 2.9
patent ... 5.2
paternal[4a]
paternal ... 4.8
paternidad[6b]
fatherhood ... 11.4
paterno[5a]
paternal ... 4.8
patético
pathetic ... 5.
patinar
skate ... 6.
patio[2b]
court ... 1.1
– de trabajo
work-yard ... 12.2
pato[5a]
duck ... 5.
patria[1b]
country ... 1.1
patriarca
patriarch ... 6.8
patriarcal[5b]
patriarchal ... 10.1
patrimonio[4b]
inheritance ... 3.9
patrio[5a]
native ... 3.2
patriota[4b]
patriot ... 5.2
patriótico[4b]
patriotic ... 4.8
patriotismo[3b]
patriotism ... 6.5
patrón[3a]
model ... 2.
– oro
(gold) standard .. 3.1
employer ... 3.7
patron ... 4.
pausa[3a]
pause (*n.*) ... 2.9
respite ... 4.5
pavimentar
pave ... 6.2
pavimento[6a]
pavement ... 5.7
pavo[4b]
turkey ... 5.6
– real, peacock ... 6.4
pavor[4b]
fear (*n.*) ... 1.4
pavoroso[5b]
terrible ... 1.8
paz[1a]
peace ... 1.
pecado[1b]
sin (*n.*) ... 2.2
pecador[3a]
sinner ... 5.1
pecar[2b]
sin (*vb.*) ... 2.4
peculiar[3b]
strange ... 1.
peculiar ... 3.6
pechera
shirt-front ... 13.
pecho[1a]
chest ... 1.9
pedagogo[6a]
teacher ... 1.

Section

picaposte
woodpecker 7.2
picar[1b]
sting 3.5
chop 4.2
picaresco[6b]
roguish 10.2
pícaro[2b]
knave 4.5
pico[2a]
point (*n.*) 1.2
beak 5.9
pichón[6b]
dove 4.4
pigeon 4.8
pie[1a]
foot .... 1.
esar de –, ponerse de –
stand .... 1.
al – de la letra
literally 2.2
dedo del –, toe 4.6
piedad[2a]
pity 2.4
piety 4.9
sin –, merciless 5.4
piedra[1a]
stone 1.4
de –, (of) stone ...... 3.
– preciosa, gem 3.6
– de albardilla
coping stone 7.2
piel[2a]
skin (*n.*) .... 2.
fur .... 5.
pierna[2b]
leg 1.9
pieza[2a]
piece .... 1.
pila[4a]
mass 1.6
trough 6.8
píldora
pill 6.8
piloto[6b]
pilot 6.8
pillo[6b]
knave 4.5
pimienta[3b]
pepper 5.9
pimiento[5b]
pepper 5.9
pincel[6b]
brush 4.6
pinchazo[7b]
prick (*n.*) 3.6
pino[4a]
steep 2.8
pine 4.9
pintar[1b]
paint (*vb.*) 1.5
pintor[3b]
painter .... 3.
pintoresco[3a]
strange .... 1.
picturesque 4.6
pintura[2b]
painting 3.2
pío[6a]
pious 2.9
pipa[6a]
pipe 3.6
pique[5b]
itch 6.9
pirámide[4b]
pyramid 5.7
pirata[5b]
pirate 6.9

Section

pisada[6a]
step .... 2.
pisar[2a]
step (*vb.*) 1.1
piso[3a]
flat (*n.*) 2.1
floor 2.5
– bajo, ground floor .. 4.4
pistola[7a]
pistol 5.9
pizarra
blackboard 5.8
slate 6.8
placa[5b]
badge 6.7
placentero[6a]
joyful 2.2
placer[1a]
please .... 1.
pleasure 1.4
plácido[4b]
quiet .... 1.
plaga[6a]
plague 4.6
plan[2b]
plan (*n.*) 1.1
plancha[5b]
iron (*n.*) 1.8
slab 4.1
planeta[3a]
planet 3.9
plano[4a]
map 1.9
flat (*adj.*) 2.7
plane 3.7
primer –, foreground .. 6.5
planta[1b]
plant (*n.*) 1.5
sole (foot) 4.3
plantar[3a]
plant (*vb.*) 2.4
plantear[6b]
state (*vb.*) 2.2
plástico
plastic 7.6
plata[1b]
money .... 1.
silver 1.4
plátano[6a]
plane tree .... 6.
banana 6.2
plateado
silvery 5.6
platear[5b]
plate 5.1
plática[5a]
talk 1.2
platillo
saucer .... 7.
plato[2a]
lista de -s
bill of fare 2.1
plate (*n.*) 2.5
dish 4.5
playa[3a]
beach 3.9
plaza[1b]
seat (*n.*) .... 1.
square (*n.*) .... 1.
plazo[3a]
term 1.8
plebe[6a]
people (common) ... 1.
mob 4.9
plegar[4a]
fold .... 4.
plegaria[6a]
prayer 2.3

Section

pleito[3a]
suit 1.8
plenitud[6a]
plenty 2.2
pleno[2b]
plenamente, all ...... 1.
full .... 1.
plenamente, fully 2.2
pliego[4a]
sheet 2.2
pliegue[5b]
fold 4.4
plomo[4a]
lead (*n.*) 2.3
pluma[1b]
pen 1.5
feather 1.9
plumaje[6a]
feather 1.9
(p)neumático
tire 7.2
población[2a]
population 2.5
poblado[5a]
village 1.2
poblar[3a]
people 4.3
pobre[1a]
poor .... 1.
imperfect 3.9
pobreza[2b]
poverty .... 4.
poco[1a]
-s, (a) few .... 1.
hace –, just .... 1.
little (*n.*) .... 1.
– a –, little by little .. 1.
a –, soon .... 1.
tan – como
(as) little (as) 2.6
– común, unusual 2.6
– ha, recently 2.8
– bondadoso, unkind .. 6.1
poder (*vb.*)[1a]
(be) able .... 1.
may .... 1.
poder (*n.*)[1b]
power .... 1.
(Great) Power ..... 3.
– mágico, magic 3.5
poderío[5a]
power .... 1.
poderoso[1b]
strong .... 1.
podrir[4b]
spoil 2.6
poema[3b]
poem 2.5
poesía[2b]
poetry 2.4
poeta[1a]
poet 1.5
poético[3b]
poetic 3.9
polaco
Polish 4.1
polar[6b]
polar 6.8
policía[4b]
police 3.7
policeman 5.8
policiaco
police .... 5.
polilla
moth 6.8
política[2a]
policy 2.4
politics 4.4

Section

político[1b]
political 1.9
politician 5.5
póliza
policy 4.6
polo[6b]
pole 4.6
polvo[1b]
dust (*n.*) 1.9
powder 2.8
pólvora[6b]
powder 2.8
polvoriento
dusty 6.1
pollino[6b]
ass 3.9
pollo[4b]
chicken 4.8
pompa[4a]
pomp 4.4
bubble 5.6
pomposo[5b]
magnificent 3.5
ponderar[4a]
consider 1.8
poner[1a]
puesto que, as (since). 1.
lay .... 1.
place (put) .... 1.
-se de pie, stand ..... 1.
– la mesa, set table ... 1.1
– reparo, object 1.9
put on 2.6
-se de hinojos, kneel .. 3.9
poniente
setting 9.6
popular[3a]
popular 4.1
popularidad[6a]
popularity 7.4
populoso[5b]
populous 7.3
poquito[1a]
little (*n.*) .... 1.
por[1a]
by (agent) .... 1.
for (in behalf of) ... 1.
for (in favor of) .... 1.
– lo tanto, therefore .. 1.
through (motion) .. 1.
through (agent) .... 1.
– conducto de
through (agent) .. 1.
sake 1.8
porcelana[4b]
china 3.7
porción[3a]
share .... 2.
porfía[4a]
obstinacy 7.2
porfiar[4b]
persist 3.8
pormenor[6b]
particular 2.3
poro[7b]
pore 7.1
porque, porqué[1a]
because .... 1.
why .... 1.
porrazo[6b]
blow 1.4
portada[5b]
front (*n.*) 1.5
portador[5b]
porter 3.3
portal[3b]
entrance 1.8
porch 2.7
portar[4a]
-se, act (behave) ..... 1.

Section
príncipe + princesa[1b]
prince.......... 1.1
princess.......... 2.9
principiar[3b]
begin.......... 1.
principio[1a]
al –, (at) first.......... 1.
principle.......... 1.9
beginning.......... 2.7
en –, (on) principle... 2.7
desde un –
(from the) beginning.......... 3.9
prisa + priesa[2a]
hurry.......... 2.4
dar –, hurry (*tr. vb.*).. 2.5
prisión[2b]
prison.......... 2.
imprisonment.......... 5.
prisionero[3b]
prisoner.......... 2.4
prisma[5a]
prism.......... 6.9
privación[5a]
want.......... 3.9
privar + privado[2a]
private (*adj.*).......... 3.
deprive.......... 3.2
privilegiar[6a]
favor (*vb.*).......... 2.1
privilegio[2b]
privilege.......... 3.7
pro[6a]
en –, for (in behalf)... 1.
proa[6a]
bow.......... 4.3
probabilidad[5b]
chances.......... 3.3
probable[3a]
probable.......... 1.7
probar[1b]
prove.......... 1.
try.......... 1.
prove (establish)... 1.4
problema[3a]
problem.......... 3.3
procedente[6b]
come from.......... 1.
proceder[1b]
act (take action)... 1.
come from.......... 1.
conduct (*n.*).......... 2.3
procedure (*n.*).......... 5.1
procedimiento[3a]
process.......... 1.7
procesión[6a]
procession.......... 4.1
proceso[4b]
suit.......... 1.8
trial.......... 2.
– de quiebra
(procedure in) bankruptcy... 7.3
proclama
proclamation.......... 7.4
proclamación
proclamation.......... 7.4
proclamar[3a]
proclaim.......... 3.5
procurador[7a]
attorney.......... 4.7
– general
attorney-general. 9.5
procurar[1a]
try.......... 1.
prodigar[6a]
lavish.......... 6.3
prodigio[3a]
wonder (*n.*).......... 1.7

Section
prodigioso[3a]
wonderful.......... 1.2
pródigo[4a]
lavish.......... 3.7
producción[3a]
production.......... 3.9
producir[1a]
produce (*vb.*).......... 1.8
produce (yield).... 3.4
productivo[6a]
fertile.......... 3.8
profitable.......... 4.1
productive.......... 6.3
producto[2b]
product.......... 2.1
proeza[5a]
exploit.......... 5.9
profanar[5b]
profane.......... 6.5
profano[5b]
profane.......... 6.3
profecía[6b]
prophecy.......... 6.6
profesar[3b]
exercise (*vb.*).......... 1.6
profesión[2b]
profession.......... 2.9
profesional[5a]
professional.......... 4.5
profesor[3a]
teacher.......... 1.
professor.......... 2.6
profeta[3b]
prophet.......... 3.1
profundidad[4b]
depth.......... 2.6
profundizar
deepen.......... 5.
profundo[1a]
deep.......... 1.
programa[4b]
program.......... 4.2
progresar[4a]
improve.......... 2.4
progress (*vb.*).......... 2.6
progresivo[6a]
progressive.......... 6.7
progreso[2b]
progress.......... 2.4
prohibición
prohibition.......... 5.
prohibir[3a]
forbid.......... 2.
prójimo[4b]
neighbor (fellow being).......... 3.4
proletario[6b]
people (common)... 1.
prolijo[4a]
superfluous.......... 4.1
prólogo[6b]
introduction.......... 3.7
preface.......... 7.3
prolongación[6b]
continuance.......... 5.9
prolongar[2b]
prolong.......... 3.6
promedio[7b]
average (*adj.*).......... 1.8
(on the) average... 3.2
promesa[3a]
promise (*n.*).......... 2.7
prometer + prometido[1b]
promise (*vb.*).......... 1.
engaged.......... 2.5
promover[6a]
further (*vb.*).......... 1.8

Section
pronombre[4b]
pronoun.......... 6.8
prontitud[4b]
speed.......... 2.5
promptitude.......... 10.
pronto[1a]
tan – como
as soon as.......... 1.
fast.......... 1.
soon.......... 1.
de –, sudden.......... 1.
de –, suddenly.......... 1.
by and by.......... 1.1
just.......... 1.3
prompt.......... 2.5
pronunciación[6b]
pronunciation.......... 7.
pronunciar[1b]
pronounce.......... 1.4
– un discurso
(make a) speech.. 1.6
propaganda[6b]
propaganda.......... 7.5
propagar[6b]
propagate.......... 7.
propicio[4a]
favorable.......... 2.2
propiedad[2a]
property.......... 1.5
property (landed).. 1.9
propietario[3b]
owner.......... 2.
propina[6b]
tip.......... 5.2
propio[1a]
own.......... 1.
same.......... 1.
proper.......... 1.4
de propia mano
(with one's own) hand.......... 3.
proponer[1b]
propose.......... 1.4
proporción[2a]
proportion.......... 2.1
proporcionar[2a]
supply.......... 1.1
proposición[4a]
proposition.......... 3.1
propósito[1a]
purpose.......... 1.
a –, fitness.......... 6.7
propuesta[6a]
proposition.......... 3.1
prorrumpir[3b]
break out.......... 2.2
prosa[3a]
prose.......... 5.3
prosaico[5a]
prosaic.......... 10.5
proscribir[5b]
proscribe.......... 9.7
proseguir[2a]
continue.......... 1.
proceed.......... 2.
prosperar[6a]
flourish.......... 4.1
prosperidad[4b]
prosperity.......... 4.4
próspero[5b]
prosperous.......... 4.7
prosternar
prostrate.......... 6.6
protagonista[6b]
actor.......... 3.9
protección[3a]
protection.......... 2.1

Section
protector[2b]
patron.......... 4.
protector.......... 6.3
proteger[3a]
protect.......... 2.1
protegido
protégé.......... 11.
protesta[3a]
protest.......... 4.1
protestante
Protestant.......... 4.4
protestar[2a]
protest.......... 4.4
provecho[2b]
advantage.......... 1.5
benefit.......... 3.4
provechoso[6a]
favorable.......... 2.2
profitable.......... 4.1
helpful.......... 5.6
proveer[2b]
supply (*vb.*).......... 1.1
provisto que
provided that.... 2.9
provenir[4b]
come from.......... 1.
providencia[3b]
providence.......... 4.3
provincia[1b]
province.......... 1.5
provinciano[6b]
provincial.......... 7.9
provisión[5a]
provision.......... 4.1
provocar[2b]
provoke.......... 2.4
proximidad[4a]
neighborhood.......... 2.9
proximity.......... 5.6
próximo[2a]
near (*adj.* and *adv.*). 1.
next.......... 1.
proximamente, soon.. 1.
proyectar[4a]
plan (*vb.*).......... 2.3
proyecto[2b]
– del gobierno
(government) bill 1.9
– de ley, draft (of a bill) 2.3
project.......... 3.5
prudencia[3a]
prudence.......... 3.7
prudente[2b]
prudent.......... 3.3
prueba[1b]
proof.......... 1.4
test.......... 1.9
prusiano
Prussian.......... 4.5
psicología[5a]
psychology.......... 8.5
psicológico[5b]
psychological.......... 9.3
publicación[5a]
publication.......... 4.6
– del estado
publication of the general staff.......... 5.1
publicar[2a]
publish.......... 2.8
publicidad
publicity.......... 7.8
público[1a]
public (*adj.*).......... 1.
public (*n.*).......... 1.4
puchero[4a]
pot.......... 2.3

Section

- realizar[2a]
  - realize … 3.5
- reanimar[7a]
  - refresh (in spirit) … 5.2
- rebajar[5b]
  - decline … 3.3
- rebanada
  - slice … 4.
- rebaño[4b]
  - drove … 3.9
- rebelarse[5b]
  - rebel … 3.6
- rebelde[3b]
  - rebel … 4.
  - rebellious … 6.4
- rebeldía[5b]
  - rebellion … 6.5
- rebelión[4b]
  - revolt … 4.4
- reborde
  - ledge … 6.8
- rebosar[4a]
  - overflow … 5.5
- recado[3b]
  - errand … 3.
  - message … 3.
- recaer[5b]
  - fall back again … 1.5
- recatar +recatado[4b]
  - hide … 1.
- recato[6a]
  - care … 1.
  - prudence … 3.7
- recelar[6a]
  - suspect … 2.9
- recelo[3a]
  - fear (*n.*) … 1.4
- receloso[6a]
  - suspect … 4.3
- receptor
  - receiver … 6.
- receso
  - estar de –
    - (have) recess … 5.8
- receta[6b]
  - receipt … 2.6
- recibidor
  - entrance hall … 5.3
- recibimiento[6b]
  - reception … 3.2
- recibir[1a]
  - get (receive) … 1.
  - admit … 1.8
- recibo[5a]
  - receipt … 3.3
  - receipts (e.g., for expenditures) … 3.3
  - receipt (for payment) … 4.9
- reciente +recién[1b]
  - recent … 2.7
  - recently … 2.8
  - -mente, recently … 2.8
- recinto[5b]
  - place … 1.
- recio[2b]
  - strong … 1.
- recíproco[6a]
  - mutual … 3.1
- recitar[4a]
  - recite … 3.9
- reclamación[6b]
  - claim (*n.*) … 1.7
  - complaint … 2.4
- reclamar[2b]
  - claim (*vb.*) … 2.3
- reclamo
  - puff … 5.8
- recluta
  - recruit … 6.4
- recobrar[2b]
  - recover … 1.9
- recoger[1a]
  - gather (collect) … 1.5
  - gather (glean) … 1.5
  - pick up … 1.5
- recogimiento[5a]
  - concentration … 7.1
- recomendación[3b]
  - recommendation … 4.5
- recomendar[3b]
  - recommend … 2.1
- recompensa[4a]
  - en –, (in) return … 1.1
  - reward (*n.*) … 2.5
- recompensar[4b]
  - reward … 3.8
- reconcentrar[4b]
  - concentrate … 4.8
- reconciliar[6b]
  - reconcile … 4.6
  - reconcile (persons) … 4.7
- reconocer[1b]
  - admit … 1.4
  - recognize … 1.4
  - no –
    - (not) recognize … 2.6
- reconocimiento[4a]
  - gratitude … 3.3
- reconstituir
  - reconstitute … 9.7
- recordar[1a]
  - remember … 1.
  - recall … 1.8
- recorrer[1b]
  - run through … 3.1
- recortar[6b]
  - carve … 3.3
  - bob … 5.8
- recrear[5a]
  - amuse … 3.5
- recreo[5a]
  - pastime … 4.8
- rectángulo
  - rectangle … 6.8
- rectificar[5a]
  - correct (*vb.*) … 2.7
- rectitud
  - righteousness … 6.9
- recto[2b]
  - direct (*adj.*) … 1.
  - direct (*adv.*) … 1.1
  - straight … 1.8
- rector[6a]
  - chancellor … 7.
- recuerdo[1b]
  - memory … 1.8
- recular
  - recoil … 6.6
- recurrir[4b]
  - turn to … 1.1
  - resort … 5.3
- recurso[2b]
  - resource … 3.6
- rechazar[2b]
  - drive back … 1.5
  - drive back (push) … 3.1
  - reject … 3.2
- rechinar[4a]
  - grate … 5.7
- red[3a]
  - net … 3.1
  - web … 3.4
- redacción[5a]
  - (editorial) staff … 5.3
- redactar[4b]
  - draw up … 3.2
  - draft … 3.6
- redactor[4b]
  - editor … 6.1
- redimir[5b]
  - redeem … 4.7
- redoblar[6b]
  - double … 4.3
- redondear
  - round off … 4.9
- redondo +redonda[2b]
  - round (*adj.*) … 1.6
- reducción
  - reduction … 5.3
- reducir +reducido[1b]
  - decline … 3.3
  - – la marcha
    - slow down … 4.4
- reelección
  - reelection … 8.4
- reemplazar[3b]
  - substitute … 2.3
- referencia[4a]
  - reference … 4.8
- referente[5b]
  - referring … 2.6
  - refer (to) … 3.1
- referir[1b]
  - tell … 1.
- refinamiento[5b]
  - excellence … 5.6
  - refinement … 6.6
- refinar[5a]
  - refine … 5.5
- reflejar[2b]
  - reflect … 4.3
- reflejo[3a]
  - reflection … 5.4
- reflexión[2b]
  - consideration … 2.4
- reflexionar[3b]
  - consider … 1.8
- reflexivo[5b]
  - pensive … 3.9
- reforma[4b]
  - reform … 3.2
- reformar[6a]
  - reform … 5.
- reforzar[5b]
  - strengthen … 3.4
- refractario
  - refractory … 9.8
- refrán[3b]
  - saying … 2.9
  - proverb … 4.9
- refrescar[5a]
  - cool … 4.9
- refresco
  - refreshment … 6.8
- refuerzo
  - reinforcement … 7.6
- refugiar[4b]
  - shelter (*vb.*) … 2.6
  - -se, (take) refuge … 3.9
- refugio[5a]
  - refuge … 3.9
- regalar[2a]
  - present (*vb.*) … 1.4
  - entertain … 2.4
- regalo[2b]
  - present … 1.7
- regar[4a]
  - spread … 1.4
  - water (*vb.*) … 2.4
- regazo[6a]
  - chest … 1.9
  - lap … 2.4
- regente
  - regent … 6.4
- régimen[4a]
  - government … 1.1
  - direction … 1.8
- regimiento[6a]
  - regiment … 3.6
- regio[4b]
  - royal … 1.5
- región[1b]
  - part (of country) … 1.
- regir[3a]
  - rule (*vb.*) … 1.
- registrar[3b]
  - look for … 1.
  - register (*vb.*) … 3.
- registro[6b]
  - record … 3.8
  - registering … 4.2
- regla[1b]
  - rule (*n.*) … 1.1
- regocijar[5a]
  - -se, rejoice … 3.2
- regocijo[3b]
  - delight … 1.
- regresar[2b]
  - come back … 1.8
- regreso[3b]
  - de –, back … 1.
  - return (*n.*) … 1.4
- regular[2b]
  - control (*vb.*) … 1.4
  - (put in) order … 1.4
  - regular … 2.
  - regulate … 4.4
- regularidad[7a]
  - regularity … 8.
- rehacer[6b]
  - do over again … 1.8
  - -se, rally … 4.7
- rehén
  - hostage … 8.2
- rehusar[6b]
  - refuse (*vb.*) … 2.3
- reina[1b]
  - queen … 1.6
- reinado[6a]
  - reign (*n.*) … 2.1
- reinar[2a]
  - reign (*vb.*) … 2.
  - rage (war, etc.) … 3.2
- reino[2a]
  - kingdom … 1.7
- reír[1b]
  - laugh … 1.
- reiterar[6b]
  - say again … 1.
- reja[3b]
  - bars … 4.6
  - – de taquilla
    - ticket window … 5.3
- rejuvenecer
  - restore … 4.4
- relación[1a]
  - report … 1.
  - account … 1.5
  - relation … 1.6
- relacionar[4a]
  - relate … 2.1
- relámpago[2b]
  - flash (lightning) … 3.3
- relatar[4a]
  - tell … 1.
- relativo[2a]
  - (in) proportion … 2.6
  - relative … 3.7
  - pertaining … 5.9

Section

retrasado
- late-comer .... 13.

retrasar[6a]
- delay (*intr. vb.*) ..... 2.
- delay (*tr. vb.*) 2.7
- -se, linger 3.6

retraso
- restoration 6.5

retratar[4b]
- painting 3.2

retrato[2a]
- painting 3.2

retroceder[3b]
- draw back 1.5
- go back 2.1

retumbar[5a]
- ring (*vb.*) 2.9

reuma
- rheumatism 7.2

reumatismo
- rheumatism 7.2

reunión[2a]
- convention 2.8
- union 3.5

reunir[1b]
- unite .... 1.
- gather (glean) 1.5
- assemble 2.8

revelación[4a]
- revelation 5.5

revelar[2b]
- reveal 2.4

reventar[3a]
- burst 1.4

reverencia[4b]
- reverence 4.1

reverendo[5b]
- reverend 4.9

revés[2b]
- (wrong) side 1.7

revestir[4a]
- clothe 1.9

revisión
- revision 6.8

revista[3a]
- review (*n.*) 2.6
- magazine .... 3.

revocación
- recall 5.8

revolotear
- flutter 5.7

revolución[2b]
- turn (*n.*) .... 3.
- revolution 3.2

revolucionario[3b]
- revolutionary ...... 5.

revolver +revuelto[2a]
- turn (*vb.*) .... 1.
- revolve 5.5

revuelta[4b]
- revolt 4.4

rey[1a]
- king .... 1.

rezar[2b]
- pray 2.2

ría[6b]
- mouth (of river) ... 2.7
- estuary 9.4

ribera[2b]
- bank 1.5

rico[1a]
- rich .... 1.

ridículo[2a]
- ridiculous 3.6

riego[5a]
- irrigation 7.3

riel
- rail 5.3

Section

rienda[4a]
- bridle 3.4

riesgo[2a]
- danger 1.5
- risk 3.4

rigidez[5b]
- stiffness 9.3

rígido[5a]
- stiff 3.2
- hacer –, (make) stiff .. 4.9

rigor[2a]
- rigor 4.2

riguroso[3b]
- exact 1.4

rima
- rhyme .... 6.

rincón[2a]
- corner 1.9
- corner (nook) 2.3

riña[5b]
- fight (*n.*) 1.1
- quarrel (*n.*) 2.5

riñón[5a]
- -es, loin 5.7
- kidney 7.3

río[1a]
- river 1.5

riqueza[1b]
- wealth 1.5

risa[1b]
- laugh (*n.*) 1.8
- laughter 3.8

risco[5a]
- cliff 4.6

risueño[3a]
- pleasant 1.1

ritmo[5a]
- rhythm 7.9

rival[3b]
- rival .... 5.

rivalidad[6b]
- rivalry 7.8

rizar[4a]
- curl 4.8

rizo[5a]
- curl 4.9

robar[1b]
- rob 2.3

roble[6a]
- oak 3.1

robusto[2b]
- strong .... 1.
- sound 1.2
- hardy 2.6

robo[5a]
- robbery 4.8

roca[2b]
- rock (*n.*) 1.7

roce[5b]
- friction 6.1

rociar[5b]
- sprinkle 3.7

rocín[6b]
- hack .... 7.

rocío[6a]
- dew 3.9

rocoso
- rocky 5.9

rodar[2a]
- roll (*tr. vb.*) 2.3
- roll (of thunder, etc.) 4.3

rodear[1b]
- go round 1.8
- surround 1.8

rodeo[6a]
- detour 8.1

Section

rodilla[2a]
- knee .... 2.
- hincar la –, kneel 3.9

roer[4a]
- gnaw 6.1

rogar[1b]
- ask (favor) .... 1.
- pray 2.2
- beg 2.7

rojo[1b]
- red .... 1.

rollo[6b]
- roll (*n.*) 2.6
- – de papel, scroll 4.6

romance[3a]
- romance 6.4

romano[3a]
- Roman 1.8

romanticismo[4b]
- romanticism 10.4

romántico[3a]
- romantic 4.3

romo
- dull 5.2

romper +roto[1a]
- break 1.1
- burst 1.4
- break out (crying, etc.) 2.2
- break (in pieces) ... 2.3
- burst (out laughing) 3.
- burst (into tears) ... 3.5

roncar[6a]
- snore 6.7

ronco[3b]
- hoarse 6.5

ronda[4b]
- rounds (military) ... 4.2
- hacer la – (make the) rounds 4.3

rondar
- haunt 5.7

ropa[1b]
- clothes 1.4

rosa[1b]
- rose 1.5

rosado[4a]
- pink 4.6

rosal[6a]
- rose bush 5.2

rosario[4a]
- beads 5.4

rosca[6b]
- screw 5.8

rostro[1b]
- face .... 1.

rota[5a]
- defeat 3.6

rótulo
- sign 3.4

rotundo[6b]
- round (*adj.*) 1.6
- circular 3.3

rozar[5a]
- graze 3.4

rubio[2a]
- fair 1.2

rubor[3b]
- blush 5.5

ruborizar(se)[6b]
- blush .... 4.

rudo[2b]
- rude 4.3

rueca[6b]
- distaff 8.2

rueda[2b]
- wheel (*n.*) 2.5
- – del timón, helm 5.6

Section

ruedo
- border 5.1

ruego[3a]
- request (*n.*) 2.1
- plea 5.3

rufián
- ruffian .... 7.

rugido[5b]
- roar 5.3

rugir[3b]
- roar 4.7

ruido[1b]
- noise 2.6

ruidoso[3b]
- loud 1.2
- noisy 5.8

ruin[4a]
- mean 1.5

ruina[2a]
- ruin (*n.*) 2.4
- decline 4.4

ruinoso[5b]
- ruinous 6.5

ruiseñor[5b]
- nightingale 6.1

rumbo[2b]
- direction .... 1.

rumor[2a]
- rumor 3.8

ruptura[6b]
- break 3.8

rural[6b]
- rural 3.3
- guardia –, constable .. 6.2

ruso[5b]
- Russian .... 3.

rústico[3a]
- rural 3.3

ruta[5a]
- road .... 1.

rutina[7a]
- routine 7.7

S

sábado[4a]
- Saturday 3.5

sábana[6b]
- sheet 4.9

saber (*vb.*)[1a]
- know (have knowledge) .... 1.
- desear –, wonder ..... 1.
- sin – lo, unknown 2.2

saber (*n.*)[3b]
- learning 3.6

sabiduría[4b]
- wisdom 2.3
- learning 3.6

sabio[1b]
- wise 1.5
- learned 1.6

sable
- saber 7.2

sabor[3a]
- taste (*n.*) 1.4

saborear[6b]
- taste (*vb.*) 1.5
- relish .... 4.

sabroso[3a]
- delicious 2.8
- savory (*adj.*) 6.9

sacar[1a]
- pull .... 1.
- draw up 1.7
- take away 2.6

Section

señalar[1b]
- mark (*vb.*) 1.
- point out 1.4
- assign 2.5

señor[1a]
- -a, lady 1.
- Mr. 1.
- -a, Mrs. 1.
- lord 1.1
- lord (title) 2.2
- -a, mistress 3.5

señoría[6b]
- lord 2.2

señorío[4b]
- dominion 3.1

señorito[1a]
- Mr. 1.
- señorita, Miss 1.1
- señorita, young lady 1.1

separación[3b]
- separation 3.4

separar[1b]
- separate 1.
- separado
  - separate (*adj.*) 1.

septentrional[6b]
- northern 2.

septiembre[3b]
- September 2.1

séptimo[5*]
- seventh 4.5

sepulcro[3a]
- grave (*n.*) 2.2

sepultar[4a]
- bury 3.1

sepultura[3a]
- grave (*n.*) 2.2

sequedad[6b]
- dryness 11.5

ser (*vb.*)[1a]
- be 1.
- llegar a –, become 1.

ser (*n.*)[1b]
- being 1.
- life 1.

serenarse[5a]
- quiet (*vb.*) 1.6

serenidad[3a]
- quiet (*n.*) 1.

sereno[2a]
- quiet 1.
- dew 3.9
- serene 6.

serie[3a]
- series 2.5

seriedad[5b]
- gravity 3.8

serio[1b]
- grave 1.4

sermón[3b]
- sermon 3.7

serpiente[4b]
- snake 3.8

servicio[1b]
- service 1.
- favor (*n.*) 1.4

servidor[2b]
- servant 1.9

servidumbre[4b]
- servant 1.9

servil
- servile 7.

servilleta[7b]
- napkin 5.5

servir[1a]
- serve 1.

sesenta[3*]
- sixty 4.

Section

sesión[4b]
- session 5.3

seso[4a]
- brain 3.3

setenta[5*]
- seventy 5.1

seto
- hedge 5.4

severidad[3b]
- rigor 4.2
- severity 4.7

severo[2a]
- severe 1.6

sexo[3a]
- sex 3.3

sexto[5*]
- sixth 3.7

si, sí[1a]
- if 1.
- self 1.
- whether 1.
- yes 1.
- itself 1.5

sidra[6a]
- cider 7.

siembra[5b]
- sowing 4.5

siempre[1a]
- always 1.

sien[4b]
- temple 4.8

sierpe[6b]
- snake 3.8

sierra[3a]
- mountain 1.5

siervo[5a]
- slave 2.2

siesta[4a]
- sleep (*n.*) 1.5
- nap 6.

siete[1*]
- seven 1.4

siglo[1a]
- century 1.4

significación[4a]
- import (*n.*) 2.2

significar[2a]
- mean 1.

significativo[6a]
- (full of) meaning 3.3

signo[3a]
- sign 1.1

siguiente[1a]
- día –, day after 1.
- next 1.

sílaba[4b]
- syllable 4.9

silbar[3a]
- whistle 4.6
- hiss 5.4

silbido[6a]
- whistle 3.9

silencio[1b]
- quiet (*n.*) 1.
- silence (*n.*) 2.2

silencioso[3a]
- silent 1.5

silueta[6a]
- outline 4.8

silla[1b]
- chair 1.8
- saddle 3.8

sillón[5b]
- chair 1.8

símbolo[3b]
- symbol 5.6

simiente[4b]
- seed 2.7

Section

simpatía[2b]
- tener – por, like 1.
- sympathy 2.8

simpático[3a]
- pleasant 1.1

simple[1b]
- simple (mere) 1.

simplificar
- (make) simple 2.1

simultáneo[6a]
- (at the) same time 1.9

sin[1a]
- – duda
  - (without) doubt 1.
- – reserva, free 1.
- without 1.
- – saber lo, – noticia de
  - unknown 2.2
- – valor, worthless 4.2
- – piedad, merciless 5.4
- – nombre, nameless 5.8
- – hilos, wireless 6.

sin embargo[1a]
- however 1.

sinceridad[3b]
- sincerity 5.9

sincero[2a]
- sincere 2.5

sindicado
- syndicate 9.3

singular[2a]
- strange 1.

siniestro[3b]
- left 1.
- sinister 5.

sino[1a]
- but 1.
- else 1.1
- fate 1.5

sinrazón[6b]
- wrong (injury) 3.1
- wrong (misdeed) 3.2

sintético[6b]
- synthetic 8.6

síntoma[7a]
- symptom 7.7

siquiera[1b]
- (at) least 1.

sirena[5a]
- siren 7.

sirviente[6a]
- servant (maid) 1.5
- servant (man) 1.9

sistema[2a]
- system 1.6
- – escolar
  - school system 4.2

sistemático
- systematic 6.9

sitio[1a]
- place 1.

situación[1b]
- state (condition) 1.
- position 1.4
- position (plight) 1.5

situar +situado[2a]
- place (*vb.*) 1.
- locate 2.

soberanía[6b]
- rule 2.

soberano[2a]
- sovereign 3.7

soberbia[3a]
- pride 2.4

soberbio[2a]
- haughty 4.7

sobornar[7a]
- bribe 6.

Section

sobra[3a]
- rest (remainder) 1.1
- de –, spare 3.
- excess 3.3

sobrar[2b]
- exceed 2.3

sobre (*prep.*)[1a]
- above (*prep.*) 1.
- – todo, above all 1.
- on 1.
- – lo cual, upon which 1.6

sobre (*n.*)[5a]
- envelope 5.6

sobrehumano[6b]
- superhuman 9.4

sobrenatural
- supernatural 8.4

sobrepasar
- surpass 4.6

sobreponer[5a]
- put over 3.

sobresalir[4b]
- (be) ahead (of) 2.7
- project 3.7

sobresalto[5b]
- de –, suddenly 1.
- start (*n.*) 1.7

sobrevenir[5a]
- happen 1.

sobrevivir
- survive 5.8

sobriedad[7a]
- moderation 3.8
- temperance 6.4

sobrino[1b]
- nephew 3.7
- sobrina, niece 4.1

sobrio[4b]
- sober 3.8

socarrón[5a]
- sly 4.2

social[1b]
- social 2.3

social democracia
- social democracy 5.3

socialista[6b]
- socialist 6.1

sociedad[1b]
- company (business) 1.
- company (social) 1.
- -es benéficas
  - charity societies 4.6

socio[4a]
- partner 3.4

socorrer[3a]
- help 1.

socorro[3a]
- help 1.1

sofá[5a]
- couch 4.1

sofocar[3b]
- choke 3.7

sol[1a]
- sun 1.
- rayo de –, sunbeam 4.3
- puesta del –, sunset 5.3
- salida del –, sunrise 5.8

solar[3a]
- luz –, sunshine 3.2

soldado[1b]
- soldier 1.

soleado
- sunny 6.

soledad[2a]
- solitude 3.6

solemne[2b]
- solemn 2.8

Section

suplir[3b]
supply 1.1

suponer +supuesto[1a]
por supuesto
(of) course 1.
suppose 1.
(so) called 1.2

suposición[5a]
basis 3.4
conjecture 4.7

supremo[2a]
supreme 2.
tribunal –
supreme court 4.3

supresión
suppression 8.4

suprimir[3a]
suppress 3.7
take out 4.1
omit 4.4

sur[5b]
south 2.2
del –, southern 2.3

surcar[6b]
plow (ship through waves) 5.4

surco[5b]
furrow 6.

surgir[2b]
emerge 4.1

suroeste
southwest 6.5

susceptible[6a]
– de, liable 6.5
susceptible 6.9

susodecir[5b]
susodicho
above (mentioned) 2.2

suspender[2a]
hang 1.1

suspensión[5a]
suspension 5.8

suspenso[4a]
(in) suspense 6.

suspirar[2a]
sigh (*vb.*) 2.6

suspiro[2b]
sigh 2.8

sustentar[3a]
support (*vb.*) 1.8

sustento[4b]
support (*n.*) 2.1

susto[2b]
fear (*n.*) 1.4

sustraer[5b]
subtract 4.5

susurrar[6b]
whisper (*vb.*) 3.1
rustle 4.6

sutil[2b]
subtle 3.

sutileza[5b]
cunning 5.1

suyo
–[1]*, his 1.1
–[3]*, hers 2.9
–[3]*, theirs 3.6

T

tabaco[4a]
tobacco 3.9

taberna[3a]
tavern 4.1

tabla[2a]
board 1.7

tablado[6b]
stage 3.

Section

taciturno[6a]
silent 1.5

tacón
heel 2.4

táctico
tactical 11.7

tacto[5a]
touch (*n.*) 2.2

tacha[5b]
fault 1.8
spot 2.2

tachar[6a]
blame 2.8
cross out 4.7

tajada
slice 4.

tal[1a]
so 1.
such 1.

tal vez[1a]
perhaps 1.

taladrar
bore 5.

talante[6b]
humor 2.4
temper 4.2

talento[2a]
talent 2.4

talón[5b]
heel 4.9

talla[7a]
stature 2.9

tallar
carve 5.6

talle[3a]
figure 1.
waist 4.4

taller[3a]
workshop 5.5

tallo[4b]
stem 2.7

tamaño[3a]
size 1.3

también[1a]
also 1.

tambor[6a]
drum 4.3

tampoco[1b]
neither (*adv.*) 1.

tan, tanto[1a]
– pronto como
as soon as 1.
so 1.
por lo –, therefore 1.
– . . . . como
as long as 1.1
– . . . . como
(as) well (as) 1.2
– . . . . como
as (good) as 1.4
as much 1.8
– como, (as) much (as) 1.9
– poco como
(as) little (as) 2.6
mientras –, meanwhile 2.8
– más
(so) much (the more) 3.6

tango[6b]
dance 3.1

tañer[6a]
play (*vb.*) 1.
ring (*vb.*) 1.4

tañido
ringing of bell 4.9

tapar[2b]
cover (*vb.*) 1.

tapia[4b]
wall 1.7

Section

tapiz[6a]
tapestry 5.8

tapón
cork 6.5

taquigrafía
shorthand 9.2

taquigráficamente
(in) shorthand 9.6

taquilla
reja de –
ticket window 5.3

tardanza[4b]
delay 3.8

tardar[1b]
delay (*tr. vb.*) 2.7

tarde (*n.* and *adv.*)[1a]
evening 1.
late 1.
buenas -s
good morning 1.1
afternoon 1.9

tardo[5b]
late 1.
slow 1.2
backward 5.4

tarea[3a]
(piece of) work 1.1

tarifa[6b]
fare 3.6
– de impuesto
tax rate 4.

tarjeta[3b]
card 2.1

tasa[6a]
measure 1.

taza[4a]
cup 4.3

té (*n.*)[5a]
tea 4.1

teatral[4b]
theatre 4.6

teatro[1b]
theatre 1.9

técnica
technique 6.6

técnico[7b]
technical 4.7

techo[2b]
roof 2.
bajo –, indoors 3.1
ceiling 3.7
paja de –, thatch 6.

tejado[4a]
roof 2.

tejedor
weaver 7.2

tejer +tejido[2b]
web 3.4
weave 4.6
knit 5.4

tejo
yew 7.2

tela[2b]
cloth 1.3
– de hilo, linen 3.6

teléfono[5b]
telephone 5.3

telegráfico[5b]
telegraph 5.3

telégrafo[5a]
telegraph 4.9

telegrama[5b]
wire 3.5

telescopio[7a]
telescope 5.4

telón[5a]
curtain (theatre) 3.8

Section

tema[2b]
subject 1.
theme 4.

temblar[1b]
tremble 1.8

temblor[4a]
trembling 4.
shiver 4.7

temblor de tierra
earthquake 6.

tembloroso[4a]
tremble 1.8

temer[1a]
(be) afraid 1.
temido, dreaded 2.4

temerario[4a]
rash 4.9

temeridad[4a]
folly 3.2

temeroso[3b]
timid 4.6

temible[4b]
terrible 1.8
dreaded 2.4

temor[1b]
fear (*n.*) 1.4

temperamento[4a]
nature (character) 1.
temper 4.2

temperatura[3a]
temperature 3.

tempestad[2b]
storm 1.6

templar +templado[2b]
temper 4.9

templo[2a]
temple 2.1

temporada[3b]
season (*n.*) 2.4

temporal[3b]
storm 1.6
temporary 3.2

temprano[2a]
early 1.1

tenaz[3b]
tenacious 8.

tenaza[6b]
-s, tongs 6.4

tendencia[4a]
leaning 1.8
tener –, tend 2.4
tendency 3.2

tender[1b]
spread 1.4

tendero[7a]
tradesman 5.7

tendón
sinew 6.

tenebroso[3b]
dark 1.

tenedor[5a]
fork 4.2

tener[1a]
have 1.
hold 1.

teniente[4b]
lieutenant 3.4

tenis
tennis 6.8

tenor[6a]
kind 1.

tensión[7b]
strain 4.1

tentación[4a]
temptation 4.4

tentador[6b]
attractive 4.

Section

trabajar[1a]
- work (*vb.*) … 1.

trabajo[1a]
- work (*n.*) … 1.
- workmanship … 3.
- patio de –, work-yard … 12.2

trabar[4a]
- fasten … 2.9

tradición[3b]
- tradition … 3.7

tradicional[4b]
- traditional … 7.8

traducción[6a]
- translation … 5.

traducir[3a]
- translate … 3.8

traer[1a]
- bring … 1.
- wear (clothes) … 1.
- bring before … 2.2

tragar[3b]
- swallow … 3.5

tragedia[4a]
- tragedy … 4.4

trágico[2b]
- tragic … 4.9

trago[5a]
- draft … 2.2

traición[3a]
- treason … 4.3

traicionar[6b]
- betray … †2.5

traidor[2b]
- traitor … 4.9

traje[1b]
- clothes … 1.4
- dress (*n.*) … 1.4
- suit … 2.7
- costume … 4.3

trampa[7a]
- hacer –, cheat … 3.1
- trap … 5.1

trance[4b]
- state (condition) … 1.

tranquear
- stride (*vb.*) … 3.3

tranquilidad[3a]
- quiet (*n.*) … 1.

tranquilizar[3b]
- quiet (*vb.*) … 1.6
- soothe … 4.3

tranquilo[1b]
- quiet … 1.

transcendencia[5b]
- importance … 1.8

transcendental[6b]
- surpassing … 6.2

transcurrir[3b]
- pass … 2.6

transeunte[6b]
- passerby … 10.9

transformación[5a]
- change (*n.*) … 2.9

transformar[2b]
- transform … 2.8

transición[6b]
- transition … 4.4

transigir[4b]
- settle … 1.8

tránsito[4b]
- crossing … 1.6

transmisión[5b]
- sending (*n.*) … 2.6

transmitir[3b]
- send … 1.

transparente[4b]
- transparent … 5.7

transponer[4b]
- transfer (*vb.*) … 2.4

transportar[5a]
- transport … 3.9
- transportado, rapt … 4.3

transporte[6b]
- transport … 3.2

transversal
- calle –, crossroad … 10.5

tranvía[4b]
- car … 2.1

trapo[4b]
- rag … 5.3

tras[1b]
- after … 1.
- (in) back (of) … 1.
- – bastidores (behind the) scene … 5.4

trasladar[2a]
- transfer (*vb.*) … 2.4

traslucir(se)[5b]
- show through … 3.4

trasnochar[6a]
- spend night … 2.7

traspasar[3a]
- cross … 1.

trastornar[3a]
- (make) mad … 2.9

trastorno[5b]
- confusion … 3.2
- upset … 6.3

tratado[4b]
- treaty … 2.6

tratamiento[4a]
- treatment … 2.8

tratar[1a]
- -se, (be a) question of … 1.
- try … 1.
- treat (*vb.*) … 1.4

trato[1b]
- bargain … 1.9
- dealing (*n.*) … 3.

través[2a]
- a –, through (motion) … 1.
- al – de, throughout … 2.8
- de –, across … 3.4

travesía[5b]
- journey … 1.

travesura[5b]
- mischief … 4.5
- prank … 5.7

travieso[4b]
- naughty … 2.3

traza[4a]
- trace (*n.*) … 2.1

trazar[2b]
- trace (out) … 1.7

trébol
- clover … 6.4

trece[5]*
- thirteen … 5.2

trecho[4a]
- distance … 1.1

tregua[5a]
- recess … 4.7

treinta[2]*
- thirty … 2.3

tremendo[2b]
- terrible … 1.8

trémulo[3a]
- tremble … 1.8

tren[2b]
- train … 1.1
- train (military) … 3.1

trenza[4b]
- braid … 6.

trepar[4b]
- climb … 2.7

tres[1]*
- three … 1.
- – veces, three times … 2.6

triángulo[6a]
- triangle … 7.

tribu[4b]
- tribe … 2.5

tribuna[6a]
- platform … 5.8

tribunal[3a]
- court … 1.4
- – supremo supreme court … 4.3

tributar[4a]
- (pay) tribute (to) … 3.2

tributo[4b]
- tax … 1.6

tricolor
- three-colored … 13.

trigo[2b]
- wheat … 2.5

trillar[6a]
- thrash … 5.9

trinchar[7b]
- carve … 3.3

trineo
- sled … 6.8
- sledge … 6.8

tripa[5a]
- entrails … 7.7

triple[6a]
- triple … 5.8

tripulación
- crew … 3.2

triste[1a]
- sad … 1.4
- bleak … 4.8

tristeza[1b]
- sadness … 3.5

triunfal[5b]
- triumphant … 4.6

triunfante[5b]
- triumphant … 4.6

triunfar[2a]
- triumph … 4.2

triunfo[1b]
- triumph … 3.1

trocar[3a]
- change (*vb.*) … 1.4

trofeo
- trophy … 6.8

trompa[5a]
- horn … 3.6

trompeta[5a]
- horn … 3.6

trompetero
- trumpeter … 8.4

tronar[5a]
- thunder … 4.2

tronco[3a]
- (tree) trunk … 2.3
- team (horses) … 3.9
- log … 4.8

trono[3a]
- throne … 2.3

tropa[2b]
- troop … 1.6

tropel[4b]
- crowd … 1.

tropezar[2a]
- stumble … 5.5

tropical[5b]
- tropic … 6.9

trópico[5b]
- tropic … 6.9

tropiezo[4b]
- error … 1.8

trotar[6a]
- trot … 5.5

trote[6a]
- trot … 4.6

trovador
- minstrel … 7.2

trozo[2b]
- piece … 1.
- slip … 3.5
- scrap … 5.5

trucha
- trout … 6.8

trueno[3a]
- thunder … 3.6

trueque[5a]
- exchange (*n.*) … 2.

tu[1]*
- thou … 1.
- thy … 1.6

tubo[4b]
- pipe … 3.2

tuerto[5b]
- blind (*adj.*) … 2.

tumba[3a]
- grave (*n.*) … 2.2

tumbar[6b]
- fell … 2.8
- tip over … 3.5

tumulto[6a]
- noise … 2.6

túnel[6b]
- tunnel … 6.4

túnica[4a]
- robe … 3.3

tupir[5a]
- stop up … 3.1

turba[5a]
- mob … 4.9

turbación[5a]
- confusion … 3.2

turbar[2a]
- embarrass … 3.2

turbio[4a]
- muddy … 5.2

turbulento[6b]
- stormy … 4.

turco[6a]
- Turkish … 5.

turista
- tourist … 6.9

turno[6b]
- por –, (in) turn … 1.
- shift … 3.5

tutear
- (use) thou-form … 13.

tutor[7a]
- guardian … 5.5

tuyo[3]*
- yours … 2.1
- thine … 2.3

U

u[1a]
- either … 1.
- or … 1.

ufano[4a]
- proud … 1.6

ujier
- usher … 7.3

ulterior[4b]
- subsequent … 4.1

Section
último[1a]
last (*adj.*) . . . . 1.
por –, (at) last . . . . 1.
latter 1.4
últimamente, lately . . . 5.1
umbral[4b]
threshold 4.2
umbroso
shady 6.1
un, uno, una[1a]
a . . . . 1.
cada –, each . . . . 1.
el – al otro, each other 1.
el – o el otro
either (one) . . . . . 1.
ni el – ni el otro
neither (one) . . . . 1.
una vez, once . . . . 1.
one (*indef. pron.*) . . . 1.
one (numeral) . . . . . 1.
unánime[6a]
unanimous . . . . 5.
undécimo
eleventh 7.2
ungir[7a]
anoint . . . . 7.
ungüento[6a]
ointment . . . . 7.
único[1a]
only (*adj.*) . . . . . . 1.
unidad[3a]
unity 3.8
unit 4.2
unit (military) 5.9
uniforme[4a]
uniform (*adj.*) 3.1
uniform (*n.*) 4.4
unión[2a]
union 1.6
union (bringing together) 3.5
unir[1a]
unite . . . . 1.
unido, united 1.5
universal[3a]
universal 3.8
universidad[3b]
university 3.3
universo[3b]
universe 5.4
untar[6a]
spread 4.5
anoint . . . . 7.
uña[3b]
nail 3.1
urbanidad[6b]
(good) manners 2.9
urbano[6a]
civil 3.2
courteous 4.3
urgencia[6b]
hurry (*n.*) 2.4
urgency 2.8
urgente[3b]
pressing 1.7
usanza[5a]
custom 1.9
usar[1a]
use . . . . 1.
uso[1b]
use (*n.*) 1.1
usted[1a]
you . . . . 1.
– mismo, yourself 2.1
usual[6a]
usual . . . . 1.
no –, unusual 2.6
usurpar[5b]
usurp 4.5
útil[2a]
useful . . . . 2.
helpful 5.6
utilidad[3a]
profit . . . . 2.
utilizar[3a]
use . . . . 1.
uva[5a]
grapes 4.1

V

vaca[2b]
cow 3.4
beef 4.1
vacaciones
holidays 5.2
vacante[6b]
vacant 2.8
vacilación[6b]
hesitation 7.3
vacilar[3a]
reel 3.1
waver 3.4
vacío[2a]
empty (*adj.*) . . . . 2.
void 5.2
vadear
wade 7.1
vado
ford 6.4
vagabundo[4b]
tramp 4.9
vagar[3b]
wander 2.7
vago[7a]
vague . . . . 4.
vaina
sheath 4.4
vaivén[4b]
motion 1.4
valenciano[6b]
English . . . . 1.
valentía[4b]
courage 1.4
valer[1a]
(be) worth . . . . 1.
valeroso[4a]
(be) brave . . . . 1.
validez
validity 5.8
valiente[1b]
(be) brave . . . . 1.
valioso[6a]
valuable 2.7
valor[1a]
value . . . . 1.
courage 1.4
sin –, worthless 4.2
válvula[7b]
valve 6.3
valla[5b]
fence 4.8
valle[2a]
valley 1.7
vanagloria[6a]
conceit 5.3
vanguardia
van 4.4
vanidad[2a]
vanity 3.3
vanidoso[6b]
vain 2.3
vano[1b]
en –, (in) vain 1.9
vain (*adj.*) 2.3
vapor[2a]
steam (*n.*) 2.5
buque de –, steamer . . 3.7
vara[3a]
yard 1.3
stick (*n.*) . . . . 2.
wand 3.2
variable[5a]
changing 4.6
variación[5a]
change (*n.*) 1.5
variar[2a]
vary 3.6
variedad[3a]
variety 3.8
vario[1a]
different . . . . 1.
-s, several . . . . 1.
varias veces
several times 1.2
various 2.6
varón[2a]
male 3.1
varonil[5b]
manly 3.8
vasallo[4a]
vassal 6.6
vasija[6b]
pot 2.3
vaso[1b]
glass . . . . 1.
vein 3.6
vasto[3a]
vast 2.8
vate[5b]
poet 1.5
vecindad[4b]
neighborhood 2.9
vecindario[6a]
neighborhood 2.9
vecino[1b]
near . . . . 1.
neighbor 1.8
adjoining 3.8
vega[6b]
plain (*n.*) 1.6
vegetación[4b]
vegetation 7.2
vegetal[4a]
vegetable 4.8
vegetable (*adj.*) . . . . 5.
vehemente[4b]
vehement 4.8
vehículo[5a]
vehicle . . . . 5.
veinte*
twenty 1.9
veinticinco[4]*
twenty-five 4.2
veinticuatro*
twenty-four 4.7
veintidós[5]*
twenty-two 4.6
veintiséis[5]*
twenty-six 4.7
vejez[2b]
old age 1.3
vela[2a]
candle 2.2
sail 3.5
velada[5b]
evening . . . . 1.
velar[2a]
watch (*vb.*) . . . . 1.
velo[3b]
veil 3.4
velocidad[4a]
speed 2.5
rate (of speed) 3.4
veloz[3a]
fast . . . . 1.
vellocino
fleece 6.4
vellón
fleece 6.4
velludo
hairy 7.8
vena[3a]
vein 3.6
vencedor[3a]
victor 3.8
vencer + vencido[1b]
overcome 2.4
vencimiento[6a]
defeat 3.6
falling due 5.2
venda[5b]
bandage 5.3
vendaval[5a]
storm 1.6
vendedor[6a]
merchant 2.2
clerk 2.7
dealer 4.8
vender[1b]
sell 1.4
– al (por) menor
retail 6.3
veneno[3b]
poison 3.1
venenoso
poisonous . . . . 6.
venerable[3b]
venerable 5.1
veneración[3b]
worship 3.6
venerar[3b]
reverence (*vb.*) 2.7
vengador[5a]
avenger 8.9
venganza[2a]
revenge 2.8
vengar[2b]
avenge 3.8
venida[4b]
arrival 2.8
venidero[4b]
next . . . . 1.
future (*adj.*) . . . . 2.
venir[1a]
come . . . . 1.
– de, come from . . . . . 1.
ir y –, ply 3.4
venta[2a]
sale 2.4
ventaja[6b]
advantage 1.6
ventajoso[6a]
favorable 2.2
profitable 4.1
ventana[1b]
window 1.4
ventero[6a]
innkeeper 5.8
ventoso
windy 6.5
ventura[2a]
fortune 1.4
venturoso[4a]
fortunate . . . . 2.
ver[1a]
see . . . . 1.
verano[2a]
summer 1.6

Section

veras[2a]
de –, really 1.4
verbal[6a]
oral 5.4
verbigracia[2b]
(for) example 1.4
verbo[1b]
verb 6.5
verdad[1a]
truth .... 1.
en –, really 1.4
verdadero[1a]
indeed .... 1.
verdaderamente
indeed .... 1.
real .... 1.
true .... 1.
verdaderamente, really 1.4
verde[1b]
green 1.5
verdor[6a]
green .... 4.
verdugo[3a]
hangman 7.3
verdura[4b]
green .... 4.
vergonzoso[4a]
shy 4.2
shameful 4.7
vergüenza[2a]
shame 3.3
verificar[2b]
check 3.8
verja[5b]
bars 4.6
versión[6a]
translation .... 5.
interpretation 5.5
verso[1b]
verse 2.7
verter[2b]
pour 2.3
vertical[5b]
upright 4.1
vertiginoso[6a]
fast .... 1.
vértigo[4a]
tener –, dizzy 6.4
vestido[1b]
clothes 1.4
dress (*n.*) 1.4
vestigio[6a]
trace (*n.*) 2.1
vestir[1a]
clothe 1.9
veterano
veteran 7.2
vetusto[5b]
ancient 2.6
vez[1a]
otra –, again .... 1.
muchas veces, often .. 1.
una –, once .... 1.
time (how many) .. 1.
a la –
(at the same) time 1.
algunas veces, de – en cuando
(at) times .... 1.
a su –, (in) turn .... 1.
varias veces
several times 1.2
a veces, algunas veces
sometimes 1.4
rara –, seldom 1.5
dos veces, two times .. 1.8
cada –, (every) time .. 2.2
tres veces
three times 2.6

Section

vez[1a]—*continued*
por primera –
(for the) first time 2.6
vía[2b]
road .... 1.
viajar[3a]
travel (*vb.*) 1.8
viaje[1a]
journey .... 1.
saco de –
bag (suitcase) 4.5
viajero[3a]
traveler 2.4
vianda[5b]
food 1.9
víbora[6a]
viper .... 7.
vibración[4a]
vibration 7.6
vibrante[6b]
vibrate 4.4
vibrar[3a]
vibrate 4.4
vicepresidente[6a]
vice-president 9.8
vicio[2a]
vice 3.2
vicioso[5b]
bad .... 1.
vicious 6.5
víctima[1b]
victim 2.2
victoria[2b]
victory .... 2.
victorioso[4b]
victorious 3.9
vida[1a]
life .... 1.
vidriera[7a]
(church) window ... 2.4
vidrio[3a]
glass 1.7
pane 3.3
viejo[1a]
old .... 1.
hierro –
(old) iron 2.3
(old) man 2.4
viento[1b]
wind 1.4
molino de –
windmill 5.4
vientre[3b]
belly 6.2
viernes[4a]
Friday 3.6
vigésimo[7*]
twentieth 7.1
vigilancia[4b]
care 3.2
vigilante[6b]
guard (*n.*) .... 2.
vigilar[4a]
watch (*vb.*) .... 1.
vigilia[5a]
vigil 6.2
vigor[3a]
force .... 1.
vigor .... 4.
vigoroso[3a]
hardy 2.6
vil[2b]
low 1.8
villa[2b]
city .... 1.

Section

villano[3b]
bad 1.2
knave 4.5
villain .... 5.
vinagre[3b]
vinegar 6.3
vincular[6b]
unite .... 1.
vínculo[4b]
tie (*n.*) 1.6
union 1.6
vino[1a]
wine 1.4
viña[4a]
vineyard 5.1
violación
violation 6.8
violencia[2a]
violence 3.6
violento[1b]
furious 1.9
violeta[5a]
violet (flower) 5.2
violet (color) 5.5
violín[5b]
violin 6.1
virgen[2a]
girl .... 1.
virgin (*n.*) 2.9
virgin (e.g., ground) 4.1
virginal[6a]
virgin 5.3
viril[5a]
manly 3.8
virilidad
manhood 6.8
virrey[6a]
viceroy 8.6
virtud[1a]
virtue 1.9
virtuoso[3b]
virtuous 4.8
viruela[6a]
smallpox 7.8
visible[3b]
visible 2.9
visión[2a]
sight .... 1.
visita[1b]
visit (*n.*) 1.4
visitante[7a]
visitor 5.1
visitar[1b]
visit (*vb.*) 1.4
vislumbrar[5b]
(catch) sight of 1.1
glance (*vb.*) 2.3
vislumbre[6b]
look .... 1.
viso[6a]
looks (*n.*) .... 1.
víspera[5b]
day before 1.4
– de Año Nuevo
(New Year's) Eve 3.8
vista[1a]
punto de –
point of view .... 1.
sight .... 1.
hasta la –, farewell .. 3.4
vistoso[4b]
beautiful .... 1.
magnificent 3.5
vital[4a]
essential 2.9
vituperio[6a]
vituperation .... 13.

Section

viudo[2a]
viuda, widow .... 3.
widower 10.3
viva[6b]
applause 3.7
viveza[6a]
life 3.8
vivienda[3b]
dwelling 2.3
viviente[4b]
alive 1.9
living 3.4
vivir[1a]
live .... 1.
vivo + vivaracho[1a]
fast .... 1.
(full of) life .... 1.
alive 1.9
vizcaíno[4a]
English .... 1.
vizconde[7b]
viscount 8.4
vocablo[4b]
word .... 1.
vocación[6a]
occupation 2.4
vocal[5b]
voter 4.6
volante[5b]
ruffle 6.1
volar[1b]
fly (*vb.*) 1.6
volcán[3a]
volcano 6.7
volcar[5a]
overthrow 3.1
tip over 3.5
voltear[7a]
tip over 3.5
voltio
volt 9.4
volumen[2b]
volume 2.9
voluntad[1a]
will (*n.*) .... 1.
voluntario[4a]
(of own) accord 3.4
voluptuoso[5a]
voluptuous 8.6
volver[1a]
– a, again .... 1.
turn .... 1.
go back 1.4
-se, turn round 1.4
come back 1.8
hacer –, call back 2.6
– a llevar
carry back 3.2
vomitar[6a]
vomit .... 5.
voraz[6a]
greedy .... 6.
votar[4b]
vote (*vb.*) 1.8
voto[2a]
vote 2.8
vow (*n.*) 4.9
hacer -s, vow (*vb.*) ... 5.2
voz[1a]
voice .... 1.
vuelo[2b]
flight 2.5
vuelta[1b]
de –, back .... 1.
return 1.4
dar la –, go round 1.8
turn (*n.*) .... 3.

† The thousand number for the indexed word was discovered to have been inaccurately entered in this section. Following is given the English key word for the entry with the correct section number.

benefit, Sec. 3.6, *should be in* Sec. 3.7
betray, Sec. 2.5, *should be in* Sec. 2.8
bride, Sec. 1.6, *should be in* Sec. 2.2
domestic (*adj.*), Sec. 2.9, *should be in* Sec. 3.5
event, Sec. 2., *should be in* Sec. 1.9
(the) faithful, Sec. 2.7, *should be in* Sec. 3.9
indulge, Sec. 5.3, *should be in* Sec. 5.2
limb, Sec. 2., *should be in* Sec. 1.9
manifest, Sec. 3.1, *should be in* Sec. 3.4

APPENDIXES

APPENDIX I

LIST OF ENGLISH PROPER NOUNS DELETED FROM THE SOURCE LIST

(233 Words)

Abraham[4b]
Adam[5a]
Albany[5a]
Albert[6]
Alexander[5a]
Alfred[6]
Alice[3b]
Alps[6]
America[2a]
Andrew[4b]
Anna[5a]
Anne[4b]
Argentina[6]
Arthur[3b]
Asia[2b]
Athens[6]
Atlantic[2b]
Australia(n)[5a]
Babylon[6]
Baltimore[4b]
Belgium[6]
Ben[6]
Benjamin[5a]
Bess[4b]
Betty[4a]
Billy (b)[3b]
Bob (b)[3b]
Boston[3b]
Brazil[6]
Britain[3b]
Broadway[6]
Brooklyn[4a]
brownie (B)[5b]
C.[6]
Caesar[3b]
Cain[6]
California[3a]
Canada[3b]
Carl[4b]
Carolina[5a]
Charles[2a]
Charley(ie)[6]
Chicago[3b]
Cinderella[5b]
Cleveland[5b]
Clifford[6]
cologne (C)[6]
Colorado[5a]
Columbia(n)[4a]
Columbus[3a]
Connecticut[5b]
Cromwell[6]
Crusoe[6]
Cupid[6]
daisy (D)[3a]
Dan[3a]
Daniel[4b]
David[3b]
Delaware[6]
Denmark[6]
Diana[6]
Dick[2b]
Donald[6]
Dorothy[5a]
Eden[5a]
Edith[5b]
Edward[3a]
Egypt[3b]
Elizabeth[4a]
Ella[5b]
Ellen[6]
Emily[6]
England[1b]
Europe[2a]
Fannie(y)[5b]
Florence[5b]
Florida[5a]
France[1b]
Francis[4b]
franklin (F)[5b]
Fred[4a]
Frederic(k)[6]
Fritz[6]
Fulton[5b]
George[2a]
Georgia[5b]
Germany[3a]
Greece[5a]
Hamilton[4a]
Hannah[6]
Hans[4b]
Harold[5a]
hazel (H)[6]
Helen[4a]
Henry[2a]
Herbert[6]
Hiawatha[6]
Holland[4b]
Homer (h)[6]
Horace[6]
Houston[5b]
Howard[6]
Hudson[3b]
Illinois[5a]
India[3a]
Indiana[5b]
Indies[5b]
Ireland[5b]
Israel[4a]
Italy[3a]
jack (J)[2a]
Jackson[5b]
Jacob[4a]
James[2a]
Jamestown[6]
Jane[5a]
Japan[4a]
jay (J)[6]
Jean (j)[5b]
jersey (J)[4a]
Jerusalem[5a]
Jim[6]
Joe[4b]
John[1a]
Johnny[5a]
Johnson[6]
Jones[6]
Joseph[3a]
Jove[5b]
Julia[6]
Kansas[6]
Kate[2b]
Lawrence[6]
Leonard[6]
Lincoln[3b]
London[2a]
Louis[4a]
Lucy[5a]
Madison[4b]
Maine[6]
Manhattan[5a]
Margaret[4b]
Margery[5a]
Marion[5a]
Martha[5b]
Martin (m)[5b]
Mary[2a]
Maryland[5b]
Massachusetts[4b]
Maud[5a]
Mediterranean[6]
Mexico[4a]
Michael[6]
Michigan[6]
Milton[6]
Mississippi[3b]
Missouri[5b]
Moses[5b]
Ned[4b]
Nell[5a]
Netherlands[5b]
New York[1b]
Nicholas[6]
Noah[6]
Norway[5b]
Ohio[4a]
Oliver[5a]
Oregon[6]
Orleans[6]
Oxford[5a]
Panama[4b]
Paris[3b]
Paul[3a]
Pennsylvania[3b]
Peru[6]
Peter[2b]
Philadelphia[3b]
Philip[3a]
Philippine[6]
Philistine[6]
Pittsburg[6]
Poland[6]
Polly[6]
Portugal[6]

Puritan[6]
Ralph[3b]
Rhine[5a]
Richard[4a]
Richmond[5b]
Robert[2b]
Robinson[6]
Roger[5b]
Rome[2b]
Ruth[3b]
sally (S)[5a]
Sam[6]
Samuel[5a]
San Francisco[5b]
Santa Claus[4a]
Sara(h)[6]
Saul[6]
Scotland[4b]
Shakespeare[6]
Simon[5a]
smith (S)[3a]
Solomon[5b]
Spain[2b]
Stanley[5a]
Stephen[5a]
sue (S)[6]
Switzerland[6]
Syria[5b]
Tennessee[5b]
Texas[4a]
Thames[6]
Thanksgiving (t)[3b]
Thomas[3a]
timothy (T)[6]
Tom[3a]
Tommy[5a]
troy (T)[6]
Ulysses[6]
U.S.[6]
Venice[6]
Venus[6]
Virginia[3a]
Wales[6]
Walter[3b]
Washington[2a]
William[2a]
Willy[6]
Wisconsin[5b]
York[6]

LIST OF ENGLISH WORDS MOVED FROM ONE THOUSAND TO ANOTHER

Words Moved up from 2a to 1b (4 Words)

accept
character
direction
feeling

Words from 3a to 2b (23 Words)

author
conscience
contrary
dispose
education
eternal
everywhere
exclaim
goodness
habit
importance
numerous
position
process
propose
recognize
relation
religion
sacred
science
sentence
somebody
surround

Words from 4a to 3b (59 Words)

admiration
agony
attract
audience
capacity
ceremony
champion
chapter
clever
comparison
complaint
compose
confirm
consideration
decree
delicious
dense
desperate
development
dignity
doubtful
endless
estimate
European
evidence
exception
exhaust
exist
genius
gleam
greatness
hardy
infinite
institute
justify
miserable
observation
parliament
peasant
poetry
political
previous
reckon
resist
reverence
risk
sample
scholar
splendor
statement
substitute
supreme
suspect
talent
traffic
transfer
unusual
victim
whoever

Words from 5a to 4b (93 Words)

actor
affirm
afflict
agreement
ambassador
amend
appreciate
arrangement
artificial
attentive
battery
beer
comedy
conclusion
confuse
consecrate
converse
dazzle
decoration
dedicate
defiance
desirable
diligent
distribution
ending
engagement
entice
eternity
expectation
experiment
expression
function
genuine
gloomy
gush
hardship
hesitate
impatient
imperfect
imprison

income
inhabitant
inheritance
instinct
landscape
likeness
manly
martyr
misfortune
mission
murderer
normal
nourish
novel
obedient
opposition
oppression
origin
painful
peninsula
pensive
performance
petition
positive
possibility
pressure
production
profession
project
prudent
quote
reception
reflection
renounce
resolution
respective
restraint
separation
sermon
shipment
solicit
sublime
summit
surpass
temporary
theirs
theme
thoughtful
torrent
transform
treaty
unable
unfold

WORDS FROM 6 TO 5b (157 WORDS)

abominable
absorb
absurd
abyss
academy
acceptance
accusation
acid
adjust
admirable
adversary
allege
alternate
amen
animate
antiquity
applaud
aspire
astonishing
awkward
axis
beckon
beget
boldness
brutal
buyer
cardinal
casual
childish
communicate
competition
condense
confirmation
contemplation
corpse
correction
countless
cowardly
creator
creditor
culture
decent
definite
deliberate
democrat
demonstrate
denounce
desirous
disagreeable
discreet
disturbance
divinity
document
edition
elevation
embarrass
emerge
enquire
enthusiastic
equality
equipment
essence
exceptional
excursion
exhibition
extol
extremity
fantastic
feminine
foliage
formation
germ
gesture
homage
immortality
ingenious
injurious
injustice
insignificant
introduction
inventor
investigate
jury
lengthen
luggage
meaning
miner
ministry
mistrust
modesty
monthly
movable
negative
niece
nobleman
noisy
nomination
painting
paragraph
parish
passionate
patriotic
pension
persecution
persist
photograph
piety
poetic
prejudice
prose
proverb
prudence
publication
purify
remorse
resource
responsible
ridiculous
rigor
robbery
romantic
rot
scandal
scruple
seduce
session
sheath
shorten
sincerity
slander
slap
stammer
statute
straighten
subsequent
subtract
successor
suffering
suggestion
sumptuous
superfluous
taint
tease
tendency
thoughtless
thunderbolt
triumphant
troublesome
trusty
unequal
upstairs
vague
vineyard
voter
weaken
wrestle
wrist

WORDS FROM 7 TO 6 (233 WORDS)

abbot
accidental
accomplishment
activity
adjacent
admirer
adversity
advertisement
aggravate
almond
ammunition
analyze
anecdote
anticipate
apparatus
approval
architect
architecture
aristocratic
artillery
aught
authorize
award
baptism
beating
blasphemy
blouse
bristle
carter
charitable
cider
circulation
civilization
cleanliness
colonel
combustion
comet
communion
complement
compromise
concentrate
conception
confederate
congratulation
conjecture
consecration
conservative
contemporary
contemptuous
continuance
contribution
coo
countryman
criticism
currency
dancer
debtor
decade
decisive
declaration
defective
delicacy
democracy
demonstration
depose
depress
descendant
determination
dialogue
digest
dimension
disadvantage
disastrous
discretion
dividend
duchess
durable
economy
electricity
eloquent
embark
embody
emerald
emphasis
employer
engrave
enjoyment
ether
ethereal
exaggerate
excellence
exclamation
expansion
farce
finance
flexible
focus
fraternal
friction
fundamental
generosity
goodwill
grandson
gravity
harmonious
Hebrew
heroine
historian
hoarse
honesty
horizontal
hospitality
humane
hydrogen
hypocrisy
identical
illusion
imaginary
impartial
impulse
incredible
indifference
indifferent
indirect
indulgence
infernal
ingenuity
inscription
insensible
inseparable
inspect
instinctive
intellectual
intensity
interpose
interpretation
interpreter
invasion
involuntary
isolate
jerk
jostle
kernel
leadership
legislation
linden
loan
logic
luxurious
magnet
manuscript
mattress
mechanical
mental
metropolis
militia
misunderstand
moderation
monarchy
naval
necktie
nucleus
oasis
oath
offensive
omission
organic
organism
paternal
patriotism
peddler
penance
perseverance
personage
personality
phenomenon
poisonous
predecessor
preference
prism
professional
prohibition
pronoun
pronunciation
protestant
publisher
pyramid
radical
ranch
ration
receiver
recruit
refinement
regiment
repetition
reproduce
reproduction
requirement
requisite
resistance
respectable
revelation
revolutionary
satire
scientific
scientist
sculpture
secondary
sensitive
severity
shipwreck
skeleton
solemnity
sovereignty
specific
spectator

structure
submission
suffrage
technical
tradesman
tragic
transition
unanimous
vehement
vehicle
venerable
vigil
vigorous
viper
volcano
wallet
zinc

LIST OF GERMAN PROPER NOUNS DELETED FROM THE SOURCE LIST

(51 Words)

Agnes[4a]
Alexander[4a]
Berliner[2b]
Bremer[6b]
Charlotte[3b]
Eduard[3b]
Egmont[4b]
Elisabeth[5a]
Felix[6b]
Ferdinand[4b]
Frankfurter[6a]
Franz[4a]
Frieda[6b]
Friedrich[2a]
Fritz[6a]
Gabriel[6b]
Georg[4a]
Hamburger[6a]
Hans[6b]
Harz[6b]
Heinrich[3b]
Heinz[5b]
Helene[5b]
Hermann[5a]
Jeronimus[6a]
Johann[3a]
Joseph[6a]
Julie[6b]
Julius[5b]
Karl[2b]
Ludwig[4a]
Maria[2b]
Marie[3b]
Max[6a]
Ottilie[5b]
Otto[6b]
Ottokar[4a]
Pan[5b]
Pariser[4a]
Paul[5a]
Peter[6a]
Philipp[4b]
Preußen[4a]
Richard[5b]
Robert[5a]
Rudolf[6a]
Rupert[5a]
Sophie[6b]
Venus[6a]
Wiener[4b]
Wilhelm[2a]

LIST OF GERMAN WORDS MOVED FROM ONE THOUSAND TO ANOTHER

Words Moved up from 3a to 2b (5 Words)

Bestandteil
erwachen
Fläche
gründlich
verhältnismäßig

From 4a to 3b (10 Words)

Ablauf
Autorität
Bach
beschaffen
Blei
eitel
Priester
unruhig
vorschieben
zuverlässig

From 5a to 4b (22 Words)

aufwärts
Botschaft
durchweg
einreichen
ersichtlich
Erwähnung
geheimnisvoll
Gewerbebetrieb
Jahrtausend
Mode
Post-
rauchen
Rüstung
senkrecht
trachten
unbegreiflich
verantwortlich
vorbringen
zerbrechen
zukünftig
zürnen
zurücktreten

From 6a to 5b (33 Words)

abfallen
achte
Anlauf
Ausgangspunkt
Auszeichnung
Bedienung
belassen
beneiden
Buße
dehnen
demokratisch
Eiche
entledigen
Garnison
gewahr
Griff
Handelskammer
langweilig
Strafgesetzbuch
umständlich
Urlaub
Vaterstadt
verabreden
verbannen
vermischen
Verwertung
Verwundete
zersetzen
zielen
zornig
Zucht
zurückrufen
zuziehen

From 7a to 6b (51 Words)

anrechnen
Ballen
Befehlshaber
Befinden
belagern
berauschen
bezaubern
Binnenschiffahrt
Check
Ebbe
Ehemann
erstlich
erträglich
Gesandtschaft
Gesellschaftsvertrag
Grausamkeit
hieher
klammern
Kommen
Konsumverein
Korporation
Krisis
löslich
Lyrik
Mäßigung
mitmachen
physikalisch
Rathaus
Rebe
Rückblick
rühmlich
Schachtel
Schall
sparsam
Staatskasse
Trompeter
trostlos
Tüchtigkeit
unbeschreiblich
ungewohnt
unrecht (*adj.*)
Unterwerfung
Verschwörung
Verwick(e)lung
Villa
Volksvertretung
Wandlung
wasserdicht
wohlbekannt
wundersam
Zuverlässigkeit

APPENDIX II

(Average Frequencies Occur in Thousands Indicated by Italics)

CONCEPTUAL ANALYSIS OF THE SUBSTANTIVES IN THE LIST

Conceptual Categories	Number of Times Concept Occurs in — First 1,000	Second 1,000	Third 1,000	Fourth 1,000	Fifth 1,000	Sixth 1,000	First Half of Seventh 1,000	Total
Total number of substantival concepts	331	524	558	600	*634*	719	352	3,718
A. Abstractions	82	100	113	111	*98*	94	108	706
1. Quality	40	47	53	39	*51*	39	53	322
a) Qualitative (e.g., goodness)	36	44	49	35	*48*	36	53	301
b) Quantitative (e.g., load)	4	3	4	*4*	3	3	0	21
2. State (e.g., quiet)	20	34	37	57	*32*	36	37	253
3. Systems	4	7	14	10	*6*	14	15	70
a) Art and science (e.g., physics)	3	2	2	6	2	*12*	10	37
b) Sociological (e.g., industry)	1	3	10	*3*	4	2	3	26
c) Ideological (e.g., religion)	0	2	2	*1*	0	0	2	7
4. Dimensional units	18	12	9	*5*	9	5	3	61
a) Numerals (e.g., five)	13	5	*5*	3	6	4	1	37
b) Measures (e.g., ton)	5	7	4	*2*	3	1	2	24
B. Activity	57	123	177	*205*	156	106	68	892
1. Continued action (e.g., journey)	12	36	46	47	*47*	35	29	252
2. Completed action	45	87	131	*158*	109	71	39	640
a) Result of action (e.g., statement)	41	84	123	*150*	102	64	38	602
b) Product of action (see D.3.*a*.ii)								
c) Single manifestation of action (e.g., kiss)	4	3	8	8	*7*	7	1	38
C. Animate beings	56	76	85	95	*125*	171	86	694
1. Characterized by	36	33	27	35	*56*	82	28	297
a) Special attribute(s)	25	24	19	31	*48*	75	20	242
i) Humans (e.g., child)	21	19	14	*15*	14	23	16	122
ii) Others than humans	4	5	5	16	34	*52*	4	120
α) Animals (e.g., horse)	3	1	4	9	*18*	12	0	47
β) Birds (e.g., eagle)	0	1	0	3	7	*17*	1	29
γ) Fish (e.g., trout)	0	1	0	0	0	*8*	1	10
δ) Insects (e.g., flea)	0	0	0	3	3	*10*	1	17
ε) Reptiles (e.g., snake)	0	0	0	1	0	*3*	1	5
ζ) Spirits, etc. (e.g., elf)	1	2	1	0	*6*	2	0	12
b) Special relationship (e.g., brother)	11	9	8	*4*	8	7	8	55
2. Person-agent	15	37	51	55	*65*	86	47	356
a) Function (occupation) (e.g., professor)	14	30	36	39	*46*	55	26	246
b) Agency (e.g., lover)	1	7	15	16	19	*31*	21	110
3. Person-member	5	6	7	5	*4*	3	11	41
a) Of group or organization (e.g., royalist)	1	1	1	1	2	*1*	6	13
b) Of sect (adherent) (e.g., Protestant)	1	1	2	1	*1*	2	3	11
c) Of race (ethnic or national) (e.g., negro)	3	4	4	*3*	1	0	2	17

Conceptual Categories	Number of Times Concept Occurs in —							
	First 1,000	Second 1,000	Third 1,000	Fourth 1,000	Fifth 1,000	Sixth 1,000	First Half of Seventh 1,000	Total
D. Spatial units (inanimate)	121	194	178	182	*250*	347	89	1,361
1. Range	22	25	16	*16*	13	21	7	123
a) Simple extension (e.g., territory)	9	11	5	*6*	5	5	1	42
b) Space characterized by special attribute(s) (e.g., city)	13	17	11	*19*	8	16	6	81
2. Function-endowed	33	70	89	87	*103*	136	41	559
a) Place where (e.g., shop)	11	21	32	*24*	21	25	10	144
b) Instruments (e.g., watch)	16	40	48	42	*57*	78	20	301
c) Containers (e.g., purse)	1	4	3	10	*12*	12	3	45
d) Clothing (e.g., skirt)	2	3	5	11	*10*	14	2	47
e) Nondescripts characterized by function only (e.g., number)	3	2	1	*0*	3	7	6	22
3. Thing characterized by	66	96	73	79	*134*	190	41	679
a) Special attribute(s)	52	80	62	72	*126*	185	38	615
i) Materials (e.g., wax)	2	3	3	*5*	5	2	3	23
ii) Thing-product (e.g., liquor)	20	23	29	30	*39*	61	8	210
iii) Natural food (e.g., cabbage)	0	5	4	6	14	*31*	4	64
iv) Plant life (except vegetables and fruit in D.3.*a*.iii) (e.g., tree)	2	6	8	4	*28*	33	5	86
v) Minerals and natural elements (e.g., gold)	10	7	7	*12*	12	21	4	83
vi) Parts of body (e.g., tail)	12	8	6	9	*23*	24	7	99
vii) Nondescripts characterized by shape only (e.g., spiral)	3	1	2	3	*3*	5	3	20
viii) Nondescripts semi-identified by quality (e.g., treasure)	3	7	3	3	*2*	8	4	30
b) Relationship (e.g., front)	14	16	11	*7*	8	5	3	64
E. Temporal units	13	31	*5*	7	5	1	1	65
1. Range (e.g., interval)	7	23	*3*	5	2	0	0	40
2. Time when (e.g., noon)	1	*3*	0	0	0	0	0	4
3. Characterized by special attribute(s) (e.g., Easter)	1	0	2	*2*	2	1	0	8
4. Measures (e.g., century)	6	5	*0*	0	1	0	1	13
M. Collectives (taken from A.1, A.3.*a*, A.3.*c*, A.4, B.1, B.2.*a*, C.1.*a*, C.1.b, C.2.*a*, C.2.*b*, C.3.*b*, C.3.*c*, D.1, D.2.*d*, D.3.*a*) (e.g., group)	22	31	43	*34*	33	20	11	194
N. Feminines (taken from C.1.*a*.i, C.1.*a*.ii, C.2.*a*, C.2.*b*) (e.g., goddess)	12	7	8	*3*	8	12	4	54

CONCEPTUAL ANALYSIS OF THE VERBS IN THE LIST

Conceptual Categories	First 1,000	Second 1,000	Third 1,000	Fourth 1,000	Fifth 1,000	Sixth 1,000	First Half of Seventh 1,000	Total
	Number of Times Concept Occurs in —							
Total number of verbal concepts	287	301	258	224	177	125	28	1,400
A. State	62	51	27	19	16	8	3	186
1. Positional	5	7	3	4	3	2	0	24
a) Subject centered (e.g., sit)	5	4	3	2	1	1	0	16
b) Subject-object relational (e.g., flank)	0	3	0	2	2	1	0	8
2. Conditional	57	44	24	15	13	6	3	162
a) Subject centered	19	14	7	6	4	3	1	54
i) Characterizing (e.g., wait)	14	12	6	5	3	3	1	44
ii) Evaluating (e.g., be right)	5	2	1	1	1	0	0	10
b) Subject-object relational	38	30	17	9	9	3	2	108
i) Comparison (e.g., equal)	3	3	4	1	2	0	1	14
ii) Association	17	10	2	1	1	2	1	34
α) Static (e.g., cost)	11	4	1	0	0	1	1	18
β) Dynamic (e.g., be engaged in)	6	6	1	1	1	1	0	16
iii) Attitudinal	18	17	11	7	6	1	0	60
α) Static (e.g., love)	16	9	6	4	2	1	0	38
β) Dynamic (e.g., celebrate)	2	8	5	3	4	0	0	22
B. Motion	38	32	25	19	15	13	3	145
1. Subject centered	29	31	20	18	15	13	3	129
a) Progressive	27	27	18	15	8	10	2	107
i) Directed (e.g., disappear)	20	18	12	10	5	5	2	72
ii) Free (e.g., swim)	7	9	6	5	3	5	0	35
b) Localized (e.g., vibrate)	2	4	2	3	7	3	1	22
2. Object centered (subject moves) (e.g., carry)	9	1	5	1	0	0	0	16
C. Action	175	216	205	186	146	104	22	1,054
1. Subject centered	36	31	43	38	39	43	5	235
a) Passive (e.g., be overcome)	4	4	3	2	0	2	0	15
b) Active	32	27	40	36	39	41	5	220
i) Transformative (e.g., shrink)	8	9	16	15	6	5	3	62
ii) Productive (e.g., foam)	2	2	2	4	6	4	0	20
iii) Utterative (e.g., roar)	7	3	5	6	11	17	1	50
iv) Manifestative (e.g., rejoice)	3	4	5	3	1	3	1	20
v) Unconfined	12	9	12	8	15	12	0	68
α) Behavioristic (e.g., breathe)	12	8	10	6	7	10	0	53
β) Effective (e.g., spin)	0	1	2	2	8	2	0	15
2. Subject-object relational	68	48	43	27	13	13	3	215
a) Perceptive (e.g., hear)	9	3	2	1	0	1	0	16
b) Solutive (e.g., decide)	16	6	7	1	2	0	0	32
c) Expressive	11	3	3	6	2	2	1	28
i) Static (e.g., represent)	3	0	2	0	0	0	0	5
ii) Dynamic (e.g., vow)	8	3	1	6	2	2	1	23
d) Emanative	19	27	24	13	5	4	1	93
i) Directed (e.g., teach)	16	23	20	12	4	1	1	77
ii) Free (e.g., spend)	3	4	4	1	1	3	0	16
e) Acquisitive (e.g., buy)	13	9	7	6	4	6	1	46

Conceptual Categories	Number of Times Concept Occurs in — First 1,000	Second 1,000	Third 1,000	Fourth 1,000	Fifth 1,000	Sixth 1,000	First Half of Seventh 1,000	Total
C. Action—*Continued*								
3. Object centered	71	137	119	121	94	48	14	604
a) Conducive	42	79	64	62	62	24	8	341
i) Causative (e.g., drown [*tr.*])	2	3	2	3	3	0	0	13
ii) Factitive, resulting in	17	37	28	42	44	15	6	189
α) Static condition (e.g., clean)	15	28	15	37	39	13	4	151
β) Dynamic state (e.g., worry)	2	9	13	5	5	2	2	38
iii) Motitive (subject does not move) (e.g., drive [horse])	10	18	19	4	3	5	1	60
iv) Locative (e.g., place)	8	10	6	6	3	1	0	34
v) Destructive (e.g., destroy)	3	7	5	7	9	3	1	35
vi) Retentive (e.g., keep)	2	4	4	0	0	0	0	10
b) Applicative	3	12	15	21	18	12	2	83
i) Supplying (e.g., clothe)	3	10	13	16	15	7	2	66
ii) Privative (e.g., strip)	0	2	2	5	3	5	0	17
c) Productive (e.g., build)	7	11	6	5	2	2	1	34
d) Directive	12	29	23	23	9	5	3	104
i) Affective (e.g., attack)	7	16	19	12	7	2	2	65
ii) With outside goal (e.g., translate)	5	13	4	11	2	3	1	39
e) Effective (e.g., cut)	7	6	11	10	3	5	0	42
D. Auxiliaries	12	2	1	0	0	0	0	15
1. Simple formants (e.g., be)	2	0	0	0	0	0	0	2
2. Modulators (e.g., be about to)	10	2	1	0	0	0	0	13
M. Secondary groupings (taken from A–C)	28	16	16	18	15	10	3	106
1. Negative and opposite (e.g., fail, displease)	3	2	1	2	2	1	0	11
2. Modes of action	21	9	8	8	3	0	1	50
a) Perdurative (e.g., walk)	4	0	2	2	2	0	0	10
b) Teleotropic (e.g., aspire)	7	2	3	1	0	0	0	13
c) Initive (e.g., start out)	3	4	2	3	0	0	1	13
d) Finitive (e.g., arrive)	7	3	1	2	1	0	0	14
3. Repetitive (e.g., say again)	2	2	0	0	0	0	1	5
4. Frequentative (e.g., flutter)	1	2	4	4	9	8	1	29
5. Reciprocal (e.g., cooperate)	0	0	0	1	0	0	0	1
6. Forms of action (intensive, diminutive) (e.g., stride, rustle)	1	1	3	3	1	1	0	10

CONCEPTUAL ANALYSIS OF THE ADJECTIVES IN THE LIST

Conceptual Categories	Number of Times Concept Occurs in — First 1,000	Second 1,000	Third 1,000	Fourth 1,000	Fifth 1,000	Sixth 1,000	First Half of Seventh 1,000	Total
Total number of adjectival concepts	188	158	170	197	175	187	117	1,192
A. Essential (predominating meaning is the essence)	130	107	117	118	112	85	70	739
1. Quantity	43	10	8	7	10	4	1	83
a) Extension	19	4	4	2	4	1	1	35
i) Temporal (e.g., eternal)	4	1	2	1	0	1	1	10
ii) Spatial (e.g., spacious)	15	3	2	1	4	0	0	25
b) Enumeration (e.g., every)	24	4	3	5	5	2	0	43
c) Frequency (e.g., daily)	0	2	1	0	1	1	0	5
2. Quality	83	85	95	86	81	55	42	527
a) Character	67	57	57	60	50	32	28	351
i) Disposition	10	19	16	25	22	19	19	130
α) Propensitive (e.g., selfish)	2	7	5	10	7	6	10	47
β) Manifestative (e.g., grateful)	8	12	11	15	15	13	9	83
ii) Evaluation	38	27	33	32	22	12	8	172
α) Static (e.g., fair, just)	33	23	23	23	13	7	5	127
β) Dynamic (e.g., industrious)	5	4	10	9	9	5	3	45
iii) Physical constitution	19	11	8	3	6	1	1	49
α) Shape (e.g., square)	0	1	3	0	0	1	0	5
β) Sensorial trait (e.g., brown)	19	10	5	3	6	0	1	44
b) State	16	28	38	26	31	23	14	176
i) Static	15	19	29	18	22	18	11	132
α) Being (e.g., silent)	8	11	14	4	5	12	6	60
β) Result of action (e.g., bent)	7	8	15	14	17	6	5	72
ii) Dynamic being (e.g., alive)	1	9	9	8	9	5	3	44
3. Activity	4	12	14	25	21	26	27	129
a) Potential	3	5	4	11	9	18	20	70
i) Active	1	2	1	5	5	3	4	21
α) Possibility (e.g., mortal)	1	1	0	3	1	3	2	11
β) Impossibility (e.g., immortal)	0	1	1	2	4	0	2	10
ii) Passive	2	3	3	6	4	15	16	49
α) Possibility (e.g., soluble)	1	2	3	3	2	7	1	19
β) Impossibility (e.g., irreparable)	1	1	0	3	2	8	15	30
b) Actual	1	7	10	14	12	8	7	59
i) Causative (e.g., instructive)	0	2	3	9	4	6	0	24
ii) Contemporary action (e.g., dying)	1	5	7	5	8	2	7	35

CONCEPTUAL ANALYSIS OF THE ADJECTIVES IN THE LIST—*Continued*

Conceptual Categories	First 1,000	Second 1,000	Third 1,000	Fourth 1,000	Fifth 1,000	Sixth 1,000	First Half of Seventh 1,000	Total
	Number of Times Concept Occurs in —							
B. Relational (predominating meaning is the relationship)	58	51	53	79	63	102	47	453
1. Comparison	39	24	9	26	10	14	6	128
a) By range	15	13	5	5	1	4	2	45
i) Temporal	5	5	2	1	1	0	1	15
α) Point (e.g., future)	4	5	2	1	0	0	1	13
β) Extension (e.g., senior)	1	0	0	0	1	0	0	2
ii) Spatial	10	8	3	4	0	4	1	30
α) Point (e.g., front)	10	7	3	4	0	3	1	28
β) Direction (e.g., westward)	0	1	0	0	0	1	0	2
b) By value (e.g., surpassing)	5	6	1	5	3	3	2	25
c) By quantity (e.g., lavish)	4	1	2	7	1	2	0	17
d) By sequence (e.g., subsequent)	7	2	1	5	4	5	2	26
e) By nature, kind (e.g., like)	8	2	0	4	1	0	0	15
2. Association	5	18	29	28	43	44	30	197
a) Conformative (e.g., theoretical)	4	6	7	11	8	14	7	57
b) Connective (e.g., church)	0	7	18	10	24	18	15	92
c) Worthiness (e.g., honorable)	0	3	1	4	4	2	3	17
d) *In re* nature (e.g., fabulous)	1	2	2	2	4	4	1	16
e) Resemblant (e.g., milky)	0	0	1	1	3	6	4	15
3. Adherence	11	5	7	15	3	17	4	62
a) Membership (e.g., Swiss)	2	3	6	12	3	15	3	44
b) Purtenance (e.g., thy)	9	2	1	3	0	2	1	18
4. Origin or constitution	3	4	8	10	7	27	7	66
a) Provenance (e.g., European)	2	2	4	8	3	12	2	33
b) Derivation (e.g., iron)	1	2	2	0	1	0	0	6
c) Provision (e.g., populous)	0	0	2	2	3	15	5	27
M. Negative (taken from A and B)	4	7	6	20	21	23	31	112
1. Denial (e.g., unfinished)	3	3	0	13	5	9	22	55
2. Opposition (e.g., unkind)	1	4	4	6	13	9	9	46
3. Privative (e.g., shapeless)	0	0	2	1	3	5	0	11

CATALOGUE OF DOVER BOOKS

Language Books and Records

GERMAN: HOW TO SPEAK AND WRITE IT. AN INFORMAL CONVERSATIONAL METHOD FOR SELF STUDY, Joseph Rosenberg. Eminently useful for self study because of concentration on elementary stages of learning. Also provides teachers with remarkable variety of aids: 28 full- and double-page sketches with pertinent items numbered and identified in German and English; German proverbs, jokes; grammar, idiom studies; extensive practice exercises. The most interesting introduction to German available, full of amusing illustrations, photographs of cities and landmarks in German-speaking cities, cultural information subtly woven into conversational material. Includes summary of grammar, guide to letter writing, study guide to German literature by Dr. Richard Friedenthal. Index. 400 illustrations. 384pp. 5⅜ x 8½. T271 Paperbound **$2.00**

FRENCH: HOW TO SPEAK AND WRITE IT. AN INFORMAL CONVERSATIONAL METHOD FOR SELF STUDY, Joseph Lemaitre. Even the absolute beginner can acquire a solid foundation for further study from this delightful elementary course. Photographs, sketches and drawings, sparkling colloquial conversations on a wide variety of topics (including French culture and custom), French sayings and quips, are some of aids used to demonstrate rather than merely describe the language. Thorough yet surprisingly entertaining approach, excellent for teaching and for self study. Comprehensive analysis of pronunciation, practice exercises and appendices of verb tables, additional vocabulary, other useful material. Index. Appendix. 400 illustrations. 416pp. 5⅜ x 8½. T268 Paperbound **$2.00**

DICTIONARY OF SPOKEN SPANISH, Spanish-English, English-Spanish. Compiled from spoken Spanish, emphasizing idiom and colloquial usage in both Castilian and Latin-American. More than 16,000 entries containing over 25,000 idioms—the largest list of idiomatic constructions ever published. Complete sentences given, indexed under single words—language in immediately useable form, for travellers, businessmen, students, etc. 25 page introduction provides rapid survey of sounds, grammar, syntax, with full consideration of irregular verbs. Especially apt in modern treatment of phrases and structure. 17 page glossary gives translations of geographical names, money values, numbers, national holidays, important street signs, useful expressions of high frequency, plus unique 7 page glossary of Spanish and Spanish-American foods and dishes. Originally published as War Department Technical Manual TM 30-900. iv + 513pp. 5⅜ x 8. T495 Paperbound **$1.75**

SPEAK MY LANGUAGE: SPANISH FOR YOUNG BEGINNERS, M. Ahlman, Z. Gilbert. Records provide one of the best, and most entertaining, methods of introducing a foreign language to children. Within the framework of a train trip from Portugal to Spain, an English-speaking child is introduced to Spanish by a native companion. (Adapted from a successful radio program of the N. Y. State Educational Department.) Though a continuous story, there are a dozen specific categories of expressions, including greetings, numbers, time, weather, food, clothes, family members, etc. Drill is combined with poetry and contextual use. Authentic background music is heard. An accompanying book enables a reader to follow the records, and includes a vocabulary of over 350 recorded expressions. Two 10″ 33⅓ records, total of 40 minutes. Book. 40 illustrations. 69pp. 5¼ x 10½. T890 The set **$4.95**

AN ENGLISH-FRENCH-GERMAN-SPANISH WORD FREQUENCY DICTIONARY, H. S. Eaton. An indispensable language study aid, this is a semantic frequency list of the 6000 most frequently used words in 4 languages—24,000 words in all. The lists, based on concepts rather than words alone, and containing all modern, exact, and idiomatic vocabulary, are arranged side by side to form a unique 4-language dictionary. A simple key indicates the importance of the individual words within each language. Over 200 pages of separate indexes for each language enable you to locate individual words at a glance. Will help language teachers and students, authors of textbooks, grammars, and language tests to compare concepts in the various languages and to concentrate on basic vocabulary, avoiding uncommon and obsolete words. 2 Appendixes. xxi + 441pp. 6½ x 9¼. T738 Paperbound **$2.45**

NEW RUSSIAN-ENGLISH AND ENGLISH-RUSSIAN DICTIONARY, M. A. O'Brien. Over 70,000 entries in the new orthography! Many idiomatic uses and colloquialisms which form the basis of actual speech. Irregular verbs, perfective and imperfective aspects, regular and irregular sound changes, and other features. One of the few dictionaries where accent changes within the conjugation of verbs and the declension of nouns are fully indicated. "One of the best," Prof. E. J. Simmons, Cornell. First names, geographical terms, bibliography, etc. 738pp. 4½ x 6¼. T208 Paperbound **$2.00**

96 MOST USEFUL PHRASES FOR TOURISTS AND STUDENTS in English, French, Spanish, German, Italian. A handy folder you'll want to carry with you. How to say "Excuse me," "How much is it?", "Write it down, please," etc., in four foreign languages. Copies limited, no more than 1 to a customer. **FREE**

Say It language phrase books

These handy phrase books (128 to 196 pages each) make grammatical drills unnecessary for an elementary knowledge of a spoken foreign language. Covering most matters of travel and everyday life each volume contains:

Over 1000 phrases and sentences in immediately useful forms — foreign language plus English.

Modern usage designed for Americans. Specific phrases like, "Give me small change," and "Please call a taxi."

Simplified phonetic transcription you will be able to read at sight.

The only completely indexed phrase books on the market.

Covers scores of important situations: — Greetings, restaurants, sightseeing, useful expressions, etc.

These books are prepared by native linguists who are professors at Columbia, N.Y.U., Fordham and other great universities. Use them independently or with any other book or record course. They provide a supplementary living element that most other courses lack. Individual volumes in:

Russian 75¢ **Italian 75¢** **Spanish 75¢** **German 75¢**
Hebrew 75¢ **Danish 75¢** **Japanese 75¢** **Swedish 75¢**
Dutch 75¢ **Esperanto 75¢** **Modern Greek 75¢** **Portuguese 75¢**
Norwegian 75¢ **Polish 75¢** **French 75¢** **Yiddish 75¢**
Turkish 75¢
English for Italian-speaking people 75¢
English for German-speaking people 75¢
English for Spanish-speaking people 75¢

Large clear type. 128-196 pages each. 3½ x 5¼. Sturdy paper binding.

Listen and Learn language records

LISTEN & LEARN is the only language record course designed especially to meet your travel and everyday needs. It is available in separate sets for FRENCH, SPANISH, GERMAN, JAPANESE, RUSSIAN, MODERN GREEK, PORTUGUESE, ITALIAN and HEBREW, and each set contains three 33⅓ rpm long-playing records—1½ hours of recorded speech by eminent native speakers who are professors at Columbia, New York University, Queens College.

Check the following special features found only in LISTEN & LEARN:

- **Dual-language recording. 812 selected phrases and sentences,** over 3200 words, spoken first in English, then in their foreign language equivalents. A suitable pause follows each foreign phrase, allowing you time to repeat the expression. You learn by unconscious assimilation.
- **128 to 206-page manual** contains everything on the records, plus a simple phonetic pronunciation guide.
- **Indexed for convenience. The only set on the market** that is completely indexed. No more puzzling over where to find the phrase you need. Just look in the rear of the manual.
- **Practical.** No time wasted on material you can find in any grammar. LISTEN & LEARN covers central core material with phrase approach. Ideal for the person with limited learning time.
- **Living, modern expressions,** not found in other courses. Hygienic products, modern equipment, shopping—expressions used every day, like "nylon" and "air-conditioned."
- **Limited objective.** Everything you learn, no matter where you stop, is immediately useful. You have to finish other courses, wade through grammar and vocabulary drill, before they help you.
- **High-fidelity recording.** LISTEN & LEARN records equal in clarity and surface-silence any record on the market costing up to $6.

"Excellent . . . the spoken records . . . impress me as being among the very best on the market," **Prof. Mario Pei,** Dept. of Romance Languages, Columbia University. "Inexpensive and well-done . . . it would make an ideal present," CHICAGO SUNDAY TRIBUNE. "More genuinely helpful than anything of its kind which I have previously encountered," **Sidney Clark,** well-known author of "ALL THE BEST" travel books.

UNCONDITIONAL GUARANTEE. Try LISTEN & LEARN, then return it within 10 days for full refund if you are not satisfied.

Each set contains three twelve-inch 33⅓ records, manual, and album.

SPANISH	the set **$5.95**	GERMAN	the set **$5.95**
FRENCH	the set **$5.95**	ITALIAN	the set **$5.95**
RUSSIAN	the set **$5.95**	JAPANESE	the set **$5.95**
PORTUGUESE	the set **$5.95**	MODERN GREEK	the set **$5.95**
MODERN HEBREW	the set **$5.95**		

Trubner Colloquial Manuals

These unusual books are members of the famous Trubner series of colloquial manuals. They have been written to provide adults with a sound colloquial knowledge of a foreign language, and are suited for either class use or self-study. Each book is a complete course in itself, with progressive, easy to follow lessons. Phonetics, grammar, and syntax are covered, while hundreds of phrases and idioms, reading texts, exercises, and vocabulary are included. These books are unusual in being neither skimpy nor overdetailed in grammatical matters, and in presenting up-to-date, colloquial, and practical phrase material. Bilingual presentation is stressed, to make thorough self-study easier for the reader.

COLLOQUIAL HINDUSTANI, A. H. Harley, formerly Nizam's Reader in Urdu, U. of London. 30 pages on phonetics and scripts (devanagari & Arabic-Persian) are followed by 29 lessons, including material on English and Arabic-Persian influences. Key to all exercises. Vocabulary. 5 x 7½. 147pp. Clothbound **$1.75**

COLLOQUIAL PERSIAN, L. P. Elwell-Sutton. Best introduction to modern Persian, with 90 page grammatical section followed by conversations, 35-page vocabulary. 139pp. Clothbound **$1.75**

COLLOQUIAL ARABIC, DeLacy O'Leary. Foremost Islamic scholar covers language of Egypt, Syria, Palestine, & Northern Arabia. Extremely clear coverage of complex Arabic verbs & noun plurals; also cultural aspects of language. Vocabulary. xviii + 192pp. 5 x 7½. Clothbound **$2.50**

COLLOQUIAL GERMAN, P. F. Doring. Intensive thorough coverage of grammar in easily-followed form. Excellent for brush-up, with hundreds of colloquial phrases. 34 pages of bilingual texts. 224pp. 5 x 7½. Clothbound **$1.75**

COLLOQUIAL SPANISH, W. R. Patterson. Castilian grammar and colloquial language, loaded with bilingual phrases and colloquialisms. Excellent for review or self-study. 164pp. 5 x 7½. Clothbound **$1.75**

COLLOQUIAL FRENCH, W. R. Patterson. 16th revision of this extremely popular manual. Grammar explained with model clarity, and hundreds of useful expressions and phrases; exercises, reading texts, etc. Appendixes of new and useful words and phrases. 223pp. 5 x 7½. Clothbound **$1.75**

COLLOQUIAL CZECH, J. Schwarz, former headmaster of Lingua Institute, Prague. Full easily followed coverage of grammar, hundreds of immediately useable phrases, texts. Perhaps the best Czech grammar in print. "An absolutely successful textbook," JOURNAL OF CZECHO-SLOVAK FORCES IN GREAT BRITAIN. 252pp. 5 x 7½. Clothbound **$3.00**

COLLOQUIAL RUMANIAN, G. Nandris, Professor of University of London. Extremely thorough coverage of phonetics, grammar, syntax; also included 70-page reader, and 70-page vocabulary. Probably the best grammar for this increasingly important language. 340pp. 5 x 7½. Clothbound **$2.50**

COLLOQUIAL ITALIAN, A. L. Hayward. Excellent self-study course in grammar, vocabulary, idioms, and reading. Easy progressive lessons will give a good working knowledge of Italian in the shortest possible time. 5 x 7½. Clothbound **$1.75**

COLLOQUIAL TURKISH, Yusuf Mardin. Very clear, thorough introduction to leading cultural and economic language of Near East. Begins with pronunciation and statement of vowel harmony, then 36 lessons present grammar, graded vocabulary, useful phrases, dialogues, reading, exercises. Key to exercises at rear. Turkish-English vocabulary. All in Roman alphabet. x + 288pp. 4¾ x 7¼. Clothbound **$4.00**

DUTCH-ENGLISH AND ENGLISH-DUTCH DICTIONARY, F. G. Renier. For travel, literary, scientific or business Dutch, you will find this the most convenient, practical and comprehensive dictionary on the market. More than 60,000 entries, shades of meaning, colloquialisms, idioms, compounds and technical terms. Dutch and English strong and irregular verbs. This is the only dictionary in its size and price range that indicates the gender of nouns. New orthography. xvii + 571pp. 5½ x 6¼. T224 Clothbound **$2.75**

LEARN DUTCH, F. G. Renier. This book is the most satisfactory and most easily used grammar of modern Dutch. The student is gradually led from simple lessons in pronunciation, through translation from and into Dutch, and finally to a mastery of spoken and written Dutch. Grammatical principles are clearly explained while a useful, practical vocabulary is introduced in easy exercises and readings. It is used and recommended by the Fulbright Committee in the Netherlands. Phonetic appendices. Over 1200 exercises; Dutch-English, English-Dutch vocabularies. 181pp. 4¼ x 7¼. T441 Clothbound **$2.25**

Literature, History of Literature

ARISTOTLE'S THEORY OF POETRY AND THE FINE ARTS, edited by S. H. Butcher. The celebrated Butcher translation of this great classic faced, page by page, with the complete Greek text. A 300 page introduction discussing Aristotle's ideas and their influence in the history of thought and literature, and covering art and nature, imitation as an aesthetic form, poetic truth, art and morality, tragedy, comedy, and similar topics. Modern Aristotelian criticism discussed by John Gassner. lxxvi + 421pp. 5⅜ x 8. T42 Paperbound **$2.00**

INTRODUCTIONS TO ENGLISH LITERATURE, edited by B. Dobrée. Goes far beyond ordinary histories, ranging from the 7th century up to 1914 (to the 1940's in some cases.) The first half of each volume is a specific detailed study of historical and economic background of the period and a general survey of poetry and prose, including trends of thought, influences, etc. The second and larger half is devoted to a detailed study of more than 5000 poets, novelists, dramatists; also economists, historians, biographers, religious writers, philosophers, travellers, and scientists of literary stature, with dates, lists of major works and their dates, keypoint critical bibliography, and evaluating comments. The most compendious bibliographic and literary aid within its price range.

Vol. I. THE BEGINNINGS OF ENGLISH LITERATURE TO SKELTON, (1509), W. L. Renwick, H. Orton. 450pp. 5⅛ x 7⅞. T75 Clothbound **$4.50**

Vol. II. THE ENGLISH RENAISSANCE, 1510-1688, V. de Sola Pinto. 381pp. 5⅛ x 7⅞. T76 Clothbound **$4.50**

Vol. III. AUGUSTANS AND ROMANTICS, 1689-1830, H. Dyson, J. Butt. 320pp. 5⅛ x 7⅞. T77 Clothbound **$4.50**

Vol. IV. THE VICTORIANS AND AFTER, 1830-1940's, E. Batho, B. Dobrée. 360pp. 5⅛ x 7⅞. T78 Clothbound **$4.50**

EPIC AND ROMANCE, W. P. Ker. Written by one of the foremost authorities on medieval literature, this is the standard survey of medieval epic and romance. It covers Teutonic epics, Icelandic sagas, Beowulf, French chansons de geste, the Roman de Troie, and many other important works of literature. It is an excellent account for a body of literature whose beauty and value has only recently come to be recognized. Index. xxiv + 398pp. 5⅜ x 8. T355 Paperbound **$2.00**

THE POPULAR BALLAD, F. B. Gummere. Most useful factual introduction; fund of descriptive material; quotes, cites over 260 ballads. Examines, from folkloristic view, structure; choral, ritual elements; meter, diction, fusion; effects of tradition, editors; almost every other aspect of border, riddle, kinship, sea, ribald, supernatural, etc., ballads. Bibliography. 2 indexes. 374pp. 5⅜ x 8. T548 Paperbound **$1.85**

MASTERS OF THE DRAMA, John Gassner. The most comprehensive history of the drama in print, covering drama in every important tradition from the Greeks to the Near East, China, Japan, Medieval Europe, England, Russia, Italy, Spain, Germany, and dozens of other drama producing nations. This unsurpassed reading and reference work encompasses more than 800 dramatists and over 2000 plays, with biographical material, plot summaries, theatre history, etc. "Has no competitors in its field," THEATRE ARTS. "Best of its kind in English," NEW REPUBLIC. Exhaustive 35 page bibliography. 77 photographs and drawings. Deluxe edition with reinforced cloth binding, headbands, stained top. xxii + 890pp. 5⅜ x 8. T100 Clothbound **$6.95**

THE DEVELOPMENT OF DRAMATIC ART, D. C. Stuart. The basic work on the growth of Western drama from primitive beginnings to Eugene O'Neill, covering over 2500 years. Not a mere listing or survey, but a thorough analysis of changes, origins of style, and influences in each period; dramatic conventions, social pressures, choice of material, plot devices, stock situations, etc.; secular and religious works of all nations and epochs. "Generous and thoroughly documented researches," Outlook. "Solid studies of influences and playwrights and periods," London Times. Index. Bibliography. xi + 679pp. 5⅜ x 8. T693 Paperbound **$2.75**

A SOURCE BOOK IN THEATRICAL HISTORY (SOURCES OF THEATRICAL HISTORY), A. M. Nagler. Over 2000 years of actors, directors, designers, critics, and spectators speak for themselves in this potpourri of writings selected from the great and formative periods of western drama. On-the-spot descriptions of masks, costumes, makeup, rehearsals, special effects, acting methods, backstage squabbles, theatres, etc. Contemporary glimpses of Molière rehearsing his company, an exhortation to a Roman audience to buy refreshments and keep quiet, Goethe's rules for actors, Belasco telling of $6500 he spent building a river, Restoration actors being told to avoid "lewd, obscene, or indecent postures," and much more. Each selection has an introduction by Prof. Nagler. This extraordinary, lively collection is ideal as a source of otherwise difficult to obtain material, as well as a fine book for browsing. Over 80 illustrations. 10 diagrams. xxiii + 611pp. 5⅜ x 8. T515 Paperbound **$3.00**

WORLD DRAMA, B. H. Clark. The dramatic creativity of a score of ages and eras — all in two handy compact volumes. Over 1/3 of this material is unavailable in any other current edition! 46 plays from Ancient Greece, Rome, Medieval Europe, France, Germany, Italy, England, Russia, Scandinavia, India, China, Japan, etc. — including classic authors like Aeschylus, Sophocles, Euripides, Aristophanes, Plautus, Marlowe, Jonson, Farquhar, Goldsmith, Cervantes, Molière, Dumas, Goethe, Schiller, Ibsen, and many others. This creative collection avoids hackneyed material and includes only completely first-rate works which are relatively little known or difficult to obtain. "The most comprehensive collection of important plays from all literature available in English," SAT. REV. OF LITERATURE. Introduction. Reading lists. 2 volumes. 1364pp. 5⅜ x 8.
Vol. 1, T57 Paperbound **$2.50**
Vol. 2, T59 Paperbound **$2.50**

MASTERPIECES OF THE RUSSIAN DRAMA, edited with introduction by G. R. Noyes. This only comprehensive anthology of Russian drama ever published in English offers complete texts, in 1st-rate modern translations, of 12 plays covering 200 years. Vol. 1: "The Young Hopeful," Fonvisin; "Wit Works Woe," Griboyedov; "The Inspector General," Gogol; "A Month in the Country," Turgenev; "The Poor Bride," Ostrovsky; "A Bitter Fate," Pisemsky. Vol. 2: "The Death of Ivan the Terrible," Alexey Tolstoy "The Power of Darkness," Lev Tolstoy; "The Lower Depths," Gorky; "The Cherry Orchard," Chekhov; "Professor Storitsyn," Andreyev; "Mystery Bouffe," Mayakovsky. Bibliography. Total of 902pp. 5⅜ x 8.
Vol. 1 T647 Paperbound **$2.25**
Vol. 2 T648 Paperbound **$2.00**

EUGENE O'NEILL: THE MAN AND HIS PLAYS, B. H. Clark. Introduction to O'Neill's life and work. Clark analyzes each play from the early THE WEB to the recently produced MOON FOR THE MISBEGOTTEN and THE ICEMAN COMETH revealing the environmental and dramatic influences necessary for a complete understanding of these important works. Bibliography. Appendices. Index. ix + 182pp. 5⅜ x 8. T379 Paperbound **$1.35**

THE HEART OF THOREAU'S JOURNALS, edited by O. Shepard. The best general selection from Thoreau's voluminous (and rare) journals. This intimate record of thoughts and observations reveals the full Thoreau and his intellectual development more accurately than any of his published works: self-conflict between the scientific observer and the poet, reflections on transcendental philosophy, involvement in the tragedies of neighbors and national causes, etc. New preface, notes, introductions. xii + 228pp. 5⅜ x 8. T741 Paperbound **$1.50**

H. D. THOREAU: A WRITER'S JOURNAL, edited by L. Stapleton. A unique new selection from the Journals concentrating on Thoreau's growth as a conscious literary artist, the ideals and purposes of his art. Most of the material has never before appeared outside of the complete 14-volume edition. Contains vital insights on Thoreau's projected book on Concord, thoughts on the nature of men and government, indignation with slavery, sources of inspiration, goals in life. Index. xxxiii + 234pp. 5⅜ x 8. T678 Paperbound **$1.65**

THE HEART OF EMERSON'S JOURNALS, edited by **Bliss Perry.** Best of these revealing Journals, originally 10 volumes, presented in a one volume edition. Talks with Channing, Hawthorne, Thoreau, and Bronson Alcott; impressions of Webster, Everett, John Brown, and Lincoln; records of moments of sudden understanding, vision, and solitary ecstasy. "The essays do not reveal the power of Emerson's mind . . . as do these hasty and informal writings," N.Y. Times. Preface by Bliss Perry. Index. xiii + 357pp. 5⅜ x 8. T477 Paperbound **$1.85**

FOUNDERS OF THE MIDDLE AGES, E. K. Rand. This is the best non-technical discussion of the transformation of Latin pagan culture into medieval civilization. Covering such figures as Tertullian, Gregory, Jerome, Boethius, Augustine, the Neoplatonists, and many other literary men, educators, classicists, and humanists, this book is a storehouse of information presented clearly and simply for the intelligent non-specialist. "Thoughtful, beautifully written," AMERICAN HISTORICAL REVIEW. "Extraordinarily accurate," Richard McKeon, THE NATION. ix + 365pp. 5⅜ x 8. T369 Paperbound **$2.00**

PLAY-MAKING: A MANUAL OF CRAFTSMANSHIP, William Archer. With an extensive, new introduction by John Gassner, Yale Univ. The permanently essential requirements of solid play construction are set down in clear, practical language: theme, exposition, foreshadowing, tension, obligatory scene, peripety, dialogue, character, psychology, other topics. This book has been one of the most influential elements in the modern theatre, and almost everything said on the subject since is contained explicitly or implicitly within its covers. Bibliography. Index. xlii + 277pp. 5⅜ x 8. T651 Paperbound **$1.75**

HAMBURG DRAMATURGY, G. E. Lessing. One of the most brilliant of German playwrights of the eighteenth-century age of criticism analyzes the complex of theory and tradition that constitutes the world of theater. These 104 essays on aesthetic theory helped demolish the regime of French classicism, opening the door to psychological and social realism, romanticism. Subjects include the original functions of tragedy; drama as the rational world; the meaning of pity and fear, pity and fear as means for purgation and other Aristotelian concepts; genius and creative force; interdependence of poet's language and actor's interpretation; truth and authenticity; etc. A basic and enlightening study for anyone interested in aesthetics and ideas, from the philosopher to the theatergoer. Introduction by Prof. Victor Lange. xxii + 265pp. 4½ x 6⅜. T32 Paperbound **$1.45**

Orientalia

ORIENTAL RELIGIONS IN ROMAN PAGANISM, F. Cumont. A study of the cultural meeting of east and west in the Early Roman Empire. It covers the most important eastern religions of the time from their first appearance in Rome, 204 B.C., when the Great Mother of the Gods was first brought over from Syria. The ecstatic cults of Syria and Phrygia — Cybele, Attis, Adonis, their orgies and mutilatory rites; the mysteries of Egypt — Serapis, Isis, Osiris, the dualism of Persia, the elevation of cosmic evil to equal stature with the deity, Mithra; worship of Hermes Trismegistus; Ishtar, Astarte; the magic of the ancient Near East, etc. Introduction. 55pp. of notes; extensive bibliography. Index. xxiv + 298pp. 5⅜ x 8.
T321 Paperbound **$2.00**

THE MYSTERIES OF MITHRA, F. Cumont. The definitive coverage of a great ideological struggle between the west and the orient in the first centuries of the Christian era. The origin of Mithraism, a Persian mystery religion, and its association with the Roman army is discussed in detail. Then utilizing fragmentary monuments and texts, in one of the greatest feats of scholarly detection, Dr. Cumont reconstructs the mystery teachings and secret doctrines, the hidden organization and cult of Mithra. Mithraic art is discussed, analyzed, and depicted in 70 illustrations. 239pp. 5⅜ x 8. T323 Paperbound **$1.85**

CHRISTIAN AND ORIENTAL PHILOSOPHY OF ART, A. K. Coomaraswamy. A unique fusion of philosopher, orientalist, art historian, and linguist, the author discusses such matters as: the true function of aesthetics in art, the importance of symbolism, intellectual and philosophic backgrounds, the role of traditional culture in enriching art, common factors in all great art, the nature of medieval art, the nature of folklore, the beauty of mathematics, and similar topics. 2 illustrations. Bibliography. 148pp. 5⅜ x 8. T378 Paperbound **$1.35**

TRANSFORMATION OF NATURE IN ART, A. K. Coomaraswamy. Unabridged reissue of a basic work upon Asiatic religious art and philosophy of religion. The theory of religious art in Asia and Medieval Europe (exemplified by Meister Eckhart) is analyzed and developed. Detailed consideration is given to Indian medieval aesthetic manuals, symbolic language in philosophy, the origin and use of images in India, and many other fascinating and little known topics. Glossaries of Sanskrit and Chinese terms. Bibliography. 41pp. of notes. 245pp. 5⅜ x 8.
T368 Paperbound **$1.75**

BUDDHIST LOGIC, F.Th. Stcherbatsky. A study of an important part of Buddhism usually ignored by other books on the subject: the Mahayana buddhistic logic of the school of Dignaga and his followers. First vol. devoted to history of Indian logic with Central Asian continuations, detailed exposition of Dignaga system, including theory of knowledge, the sensible world (causation, perception, ultimate reality) and mental world (judgment, inference, logical fallacies, the syllogism), reality of external world, and negation (law of contradiction, universals, dialectic). Vol. II contains translation of Dharmakirti's Nyayabindu with Dharmamottara's commentary. Appendices cover translations of Tibetan treatises on logic, Hindu attacks on Buddhist logic, etc. The basic work, one of the products of the great St. Petersburg school of Indian studies. Written clearly and with an awareness of Western philosophy and logic; meant for the Asian specialist and for the general reader with only a minimum of background. Vol. I, xii + 559pp. Vol. II, viii + 468pp. 5⅜ x 8½.
T955 Vol. I Paperbound **$2.50**
T956 Vol. II Paperbound **$2.50**
The set **$5.00**

THE TEXTS OF TAOISM. The first inexpensive edition of the complete James Legge translations of the Tao Te King and the writings of Chinese mystic Chuang Tse. Also contains several shorter treatises: the T'ai Shang Tractate of Actions and Their Retributions; the King Kang King, or Classic of Purity; the Yin Fu King, or Classic of the Harmony of the Seen and Unseen; the Yu Shu King, or Classic of the Pivot of Jade; and the Hsia Yung King, or Classic of the Directory for a Day. While there are other translations of the Tao Te King, this is the only translation of Chuang Tse and much of other material. Extensive introduction discusses differences between Taoism, Buddhism, Confucianism; authenticity and arrangement of Tao Te King and writings of Chuang Tse; the meaning of the Tao and basic tenets of Taoism; historical accounts of Lao-tse and followers; other pertinent matters. Clarifying notes incorporated into text. Originally published as Volumes 39, 40 of SACRED BOOKS OF THE EAST series, this has long been recognized as an indispensible collection. Sinologists, philosophers, historians of religion will of course be interested and anyone with an elementary course in Oriental religion or philosophy will understand and profit from these writings. Index. Appendix analyzing thought of Chuang Tse. Vol. I, xxiii + 396pp. Vol. II, viii + 340pp. 5⅜ x 8½.
T990 Vol. I Paperbound **$2.25**
T991 Vol. II Paperbound **$2.25**

Art, History of Art, Antiques, Graphic Arts, Handcrafts

ART STUDENTS' ANATOMY, E. J. Farris. Outstanding art anatomy that uses chiefly living objects for its illustrations. 71 photos of undraped men, women, children are accompanied by carefully labeled matching sketches to illustrate the skeletal system, articulations and movements, bony landmarks, the muscular system, skin, fasciae, fat, etc. 9 x-ray photos show movement of joints. Undraped models are shown in such actions as serving in tennis, drawing a bow in archery, playing football, dancing, preparing to spring and to dive. Also discussed and illustrated are proportions, age and sex differences, the anatomy of the smile, etc. 8 plates by the great early 18th century anatomic illustrator Siegfried Albinus are also included. Glossary. 158 figures, 7 in color. x + 159pp. 5⅝ x 8⅜. T744 Paperbound **$1.50**

AN ATLAS OF ANATOMY FOR ARTISTS, F Schider. A new 3rd edition of this standard text enlarged by 52 new illustrations of hands, anatomical studies by Cloquet, and expressive life studies of the body by Barcsay. 189 clear, detailed plates offer you precise information of impeccable accuracy. 29 plates show all aspects of the skeleton, with closeups of special areas, while 54 full-page plates, mostly in two colors, give human musculature as seen from four different points of view, with cutaways for important portions of the body. 14 full-page plates provide photographs of hand forms, eyelids, female breasts, and indicate the location of muscles upon models. 59 additional plates show how great artists of the past utilized human anatomy. They reproduce sketches and finished work by such artists as Michelangelo, Leonardo da Vinci, Goya, and 15 others. This is a lifetime reference work which will be one of the most important books in any artist's library. "The standard reference tool," AMERICAN LIBRARY ASSOCIATION. "Excellent," AMERICAN ARTIST. Third enlarged edition. 189 plates, 647 illustrations. xxvi + 192pp. 7⅞ x 10⅝. T241 Clothbound **$6.00**

AN ATLAS OF ANIMAL ANATOMY FOR ARTISTS, W. Ellenberger, H. Baum, H. Dittrich. The largest, richest animal anatomy for artists available in English. 99 detailed anatomical plates of such animals as the horse, dog, cat, lion, deer, seal, kangaroo, flying squirrel, cow, bull, goat, monkey, hare, and bat. Surface features are clearly indicated, while progressive beneath-the-skin pictures show musculature, tendons, and bone structure. Rest and action are exhibited in terms of musculature and skeletal structure and detailed cross-sections are given for heads and important features. The animals chosen are representative of specific families so that a study of these anatomies will provide knowledge of hundreds of related species. "Highly recommended as one of the very few books on the subject worthy of being used as an authoritative guide," DESIGN. "Gives a fundamental knowledge," AMERICAN ARTIST. Second revised, enlarged edition with new plates from Cuvier, Stubbs, etc. 288 illustrations. 153pp. 11⅜ x 9. T82 Clothbound **$6.00**

THE HUMAN FIGURE IN MOTION, Eadweard Muybridge. The largest selection in print of Muybridge's famous high-speed action photos of the human figure in motion. 4789 photographs illustrate 162 different actions: men, women, children—mostly undraped—are shown walking, running, carrying various objects, sitting, lying down, climbing, throwing, arising, and performing over 150 other actions. Some actions are shown in as many as 150 photographs each. All in all there are more than 500 action strips in this enormous volume, series shots taken at shutter speeds of as high as 1/6000th of a second! These are not posed shots, but true stopped motion. They show bone and muscle in situations that the human eye is not fast enough to capture. Earlier, smaller editions of these prints have brought $40 and more on the out-of-print market. "A must for artists," ART IN FOCUS. "An unparalleled dictionary of action for all artists," AMERICAN ARTIST. 390 full-page plates, with 4789 photographs. Printed on heavy glossy stock. Reinforced binding with headbands. xxi + 390pp. 7⅞ x 10⅝. T204 Clothbound **$10.00**

ANIMALS IN MOTION, Eadweard Muybridge. This is the largest collection of animal action photos in print. 34 different animals (horses, mules, oxen, goats, camels, pigs, cats, guanacos, lions, gnus, deer, monkeys, eagles—and 21 others) in 132 characteristic actions. The horse alone is shown in more than 40 different actions. All 3919 photographs are taken in series at speeds up to 1/6000th of a second. The secrets of leg motion, spinal patterns, head movements, strains and contortions shown nowhere else are captured. You will see exactly how a lion sets his foot down; how an elephant's knees are like a human's—and how they differ; the position of a kangaroo's legs in mid-leap; how an ostrich's head bobs; details of the flight of birds—and thousands of facets of motion only the fastest cameras can catch. Photographed from domestic animals and animals in the Philadelphia zoo, it contains neither semiposed artificial shots nor distorted telephoto shots taken under adverse conditions. Artists, biologists, decorators, cartoonists, will find this book indispensable for understanding animals in motion. "A really marvelous series of plates," NATURE (London). "The dry plate's most spectacular early use was by Eadweard Muybridge," LIFE. 3919 photographs; 380 full pages of plates. 440pp. Printed on heavy glossy paper. Deluxe binding with headbands. 7⅞ x 10⅝. T203 Clothbound **$10.00**

CATALOGUE OF DOVER BOOKS

ART ANATOMY, William Rimmer, M.D. Often called one of America's foremost contributions to art instruction, a work of art in its own right. More than 700 line drawings by the author, first-rate anatomist and dissector as well as artist, with a non-technical anatomical text. Impeccably accurate drawings of muscles, skeletal structure, surface features, other aspects of males and females, children, adults and aged persons show not only form, size, insertion and articulation but personality and emotion as reflected by physical features usually ignored in modern anatomical works. Complete unabridged reproduction of 1876 edition slightly rearranged. Introduction by Robert Hutchinson. 722 illustrations. xiii + 153pp. 7¾ x 10¾.
T908 Paperbound **$2.00**

ANIMAL DRAWING: ANATOMY AND ACTION FOR ARTISTS, C. R. Knight. The author and illustrator of this work was "the most distinguished painter of animal life." This extensive course in animal drawing discusses musculature, bone structure, animal psychology, movements, habits, habitats. Innumerable tips on proportions, light and shadow play, coloring, hair formation, feather arrangement, scales, how animals lie down, animal expressions, etc., from great apes to birds. Pointers on avoiding gracelessness in horses, deer; on introducing proper power and bulk to heavier animals; on giving proper grace and subtle expression to members of the cat family. Originally titled "Animal Anatomy and Psychology for the Artist and Layman." Over 123 illustrations. 149pp. 8¼ x 10½. T426 Paperbound **$2.00**

DESIGN FOR ARTISTS AND CRAFTSMEN, L. Wolchonok. The most thorough course ever prepared on the creation of art motifs and designs. It teaches you to create your own designs out of things around you — from geometric patterns, plants, birds, animals, humans, landscapes, and man-made objects. It leads you step by step through the creation of more than 1300 designs, and shows you how to create design that is fresh, well-founded, and original. Mr. Wolchonok, whose text is used by scores of art schools, shows you how the same idea can be developed into many different forms, ranging from near representationalism to the most advanced forms of abstraction. The material in this book is entirely new, and combines full awareness of traditional design with the work of such men as Miro, Léger, Picasso, Moore, and others. 113 detailed exercises, with instruction hints, diagrams, and details to enable you to apply Wolchonok's methods to your own work. "A great contribution to the field of design and crafts," N. Y. SOCIETY OF CRAFTSMEN. More than 1300 illustrations. xv + 207pp. 7⅞ x 10¾. T274 Clothbound **$4.95**

HAWTHORNE ON PAINTING. A vivid recreation, from students' notes, of instruction by Charles W. Hawthorne, given for over 31 years at his famous Cape Cod School of Art. Divided into sections on the outdoor model, still life, landscape, the indoor model, and water color, each section begins with a concise essay, followed by epigrammatic comments on color, form, seeing, etc. Not a formal course, but comments of a great teacher-painter on specific student works, which will solve problems in your own painting and understanding of art. "An excellent introduction for laymen and students alike," Time. Introduction. 100pp. 5⅜ x 8.
T653 Paperbound **$1.00**

THE ENJOYMENT AND USE OF COLOR, Walter Sargent. This book explains fascinating relations among colors, between colors in nature and art; describes experiments that you can perform to understand these relations more thoroughly; points out hundreds of little known facts about color values, intensities, effects of high and low illumination, complementary colors, color harmonies. Practical hints for painters, references to techniques of masters, questions at chapter ends for self-testing all make this a valuable book for artists, professional and amateur, and for general readers interested in world of color. Republication of 1923 edition. 35 illustrations, 6 full-page plates. New color frontispiece. Index. xii + 274pp. 5⅜ x 8. T944 Paperbound **$2.25**

DECORATIVE ALPHABETS AND INITIALS, ed. by Alexander Nesbitt. No payment, no permission needed to reproduce any one of these 3924 different letters, covering 1000 years. Crisp, clear letters all in line, from Anglo-Saxon mss., Luebeck Cathedral, 15th century Augsburg; the work of Dürer, Holbein, Cresci, Beardsley, Rossing Wadsworth, John Moylin, etc. Every imaginable style. 91 complete alphabets. 123 full-page plates. 192pp. 7¾ x 10¾.
T544 Paperbound **$2.25**

THREE CLASSICS OF ITALIAN CALLIGRAPHY, edited by Oscar Ogg. Here, combined in a single volume, are complete reproductions of three famous calligraphic works written by the greatest writing masters of the Renaissance: Arrighi's OPERINA and IL MODO, Tagliente's LO PRESENTE LIBRO, and Palatino's LIBRO NUOVO. These books present more than 200 complete alphabets and thousands of lettered specimens. The basic hand is Papal Chancery, but scores of other alphabets are also given: European and Asiatic local alphabets, foliated and art alphabets, scrolls, cartouches, borders, etc. Text is in Italian. Introduction. 245 plates. x + 272pp. 6⅛ x 9¼. T212 Paperbound **$2.25**

CALLIGRAPHY, J. G. Schwandner. One of the legendary books in the graphic arts, copies of which brought $500 each on the rare book market, now reprinted for the first time in over 200 years. A beautiful plate book of graceful calligraphy, and an inexhaustible source of first-rate material copyright-free, for artists, and directors, craftsmen, commercial artists, etc. More than 300 ornamental initials forming 12 complete alphabets, over 150 ornate frames and panels, over 200 flourishes, over 75 calligraphic pictures including a temple, cherubs, cocks, dodos, stags, chamois, foliated lions, greyhounds, etc. Thousand of calligraphic elements to be used for suggestions of quality, sophistication, antiquity, and sheer beauty. Historical introduction. 158 full-page plates. 368pp. 9 x 13.
T475 Clothbound **$10.00**

THE HISTORY AND TECHNIQUE OF LETTERING, A. Nesbitt. The only thorough inexpensive history of letter forms from the point of view of the artist. Mr. Nesbitt covers every major development in lettering from the ancient Egyptians to the present and illustrates each development with a complete alphabet. Such masters as Baskerville, Bell, Bodoni, Caslon, Koch, Kilian, Morris, Garamont, Jenson, and dozens of others are analyzed in terms of artistry and historical development. The author also presents a 65-page practical course in lettering, besides the full historical text. 89 complete alphabets; 165 additional lettered specimens. xvii + 300pp. 5⅜ x 8. T427 Paperbound **$2.00**

FOOT-HIGH LETTERS: A GUIDE TO LETTERING (A PRACTICAL SYLLABUS FOR TEACHERS), M. Price. A complete alphabet of Classic Roman letters, each a foot high, each on a separate 16 x 22 plate—perfect for use in lettering classes. In addition to an accompanying description, each plate also contains 9 two-inch-high forms of letter in various type faces, such as "Caslon," "Empire," "Onyx," and "Neuland," illustrating the many possible derivations from the standard classical forms. One plate contains 21 additional forms of the letter A. The fully illustrated 16-page syllabus by Mr. Price, formerly of the Pratt Institute and the Rhode Island School of Design, contains dozens of useful suggestions for student and teacher alike. An indispensable teaching aid. Extensively revised. 16-page syllabus and 30 plates in slip cover, 16 x 22. T239 Clothbound **$6.00**

THE STYLES OF ORNAMENT, Alexander Speltz. Largest collection of ornaments in print—3765 illustrations of prehistoric, Lombard, Gothic, Frank, Romanesque, Mohammedan, Renaissance, Polish, Swiss, Rococo, Sheraton, Empire, U. S. Colonial, etc., ornament. Gargoyles, dragons, columns, necklaces, urns, friezes, furniture, buildings, keyholes, tapestries, fantastic animals, armor, religious objects, much more, all in line. Reproduce any one free. Index. Bibliography. 400 plates. 656pp. 5⅝ x 8⅜. T557 Paperbound **$2.50**

HANDBOOK OF DESIGNS AND DEVICES, C. P. Hornung. This unique book is indispensable to the designer, commercial artist, and hobbyist. It is not a textbook but a working collection of 1836 basic designs and variations, carefully reproduced, which may be used without permission. Variations of circle, line, band, triangle, square, cross, diamond, swastika, pentagon, octagon, hexagon, star, scroll, interlacement, shields, etc. Supplementary notes on the background and symbolism of the figures. "A necessity to every designer who would be original without having to labor heavily," ARTIST AND ADVERTISER. 204 plates. 240pp. 5⅜ x 8. T125 Paperbound **$2.00**

THE UNIVERSAL PENMAN, George Bickham. This beautiful book, which first appeared in 1743, is the largest collection of calligraphic specimens, flourishes, alphabets, and calligraphic illustrations ever published. 212 full-page plates are drawn from the work of such 18th century masters of English roundhand as Dove, Champion, Bland, and 20 others. They contain 22 complete alphabets, over 2,000 flourishes, and 122 illustrations, each drawn with a stylistic grace impossible to describe. This book is invaluable to anyone interested in the beauties of calligraphy, or to any artist, hobbyist, or craftsman who wishes to use the very best ornamental handwriting and flourishes for decorative purposes. Commercial artists, advertising artists, have found it unexcelled as a source of material suggesting quality. "An essential part of any art library, and a book of permanent value," AMERICAN ARTIST. 212 plates. 224pp. 9 x 13¾. T20 Clothbound **$10.00**

1800 WOODCUTS BY THOMAS BEWICK AND HIS SCHOOL. Prepared by Dover's editorial staff, this is the largest collection of woodcuts by Bewick and his school ever compiled. Contains the complete engravings from all his major works and a wide range of illustrations from lesser-known collections, all photographed from clear copies of the original books and reproduced in line. Carefully and conveniently organized into sections on Nature (animals and birds, scenery and landscapes, plants, insects, etc.), People (love and courtship, social life, school and domestic scenes, misfortunes, costumes, etc.), Business and Trade, and illustrations from primers, fairytales, spelling books, frontispieces, borders, fables and allegories, etc. In addition to technical proficiency and simple beauty, Bewick's work is remarkable as a mode of pictorial symbolism, reflecting rustic tranquility, an atmosphere of rest, simplicity, idyllic contentment. A delight for the eye, an inexhaustible source of illustrative material for art studios, commercial artists, advertising agencies. Individual illustrations (up to 10 for any one use) are copyright free. Classified index. Bibliography and sources. Introduction by Robert Hutchinson. 1800 woodcuts. xiv + 247pp. 9 x 12. T766 Clothbound **$10.00**

A HANDBOOK OF EARLY ADVERTISING ART, C. P. Hornung. The largest collection of copyright-free early advertising art ever compiled. Vol. I contains some 2,000 illustrations of agricultural devices, animals, old automobiles, birds, buildings, Christmas decorations (with 7 Santa Clauses by Nast), allegorical figures, fire engines, horses and vehicles, Indians, portraits, sailing ships, trains, sports, trade cuts — and 30 other categories! Vol. II, devoted to typography, has over 4000 specimens: 600 different Roman, Gothic, Barnum, Old English faces; 630 ornamental type faces; 1115 initials, hundreds of scrolls, flourishes, etc. This third edition is enlarged by 78 additional plates containing all new material. "A remarkable collection," PRINTERS' INK. "A rich contribution to the history of American design," GRAPHIS.
Volume I, Pictorial. Over 2000 illustrations. xiv + 242pp. 9 x 12. T122 Clothbound **$10.00**
Volume II, Typographical. Over 4000 specimens. vii + 312pp. 9 x 12. T123 Clothbound **$10.00**
Two volume set, T121 Clothbound, only **$18.50**

THE 100 GREATEST ADVERTISEMENTS, WHO WROTE THEM AND WHAT THEY DID, J. L. Watkins. 100 (plus 13 added for this edition) of most successful ads ever to appear. "Do You Make These Mistakes in English," "They laughed when I sat down," "A Hog Can Cross the Country," "The Man in the Hathaway Shirt," over 100 more ads that changed habits of a nation, gave new expressions to the language, built reputations. Also salient facts behind ads, often in words of their creators. "Useful . . . valuable . . . enlightening," Printers' Ink. 2nd revised edition. Introduction. Foreword by Raymond Rubicam. Index. 130 illustrations. 252pp. 7¾ x 10¾. T540 Paperbound **$2.50**

THE DIDEROT PICTORIAL ENCYCLOPEDIA OF TRADES AND INDUSTRY, MANUFACTURING AND THE TECHNICAL ARTS IN PLATES SELECTED FROM "L'ENCYCLOPEDIE OU DICTIONNAIRE RAISONNE DES SCIENCES, DES ARTS, ET DES METIERS" OF DENIS DIDEROT, edited with text by C. Gillispie. The first modern selection of plates from the high point of 18th century French engraving, Diderot's famous Encyclopedia. Over 2000 illustrations on 485 full-page plates, most of them original size, illustrating the trades and industries of one of the most fascinating periods of modern history, 18th century France. These magnificent engravings provide an invaluable source of fresh, copyright-free material to artists and illustrators, a lively and accurate social document to students of cultures, an outstanding find to the lover of fine engravings. The plates teem with life, with men, women, and children performing all of the thousands of operations necessary to the trades before and during the early stages of the industrial revolution. Plates are in sequence, and show general operations, closeups of difficult operations, and details of complex machinery. Such important and interesting trades and industries are illustrated as sowing, harvesting, beekeeping, cheesemaking, operating windmills, milling flour, charcoal burning, tobacco processing, indigo, fishing, arts of war, salt extraction, mining, smelting iron, casting iron steel, extracting mercury, zinc, sulphur, copper, etc., slating, tinning, silverplating, gilding, making gunpowder, cannons, bells, shoeing horses, tanning, papermaking, printing, dying, and more than 40 other categories. Besides being a work of remarkable beauty and skill, this is also one of the largest collections of working figures in print. 920pp. 9 x 12. Heavy library cloth. T421 Two volume set **$18.50**

THE HANDBOOK OF PLANT AND FLORAL ORNAMENT, R. G. Hatton. One of the truly great collections of plant drawings for reproduction: 1200 different figures of flowering or fruiting plants—line drawings that will reproduce excellently. Selected from superb woodcuts and copperplate engravings appearing mostly in 16th and 17th century herbals including the fabulously rare "Kreuter Büch" (Bock) "Cruijde Boeck" (Dodoens), etc. Plants classified according to botanical groups. Also excellent reading for anyone interested in home gardening or any phase of horticulture. Formerly "The Craftsman's Plant-Book: or Figures of Plants." Introductions. Over 1200 illustrations. Index. 548pp. 6⅛ x 9¼. T649 Paperbound **$3.00**

HANDBOOK OF ORNAMENT, F. S. Meyer. One of the largest collections of copyright-free traditional art in print. It contains over 3300 line cuts from Greek, Roman, Medieval, Islamic, Renaissance, Baroque, 18th and 19th century sources. 180 plates illustrate elements of design with networks, Gothic tracery, geometric elements, flower and animal motifs, etc., while 100 plates illustrate decorative objects: chairs, thrones, daises, cabinets, crowns, weapons, utensils, vases, jewelry, armor, heraldry, bottles, altars, and scores of other objects. Indispensable for artists, illustrators, designers, handicrafters, etc. Full text. 3300 illustrations. xiv + 548pp. 5⅜ x 8. T302 Paperbound **$2.50**

COSTUMES OF THE GREEKS AND ROMANS, Thomas Hope. Authentic costumes from all walks of life in Roman, Greek civilizations, including Phrygia, Egypt, Persia, Parthia, Etruria, in finely drawn, detailed engravings by Thomas Hope (1770-1831). Scores of additional engravings of ancient musical instruments, furniture, jewelry, sarcophagi, other adjuncts to ancient life. All carefully copied from ancient vases and statuary. Textual introduction by author. Art and advertising personnel, costume and stage designers, students of fashion design will find these copyright-free engravings a source of ideas and inspiration and a valuable reference. Republication of 1st (1812) edition. 300 full-page plates, over 700 illustrations. xliv + 300pp. 5⅝ x 8⅜. T21 Paperbound **$2.00**

PRINCIPLES OF ART HISTORY, H. Wölfflin. Analyzing such terms as "baroque," "classic," "neoclassic," "primitive," "picturesque," and 164 different works by artists like Botticelli, van Cleve, Durer, Hobbema, Holbein, Hals, Rembrandt, Titian, Brueghel, Vermeer, and many others, the author establishes the classifications of art history and style on a firm, concrete basis. This classic of art criticism shows what really occurred between the 14th century primitives and the sophistication of the 18th century in terms of basic attitudes and philosophies. "A remarkable lesson in the art of seeing," SAT. REV. OF LITERATURE. Translated from the 7th German edition. 150 illustrations. 254pp. 6⅛ x 9¼. T276 Paperbound **$2.00**

AFRICAN SCULPTURE, Ladislas Segy. First publication of a new book by the author of critically acclaimed AFRICAN SCULPTURE SPEAKS. It contains 163 full-page plates illustrating masks, fertility figures, ceremonial objects, etc., representing the culture of 50 tribes of West and Central Africa. Over 85% of these works of art have never been illustrated before, and each is an authentic and fascinating tribal artifact. A 34-page introduction explains the anthropological, psychological, and artistic values of African sculpture. "Mr. Segy is one of its top authorities," NEW YORKER. 164 full-page photographic plates. Bibliography. 244pp. 6 x 9. T396 Paperbound **$2.00**

DESIGN MOTIFS OF ANCIENT MEXICO, J. Enciso. This unique collection of pre-Columbian stamps for textiles and pottery contains 766 superb designs from Aztec, Olmec, Totonac, Maya, and Toltec origins. Plumed serpents, calendrical elements, wind gods, animals, flowers, demons, dancers, monsters, abstract ornament, and other designs. More than 90% of these illustrations are completely unobtainable elsewhere. Use this work to bring new barbaric beauty into your crafts or drawing. Originally $17.50. Printed in three colors. 766 illustrations, thousands of motifs. 192pp. 7⅞ x 10¾. T84 Paperbound **$1.85**

DECORATIVE ART OF THE SOUTHWEST INDIANS, D. S. Sides. A magnificent album of authentic designs (both pre- and post-Conquest) from the pottery, textiles, and basketry of the Navaho, Hopi, Mohave, Santo Domingo, and over 20 other Southwestern groups. Designs include birds, clouds, butterflies, quadrupeds, geometric forms, etc. A valuable book for folklorists, and a treasury for artists, designers, advertisers, and craftsmen, who may use without payment or permission any of the vigorous, colorful, and strongly rhythmic designs. Aesthetic and archeological notes. 50 plates. Bibliography of over 50 items. xviii + 101pp. 5⅝ x 8⅜. T139 Paperbound **$1.00**

PAINTING IN THE FAR EAST, Laurence Binyon. Excellent introduction by one of greatest authorities on subject studies 1500 years of oriental art (China, Japan; also Tibet, Persia), over 250 painters. Examines works, schools, influence of Wu Tao-tzu, Kanaoka, Toba Sojo, Masanobu, Okio, etc.; early traditions; Kamakura epoch; the Great Decorators; T'ang Dynasty; Matabei, beginnings of genre; Japanese woodcut, color print; much more, all chronological, in cultural context. 42 photos. Bibliography. 317pp. 6 x 9¼. T520 Paperbound **$2.25**

ON THE LAWS OF JAPANESE PAINTING, H. Bowie. This unusual book, based on 9 years of profound study-experience in the Late Kano art of Japan, remains the most authentic guide in English to the spirit and technique of Japanese painting. A wealth of interesting and useful data on control of the brush; practise exercises; manufacture of ink, brushes, colors; the use of various lines and dots to express moods. It is the best possible substitute for a series of lessons from a great oriental master. 66 plates with 220 illustrations. Index. xv + 177pp. 6⅛ x 9¼. T30 Paperbound **$2.00**

THE MATERIALS AND TECHNIQUES OF MEDIEVAL PAINTING, D. V. Thompson. Based on years of study of medieval manuscripts and laboratory analysis of medieval paintings, this book discusses carriers and grounds, binding media, pigments, metals used in painting, etc. Considers relative merits of painting al fresco and al secco, the procession of coloring materials, burnishing, and many other matters. Preface by Bernard Berenson. Index. 239pp. 5⅜ x 8. T327 Paperbound **$1.85**

THE CRAFTSMAN'S HANDBOOK, Cennino Cennini. This is considered the finest English translation of IL LIBRO DELL' ARTE, a 15th century Florentine introduction to art technique. It is both fascinating reading and a wonderful mirror of another culture for artists, art students, historians, social scientists, or anyone interested in details of life some 500 years ago. While it is not an exact recipe book, it gives directions for such matters as tinting papers, gilding stone, preparation of various hues of black, and many other useful but nearly forgotten facets of the painter's art. As a human document reflecting the ideas of a practising medieval artist it is particularly important. 4 illustrations. xxvii + 142pp. D. V. Thompson translator. 6⅛ x 9¼. T54 Paperbound **$1.35**

VASARI ON TECHNIQUE, G. Vasari. Pupil of Michelangelo and outstanding biographer of the Renaissance artists, Vasari also wrote this priceless treatise on the technical methods of the painters, architects, and sculptors of his day. This is the only English translation of this practical, informative, and highly readable work. Scholars, artists, and general readers will welcome these authentic discussions of marble statues, bronze casting, fresco painting, oil painting, engraving, stained glass, rustic fountains and grottoes, etc. Introduction and notes by G. B. Brown. Index. 18 plates, 11 figures. xxiv + 328pp. 5⅜ x 8. T717 Paperbound **$2.25**

METHODS AND MATERIALS OF PAINTING OF THE GREAT SCHOOLS AND MASTERS, C. L. Eastlake. A vast, complete, and authentic reconstruction of the secret techniques of the masters of painting, collected from hundreds of forgotten manuscripts by the eminent President of the British Royal Academy: Greek, Roman, and medieval techniques; fresco and tempera; varnishes and encaustics; the secrets of Leonardo, Van Eyck, Raphael, and many others. Art historians, students, teachers, critics, and laymen will gain new insights into the creation of the great masterpieces; while artists and craftsmen will have a treasury of valuable techniques. Index. Two volume set. Total of 1025pp. 5⅜ x 8.
T718 Paperbound **$2.25**
T719 Paperbound **$2.25**
The set **$4.50**

BYZANTINE ART AND ARCHAEOLOGY, O. M. Dalton. Still the most thorough work in English—both in breadth and in depth—on the astounding multiplicity of Byzantine art forms throughout Europe, North Africa, and Western Asia from the 4th to the 15th century. Analyzes hundreds of individual pieces from over 160 public and private museums, libraries, and collections all over the world. Full treatment of Byzantine sculpture, painting, mosaic, jewelry, textiles, etc., including historical development, symbolism, and aesthetics. Chapters on iconography and ornament. Indispensable for study of Christian symbolism and medieval art. 457 illustrations, many full-page. Bibliography of over 2500 references. 4 Indexes. xx + 727pp. 6⅛ x 9¼. T776 Clothbound **$8.50**

METALWORK AND ENAMELLING, H. Maryon. This is probably the best book ever written on the subject. Prepared by Herbert Maryon, F.S.A., of the British Museum, it tells everything necessary for home manufacture of jewelry, rings, ear pendants, bowls, and dozens of other objects. Clearly written chapters provide precise information on such topics as materials, tools, soldering, filigree, setting stones, raising patterns, spinning metal, repoussé work, hinges and joints, metal inlaying, damascening, overlaying, niello, Japanese alloys, enamelling, cloisonné, painted enamels, casting, polishing, coloring, assaying, and dozens of other techniques. This is the next best thing to apprenticeship to a master metalworker. 363 photographs and figures. 374pp. 5½ x 8½. T183 Clothbound **$8.50**

SILK SCREEN TECHNIQUES, J. I. Biegeleisen, Max A. Cohn. A complete-to-the-last-detail copiously illustrated home course in this fast growing modern art form. Full directions for building silk screen out of inexpensive materials; explanations of five basic methods of stencil preparation—paper, blockout, tusche, film, photographic—and effects possible: light and shade, washes, dry brush, oil paint type impastos, gouaches, pastels. Detailed coverage of multicolor printing, illustrated by proofs showing the stages of a 4 color print. Special section on common difficulties. 149 illustrations, 8 in color. Sources of supply. xiv + 187pp. 6⅛ x 9¼. T433 Paperbound **$1.75**

A HANDBOOK OF WEAVES, G. H. Oelsner. Now back in print! Probably the most complete book of weaves ever printed, fully explained, differentiated, and illustrated. Includes plain weaves; irregular, double-stitched, and filling satins; derivative, basket, and rib weaves; steep, undulating, broken, offset, corkscrew, interlocking, herringbone, and fancy twills; honeycomb, lace, and crepe weaves; tricot, matelassé, and montagnac weaves; and much more. Translated and revised by S. S. Dale, with supplement on the analysis of weaves and fabrics. 1875 illustrations. vii + 402pp. 6 x 9¼. T209 Clothbound **$5.00**

BASIC BOOKBINDING, A. W. Lewis. Enables the beginner and the expert to apply the latest and most simplified techniques to rebinding old favorites and binding new paperback books. Complete lists of all necessary materials and guides to the selection of proper tools, paper, glue, boards, cloth, leather, or sheepskin covering fabrics, lettering inks and pigments, etc. You are shown how to collate a book, sew it, back it, trim it, make boards and attach them in easy step-by-step stages. Author's preface. 261 illustrations with appendix. Index. xi + 144pp. 5⅜ x 8. T169 Paperbound **$1.45**

BASKETRY, F. J. Christopher. Basic introductions cover selection of materials, use and care of tools, equipment. Easy to follow instructions for preparation of oval, oblong trays, lidded baskets, rush mats, tumbler holders, bicycle baskets, waste paper baskets, many other useful, beautiful articles made of coiled and woven reed, willow, rushes, raffia. Special sections present in clear, simple language and numerous illustrations all the how-to information you could need: linings, skein wire, varieties of stitching, simplified construction of handles, dying processes. For beginner and skilled craftsman alike. Edited by Majorie O'Shaugnessy. Bibliography. Sources of supply. Index. 112 illustrations. 108pp. 5 x 7¼. T903 Paperbound **$1.00**

THE ART OF ETCHING, E. S. Lumsden. Everything you need to know to do etching yourself. First two sections devoted to technique of etching and engraving, covering such essentials as relative merits of zinc and copper, cleaning and grounding plates, gravers, acids, arrangement of etching-room, methods of biting, types of inks and oils, mounting, stretching and framing, preserving and restoring plates, size and color of printing papers, much more. A review of the history of the art includes separate chapters on Dürer and Lucas van Leyden, Rembrandt and Van Dyck, Goya, Meryon, Haden and Whistler, British masters of nineteenth century, modern etchers. Final section is a collection of prints by contemporary etchers with comments by the artists. Professional etchers and engravers will find this a highly useful source of examples. Beginners and teachers, students of art and printing will find it a valuable tool. Index. 208 illustrations. 384pp. 5⅜ x 8. T49 Paperbound **$2.50**

WHITTLING AND WOODCARVING, E. J. Tangerman. What to make and how to make it for even a moderately handy beginner. One of the few works that bridge gap between whittling and serious carving. History of the art, background information on selection and use of woods, grips, types of strokes and cuts, handling of tools and chapters on rustic work, flat toys and windmills, puzzles, chains, ships in bottle, nested spheres, fans, more than 100 useful, entertaining objects. Second half covers carving proper: woodcuts, low relief, sculpture in the round, lettering, inlay and marquetry, indoor and outdoor decorations, pierced designs, much more. Final chapter describes finishing, care of tools. Sixth edition. Index. 464 illustrations. x + 239pp. 5½ x 8⅛. T965 Paperbound **$1.75**

THE PRACTICE OF TEMPERA PAINTING, Daniel V. Thompson, Jr. A careful exposition of all aspects of tempera painting, including sections on many possible modern uses, propensities of various woods, choice of material for panel, making and applying the gesso, pigments and brushes, technique of the actual painting, gilding and so on—everything one need know to try a hand at this proven but neglected art. The author is unquestionably the world's leading authority on tempera methods and processes and his treatment is based on exhaustive study of manuscript material. Drawings and diagrams increase clarity of text. No one interested in tempera painting can afford to be without this book. Appendix, "Tempera Practice in Yale Art School," by Lewis E. York. 85 illustrations by York; 4 full-page plates. ix x 149pp. 5⅜ x 8½. T343 Paperbound **$1.50**

The more difficult books are indicated by an asterisk (*)

Books Explaining Science and Mathematics

WHAT IS SCIENCE?, N. Campbell. The role of experiment and measurement, the function of mathematics, the nature of scientific laws, the difference between laws and theories, the limitations of science, and many similarly provocative topics are treated clearly and without technicalities by an eminent scientist. "Still an excellent introduction to scientific philosophy," H. Margenau in PHYSICS TODAY. "A first-rate primer . . . deserves a wide audience," SCIENTIFIC AMERICAN. 192pp. 5⅜ x 8. S43 Paperbound **$1.25**

THE NATURE OF PHYSICAL THEORY, P. W. Bridgman. A Nobel Laureate's clear, non-technical lectures on difficulties and paradoxes connected with frontier research on the physical sciences. Concerned with such central concepts as thought, logic, mathematics, relativity, probability, wave mechanics, etc. he analyzes the contributions of such men as Newton, Einstein, Bohr, Heisenberg, and many others. "Lucid and entertaining . . . recommended to anyone who wants to get some insight into current philosophies of science," THE NEW PHILOSOPHY. Index. xi + 138pp. 5⅜ x 8. S33 Paperbound **$1.25**

EXPERIMENT AND THEORY IN PHYSICS, Max Born. A Nobel Laureate examines the nature of experiment and theory in theoretical physics and analyzes the advances made by the great physicists of our day: Heisenberg, Einstein, Bohr, Planck, Dirac, and others. The actual process of creation is detailed step-by-step by one who participated. A fine examination of the scientific method at work. 44pp. 5⅜ x 8. S308 Paperbound **75¢**

THE PSYCHOLOGY OF INVENTION IN THE MATHEMATICAL FIELD, J. Hadamard. The reports of such men as Descartes, Pascal, Einstein, Poincaré, and others are considered in this investigation of the method of idea-creation in mathematics and other sciences and the thinking process in general. How do ideas originate? What is the role of the unconscious? What is Poincaré's forgetting hypothesis? are some of the fascinating questions treated. A penetrating analysis of Einstein's thought processes concludes the book. xiii + 145pp. 5⅜ x 8. T107 Paperbound **$1.25**

THE NATURE OF LIGHT AND COLOUR IN THE OPEN AIR, M. Minnaert. Why are shadows sometimes blue, sometimes green, or other colors depending on the light and surroundings? What causes mirages? Why do multiple suns and moons appear in the sky? Professor Minnaert explains these unusual phenomena and hundreds of others in simple, easy-to-understand terms based on optical laws and the properties of light and color. No mathematics is required but artists, scientists, students, and everyone fascinated by these "tricks" of nature will find thousands of useful and amazing pieces of information. Hundreds of observational experiments are suggested which require no special equipment. 200 illustrations; 42 photos. xvi + 362pp. 5⅜ x 8. T196 Paperbound **$2.00**

***MATHEMATICS IN ACTION, O. G. Sutton.** Everyone with a command of high school algebra will find this book one of the finest possible introductions to the application of mathematics to physical theory. Ballistics, numerical analysis, waves and wavelike phenomena, Fourier series, group concepts, fluid flow and aerodynamics, statistical measures, and meteorology are discussed with unusual clarity. Some calculus and differential equations theory is developed by the author for the reader's help in the more difficult sections. 88 figures. Index. viii + 236pp. 5⅜ x 8. T440 Clothbound **$3.50**

SOAP-BUBBLES: THEIR COLOURS AND THE FORCES THAT MOULD THEM, C. V. Boys. For continuing popularity and validity as scientific primer, few books can match this volume of easily-followed experiments, explanations. Lucid exposition of complexities of liquid films, surface tension and related phenomena, bubbles' reaction to heat, motion, music, magnetic fields. Experiments with capillary attraction, soap bubbles on frames, composite bubbles, liquid cylinders and jets, bubbles other than soap, etc. Wonderful introduction to scientific method, natural laws that have many ramifications in areas of modern physics. Only complete edition in print. New Introduction by S. Z. Lewin, New York University. 83 illustrations; 1 full-page color plate. xii + 190pp. 5⅜ x 8½. T542 Paperbound **95¢**

CATALOGUE OF DOVER BOOKS

THE STORY OF X-RAYS FROM RÖNTGEN TO ISOTOPES, A. R. Bleich, M.D. This book, by a member of the American College of Radiology, gives the scientific explanation of x-rays, their applications in medicine, industry and art, and their danger (and that of atmospheric radiation) to the individual and the species. You learn how radiation therapy is applied against cancer, how x-rays diagnose heart disease and other ailments, how they are used to examine mummies for information on diseases of early societies, and industrial materials for hidden weaknesses. 54 illustrations show x-rays of flowers, bones, stomach, gears with flaws, etc. 1st publication. Index. xix + 186pp. 5⅜ x 8. T622 Paperbound **$1.35**

SPINNING TOPS AND GYROSCOPIC MOTION, John Perry. A classic elementary text of the dynamics of rotation — the behavior and use of rotating bodies such as gyroscopes and tops. In simple, everyday English you are shown how quasi-rigidity is induced in discs of paper, smoke rings, chains, etc., by rapid motions; why a gyrostat falls and why a top rises; precession; how the earth's motion affects climate; and many other phenomena. Appendix on practical use of gyroscopes. 62 figures. 128pp. 5⅜ x 8. T416 Paperbound **$1.00**

SNOW CRYSTALS, W. A. Bentley, M. J. Humphreys. For almost 50 years W. A. Bentley photographed snow flakes in his laboratory in Jericho, Vermont; in 1931 the American Meteorological Society gathered together the best of his work, some 2400 photographs of snow flakes, plus a few ice flowers, windowpane frosts, dew, frozen rain, and other ice formations. Pictures were selected for beauty and scientific value. A very valuable work to anyone in meteorology, cryology; most interesting to layman; extremely useful for artist who wants beautiful, crystalline designs. All copyright free. Unabridged reprint of 1931 edition. 2453 illustrations. 227pp. 8 x 10½. T287 Paperbound **$3.00**

A DOVER SCIENCE SAMPLER, edited by George Barkin. A collection of brief, non-technical passages from 44 Dover Books Explaining Science for the enjoyment of the science-minded browser. Includes work of Bertrand Russell, Poincaré, Laplace, Max Born, Galileo, Newton; material on physics, mathematics, metallurgy, anatomy, astronomy, chemistry, etc. You will be fascinated by Martin Gardner's analysis of the sincere pseudo-scientist, Moritz's account of Newton's absentmindedness, Bernard's examples of human vivisection, etc. Illustrations from the Diderot Pictorial Encyclopedia and De Re Metallica. 64 pages. **FREE**

THE STORY OF ATOMIC THEORY AND ATOMIC ENERGY, J. G. Feinberg. A broader approach to subject of nuclear energy and its cultural implications than any other similar source. Very readable, informal, completely non-technical text. Begins with first atomic theory, 600 B.C. and carries you through the work of Mendelejeff, Röntgen, Madame Curie, to Einstein's equation and the A-bomb. New chapter goes through thermonuclear fission, binding energy, other events up to 1959. Radioactive decay and radiation hazards, future benefits, work of Bohr, moderns, hundreds more topics. "Deserves special mention . . . not only authoritative but thoroughly popular in the best sense of the word," Saturday Review. Formerly, "The Atom Story." Expanded with new chapter. Three appendixes. Index. 34 illustrations. vii + 243pp. 5⅜ x 8. T625 Paperbound **$1.60**

THE STRANGE STORY OF THE QUANTUM, AN ACCOUNT FOR THE GENERAL READER OF THE GROWTH OF IDEAS UNDERLYING OUR PRESENT ATOMIC KNOWLEDGE, B. Hoffmann Presents lucidly and expertly, with barest amount of mathematics, the problems and theories which led to modern quantum physics. Dr. Hoffmann begins with the closing years of the 19th century, when certain trifling discrepancies were noticed, and with illuminating analogies and examples takes you through the brilliant concepts of Planck, Einstein, Pauli, Broglie, Bohr, Schroedinger, Heisenberg, Dirac, Sommerfeld, Feynman, etc. This edition includes a new, long postscript carrying the story through 1958. "Of the books attempting an account of the history and contents of our modern atomic physics which have come to my attention, this is the best," H. Margenau, Yale University, in "American Journal of Physics." 32 tables and line illustrations. Index. 275pp. 5⅜ x 8. T518 Paperbound **$1.50**

SPACE AND TIME, E. Borel. Written by a versatile mathematician of world renown with his customary lucidity and precision, this introduction to relativity for the layman presents scores of examples, analogies, and illustrations that open up new ways of thinking about space and time. It covers abstract geometry and geographical maps, continuity and topology, the propagation of light, the special theory of relativity, the general theory of relativity, theoretical researches, and much more. Mathematical notes. 2 Indexes. 4 Appendices. 15 figures. xvi + 243pp. 5⅜ x 8. T592 Paperbound **$1.45**

FROM EUCLID TO EDDINGTON: A STUDY OF THE CONCEPTIONS OF THE EXTERNAL WORLD, Sir Edmund Whittaker. A foremost British scientist traces the development of theories of natural philosophy from the western rediscovery of Euclid to Eddington, Einstein, Dirac, etc. The inadequacy of classical physics is contrasted with present day attempts to understand the physical world through relativity, non-Euclidean geometry, space curvature, wave mechanics, etc. 5 major divisions of examination: Space; Time and Movement; the Concepts of Classical Physics; the Concepts of Quantum Mechanics; the Eddington Universe. 212pp. 5⅜ x 8. T491 Paperbound **$1.35**

History of Science and Mathematics

THE STUDY OF THE HISTORY OF MATHEMATICS, THE STUDY OF THE HISTORY OF SCIENCE, G. Sarton. Two books bound as one. Each volume contains a long introduction to the methods and philosophy of each of these historical fields, covering the skills and sympathies of the historian, concepts of history of science, psychology of idea-creation, and the purpose of history of science. Prof. Sarton also provides more than 80 pages of classified bibliography. Complete and unabridged. Indexed. 10 illustrations. 188pp. 5⅜ x 8. T240 Paperbound **$1.25**

A HISTORY OF PHYSICS, Florian Cajori, Ph.D. First written in 1899, thoroughly revised in 1929, this is still best entry into antecedents of modern theories. Precise non-mathematical discussion of ideas, theories, techniques, apparatus of each period from Greeks to 1920's, analyzing within each period basic topics of matter, mechanics, light, electricity and magnetism, sound, atomic theory, etc. Stress on modern developments, from early 19th century to present. Written with critical eye on historical development, significance. Provides most of needed historical background for student of physics. Reprint of second (1929) edition. Index. Bibliography in footnotes. 16 figures. xv + 424pp. 5⅜ x 8. T970 Paperbound **$2.00**

A HISTORY OF ASTRONOMY FROM THALES TO KEPLER, J. L. E. Dreyer. Formerly titled A HISTORY OF PLANETARY SYSTEMS FROM THALES TO KEPLER. This is the only work in English which provides a detailed history of man's cosmological views from prehistoric times up through the Renaissance. It covers Egypt, Babylonia, early Greece, Alexandria, the Middle Ages, Copernicus, Tycho Brahe, Kepler, and many others. Epicycles and other complex theories of positional astronomy are explained in terms nearly everyone will find clear and easy to understand. "Standard reference on Greek astronomy and the Copernican revolution," SKY AND TELESCOPE. Bibliography. 21 diagrams. Index. xvii + 430pp. 5⅜ x 8. S79 Paperbound **$2.25**

A SHORT HISTORY OF ASTRONOMY, A. Berry. A popular standard work for over 50 years, this thorough and accurate volume covers the science from primitive times to the end of the 19th century. After the Greeks and Middle Ages, individual chapters analyze Copernicus, Brahe, Galileo, Kepler, and Newton, and the mixed reception of their startling discoveries. Post-Newtonian achievements are then discussed in unusual detail: Halley, Bradley, Lagrange, Laplace, Herschel, Bessel, etc. 2 indexes. 104 illustrations, 9 portraits. xxxi + 440pp. 5⅜ x 8. T210 Paperbound **$2.00**

PIONEERS OF SCIENCE, Sir Oliver Lodge. An authoritative, yet elementary history of science by a leading scientist and expositor. Concentrating on individuals—Copernicus, Brahe, Kepler, Galileo, Descartes, Newton, Laplace, Herschel, Lord Kelvin, and other scientists—the author presents their discoveries in historical order, adding biographical material on each man and full, specific explanations of their achievements. The full, clear discussions of the accomplishments of post-Newtonian astronomers are features seldom found in other books on the subject. Index. 120 illustrations. xv + 404pp. 5⅜ x 8. T716 Paperbound **$1.65**

THE BIRTH AND DEVELOPMENT OF THE GEOLOGICAL SCIENCES, F. D. Adams. The most complete and thorough history of the earth sciences in print. Geological thought from earliest recorded times to the end of the 19th century—covers over 300 early thinkers and systems: fossils and hypothetical explanations of them, vulcanists vs. neptunists, figured stones and paleontology, generation of stones, and similar topics. 91 illustrations, including medieval, renaissance woodcuts, etc. 632 footnotes and bibliographic notes. Index. 511pp. 5⅜ x 8. T5 Paperbound **$2.25**

THE STORY OF ALCHEMY AND EARLY CHEMISTRY, J. M. Stillman. "Add the blood of a red-haired man"—a recipe typical of the many quoted in this authoritative and readable history of the strange beliefs and practices of the alchemists. Concise studies of every leading figure in alchemy and early chemistry through Lavoisier, in this curious epic of superstition and true science, constructed from scores of rare and difficult Greek, Latin, German, and French texts. Foreword by S. W. Young. 246-item bibliography. Index. xiii + 566pp. 5⅜ x 8. S628 Paperbound **$2.45**

HISTORY OF MATHEMATICS, D. E. Smith. Most comprehensive non-technical history of math in English. Discusses the lives and works of over a thousand major and minor figures, from Euclid to Descartes, Gauss, and Riemann. Vol. I: A chronological examination, from primitive concepts through Egypt, Babylonia, Greece, the Orient, Rome, the Middle Ages, the Renaissance, and up to 1900. Vol. 2: The development of ideas in specific fields and problems, up through elementary calculus. Two volumes, total of 510 illustrations, 1355pp. 5⅜ x 8. Set boxed in attractive container. T429,430 Paperbound the set **$5.00**

CATALOGUE OF DOVER BOOKS

A CONCISE HISTORY OF MATHEMATICS, D. Struik. A lucid, easily followed history of mathematical ideas and techniques from the Ancient Near East up to modern times. Requires no mathematics but will serve as an excellent introduction to mathematical concepts and great mathematicians through the method of historical development. 60 illustrations including Egyptian papyri, Greek mss., portraits of 31 eminent mathematicians. Bibliography. xix + 299pp. 5⅜ x 8. T255 Paperbound **$1.75**

A SHORT ACCOUNT OF THE HISTORY OF MATHEMATICS, W. W. Rouse Ball. Last previous edition (1908) hailed by mathematicians and laymen for lucid overview of math as living science, for understandable presentation of individual contributions of great mathematicians. Treats lives, discoveries of every important school and figure from Egypt, Phoenicia to late nineteenth century. Greek schools of Ionia, Cyzicus, Alexandria, Byzantium, Pythagoras; primitive arithmetic; Middle Ages and Renaissance, including European and Asiatic contributions; modern math of Descartes, Pascal, Wallis, Huygens, Newton, Euler, Lambert, Laplace, scores more. More emphasis on historical development, exposition of ideas than other books on subject. Non-technical, readable text can be followed with no more preparation than high-school algebra. Index. 544pp. 5⅜ x 8. S630 Paperbound **$2.00**

ON MATHEMATICS AND MATHEMATICIANS, R. E. Moritz. A ten year labor of love by the discerning and discriminating Prof. Moritz, this collection has rarely been equalled in its ability to convey the full sense of mathematics and the personalities of great mathematicians. A collection of anecdotes, aphorisms, reminiscences, philosophies, definitions, speculations, biographical insights, etc., by great mathematicians and writers: Descartes, Mill, De Morgan, Locke, Berkeley, Kant, Coleridge, Whitehead, Sylvester, Klein, and many others. Also, glimpses into the lives of mathematical giants from Archimedes to Euler, Gauss, and Weierstrass. To mathematicians, a superb book for browsing; to writers and teachers, an unequalled source of quotation; to the layman, an exciting revelation of the fullness of mathematics. Extensive cross index. 410pp. 5⅜ x 8. T489 Paperbound **$1.95**

SIR ISAAC NEWTON: A BIOGRAPHY, Louis Trenchard More. Standard, definitive biography of Newton, covering every phase of his life and career in its presentation of the renowned scientific genius as a living man. Objective, critical analysis of his character as well as a careful survey of his manifold accomplishments in many areas of science, and in theology, history, politics, finance. Text includes letters by Newton and acquaintances, many other papers, some translated from Latin to English by the author. Scientists, teachers of science will especially be interested in this book, which will appeal to all readers concerned with history of ideas, development of science. Republication of original (1934) edition. 1 full-page plate. Index. xii + 675pp. 5⅜ x 8½. S79 Paperbound **$2.50**

GUIDE TO THE LITERATURE OF MATHEMATICS AND PHYSICS, N. G. Parke III. Over 5000 entries included under approximately 120 major subject headings, of selected most important books, monographs, periodicals, articles in English, plus important works in German, French, Italian, Spanish, Russian (many recently available works). Covers every branch of physics, math, related engineering. Includes author, title, edition, publisher, place, date, number of volumes, number of pages. A 40-page introduction on the basic problems of research and study provides useful information on the organization and use of libraries, the psychology of learning, etc. This reference work will save you hours of time. 2nd revised edition. Indices of authors, subjects. 464pp. 5⅜ x 8. S447 Paperbound **$2.49**